BUSINESS ESSENTIALS

BUSINESS ESSENTIALS

EIGHTH CANADIAN EDITION

RONALD J. EBERT
UNIVERSITY OF MISSOURI-COLUMBIA

RICKY W. GRIFFIN
TEXAS A&M UNIVERSITY

FREDERICK A. STARKE
UNIVERSITY OF MANITOBA

GEORGE DRACOPOULOS
VANIER COLLEGE AND MCGILL UNIVERSITY

PEARSON

Toronto

Editorial Director: Claudine O'Donnell
Acquisitions Editor: Carolin Sweig
Marketing Manager: Lisa Gillis
Program Manager: Karen Townsend
Project Manager: Jessica Hellen
Developmental Editor: Paul Donnelly
Media Developer: Kelli Cadet
Production Services: Mohinder Singh, iEnergizer Aptara®, Ltd.
Permissions Project Manager: Joanne Tang
Photo Permissions Research: Melody English, Integra
Text Permissions Research: Renae Horstman, Integra
Interior and Cover Designer: Anthony Leung
Canadian Skyline Image: Mary Beth MacLean
Cover Image: © peshkova - Fotolia.com
Vice-President, Cross Media and Publishing Services: Gary Bennett

10 9 8 7 6 5 4 3 2 1 [V0RJ]

Library and Archives Canada Cataloguing in Publication

Ebert, Ronald J., author

Business essentials / Ronald J. Ebert (University of Missouri-Columbia), Ricky W. Griffin (Texas A&M University), Frederick A. Starke (University of Manitoba), George Dracopoulos (Vanier College and McGill University).—Eighth Canadian edition.

Includes bibliographical references and index.

ISBN 978-0-13-400009-1 (paperback)

1. Industrial management—Textbooks. 2. Business enterprises—Textbooks. 3. Industrial management—Canada—Textbooks. 4. Business enterprises—Canada—Textbooks. I. Griffin, Ricky W., author II. Starke, Frederick A., 1942-, author III. Dracopoulos, George, 1970-, author IV. Title.

HD70.C3E32 2016 658 C2015-906519-4

ISBN 978-0-13-400009-1

To Fran, for bringing a lifetime of friendship, fun, and love into our family.

—R.J.E.

For Paul and Sherry–Friends for life.

—R.W.G.

To Ann, Eric, and Grant.

—F.A.S.

To Nitsa and Costa Dean.

—G.D.

BRIEF CONTENTS

PART 1
INTRODUCING THE CONTEMPORARY BUSINESS WORLD 2

01
UNDERSTANDING THE CANADIAN BUSINESS SYSTEM 3

02
THE ENVIRONMENT OF BUSINESS 23

03
CONDUCTING BUSINESS ETHICALLY AND RESPONSIBLY 45

04
ENTREPRENEURSHIP, SMALL BUSINESS, AND NEW VENTURE CREATION 73

05
THE GLOBAL CONTEXT OF BUSINESS 97

PART 2
THE BUSINESS OF MANAGING 120

06
MANAGING THE BUSINESS ENTERPRISE 121

07
ORGANIZING THE BUSINESS ENTERPRISE 147

08
MANAGING HUMAN RESOURCES AND LABOUR RELATIONS 169

09
MOTIVATING, SATISFYING, AND LEADING EMPLOYEES 197

PART 3
MANAGING OPERATIONS AND INFORMATION 228

10
OPERATIONS MANAGEMENT, PRODUCTIVITY, AND QUALITY 229

11
UNDERSTANDING ACCOUNTING 255

PART 4
PRINCIPLES OF MARKETING 290

12
UNDERSTANDING MARKETING PRINCIPLES AND DEVELOPING PRODUCTS 291

13
PRICING, PROMOTING, AND DISTRIBUTING PRODUCTS 317

PART 5
MANAGING FINANCIAL ISSUES 342

14
MONEY AND BANKING 343

15
FINANCIAL DECISIONS AND RISK MANAGEMENT 365

CONTENTS

PART 1
INTRODUCING THE CONTEMPORARY BUSINESS WORLD 2

01 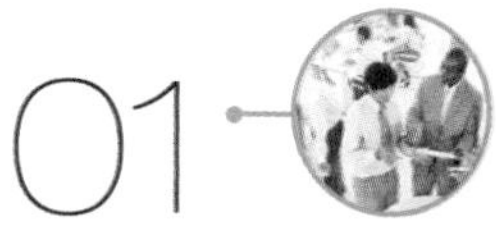

UNDERSTANDING THE CANADIAN BUSINESS SYSTEM 3

Combining the Whopper and the Timbit 3

LO-1 The Idea of Business and Profit 4

LO-2 Economic Systems Around the World 5

Factors of Production 5
Types of Economic Systems 5

ENTREPRENEURSHIP AND NEW VENTURES Riversong: Revolutionary Canadian Guitars 6

THERE'S AN APP FOR THAT! 8

LO-3 Interactions Between Business and Government 9

How Government Influences Business 9
How Business Influences Government 11

LO-4 The Canadian Market Economy 12

Demand and Supply in a Market Economy 12

LO-5 Private Enterprise and Competition 14

Degrees of Competition 14

E-BUSINESS AND SOCIAL MEDIA SOLUTIONS Taking a Bite out of Internet Radio 15

Summary of Learning Objectives 16
Questions and Exercises 17
Team Exercises 17
BUSINESS CASE 1 19

CHAPTER SUPPLEMENT 01 21

02 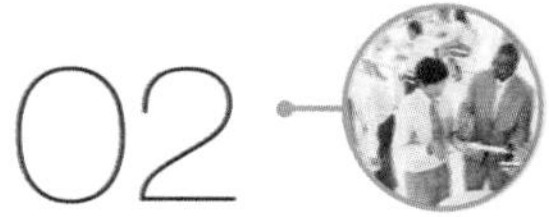

THE ENVIRONMENT OF BUSINESS 23

Supermarket Battles: Then There Were Three 23

LO-1 Organizational Boundaries and Environments 25

Organizational Boundaries 25
Multiple Organizational Environments 26

LO-2 The Economic Environment 26

Economic Growth 27

THERE'S AN APP FOR THAT! 29

Economic Stability 30
Managing the Canadian Economy 31

LO-3 The Technological Environment 31

Research and Development (R&D) 31
Product and Service Technologies 32

THE GREENING OF BUSINESS Here Comes the Hydrogen Fuel Cell ... Again 32

ENTREPRENEURSHIP AND NEW VENTURES Selling Magic in a Connected World 33

LO-4 The Political–Legal Environment 33

LO-5 The Socio-Cultural Environment 34

Customer Preferences and Tastes 34
Ethical Compliance and Responsible Business Behaviour 34
The Business Environment 34
The Industry Environment 34

MANAGING IN TURBULENT TIMES The Impact of the Physical Environment 35

LO-6 Emerging Challenges and Opportunities in the Business Environment 36

Outsourcing 36
The Growing Role of Social Media 37
Business Process Management 37

E-BUSINESS AND SOCIAL MEDIA SOLUTIONS Staying Connected in the Skies 37

LO-7 Redrawing Corporate Boundaries 38

Mergers and Acquisitions 38
Divestitures and Spinoffs 38
Employee-Owned Corporations 38
Strategic Alliances 39
Subsidiary and Parent Corporations 39

Summary of Learning Objectives 39
Questions and Exercises 40
Team Exercises 41
BUSINESS CASE 2 42

03 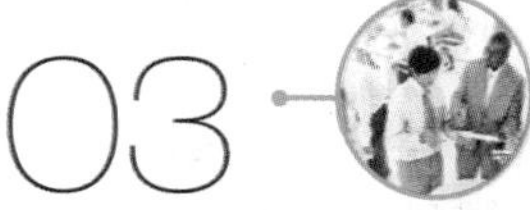

CONDUCTING BUSINESS ETHICALLY AND RESPONSIBLY 45

What's Happening in the Fair Trade Movement? 45

Ethics in the Workplace 47

LO-1 Individual Ethics 47
Managerial Ethics 48
Assessing Ethical Behaviour 49
Encouraging Ethical Behaviour in Organizations 50

LO-2 Corporate Social Responsibility 51

LO-3 The Stakeholder Model of Responsibility 52

THERE'S AN APP FOR THAT! 53

ENTREPRENEURSHIP AND NEW VENTURES Creating Games with a Social Twist 55
MANAGING IN TURBULENT TIMES Should We Pay Whistle-Blowers? 56
THE GREENING OF BUSINESS Some Frustrations in the Green Movement 60

Implementing Social Responsibility Programs 60
LO-4 Approaches to Social Responsibility 60
Managing Social Responsibility Programs 61

LO-5 Social Responsibility and the Small Business 62

Summary of Learning Objectives 63
Questions and Exercises 64
Team Exercises 64
BUSINESS CASE 3 65

CHAPTER SUPPLEMENT 02 68

04 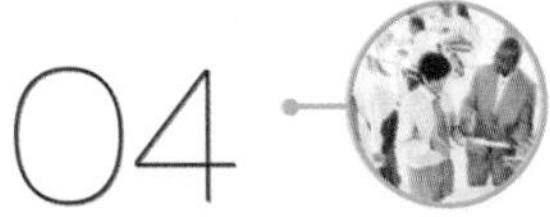

ENTREPRENEURSHIP, SMALL BUSINESS, AND NEW VENTURE CREATION 73

Mr. Ma: King of the Canadian Food Court! 73

Small Business, New Venture Creation, and Entrepreneurship 75
LO-1 Small Business 75
The New Venture/Firm 76
Entrepreneurship 76

LO-2 The Role of Small and New Businesses in the Canadian Economy 76
Small Businesses 77
New Ventures 77

LO-3 The Entrepreneurial Process 78
Identifying Opportunities 78
E-BUSINESS AND SOCIAL MEDIA SOLUTIONS Teenage Innovator, Entrepreneur, and Multimillionaire 79
ENTREPRENEURSHIP AND NEW VENTURES Harvard Dropout Turned Billionaire 80
Accessing Resources 82
THERE'S AN APP FOR THAT! 83
Building the Right Team 83
Assessing the Fit Between Elements in the Entrepreneurial Process 84
THE GREENING OF BUSINESS Small Businesses Go Green 85

Start-up and Beyond 85
LO-4 Starting up a Small Business 85

LO-5 Success and Failure in Small Business 87
Reasons for Success 87
Reasons for Failure 87
LO-6 Forms of Business Ownership 88

Summary of Learning Objectives 91
Questions and Exercises 93
Team Exercises 93
BUSINESS CASE 4 94

05 

THE GLOBAL CONTEXT OF BUSINESS 97

Not My Cup of Tea 97

The Contemporary Global Economy 99
LO-1 The Major World Marketplaces 100
LO-2 Emerging Markets: BRICS and Beyond 100
LO-3 Forms of Competitive Advantage 101
The Balance of Trade 103
The Balance of Payments 103
Exchange Rates 103
THERE'S AN APP FOR THAT! 104

LO-4 International Business Management 104
Going International 104
Levels of Involvement in International Business 105
International Organizational Structures 106
ENTREPRENEURSHIP AND NEW VENTURES Bugatti-Sedona: Charting a New Path 107

LO-5 Barriers to International Trade 108
Social and Cultural Differences 108
Economic Differences 108
Legal and Political Differences 108

LO-6 Overcoming Barriers to Trade 110
General Agreement on Tariffs and Trade (GATT) 110
World Trade Organization 111
The European Union 111
The North American Free Trade Agreement 111
MANAGING IN TURBULENT TIMES The Urge to Move 112
Major Agreements in the Works: TPP and CETA 112
Other Free Trade Agreements 112

Summary of Learning Objectives 113
Questions and Exercises 114
Team Exercises 114
BUSINESS CASE 5 115

Crafting a Business Plan 117
CBC VIDEO CASE 1-1 118
BUSINESS TODAY VIDEO CASE 1-1 118
BUSINESS TODAY VIDEO CASE 1-2 119

PART 2
THE BUSINESS OF MANAGING 120

06 

MANAGING THE BUSINESS ENTERPRISE 121

Google Keeps Growing 121

Who Are Managers? 123

LO-1 The Management Process 123
Planning 123
Organizing 124

Leading 124
Controlling 124
E-BUSINESS AND SOCIAL MEDIA SOLUTIONS The Truth About Your Online Customer Service 125
Management: Science or Art? 125
Becoming a Manager 125
MANAGING IN TURBULENT TIMES Challenges Facing Managers 126
What Should You Expect in a Management Job? 126
LO-2 Types of Managers 127
Levels of Management 127
Areas of Management 128
LO-3 Management Roles and Skills 129
Management Roles 129
Basic Management Skills 129
LO-4 Strategic Management 133
Setting Business Goals 133
Formulating Strategy 134
THE GREENING OF BUSINESS Some Complications in Setting Green Goals 134
THERE'S AN APP FOR THAT! 135
Levels of Strategy 136
LO-5 Contingency Planning and Crisis Management 137
Contingency Planning 137
Crisis Management 138
LO-6 Management and the Corporate Culture 138
Communicating the Culture and Managing Change 139
Summary of Learning Objectives 140
Questions and Exercises 141
Team Exercises 141
BUSINESS CASE 6 143

ORGANIZING THE BUSINESS ENTERPRISE 147
Time to Reorganize! 147
What Is Organizational Structure? 150
LO-1 Determinants of Organizational Structure 150
The Chain of Command 151
The Building Blocks of Organizational Structure 151
LO-2 Specialization 151
Departmentalization 152
Establishing the Decision-Making Hierarchy 153
LO-3 Assigning Tasks 154
Performing Tasks 154
Distributing Authority 155
Three Forms of Authority 155
LO-4 Basic Organizational Structures 157
The Functional Structure 157
The Divisional Structure 158
Project Organization 158
International Organization Structures 160
Organizational Design for the Twenty-First Century 160
Boundaryless Organization 160
THE GREENING OF BUSINESS Green Roof Structures 161
Team Organization 161
Virtual Organization 161
Learning Organization 161
LO-5 The Informal Organization 162
Informal Groups 162
The Organizational Grapevine 163
THERE'S AN APP FOR THAT! 163
MANAGING IN TURBULENT TIMES Gossip on the Grapevine 163
Summary of Learning Objectives 164
Questions and Exercises 165
Team Exercises 165
BUSINESS CASE 7 167

MANAGING HUMAN RESOURCES AND LABOUR RELATIONS 169
Can Different Generations Work Together? 169
LO-1 The Foundations of Human Resource Management 171
The Strategic Importance of HRM 171
Human Resource Planning 171
LO-2 Recruiting Human Resources 172
Selecting Human Resources 173
THERE'S AN APP FOR THAT! 173
THE GREENING OF BUSINESS "Green" Jobs in Surprising Places 174
LO-3 Developing Human Resources 175
New Employee Orientation 176
Training and Development 176
ENTREPRENEURSHIP AND NEW VENTURES LinkedIn: Strengthening Your Ability to Connect 177
Team Building and Group-Based Training 177
Evaluating Employee Performance 177
LO-4 Compensation and Benefits 178
Determining Basic Compensation 179
Incentive Programs 179
Benefits 180
LO-5 The Legal Context of HRM 181
Equal Employment Opportunity 181
Comparable Worth 181
Sexual Harassment 182
Employee Safety and Health 182
Retirement 182
MANAGING IN TURBULENT TIMES Defined Benefit Versus Defined Contribution Pension Plans 183

LO-6 New Challenges in the Changing Workplace 183
Managing Workforce Diversity 183
Managing Knowledge Workers 184
Managing Contingent Workers 184

LO-7 Dealing with Organized Labour 185
The Development of Canadian Labour Unions 185
Unionism Today 185
The Future of Unions 186

LO-8 The Legal Environment for Unions in Canada 186
Federal Legislation—The Canada Labour Code 186
Provincial Labour Legislation 187
Union Organizing Strategy 187
Union Security 188
Types of Unions 188

LO-9 Collective Bargaining 189
Reaching Agreement on the Contract's Terms 189
Contract Issues 189
When Bargaining Fails 190
Conciliation, Mediation, and Arbitration 191

Summary of Learning Objectives 191
Questions and Exercises 193
Team Exercises 193
BUSINESS CASE 8 194

09 MOTIVATING, SATISFYING, AND LEADING EMPLOYEES 197

Satisfaction, Productivity, and Employee Engagement 197

LO-1 Forms of Employee Behaviour 200

LO-2 Individual Differences Among Employees 201
Personality 201
Other Personality Traits 202
Attitudes at Work 202
E-BUSINESS AND SOCIAL MEDIA SOLUTIONS Employers Are Judging Your Social Life 203

LO-3 Matching People and Jobs 204
Psychological Contracts 204
The Person–Job Fit 204

Motivation in the Workplace 204
Classical Theory 205
Early Behavioural Theory 205

LO-4 The Human Resources Model: Theories X and Y 205
Contemporary Motivation Theory 207

LO-5 Strategies for Enhancing Motivation 208
Reinforcement/Behaviour Modification 208
Goal-Setting Theory 208
MANAGING IN TURBULENT TIMES Carrot or Stick? 209
Participative Management and Empowerment 210
Team Management 210
Job Enrichment and Redesign 211
Modified Work Schedules 211
THE GREENING OF BUSINESS The Four-Day Workweek and Telecommuting: Are They Really Green? 213

LO-6 Leadership and Motivation 214
Leadership and Power 214

LO-7 Approaches to Leadership 215
THERE'S AN APP FOR THAT! 216

LO-8 Recent Trends in Leadership 217

Summary of Learning Objectives 219
Questions and Exercises 221
Team Exercises 222
BUSINESS CASE 9 222

Crafting a Business Plan 224
CBC VIDEO CASE 2-1 225
BUSINESS TODAY VIDEO CASE 2-1 226
BUSINESS TODAY VIDEO CASE 2-2 227

PART 3 MANAGING OPERATIONS AND INFORMATION 228

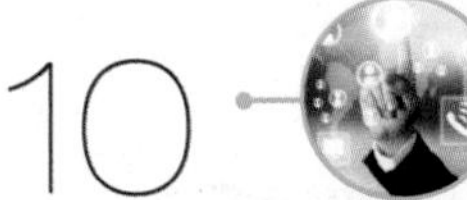

10 OPERATIONS MANAGEMENT, PRODUCTIVITY, AND QUALITY 229

Big Changes in Canadian Manufacturing 229

LO-1 What Does "Operations" Mean Today? 232
Changes in Operations 232

Creating Value Through Operations 232
LO-2 Differences Between Service and Manufacturing Operations 232
THE GREENING OF BUSINESS Producing Green Energy 233
LO-3 Operations Processes 235
Business Strategy As the Driver of Operations 236

LO-4 Operations Planning 237
Capacity Planning 237
Location Planning 237
Layout Planning 237
MANAGING IN TURBULENT TIMES Will Robots Take Your Job? 239
Quality Planning 240
Methods Planning 240

Operations Scheduling 240
The Master Operations Schedule 240
Detailed Schedules 241
Staff Schedules and Computer-Based Scheduling 241
Project Scheduling 241

Operations Control 243
Materials Management 243
Production Process Control 243

LO-5 The Productivity–Quality Connection 244
Meeting the Productivity Challenge 244

Meeting the Quality Challenge 245
LO-6 Managing for Quality 245
THERE'S AN APP FOR THAT! 246
Tools for Quality Assurance 247

Summary of Learning Objectives 250
Questions and Exercises 251
Team Exercises 251
BUSINESS CASE 10 252

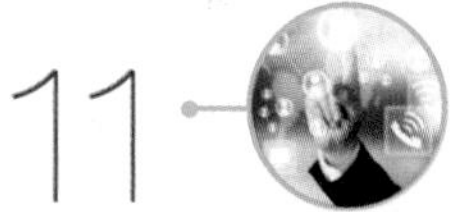

11 UNDERSTANDING ACCOUNTING 255

Searching for Stolen Maple Syrup: Accounting for Missing Inventory 255

What Is Accounting, and Who Uses Accounting Information? 257

LO-1 Who Are Accountants and What Do They Do? 258
Financial Versus Managerial Accounting 258
Professional Accountants 258
THERE'S AN APP FOR THAT! 259
Accounting Services 259
Private Accountants 260

LO-2 The Accounting Equation 261
Assets and Liabilities 261
Owners' Equity 261

LO-3 Financial Statements 262
Balance Sheets 262
LO-4 Income Statements 263
ENTREPRENEURSHIP AND NEW VENTURES Accounting Practices for the Small Business 264
Statements of Cash Flows 265
The Budget: An Internal Financial Statement 265

LO-5 Analyzing Financial Statements 266
Solvency Ratios: Borrower's Ability to Repay Debt 266
MANAGING IN TURBULENT TIMES The Fairness Dilemma: What Is an Asset's Real Value? 266
Profitability Ratios: Earnings Power for Owners 267
Activity Ratios: How Efficiently Is the Firm Using Its Resources? 267

LO-6 Bringing Ethics into the Accounting Equation 268
Why Accounting Ethics? 268

LO-7 The Evolving Role of the Modern Accountant 269

Summary of Learning Objectives 270
Questions and Exercises 271
Team Exercises 272
BUSINESS CASE 11 273

CHAPTER SUPPLEMENT 03 274

Crafting a Business Plan 287
CBC VIDEO CASE 3-1 288
BUSINESS TODAY VIDEO CASE 3-1 288
BUSINESS TODAY VIDEO CASE 3-2 289

PART 4
PRINCIPLES OF MARKETING 290

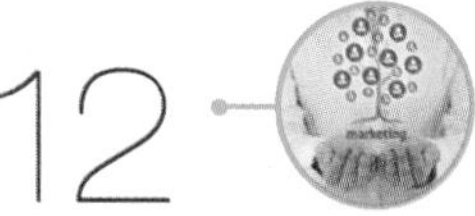

12 UNDERSTANDING MARKETING PRINCIPLES AND DEVELOPING PRODUCTS 291

P&G Marketing: Dealing with a Shrinking Middle Class 291

LO-1 What Is Marketing? 293
Delivering Value 293
Goods, Services, and Ideas 293
Relationship Marketing and Customer Relationship Management 294
The Marketing Environment 294
THE GREENING OF BUSINESS Feeling the Pressure for "Green" 295

LO-2 Developing the Marketing Plan 296
Strategy: The Marketing Mix 297
THERE'S AN APP FOR THAT! 297
Product 297
Pricing 297
Place (Distribution) 298
Promotion 298

LO-3 Marketing Strategy: Market Segmentation, Target Marketing, and Positioning 298
Identifying Market Segments 299

LO-4 Marketing Research 300
The Research Process 301
Research Methods 301

LO-5 Understanding Consumer Behaviour 301
E-BUSINESS AND SOCIAL MEDIA SOLUTIONS Retailers Are Watching and Tracking You 302
Influences on Consumer Behaviour 302
The Consumer Buying Process 303

LO-6 Organizational Marketing and Buying Behaviour 303
Business Marketing 303
B2B Buying Behaviour 304

LO-7 What Is a Product? 304
The Value Package 304
Classifying Goods and Services 304
The Product Mix 305

LO-8 Developing New Products and Branding 305
The New Product Development Process 306
Product Life Cycle 307
ENTREPRENEURSHIP AND NEW VENTURES This Business Is Appsolutely Booming 307
Identifying Products: Branding and Packaging 309
Packaging Products 310
Labelling Products 310

Summary of Learning Objectives 311
Questions and Exercises 313
Team Exercises 313
BUSINESS CASE 12 314

13

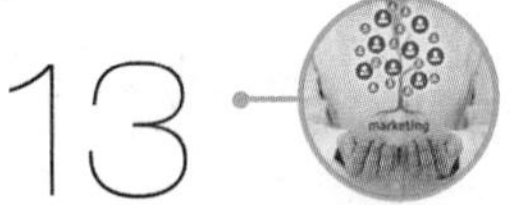

PRICING, PROMOTING, AND DISTRIBUTING PRODUCTS 317

Premium Pricing, Rising Market Share 317

LO-1 Determining Prices 319
Pricing to Meet Business Objectives 319
Price-Setting Tools 319

LO-2 Pricing Strategies and Tactics 321
Pricing Strategies 321
Pricing Tactics 321
THERE'S AN APP FOR THAT! 321

LO-3 Promoting Products and Services 322
Promotional Strategies 322
The Promotional Mix 322

LO-4 Advertising Promotions and Media 323
Advertising Media 323
ENTREPRENEURSHIP AND NEW VENTURES Promoting Music Artists 326

LO-5 Personal Selling, Sales Promotions, Direct (or Interactive) Marketing, Public Relations, and Publicity 326
Personal Selling 326
Sales Promotions 327
Publicity and Public Relations 327
MANAGING IN TURBULENT TIMES Direct Mail: Back from a Slow Death? 328

LO-6 The Distribution Mix 329
Intermediaries and Distribution Channels 329
Distribution Strategies 330
Channel Conflict and Channel Leadership 330

LO-7 The Role of Intermediaries 330
Wholesaling 330
Retailing 331
E-BUSINESS AND SOCIAL MEDIA SOLUTIONS Bye-Bye Cash Registers, Hello Tablets! 331

LO-8 Physical Distribution 333
Warehousing Operations 333
Transportation Operations 333
Distribution Through Supply Chains as a Marketing Strategy 333
THE GREENING OF BUSINESS Unexpected Outcomes 334

Summary of Learning Objectives 334
Questions and Exercises 336
Team Exercises 337
BUSINESS CASE 13 338

Crafting a Business Plan 339
CBC VIDEO CASE 4-1 339
BUSINESS TODAY VIDEO CASE 4-1 340
BUSINESS TODAY VIDEO CASE 4-2 341

PART 5

MANAGING FINANCIAL ISSUES 342

14

MONEY AND BANKING 343

Canadian Mortgages: Bulls, Bears, and Banks 343

LO-1 What Is Money? 345
The Characteristics of Money 346
The Functions of Money 346
The Spendable Money Supply: M-1 346
M-1 Plus the Convertible Money Supply: M-2 347
Credit Cards and Debit Cards: Plastic Money? 347

LO-2 The Canadian Financial System 347
Financial Institutions 348

Financial Pillar #1—Chartered Banks 348
Services Offered by Banks 348
THERE'S AN APP FOR THAT! 349
E-BUSINESS AND SOCIAL MEDIA SOLUTIONS When Cash Gets Scarce, Businesses Switch to Internet Bartering 350
Bank Loans 350
Banks as Creators of Money 350
Other Changes in Banking 351
LO-3 The Bank of Canada 351

LO-4 Financial Pillar #2—Alternate Banks 353
Trust Companies 353
Credit Unions/Caisses Populaires 353

Financial Pillar #3—Specialized Lending and Savings Intermediaries 353
Life Insurance Companies 353
Factoring Companies 353
Financial Corporations 353
Venture Capital Firms 354
Pension Funds 354

Financial Pillar #4—Investment Dealers 354

Other Sources of Funds 354
Government Financial Institutions and Granting Agencies 354
International Sources of Funds 355

LO-5 International Banking and Finance 355
Currency Values and Exchange Rates 355
The International Payments Process 356
The International Bank Structure 356
MANAGING IN TURBULENT TIMES What's the Deal with Bitcoin? 357

Summary of Learning Objectives 358
Questions and Exercises 359
Team Exercises 359
BUSINESS CASE 14 360

CHAPTER SUPPLEMENT 04 362

15 

FINANCIAL DECISIONS AND RISK MANAGEMENT 365

Piles of Cash 365

LO-1 The Role of the Financial Manager 367

Objectives of the Financial Manager 367
Responsibilities of the Financial Manager 367

LO-2 Why Businesses Need Funds 368

Short-Term (Operating) Expenditures 368
Long-Term (Capital) Expenditures 369

LO-3 Sources of Short-Term Funds 369

Trade Credit 369
Secured Short-Term Loans 370
Unsecured Short-Term Loans 370

LO-4 Sources of Long-Term Funds 371

Debt Financing 371

THE GREENING OF BUSINESS Green Bonds 372

LO-5 Equity Financing 373
Hybrid Financing: Preferred Stock 374
Choosing Between Debt and Equity Financing 375
The Risk-Return Relationship 375

Securities Markets 377

Investment Banking 377
Stock Exchanges 377
LO-6 Buying and Selling Securities 378
Financing Securities Purchases 380

E-BUSINESS AND SOCIAL MEDIA SOLUTIONS Stock Trading at Your Fingertips 381

LO-7 Other Investments 382

Mutual Funds 382

MANAGING IN TURBULENT TIMES Short Selling: Herbalife and Sino-Forest 382

Exchange-Traded Funds 383
Hedge Funds 383
Commodities 383

THERE'S AN APP FOR THAT! 383

Securities Regulation 384

Financial Management for Small Businesses 384

Establishing Bank Credit and Trade Credit 384

ENTREPRENEURSHIP AND NEW VENTURES Crowdfunding: Some Changes in the Works 385

Venture Capital 385
Planning for Cash-Flow Requirements 385

LO-8 Risk Management 386

Coping with Risk 386

Summary of Learning Objectives 387
Questions and Exercises 389
Team Exercises 389
BUSINESS CASE 15 390

CHAPTER SUPPLEMENT 05 392

Crafting a Business Plan 394
CBC VIDEO CASE 5-1 394
BUSINESS TODAY VIDEO CASE 5-1 395
BUSINESS TODAY VIDEO CASE 5-2 395

Endnotes and Source Notes 397
Name and Organization Index 423
Subject Index 434

PREFACE

HELPING STUDENTS BUILD A SOLID BUSINESS KNOWLEDGE FOUNDATION

Welcome to the eighth Canadian edition of *Business Essentials*. If you're like many students, you may be starting this term with some questions about why you're here. You may be taking this course at a community college, CEGEP, or university, and you may be taking it in a traditional classroom setting or online. Whatever the case, you may be wondering just what you're supposed to get from this course and how it will benefit you—in short, "How will this help me?"

This is a survey course designed to introduce you to the exciting and challenging world of business, both in Canada and elsewhere. It is designed to fit the needs of a wide variety of students. You may be taking it as the first step toward earning a degree in business, or you may be thinking about business and want to know more about it, or you may know you want to study business but are unsure of the area you want to pursue. You may plan to major in another field but want some basic business background and are taking this course as an elective. Or you may be here because this course is required or a prerequisite for another course. Whatever your situation, this course will be helpful to you.

If you don't have a lot of work experience, you might be uncertain regarding what the business world is all about. If you have a lot of work experience, you might be a bit skeptical about what you can actually learn from an introductory course. One of our biggest challenges is to write a book that meets the needs of such a diverse student population, especially when we acknowledge the legitimacy of your right to ask, "How will this help me?" We also want to do our best to ensure that you find the course challenging, interesting, and useful. To achieve this goal, we think it is helpful to use the old metaphor about people wearing different "hats" as they go through life. Every individual has different roles to play in different settings. For example, your roles might include student, child, spouse, employee, friend, and/or parent. You can think of each of these as requiring a different hat—when you play the role of a student, for example, you wear one hat, but when you leave campus and go to your part-time job, you put on a different one. From the perspective of studying and interfacing with the world of *business*, there are at least four distinct "hats" that you might wear:

- *The employee hat.* One hat is "worn" as an employee working for a business. Most people wear this hat throughout their working career. To wear it successfully, you will need to understand your "place" in the organization—your job duties and responsibilities, how to get along with others, how to work with your boss, what your organization is all about, and so on. You'll begin to see how best to wear this hat as you learn more about organizing business enterprises in Chapter 7 and how organizations manage their human resources in Chapter 8, and as in several other places in this book.
- *The employer or boss hat.* Another business hat many people wear is as an employer or boss. Whether you start your own business or get promoted within someone else's, people will be working for you. You'll still need to know your job duties and responsibilities, but you'll also need to understand how to manage other people—how to motivate and reward them, how to lead them, how to deal with conflict among them, and the legal parameters that may affect how you treat them. Chapters 3, 6, 8, and 9 provide a lot of information about how you can best wear this hat, although information about the role of employer is found throughout the book.
- *The consumer hat.* Even if you don't work for a business, you will still wear the hat of a consumer. Whenever you fill your car with Petro-Canada gasoline, purchase something on Amazon, buy clothes at Zara or Reitmans, or download a song from iTunes, you're consuming products or services created by businesses. To wear this hat effectively, you need to understand how to assess the value of what you're buying, your rights as a consumer, and so on. We discuss how you can best wear this hat in Chapters 1, 3, 12, and 13.
- *The investor hat.* The final business hat many people wear is that of an investor. You may buy your own business or work for a company that allows you to buy its stock. You may also invest in other companies through the purchase of stocks or shares of a mutual fund. In order for you to invest wisely, you must understand some basics, such as financial markets, business earnings, and the costs of investment. Chapters 4, 11, 14, and 15 will help you learn how to best wear this hat.

Most people wear more than one of these hats at the same time. Regardless of how many hats you wear or when you may be putting them on, you will interact with many different businesses in different ways. Knowing how to best wear all of these hats is what this book is all about.

The world is populated with a breathtaking array of businesses and business opportunities. Big and small businesses, established and new businesses, broad-based and niche businesses, successful and unsuccessful businesses, global and domestic businesses—regardless of where your future plans take you, we hope you will look back on this course as one of your positive first steps.

Keep in mind that what you get out of this course depends on at least three factors. One is this book, and the information about business you will acquire as a result of reading it. Another is your instructor, a dedicated professional who wants to help you grow and develop intellectually and academically. The third is YOU. Learning is an active process that requires you to be a major participant. Simply memorizing the key terms and concepts in this book might help you achieve an acceptable course grade, but true learning requires that you read, study, discuss, question, review, experience, evaluate—and wear the four hats—as you go along. Tests and homework are necessary, but we hope you will finish this course with new knowledge and increased enthusiasm for the world of business. Your instructor will do his or her part to facilitate your learning. The rest, then, is up to you. We wish you success.

CHAPTER MATERIAL

NEW & UPDATED! Chapter Opening Cases Each chapter begins with a description of a problem or opportunity that is facing a Canadian company, or a general issue that impacts many different businesses in Canada. These chapter opening cases help students to bridge the gap between theory and practice. Topics include supermarket mergers, the fair trade movement, stories about Canadian entrepreneurs, corporate reorganizations, changes in Canadian manufacturing, new product marketing, credit-card traps, and many others that will be of great interest to students. Questions for Discussion at the end of each opening case direct student attention to important issues in the chapter that they should consider.

Google Keeps Growing

Eric Carr/Alamy

Sergey Brin and Larry Page met at Stanford University in 1995, when both were graduate students in computer science. At the time, Page was working on a software development project that was designed to create an index of websites by scouring sites for keywords and other linkages. Brin joined him on the project, and when they were satisfied that they had developed something with commercial value, they tried to license the technology to other search companies. As luck would have it, they couldn't find a buyer and settled instead for procuring enough investment capital to keep refining and testing their product.

In 2000, Brin and Page ran across the description of a business model on the concept of selling advertising in the form of sponsored links and search-specific advertisements. They adapted it to their own concept and went into business for themselves, eventually building Google into the world's largest search engine. Google processes more than 11 billion searches a month by a user base of 380 million people in 181 different countries using 146 languages. Following an initial public offering (IPO) in 2004, the company's market capitalization increased to more than $43 billion by 2012, when Google controlled about two-thirds of the search market. That was more than Microsoft and Yahoo combined.

Google is much more than a search engine. Services include searches for news, shopping, local businesses,

NEW & UPDATED! There's an App for That! Each chapter includes a description of several useful apps related to the chapter material. These apps allow students to understand business concepts in new and dynamic ways.

THERE'S AN APP FOR THAT!

APP DETAILS	PLATFORMS
1. **McKinsey Insights** **Source:** McKinsey and Company **Key Features:** The latest thinking on the biggest issues facing senior executives, everything from leadership and corporate strategy to globalization and technology's impact on business and society.	Apple, Android
2. **SWOT Chart** **Source:** K. Kaleeswaran **Key Features:** Strategic planning method used to evaluate strengths, weaknesses, opportunities, and threats.	Apple, BlackBerry, Windows
3. **Goal Tracker: SmartGoals** **Source:** MSurf Lab **Key Features:** Tool to help you set SMART (specific, measurable, attainable, reasonable and timely) goals.	Android

APP DISCOVERY EXERCISE

Since app availability changes, conduct your own search for the "Top Three" management apps and identify the key features.

NEW & UPDATED! Boxed Inserts on Key Topics The text contains four series of boxed inserts positioned at strategic points in the chapters. The first—*E-Business and Social Media Solutions*—describes how rapidly changing technology has provided business firms with many new ways to connect with customers. The second—*Managing in Turbulent Times*—explains how businesses in Canada and elsewhere are trying to cope with the volatility and uncertainty that exists in the contemporary business world. The third—*Entrepreneurship and New Ventures*—provides real-life examples of entrepreneurs who saw an opportunity to provide a new product or service in the marketplace, and the activities they carried out in order to be successful. The fourth—*The Greening of Business*—analyzes the steps businesses are taking to be more environmentally friendly. Critical thinking questions appear at the end of each boxed insert to motivate students to think about what they have read.

E-BUSINESS AND SOCIAL MEDIA SOLUTIONS

The Truth About Your Online Customer Service

Effective decision making requires good, timely information. Retailers in particular are constantly monitoring trends and competitor actions in order to improve their standing with consumers.

Online purchases keep increasing as shoppers enjoy easy access to more and more products from the comfort of home. However, poor customer service can disappoint and anger customers, resulting in lost sales. So how good is a company's online customer service, especially compared to that of its online competitors? StellaService Inc. answered that question by providing a better way to measure online service, enabling it to become a market winner for online shoppers and retailers alike.

Following its start-up in 2010, StellaService (Stella) spent two years gathering data on customer satisfaction with thousands of online retailers, including giants like Amazon.com. They measure satisfaction in four service areas—phone support, email support, delivery, and returns/refunds—for each retailer. Each area includes from 9 to as many as 25 different measurements. Phone support, for example, considers speed of answering the call and respondent's knowledge of the product among its nine measurements. Delivery measurements include delivery time and product accuracy. By combining the various measurements, consumers can find summary scores for each of the four service areas. Results provide rankings of competitors showing where each retailer currently stands relative to competitors in each of the four areas of service. Rankings allow period-to-period tracking, revealing trends for improvements in each of the areas across time for each company.

With these measurements Stella hopes to better inform consumers on the range of customer service they can expect from online retailers. Knowing that success hinges on the validity and believability of their methods, Stella uses an independent third-party rating system. "Secret shoppers" (trained employees) use strict and controlled measurement methods as they engage online retailers via emails, phone calls, and live chats to purchase, await deliveries, or make returns for refunds. As added assurance for validity the company maintains a "Customer Service Measurement Process Audit" detailing its measurements and procedures for gathering and processing data, with specific steps to assure accuracy and validity.

Recently, in its Independent Auditing Report, KPMG stated that Stella's methodologies are complying with their stated policies. This confirmation should help in Stella's latest move: offering subscription services to retailers. Subscribers can, for the first time, receive measured data showing their standing, along with competitors, on phone support, email support, delivery, and returns/refunds. This service allows retailers to base decisions on objective and independent information about their online customer service. It looks like the company is on to something. They have already enlisted major retailers like Walmart and Ralph Lauren, raised more than US$22 million in venture capital, and received the greatest compliment (as well as a financial boost) when Google licensed StellaService's data in order to rate retailers on its search engine.

CRITICAL THINKING QUESTIONS

1. How do the results of customer service reports influence a manager's decisions? In answering this question refer to Figure 6.1 (the control process).

NEW! Examples of Business Practice In addition to the boxed inserts, each chapter contains numerous examples of how actual Canadian and international businesses operate so that students can gain a better understanding of the dynamics of business practice in both Canada and elsewhere. These examples—which range in length from one sentence to several paragraphs—help students understand concepts that are discussed in the text.

NEW & UPDATED! Key Terms In each chapter, the key terms that students should know are highlighted in the text and defined in the margin.

NEW & UPDATED! Figures and Tables The latest available data appear in tables and figures throughout the text.

END-OF-CHAPTER MATERIAL

UPDATED! Summary of Learning Objectives The material in each chapter is concisely summarized, using the learning objectives as the organizing scheme. This helps students understand the main points that were presented in the chapter.

NEW & UPDATED! Assisted-Grading Writing Assignments Two types of questions are included at the end of each chapter: *analysis questions* (which require students to think beyond simple factual recall and apply the concepts they have read about) and *application exercises* (which ask students to apply what they have learned). The exercises, designed to help students increase their understanding of how business firms actually operate, require students to engage in practical activities such as interviewing managers about concepts and issues discussed in the chapter. Selected end-of-chapter questions (identified by the symbol >>>) have been built as *assisted-graded assignments* within MyBizLab to help assess students' written communication skills. Each question is built with marking rubrics to help facilitate the grading of these assignments.

QUESTIONS AND EXERCISES

QUESTIONS FOR ANALYSIS

1. How are the four *functions* of management related to the five *skills* of management? Use examples to clarify your answer.
2. What is the relationship between Mintzberg's *roles* of management and the more traditional *functions* of management? Use examples to clarify your answer.
3. Identify the managers by level and area at your college or university.
4. Can you identify any organizations where the technical skills of top managers are more important than human relations or conceptual skills? Can you identify organizations in which conceptual skills are not important at all?
5. What differences might you expect to find in the corporate cultures of a 100-year-old manufacturing firm based in Winnipeg and a 5-year-old e-commerce firm based in Ottawa?
6. Consider the various corporate-level strategies discussed in the chapter (concentration, growth, integration, diversification, investment, reduction). What is the relationship between these various strategies? Are they mutually exclusive? Complementary? Explain.

APPLICATION EXERCISES

7. Interview a manager at any level of a local company. Identify the manager's job according to level and area. Explain what planning, organizing, directing, and controlling mean in terms of the manager's job. Give examples. Also indicate which management skills are most important for the manager's job.
8. Review the example of the decisions made by Airbus and Boeing regarding new large aircraft. Then research the most current information on the status of the two planes. Which company seems to have made the better decision?
9. Interview an administrator at your college or university and get that person's views on the school's strengths and weaknesses and on the threats and opportunities the school is facing. Then use this information to write up a SWOT analysis for the school.
10. Select any organization of which you are a member (your company, your family, your place of worship, or a club). Explain the relevance of the management functions of planning, organizing, directing, and controlling for that organization.

NEW & UPDATED! Building Your Business Skills Exercise This feature asks students to examine some specific aspect of business. While working in a group context, students gather data about an interesting business issue, and then develop a written report or a class presentation based on the information that was gathered. Each exercise begins with a list of goals, a description of the situation, a step-by-step methodology for proceeding, and follow-up questions to help students focus their responses to the challenge.

NEW & UPDATED! Exercising Your Ethics: Team Exercise A team ethics exercise describes a situation that involves an ethical dilemma. Students are then asked several questions that focus on how to approach and resolve the dilemma. In the exercise, students take on the role of employee, owner, customer, or investor and examine a chapter-related business ethics dilemma through the perspective of that role. By working as a team, students learn how to cooperate, see an ethical dilemma from various points of view, and decide what outcome is ultimately best in each situation.

NEW & UPDATED! End-of-Chapter Case Each chapter concludes with a case study that focuses on a real Canadian or international company. The cases are designed to help students apply the chapter material to a company or an issue currently in the news. At the end of each case, several Questions for Discussion guide students in their analysis.

BUSINESS CASE 6

CORPORATE CULTURE

Corporate culture is sometimes defined simply as "the way we do things around here." A corporate culture can emphasize a variety of things. Consider the following examples:

- At Telus Corp., *customer service* is the cornerstone of its culture; during one quarter in 2014, the company attracted 113 000 new customers, more than either BCE or Rogers.
- At competitor Rogers Communications, the culture emphasizes the *well-being of employees*; this includes offering employees discounts on products.
- At CIBC, the culture includes three core values: teamwork, trust, and accountability; these three values create a culture of providing high quality service to *customers*.
- At MEG Energy, the corporate culture encourages all employees to share *innovative ideas*; this leads to advancements in sustainable technology.

nikitos77/Fotolia

Two interesting questions arise regarding corporate culture:

1. What happens if two companies with widely differing cultures merge?
2. What happens if there is a culture clash within an organization? That is, what if top managers disagree with lower-level employees about the kind of culture the organization should have?

MERGING COMPANIES WITH DIFFERENT CULTURES

During the past few years, there have been several high-profile mergers between companies with different cultures, and these combinations often caused difficulties.

Vale and Glencore Plc. In 2014, the Brazilian mining company Vale and the Swiss miner Glencore Plc discussed merging their nickel assets in Sudbury. But the idea was finally abandoned when it became clear that the two companies had significantly different corporate cultures. One point of concern was each company's view of risk: Vale's culture was risk-averse, while Glencore's culture was much more risk-seeking. There were also disagreements about how to share the costs of the merger. This is an interesting situation, because a few years earlier Inco and Falconbridge had talked about combining their Sudbury assets, but then Inco was purchased by Vale, and Xstrata purchased Falconbridge. Then Glencore bought Xstrata.

Vale and Inco. When Vale bought Inco, there was also a "culture clash." Shortly after the purchase, there was a meeting of executives of both companies, but the meeting ended suddenly when one of the Brazilian managers lost his temper. That was the first sign the cultures of the companies were different enough that problems were going to be evident. Over the next few months, many Canadian managers, engineers, and operating staff left the company. For example, of 29 managers who were involved in a strategy session shortly after the merger, only 6 were still there a few months later.

In retrospect, it is clear that the cultures of the companies were quite different prior to the takeover. At Inco, there was a constant exchange of ideas, and decentralized decision making was encouraged by top management. But at Vale, top managers gave orders and expected them to be followed. Not surprisingly, Vale encountered resistance from Inco executives who did not agree with that approach. There were also differences in the products the companies focused on before Vale bought Inco. Vale's focus was on iron ore, a basic commodity mined using a relatively simple technology. But the underground mining of nickel, a key ingredient in stainless steel, is a more complex undertaking. One Inco manager likened nickel mining to having a PhD, while iron ore mining was like having a high school diploma. Canadian managers obviously felt some disdain for their new Brazilian bosses.

The cultural differences between the two companies were not limited to the top level of management. Some years earlier, the miner's union had given up annual wage increases in return for a bonus based on the price of nickel. When the price of nickel soared, workers

END-OF-PART MATERIAL

NEW! Video Cases Several video cases are presented at the end of each of the five major parts of the text. Some of the videos are from the CBC *Dragons Den* series, others from Pearson's *Business Today* series. The instructor can show them in class and then either conduct a discussion using the questions at the end of the written case summary as a guide or ask students to complete a written assignment that requires answering the questions at the end of the case. This approach adds a positive dynamic to classes, because students will be able to relate text material to actual Canadian business situations.

CBC VIDEO CASE 3-1

ZERONEXT

THE COMPANY

Mathieu Desjardins and Claude Pinet, entrepreneurs from Montreal, are trying to change the look—indeed the very thinking—behind wine cooler technology. The Renoir is a design-driven, wall-mounted, silent fridge that stores 30 bottles and displays them like a piece of artwork. This is not like the standard appliance it attempts to replace. It is unique not only in aesthetic design but also in functional design, with side access panels and cutting-edge electronic cooling that does not require a compressor. It is silent . . . it is beautiful . . . and it comes with five optional art frames to complete the look. The Renoir retails for about $4500. For more details on the company, go to zeronext.com.

THE PITCH

The owners of Zeronext asked for $500 000 in return for 20 percent ownership of the company (valued at $2 500 000). Zeronext has projected sales of approximately $1 million dollars (by year-end). Mathieu and Claude are seeking the investment and the support of the dragons to help them expand and to address existing interest in Europe and the United States.

THE DRAGONS' POINT OF VIEW

The dragons seemed very interested in the product, and they loved the design, but the consensus was that Zeronext should have charged a higher price in order to increase the margins after Mathieu revealed that the Renoir had a 40 percent markup (when sold to distributors). Arlene was concerned; she indicated that they probably only ended up with 10 percent on the bottom line. Claude said that the margins were going to improve in the coming months because of the economies of scale, which are associated with higher sales volume. However, the dragons insisted that they should increase the price by a few hundred dollars. This is a premium product and charging $4999 rather than $4499 would probably not make a huge difference to consumer demand but it would mean a lot to the company's bottom line.

Vikram Vij began the process of negotiation by offering to pay the $500 000 asking price for a 35 percent stake rather than 20 percent. He also seemed confident that this product would be a good fit for luxury condo builders in Vancouver. Soon after, Michael Wekerle increased the stakes when he offered $1 000 000 for 40 percent; he also asked Jim Treliving to join him on the deal. He believed that this product should be targeted at high-end hotels. Jim Treliving agreed to join forces with Michael. Arlene Dickinson said she loved the product but only as a potential consumer not as an investor. Finally, Dave Chilton told the owners not to give up the extra equity; he offered exactly what they asked: $500 000 for 20 percent.

THE OUTCOME

After discussing the pros and cons of the offers, the entrepreneurs decided that they would indeed give up 40 percent of the company for $1 million to Jim Treliving and Michael Wekerle. They believed that giving up the higher percentage was worth it if the extra funding could help them expand quicker into the U.S. market.

QUESTIONS FOR DISCUSSION

1. In this section of the course we cover key accounting terms such as *revenues, expenses, margins,* and *markups*. Trace the discussion that the owners had with the dragons, and highlight the key accounting terms and how they were used by the dragons to help them make their points and analyze the situation.
2. Do you think the owners did a good job in this pitch? (From an accounting point of view? From an operations point of view?) What was the high point and what was the low point from the owners' perspective?
3. Do you think it was wise for the owners of Zeronext to sell 40 percent equity in the company? In the short term? In the long term? (Support your answers.)

Source: "ZeroNext," *Dragons' Den*, Season 9, Episode 19 (April 22, 2015).

BUSINESS TODAY VIDEO CASE 3-1

RUDI'S BAKERY

Rudi's Organic Bakery operates a state-of-the-art, small-batch bakery. The company bakes about 16 million loaves of bread annually and ships its products across the country. When Hanno Holm, the chief operating officer, first started working at Rudi's, there was a lot of discussion among employees that there was a quality problem due to excessive variation in the colour of the loaves being made. In one three-month period, about 4.5 million loaves were produced, and the company received just 60 complaints. But none of those complaints were actually about the *colour* of the bread; they were about *bubbles* in the bread.

Holm realized that the company had to define quality the same way consumers defined it, and in this case it meant that Rudi's had to focus on reducing the number of bubbles instead of the colour. Since the bubbles could be seen in uncut loaves, they had to develop a system for solving the problem. With some research they found they could buy a machine that broke air bubbles as the loaves were being produced. The result was a more uniform mass of dough and far fewer bubbles. This reduced consumer complaints. Holm says that quality management means focusing on how to solve quality problems that consumers talk about, not just ones that workers talk about.

QUESTIONS FOR DISCUSSION

1. How is "quality" defined in the text? Is Hanno Holm's definition of quality consistent with the text definition? Explain.
2. How is the concept of total quality management relevant here?
3. What different tools for quality assurance are available to managers? Which ones would be most appropriate for Rudi's bakery?

Crafting a Business Plan The business plan project is tailor-made to match and reinforce text content. It is *software-independent* and provides students with an easy-to-understand template that they work from as they create their business plans. The business plan project is divided into logical sections, and each part (e.g., marketing, production, finance, and so on) is located at the end of the section where that material is covered. With the five parts of the business plan distributed throughout the book, students can gradually apply the concepts they've learned in the chapters to their business plans throughout the course.

SUPPLEMENTAL CONTENT

There are five supplements to the text.

- The first supplement—**A Brief History of Business in Canada**—is found at the end of Chapter 1. The material in this supplement (summarized in the text and included in its entirety online in MyBizLab) outlines the development of business activity in Canada over the past 300 years.

- The second supplement—**Business Law**—is found at the end of Chapter 3. It includes key topics such as contracts, the concept of agency, warranties, copyrights and trademarks, and bankruptcy.
- The third supplement—**Using Technology to Manage Information in the Internet and Social Media Era**—is included at the end of Chapter 11. It focuses on the impact IT has had on the business world, the IT resources businesses have at their disposal, the threats that information technology pose for businesses, and how businesses protect themselves from these threats. There is also an important section on the role of social media platforms in the modern business world.
- The fourth supplement—**Managing Your Personal Finances: A Synopsis**—is found at the end of Chapter 14. The material in this supplement (briefly summarized in the text and included in its entirety online in MyBizLab) presents a down-to-earth, hands-on approach that will help students manage their personal finances. Included in the supplement is a worksheet for determining personal net worth, insightful examples demonstrating the time value of money, a method for determining how much money to invest now in order to build a nest egg of a certain size, suggestions on how to manage credit-card debt, guidelines for purchasing a house, and a personalized worksheet for setting financial goals.
- The fifth supplement—**Insurance as Risk Management**—is found at the end of Chapter 15. It provides information on insurable versus uninsurable risks, the different types of insurance products available, and special forms of business insurance.

CHAPTER SUPPLEMENT 03

Using Technology to Manage Information in the Internet and Social Media Era

Throughout the text, we examine how the internet and the emergence of social media have improved communications, revolutionized distribution, augmented human resource practices, revolutionized industries (and threatened others), developed new marketing communication channels, and changed the most basic business systems. In this supplement, we will begin by providing additional information about the internet and social media. We will also examine the evolving role of technology in managing information.

INTERNET USAGE

Before we look into the specific impact of the internet on business, let's examine some of the key Canadian internet statistics. As regards speed, Hong Kong has the fastest internet connections in the world; Canada ranks 17th.[1] However, Canada ranks ninth among G20 countries in terms of internet contribution to GDP. Canadian also spend an average of 36.3 hours per month on their computers (not including the vast amount of time spent on mobile devices) which ranks first in the world.[2] In addition, 94 percent of Canadians who live in households with incomes above $85 000 are connected (only 56 percent for households with incomes below $30 000 per year).[3] These figures will continue to increase for the next few years.

The federal government has also set its sights on increasing and improving the connectivity in rural settings. The improved infrastructure will help increase rural access, build further opportunities for companies wishing to sell to rural Canadian clients, and provide more incentive and opportunity for small businesses to operate in rural settings.[4]

THE IMPACT OF INFORMATION TECHNOLOGY (IT)

No matter where we go, we can't escape the impact of **information technology (IT)**—the various devices for creating, storing, exchanging, and using information in diverse modes, including images, voice, multimedia, and business data. We see ads all the time for the latest smartphones, laptops, iPads and other tablets, and software products, and most of us connect daily to the internet (many of you never disconnect).

INFORMATION TECHNOLOGY (IT) The various devices for creating, storing, exchanging, and using information in diverse modes, including visual images, voice, multimedia, and business data.

E-COMMERCE Buying and selling processes that make use of electronic technology.

INTERNET MARKETING The promotional efforts of companies to sell their products and services to consumers over the internet.

Email, texting, and instant messaging have become staples in business, and even such traditionally "low tech" businesses as hair salons and garbage collection companies are becoming dependent on the internet, computers, and networks. As consumers, we interact with databases every time we withdraw money from an ATM, order food at McDonald's, use an Apple or Android application to order food or movie tickets, or check on the status of a package at UPS or FedEx.

IT has had an immense effect on businesses—in fact, the growth of IT has changed the very structure of business organizations. Its adoption has altered workforces in many companies, contributed to greater flexibility in dealing with customers, and changed how employees interact with each other. E-commerce has created new market relationships around the globe.

We begin by looking at how businesses are using IT to bolster productivity, improve operations and processes, create new opportunities, and communicate and work in ways not possible before.

THE IMPACT OF THE INTERNET ON MARKETING

E-commerce refers to buying and selling processes that make use of electronic technology, while **internet marketing** refers to the promotional efforts of companies to sell their products and services to consumers over the internet.[5]

Photoshot/Newscom

In 2015, Barack Obama was still an avid BlackBerry user. Despite calls for him to join the iPhone crowd, he resisted. The BlackBerry provides a superior encryption system for secure messaging with advisors and colleagues.

WHAT'S NEW IN THE EIGHTH CANADIAN EDITION?

New content has been included in all chapters. An illustrative (but not exhaustive) list follows:

Chapter 1—New material on the government as a regulator, the activities of the Competition Bureau and its concerns about anti-competitive behaviour, the debate about the advisability of government bailouts of companies, public–private partnerships (so-called P3s), problems in the provision of essential services to Canadians (e.g., increasing electricity rates in the province of Ontario), and Canada's supply management system.

Chapter 2—New information on the business cycle, the CPI measure, and mergers and acquisitions.

Chapter 3—New information on corruption and bribes in international business activity, a survey of global managers indicating their perception of corruption in various countries, how to incorporate various ethical norms into management decision making, the fair trade movement, price fixing, and counterfeit goods.

Chapter 4—New information on small business employment, issues in taking over a family business, and the top corporations in Canada.

Chapter 5—New information about the BRICS nations and the Comprehensive Economic and Trade Agreement (CETA).

Chapter 6—New information on the planning process managers at McDonald's use to try to improve the company's performance, what is expected in a manager's job, how social media makes the activities of managers more visible to the public, the importance of managers having "soft" skills" (as opposed to technical skills), decision-making skills, and the importance of contingency planning.

Chapter 7—New information on the obstacles to effective delegation of authority, "tall" and "flat" organization structures, and structural issues that Canadian companies must address when they "go global."

Chapter 8—New information on the concept of the realistic job preview, behaviour-based interviewing, the legal status of random drug testing of employees, needs analysis in making training decisions, mentoring programs, guidelines for ensuring performance appraisal is effective, workforce management systems, retirement trends in Canada, workforce diversity, the development of Canadian labour unions, union membership in Canada, and union organizing strategies and their success rate.

Chapter 9—New material on personality traits (including concepts such as locus of control, self-efficacy, and authoritarianism), attitudes (including cognition, affect, and intention), McClelland's acquired needs theory, the concept of power (legitimate, reward, coercive, expert, and referent power), and three leadership theories (path-goal, decision-tree, and leader–member exchange theories).

Chapter 10—New material on the difference between "make-to-order" and "make-to-stock" production strategies, capacity planning, process and product layouts, operations scheduling, international productivity comparisons, and supply chain disruptions.

Chapter 11—Updated information about the new CPA accounting designation, the transition process currently taking place, and the evolving role of the modern accountant.

Chapter 12—New material on the steps in developing a marketing plan, marketing strategy, and market research.

Chapter 13—New information on the unique challenges faced by e-businesses in pricing their products, online consumer engagement, mobile and other advertising media, direct (interactive) marketing, publicity, and public relations.

Chapter 14—New information on plastic money (credit cards and debit cards), the top banks and credit unions in Canada, and the Big Mac Index statistics.

Chapter 15—New information on financial planning, managing risk with diversification, return on investment, the time value of money, fantasy stock markets, mutual funds, and securities regulation.

SUPPLEMENTS

MyBizLab MyBizLab delivers **proven results** in helping individual students succeed. It provides **engaging experiences** that personalize, stimulate, and measure learning for each student. For the second Canadian edition, MyBizLab includes powerful new learning resources, including a new set of online lesson presentations to help students work through and master key business topics, a completely restructured Study Plan for student self-study, and a wealth of engaging assessment and teaching aids to help students and instructors explore unique learning pathways. MyBizLab online resources include:.

- **NEW Interactive Lesson Presentations.** Students can now study key chapter topics and work through interactive assessments to test their knowledge and mastery of business concepts. Each presentation allows students to explore through expertly designed steps of reading, practising, and testing to ensure that students not only experience the content, but truly engage with each topic. Instructors also have the ability to assign quizzes, projects, and follow-up discussion questions relating to the online lessons to further develop the valuable learning experiences from the presentations.
- **NEW Study Plan.** MyBizLab offers students an engaging and focused self-study experience that is driven by a powerful new Study Plan. Students work through assessments in each chapter to gauge their understanding and target the topics that require additional practice. Along the way, they are recognized for their mastery of each topic and guided toward resources in areas that they might be struggling to understand.
- **NEW Dynamic Study Modules.** These new study modules allow students to work through groups of questions and check their understanding of foundational business topics. As students work through questions, the Dynamic Study Modules assess their knowledge and only show questions that still require practice. Dynamic Study Modules can be completed online using your computer, tablet, or mobile device.
- **BizSkills and Decision-Making Simulations.** BizSkills are real-world scenarios that invite students to assume the role of a decision maker at a company to apply the concepts they have just learned. Decision-Making Mini-Simulations walk students through key business decision-making scenarios to help them understand how business decisions are made. Students are asked to make important decisions relating to core business concepts. At each point, students receive feedback to help them understand the implications of their choices in the business environment. Both types of simulations can now be assigned by instructors and graded directly through MyBizLab.
- **NEW Business Today Video Database.** Business Today is a dynamic and expanding database of videos that covers the disciplines of business, marketing, management, and more. In addition to the videos that have been specifically correlated to this text, you will find new videos posted regularly. Check back regularly to see up-to-date video examples that are perfect for classroom use.
- **NEW Learning Catalytics.** Learning Catalytics is a "bring your own device" student engagement, assessment, and classroom intelligence system. It allows instructors to engage students in class with a variety of question types designed to gauge student understanding.
- **Glossary Flashcards.** The Glossary Flashcards provide a targeted review of the Key Terms in each chapter. They allow learners to select the specific terms and chapters that they would like to study. The cards can also be sorted by Key Term or by definition to give students greater flexibility when studying.
- **Business Plan Project.** A simple, concise Business Plan Project is available on MyBizLab for instructors to share with their students.
- **NEW Canadian Sketch Animation Series.** Explore a NEW animation series that presents key marketing and business concepts from a uniquely Canadian perspective. This interesting and lively series of videos will help your students grasp course concepts that they find difficult.
- **Problem-Based Learning Assignments.** Problem-Based Learning assignments encourage students to ask questions, think critically, solve problems and, if working in a group, engage with others. Problem-Based Learning assignments help students assume responsibility for their own learning, helping them to exercise leadership, and facilitate their ability to apply their knowledge. Students who actively participate in their own learning process are better able to link concept to application.

eText The Pearson eText gives students access to their textbook anytime, anywhere. In addition to enabling note taking, highlighting, and bookmarking, the Pearson eText offers interactive and sharing features. Rich media options may include videos, animations, interactive figures, and built-in assessments, all embedded in the text. Instructors can share their comments or highlights, and students can add their own, creating a tight community of learners within the class.

The Pearson eText may include a responsive design for easy viewing on smartphones and tablets. Many of these eTexts now have configurable reading settings, including resizable type and night-reading mode.

ADDITIONAL INSTRUCTOR RESOURCES

Instructor resources are password-protected and available for download via www.pearsoncanada.ca/highered.

UPDATED! Test Bank The updated Test Bank, in Microsoft Word format, contains approximately 4000 multiple-choice, critical thinking, true/false, short-answer, and essay questions. Bloom's Taxonomy tagging and textbook page references tied to each question will help in assessing students. This robust Test Bank is also available in computerized format (see below).

Computerized Test Bank Pearson's computerized test banks allow instructors to filter and select questions to create quizzes, tests, or homework. Instructors can revise questions or add their own, and may be able to choose print or online options. These questions are also available in Microsoft Word format.

UPDATED! Instructor's Resource Manual The Instructor's Resource Manual contains chapter synopses, chapter outlines, teaching tips, in-class exercises, solutions to case studies, and answers to the critical thinking questions found at the end of each boxed insert. The manual also provides answers to the end-of-chapter exercises, including Building Your Business Skills and Exercising Your Ethics. Answers are also provided for the Questions for Discussion at the end of the CBC and Business Today video cases in each of the five major parts of the text.

UPDATED! PowerPoint® Presentations PowerPoint Presentations offer an average of 40 slides per chapter, outlining the key points in the text. Improved visuals, unique examples, and quick-check questions are provided. The slides also include lecture notes, summaries, and suggestions for student activities or related questions from the text.

Learning Solutions Managers Pearson's Learning Solutions Managers work with faculty and campus course designers to ensure that Pearson technology products, assessment tools, and online course materials are tailored to meet your specific needs. This highly qualified team is dedicated to helping schools take full advantage of a wide range of educational resources, by assisting in the integration of a variety of instructional materials and media formats. Your local Pearson Canada sales representative can provide you with more details on this service program.

Your Pearson Education Canada Sales Representative Your Pearson sales rep is always available to ensure you have everything you need to teach a winning course. Armed with experience, training, and product knowledge, he or she will support your assessment and adoption of any of the products, services, and technology outlined here to ensure our offerings are tailored to suit your individual needs and the needs of your students. Whether it's getting instructions on TestGen software or specific content files for your new online course, your representative is there to help. Ask your Pearson sales representative for details.

ACKNOWLEDGMENTS

We owe special thanks to Rodney Rawlings, copyeditor; Jessica Hellen, Project Manager; Carolin Sweig, Acquisitions Editor; Karen Townsend, Program Manager; Paul Donnelly, Developmental Editor; and others at Pearson Canada who assisted with the production, marketing, and sales of this edition.

We also appreciate the insights and suggestions of the following individuals, who provided feedback on the seventh edition or reviewed the manuscript for the new edition:

Matt Archibald, University of Ottawa
Robert Maher, University of New Brunswick
Jeff May, McMaster University
Bill McConkey, University of Toronto Scarborough
Carolan McLarney, Dalhousie University
Frank Saccucci, MacEwan University
Les Schiller, Dawson College

ABOUT THE AUTHORS

Ronald J. Ebert is Emeritus Professor at the University of Missouri–Columbia where he lectures in the Management Department and serves as advisor to students and student organizations. Dr. Ebert draws upon more than 30 years of teaching experience at such schools as Sinclair College, University of Washington, University of Missouri, Lucian Blaga University of Sibiu (Romania), and Consortium International University (Italy). His consulting alliances include such firms as Mobay Corporation, Kraft Foods, Oscar Mayer, Atlas Powder, and John Deere. He has designed and conducted management development programs for such diverse clients as the American Public Power Association, the United States Savings and Loan League, and the Central Missouri Manufacturing Training Consortium.

His experience as a practitioner has fostered an advocacy for integrating concepts with best business practices in business education. The five business books he has written have been translated into Spanish, Chinese, Malaysian, and Romanian. Dr. Ebert has served as the editor of the *Journal of Operations Management*. He is a past president and fellow of the Decision Sciences Institute. He has served as consultant and external evaluator for *Quantitative Reasoning for Business Studies* an introduction-to-business project sponsored by the National Science Foundation.

Ricky W. Griffin is Distinguished Professor of Management and holds the Blocker Chair in Business in the Mays School of Business at Texas A&M University. Dr. Griffin currently serves as executive associate dean. He previously served as head of the Department of Management and as director of the Center for Human Resource Management at Texas A&M. His research interests include workplace aggression and violence, executive skills and decision making, and workplace culture. Dr. Griffin's research has been published in such journals as *Academy of Management Review*, *Academy of Management Journal*, *Administrative Science Quarterly*, and *Journal of Management*. He has also served as editor of *Journal of Management*. Dr. Griffin has consulted with such organizations as Texas Instruments, Tenneco, Amoco, Compaq Computer, and Continental Airlines.

Dr. Griffin has served the Academy of Management as chair of the organizational behaviour division. He also has served as president of the southwest division of the Academy of Management and on the board of directors of the Southern Management Association. He is a fellow of both the Academy of Management and the Southern Management Association. He is also the author of several successful textbooks, each of which is a market leader. In addition, they are widely used in dozens of countries and have been translated into numerous foreign languages, including Spanish, Polish, Malaysian, and Russian.

Frederick A. Starke is Emeritus Professor of Organizational Behaviour in the Asper School of Business at the University of Manitoba. He has taught courses in organizational behaviour, organization theory, decision making, and marketing. He has served in several administrative positions, including Head of the Department of Business Administration (from 1982 to 1987 and from 1989 to 1994), and as Associate Dean of the Asper School of Business (from 1996 to 2005).

Dr. Starke earned his BA and MBA from Southern Illinois University and his PhD in Organizational Behavior from Ohio State University. He has published research articles in such scholarly journals as *Administrative Science Quarterly*, *Journal of Applied Psychology*, *Academy of Management Journal*, *Journal of Management Studies*, and *Journal of Business Venturing*. He has written articles for professional journals, such as the *Journal of Systems Management*, *Information Executive*, and the *Canadian Journal of Nursing Administration*. Dr. Starke also writes textbooks that are used by university and community college students in business programs across Canada. These titles include *Organizational Behaviour*, *Business Essentials*, *Management*, and *Business*. Dr. Starke also presents seminars on the topics of decision making and goal setting to practising managers in both the public and private sectors.

George Dracopoulos is a member of the Business Administration department at Vanier College. In the past, he has served as chairman of the department but is now devoting significant energy to his role as the International Business Exchange Coordinator. In the past decade, George has created links and built bridges with universities and businesses throughout France and Belgium. To date, hundreds of students have benefitted from these initiatives. He is also the co-organizer and co-founder of the national BDC/Vanier Marketing Case Competition and was recently awarded with the distinction as the Vanier VIP for his dedication and devotion to the community.

Mr. Dracopoulos also serves as a lecturer at McGill University, teaching traditional and online courses. He recently worked on an online broadcast pilot-project and has built courses geared primarily towards aboriginal students. He was honoured (among a select group) as Professor of the Year by a McGill University publication for his work in the Desautels Faculty of Management. He earned his MBA at McGill, and a graduate Diploma in Education and Graduate Degree in Applied Management. He earned his BA at Concordia University. Mr. Dracopoulos is an advocate of experiential learning and dedicates a significant amount of class time to hands-on projects. His primary interests are in the fields of marketing and management. While completing his university education, he spent a semester abroad studying management globalization issues in Europe. He has also spent a considerable amount of time coaching high-level sports and organizing events.

Outside his teaching career, Mr. Dracopoulos has worked in marketing and sales positions and provides marketing and management solutions (e.g., brand audits, customer relationship surveys, strategic consultations, IMC campaigns, and so on). He has also built web-based materials and training documents for clients in various industries, including aviation/IT solutions, publishing, office supplies, sound and music products, and higher education. Mr. Dracopoulos has been invited to provide motivational speeches and/or keynote addresses at major events across North America on topics such as Connecting with Millennials, Effective Communication, and Transformational Leadership.

In addition to this text, he has worked on many publishing projects, including *Business in Action* In-Class Edition, second Canadian edition (2009), co-authored with Courtland L. Bovée and John V. Thill, and *Business*, eighth Canadian edition (2014), co-authored with Ricky Griffin, Ronald J. Ebert, Frederick Starke, and Melanie Lang.

BUSINESS ESSENTIALS

PART 1 INTRODUCING THE CONTEMPORARY BUSINESS WORLD

Rawpixel/Fotolia

LO

AFTER READING THIS CHAPTER, YOU SHOULD BE ABLE TO:

LO-1 Define the nature of Canadian *business* and identify its main goals.

LO-2 Describe different types of global *economic systems* according to the means by which they control the *factors of production* through *input* and *output markets*.

LO-3 Describe the interactions between business and government in Canada.

LO-4 Show how *demand* and *supply* affect resource distribution in Canada.

LO-5 Identify the elements of *private enterprise*, and explain the various *degrees of competition* in the Canadian economic system.

Combining the Whopper and the Timbit

James Hackland/Alamy

joel zatz/Alamy

In August 2014, U.S.-based Burger King and Canadian-based Tim Hortons announced plans to merge. But there was a big surprise: the new company—named Restaurant Brands International—would have its headquarters in Canada, not in the United States. Annual sales would be more than $23 billion, making it the third-largest company in the fast food industry. The announcement generated a great deal of debate and concern in both Canada and the United States.

To obtain approval for the merger from Investment Canada, the new company agreed to keep the Tim Hortons brand separate from the Burger King brand, to maintain significant employment levels at Tim Hortons, to guarantee that at least 50 percent of the Tim Hortons board of directors would be Canadians, and to maintain Tim Hortons' pre-merger level of charity work in Canada.

Approval for the merger also had to be obtained from the Canadian Competition Bureau. The Bureau concluded that the merger would not reduce competition in the industry because there are so many competing fast food restaurant chains. But the Canadian Centre for Policy Alternatives

Understanding *the* Canadian Business System

CHAPTER 01

predicted that there would be big layoffs and a lot of cost-cutting once the merger was complete. They based that claim on the fact that in past takeovers, 3G Capital—which is Burger King's majority shareholder—had approved significant layoffs and cost-cutting in other takeovers.

In the United States, the announcement was greeted with hostility because Burger King is such a prominent brand, and because it was perceived that Burger King was moving to Canada to avoid the high corporate tax rate in the United States. When a U.S. company merges with a company in a foreign country that has lower tax rates and then moves its headquarters to that foreign country, it is called an "inversion." Because the corporate tax rate in the United States is higher than the corporate tax rate in Canada, the move made sense for Burger King (although both Burger King and Tim Hortons say that taxes were not the reason for the merger). The U.S. government was so concerned about this trend that in September 2014 the U.S. Treasury Secretary imposed new restrictions on U.S. companies that move abroad for tax purposes.

In December 2014, Tim Hortons shareholders voted to approve the merger. The CEO of Burger King would be the CEO of the new company, and the CEO of Tim Hortons would serve as the vice-chairman. Also in December 2014, the Ontario Superior Court of Justice issued a final order to approve the merger.

The merger should help Tim Hortons achieve one of its long-time goals: increased market penetration in the giant U.S. market. For the last decade, Tim Hortons has pursued a growth strategy by expanding into the United States. Just three months before the merger was announced, Tim Hortons announced a strategic plan that included opening 300 new outlets in the United States. The merger would accelerate Tim Hortons' growth in the United States, because its brand could take advantage of Burger King's greater knowledge of regional U.S. markets and distribution networks.

HOW WILL THIS HELP ME?

All businesses are subject to the influences of economic forces. But these same economic forces also provide astute managers and entrepreneurs with opportunities for profits and growth. The ideas presented in this chapter will help you to better understand (1) how *managers* deal with the challenges and opportunities resulting from economic forces and (2) how *consumers* deal with the challenges and opportunities of price fluctuations.

Rob Byron/Fotolia

QUESTIONS FOR DISCUSSION

1. What are the advantages of the merger for Burger King? For Tim Hortons? What are the potential disadvantages for each company?
2. What kind of economic system is evident in Canada? What roles does government play in the economic system? How are those roles evident in the Burger King–Tim Hortons merger?
3. Are the restrictions that were imposed on the merger by the Canadian government consistent with our economic system? What potential problems might arise as a result of these restrictions?

LO-1 THE IDEA OF BUSINESS AND PROFIT

The opening case illustrates the dynamic and rapidly changing nature of modern business activity and the opportunities and challenges that are evident. It also shows how business managers must pay attention to many different issues, including corporate strategy, brand strategy, business–government relations, international business opportunities, mergers, marketing strategy, and many other concepts that you will read about in this text.

Let's begin by asking what you think of when you hear the word *business*. Do you think of large corporations like Shoppers Drug Mart and Walmart, or smaller companies like your local supermarket or favourite restaurant? Do you think about successful companies like Netflix and CN, or less successful companies like Bombardier or Barrick Gold? Each of these firms is a **business**—an organization that produces or sells goods or services in an effort to make a profit. Businesses produce most of the goods and services that we consume, and they employ many of the working people in Canada. Taxes that businesses pay help to support governments at all levels. In addition, businesses help support charitable causes and provide community leadership. A study by *Forbes* magazine ranked Canada (out of 134 countries) as the world's top country in which to do business.[1]

Profit is what remains after a business's expenses have been subtracted from its revenues. Profits reward the owners of businesses for taking the risks involved in investing their time and money. Profits can be very large if a company produces something that consumers really like. For example, the multi-part film *Hunger Games* has generated large profits for Lions Gate (the first film in the series generated box office receipts of $155 million in just its first week).

Many organizations in Canada do not try to make a profit. These **not-for-profit organizations** use the funds they generate from government grants or the sale of goods or services to provide services to the public. Charities, educational institutions, hospitals, labour unions, and government agencies are examples of not-for-profit organizations. Business principles are helpful to these not-for-profit organizations as they try to achieve their service goals.

BUSINESS An organization that seeks to earn profits by providing goods and services.

PROFIT What remains (if anything) after a business's expenses are subtracted from its sales revenues.

NOT-FOR-PROFIT ORGANIZATION An organization that provides goods and services to customers, but does not seek to make a profit while doing so.

LO-2 ECONOMIC SYSTEMS AROUND THE WORLD

A Canadian business is different in many ways from one in China, and both are different from businesses in Japan, France, or Peru. A major determinant of how organizations operate is the kind of economic system that characterizes the country in which they do business. An **economic system** allocates a nation's resources among its citizens. Economic systems differ in terms of who owns and controls these resources, known as the "factors of production."

Factors of Production

The key difference between economic systems is the way in which they manage the **factors of production**—the basic resources that a country's businesses use to produce goods and services. The factors of production are: labour, capital, entrepreneurs, natural resources, and information.[2]

LABOUR

The people who work for a company represent the first factor of production—*labour*. Sometimes called human resources, labour is the mental and physical capabilities of people. Carrying out the business of a huge company, such as Imperial Oil, requires a labour force with a wide variety of skills ranging from managers to geologists to truck drivers.

CAPITAL

Capital refers to the funds that are needed to start a business and to keep it operating and growing. For example, Imperial Oil needs capital to pay for its annual drilling costs, which run into the millions of dollars each year. Major sources of capital for businesses are personal investment by owners, the sale of stock to investors, profits from the sale of products and services, and funds borrowed from banks and other lending institutions.

ENTREPRENEURS

Entrepreneurs are people who accept the opportunities and risks involved in creating and operating businesses. Mike Lazaridis (BlackBerry), Sergey Brin and Larry Page (Google), Michael Dell (Dell), and Mark Zuckerberg (Facebook) are well-known entrepreneurs. The boxed insert entitled "Riversong: Revolutionary Canadian Guitars" describes the activities of one Canadian entrepreneur.

NATURAL RESOURCES

Natural resources include all physical resources such as land, water, mineral deposits, and trees. Imperial Oil makes use of a wide variety of natural resources. It obviously has vast quantities of crude oil to process each year. But Imperial Oil also needs the land where the oil is located, as well as land for its refineries and pipelines.

INFORMATION

Information includes the specialized knowledge and expertise of people who work in businesses, as well as information that is found in market forecasts and various other forms of economic data. Information is a key factor of production, because unlike land, labour, and capital, information can be shared without being diminished. For example, if two people exchange apples, they still each have only one apple, but if two people exchange ideas, each person now has two ideas instead of one.[3]

Types of Economic Systems

Different types of economic systems manage the factors of production in different ways. In some systems, ownership is private; in others, the factors of production are owned by the government. Economic systems also differ in the ways decisions are made about production and allocation. A **command economy**, for example, relies on a centralized government to control all or most factors of production and to make all or most production and allocation decisions. In a **market economy**, individuals—producers and consumers—make production and allocation decisions through the mechanism of supply and demand.

ECONOMIC SYSTEM The way in which a nation allocates its resources among its citizens.

FACTORS OF PRODUCTION The resources used to produce goods and services: labour, capital, entrepreneurs, and natural resources.

COMMAND ECONOMY An economic system in which government controls all or most factors of production and makes all or most production decisions.

MARKET ECONOMY An economic system in which individuals control all or most factors of production and make all or most production decisions.

Wang Chengyun/PhotoShot

UPPA/PhotoShot

foodfolio/Alamy Stock Photo

Starbucks uses various factors of production, including labour (a Starbucks barista), entrepreneurs (CEO Howard Schultz), and natural resources (such as coffee beans).

ENTREPRENEURSHIP AND NEW VENTURES

Riversong: Revolutionary Canadian Guitars

Mike Miltimore grew up working in a successful family business (Lee's Music stores) in British Columbia, and he learned a lot about the inner workings of musical instruments. He came up with the Riversong guitar idea after he considered customer feedback about guitars. He knew that most guitars have a design flaw: a joint where the neck meets the body. Since manufacturers often use different types of wood that have different expansion and contraction rates, in time these weaknesses impact the performance of the instrument. Mike therefore decided to eliminate the joint and make a guitar whose neck runs all the way to the base of the instrument.

Mike's original goal for Riversong was "to take over the world one guitar at a time." To achieve this, Mike had to address two fundamental business questions: (1) Could he build demand for a new brand in an industry dominated by popular names like Gibson, Martin, Taylor, and Godin? and (2) could he supply enough guitars if his promotional efforts succeeded?

With regard to building demand for his brand, by 2013 Mike's new design had earned significant buzz when he finished second in the Business Development Bank of Canada (BDC) Young Entrepreneurs competition. His award also gave him access to $25 000 worth of consulting services, which provided him with insights about social media strategies and helped him create an online store. Mike also went to the National Association of Music Merchants (NAMM) trade show and met important industry players, including current and international dealers. He recently signed a licensing deal with EMD music, one of the top European companies in the distribution of musical instruments and accessories with a client base of more than 2000 retailers. The deal means that the Riversong guitar neck technology will be used in some of EMD's internationally branded guitars (e.g., James Neligan). EMD will also simultaneously distribute guitars under the Riversong brand. In 2015, Riversong won an A'Design Award as the top acoustic guitar among 10 000 entries considered.

In terms of increasing supply, Mike has reduced the usual 100-hour manufacturing process to about 24 hours by using computer numerical control machines to cut the profile of the guitars and a custom bending machine for the sides. A new production facility is also part of his plan.

Like any true entrepreneur, Mike is always seeking new opportunities. His latest creation is a five-ply wooden guitar pick that promises to deliver three distinct tones to the guitar. He already has a patent pending on this product and he will be promoting it at a music store near you in the very near future.

Riversong Guitars

CRITICAL THINKING QUESTION

1. What else does Mike Miltimore need to do to get his brand noticed in an industry that is dominated by well-known brands with long and storied histories?

Based on a case written by Christopher Ross, John Molson School of Business, Concordia University, "Riversong Guitars," Vanier/BDC Case Competition.

COMMAND ECONOMIES

The two most basic forms of command economies are communism and socialism. As originally proposed by nineteenth-century German economist Karl Marx, **communism** is a system in which the government owns and operates all sources of production. Marx envisioned a society in which individuals would ultimately contribute according to their abilities and receive economic benefits according to their needs. He also expected government ownership of production factors to be only temporary. But Marx's predictions were faulty. During the past 30 years, most countries have abandoned communism in favour of a more market-based economy. Even countries that still claim to be communist (e.g., China, Vietnam, and Cuba) now contain elements of a market-based economy.

In a less extensive command economic system called *socialism*, the government owns and operates only selected major industries. Smaller businesses such as clothing stores and restaurants may be privately owned. Although workers in socialist countries are usually allowed to choose their occupations or professions, a large proportion generally work for the government. Many government-operated enterprises are inefficient, since management positions are frequently filled on the basis of political considerations rather than ability. Extensive public welfare systems have also resulted in very high taxes. Because of these factors, socialism is generally declining in popularity.[4]

MARKET ECONOMIES

A **market** is a mechanism for exchange between the buyers and sellers of a particular good or service. For example, the internet is a technologically sophisticated market that brings buyers and sellers together through e-commerce. People usually think of e-commerce as being business-to-consumer (B2C) transactions, such as buying books over the internet for personal use. But business-to-business (B2B) transactions actually far exceed B2C transactions in dollar value. B2B involves businesses joining together to create e-commerce companies that make them more efficient when they purchase the goods and services they need.

In a market economy, B2C and B2B exchanges take place without much government involvement. To understand how a market economy works, consider what happens when a customer goes to a fruit stand to buy apples. Assume that one vendor is selling apples for $1 per kilogram, and another is charging $1.50. Both vendors are free to charge what they want, and customers are free to buy what they want. If both vendors' apples are of the same quality, the customer will likely buy the cheaper ones. But if the $1.50 apples are fresher, the customer may buy them instead. Both buyers and sellers enjoy freedom of choice.

A GlobeScan poll of over 20 000 people in 20 different countries asked people whether they agreed with the following statement: "The free market economy is the best system." Where do you think the highest support was found? Not in Canada, the United States, Germany, or Japan, but in communist *China*, where 74 percent of people polled agreed with the statement.[5] In spite of the Chinese government's strong support of the communist economic ideology, the country's private sector has become incredibly productive. It is estimated that China produces 60 percent of all the toys in the world.[6] It is also a vast market for many of the products that Canadian firms produce—chemicals, ores, cereals, and wood products. Changes are also occurring in communist Cuba, where more private initiative is being encouraged, and the role of the state is being reduced in some sectors.[7] The recent attempts to normalize relations between the United States and Cuba may cause even more movement toward a market economy in Cuba.

COMMUNISM A type of command economy in which the government owns and operates all industries.

MARKET An exchange process between buyers and sellers of a particular good or service.

INPUT MARKET Firms buy resources that they need in the production of goods and services.

OUTPUT MARKET Firms supply goods and services in response to demand on the part of consumers.

Input and Output Markets

A useful model for understanding how the factors of production work in a pure market economy is shown in Figure 1.1.[8] In the **input market**, firms buy resources from households, which then supply those resources. In the **output market**, firms supply goods and services in response to demand on the part of the households. The activities of these two markets create a circular flow. Ford Motor Co., for example, buys labour directly from households, which may also supply capital from accumulated savings in the form of stock purchases. Consumer buying patterns provide information that helps Ford decide which models to produce and which to discontinue. In turn, Ford uses these inputs in various ways and becomes a supplier to households when it designs and produces various kinds of automobiles, trucks, and sport-utility vehicles and offers them for sale to consumers.

Individuals are free to work for Ford or an alternative employer and to invest in Ford stock or alternative forms of saving or consumption. Similarly, Ford can create whatever vehicles it chooses and price them at whatever value it chooses. Consumers are free to buy their next car

The People's Republic of China has used a planned economic model for many years, but is now moving toward a mixed market economy. But Hong Kong has been using the mixed market model for years. These signs on a busy Hong Kong street are promoting a variety of goods and services provided by merchants along the street.

Geoff A Howard/Alamy Stock Photo

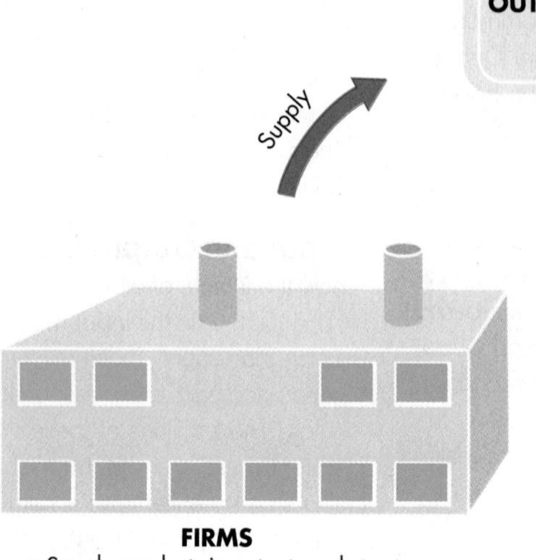

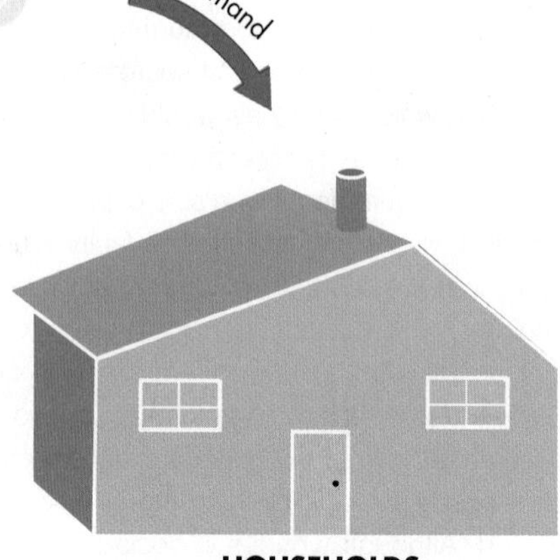

>>> **FIGURE 1.1** Circular flow in a market economy

from Ford, Toyota, BMW, or any other manufacturer. The political basis for the free market economy is called **capitalism**, which allows private ownership of the factors of production and encourages entrepreneurship by offering profits as an incentive. This process contrasts markedly with that of a command economy, in which individuals may be told where they can and cannot work, companies may be told what they can and cannot manufacture, and consumers may have little or no choice as to what they purchase or how much they pay for items.

MIXED MARKET ECONOMIES

Command and market economies are two extremes, or opposites. In reality, most countries rely on some form of **mixed market economy** that features characteristics of both command and market economies. One trend in mixed market economies that began in the 1990s is **privatization**—converting government enterprises into privately owned companies. In Canada, for example, the air traffic control system was privatized, and the federal government sold several other corporations, including Canadian National Railway and Air Canada. The Netherlands privatized its TNT Post Group N.V., and India privatized 18 different industries, including iron, steel, machinery, and telecommunications.[9] The Organisation for Economic Co-operation and Development (OECD) said that Canada Post's monopoly should be ended and it should be privatized.[10] But the worldwide recession in 2008–2009 slowed the privatization trend. Government bailouts of Chrysler and GM in both Canada and the United States meant that government was once again a part-owner of some business firms. A few countries are even pursuing a policy of *nationalization*—converting private firms into government-owned firms. Venezuela, for example, nationalized its telecommunications industry.

CAPITALISM An economic system in which markets decide what, when, and for whom to produce.

MIXED MARKET ECONOMY An economic system with elements of both a command economy and a market economy; in practice, typical of most nations' economies.

PRIVATIZATION The transfer of activities from the government to the private sector.

THERE'S AN APP FOR THAT!

APP DETAILS	PLATFORMS
1. **The Economist App** **Source:** The Economist **Key Features:** Free access to the editor's top six must-read articles; access to the full magazine for subscribers	Apple, Android, BlackBerry
2. **Economics App** **Source:** WAGmob **Key Features:** On-the-go learning—interactive tutorials, quizzes, and flashcards on key economic terms and theories	Apple, Android, BlackBerry
3. **IB Smart Economics** **Source:** IB Smart **Key Features:** Fun, interactive games designed to aid learning	Apple

APP DISCOVERY EXERCISE

Since app availability changes, conduct your own search for "Top 3" economic statistics apps and identify the key features.

Deregulation means a reduction in the number of laws affecting business activity and in the powers of government enforcement agencies. This trend also developed during the 1990s, and deregulation occurred in many industries, including airlines, banking, pipelines, trucking, and communications. A study by the Conference Board of Canada showed that deregulation (in tandem with privatization and increased competition) caused a sharp increase in productivity in sectors like freight and airlines.[11] But this trend has also slowed due to the 2008–2009 recession. For example, laws regulating business activity in the financial sector have been tightened up.

DEREGULATION A reduction in the number of laws affecting business activity.

LO-3 INTERACTIONS BETWEEN BUSINESS AND GOVERNMENT

In Canada's mixed market economy, there are many important interactions between business and government. The ways in which government influences business and the ways business influences government are described below.

How Government Influences Business

Government plays several key roles in the Canadian economy, and each of these roles influences business activity in some way. The roles government plays are as follows.

GOVERNMENT AS A CUSTOMER

Government buys thousands of different products and services from business firms, including office supplies, office buildings, computers, battleships, helicopters, highways, water treatment plants, and management and engineering consulting services. Many businesses depend on government purchasing, if not for their survival then at least for a certain level of prosperity. Total government expenditures in 2013 were $235.3 billion.[12]

GOVERNMENT AS A COMPETITOR

Government also competes with business through Crown corporations, which are accountable to a minister of parliament for their conduct. Crown corporations like Hydro-Quebec and Canada Post generate billions of dollars of revenue and account for significant economic activity in Canada. Crown corporations exist at both the provincial and federal levels.

GOVERNMENT AS REGULATOR

Federal and provincial governments in Canada regulate many aspects of business activity through administrative boards, tribunals, and commissions, but there is a continuing debate about how much influence government regulators have, and how much they *should* have. For many years, the Canadian Wheat Board regulated the price of wheat and prohibited farmers from selling their wheat directly to U.S. elevators. Instead, farmers were required to sell their wheat through the Wheat Board. But that all changed in 2011 when the Conservative government introduced legislation to allow farmers to sell their wheat without going through the Wheat Board.

Another example of regulation is the *Canadian Radio-television and Telecommunications Commission (CRTC)*, which issues and renews broadcast licences. Because of rapid technological changes in broadcasting, the CRTC is facing a complex environment for regulation. In 2014, it conducted hearings that focused on Canadian-content rules and how competition from online video providers like Netflix was affecting Canadian television and cable companies. During the hearings, Netflix was told to submit information about its Canadian subscribers, but it refused to do so, arguing that the CRTC didn't have any jurisdiction over online media. Faced with this refusal, the CRTC decided to simply drop the matter. This approach didn't bring any clarity to the issue of what kind of jurisdiction the CRTC has in enforcing Canadian-content rules.[13] Critics argue that the CRTC is obsolete, and that it cannot achieve its goal of a level playing field because the internet is being used to circumvent Canadian laws.[14]

Provincial governments also have regulatory bodies. For example, prior to 2011, the provinces of Quebec and British Columbia allowed mixed martial arts events such as the UFC, while Ontario did not. But Ontario began allowing these events in 2011.

The reasons for regulating business activity include protecting competition, protecting consumers, achieving social goals, and protecting the environment.

Promoting Competition Competition is crucial to a market economy, so government regulates business activity to ensure that healthy competition exists among business firms. Without these restrictions, a large company with vast resources could cut its prices and drive smaller firms out of the market. The guidelines for Canada's competition policy are contained in the **Competition Act**, which prohibits a variety of practices (see Table 1.1).

The Act prohibits agreements among companies that are designed to reduce competition. Formerly, the government had to prove that such agreements actually reduced competition, but recent changes to the legislation mean that the mere existence of a conspiracy is assumed to be proof that competition has been reduced.[15] Another major change is the dramatically increased fines for misleading marketing practices by corporations (formerly $100 000 for the first offence, now $10 million).[16]

After Loblaw Cos. Ltd. acquired Shoppers Drug Mart, the Competition Bureau imposed limits on how much the company could squeeze Shoppers' suppliers by demanding that those suppliers reduce their prices. Loblaw was also required to sell 18 stores and 9 pharmacies because the Bureau was concerned about anti-competitive

COMPETITION ACT Prohibits a variety of business practices that lessen competition.

TABLE 1.1 The Competition Act

Section 45	Prohibits conspiracies and combinations formed for the purpose of unduly lessening competition in the production, transportation, or storage of goods. Persons convicted may be imprisoned for up to five years, fined up to $1 million, or both.
Section 50	Prohibits illegal trade practices. A company may not, for example, cut prices in one region of Canada while selling at a higher price everywhere else if this substantially lessens competition. A company may not sell at "unreasonably low prices" if this substantially lessens competition. (This section does not prohibit credit unions from returning surpluses to their members.)
Section 51	Prohibits giving allowances and rebates to buyers to cover their advertising expenses, unless these allowances are made available proportionally to other purchasers who are in competition with the buyer given the rebate.
Section 52	Prohibits marketing (promotion) activities that are false or misleading. Includes telemarketing activities.
Section 53	Prohibits the deceptive notice that a person has won a prize if the recipient is asked to pay money as a condition of winning the prize.
Section 54	Prohibits charging the higher price when two prices are shown on a product.
Section 55.1	Prohibits pyramid selling (a participant in the plan receives compensation for recruiting other individuals into the plan).
Section 61	Prohibits resale price maintenance. No person who produces or supplies a product can attempt to influence upward, or discourage reduction of, the price of the good in question. It is also illegal for the producer to refuse to supply a product to a reseller simply because the producer believes the reseller will cut the price.
Section 74	Prohibits bait-and-switch selling. No person can advertise a product at a bargain price if there is no supply of the product available to the consumer. (This tactic baits prospects into the store, where salespeople switch them to higher-priced goods.) This section also controls the use of contests to sell goods and prohibits the sale of goods at a price higher than the advertised one.

practices.[17] In another case, the Bureau alleged that Keurig Green Mountain Coffee used anti-competitive practices to maintain its market dominance by telling stores and consumers that only Keurig cups would work with their coffee machines. Keurig said the company had to control the quality of the "Keurig experience," and that the allegations were without merit.[18]

Businesses often complain that the Competition Bureau is too slow in making decisions, and that it makes decisions that are unfriendly to business. One highly visible recent case has pitted the Competition Bureau against the Canadian Real Estate Association (CREA). The dispute began in 2010 when the Bureau alleged that CREA was acting in an anti-competitive manner because it was refusing to allow online, low-cost real estate brokers access to its Multiple Listing Service (MLS). In 2011, the Bureau also told the Toronto Real Estate Board (TREB) that its practices were anti-competitive because brokers weren't being allowed to share information over the internet. TREB appealed the ruling, but as of mid-2015, the case had still not been settled.[19]

Protecting Consumers The federal government has initiated many programs that protect consumers. Consumer and Corporate Affairs Canada administers many of these. Important legislation includes the *Tobacco Act* (which prohibits cigarette advertising on billboards and in stores), the *Weights and Measures Act* (which sets standards of accuracy for weighing and measuring devices), the *Consumer Packaging and Labelling Act* (which stipulates labelling requirements for products), the *Textile Labelling Act* (which regulates the labelling, sale, importation, and advertising of consumer textile articles), and the *Food and Drug Act* (which prohibits the sale of food that contains any poisonous or harmful substances). In 2011, the *Canada Consumer Product Safety Act* (which replaced the former *Hazardous Products Act*) came into force. It requires poisonous, flammable, explosive, or corrosive products to be appropriately labelled. In addition to federal regulations, consumers are also protected by provincial and municipal bylaws (e.g., "no smoking" bylaws).

Achieving Social Goals Social goals, which promote the well-being of Canadian society, include things like universal access to health care, safe workplaces, employment insurance, and decent pensions. All of these goals require the interaction of business firms and the Canadian government. But the decisions of foreign governments—as they pursue their own social goals—can also affect Canadian businesses. For example, when the U.S. government introduced legislation making it difficult for online gambling companies to operate in the United States, the stock prices of Canadian firms like Cryptologic Inc. and Chartwell Technology dropped.[20]

Hazardous products must have warning labels to protect consumers who use them.

Branko Miokovic/Getty Images

Protecting the Environment Government legislation designed to protect the environment includes the *Canada Water Act* (which controls water quality in fresh and marine waters), the *Fisheries Act* (which controls the discharge of any harmful substance into water), and the *Environmental Contaminants Act* (which establishes regulations for airborne substances that are a danger to human health or the environment).

GOVERNMENT AS A TAXATION AGENT

Taxes are imposed and collected by the federal, provincial, and local governments. *Revenue taxes* (e.g., income taxes) are levied by governments primarily to provide revenue to fund various services and programs. *Progressive revenue taxes* are levied at a higher rate on higher-income taxpayers and at a lower rate on lower-income taxpayers. *Regressive revenue taxes* (e.g., sales tax) are levied at the same rate regardless of a person's income. They cause poorer people to pay a higher percentage of their income for these taxes than rich people pay. *Restrictive taxes* (e.g., taxes on alcohol, tobacco, and gasoline) are levied partially for the revenue they provide, but also because legislative bodies believe that the products in question should be controlled.

GOVERNMENT AS A PROVIDER OF INCENTIVES AND FINANCIAL ASSISTANCE

Federal, provincial, and municipal governments offer incentive programs that attempt to stimulate economic development. The Province of Quebec, for example, has attracted video game companies like Ubisoft by giving them multimillion-dollar subsidies if they locate in the province.[21] The Provinces of Ontario and British Columbia have given hundreds of millions of dollars in subsidies to film companies to motivate them to make major films in those provinces.[22]

The most publicized example of government incentives was the bailout of General Motors Canada and Chrysler Canada in 2009, when the federal government and the province of Ontario provided US$13.7 billion in loans and share purchases. Supporters of the bailout argued that Canadians were better off as a result of the bailouts because thousands of jobs were saved. Critics of the bailout argued that it cost far too much to save those jobs. Even with the bailout, Canada dropped from 8th to 16th in in the world for car production during the period 1999–2014.[23]

Industry Canada offers many different programs designed to help small businesses. The Canada Business program, for example, provides information on government programs, services, and regulations in order to improve the start-up and survival rates of small and medium-sized businesses. It also encourages businesses to focus on sound business planning and the effective use of market research. The Department of Foreign Affairs and International Trade (DFAIT) helps Canadian companies doing business internationally by promoting Canada as a good place in which to invest and carry on business activities. It also assists in negotiating and administering trade agreements.

Governments also offer incentives through the many services they provide to business firms through government organizations. Examples include the Export Development Corporation (which assists Canadian exporters by offering export insurance against non-payment by foreign buyers and long-term loans to foreign buyers of Canadian products), Natural Resources Canada (which provides geological maps of Canada's potential mineral-producing areas), and Statistics Canada (which provides data and analysis on almost every aspect of Canadian society). Industry Canada offers many different programs designed to help small businesses.

There are many other government incentive programs, including municipal tax rebates for companies that locate in certain areas, design assistance programs, and remission of tariffs on certain advanced technology production equipment. Government incentive programs may or may not have the desired effect of stimulating the economy. They may also cause difficulties with our trading partners, as we shall see in Chapter 5. Some critics argue as well that business firms are too willing to accept government assistance—either in the form of incentives or bailouts—and that managers should put more emphasis on innovation and creativity so business firms can better cope with economic difficulties when they arise, as they did during the 2008–2009 recession.

GOVERNMENT AS A PROVIDER OF ESSENTIAL SERVICES

The various levels of government facilitate business activity through the services they supply. The federal government provides highways, the postal service, the minting of money, the armed forces, and statistical data on which to base business decisions. It also tries to maintain stability through fiscal and monetary policy (discussed in Chapter 2). Provincial and municipal governments provide streets, sewage and sanitation systems, police and fire departments, utilities, hospitals, and education. All of these activities create the kind of stability that encourages business activity.

In public–private partnerships (called P3s), the government pays a private sector company to build, finance, and operate organizations like hospitals and transit lines. But studies show that P3s cost more money than the traditional approach in which the government puts up the money and then hires contractors to do the necessary work.[24]

There is general agreement that governments should provide essential services like utilities, but governments may make controversial decisions when doing so. In Ontario, for example, the provincial government's decisions about electricity generation have resulted in steep increases in the cost of electricity for consumers. In 2003, the typical consumer paid 6.5 cents per kilowatt hour (kWh), but by 2014 the cost had risen to 17.9 cents. Critics claim that Ontario unwisely agreed to pay subsidies to encourage wind and solar power, and that that is a key reason why electric bills have increased for customers.[25]

How Business Influences Government

Businesses also try to influence the government through the use of lobbyists, trade associations, and advertising (see Figure 1.2). A **lobbyist** is a person hired by a company or industry to represent that company's interests with government officials. The Canadian Association

LOBBYIST A person hired by a company or an industry to represent its interests with government officials.

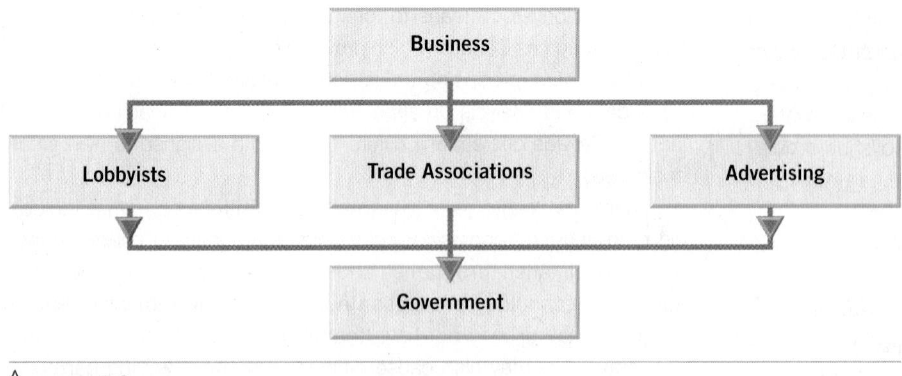

FIGURE 1.2

of Consulting Engineers, for example, regularly lobbies the federal and provincial governments to make use of the skills possessed by private-sector consulting engineers on projects like city water systems. Some business lobbyists have training in the particular industry, public relations experience, or a legal background. A few have served as legislators or government regulators.

The federal *Lobbying Act* requires lobbyists to register with the Commissioner of Lobbying so it is clear which individuals are being paid for their lobbying activity. It also sets rules for accountability and transparency and requires lobbyists to report detailed information about their communications with what are known as Designated Public Office Holders (DPOHs).[26] For many lobbying efforts, there are opposing points of view. For example, the Canadian Cancer Society and the Tobacco Institute present very different points of view on cigarette smoking and cigarette advertising.

Employees and owners of small businesses that cannot afford lobbyists often join **trade associations**, which may act as an industry lobby to influence legislation. They also conduct training programs relevant to the particular industry, and they arrange trade shows at which members display their products or services to potential customers. Most publish newsletters featuring articles on new products, new companies, changes in ownership, and changes in laws affecting the industry.

Corporations can influence legislation indirectly by influencing voters. A company can, for example, launch an advertising campaign designed to get people to write their MPs, MPPs, or MLAs demanding passage—or rejection—of a particular bill that is before parliament or the provincial legislature.

TRADE ASSOCIATION An organization dedicated to promoting the interests and assisting the members of a particular industry.

LO-4 THE CANADIAN MARKET ECONOMY

Understanding the complex nature of the Canadian economic system is essential to understanding Canadian business. In this section, we will examine the workings of our market economy, including markets, demand, supply, private enterprise, and degrees of competition.

Demand and Supply in a Market Economy

In economic terms, a **market** is not a specific place, like a supermarket, but an exchange process between buyers and sellers. Decisions about production in a market economy are the result of millions of exchanges. How much of what product a company offers for sale and who buys it depends on the laws of demand and supply.

THE LAWS OF SUPPLY AND DEMAND

In a market economy, decisions about what to buy and what to sell are determined primarily by the forces of demand and supply. **Demand** is the willingness and ability of buyers to purchase a product or service. **Supply** is the willingness and ability of producers to offer a good or service for sale. The **law of demand** states that buyers will purchase (demand) more of a product as its price drops. Conversely, the **law of supply** states that producers will offer (supply) more for sale as the price rises.[27]

DEMAND AND SUPPLY SCHEDULES

To appreciate these laws in action, consider the market for pizza in your town. If everyone is willing to pay $25 for a pizza (a relatively high price), the local pizzeria will produce a large supply. If, however, everyone is willing to pay only $5 (a relatively low price), the restaurant will make fewer pizzas. Through careful analysis, we can determine how many pizzas will be sold at different prices. These results, called a **demand and supply schedule**, are obtained from marketing research and other systematic studies of the market. Properly applied, they help managers understand the relationships among different levels of demand and supply at different price levels.

MARKET An exchange process between buyers and sellers of a particular good or service.

DEMAND The willingness and ability of buyers to purchase a product or service.

SUPPLY The willingness and ability of producers to offer a good or service for sale.

LAW OF DEMAND The principle that buyers will purchase (demand) more of a product as price drops.

LAW OF SUPPLY The principle that producers will offer (supply) more of a product as price rises.

DEMAND AND SUPPLY SCHEDULE Assessment of the relationships between different levels of demand and supply at different price levels.

DEMAND AND SUPPLY CURVES

The demand and supply schedule can be used to construct demand and supply curves for pizza. A **demand curve** shows how many products—in this case, pizzas—will be demanded (bought) at different prices. A **supply curve** shows how many pizzas will be supplied (cooked) at different prices.

Figure 1.3 shows the hypothetical demand and supply curves for pizzas in our illustration. As you can see, demand increases as price decreases, and supply increases as price increases. When the demand and supply curves are plotted on the same graph, the point at which they intersect is the **market price**, or **equilibrium price**—the price at which the quantity of goods demanded and the quantity of goods supplied are equal. In Figure 1.3, the equilibrium price for pizzas is $10. At this point,

DEMAND CURVE Graph showing how many units of a product will be demanded (bought) at different prices.

SUPPLY CURVE Graph showing how many units of a product will be supplied (offered for sale) at different prices.

MARKET PRICE (EQUILIBRIUM PRICE) Profit-maximizing price at which the quantity of goods demanded and the quantity of goods supplied are equal.

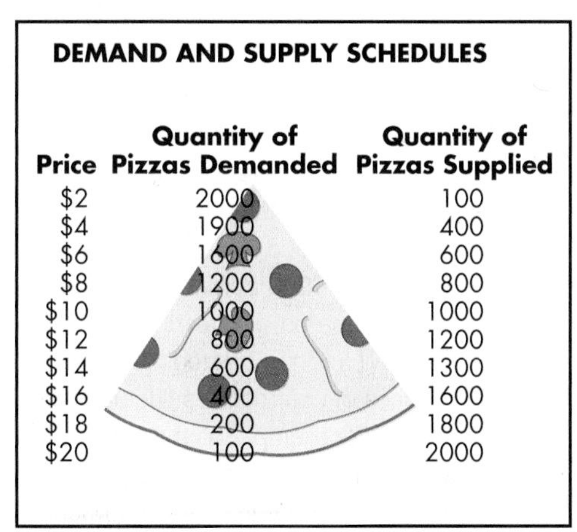

DEMAND AND SUPPLY SCHEDULES

Price	Quantity of Pizzas Demanded	Quantity of Pizzas Supplied
$2	2000	100
$4	1900	400
$6	1600	600
$8	1200	800
$10	1000	1000
$12	800	1200
$14	600	1300
$16	400	1600
$18	200	1800
$20	100	2000

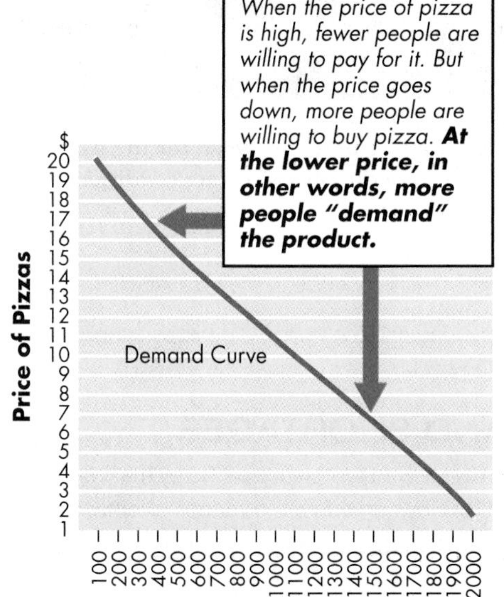

When the price of pizza is high, fewer people are willing to pay for it. But when the price goes down, more people are willing to buy pizza. **At the lower price, in other words, more people "demand" the product.**
Demand Curve
Price of Pizzas
Quantity of Pizzas Demanded

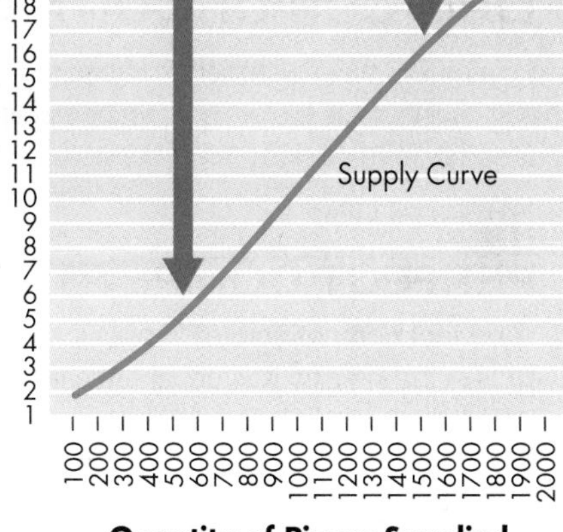

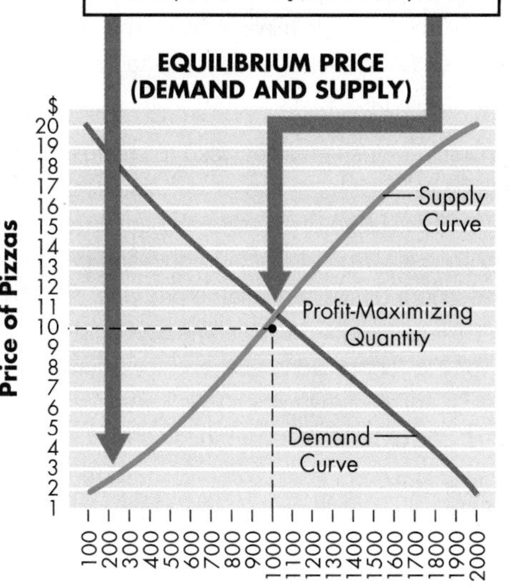

FIGURE 1.3 Demand and supply

Source: Adapted from Karl E. Case and Ray C. Fair, *Principles of Economics*, 8th ed., updated (Upper Saddle River, NJ: Prentice Hall, 2007).

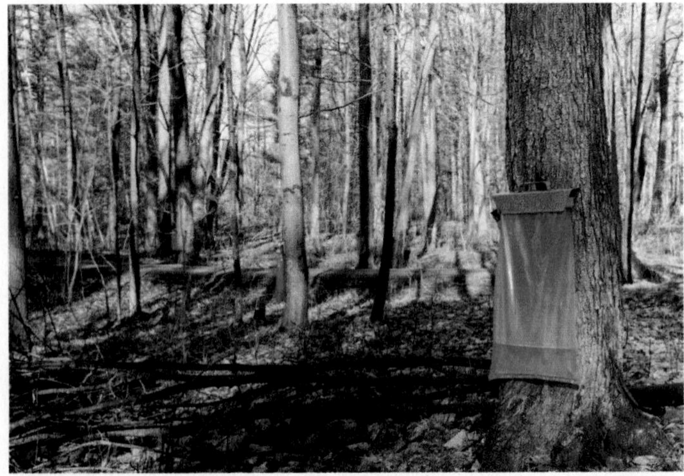

Canada is the dominant supplier of maple syrup for the world market. But variable weather conditions can create conditions of either surplus or shortage.

James_Pintar/Fotolia

the quantity of pizzas demanded and the quantity of pizzas supplied are the same—1000 pizzas per week.

SURPLUSES AND SHORTAGES

What would happen if the owner tried to increase profits by making more pizzas to sell? Or, what if the owner wanted to reduce overhead, cut back on store hours, and reduced the number of pizzas offered for sale? In either case, the result would be an inefficient use of resources. For example, if the restaurant supplies 1200 pizzas and tries to sell them for $10 each, 200 pizzas will not be purchased. The demand schedule clearly shows that only 1000 pizzas will be demanded at this price. The pizza maker will therefore have a **surplus**—a situation in which the quantity supplied exceeds the quantity demanded. The restaurant will thus lose the money that it spent making those extra 200 pizzas.

Conversely, if the pizzeria supplies only 800 pizzas, a *shortage* will result, because the quantity demanded will be greater than the quantity supplied. The pizzeria will "lose" the extra money it could have made by producing 200 more pizzas. Even though consumers may pay more for pizzas because of the shortage, the restaurant will still earn lower profits than it would have if it had made 1000 pizzas. In addition, it may risk angering customers who cannot buy pizzas. To optimize profits, therefore, all businesses must constantly seek the right combination of price charged and quantity supplied. This "right combination" is found at the equilibrium point.

These supply and demand ideas apply to all sorts of commodities. Canada produces about 80 percent of the world's maple syrup, but its price fluctuates because weather influences the supply that is available.[28] The price of expensive truffles (an edible root) is also affected by the weather. Prices recently declined from about $5000 a pound to $2000 a pound because good growing conditions caused large harvests of the product in 2014.[29]

The economic activity of a single large country can have an influence on the price of commodities by increasing demand for the commodity. The rapid increase in automobile sales in China has caused the price of palladium (which is used in cars' catalytic converters) to increase from $400 per ounce to $900 dollars per ounce. China has also reduced its exports of the so-called "rare earth" metals like cerium, lanthanum, and neodymium, and this has created concerns about a supply shortage.[30]

When prices of commodities fluctuate, there are often unanticipated consequences. For example, as the price of stainless steel and aluminum rose during the last few years, thieves began stealing items such as beer kegs, railway baggage carts, railroad tracks, light poles, and highway guard rails. These items were then sold to scrap yards for cash.[31]

SURPLUS Situation in which quantity supplied exceeds quantity demanded.

LO-5 PRIVATE ENTERPRISE AND COMPETITION

Market economies rely on a **private enterprise** system—one that allows individuals to pursue their own interests with minimal government restriction. Private enterprise requires the presence of four elements: private property rights, freedom of choice, profits, and competition.

- *Private property*. Ownership of the resources used to create wealth is in the hands of individuals.[32]
- *Freedom of choice*. You can sell your labour to any employer you choose. You can also choose which products to buy, and producers can usually choose whom to hire and what to produce.
- *Profits*. The lure of profits (and freedom) leads some people to abandon the security of working for someone else and to assume the risks of entrepreneurship. Anticipated profits also influence individuals' choices of which goods or services to produce.
- *Competition*. Competition is evident when two or more businesses vie for the same resources or customers. While profits motivate individuals to *start* businesses, competition motivates them to *operate* their businesses efficiently. Competition forces businesses to make products better and/or cheaper.

PRIVATE ENTERPRISE An economic system characterized by private property rights, freedom of choice, profits, and competition.

PERFECT COMPETITION A market or industry characterized by a very large number of small firms producing an identical product so that none of the firms has any ability to influence price.

Degrees of Competition

Economists have identified four basic degrees of competition within a private enterprise system: perfect competition, monopolistic competition, oligopoly, and monopoly.

PERFECT COMPETITION

In **perfect competition**, all firms in an industry are small, the number of firms in the industry is large, and the products produced by the different firms are virtually identical. Under these conditions, no single firm is powerful enough to influence prices, so they are determined by the market forces of supply and demand. Canadian agriculture is a good example of perfect competition. The wheat produced on one farm is the same as that on another. Both producers and buyers are aware of prevailing market prices. It is relatively easy to start producing wheat and relatively easy to stop when it's no longer profitable.

MONOPOLISTIC COMPETITION

In **monopolistic competition**, there are fewer sellers, but still many buyers. Businesses may be large or small, and small clothing stores can compete successfully with large apparel retailers such as Liz Claiborne and Limited Brands. Whatever their size, sellers try to make their products at least *seem* different from those of competitors, and this product differentiation gives sellers some control over prices. For instance, even though a Sears shirt may look pretty much like a Ralph Lauren Polo shirt, the latter can be priced $20 higher than the Sears shirt. Other differentiating strategies include brand names (Tide and Cheer) and advertising (Coca-Cola and Pepsi).

OLIGOPOLY

When an industry has only a handful of very large sellers, an **oligopoly** exists. Competition is fierce because the actions of any one firm in an oligopolistic market can significantly affect the sales of all other firms.[33] Most oligopolistic firms avoid price competition because it reduces profits. For example, the four major cereal makers (Kellogg, General Mills, General Foods, and Quaker Oats) charge roughly the same price for their cereals. Rather than compete on price, they emphasize advertising, which claims that their cereals are better tasting or more nutritious than the competitions'. Entry into an oligopolistic market is difficult because large capital investment is usually necessary. Thus, oligopolistic industries (such as the automobile, rubber, and steel industries) tend to stay oligopolistic. As the trend toward globalization continues, it is likely that more global oligopolies will come into being.[34]

The boxed insert entitled "Taking a Bite out of Internet Radio" describes the intense competition that exists for technology companies like Apple and Samsung.

Consumers often buy products under conditions of monopolistic competition. For example, there are few differences between various brands of toothpaste, cold tablets, detergents, canned goods, and soft drinks.

Danr13/Fotolia

MONOPOLISTIC COMPETITION A market or industry characterized by a large number of firms supplying products that are similar but distinctive enough from one another to give firms some ability to influence price.

OLIGOPOLY A market or industry characterized by a small number of very large firms that have the power to influence the price of their product and/or resources.

E-BUSINESS AND SOCIAL MEDIA SOLUTIONS

Taking a Bite out of Internet Radio

Apple is one of the most innovative companies in the world; it has helped transform the computer, smartphone, tablet, and music industries. However, in recent years, competitors like Samsung (in the smartphone market) are cutting into Apple's pie. Samsung controlled only 4 percent of the smartphone market in 2010 but controlled 24 percent by 2015. The dominant position achieved by Apple iTunes (after the digital revolution) is now under threat by streaming services.

Streaming radio is the fastest-growing form of music listening. In late 2013, Apple rolled out the iTunes Radio service with more than 200 stations and, like competitor Pandora, the ability of users to create custom stations to fit their musical tastes. The service also integrates with the Siri mobile assistant, allowing users to ask Siri, "Who plays this song?" (just like Shazam). There is a free ad-supported option, as well as a yearly ad-free option for $24.99. Apple's service will try to leverage its built-in library of 43 million songs and customer loyalty associated with the iTunes Store.

Apple has no shortage of competition in this venture, and they were late to enter the market. Market leader Pandora offers a free ad-supported version and a subscription service for $36 per year. It is available on Android, BlackBerry, and iPhone. Spotify has an average audience of 60 million users.

So why is Apple making this "me too" move now? Music downloads are down by about 15 percent and Apple is losing its grip on the music industry as newer streaming competitors like Beats Music and Songza gain momentum. According to one music label, iTunes' share of company revenue has declined from 70 percent in 2012 to less than 50 percent.

Industry analysts are divided in their opinion of Apple's new venture. Ken Volkman, chief technical officer at SRV Network, concludes: "They have a large and loyal customer base established and the capability to be competitive with advertising revenue rates, both providing great incentive for music publishers." But Rocco Pendola, from the finance site The Street, told CNN that "iTunes Radio is a Pandora knockoff. It absolutely will not come close to Pandora in terms of functionality and user experience. It can't possibly do that. Pandora is a 13-year-old company. Apple is just doing what everyone else has done—copying it."

In Canada, iTunes Radio has a slightly easier task. Thanks to the Canadian government (the CRTC in particular), some top streaming services like Pandora and Hulu are banned as they are not licensed Canadian music distributors. While the future of iTunes Radio is uncertain, it is clear that the future of internet radio is bright. Will Apple surge past its competitors or fade into the background? Time will tell.

CRITICAL THINKING QUESTIONS

1. In terms of degrees of competition, how would you describe the market for internet radio? Do you think this will change in the next five years? If so, how?
2. Do you think that Apple will be successful in this new venture? Do you think it was a wise decision for them to enter the already crowded market?

MONOPOLY

When an industry or market has only one producer, a **monopoly** exists. Being the only supplier gives a firm complete control over the price of its product. Its only constraint is how much consumer demand will fall as its price rises. For centuries, wine bottles were sealed using natural cork made from tree bark. But a new technology allows wine bottles to be sealed with plastic corks that are cheaper and work just as well. The natural wine cork industry has lost its monopoly.[35] In Canada, laws such as the Competition Act forbid most monopolies. So-called *natural monopolies*—such as provincial electric utilities—are closely watched by provincial utilities boards, and the assumption that there is such a thing as a natural monopoly is increasingly being challenged. For example, the volume of mail that Canada Post handles has declined, and it has been annually losing millions of dollars in recent years.[36] There have been repeated calls to end its monopoly on letters weighing less than 500 grams (competition from companies like FedEx and UPS is allowed for parcels and express mail). During the ten years after it became a Crown corporation, Canada Post has raised its rates by 41 percent. By contrast, postal rates have dropped in countries where the post office has been privatized (e.g., Germany and the Netherlands).[37]

Producers in several industries in Canada operate under a system called *supply management*, which has some of the characteristics of a monopoly. Domestic production quotas are established for commodities like dairy products, maple syrup, eggs, chickens, and turkeys. Producers of these commodities are not allowed to produce more than the quota they have been granted. To prevent foreign competitors from entering the market, high tariffs are charged on imports of these commodities (e.g., the tariff on butter is 299 percent, on cheese 246 percent, and on milk 241 percent).[38] The supply management system continues to operate in spite of evidence that it increases costs to consumers, encourages smuggling, reduces innovation, and inhibits exports.

MONOPOLY A market or industry with only one producer, who can set the price of its product and/or resources.

MyBizLab

Study, practise, and explore real business situations with these helpful resources:

- **Interactive Lesson Presentations:** Work through interactive presentations and assessments to test your knowledge of business concepts.
- **Study Plan:** Check your understanding of chapter concepts with self-study quizzes.
- **Dynamic Study Modules:** Work through adaptive study modules on your computer, tablet, or mobile device.
- **Simulations:** Practise decision-making in simulated business environments.
- **Videos:** Learn more about the business practices and strategies of real companies.

SUMMARY OF LEARNING OBJECTIVES

LO-1 DEFINE THE NATURE OF CANADIAN *BUSINESS* AND IDENTIFY ITS MAIN GOALS.

Businesses are organizations that produce or sell goods or services to make a profit. *Profits* are the difference between a business's revenues and expenses. The prospect of earning profits encourages individuals and organizations to open and expand businesses. The benefits of business activities also extend to wages paid to workers and to taxes that support government functions.

LO-2 DESCRIBE DIFFERENT TYPES OF GLOBAL *ECONOMIC SYSTEMS* ACCORDING TO THE MEANS BY WHICH THEY CONTROL THE *FACTORS OF PRODUCTION* THROUGH *INPUT* AND *OUTPUT MARKETS*.

An *economic system* is a nation's system for allocating its resources among its citizens. Economic systems differ in terms of who owns or controls the five basic *factors of production*: labour, capital, entrepreneurs, natural resources, and information. In *command economies*, the government controls all or most of these factors. In *market economies*, which are based on the principles of capitalism, individuals and businesses control the factors of production and exchange them through input and output markets. Most countries today have *mixed market economies* that are dominated by one of these systems, but include elements of the other. The processes of *deregulation* and *privatization* are important means by which many of the world's planned economies are moving toward mixed market systems.

LO-3 DESCRIBE THE INTERACTIONS BETWEEN BUSINESS AND GOVERNMENT IN CANADA.

Government plays many important roles within the Canadian economic system, and, in so doing, it influences business firms. Government can play the role of *customer*, *competitor*, *regulator*, *taxation agent*, *provider of incentives*, and *provider of essential services*. Businesses can influence government by lobbying, joining trade associations, and trying to convince voters to support or oppose certain regulations.

LO-4 SHOW HOW *DEMAND* AND *SUPPLY* AFFECT RESOURCE DISTRIBUTION IN CANADA.

The Canadian economy is strongly influenced by markets, demand, and supply. *Demand* is the willingness and ability of buyers to purchase a good or service. *Supply* is the willingness and ability of producers to offer goods or services for sale. Demand and supply work together to set a *market* or *equilibrium price*—the price at which the quantity of goods demanded and the quantity of goods supplied are equal.

LO-5 IDENTIFY THE ELEMENTS OF *PRIVATE ENTERPRISE*, AND EXPLAIN THE VARIOUS *DEGREES OF COMPETITION* IN THE CANADIAN ECONOMIC SYSTEM.

The Canadian economy is founded on the principles of *private enterprise*: private property rights, freedom of choice, profits, and competition. Degrees of competition vary because not all industries are equally competitive. Under conditions of *pure competition*, numerous small firms compete in a market governed entirely by demand and supply. In *monopolistic competition*, there are a smaller number of sellers, and each one tries to make its product seem different from the products of competitors. An *oligopoly* involves only a handful of sellers who fiercely compete with each other. A *monopoly* involves only one seller.

QUESTIONS AND EXERCISES

QUESTIONS FOR ANALYSIS

1. On various occasions, government provides financial incentives to business firms. For example, the Canadian government provided export assistance to Bombardier Inc. with its Technology Transfer Program. Is this consistent with a basically free market system? Explain how this might distort the system.
2. In recent years, many countries have moved from planned economies to market economies. Why do you think this has occurred? Can you envision a situation that would cause a resurgence of planned economies?
3. In your opinion, what industries in Canada should be regulated by the government? Defend your arguments.
4. Familiarize yourself with a product or service that is sold under conditions of pure competition. Explain why it is an example of pure competition and identify the factors that make it so. Then do the same for a product in each of the other three competitive situations described in the chapter (monopolistic competition, oligopoly, and monopoly).
5. Analyze how the factors of production (labour, capital, entrepreneurs, natural resources, and information resources) work together for a product or service of your choice.
6. Government plays a variety of roles in the Canadian mixed economy (customer, regulator, taxation agent, provider of services, and so on). Consider each of the roles discussed in this chapter and state your view as to whether government involvement in each role is excessive, insufficient, or about right. What criteria did you use to make your assessments?

APPLICATION EXERCISES

7. For a product that is not discussed in this chapter, find an example where a surplus led to decreased prices. Then find an example where a shortage led to increased prices. What eventually happened in each case? Why? Is what happened consistent with what economic theory predicts?
8. Choose a locally owned business. Interview the owner to find out (1) how demand and supply affect the business, (2) how the business uses the factors of production, and (3) how the owner acquires each factor of production.
9. Visit a local shopping mall or shopping area. List each store that you see and determine what degree of competition it faces in its immediate environment. For example, if there is only one store in the mall that sells shoes, that store represents a monopoly. Note those businesses with direct competitors (e.g., two jewellery stores) and show how they compete with one another.
10. Pick a specific product that you use. Explain how the factors of production work together to make that product available.

TEAM EXERCISES

BUILDING YOUR BUSINESS SKILLS

ANALYZING THE PRICE OF DOING BUSINESS

GOAL

To encourage students to understand how competition affects a product's price.

SITUATION

Assume that you are the owner of a local gym and fitness studio. You've worked hard to build a loyal customer base and your facility is top-notch, with the latest equipment and a variety of classes for customers at all fitness levels. Within your geographical area, there are three other gyms, each charging the same price ($40 per month for individuals, $60 per month for couples, and $75 per month for families). However, you've become concerned because one of your competitors has just announced that they are reducing membership costs by $10 per month for each of the three categories of memberships. Rumour has it that another facility plans to follow suit in the near future. You can't afford to get into a price war because you are just barely making a profit at your current price structure.

METHOD

Divide into groups of four or five people. Each group is to develop a general strategy for handling competitors' price changes. In your discussion, take the following factors into account:

- how the demand for your product is affected by price changes
- the number of competitors selling the same or a similar product
- the methods—other than price—you can use to attract new customers and/or retain current customers

ANALYSIS

Develop specific pricing strategies based on each of the following situations:

- A month after dropping prices by $10 per month, one of your competitors returns to your current pricing level.
- Two of your competitors drop their prices even further, reducing membership costs by a further $5 per month. As a result, your business falls off by 25 percent.
- One of your competitors announces that it will keep its prices low, but it will charge members $2 per session for high-demand classes such as Pilates.
- Each of the competitors that lowered their price makes an adjustment, with reduced rates for families and couples, but they plan to return to $40 per month for singles.
- All four providers (including you) have reduced their monthly fees. One gym goes out of business, and you know that another is in poor financial health.

FOLLOW-UP QUESTIONS

1. Discuss the role that various inducements other than price might play in affecting demand and supply in the market.
2. Is it always in a company's best interest to feature the lowest prices?
3. Eventually, what form of competition is likely to characterize this market?

EXERCISING YOUR ETHICS

MAKING THE RIGHT DECISION

THE SITUATION

The rural municipality of Hanover recently received a proposal from a large international mining company that wants to build a processing facility in Hanover. The company has mining operations in two adjacent provinces, and it wants to process the output from those mines in Hanover.

THE DILEMMA

The municipality of Hanover has about 50 000 inhabitants. It has been economically depressed for more than 20 years. Way back in the 1950s, a large textile factory was established in the municipality, and it provided hundreds of jobs. New homes were built, many new business opened, and the town prospered. But in 1991, the factory closed and all production was moved overseas to save on labour costs. As a result, unemployment has been high and housing values have plummeted. Many stores have closed, and residents often must travel considerable distances for jobs and to buy certain products.

The proposed processing facility will create 400 new jobs during the one-year construction period, and when the plant is operational, there will be 300 new full-time jobs with excellent pay and benefits. Some managers may be transferred in from other locations, but most of these new jobs would be filled by current residents of Hanover.

Virtually everyone in Hanover has an opinion on the proposed processing facility, but there is a lot of disagreement. Residents enjoy the quiet nature of the area and are concerned about heavy truck traffic once the plant starts operating. On the other hand, local store owners, many of whom are just barely making a profit, look forward to the economic boom that will take place, and they strongly support the proposed facility. The municipality is considering three options:

- approve the construction of the processing facility based on the potential positive economic impact
- reject the proposal and seek out other types of new business opportunities
- accept the proposal for the processing facility, but place conditions on its size, location, and operations

TEAM ACTIVITY

Assemble groups of four students and assign each group member to one of the following roles:

- council member for the municipality of Hanover
- mining company executive
- local storeowner
- environmental activist

ACTION STEPS

1. Before discussing the situation with your group, and from the perspective of your assigned role, decide which of the three options is the best choice. Write down the reasons for your position.
2. Before discussing the situation with your group, and from the perspective of your assigned role, determine the underlying ethical issues, if any, in this situation. Write down the issues.
3. Gather your group together and reveal, in turn, each member's comments on the best choice of the three options. Next, reveal the ethical issues listed by each member.
4. Appoint someone to record the main points of agreement and disagreement within the group. How do you explain the results? What accounts for any disagreement?
5. From an ethical standpoint, what does your group conclude is the most appropriate action that should be taken by the municipality of Hanover in this situation?
6. Develop a group response to the following question: Can your team identify other solutions that might help the municipality of Hanover reach a consensus on this issue?

BUSINESS CASE 1

WHERE ARE GASOLINE PRICES HEADED?

What did you pay for the most recent cup of coffee you bought? Whatever you paid, it probably wasn't much different from what you paid the time before that. For most products, prices don't fluctuate very much in the short run. But there is one glaring exception: the price of gasoline. You never know how much you're going to pay when you pull up to the pump. In early 2014, prices across Canada were approximately $1.24 per litre, but by the beginning of 2015, they had dropped to less than 90 cents per litre in some provinces. In the United States during the same period, prices dropped from $3.75 per gallon to just $1.93 per gallon. Since gasoline is such a crucial commodity for Canadians and Americans, these fluctuations have a big effect on consumer spending and hence on the overall economy.

The most general reason why gas prices fluctuate relates to the supply of gas available; that is, gas prices increase when *supply* declines and decrease when supply increases. Increased supply has been the biggest factor in the recent sharp decline in oil prices (from about $110 per barrel in June 2014 to about $53 per barrel in April 2015). To add to the impact of greater supply, OPEC announced in 2014 that it would continue to pump large amounts of oil. Observers concluded that OPEC (whose oil production costs are relatively low) was adopting this strategy because it wanted to drive out foreign producers who had higher costs and couldn't make any profits if oil prices were low.

Gas prices are also influenced by other factors. For example, when the global economy is booming, there is increased demand for oil to support increased economic activity. In 2014, growth in many economies (particularly in the European Union) began to slow down, and the demand for oil moderated. Another factor is political instability. Some of the key producers of oil are located in countries that suffer frequent political upheavals (e.g., Venezuela, Nigeria, Iraq, and Iran). This affects the amount of oil produced and contributes to either an increased or a decreased supply in the world market. Yet another factor is technological breakthroughs that enhance our ability to extract more oil and thus increase supply.

What does all this mean for the future of gas prices? Before making any predictions, it is important to understand some facts about the supply of oil. Just a few years ago, the so-called "peak-oil" theory was very popular. It said that world oil production had peaked and was going to rapidly decline and cause a major shortfall in the amount of oil that was available. Supporters of this idea presented certain facts to show that "peak oil" was imminent:

Calin Tatu/Fotolia

- Output from existing oil fields around the world is declining, and that means that 3–4 million barrels a day of new oil will have to be found for global oil production just to remain steady.
- Top-level executives in the oil industry say that there is a limit to how much oil can be produced each year (about 100 million barrels per day).
- Oil production will peak because of factors such as restricted access to oil fields, shortages of oil field workers, rapidly increasing costs, political crises, and complex oil field geology.
- New oil discoveries have declined sharply.

Opponents of peak-oil theory accepted these facts, but rejected the idea that a crisis was coming. They argued that other, more important facts had been completely ignored by the theory's supporters:

- The world's "ultimate recoverable reserves" (URR) are growing at an increasing rate. For example, during the period 1957–2006, URR grew at an annual rate of 2.4 percent, but from 2000 to 2007 the rate was 6 percent. The URR was 1.6 trillion barrels in 1995 and was predicted to rise to 3.3 trillion barrels by 2025, but it had already reached 3.2 trillion barrels in 2006, many years ahead of schedule.
- New oil discoveries were made in 2010 and 2011 off the coast of Brazil and in the Gulf of Mexico, and North American oil production has increased dramatically because of the Alberta oil sands and the Bakken oil field in North Dakota.
- In 1979, the "life index" of oil was estimated to be about 35 years (at 1979 consumption rates). That meant we would experience an oil crisis early in the twenty-first century. But by 2003, the life index had actually risen to 40 years, and by 2007 it had risen to 45 years. These increases have occurred even though oil consumption rates now far exceed those of 1979.
- As oil prices increase, greater amounts of oil will be economically extracted from formations such as the Alberta oil sands, alternative sources of fuel will be developed, and new technologies for extracting oil will be developed.

At the moment, the opponents of peak oil have the upper hand. Dramatic increases in supply have occurred in recent years, and there is even talk that the United States may become self-sufficient in oil by 2020. This was considered impossible just a few years ago.

Brian Crowley, the Managing Director of the Macdonald-Laurier Institute, says that we must look at both the supply and demand side when trying to predict the price of gasoline. The "supply" of oil (or any other natural resource) doesn't simply mean the physical amount found in the earth; it also includes the application of human ingenuity in finding better ways to use it. So, while it is absolutely true that there is a finite quantity of oil, we will not run out of oil any time soon because we are becoming more and more efficient at using it. To see the magnitude of this, consider another commodity: copper. Years ago, there were miles of overhead copper telephone wires along roadways, but with the development of fibre optics, the reach of the telephone increased without any increase in the need for copper.

As you can now appreciate, what all this means for the price of gas at the pump is difficult to predict. Many cycles of increasing and decreasing prices have occurred during that last 100 years, but the timing and duration of these cycles varies. This is probably not what you wanted to hear, but it is the reality that we must all cope with. The same kinds of fluctuations are occurring with another fossil fuel: natural gas. As recently as 2008, natural gas reserves didn't seem to be very large. But then a new technology was developed to tap "shale gas" (natural gas that is trapped in sedimentary rocks). This new technology involves pumping water, sand, and chemicals into the ground under high pressure to fracture the rock and release the natural gas (the process is called "fracking"). The U.S.-based Energy Information Administration (EIA) released a report stating that total recoverable natural gas (including conventional natural gas and shale gas) was 4.244 quadrillion cubic feet. At present consumption rates, the supply will last 575 years. In the future, even more dramatic gains may be made. For example, a successful field trial was announced in 2012 using a technology to extract natural gas from methane hydrates (chunks of ice that trap natural gas). This type of natural gas is the most abundant fossil fuel, and the numbers are staggering. For example, the United States currently produces 21 trillion cubic feet (21 tcf) of natural gas and shale gas annually. But it is estimated that there is *330 000* tcf of methane hydrates in the United States, enough to last 3000 years. Japanese researchers have a goal of commercially producing natural gas hydrates by 2019.

QUESTIONS FOR DISCUSSION

1. Consider the arguments in support of peak-oil theory and the arguments against it. Then draw a graph that shows your predictions of world oil production from now until the year 2100 (measure annual world oil production in billions of barrels on the vertical axis and time on the horizontal axis). Defend your predictions.
2. What do your predictions imply about the price of gas at the pump over time?
3. It appears that the supply of oil and natural gas is very large. Discuss some potential problems that might arise even with such a large supply.
4. Consider the following statement: *There are so many uncertainties that must be taken into account when trying to predict the supply of, and demand for, oil that it is impossible to have any confidence in anyone's predictions.* Do you agree or disagree? Explain your reasoning.

CHAPTER SUPPLEMENT 01

A Brief History of Business in Canada

In this supplement, we summarize the broad outlines of the development of business activity in Canada. A more detailed discussion of the development of Canadian business activity is found online in MyBizLab.

THE EARLY YEARS

Business activity and profit from commercial fishing were the motivation for the first European involvement in Canada. Beginning in the 1500s, French and British adventurers began trading with the native peoples. The governments of these countries were strong supporters of the mercantilist philosophy, and colonists were expected to export raw materials like beaver pelts and lumber at low prices to the mother country. Attempts to develop industry in Canada were hindered by England and France, which enjoyed large profits from mercantilism.

THE FACTORY SYSTEM AND THE INDUSTRIAL REVOLUTION

British manufacturing took a great leap forward around 1750 with the coming of the *Industrial Revolution*. This revolution was made possible by advances in technology and by the development of the *factory system*. Instead of hundreds of workers turning out items one at a time in their cottages, the factory system brought together in one place all of the materials and workers required to produce items in large quantities, along with newly created machines capable of *mass production*. In spite of British laws against the export of technology and manufacturing to North America, modest manufacturing operations were evident in sawmills, breweries, grist mills for grinding grain, tanneries, woollen mills, shoemakers' shops, and tailors' shops. These operations became so successful that by 1800 exports of manufactured goods were more important than exports of fur.

THE ENTREPRENEURIAL ERA

In the last half of the nineteenth century, entrepreneurs emerged who were willing to take risks in the hope of earning large profits. Some individuals became immensely wealthy through their aggressive business dealings. But the size and economic power of some firms meant that other businesses had difficulty competing against them. At the same time, some business executives decided that it was more profitable to collude than to compete. They decided among themselves to fix prices and divide up markets. Hurt by these actions, Canadian consumers called for more regulation of business.

THE PRODUCTION ERA

Henry Ford's introduction of the moving assembly line in the United States in 1913 ushered in the *production era*. The Scientific Management Movement focused management's attention on production. Increased efficiency via the "one best way" to accomplish tasks became a major management goal. During the production era, less attention was paid to selling and marketing than to technical efficiency when producing goods. The growth of corporations and improved production output resulting from assembly lines sometimes came at the expense of worker freedom. To restore some balance within the overall system, both government and labour had to develop and grow.

THE SALES AND MARKETING ERAS

By the 1930s, business's focus on production had resulted in spectacular increases in the amount of goods and services available for sale. As a result, buyers had more choices and producers faced greater competition in selling their wares. According to the ideas of that time, a business's profits and success depended on hiring the right salespeople, advertising heavily, and making sure products were readily available. In the marketing era (the 1950s and 1960s), businesses increasingly used market research to determine what customers wanted, and then made it for them.

THE FINANCE ERA

In the finance era (the 1980s), there was a sharp increase in mergers and in the buying and selling of business enterprises. Some people now call it the "decade of greed." During the finance era, there was a great deal of financial manipulation of corporate assets by so-called corporate raiders.

THE GLOBAL ERA

During the past two decades, we have witnessed the emergence of the global economy and further dramatic technological advances in production, computer technology, information systems, and communication capabilities. While some Canadian businesses have been hurt by foreign imports, numerous others have profited by exploring new foreign markets themselves. Global and domestic competition has also forced all businesses to work harder than ever to cut costs, increase efficiency, and improve product and service quality.

THE INTERNET ERA

The rapid increase in internet usage has facilitated global business activity. Both large and small businesses are not restricted to thinking only in terms of local markets. Web-based services that are offered through a web browser are helping businesses "go global."

Rawpixel/Fotolia

LO

AFTER READING THIS CHAPTER, YOU SHOULD BE ABLE TO:

- LO-1 Explain the concepts of *organizational boundaries and multiple organizational environments*.
- LO-2 Explain the importance of the *economic environment* to business and identify the factors used to evaluate the performance of an economic system.
- LO-3 Describe the *technological environment* and its role in business.
- LO-4 Describe the *political–legal environment* and its role in business.
- LO-5 Describe the *socio-cultural environment* and its role in business.
- LO-6 Identify emerging challenges and opportunities in the *business environment*.
- LO-7 Understand recent trends in the *redrawing of corporate boundaries*.

Supermarket Battles: Then There Were Three

Whether you know it or not, there are essentially three major supermarket chains left in Canada: (1) Loblaws, (2) Sobeys, and (3) Metro. Even if you shop at a retail outlet operating under another banner, chances are it is owned by one of these three. For example, are you wondering why Safeway was not mentioned? It was recently purchased by Sobeys. There have been many acquisitions in the past few years as the threats from Walmart and upscale supermarkets and from evolving online grocers intensify. This Canadian consolidation has had a major impact on manufacturers, suppliers, and ultimately the consumer. Let's look at the facts before analyzing the consequences.

Loblaws

Loblaws was founded nearly 100 years ago. It is headquartered in Brampton, Ontario, and is a division of Loblaws Companies Limited. Today it has over 2300 retail outlets and 192 000 employees. After years of building up its grocery business and establishing different retail brands,

Pat Holmes/Alamy Stock Photo

Loblaws shifted gears when it bought Shoppers Drug Mart for $12.4 billion. It is no coincidence that this move occurred at a time when drugstores were transforming into megastores with increased shelf space being allocated to groceries. Loblaws also announced plans to spend $1.2 billion for new stores and renovations to existing ones.

Loblaws Family of Retail Brands: Atlantic Superstore, Box, Dominion, Extra Foods, Fortinos, Loblaws City Market, Independent City Market, No Frills, Real Canadian Superstore, Save Easy, Maxi & Cie, Provigo, Your Independent Grocer, Valu-mart, Zehrs Markets.

The Environment *of* Business

CHAPTER 02

CNW Group/SOBEYS INC./Newscom

Sobeys Inc.

Sobeys Inc. (owned by Empire Co. Ltd.) was founded over 100 years ago and has headquarters in Stellarton, Nova Scotia. Sobeys has over 1500 stores with outlets in all ten provinces. It has over 125 000 employees and franchise affiliates. Sobeys made major waves with the purchase of Safeway for $5.8 billion. In 2015, the company announced higher profits due in large part to the acquisition of Sobeys and the estimated $200 million in related annual cost savings from improved operational efficiency.

Sobeys Family of Retail Brands: BoniChoix, FreshCo., Foodland, IGA, Price Chopper, Safeway, Thrifty Foods, Les Marchés Tradition.

By understanding the material in this chapter, you'll be better able to assess (1) the impact that events outside a business can have on its *owners* and *managers*, (2) how environmental change impacts you as a *consumer*, and (3) the challenges and opportunities that environmental change provides to you as an employee or an *investor*.

Metro Inc.

Metro is a distant third to Sobeys and Loblaws. However, the Montreal-based company has 800 outlets and 65 000 employees. These statistics demonstrate that Metro is another important force in the Canadian grocery business. Even if it does not have a true national reach like the other two, Metro has a major presence in Ontario and Quebec.

Metro Family of Retail Brands: Food Basics, Metro, SuperC, Marché Richelieu, Marché Ami, Marché Extra and Adonis.

Torontonian/Alamy

What Does This Consolidation Mean?

After acquiring Shoppers Drug Mart, Loblaws sent a notice to its suppliers telling them that it would not accept any price increases for a full year. Similarly, after the Safeway deal, Sobeys actually demanded a 1 percent price cut from its suppliers; to make matters worse they demanded the reduction retroactively (going back three months). Suppliers were obviously not pleased, but when dealing with a company that controls a thousand or more stores and billions in consumer purchases, what can you do? These mega companies have power and they are not afraid to flex their muscles.

Andres Rodriguez/Fotolia

In addition, they are pushing their own private-label brands (e.g., President's Choice at Loblaws), which means shelf space is now much tougher to acquire.

External Threats and Opportunities

So, since suppliers are being squeezed, that should translate into cheaper prices for consumers, right? The short answer is . . . maybe. You can only push so far. Legitimate increases in costs will find their way to the aisles. In a business where margins are very tight, external shocks are extremely important. At the beginning of 2015, Metro's CEO Eric La Fleche provide an interesting explanation of why his company realized increased profits that year. He said that lower fuel prices, in the previous six-month period, had led to increased consumer spending in Metro supermarkets. While economists were worried about the impact of the weak price of oil on the economy, supermarkets were seeing benefits because customers had an extra \$20–\$30 per week in their pockets to spend. However, on the downside, the corresponding fall in the Canadian dollar (against the U.S. dollar) was leading to increases in the price for imported meat and produce, which meant consumers would have to pay more.

Final Thoughts

Next time you are pushing a cart at your favorite grocery store, you will realize there is a great battle for your consumer dollar. Every square centimetre of shelf space earned by a manufacturer represents hard-fought territory. The external environment plays a key role in the potential profitability for supermarket chains and the suppliers that provide the products. This is a tough business operated on a low-margin, high-volume basis.

It is a very delicate balancing act.

QUESTIONS FOR DISCUSSION

1. What are the biggest challenges to long-term success and profitability for Loblaws, Sobeys, and Metro?
2. The three main players in the Canadian grocery market each operate under various brands. Why do you think they still use all those different brand names? Why don't they just rebrand all their stores?
3. What are the main challenges for suppliers as the industry continues to consolidate?
4. How do the external factors other than competition (economy, technology, socio-cultural, political–legal) impact the grocery business?

LO-1 ORGANIZATIONAL BOUNDARIES AND ENVIRONMENTS

All businesses, regardless of their size, location, or mission, operate within a larger external environment that plays a major role in determining their success or failure. The **external environment** consists of everything outside an organization that might affect it. Managers must understand the key features of the external environment and then operate proactively to compete within it.

To better explain the environment of business, we begin by discussing organizational boundaries and multiple organizational environments.

Organizational Boundaries

An *organizational boundary* separates the organization from its environment. Consider the simple case of a neighbourhood grocery store that includes a retail customer area, a storage room, and the owner/manager's office. In many ways, the store's boundary coincides with its physical structure; when you walk through the door, you're crossing the boundary into the business and, when you go back onto the sidewalk, you cross the boundary back into the environment. But this is an oversimplification. During the business day, distributors of soft drinks, snack foods, ice, and bread products may enter the store, inventory their products, and refill coolers and shelves just as if they were employees. These distributors are normally considered part of the environment rather than the organization, but while inside the store they are essentially part of the business. Customers may even assume these distributors are store employees and ask them questions as they restock shelves.

Now consider the case of a large domestic business (such as GM Canada) owned by an even-larger international corporation (U.S.–based General Motors). The domestic business has a complex network of relationships with other businesses, like Magna International, that conduct research and build components for GM. GM Canada also deals with companies that supply tires, glass, steel, and engines. But GM Canada also functions within the boundaries of its international parent, which has its own network of business relationships, some overlapping and some distinct from GM Canada's network.

EXTERNAL ENVIRONMENT Everything outside an organization's boundaries that might affect it.

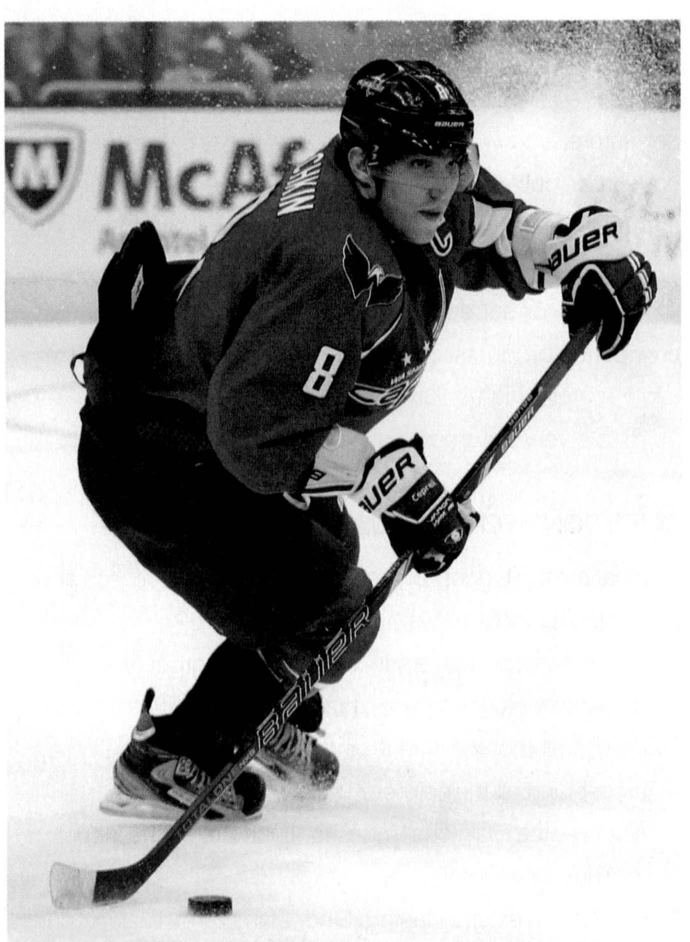

<<< Bauer has 52 percent market share of the global hockey equipment market. The company must constantly stay ahead of the technological race with its competitors for products like composite sticks.

Alex Brandon/AP Images

Multiple Organizational Environments

Organizations have multiple environments. Some, like current economic conditions, affect the performance of almost every business. But other dimensions of the environment are much more specific. The neighbourhood grocery store, for example, will be influenced not only by an increase in unemployment in its area but also by the pricing and other marketing activities of its nearest competitors. Major organizations like Bauer Performance Sports Limited (which owns a 52 percent market share of the global hockey equipment market) must contend with external factors beyond its control, such as competitive actions by companies like Reebok and Easton, as well as stay ahead of the technological race for new composite sticks. However, its success may also be impacted by unexpected issues that can hurt revenues like the recent hockey lockout.[1]

Figure 2.1 shows the major elements of the external environment: economic conditions, technology, political–legal considerations, social issues, the global environment, issues of ethical and social responsibility, the business environment itself, and emerging challenges and opportunities. We will cover ethical and global issues in detail in Chapters 3 and 5 respectively, so we discuss them here only as they relate directly to the other areas in this chapter.

LO-2 THE ECONOMIC ENVIRONMENT

The **economic environment** refers to the conditions of the economic system in which an organization operates.[2] In recent years, the economic environment has been characterized by low growth, fairly steady unemployment rates, and low inflation. During periods of rising unemployment, people are less likely to make unnecessary purchases and they may delay the purchase of a new car or new furniture. The fear of potential job loss or an uncertain paycheque is a very powerful enemy of the economy. It's only rational to reduce your spending in tougher times, but this also means that less needs to be produced and this can ultimately lead to more job losses for the economy as a whole. In a positive economic period, momentum pushes unemployment down as consumers spend more.

Despite low overall inflation, rising costs have put economic pressure on businesses in many sectors. Restaurants and grocery stores have increased prices or reduced package

ECONOMIC ENVIRONMENT Conditions of the economic system in which an organization operates.

<<< The tougher economic times have led to a growth in the popularity of the various dollar-store retailers across the nation.

Kathy deWitt/Alamy

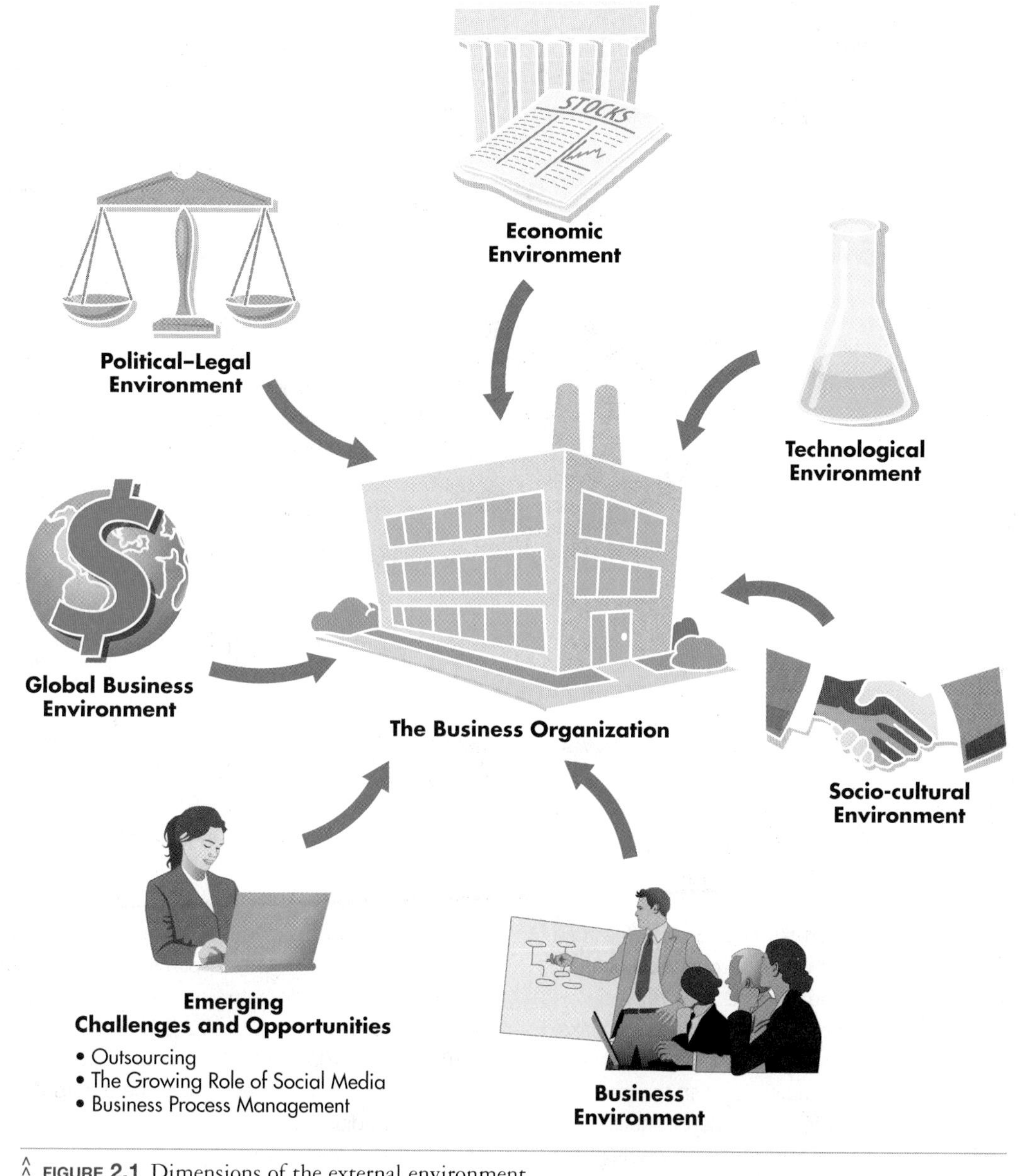

FIGURE 2.1 Dimensions of the external environment

sizes to compete and survive. For example, Loblaws raised the price of its President's Choice Granola cereal from $4.99 to $5.79, while shrinking the package from 800 to 750 grams.[3] Many companies that cater to low-cost interests of consumers, such as Dollarama and Costco, have thrived in the tough economic times as consumers have searched for cheaper prices. Dollarama, which has 917 stores across Canada, realized a 15 percent increase in profits in 2014.[4]

Economic Growth

At one time, about half of the Canadian population was involved in producing the food that we eat. Today, less than 2.5 percent of the population works in agriculture, because agricultural efficiency has improved so much that far fewer people are needed to produce the food we need. We can therefore say that agricultural production has grown because the total output of the agricultural sector has increased. We can apply the same idea to a nation's economic system, but the computations are much more complex, as we shall see.

AGGREGATE OUTPUT AND THE STANDARD OF LIVING

How do we know whether an economic system is growing? The main measure of growth is **aggregate output**: the total quantity of goods and services produced by an economic system during a given period.[5] To put it simply, an increase in aggregate output is economic growth.[6] When output grows more quickly than the population, two things usually follow: output per capita (the quantity of goods and services per person) goes up and the system provides relatively more of the goods and services that people want.[7] And when these two things occur, people living in an economic system benefit from a higher *standard of living*—the total quantity and quality of goods and services they can purchase with the currency used in their economic system.

AGGREGATE OUTPUT Total quantity of goods and services produced by an economic system during a given period.

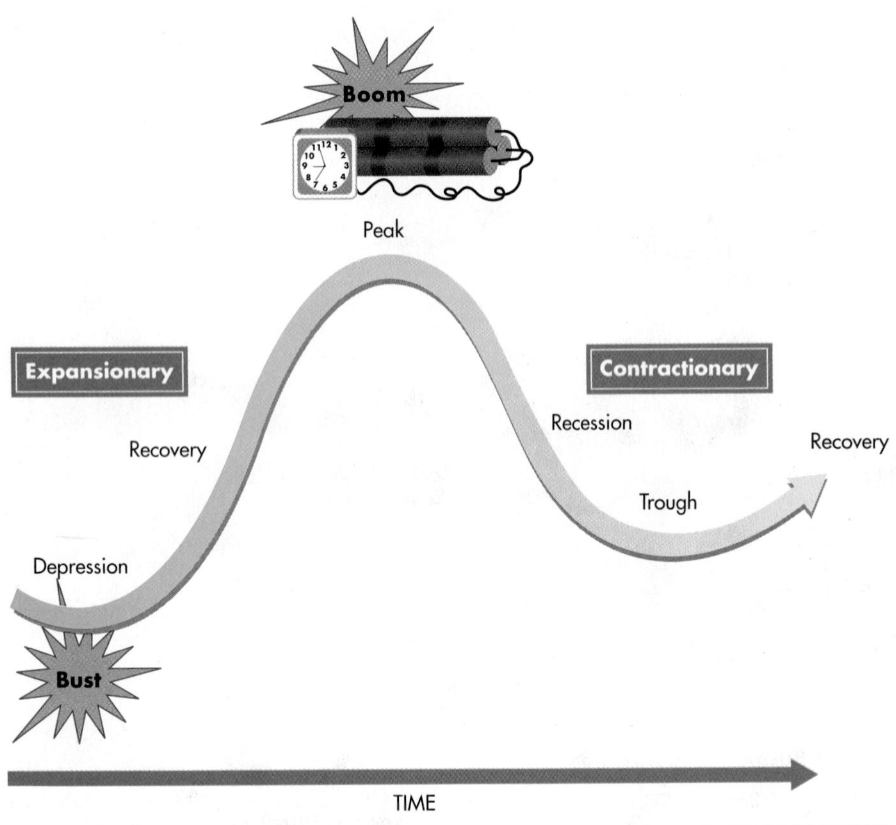

FIGURE 2.2 The business cycle

Today, GDP is the key measure of economic growth because it tracks an economy's performance over time. However, some argue that such measures are flawed. According to one study, more attention should be paid to other indicators, like rising debt. An article in the magazine *The Economist* even referred to GDP as "grossly deceptive product."[12]

Real Growth Rates GDP is the preferred method of calculating national income and output. The real growth rate of GDP—the growth rate of GDP adjusted for inflation and changes in the value of the country's currency—is what counts. Remember that growth depends on output increasing at a faster rate than population. If the growth rate of GDP exceeds the rate of population growth, then our standard of living should be improving.

GDP per Capita **GDP per capita** means GDP per person. We get this figure by dividing total GDP by the total population of a country. As a measure of economic well-being of the average person, GDP per capita is a better measure than GDP. Macao SAR China has the highest GDP per capita (approximately US$142 599), followed by Qatar (US$136 727), Luxembourg (US$90 410), and Singapore (US$78 763). Canada's per capita GDP is (US$42 247).[13]

THE BUSINESS CYCLE

The growth (and contraction) pattern of short-term ups and downs in an economy is called the **business cycle**. It has four recognizable phases: peak, recession, trough, and recovery (see Figure 2.2). A recession is usually defined as two consecutive quarters when the economy shrinks, but it is probably more helpful to say that a recession starts just after the peak of the business cycle is reached and ends when the trough is reached.[8] A depression occurs when the trough of the business cycle extends two or more years. Periods of expansion and contraction can vary from several months to several years.

GROSS DOMESTIC PRODUCT AND GROSS NATIONAL PRODUCT

The term **gross domestic product (GDP)** refers to the total value of all goods and services produced within a given period by a national economy through domestic factors of production. Canada's GDP in 2014 was $1.825 trillion.[9] Global GDP was approximately $76 trillion; the top five countries were the United States, China, Japan, Germany, and France.[10] If GDP rises, a nation experiences economic growth.

GDP measures all business activity within a nation's borders and it has widely replaced **gross national product (GNP)**, which refers to the total value of all goods and services produced by a national economy within a given period regardless of where the factors of production are located. For example, Bombardier is a Canadian company, but all of the manufacturing that occurs in its foreign plants (Kansas, Mexico, Ireland, and, more recently, Morocco) is included in Canadian GNP—but not in GDP—because its output is not produced in Canada. Conversely, those figures are included in the GDP of those nations (U.S., Mexico, Ireland, and Morocco respectively) but not their GNP—because they are produced inside their borders by a Canadian company.[11]

Real GDP **Real GDP** means that GDP has been adjusted. To understand why adjustments are necessary, assume that pizza is the only product in an economy. Assume that in 2015, a pizza cost $10 and, in 2016, it cost $11. In both years, exactly 1000 pizzas were produced. In 2015, the GDP was $10 000 ($10 × 1000); in 2016, the GDP was $11 000 ($11 × 1000). Has the economy grown? No. Since 1000 pizzas were produced in both years, aggregate output remained the same. If GDP is not adjusted for 2016, it is called *nominal GDP*, that is, GDP measured in current dollars.[14]

Purchasing Power Parity In our example, current prices would be 2016 prices. On the other hand, we calculate real GDP when we account for changes in currency values and price changes. When we make this adjustment, we account for both GDP and **purchasing power parity**—the principle that exchange rates are set so that the prices of similar

BUSINESS CYCLE Pattern of short-term ups and downs (expansions and contractions) in an economy.

GROSS DOMESTIC PRODUCT (GDP) Total value of all goods and services produced within a given period by a national economy through domestic factors of production.

GROSS NATIONAL PRODUCT (GNP) Total value of all goods and services produced by a national economy within a given period regardless of where the factors of production are located.

GDP PER CAPITA Gross domestic product per person.

REAL GDP GDP calculated to account for changes in currency values and price changes.

PURCHASING POWER PARITY Principle that exchange rates are set so that the prices of similar products in different countries are about the same.

products in different countries are about the same. Purchasing power parity gives us a much better idea of what people can actually buy. In other words, it gives us a better sense of standards of living across the globe.

PRODUCTIVITY

A major factor in the growth of an economic system is **productivity**, which is a measure of economic growth that compares how much a system produces with the resources needed to produce it. Let's say, for instance, that it takes 1 Canadian worker and 50 Canadian dollars to make 10 pairs of leather boots in an 8-hour workday. Let's also say that it takes 1.2 Spanish workers and the equivalent of $60 (in euros, the official currency used in Spain) to make 10 pairs of equivalent leather boots in the same 8-hour workday. We can say, then, that the Canadian boot manufacturing industry is more productive than the Spanish boot manufacturing industry.

The two factors of production in this simple case are labour and capital. According to the Organisation for Economic Co-operation and Development (OECD) rankings, Canada stood in 12th place with a productivity ratio of 76.8 percent compared to the United States. Luxembourg and Norway were the most productive nations at 171.2 and 121.6 percent respectively. Switzerland (108.4) was also classified above the benchmark U.S. statistics.[15] If more products are being produced with fewer factors of production, what happens to the prices of these products? They go down. As a consumer, therefore, you would need less of your currency to purchase the same quantity of these products. Thus, your standard of living—at least with regard to these products—has improved.

THE BALANCE OF TRADE AND THE NATIONAL DEBT

There are several factors that can help or hinder the growth of an economic system, but here we focus on just two of them: balance of trade and the national debt.

Balance of Trade

The **balance of trade** is the economic value of all the products that a country exports minus the economic value of its imported products. Canada traditionally has a positive balance of trade. It is usually a creditor nation rather than a debtor nation. For example, Canada received $43 to $47 billion more from exports than it spent on imports annually from 2006 to 2008, but a long trend was reversed in 2009 when Canada had a trade deficit of $6 billion due mainly to the sharp rise in the Canadian dollar relative to the U.S. dollar. In 2014, a surplus was once again registered, at $4.4 billion; however, it was no coincidence that the Canadian dollar dropped that year significantly, leading to a boost in exports.[16] A trade deficit negatively affects economic growth, because the money that flows out of a country can't be used to invest in productive enterprises, either at home or overseas.

The balance of trade looks at the all products, including popular imports like the Sony PlayStation Four (PS4). Of course, Sony is a very popular Japanese game console manufacturer that makes products in Japan and China.

Ian Langsdon/EPA/Alamy

National Debt

A country's **national debt** is the amount of money the government owes its creditors. Like a business, the government takes in revenues (e.g., taxes) and has expenses (e.g., military spending, social programs). For many years, the government of Canada incurred annual **budget deficits**, that is, it spent more money each year than it took in. These accumulated annual deficits created a huge national debt (estimated above $615 billion at the beginning of 2015).This figure amounts to approximately $17 500 per citizen.[17]

How does the national debt affect economic growth? When the government of Canada sells bonds to individuals and organizations (both at home and overseas), this affects economic growth because the Canadian government competes with every other potential borrower—individuals, households, businesses, and other organizations—for the available supply of loanable money. The more money the government borrows, the less money is available for the private borrowing and investment that increases productivity.

Take a look at the following There's an App for That! feature that outlines three economics apps.

THERE'S AN APP FOR THAT!

APP DETAILS	PLATFORMS
1. **National Debt** **Source:** Caramba App Development **Key Features:** Provides insight into the national debts of more than 180 countries.	Apple
2. **The Economist World in Figures** **Source:** The Economist **Key Features:** facts and figures for 190 sovereign states (GDP, inflation, population etc.)	Apple, Android, Windows
3. **Gross Domestic Product** **Source:** Samuel Bryant **Key Features:** GDP referenced by year and country.	Apple, Android

APP DISCOVERY EXERCISE

Since app availability changes, conduct your own search for the "Top Three" economics apps and identify the key features.

PRODUCTIVITY Measure of economic growth that compares how much a system produces with the resources needed to produce it.

BALANCE OF TRADE The total of a country's exports (sales to other countries) minus its imports (purchases from other countries).

NATIONAL DEBT The total amount of money that a country owes its creditors.

BUDGET DEFICITS The result of the government spending more in one year than it takes in during that year.

Economic Stability

A key goal of an economic system is *stability*, a condition in which the amount of money available in an economic system and the quantity of goods and services produced in it are growing at about the same rate. Several factors threaten stability—namely, inflation, deflation, and unemployment.

INFLATION

Inflation is evident when the amount of money injected into an economic system outstrips the increase in actual output. When inflation occurs, people have more money to spend, but there will still be the same quantity of products available for them to buy. As they compete with one another to buy available products, prices go up. Before long, high prices will erase the increase in the amount of money injected into the economy. Purchasing power, therefore, declines.

Inflation varies widely across countries. One dramatic example occurred in Zimbabwe in 2008, when inflation reached an astonishing annual rate above 40 million percent (most countries have rates between 2 and 15 percent). One Zimbabwean dollar from 2005 would have been worth 1 trillion Zimbabwean dollars in 2008. Many workers simply stopped going to their jobs, because their pay was not enough to cover their bus fare.[18] The problem was finally solved when the government began allowing people to pay their bills using other currencies, like the U.S. dollar or the South African rand.[19] Inflation was 3.9 percent at the beginning of 2015 in South Africa (the rand is a more stable measure of value in the region).[20]

Measuring Inflation: The CPI

The **Consumer Price Index (CPI)** measures changes in the cost of a "basket" of goods and services that a typical family buys. What is included in the basket has changed over the years. For example, the first CPI in 1913 included items like coal and spirit vinegar, while today it includes bottom-freezer fridges, flat-screen TVs, energy-saving light bulbs, and laser eye surgery.[21] These changes in the CPI reflect changes that have occurred in the pattern of consumer purchases. Figure 2.3 shows how inflation has varied over the past 30 years in Canada.

As mentioned earlier, despite the fact that official inflation rates, as measured by the CPI, have remained low, price pressure (caused by issues like increased fuel prices) put great strain on companies in all sectors. Food manufacturers are particularly vulnerable. In recent years, Maple Leaf Foods has increased prices based on rising costs for inputs such as corn and wheat, which have risen 95 percent and 102 percent, respectively, in one 12-month period alone.[22] At the beginning of 2015, inflationary forces appeared to be reversing, because lower oil prices should logically mean lower transport costs; however, as discussed in the opening case, the slump in the Canadian dollar meant it had become more expensive to buy goods from the United States. Translation: meat, fish, seafood, and vegetables were expected to rise 3 to 5 percent that year.[24]

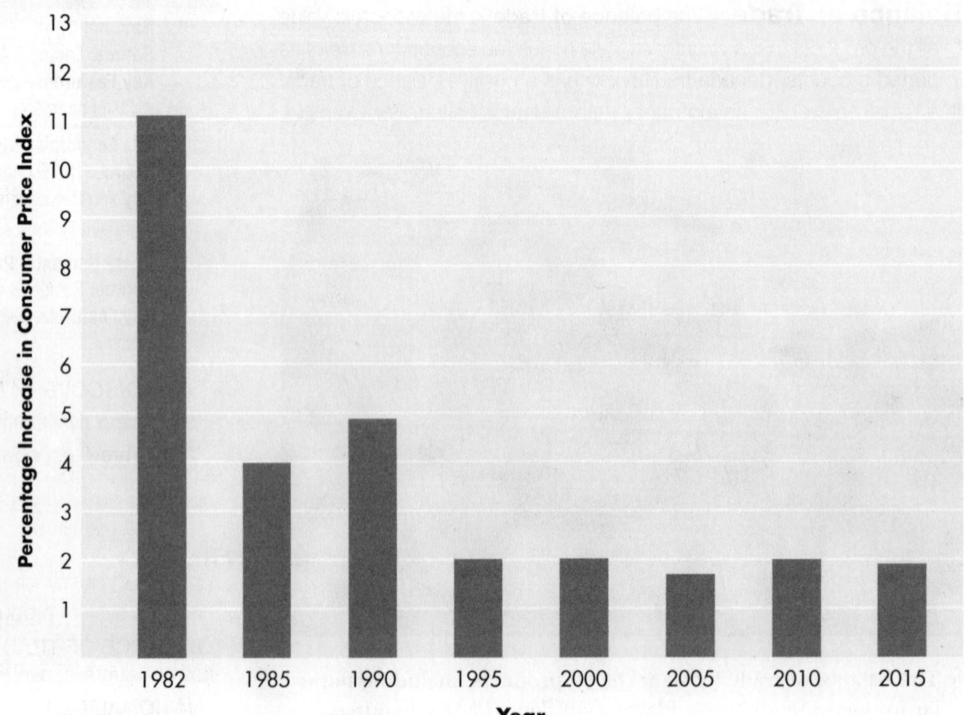

>>> **FIGURE 2.3** Price increases in Canada[23]

During the past 20 years, the rate of price increases in Canada has been low and quite stable.

DEFLATION

Deflation (falling prices) is evident when the amount of money injected into an economic system lags behind increases in actual output. Prices may fall because industrial productivity is increasing and cost savings are being passed on to consumers (this is good), or because consumers have high levels of debt and are therefore unwilling to buy very much (this is bad).

UNEMPLOYMENT

At the beginning of 2015, there were 8.1 million men and 7.2 million women (over age 25) working in Canada's labour force.[25] But there were many additional people who wanted a job but could not get one. **Unemployment** is the level of joblessness among people actively seeking work. There are various types of unemployment: *frictional unemployment* (people are out of work temporarily while looking for a new job), *seasonal unemployment* (people are out of work because of the seasonal nature of their jobs), *cyclical unemployment* (people are out of work because of a downturn in the business cycle), and *structural unemployment* (people are unemployed because they lack the skills needed to perform available jobs). Unemployment rates have varied greatly over

INFLATION Occurrence of widespread price increases throughout an economic system.

CONSUMER PRICE INDEX (CPI) Measure of the prices of typical products purchased by consumers living in urban areas.

DEFLATION A period of generally falling prices.

UNEMPLOYMENT The level of joblessness among people actively seeking work in an economic system.

the years, as Figure 2.4 shows, the rates for men generally being higher than the rates for women. At the beginning of 2015, the Canadian unemployment rate stood at 6.8 percent.[26]

When unemployment is low, there is a shortage of labour available for businesses. As businesses compete with one another for the available supply of labour, they raise the wages they are willing to pay. Then, because higher labour costs eat into profit margins, businesses raise the prices of their products. If prices get too high, consumers will respond by buying less. Businesses will then reduce their workforces because they don't need to produce as much. But this causes unemployment to go up and the cycle starts all over again.

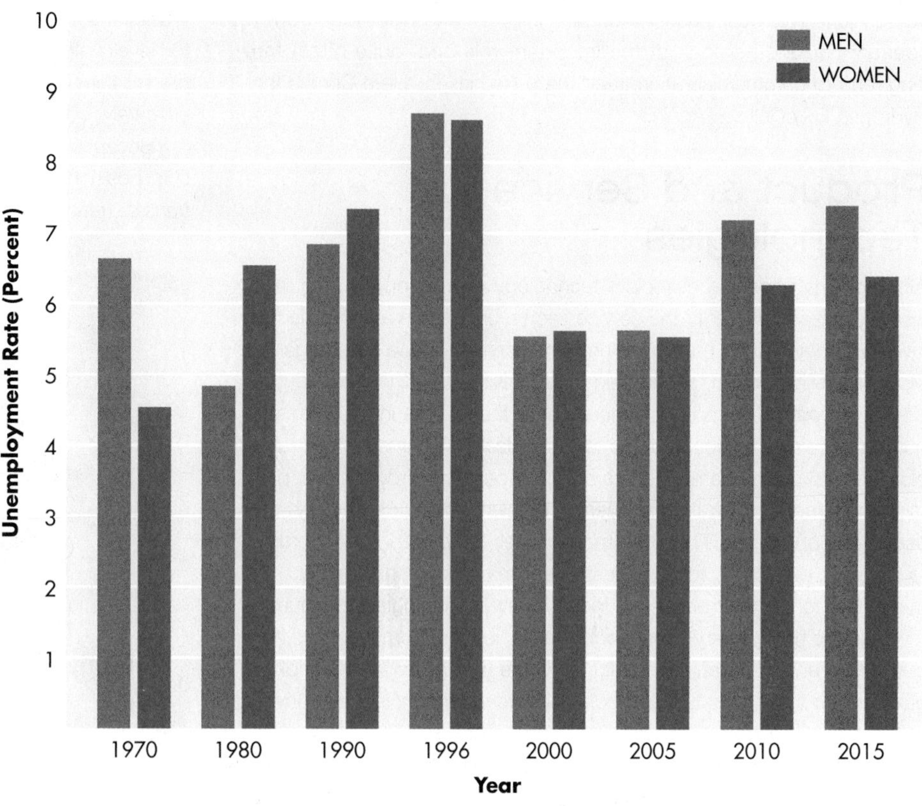

FIGURE 2.4 Historical unemployment rate[27]

Managing the Canadian Economy

The federal government manages the Canadian economic system through two sets of policies: fiscal and monetary. **Fiscal policies** involve the collection and spending of government revenues. For example, when the growth rate of the economy is decreasing, tax cuts will normally stimulate renewed economic growth. **Monetary policies** focus on controlling the size of the nation's money supply. Working primarily through the Bank of Canada (see Chapter 14), the government can influence the ability and willingness of banks throughout the country to lend money. The power of the Bank of Canada to make changes in the supply of money is the centrepiece of the Canadian government's monetary policy. The principle is fairly simple:

- Higher interest rates make money more expensive to borrow and thereby reduce spending by companies that produce goods and services and consumers who buy them. When the Bank of Canada restricts the money supply, we say it is practising a "tight" monetary policy.
- Lower interest rates make money less expensive to borrow and thereby increase spending by both companies that produce goods and services and consumers who buy them. When the Bank of Canada loosens the money supply, we say it is practising an "easy" monetary policy. During a financial crisis central banks tend to cut their interest rates in an attempt to stimulate their countries' economies.

FISCAL POLICIES Policies whereby governments collect and spend revenues.

MONETARY POLICIES Policies whereby the government controls the size of the nation's money supply.

LO-3 THE TECHNOLOGICAL ENVIRONMENT

As applied to the environment of business, *technology* generally includes all the ways firms create value for their constituents. Technology includes human knowledge, work methods, physical equipment, electronics and telecommunications, and various processing systems that are used to perform business activities.

Research and Development (R&D)

Technological improvements and innovation in general are important contributors to the economic development of a country. The innovation process includes **research and development (R&D)**, which provides new ideas for products, services, and processes (see Chapter 12). There are two types of R&D. *Basic (or pure) R&D* involves improving knowledge in an area without a primary focus on whether any discoveries that might occur are immediately marketable. For example, chemists in a laboratory might examine how certain chemical compounds behave. The knowledge gained from this activity might or might not result in a marketable product. *Applied R&D*, on the other hand, means focusing specifically on how a technological innovation can be put to use in the making of a product or service that can be sold in the marketplace.

The Canadian private sector accounts for about 52 percent of R&D, the government 10 percent, and universities 38 percent.[28] In the private

RESEARCH AND DEVELOPMENT (R&D) Those activities that are necessary to provide new products, services, and processes.

sector, just 100 businesses account for over half of all R&D money spent.[29] For another look at the important role and (quite often) the long road to commercialization, read the boxed insert "Here Comes the Hydrogen Fuel Cell . . . Again."

Product and Service Technologies

Although many people associate technology with manufacturing, it is also a significant factor in the service sector. Just as an automobile follows a predetermined pathway along an assembly line, a hamburger at McDonald's is cooked, assembled, and wrapped as it moves along a predefined path. The rapid advancement of the internet into all areas of business is also a reflection of the technological environment. For example, Starbucks Canada now offers a mobile payment program that permits consumers to use their phones as an electronic wallet through the use of an app and a QR code to pay for their "latte grande." According to a senior executive, today's customers may forget their wallet, but they never forget their phones.[30] Indeed, new technologies continue to revolutionize nearly every aspect of business, ranging from the ways that customers and companies interact to where, when, and how employees perform their work. Social media and internet technology are now a major part of the job search and recruitment process.

Companies must constantly be on the lookout for technological breakthroughs that might make their current products or services obsolete and thereby threaten their survival. Many breakthroughs do not come from direct competitors or even from the company's own industry. Technology is the basis of competition for some companies, especially when their goal is to be the technology leader in their industry. Apple revolutionized the home computer business and transformed the smartphone and music industries. More recently, the company has invested its resources to develop the Apple Watch. Will it be a smashing success? Analysts predict they could sell as many as 15 million units in the first year. Well, ultimately, consumers will decide its fate.

Because of the rapid pace of new developments, keeping a leadership position based on technology is increasingly difficult. *Technology transfer* refers to the process of getting a new technology out of the lab

Apple is betting consumers will flock to the new Apple Watch like they have to their other star products. Will the device deliver the promised benefits to the consumer and to the company's bottom line? Time will tell.

Pawan Kumar/Alamy

THE GREENING OF BUSINESS

Here Comes the Hydrogen Fuel Cell . . . Again

In November 2014, Hyundai Corp. began offering its Tucson model automobile to drivers in British Columbia. The car is powered by a hydrogen fuel cell. Toyota Motor Co. also unveiled a fuel cell car at the Los Angeles Auto Show earlier in November. The hydrogen fuel cell combines hydrogen (one of Earth's most common elements) with oxygen to produce electricity. The only exhaust is warm water. This looks like a great "green" technology that might power millions of cars. These developments have increased investor interest in the hydrogen fuel cell. Hydrogenics Corp. (based in Mississauga) makes fuel cells, and financial analysts predicted it would make a profit by the end of 2014. Another fuel cell maker, Plug Power Inc., saw its stock price increase by 1000 percent during 2012 and 2013. Does this mean that the long-awaited fuel cell revolution is upon us? Well, maybe.

Caution is in order, because we've heard this hype before. Back in the early 1990s, Vancouver-based Ballard Power Systems generated great excitement when it announced it was going to develop a fuel cell that would solve the world's energy problems and save the environment at the same time. Initially, enthusiasm for the hydrogen fuel cell was high, and by 2000 Ballard's stock price had soared to $170 per share. But nearly 25 years have passed, and the hydrogen fuel cell is still not widely used in automobiles. Skeptics (and investors) wonder if the fuel cell will ever be available to the mass market. In 2014, Ballard's stock was trading at about $5 per share.

What happened? Why has the fuel cell—which looks like a fantastic product—taken so long to develop? There are many reasons: insufficient numbers of hydrogen refuelling stations, safety concerns, expensive hydrogen fuel, and strong competition from both electric cars and from cars powered by the traditional internal combustion engine. The fuel cell may become commercially viable sometime in the next decade, but progress is slow. The biggest impediments to sales appear to be the high price of the car and the lack of hydrogen fuelling stations. Maybe the technology will eventually become popular. Keep in mind what critics said when internal combustion–powered automobiles were introduced early in the twentieth century: "They'll never become popular because there would have to be gas stations all over the place." Well, now we have gas stations all over the place.

CRITICAL THINKING QUESTION

1. Consider the following statement: *If the fuel cell had any value, it would have been fully developed by now and there would be many cars on the road that are powered by fuel cells.* Do you agree or disagree? Explain your reasoning.

ENTREPRENEURSHIP AND NEW VENTURES

Selling Magic in a Connected World

Regardless of the industry, entrepreneurs are opportunity-seekers. They see what others don't see. Ever since Philp Murad was a young child he spent his time trying to ensure that people could not see what he saw because he is a magician. He spent countless hours mastering his craft in creating illusions and fostering a sense of wonder for his audience. That training clearly sharpened his perception, and in combination with his entrepreneurial ambition, it led Philip down the path to becoming a pioneer in internet marketing. He no longer performs as a magician, but his Philip & Henry Productions actually books a large volume of shows across North America every year. They represent more than 800 magicians in Canada and the United States and arrange over 3000 shows per year at children's parties, daycares, schools, and corporate events.

The company was created back in 1998 with a dream. By 2015, it had over 20 full-time employees based in its Canadian and U.S. offices. The primary value the company offers customers is derived from a central screening process and a commitment to quality events. Philip & Henry Productions books the talent and provides peace of mind. The company name and reputation is attached to each show, so there is an important selection procedure before any magician is booked. The client knows they are dealing with a reputable organization that is ultimately accountable for good performances.

Why do independent magicians associate themselves with Philip & Henry? Bookings! The company was an early adopter of internet marketing and still invests significant funds in promoting magic. In fact, it spends approximately $25 000 per month on Google AdWords. The volume of events provides them with the financial leverage to be highly visible when someone goes online looking to hire a magic act. Philip & Henry provides continent-wide service, with mostly local entertainers. In essence they create a win-win-win situation. This is the magic formula for long-term success in the entertainment field.

CRITICAL THINKING QUESTION

1. Philip & Henry Productions owes much of its success to internet marketing. How can the company use modern-day social media tools to continue to expand and to help increase repeat business?

Based on a case written by Eric Dolansky, Brock University, Goodman School of Business, "Selling Magic Online," Vanier/BDC Case Competition 2015.

and into the marketplace where it can generate profits for the company. Efficient technology transfer means an increased likelihood of business success, as discussed above. A related challenge is meeting the constant demand to decrease cycle time—the time from beginning to end that it takes a firm to accomplish some recurring activity or function. Since businesses are more competitive if they can decrease cycle times, many companies now focus on decreasing cycle times in areas such as developing products, making deliveries, and collecting credit payments.

Read the Entrepreneurship and New Ventures Box entitled "Selling Magic in a Connected World" to see how one organization uses technological advancements to get noticed and to serve magicians and consumers.

LO-4 THE POLITICAL–LEGAL ENVIRONMENT

The **political–legal environment** reflects the relationship between business and government, including government regulation of business. The legal system defines what an organization can and can't do. Although Canada is a free-market economy, there is still significant regulation of business activity, as we saw in Chapter 1. At times, government policy can be tremendously advantageous to businesses. The Yukon government has not raised taxes (royalties) on the extraction of gold since 1906. So the 2.5 percent export royalty is still based on a price per ounce of gold of $15, which translates into a royalty of just 37.5 cents an ounce at a time when gold is Selling at approximately $1200 per ounce. This is an extreme example of business-friendly practices.[31] On the other hand, Shoppers Drug Mart has been very vocal about its opposition to Ontario government regulations that have cut the price of generic drug payments to as low as 20 percent of the original brand name product's cost, down from 50 percent. This regulation is saving the province $55 million in costs, but has hurt profits for pharmacies.[32]

Society's general view of business (pro or anti) is also important. During periods of anti-business sentiment, companies may find their competitive activities restricted. Political stability is also an important consideration, especially for multinational firms. No business wants to set up shop in another country unless trade relationships with that country are relatively well defined and stable. Thus, Canadian firms are more likely to do business in England than in Haiti. Relations between sovereign governments can also affect business activity. Former CEO of Toronto-based Sherritt International Ian Delaney struck a mining deal with Fidel Castro a couple of decades ago that helped Sherritt become one of the largest foreign investors in Cuba. This decision also led to Mr. Delaney being blacklisted in the United States, however, because of the American embargo of that country.[33] On a smaller scale, similar issues also pertain to assessments of local and provincial governments. A new mayor or provincial leader can affect many organizations, especially small firms that do business in a single location and are subject to zoning restrictions, property and school taxes, and the like.

POLITICAL–LEGAL ENVIRONMENT Conditions reflecting the relationship between business and government, usually in the form of government regulation.

LO-5 THE SOCIO-CULTURAL ENVIRONMENT

The **socio-cultural environment** includes the customs, values, attitudes, and demographic characteristics of the society in which a company operates. It influences the customer preferences for goods and services, and what standards of business conduct are seen as acceptable.

Customer Preferences and Tastes

Customer preferences and tastes vary both across and within national boundaries. In some countries, consumers are willing and able to pay premium prices for designer clothes with labels such as Armani. But the same clothes have virtually no market in other countries. Product usage also varies between nations. In China, bicycles are primarily seen as a mode of transportation, but in Canada they are marketed primarily for recreational purposes. While differences in tastes across national borders are sometimes clear and obvious, it is important to avoid stereotypical assumptions. Would you be surprised to hear that Canadian lingerie retailers like La Senza and La Vie en Rose have a significant presence in the Middle East? Behind the conservative, strict, exterior dress code, there is a significant market for lingerie.[34] Consumer preferences and tastes also change over time. In response to concerns about nutrition and health, McDonald's added salads to its menus and experiments with other low-fat foods.

For another example of the influence of the external environment read the Managing in Turbulent Times Box entitled "The Impact of the Physical Environment."

Ethical Compliance and Responsible Business Behaviour

An especially critical element of the socio-cultural environment is the practice of ethical conduct and social responsibility. Keeping up with today's increasingly fast-paced business activities is putting a strain on the accounting profession's traditional methods for auditing, financial reporting, and time-honoured standards for professional ethics. The stakeholders of business firms—employees, stockholders, consumers, labour unions, creditors, and the government—are entitled to a fair accounting so they can make enlightened personal and business decisions, but they often get a blurred picture of a firm's competitive health.

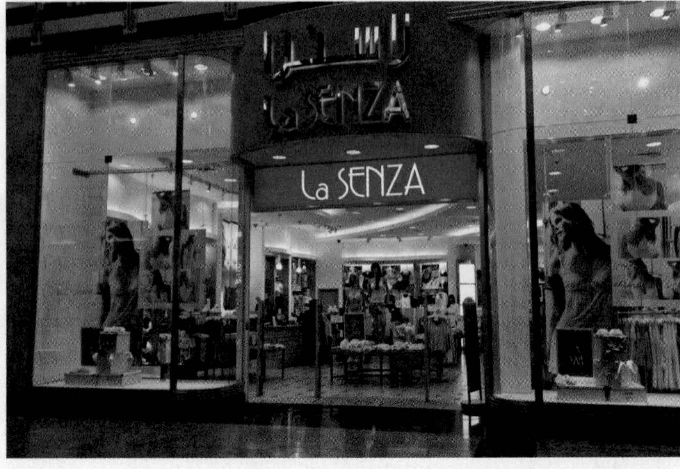

La Senza has made inroads in the Middle East. Despite strict rules about dress code, there is a thriving business for undergarments in places like Saudi Arabia.

Megapress/Alamy

Walmart has a reputation for low prices, but the company has had a very rocky relationship with its employees. For example, Walmart recently agreed to pay US$86 million to settle a lawsuit from 232 000 employees in California. A few years ago, when the company bought out a South African retailer named Massmart, the company agreed to respect the union contracts to close the deal. However, the South African union did not stop there—they also publicly urged Walmart to end its adversarial approach with employees in the United States.[35] Walmart Canada, also, has had a very spotty history, and a court ruling found the company guilty of unfair labour practices in its attempt to block a union drive in Weyburn, Saskatchewan.[36] The BC Labour Relations Board also found Walmart guilty of interfering with the formation of a union in Quesnel, British Columbia.[37]

The Business Environment

Business today is faster-paced, more complex, and more demanding than ever before. As businesses aggressively try to differentiate themselves, there has been a trend toward higher-quality products, planned obsolescence, and product life cycles measured in weeks or months rather than years. This, in turn, has created customer expectations of instant gratification. Final consumers and business customers want high-quality goods and services—often customized—for lower prices and with immediate delivery. Sales offices, service providers, and production facilities are shifting geographically as new markets and resources emerge in other countries. Employees want flexible working hours and opportunities to work at home. Shareholders' expectations also add pressure for productivity increases, growth in market share, and larger profits. At the same time, however, a more vocal public demands more honesty, fair competition, and respect for the environment.

A C-Suite survey found that the three most important issues facing Canadian businesses are (1) the value of the Canadian dollar, (2) a skilled labour shortage, and (3) the environment. These three issues are all important elements of the business environment.[38]

The Industry Environment

Every business firm operates in a specific industry, and every industry has different characteristics. The intensity of the competition in an industry has a big influence on how a company operates. To be effective, managers must understand the competitive situation, and then develop a strategy to exploit opportunities in the industry.

One of the most popular tools to analyze competitive situations in an industry is Michael Porter's five forces model.[39] The model (see Figure 2.5) helps managers analyze five important sources of competitive pressure and then decide what their competitive strategy should be. We briefly discuss each of the elements of the model in the following paragraphs.

SOCIO-CULTURAL ENVIRONMENT Conditions including the customs, values, attitudes, and demographic characteristics of the society in which an organization functions.

MANAGING IN TURBULENT TIMES

The Impact of the Physical Environment

The economic, technological, socio-cultural, legal–political, and business environments all affect how business is conducted in Canada. But another environment, the physical one, can also have an impact. Consider how the weather during the winter of 2013–2014 negatively affected business activity:

- Steel production fell 10 percent at Essar Steel Algoma Inc. in Sault Ste. Marie because ice on the St. Marys River prevented shipments of iron ore by water.
- Fourth-quarter sales at Rona Inc. fell short of expectations because the cold weather kept more shoppers at home.
- Natural gas prices rose because demand for natural gas surged with the onset of cold weather.
- Insurance companies raised rates for homeowners insurance by 15–20 percent because of increased claims for flooding, ice damage, and hail; claims like these can represent half of all claims made to insurance companies.
- Pearson Airport in Toronto shut down when wind chill temperatures reached –40C; the shutdown was necessary because of the cold weather's effect on both equipment and personnel who have to work outside.
- Cattle in feedlots lose weight in cold weather as they expend extra energy trying to stay warm; farmers therefore receive less revenue from the cattle they sell.
- Canadian railroads were forced to run shorter trains and pay more for fuel as a result of the cold weather.

The physical environment might also affect business activity positively. Consider these examples:

- Canadian Tire capitalized on the cold weather by airing an advertisement showing how its MotoMaster battery worked in a truck made from blocks of ice.
- Advertisements on The Weather Network are coordinated with weather conditions; for example, Troy-Bilt, a manufacturer of snow blowers, sponsors the "Storm Watch" program and its advertisements run when a snowstorm hits.
- Restaurants with patios have increased business when summer weather is nice (but, of course, business activity declines when the weather is bad).
- Snow is not always bad for business; ski resorts, for example, are a lot busier after a big snowfall (but, of course, they are not so busy if the snow doesn't materialize).
- Many other retailers, consumer goods companies, and restaurants adjust their advertisements depending on the weather.

In the most general sense, climate change can have a major impact on businesses around the world because a change in the climate will create winners and losers. If the climate warms, for example, a place like Greenland will benefit livestock farmers because there will be increased pasture land. But rising temperatures may hurt Inuit seal hunters because of thinning ice. If the climate cools, the reverse will happen. Another example: If the climate warms, potato farmers in the Andes of South America can produce their crops at higher mountain elevations. But these higher temperatures will also melt mountain glaciers, and that may cause water shortages at lower elevations in the summer.

CRITICAL THINKING QUESTIONS

1. How important is the physical environment compared to the other environments of business discussed in this chapter?
2. Give three more examples of how a warming climate can negatively affect business activity. Then give another three examples of how a warming climate can positively affect business activity. Finally, do the same analysis for a cooling climate.

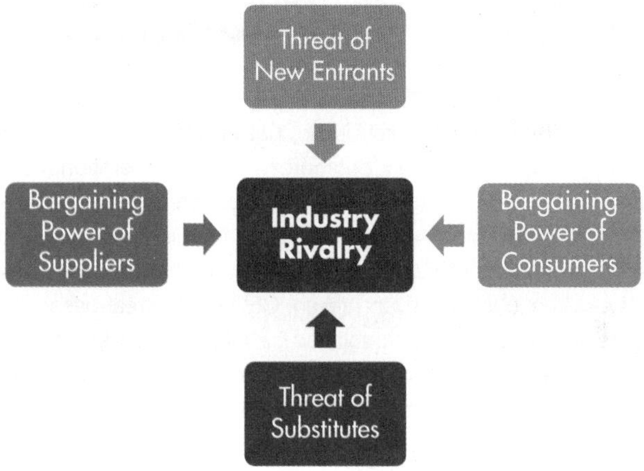

Threat of New Entrants

Bargaining Power of Suppliers

Industry Rivalry

Bargaining Power of Consumers

Threat of Substitutes

FIGURE 2.5 Michael Porter's five forces model

RIVALRY AMONG EXISTING COMPETITORS

The amount of rivalry among companies varies across industries. Rivalry can be seen in activities like intense price competition, elaborate advertising campaigns, and an increased emphasis on customer service. For many years, Tim Hortons has dominated the Canadian coffee industry with its extensive coverage of the market and strong brand equity. More recently, however, we have seen some stronger competitive efforts from the likes of Starbucks and McDonald's. In particular, McDonald's has made some aggressive moves (like free coffee for a week, adding fireplaces and Wi-Fi to McCafé locations, and so on.) to gain market share.[40]

THREAT OF POTENTIAL ENTRANTS

When new competitors enter an industry, they may cause big changes. If it is easy for new competitors to enter a market, competition will likely be intense and the industry will not be very attractive. Some industries (e.g., automobile manufacturing) are very capital-intensive and are therefore difficult to enter, but others (e.g., home cleaning or lawn care services) are relatively easy to enter.

Target may have failed to make a lasting impact on the Canadian retail landscape but others are making inroads. The new threat is to upscale retailers like Holt Renfrew with the entry of Nordstrom Inc. Unlike Target, this American retailer is taking it slowly by opening one store initially in Calgary, a second one in Ottawa, and a third in Vancouver. In total, Nordstrom plans to open six outlets by 2017.[41]

Nordstrom is taking it slowly, but it is committed to building its presence in Canada. For now, it has experienced losses of $32 million in 2014 and projected a loss of $60 million in 2015. Entering a new market is not easy.

RosalreneBetancourt 9/Alamy

SUPPLIERS

The amount of bargaining power suppliers have in relation to buyers helps determine how competitive an industry is. When there are only a few suppliers in an industry, they tend to have great bargaining power. The power of suppliers is influenced by the number of substitute products available (i.e., products that perform the same or similar functions). When there are few substitute products, suppliers obviously have more power.

BUYERS

When there are only a few buyers and many suppliers, the buyers have a great deal of bargaining power. Retail powerhouse Walmart, for example, is often described as a buyer that puts tremendous pressure on its suppliers to reduce their prices. It can do this because it buys so much from them. In another example, when Canadian Tire purchased Forzani (owner of Sport Chek and Hockey Experts stores) for $771 million a few years ago, it was not necessarily good news for hockey equipment maker Bauer Performance Sports Ltd. When two of your biggest customers merge, it alters the power relationship somewhat. Bauer CEO Scott Davis indicated that this merger may lead to price pressure on his company.[42]

SUBSTITUTES

If there are many substitute products available, the industry is more competitive. For example, various synthetic fibres can be used as substitutes for cotton. The internet has changed the way people pay bills. Because of online banking, people send a lot less mail than they did in the past and thus spend less on stamps as well. Even the federal government recently announced that it would stop issuing pension cheques by mail in 2016. This is bad news for Canada Post, as the threat from substitutes is expected to reduce mail volume by another 50 percent in the next decade.[43]

LO-6 EMERGING CHALLENGES AND OPPORTUNITIES IN THE BUSINESS ENVIRONMENT

The most successful firms are dealing with challenges and opportunities in today's business environment by focusing on their *core competencies*—the skills and resources with which they compete best and create the most value for owners. They outsource non-core business processes and pay suppliers and distributors to perform them, thereby increasing their reliance on suppliers. These new business models call for unprecedented coordination—not only among internal activities, but also among customers, suppliers, and strategic partners—and they often involve globally dispersed processes and supply chains.

In this section, we discuss some of the most popular steps that companies have taken to respond to challenges and opportunities in the business environment. These include outsourcing, the growing role of social media, and business process management.

Outsourcing

Outsourcing is the strategy of paying suppliers and distributors to perform certain business processes or to provide needed materials or services. For example, the cafeteria in a museum may be important to employees and customers, but the museum's primary focus is on exhibits that will interest the general public, not on food-service operations. That's why museums usually outsource cafeteria operations to food-service management companies. The result is more attention to museum exhibits and better food service for customers. Firms today outsource numerous activities, including payroll, employee training, and research and development. When Levon Afeyan, CEO of Montreal-based Seatply Products Inc., searched for a solution to fight low-cost providers from China while fending off local competitors providing premium products, he turned to an outsourcing partner in Malaysia. His seat component company now manufacturers about half of its product there; it also buys over 80 percent of its partner's output. The partnership has permitted his business to fight the competition under the new, increasingly competitive environment.[44]

OUTSOURCING Strategy of paying suppliers and distributors to perform certain business processes or to provide needed materials or services.

The Growing Role of Social Media

Social media sites and applications, such as Facebook and Snapchat are now an important part of everyday life for consumers (especially the youth market). Companies are addressing this new reality by providing content and creating various links to connect with consumers. Most organizations are being careful about their online presence, because they don't want it to be seen as an imposition, but rather a natural extension of their real-world relationship with clients. As we discuss throughout this book in the E-Business and Social Media Solutions boxes, some companies are making strong inroads as this new model evolves and companies learn to deal with an empowered consumer base.

Viral marketing predates the social media craze and first gained prominence through basic email transfer; it describes word of mouth that spreads information like a virus from customer to customer and relies on the internet to replace face-to-face communications. Messages about new cars, sports events, and numerous other goods and services travel on the internet among potential customers, who pass the information on. Using various formats—games, contests, and instant messaging—marketers encourage potential customers to try out products and tell other people about them.[45] Viral marketing works because people increasingly rely on social media for information they used to get from radio and newspapers, and because the customer becomes a participant in the process of spreading the word by forwarding information to friends and followers.

With this social media revolution it is not surprising that people can't bear to be out of the social loop even on an airline flight. Read the E-Business and Social Media Solutions box called "Staying Connected in the Skies" for more information.

Snapchat is a popular photo messaging application that allows users to share. On average over 700 million videos and photos are shared per day. Users set a time limit of one to ten seconds for their snaps. After that time the message is deleted.

ZoomTeam/Fotolia

Business Process Management

A *process* is any activity that adds value to some input, transforming it into an output for a customer (whether external or internal).[46] For example, human resources departments perform interviewing and hiring processes, payroll departments perform the employee-payment process,

E-BUSINESS AND SOCIAL MEDIA SOLUTIONS

Staying Connected in the Skies

In this day and age, many people start to feel a sense of withdrawal when they are away from their smartphones for more than a few minutes. The thought of being "off the grid" is a source of anxiety for some.

For others, disconnecting is the definition of relaxation; and until recently, airplane flights represented one of the last remaining places where people could just forget about social media friends, work emails, and day-to-day routine (for a few hours anyway).

No more! You may be familiar with the in-flight internet service called Gogo. The company's roots go back 25 years, when it first developed technology for in-flight phone services. Gogo is now available on ten major airlines including Air Canada. The company uses a network of cell towers to provide internet access to passengers on more than 6600 planes. At this time, Air Canada is only able to offer this service on its A319 airplanes travelling to destinations within Canada, the United States, and Mexico. But there are already plans to add the service to their A320, A321, and E190 planes. So if you are one of those people who can't stand to be disconnected, you are in luck. Slowly but surely, the skies are becoming connection-friendly.

Over the years, Gogo has grown through attention to innovation, as well as debt and equity financing. However, the enormous technology costs associated with expanding their network has resulted in losses every year. Gogo realizes that international expansion is critical to their long-term plan. Though they can achieve greater saturation of the domestic U.S. market by having their equipment installed on more planes, international expansion is the key to turning a profit. The company has begun this effort, recently signing a new agreement with Delta to install their equipment on all 170 planes in their international fleet.

Executing such a full vision takes a lot of money, so it was only natural that the company should turn to the stock market. Gogo's initial public offering back in 2011 resulted in the sale of 11 million shares at $17 each—$187 million to fund their international expansion. Although the price of the stock fell quickly over the following month, down to just more than $12 within weeks, as of March 2015 the stock stood at $21.

Should Gogo successfully penetrate the international market, investors might see a huge return. Only time will tell if this risky investment will pay off.

QUESTIONS FOR DISCUSSION

1. So where do you stand? Do you think communications in mid-flight are an unnecessary distraction or does the thought of connecting in flight please you? How much are you willing to pay for that service?
2. Given the risk, what would motivate an investor to purchase stock in Gogo?

the purchasing department performs the process of ordering materials, accounting performs the financial reporting process, and marketing performs the process of taking orders from customers.

Business process management means moving away from organizing around departments and moving toward organizing around process-oriented team structures that cut across old departmental boundaries. Often, companies begin by asking, "What must we do well to stay in business and win new orders?" Next, they identify the major processes that must be performed well to achieve these goals. Then they organize resources and skills around those essential processes. By organizing according to processes rather than functional departments, decision making is faster and more customer-oriented, materials and operations are coordinated, and products get to customers more rapidly.[47]

BUSINESS PROCESS MANAGEMENT Approach by which firms move away from department-oriented organization and toward process-oriented team structures that cut across old departmental boundaries.

LO-7 REDRAWING CORPORATE BOUNDARIES

Successful companies are responding to challenges in the external environment by redrawing traditional organizational boundaries and by joining together with other companies to develop new goods and services. Several trends have become evident in recent years: acquisitions and mergers, divestitures and spinoffs, employee-owned corporations, strategic alliances, and subsidiary/parent corporations.

Mergers and Acquisitions

In an **acquisition**, one firm simply buys another firm. For example, the Hudson's Bay Company (HBC) purchased Saks Inc. (Saks Fifth Avenue) for US$2.4 billion.[48] The transaction is similar to buying a car that becomes your property. In contrast, a **merger** is a consolidation of two firms, and the arrangement is more collaborative. In 2014, mergers and acquisitions in Canada had a total value of $229 billion. This was higher than average with Burger King's takeover of Tim Hortons (worth $13.2 billion) leading the way followed by Repsol SA's takeover of Talisman Energy (for $13 billion).[49]

When the companies are in the same industry, as when Molson Inc. merged with Adolph Coors Co., it is called a *horizontal merger*. When one of the companies in the merger is a supplier or customer to the other, it is called a *vertical merger*. When the companies are in unrelated businesses, it is called a *conglomerate merger*.

A merger or acquisition can take place in one of several ways. In a *friendly takeover*, the acquired company welcomes the acquisition, perhaps because it needs cash or sees other benefits in joining the acquiring firm. But in a *hostile takeover*, the acquiring company buys enough of the other company's stock to take control even though the other company is opposed to the takeover.

Montreal-based Couche-Tard has plenty of experience in the merger and takeover game. In the past two decades it has acquired Mac's, Dairy Mart, and Winks, to become the nation's top convenience chain. However, their ambitions have stretched much further. In fact, it is one of the biggest convenience store operators in North America with over 6314 stores. The company also owns 2233 outlets in Europe (most under their Statoil brand). Finally, Couche-Tard has 4600 independent stores operated worldwide (under their Circle K brand).[50]

Companies that want to fight a takeover attempt have options. A **poison pill** is a defence tactic management adopts to make a firm less attractive to an actual or potential hostile suitor in a takeover attempt. The objective is to make the "pill" so distasteful that a potential acquirer will not want to swallow it. Air Canada recently announced plans to institute a poison pill provision that would give all Class A and Class B shareholders the right to purchase stocks, at a discounted price, the moment any group or person announces the intention to buy more than 20 percent of the outstanding shares.[51]

Divestitures and Spinoffs

A **divestiture** occurs when a company decides to sell part of its existing business operations to another corporation. When Pfizer Inc. decided to divest its infant-nutrition and animal-health units, competitors jumped at the chance. Nestlé and Groupe Danone both showed interest in the strong infant-nutrition assets and Nestlé eventually won the auction with a US$11.85 billion bid.[52]

In other cases, a company might set up one or more corporate units as new, independent businesses because a business unit might be more valuable as a separate company. This is known as a **spinoff**. For example, PepsiCo spun off Pizza Hut, KFC, and Taco Bell into a new, separate corporation known as Yum! Brands Inc.

Employee-Owned Corporations

Corporations are sometimes owned by the employees who work for them. The current pattern is for this ownership to take the form of *employee stock ownership plans* or ESOPs. A corporation might decide to set up an ESOP to increase employee motivation or to fight a hostile takeover attempt. The company first secures a loan that it then uses to buy shares of its stock on the open market. Some of the future profits made by the corporation are used to pay off the loan. The stock, meanwhile, is controlled by a bank or other trustee. Employees gradually gain ownership of the stock, usually on the basis of seniority. But even though they might not have physical possession of the stock for a while, they control its voting rights immediately.

ACQUISITION The purchase of a company by another, larger firm, which absorbs the smaller company into its operations.

MERGER The union of two companies to form a single new business.

POISON PILL A defence management adopts to make a firm less attractive to an actual or potential hostile suitor in a takeover attempt.

DIVESTITURE Occurs when a company sells part of its existing business operations to another company.

SPINOFF Strategy of setting up one or more corporate units as new, independent corporations.

A survey of 471 Canadian and U.S. companies, conducted by Western Compensation & Benefits Consultants of Vancouver, found that three-quarters of the companies that have adopted ESOPs have experienced improvement in both sales and profits. Charlie Spiring, the CEO of Wellington West Holdings Inc., says that one of the fundamental principles of his business is employee ownership. People really have to be entrepreneurs to work well in the company.[53]

Strategic Alliances

A **strategic alliance**, or joint venture, involves two or more enterprises cooperating in the research, development, manufacture, or marketing of a product. For example, Rogers and Walmart have teamed up to launch a new 100-page magazine called *Walmart Live Better.* The circulation will be approximately 1 million copies per issue (six editions per year) distributed inside Walmart stores.[54] Companies form strategic alliances for two main reasons: (1) to help spread the risk of a project and (2) to get something of value (like technological or industry expertise) from their strategic partner.

Subsidiary and Parent Corporations

A *subsidiary corporation* is one that is owned by another corporation. The corporation that owns the subsidiary is called the *parent corporation*. For example, the Hudson's Bay Company (HBC) is the parent corporation of Home Outfitters.

STRATEGIC ALLIANCE An enterprise in which two or more persons or companies temporarily join forces to undertake a particular project.

MyBizLab

Study, practise, and explore real business situations with these helpful resources:

- **Interactive Lesson Presentations:** Work through interactive presentations and assessments to test your knowledge of business concepts.
- **Study Plan:** Check your understanding of chapter concepts with self-study quizzes.
- **Dynamic Study Modules:** Work through adaptive study modules on your computer, tablet, or mobile device.
- **Simulations:** Practise decision-making in simulated business environments.
- **Videos:** Learn more about the business practices and strategies of real companies.

SUMMARY OF LEARNING OBJECTIVES

LO-1 EXPLAIN THE CONCEPTS OF ORGANIZATIONAL BOUNDARIES AND MULTIPLE ORGANIZATIONAL ENVIRONMENTS.

All businesses operate within a larger *external environment* consisting of everything outside an organization's boundaries that might affect it. An *organizational boundary* is that which separates the organization from its environment. Organizations have multiple environments: economic conditions, technology, political–legal considerations, social issues, the global environment, issues of ethical and social responsibility, the business environment itself, and numerous other emerging challenges and opportunities.

LO-2 EXPLAIN THE IMPORTANCE OF THE ECONOMIC ENVIRONMENT TO BUSINESS AND IDENTIFY THE FACTORS USED TO EVALUATE THE PERFORMANCE OF AN ECONOMIC SYSTEM.

The *economic environment* is the economic system in which business firms operate. The key goals of the Canadian system are economic growth, economic stability, and full employment. *Gross domestic product* (GDP) is the total value of all goods and services produced within a given period by a national economy domestically. The government manages the economy through *fiscal and monetary policies*.

LO-3 DESCRIBE THE TECHNOLOGICAL ENVIRONMENT AND ITS ROLE IN BUSINESS.

Technology refers to all the ways firms create value for their constituents, including human knowledge, work methods, physical equipment, electronics and telecommunications, and various processing systems. The innovation process includes *research and development (R&D)*, which provides new ideas for products, services, and processes. There are two general categories of business-related technologies: *product and service technologies* and *business process technologies*.

LO-4 DESCRIBE THE POLITICAL–LEGAL ENVIRONMENT AND ITS ROLE IN BUSINESS.

The *political–legal environment* reflects the relationship between business and government. The legal system defines what an organization can and can't do. Various government agencies regulate important areas such as advertising practices, safety and health considerations, and acceptable standards of business conduct. Pro- or anti-business sentiment in government can further influence business activity.

LO-5 DESCRIBE THE SOCIO-CULTURAL ENVIRONMENT AND ITS ROLE IN BUSINESS.

The *socio-cultural environment* includes the customs, values, and demographic characteristics of society. Socio-cultural processes determine the goods and services as well as the standards of business conduct that a society values and accepts. The shape of the market, the political influence, and the attitudes of its workforce are only a few of the many ways in which culture can affect an organization.

LO-6 IDENTIFY EMERGING CHALLENGES AND OPPORTUNITIES IN THE BUSINESS ENVIRONMENT.

Successful companies focus on their core competencies. The innovative ways in which companies respond to emerging challenges and opportunities include *outsourcing*, *the role of social media*, and *business process management*.

LO-7 UNDERSTAND RECENT TRENDS IN THE REDRAWING OF CORPORATE BOUNDARIES.

An *acquisition* occurs when one firm buys another. A *merger* occurs when two firms combine to create a new company. A *divestiture* occurs when a corporation sells a part of its existing business operations or sets it up as a new and independent corporation. When a firm sells part of itself to raise capital, the strategy is known as a *spinoff.* The *ESOP* plan allows employees to own a significant share of the corporation through trusts established on their behalf. In a *strategic alliance*, two or more organizations collaborate on a project for mutual gain.

QUESTIONS AND EXERCISES

QUESTIONS FOR ANALYSIS

1. Why is it important for managers to understand the environment in which their businesses operate?
2. It has been argued that inflation is both good and bad. Explain. Are government efforts to control inflation well-advised? Explain.
3. What are the benefits and risks of outsourcing? What, if anything, should be done about the problem of Canadian companies outsourcing jobs to foreign countries? Defend your answer.
4. Explain how current economic indicators such as inflation and unemployment affect you personally. Explain how they affect managers.
5. At first glance, it might seem as though the goals of economic growth and stability are inconsistent with one another. How can this apparent inconsistency be reconciled?
6. What is the current climate in Canada regarding the regulation of business? How might it affect you if you were a manager today?

APPLICATION EXERCISES

7. Select two businesses you are familiar with. Identify the major elements of their external environments that are most likely to affect them in important and meaningful ways.
8. Assume you are the owner of an internet pharmacy that sells prescription drugs to U.S. citizens. Analyze the factors in the external environment (economic, technological, political–legal, and socio-cultural) that might facilitate your company's activities. Analyze the factors in the external environment that might threaten your company's activities.
9. Select a technology product, such as the Samsung Galaxy smartphone or Amazon's Kindle e-reader, and research how the various environments of business (economic, technological, socio-cultural, global, political–legal, and general business) are currently impacting the sales possibilities of the product or service.
10. Interview two business owners or managers. Ask them to answer the following questions: (a) What business functions, if any, do they outsource? (b) Are they focusing more attention on business process management now than in the past? (c) How have internet applications and the growth of social media changed the way they conduct business?

BUILDING YOUR BUSINESS SKILLS

FEELING THE HEAT FROM BAD RESULTS: PRAYING FOR GOOD WEATHER

PURPOSE OF THE ASSIGNMENT

To help students identify the important role played by uncontrollable natural events on the bottom line.

THE SITUATION

Rona Inc. is a Canadian home improvement giant with over $4 billion in annual sales coming from over 500 corporate, franchise, and affiliate stores. It is the largest Canadian retailer of hardware, home renovation, and gardening products and has a roster of over 24 000 employees. Despite its impressive growth, good strategic decisions in the past decade, and locations across the nation, Rona's results are still largely susceptible to natural weather patterns. For example, in the first quarter of a recent year, the retailer lost 23 cents per share based on a 12.6 percent decline in same-store sales from the previous year. The reason, according to the CEO, was that "spring failed to materialize." The extra-long winter that year meant that customers did not rush out to buy things like home gardening supplies, which traditionally pad the bottom line during this sales period. Labour costs remained high while staff had fewer customers to serve. The incentive to discount to attract sales was strong, but company officials stated that they would avoid such tactics. However, the extra buildup of inventory has a direct holding cost; additionally, analysts were worried that the company would likely need to discount (and drastically slash profit margins) to rid itself of the extra stock once the shortened season arrived.[55]

Weather patterns can play an important role in the short-term success or failure of many businesses and clearly Rona was affected by this uncontrollable factor in this case.

ASSIGNMENT

Divide up into groups of four or five students. Each group should begin by doing the following:

Step 1 Identify three *big companies* that might be *positively* affected by warmer-than-usual weather during a particular season.

Step 2 Identify three *big companies* that might be *negatively* affected by warmer-than-usual weather patterns during a particular season. If it is appropriate, a company can appear on both lists.

Step 3 Now respond to the following items:

1. For each company that you identify, describe the specific effects on each business.
2. Describe the most logical organizational response to these effects for each company.
3. What kinds of plans, if any, should each organization develop in the event of similar future events?

ALTERNATIVE ASSIGNMENT

Conduct the same exercise on *small businesses* and *entrepreneurs* and highlight some of the unique challenges that they face. Then proceed with Steps 1–3 above.

QUESTIONS FOR DISCUSSION

1. How could Rona better prepare for and handle negative weather patterns?
2. Are unfavourable natural weather patterns more dangerous for major retailers like Rona or for small businesses? Provide at least one argument on each side before making a choice.
3. Is it possible for a manager to spend too much time trying to anticipate future events? Why or why not?

EXERCISING YOUR ETHICS

PRESCRIBING A DOSE OF COMPETITIVE MEDICINE

THE SITUATION

You are a businessperson in a small town, where you run one of two local pharmacies. The population and economic base are fairly stable. Each pharmacy controls about 50 percent of the market. Each is reasonably profitable, generating solid if unspectacular revenues.

THE DILEMMA

You have just been approached by the owner of the other pharmacy. He has indicated an interest either in buying your pharmacy or in selling his to you. He argues that neither company can substantially increase profits and complains that if one pharmacy raises its prices, customers will simply go to the other one. He tells you outright that if you sell to him, he plans to raise prices by 10 percent.

He believes that the local market will have to accept the increase for two reasons: (1) the town is too small to attract national competitors, such as Shoppers Drug Mart and (2) local customers can't go elsewhere to shop because the nearest town with a pharmacy is 50 kilometres away.

TEAM ACTIVITY

Form groups of four and assign two members to represent the company that is making the proposition and two members to represent the company that was approached. Answer the questions for discussion found below and then role-play a discussion between the two company owners. Are there alternative solutions? Do they cross ethical lines?

QUESTIONS FOR DISCUSSION

1. What are the roles of supply and demand in this scenario?
2. What are the underlying ethical issues?
3. What would you do if you were actually faced with this situation?

BUSINESS CASE 2

NETFLIX: VIDEO STREAMING REVOLUTION

For about two decades, Blockbuster was the premier name in the video rental business. At its peak, it had 9000 retail stores and 60 000 employees. But Blockbuster's days were numbered with the introduction of Netflix (and other streaming services). In 2011, the company filed for bankruptcy. By 2014 it shut its retail doors for good. The brand was purchased by Dish Network, who planned to use it for their on-the-go service; however, the reign of the retail video king was over. According to experts like Kaan Yigit, president of Consultancy Solutions Research Group, we had entered the Netflix decade.

NETFLIX'S INNOVATIVE MODELS

Netflix represents the great promise of technology, but is also a perfect example of the challenge of doing business in a technological age. Here is a company that was created approximately 20 years ago and yet it has already changed its core business model twice. The initial success story was based on DVD home delivery service in the United States, a novel idea at the time. While competitors like Blockbuster were stuck with big retail locations and high rental space costs, Netflix was able to provide subscribers with a reliable home delivery service at an economical price. But the initial success would soon have faded if Netflix had not evolved with the times. It quickly jumped on the next game-changing opportunity: the video-on-demand streaming business.

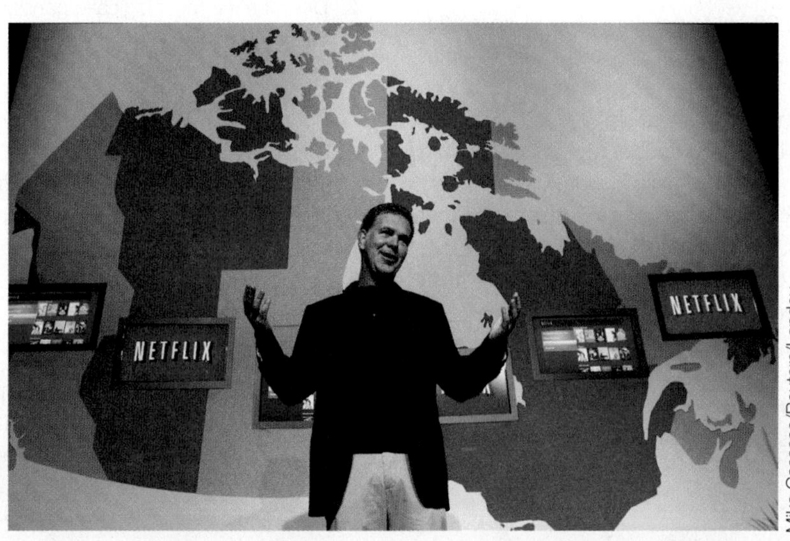

Mike Cassese/Reuters/Landov

COMPETITIVE FORCES

Netflix had become a poster child for online success. It was also a model that new competitors and suppliers quickly copied and/or exploited. One of the reasons for that success was the company's ability to charge a low monthly flat fee of just US$7.99. As a pioneer, Netflix had negotiated favourable content-rights deals with movie studios and TV show producers. But soon problems began to surface. Canadian customers complained about the limited selection on the Canadian site compared to the U.S. site. In addition, the TV and movie studios started using Netflix to apply competitive pressure and increase prices charged to TV stations looking to buy content. This meant that Netflix, in turn, also had to pay more. The cost to acquire rights to stream video content increased eightfold in one year alone. In addition, Netflix had been unsuccessful in renewing certain rights agreements. It also lost its exclusive distribution deal from EPIX, a joint-venture company that licenses movies from Paramount, MGM, and Lions Gate; EPIX licensed the films to Amazon Prime Video. To make matters worse, new threats were coming in many forms:

- Traditional cable and satellite providers like Bell, Videotron, Shaw, and Rogers had launched their own direct video-on-demand services to subscribers.
- Astral Media Inc. possessed exclusive rights to distribute HBO programming in eastern Canada and refused to sell Netflix the rights to its popular shows like *True Blood*. To make matters worse, it launched its own HBO Go streaming service.
- Apple TV was another important threat.

The list goes on and on.

GOVERNMENT REGULATION

Success is often based on how well a firm plays by the prescribed rules, but rules can be changed. Netflix's competitors put pressure on the Canadian Radio-television and Telecommunications Commission (CRTC) to fight the threat of "over-the-top" internet streaming services. The CRTC initially resisted making a ruling; however, more recently Netflix and the CRTC have been at odds. In fact, Netflix refused to provide the commission with information about how much money it had spent on Canadian programming as well as other statistics. Clearly, it is not a good idea to fight a powerful government organization, but Neflix felt this information was private and sensitive.

Netflix also faced a major threat from the U.S. government. The Federal Communications Commission (FCC) was seriously considering a new rule allowing internet providers to provide preferential treatment for clients that have higher bandwidth needs (like Netflix). This preferential treatment would come at a higher cost. Netflix and other major industry players were ready to fight to protect "net neutrality" (which corresponded with their interests).

STRATEGIC CHOICES

At the beginning of 2015, Netflix had over 57 million subscribers and was present in 50 countries. Its initial success had been based on quick manoeuvring, but the industry was shifting yet again. To counter some of the challenges, Netflix invested heavily in creating a show called *House of Cards*—a move that clearly demonstrated their concern about content issues and another sign of their ability to adapt. More recently, Netflix created a partnership, in Canada, with Rogers and Shaw Communications (through their Shomi joint venture), to create a Canadian thriller called *Between*.

What direction should Netflix take now? Who or what is the greatest threat to the long-term profitability of the company? Should Netflix consider more affiliations or a potential merger? These are just some of the questions Netflix executives must answer if the company is to continue to grow and survive. One thing is certain, external threats continue to appear from all angles.

QUESTIONS FOR DISCUSSION

1. What are the primary external threats for Netflix in the short term? How about in the long term?
2. What do you think of Netflix's move to create new media content? What are the advantages and disadvantages of this strategic move?
3. Do some research on "net neutrality?" Debate the pros and cons of this concept.

Rawpixel/Fotolia

LO

AFTER READING THIS CHAPTER, YOU SHOULD BE ABLE TO:

LO-1 Explain how individuals develop their personal *codes of ethics* and why ethics are important in the workplace.

LO-2 Distinguish *ethics* from *social responsibility* and identify *organizational stakeholders*.

LO-3 Show how the concept of social responsibility applies both to environmental issues and to a firm's relationships with customers, employees, and investors.

LO-4 Identify four general *approaches to social responsibility* and describe the four steps a firm must take to implement a *social responsibility program*.

LO-5 Explain how issues of social responsibility and ethics affect small businesses.

What's Happening in the Fair Trade Movement?

The "fair trade" movement tries to ensure that small farmers in developing countries receive fair prices for their crops. Canadian consumers know about fair trade products such as coffee and chocolate, but the fair-trade logo can also be found on many other products, including sugar, cotton, rice, gold, and cut flowers. Several fair-trade programs are sponsored by Fairtrade Labelling Organizations International (FLO), a global non-profit network of fair-trade groups headquartered in Germany. FLO works with cooperatives representing producers of commodities like coffee in Latin America and chocolate in Africa to establish standards for the producers' products and operations, and pushes for socially relevant policies such as enforcing child labour laws and providing education and health care services. In return, FLO guarantees producers a "Fairtrade Minimum Price" for their products. If the market price falls below that level, FLO covers the difference. If the market exceeds that price, FLO pays producers a premium.

The money to do this comes from the importers, manufacturers, and distributors who buy and sell commodities from FLO-certified producers. These companies are, in turn, monitored by a network of FLO-owned organizations called TransFair, which ensures that FLO criteria are met and that FLO-certified producers receive the fair prices guarantee by FLO. Products that meet the appropriate FLO-TransFair criteria bear labels attesting they are "Fair Trade Certified."

Importers, manufacturers, and distributors have an incentive not only to adopt FLO-TransFair standards, but also to incur the costs of subsidizing overseas producers, because they get the right to promote their products as fair trade. And these categories typically command premium retail prices. When consumers know that they are supporting programs to empower farmers in developing countries, sellers and resellers can charge higher prices. A 100 g chocolate bar labelled "organic fair trade" may sell for $3.49, compared to about $1.50 for one that's not.

Conducting Business Ethically *and* Responsibly

CHAPTER 03

The fair-trade movement came about partly because of significant negative publicity about the bad working conditions of workers who pick cocoa beans in Ivory Coast, a small Africa country that provides over 40 percent of the world's chocolate. Most of it is produced on small farms scattered throughout the country. Chocolate comes from small beans that grow on cocoa trees, and it takes about 400 beans to make a pound of chocolate. To harvest the beans, labourers must chop them from the trees, slice them open, scoop out the beans, spread them on mats, and cover them to ferment. Once the beans are fermented, they're dried, packed in bags, and carried to waiting trucks. At that point, they've entered the supply chain that will take them to Canada, the United States, or Europe, where they'll be turned into all sorts of chocolate products, including Snickers candy bars and Breyer's Double Fudge Brownie ice cream.

HOW WILL THIS HELP ME?

There is a growing dilemma in the business world today: the economic imperatives (real or imagined) facing managers versus pressures to function as good citizens. By understanding the material in this chapter, you will be better able to assess ethical and social responsibility issues that you will face as an *employee* and as a *boss* or *business owner*. It will also help you understand the ethical and social responsibility actions of businesses you deal with as a *consumer* and as an *investor*.

Kaband/Shutterstock

Reports issued by the United Nations Children's fund say that much of the labour involved in Ivory Coast chocolate production is performed by boys ranging in age from 12 to 16. These child labourers—perhaps as many as 15 000 of them—work 12 hours a day, seven days a week. They are often beaten to maintain productivity quotas, and they sleep on bare wooden planks in cramped rooms. Most of them were tricked or sold into forced labour, many by destitute parents who couldn't afford to feed them. Efforts to alleviate the problem have met with little success.

Enslaving children became business as usual in the Ivory Coast cocoa industry because the country is heavily dependent on world market prices for cocoa (one-third of the country's economy is based on cocoa exports). Since cocoa prices fluctuate significantly on global markets, profitability in the cocoa industry depends on prices over which farmers have no control. To improve their chances of making a profit, producers look for ways to cut costs, and the use of slave labour is one way to do that.

The action the fair-trade movement has taken to protect these and other workers in developing countries is a positive step, but two recent developments are creating concerns about its effectiveness. First, a split has developed in the movement that may dilute what the term "fair trade" means. There are now two competing organizations: the original Fairtrade International (which allows only democratically organized groups of farmers

Chunumunu/Fotolia

to be certified) and a new Fair Trade USA (which allows commodities from privately owned businesses to be certified). Consumers may be confused by the competing labels, because products that don't meet the standards of Fairtrade International are appearing on the shelves of Canadian stores with the Fair Trade USA label on them.

The second development is a very surprising study from the School of Oriental and African Studies (SOAS) at London University. The study found that workers at Fairtrade farms were actually paid less than workers on non-Fairtrade farms. In addition, workers at Fairtrade farms were required to pay bribes in order to get jobs, suffered abusive treatment on the job, were exposed to harmful pesticides, and received less sick leave, fewer paid holidays, and poor health and safety training. The Fairtrade Foundation said there were flaws in the study.

Other critics of fair trade agree in principle with those who advocate its use, but contend that consumers don't need to be paying higher prices for fair-trade products. They point out that, according to TransFair's own data, cocoa farmers get only 3 cents of the $3.49 that a socially conscious consumer pays for a fair trade–certified candy bar. Most of the premium goes to intermediaries. Other critics say that sellers of fair-trade products are taking advantage of consumers who are socially conscious, but not price-conscious. They point out that if sellers priced that $3.49 candy bar for $2.49 instead, farmers would still get just 3 cents per bar. The price is inflated to $3.49 simply because there is a small segment of the market willing to pay that price.

QUESTIONS FOR DISCUSSION

1. Do you think fair-trade is a good solution to child labour and related problems? Explain.
2. Are you willing to pay more for fair-trade products? Why or why not?
3. Under what circumstances could unethical parties abuse the fair trade concept?

ETHICS IN THE WORKPLACE

The situation described in the opening case clearly demonstrates the controversy that often arises when dealing with the issue of ethics in business. **Ethics** are beliefs about what is right and wrong or good and bad. An individual's personal values and morals—and the social context in which they occur—determine whether a particular behaviour is perceived as ethical or unethical. In other words, *ethical behaviour* is behaviour that conforms to individual beliefs and social norms about what is right and good. *Unethical behaviour* is behaviour that individual beliefs and social norms define as wrong and bad. **Business ethics** is a term often used to refer to ethical or unethical behaviours by a manager or employee of a business.

LO-1 Individual Ethics

Because ethics are based on both individual beliefs and social concepts, they vary from person to person, from situation to situation, and from culture to culture. But there are some commonalities. For example, most societies view stealing as wrong. But what if you happen to see someone drop a $20 bill in a store? Most people would probably say that it would be ethical to return it to the owner, but some might think it is OK to keep it. There will be even less agreement if you find $20 and don't know who dropped it. Should you turn it in to the lost-and-found department? Or, since the rightful owner isn't likely to claim it, can you just keep it?

It is important to make the distinction between *unethical* and *illegal* behaviour. A given behaviour may be ethical and legal (e.g., providing high-quality products to consumers), ethical and illegal (e.g., breaking the law in a totalitarian regime in order to carry out humanitarian efforts), unethical and legal (e.g., paying low wages to workers at a company facility in a foreign country), or unethical and illegal (e.g., "cooking the books" to make a company's financial situation look better than it really is). Some of these distinctions are controversial. Consider the case of Netsweeper, a Canadian company that sells web-filtering products that block pornography and computer viruses. That sounds good, but what if these products are used by a repressive government to block information it doesn't want its citizens to see (e.g., information on human rights)? While it is perfectly legal for Netsweeper to sell the software, critics argue that the sales are unethical because the company knows its products can be misused.[1]

Making ethical judgments is also complicated by the fact that practices that are legal in one country may not be legal in another. For example, selling Nazi memorabilia online is legal in the United States, but not in Germany. In some cultures, ethically ambiguous practices are hallmarks of business activity. Brazilians, for example, apply the philosophy of *jeitinho*—meaning "to find a way"—by using personal connections, bending the rules, or making a "contribution."[2] If you need to get an official document, you might start out determined to take all the proper bureaucratic steps to get it. However, if you find yourself in a complex maze of rules and regulations and think you'll never get your document, you may resort to *jeitinho* to get the job done.

ETHICS Individual standards or moral values regarding what is right and wrong or good and bad.

BUSINESS ETHICS Ethical or unethical behaviours by a manager or employee of an organization.

INDIVIDUAL VALUES AND CODES

The ethical views of individuals in a business—managers, employees, agents, and other legal representatives—are determined by a combination of factors. We start to form ethical standards as children in response to our perceptions of the behaviour of parents and other adults. When we enter school, peers and the entertainment media also shape our lives and contribute to our ethical beliefs and our behaviour. We also develop values and morals that influence our behaviour. If you put financial gain at the top of your priority list, you may develop a code of ethics that supports the pursuit of material comfort. But if you put a high priority on family and friends, you'll probably adopt different standards.

Because ethics are both personally and culturally defined, differences of opinion arise as to what is ethical or unethical. For example, people who would never think of stealing a candy bar from a grocery store may think it perfectly legitimate to take home pens and pads of paper from their workplace. Many otherwise law-abiding citizens have no qualms about using radar detectors to avoid speeding tickets. In each situation, people will use different standards of ethics and will argue that their actions are ethical. These difficulties have led some observers to conclude that individuals can rationalize almost any behaviour as ethical.

Managerial Ethics

Managerial ethics are the standards of behaviour that guide individual managers in their work.[3] Although ethics can affect managerial work in any number of ways, it's helpful to classify behaviour in terms of three broad categories.

BEHAVIOUR TOWARD EMPLOYEES

There are important ethical questions with regard to issues like hiring and firing, wages and working conditions, and privacy. In Canada, ethical and legal guidelines state that hiring and firing decisions should be based solely on a person's ability to perform a job. A manager who discriminates against any ethnic minority in hiring therefore exhibits both unethical and illegal behaviour. But what about the manager who hires a friend or relative when someone else might be more qualified? Such decisions may not be illegal, but in Canada they may be seen as objectionable on ethical grounds. But they are not necessarily seen as unethical in some other countries.

Wages and working conditions are also areas for debate. Consider a manager who pays a worker less than what is deserved because the manager knows that the employee can't afford to quit. While some people will see that behaviour as unethical, others will see it as simply smart business.

Protecting the privacy of employees is another area where there are ethical implications. In Canada, the Personal Information Protection and Electronic Documents Act (PIPEDA) requires organizations to obtain consent before they collect, use, or disclose information about individuals. Many people see these guidelines are necessary and useful, but others view them as yet another example of bureaucratic red tape and government interference in business.

BEHAVIOUR TOWARD THE ORGANIZATION

Ethical issues also arise with respect to employee behaviour toward employers. A **conflict of interest** occurs when an activity benefits an employee at the expense of the employer. For example, suppose the shoe buyer for a large department store chain accepts a free vacation from a shoe manufacturer. If the manufacturer then asks the buyer to increase the size of an order, the buyer may feel an obligation to do so. The buyer might also conclude that more large orders will result in another vacation next year. Most companies have policies that forbid buyers from accepting gifts from suppliers. Businesses in highly competitive industries—software or fashion apparel, for example—have safeguards against designers selling company secrets to competitors. Relatively common problems in the general area of honesty include behaviour such as stealing supplies, padding expense accounts, and using a business phone to make personal long-distance calls. Most employees are honest, but organizations must be vigilant.

BEHAVIOUR TOWARD OTHER ECONOMIC AGENTS

Ethical disputes often arise in the relationship between a company and its customers, competitors, stockholders, suppliers, dealers, and unions. In 2012, for example, Caterpillar Inc. demanded that union workers at its London, Ontario, factory take a 50 percent wage cut in order to help the company's operations become more cost-effective. When the union refused, the company closed the plant and moved the production to the United States. Some people feel that it is unethical for a company to give employees an ultimatum like Caterpillar did, because it seems outrageous and is an attempt to make an offer to employees that the company knows they will not accept. Others would disagree and say the company has to do what it thinks is economically necessary. Another example: Businesses in the pharmaceuticals industry are often criticized because of the high prices of drugs. The companies argue that high prices are needed to cover the cost of developing new drugs, but critics argue that the companies are engaging in *price gouging* (charging unreasonably high prices).[4]

After a WestJet executive accessed Air Canada's confidential reservations database, WestJet admitted its actions were unethical and paid Air Canada $5 million.[5] Most people would probably see the WestJet incident as a fairly clear case of unethical behaviour. But what if a manager is given confidential information by an unhappy former employee of a competitor who wants to get revenge on his former employer? Is it acceptable in that case for the manager to use the information? Some people would say it's still unethical, but others might argue that since the manager didn't go looking for the information, it's acceptable to use it.[6]

Difficulties may also arise because business practices vary globally. In some countries, bribes are a normal part of doing business, but in Canada (and increasingly in other countries as well), bribes are seen as clearly unethical and illegal. Several employees at SNC-Lavalin Group's Candu Energy were fired as a result of allegations of corruption, both in Canada and elsewhere,[7] and in 2015 the RCMP charged the company with offering millions of dollars in bribes to Libyan government officials.[8] In 2014, China fined drug maker GlaxoSmithKline $489 million for bribing doctors,[9] and Alstom SA, a French company, agreed to pay $772 million in fines as a result of a widespread bribery scheme that was used to help the company win energy contracts in various countries.[10]

A 2014 survey of global managers found that an average of 40 percent of managers felt that corruption was widespread in their

MANAGERIAL ETHICS Standards of behaviour that guide individual managers in their work.

CONFLICT OF INTEREST Occurs when an activity benefits the employee at the expense of the employer.

Antony Nettle/Alamy

David Osborn/Alamy Stock Photo

The intense competition between Air Canada and WestJet motivated a WestJet executive to access Air Canada's confidential reservations database in hopes of gaining a competitive edge.

country (only 20 percent of Canadian managers perceived that corruption was widespread in Canada).[11] The Organisation for Economic Co-operation and Development (OECD) has expressed concerns about loopholes in Canada's bribery laws and the lack of enforcement of bribery penalties.[12] (See Chapter 5 for more information about the issue of bribery.)

Assessing Ethical Behaviour

We can determine whether a particular action or decision is ethical or unethical by using a three-step model to systematically apply ethical judgments to situations that may arise during the course of business activities.[13]

1. Gather the relevant factual information.
2. Determine the most appropriate moral values.
3. Make an ethical judgment based on the rightness or wrongness of the proposed activity or policy.

Let's see how this process might work for a common dilemma faced by managers: expense account claims. Companies routinely cover work-related expenses of employees when they are travelling on company business and/or entertaining clients for business purposes. Common examples of such expenses include hotel bills, meals, rental cars, and so forth. Employees are expected to claim only those expenses that are work-related. Suppose we have the following factual information (Step 1): A manager takes a client to dinner while travelling on business and spends $100; submitting a receipt for that dinner and expecting to be reimbursed for $100 is clearly appropriate. Suppose, however, the manager also has a $100 dinner the next night in that same city with a good friend for purely social purposes. Submitting the receipt for full reimbursement would be seen by most managers as unethical (but some might rationalize that it is acceptable because they are underpaid and this is a way to increase their pay).

Given this information, we need to determine the most appropriate moral values (Step 2). There are four commonly used ethical norms we can use to make this determination:

Utility. Does a particular act optimize what is best for those who are affected by it?

Rights. Does it respect the rights of the individuals involved?

Justice. Is it consistent with what we regard to be fair?

Caring. Is it consistent with people's responsibilities to each other?

Figure 3.1 incorporates these ethical norms into a model of ethical decision making. Now, let's return to the case of the expense account and make an ethical judgment (Step 3). The *utility* norm would acknowledge that the manager benefits from padding an expense account, but co-workers and owners do not. Likewise, inflating an expense account does not respect the *rights* of others. It is also *unfair* and compromises the manager's *responsibilities* to others. This particular act, then, appears to be clearly unethical. But now suppose that the manager happens to lose the receipt for the legitimate dinner but does not lose the receipt for the social dinner. Would it be ethical to submit the illegitimate receipt because the manager is only doing so to be reimbursed for what he or she is entitled to? Or is submitting the other receipt unethical under any circumstances? Changes in the factual information about the case may make ethical issues more or less clear-cut.

Technological innovations have ceated all sorts of new ethical dilemmas: cloning, satellite reconnaissance, email snooping, and bio-engineered foods, to name just a few. In 2015, it was discovered that Volkswagen had installed software on its diesel vehicles that could sense when the engine was being tested to see if it adhered to emissions regulations established by the Environmental Protection Agency in the U.S. The software caused the engine to function in such a way that it would pass inspection, but only for the brief time when it was being tested. For every innovation that promises convenience or safety, there seems to be a related ethical issue. The internet and email, for example, are convenient and efficient, but they present business people with a variety of ethics-related problems. For example, a manager in one company sent false emails to his workers, pretending to be a recruiter from a competing firm. Any employees who responded to the emails were skipped for promotion. Electronic communication also makes it possible to run swindles with greater efficiency than ever before. During the past few years, several individuals have been convicted for running Ponzi schemes.[14]

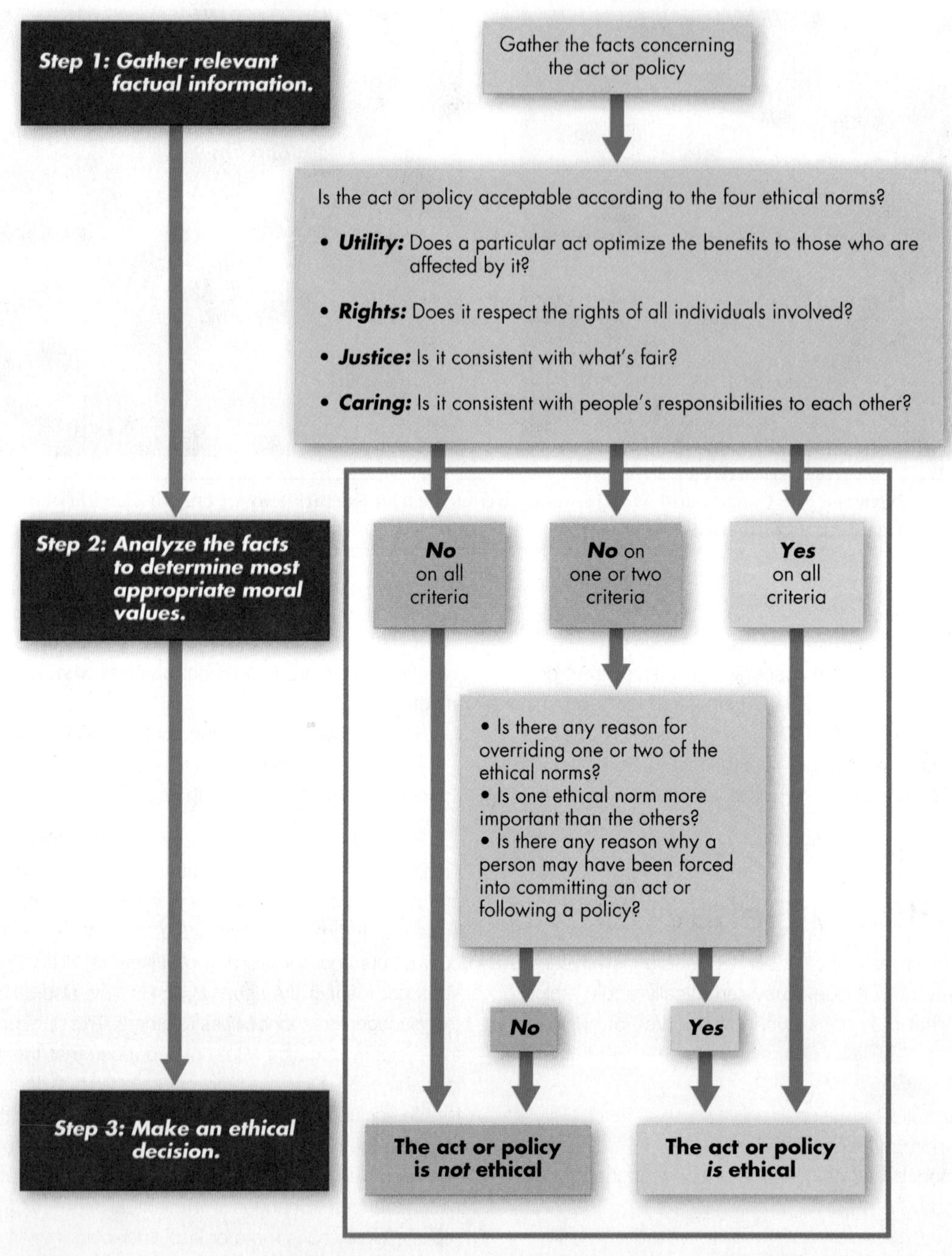
Step 1: Gather relevant factual information.
Gather the facts concerning the act or policy
Is the act or policy acceptable according to the four ethical norms?
• Utility: Does a particular act optimize the benefits to those who are affected by it?
• Rights: Does it respect the rights of all individuals involved?
• Justice: Is it consistent with what's fair?
• Caring: Is it consistent with people's responsibilities to each other?
Step 2: Analyze the facts to determine most appropriate moral values.
No on all criteria
No on one or two criteria
Yes on all criteria
• Is there any reason for overriding one or two of the ethical norms?
• Is one ethical norm more important than the others?
• Is there any reason why a person may have been forced into committing an act or following a policy?
No
Yes
Step 3: Make an ethical decision.
The act or policy is not ethical
The act or policy is ethical

FIGURE 3.1 Model of Ethical Judgment Making

Encouraging Ethical Behaviour in Organizations

To promote ethical behaviour, managers must understand *why* unethical behaviour occurs in the first place. Three general factors have been identified as important in causing individuals to behave in unethical ways: *pressure* (the employee has some problem that cannot be solved through legitimate means), *opportunity* (the employee uses his or her position in the organization to secretly solve the problem), and *rationalization* (the employee sees him- or herself as basically an ethical person caught up in an unfortunate situation).[15] To reduce the chance of unethical behaviour, organizations should *demonstrate top management commitment to ethical standards, adopt written codes of ethics*, and *provide ethics training to employees*.

DEMONSTRATE TOP MANAGEMENT COMMITMENT TO VALUES AND HIGH ETHICAL STANDARDS

It is crucial that top management demonstrate a serious a public commitment to high ethical standards. For example, Mountain Equipment Co-op is publicly committed to the concept of *ethical sourcing*, which means monitoring factories that produce its products to make sure that those factories are providing good working conditions for their employees, Without this ethical "tone at the top," lower-level employees are not likely to take ethics very seriously.

Figure 3.2 illustrates the essential role corporate ethics and values should play in corporate policy. It shows that business strategies and practices can change frequently and business objectives may change

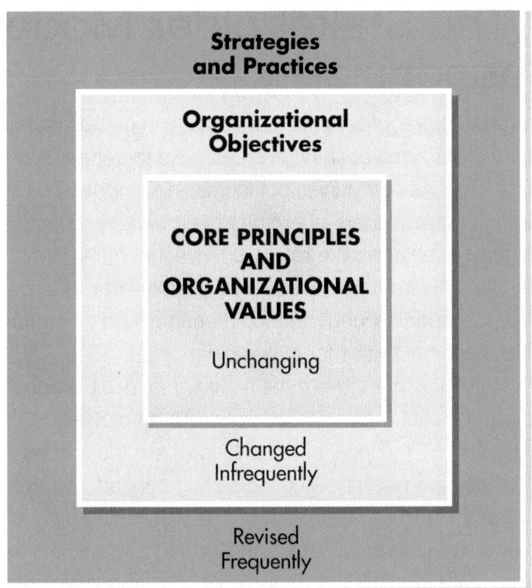

FIGURE 3.2 Core principles and organizational values

Source: Baron, David P. *Business and Its Environment*, 4th edition, © 2003. Reprinted by permission of Pearson Education, Inc., Upper Saddle River, NJ.

occasionally, but an organization's core principles and values should remain the same. For example, Google's core principle is "Don't Be Evil." Google adapts its strategies and practices to meet the challenges posed by the rapidly changing technology industry, but Google must do so in a way that does not violate its core principle.

ADOPT WRITTEN CODES OF ETHICS

A written code of ethics formally acknowledges that a company intends to do business in an ethical manner. Codes of ethics increase public confidence in a company, improve internal operations, and help managers respond on those occasions when there are problems with illegal or unethical employee behaviour. About two-thirds of Canada's largest corporations have codes of ethics (90 percent of large U.S. firms do). More and more regulatory and professional associations in Canada are recommending that corporations adopt codes of ethics. The Canada Deposit Insurance Corporation, for example, requires that all deposit-taking institutions have a code of conduct that is periodically reviewed and ratified by the board of directors. The Canadian Competition Bureau, the Canadian Institute of Chartered Accountants, and the Ontario Human Rights Commission are all pushing for the adoption of codes of ethics by corporations.[16] Many Canadian and U.S. firms are also adding a position called "ethics director" or "ethics officer."

If codes of ethics are to be effective, there must be a control system and consistent enforcement when unethical behaviour occurs. Employees will then know that the company is serious about its pursuit of high ethical standards. This is exactly what did *not* happen in the infamous Enron case. Enron had a code of ethics, but managers did not follow it. On one occasion, Enron's board of directors voted to set aside the code in order to complete a deal that would have violated it. After the deal was completed, they then voted to reinstate the code.

PROVIDE ETHICS TRAINING

Can business ethics be "taught," either in the workplace or in schools? Business schools are important players in the debate about ethics, as they sensitize students to academic integrity issues like plagiarism and cheating and how these unethical activities harm students and the educational system. But most analysts agree that companies must take the lead in educating employees about ethics. Imperial Oil, for example, conducts workshops that help employees put Imperial's ethics statement into actual practice. More and more firms are doing ethics training where managers are reminded of the importance of ethical decision making, and are updated on the most current laws and regulations that are relevant for their firm. Mary Gentile, a management consultant, says that employees know the difference between right and wrong, but they occasionally behave in an unethical fashion because they don't know how to resist pressure from peers and bosses to behave unethically.[17] She provides suggestions to help individuals resist such pressure and to act out their ethical values. Some ethics training programs take a more dramatic approach; ethics seminars are taught by former executives who have spent time in prison for their own ethical misdeeds.[18]

Dealing with ethical issues is not a simple matter, and many companies struggle with ethical dilemmas. This is particularly true for those that operate internationally. On several occasions, dangerous working conditions have been discovered in factories in developing countries that produce goods for Western retailers. In 2013, over 1100 workers were killed when a garment factory in Bangladesh collapsed. Soon after the disaster, the Worker Rights Consortium circulated a photo of a Joe Fresh label in the debris.[19] In 2011, allegations were made that some products sold by Victoria's Secret contained cotton that had been produced using child labour.[20]

LO-2 CORPORATE SOCIAL RESPONSIBILITY

Corporate social responsibility (CSR) refers to the way in which a business tries to balance its commitments to important individuals and groups in its external environment. Mountain Equipment Co-op (MEC) is an example of an organization with a strong sense of social responsibility. The company does not simply try to maximize shareholder wealth, but rather seeks a balance between financial and social/environmental goals. To demonstrate its concern for social responsibility, MEC provides a safe and healthy workplace for employees, audits suppliers who produce the products it sells, minimizes the negative impact of manufacturing and packaging on the environment, ensures that waste is disposed of in an environmentally responsible manner, treats workers with dignity, pays workers fairly, and emphasizes energy efficiency, pollution control, and recycling potential in MEC buildings.[21]

Another example of social responsibility in action is the **fair-trade movement**, described in the opening case. The movement was motivated

CORPORATE SOCIAL RESPONSIBILITY The idea that a business should balance its commitments to individuals and groups that are directly affected by the organization's activities.

FAIR-TRADE MOVEMENT A movement designed to help workers in developing countries receive fair payments for their work.

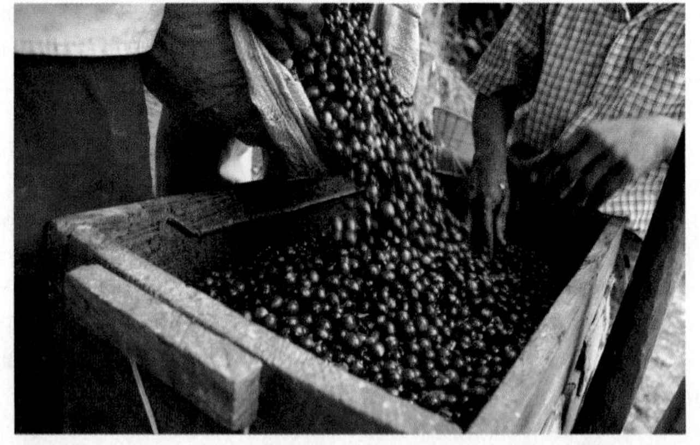

Starbucks helps local farmers gain access to credit, develops and maintains sustainability of the coffee crop, and builds farmer support centres in Latin America and Africa to provide local farmers with agricultural and technical education support.

haak78/Shutterstock

by concerns that workers in developing countries who produce commodities like coffee were not receiving fair payment for their products. Companies in developed countries who are concerned about this problem work with non-profit organizations like the Fairtrade Foundation and the Rainforest Alliance, who certify that farming co-operatives are paying workers fairly and not damaging the environment. More than 5000 companies—including Kraft Foods, Avon, and Starbucks—sell products with a Fairtrade or Rainforest Alliance logo on them.[22]

LO-3 The Stakeholder Model of Responsibility

Organizational stakeholders are individuals and groups that are directly affected by the practices of an organization and therefore have a stake in its performance.[23] As companies put increasing emphasis on their social responsibility to stakeholders, there has been a move to go beyond traditional *financial* measures like return on investment. A new measure—called the Social Return on Investment (SROI)—has been developed which helps companies understand, manage, and communicate the *social* value of their activities for stakeholders.[24]

Most companies that strive to be socially responsible concentrate on the following stakeholders: (1) customers, (2) employees, (3) investors, (4) suppliers, and (5) the local communities where they do business (see Figure 3.3). They are also showing increasing concern for protecting the natural environment.

While everyone seems to accept the idea that attention must be paid to organizational stakeholders, there is debate about which should be given the most attention. One view, called *managerial capitalism*, is that a company's only responsibility is to make as much money as possible for its *shareholders*, as long as the company doesn't break any laws.

ORGANIZATIONAL STAKEHOLDERS Groups, individuals, and organizations that are directly affected by the practices of an organization and that therefore have a stake in its performance.

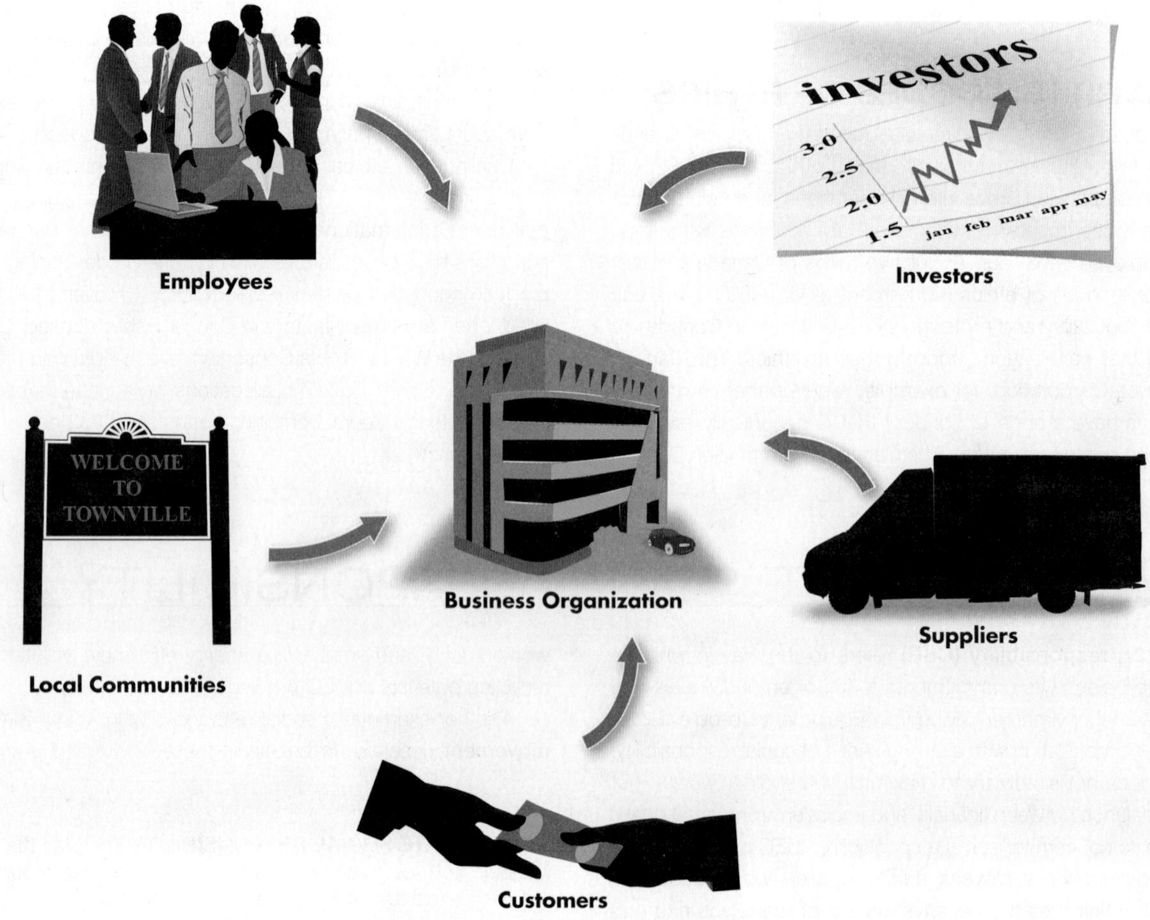

FIGURE 3.3 Major corporate stakeholders

This view has been strongly challenged by an opposing view that says that companies must be responsible to a variety of stakeholders, including *customers*, *employees*, *investors*, *suppliers*, and the *local communities* in which they do business. Opponents of CSR claim that it is being imposed on businesses by a coalition of environmentalists, while supporters of CSR claim that companies have become interested in CSR because that is what consumers prefer.[25]

RESPONSIBILITY TOWARD CUSTOMERS

There are three key areas that are currently in the news regarding the social responsibility of business toward customers: *consumer rights*, *unfair pricing*, and *ethics in advertising*.

Consumer Rights

Consumerism is a movement dedicated to protecting the rights of consumers in their dealings with businesses. Consumers have the following rights:

1. *The right to safe products.* The right to safe products is not always honoured. In 2008, 20 people died after eating listeria-contaminated meat made by Maple Leaf Foods. Sales dropped by nearly 50 percent once this became public.[26] The government of China has become concerned that negative publicity about faulty toys and contaminated pet food and toothpaste has damaged the "Made in China" label. In a surprising development, Mattel Inc. apologized to China for claiming that a recall of 18 million playsets with dangerous magnets was necessitated by poor quality control at one of its Chinese suppliers. Mattel eventually admitted that its own product design was flawed.[27]
2. *The right to be informed about all relevant aspects of a product.* Food products must list their ingredients, clothing must be labelled with information about its proper care, and banks must tell you exactly how much interest you are paying on a loan.
3. *The right to be heard.* Procter & Gamble puts a toll-free number on many of its products that consumers can call if they have questions or complaints. Many other retailers offer money-back guarantees if consumers are not happy with their purchase.
4. *The right to choose what they buy.* Central to this right is free and open competition among companies. In times past, companies divided up a market so that firms did not have to truly compete against each other. Such practices are illegal today and any attempts by business to block competition can result in fines or other penalties.
5. *The right to be educated about purchases.* All prescription drugs now come with detailed information regarding dosage, possible side effects, and potential interactions with other medications.
6. *The right to courteous service.* This right is hard to legislate, but as consumers become increasingly knowledgeable, they are more willing to complain about bad service. Consumer hotlines can also be used to voice service-related issues.

THERE'S AN APP FOR THAT!

APP DETAILS	PLATFORMS
1. **Ethical Barcode** **Source:** David Hamp-Gonsalves **Key Features:** Exposes the environmental, social, and ethical ramifications of the products you buy.	Apple, Android
2. **The Eco Activist** **Source:** Bright Beam **Key Features:** Built-in carbon footprint calculator; you can get a fast estimate, or a deeper, more accurate calculation of your carbon footprint, as well as your family/household's result.	Android
3. **iRecycle** **Source:** Earth 911 Inc. **Key Features:** iRecycle provides access to more than 1600 000 ways to recycle over 350 materials.	Apple, Android

APP DISCOVERY EXERCISE

Since app availability changes, conduct your own search for the "Top Three" socially responsible and green business apps and identify the key features.

Unfair Pricing

Interfering with competition can also mean illegal pricing practices. *Collusion* among companies—including getting together to "fix" prices—is against the law. Arctic Glacier Inc. of Winnipeg was one of several companies served with subpoenas by the U.S. government during an investigation of collusion in the U.S. market for packaged ice. Arctic eventually paid $12.5 million in fines.[28] The Canadian Competition Bureau launched an investigation after hearing allegations from a confidential informant that Mars, Hershey, Nestlé, and Cadbury had teamed up in a price-fixing scheme.[29] In 2012, three gas companies in Kingston and Brockville—Canadian Tire, Pioneer Energy, and Mr. Gas Ltd.—were fined a total of $2 million by the Competition Bureau for fixing gas prices.[30] Other countries are also concerned about price fixing. In Germany, the competition watchdog recently fined companies in three different industries—meat, sugar, and beer—for conspiring to fix prices. The fines totalled more than $700 million.[31]

In 2010, new laws came into effect that were designed to make it easier for the Competition Bureau to convict price-fixers (since 1980, only three price-fixing convictions were secured in the 23 cases that came before the Bureau). The maximum prison sentence for price fixing has been tripled to 14 years, and the maximum fine increased from $10 million to $25 million.[32]

Ethics in Advertising

There are several ethical issues in advertising, including truth-in-advertising claims, the advertising of counterfeit brands, the use of stealth advertising, and advertising that is morally objectionable.

Truth in advertising has long been regulated in Canada, but an increased emphasis on this issue is now becoming more noticeable on the international scene as well. For example, Chinese government officials investigated Procter & Gamble's claim that its Pantene shampoo made hair "10 times stronger." This came shortly after Procter & Gamble was ordered to pay a $24 000 fine after one consumer complained that SK-II skin cream was not the "miracle water" it claimed to be and did not make her skin "look 12 years younger in 28 days."[33]

Advertising of counterfeit brands is a problem in many different product lines, including perfume, luggage, pharmaceuticals, designer clothing, shoes, cigarettes, watches, sports memorabilia, golf clubs, and fine wines, to name just a few. Because cancer drugs are so expensive, fake versions have started to appear in various countries.[34] In 2011, fake jerseys of the reborn Winnipeg Jets hockey team were seized by the RCMP.[35] In

CONSUMERISM A social movement that seeks to protect and expand the rights of consumers in their dealings with businesses.

Counterfeit goods being sold on a street in Rome, Italy.

AHMAD FAIZAL YAHYA/Shutterstock

2014, Lululemon filed a lawsuit against several China-based companies, alleging that they were selling fake versions of its popular yoga pants online.[36] In 2015, the government of China charged that Alibaba, the e-commerce giant, was not doing enough to prohibit the sale of fake goods on its websites.[37]

Counterfeiting has moved beyond the manufacturing of individual products. In China and in New York City, fake Apple stores have popped up, complete with sales assistants wearing blue T-shirts with the Apple logo and signs advertising the latest Apple products.[38] In the Chinese city of Kunming, an Ikea knockoff store called 11 Furniture duplicates Ikea's well-known blue-and-yellow look and has essentially pirated the entire Ikea brand experience.[39]

The International Chamber of Commerce estimated the value of global trade in counterfeit goods at $1.7 trillion dollars in 2014.[40] Counterfeiting is obviously harmful to the companies that have spent a lot of time and money developing brand name goods for sale. While it might seem consumers benefit because they get low prices for goods that look like the real thing, in fact consumers often pay far too much for counterfeit goods because they are of very low quality. As well, some are downright dangerous to use. While a fake handbag simply costs money, fake pharmaceuticals, electrical products, and motorcycles can kill people who use them.[41] Nearly one-third of the counterfeit goods seized in Canada in one recent year were deemed by the RCMP to be harmful to the user.[42]

Stealth (undercover) advertising, a variation of viral marketing (see Chapter 2), involves companies paying individuals to extol the virtues of their products to other individuals who are not aware that they are listening to a paid spokesperson for the company. For example, Student Workforce hires individuals who are 18 to 30 years old to market products to other people in the same age bracket.[43] One advertising agency hired models to pose as tourists. These models asked real tourists to take their picture with a new Sony Ericsson camera cell phone. The models then talked up the advantages of the new product to the unsuspecting real tourists. The ethics of this are questionable when the paid individuals do not reveal that they are being paid by a company, so the recipient of the advertising is not aware that it is advertising. Commercial Alert, a U.S.-based consumer protection group, wants a government investigation of these undercover marketing tactics.[44]

Morally objectionable advertising offends the average person's sense of what is reasonable. Advertisements that have been criticized include Victoria's Secret models in skimpy underwear, campaigns by tobacco and alcohol companies that target young people, and the way women are portrayed in some video games (some new products are coming on the market to rectify this latter situation; see the boxed insert entitled "Silicon Sisters").

<<< Of all roadway accidents, 25 percent are distraction-related, and the biggest distractions for motorists are handheld gadgets: smartphones, pagers, and the like. In fulfilling their responsibility to consumers, some companies are conducting tests that yield important data about roadway accidents. Ford Motor Co., for example, has a Virtual Test Track Experiment simulator that determines how often drivers get distracted. Under normal circumstances, an adult driver will miss about 3 percent of the simulated "events" (like an ice patch or a deer on the road) that show up in the virtual road trip. If they're on the cell phone, they miss about 14 percent. But teenagers miss a scary 54 percent of the events.

Elena Elisseeva/Shutterstock

RESPONSIBILITY TOWARD EMPLOYEES

In Chapter 8, we describe the human resource management activities essential to a smoothly functioning business. These same activities—recruiting, hiring, training, promoting, and compensating—are also the basis for socially responsible behaviour toward employees. Socially responsible companies hire and promote new workers without regard to race, sex, or other irrelevant factors, provide a safe and non-bullying workplace, do not tolerate abusive managers or managers who sexually harasses subordinates, promote a work–life balance among employees, emphasize employee mental health, and pay a living wage.

Progressive companies go well beyond legal requirements, hiring and training the so-called hardcore unemployed (people with little education and training and a history of unemployment) and those who have disabilities. Bank of Montreal, for example, sponsors a community college skills upgrading course for individuals with hearing impairments. Royal Bank provides managers with discrimination awareness training. Rogers Communications provides individuals with mobility restrictions with telephone and customer-service job opportunities.[45]

Businesses also have a responsibility to respect the privacy of their employees, though there is some controversy about exactly how much control companies should have in areas like drug testing and computer monitoring. When Canadian National Railway instituted drug testing for train, brake, and yard employees, 12 percent failed. Trucking companies have found that nearly one-third of truckers who had an accident were on drugs.[46] It seems likely that safety will be compromised when employees in transportation companies use drugs, but there is controversy about what kind of testing is appropriate.

Differences of opinion are also evident with regard to the computer monitoring of employees while they are at work. New software programs allow bosses to see things like employees' Facebook comments and their opinions about pubs on Foursquare. Social Sentry, a tracking system developed by Social Logix, records employee social media activity

ENTREPRENEURSHIP AND NEW VENTURES

Creating Games with a Social Twist

Video games—which often portray young women in a negative light—have been largely created by young men with the young male consumer in mind. More often than not, these games play to low-level, base emotions. According to the Entertainment Software Association of Canada, approximately 59 percent of Canadians play video games and about 39 percent of those people are women. Meeting the specific needs of female gamers is a huge market opportunity that has so far been largely ignored. Silicon Sisters Interactive was created by two women to address this opportunity and to change the face of gaming.

Think of it as gaming with a social consciousness: gaming by women, for the female market, with images girls can aspire to, and women can relate to. So put away the guns and explosives—let's talk about a new model for a largely ignored market segment.

The two women behind Silicon Sisters Interactive have first-hand knowledge and experience in all aspects of the gaming industry. Brenda Bailey Gershkovitch, the CEO, focuses on the business side. She earned her stripes as the former COO of Deep Fried Entertainment while working on games like *MLB Superstars, Shadow Play,* and *Fantasy All Stars.* She is also on the board of directors of the Game Developers Conference of Canada. Kristen Forbes, the COO, is responsible for production. Kristen gained experience as an Executive Producer at Radical Entertainment where she worked on games like *Crash of the Titans, Scarface, The Incredible Hulk,* and *The Simpsons: Hit & Run.*

The shift from gaming consoles to new social gaming platforms (e.g., Facebook) has created an opportunity to connect and create scenarios for collaboration and group interaction. The gaming world is no longer stuck in a dark basement. The success of games like *FarmVille* (especially among older women) and social forums like Club Penguin (designed for kids up to 12 years old) have led the way. With this in mind, the women behind Silicon Sisters have created games like *School 26* and *Everlove.*

School 26 is a unique, casual game designed for girls aged 12 to 16. It follows Kate, a student whose family moves often, making it hard for her to maintain friendships. As she enrolls in her 26th new school, she makes a deal with her parents: if she makes good friends here, the family will stay put. Now the player has to help Kate use intuition, empathy, and strategy to build friendships and navigate the moral dilemmas (peer pressure, romance, and so on) of high school.

Everlove is a social gaming product aimed at women aged 35 to 50, a blend of romance novels and gaming served on a smartphone or tablet.

Will Silicon Sisters Interactive become the next big gaming company? Perhaps, and it is already changing the face of gaming by thinking about the needs of a large market segment that has been largely ignored. That is a really good start.

Recently, at a gaming industry event, the Silicon Sisters approach received support not simply because of its social message but also because of its business potential. George Lucas, the famous director of the movie *Star Wars*, said he thinks the "big game of the next five years will be a game . . . aimed at women and girls." For Brenda and Kristen these comments are music to their ears, and they fully intend to be at the front of the line to change the landscape and be a legitimate voice for female gamers.

CRITICAL THINKING QUESTIONS

1. What do you think of the potential for gaming products aimed at female consumers?
2. What themes or topics would you recommend for this underserved market?

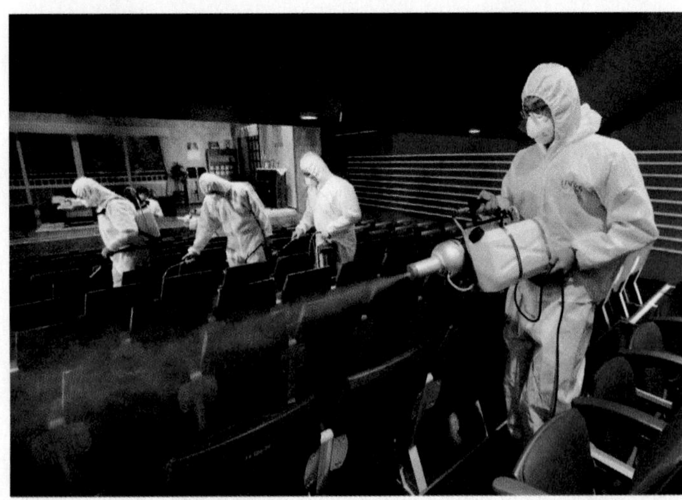

The safety of workers is an important consideration for all organizations. The required use of protective clothing when dealing with toxic substances is just one example of precautions that companies can take to protect workers while they are on the job.

Ahn Young-joon/The Canadian Press

from work or home. The program looks for workers who leak sensitive company information or badmouth the company.[47] Workers shouldn't damage the reputation of the company they work for, but there is no consensus on what constitutes going "too far."

Whistle-Blowers Respecting employees as people also means respecting their behaviour as ethically responsible individuals. Employees who discover that their company has been engaging in practices that are illegal, unethical, and/or socially irresponsible should be able to report the problem to higher-level management and be confident that managers will stop the questionable practices. If no one in the organization will take action, the employee might decide to inform a regulatory agency or the media. At this point, the person becomes a **whistle-blower**—an employee who discovers and tries to put an end to a company's unethical, illegal, and/or socially irresponsible actions by publicizing them.

John Kopchinski, a sales representative at pharmaceutical giant Pfizer, blew the whistle after he learned that Pfizer was promoting certain drugs for unapproved uses. He received $5.1 million from the U.S. government for his efforts.[48] In Canada, WestJet employee Melvin Crothers discovered that a fellow WestJet employee was somehow accessing a restricted Air Canada website in order to obtain data about Air Canada's "load factor" (the proportion of seats filled) on certain flights. It turned out that the employee had formerly worked for Air Canada, but his access to confidential Air Canada data had inadvertently not been cancelled. After discovering this, Crothers had a conversation with a former WestJet president who was heading up an Air Canada discount airline, which led

WHISTLE-BLOWER An individual who calls attention to an unethical, illegal, and/or socially irresponsible practice on the part of a business or other organization.

MANAGING IN TURBULENT TIMES

Should We Pay Whistle-Blowers?

When Eric Ben-Artzi, a risk analyst for Deutsche Bank, came to the conclusion that his company was overvaluing billions of dollars of derivatives, he discussed his concerns with his bosses. When they didn't pay attention, he filed a whistle-blower complaint with the U.S. Securities and Exchange Commission (SEC). Eric was let go a few months later, and has now filed a wrongful dismissal lawsuit against Deutsche. If Eric's claims are shown to be correct, he could receive millions of dollars in compensation. When the SEC levies a fine of $1 million or more, a whistle-blower who provided helpful information in the case can receive between 10 and 30 percent of the fine. One whistle-blower received $30 million.

In Canada, whistle-blower programs like the one established by the Investment Industry Regulatory Organization of Canada (IIROC) do not pay whistle-blowers for reporting illegal acts. Rather, attention in Canada has focused on protecting whistle-blowers from retaliation by the companies they reported. In 2013, the SEC received 62 tips from Canadian whistle-blowers (out of a total of 3238 tips).

In 2015, the Ontario Securities Commission proposed an incentive-based system for paying whistle-blowers which would cap payments at $1.5 million. Here is a key question that is part of their deliberations: Are there unanticipated negative consequences that might arise as from such payment? There are two opposing views on this question (naturally!).

Supporters say it is a good idea because whistle-blowers face a great deal of hostility and harassment from their companies when they report managerial misconduct. Companies also try to publicly discredit the whistle-blower, and this likely reduces the person's future job prospects. Because "speaking truth to power" is risky, whistle-blowers should be compensated. It's also true that the government can recover large sums of money from companies that behave badly if whistle-blowers come forward.

Opponents argue that if whistleblowers are paid, they will have an incentive to bypass existing compliance programs and go straight for the money. They also argue that whistle-blowers may make questionable charges as they put their own financial interests ahead of the interests of the company they work for. There may also be a "rush to judgment" about a situation. For example, at French carmaker Renault, three high-ranking executives were fired after an anonymous tip that they had stashed bribe money in a Swiss bank. The three executives were eventually exonerated, but they were subjected to considerable stress and the company experienced a public humiliation.

CRITICAL THINKING QUESTIONS

1. In your own words, state the pros and cons of paying whistle-blowers for the information they provide.
2. On balance, do you think it is a good idea to pay whistle-blowers? Explain your reasoning.

to Air Canada filing a lawsuit against WestJet. Crothers resigned from WestJet four days later.[49]

Whistle-blowers are often demoted or fired when they take their accusations public. Even if they retain their jobs, they may still be treated as outsiders and suffer resentment or hostility from co-workers. One recent study found that about half of all whistle-blowers eventually get fired, and about half of those who get fired subsequently lose their homes and/or families.[50]

Federal legislation to protect whistle-blowers was introduced in Canada in 2003. In 2009, the Investment Industry Regulatory Organization of Canada (IIROC) opened a whistle-blower hotline as a result of an increased incidence of securities fraud such as Ponzi schemes in both Canada and the United States. Calls regarding market fraud are forwarded to four of the top people at the IIROC so that swift action can be taken.[51] The boxed insert entitled "Should We Pay Whistle-Blowers?" analyzes an interesting issue in whistle-blowing.

RESPONSIBILITY TOWARD INVESTORS

It might sound odd to say that managers can be irresponsible toward investors, since the investors are the owners of the company, but managers behave irresponsibly when they pay themselves outlandish salaries and bonuses or spend large amounts of company money for their own personal comfort. If managers do not use the firm's financial resources in a responsible way, the ultimate losers are the owners, since they do not receive the earnings, dividends, or capital appreciation due to them. Financial mismanagement can take many forms, including *improper financial management, misrepresentation of finances*, *cheque kiting*, and *insider trading*.

Improper Financial Management

This can take many forms, including executives making bad financial decisions, paying executives outlandish salaries and bonuses, or sending them on extravagant "retreats" to exotic resorts. For example, managers at American International Group became involved in very-high-risk insurance that caused the company to be on the hook for billions of dollars. The U.S. government ended up giving hundreds of billions of dollars to the company to keep it afloat. In many of these situations, creditors don't have much leverage and shareholders have few viable options. Trying to force a management changeover is not only difficult, but it can also drive down the price of the company's stock, a penalty shareholders are usually unwilling to assign themselves.

Misrepresentation of Finances

Occasionally, managers are guilty of misrepresenting a company's financial condition. In Canada, one of the most highly publicized cases involved Garth Drabinsky and Myron Gottlieb, the top managers at Livent Inc. In 2006, Ken Lay, the CEO of Enron, was convicted of conspiracy and securities fraud, but he died before he was sentenced. In 2007, Conrad Black, CEO of Hollinger International, was convicted of fraud and obstruction of justice and was sentenced to six and a half years in prison. In December 2008, Bernie Madoff pleaded guilty to swindling investors in a $50 billion fraud. He is likely to spend the rest of his life in prison.[52] In 2012, R. Allen Stanford was found guilty of wasting investor money on yachts, failing businesses, and cricket tournaments. He was sentenced to 110 years.[53]

Cheque Kiting

This involves writing a cheque from one account, depositing it in a second account, and then immediately spending money from the second account while the money from the first account is still in transit. A cheque from the second account can also be used to replenish the money in the first account, and the process starts all over again. This practice obviously benefits the person doing the kiting, but it is irresponsible because it involves using other people's money without paying for it. In 2012, the Bank of Montreal sued several U.S. and Canadian businesspeople, alleging that they ran a cheque kiting scheme that cost BMO $20 million.[54]

Insider Trading

Using confidential information to gain from the purchase or sale of stock is called **insider trading**. The trader uses information not available to the general investor by either buying stock just before its price goes up or selling stock just before its stock goes down. The Alberta securities regulator charged several executives at Grand Cache Coal Corp. with insider trading for selling company stock before the company disclosed negative news about its sales.[55] Raj Rajaratnam, the co-founder of Galleon Group, was sentenced to 11 years in prison for insider trading,[56] and Matthew Martoma, who worked for an affiliate of SAC Capital Advisors, was sentence to 9 years.[57] One study showed that there was "abnormal" trading in 25 percent of takeover deals between 1996 and 2012.[58] Critics say that the government is not doing nearly enough to stop insider trading, but the offence can be hard to prove because evidence is often circumstantial.[59]

RESPONSIBILITY TOWARD SUPPLIERS

Businesses that are socially responsible take care when managing their relationships with their suppliers, because they recognize the importance of mutually beneficial partnership arrangements. Thus, they keep suppliers informed about the company's plans, and they negotiate delivery schedules and prices that are acceptable to both firms. Some firms go so far as to allow suppliers access to the firm's internal records so the supplier can better serve the firm. Toyota and Amazon.com are among the companies acknowledged to have excellent relationships with their suppliers.

In contrast, some large retailers put intense pressure on their suppliers to lower their prices. If the supplier cannot get the price down to the level the retailer demands, the retailer drops the supplier and finds another one that will meet the price. The retailer does this so it will be able to charge low prices to consumers and thereby improve its market share. Consumers like the low prices, but suppliers may have difficulty surviving because they cannot cover their costs.

RESPONSIBILITY TOWARD LOCAL AND INTERNATIONAL COMMUNITIES

Businesses can demonstrate socially responsible behaviour in their local communities by contributing to local programs like community hockey, by donating to charities such as the United Way, and by many other actions that support an improved quality of life for people who live in the local community where the business operates.

Corporate Charitable Donations

Many companies donate money and time to different causes. For example, in 2014 the "Celebration of Giving" program at Telus generated $46 million of donations to charities, and Telus employees donated 15 000 hours of volunteer work.[60] At AltaGas, employees can take two paid days off per year to

INSIDER TRADING The use of confidential information to gain from the purchase or sale of stock.

volunteer at a charity of their choice.[61] Every four months, Whole Foods (Toronto) donates 5 percent of one day's sales to a designated non-profit organization.[62] Unilever Canada gives employees four afternoons a year for community activities.[63] Mars Canada sets aside one day each year for employees to volunteer. In 2013, Tim Hortons' Children's Foundation started construction on a camp for underprivileged children at Sylvia Lake in Manitoba. The Foundation also has a Youth Leadership Program that is currently offered at two sites in Ontario.[64] A survey of 93 large Canadian companies found that 97 percent made a charitable contribution of some sort and that the median value of their contributions was $340 000.[65] More than 80 percent of the companies said that they made contributions because it was a good thing to do, irrespective of any financial benefits they might achieve from giving.[66]

The stakeholder model can also provide some helpful insights into the conduct of managers in international business. In particular, organizations should acknowledge their commitment to their stakeholders in each country where it does business. Daimler, for example, has investors not only in Germany, but also in Canada, the United States, Japan, and various other countries. It also has suppliers, employees, and customers in multiple countries, so its actions affect communities in many different countries. International businesses must also address their responsibilities in areas such as wages, working conditions, and environmental protection across different countries (that have varying laws and norms). ExxonMobil, for example, has helped build hospitals and expand schools in Angola, and it also supports a local anti-malaria program.

RESPONSIBILITY TOWARD THE ENVIRONMENT

Controlling **pollution**—the injection of harmful substances into the environment—is a significant social responsibility challenge for business firms. Air, water, and land pollution are the focus of most anti-pollution efforts by business and governments.

Air Pollution *Air pollution* results when a combination of factors lowers air quality. Large amounts of chemicals such as the carbon monoxide emitted by automobiles contribute to air pollution. So do smoke and other chemicals emitted by manufacturing plants. The rapid industrialization of developing countries has led to increased concerns about air pollution. In China, for example, 100 coal-fired power plants are being built every year, and each plant uses 1.2 million tonnes of coal and throws off 3.7 million tons of carbon dioxide. Only 5 percent of the coal-fired power plants in China are equipped with pollution-control equipment.[67] Many industrial companies were forcibly shut down by the Chinese government in advance of the 2008 Olympics in an attempt to improve air quality.

High pollution levels in the city centre of Shanghai, China. Air pollution is a major problem in some large cities in China because power plants and factories have not installed proper pollution controls.

oceanfishing/Shutterstock

The Kyoto Summit in 1997 was an early attempt by various governments to reach an agreement on ways to reduce the threat of pollution. Australia is the world's largest greenhouse gas emitter per capita, contributing 7.3 percent of the world's total. The United States (at 6.5 percent) and Canada (at 6.4 percent) are close behind. Canada is the only one of the three leading emitters that signed the 1997 Protocol, but in 2006 the Conservative government said Canada would not be able to meet its targets for reducing pollution, and that it would continue with the Protocol only if the targets were renegotiated.[68] The 2009 meetings in Copenhagen on this issue ended without an agreement.

The United Nations has promoted a "cap and trade" system, in which companies in industrialized countries can buy carbon credits, which essentially give them the right to pollute the atmosphere with carbon dioxide. The money collected is then used to help fund clean-air projects in developing countries that would not otherwise be affordable.[69] In 2013, the province of Quebec and the state of California introduced compulsory cap-and-trade rules in an attempt to reduce greenhouse gas emissions. Quebec has set a goal to reduce emissions to 25 percent below 1990 levels.[70] But critics of cap and trade say that the scheme is an open invitation to fraudsters. Suppose, for example, that an Indonesian forest operator sells a carbon permit to a German manufacturing firm that is releasing too much CO_2 into the atmosphere. That one transaction is fine, but what if the Indonesian firm sells the same carbon permit to manufacturers in other countries? That will make it appear like a lot more carbon dioxide has been reduced than is actually the case. Multibillion-dollar fraud has already occurred in the European Union's carbon trading market, and Europol's Criminal Finances and Technology section estimates that up to 90 percent of all carbon market volume in certain EU nations is fraudulent.[71]

Figure 3.4 shows world atmospheric carbon dioxide levels for the period between 1750 and 2000, and it offers three possible scenarios for future levels under different sets of conditions. Energy supplies are measured in exajoules—one of which is roughly the annual energy consumption of a large metropolitan area like New York or London. Under the lowest, or best-case, scenario, by 2100 the population would only grow to 6.4 billion people, economic growth would be no more than 1.2 to 2 percent a year, and energy supplies would require only 8000 exajoules of conventional oil. However, under the highest, or worst-case, scenario, the population would increase to 11.3 billion people, annual economic growth would be between 3 and 3.5 percent, and energy supplies would require as much as 18 400 exajoules of conventional oil.

Concerns about the negative effect of air pollution has led to an increasing emphasis on the development of clean, renewable energy such as wind, solar, and hydroelectric power as a way to reduce the pollution caused by burning fossil fuels. In terms of capacity, Canada ranks in the top five countries in the world for hydroelectric power generation. In terms of total investment in renewable energy, Canada ranks sixth.[72]

POLLUTION The introduction of harmful substances into the environment.

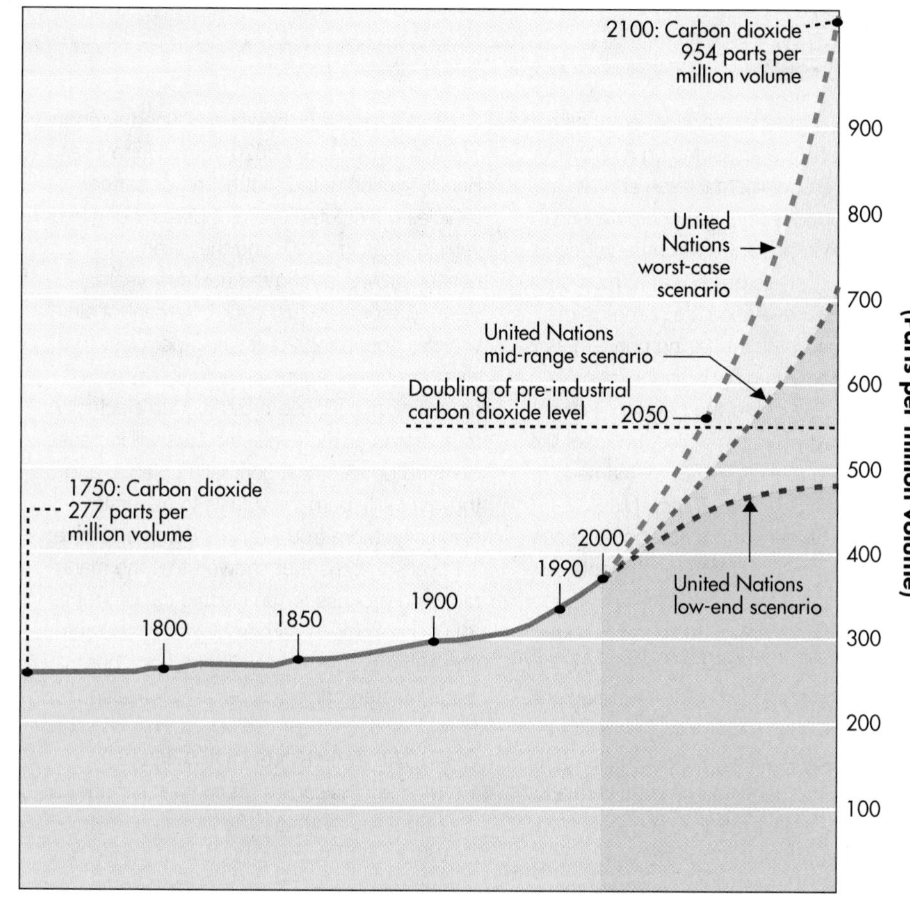

FIGURE 3.4 CO_2 emissions, past and future

There is currently an intense debate about whether *global warming*—an increase in the earth's average temperature—is occurring because of increased air pollution. Supporters and skeptics alike provide evidence to prove their point. If global warming occurs, it will benefit some people and hurt others. In normally icy Greenland, for example, a warming climate will result in a longer growing season for grain and vegetables, and farmers may start raising cattle because of the increased forage that would be available in the summertime. But warming would also melt some of the world's glaciers and cause sea levels to rise and flood some coastal cities.[73]

In difficult economic times, the general public is less willing to make personal sacrifices in order to battle climate change. A poll of 12 000 people in 11 countries showed that less than half of the respondents were willing to make lifestyle changes to reduce carbon emissions, and only 20 percent said they would be willing to spend extra money to fight climate change.[74]

Water Pollution For many years, businesses and municipalities dumped their waste into rivers, streams, and lakes with little regard for the effects. Thanks to new, stricter legislation and increased awareness on the part of businesses, water quality is improving in many areas. But water pollution is still a concern, and several high-profile oil spills—like the BP disaster in the Gulf of Mexico in 2010—have occurred. Pollution of the oceans by both cargo and passenger ships is a continuing problem.

Land Pollution *Toxic wastes* are dangerous chemical and/or radioactive by-products of various manufacturing processes that are harmful to humans and animals. In 2010, oil-sands giant Syncrude was found guilty of causing the death of 1600 ducks that landed in a tailing pond they had mistaken for a small lake. The company faced fines of up to $800 000 under the federal Migratory Birds Act and the Alberta Environmental Protection and Enhancement Act.[75]

Changes in forestry practices, limits on certain types of mining, and new forms of solid waste disposal are all attempts to address the issue of toxic waste. An entire industry—**recycling**—has developed as part of increased consciousness about land pollution. For example, MET Fine Printers in Vancouver, which used to spend $3000 each month on waste disposal, reduced that cost to just $300 after introducing a recycling program.[76] Vancouver-based Plastic Bank recycles plastic to produce "Social Plastic" products, and in the process provides employment to marginalized workers in Latin America and the Caribbean.[77] Plant and animal waste can be recycled to produce energy; this is referred to as *biomass*. Waste materials like sawdust, manure, and sludge are increasingly being turned into useful products. Ensyn Corp., for example, converts sawdust into liquid fuel by blasting wood waste with a sand-like substance that is heated. What's left is bio-oil.[78]

Canadian businesses are now routinely reducing various forms of pollution. However, the road to environmental purity is not easy. Under the Canadian and Ontario Environmental Protection Acts, pollution liability for a business firm can run as high as $2 million per day. To avoid such fines, companies must prove that they showed diligence in avoiding an environmental disaster such as an oil or gasoline spill.[79] The Environmental Choice program, sponsored by the federal government, licenses products that meet environmental standards set by the Canadian Standards Association. Firms whose products meet these standards can put the logo—three doves intertwined to form a maple leaf—on their products.[80]

An interesting problem that highlights some of the complexities in both waste disposal and recycling involves wooden pallets—those splintery wooden platforms used to store and transport consumer goods. Pallets are very recyclable, but since the cost of new ones is so low, many companies just toss used ones aside and buy new ones. Ironically, some environmentalists argue that abandoned pallets actually serve a useful purpose because in urban areas, they often become refuge for animals such as raccoons and abandoned pets.[81]

Canadian firms that do business abroad are increasingly being confronted with environmental issues. In many cases, there is opposition to a project by local residents because they fear that some sort of pollution will result. For example, Calgary-based TVI Pacific Inc.'s planned open-pit mine and cyanide processing plant in the Philippines led to violent clashes between the company and the Subanon people. In Peru, indigenous groups threatened violence if Talisman Energy continued drilling for oil on their land.[82] Multinational firms have also been publicly criticized. For example, Nestlé has received negative publicity on YouTube,

RECYCLING The reconversion of waste materials into useful products.

THE GREENING OF BUSINESS

Some Frustrations in the Green Movement

Consumers interested in buying products that are environmentally friendly face two key problems. The first is that companies often make misleading claims about the green characteristics of their products. A study of 5296 products by TerraChoice, an environmental marketing company, found that there was at least one misleading green claim on 95.6 percent of the products they studied. The study also found that 100 percent of toy manufacturers and 99.2 percent of baby-product makers were guilty of "greenwashing" (misleading consumers about the environmental benefits of a product). Having a product certified by a recognized, independent third party reduced the incidence of greenwashing, but fake certifications are readily available on the internet. TerraChoice identified several green "sins," including (1) making an environmentally friendly claim but providing no proof, (2) making vague claims (e.g., saying that a product is "all natural"), (3) making a green claim for a product that is inherently harmful (e.g., cigarettes), and (4) emphasizing a product's positive attributes on a relatively unimportant environmental issue and downplaying a product's negative characteristics on a far more important environmental issue. However, progress is being made; more and more products have accurate green claims.

The second problem facing consumers is that green products can be very expensive. Governments subsidize the development of electric and hybrid automobiles, but cars like Chevy's hybrid rechargeable Volt (named Car of the Year by *Motor Trend*), Nissan's all-electric Leaf, and Ford's all-electric Focus are expensive enough that many people cannot afford them. A hybrid car like the Prius, for example, costs about 30 percent more than an equivalent gasoline-powered car, and battery-powered cars are 50 to 100 percent higher. Even with fuel savings, it would take more than ten years for your purchase of an electric or hybrid car to break even with a car like the Ford Fiesta. Gasoline-powered automobiles also outperform electric and hybrid cars on dimensions that are important to consumers (cost, driving range, and power). Consulting firm J.D. Power produced a report entitled "Drive Green 2020: More Hope Than Reality" which noted that hybrid or battery vehicles constituted only 2.2 percent of global vehicle sales in 2010, and that even with healthy growth during the next few years, they will represent just over 7 percent of all vehicles sold by 2020. It's also not clear that electric-powered cars will actually mean less air pollution, because providing the electricity to recharge all those electric cars will increase demand on electrical generating plants, and they typically burn fossil fuels to generate electricity. More troubling is a comprehensive life cycle analysis that showed that the manufacturing process for an electric car produces 30 000 pounds of carbon dioxide emissions (the same process for an internal combustion–powered car produces 14 000 pounds).

CRITICAL THINKING QUESTIONS

1. Why are misleading green claims made for so many products?
2. What are the pros and cons of having government actively involved in subsidizing the development of green products?

Facebook, and Twitter claiming that the company is contributing to destruction of Indonesia's rainforest because it purchases palm oil from an Indonesian company that has cleared the rainforest to make way for a palm oil plantation.[83]

The boxed insert entitled "Some Frustrations in the Green Movement" describes some difficulties that are evident as companies and consumers try to behave in a more environmentally friendly way.

IMPLEMENTING SOCIAL RESPONSIBILITY PROGRAMS

Thus far, we have discussed corporate social responsibility (CSR) as if there is agreement on how companies should behave in most situations. In fact, differences of opinion exist as to the appropriateness of CSR as a business goal. Some people oppose any business activity that cuts into investor profits, while others argue that CSR must take precedence over profits.

Even people who share a common attitude toward CSR by business may have different reasons for their beliefs, and this influences their view about how social responsibility should be implemented. Some people fear that if businesses become too active in social concerns, they will gain too much control over how those concerns are addressed. They point to the influence many businesses have been able to exert on the government agencies that are supposed to regulate their industries. Other critics of business-sponsored social programs argue that companies lack the expertise needed. They believe that technical experts, not businesses, should decide how best to clean up a polluted river, for example.

Supporters of CSR believe that corporations are citizens just like individuals and therefore should help improve our lives. Others point to the vast resources controlled by businesses and note that, since businesses often create many of the problems social programs are designed to alleviate, they should use their resources to help. Still others argue that CSR is wise because it pays off for the firm in terms of good public relations.

The late Max Clarkson, formerly a top-level business executive and director of the Centre for Corporate Social Performance and Ethics at the University of Toronto, designed and applied a CSR rating system for companies. He found that companies that had the highest marks on ethics and CSR also had the highest financial performance.[84]

LO-4 Approaches to Social Responsibility

Given these differences of opinion, it is little wonder that corporations have adopted a variety of approaches to social responsibility. As Figure 3.5 illustrates, the four stances an organization can take concerning its obligations to society fall along a continuum ranging from the lowest

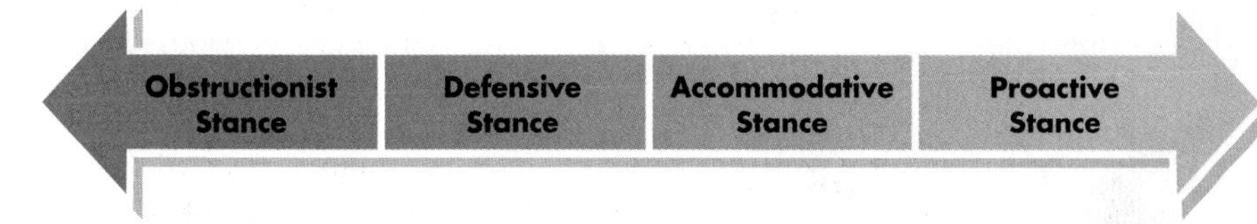

<<< **FIGURE 3.5** Spectrum of approaches to social responsibility

to the highest degree of socially responsible practices. Keep in mind that organizations do not always fit neatly into one category or another. The Ronald McDonald House program has been widely applauded, for example, but McDonald's has also come under fire for allegedly misleading consumers about the nutritional value of its food products. The Exercising Your Ethics exercise at the end of this chapter gives you an opportunity to think about the pros and cons of the various stances toward CSR.

OBSTRUCTIONIST STANCE

Businesses that take an *obstructionist stance* to social responsibility do as little as possible to solve social or environmental problems. When they cross the ethical or legal line that separates acceptable from unacceptable practices, their typical response is to deny or cover up their actions. Firms that adopt this position have little regard for ethical conduct and will generally go to great lengths to hide wrongdoing.

DEFENSIVE STANCE

An organization adopting a *defensive stance* will do everything required of it legally, but nothing more. Such a firm, for example, would install pollution-control equipment dictated by law, but would not install higher-quality equipment even though it might further limit pollution. Managers who take a defensive stance insist that their job is to generate profits. Tobacco companies in Canada and the United States generally take this position in their marketing efforts, since they are legally required to include warnings to smokers on their products and to limit advertising to prescribed media. They follow these rules to the letter of the law, but use more aggressive marketing methods in countries that have no such rules.

ACCOMMODATIVE STANCE

A firm that adopts an *accommodative stance* meets its legal and ethical requirements, but will also go further in certain cases. Such firms may agree to participate in social programs, but solicitors must convince them that these programs are worthy of funding. Many organizations respond to requests for donations to community hockey teams, Girl Guides, youth soccer programs, and so forth. The point, however, is that someone has to knock on the door and ask; accommodative organizations do not necessarily or proactively seek avenues for contributing.

PROACTIVE STANCE

Firms that adopt a *proactive stance* take to heart the arguments in favour of CSR. They view themselves as good citizens of society and they proactively seek opportunities to contribute. The most common—and direct—way to implement this stance is by setting up a foundation to provide direct financial support for various social programs.

Managing Social Responsibility Programs

The management of social responsibility programs can be done at both the formal and informal level.

FORMAL ACTIVITIES

At the *formal level*, top management must state strong support for CSR and make it a factor in strategic planning. Without the support of top management, no program can succeed. A specific executive must be given the authority to act as the director of the firm's social agenda. This individual monitors the program and ensures that its implementation is consistent with the policy statement and the strategic plan. Some companies appoint a committee of top managers to develop plans that detail the level of support that will be provided for the firm's social responsibility initiatives. For example, the company may decide to set aside a percentage of profits for social programs. Levi Strauss has a policy of giving 2.4 percent of its pre-tax earnings to worthy causes.

All of the organization's formal activities are summarized in a **social audit,** which is a systematic analysis of how a firm is using funds earmarked for its social-responsibility goals, and how effective these expenditures have been.[85] An important related element in a social responsibility program is the idea of **sustainable development**, which means pursuing activities that meet current needs, but which will not put future generations at a disadvantage when they attempt to meet their needs. Canadian businesses publish sustainability reports that explain how the company is performing on issues such as the environment, employee relations, workplace diversity, and business ethics. A study by Ottawa-based Stratos Inc. found that 60 percent of the 100 largest Canadian companies report at least some sustainability performance information.[86] For example, Artopex Inc., a furniture manufacturer in Quebec, has an active sustainability program.[87] Baxter Corp., a medical products company, publishes an annual Global Sustainability Report measuring the company's progress on nine sustainable priorities, including reductions in its carbon footprint.[88] Social audits and sustainability reports together constitute *triple-bottom-line reporting*—measuring the social, environmental, and economic performance of a company. Vancouver City Savings Credit Union (Vancity) uses triple-bottom-line reporting.[89] Companies that adopt mandatory sustainability reporting requirements see positive effects on corporate performance.[90]

SUSTAINABLE DEVELOPMENT Activities that meet current needs, but will not put future generations at a disadvantage when they try to meet their needs.

SOCIAL AUDIT A systematic analysis of how a firm is using funds earmarked for social-responsibility goals and how effective these expenditures have been.

<<< Ronald McDonald House helps the families of children who are in hospital care. It is supported by McDonald's and is an excellent example of socially responsible behaviour by a business.

Enigma/Alamy

The Global 100 list of the most sustainable corporations in the world is based on factors like energy productivity (the ratio of sales to energy consumption) and water productivity (sales to water usage). In the 2015 ranking, Biogen Idec was first, Allergan second, and Adidas third. Several Canadian companies made the list, including Tim Hortons (ranked #11), Teck Resources (#29), Telus (#37), and Bombardier (#57).[91]

INFORMAL ACTIVITIES

At the *informal level*, the culture of the organization (see Chapter 6) is very important in either inhibiting or facilitating social responsibility activities. Although members of the organization may not actually talk much about the culture, it can have a strong influence on their attitudes and behaviour, including their view of social responsibility. When organizational leaders demonstrate ethical leadership as part of the organizational culture, that will also convey to employees that socially responsible behaviour is valued.

Whistle-blowing behaviour by employees is another facet of informal activities that can enhance social responsibility (even though some members of top management may view such behaviour negatively). How an organization responds to whistle-blowing gives some insight into its actual stance on social responsibility. An employee who observes questionable behaviour usually reports the incident to his or her boss first. If nothing is done, the whistle-blower may then take more formal steps and report to higher-level managers or to an ethics committee. Eventually, the person may have to go to a regulatory agency or even the media to be heard. Whistle-blowing typically does not become a truly formal activity until the employee cannot get any satisfaction within the company.

LO-5 SOCIAL RESPONSIBILITY AND THE SMALL BUSINESS

In the most general sense, small businesses face many of the same ethical and social-responsibility issues as large businesses. But small business owners face many specific ethical dilemmas that have an immediate (and perhaps profound) effect on their business. For example, as the owner of a small garden supply store, how would you respond to a building inspector's suggestion that a cash payment would "expedite" your application for a building permit? As the manager of a nightclub, would you call the police, refuse service, or sell liquor to a customer whose ID card looked forged? Or, as the owner of a small medical laboratory, would you call the board of health to make sure that it has licensed the company you want to contract with to dispose of the lab's medical waste? As the owner of a small manufacturing firm, are you justified in overcharging by 5 percent a customer whose purchasing agent is lax? As the owner of a small computer services company, should you pad your income statement a bit to increase the chance that you will get a much-needed bank loan?

Other dilemmas present themselves to small business owners in the form of social responsibility issues. For example, can a small business afford to pursue CSR objectives? Should it sponsor hockey teams, make donations to the United Way, and buy light bulbs from the Lion's Club? Should it join the chamber of commerce and support the Better Business Bureau because it is the responsible thing to do or just because it is good business? Most of these decisions have financial implications, and the owners of many small firms feel that they do not have any financial flexibility.

MyBizLab

Study, practise, and explore real business situations with these helpful resources:

- **Interactive Lesson Presentations:** Work through interactive presentations and assessments to test your knowledge of business concepts.
- **Study Plan:** Check your understanding of chapter concepts with self-study quizzes.
- **Dynamic Study Modules:** Work through adaptive study modules on your computer, tablet, or mobile device.
- **Simulations:** Practise decision-making in simulated business environments.
- **Videos:** Learn more about the business practices and strategies of real companies.

SUMMARY OF

LEARNING OBJECTIVES

LO-1 EXPLAIN HOW INDIVIDUALS DEVELOP THEIR PERSONAL *CODES OF ETHICS* AND WHY ETHICS ARE IMPORTANT IN THE WORKPLACE.

Individual *codes of ethics* are derived from social standards of right and wrong. Ethical behaviour is behaviour that conforms to generally accepted social norms concerning beneficial and harmful actions. Because ethics affect the behaviour of individuals on behalf of the companies that employ them, many firms are adopting formal statements of ethics. Unethical behaviour can result in loss of business, fines, and even imprisonment.

LO-2 DISTINGUISH *ETHICS* FROM *SOCIAL RESPONSIBILITY* AND IDENTIFY *ORGANIZATIONAL STAKEHOLDERS.*

Ethics are individual beliefs about what is right and wrong, while *social responsibility* refers to the way a firm attempts to balance its commitments to organizational stakeholders. Stakeholders are individuals, groups, and organizations that are directly affected by the practices of an organization and that, therefore, have a stake in its performance. The stakeholders that businesses usually pay the most attention to are *investors*, *employees*, *customers*, and *local communities*. Businesses formerly paid almost exclusive attention to investors, but public pressure and government regulations have forced businesses to consider other stakeholders as well.

LO-3 SHOW HOW THE CONCEPT OF SOCIAL RESPONSIBILITY APPLIES BOTH TO ENVIRONMENTAL ISSUES AND TO A FIRM'S RELATIONSHIPS WITH CUSTOMERS, EMPLOYEES, AND INVESTORS.

Social responsibility toward the environment requires firms to minimize pollution of air, water, and land. Social responsibility toward customers requires firms to provide products of acceptable quality, to price products fairly, and to respect consumers' rights. Social responsibility toward employees requires firms to respect workers both as resources and as people who are more productive when their needs are met. Social responsibility toward investors requires firms to manage their resources and to represent their financial status honestly.

LO-4 IDENTIFY FOUR GENERAL *APPROACHES TO SOCIAL RESPONSIBILITY* AND DESCRIBE THE FOUR STEPS A FIRM MUST TAKE TO IMPLEMENT A *SOCIAL RESPONSIBILITY PROGRAM.*

An *obstructionist* stance on social responsibility is taken by a firm that does as little as possible to address social or environmental problems and that may deny or attempt to cover up problems that may occur. The *defensive* stance emphasizes compliance with legal minimum requirements. Companies adopting the *accommodative* stance go beyond minimum activities, if asked. The *proactive* stance commits a company to actively seeking to contribute to social projects. Implementing a social responsibility program entails four steps: (1) drafting a policy statement with the support of top management, (2) developing a detailed plan, (3) appointing a director to implement the plan, and (4) conducting social audits to monitor results.

LO-5 EXPLAIN HOW ISSUES OF SOCIAL RESPONSIBILITY AND ETHICS AFFECT SMALL BUSINESSES.

Managers and employees of small businesses face many of the same ethical questions as their counterparts at larger firms; they also face the same issues of social responsibility and the same need to decide on an approach to social responsibility. The differences are primarily differences of scale.

QUESTIONS AND EXERCISES

QUESTIONS FOR ANALYSIS

1. In what ways do you think your personal code of ethics might clash with the practices of some companies? How might you resolve these differences?
2. What kind of company wrong doing would most likely prompt you to be a whistle-blower? What kind of wrong doing would be least likely? Explain the difference.
3. In your opinion, which area of social responsibility is most important to you? Why? Are there areas other than those noted in this chapter that you consider important as well? Describe these areas, and indicate why they are important.
4. Identify some specific social responsibility issues that might be faced by small business managers and employees in each of the following areas: environment, customers, employees, and investors.
5. Choose a product or service and explain the social responsibility concerns that are likely to be evident in terms of the environment, customers, employees, and investors.
6. Analyze the forces that are at work from both a company's perspective and a whistle-blower's perspective. Given these forces, what characteristics would a law to protect whistle-blowers have to have to be effective?

APPLICATION EXERCISES

7. Write a one-paragraph description of an ethical dilemma you faced recently (including the outcome). Analyze the situation using the ideas presented in this chapter. Make particular reference to the ethical norms of utility, rights, justice, and caring in terms of how they impacted the situation. What would each of these suggest about the correct decision? Is this analysis consistent with the outcome that actually occurred? Why or why not?
8. Go to the website of the Center for Ethics and Business at Loyola Marymount University (lmu.edu/Page23849.aspx) and take the quiz entitled "What's Your Ethical Style?" Analyze what your score implies about how you are likely to react when you are faced with an ethical dilemma.
9. Develop a list of the major stakeholders of your college or university. What priority does the school assign to these stakeholders? Do you agree or disagree with this priority? Explain your reasoning.
10. Interview the owner of a local small business. Ask the owner to (a) describe the kinds of socially responsible activities the company is currently involved in and (b) identify the factors that facilitate and inhibit socially responsible behaviour in small businesses.

TEAM EXERCISES

BUILDING YOUR BUSINESS SKILLS

TO LIE OR NOT TO LIE: THAT IS THE QUESTION

METHOD

Step 1 Working with four other students, discuss ways in which you would respond to the following ethical dilemmas. When there is a difference of opinion among group members, try to determine the specific factors that influence different responses.

GOAL

To encourage students to apply general concepts of business ethics to specific situations.

BACKGROUND

Workplace lying, it seems, has become business as usual. According to one survey, one-quarter of working adults said that they had been asked to do something illegal or unethical on the job. Four in ten did what they were told. Another survey of more than 2000 secretaries showed that many employees face ethical dilemmas in their day-to-day work.

- Would you lie about your supervisor's whereabouts to someone on the phone?
- Would you lie about who was responsible for a business decision that cost your company thousands of dollars to protect your own or your supervisor's job?
- Would you inflate sales and revenue data on official company accounting statements to increase stock value?
- Would you say that you witnessed a signature when you did not if you were acting in the role of a notary?
- Would you keep silent if you knew that the official minutes of a corporate meeting had been changed?
- Would you destroy or remove information that could hurt your company if it fell into the wrong hands?

Step 2 Research the commitment to business ethics at Johnson & Johnson (www.jnj.com) and Texas Instruments (www.ti.com/corp/docs/csr/2012/corpgov/ethics/accountability.shtml) by clicking on their respective websites. As a group, discuss ways in which these statements are likely to affect the specific behaviours mentioned in Step 1.

Step 3 Working with group members, draft a corporate code of ethics that would discourage the specific behaviours mentioned in Step 1. Limit your code to a single typewritten page, but make it sufficiently broad to cover different ethical dilemmas.

FOLLOW-UP QUESTIONS

1. What personal, social, and cultural factors do you think contribute to lying in the workplace?
2. Do you agree or disagree with the following statement? *The term business ethics is an oxymoron.* Support your answer with examples from your own work experience or that of a family member.
3. If you were your company's director of human resources, how would you make your code of ethics a "living document"?
4. If you were faced with any of the ethical dilemmas described in Step 1, how would you handle them? How far would you go to maintain your personal ethical standards?

EXERCISING YOUR ETHICS

ON THE VERGE OF COLLAPSE

THE SITUATION

In 2013, the eight-storey Rana Plaza collapsed in Bangladesh. The building was home to five garment factories that produced apparel for a variety of foreign retailers. More than 1000 people died in the collapse, and more than 2500 were rescued, many with severe injuries. Foreign companies found it financially beneficial to work with manufacturers in Bangladesh because wage rates were low.

After the building collapsed, consumer groups began encouraging people to boycott companies with production in Bangladesh. You are the vice-president of Operations for Luxury Brands, a high-end manufacturer of men's and women's apparel. For the past five years, your company has worked closely with several manufacturers in Bangladesh. These partnerships have allowed your company to generate substantial profits. However, your company's risk manager is concerned about continuing to do business in Bangladesh given the negative press about unsafe working conditions and extremely low wages.

TEAM ACTIVITY

Assemble a group of four students and assign each group member to one of the following roles:

- Vice-President of Operations for Luxury Brands
- Owner of a factory in Bangladesh
- An employee from the factory in Bangladesh
- Head of a consumer advocacy group

ACTION STEPS

1. From the perspective of your assigned role, and before hearing any of your group's comments on this situation, decide what Luxury Brands should do. Write down the reasons for your decision.
2. From the perspective of your assigned role, and before hearing any of your group's comments on this situation, decide what the underlying ethical issues are in this situation. Write down the issues.
3. Gather your group together and reveal, in turn, each member's comments on their choices. Next, reveal the ethical issues listed by each member.
4. Appoint someone to record the main points of agreement and disagreement within the group. How do you explain the results? What accounts for any disagreements?
5. From an ethical standpoint, what does your group conclude is the most appropriate choice for the company in this situation?

BUSINESS CASE 3

THE PROBLEM OF CONSUMER SKEPTICISM

In recent years, a consensus seems to be developing that it is important to care for the environment. This "green movement" has motivated many companies to publicize what they are doing to be more eco-friendly. Coca-Cola, for example, pushed its new green image at the 2010 Winter Olympics with its "environmental call to action." Market research suggested that Coke had a lot of work to do to polish up its green image, particularly among consumers in the 13 to 29 age group. Critics have accused Coke of wasting water (it takes 250 litres of water to make one litre of Coca-Cola) and creating a lot of waste for landfills (75 percent of plastic bottles that contain Coca-Cola products end up in landfills). Coke therefore developed a new, eco-friendly container (called the PlantBottle) that is made partly from sugar cane and molasses. The new bottle produces 30 percent fewer emissions because less oil is used in making it.

Bill Brooks/Alamy

You might think any attempt by a company to be more eco-friendly would be viewed positively by those who are concerned about protecting the environment. But that isn't the case. Skeptics say that the new Coke bottle really doesn't accomplish much, because it is still mostly plastic. They note that even though plastic bottles are recyclable, most consumers just throw them out, so simply giving consumers access to plastic bottles is a bad idea.

The criticism that Coca-Cola is getting is not unusual. The fact is that almost any proposed green idea can become caught up in controversy that inhibits the progress of green practices. For example, consider the idea of green roofs—that is, planting vegetation on the roofs of buildings (see photo). Some companies have had green roofs for years (e.g., the green roof on the Manulife Centre parkade in Toronto has been there 25 years, and the trees are now three storeys high), but the idea is just now starting to really catch on. Toronto's city council passed a bylaw that mandates green roofs on new commercial buildings and high-rise residential buildings. Starting in 2010, such buildings had to have at least part of their roof space devoted to green plantings. It is estimated that a green roof of 350 square metres with 75 percent of its area in greenery would reduce the "heat-island effect" by 26 percent and reduce rainwater runoff by 38 percent. This sounds promising, but critics argue that the new bylaw may actually inhibit the progress of the green movement because it will increase building development costs and limit the options developers can choose from when they are trying to make buildings more environmentally friendly.

The bylaw is seen as one more problem that developers must solve before they can build. And during those periods when the economy is in a fragile state, that is a problem. The recession of 2008 to 2009, for example, caused many businesses to put eco-friendly plans on hold. Horizon Air, a U.S.-based airline, had planned to replace its regional jets with new Q400 turboprops made by Bombardier. The new planes burn 30 percent less fuel and therefore produce fewer emissions. But the economic slowdown forced the company to put those plans on hold. Another example: Clear Skies Solar cancelled plans to build a 1 megawatt solar plant because it couldn't get enough financial backing. The plans were cancelled even though government grants are available for the development of solar power.

Consumer attitudes about eco-friendly behaviour can also limit the success of green products. A survey by the Boston Consulting Group in Toronto showed that one-third of Canadians say they often purchase environmentally friendly products, but 78 percent are unwilling to pay the higher price that is often evident for green products. Another online survey of 1000 Canadians showed that people are willing to do certain small things (e.g., buying environmentally friendly light bulbs), but they are skeptical about adopting bigger measures. A third study, conducted by Procter & Gamble (P&G), showed that consumers are reluctant to spend more money just because a product is eco-friendly. Only 10 percent of consumers who were surveyed said they would pay a higher price (or accept a performance decrease) for a product that would benefit the environment. What's worse, 75 percent said they would not accept *any* tradeoff. So P&G is now focusing on developing sustainable innovation products that are more eco-friendly than earlier products, but that cost about the same price and have the same quality.

Another survey of 10 000 people from Canada and nine other countries analyzed the willingness of consumers to pay a premium for things like improved water quality, renewable (green) energy, and organic food. Here are some illustrative results:

- For improved water quality: on average, respondents were willing to pay a 7.5 percent premium on the median amount of their water bill.
- For renewable energy: 50 percent of respondents said they weren't willing to pay *any* premium, 48 percent were willing (on average) to pay a 5 percent premium; 2 percent were willing to pay a 30 percent premium.
- For organic food: 30 percent said they weren't willing to pay *any* premium; one-third said they would pay a premium between 1 and 5 percent; 2 percent were willing to pay a 50 percent premium.

The level of acceptance of green products has also been influenced by individuals who argue that the green movement has gone too far, and that too many consumers are suffering from eco obsessive-compulsive disorder (consumers being compulsively obsessed with being green in terms of the products they buy). Skeptics argue, for example, that the green movement negatively affects economic growth and increases unemployment. One study in Spain showed that every "green" job that was created destroyed 2.2 jobs elsewhere in the economy. The study concluded that government spending on renewable energy was only half as effective at creating new jobs as an equivalent amount of spending by the private sector.

Consumers may also be reluctant to spend money on eco-friendly products because they are confused by the green claims being made by various companies. The Boston Consulting Group study mentioned above also found that consumers are confused about the green options that are available because there is such a wide array of eco-labels on products. Ecolabelling.org is a Vancouver-based company that has identified 274 eco-labels, 23 of them originating in Canada. There are labels touting compostable products, fair-trade products, energy-efficient products, forest stewardship products, lake-friendly products, and organic products. These eco-labels are supposed to help consumers sift through environmental claims, but what do these labels actually mean? How can shoppers know which products are really eco-friendly and which ones are simply hype? The only thing that seems reasonably certain is that consumers are willing to pay a price premium in the short run if it leads to obvious long-term gains (e.g., an energy-efficient refrigerator costs more than a regular one, but it saves money in the long run due to lower electric bills).

There are people trying to help consumers sort through the maze of conflicting claims. Dara O'Rourke, a university professor, has developed a website called GoodGuide that allows consumers to identify the ingredients found in the products they buy. The website reports on both the environmental impact of products as well as their health effects. Website visitors enter a product name and get a score. The higher the score, the safer and more environmentally friendly the product is. O'Rourke's goal is to help consumers get past the green claims of companies to the facts. The goal is to really change the system. Instead of having companies telling consumers what to believe about their products, the idea is to have consumers tell companies what is important to them in the products they buy.

Consumers may also become confused as they try to balance contradictory objectives about products. This problem can be clearly seen in automobile products. On the one hand, we need to sharply reduce carbon emissions by discouraging the use of gas-guzzling cars. This goal could be achieved by raising fuel-efficiency standards. But a study by the Boston Consulting Group concluded that fuel-saving improvements that reduce emissions by 40 percent would also raise the price of the average car by $2000. On the other hand, the governments of both the United States and Canada are giving billions of dollars to Chrysler and General Motors in an attempt to save jobs at two companies that have historically produced gas-guzzling cars. These billions of dollars would move us toward the goal of reduced carbon emissions if Chrysler and General Motors could start producing green cars at a price consumers could afford, but industry experts say they can't (at least not in the near term). GM's all-electric car, the Volt, is too expensive to be purchased by a lot of consumers, and GM's financial problems mean that it cannot risk the kind of money it formerly would have on a new product. It is also true that when gas prices are relatively low, consumers don't seem overly interested in green cars. Profit margins are small on green cars, and that is yet another limiting factor.

To cope with all this complexity, consumers need a good measure of ecological intelligence to help them make the distinction between style and substance in ecological claims. One proposal is for consumers to use something called Life Cycle Analysis, which calculates the carbon footprint of various activities (e.g., a round-trip flight from Vancouver to Hong Kong, or a bouquet of flowers flown to Toronto from Kenya). But there is no guarantee that providing such detailed information would cause consumers to change their purchasing patterns. Organic foods and so-called "fair trade" products have been around for years, yet most people ignore them.

QUESTIONS FOR DISCUSSION

1. Summarize in your own words the major factors that can inhibit the progress toward greener practices on the part of businesses and consumers.

2. Electric cars create far less pollution than cars powered by the internal combustion engine. In spite of their environmentally friendly nature, it may be quite a few years before there are a lot of electric cars on the road. Why might this be so?
3. Consider the following statement: *It is not worthwhile to provide consumers with detailed information about the content of products or the carbon footprint of various activities, because most consumers simply won't use the information. Consumers are struggling to get along financially from day to day, and they don't have the time or inclination to use such information.* Do you agree or disagree? Explain your reasoning.

CHAPTER SUPPLEMENT 02

Business Law

Law means the set of rules and standards that a society agrees upon to govern the behaviour of its citizens. Both the British and the French influenced the development of law in Canada. In 1867, the British North America (BNA) Act created the nation of Canada. The BNA Act was "patriated" to Canada in 1982 and is now known as the Constitution Act. This act divides legislative powers in Canada between the federal and provincial governments.

SOURCES OF LAW

The law in Canada has evolved and changed in response to our norms and values. Our laws have arisen from three sources: (1) customs and judicial precedents (the source of common law), (2) the actions of provincial and federal legislatures (the source of statutory law), and (3) rulings by administrative bodies (the source of administrative law).

Common law is the unwritten law of England, derived from ancient precedents and judges' previous legal opinions. Common law is based on the principle of equity, the provision to every person of a just and fair remedy. Canadian legal customs and traditions derive from British common law. All provinces except Quebec, which uses the French Civil Code, have laws based on British common law, and court decisions are often based on precedents from common law. That is, decisions made in earlier cases that involved the same legal point will guide the court.

Statutory law is written law developed by city councils, provincial legislatures, and parliament. Most law in Canada today is statutory law.

Administrative law is the rules and regulations that government agencies and commissions develop based on their interpretations of statutory laws. For example, Consumer and Corporate Affairs Canada develops regulations on false advertising using federal legislation.

THE COURT SYSTEM

In Canada, the judiciary branch of government has the responsibility of settling disputes among organizations or individuals by applying existing laws. Both provincial and federal courts exist to hear both criminal and civil cases. The Supreme Court of Canada is the highest court in Canada. It decides whether to hear appeals from lower courts.

BUSINESS LAW

Business firms, like all other organizations, are affected by the laws of the country. **Business law** refers to laws that specifically affect how business firms are managed. Some laws affect all businesses, regardless of size, industry, or location. For example, the Income Tax Act requires businesses to pay income tax. Other laws may have a greater impact on one industry than on others. For example, pollution regulations are of much greater concern to Vale, a mining corporation, than they are to Carlson Wagonlit Travel.

Business managers should have at least a basic understanding of the following nine important concepts in business law:

1. contracts
2. agency
3. bailment
4. property
5. warranty
6. trademarks, patents, and copyrights
7. torts
8. negotiable instruments
9. bankruptcy

CONTRACTS

Agreements about transactions are common in a business's day-to-day activity. A **contract** is an agreement between two parties to act in a specified way or to perform certain acts. A contract might, for example, apply to a customer buying a product from a retail establishment or to two manufacturers agreeing to buy products or services from each other. A contract may be either **express** or **implied**. An express contract clearly specifies (either orally or in writing) the terms of an agreement. By contrast, an implied contract depends on the two parties' behaviours. For example, if you hire a fishing guide to help you catch fish, you have an implied contract that obligates you to pay the fishing guide for the service you receive.

A valid contract includes several elements:

- *An agreement.* All parties must consciously agree to the contract.
- *Consideration.* The parties must exchange something of value (e.g., time, products, services, money, and so on).
- *Competence.* All parties to the contract must be legally able to enter into an agreement. Individuals who are below a certain age or who are legally insane, for example, cannot enter into legal agreements.

LAW The set of rules and standards that a society agrees upon to govern the behaviour of its citizens.

COMMON LAW The unwritten law of England, derived from precedent and legal judgments.

STATUTORY LAW Written law developed by city councils, provincial legislatures, and parliament.

ADMINISTRATIVE LAW The rules and regulations that government agencies and commissions develop based on their interpretations of statutory laws.

BUSINESS LAW Laws that specifically affect how business firms are managed.

CONTRACT An agreement between two parties to act in a specified way or to perform certain acts.

EXPRESS CONTRACT Clearly specifies the terms of an agreement.

IMPLIED CONTRACT Specifies the necessary behaviours of the parties to the contract.

- *Legal purpose.* What the parties agree to do for or with each other must be legal. An agreement between two manufacturers to fix prices is not legal.

The courts will enforce a contract if it meets the criteria described above. Most parties honour their contracts, but occasionally one does not do what it was supposed to do. **Breach of contract** occurs when a party to an agreement fails, without legal reason, to live up to the agreement's provisions. The party that has not breached the contract has three alternatives under the law in Canada: (1) discharge, (2) sue for damages, or (3) require specific performance.

An example will demonstrate these three alternatives. Suppose that Barrington Farms Inc. agrees to deliver 100 dozen long-stemmed roses to the Blue Violet Flower Shop the week before Mother's Day. One week before the agreed-upon date, Barrington informs Blue Violet that it cannot make the delivery until after Mother's Day. Under the law, the owner of Blue Violet can choose among any of the following actions.

1. *Discharge.* Blue Violet can also ignore its obligations in the contract. That is, it can contract with another supplier.
2. *Sue for damages.* Blue Violet can legally demand payment for losses caused by Barrington's failure to deliver the promised goods on time. Losses might include any increased price Blue Violet would have to pay for the roses or court costs incurred in the damage suit.
3. *Require specific performance.* If monetary damages are not sufficient to reimburse Blue Violet, the court can force Barrington to live up to its original contract.

AGENCY

In many business situations, one person acts as an agent for another person. Well-known examples include actors and athletes represented by agents who negotiate contracts for them. An **agency–principal relationship** is established when one party (the agent) is authorized to act on behalf of another party (the principal).

The agent is under the control of the principal and must act on behalf of the principal and in the principal's best interests. The principal remains liable for the acts of the agent as long as the agent is acting within the scope of authority granted by the principal. A salesperson for IBM, for example, is an agent for IBM, the principal.

BAILMENT

Many business transactions are not covered by the agency–principal relationship. For example, suppose that you take your car to a mechanic to have it repaired. Because the repair shop has temporary possession of something you own, it is responsible for your car. This is a bailor–bailee relationship. In a **bailor–bailee relationship**, the bailor (e.g., the car owner) gives possession of his or her property to the bailee (e.g., the repair shop) but retains ownership of the item. A business firm that stores inventory in a public warehouse is in a bailor–bailee relationship. The business firm is the bailor and the warehouse is the bailee. The warehouse is responsible for storing the goods safely and making them available to the manufacturer upon request.

THE LAW OF PROPERTY

Property includes anything of tangible or intangible value that the owner has the right to possess and use. **Real property** is land and any permanent buildings attached to that land. **Personal property** is tangible or intangible assets other than real property. Personal property includes cars, clothing, furniture, money in bank accounts, stock certificates, and copyrights.

TRANSFERRING PROPERTY

From time to time, businesses and individuals need to transfer property to another person or business. A **deed** is a document that shows ownership of real property. It allows the transfer of title of real property.

A **lease** grants the use of an asset for a specified period of time in return for payment. The business or individual granting the lease is the lessor and the tenant is the lessee. For example, a business (the lessee) may rent space in a mall for one year from a real estate development firm (the lessor).

A **title** shows legal possession of personal property. It allows the transfer of title of personal property. When you buy a snowmobile, for example, the former owner signs the title over to you.

WARRANTY

When you buy a product or service, you want some assurance that it will perform satisfactorily and meet your needs. A **warranty** is a promise that the product or service will perform as the seller has promised it will.

There are two kinds of warranties—express and implied. An **express warranty** is a specific claim that the manufacturer makes about a product. For example, a warranty that a screwdriver blade is made of case-hardened steel is an express warranty. An **implied warranty** suggests that a product will perform as the manufacturer claims it will. Suppose that you buy an outboard motor for your boat and the engine burns out in one week. Because the manufacturer implies by selling the motor that it will work for a reasonable period of time, you can return it and get your money back.

Because opinions vary on what is a "reasonable" time, most manufacturers now give limited-time warranties on their products. For example, they will guarantee their products against defects in materials or manufacture for six months or one year.

BREACH OF CONTRACT When one party to an agreement fails, without legal reason, to live up to the agreement's provisions.

AGENCY–PRINCIPAL RELATIONSHIP Established when one party (the agent) is authorized to act on behalf of another party (the principal).

BAILOR–BAILEE RELATIONSHIP In a bailor–bailee relationship, the bailor (the property owner) gives possession of his or her property to the bailee (a custodian) but retains ownership of the item.

PROPERTY Anything of tangible or intangible value that the owner has the right to possess and use.

REAL PROPERTY Land and any permanent buildings attached to that land.

PERSONAL PROPERTY Tangible or intangible assets other than real property.

DEED A document that shows ownership of real property.

LEASE Grants the use of an asset for a specified period of time in return for payment.

TITLE Shows legal possession of personal property.

WARRANTY A promise that the product or service will perform as the seller has promised it will.

EXPRESS WARRANTY A specific claim that the manufacturer makes about a product.

IMPLIED WARRANTY A suggestion that a product will perform as the manufacturer claims it will.

TRADEMARKS, PATENTS, AND COPYRIGHTS

Because developing brand names is very expensive, companies do not want others using their brand name and confusing consumers. Many companies therefore apply to the Canadian government and receive a **trademark**, which is the exclusive legal right to use a brand name. Trademarks are granted for 15 years and may be renewed for further periods of 15 years, but only if the company continues to protect its brand name. In 2008, a European court ruled that the construction toys made by LEGO could no longer be protected by trademark law. Montreal-based Mega Brands Inc., which makes a competitive product called Mega-Bloks, had challenged LEGO's trademark.[92]

Just what can be trademarked is not always clear. If the company allows the name to lapse into common usage, the courts may take away protection. Common usage occurs when the company fails to use the ® (registered) symbol for its brand. It also occurs if the company fails to correct those who do not acknowledge the brand as a trademark. Windsurfer, a popular brand of sailboards, lost its trademark, and the name can now be used by any sailboard company. The same thing has happened to other names that were formerly brand names—trampoline, yo-yo, thermos, snowmobile, kleenex, and aspirin. But companies like Xerox, Coca-Cola, Jell-O, and Scotch tape have successfully defended their brand names.

A **patent** protects an invention or idea for a period of 20 years. The cost is $1600 to $2500 and it takes 18 months to three years to secure a patent from the Canadian Intellectual Property Office.[93] Patents can be very valuable. In 2006, BlackBerry agreed to pay $612.5 million to NTP Inc., a U.S. firm that claimed BlackBerry was infringing on some patents that NTP held.[94] In 2010, BlackBerry was found not guilty by a judge in the United Kingdom for a claim by Motorola.[95] In yet another patent dispute, Pfizer Inc. reached an agreement in 2008 with an Indian generic drug maker that kept a cheaper version of the cholesterol-lowering drug Lipitor out of the U.S. market until 2011. Sales revenues of Lipitor are about US$13 billion annually, so this was a very important deal for Pfizer.[96]

Copyrights give exclusive ownership rights to the creators of books, articles, designs, illustrations, photos, films, and music. Computer programs and even semiconductor chips are also protected. Copyrights extend to creators for their entire lives and to their estates for 50 years thereafter. Copyrights apply to the tangible expressions of an idea, not to the idea itself. For example, the idea of cloning dinosaurs from fossil DNA cannot be copyrighted, but Michael Crichton, the author of *Jurassic Park*, could copyright his novel because it is the tangible result of the basic idea.

There is much debate about how copyrights apply to material that appears on the internet. In 2005, the U.S.-based Authors Guild and several publishers sued Google, claiming that its book-scanning project was infringing on their copyrights. In 2008, Google agreed to pay US$125 million to settle the lawsuits. Google can now make available millions of books online.[97] The issue of file sharing is making copyright a big issue these days. New laws and new interpretations of old ones will redefine the role of copyright over the next few years.

TORTS

A **tort** is a wrongful civil act that one party inflicts on another and that results in injury to the person, to the person's property, or to the person's good name. An **intentional tort** is a wrongful act intentionally committed. If a security guard in a department store suspects someone of shoplifting and uses excessive force to prevent him or her from leaving the store, the guard might be guilty of an intentional tort. Other examples are libel, embezzlement, and patent infringement.

Negligence is a wrongful act that inadvertently causes injury to another person. For example, if a maintenance crew in a store mops the floors without placing warning signs in the area, a customer who slips and falls might bring a negligence suit against the store.

In recent years, the most publicized area of negligence has been product liability. **Product liability** means that businesses are liable for injuries caused to product users because of negligence in design or manufacturing. **Strict product liability** means that a business is liable for injuries caused by their products even if there is no evidence of negligence in the design or manufacture of the product.

NEGOTIABLE INSTRUMENTS

Negotiable instruments can be transferred among individuals and business firms. Cheques, bank drafts, and certificates of deposit are examples of negotiable instruments. The Bills of Exchange Act specifies that a negotiable instrument must:

- be written
- be signed by the person who puts it into circulation (the maker or drawer)
- contain an unconditional promise to pay a certain amount of money
- be payable on demand
- be payable to a specific person (or to the bearer of the instrument)

Negotiable instruments are transferred from one party to another through an endorsement. An **endorsement** means signing your name to a negotiable instrument—this makes it transferable to another person or organization. If you sign only your name on the back of a cheque, you are making a blank endorsement. If you state that the instrument is being transferred to a specific person, you are making a special endorsement. A qualified endorsement limits your liability if the instrument is not backed up by sufficient funds. For example, if you get a cheque from a friend and want to use it to buy a new stereo, you can write "Without Recourse" above your name. If your friend's cheque bounces, you have no liability. A restrictive endorsement limits the negotiability of the instrument. For example, if you write "For Deposit Only" on the back of a cheque and it is later stolen, no one else can cash it.

TRADEMARK The exclusive legal right to use a brand name.

PATENT Protects an invention or idea for a period of 20 years.

COPYRIGHT Exclusive ownership rights granted to creators for the tangible expression of an idea.

TORT A wrongful civil act that one party inflicts on another and that results in injury to the person, to the person's property, or to the person's good name.

INTENTIONAL TORT A wrongful act intentionally committed.

NEGLIGENCE A wrongful act that inadvertently causes injury to another person.

PRODUCT LIABILITY The liability of businesses for injuries caused to product users because of negligence in design or manufacturing.

STRICT PRODUCT LIABILITY The liability of businesses for injuries caused by their products even if there is no evidence of negligence in the design or manufacture of the product.

NEGOTIABLE INSTRUMENTS Instruments like cheques, bank drafts, and certificates of deposit that can be transferred among individuals and business firms.

ENDORSEMENT Signing your name to a negotiable instrument, making it transferable to another person or organization.

BANKRUPTCY

At one time, individuals who could not pay their debts were jailed. Today, however, both organizations and individuals can seek relief by filing for **bankruptcy**, which is the court-granted permission to not pay some or all of their debts.

Thousands of individuals and businesses file for bankruptcy every year. They do so for various reasons, including cash-flow problems, reduced demand for their products, or some other problem that makes it difficult or impossible for them to resolve their financial problems. In recent years, large businesses like Eaton's, Olympia & York, and Enron have sought the protection of bankruptcy laws. Three main factors account for the increase in bankruptcy filings:

1. the increased availability of credit
2. the "fresh-start" provisions in current bankruptcy laws
3. the growing acceptance of bankruptcy as a financial tactic

In Canada, jurisdiction over bankruptcy is provided by the Bankruptcy and Insolvency Act. An **insolvent person (or company)** is defined as one who cannot pay current obligations to creditors as they come due, or whose debts exceed their assets. A **bankrupt person (or company)** is one who has either made a voluntary application to start bankruptcy proceedings (voluntary bankruptcy) or been forced by creditors into bankruptcy (involuntary bankruptcy) by a process referred to as a *receiving order*. A person who is insolvent may or may not be bankrupt, and a person who is bankrupt may or may not be insolvent, as there are other bases for bankruptcy under the Act. Another procedure under the Act is referred to as a proposal, which can delay or avoid liquidation by providing the debtor with time to reorganize affairs and/or propose a payment schedule to creditors.

Business bankruptcy under the Act may be resolved or avoided by one of three methods:

1. Under a liquidation plan, the business ceases to exist. Its assets are sold and the proceeds are used to pay creditors.
2. Under a repayment plan, the bankrupt company works out a new payment schedule to meet its obligations. The time frame is usually extended, and payments are collected and distributed by a court-appointed trustee.
3. Reorganization is the most complex form of business bankruptcy. The company must explain the sources of its financial difficulties and propose a new plan for remaining in business. Reorganization may include a new slate of managers and a new financial strategy. A judge may also reduce the firm's debts to ensure its survival. Although creditors naturally dislike debt reduction, they may agree to the proposal, since getting, say, 50 percent of what you are owed is better than getting nothing at all.

THE INTERNATIONAL FRAMEWORK OF BUSINESS LAW

Laws vary from country to country, and many businesses today have international markets, suppliers, and competitors. Managers in such businesses need a basic understanding of the international framework of business law that affects the ways in which they can do business. Issues such as pollution across borders are matters of **international law**—the very general set of co-operative agreements and guidelines established by countries to govern the actions of individuals, businesses, and nations themselves.

International law has several sources. One source is custom and tradition. Among countries that have been trading with one another for centuries, many customs and traditions governing exchanges have gradually evolved into practice. Although some trading practices still follow ancient unwritten agreements, there has been a clear trend in recent years to approach international trade within a formal legal framework. Key features of that framework include a variety of formal trade agreements (see Chapter 5).

Organizations such as the WTO and EU also provide legal frameworks within which participating nations agree to abide.

BANKRUPTCY The court-granted permission for organizations or individuals to not pay some or all of their debts.

INSOLVENT PERSON (OR COMPANY) One who cannot pay current obligations to creditors as they come due, or whose debts exceed their assets.

BANKRUPT PERSON (OR COMPANY) One who has either made a voluntary application to start bankruptcy proceedings (voluntary bankruptcy) or has been forced by creditors into bankruptcy (involuntary bankruptcy) by a process referred to as a receiving order.

INTERNATIONAL LAW The very general set of co-operative agreements and guidelines established by countries to govern the actions of individuals, businesses, and nations themselves.

Rawpixel/Fotolia

CHAPTER 04

Entrepreneurship, Small Business, and New Venture Creation

LO

AFTER READING THIS CHAPTER, YOU SHOULD BE ABLE TO:

LO-1 Explain the meaning and interrelationship of the terms *small business*, *new venture creation*, and *entrepreneurship*.

LO-2 Describe the role of *small and new businesses* in the Canadian economy.

LO-3 Explain the entrepreneurial process and describe its three key elements.

LO-4 Describe three alternative strategies for becoming a business *owner—starting from scratch*, *buying an existing business*, and *buying a franchise*.

LO-5 Identify four key *reasons for success* in small businesses and four key *reasons for failure*.

LO-6 Describe four forms of *legal organization* for a business and discuss the advantages and disadvantages of each.

Mr. Ma: King of the Canadian Food Court!

In previous chapters we have examined companies that thrive in traditional industries and we have highlighted technology-based success stories. Regardless of the industry, pure entrepreneurs share a passion and commitment for their businesses. Stanley Ma is one of those individuals.

Who is he? You might not know the name, but you have probably had a meal at one (if not dozens) of his 2800 restaurants across the nation. He is the undisputed king of the food court. He built the MTY Group into a major force in the food service sector, and in 2015 their franchisees actually employed over 25 000 people. Some of you may have even worked at one of their locations at some point in your life.

The MTY Group has restaurants that operate under 37 separate banners (32 wholly owned and 5 under exclusive licences)—Mr. Sub, Thai Express, Country Style, Jugo Juice, KimChi, Tiki-Ming, Cultures, and Yogen Früz, to name a few. In total, MTY has revenues that surpass $115 million

Armand Trottier/Montreal La Presse/The Canadian Press

and system-wide sales (which include franchisee revenues) of approximately $1 billion annually.

Origins of a Success Story

It all began way back in 1979 when a young entrepreneur named Stanley Ma opened his first restaurant serving

Chinese and Polynesian food. By 1983 Mr. Ma had made his first steps into the world of franchising after launching Tiki-Ming. This was the path that would eventually lead to exponential growth. The organic expansion phase lasted from 1988 until 2008; it was centred on internal development of new restaurant concepts. During that time 13 brands were created and nurtured from within. However, during the past few years of that time period, Mr. Ma and his team began to simultaneously focus on expansion through acquisition. In fact, from 2001 until 2013 MTY spent over $170 million acquiring 22 restaurant brands. Another key moment occurred in 2010 when MTY was listed on the Toronto Stock Exchange.

In recent years, additional acquisitions have enabled MTY to add to the roster names like Van Houtte Coffee, Koryo Korean BBQ, Manchu Wok, SenseAsian, Wasabi Grill and Noodle, Extreme Pita, and Mr. Burrito.

HOW WILL THIS HELP ME?

A recent Gallup poll suggests that almost half of the young people surveyed were interested in entrepreneurship.[1] Even if you are not among that number, you will still be called on to interact with small businesses and entrepreneurs as a customer, as an investor, or as a client. You may also be trying to sell products or services to small businesses and entrepreneurs. One key to understanding entrepreneurship is to understand entrepreneurs themselves and what it takes for them to succeed. As an investor, you should also be better prepared to assess the market potential for new and up-and-coming businesses. This chapter will discuss these and additional issues important for starting and owning a business, including the business plan, the reasons for success and failure, and the advantages and disadvantages of different kinds of ownership. Let's start by defining a small business and identifying its importance in the Canadian economy.

New Horizons

Some of the new acquisitions have provided MTY with a growing footprint in the United States, but Mr. Ma is now looking beyond North American options. Look at some of the new MTY franchise locations that have opened their doors abroad: Sushi Shop in Qatar, Tiki-Ming in Lebanon, Vanelli's in Kuwait, Sukiyaki in the United Arab Emirates, Tandori in Bahrain, Pad Thai in Saudi Arabia, Extreme Pita in Australia, and many more. As you can see, it is not simply an expansion of a single restaurant concept to a strategic market; it is actually an expansion of the various brands under the MTY banner, with the supporting expertise, appearing where opportunities arise and where franchisees can be expected to thrive.

Despite the successful expansion, clearly this entrepreneur still has a passion for what he does. Recently, while eating lunch at a food court that houses about 20 of his restaurant banners, he was quoted as saying that all of his brands were like his children and he could not pick a favourite. Like any good parent (and entrepreneur) he still spends significant time observing his children and trying to find new ways to improve their chances of success.

Minerva Studio/Fotolia

QUESTIONS FOR DISCUSSION

1. From what you have read, how does Mr. Ma fit the profile of an entrepreneur?
2. What are the reasons for Mr. Ma's success where so many others have failed (particularly in the food service business)?
3. How does the case demonstrate the important relationships between franchisors and franchisees in the modern business world? Describe the role each side plays in the success of the other.
4. How does the decision to list MTY on the Toronto Stock Exchange relate to the overall strategy pursued by MTY in recent years?

SMALL BUSINESS, NEW VENTURE CREATION, AND ENTREPRENEURSHIP

In this chapter we examine established companies with an enduring entrepreneurial spirit (MTY), exciting growth-oriented newcomers (Facebook and Beyond the Rack), major family organizations that have stood the test of time (Kal Tire), and a host of small organizations with dreams and aspirations. Each of these examples gives us a glimpse of an important element of the Canadian business landscape. We begin by examining the lifeblood of an economy: small business, entrepreneurship, and new ventures.

Self-employed Canadians account for 15.5 percent of the workforce.[2] Every day, approximately 380 businesses are started in Canada.[3] New firms create the most jobs, are noted for their entrepreneurship, and are typically small.[4] But does this mean most small businesses are entrepreneurial? Not necessarily.

The terms *small business*, *new venture*, and *entrepreneurship* are closely linked, but each idea is distinct. In the following paragraphs we will explain these terms to help you understand these topics and how they are interrelated.

LO-1 Small Business

Defining a "small" business can be a bit tricky. Various measures might be used, including the number of people the business employs, the company's sales revenue, the size of the investment required, or the type of ownership structure the business has. Some of the difficulties in defining a small business can be understood by considering the way the Canadian government collects and reports information on small businesses.

Industry Canada is the main federal government agency responsible for small business. In reporting small business statistics, the government relies on two distinct sources of information, both provided by Statistics Canada: the *Business Register* (which tracks businesses) and the *Labour Force Survey* (which tracks individuals). To be included in the Register, a business must have at least one paid employee, have annual sales revenues of $30 000 or more, or be incorporated (we describe incorporation later in this chapter). A goods-producing business in the *Register* is considered small if it has fewer than 100 employees, while a service-producing business is considered small if it has fewer than 50 employees. The *Labour Force Survey* uses information from individuals to make estimates of employment and unemployment levels. Individuals are classified as self-employed if they are working owners of a business that is either incorporated or unincorporated, if they work for themselves but do not have a business (some musicians would fall into this category), or if they work without pay in a family business.[5] In its publication *Key Small Business Statistics* (www.strategis.gc.ca/sbstatistics), Industry Canada reports that there are 2.2 million "business establishments" in Canada and about 2.7 million people who are "self-employed."[6] There is no way of identifying how much overlap there is in these two categories, but we do know that an unincorporated business operated by a self-employed person (with no employees) would not be counted among the 2.2 million businesses in the *Register*. This is an important point, because the majority of businesses in Canada have no employees (just the owner), nor are they incorporated.

For our purposes, we define a **small business** as an owner-managed business with fewer than 100 employees. We do so because it enables us to make better use of existing information, and because you are now aware of how definitions can affect our understanding of small businesses. According to Industry Canada's statistics, small business have contributed between 25 to 30 percent of Canada's GDP over the past decade.[7]

Each year, the Queen's Centre for Business Venturing develops a ranking of the top 50 small and medium-sized employers to work for in conjunction with Aon Hewitt and *Profit* magazine. The top ten firms in the 2015 study are shown in Table 4.1. Each of these companies exhibited superiority in employee recognition, managing performance, career opportunities, and organizational reputation.[8]

SMALL BUSINESS An independently owned and managed business that does not dominate its market.

>>> **TABLE 4.1** Top Small and Medium-Sized Employers in Canada, 2015

	Company	Industry	Location
1.	D.L.G.L. Ltd.	Human resources software	Blainville, Quebec
2.	Klick Health	Staffing and human resources services	Toronto, Ontario
3.	Habanero Consulting Group	Information technology consulting	Vancouver, British Columbia
4.	DevFacto Technologies Inc.	Information technology consulting	Edmonton, Alberta
5.	Protegra Inc.	Business performance consulting and software development	Winnipeg, Manitoba
6.	iGate Global Solutions Ltd.	Consulting, information technology and business process outsourcing services	Toronto, Ontario
7.	Cybertech Automation Inc. and i-Gen Solutions Inc.	Engineering and industrial information technology services	Edmonton, Alberta
8.	OACIQ	Real estate	Brossard, Quebec
9.	ISL Engineering and Land Services Ltd.	Engineering consulting	Edmonton, Alberta
10.	Intelex Technologies Inc.	Software for environment, health, safety, and quality	Toronto, Ontario

The New Venture/Firm

Various criteria can also be used to determine when a new firm comes into existence. Three of the most common are when it was formed, whether it was incorporated, and whether it sold goods and/or services.[9] A business is considered to be new if it has become operational within the previous 12 months, if it adopts any of the main organizational forms (proprietorship, partnership, corporation, or co-operative), and if it sells goods or services. Thus, we define a **new venture** as a recently formed commercial organization that provides goods and/or services for sale.

Entrepreneurship

Entrepreneurship is the process of identifying an opportunity in the marketplace and accessing the resources needed to capitalize on it.[10] People start new businesses because they want to control their own destiny and prefer to take a chance rather than looking for a secure job. **Entrepreneurs** are people who recognize and seize these opportunities.

For example, Mark Zuckerberg created Facebook, and in 2015 it had over 1.3 billion active users, if you include the company's active users under its other key properties WhatsApp (500 million), Instagram (200 million) and Messenger (200 million). While there is clearly overlap, that total of 2.2 billion active users represents roughly one-third of the planet's population. Zuckerberg worked long hours, and he is constantly tailoring the website to suit its expanding audience.[11]

In another example, far from Silicon Valley, we find a different tale of entrepreneurial success. After growing up in Toronto and studying in Montreal, Elena Rosenfeld left life in the big city behind to set up shop in the small town of Invermere, British Columbia. She and her partner Leo Johnson started Kicking Horse Coffee from their garage with the mission of selling fair-trade organic coffee. Today, nearly two decades later, the company operates a huge, 60 000 square foot facility out of the town they fell in love with. The company employs 70 people and sells coffee across the country and in the United States.[12]

Every year, the Heritage Foundation publishes an index of economic freedom, which assesses the extent to which entrepreneurs have freedom to pursue new business opportunities. In 2015, the top three countries were Hong Kong, Singapore, and New Zealand, with freedom scores of 89.6, 89.4, and 82.1 respectively. Canada ranked sixth with a score of 79.1 and North Korea ranked last with a score of 1.3.[13]

Small businesses often provide an environment to use personal attributes—such as creativity—that have come to be associated with entrepreneurs.[14] Because starting a business involves dealing with a great deal of uncertainty, ambiguity, and unpredictability, every new venture founder needs to exercise some of the personal attributes that entrepreneurs are noted for. But do not assume that only small business owners exhibit entrepreneurial characteristics.[15] Many successful managers in large organizations in both the public and private sectors also exhibit similar characteristics. Entrepreneurship therefore occurs in a wide range of contexts—not just in small or new commercial firms, but also in old firms, in large firms, in firms that grow slowly, in firms that grow rapidly, in non-profit organizations, and in the public sector.[16]

Kicking Horse Coffee is a small-town success story with a large reach across Canada and in the United States. Entrepreneurs Elena Rosenfeld and Leo Johnson have managed to build a solid business out of selling organic fair-trade coffee.

Kicking Horse Coffee Co. Ltd.

People who exhibit entrepreneurial characteristics and create something new within an existing firm or organization are called **intrapreneurs**. Procter & Gamble, 3M, and Xerox encourage intrapreneurship by having divisions that focus on creating new products for specific markets. At Telus, a recent redesign of the company website was accomplished by a small intrapaneurial team that was given the mandate to operate in creative manner autonomous from the bureaucratic structure that characterizes large companies.[17] A key difference between intrapreneurs and entrepreneurs is that intrapreneurs typically don't have to concern themselves with getting the resources needed to bring the new product to market, since big companies tend to have the necessary resources already available.

As we explore the entrepreneurial process later in this chapter, we will do so within a new venture context. We begin by outlining the role of small and new businesses in the Canadian economy.

NEW VENTURE A recently formed commercial organization that provides goods and/or services for sale.

ENTREPRENEURSHIP The process of identifying an opportunity in the marketplace and accessing the resources needed to capitalize on it.

ENTREPRENEUR A business person who accepts both the risks and the opportunities involved in creating and operating a new business venture.

INTRAPRENEURS People who create something new within an existing large firm or organization.

LO-2 THE ROLE OF SMALL AND NEW BUSINESSES IN THE CANADIAN ECONOMY

As we will see in this section, small and new businesses play a key role in the Canadian economy. However, the recognition of this role has really only been acknowledged in the past two decades. Previously, large businesses were the focus of attention in terms of economic impact within industrialized nations.

Small Businesses

It may surprise you to learn that 98.2 percent of all businesses in Canada are small (they have fewer than 100 employees), and more than half of them have fewer than 5 employees. Medium-sized businesses (100–499 employees) make up 1.6 percent of employer businesses, and large businesses (those with 500 or more employees) represent just 0.2 percent.[18] This pattern is consistent across all provinces. While one large business has many more employees than one small business, as a group small businesses provide more jobs than large ones. They also lead the way when it comes to innovation and new technology, and account for 30 percent of Canadian GDP.

Ontario and Quebec together account for the largest proportion of business establishments in Canada (about 57 percent), followed by the western provinces (36 percent) and the Atlantic provinces (7 percent). Northwest Territories, Yukon, and Nunavut represent just 0.3 percent of Canada's businesses.[19]

While the previous figures profile the number of businesses in Canada by size, we now look at how many people work in small versus medium- and large-sized businesses. According to Statistics Canada, in 2015 there were 11 569 400 employees in the **private sector** (the part of the economy consisting of companies and organizations not owned or controlled by government).[20] In all industries, at least half the workforce is employed by small business. In addition, small businesses account for over 80 percent of employment in four industries; agriculture, other services, accommodation and food services, and construction. (See Figure 4.1.)[21]

New Ventures

Not only are new firms the main source of job creation, but they are also responsible for the vast majority of new products and services. From 2002 to 2012, small businesses created 77.7 percent of all private-sector jobs in Canada (on average 100 000 per year).[22]

Women are playing a more prominent role than ever before in starting new ventures (see Figure 4.2). More and more women are starting

PRIVATE SECTOR The part of the economy made up of companies and organizations not owned or controlled by the government.

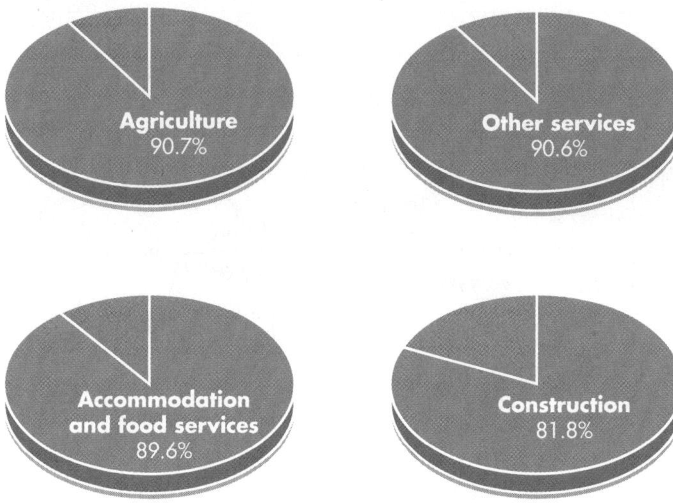

FIGURE 4.1 Small business employment

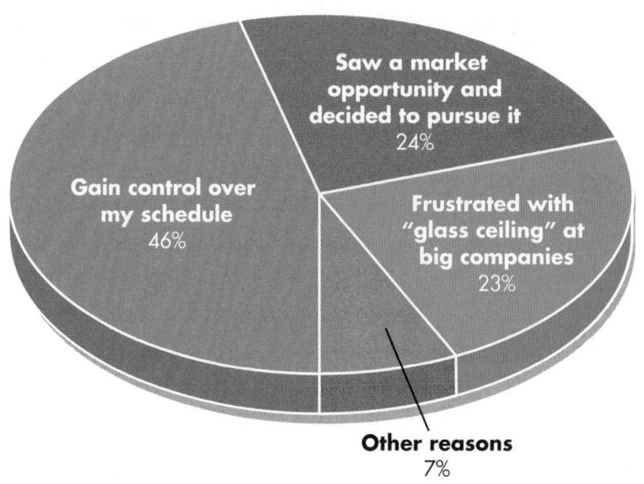

FIGURE 4.2 Reasons women give for starting their own businesses

and successfully operating their own small businesses, and they now account for half of all new businesses formed. But, on a negative note, women lead only 12 percent of the small and medium-sized businesses that export goods and services.[23]

Female entrepreneurs are honoured every year at the RBC Canadian Woman Entrepreneur Awards. Previous winners have been Jennifer Carlson (Calgary-based Baby Gourmet, Emily (Shi Yu) Zhang (Vancouver-based Willowest Hospitality Furnishings), Cora Tsouflidou (Montreal-based Cora Franchise Group), and Cathy Buckingham (Barrie, Ontario–based TNR Industrial Doors).[24]

Women who run businesses from their homes are sometimes called "mompreneurs."[25] The Mompreneur Networking Group organizes seminars and publishes *Mompreneur*, a free magazine that helps women who want to start a business.

Many young entrepreneurs are also involved in creating new ventures in Canada. Consider the following examples:

- Shep Ysselstein was the grand prize winner of the BDC Young Entrepreneurs Award in 2014 for Gunn's Hill Artisan Cheese in Ontario. The $100 000 grand prize has helped him get a great head

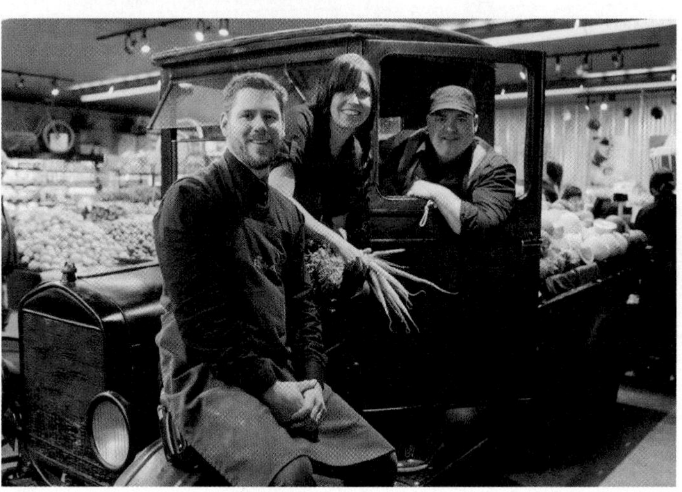

Daisy and Adam Orser were also previous winners of the BDC Young Entrepreneur award. Their Victoria, B.C.–based company Root Cellar Village Green Grocer is capitalizing on the movement for fresh local produce and healthier lifestyles.

The Root Cellar, Left- Phil Lafreniere, Middle-Daisy Leslie Orser, Right- Adam A. Orser

start and build a brand name through the exposure and new contacts with marketing specialists at the BDC.

- Zane Kelsall won the prize two years earlier for his Two If by Sea Café concept in Halifax.
- Rachel Mielke, from Regina, Saskatchewan, transformed her Hillberg & Burk designer jewellery brand from a high-school hobby into a successful business. She makes her hand-made jewellery out of sterling silver, semi-precious stones, and Swarovski crystals. Her designs have ended up in the Academy Award gift bags and her company was featured on *Dragon's Den*.[26]

LO-3 THE ENTREPRENEURIAL PROCESS

The entrepreneurial process is like a journey (see Figure 4.3). It is influenced by the social, economic, political, and technological factors in the broader environment, but we will focus our attention on understanding the three key elements in the entrepreneurial process—the entrepreneur, the opportunity, and resources—and how they interact. As these key elements interact, they may or may not be well matched. For example, if an entrepreneur identifies an opportunity for a new health service but does not have the relevant background and skills to deliver the service, the business may never get off the ground. However, if all the elements are harmonious, the new business will likely become operational at some point.

Since the entrepreneur is at the heart of the entrepreneurial process, considerable attention has been paid to identifying the personal characteristics of entrepreneurs. Research shows that these characteristics are wide-ranging. Some are behavioural (e.g., taking initiative), others are personality traits (e.g., independence), and still others are skills (e.g., problem solving).[27] Some people think entrepreneurs are rare, but their characteristics have been found to be widely distributed in the population.[28] We also know that personal characteristics often have less impact on a person's action than the situation a person is in.[29] What is really important is not who the person is but what the person does.[30] Entrepreneurs must (1) identify an opportunity and (2) access resources.

Identifying Opportunities

Identifying opportunities involves generating ideas for new (or improved) products, processes, or services, screening those ideas, and developing the best ones.

IDEA GENERATION

Typically, generating ideas involves abandoning traditional assumptions about how things work and how they ought to be, and seeing what others do not. If the prospective new (or improved) product, process, or service can be profitably produced and is attractive relative to other potential venture ideas, it might present an opportunity. For example, Kevin Systrom developed an app to allow people to virtually check in at locations visited and broadcast that to a person's social network. The idea eventually changed and evolved into a photo-sharing service, and Kevin's ability to pivot and evolve led to the creation of Instagram, which he sold to Facebook for $1 billion.[31] For another interesting example of success in this modern age, take another look at the box entitled "Teenage Innovator, Entrepreneur, and Multimillionaire."

Where do ideas come from? Most new ventures do not emerge from a deliberate search for viable business ideas. Rather, the majority originate from events relating to work or everyday life.[32] In fact, work

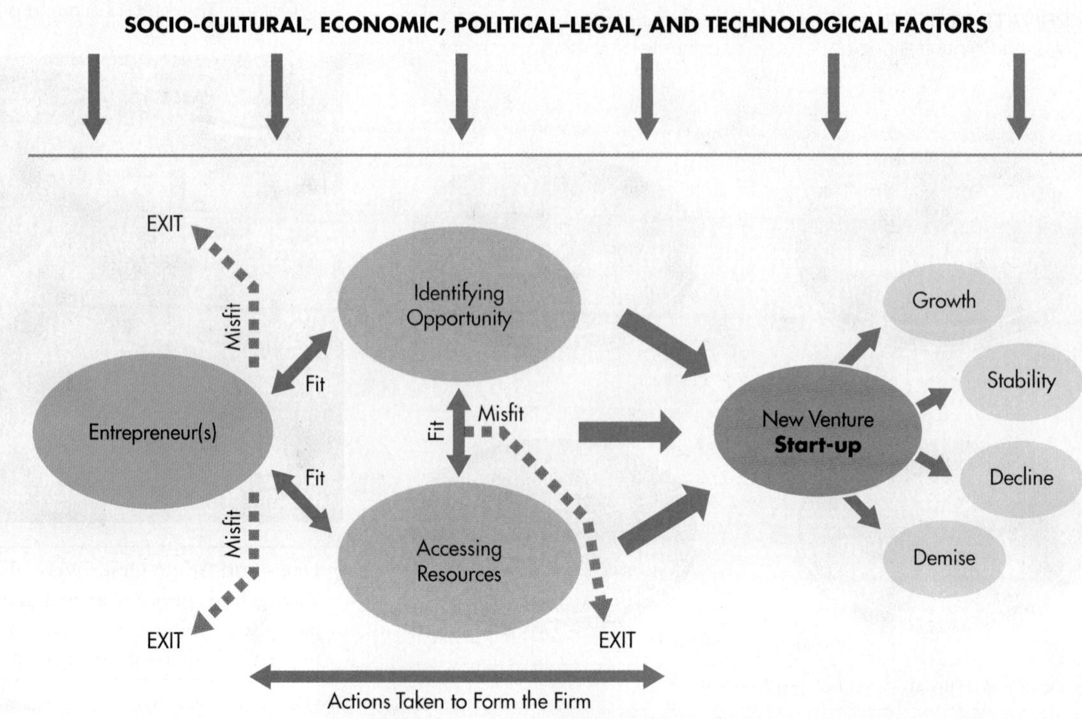

>>> **FIGURE 4.3** The Entrepreneurial Process in a New Venture

experience is the most common source of ideas, accounting for 45 to 85 percent of those generated. This happens because as employees of a company, prospective entrepreneurs are familiar with the product or service, the customers, the suppliers, and the competitors. They are also aware of marketplace needs, can relate those needs to personal capabilities, and can determine whether they are capable of producing products or services that can fill the void.

Other frequent sources of new venture ideas include a personal interest/hobby (16 percent) or a chance happening (11 percent).[33] The latter refers to a situation in which a venture idea comes about unexpectedly. For example, while on vacation in another country you might try a new snack food that you feel would be in demand if introduced to the Canadian market.

SCREENING

Entrepreneurs often generate many ideas, and screening them is a key part of the entrepreneurial process. The faster you can weed out the "dead-end" venture ideas, the more time and effort you can devote to the ones that remain. The more of the following characteristics an idea has, the greater the opportunity it presents.

The Idea Creates or Adds Value for the Customer A product or service that creates or adds value for the customer is one that solves a significant problem or meets a significant need in new or different ways. Consider Polar Mobile, a Toronto-based developer of mobile applications that has made great strides since launching a few years ago. Polar provides a software platform called MediaEverywhere™ that makes it easy for media companies to launch apps for all types of smartphones and tablet devices. Polar must be doing something right, because major companies are finding value in this relatively new company. In 2015, just eight years since it was established, Polar had over 600 customers in 12 countries. Its long list of media clients included *Forbes, The Economist,* and *Rolling Stone.* It seems like Polar has clearly shown the capacity to add value based on this impressive list of partners.[34]

E-BUSINESS AND SOCIAL MEDIA SOLUTIONS

Teenage Innovator, Entrepreneur, and Multimillionaire

At just 17 years of age, Nick D'Aloisio was living the modern-day entrepreneurial dream. He had identified an opportunity in the mobile app world and turned it into a $30-million-dollar payday from Yahoo. The acquisition of Nick's company fit a deliberate strategy at Yahoo. In the past couple of years, Yahoo had purchased a series of small companies in emerging business categories. According to CEO Marissa Meyer, the transactions were helping Yahoo attract more engineers with expertise in creating services for the valuable smartphone and tablet platforms.

Mr. D'Aloisio appeared to have been bitten by the entrepreneurial bug quite early in his life. He started his company at just 15 years of age, creating several apps, with Summly as his biggest hit (before his 18th birthday, anyway). The app uses complex algorithms to compile and simplify news articles for easy viewing on a smartphone. In other words, it is an easy way to get news on the go. From the publishers' perspective, it can drive traffic to content for a new generation of people who are on the move and don't necessarily have traditional subscriptions. Before Yahoo approached Nick, Summly had already been downloaded more than 750 000 times. Clearly, Summly had gained acceptance in a very crowded competitive environment. Just like a small retailer or a manufacturer of goods, the consumer is the one who decides if your offer is worthwhile. In

At 17 he sold his innovation to Yahoo for $30 million. By the age of 19 he was a key member of the Yahoo Mobile engineering team. What's next for this innovator?

Britta Pedersen/dpa picture alliance/Alamy

this case, they vote with downloads, not necessarily dollars. But Yahoo identified potential for a long-term revenue-generating model from this app. According to Adam Cahan, a senior vice-president at Yahoo, after the purchase, Summly was taken down while Nick D'Aloisio and a small team integrated the features into existing Yahoo products.

In a clear sign of the times and his age, Nick talked about what a great honour it was to work for a classic internet company. You see, Nick is younger than Yahoo. He may be young, but he clearly sees himself as more than a one-trick wonder. He planned to invest his money wisely, but also talked about his interest in becoming an angel investor at some point. Nick had already earned more than just programming experience. A year before the Yahoo payday, Nick had convinced some big-time investors to support his company; he had raised $1.5 million in funding from Zynga's CEO Mark Pincus and a Hong Kong–based businessman. Entrepreneurs must identify opportunities and seize them. Clearly, Nick D'Aloisio had proven he could do just that.

Nick was also quick to point out that his parents were a strong driving force behind his success by encouraging his entrepreneurial passion and supporting his dreams. However, as he approached the important age of 18, he had commitments to Yahoo and some long-term decisions to make. Should he become an intrapreneur (working within Yahoo or another company) or should he take advantage of this experience to eventually continue on his path as an independent internet entrepreneur? Only time will tell. But at 17, when most people his age are looking for internships, Nick D'Aloisio had earned some very interesting options.

Two years later, at the age of 19, he was named *Wall Street Journal*'s Innovator of the Year. For now, D'Aloisio is working as a key full-time member of Yahoo's mobile engineering team. It should be interesting to see what else he accomplishes before his 25th or even his 20th birthday.

CRITICAL THINKING QUESTIONS

1. If you were in Nick's shoes, what would you do? Would you be satisfied working with a great internet organization like Yahoo or would you take the money and go off on your own? Do you consider yourself an entrepreneur at heart?

The Idea Provides a Competitive Advantage That Can Be Sustained A competitive advantage exists when potential customers see the product or service as better than that of competitors. Sustaining a competitive advantage involves maintaining it in the face of competitors' actions or changes in the industry. All other things being equal, the longer markets are in a state of flux, the greater the likelihood of being able to sustain a competitive advantage. The inability to develop a competitive advantage is a common fatal flaw in many new ventures.[35]

Cameron Piron founded Toronto-based Sentinelle Medical and spent ten years developing a better cancer detection technology and another two years convincing General Electric to use it in its MRI machines. For his efforts he received the Ontario Government Innovation Award. By 2015 the technology had proven successful and demonstrated a clear marketplace advantage. The company has been acquired by Invivo (a Philips health-care company) because of this technology.[36]

The Idea Is Marketable and Financially Viable While it is important to determine whether there are enough customers willing to buy the product or service, it is also important to determine whether sales will lead to profits.[37] Estimating the market demand requires an initial understanding of who the customers are, what their needs are, and how the product or service will satisfy their needs better than competitors' products will. Customers define the competition in terms of who can satisfy their needs best. However, success also requires a thorough understanding of the key competitors who can provide similar products, services, or benefits to the target customer.

After learning about the competition and customers, the entrepreneur must prepare a **sales forecast**, which is an estimate of how much of a product or service will be purchased by the prospective customers for a specific period of time—typically one year. Total sales revenue is estimated by multiplying the units expected to be sold by the selling price. The sales forecast forms the foundation for determining the financial viability of the venture and the resources needed to start it.

Determining financial viability involves preparing financial forecasts, two-to-three-year projections of a venture's future financial position and performance. They typically consist of an estimate of start-up costs, a cash budget, an income statement, and a balance sheet (see Chapter 11 for more details about these financial documents). These projections serve as the basis for decisions regarding whether to proceed with the venture, and if so the amount and type of financing to be used in financing it.

The Idea Has Low Exit Costs The final consideration is the venture's exit costs. Exit costs are low if a venture can be shut down without a significant loss of time, money, or reputation.[38] If a venture is not expected to make a profit for a number of years, its exit costs are high, since the project cannot be reasonably abandoned in the short term.

SALES FORECAST An estimate of how much of a product or service will be purchased by prospective customers over a specific period.

ENTREPRENEURSHIP AND NEW VENTURES

Harvard Dropout Turned Billionaire

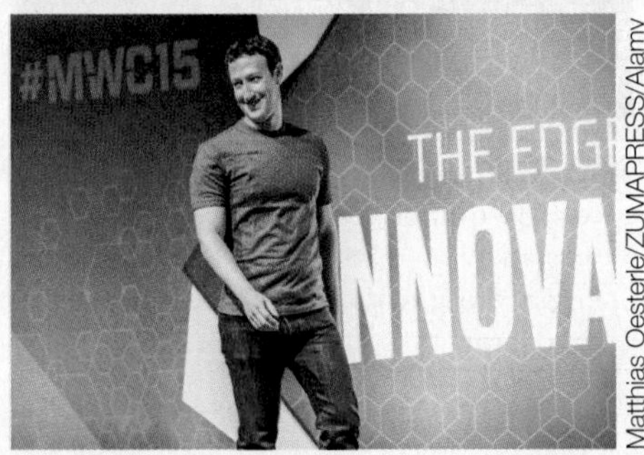

Matthias Oesterle/ZUMAPRESS/Alamy

This immensely popular social networking story, about a site conceived by Harvard sophomore Mark Zuckerberg in February 2004, has been described in films and become an inspiration for a generation of tech-savvy young people looking to create the next big thing. As the story goes, Facebook proved so popular that it quickly expanded to other schools. By November 2004, the site boasted 1 million users. A mere 18 months later, membership had ballooned to 7 million at 2100 colleges and 22 000 high schools. When Facebook began accepting non-students in October 2006, membership doubled from 12 million to 24 million in just 8 months. Today, Facebook is one of the most visited sites on the internet with over 1.3 billion active users, more than half of them visiting daily.

Although Facebook began as a non-commercial enterprise, it wasn't long before Zuckerberg realized that if he had more cash he could convert it into a business. PayPal co-founder Peter Thiel invested $500 000 in 2004, and substantial investments of additional venture capital followed. The new company lost $3.6 million in fiscal 2005, but with projected revenues of $150 million in 2007, Microsoft paid $240 million for a 1.6 percent stake, pushing its valuation to $15 billion. When Facebook started trading its stock in 2012, Zuckerberg became a billionaire.

But interestingly, from a pure business standpoint, Facebook had a persistent problem for nearly a decade with monetization—how to make a profit. For example, in 2009 approximately 90 percent of the company's total revenue came from advertising, with another small percentage coming from sales of virtual gifts, little icons that pop up in certain Facebook programs and that users can exchange for about $1. That year, Facebook sold about $3 million worth of virtual gifts every month, but revenues for the year—about $260 million—fell short of the company's $300 million projection. It was time to get serious about profit. Even in 2012, Facebook could only manage profits of $32 million on $5 billion in sales revenue.

However, the company seems to have turned the corner in the most basic metric by posting profit of approximately $1.5 billion in 2013 from approximately $7 billion in revenues, and nearly $3 billion in profit from $12.5 billion in sales/revenues in 2014. The move from social media sensation to sustainable, profitable company had taken time, but the future possibilities seemed endless.

Facebook is now on constant lookout for new ways to entertain and gain revenues from their user base. With the acquisitions of Instagram (for $1 billion) in 2012 and WhatsApp (for $19 billion) in 2014, clearly Facebook has shifted gears. It has come a long way from the dorm room where it all began.

CRITICAL THINKING QUESTIONS

1. What are some of the key entrepreneurial traits displayed by Marc Zuckerberg in building Facebook?
2. Why do you think the road to profitability was such a long one for Facebook?

DEVELOPING THE OPPORTUNITY

As the "dead-end" venture ideas are weeded out, a clear notion of the business concept and an entry strategy for pursuing it must be developed. The business concept often changes from the original plan. Some new ventures develop entirely new markets, products, and sources of competitive advantage once the needs of the marketplace and the economies of the business are understood. So, while a vision of what is to be achieved is important, it is equally important to incorporate new information and to be on the lookout for unanticipated opportunities. Take a look at the box entitled "Harvard Dropout Turned Billionaire."

New ventures use one or more of three main entry strategies: they introduce a totally new product or service, they introduce a product or service that will compete directly with existing competitive offerings but add a twist (customization of the standard product), or they franchise.[39] A **franchise** is an arrangement in which a buyer (franchisee) purchases the right to sell the product or service of the seller (franchiser). We discuss franchising in more detail later in the chapter.

When capital requirements are high, such as when a manufacturing operation is being proposed, there is a need for considerable research and planning. Similarly, if product development or operations are fairly complex, research and analysis will be needed to ensure that the costs associated with effectively coordinating tasks will be minimized. In these circumstances, or when the aim is to attract potential investors, a comprehensive written business plan is required. A **business plan** is a document that describes the entrepreneur's proposed business venture, explains why it is an opportunity, and outlines its marketing plan, its operational and financial details, and its managers' skills and abilities.[40] The contents of a business plan are shown in Table 4.2.

If market conditions are changing rapidly, the benefits gained from extensive research and planning diminish quickly. By the time the entrepreneur is ready, new competitors may have entered the market, prices may have changed, a location may no longer be available, and so on. Similarly, if the product is highly innovative, market research is of less value, since the development of entirely new products involves creating needs and wants rather than simply responding to existing needs.

Contrary to what many people think, planning does not have to be completed before action is taken. For example, if an electrical contracting business is being proposed in an area where there is a shortage of tradespeople, it would be important to seek out qualified employees prior to conducting other analyses that are needed to complete the business plan. Such early action also helps to build relationships that can be drawn on later. Obviously, some ventures do not lend themselves to early action, particularly those that are capital intensive. Since most entrepreneurs have limited resources, it is

FRANCHISE An arrangement that gives franchisees (buyers) the right to sell the product of the franchiser (the seller).

BUSINESS PLAN Document in which the entrepreneur summarizes her or his business strategy for the proposed new venture and how that strategy will be implemented.

TABLE 4.2 A Business Plan

A well-written business plan is formally structured, is easy to read, and avoids confusion. Organizing the information into sections makes it more manageable. The amount of detail and the order of presentation may vary from one venture to another and according to the intended audience (if the plan is intended for potential investors it will require more detail than if it is intended for internal use by the entrepreneur). An outline for a standard business plan is provided below.

I.	**Cover Page.** Name of venture and owners, date prepared, contact person, his/her address, telephone and fax numbers, email address, Facebook link, and name of organization the plan is being presented to. The easier it is for the reader to contact the entrepreneur, the more likely the contact will occur.
II.	**Executive Summary.** One-to-three-page overview of the total business plan. Written after the other sections are completed, it highlights their significant points and aims to create enough excitement to motivate the reader to continue.
III.	**Table of Contents.** Lists major sections with page numbers for both the body and the appendices of the plan.
IV.	**Company Description.** Identifies the type of company: manufacturing, retail, and so on. Also describes the proposed form of organization: sole proprietorship, partnership, corporation, or co-operative. A typical organization of this section is as follows: name and location, company objectives, nature and primary product or service of the business, current status (start-up, buyout, or expansion) and history, if applicable, and legal form of organization.
V.	**Product or Service Description.** Describes the product or service and indicates what is unique about it. Explains the value added for customers—why people will buy the product or service, features of the product or service providing a competitive advantage, legal protection (patents, copyrights, trademarks, if relevant), and dangers of technical or style obsolescence.
VI.	**Marketing.** Has two key parts, the market analysis and the marketing plan. The market analysis convinces the reader that the entrepreneur understands the market for the product or service and can deal effectively with the competition to achieve sales projections. The marketing plan explains the strategy for achieving sales projections.
VII.	**Operating Plan.** Explains the type of manufacturing or operating system to be used. Describes the facilities, labour, raw materials, and processing requirements.
VIII.	**Management.** Identifies the key players—the management team, active investors, and directors—and cites the experience and competence they possess. Includes a description of the management team, outside investors and directors and their qualifications, outside resource people, and plans for recruiting and training employees.
IX.	**Financial Plan.** Specifies financial needs and expected financing sources. Presents projected financial statements, including cash budget, balance sheet, and income statement.
X.	**Supporting Details/Appendix.** Provides supplementary materials to the plan such as résumés and other supporting data.

important to concentrate on the issues that can be dealt with, and that will help determine whether to proceed and how to proceed.[41]

Accessing Resources

Typically, entrepreneurs acquire the various resources needed to make the venture a reality by **bootstrapping**, which means "doing more with less." Usually the term refers to financing techniques whereby entrepreneurs make do with less and use other people's resources wherever they can. However, bootstrapping can also refer to the acquisition of other types of resources, such as people, space, equipment, or materials loaned or provided free by customers or suppliers.

FINANCIAL RESOURCES

There are two main types of financing—debt and equity (see Chapter 15). Since a business is at its riskiest point during the start-up phase, equity is usually more appropriate and accessible than debt. However, most new venture founders prefer debt, because they are reluctant to give up any control to outsiders. To obtain debt financing, the entrepreneur must have an adequate equity investment in the business—typically 20 percent of the business's value—and collateral (or security).

Collateral refers to items (assets) owned by the business (such as a building and equipment) or by the individual (such as a house or car) that the borrower uses to secure a loan or other credit. These items can be seized by the lender if the loan isn't repaid according to the specified terms. To lenders, equity investment demonstrates the commitment of the entrepreneur, as individuals tend to be more committed to a venture if they have a substantial portion of what they own invested in it.

The most common sources of equity financing are:

1. *Personal savings.* New venture founders draw heavily on their own finances to start their businesses. Most save as much as they can in preparation for start-up.
2. *Love money.* This type of financing includes investments from friends, relatives, and business associates. It is called "love money" because it is often given more on the basis of the relationship than on the merit of the business concept.
3. *Private investors.* One popular source of equity is informal capital from private investors called *angels*. Usually, these persons are financially well off; many are successful entrepreneurs. For example, Gerry Pond provided financial support to Chris Newton in developing Radian6 and Q1 Labs. After a couple of years, the spectacular sale of these two firms accounted for over a billion dollars and created 50 millionaires in New Brunswick. For his contribution Mr. Pond was named Canadian Angel Investor of the Year.[42]
4. *Venture capitalists.* Investments by venture capitalists come from professionally managed pools of investor money (venture capital). Since the risk of receiving little or no return on investment is high, only deals that present an attractive, high-growth business opportunity with a return between 35 and 50 percent are considered. Very few new ventures meet this criterion. Venture capital investment in Canada has been fairly steady, totalling $2 billion in 2013 and $1.9 billion in 2014—figures way below the $48 billion estimated in the U.S. in 2014 (even on a per capita population basis)—so angels are very important in providing start-up money to Canadian entrepreneurs.[43]

The most common sources of debt financing are:

1. *Financial institutions.* While commercial banks are the main providers of debt financing for established small businesses, it is usually hard for a new business to get a loan. Banks are risk-averse and new businesses are considered very risky. Typically, entrepreneurs have more luck obtaining financing for a new venture with a personal loan (as opposed to a business loan). The most common way to obtain a personal loan is to mortgage a house or borrow against the cash value of a life insurance policy. In addition to commercial banks, other sources of debt financing include trust companies, co-operatives, finance companies, credit unions, and government agencies.
2. *Suppliers.* Another source of financing is suppliers who provide goods (i.e., inventory) or services to the entrepreneur with an agreement to bill them later. This is referred to as *trade credit*. Trade credit can be helpful in getting started, because inventory can be acquired without paying cash, freeing up money to pay other start-up costs. This type of financing is short-term; 30 days is the usual payback period. The amount of trade credit available to a new firm depends on the type of business and the supplier's confidence in the firm. Frequently, though, a new business has trouble getting trade credit since its capacity to repay has not been demonstrated.

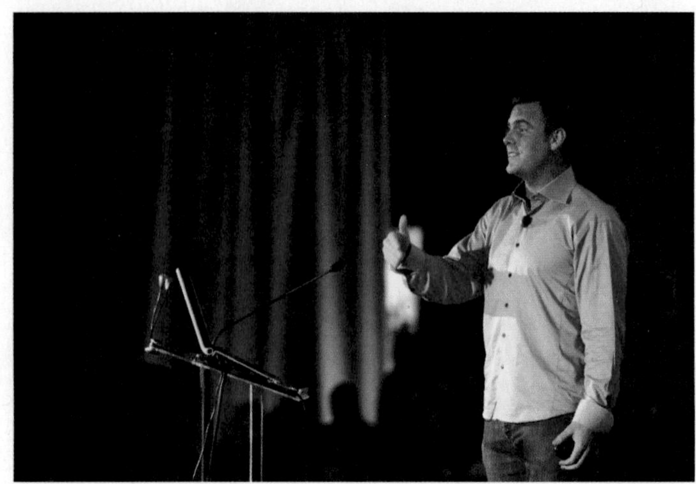

New Brunswick appears to be a hotbed of angel investing, as Dan Martell won the Canadian Angel Investor of the Year award for his support of 18 start-ups one year after Gerry Pond won the same award.

Tim Wagner/ZUMApress/Newscom

Besides these conventional sources of financing, the possibilities for bootstrap financing are endless. For example, an entrepreneur might require an advance payment from customers. Equipment can be leased rather than purchased (which reduces the risk of obsolete equipment). Office furniture can be rented, premises can be shared, and manufacturing can be subcontracted, thereby avoiding the expense of procuring material, equipment, and facilities. All of these activities free up cash that can then be used for other purposes. The need for cost reduction services is clear; Regus PLC, a temporary rental space company, based in Dallas, has opened 30 office centres in Canada in the past decade. It has locations in cities across the nation: Calgary, Edmonton, Winnipeg, Regina, Montreal, Toronto, Ottawa, Vancouver, Victoria, and Halifax. Regus is present in smaller cities and regions as well.[44]

BOOTSTRAPPING Doing more with less.

COLLATERAL Assets that a borrower uses to secure a loan or other credit, and that are subject to seizure by the lender if the loan isn't repaid according to the specified repayment terms.

THERE'S AN APP FOR THAT!

APP DETAILS	PLATFORMS
1. **Expensify** **Source:** Expensify **Key Features:** Keeping track of your expenses while on a business trip.	Apple, Android, BlackBerry, Windows
2. ***Entrepreneur* Magazine** **Source:** Entrepreneur Media **Key Features:** Looks at innovative approaches to businesses that create lasting opportunities.	Apple, Android, Windows
3. ***Success* Magazine** **Source:** Success Partners **Key Features:** A magazine that focuses on successful entrepreneurs and Intrapreneurs.	Apple, Android

APP DISCOVERY EXERCISE

Since app availability changes, conduct your own search for the "Top Three" entrepreneurship and small business apps and identify the key features.

OTHER RESOURCES

Businesses have other resources to help them with financing, legal, marketing, or operational advice or support. The federal and provincial governments have a wide range of financial assistance programs for small businesses. Among the various forms of assistance are low-interest loans, loan guarantees, interest-free loans, and wage subsidies. We examine three sources of information and assistance below: Business Development Bank of Canada, business incubators, and the internet.

Business Development Bank of Canada The Business Development Bank of Canada (BDC) has a mandate to help develop Canadian businesses, with a particular focus on small and medium-sized companies. It provides financing, venture capital, and consulting strategies. The BDC provides services to over 30 000 businesses from coast to coast and serves them through over 100 branch offices. The BDC is a financial institution wholly owned by the Government of Canada. Information can be found at www.bdc.ca or by calling 1-877-BDC-Banx.[45]

Incubators Business **incubators** provide new businesses ("newborns") with support to help nurture them into a successful future. The type of support varies, but some key forms of assistance include consulting services, legal advice, accounting services, business contacts, clerical services, and office space. According to the Canadian Association of Business Incubation (CABI), business survival rates are greatly improved by getting involved with an incubator. Survival rates after five years stand at about 80 percent, far above the average rates for businesses that don't use incubators. You can learn more by visiting www.cabi.ca. Take a look at Table 4.3 for examples of incubators across the country.

The Internet There are countless resources available online that can help budding entrepreneurs gather research information, write a business plan, and access government grants. The banks all have unique sites dedicated to small business and entrepreneurship resources. For example, Royal Bank of Canada (RBC) has a great site that provides checklists, business plan formats and samples, and advice on selecting business structures and more (www.rbcroyalbank.com/business/startingabusiness/index.html). There are also government sites such as the Canada Business Network dedicated to providing information and advice on every aspect of starting a business, including accessing government grants (www.canadabusiness.ca/eng).

Building the Right Team

A business might be owned by one person, but entrepreneurship is not a solo process. There are various stakeholders who can provide resources to the venture. When ownership is shared, decisions must be made regarding how much each stakeholder will own, at what cost, and under what conditions. The form of legal organization chosen affects whether ownership can be shared and whether resources can be accessed.

INCUBATORS Facilities that support small businesses during their early growth phase by providing basic services, office space, legal advice, and more.

Helen Sessions/Alamy Stock Photo

>>> **TABLE 4.3** Business Incubators Across Canada[46]

Name	Industry Sector	Location
SFU Venture Connections	Mixed use	Vancouver, British Columbia
AcceleratorYYC	Digital media, creativity	Calgary, Alberta
CIC Manitoba	Manufacturing	Winnipeg, Manitoba
Toronto Fashion Incubator	Fashion	Toronto, Ontario
Genesis Centre	Technology (software)	St. John's, Newfoundland
Aerospace & Defence Park	Aerospace	Fredericton, New Brunswick
Innovacorp	Technology	Halifax, Nova Scotia
Springboard West Innovations	Mixed use	Regina, Saskatchewan
BIO | FOOD | TECH	Food processing	Charlottetown, Prince Edward Island
J.-Armand Bombardier Incubator	Technology	Montreal, Quebec

Jennifer Borton/DigitalVision Vectors/Getty Images

Deciding whether to share ownership by forming a venture team involves consideration of two main issues:

- *The size and scope of the venture.* How many people does the venture require? Can people be hired to fill the key roles as they are required?
- *Personal competencies.* What are the talents, know-how, skills, track record, contacts, and resources that the entrepreneur brings to the venture? How do they match with what the venture needs to succeed?

The nature of the team depends upon the match between the lead entrepreneur and the opportunity and how quickly and aggressively he or she plans to proceed. Most teams tend to be formed in one of two ways: (1) one person has an idea (or wants to start a business), and then several associates join the team in the first few years of operation, or (2) an entire team is formed at the outset based on such factors as a shared idea, a friendship, or an experience.

As you will see in the closing case featuring Beyond the Rack, the ideal team consists of people with complementary skills covering the key areas of business (i.e., marketing, finance, production). Small founding teams tend to work better than big ones. It is quite common for the initial team to consist of just two people—a craftsperson and a salesperson.

If the entrepreneur does not intend to establish a high-growth venture, going solo may be a realistic option. Some new venture founders bring on additional team members only as the business can afford them. Most successful solo businesses are simple ventures (e.g., retail stores or service providers).[47] The odds for survival, growth, profitability, and attracting capital are increased by a team approach.[48]

Assessing the Fit Between Elements in the Entrepreneurial Process

Assessing the fit between the various elements in the entrepreneurial process is an ongoing task, since the shape of the opportunity, and consequently the resources and people needed to capitalize on it, typically change as the opportunity is developed. It is the entrepreneur who stands to gain the most by attending to these fits and any changes they may require, although other stakeholders, such as investors, will be considering them as well.

THE ENTREPRENEUR–OPPORTUNITY FIT

The entrepreneur needs to decide whether the opportunity is something he or she can do and wants to do. A realistic self-assessment is important. Prospective ventures that are of limited personal interest and require skills and abilities that do not fit the entrepreneur should be quickly eliminated. No matter how good the product or service concept is, as the opportunity changes shape it may demand skills a single entrepreneur lacks. This may prompt a decision to acquire the needed skills either by forming a team or by getting further training.

THE OPPORTUNITY–RESOURCES FIT

Assessing the opportunity–resources fit involves determining whether the resources needed to capitalize on the opportunity can be acquired. When challenges or risks appear, the aim is to determine whether they can be resolved and to deal with them quickly. For example, if the venture requires a greater financial investment than originally anticipated, this does not necessarily mean that the venture should be abandoned. Other options, such as taking on partners or leasing rather than building a facility, may be viable. Of course, some ventures may not be viable regardless of the alternatives considered.

THE ENTREPRENEUR–RESOURCES FIT

Once the resource requirements of the venture have been determined, the entrepreneur needs to assess whether he or she has the capacity to meet those requirements. For example, an entrepreneur with a strong reputation for software development will have an easier time attracting employees for a venture specializing in software than someone with no track record. If that same entrepreneur is well connected with people in the industry, he or she will be more likely to gain commitments from customers, and in turn, investors.

Small businesses are increasingly seeing the need and investing in resources that promote environmentally friendly practices. Read box entitled "Small Businesses Go Green."

THE GREENING OF BUSINESS

Small Businesses Go Green

A survey conducted by Ipsos Reid showed that half of Canadian small business owners currently have, or are considering implementing, a green plan for their business. Of those that already have a plan, the majority emphasize the reduction of energy costs. Actual spending on green initiatives, however, has been low (less than $500 during the last two years).

Many small businesses in Canada have already taken some easy-to-implement actions to become greener (e.g., changing to energy-efficient lighting, turning off photocopiers and computers overnight, using recycled paper, buying eco-friendly cleaning supplies, and using pens made of compostable material instead of plastic). Other environmentally friendly strategies have also emerged. Consider cargo bicycles, which have been popular for many years in places like China and India, but are now becoming popular in North America as environmental consciousness rises and traffic congestion in large cities increases. Here are some examples:

- Toronto-based Vert Catering uses a cargo bicycle to deliver food to its customers.
- Vancouver entrepreneurs launched SHIFT Urban Cargo Delivery, which is designed to fill the gap between bike couriers and delivery trucks. SHIFT delivers everything from office supplies to small furniture. Their cargo bicycles have an electric assist to help with heavy loads.
- Green Gardeners uses cargo bikes to transport garden tools to client sites.
- Featherstone Two Wheels Green Delivery saves $7000–$9000 in insurance and maintenance costs every year by using cargo bicycles instead of cars.

Small businesses can take other actions to save money and go green at the same time. For example, The Auto West Group BMW auto dealership in Richmond, B.C., installed a wind turbine to generate electricity. The turbine—which reduces the company's power bill—is just one of many green initiatives for this company (it already had one of the greenest buildings in British Columbia, and had installed solar panels, geo-thermal heating and cooling technology, and a rooftop garden).

Help for small businesses that wish to "go green" is available from diverse organizations such as Investeco Capital Corp. (a private equity group that launched a $40 million fund to help small and medium-sized food companies to operate sustainably), Gobi Carbon Management Solutions (which developed software to help small businesses identify their emissions sources and make suggestions for saving money), and the federal government's EcoAction program website, (which contains information about programs that help organizations reduce energy costs).

CRITICAL THINKING QUESTIONS

1. Find a small business in your local area that is committed to being eco-friendly. Why did the owner decide to commit to having an eco-friendly business?
2. Consider the following statement: *Because the failure rate of small businesses is high, small business owners must focus all their energies on trying to survive. They therefore do not have the time or the money to implement green practices.* Do you agree or disagree? Explain your reasoning.

START-UP AND BEYOND

Entrepreneurs must make the right start-up decisions, but they must also pay attention to how the business will be run once it is started. In this section, we examine three important topics relevant to these issues. First, we describe the three main ways entrepreneurs start up a small business. Next, we look at the four main organizing options available to entrepreneurs. We conclude the chapter with a look at the reasons for success and failure in small business.

LO-4 Starting up a Small Business

Most entrepreneurs start up a small business in one of three ways: they start from scratch, they buy an existing business, or they buy a franchise. We have already examined the "starting from scratch" alternative in detail in the preceding section, so we turn now to the latter two alternatives.

BUYING AN EXISTING BUSINESS

About one-third of all new businesses started in the past decade were bought from someone else. Many experts recommend buying an existing business because it increases the chances of success; it has already proven its ability to attract customers and has established relationships with lenders, suppliers, and other stakeholders. The track record also gives potential buyers a clearer picture of what to expect than any estimate of a new business's prospects.

But an entrepreneur who buys someone else's business may not be able to avoid certain problems. For example, there may be uncertainty about the exact financial shape the business is in, the business may have a poor reputation, the location may be poor, or it may be difficult to determine an appropriate purchase price.

Taking Over a Family Business Taking over a family business poses both opportunities and challenges. On the positive side, a family business can provide otherwise unobtainable financial and management resources—it often has a valuable reputation that can result in important community and business relationships, employee loyalty is often high, and an interested, unified family management and shareholders group may emerge. On the other hand, there may be disagreements over which family members assume control. Choosing an appropriate successor is a key issue for continuity, but it is also a key source of conflict. In addition, if a parent sells his or her interest in the business, the price to be paid may be an issue. Expectations can also be problematic, as some family members may feel that they have a right to a job, promotion, and an impressive title based on birth rights.[49] Handling disagreements among family members about the future of the business can be a challenge. How do you fire a loved one if things are not working out?[50]

Plenty of companies have thrived for more than one generation. For example, Kal Tire is headed by a second generation leader named Robert Foord. He took over from his late father, Tom Foord. Kal Tire was

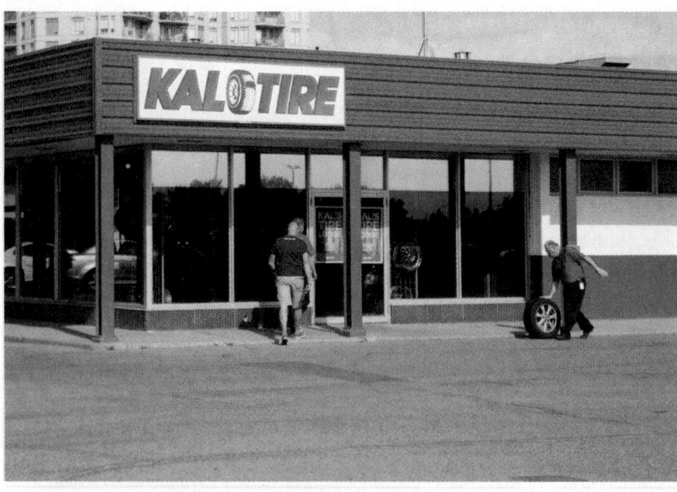

^ Kal Tire is a positive example of a family business that has stood the test of time and grown into a major company.

Rosanne Tackaberry/Alamy

^ Franchising is very popular in Canada. It offers individuals who want to run their own business an opportunity to establish themselves quickly in a local market.

Steve Russell/Getty Images

started in 1953, in Vernon, B.C., and now has over 250 locations, 5400 employees, and annual sales of $1.4 billion. Among that large roster of employees, you can clearly trace the family tree: Tom Foord's five siblings, along with their spouses, children, and grandchildren.[51]

BUYING A FRANCHISE

If you drive around any Canadian town or city, you will notice retail outlets with names like McDonald's, RE/MAX, Canadian Tire, Chez Cora, and Tim Hortons. These diverse businesses have one thing in common—they are all franchises, operating under licences issued by parent companies to entrepreneurs who own and manage them. Depending on how it is defined, franchising now accounts for 40 percent of retail sales in Canada. There are approximately 78 000 franchise establishments in Canada that employ over 1 million people and account for over 10 percent of Canadian GDP.[52]

Franchising continues to increase in importance for large and small ambitious companies. For example, Doug Bourgoyne, founder of FrogBox, an eco-friendly moving box rental company, has used this approach to expand. The company was even featured on *Dragon's Den*. After this major exposure, he received 1500 applications for franchises in Canada.[53]

A **franchising agreement** outlines the duties and responsibilities of each party. It indicates the amount and type of payment that franchisees must make to the franchiser. These franchise agreements have become increasingly complicated, often 60 or even 100 pages long. Tim Hortons avoids this trend with a streamlined contract of about 26 pages.[54] Franchisees usually make an initial payment for the right to operate an outlet. They also make royalty payments to the franchiser ranging from 2 to 30 percent of the franchisee's annual revenues or profits. The franchisee may also pay an advertising fee to the franchiser. Franchise fees vary widely, from $23 500 for a Mad Science franchise, to over $1 million for a Burger King franchise, to hundreds of millions for a professional sports franchise.

The Advantages of Franchising

Both franchisers and franchisees benefit from the franchising way of doing business (see Table 4.4).

The Disadvantages of Franchising

There are two sides to any story. Table 4.4 clearly outlines the obvious advantages. However, many experienced people will tell you that buying a franchise is like buying a job. The agreements are long, because franchisers want to protect their image and recipes and want franchisees to follow their rules. If they don't abide by the agreement, franchisees may be sued. So if you have a great new breakfast menu idea for your outlet and have creative promotional ideas, franchising may not be for you. If things go well it can be rewarding, but it is important to do your homework—there are many disappointed franchise owners out there.

You should carefully read the agreement and ensure that your territory is protected and that you have the right of first refusal on new potential stores within a certain distance (e.g., 10–15 kilometres or exclusivity of your particular town). Some franchisees have been shocked to see their franchiser place a new franchisee a few blocks away or even across the street. Franchisees can benefit from support and advertising, but that does not come for free. For example, a Harvey's franchisee pays a 5 percent royalty fee and a 4 percent advertising fee (based on gross sales), and these fees are payable each week in addition to regular operating costs and rent.[56] This after paying anywhere from $650 000 to $950 000 for a free-standing outlet. Plenty of franchisees who belong to popular chains that are barely surviving are wondering whatever happened to that promised success.

In response to these issues, the provincial governments of Manitoba, Alberta, Ontario, New Brunswick, and Prince Edward Island have created laws to protect franchisees through Franchise Disclosure Documents (FDD) that provide clear details of the agreement and helps protect franchisees in these jurisdictions.[57]

Is Franchising for You?

Do you think you would be happy being a franchisee? The answer depends on a number of factors, including your willingness to work hard, your ability to find a good franchise to buy, and the financial resources you possess. If you are thinking seriously of going into franchising, you should consider several areas of costs you will incur:

- the franchise sales price
- expenses that will be incurred before the business opens
- training expenses
- operational expenses for the first six months
- personal financial needs for the first six months
- emergency needs

FRANCHISING AGREEMENT Stipulates the duties and responsibilities of the franchisee and the franchiser.

TABLE 4.4 The Benefits of Franchising

For the Franchiser	For the Franchisee
• The franchiser can attain rapid growth for the chain by signing up many franchisees in many different locations.	• Franchisees own a small business that has access to big business management skills.
• Franchisees share in the cost of advertising.	• The franchisee does not have to build up a business from scratch.
• The franchiser benefits from the investment money provided by franchisees.	• Franchisee failure rates are lower than when starting one's own business.
• Advertising money is spent more efficiently.	• A well-advertised brand name comes with the franchise and the franchisee's outlet is instantly recognizable.
• Franchisees are motivated to work hard for themselves, which creates profit for the franchiser.	• The franchiser may send the franchisee to a training program run by the franchiser (e.g., the Canadian Institute of Hamburgerology run by McDonald's).
• The franchiser is freed from all details of a local operation, which are handled by the franchisee.	• The franchiser may visit the franchisee and provide expert advice on how to run the business. Burger King has 145 coaches who travel to franchisees to improve everything from cooking techniques to cost-cutting measures.[55]
• Economies in buying allow franchisees to get lower prices for the raw materials they must purchase.	
• Financial assistance is provided by the franchiser in the form of loans; the franchiser may also help the franchisee obtain loans from local sources.	
• Franchisees are their own bosses and get to keep most of the profit they make.	

LO-5 SUCCESS AND FAILURE IN SMALL BUSINESS

Of every 100 small businesses that begin operation, 85 will still be operating after one year, 70 after three years, and 51 after five years.[58] A study conducted by CIBC World Markets found that small businesses with above-average revenue growth were run by owners who had more education, used professional advisers, adopted the corporate form of ownership, did outsourcing work for other companies, had a high level of internet connectivity, and used the internet to sell outside Canada.[59]

Reasons for Success

Beyond the specific findings like the CIBC study, four general factors typically are cited to explain the success of small-business owners:

1. *Hard work, drive, and dedication.* Small business owners must be committed to succeeding and be willing to put in the time and effort to make it happen. Long hours and few vacations generally characterize the first few years of new business ownership.
2. *Market demand for the product or service.* Careful analysis of market conditions can help small business people assess the probable reception of their products. If the area around a college has only one pizza parlour, a new pizzeria is more likely to succeed than if there are already ten in operation.
3. *Managerial competence.* Successful small business people have a solid understanding of how to manage a business. They may acquire competence through training (taking courses), experience, or using the expertise of others. Few, however, succeed alone or straight out of school. Most spend time in successful companies or partner with others to bring expertise to a new business.
4. *Luck.* Luck also plays a role in the success of some firms. For example, after one entrepreneur started an environmental clean-up firm, he struggled to keep his business afloat. Then the government committed a large sum of money to toxic waste clean-up. He was able to get several large contracts, and his business is now thriving.

Reasons for Failure

Small businesses fail for many specific reasons. Entrepreneurs may have no control over some of these factors (e.g., weather, accidents), but they can influence most items on the list. Although no pattern has been established, four general factors contribute to failure:

1. *Managerial incompetence or inexperience.* Some entrepreneurs overestimate their own managerial skills, or believe that hard work alone ensures success. If managers don't know how to make basic business decisions or don't understand basic management principles, they aren't likely to succeed.
2. *Neglect.* Some entrepreneurs try to launch ventures in their spare time, and others devote only limited time to new businesses. But starting a small business demands an overwhelming time commitment.
3. *Weak control systems.* Effective control systems keep a business on track and alert managers to potential trouble. If the control systems don't signal potential problems, the business may be in serious trouble before obvious difficulties are spotted.
4. *Insufficient capital.* Some entrepreneurs are overly optimistic about how soon they'll start earning profits. In most cases, it takes months or even years. Amazon.com didn't earn a profit for ten years, but obviously still required capital to pay employees and cover expenses. Experts say you need enough capital to operate six months to a year without earning a profit.[60]

LO-6 Forms of Business Ownership

Before embarking on the road to success and facing all the potential problems an entrepreneur must consider the best form of ownership: sole proprietorship, partnership, corporation, or co-operative. Whether they intend to run small farms, large factories, or online e-tailers, they must decide which one best suits their goals.

THE SOLE PROPRIETORSHIP

The **sole proprietorship** is a business owned and operated by one person. Legally, if you set up a business as a sole proprietorship, your business is considered to be an extension of yourself (and not a separate legal entity). Though usually small, a sole proprietorship may be as large as a steel mill or as small as a lemonade stand. While the majority of businesses in Canada are sole proprietorships, they account for only a small proportion of total business revenues.

Advantages of a Sole Proprietorship Freedom may be the most important benefit of a sole proprietorship. Sole proprietors answer to no one but themselves, since they don't share ownership. A sole proprietorship is also easy to form. If you operate the business under your own name, with no additions, you don't even need to register your business name to start operating as a sole proprietor—you can go into business simply by putting a sign on the door. The simplicity of legal set-up procedures makes this form appealing to self-starters and independent spirits, as do the low start-up costs.

Another attractive feature is the tax benefits. Most businesses suffer losses in their early stages. Since the business and the proprietor are legally one and the same, these losses can be deducted from income the proprietor earns from personal sources other than the business.

Disadvantages of a Sole Proprietorship A major drawback is **unlimited liability**, which means that a sole proprietor is personally liable (responsible) for all debts incurred by the business. If the business fails to generate enough cash, bills must be paid out of the owner's pocket. Another disadvantage is lack of continuity; a sole proprietorship legally dissolves when the owner dies. Finally, a sole proprietorship depends on the resources of one person whose managerial and financial limitations may constrain the business. Sole proprietors often find it hard to borrow money to start up or expand. Many bankers fear that they won't be able to recover loans if the owner becomes disabled.

THE PARTNERSHIP

A **partnership** is established when two or more individuals (partners) agree to combine their financial, managerial, and technical abilities for the purpose of operating a business for profit. This form of ownership is often used by professionals such as accountants, lawyers, and engineers. Partnerships are often an extension of a business that began as a sole proprietorship. The original owner may want to expand, or the business may have grown too big for a single person to handle.

There are two basic types of partners in a partnership. **General partners** are actively involved in managing the firm and have unlimited liability. **Limited partners** don't participate actively in the business, and their liability is limited to the amount they invested in the partnership. A *general partnership* is the most common type and is similar to the sole proprietorship in that all the (general) partners are jointly liable for the obligations of the business. The other type, the *limited partnership*, consists of at least one general partner (who has unlimited liability) and one or more limited partners. The limited partners cannot participate in the day-to-day management of the business or they risk the loss of their limited liability status.

Advantages of a Partnership The most striking advantage of a general partnership is the ability to grow by adding talent and money. Partnerships also have an easier time borrowing funds than sole proprietorships. Banks and other lending institutions prefer to make loans to enterprises that are not dependent on a single individual. Partnerships can also invite new partners to join by investing money.

Like a sole proprietorship, a partnership is simple to organize, with few legal requirements. Even so, all partnerships must begin with an agreement of some kind. It may be written, oral, or even unspoken. Wise partners, however, insist on a written agreement to avoid trouble later. This agreement should answer such questions as:

- Who invested what sums of money in the partnership?
- Who will receive what share of the partnership's profits?
- Who does what and who reports to whom?
- How may the partnership be dissolved?
- How will leftover assets be distributed among the partners?
- How would surviving partners be protected from claims by surviving heirs if a partner dies?
- How will disagreements be resolved?

The partnership agreement is strictly a private document. No laws require partners to file an agreement with any government agency. Nor are partnerships regarded as legal entities. In the eyes of the law, a partnership is nothing more than two or more people working together. The partnership's lack of legal standing means that the partners are taxed as individuals.

Disadvantages of a Partnership Unlimited liability is also the biggest disadvantage of a general partnership. By law, each partner may be held personally liable for all debts of the partnership. And if any partner incurs a debt, even if the other partners know nothing about it, they are all liable if the offending partner cannot pay up. Another problem with partnerships is the lack of continuity. When one partner dies or pulls out, a partnership dissolves legally, even if the other partners agree to continue the business.

A related drawback is the difficulty of transferring ownership. No partner may sell out without the other partners' consent. Thus, the life of a partnership may depend on the ability of retiring partners to find someone compatible with the other partners to buy them out. Finally, a partnership provides little or no guidance in resolving conflicts between the partners.

SOLE PROPRIETORSHIP Business owned and usually operated by one person who is responsible for all of its debts.

UNLIMITED LIABILITY A person who invests in a business is liable for all debts incurred by the business; personal possessions can be taken to pay debts.

PARTNERSHIP A business with two or more owners who share in the operation of the firm and in financial responsibility for the firm's debts.

GENERAL PARTNER A partner who is actively involved in managing the firm and has unlimited liability.

LIMITED PARTNER A partner who generally does not participate actively in the business, and whose liability is limited to the amount invested in the partnership.

For example, suppose one partner wants to expand the business rapidly and the other wants it to grow slowly. If under the partnership agreement the two are equal, it may be difficult for them to decide what to do.

THE CORPORATION

When you think of corporations you probably think of giant businesses such as Air Canada, Walmart, or Telus. The very word "corporation" suggests bigness and power. Yet the tiny corner retailer has as much right to incorporate as a giant oil refiner. Both of them have the same basic characteristics that all corporations share—legal status as a separate entity, property rights and obligations, and an indefinite lifespan. (See Table 4.5 for a list of the top ten corporations in Canada.)

A corporation has been defined as "an artificial being, invisible, intangible, and existing only in contemplation of the law." As such, corporations may sue and be sued; buy, hold, and sell property; make products and sell them to consumers; and commit crimes and be tried and punished for them. Simply defined, a **corporation** is a business that is a separate legal entity, that is liable for its own debts, and whose owners' liability is limited to their investment.

Shareholders—investors who buy shares of ownership in the form of stock—are the real owners of a corporation. (The different kinds of stockholders are described in Chapter 15.) Profits may be distributed to stockholders in the form of dividends, although corporations are not required to pay dividends. Instead, they often reinvest any profits in the business. Common stockholders have the last claim to any assets if the company folds. Dividends on **common stock** are paid on a per-share basis (if a dividend is declared). Thus, a shareholder with ten shares receives ten times the dividend paid a shareholder with one share. When investors cannot attend a shareholders' meeting, they can grant voting authority to someone who will attend. This procedure, called *voting by proxy*, is how almost all individual investors vote.

The **board of directors** is the governing body of a corporation. Its main responsibility is to ensure that the corporation is run in the best interests of the shareholders. The directors choose the president and other officers of the business and delegate the power to run the day-to-day activities of the business to those officers. The directors set policy on paying dividends, on financing major spending, and on executive salaries and benefits. Large corporations tend to have large boards with as many as 20 or 30 directors, whereas smaller corporations tend to have no more than five directors. Usually, these are people with personal or professional ties to the corporation, such as family members, lawyers, and accountants. Every year, the *Globe and Mail* analyzes the governance practices of Canadian companies in four areas: board composition, compensation, shareholder rights, and disclosure. The top-ranked companies in 2014 were the Bank of Montreal, Sun Life Financial Inc., and the Bank of Nova Scotia.[62]

Inside directors are employees of the company and have primary responsibility for the corporation. They are top managers, such as the president and executive vice-presidents. *Outside directors* are not employees of the corporation. Attorneys, accountants, university officials, and executives from other firms are commonly used as outside directors.

Corporate officers are the top managers hired by the board to run the corporation on a day-to-day basis. The **chief executive officer (CEO)** is responsible for the firm's overall performance. Other corporate officers typically include the president, who is responsible for internal management, and various vice-presidents, who oversee functional areas such as marketing or operations.

Types of Corporations

A **public corporation** is one whose shares of stock are widely held and available for sale to the general public. Anyone who has the funds to pay for them can buy shares of

TABLE 4.5 Top 10 Corporations in Canada, 2014[61]

Company	Sales Revenues (in billions of $)
1. Suncor Energy Inc.	42.4
2. Magna International	36.1
3. Royal Bank of Canada	35.9
4. Alimentation Couche-Tard	35.6
5. George Weston Ltd.	33.6
6. Enbridge Inc.	33.1
7. Imperial Oil	32.9
8. Loblaw Companies	32.4
9. Toronto-Dominion Bank	30.7
10. Power Corp. Of Canada	29.7

CORPORATION A business considered by law to be a legal entity separate from its owners with many of the legal rights and privileges of a person; a form of business organization in which the liability of the owners is limited to their investment in the firm.

SHAREHOLDERS Investors who buy shares of ownership in the form of stock.

COMMON STOCK Shares whose owners usually have last claim on the corporation's assets (after creditors and owners of preferred stock) but who have voting rights in the firm.

BOARD OF DIRECTORS A group of individuals elected by a firm's shareholders and charged with overseeing, and taking legal responsibility for, the firm's actions.

CHIEF EXECUTIVE OFFICER (CEO) The highest-ranking executive in a company or organization.

PUBLIC CORPORATION A business whose stock is widely held and available for sale to the general public.

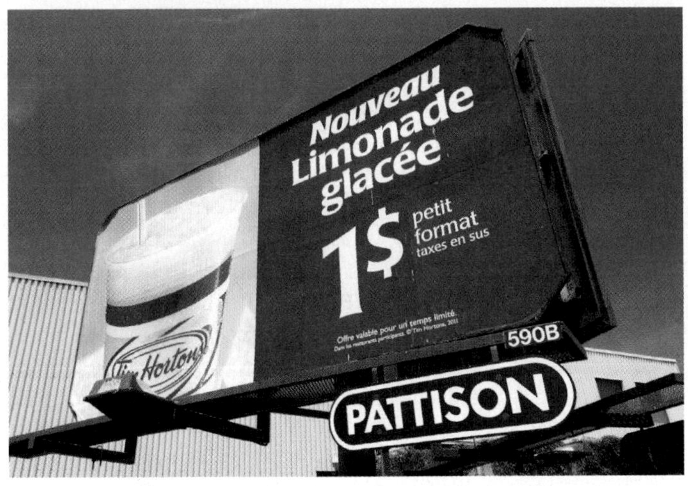

If you are from British Columbia, you know the Pattison name well but the reach goes across the country and beyond. The company built by this 84-year-old pure entrepreneur has created an empire that employs over 31 000 employees and earned approximately $8 billion in 2014.

Pierre Rochon/Alamy Stock Photo

companies such as Petro-Canada, Bombardier, or Air Canada. The stock of a **private corporation**, on the other hand, is held by only a few people and is not generally available for sale. The controlling group may be a family, employees, or the management group. Pattison and Cirque du Soleil are two well-known Canadian private corporations.

Most new corporations start out as private corporations, because few investors will buy an unknown stock. As the corporation grows and develops a record of success, it may issue shares to the public to raise additional money. This is called an **initial public offering (IPO)**. IPOs are not very attractive to investors during stock market declines, but they become more popular when stock markets recover. According to a PWC report, IPOs in Canada raised over $3.5 billion in 2015.[63] A public corporation can also "go private," which is the reverse of going public. **Private equity firms** buy publicly traded companies and then take them private. They often make major changes to company operations in order to increase its value.

About a decade ago, many corporations converted to an **income trust** structure, which allowed them to avoid paying corporate income tax if they distributed all or most of their earnings to investors. However, the federal government changed the rules and began taxing income trusts more like corporations a few years ago. This caused a significant decline in the market value of income trusts and put an end to the rush to convert.[64] Income trusts distribute much of their cash flow to investors each month.[65]

Formation of the Corporation

The two most widely used methods of forming a corporation are federal incorporation under the Canada Business Corporations Act and provincial incorporation under any of the provincial corporations acts. The former is used if the company is going to operate in more than one province; the latter is used if the founders intend to carry on business in only one province. Except for banks and certain insurance and loan companies, any company can be federally incorporated under the Canada Business Corporations Act. To do so, articles of incorporation must be drawn up. These articles include such information as the name of the corporation, the type and number of shares to be issued, the number of directors the corporation will have, and the location of the company's operations. The specific procedures and information required for provincial incorporation vary from province to province.

All corporations must attach the word "Limited" (Ltd./Ltée), "Incorporated" (Inc.), or "Corporation" (Corp.) to the company name to indicate clearly to customers and suppliers that the owners have limited liability for corporate debts. The same sorts of rules apply in other countries. British firms, for example, use PLC for "public limited company" and German companies use AG for "Aktiengesellschaft" (corporation).

Advantages of Incorporation

The biggest advantage of the corporate structure is **limited liability**, which means that the liability of investors is limited to their personal investment in the corporation. In the event of failure, the courts may seize a corporation's assets and sell them to pay debts, but the courts cannot touch the investors' personal possessions. If, for example, you invest $25 000 in a corporation that goes bankrupt, you may lose your $25 000, but no more. In other words, $25 000 is the extent of your liability.

Another advantage of a corporation is continuity. Because it has a legal life independent of its founders and owners, a corporation can, in theory, continue forever. Shares of stock may be sold or passed on to heirs, and most corporations also benefit from the continuity provided by professional management. Finally, corporations have advantages in raising money. By selling **stock**, they expand the number of investors and available funds. The term "stock" refers to a share of ownership in a corporation. Continuity and legal status tend to make lenders more willing to grant loans to corporations.

Disadvantages of Incorporation

One of the disadvantages for a new firm in forming a corporation is the cost (approximately $2500). In addition, corporations also need legal help in meeting government regulations, because they are far more heavily regulated than proprietorships or general partnerships. Some people say that **double taxation** is another problem with the corporate form of ownership. By this they mean that a corporation must pay income taxes on its profits, and then shareholders must also pay personal income taxes on the **dividends** they receive from the corporation. The dividend a corporation pays is the amount of money, normally a portion of the profits that is distributed to the shareholders. Since dividends paid by the corporation are paid with after-tax dollars, this amounts to double taxation. Others point out that shareholders get a dividend tax credit, which largely offsets double taxation.

THE CO-OPERATIVE

A **co-operative** is an incorporated form of business organized, owned, and democratically controlled by the people who use its products and services, and whose earnings are distributed on the basis of use of the co-operative rather than level of investment. As such, it is formed to benefit its owners in the form of reduced prices and/or the distribution of surpluses at year-end. Some popular forms of co-operatives include: consumer co-operatives like Mountain Equipment Co-op and financial co-operatives like Vancity.

The process works like this. Suppose a group of farmers believe they can get cheaper fertilizer prices if they form their own company and purchase in large volumes. They might then form a co-operative, which can be either federally or provincially chartered. Prices are generally lower to buyers and, at the end of the fiscal year, any surpluses are distributed to members on the basis of how much they purchased. If Farmer Jones bought 5 percent of all co-op sales, he would receive 5 percent of the surplus.

PRIVATE CORPORATION A business whose stock is held by a small group of individuals and is not usually available for sale to the general public.

INITIAL PUBLIC OFFERING (IPO) Selling shares of stock in a company for the first time to a general investing public.

PRIVATE EQUITY FIRMS Companies that buy publicly traded companies and then make them private.

INCOME TRUST A structure allowing companies to avoid paying corporate income tax if they distribute all or most of their earnings to investors.

LIMITED LIABILITY Investor liability is limited to their personal investments in the corporation; courts cannot touch the personal assets of investors in the event that the corporation goes bankrupt.

STOCK A share of ownership in a corporation.

DOUBLE TAXATION A corporation must pay income taxes on its profits, and then shareholders must also pay personal income taxes on the dividends they receive from the corporation.

DIVIDENDS The amount of money, normally a portion of the profits that is distributed to the shareholders.

CO-OPERATIVE An organization that is formed to benefit its owners in the form of reduced prices and/or the distribution of surpluses at year-end.

>>> **TABLE 4.6** A Comparison of Four Forms of Business Ownership

Characteristic	Sole Proprietorship	Partnership	Corporation	Co-operative
Protection against liability for bad debts	Low	Low	High	High
Ease of formation	High	High	Medium	Medium
Permanence	Low	Low	High	High
Ease of ownership transfer	Low	Low	High	High
Ease of raising money	Low	Medium	High	High
Freedom from regulation	High	High	Low	Medium
Tax advantages	High	High	Low	High

The co-operative's start-up capital usually comes from shares purchased by the co-operative's members. Sometimes all it takes to qualify for membership in a co-operative is the purchase of one share with a fixed (and often nominal) value. Federal co-operatives, however, can raise capital by issuing investment shares to members or non-members. Co-operatives, like investor-owned corporations, have directors and appointed officers.

In terms of numbers, co-operatives are the least important form of ownership. However, they are of significance to society and to their members and may provide services that are not readily available or that cost more than the members would otherwise be willing to pay. Table 4.6 compares the various forms of business ownership using different characteristics.

Advantages of a Co-operative Co-operatives have many of the same advantages as investor-owned corporations, such as limited liability of owners and continuity. A key benefit of a co-operative relates to its structure. Each member has only one vote in the affairs of the co-operative, regardless of how many shares he or she owns. This system prevents voting and financial control of the business by a few wealthy individuals. This is particularly attractive to the less-wealthy members of the co-operative.

Unlike corporations, which are not allowed a tax deduction on dividend payments made to shareholders, co-operatives are allowed to deduct patronage refunds to members out of before-tax income. Thus, income may be taxed only at the individual member level rather than at both the co-operative and member level.[66]

Disadvantages of a Co-operative One of the main disadvantages of co-operatives relates to attracting equity investment. Since the benefits from being a member of a co-operative arise through the level of use of the co-operative rather than the level of equity invested, members do not have an incentive to invest in equity capital of the co-operative. Another drawback is that democratic voting arrangements and dividends based purely on patronage discourage some entrepreneurs from forming or joining a co-operative.

MyBizLab

Study, practise, and explore real business situations with these helpful resources:

- **Interactive Lesson Presentations:** Work through interactive presentations and assessments to test your knowledge of business concepts.
- **Study Plan:** Check your understanding of chapter concepts with self-study quizzes.
- **Dynamic Study Modules:** Work through adaptive study modules on your computer, tablet, or mobile device.
- **Simulations:** Practise decision-making in simulated business environments.
- **Videos:** Learn more about the business practices and strategies of real companies.

SUMMARY OF LEARNING OBJECTIVES

LO-1 EXPLAIN THE MEANING AND INTERRELATIONSHIP OF THE TERMS *SMALL BUSINESS, NEW VENTURE CREATION,* AND *ENTREPRENEURSHIP.*

A *small business* has fewer than 100 employees. A new firm is one that has become operational within the previous 12 months, has adopted any of four main organizational forms—sole proprietorship, partnership, corporation, or co-operative—and sells goods or services. *Entrepreneurship* is the process of identifying an opportunity in the marketplace and accessing the resources needed to capitalize on it. In relation to small and/or new businesses, entrepreneurship is the process by which a small business or a new business is created.

LO-2 DESCRIBE THE ROLE OF *SMALL AND NEW BUSINESSES* IN THE CANADIAN ECONOMY.

While 98 percent of employer businesses in Canada are small (fewer than 100 employees), about half of the total private-sector labour force work for *small businesses*. The distribution of employment by size of firm varies across industries. The small-business sector's capacity for entrepreneurship and innovation accounts for much of the job creation; this sector contributes to the economy, with start-ups accounting for most of the growth. Women are playing a major role in the growth of small businesses. *New businesses* are also important to the Canadian economy, because they are the main source of new products and services.

LO-3 EXPLAIN THE *ENTREPRENEURIAL PROCESS* AND DESCRIBE ITS THREE KEY ELEMENTS.

The *entrepreneurial process* occurs within a social, political, and economic context and consists of three key elements: the entrepreneur, the opportunity, and resources. Entrepreneurs typically access the various resources needed by bootstrapping—doing more with less. These resources are both financial and non-financial. Two types of financing—debt and equity—can be accessed from a range of sources.

LO-4 DESCRIBE THREE ALTERNATIVE STRATEGIES FOR BECOMING A BUSINESS OWNER—*STARTING FROM SCRATCH*, *BUYING AN EXISTING BUSINESS*, AND *BUYING A FRANCHISE*.

It is necessary to work through the entrepreneurial process in order to *start a business from scratch*. Whether start-up efforts will result in a new business often depends upon how well matched the entrepreneur's skills and abilities are with the opportunity and the resources required, as well as how well matched the opportunity and resources are. Generally, when someone *buys an existing business*, the odds of success are better because it has existing customers, established relationships (e.g., lenders, suppliers), and an existing track record. Potential buyers have a clearer picture of what to expect. However, the business may have a poor reputation or poor location, and it may be difficult to determine an appropriate purchase price. A special case of buying an existing business involves family businesses, which pose both opportunities and challenges. In *buying a franchise*, the buyer (franchisee) purchases the right to sell the product or service of the seller (franchiser) according to the terms of the franchising agreement. In return, the franchiser provides assistance with the business's start-up as well as with ongoing operations once the business opens its doors.

LO-5 IDENTIFY FOUR KEY *REASONS FOR SUCCESS* IN SMALL BUSINESSES AND FOUR KEY *REASONS FOR FAILURE*.

Four basic factors explain most small-business success: (1) hard work, drive, and dedication, (2) market demand for the products or services being provided, (3) managerial competence, and (4) luck. Four factors contribute to small-business failure: (1) managerial incompetence or inexperience, (2) neglect, (3) weak control systems, and (4) insufficient capital.

LO-6 DESCRIBE FOUR FORMS OF *LEGAL ORGANIZATION* FOR A BUSINESS AND DISCUSS THE ADVANTAGES AND DISADVANTAGES OF EACH.

Sole proprietorships are owned and operated by one person, are easy to set up, have low start-up costs, and get tax benefits—and their owners enjoy freedom. However, they have unlimited liability, a lack of continuity, and limited resources.

Under a general partnership, all partners have unlimited liability. Partnerships may lack continuity, and transferring ownership may be difficult. On the positive side, partnerships can grow by adding new talent and money, partners are taxed as individuals, and banks prefer to make loans to enterprises that are not dependent on one individual. All partnerships should have a partnership agreement.

Corporations are separate legal entities; they have property rights and obligations, and they have indefinite life spans. They may sue and be sued; buy, hold, and sell property; make and sell products; and commit crimes and be tried and punished for them. The biggest advantage of incorporation is limited liability. Other advantages include continuity, professional management, and improved ability to raise money by selling stock. Disadvantages of the corporation include high start-up costs, complexity, and double taxation. The vast majority of corporations are privately held. In forming a corporation, a business will incorporate federally if it is going to operate in more than one province and provincially if it is going to operate in only one province.

A co-operative is an organization that is formed to benefit its owners in the form of reduced prices and/or the distribution of surpluses at year-end. On the positive side, co-operatives are democratically controlled, enjoy limited liability and continuity, and are not subject to double taxation. The main disadvantages include difficulty in raising equity.

QUESTIONS AND EXERCISES

QUESTIONS FOR ANALYSIS

1. After considering the characteristics of entrepreneurs, do you think that you would be a good candidate to start your own business? Why or why not?
2. If you were going to open a new business, what type of business would it be? Why?
3. Which industries are easiest for a small business to enter? Which are hardest? Why?
4. Would you prefer to buy an existing business or start from scratch? Why?
5. Why might a private corporation choose to remain private? Why might it choose to "go public"?
6. Consider a new product or service that has recently become available for purchase by consumers. To what extent did this product or service possess the "screening" characteristics that are described in the chapter (adding value, providing competitive advantage, and so on)?

APPLICATION EXERCISES

7. There are thousands of mobile applications on the various mobile platforms (you probably use some of them on a weekly or daily basis). Identify an idea for a new application that can serve a consumer need that is currently unmet or can be improved upon.
8. Interview the owner/manager of a sole proprietorship or a general partnership. What characteristics of that business form led the owner to choose it? Does he or she ever plan on changing the form of the business?
9. Identify two or three of the fastest-growing businesses in Canada during the last year. What role has entrepreneurship played in the growth of these firms?
10. Although more than half of all small businesses don't survive five years, franchises have a much better track record. However, it can be difficult to buy a franchise. Research a popular food industry franchise, such as Subway, and detail the requirements for net worth and liquid cash for the franchisee as well as up-front and annual fees.

TEAM EXERCISES

BUILDING YOUR BUSINESS SKILLS

A TASTY IDEA

GOAL

To encourage you to identify options for financing a new business.

BACKGROUND INFORMATION

Suppose that you and three friends from college would like to open a new restaurant. Collectively, you have almost 20 years of experience in the restaurant industry and, with lots of new houses in the area, you think that there's an opportunity to make a lot of money if you can offer interesting food at good prices. You've even identified a great location, but you realize that it's going to take a lot of money to get this business off the ground. As recent college graduates, you don't have a lot of money, so you're looking for the best source of funding. Realistically, you realize that you're going to need at least $100 000 to sustain operations until your business starts to return a profit.

METHOD

Step 1 Individually or in a group of two or three students, brainstorm a list of options for financing. You'll want to do a little online research to find out more about some of the loan programs identified in the text.

Step 2 For each of the funding options, develop a list of pros and cons. Be sure to consider all the implications of each form of financing, considering interest rates, repayment options, and eligibility requirements.

FOLLOW-UP QUESTIONS

1. Before getting financing, what will be expected of you and your business partners?
2. Which source of financing would be best for you and your partners? Why?
3. What form of business ownership would be most appropriate for your new restaurant and why?

EXERCISING YOUR ETHICS

BREAKING UP IS HARD TO DO

THE SITUATION

Connie and Mark began a 25-year friendship after finishing college and discovering their mutual interest in owning a business. Established as a general partnership, their home-furnishings centre is a successful business that has been sustained for 20 years by a share-and-share-alike relationship. Start-up cash, daily responsibilities, and profits have all been shared equally. The partners both work four days each week except when busy seasons require both of them to be in the store. Shared goals and compatible personalities have led to a solid give-and-take relationship that helps them overcome business problems while maintaining a happy interpersonal relationship.

The division of work is a natural match and successful combination because of the partners' different but complementary interests. Mark buys the merchandise and maintains up-to-date contacts with suppliers; he also handles personnel matters (hiring and training employees). Connie manages the inventory, buys shipping supplies, keeps the books, and manages the finances. Mark does more selling, with Connie helping out only during busy seasons. Both partners share in decisions about advertising and promotions. Mark has taken a particular interest in learning the latest social media tools and has begun to implement these strategies successfully.

THE DILEMMA

Things began changing two years ago, when Connie became less interested in the business and got more involved in other activities. Whereas Mark's enthusiasm remained high, Connie's time was increasingly consumed by travel, recreation, and community-service activities. At first, she reduced her work commitment from four to three days a week. Then she indicated that she wanted to cut back further, to just two days. "In that case," Mark replied, "we'll have to make some changes."

Mark insisted that profit sharing be adjusted to reflect his larger role in running the business from the original 50-50. This was not addressed immediately; however, he also proposed that Connie's monthly salary be cut in half (from $4000 to $2000). Connie agreed. He recommended that the $2000 savings be shifted to his salary because of his increased workload, but this time Connie disagreed, arguing that Mark's current $4000 salary already compensated him for his contributions. She proposed to split the difference, with Mark getting a $1000 increase and the other $1000 going into the firm's cash account. Mark said no and insisted on a full $2000 raise. To avoid a complete falling out, Connie finally gave in, even though she thought it unfair for Mark's salary to jump from $4000 per month to $6000. At that point, she made a promise to herself: "To even things out, I'll find a way to get $2000 worth of inventory for personal use each month and I won't give in on any future profit-sharing adjustments."

TEAM ACTIVITY

Assemble a group of four students and divide the four into two pairs and answer the questions from one of the following perspectives:

- Mark's perspective
- Connie's perspective

QUESTIONS TO ADDRESS

1. Identify the ethical issues, if any, regarding Mark's and Connie's respective positions on Mark's proposed $2000 salary increase.
2. What kind of salary and profit adjustments do you think would be fair in this situation? Explain why.
3. There is another way for Mark and Connie to solve their differences—because the terms of participation have changed, it might make sense to dissolve the existing partnership. What do you recommend in this regard?

BUSINESS CASE 4

ENTREPRENEURIAL SPIRIT: BEYOND THE RACK

Beyond the Rack (BTR) was established in 2009 by two ambitious entrepreneurs named Yona Shtern and Robert Gold, along with two full-time employees. By 2015, BTR had over 13 million members (across North America) and had created working relationships with over 5000 brands. The company now operates out of offices in Montreal, Toronto, New York, and Las Vegas, and sends approximately 3 billion emails a year to its members. Like most successful teams, the two entrepreneurs possess complementary skills. Mr. Shtern is the CEO, who spends time taking care of the marketing and merchandising and actively seeks financing, while Mr. Gold is in charge of day-to-day operations.

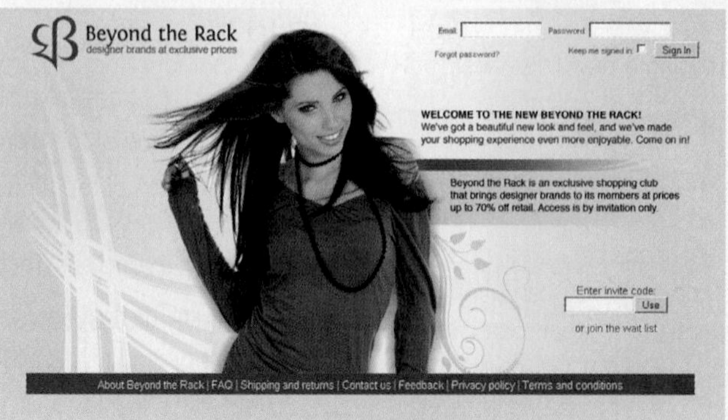

© n8n photo/Alamy

BUSINESS MODEL

The model was inspired by two highly successful European sites, Gilt and Vente-privee. BTR obtains the rights to sell authentic designer brands at major discounted prices (up to 80 percent off retail) exclusively to its members. It is a private shopping club that hosts limited-time, limited-quantity online events. Every day, members can expect up to 15 new events, usually starting at 11 a.m. Eastern Time and lasting 48 hours. Once the event is over, the merchandise is no longer available. The whole model is built on speed. BTR does not use a traditional retail approach—it does not buy large quantities of stock, ship it to its warehouse, and hope to sell it. At the prices they are offering, this approach would be unfeasible. Instead, they acquire the rights to sell a specific quantity of discounted products. Once the event is over and the members have committed to purchasing the units, BTR orders the physical quantities and then ships them to members around North America. In other words, products do not come to the premises unless member orders are placed. Beyond the Rack has created an efficient win-win-win scenario: (1) customers get designer products at great prices; (2) the designer brands have an efficient way to dispose of excess end-of-season items (from a branding point of view this approach is favourable—it's better to sell to this private club than to have expensive brands sit in cluttered racks in stores like Winners, for example); and (3) BTR earns an attractive margin as the facilitator. It's quick, it's efficient, and it's online.

FINANCING

Successful entrepreneurs need more than a good idea; they also require the willingness to take a risk and the energy to work hard, as well as access to financing. If you are opening a small mom-and-pop store, you may need to dip in to your savings or take out a loan to buy equipment and build a storefront. However, when your goals are set high, like becoming the premier online shopping club in North America, you need to be creative and you must convince individuals and organizations to provide major financing to support growth. This is exactly what Yona Shtern and his team have done. In their first six years, BTR had already managed to attract more than $75 million in financing from major investors and organizations such as BDC Venture Capital Inc., Export Development Canada, Highland Capital Partners LLC, Oleg Tscheltzoff and Oliver Jung (two European internet entrepreneurs), Montreal StartUp (a venture fund), and David Chamandy (an "angel investor").

GROWTH AND EXPANSION

In only its second year of operation, BTR acquired selected assets of New York–based BeautyStory.com. This move added to the solid base of members (a key figure for BTR's growth and bargaining power) and strengthened the already successful beauty division. This was yet another important milestone in its brief history. However, as companies grow and structures are put in place, the entrepreneurial spirit of an organization runs the risk of being smothered by bureaucracy. Its trademark creativity, flexibility, and passion will be necessary for BTR to sustain its spirit and continue to grow in the dynamic online world. The team at BTR spirit of the organization. For example, each month all employees, regardless of their official position, spend some time completing orders in the fulfillment centre. The core message of this approach: "You may be a marketer or an accountant but without these orders and the ultimate satisfaction of the end consumer, there is no business. Never forget who we are."

THE FUTURE

In the next few years, Beyond the Rack will surely experience new challenges and will need to secure additional financing to reach its objectives. Despite BTR's 13 million members the company has yet to make a profit. While it is true that many internet (and most social media) companies have taken years before becoming profitable (e.g., Facebook) it is still the most important long-term metric. In addition, initial success inevitably brings more competition which further complicate matters. For example, Amazon launched MyHabit.com a couple of years ago to compete with companies like Gilt and BTR. What does the future hold for Beyond the Rack? That is unclear. However, the brief history of the firm is impressive. For these internet entrepreneurs, future success, as is the case for more traditional companies, will be based on their ability to satisfy the needs of their brand suppliers and consumers alike, and of course, eventually generate substantial profits for themselves and for all of the investors that have backed them financially and shown faith in the concept.

QUESTIONS FOR DISCUSSION

1. Entrepreneurs are vital for the success of a free-market economy. Highlight the entrepreneurial process and describe some of the key entrepreneurial characteristics as they relate to this case.
2. Describe some of the major challenges that the entrepreneurs behind Beyond the Rack face.
3. What does this case reveal about the importance of financing a successful growth-oriented start-up business?

Rawpixel/Fotolia

LO

AFTER READING THIS CHAPTER, YOU SHOULD BE ABLE TO:

LO-1 Describe the growing complexity in the *global business environment* and identify the *major world marketplaces*.

LO-2 Identify the evolving role of *emerging markets* and highlight the importance of the *BRICS nations*.

LO-3 Explain how different forms of *competitive advantage*, *import–export balances*, *exchange rates*, and *foreign competition* determine how countries and businesses respond to the international environment.

LO-4 Discuss the factors involved in conducting business internationally and in selecting the appropriate levels of *international involvement* and *organizational structure*.

LO-5 Describe some of the ways in which *social*, *cultural*, *economic*, *legal*, *and political differences* act as barriers to international trade.

LO-6 Explain how *free trade agreements* assist world trade.

Not My Cup of Tea

China is famous for its love of tea. Over thousands of years, tea has been the beverage of choice. This, however, did not deter Starbucks from entering one of the fastest-growing consumer markets in the world. The company's global expansion actually began when Starbucks opened its first store outside the United States in Vancouver back in 1987. Today there are over 21 000 locations in 66 countries, including more than 7000 in the United States and over 1000 in Canada.

Winning over customers in Canada, with a recipe that works in the United States, is a bit easier than winning over diverse global consumers. Starbucks has clearly managed to learn a few lessons along the way and understands the process better than most. Starbucks opened in Taipei, Taiwan, in 1998 and the first mainland store was opened in Beijing in 1999. By 2015 there were over 1500 locations in 90 Chinese cities and over 25 000 employees in the country.

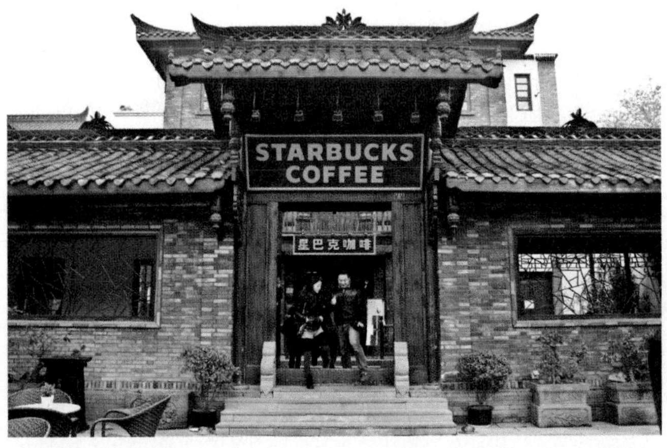

Starbucks has made a name for itself in China and the company is integrating into the Chinese landscape.

Guo qichang/Imaginechina/AP Images

Starbucks analyzed the Chinese market and found that their brand was valued, not only for their food and beverage offerings, but also for the atmosphere. Chinese consumers enjoyed the opportunity to meet with friends and business

The Global Context *of* Business

CHAPTER 05

partners in a comfortable location and appreciated the upbeat music and sleek interiors. While kiosks have become popular in the United States and Canada, some Chinese Starbucks locations are as large as 350 square metres.

Starbucks has customized its product offerings by introducing products like the Green Tea Frappuccino® Blended Crème. However, not all Chinese consumers are fans. Cheng Xiaochen, an English teacher who likes to meet students at Starbucks, exclaims, "It's a good place to meet people, but the coffee is so bitter it tastes like Chinese medicine." Responding to Mr. Cheng and others like him, the company offers mint hot chocolate and red bean Frappuccino. Food offerings have also been customized to the Chinese market, with Hainan chicken sandwiches and rice wraps.

Starbucks is constantly looking to uncover needs and adapt to local tastes. It recently partnered with Tingyi Holdings (China's #2 soft-drink seller) to manufacture and distribute ready-to-go drinks. Tingyi has an existing, highly developed distribution network that can reach across the entire nation (rural and urban). In addition, Tingyi provides real insights into local consumer tastes.

Starbucks acknowledges that employees are at the centre of its success and makes a considerable investment in training, developing, and retaining these employees. However, it faced a challenge in an achievement-oriented Chinese culture, where parents aspire for their children to take jobs in traditionally successful fields such as financial services and banking. In response, it launched a family forum, which provided stories from managers who have worked their way up the career ladder with the company.

Starbucks has worked to extend every component of its corporate culture into its expansion. The company has brought its long tradition of community involvement to China. Through a $5 million grant to the Starbucks China Education Project, it aims to give students and teachers in rural areas more access to clean drinking water, and provide relief from natural disasters like the Sichaun earthquake. Starbucks has demonstrated that long-term commitment and sensitivity to international market conditions are the keys to success.

Finally, the lessons learned around the world inspire new products and new opportunities back home. A few years ago, Starbucks bought the Teavana retail brand along with their 300 retail stores for over US$600 million. Currently, the brand has locations only in the United States, Canada, and Mexico; but for the next few years, it at least has an asset to battle growing local North American tea brands (like David's Tea here).

HOW WILL THIS HELP ME?

As we will see in this chapter, global forces—business as well as political—affect each and every one of us daily. As you begin your business career, regardless of whether you see yourself living abroad, working for a big company, or starting your own business, the global economy will affect you in a variety of ways. Exchange rates for different currencies and global markets for buying and selling are all of major importance to everyone, regardless of their role or perspective. As a result, this chapter will better enable you to (1) understand how global forces affect you as a customer, (2) understand how globalization affects you as an employee, and (3) assess how global opportunities and challenges can affect you as a business owner and as an investor. You will also gain insight into how wages and working conditions in different regions are linked to what we buy and the prices we pay.

We begin with an exploration of the major world marketplaces and trade agreements that affect international business. We will examine some of the social, cultural, economic, legal, and political factors that affect international business. We will highlight several factors that help determine how countries and businesses respond to international opportunities and challenges. We will also describe some of the decisions managers must make if they intend to compete effectively in international markets.

Mocker bat/Fotolia

Can Starbucks sell the Teavana brand in China? You can bet that at some point they will try, but first they might want to build the brand name closer to home.

QUESTIONS FOR DISCUSSION

1. What motivates companies like Starbucks to expand into international markets with little perceived interest for their product?
2. How has Starbucks adapted to Chinese culture?
3. Are you concerned that Starbucks' expansion into China threatens their traditional culture? Why or why not?
4. If China wished to slow Starbucks' expansion, what legal barriers would be most helpful? How would these barriers affect Chinese consumers and businesses?

THE CONTEMPORARY GLOBAL ECONOMY

The total volume of world trade is immense—nearly $19 trillion in merchandise trade each year.[1] The world economy is increasingly transforming into a single, interdependent system in a process called **globalization**.

Even so, we often take for granted the diversity of goods and services available as a result of international trade. Your tablet, smartphone, clothing, and even the roast lamb on your dinner table may all be **imports**—that is, products made or grown abroad, but sold in Canada. At the same time, the success of many Canadian firms depends on **exports**—products made or grown domestically and shipped abroad.

Major companies like McDonald's, Apple, and Bombardier have found international markets to be a fruitful area for growth. But firms sometime stumble when they try to expand abroad. Home Depot closed most of the stores it opened in China, for example, because labour costs are so low there few homeowners are interested in do-it-yourself projects. Similarly, Best Buy closed its stores in China because consumers there tend to buy their electronics goods at lower prices from local or online merchants.[2]

And the impact of globalization doesn't stop with firms looking to open locations abroad or having to close locations that fail. Small firms with no international operations (such as an independent coffee shop) may still buy from international suppliers, and even individual contractors or self-employed people can be affected by fluctuations in exchange rates.

International trade has become increasingly central to the fortunes of most nations of the world, as well as businesses. In the past, many nations followed strict policies to protect domestic companies, while today most countries are aggressively encouraging international trade. They are opening their borders to foreign businesses, offering incentives for their own domestic businesses to expand internationally, and making it easier for foreign firms to partner with local firms through various alliances. Today, it is not simply a question of Western nations pushing trade abroad. China is making major inroads and increasing its economic and political influence in Africa with major deals with Nigeria, South Africa, Ethiopia, and Zambia. China is now the largest trading partner in the region with trade totalling more than $114 billion, just ahead of the United States.[3] It also took the title from Germany as the world's top merchandise exporter a few years ago with total exports of over $2 trillion annually.[4]

GLOBALIZATION Process by which the world economy is becoming a single interdependent system.

IMPORT Product made or grown abroad but sold domestically.

EXPORT Product made or grown domestically but shipped and sold abroad.

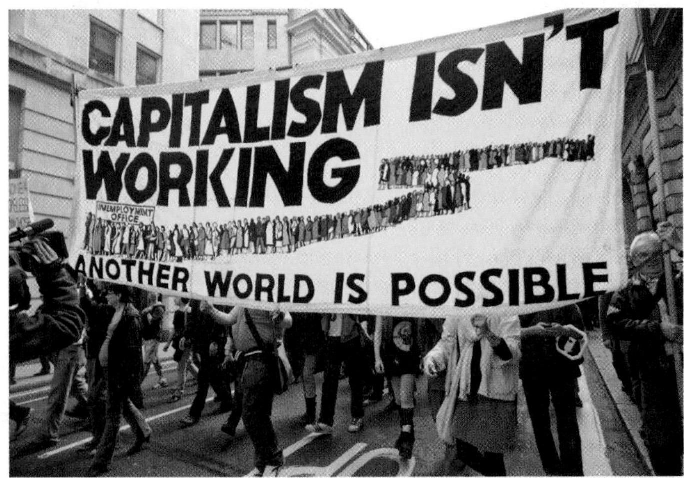

Some globalization protestors fear multinational companies will wipe out small domestic businesses and prioritize profits over fair wages and human rights.

Peter Marshall/Alamy

Several forces have combined to spark and sustain globalization. For one thing, governments and businesses have simply become more aware of the benefits of globalization to their countries and stockholders. For another, new technologies have made travel, communication, and commerce easier, faster, and cheaper. The cost of overseas phone calls and seaborne shipping costs per tonne have both declined sharply over the past several decades. Likewise, transatlantic travel takes only a few hours by air. The internet has torn down barriers for large and small companies. Finally, there are competitive pressures; sometimes a firm simply must enter foreign markets just to keep up with its competitors.

Globalization has critics who claim that businesses exploit workers in less-developed countries and avoid domestic environmental and tax regulations. They also charge that globalization leads to the loss of cultural heritage and benefits the rich more than the poor. As a result, many international gatherings of global economic leaders (such as the G8 and G20) have been marked by protests. But despite fears, globalization is part of our evolving existence.

LO-1 The Major World Marketplaces

Managers involved with international businesses need to have a solid understanding of the global economy, including the major world marketplaces. This section examines some fundamental economic distinctions between countries based on wealth and then looks at some of the world's major international marketplaces.

DISTINCTIONS BASED ON WEALTH

The World Bank, an agency of the United Nations, uses *per-capita income*, average income per person, to make distinctions among countries. Its current classification method consists of four different categories of countries:[5]

1. *High-income countries.* Annual per-capita income greater than US$12 746. They include Canada, the United States, most countries in Europe, Australia, Japan, South Korea, Israel, Kuwait, the United Arab Emirates, and Oman.
2. *Upper-middle-income countries.* Annual per-capita income between US$4126 and US$12 745. This group includes China, Colombia, Lebanon, Turkey, Argentina, and South Africa.
3. *Low-middle-income countries.* Annual per-capita income between US$1046 and US$4125. This group includes Ukraine, Philippines, Armenia, Guatemala, and Vietnam.
4. *Low-income countries* (often called *developing countries*). Annual per-capita income of US$1045 or less. Malawi, Bangladesh, Haiti, and Afghanistan are among the countries in this group. Due to low literacy rates, weak infrastructures, unstable governments, and related problems, these countries are less attractive for international business.

GEOGRAPHIC CLUSTERS

The world economy is evolving quickly with emerging markets playing an ever-increasing role. However, it still revolves greatly around three major marketplaces: North America, Europe, and Asia. These clusters include relatively more of the upper-middle-income and high-income nations, but relatively few low-income and low-middle-income countries. For instance, because Africa consists primarily of low-income and low-middle-income countries, it is not generally seen as a major marketplace. The three key geographic regions are home to most of the world's largest economies, biggest corporations, influential financial markets, and highest-income consumers.

North America The United States dominates the North American business region. It is the single largest national marketplace and has been the most stable economy in the world for decades, but the U.S has major problems due to many issues (e.g., a huge increase in the nation's debt load). Canada also plays a major role in the global economy. Moreover, the United States and Canada are each other's largest trading partners. Many U.S. firms, such as General Motors and Procter & Gamble, have maintained successful Canadian operations for decades, and many Canadian firms, such as Scotiabank, are also major international competitors.

Mexico has become a major manufacturing centre, especially along the U.S. border, where cheap labour and low transportation costs have encouraged many firms from the United States and other countries to build factories. The auto industry has been very active, with Daimler, General Motors, Volkswagen, Nissan, and Ford all running large assembly plants, and major suppliers have also built facilities in the region. But Mexico's role as a low-cost manufacturing hub has been threatened as some companies have shifted production to China instead.[6]

Europe Europe was traditionally divided into two regions—Western and Eastern. Western Europe, dominated by Germany, the United Kingdom, France, Spain, and Italy, has long been a mature but fragmented marketplace. But the transformation of this region, via the European Union (EU) (discussed later in this chapter), into an integrated economic system has further increased its importance. Major international firms such as Unilever, Renault, Royal Dutch Shell, Michelin, Siemens, and Nestlé are headquartered in Western Europe. Eastern Europe, once primarily communist, has also gained importance, both as a marketplace and as a producer. Multinational corporations such as Nestlé and General Motors have set up operations in Poland. Ford, General Motors, and Volkswagen have built new factories in Hungary. However, governmental instability has slowed development in Bulgaria, Albania, Romania, and other nations.

In recent years, the traditional view of Europe has been severely altered by the European Union, the common currency, and a clear divide between Northern Europe (led by Germany, the Netherlands, and, to a lesser extent, France) and Southern Europe (including Spain, Italy, Greece, and Portugal).

Asia Pacific Asia Pacific consists of Japan, China, Thailand, Malaysia, Singapore, Indonesia, South Korea, Taiwan, the Philippines, Vietnam, and Australia (which is technically not in Asia, but is included because of proximity). Fuelled by strong entries in the automobile, electronics, and banking industries, the economies of these countries have grown rapidly in the past three decades.

As the trends indicate, Asia Pacific is a growing force in the world economy. The Japanese dominate the region through firms like Toyota, Toshiba, and Nippon Steel. However, South Korea (Samsung and Hyundai), Taiwan (China National Petroleum Corporation and manufacturing for foreign firms), and Hong Kong (a major financial centre) are also successful players in the global economy. China, the world's most densely populated country, has emerged as an important market and now boasts the world's second-largest economy behind that of the United States, after recently surpassing Japan.[7] In all three key regions, technology is playing an increasingly important role.

LO-2 Emerging Markets: BRICS and Beyond

The term *BRIC* denotes a group of four increasingly important nations in global trade: Brazil, Russia, India, and China. The BRIC concept was first used by Goldman Sachs in 2001; since that time, BRIC investment funds have become an important group for money managers and international analysts. These four nations have begun to act like a unit, holding unofficial summits and discussing common strategies.

The status of these four nations has risen in international trade for different reasons. Brazil is strong in commodities and agriculture, Russia is a powerful energy supplier, and China is a major hub of manufacturing activity. India has become a leading service provider at various levels ranging from basic customer service call centres to engineering solutions providers. The growth and quick market development of the consumer market in these nations is also providing great

<<< **The BRICS nations are a force to be respected in the modern global economy.**

Baur/Shutterstock

sales opportunities for foreign companies that manufacture cars and high-end clothing brands, etc.[8]

The old international trading patterns and activities are changing. In the past, Western companies used less-developed markets to acquire natural resources supplies and to carry out simple assembly tasks. But the BRIC nations now demonstrate relationships that are much more complex. A clear signal of this shift was evident a few years ago when Indian carmaker Tata acquired Jaguar and Land Rover from Ford. This was not quite business as usual in the traditional sense.[9]

A few years ago, the initial group of four extended an invitation to South Africa to form a group called **BRICS**. The move was surprising to many analysts, because there seemed to better candidates for admission. However, it was clear that the informal group was developing into an important political club with its own goals. South Africa is rich in minerals and other resources, something that these emerging markets need to sustain growth. In addition, the new member, with over a billion potential consumers, serves as a gateway to the African continent.[10]

In an even stronger sign of the changing times, a formal BRICS meeting was held in Durban, South Africa, to negotiate a $100 billion reserve fund to protect their currencies and a $50 billion seed-capital plan (i.e., to promote new businesses). In addition, they negotiated details for the creation of a development bank to compete with the World Bank. Emerging economies are clearly not relying on "old world" economies, and the BRICS nations clearly have their own, independent agenda. The New Development Bank (as it is called) will be based in China with the first regional office in South Africa. The first chair of the board of Governors will be Russian and the first chair of the board of directors will be from India.[11]

BRICS A term denoting a group of five important and powerful emerging markets in the business world: Brazil, Russia, India, China, and South Africa.

While the BRICS nations have received a lot of publicity, there are tremendous opportunities in other emerging nations, including Thailand, Indonesia, South Korea, and Ukraine, to name just a few. According to the Global Institute of Research, the opportunity in emerging markets amounts to annual projected consumption of $30 trillion by 2025.[12] A new world order is evolving, and "old" economic powers like the United States, Japan, Germany, and even Canada are going to need to adapt.

LO-3 Forms of Competitive Advantage

No country can produce all the goods and services its people need. Thus, countries export products they can make more efficiently or cheaper than other countries. The proceeds are then used to import products they cannot produce effectively. However, this principle does not fully explain why nations export and import. Such decisions depend on the kinds of advantages a particular country may enjoy regarding its abilities to create and/or sell various products and resources.[13] Traditionally, economists have focused on absolute and comparative advantage to explain international trade. But because this approach focuses narrowly on such factors as natural resources and labour costs, the more contemporary view of national competitive advantage has emerged.

^^ **The establishment of the New Development bank is a clear sign of the times and the emerging BRICS nations have announced their ever-growing influential role in world economics.**

ITAR-TASS Photo Agency/Alamy Stock Photo

ABSOLUTE ADVANTAGE

An **absolute advantage** exists when a country can produce something more efficiently than any other country—in other words, if it can produce a larger output of goods or services using the same or fewer input resources. The concept was first proposed by economist Adam Smith in 1776. Saudi oil, Brazilian coffee beans, and Canadian timber approximate absolute advantage. The theory is simple; countries should focus on producing goods and services that they have an absolute advantage in and buy products that they do not produce more efficiently than other nations.[14] Canada exports timber because of its natural strengths, and imports bananas because the climate here does not permit farmers to grow bananas efficiently. If trade were limited to two countries, you might negotiate which nation should produce which items for the greater good. However, the global economy is a complex network and most decisions are not that simple. In addition, true absolute advantage is very rare; the vast majority are actually relative.

COMPARATIVE ADVANTAGE

A country has a **comparative advantage** in goods that it can produce more efficiently or better than other goods. For example, if businesses in a given country can make computers more efficiently than they can make automobiles, that nation's firms have a comparative advantage in computer manufacturing. Canada has a comparative advantage in farming (because of fertile land and a temperate climate), while South Korea has a comparative advantage in electronics manufacturing (because of efficient operations and cheap labour). As a result, Canadian firms export grain to South Korea and import electronic equipment from South Korea. All countries have a comparative advantage in some products, but no country has a comparative advantage in all products.

Developed countries tend to have a comparative advantage in making high-tech products, while developing countries tend to have a comparative advantage in making products that require lots of low-cost labour. For example, in the past two decades, most of the textile manufacturing jobs in Canada (and elsewhere) have moved to China. But the race to the bottom (in terms of labour costs) now sees countries like Cambodia, Bangladesh, and Vietnam taking manufacturing jobs away from China. Why? In Cambodia, textile workers are paid $76 for a 60-hour week, while in China the wages range from $280 to $460. In other words, Cambodia is just like China was 20 years ago—bad news for Chinese manufacturing.[15]

This race to the lowest cost has not come without consequences. In 2013, a building that housed garment manufacturers in Bangladesh collapsed suddenly, killing over 1000 people. A year later, Bangladesh was still producing more than US$22 billion in garment exports, but many of the companies (like H&M) that they supplied were asking new safety questions. An international group inspected and found flaws in over 1000 additional garment plants. Seventeen of those plants were shut down and major repairs were completed on more than 100.[16]

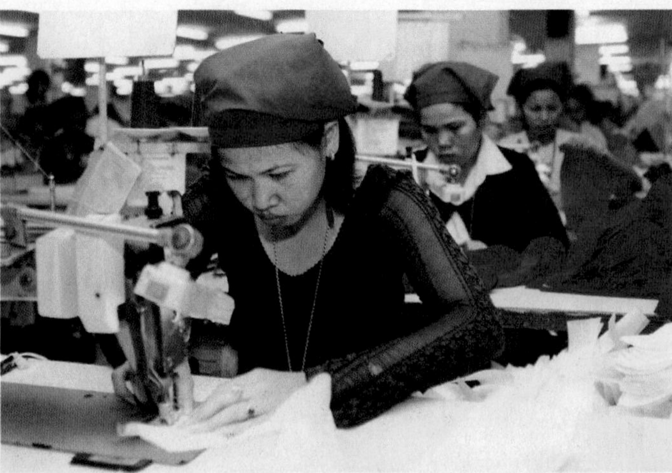

Chinese textile workers are learning what North American textile workers learned years ago. Manufacturers are increasingly moving textile manufacturing to lower-cost locations like Cambodia, where workers (like the ones seen in this photo) earn on average $76 for a 60-hour week as opposed to $280–$460 in China.

Khem SOVANNARA/Newscom

NATIONAL COMPETITIVE ADVANTAGE

In more recent years, the theory of national competitive advantage has become a more widely accepted model of why nations engage in international trade.[17] **National competitive advantage** is based on four conditions:

1. *Factor conditions* are the factors of production that we identified in Chapter 1 (labour, capital, entrepreneurs, natural resources, and information).
2. *Demand conditions* reflect a large domestic consumer base that promotes strong demand for innovative products.
3. *Related and supporting industries* include strong local or regional suppliers and/or industrial customers.
4. *Strategies, structures, and rivalries* refer to firms and industries that stress cost reduction, product quality, higher productivity, and innovative new products.

When all of these conditions exist in an industry, the companies in that industry are motivated to be very innovative and to excel. This also increases the likelihood that they will engage in international business. Japan, for instance, has strong domestic demand for automobiles. Its automobile producers have well-developed supplier networks, and Japanese firms have competed intensely with each other for decades. This set of circumstances explains why Japanese automobile companies such as Toyota, Honda, Nissan, and Mazda are generally successful in foreign markets.

International competitiveness refers to the ability of a country to generate more wealth than its competitors in world markets. Every year, the World Economic Forum publishes a global competitiveness ranking. The ranking is based on both hard economic data and a poll of business leaders. In 2015, the top three countries on the list were Switzerland, Singapore, and the United States. Canada ranked 15th; its high taxes, regulated industries, relatively large bureaucracy, and overly conservative capital market structure were listed as reasons for a lower rating.[18]

ABSOLUTE ADVANTAGE The ability to produce something more efficiently than any other country.

COMPARATIVE ADVANTAGE The ability to produce some products more efficiently than others.

NATIONAL COMPETITIVE ADVANTAGE International competitive advantage stemming from a combination of factor conditions; demand conditions; related and supporting industries; and firm strategies, structures, and rivalries.

INTERNATIONAL COMPETITIVENESS Competitive marketing of domestic products against foreign products.

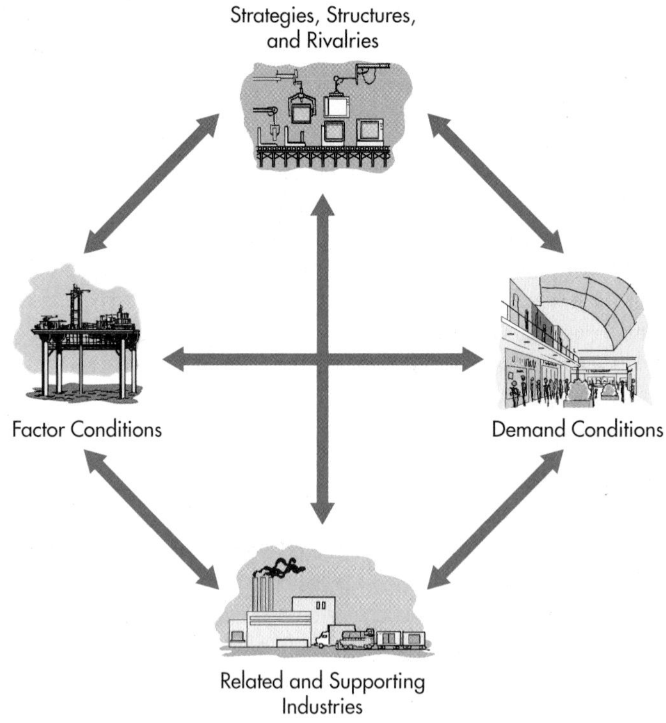

FIGURE 5.1 Attributes of national competitive advantage

TABLE 5.1 Canadian Balance of Trade (Total + Selected Country Breakdown), 2014[20]

Country	Exports to ($billions)	Imports from ($billions)	Balance of Trade (Surplus or Deficit)
United States	$400	$350.7	+$49.3
European Union	$40.5	$49.3	−$8.8
China	$20.6	$35.6	−$15
Mexico	$6.8	$17.2	−$10.4
Japan	$11.1	$9.2	−$1.9
All others	$49.8	$62.2	−$12.4
Total	**$528.8**	**$524.2**	**+$4.6**

The Balance of Trade

A country's **balance of trade** is the difference in value between its total exports and its total imports. A country that exports more than it imports has a favourable balance of trade, or a **surplus**. A country that imports more than it exports has an unfavourable balance of trade, or a **deficit**. In 2014 Canada had a trade surplus of $4.6 billion. As you can see from Table 5.1 the main reason for surplus is the trading relationship with the United States. Canada exports more to the United States than it imports from it. For years, economists had warned against Canada's dependence on the United States. A few years ago, this was clearly proven when the Canadian dollar rose sharply (and actually surpassed the U.S. dollar); Canada's nearly $47 billion surplus in 2008 turned into a deficit because of a major decline in exports to the United States. Deficits were also registered in 2009, 2010, 2012, and 2013. It was no coincidence that the trade deficit returned to a surplus in 2014 when the Canadian dollar fell from near-parity to the $0.80 cent range that year.[19]

The Balance of Payments

Even if a country has a favourable balance of trade, it can still have an unfavourable balance of payments. A country's **balance of payments** is the difference between money flowing into the country and money flowing out as a result of trade and other transactions. An unfavourable balance means more money is flowing out than in. For Canada to have a favourable balance of payments for a given year, the total of our exports, foreign-tourist spending in this country, foreign investments here, and earnings from overseas investments must be greater than the total of our imports, Canadian-tourist spending overseas, our foreign aid grants, our military spending abroad, the investments made by Canadian firms abroad, and the earnings of foreigners from their investments in this country. Canada has had an unfavourable balance of payments for the past two decades; in 2014, it amounted to $44 billion.[21]

Exchange Rates

An **exchange rate** is the rate at which the currency of one nation can be exchanged for another.[22] For example, if the exchange rate between

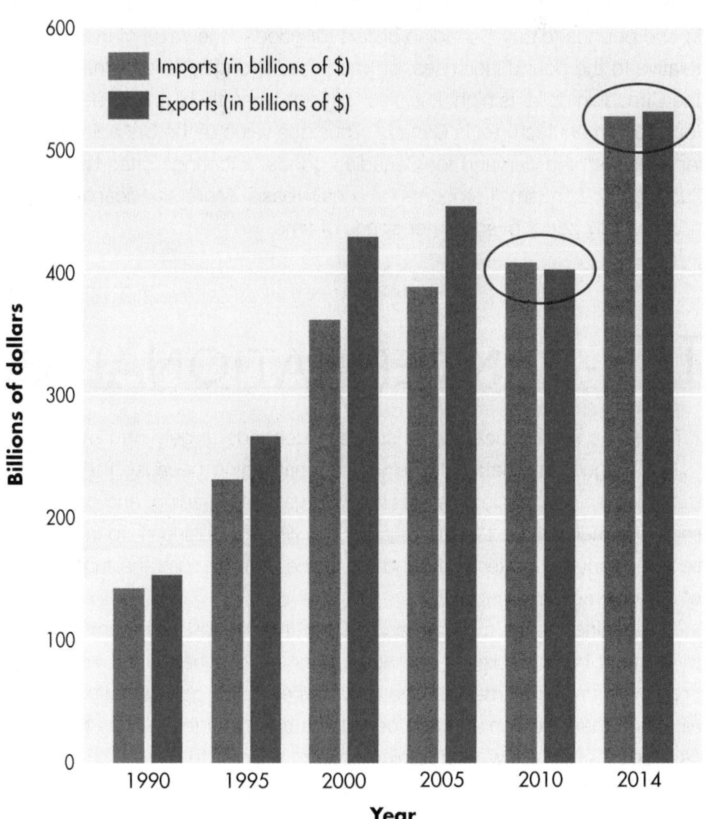

FIGURE 5.2 Canadian imports and exports of merchandise

BALANCE OF TRADE The economic value of all the products that a country exports minus the economic value of all the products it imports.

SURPLUS Situation in which a country exports more than it imports, creating a favourable balance of trade.

DEFICIT Situation in which a country's imports exceed its exports, creating a negative balance of trade.

BALANCE OF PAYMENTS Flow of all money into or out of a country.

EXCHANGE RATE Rate at which the currency of one nation can be exchanged for the currency of another nation.

THERE'S AN APP FOR THAT!

APP DETAILS	PLATFORMS
1. **XE Currency App** **Source:** XE.COM Inc. **Key Features:** Allows you to access live rates for every currency in the world.	Apple, Android, BlackBerry, Windows
2. **Business Anywhere APK** **Source:** Lothar Katz **Key Features:** Provides information for countries around the world: current time, up-to-date exchange rates, weather information, business competitiveness and labour data, and much more.	Apple, Android, BlackBerry, Windows
3. **International Business Guide** **Source:** Avant Web Solutions **Key Features:** Offers up-to-date information and economic profile of the hottest upcoming investment destinations and comprehensive insight into trading, investment opportunities, and current business climate (with a focus on Eurasia).	Apple, Android

APP DISCOVERY EXERCISE

Since app availability changes, conduct your own search for the "Top Three" global business apps and identify the key features.

Canadian dollars and British pounds is 1 to 1.85, this means that it costs $1.85 in Canadian dollars to "buy" one British pound. Alternatively, it would cost only 0.54 of a British pound to "buy" one Canadian dollar. This exchange rate means that 0.54 of a British pound and one Canadian dollar should have exactly the same purchasing power.

The value of one country's currency relative to another varies with market conditions. For example, when many English citizens want to spend pounds to buy Canadian dollars (or goods), the value of the dollar relative to the pound increases, or becomes "stronger," and demand for the Canadian dollar is high. It is also "strong" when there is high demand for goods manufactured in Canada. Thus, the value of the Canadian dollar rises with the demand for Canadian goods. Exchange rates typically fluctuate by very small amounts on a daily basis. More significant variations usually occur over greater spans of time.

One of the most significant developments in foreign exchange has been the introduction of the **euro**—a common currency among 18 members of the European Union (Denmark, Sweden, and the United Kingdom and other EU members do not participate). The euro was officially introduced back in 2002. It quickly became as important as the U.S. dollar and the Japanese yen in international commerce. The euro rose in value against the U.S. and Canadian dollars and stood as high as $1.73 against the Canadian dollar in 2008; however, there was a sharp drop when the European crisis began in 2010, and it has dropped to as low as $1.25. It was valued at around $1.45 in late 2015. The primary reason for the initial drop was the economic instability that raised concern about the long-term survival of the currency.

EXCHANGE RATES AND COMPETITION

Companies that conduct international operations must watch exchange-rate fluctuations closely, because these changes affect overseas demand for their products and can be a major factor in international competition. In general, when the value of a country's domestic currency rises—becomes "stronger"—companies based there find it harder to export products to foreign markets and it is easier for foreign companies to enter local markets. It also makes it more cost-efficient for domestic companies to move production operations to lower-cost sites in foreign countries. When the value of a country's currency declines—becomes "weaker"—just the opposite patterns occur. Thus, as the value of a country's currency falls, its balance of trade should improve because domestic companies should experience a boost in exports. There should also be a corresponding decrease in the incentives for foreign companies to ship products into the domestic market.

These dollar fluctuations have also had a huge impact on businesses. Canadian companies find it harder to compete internationally when the dollar rises (because Canadian products become more expensive in foreign currencies). However, on the flip side, companies, like Nova Scotia–based High Liner Foods (which buys most of its raw fish on the world markets in U.S. dollars) sees a net benefit from a stronger Canadian dollar.[23]

EURO A common currency shared among most of the members of the European Union.

LO-4 INTERNATIONAL BUSINESS MANAGEMENT

Wherever a firm is located, its success depends largely on how well it is managed. International business is challenging because the basic management responsibilities—planning, organizing, leading, and controlling—are much more difficult to carry out when a business operates in several markets scattered around the globe. (We discuss the functions of management in Chapter 6.)

Managing means making decisions. In this section, we examine the three most basic decisions managers must make when faced with the prospect of a global market. The first is whether to "go international" at all. Often that decision is made because a company feels it has to shift its production to a low-cost foreign country in order to remain competitive. Once that decision has been made, managers must decide on the company's level of international involvement and on the organizational structure that will best meet its global needs.

Going International

The world economy is slowly transforming into one large global village. As Figure 5.3 shows, several factors enter into the decision to go international. One overriding factor is the business climate in other nations. Even experienced firms have encountered cultural, legal, and economic roadblocks, as we shall see later in this chapter. In considering international expansion, a company should also consider at least two other questions: Is there a demand for its products abroad? If so, do those products have to be adapted for international consumption?

GAUGING INTERNATIONAL DEMAND

Products seen as vital in one country may be useless in another. Snowmobiles are popular for transportation and recreation in Canada

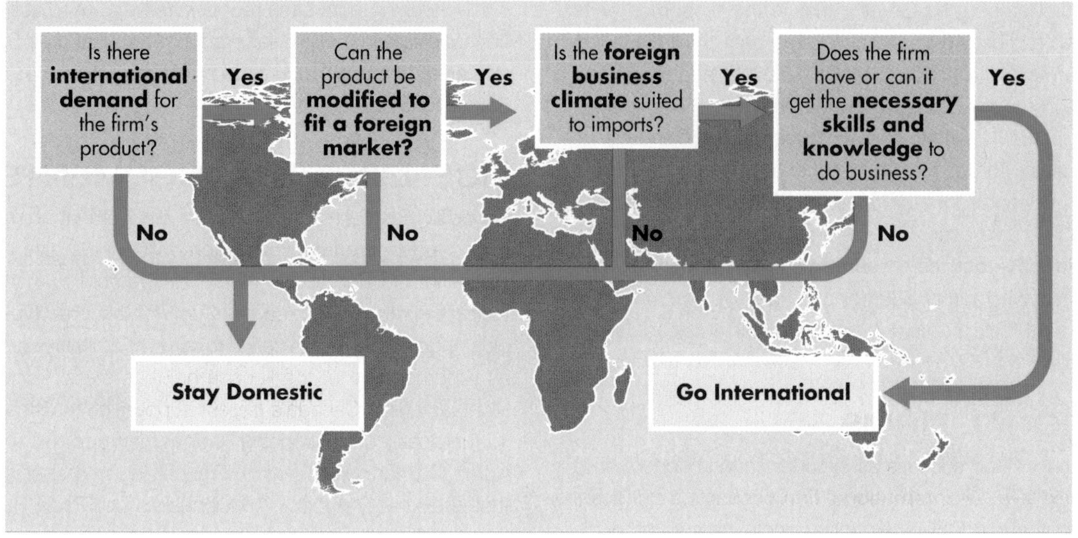

<<< **FIGURE 5.3** Going international

and the northern United States, but there would be no demand at all for them in Central America. Although this is an extreme example, the point is quite basic to the decision to go international. Specifically, foreign demand for a company's product may be greater than, the same as, or weaker than domestic demand. Even when there is demand, advertising may still need to be adjusted. For instance, in Canada, bicycles and small motorcycles are mainly used for recreation, but in many parts of Asia they are seen as transportation. Market research and/or the prior market entry of competitors may indicate whether there is an international demand for a firm's products.

Some products—like smartphones, Hollywood movies, and video games—are popular all over the world. Movies like *The Hunger Games* and *The Avengers* earn significant revenues in North America, but generate even more revenues overseas.

ADAPTING TO CUSTOMER NEEDS

If there is international demand for its product, a firm must still figure out whether to adapt the product. If they decide to do so, they must figure out how to change the product to meet the special demands and expectations of foreign customers. For example, New Brunswick–based McCain Foods Limited has worked hard to build market share in South Africa. It even developed single-sized portions of frozen vegetables to serve customers that do not have proper refrigeration.[24] KFC's dishes in China come with a side order of rice and hot soy milk.[25] They must be doing something right, because, at last count, the company had over 4800 outlets in China.[26] Likewise, McDonald's restaurants sell beer in Germany and meatless sandwiches in India to accommodate local tastes and preferences.

Levels of Involvement in International Business

After a firm decides to go international, it must decide on the level of its international involvement. Several options are available. At the most basic level, it may act as an exporter or importer, organize as an international firm, or operate as a multinational firm. Most of the world's largest industrial firms are multinationals.

EXPORTERS AND IMPORTERS

An **exporter** is a firm that makes products in one country and then distributes and sells them in others. An **importer** buys products in foreign markets and then imports them for resale in its home country. These approaches represent the lowest level of involvement in international operations and are excellent ways to learn the fine points of global business. Exporters and importers tend to conduct most of their business in their home nations. It is not just large companies that are exporting; small firms also export products and services.

EXPORTER Firm that distributes and sells products to one or more foreign countries.

IMPORTER Firm that buys products in foreign markets and then imports them for resale in its home country.

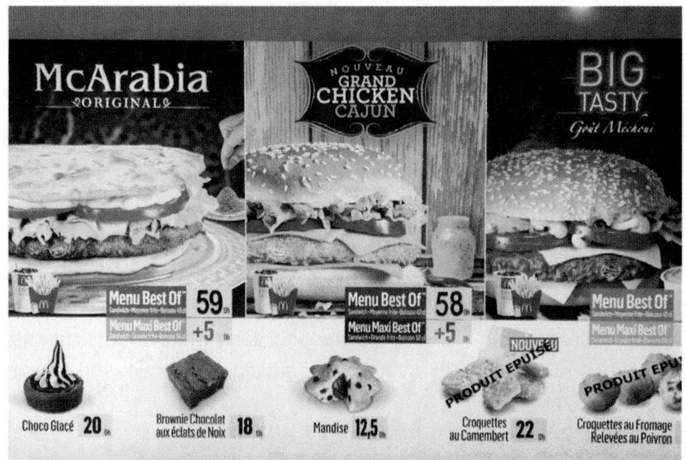

^ McDonald's adapts their menu offerings in different regions of the world to address unique tastes and expectations and to better satisfy their consumers.

Bill Bachmann/Alamy Stock Photo

Canada ranks first among the G8 countries in the proportion of its production exported (almost 40 percent).[27] Large and small Canadian firms export products and services. McCain Foods began in New Brunswick, but the company has a worldwide presence. For example, McCain holds a 75 percent market share for "oven fries" in Germany.

On a smaller scale, Target Marine Hatcheries, based in Sechelt, British Columbia, is Canada's lone producer of certified-organic farmed sturgeon. Their tanks have over 200 000 Fraser River sturgeon, and the company can produce between 1 and 2 tonnes of caviar per year. The product retails anywhere from $88 (for a 30 gram tin) to $4320 (for a 1.8 kilogram tin) and they are sold to clients as far away as Japan, Europe, and Australia.[28]

INTERNATIONAL FIRMS

As firms gain experience and success as exporters and importers, they may move to the next level. An **international firm** conducts a significant portion of its business abroad. Hershey, for example, sells its products in 90 foreign countries, and it buys ingredients for its chocolates from several foreign suppliers. But it manufactures the vast majority of its products in the United States (there is one plant in Mexico). In fact, most of that manufacturing occurs in Pennsylvania.[29] So an international firm may be large and influential in the global economy, but remain basically a domestic firm with international operations. Its central concern is its own domestic market.

MULTINATIONAL FIRMS

Most **multinational firms** do not think of themselves as having domestic and international divisions. Instead, planning and decision making are geared toward global markets.[30] The locations of headquarters are almost irrelevant. Royal Dutch Shell, Nestlé, IBM, and Ford are well-known multinationals.

The economic importance of multinational firms should not be underestimated. Consider the economic impact of the 500 largest multinational corporations: they employ millions of people; buy supplies, parts, equipment, and materials from thousands of other firms; and pay billions of dollars in taxes. Moreover, their activities and products affect the lives of hundreds of millions of consumers, competitors, and investors (sometimes not in a very positive way). Organized protests against the activities of multinational corporations have become quite common. In 2014, Walmart ranked first in the Fortune 500 Global rankings of multinationals with $476 billion in revenues.[31]

International Organizational Structures

Different levels of involvement in international business require different kinds of organizational structure. For example, a structure that would help coordinate an exporter's activities would be inadequate for the activities of a multinational firm. In this section, we briefly consider the international organizational strategies, including independent agents, licensing arrangements, branch offices, strategic alliances, and foreign direct investment.

INDEPENDENT AGENTS

An **independent agent** is a foreign individual or organization that agrees to represent an exporter's interests in foreign markets. Independent agents often act as sales representatives—they sell the exporter's products, collect payment, and ensure that customers are satisfied. Independent agents often represent several firms at once and usually do not specialize in a particular product or market. Levi Strauss uses agents to market clothing products in many small countries in Africa, Asia, and South America.

LICENSING ARRANGEMENTS

Canadian companies seeking more involvement in international business may choose **licensing arrangements**. Firms give individuals or companies in a foreign country the exclusive right to manufacture or market their products in that area. In return, the exporter typically receives a fee plus ongoing payments called *royalties*.[32] Royalties are usually calculated as a percentage of the licence holder's sales. For example, Can-Eng Manufacturing, Canada's largest supplier of industrial furnaces, exports its furnaces under licensing arrangements to Japan, Brazil, Germany, Korea, Taiwan, and Mexico. Franchising is a special form of licensing that is also very popular.[33] McDonald's and Pizza Hut franchise around the world. Similarly, Accor SA, a French hotel chain, franchises its Ibis, Sofitel, and Novotel hotels.

BRANCH OFFICES

Instead of developing relationships with foreign companies or independent agents, a firm may simply send some of its own managers to overseas branch offices. A company has more direct control over branch managers than agents or licence holders. **Branch offices** also provide a more visible public presence in foreign countries. Potential customers tend to feel more secure when a business has branch offices in their country.

When a business operates branches, plants, or subsidiaries in several countries, it may assign one plant or subsidiary the responsibility for researching, developing, manufacturing, and marketing one product or line of products. This is known as *world product mandating*.

STRATEGIC ALLIANCES

The concept of a strategic alliance was introduced in Chapter 2. In international business, it *strategic alliance* means that a company finds a partner in a foreign country where it would like to conduct business. Each party agrees to invest resources and capital in a new business or else to cooperate in some way for mutual benefit. This new business—the alliance—is then owned by the partners, which divide its profits.

The number of strategic alliances among major companies has increased significantly over the past decade and is likely to grow further. In many countries, including India, and China, laws make alliances virtually the only way to do business within their borders.[34] Whirlpool, the world's largest manufacturer of home appliances, has partnered with Hisene Kelon Electrical Holdings Co. in China to manufacture appliances locally. In addition, the company has signed a preferential distribution

INTERNATIONAL FIRM Firm that conducts a significant portion of its business in foreign countries.

MULTINATIONAL FIRM Firm that designs, produces, and markets products in many nations.

INDEPENDENT AGENT Foreign individual or organization that agrees to represent an exporter's interests.

LICENSING ARRANGEMENT Arrangement in which firms choose foreign individuals or organizations to manufacture or market their products in another country.

BRANCH OFFICE A location that an exporting firm establishes in a foreign country to sell its products more effectively.

ENTREPRENEURSHIP AND NEW VENTURES

Bugatti-Sedona: Charting a New Path

When you think of entrepreneurs, you might have an image of someone creating a start-up company who is bringing a new concept to market. You might not instantly think about the entrepreneurs behind established companies, like Montreal-based Bugatti-Sedona that has been designing, importing and selling business bags, accessories, briefcases, and luggage since 1940. But to stay in business that long requires entrepreneurial passion and key ingredients such as time, effort, creativity, and adaptability.

In 2013, when Julius Lis decided to sell his company, he searched for individuals that could move the company forward. He sold it to two ambitions entrepreneurs. Andrew Hattem (President) who brings 30 years of import and sales experience to the table and Benoit Larose (Executive Vice-President) who has over 15 years of business experience with Reebok-CCM's hockey division; he is also a former Detroit Red Wing draft pick, so he knows how to battle in the trenches. From day one of the new regime, it was clearly not business as usual; the goal was international expansion and building upon the current base.

In describing the transition Benoit Larose said, "we bought a brand that had been living on Canadian soil for decades, but while conducting our due diligence we saw great opportunities waiting to be captured. We have executed some of them already but we have plans to position Bugatti and our other brands to achieve new heights."

Bugatti-Sedona is in major expansion mode as they look to expand their sales in the United States and capitalize on new partnerships abroad.

Hand-out/BUGATTI-SEDONA INC./Newscom

Acquisitions and Strategic Alliance

Acquiring the Bugatti name was just the first step. The partners sought to significantly increase the value of the company and maximize selling opportunities by purchasing licences to open up markets and by purchasing other companies and brands to expand the product and retail account base:

- In 2013, Bugatti-Sedona acquired the Distribution License of Bugatti (The European Brand) for the North American market.
- In 2014, they acquired Bond Street and Stebco; the core of the distribution for these brands (80%) is in the United States under the office supply business channel.
- In September of 2014, Bugatti-Sedona becomes the main Global Licensee of Bugatti (The European Brand). Thus creating a division that is based in Manheim, Germany called Traveller-Sedona GbbH.
- In April of 2015, Bugatti-Sedona and Joanel Inc. (owners of Mouffon, Joanel, and Ugo Santini brands) formed a strategic alliance in which Joanel would help Bugatti in the areas of brand design and Bugatti would support Joanel by utilizing its strong distribution network.

EDC Support + Building Buzz

To achieve their expansion goals, Bugatti-Sedona applied for and received support from Export Development Canada in the form of $1.5 million dollars in financing guarantees. The EDC essentially enabled their bank (Desjardins) to manage the capital risk. According to Christian Dallaire (Vice-President of Small Business Solutions EDC) "This is a great example of what going global can do for your business."

In 2015, the company also got an unexpected brand-building boost when one of their bags was selected for the prestigious Golden Globe Ceremony Gift Bag.

So what's next? How will the firm capitalize on the additional products, brands, and market access? Time will tell. But if the first two years, under new ownership, is any indication, it should be interesting to follow.

CRITICAL THINKING QUESTIONS

1. Based on what you have read, how does this case demonstrate the complexity of being an entrepreneur in a global context?
2. Describe the various forms of international expansion discussed in this case and list the pros and cons of each tool.

agreement with Suning Appliance Co., which owns 1700 retail stores in 300 Chinese cities.[35] This approach eases the way into new markets; alliances also give firms greater control over their foreign activities than independent agents and licensing arrangements. (All partners in an alliance retain some say in its decisions.) Perhaps most important, alliances allow firms to benefit from the knowledge and expertise of their foreign partners.

The Entrepreneurship and New Ventures box called "Bugatti-Sedona: Charting a New Path" provides an example of a firm that is actively involved in exporting, licensing, and employing strategic alliances.

FOREIGN DIRECT INVESTMENT

The term **foreign direct investment (FDI)** means buying or establishing tangible assets (e.g., a manufacturing plant) in another country.[36] For example, Bombardier built a manufacturing facility in Casablanca, Morocco.[37] The Royal Bank of Canada recently purchased Los Angeles–based City National Corp. for US$5.4 billion.[38] However, despite such moves, a debate has been going on for years about how FDI by foreign firms in Canada affects Canadians. Recently, foreign buyouts of major Canadian firms like Inco, Four Seasons Hotels, Cirque du Soleil, and Alcan have caused some Canadian business leaders to express concern. The most general fear is that such buyouts will damage the economy because head offices will move to foreign countries and major decisions will be made there, not in Canada.

Investment Canada has a mandate to help attract foreign investment to the nation and, in the past three decades, foreign direct investment in Canada has been growing steadily; it now averages over $600 billion annually. More than half of that amount is flowing from the United States; however, nearly half of FDI flowing from Canadian firms goes to the United States as well.[39]

FOREIGN DIRECT INVESTMENT (FDI) Buying or establishing tangible assets in another country.

LO-5 BARRIERS TO INTERNATIONAL TRADE

Whether a business is selling to just a few foreign markets or is a true multinational, a number of differences between countries will affect its international operations. How a firm responds to and manages social, economic, and political issues will go a long way toward determining its success.

Social and Cultural Differences

Any firm involved in international business needs to understand something about the society and culture in the countries it plans to operate in. Unless a firm understands these cultural differences—either itself or by acquiring a partner that does—it will probably not be successful in its international activities.

Some differences are relatively obvious. Language itself can be an important factor. Beyond the barriers posed by people who speak different languages, subtle differences in meaning can also play a major role. Language barriers can cause inappropriate naming of products. For example, Imperial Oil markets gasoline under the brand name Esso in Canada. When the firm tried to sell its gasoline in Japan, it learned that *esso* means "stalled car" in Japanese. Many differences are discovered the hard way. In Japanese, the word *hai* (pronounced "hi") means "yes." In conversation, however, this word is used much like people in the United States use "uh-huh"; it moves a conversation along or shows the person with whom you are talking that you are paying attention. So when does *hai* mean "yes" and when does it mean "uh-huh"? This turns out to be a relatively difficult question to answer. If a Canadian manager asks a Japanese manager if he agrees to some trade arrangement, the Japanese manager is likely to say, "*Hai*"—but this may mean "Yes, I agree" or "Yes, I understand" or "Yes, I am listening." Many Canadian managers get frustrated in negotiations because they believe that the Japanese continue to raise issues already settled (because the Japanese managers seem to have said yes). What many of these managers fail to recognize is that yes does not always mean yes in Japan.

The average physical stature of people in different countries can make a difference. For example, the Japanese are slimmer and shorter on average than Canadians, an important consideration for firms that intend to sell clothes. Differences in the average age of the local population can also impact product development and marketing. Countries with growing populations tend to have a high percentage of young people. Thus, electronics and fashionable clothing would likely do well. Countries with stable or declining populations tend to have more old people. Generic pharmaceuticals might be more successful in such markets.

A wide range of subtle value differences can also have an important impact. For example, many Europeans shop daily. To Canadians, used to weekly trips to the supermarket, the European pattern may seem like a waste of time. But for Europeans, shopping is not just "buying food." It is also meeting friends, exchanging political views, gossiping, and socializing. What implications does this kind of shopping have for firms selling in European markets? People who go shopping every day do not need the large refrigerators and freezers common in North America. In Canada, prepared and frozen foods are important, but Europeans often prefer to buy fresh ingredients to do their own food preparation. These differences are gradually disappearing, however, so firms need to be on the lookout for opportunities as they emerge.

Business activity can be influenced by even more subtle behavioural differences than this. For example, crossing your legs in a business meeting in Saudi Arabia is inappropriate, because showing the sole of your foot is viewed as an insult to the other people in the room. In Portugal, it is considered rude to discuss business during dinner, and in Taiwan tapping your fingers on the table is a sign of appreciation for a meal. In China, don't give a businessman a green hat and don't wrap a gift in white or black (a green hat on a Chinese man is said to indicate that his wife is unfaithful, and black and white are associated with death). Deals can be lost on the basis of cultural misunderstandings. Local dos and don'ts are important in international business activity. Do your homework.[40]

Economic Differences

Although cultural differences are often subtle, economic differences can be fairly pronounced. In dealing with economies like those of France and Sweden, firms must be aware of the extent of government involvement. For example, the French government is heavily involved in all aspects of airplane design and manufacturing. Similarly, a foreign firm doing business in a pure command economy must understand the unfamiliar relationship of government to business. Another very important consideration is the level of economic development and the financial infrastructure in a country. What percentage of retail transactions are completed by credit card? Is financing readily available? Is it a cash economy? And so on.

Navigating the economic differences and identifying the global opportunities is a major challenge for today's corporations. Growth is quite often fuelled by nations across the globe. For instance, luxury goods manufacturers can see major benefits as economies grow and a taste for global brands increases. Swiss watchmaker Patek Philippe experienced growth of approximately 20 percent in two consecutive years, due largely to growing demand in China, where Swiss watches are often given to government officials.[41]

Legal and Political Differences

Legal and political differences are often closely linked to the structure of the economic systems in different countries. These issues include tariffs and quotas, local-content laws, and business-practice laws.

QUOTAS, TARIFFS, AND SUBSIDIES

Even free-market economies often use some form of quota and/or tariff that affects the prices and quantities of foreign-made products in those nations. A **quota** restricts the total number of certain products that can be imported into a country. It indirectly raises the prices of those imports by reducing their supply. The ultimate form of quota is an **embargo**, a government order forbidding exportation and/or importation of a particular product—or even all the products—of a particular country.

A **tariff** is a tax charged on imported products. Tariffs directly affect the prices of products, effectively raising the price of imports to consumers. Tariffs raise money for the government and somewhat discourage the sale of imported products. Governments from around the world impose quotas and tariffs. For example, Italy imposes high tariffs on imported electronic goods. A couple of years ago, the Canadian government announced a reduction in tariffs on sporting goods and baby clothes, which could lead to potential annual savings of $76 million for consumers. However, at the same time, the government announced higher tariffs on goods imported

QUOTA A restriction by one nation on the total number of products of a certain type that can be imported from another nation.

EMBARGO A government order forbidding exportation and/or importation of a particular product.

TARIFF A tax levied on imported products.

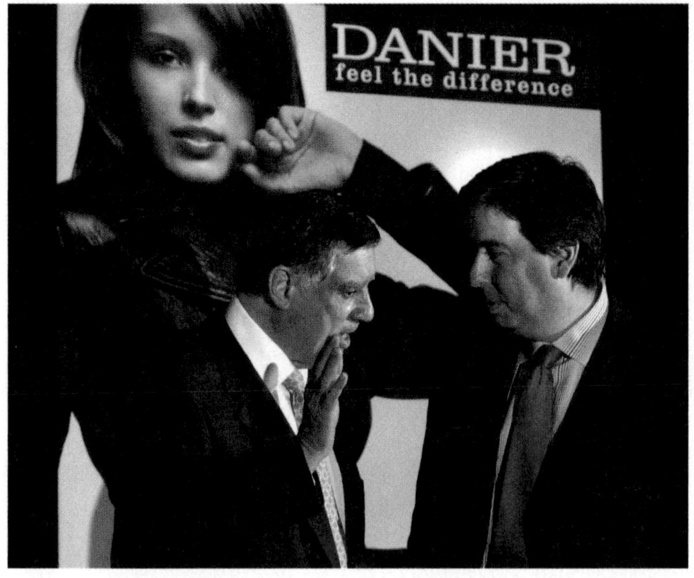

New, tougher tariffs imposed on goods imported from 72 countries translate directly into an estimated additional cost of $1.2 million for Danier Leather.

Dick Loek/Getty Images

Subsidies are designed to support domestic companies; however, in this free-trade era, governments are increasingly generous with foreign firms that can help develop local industries and provide local jobs. A few years ago Warner Bros. opened up a new studio to develop high-end video games in Montreal. Local talent, reputation, and knowledge were key factors, but government funding helped close the deal. The Quebec government provided $7.5 million to get the studio off the ground.

Jae C. Hong/AP Images

from 72 countries which could lead to a $330 million increase in costs for Canadian shoppers. For example, the new rules will cost Danier Leather an estimated $1.2 million a year (or about $10–$20 per jacket). You can bet this extra cost will be passed along to the consumer.[42]

A **subsidy** is a government payment given to a domestic business to help it compete with foreign firms. When the government of a country pays subsidies to one of its domestic companies or industries, this can have a negative effect on producers in other countries. Bombardier has received subsidies from both federal and provincial governments. These funds, or sometimes low-interest loans, have helped the company compete and develop its major projects. In late 2015, the Quebec government announced it would invest $1 billion for a 49.5% stake in the new C-Series line of planes. This angered unions representing public workers who were being asked to accept a 3 year wage freeze during the same time period. The federal government was also being pressured to put in another billion dollars.[43] The company and its main rival, Brazil-based Embraer, have accused each other of receiving excessive unfair government support, which has led to official disputes at the World Trade Organization (more information about the WTO is available at the end of the chapter).

Protectionism—the practice of protecting domestic business at the expense of free market competition—has advocates and critics. Supporters argue that tariffs and quotas protect domestic firms and jobs. In particular, they protect new industries until they are able to compete internationally. Some claim they are necessary because other nations have such measures. Still others justify protectionism in the name of national security and argue that advanced technology should not be sold to potential enemies.

But opponents of protectionism are equally vocal. They note that protectionism reduces competition and drives up prices. It is also a cause of friction between nations. The opponents maintain that while jobs in some industries would be lost if protectionism ceased, jobs in other industries would expand if all countries abolished tariffs and quotas.

At times, protectionism takes on an almost comic dimension. Many of you may enjoy Cheetos Cheesy snacks, but you have probably never realized that the brand has been in trouble with the law. A few years back, the company, Frito-Lay, incorrectly labelled several shipments of Cheetos from the United States into Canada as cardboard boxes. When the company realized the error they immediately informed the authorities; but, since neither cardboard boxes nor Cheetos snacks were subject to tariff, they figured there was no real problem. They were wrong. The Canada Border Services Agency hit them with a retroactive 11 percent tariff on all the shipments going back three years. For five additional years, the agency refused to consider changing its decision. A tribunal eventually deemed this an excessive example of protectionism; Frito-Lay had been taken on an "administrative ride" for an innocent clerical mistake.[44]

LOCAL-CONTENT LAWS

A country can affect how a foreign firm does business there by enacting **local-content laws** that require products sold in a particular country to be at least partly made in that country. These laws typically mean that firms seeking to do business there must either invest directly or have a local joint-venture partner. In this way, some of the profits in a foreign country are shared with the people who live there.

Many countries have local-content laws. In a fairly extreme case, Venezuela forbids the import of any product if a similar product is made there. A few years ago, Venezuela's president said he would cancel all mining licences and stop issuing new ones to foreign companies. This move was designed to protect the many small, local miners. Oil and gas licences held by foreign companies had already been cancelled. These actions make foreign companies more reluctant to invest in Venezuela.[45]

Local-content laws might even exist within a country, and when they do they act just like trade barriers. In Canada, for example, a low bid on a bridge in British Columbia was rejected because the company that had made the bid was from Alberta; the job was given to a B.C. company. A window

SUBSIDY A government payment to help domestic business compete with foreign firms.

PROTECTIONISM Protecting domestic business at the expense of free market competition.

LOCAL-CONTENT LAWS Laws requiring that products sold in a particular country be at least partly made in that country.

manufacturer from New Brunswick lost a contract in Nova Scotia despite having made the lowest bid; the job went to a company in Nova Scotia.

The Agreement on Internal Trade (AIT) requires all ten provinces to remove barriers to agricultural trade. However, internal conflicts are still common. According to Perrin Beatty, former president of the Canadian Chamber of Commerce, interprovincial trade barriers are putting Canadian companies at a huge disadvantage. This has to change if they are to survive and thrive in a global marketplace.[46]

BUSINESS-PRACTICE LAWS

Many businesses entering new markets encounter problems in meeting strict regulations and bureaucratic barriers. Such practices are affected by the **business-practice laws** that host countries set in their jurisdictions. They can be frustratingly effective. Walmart left Germany and South Korea because the company did not effectively adapt to local tastes or rules and was unable to achieve economies of scale.[47] In Germany, for example, it had to stop refunding price differences on items sold for less by other stores because the practice is illegal in that country. In another case, Google agreed to pay $500 million to settle a case with the U.S. government over advertising revenue earned from Canadian online pharmacies; the government had accused the company of enabling the illegal importation of drugs.[48]

Bribes to government officials to get business is another problem area. In 2013, SNC-Lavalin executives Ben Aissa and Stefane Roy were accused of paying $160 million to Saadi Gadhafi and other Libyan officials (under the old regime) to secure over $2 billion worth of contracts in Libya (to build an airport, a prison, and a water filtration plant) over a ten-year span.[49] Canada's Corruption of Foreign Public Officials Act prohibits bribery of foreign officials; but as more Canadian companies do business abroad they find themselves competing against companies only too happy to pay bribes. In an attempt to create fairer competition among multinational companies, ministers from the Organisation for Economic Co-operation and Development (OECD) agreed in 1997 to criminalize bribery of foreign public officials.[50]

Transparency International (TI) publishes a "Corruption Perceptions Index," which ranks countries on the basis of the amount of corruption perceived to exist according to ratings by business people, academics, and risk analysts. The index showed that the least corrupt countries are Denmark, New Zealand, and Finland, and the most corrupt Somalia, North Korea, Afghanistan, and Sudan. Canada ranked tenth.[51]

Cartels and Dumping A **cartel** is an association of producers whose purpose is to control the supply and price of a commodity. The most famous cartel is the Organization of the Petroleum Exporting Countries (OPEC). It has given oil-producing countries great power in the past 40 years although it has been weakened in recent years. At various times, other cartels have been evident in diamonds, shipping, and coffee. While nothing much can be done when governments form a cartel like OPEC, private-sector businesses can be prosecuted for doing so. Canada was involved in a potash cartel with Belarus and Russia (these three nations account for almost 80 percent of potash production), but when Uralkali (a Belarussian company) quit the cartel the price of Potash fell from $400 to $300 per tonne.[52]

Many countries forbid **dumping**—selling a product abroad for less than the comparable price charged in the home country. Antidumping legislation typically defines dumping as occurring if products are being sold at prices less than fair value, or if the result unfairly harms domestic industry. Recently, the U.S. imposed duties of 10.36 to 15.78 percent on steel pipes produced in China. China denounced this protectionist approach.[53] However, the United States is not alone in its concerns; India has accused China of dumping products on the Indian market that it can't sell elsewhere.[54]

BUSINESS-PRACTICE LAW Law or regulation governing business practices in given countries.

CARTEL Any association of producers whose purpose is to control supply of and prices for a given product.

DUMPING Selling a product for less abroad than in the producing nation.

LO-6 OVERCOMING BARRIERS TO TRADE

Despite the barriers to trade described so far, international trade is flourishing. This is because both organizations and free-trade treaties exist to promote trade. The most significant of these are the General Agreement on Tariffs and Trade (GATT), the World Trade Organization (WTO), the European Union (EU), and the North American Free Trade Agreement (NAFTA). We will also examine new potential agreements that promise to make a big impact: The Trans Pacific Partnership (TPP) and the Canada-European Union Comprehensive Economic and Trade Agreement (CETA).

General Agreement on Tariffs and Trade (GATT)

Governments typically view exports as good (because they create jobs in the country) and imports as bad (because they cause job losses in the country). Consequently, governments may be tempted to build trade barriers to discourage imports. But if every country does it, international trade is damaged. To avoid this problem, the **General Agreement on Tariffs and Trade (GATT)** was signed after World War II. Its purpose was to reduce or eliminate trade barriers, such as tariffs and quotas, by encouraging nations to protect domestic industries within agreed-upon limits and to engage in multilateral negotiations.

While 92 countries signed GATT, not all complied with its rules. The United States was one of the worst offenders. A revision of GATT went into effect in 1994, but many issues remained unresolved—for example, the opening of foreign markets to most financial services.

World Trade Organization

On January 1, 1995, the **World Trade Organization (WTO)** came into existence as the successor to GATT. The 160 member countries are required to open markets to international trade, and the WTO is empowered to pursue three goals:

1. promote trade by encouraging members to adopt fair trade practices
2. reduce trade barriers by promoting multilateral negotiations
3. establish fair procedures for resolving disputes among members

GENERAL AGREEMENT ON TARIFFS AND TRADE (GATT) International trade agreement to encourage the multilateral reduction or elimination of trade barriers.

WORLD TRADE ORGANIZATION (WTO) Organization through which member nations negotiate trading agreements and resolve disputes about trade policies and practices.

The WTO is overseeing reductions in import duties on thousands of products that are traded between countries. Canada, the United States, and the European Union are founding members of the WTO.[55] Unlike GATT, the WTO's decisions are binding, and many people feared that it would make sweeping decisions and boss countries around. Those fears were overstated.[56] The WTO has served its role as a ruling body but appeals can often drag on for years. For example, Boeing won a ruling against Airbus because it received US$4.1 billion in loans from European governments while developing its A380 jets. Despite the ruling, there appears to be even more money being given to Airbus for development of the A350. It has been over five years since the case was first presented, and it might be years before Boeing sees any rewards from the ruling.[57]

New free—trade agreements are promising to change the landscape once again (see descriptions of TPP and CETA below). Many senior trade officials are openly questioning the long-term relevance of the WTO if the members don't make adjustments. Many of the new agreements have more modern, faster rules such as better coordination of standards and regulations (which sometimes act as obstacles to trade).[58]

The European Union

Originally called the Common Market, the **European Union (EU)** initially included only the principal Western European nations like Italy, Germany, France, and the United Kingdom. But by 2015, 28 countries belonged to the EU (see Figure 5.4). Other countries are in the process of applying for membership, including Serbia and Turkey. The EU has eliminated most quotas and set uniform tariff levels on products imported and exported within its group. The EU is the largest free marketplace in the world and produces nearly one-quarter of total global wealth.[59]

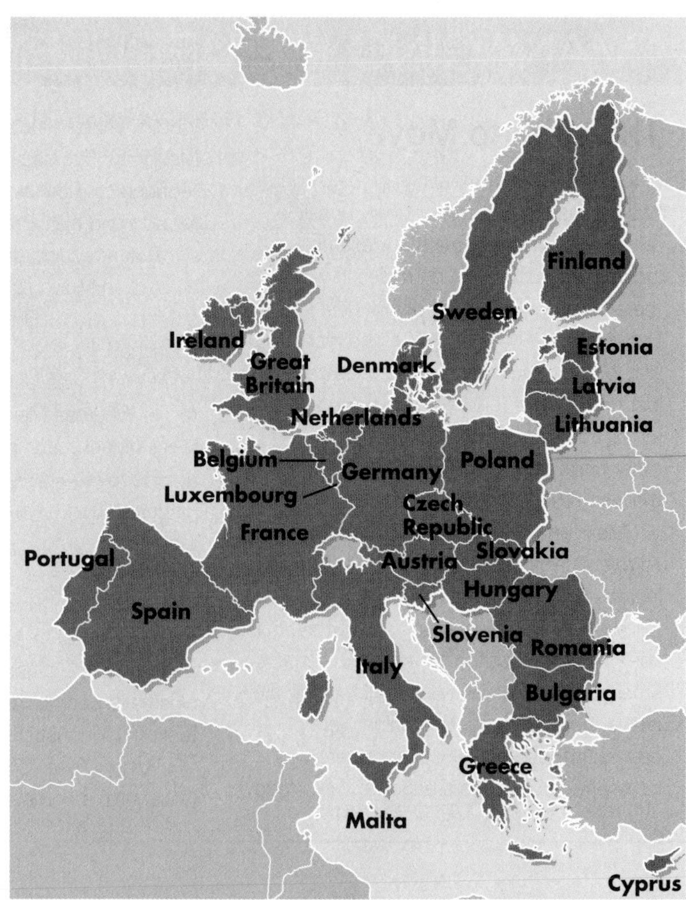

FIGURE 5.4 The nations of the European Union

The North American Free Trade Agreement

On January 1, 1994, the **North American Free Trade Agreement (NAFTA)** took effect. Its objective was to create a free trade area for Canada, the United States, and Mexico. It eliminates trade barriers, promotes fair competition, and increases investment opportunities.

Surveys conducted before the deal showed a majority of Canadians opposed to NAFTA. They feared jobs would be lost or Canada's sovereignty threatened, and that Canada would be flooded with products manufactured in Mexico, where wages are much lower. Supporters of NAFTA argued that the agreement would open up U.S. markets for Canadian products and create more employment, would create more employment possibilities for women, and would not threaten Canada's sovereignty.

What has actually happened since NAFTA took effect? A group of economists at the Canadian Economics Association concluded that free trade has not been as good for Canada as predicted by its supporters, nor as bad as predicted by its detractors.[60] Several specific effects are noticeable:

- NAFTA has created a much more active North American market.
- Direct foreign investment has increased in Canada.
- U.S. imports from (and exports to) Mexico have increased.
- Canada has become an exporting powerhouse.
- Trade between the United States and Canada rose sharply, and Canada enjoys a large trade surplus with the United States. Canada has become an exporting powerhouse.

In the past few years, there has been evidence that the benefits of NAFTA are slowly being eroded by ever-increasing delays at border crossings because of security concerns. The manufacturing drain continues, with most jobs being lost overseas. Meanwhile, between 2009 and 2015 seven car assembly plants were built in Mexico; no plants were built in the United States or Canada.[61]

On the positive side, there is now an extensive Canadian presence in Mexico in everything from mining, to auto parts, to banking. For example, as we will see in the closing case, Scotiabank, the most international Canadian bank, has made great inroads in Mexico with over 2 million Mexican clients.[62] There is also a renewed effort to increase direct trade between Mexico and Canada. Mexico recently eliminated nearly 14 000 rules and regulations to improve trade competitiveness. At the time, trade minister Bruno Ferrari called on Canada to increase its relationship with Mexico and help ensure that the $20 billion in trade between the nations continues to increase over the next decade.[63]

As you will see in the Managing in Turbulent Times feature "The Urge to Move," the conditions for greater North American trade may be turning more favourable (especially for Mexico).

EUROPEAN UNION (EU) Agreement among major Western European nations to eliminate or make uniform most trade barriers affecting group members.

NORTH AMERICAN FREE TRADE AGREEMENT (NAFTA) Agreement to gradually eliminate tariffs and other trade barriers among the United States, Canada, and Mexico.

MANAGING IN TURBULENT TIMES

The Urge to Move

In today's highly competitive global economy, businesses must strive for every possible advantage. Manufacturers, for example, locate their factories in countries in which there is an ample supply of low-cost labour. During the 1980s and 1990s, the place to be was Mexico. Hundreds of factories were built just cross the U.S.-Mexican border, and thousands of workers came to the region from other parts of Mexico for employment. But in the late 1990s the world started to shift.

Mexican prosperity, fuelled in part by its role as a centre of manufacturing, led to increases in the cost of living, and that was followed by wage increases so workers could keep up. At about the same time, China emerged as an attractive manufacturing alternative, because wages in China were about one-sixth those in Mexico, and there was no shortage of workers eager to take steady jobs in Chinese factories. China's boom was Mexico's bust, as one company after another reduced or eliminated manufacturing in Mexico and moved to China.

But in recent years, things have started to tilt back in Mexico's favour. Why? There are several reasons. First, as China's economy flourished, its labour costs increased to the point that it was less of a bargain than it used to be. Whereas Mexican wages were six times higher than wages in China ten years ago, today they are only about 40 percent higher. Second, when shipping costs are factored in, producing in Mexico now costs about the same as in China. Third, time differences between North America and China can make it difficult to schedule videoconferences and telephone calls. Finally, several companies have been burned by China's lack of protection for industrial and intellectual property.

Roger Moser is the president of Casabella, a company that makes a line of cleaning products and kitchen gadgets. Moser had all of the firm's manufacturing centred in Mexico in the 1990s, but moved it to China in 2002. Now, however, Casabella is in the process of moving its manufacturing work from China back to Mexico. Another company, Manufacturing Marvel, produces toys in both China and Mexico, but it is considering moving everything to Mexico. A company official said that counterfeiting of its products in China was on the upswing, and that also played a role in its decision.

CRITICAL THINKING QUESTIONS

1. Consider the following statement: *Because of intense international competition, companies really don't have any alternative but to locate their manufacturing facilities in countries with low wages so that they can lower their cost structure and be more competitive in global markets.* Do you agree or disagree? Defend your answer.

Major Agreements in the Works: TPP and CETA

Canada is actively seeking more open trade and participating in major new agreements.

- *The Trans-Pacific Partnership* has 12 members states including: Canada, the U.S, Australia, Brunei Darassalum, Chile, Japan, Malaysia, Mexico, New Zealand, Peru, Singapore and Vietnam. It is a comprehensive agreement that will increase Canada's foothold in Asia-Pacific. This region may account for two-thirds of the world's middle class by 2030, and one-half of global gross domestic product (GDP) by 2050.[63] However, TPP has many domestic opponents including farmers, the auto sector and other groups. It is expected to be implemented in 2016 but a lot can change when 12 governments are involved.
- *Canada–European Union Comprehensive Economic and Trade Agreement (CETA)* Canada is negotiating a comprehensive deal with the EU. The 28 member states account for 500 million people and annual economic activity of almost $18 trillion. After making a deal with the US two decades ago Canada is trying to further strengthen its relationship with the EU which is now the world's largest economy, bigger than the United States.[64]

Other Free Trade Agreements Around the World

On January 1, 1995, a free-trade agreement known as Mercosur went into effect between Argentina, Brazil, Uruguay, and Paraguay; Venezuela became the fifth member in 2012. Within the first decade of its existence, tariffs had been eliminated on 80 percent of the goods traded between the original members.

Around the world, groups of nations are banding together to form regional trade associations for their own benefit. Some examples include

- the ASEAN Free Trade Area (see Figure 5.5)

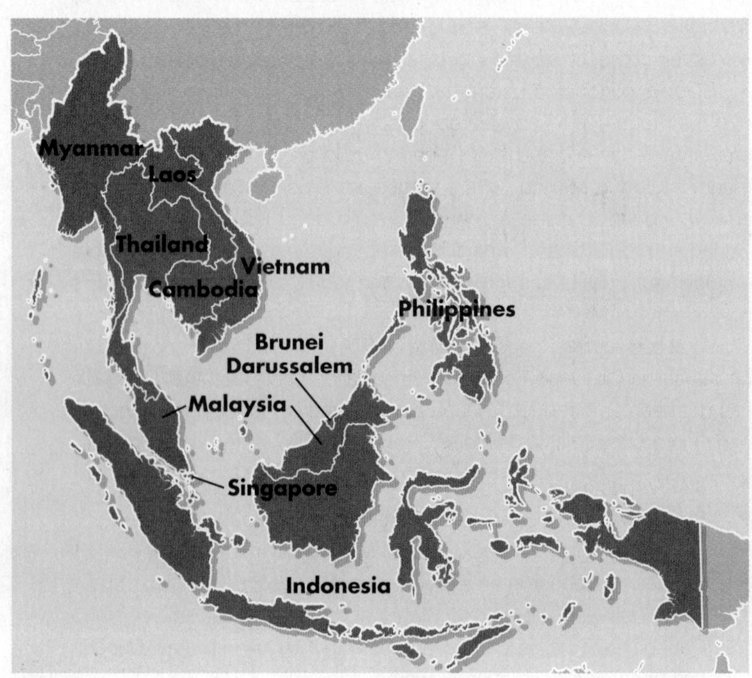

FIGURE 5.5 The nations of the Association of Southeast Asian Nations (ASEAN)

- the Economic Community of Central African States (many nations in equatorial Africa)
- the Gulf Cooperation Council (Bahrain, Kuwait, Oman, Qatar, Saudi Arabia, and United Arab Emirates)
- the Asia-Pacific Economic Cooperation (many nations of the Pacific Rim, as well as the United States, Canada, and Mexico)

MyBizLab

Study, practise, and explore real business situations with these helpful resources:

- **Interactive Lesson Presentations:** Work through interactive presentations and assessments to test your knowledge of business concepts.
- **Study Plan:** Check your understanding of chapter concepts with self-study quizzes.
- **Dynamic Study Modules:** Work through adaptive study modules on your computer, tablet, or mobile device.
- **Simulations:** Practise decision-making in simulated business environments.
- **Videos:** Learn more about the business practices and strategies of real companies.

SUMMARY OF LEARNING OBJECTIVES

LO-1 DESCRIBE THE GROWING COMPLEXITY IN THE *GLOBAL BUSINESS ENVIRONMENT* AND IDENTIFY THE *MAJOR WORLD MARKETPLACES*.

The world economy is changing and emerging markets are playing a bigger role. However, world trade still revolves greatly around three major marketplaces: North America, Europe, and Asia.

LO-2 IDENTIFY THE EVOLVING ROLE OF *EMERGING MARKETS* AND HIGHLIGHT THE IMPORTANCE OF THE *BRICS NATIONS*.

Old international trading patterns and activities are changing. In the past, Western companies used less-developed markets to acquire natural resources and to carry out simple assembly tasks. While this is still evident in international trade, the relationships have become much more complex, and many former have-nots are now exploiting relationships for their own gain. There are great opportunities in places like Thailand, Indonesia, South Korea, and Ukraine. However, the *BRICS nations* are getting most of the attention. *BRICS* stands for *Brazil, Russia, India, China, and South Africa*.

LO-3 EXPLAIN HOW DIFFERENT FORMS OF *COMPETITIVE ADVANTAGE*, *IMPORT–EXPORT BALANCES*, *EXCHANGE RATES*, AND *FOREIGN COMPETITION* DETERMINE HOW COUNTRIES AND BUSINESSES RESPOND TO THE INTERNATIONAL ENVIRONMENT.

With an *absolute advantage*, a country engages in international trade because it can produce a good or service more efficiently than any other nation. Countries usually trade because they enjoy *comparative advantages*; they can produce some items more efficiently than they can produce other items. A country that exports more than it imports has a favourable *balance of trade*, while a country that imports more than it exports has an unfavourable balance of trade. If the *exchange rate* decreases, our exports become less expensive for other countries, so they will buy more of what we produce. The reverse happens if the value of the Canadian dollar increases. Changes in the exchange rate, therefore, have a strong impact on our international competitiveness.

LO-4 DISCUSS THE FACTORS INVOLVED IN CONDUCTING BUSINESS INTERNATIONALLY AND IN SELECTING THE APPROPRIATE LEVELS OF *INTERNATIONAL INVOLVEMENT* AND *INTERNATIONAL ORGANIZATIONAL STRUCTURE*.

In deciding whether to do business internationally, a firm must determine whether a market for its product exists abroad and whether the firm has the skills and knowledge to manage such a business. Firms must also assess the business climates in other nations and the preferred *level of international involvement: (1) exporter or importer, (2) international firm, or (3) multinational firm*. The choice will influence the organizational structure of its international operations, specifically its use of *independent agents, licensing arrangements, branch offices, strategic alliances, and direct investment*.

LO-5 DESCRIBE SOME OF THE WAYS IN WHICH *SOCIAL, CULTURAL, ECONOMIC, LEGAL, AND POLITICAL DIFFERENCES* ACT AS BARRIERS TO INTERNATIONAL TRADE.

Social and cultural differences that can serve as barriers to trade include language, social values, and traditional buying patterns. Differences in economic systems may force businesses to establish close relationships with foreign governments before they are permitted to do business abroad. *Quotas, tariffs, subsidies, and local-content laws* offer protection to local industries. Differences in *business-practice laws* can make standard business practices in one nation illegal in another.

LO-6 EXPLAIN HOW *FREE TRADE AGREEMENTS* ASSIST WORLD TRADE.

Several trade agreements have attempted to eliminate restrictions on free trade internationally. The *World Trade Organization (WTO)* has 160 members with the mandate to help open up markets to international trade. *The European Union (EU)* has eliminated virtually all trade barriers among the 28 member nations. *The North American Free Trade Agreement (NAFTA)* eliminates many of the barriers to free trade among the United States, Canada, and Mexico.

QUESTIONS AND EXERCISES

QUESTIONS FOR ANALYSIS

1. What are the advantages and disadvantages of globalization from a Canadian consumer's point of view? From a Canadian manufacturer's point of view?
2. Assume you are the manager of a small firm seeking to enter the international arena. What information would you need about the market you're thinking of entering?
3. Do you think a firm operating internationally is better advised to adopt a single standard of ethical conduct or to adapt to local conditions? Under what conditions might each approach be preferable?
4. Explain how it is possible for a country to have a positive balance of trade and a negative balance of payments.
5. Explain how the economic system of a country affects foreign firms interested in doing business there.
6. The EU includes most of the Western European countries, but some (such as Switzerland) have chosen not to join. Why might that be? What are the implications for countries that do not join?

APPLICATION EXERCISES

7. Interview the manager of a local firm that does at least some business internationally. Identify reasons why the company decided to "go international," as well as the level of the firm's involvement and the organizational structure it uses for its international operations.
8. Select a familiar product. Conduct some research of the culture of India and identify the problems that might arise in trying to market this product to India's citizens.
9. What attributes of your province or region (cultural, geographical, economic, and so on) would be of interest to a foreign firm thinking about locating there? Visit provincial government sites and find resources that are available for businesses to help them invest in your province. Identify a company that has recently invested in your province. What reasons did it give for its decision?
10. Visit the website of a major global company such as Coca-Cola and enter some of its international sites. Make sure to choose countries from different parts of the world. What are some of the differences that you see in the websites? Identify some of the similar themes and report your findings.

TEAM EXERCISES

BUILDING YOUR BUSINESS SKILLS

WEIGHING THE TRADE-OFFS

GOAL

To encourage students to understand the reasons why companies shift labour offshore and to understand the perspective of all of the stakeholders in such a major decision.

THE SITUATION

Able Systems is a software company specializing in technology solutions for the food industry, including supermarkets and restaurants. All of your customers are located in Canada and operate nearly 24 hours a day. You provide excellent phone support for customers who have an issue, but your expenses are increasing and you're looking for ways to contain costs.

Able Systems has tried to reduce ever-increasing phone support costs by limiting the number of specialists working on each shift, but long wait times have angered customers. Because of the technical and problem-solving skills needed to provide remote support, hiring less-qualified employees is just not an option. Looking at competitors, you've noticed that many have offshored their operations—hiring employees in other countries to provide support. Because of a large number of English speakers and an adequate supply of applicants with the education needed for a support position, you are considering setting up a phone support centre in Jamaica.

This solution is not without concerns. If you offshore your support operation, you will have to lay off most of the support employees. You're willing to provide outplacement services to make sure that they can find new jobs, but you're still concerned about the impact of layoffs on your remaining employees. A group of programmers who heard of this proposal have begun to wonder if their jobs are next. Additionally, local elected officials are concerned about the impact of layoffs on the local economy. Your boss is pressuring you for a recommendation and you're weighing the pros and cons of both options.

METHOD

Step 1 Assemble a group of four students and assign each group member to one of the following roles:

- CEO of the Able Systems
- programmer at Able Systems
- liaison from a technical college in Jamaica who has graduates looking for jobs in their country
- local government official

Step 2 Each member should write down notes to express the position of their particular role. Before hearing any of your group's comments on this situation, and from the perspective of your assigned role, do you think that phone support should be offshored to Jamaica? Write down the reasons for your position.

Step 3 Gather your group together and reveal, in turn, each member's comments on whether phone support should be offshored. Appoint someone to record main points of agreement and disagreement within the group.

FOLLOW-UP QUESTIONS

1. Considering the interests of all stakeholders, what is the best option in this situation?
2. Develop a group response to the following question: Can your team identify other solutions to this dilemma?

EXERCISING YOUR ETHICS

PAYING ATTENTION TO FOREIGN PRACTICES

THE SITUATION

Assume you're an up-and-coming manager in a regional Canadian distribution company. Firms in your industry are just beginning to enter foreign markets, and you've been assigned to head up your company's new operations in a Latin American country. Because at least two of your competitors are also trying to enter this same market, your boss wants you to move as quickly as possible. You also sense that your success in this assignment will likely determine your future with the company.

You have just completed meetings with local government officials, and you're pessimistic about your ability to get things moving quickly. You've learned, for example, that it will take ten months to get a building permit for a needed facility. Moreover, once the building is up, it will take another six months to get utilities. Finally, the phone company says that it might take up to six additional months to get high-speed internet access.

THE DILEMMA

Various officials have indicated that time frames could be considerably shortened if you were willing to pay special "fees." You realize that these "fees" are bribes, and you're well aware that the practice of paying such "fees" is both unethical and illegal in Canada. In this foreign country, however, it's not illegal and not even considered unethical. Moreover, if you don't pay and one of your competitors does, you'll be at a major competitive disadvantage. In any case, your boss isn't likely to understand the long lead times necessary to get the operation running. Fortunately, you have access to a source of funds you could spend without the knowledge of anyone in the home office.

TEAM ACTIVITY

Assemble a group of four students and divide the four into two pairs and answer the questions from one of the following perspectives:

- your perspective as an employee who is being tasked with the authority to complete the job
- the perspective of the boss (assume that despite your assumptions this manager is actually well aware of the business practices in this country)

QUESTIONS TO ADDRESS

1. What are the key ethical issues in this situation?
2. What do you think most managers would do in this situation?
3. What would you do?

BUSINESS CASE 5

SCOTIABANK'S GLOBAL FOOTPRINT

If you take a cruise to the Caribbean, you might be surprised to see some familiar Canadian banks at the major ports and as a visible presence in various towns. Scotiabank is a leader in the industry with over 370 branches in the Caribbean, including locations in Aruba, Jamaica, and Barbados. This is, however, just a small glimpse of the international reach of the company. Scotiabank has been conducting international business for well over 100 years and earns a great deal of its profits from these operations. The company profile proudly states that it is the most international of the big Canadian banks.

Scotiabank was founded in 1832 in Halifax, Nova Scotia, and now has over 3000 branches in 57 countries. It employs over 86 000 people while providing a wide range of services to more than 21 million customers (14 million in international markets). While competitors like TD and BMO have set their sights on expanding in the more familiar U.S. market, Scotiabank took a more speculative expansion approach. It continues to build a strong presence in Central America, Mexico, Latin America, and Asia. As you will see, Scotiabank has various models around the world, designed to respect local laws and adapt to local challenges.

AP Photo/McDonald's Corp.

For instance, in Mexico, the approach is direct and aggressive; Scotiabank has invested through a holding company called Grupo Financiero Scotiabank Inverlat, S.A. de C.V., which owns two subsidiaries. Scotiabank Inverlat is Mexico's seventh-largest bank with over 600 full-service commercial branches and 1300 ATMs. The second is Scotiabank Inverlat Casa de Bolsa, an investment bank, which specializes in equity trading, investment advice, and corporate financing through 45 branches in major Mexican cities. Satisfying customers from different regions of the world requires knowledge of distinct local cultures and economic systems and respect for the unique needs of each market. Managing a portfolio as wide and complicated as Scotiabank's can be extremely challenging, but the company is clearly devoted to its global mission.

Many investments in international markets are designed for long-term gains while sacrificing profits in the short term. However, international banking is nothing new at Scotiabank, and this division is a profit driver for the firm today. Of course, having a presence in markets around the world also means that the bank has increased exposure to risks from around the world. This is particularly dangerous in unstable economic times.

Scotiabank has no intention of slowing down. In recent years, the expansion plan has included 22 acquisitions in Central and South America, with a particular emphasis on Colombia, Peru, and Chile. In fact, Scotiabank has set a target to capture 10 percent of the Chilean market. It recently bought Banco Sud Americano and its 142 full-service branches in that country. Scotiabank also acquired a majority stake in Banco Colpatria in a $1 billion deal in Colombia. However, such acquisitions are getting more difficult to complete. As a pioneer, Scotiabank was able to make major purchases at very reasonable acquisition prices; but today more international banks are investing in this region and the prices are getting higher. Nobody ever said it was easy!

There are tremendous prospects in Asia. Scotiabank has operations in key Asian markets including Japan, Korea, and India. Perhaps the greatest opportunities today, and probably for the next 100 years, are in China. A few years ago, Scotiabank tried to deepen its roots in China by acquiring a 19.99 percent stake in the Bank of Guangzhou for $719 million. This bank has a network of 84 branches in China's third-largest city. Why 19.99 percent? Doing business internationally often means navigating local rules and regulations. Foreign companies are not allowed to own more than 19.99 percent in any Chinese bank. This move followed a purchase of 14.8 percent of the Xi'an City Commercial Bank for $162 million two years earlier. Foreign laws must be understood and respected but even when that is understood it does not mean that the transactions are simple. After more than two years of negotiations Scotiabank actually withdrew its bid for the Bank of Guangzhou.

International growth must always be weighed against the specific challenges in each market (economic, legal, political, and so on). Regardless of the latest conditions, Scotiabank has shown its commitment to working with foreign companies, complying with foreign government rules in the quest to grow, and continuing to transform from Canada's leading international bank into Scotiabank-Global bank.

QUESTIONS FOR DISCUSSION

1. In this chapter, you have read about the different ways a company can enter foreign markets. List and describe the effectiveness of various approaches used by Scotiabank across the globe.
2. Describe the key obstacles faced by banks when they try to do business in a foreign nation.
3. Free-trade agreements are simplifying trade across the globe, but clearly there are major challenges for Scotiabank in growing their footprint. Do you believe the banking industry needs to have more open regulations to allow companies like Scotiabank to expand further across the globe?

PART 1: THE CONTEMPORARY BUSINESS ENVIRONMENT

GOAL OF THE EXERCISE

In Chapter 4, we discussed how the starting point for virtually every new business is a business plan. Business plans describe the business strategy for any new business and demonstrate how that strategy will be implemented. One benefit of a business plan is that in preparing it, would-be entrepreneurs must develop their idea on paper and firm up their thinking about how to launch their business before investing time and money in it. In this exercise, you'll get started on creating your own business plan.

EXERCISE BACKGROUND: PART 1 OF THE BUSINESS PLAN

The starting point for any business plan is coming up with a "great idea." This might be a business that you've already considered setting up. If you don't have ideas for a business already, look around. What are some businesses that you come into contact with on a regular basis? Restaurants, childcare services, and specialty stores are a few examples you might consider. You may also wish to create a business connected with a talent or interest you have, such as crafts, cooking, or car repair. It's important that you create a company from scratch rather than use a company that already exists. You'll learn more if you use your own ideas.

Once you have your idea, your next step is to create an "identity" for your business. This includes determining a name for your business and a concept of what your business will do, and identifying the type of ownership your business will take, a topic we discussed in Chapter 4. The first part of the plan also briefly looks at who your ideal customers are, how your business will stand out from the crowd, and how the business will interact with the community and demonstrate social responsibility (these last topics were discussed in Chapter 3). Finally, almost all business plans today include a perspective on the impact of global business.

YOUR ASSIGNMENT

MyBizLab

STEP 1

To complete this assignment, you first need to download the Business Plan Student Template file from this text's MyBizLab. This is a Microsoft Word file you can use to complete your business plan. For this assignment, you will fill in Part 1 of the plan.

STEP 2

Once you have the Business Plan Student Template file, you can begin to answer the following questions in Part 1: The Contemporary Business World.

1. What is the name of your business?

   Hint: *When you think of the name of your business, make sure it captures the spirit of the business you're creating.*

2. What will your business do?

   Hint: *Imagine that you are explaining your idea to a family member or a friend. Keep your description to 30 words or fewer.*

3. What form of business ownership (sole proprietorship, partnership, or corporation) will your business take? Why did you choose this form?

   Hint: *For more information on types of business ownership, refer to the discussion in Chapter 4.*

4. Briefly describe your ideal customer. What are they like in terms of age, income level, and so on?

   Hint: *You don't have to give too much detail in this part of the plan; you'll provide more details about customers and marketing in later parts of the plan.*

5. Why will customers choose to buy from your business instead of your competition?

   Hint: *In this section, describe what will be unique about your business. For example, is the product special, or will you offer the product at a lower price?*

6. All businesses have to deal with ethical issues. One way to address these issues is to create a code of ethics. List three core principles your business will follow.

   Hint: *To help you consider the ethical issues that your business might face, refer to the discussion in Chapter 3.*

7. A business shows social responsibility by respecting all its stakeholders. What steps will you take to create a socially responsible business?

   Hint: *Refer to the discussion of social responsibility in Chapter 3. What steps can you take to be a "good citizen" in the community? Also consider how you may need to be socially responsible toward your customers and, if applicable, investors, employees, and suppliers.*

8. Will you sell your product in another country? If so, what countries and why? What challenges will you face?

   Hint: *To help you consider issues of global business, refer to this chapter. Consider how you will expand internationally (e.g., independent agent, licensing). Do you expect global competition for your product? What advantages will foreign competitors have?*

Note: Once you have answered the questions, save your Word document. You'll be answering additional questions in later chapters.

CBC VIDEO CASE 1-1

CBC

VELOFIX

THE COMPANY

Chris Guillemet and Boris Martin, two Vancouver-based entrepreneurs, have built an interesting mobile bike repair business called Velofix. They do not have a traditional retail outlet, nor do they have the costs associated with renting a physical location. Instead, they invest their funds in shiny vans that offer convenience to the consumer. You no longer need to fit your bike into your car trunk or SUV and go halfway across town to drop it off. If you need a tuneup or a bike repair, Velofix will come to you. Call or make an online booking and they will fix your bike on location. Most repairs take 60–90 minutes. It's quick, it's convenient. A basic tuneup costs around $69, which is competitive with typical bike shops. According to the partners, pretty much anything that can be found in a retail store can be found in the van. For more details on the company, go to www.velofix.com.

The entrepreneurs have big plans, so if you don't live in Vancouver, don't worry—the Velofix franchising model is on the march. On this day, the entrepreneurs are joined by Canadian Olympic gold-medal triathlete Simon Whitfield, who owns the Victoria, British Columbia, franchise. This model costs the franchisee far less in start-up costs. The fee is $25 000, with another $50 000–$55 000 in buildup fees. In addition, there are royalties of 8 percent and an additional 2 percent for marketing fees. That compares favourably to the quoted costs of up to $750 000 for a prime retail location.

THE PITCH

Chris and Boris asked for $300 000 in return for 20 percent ownership in the company (valued at $1 500 000). This investment would help the entrepreneurs scale the business and increase marketing.

THE DRAGONS' POINT OF VIEW

Clearly, the dragons were impressed with the model and interested in the proposal. Jim Treliving made them an offer of $300 000 for 25 percent, and that was quickly followed by an offer from Michael Wekerle of $400 000 for 25 percent. The other dragons quickly bowed out. Dave Chilton was worried that the model would be copied by others, which would make things more difficult for Velofix. In her final words Arlene Dickinson pointed out that she thought the 2% marketing fee was too low and they would not generate enough money. According to Arlene, Velofix would need to find significant marketing funds in the near future in order to achieve their desired expansion and to build brand equity.

THE OUTCOME

After going into the Velofix van for a quick huddle, the partners came out with a counteroffer for Jim Treliving. They asked him to reduce his percentage from 25 percent to 20 percent for $300 000; in other words, they went back to their initial pitch. After a few moments of consideration, Jim took the deal. Even though they had a better offer from Michael, it was clear that they wanted Jim's franchising experience on their side.

QUESTIONS FOR DISCUSSION

1. After watching this video, describe the possible advantages and disadvantages of franchising as they relate to Velofix. Do you think it is a good investment for franchisees today?
2. In this chapter, we discussed the importance of selecting the right type of partners to work with. What lessons can we take away from this video? Do you think these entrepreneurs made the right choice?
3. Assume you were a traditional retail bike shop in your city, and conduct an external analysis. What are the primary threats and opportunities in the marketplace today? How might traditional bike shops deal with the threat from a new company like Velofix?
4. If you were one of the owners of Velofix, what tools and approaches would you use to help build your marketing presence across Canada and the United States?
5. Are the dragons angel investors or venture capitalists?

Source: "Velofix," *Dragons' Den*, Season 9, Episode 7 (November 27, 2014).

BUSINESS TODAY VIDEO CASE 1-1

MCDONALD'S EYEING NATURAL CHICKEN

Over the next two years, McDonald's plans to phase out the purchase of chicken products treated with antibiotics commonly used by humans. Insiders believe McDonald's is attempting to update its image and better compete with fast casual restaurants like Chipotle. This move seems to be in line with the trend toward healthy eating and the rise of consumer interest in natural ingredients.

In chapter 3 we discussed various approaches to dealing with social responsibility ranging from the obstructionist stance (in which an organization does as little as possible to solve social or environmental issues), to a defensive stance, to an accommodative stance, and finally to a proactive stance (in which an organization actively seeks opportunities to be socially responsible). With this latest move, it appears as though McDonald's is making a choice to create positive change.

McDonald's wants to create an image as a more health-conscious brand that is transparent with its customers. It has allowed the media to tour and film its many plants and allowed consumers to ask questions. Has any of this worked in McDonald's favour? What else, if anything, can McDonald's do to enhance its image as a health-conscious brand? Should it try to compete with the fast casual industry (e.g., Chipotle etc.)? Rick Newman, columnist for Yahoo Finance, discusses how this change might impact McDonald's and the fast food industry.

QUESTIONS FOR DISCUSSION

1. What factors have contributed to this decision? In answering this question, relate your response to the external environment of business.
2. How will McDonald's move toward natural chicken affect the fast-food industry? What are the ethical implications?
3. Do you think customers will respond positively to McDonald's planned changes?

BUSINESS TODAY VIDEO CASE 1-2

AMAZON CRACKS DOWN ON FAKE REVIEWS

Do you check online reviews before purchasing an item? If you are like most people, you probably give them considerable attention, particularly when they are very positive or negative. The rating next to a movie listings might have a big impact on your choice. Have you ever told a friend "Don't go see that movie—it is 5.5" (out of 10) even though you have not watched it yourself? We use online references and critiques to guide our daily selections ranging from movies, to hotels, to appliances, to purchases on sites like Amazon.

But how valid are such reviews? Do you take them for granted? Do you look to see how many reviewers have actually evaluated an item? Clearly five reviewers should not carry the same weight as five thousand (to account for bias and to ensure we have a representative sample).

Beyond the numbers, there is another factor to consider. Would you be shocked to learn that between 10 and 30 percent of all reviews are fabricated? Many of those are written by unethical company owners (or their friends and family) in order to influence you to pick a particular hotel, bar, or restaurant. If a business has 16 reviews, and 10 are fake positive ones that might have a major influence on your decision, you might make a misguided choice based on false information.

Consumer reviews are one advantage online retailers have over physical stores. So this tool is of vital importance to companies like Amazon. As this video indicates, Amazon plans to use sophisticated new technology to comb through user writeups and weed out deceptive reviews. It cannot catch everything, but with its sophisticated programs the company will surely continue be a leader in fighting the villains in the fake-review game.

QUESTIONS FOR DISCUSSION

1. How does this video demonstrate the power of technology and the dangers that are ever-present in this technological age?
2. Briefly describe the concerns regarding online reviews and highlight the ethical implications from a consumer and a business point of view.
3. How is Amazon planning to alleviate the problem of fabricated reviews? Why are accurate reviews so important to online retailers?

PART 2 THE BUSINESS OF MANAGING

micromonkey/Fotolia

LO

AFTER READING THIS CHAPTER, YOU SHOULD BE ABLE TO:

LO-1 Describe the four activities that constitute the *management process*.

LO-2 Identify *types of managers* by level and area.

LO-3 Describe the five basic *management skills*.

LO-4 Explain the importance of *goal setting* and *strategic management* in organizational success.

LO-5 Discuss *contingency planning* and *crisis management* in today's business world.

LO-6 Explain the idea of *corporate culture* and why it is important.

Google Keeps Growing

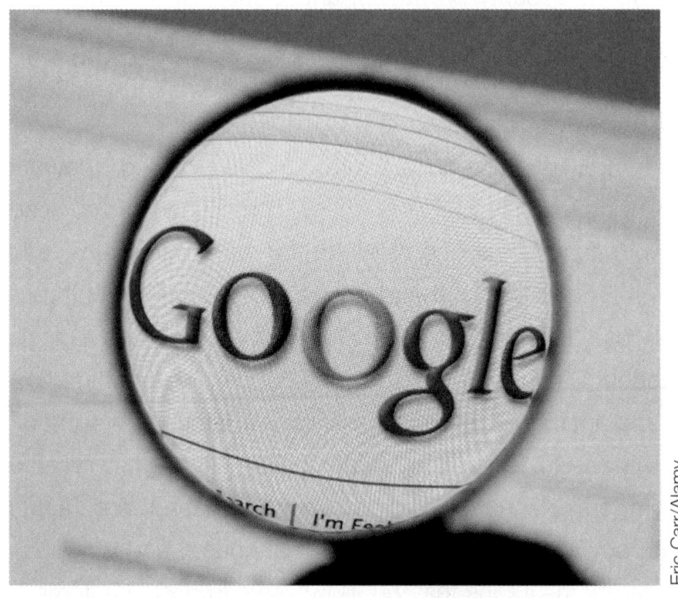

Eric Carr/Alamy

Sergey Brin and Larry Page met at Stanford University in 1995, when both were graduate students in computer science. At the time, Page was working on a software development project that was designed to create an index of websites by scouring sites for keywords and other linkages. Brin joined him on the project, and when they were satisfied that they had developed something with commercial value, they tried to license the technology to other search companies. As luck would have it, they couldn't find a buyer and settled instead for procuring enough investment capital to keep refining and testing their product.

In 2000, Brin and Page ran across the description of a business model on the concept of selling advertising in the form of sponsored links and search-specific advertisements. They adapted it to their own concept and went into business for themselves, eventually building Google into the world's largest search engine. Google processes more than 11 billion searches a month by a user base of 380 million people in 181 different countries using 146 languages. Following an initial public offering (IPO) in 2004, the company's market capitalization increased to more than $43 billion by 2012, when Google controlled about two-thirds of the search market. That was more than Microsoft and Yahoo combined.

Google is much more than a search engine. Services include searches for news, shopping, local businesses,

Managing *the* Business Enterprise

interactive maps, and discussion groups as well as blogs, web-based email and voice mail, and a digital photo-management system. You can access the results of any Google search from the Google website, from your own browser's toolbar, from your Windows taskbar, and from wireless devices such as smartphones and tablets. Google estimates 15 percent of the searches conducted each day are new, never having been searched before.

HOW WILL THIS HELP ME?

From the perspective of a *manager*, after reading this chapter you will have a clearer understanding of how to effectively carry out various management responsibilities. From the perspective of a *consumer* or *investor*, you'll be better able to assess and appreciate the quality of management in various companies.

How did two young computer scientists build this astoundingly successful company, and where will they take it in the future? Brin and Page remain in the forefront of Google's search for technological innovations. They believe in the power of mathematics and have developed unique algorithms for just about every activity in the firm. One of the most successful is an algorithm for auctioning advertising placements that ensures the highest possible prices.

Brin and Page have also been remarkably successful in attracting talented and creative employees and providing them with a work environment and culture that fosters the kind of productivity and innovation for which they were hired. Although the founders avoid formal strategic planning, they have managed to diversify extensively through acquisitions and key alliances. Typically, Google absorbs an acquired company and then improves on its technology, thereby adding variety to its own online offerings. Recent acquisitions include YouTube (a leader in online video sharing), Postini (a leader in communications security products), and DoubleClick (a leader in online advertisement services). Strategic alliances include those with foreign online service providers that offer Google searches on their sites.

For the immediate future, Google plans to follow its basic proven recipe for success, competing head to head with financial service providers for stock information and with iTunes for music and videos. Also committed to the in-house development of new features and services, Google spent $2.8 billion on research and development in 2012 and another $1 billion to acquire new information technology assets. Innovations in the works include an automated universal language translator for translating documents in any language into any other language, and personalized home pages that will allow users to design automatic searches and display the results in personal "newspapers." Nobody knows for sure what else is on the drawing board. In fact, outsiders—notably potential investors—often criticize Google for being a "black box" when they want a few more details about its long-range strategy. "We don't talk about our strategy," says Page, "because it's strategic. I would rather have people think we're confused than let our competitors know what we're going to do."

se media/Fotolia

QUESTIONS FOR DISCUSSION

1. What are the functions of management? How are these functions illustrated in this case?
2. What are the *skills* of management? Which skills are most exemplified in Sergey Brin and Larry Page?
3. What role do goals and strategy play at Google?
4. Describe the corporate culture at Google.

WHO ARE MANAGERS?

As top managers, John Fallon, CEO of Pearson PLC (left), Calin Rovinescu, CEO of Air Canada (centre), and Galen Weston, Jr., CEO of Loblaw Companies (right) are important resources for their companies. They set the strategic direction for their companies and provide leadership to other managers. They are also accountable to shareholders, employees, customers, and other key constituents for the performance and effectiveness of their businesses.

epa european pressphoto agency b.v./Alamy; Images Distribution/Agence Quebec Presse/Newscom; Mark Blinch/Reuters/Landov

Managers are the people who plan, organize, lead, and control the operations of an organization. All businesses depend on effective management. Regardless of the type of organization they work in, managers perform many of the same basic functions, are responsible for many of the same tasks, and have many of the same responsibilities. Although our focus is on managers in business settings, management is important for all kinds of organizations, including charities, religious organizations, community organizations, educational institutions, and government agencies. The prime minister of Canada, the president of the University of Toronto, the executive director of the United Way, the dean of your business school, and the chief administrator of your local hospital are all managers. Regardless of the nature and size of an organization, managers are among its most important resources.

MANAGERS The people who plan, organize, lead, and control the operations of an organization.

LO-1 THE MANAGEMENT PROCESS

Management is the process of planning, organizing, leading, and controlling an enterprise's financial, physical, human, and information resources to achieve the organization's goals. There are two important overall points to keep in mind when thinking about the management process. First, the planning, organizing, leading, and controlling aspects of a manager's job are interrelated. This means that a manager is likely to be engaged in all these activities during the course of any given business day.

Second, there is a difference between management effectiveness and management efficiency. *Efficiency* means achieving the greatest level of output with a given amount of input. *Effectiveness*, on the other hand, means achieving organizational goals that have been set. Thus, efficiency means doing things right, while effectiveness means doing the right things. A manager who focuses on being effective will likely also be efficient, but a manager who focuses on being efficient may or may not be effective.

MANAGEMENT The process of planning, organizing, leading, and controlling a business's financial, physical, human, and information resources in order to achieve its goals.

PLANNING That portion of a manager's job concerned with determining what the business needs to do and the best way to achieve it.

Planning

Planning is the process of determining the firm's goals and developing a strategy for achieving those goals. The planning process involves five steps:

- *Step 1.* Goals are established for the organization. A commercial airline, for example, may set a goal to fill 90 percent of the seats on each flight.
- *Step 2.* Managers identify whether a gap exists between the company's desired and actual position. For example, the airline may analyze load data and find that only 73 percent of the seats on the average flight are filled.
- *Step 3.* Managers develop plans to achieve the desired objectives. For example, the airline may reduce fares on heavily travelled routes in order to increase the percentage of the seats that are filled.
- *Step 4.* The plans that have been decided upon are implemented. For example, the fare from Toronto to Montreal may be reduced by 10 percent.
- *Step 5.* The effectiveness of the plan is assessed. The airline would measure the percentage of seats that were filled after the change was implemented to determine whether the goal was reached.

McDonald's experience in Canada over the past 15 years demonstrates the importance of the planning process. Until 2002, the company was the largest fast-food chain in Canada. But then it was overtaken by Tim Hortons. In response to this development, McDonald's set a goal to reinvent itself and begin to grow again (step 1). The gap between where McDonald's was and where it wanted to be (step 2) was obvious, so McDonald's top managers developed a strategic plan (called "Plan to Win") in order to achieve the new objective (step 3). This involved developing many new menu items (like the Angus Burger, new salads, and snack wraps), renovating restaurants to look more like contemporary cafés or bistros (with polished stone tabletops and fireplaces), letting franchisees target local tastes with their menus (like the McLobster sandwich in the Maritimes), and staying open longer (60 percent of McDonald's restaurants are now open 24 hours a day). These plans were implemented beginning in 2003 and 2004 (step 4). The plan was effective (step 5). Sales were $2.9 billion in 2008 (a record) and $3 billion in 2009 (another record).[1] But by 2012, McDonald's began experiencing declining sales, caused by intense competition and consumer preferences for healthier foods. That trend continued through 2013 and 2014. In response to these problems, McDonald's developed a new plan: simplifying its menu and eliminating slow-selling items.[2] Whether the latest plan will be effective remains to be seen.

Organizing

Organizing involves mobilizing the resources required to complete a particular task (this topic is examined in detail in Chapter 7). The importance and complexity of the organizing function can be seen by considering the restructuring that has taken place at Hewlett-Packard in recent years. HP had long prided itself on being a corporate confederation of individual businesses. Each business made its own decisions quickly and efficiently, and the competition kept each unit on its toes. This structure served the firm well for many years. But as time passed, HP somehow lost its competitive edge. The decision was then made to centralize company activities and develop an integrated, organization-wide internet strategy. A reorganized HP then bounced back, at least for a few years.[3] But when HP began again to experience profitability problems in its PC division in 2005, then-CEO Carly Fiorina decided to combine the PC and printing divisions in order to increase hardware sales to customers. Although Fiorina's successor Mark Hurd undid these changes, when Hurd left a few years later the new CEO Meg Whitman reinstated them.[4]

Leading

Leading (or directing) involves the interactions between managers and their subordinates as they both work to meet the firm's objectives. Legendary leaders like Sam Walton (Walmart), Clive Beddoe (WestJet), and Steve Jobs (Apple) were able to unite their employees in a clear and targeted manner, and motivate them to work in the best interests of the company. While managers have the power to give orders and demand results, leading goes beyond merely giving orders. Leaders must also have the ability to motivate their employees to set challenging goals and to work hard to achieve them. This means that employees will respect their leaders, trust them, and believe that by working together both company and employees will benefit. We discuss leadership in detail in Chapter 10.

ORGANIZING That portion of a manager's job concerned with mobilizing the necessary resources to complete a particular task.

LEADING (OR DIRECTING) That portion of a manager's job concerned with guiding and motivating employees to meet the firm's objectives.

CONTROLLING That portion of a manager's job concerned with monitoring the firm's performance and, if necessary, acting to bring it in line with the firm's goals.

Controlling

Controlling is the process of monitoring a firm's performance to make sure that it is meeting its goals. Managers at WestJet and Air Canada, for example, focus relentlessly on numerous indicators of performance that they can measure and adjust. Everything, from on-time arrivals to baggage-handling errors to the number of empty seats on an airplane to surveys of employee and customer satisfaction, are regularly and routinely monitored. If on-time arrivals start to slip, managers focus on the problem and get it fixed. No single element of the firm's performance can slip too far before it is noticed and fixed.

Figure 6.1 illustrates the control process, which begins when management establishes standards (often for financial performance). If, for example, a company sets a goal of increasing its sales by 20 percent over the next five years, an appropriate standard to assess progress toward that goal might be an increase of about 4 percent a year. Managers then measure actual performance each year against standards. If the two amounts agree, the organization continues on its present course. If they vary significantly, however, one or the other needs adjustment. If sales have increased 3.9 percent by the end of the first year, things are probably fine. But if sales have dropped 1 percent, some revision in plans is needed.

Consider how controlling applies to the courses you are now taking. The instructor first indicates the knowledge areas where you must show competence and the level of competence you must show. Next,

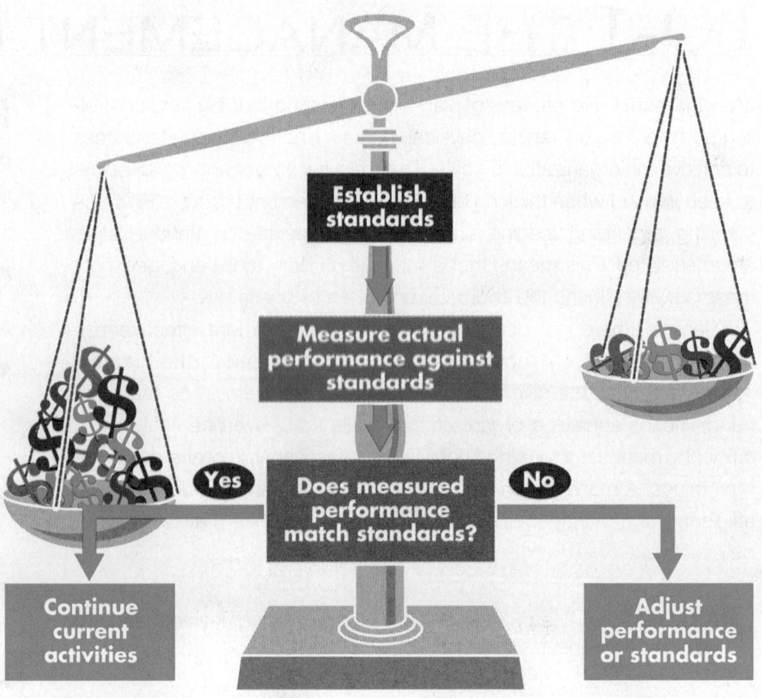

FIGURE 6.1 The control process

E-BUSINESS AND SOCIAL MEDIA SOLUTIONS

The Truth About Your Online Customer Service

Effective decision making requires good, timely information. Retailers in particular are constantly monitoring trends and competitor actions in order to improve their standing with consumers.

Online purchases keep increasing as shoppers enjoy easy access to more and more products from the comfort of home. However, poor customer service can disappoint and anger customers, resulting in lost sales. So how good is a company's online customer service, especially compared to that of its online competitors? StellaService Inc. answered that question by providing a better way to measure online service, enabling it to become a market winner for online shoppers and retailers alike.

Following its start-up in 2010, StellaService (Stella) spent two years gathering data on customer satisfaction with thousands of online retailers, including giants like Amazon.com. They measure satisfaction in four service areas—phone support, email support, delivery, and returns/refunds—for each retailer. Each area includes from 9 to as many as 25 different measurements. Phone support, for example, considers speed of answering the call and respondent's knowledge of the product among its nine measurements. Delivery measurements include delivery time and product accuracy. By combining the various measurements, consumers can find summary scores for each of the four service areas. Results provide rankings of competitors showing where each retailer currently stands relative to competitors in each of the four areas of service. Rankings allow period-to-period tracking, revealing trends for improvements in each of the areas across time for each company.

With these measurements Stella hopes to better inform consumers on the range of customer service they can expect from online retailers. Knowing that success hinges on the validity and believability of their methods, Stella uses an independent third-party rating system. "Secret shoppers" (trained employees) use strict and controlled measurement methods as they engage online retailers via emails, phone calls, and live chats to purchase, await deliveries, or make returns for refunds. As added assurance for validity the company maintains a "Customer Service Measurement Process Audit" detailing its measurements and procedures for gathering and processing data, with specific steps to assure accuracy and validity.

Recently, in its Independent Auditing Report, KPMG stated that Stella's methodologies are complying with their stated policies. This confirmation should help in Stella's latest move: offering subscription services to retailers. Subscribers can, for the first time, receive measured data showing their standing, along with competitors, on phone support, email support, delivery, and returns/refunds. This service allows retailers to base decisions on objective and independent information about their online customer service. It looks like the company is on to something. They have already enlisted major retailers like Walmart and Ralph Lauren, raised more than US$22 million in venture capital, and received the greatest compliment (as well as a financial boost) when Google licensed StellaService's data in order to rate retailers on its search engine.

CRITICAL THINKING QUESTIONS

1. How do the results of customer service reports influence a manager's decisions? In answering this question refer to Figure 6.1 (the control process).

he or she measures your performance, usually through assignments and exams. The instructor then determines whether your performance meets the standard. If your performance is satisfactory (or unsatisfactory), you receive feedback in the form of a passing (or failing) grade in the course.

Control can also show where performance is better (or worse) than expected and can serve as a basis for providing rewards or reducing costs. For example, when the distributor of the surprise hit movie *The March of the Penguins* saw how popular the movie was becoming, the firm was able to increase advertising and distribution, making the niche movie into a major commercial success. In contrast, when the sales of the Chevrolet Super Sport Roadster (a classic, late-1940s pickup-style vehicle with a two-seat roadster design) were much lower than expected, production of the vehicle was suspended.

The boxed insert entitled "The Truth About Your Online Customer Service" illustrates how important the control process is for managers.

Management: Science or Art?

Many management problems can be approached in ways that are rational, logical, objective, and systematic. Managers can use quantitative models and decision-making techniques to arrive at "correct" decisions. This approach is especially useful when managers deal with relatively routine and well-defined issues. But managers also make many decisions that are not routine, and when doing so they must rely heavily on interpersonal skills and on abstract conceptual thinking. Thus, effective management is a blend of science and art, and successful executives recognize the importance of combining both the science and art of management as their carry out the functions of management.[5] The boxed feature entitled "Challenges Facing Managers" describes some issues managers have to deal with as they blend the art and science of management.

BECOMING A MANAGER

How do you acquire the skills necessary to blend the science and art of management? Although there are many variations, the most common path involves a combination of *education* and *experience*.

If you are reading this text, you are probably doing so because you are enrolled in a management course at a community college or university. When you complete the course, you will have a foundation for developing your management skills in more advanced courses. A degree or diploma has become almost a requirement for career advancement in business, and MBA degrees are increasingly common among successful managers. Even after obtaining a degree, managers have not

MANAGING IN TURBULENT TIMES

Challenges Facing Managers

It isn't easy being a manager today. The passion for "lean and mean" organizations means that there are fewer workers to do more work. Globalization means that managers must keep informed about cross-cultural differences. Knowledge industries present unique management challenges which require greater communication skills and more flexibility. Advances in technology have opened new channels of communication. Now, more than ever, managers must be able to do just about everything, and do more of it.

One challenge is maintaining the energy required to complete their tasks. Most corporate leaders work 80 to 100 hours every week, and a lot of them have adopted regimens that allow them to rebuild and refresh so they can keep up the pace. Carlos Ghosn, the president of Renault *and* the CEO of Nissan, believes in regular respites from his workweek routine. "I don't bring my work home. I play with my four children and spend time with my family on weekends," says Ghosn. "I come up with good ideas as a result of becoming stronger after being recharged." Marissa Mayer, the CEO of Yahoo, takes a week-long vacation three times a year. Many leaders report that playing racquetball, running marathons, practising yoga, or just getting regular exercise helps them recover from overwork.

Another challenge is the control of large information flows. Starbucks CEO Howard Schultz receives a morning voice mail summarizing the previous day's sales results, and he reads three newspapers a day. Marissa Mayer watches the news all day. Carlos Ghosn, whose schedule requires weekly intercontinental travel, uses bilingual assistants to screen and translate information: one assistant for Europe (where Renault is located), one for Japan (home of Nissan), and one for the United States (where Ghosn often has to be when he doesn't have to be in Europe or Japan). Clothing designer Vera Wang also uses an assistant to filter information. "The barrage of calls is so enormous," she says, "that if I just answered calls I'd do nothing else. . . . If I were to go near email, there'd be even more obligations, and I'd be in [a mental hospital] with a white jacket on."

Another challenge is dealing with risk. Steve Jobs, the former CEO of Apple, was willing to take big risks. He demonstrated that he could see beyond the present and motivated his employees by sharing his compelling vision. But Jobs could be brutal when dealing with employees who failed to successfully implement his vision. Jobs was so disappointed by flaws in the MobileMe email system that he fired the manager leading that program (in front of a crowd of employees).

CRITICAL THINKING QUESTIONS

1. In what ways has information technology changed the work of managers?
2. Think about your job or one you used to have. What were the main challenges your manager had to deal with? How did he or she cope?

seen the end of their formal management education. Many middle and top managers periodically return to campus to participate in executive or management development programs. Large companies often have in-house training programs for furthering the education of their mangers. Some firms (McDonald's and Shell Oil) have even created corporate universities for this purpose. There is also a trend toward online education.

The primary advantage of education as a source of management skills is that you can follow a well-developed program of study and become familiar with current research and thinking on management. This text, for example, will give you a solid foundation for enhancing your management skills. However, management education is often general (in order to meet the needs of a variety of students), so specific know-how may be hard to obtain. This is where experience comes in. The day-to-day experiences that managers have as they try to achieve company goals and keep their subordinates productive and happy are crucial in improving their effectiveness. Because companies recognize the importance of experience, they assign people to a variety of jobs. Over time, individuals are exposed to most of the major aspects of the organization. In this way, managers learn by experience.

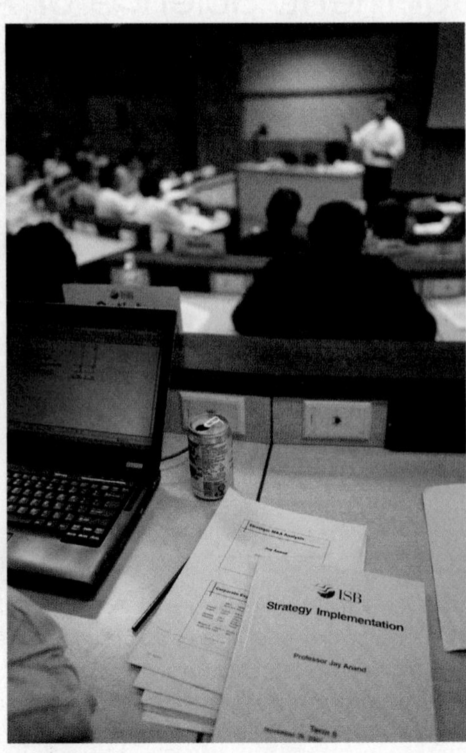

<<< **Education plays a vital role in becoming a manager. Prospective managers usually complete at least one degree in business, taking courses in finance, marketing, accounting, management, and other areas.**

Marco Cristofori/Alamy Stock Photo

What Should You Expect in a Management Job?

Managers need to be aware of the expectations that the organization has for them. Put simply, managers are expected to focus on completing tasks in an effective manner, and they are not supposed to worry about whether they are working too many hours per week. Non-managerial employees typically receive overtime pay when they work more than a 40-hour week, or when they work weekends or holidays. If a person who has been a non-manager is promoted into a management job, he or she may be dismayed to find there is no overtime pay no matter how many hours per week they work.

Under the terms of the Canada Labour Code, individuals in supervisory roles are not entitled to overtime pay for work beyond 40 hours per week. But this provision has been challenged in recent years. In 2010, a $250 million overtime class action lawsuit was launched by 1500 first-line supervisors at Canadian National Railway who oversee the movement of trains and the maintenance of track. The supervisors said they had to work 50 hours a week on average, and sometimes as much as 90 hours per week. An important issue in this case was whether a person designated as a "supervisor" can claim overtime. In other words, the case hinges on whether first-line supervisors at CN are properly classified as "managers" and whether they actually have managerial duties. In June 2012, the Ontario Court of Appeals denied certification of the CN case and concluded that it wouldn't work as a class action lawsuit because it depended on the definition of "manager" and "employee," and that would have to be determined on a case-by-case basis.[6]

It is not just groups of employees who are filing lawsuits. Massimo Sanago, the executive chef at the Glendale Golf and Country Club in Hamilton, had the responsibility of managing kitchen operations. But because of staff shortages, he spent over half his time cooking. He also had to work long hours to finish all his other work. Glendale gave him a $5000 bonus in recognition of his efforts, but he felt that was insufficient, so he filed a claim for overtime pay with the Ministry of Labour. Glendale disputed the claim, arguing Sanago was a manager and that he did not qualify for overtime pay because he performed cooking duties only on an emergency basis. But the Ontario Labour Relations Board ruled that the company had to pay him overtime.

Lawsuits against employers are partly the result of the way labour laws are written. For example, unless a person's occupation is specifically excluded by legislation, that person is entitled to overtime pay for each hour they work beyond the provincial maximum (in Ontario, that is 44 hours per week). In Ontario, occupations such as lawyers, accountants, dentists, veterinarians, farmers, salespeople, gardeners, janitors, taxi drivers, and IT professionals are excluded. Critics of the legislation argue that the first five occupations make some sense because they require independent work, but it makes little sense to exclude the latter four occupations.

LO-2 TYPES OF MANAGERS

Although all managers plan, organize, lead, and control, not all managers have the same degree of responsibility for each activity. Moreover, managers differ in the specific application of these activities. Thus, we can differentiate between managers on the basis of their level of responsibility and their area of responsibility.

Levels of Management

The three basic levels of management are top, middle, and first-line management. As Figure 6.2 shows, in most firms there are more middle managers than top managers and more first-line managers than middle managers. Moreover, as the categories imply, the authority of managers and the complexity of their duties increase as we move up the pyramid.

TOP MANAGERS

The executives who guide the fortunes of companies are **top managers**. Common titles for top managers are president, vice-president, chief operating officer (COO), chief executive officer (CEO), and chief financial officer (CFO). Top managers are responsible to the board of directors and shareholders of the firm for its overall performance and effectiveness. They set general policies, formulate strategies, oversee significant decisions, and represent the company in its dealings with other businesses and government.[7] Sometimes a corporation will have co-presidents. For example, James Gowans and Kelvin Dushnisky are co-presidents at Barrick Resources.[8]

While top managers have a lot of authority, they also have something of an image problem. One study ranked CEOs very low on the "trust" dimension, and this means that some of Canada's most successful people have low credibility.[9] Social media have also made the actions of top managers (and others) much more visible. Desmond Hague, the CEO of food services company Centerplate, was forced to resign after an elevator security video showed him kicking a dog.[10]

TOP MANAGERS Those managers responsible for a firm's overall performance and effectiveness and for developing long-range plans for the company.

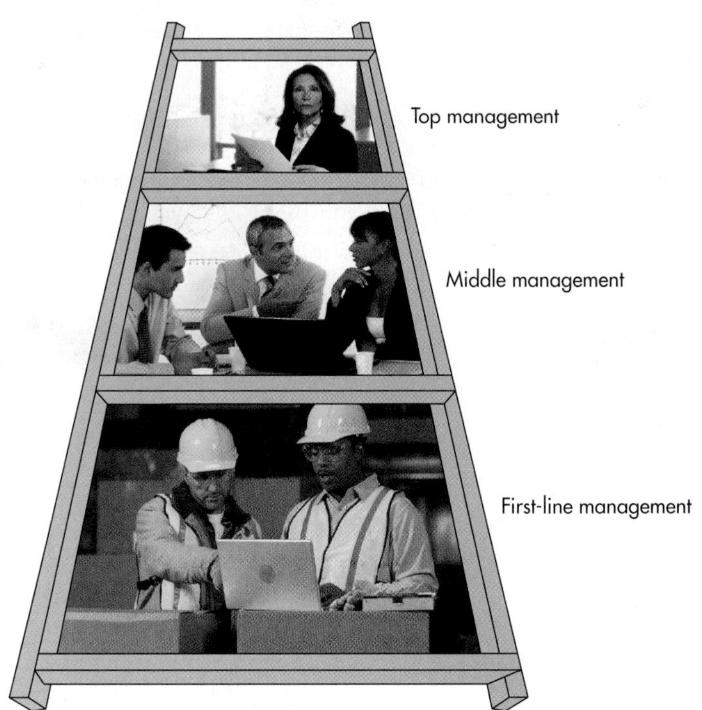

FIGURE 6.2 Organizations have three basic levels of management

(Top to Bottom) Adrian Weinbrecht/Alamy; auremar/Fotolia; Hurst Photo/Shutterstock

MIDDLE MANAGERS

Although below the ranks of the top executives, **middle managers** still occupy positions of considerable autonomy and importance. Titles such as plant manager, operations manager, and division manager are typical of middle-management positions. The producer of a Lion's Gate film like *Precious* is a middle manager. In general, middle managers are responsible for implementing the strategies, policies, and decisions made by top managers. For example, if top management decides to bring out a new product in 12 months or to cut costs by 5 percent, middle management will have to decide to increase the pace of new product development or to reduce the plant's workforce.

FIRST-LINE MANAGERS

First-line managers spend most of their time working with and supervising the employees who report to them. Common titles include supervisor, office manager, and group leader. A transit supervisor who monitors bus schedules, passenger safety, and the behaviour of bus drivers is a first-line supervisor. So is the flight-services manager for a specific Air Canada flight. Table 6.1 summarizes the duties of the three basic levels of management.

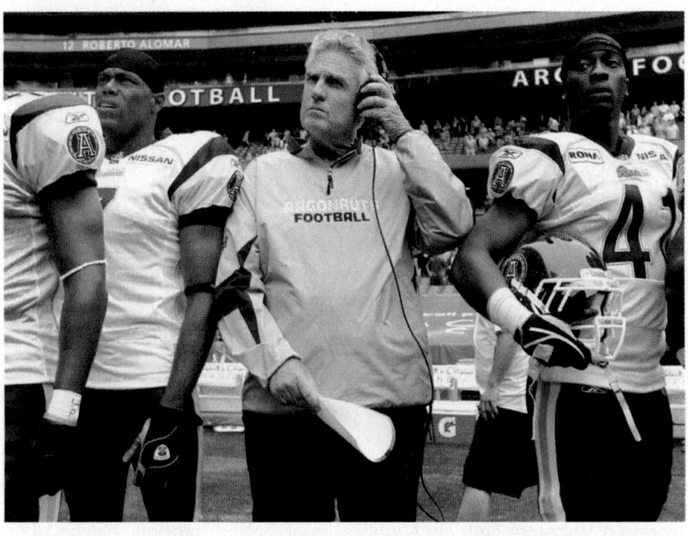

^^ Managers are needed in all kinds of business firms, including professional sports teams. A head coach is a first-line manager responsible for the day-to-day success of the team.

Darren Calabrese/AP Images

Areas of Management

Within any large company, the top, middle, and first-line managers work in a variety of areas, including human resources, operations, information, marketing, and finance.

HUMAN RESOURCE MANAGERS

Human resource managers can be found in most companies; they hire employees, train them, evaluate their performance, decide how they should be compensated, and deal with labour unions (if the workforce is unionized). Large firms may have several human resource departments, each dealing with specialized activities. Imperial Oil, for example, has separate departments to deal with recruiting and hiring, wage and salary levels, and labour relations. Smaller firms may have a single department, while very small organizations may have a single person responsible for all human resource activities. Chapters 8 and 9 address human resource management issues.

MIDDLE MANAGERS Those managers responsible for implementing the decisions made by top managers.

FIRST-LINE MANAGERS Those managers responsible for supervising the work of employees.

OPERATIONS MANAGERS

Operations managers are responsible for a company's system for creating goods and services. This includes production control, inventory control, and quality control, among other duties. Manufacturing companies like Steelcase, Bristol Aerospace, and Sony need operations managers at many levels. Such firms typically have a vice-president for operations (top), plant managers (middle), and supervisors (first-line). In recent years, sound operations management practices have also become increasingly important to service-producing organizations like hospitals, the government, and colleges and universities. Operations management is the subject of Chapter 10.

>>> **TABLE 6.1** The three levels of management

Level	Examples	Responsibilities
Top managers	President, vice-president, treasurer, chief executive officer (CEO), chief financial officer (CFO)	• Responsible for the overall performance and effectiveness of the firm • Set general policies, formulate strategies, and approve all significant decisions • Represent the company in dealings with other firms and with government bodies
Middle managers	Plant manager, operations manager, division manager, regional sales manager	• Responsible for implementing the strategies of and working toward the goals set by top managers
First-line managers	Supervisor, office manager, project manager, group leader, sales manager	• Responsible for supervising the work of employees who report to them • Ensure employees understand and are properly trained in company policies and procedures

INFORMATION MANAGERS

Dramatic increases in both the amount of information available to managers and the ability to manage it have led to the emergence of *information managers*. These persons are responsible for designing and implementing various systems to gather, process, and disseminate information. Federal Express, for example, has a chief information officer. Middle managers engaged in information management help design information systems for divisions or plants. Computer systems managers within smaller businesses or operations are first-line managers. Information management is discussed in the Chapter 11 Supplement.

MARKETING MANAGERS

Marketing includes the development, pricing, promotion, and distribution of products and services. *Marketing managers* are responsible for getting these products and services to buyers. Marketing is especially important for firms producing consumer products, such as Procter & Gamble, Coca-Cola, and Sun Ice. These firms may have large numbers of marketing managers at various levels. For example, a large firm will probably have a vice-president for marketing (top manager), regional marketing managers (middle managers), and several district sales managers (first-line managers). We examine marketing in Chapters 12–13.

FINANCIAL MANAGERS

Management of a firm's finances is extremely important to its survival. Nearly every company has *financial managers* to plan and oversee its financial resources. Levels of financial management may include a vice-president for finance (top), a division controller (middle), and an accounting supervisor (first-line). For large financial institutions, effective financial management is the company's reason for being. Chapters 14 and 15 describe financial management in detail.

OTHER MANAGERS

Some firms have more specialized managers. Chemical companies like CIL have *research and development managers*, for example, whereas companies like Petro-Canada and Apple have *public relations managers*. The range of possibilities is almost endless, and the areas of management are limited only by the needs and imagination of the company.

LO-3 MANAGEMENT ROLES AND SKILLS

Regardless of their level or area within an organization, all managers must play certain roles and possess certain skills if they are to be successful. In this section, we first describe the basic roles that managers play, and then describe the skills they need to be effective.

Management Roles

Describing managers' jobs by referring to functions like planning, organizing, leading, and controlling gives us a good *general* picture of what managers do, but it may not give a clear idea of the *specific* activities managers are involved in. The answer to the question "What do managers actually do?" is that they play a variety of roles. The work of Henry Mintzberg of McGill University illustrates the roles approach to management. In a now-classic work, Mintzberg conducted a detailed study of the work of five chief executive officers and found that (1) they worked at an unrelenting pace, (2) their activities were characterized by brevity, variety, and fragmentation, (3) they preferred "live" action and emphasized work activities that were current, specific, and well defined, and (4) they were attracted to verbal media.[11]

Mintzberg believes that a manager's job can be described as ten roles (in three general categories) that must be performed. The manager's formal authority and status give rise to three *interpersonal roles*: (1) figurehead (duties of a ceremonial nature, such as attending a subordinate's wedding), (2) leader (being responsible for the work of the unit), and (3) liaison (making contact outside the vertical chain of command). These interpersonal roles give rise to three *informational roles*: (1) monitor (scanning the environment for relevant information), (2) disseminator (passing information to subordinates), and (3) spokesperson (sending information to people outside the unit).

The interpersonal and informational roles allow the manager to carry out four *decision-making roles*: (1) entrepreneur (improving the performance of the unit), (2) disturbance handler (responding to high-pressure disturbances, such as a strike at a supplier), (3) resource allocator (deciding who will get what in the unit), and (4) negotiator (working out agreements on a wide variety of issues, such as the amount of authority an individual will be given).

Basic Management Skills

Effective managers must have several skills, including technical, human relations, conceptual, time management, and decision-making skills.

Managers play a variety of important roles. One key interpersonal role is that of figurehead. These managers, for example, are cutting a ribbon symbolizing the opening of a new business.

Ryan Miller/Getty Images

TECHNICAL SKILLS

Technical skills allow managers to perform specialized tasks. A secretary's ability to type, an animator's ability to draw a cartoon, and an accountant's ability to audit a company's records are all technical skills. People develop their technical skills through education and experience. The secretary, for example, probably took an office systems technology course and has had many hours of practice both on and off the job. The animator may have had training in an art school and probably learned a great deal from experienced animators on the job. The accountant earned a university degree and a professional certification.

As Figure 6.3 shows, technical skills are especially important for first-line managers. Most first-line managers spend considerable time helping employees solve work-related problems, monitoring their performance, and training them in more efficient work procedures. They need a basic understanding of the jobs they supervise. As a manager moves up the corporate ladder, however, technical skills become less and less important. Top managers, for example, often need only a general familiarity with the mechanics of basic tasks performed within the company. A top manager at Disney, for example, probably can't draw Mickey Mouse or build a ride for Disney World.

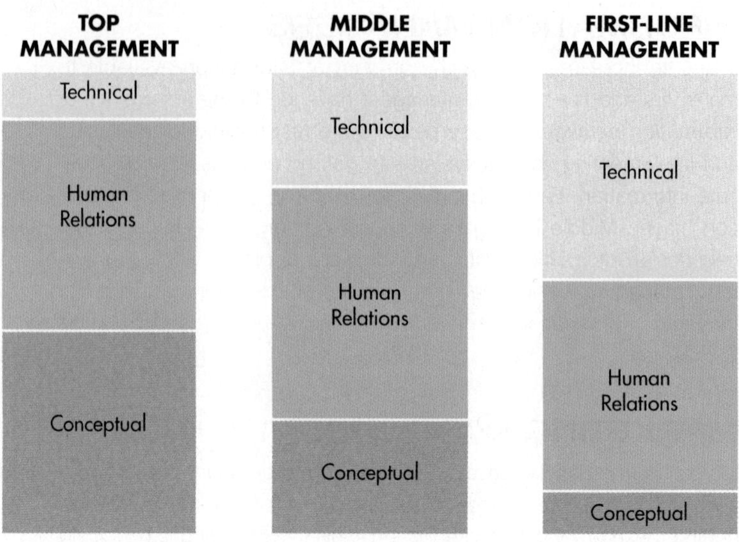

FIGURE 6.3 Different levels in an organization require different combinations of managerial skills

HUMAN RELATIONS SKILLS

Human relations skills help managers lead, motivate, communicate with, and get along with their subordinates. Managers with poor human relations skills will likely have conflicts with subordinates, cause valuable employees to quit or transfer, and contribute to poor morale. Figure 6.3 shows that human relations skills are important at all levels of management. This is true because all managers in the hierarchy act as "bridges" between their bosses, their subordinates, and other managers at the same level in the hierarchy. A study by DDI Canada found that the top reason for managerial failure was poor people skills,[12] and a study by Google found that technical expertise ranked last among a list of eight "Habits of Highly Effective Google Managers." At the top of the list were even-tempered bosses who made time for one-on-one meetings and who helped subordinates work through problems.[13] Rob Quinn, a partner at executive search firm Odgers Berndtson, says that, to be successful, managers must have good self-awareness, have superb written and verbal communication skills, and be critical thinkers—all of which are so-called "soft" skills, not technical skills.[14]

To improve their insight into employee needs and company operations, some managers work alongside lower-level employees temporarily. For example, the CEO of ING Direct sits beside call centre agents and personally answers caller inquiries.[15] When the CEO of 7-Eleven (Joseph De Pinto) worked undercover at a 7-Eleven outlet, he discovered how hard the people worked and why the location was selling so much coffee. Larry O'Donnell, the CEO of Waste Management, did jobs like sorting trash, picking up paper at a landfill, and cleaning portable toilets. The experience taught him the pressure for production that employees had to cope with, and he introduced changes based on what he had learned.[16]

TECHNICAL SKILLS Skills associated with performing specialized tasks within a firm.

HUMAN RELATIONS SKILLS Skills in understanding and getting along with people.

CONCEPTUAL SKILLS Abilities to think in the abstract, diagnose and analyze various situations, and see beyond the present situation.

TIME MANAGEMENT SKILLS Skills associated with the productive use of time.

CONCEPTUAL SKILLS

Conceptual skills refer to a person's ability to think in the abstract, to diagnose and analyze various situations, and to see beyond the present situation. Conceptual skills help managers recognize new market opportunities and threats. For example, in e-commerce businesses, conceptual skills help managers foresee how a particular business application will be affected by, or can be translated to, the internet. Figure 6.3 shows that top managers depend most on conceptual skills, and first-line managers least, but that some conceptual skills are needed in almost any management job.

TIME MANAGEMENT SKILLS

Time management skills refer to the productive use that managers make of their time. Effective time management is particularly important for highly paid top managers. For example, in 2014 the total compensation paid to Steven Williams, the CEO of Suncor Energy, was $12.8 million.[17] Assuming that he worked 50 hours a week and took two weeks' vacation, Regent earned about $5120 per hour, or about $85 per minute. Any time that Williams wastes represents a large cost to Suncor and its shareholders.

To manage time effectively, managers must address four leading causes of wasted time:

- *Paperwork.* Some managers spend too much time deciding what to do with letters and reports. Most documents of this sort are routine and can be handled quickly. Managers must learn to recognize those documents that require more attention.
- *The telephone.* Experts estimate that managers are interrupted by the telephone every five minutes. To manage time more effectively, they suggest having a secretary screen all calls and setting aside a certain block of time each day to return the important ones.
- *Meetings.* Many managers spend as much as four hours per day in meetings. To help keep this time productive, the person handling the meeting should specify a clear agenda, start on time, keep everyone focused on the agenda, and end on time.
- *Email.* With the introduction of devices like the BlackBerry, managers are relying more heavily on email and other forms of electronic communication. But many email messages are not important, and some are downright trivial. As the number of electronic messages grows, the potential time wasted also increases.

DECISION-MAKING SKILLS

Decision-making skills help managers define problems or opportunities, and to select the best course of action. Decision making is a critical management skill because it affects all of the functions of management. Managers must deal with three basic decision characteristics. First, managers must make both *problem decisions* (there is a specific problem that must be resolved) and *opportunity decisions* (there is no specific problem but rather an opportunity presents itself).

Second, the decisions that managers make are either *programmed decisions* (those that are made frequently and are highly structured) or *non-programmed decisions* (those that are made infrequently and are poorly structured).

Third, managers make decisions under several different risk conditions. In the condition of *certainty*, the manager knows what alternatives are available and what conditions are associated with each alternative. For example, when a company like Singapore Airlines decides to buy new jumbo jets, it knows there are only two alternatives (Boeing and Airbus), and it knows the price of each plane. In the condition of *risk*, the alternatives may be known, but their costs are simply probabilities rather than certainties. For example, when a labour negotiator receives a "final" offer from the union before a strike deadline, the two alternatives are to accept or reject the offer. If the offer is accepted, a strike will be avoided, but perhaps the company will find that it has accepted a deal that is very costly. If the offer is rejected, a strike may occur, but the company may eventually be able to get a deal that is less costly. In the condition of *uncertainty*, the manager does not know all of the possible alternatives or the outcomes associated with each alternative. For example, a company that wants to manufacture a new product may not know how many different manufacturing technologies (if any) will work, nor the costs associated with each.

DECISION-MAKING SKILLS Skills in defining problems and selecting the best courses of action.

Table 6.2 shows the steps in the rational decision-making process. The key elements of each step are described below.

Recognizing and Defining the Decision Situation

The first step in rational decision making is recognizing that a decision is necessary. There must be some stimulus or spark to initiate this process. For example, when equipment malfunctions, managers must decide whether to repair or replace it. The stimulus for a decision may be either a problem or an opportunity. A manager facing cost overruns on a project is faced with a problem decision, while a manager trying to decide how to invest surplus funds is faced with an opportunity decision.

Understanding precisely what the problem or opportunity is comes from careful analysis and thoughtful consideration of the situation. Consider the international air travel industry. Because of the growth of international travel related to business, education, and tourism, global carriers like Singapore Airlines, KLM, JAL, British Airways, and American Airlines need to increase their capacity for international travel. Because most major international airports are already operating at or near capacity, adding a significant number of new flights to existing schedules is not feasible. As a result, the most logical alternative is to increase capacity on existing flights. Thus, Boeing and Airbus, the world's only manufacturers of large commercial aircraft, recognized an important opportunity and defined their decision situation as how best to respond to the need for increased global travel capacity.[18]

Identifying Alternatives Once the need for a decision has been recognized and defined, the second step is to identify possible alternative courses of effective action. In general, the more important the decision, the more attention is directed to developing alternatives. If the decision involves a multimillion-dollar relocation, a great deal of time and expertise should be devoted to identifying alternatives, but if the decision

>>> **TABLE 6.2** Steps in the rational decision-making process

	Step	Detail	Example
1.	Recognizing and defining the decision situation	Some stimulus indicates that a decision must be made. The stimulus may be positive or negative.	The plant manager sees that employee turnover has increased by 5 percent.
2.	Identifying alternatives	Both obvious and creative alternatives are desired. In general, the more important the decision, the more alternatives should be generated.	The plant manager can increase wages, increase benefits, or change hiring standards.
3.	Evaluating alternatives	Each alternative is evaluated to determine its feasibility, its satisfactoriness, and its consequences.	Increasing benefits may not be feasible. Increasing wages and changing hiring standards may satisfy all conditions.
4.	Selecting the best alternative	Consider all situational factors and choose the alternative that best fits the manager's situation.	Changing hiring standards will take an extended period of time to cut turnover, so increase wages.
5.	Implementing the chosen alternative	The chosen alternative is implemented into the organizational system.	The plant manager may need permission from corporate headquarters. The human resource department establishes a new wage structure.
6.	Following up and evaluating the results	At some time in the future, the manager should ascertain the extent to which the alternative chosen in step 4 and implemented in step 5 has worked.	The plant manager notes that six months later, turnover dropped to its previous level.

involves choosing a name for the company softball team, many fewer resources should be devoted to the task (although there might be a lot of arguing about what the name should be!).

Managers must accept that factors such as legal restrictions, moral and ethical norms, and available technology can limit their alternatives. For example, after assessing the question of how to increase international airline capacity, Boeing and Airbus identified three alternatives: they could independently develop new large planes, they could collaborate in a joint venture to create a single new large plane, or they could modify their largest existing planes to increase capacity.

Evaluating Alternatives Once alternatives have been identified, they must be thoroughly evaluated to increase the chance that the alternative finally chosen will be successful. Some alternatives may not be feasible because of legal or financial barriers. Limited human, material, and information resources may make other alternatives impractical. During its analysis of alternatives, Airbus concluded that it would be at a disadvantage if it tried to simply enlarge its existing planes, because the competitive Boeing 747 was already the largest aircraft being made and could readily be expanded. Boeing was concerned about the risk inherent in building a new and even larger plane, even if it shared the risk with Airbus as a joint venture.

Selecting the Best Alternative Choosing the best available alternative is a key activity in decision making. Even though many situations do not lend themselves to objective mathematical analysis, managers can often develop subjective estimates for choosing an alternative. Decision makers should also remember that finding multiple acceptable alternatives may be possible, so selecting just one alternative and rejecting all the others might not be necessary. For example, Airbus proposed a joint venture with Boeing, but Boeing decided that its best course of action was to modify its existing 747 to increase its capacity. Airbus then decided to proceed on its own to develop and manufacture a new jumbo jet called the A380. Meanwhile, Boeing decided that, in addition to modifying its 747, it would also develop a new plane (the 787).

Implementing the Chosen Alternative After an alternative has been selected, managers have to implement it. Boeing implemented its chosen alternative by setting its engineers to work expanding the capacity of its existing 747 by adding 30 feet to the plane's body. Airbus engineers developed design concepts for a new jumbo jet equipped with escalators and elevators, and capable of carrying 655 passengers. Airbus's development costs were estimated to exceed $12 billion.

One of the key considerations during implementation is employee resistance to change. The reasons for such resistance include insecurity, inconvenience, and fear of the unknown. Managers must also recognize that even when all alternatives have been evaluated as precisely as possible and the consequences of each alternative have been weighed, unanticipated consequences are still likely. For example, both Boeing and Airbus experienced unexpected delays in bringing their new planes to market.

After a long decision-making process, Airbus decided to design its own new jumbo jet. Boeing, meanwhile, went through a similar decision-making process, but concluded that the risks were too great to gamble on such an enormous project. Instead, the company decided to modify its existing 747 design and develop a new fuel-efficient aircraft called the 787.

Oliver Fantitsch/AP Images

Following Up and Evaluating the Results The final step in the decision-making process requires managers to evaluate the effectiveness of their decision—that is, they should make sure that the chosen alternative has served its original purpose. If an implemented alternative appears not to be working, they can respond in several ways. Another previously identified alternative (the original second or third choice, for example) could be adopted. Or they might recognize that the situation was not correctly defined to begin with and start the process all over again. Or they might decide that the original alternative was in fact appropriate but either has not yet had time to work or should be implemented in a different way.

Both Boeing and Airbus had difficulties with their decisions during follow-up. The Airbus A380 made its first commercial flight almost a decade ago, but delays pushed back its production schedule. The plane has also been hampered by technical problems. Boeing's expanded 747 was launched on schedule, but its 787 Dreamliner experienced numerous delays well as some serious technical problems. For example, its lithium-ion batteries sometimes started fires during flights and the plane was grounded by the U.S. Federal Aviation Administration for several months during 2013.[19]

BEHAVIOURAL ASPECTS OF DECISION MAKING

Most managers try to be logical when they make decisions. But even when they try, they may not succeed. When Starbucks opened its first coffee shops in New York, it relied on scientific marketing research, taste tests, and rational deliberation in making a decision to emphasize drip over espresso coffee. However, that decision proved wrong when it became clear that New Yorkers strongly preferred the same espresso-style coffees that were Starbucks' mainstays in the west. Hence, the firm had to reconfigure its stores hastily to meet customer preferences.

To complicate matters, non-logical and emotional factors often influence managerial decision making. These factors include *organizational politics*, *intuition*, *escalation of commitment*, and *risk propensity*.

Organizational Politics The term *organizational politics* refers to the actions that people take as they try to get what they want. These actions may or may not be beneficial to the organization, but they do influence decision making, particularly if the person taking the action is a powerful manager. A study of 293 Canadian office workers found that 71 percent believed that office politics was at least somewhat necessary in order to get ahead in their organization.[20]

Intuition Managers sometimes decide to do something because it "feels right" or they have a "hunch." *Intuition* is usually based on years of experience and practice in making decisions in similar situations. Such an inner sense may actually help managers make an occasional decision without going through a rational sequence of steps. For example, the New York Yankees once contacted three major sneaker manufacturers—Nike, Reebok, and Adidas—and informed them that they were interested in signing a sponsorship deal. While Nike and Reebok were carefully and rationally assessing the possibilities, managers at Adidas quickly responded to the idea and ended up hammering out a contract while the competitors were still analyzing details.[21] These occasional successes can be very dramatic, but they should not cause managers to rely too heavily on intuition.

Escalation of Commitment When a manager makes a decision and then remains committed to its implementation in spite of clear evidence that it was a bad decision, *escalation of commitment* has occurred.[22] A good example of this is Expo 86, the world's fair held in British Columbia. When the project was first conceived, the deficit was projected at about $56 million. Over the next few years, the projected deficit kept rising until it was over $300 million. In spite of that, the project went forward.

Managers can avoid such overcommitment by setting specific goals ahead of time regarding the time and money they are willing to spend on a given project. This makes it harder for managers to interpret unfavourable news in a positive light.

Risk Propensity *Risk propensity* refers to how much a manager is willing to gamble when making decisions. Managers who are very cautious when making decisions are more likely to avoid mistakes, and they are unlikely to make decisions that lead to big losses (or big gains). Other managers are extremely aggressive in making decisions and are willing to take risks.[23] They rely heavily on intuition, reach decisions quickly, and often risk big money on their decisions. These managers are more likely than their conservative counterparts to achieve big successes, but they are also more likely to incur greater losses.[24] The organization's culture is a prime ingredient in fostering different levels of risk propensity.

LO-4 STRATEGIC MANAGEMENT

Strategic management is the process of effectively aligning the organization with its external environment. The starting point in strategic management is setting **goals** that a business wants to achieve. Every business needs goals. Remember, however, that deciding what it intends to do is only the first step for an organization. Managers must also make decisions about what actions will and will not achieve company goals. Decisions cannot be made on a problem-by-problem basis or merely to meet needs as they arise. In most companies, a broad program underlies those decisions. That program is called a **strategy**—the broad set of organizational plans for implementing the decisions made for achieving organizational goals.

Setting Business Goals

Goals are performance targets, the means by which organizations and their managers measure success or failure at every level. They indicate *what* results are desired, in contrast to plans, which indicate *how* these goals are to be achieved. Managers must understand the purposes of goal setting and the kinds of goals that need to be set.

THE PURPOSES OF GOAL SETTING

There are four main purposes in organizational goal setting:

1. *Goal setting provides direction, guidance, and motivation for all managers.* WestJet's goal is to challenge Air Canada for the top spot in domestic air travel by 2016.[25]
2. *Goal setting helps firms allocate resources.* Areas that are expected to grow will get first priority. Thus, 3M allocates more resources to new projects with large sales potential than it allocates to mature products with low growth potential.
3. *Goal setting helps to define corporate culture.* General Electric's goal is to have each of its divisions be #1 or #2 in its industry. The result is a competitive corporate culture that rewards success and has little tolerance for failure.
4. *Goal setting helps managers assess performance.* At Port Metro Vancouver, the goal for container "dwell time"—the time containers sit on the dock—is three days (the North American standard). In January 2010 the dwell time was 3.7 days, but by November 2011 it had been reduced to 2.5 days. Setting specific goals like this helps managers assess their performance.[26]

Goal setting is effective for individuals as well as organizations. For example, when students set goals, they achieve higher grades, lower their chance for dropping out of school, and experience greater well-being as adults. Unfortunately, less than half of the students aged 10 to 18 are aggressively pursuing goals.[27]

KINDS OF GOALS

Goals differ from company to company, depending on the firm's vision and mission. Every organization has a **vision** (or **purpose**) that indicates why it exists and what kind of organization it wants to be. For example, businesses seek profit, universities discover and transmit new knowledge, and government agencies provide services to the public. Most organizations also have a **mission statement**—a statement of how they will achieve their purpose. DaimlerChrysler's mission statement emphasizes "delighted customers," while Atco Ltd.'s mission is to provide products and services to the energy and resource industries and to invest in energy-related assets in North America. Mission statements often include some statement about the company's core values and its commitment to ethical behaviour.

STRATEGIC MANAGEMENT The process of helping an organization maintain an effective alignment with its environment.

GOALS Objectives that a business plans to attain.

STRATEGY The broad set of organizational plans for implementing the decisions made for achieving organizational goals.

VISION (OR PURPOSE) A statement indicating why an organization exists and what kind of organization it wants to be.

MISSION STATEMENT An organization's statement of how it will achieve its purpose in the environment in which it conducts its business.

Two business firms can have the same vision—for example, to sell watches at a profit—yet have very different missions. Timex sells low-cost, reliable watches in outlets ranging from department stores to corner drugstores. Rolex, on the other hand, sells high-quality, high-priced fashion watches through selected jewellery stores. Regardless of a company's purpose and mission, it must set long-term, intermediate, and short-term goals.

- *Long-term goals* relate to extended periods of time—typically five years or more into the future. American Express, for example, might set a long-term goal of doubling the number of participating merchants during the next ten years.
- *Intermediate goals* are set for a period of one to five years into the future. When Kazuo Hirai became CEO of Sony in 2012, he was determined to improve the performance of the consumer electronics company. He therefore set a sales target of US$105 billion for the division that makes medical equipment and electric car batteries. The goal was to be achieved in two years. He also set a goal to triple revenue in the mobile phone division.[28]
- Like intermediate goals, *short-term goals*—which are set for one year or less—are developed for several different areas. Increasing sales by 2 percent this year, cutting costs by 1 percent next quarter, and reducing turnover by 4 percent over the next six months are all short-term goals.

SMART GOALS Goals that are Specific, Measurable, Achievable, Relevant, and Time-framed.

STRATEGY FORMULATION Creation of a broad program for defining and meeting an organization's goals.

STRATEGIC GOALS Long-term goals derived directly from the firm's mission statement.

Whatever the time frame of the goals set, research shows that managers who set **SMART goals** (goals that are Specific, Measurable, Achievable, Relevant, and Time-framed) have higher performance than managers who don't. The boxed insert entitled "Some Complications in Setting Green Goals" describes a few dilemmas managers face when they set goals that take the environment into account.

Formulating Strategy

After a firm has set its goals, it must develop a strategy for achieving them. In contrast to planning, strategy is wider in scope and is a broad program that describes how a business intends to meet its goals, how it will respond to new challenges, and how it will meet new needs. For example, Brookfield Asset Management's strategy is to buy high-quality assets at less than replacement cost.[29] **Strategy formulation** involves three basic steps: (1) setting strategic goals, (2) analyzing the organization and its environment, and (3) matching the organization and its environment (see Figure 6.4).

STEP 1: SETTING STRATEGIC GOALS

Strategic goals are long-term goals derived directly from the firm's mission statement. When Martin Winterkorn took over as CEO of Volkswagen, he set a clear strategic goal for the company to become more successful and more profitable. By 2013, Volkwagen was making big profits and was the third-largest car producer in the world. But the emission scandal of 2015 (see Chapter 3, p. 49) hurt the company's reputation, and led to Winterkorn's resignation. The company will now have to reconsider its strategic goals.

THE GREENING OF BUSINESS

Some Complications in Setting Green Goals

Many private-sector businesses set goals to improve their performance with respect to sustainability and environmental protection. Here are some examples:

- Scotiabank set a goal to be in the top 10 percent of the companies listed on the Dow Jones sustainability World Index.
- Employees on different floors of the Air Miles building in Toronto competed to see who could reduce energy usage the most in a specific month.
- Co-operators Life Insurance Co. set a goal to reduce emissions from business travel and climate control by 50 percent.
- Dillon Consulting Ltd. (Toronto) set a goal to invest 1 percent of revenue into social, environmental, and community initiatives.

When companies set goals like these, it is generally assumed that they have enough control over their corporate activities that they can achieve the goals. And a lot of the time they actually do achieve the goals. But on various occasions factors in the external environment interfere with the achievement of green goals. This is true for both business firms and government agencies. For example, in 2007 the province of British Columbia set a goal to reduce greenhouse gas (GHG) emissions 33 percent by 2020. But now there are concerns that this goal will not be reached because of the rather sudden growth in the natural gas industry and the emissions that will result. Another example is the federal government's goal for reducing fuel consumption in cars from 8.6 litres of gas per 100 kilometres in 2010 to 5.1 litres by 2025. But the dramatic decline in gas prices that occurred in 2014 increased consumer interest in buying bigger, gas-guzzling cars. So that goal may not be reached either.

Private-sector companies can also run into unexpected problems. In 2014, Canada's Oil Sands Innovation Alliance (COSIA) announced that it would not be able to meet its goal of reducing GHG emissions because they had run into unexpected complexities when trying to share new technologies. The Alliance also set a goal to reduce the amount of fresh water used to produce a barrel of oil by 50 percent by 2022. That goal may be more achievable since it depends largely on applying a more efficient technology to the production process.

CRITICAL THINKING QUESTIONS

1. What are the advantages of setting green goals? Are there disadvantages? Explain.
2. Describe some of the uncertainties that must be taken into account when a business or a government agency sets green goals.

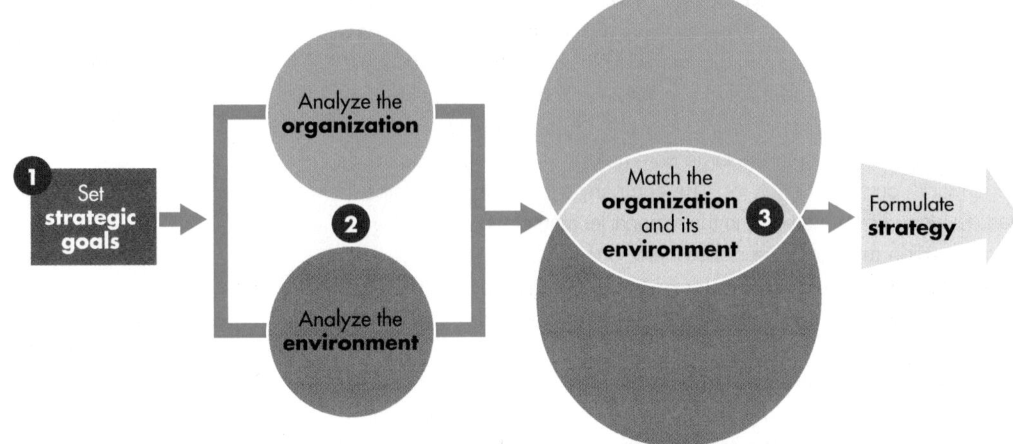

>>> **FIGURE 6.4** Strategy formulation

STEP 2: ANALYZING THE ORGANIZATION AND ITS ENVIRONMENT

After strategic goals have been set managers assess both their organization and its environment using a **SWOT analysis**. This involves identifying organizational Strengths and Weaknesses, and identifying environmental Opportunities and Threats. Strengths and weaknesses are factors internal to the firm, and are assessed using *organizational analysis*. Strengths might include surplus cash, a dedicated workforce, an ample supply of managerial talent, technical expertise, or weak competitors. For example, Pepsi's strength in beverage distribution through its network of soft-drink distributors was successfully extended to distribution of its Aquafina brand of bottled water. Weaknesses might include a cash shortage, aging factories, and a poor public image. Garden.com's reliance on the internet-based e-tailing model was its downfall when the dot-com bubble burst.

Opportunities and threats are factors external to the firm and are assessed using *environmental analysis*. Opportunities include things like market demand for new products, favourable government legislation, or shortages of raw materials that the company is good at producing. For example, when Pepsi managers recognized a market opportunity for bottled water, they moved quickly to launch their Aquafina brand and position it for rapid growth. Threats include new products developed by competitors, unfavourable government regulations, and changes in consumer tastes. For example, online music services such as iTunes proved a major threat to manufacturers of CDs and CD players. Likewise, the emergence of digital photography dramatically weakened companies tied to print photography. The Province of Ontario introduced a new law that reduced the revenue pharmacies received for dispensing prescription drugs. Some external threats are unpredictable, like the volcanic eruption in Iceland in 2010 that halted air travel in Europe for a week. Commercial airlines lost hundreds of millions of dollars of revenue, while alternative service providers like trains saw demand for their services soar.

THERE'S AN APP FOR THAT!

APP DETAILS	PLATFORMS
1. **McKinsey Insights** **Source:** McKinsey and Company **Key Features:** The latest thinking on the biggest issues facing senior executives, everything from leadership and corporate strategy to globalization and technology's impact on business and society.	Apple, Android
2. **SWOT Chart** **Source:** K. Kaleeswaran **Key Features:** Strategic planning method used to evaluate strengths, weaknesses, opportunities, and threats.	Apple, BlackBerry, Windows
3. **Goal Tracker: SmartGoals** **Source:** MSurf Lab **Key Features:** Tool to help you set SMART (specific, measurable, attainable, reasonable and timely) goals.	Android

APP DISCOVERY EXERCISE

Since app availability changes, conduct your own search for the "Top Three" management apps and identify the key features.

STEP 3: MATCHING THE ORGANIZATION AND ITS ENVIRONMENT

The final step in strategy formulation is matching environmental threats and opportunities with corporate strengths and weaknesses. Matching companies with their environments lays the foundation for successfully planning and conducting business. A firm should attempt to leverage its strengths so as to capitalize on opportunities and counteract threats. It should also attempt to shield its weaknesses, or at least not allow them to derail other activities. For example, knowing how to distribute consumer products (a strength) allows Pepsi to add new businesses and extend existing ones that use the same distribution models. But a firm that lacked a strong understanding of consumer product distribution would be foolish to add new products whose success relied on efficient distribution. Just because two companies are in the same industry does not mean they will use the same strategies. The Toronto-Dominion Bank, for example, aggressively expanded into the U.S. retail banking industry by acquiring U.S. banks, but the Royal Bank of Canada has been much less aggressive in this area.[30]

SWOT ANALYSIS Identification and analysis of organizational strengths and weaknesses and environmental opportunities and threats as part of strategy formulation.

An Example of Strategy Formulation: Bombardier For many years, Montreal-based Bombardier's strategy has been to compete in the small commercial jet market (step 1). After analyzing consumer demand for air travel and the company's own internal capabilities (step 2), Bombardier decided in 2004 to go head-to-head with Airbus and Boeing in the large commercial jet market. To do so, it began work on the CSeries jet. The company felt that the strengths it had developed over the years in the regional jet market would match well with the opportunities in the external environment (step 3). Bombardier estimated that it would achieve a significant market share in the large jet market, and this would mean huge sales revenues and profits for the company,

It's one thing to formulate a strategy, but quite another to successfully implement it, and Bombardier has run into three significant implementation problems. First, development of the new CSeries jet has taken much longer than anticipated. The plane was supposed to be delivered by late 2013, but will not actually be available until at least 2015. Second, the estimated development costs (about $3.4 billion) were too low. Bombardier will actually spend at least $4.4 billion on the CSeries jet. Third, sales of the new jet have not been as high as anticipated, partly because Boeing and Airbus improved their existing planes and have been aggressively offering discounts to buyers.[31] Industry observers are not surprised by these developments, and point out that Bombardier's original decision to compete head-on with Boeing and Airbus was very risky. It is not clear how all of this will work out for Bombardier.

A HIERARCHY OF PLANS

In the most general terms, the three-step strategy formulation process requires a hierarchy of plans on three different levels. Each level reflects plans for which managers at that level are responsible. These levels constitute a hierarchy because implementing plans is practical only when there is a logical flow from one level to the next. **Strategic plans** reflect decisions about resource allocations, company priorities, and the steps needed to meet strategic goals, and are usually set by top management. In 2010, Maple Leaf Foods developed a five-year strategic plan designed to increase its earnings by more than 75 percent by 2015.[32] **Tactical plans** are shorter-range ones concerned with implementing specific aspects of the company's strategic plan; they typically involve upper and middle management. Coca-Cola's decision to increase sales in Europe by building European bottling facilities is an example of tactical planning. **Operational plans**, developed by middle and lower-level managers, set short-term targets for daily, weekly, or monthly performance.

STRATEGIC PLANS Plans that reflect decisions about resource allocations, company priorities, and steps needed to meet strategic goals.

TACTICAL PLANS Generally, short-range plans concerned with implementing specific aspects of a company's strategic plans.

OPERATIONAL PLANS Plans setting short-term targets for daily, weekly, or monthly performance.

CORPORATE-LEVEL STRATEGY Identifies the various businesses a company will be in, and how these businesses will relate to each other.

BUSINESS-LEVEL (COMPETITIVE) STRATEGY Identifies the ways a business will compete in its chosen line of products or services.

FUNCTIONAL STRATEGIES Identify the basic courses of action each department in the firm will pursue so that it contributes to the business's overall goals.

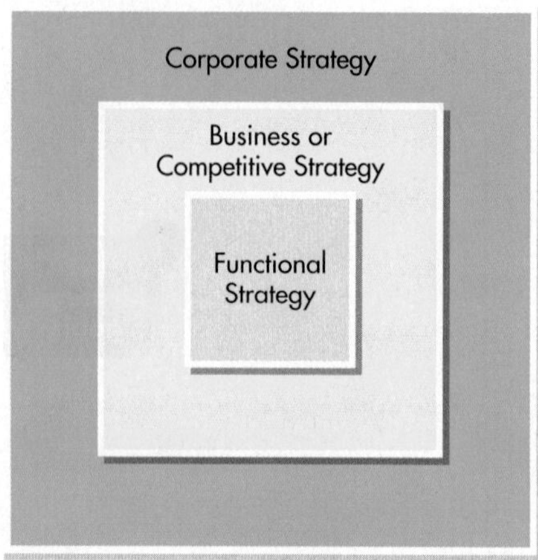

FIGURE 6.5 Hierarchy of strategy

Source: Based on Thomas L. Wheelen and J. David Hunger, *Strategic Management and Business Policy*, 8th ed. (Upper Saddle River, NJ: Prentice Hall, 2002), 14.

McDonald's, for example, establishes operational plans when it explains precisely how Big Macs are to be cooked, warmed, and served.

Levels of Strategy

There are three levels of strategy in a business firm (see Figure 6.5). A **corporate-level strategy** identifies the various businesses a company will be in and how they will relate to each other. A **business-level (competitive) strategy** identifies the ways a business will compete in its chosen line of products or services. **Functional strategies** identify the basic courses of action each department will pursue so that it contributes to the business's overall goals.

CORPORATE-LEVEL STRATEGIES

A company might pursue any of several different corporate-level strategies: concentration, growth, integration, diversification, and investment reduction.

Concentration A *concentration strategy* involves focusing the company on one product or product line that it knows very well. Organizations that have successfully pursued a concentration strategy include McDonald's and Canadian National Railway.

Growth Companies have several growth strategies available to them, including *market penetration* (boosting sales of present products by more aggressive selling in the firm's current markets), *geographic expansion* (expanding operations in new geographic areas), and *product development* (developing improved products for current markets). These three strategies focus on internal activities that will result in growth.

Integration There are two basic integration strategies. *Horizontal integration* means acquiring control of competitors in the same or similar markets with the same or similar products. For example, Hudson's Bay owns Home Outfitters (Déco Découverte in Quebec). Bauer Performance Sports Ltd., famous for its hockey sticks, is growing by acquiring other sport-related companies like Easton, which makes baseballs.[33] *Vertical integration* means owning or controlling the inputs to the firm's processes and/or the channels through which the products or services are distributed. Oil companies like Shell not only drill and produce their own oil, but also sell it through company-controlled outlets across Canada. These two strategies focus on external activities that will result in growth.

Target used a horizontal integration strategy when it entered the Canadian market. It purchased over 200 Zellers stores and then remade them in the Target style. But Target's strategy was not successful and it withdrew from the Canadian market in 2015.

Jonathan Larsen/Diadem Images/Alamy

Diversification *Diversification* helps the firm avoid the problem of having all of its eggs in one basket by spreading risk among several products or markets. *Related diversification* means adding new, but related, products or services to an existing business. For example, Maple Leaf Gardens Ltd., which already owned the Toronto Maple Leafs, acquired the Toronto Raptors basketball team. *Conglomerate diversification* means diversifying into products or markets that are not related to the firm's present businesses. Eastman Kodak was the leader for many years in the film-based photography business, but it fell on hard times when digital cameras were introduced (Kodak invented the digital camera in the 1970s, but somehow never capitalized on the idea). Kodak then adopted a diversification strategy in an attempt to survive (and tried to reinvent itself as a printing and graphics company), but it fell into bankruptcy anyway.[34]

Investment Reduction *Investment reduction* means reducing the company's investment in one or more of its lines of business. One investment-reduction strategy is *retrenchment*, which means the reduction of activity or operations. One of the most famous examples of retrenchment occurred in 2015, when Target withdrew from the Canadian market after failing to attract enough customers to its retail stores.[35] *Divestment* involves selling or liquidating one or more of a firm's businesses. For example, BCE sold its Yellow Pages and White Pages for $4 billion.

BUSINESS-LEVEL (COMPETITIVE) STRATEGIES

Whatever corporate-level strategy a firm decides on, it must also have a competitive strategy. A **competitive strategy** is a plan to establish a profitable and sustainable competitive position.[36] Michael Porter identifies three competitive strategies. *Cost leadership* means becoming the low-cost leader in an industry. Walmart is the best-known industry cost leader. Montreal-based Gildan Activewear is dedicated to achieving the lowest possible costs in producing its T-shirts.[37] A firm using a *differentiation strategy* tries to be unique in its industry along some dimension that is valued by buyers. For example, Caterpillar emphasizes durability, Volvo safety, Apple user-friendly products, and Mercedes-Benz quality. A *focus strategy* means selecting a market segment and serving the customers in that market niche better than competitors. Before it was acquired by Nexfor, Fraser Inc. focused on producing the high-quality, durable, lightweight paper used in bibles.

FUNCTIONAL STRATEGIES

Each business's choice of a competitive strategy (cost leadership, differentiation, or focus) is translated into supporting functional strategies for each of its departments to pursue. A functional strategy is the basic course of action that each department follows so that the business accomplishes its overall goals. To implement its cost-leadership strategy, for example, Walmart's distribution department pursued a functional strategy of satellite-based warehousing that ultimately drove distribution costs down below those of its competitors.

COMPETITIVE STRATEGY A plan to establish a profitable and sustainable competitive position.

LO-5 CONTINGENCY PLANNING AND CRISIS MANAGEMENT

Business environments are often difficult to predict because unexpected events may occur. Two common methods of dealing with the unforeseen are *contingency planning* and *crisis management*.

Contingency Planning

Contingency planning means identifying in advance changes that might occur that would affect a business and developing a plan to respond to such changes. For example, airlines know that snowstorms at, say, Toronto's Pearson International Airport are likely, so they develop contingency plans for coping with that eventuality. These plans typically involve rescheduling flights into neighbouring airports and providing passengers

CONTINGENCY PLANNING Identifying aspects of a business or its environment that might require changes in strategy.

Commercial airlines have contingency plans to deal with problems like major snowstorms. Here, a plane is de-iced to ensure that dangerous ice does not build up on its exterior surfaces. Contingency plans also involve making sure that planes are not stranded at airports that are experiencing snow delays.

chalabala/Fotolia

Crisis management involves an organization's methods for dealing with emergencies. Here, Red Cross volunteers provide help to hurricane victims.

Boris Grdanoski/The Canadian Press

with ground transportation into Toronto. Assessing the costs and benefits of these and other options ahead of time helps managers cope with problems when they arise. This sounds like a good idea, but sometimes it can be hard to put into practice. For example, in January 2014, ice and cold weather forced the closure of Pearson International. This resulted in major flight delays and inconvenienced thousands of passengers.[38]

Crisis Management

Crisis management means dealing with an emergency that demands an immediate response. Crisis management plans outline who will be in charge in different kinds of circumstances, how the organization will respond, and the plans that exist for assembling and deploying crisis-management teams.

CRISIS MANAGEMENT An organization's methods for dealing with emergencies.

Business crises are more common than you might think. Consider these recent examples:

- In 2014 Malaysian Airlines faced a crisis when one of its flights simply disappeared (perhaps in the southern Indian Ocean).
- In 2013, Boeing faced a crisis when batteries in the 787 Dreamliner caught fire.
- In 2013, Carnival Corp. faced a crisis when one of its cruise ships lost power and stranded 4000 passengers at sea for four days with no working toilets.
- In 2010, BP faced a crisis when an explosion at a drilling rig in the Gulf of Mexico resulted in the death of 11 workers and caused a huge oil spill.
- In 2009, Toyota faced a crisis when consumers claimed that some models of its cars were accelerating out of control.
- In 2008, Maple Leaf Foods faced a crisis when listeria (tainted meat) was discovered at one of its processing plants. Maple Leaf quickly recalled 686 000 kilograms of meat (an action that cost the company $19 million).

LO-6 MANAGEMENT AND THE CORPORATE CULTURE

Just as every individual has a unique personality, every company has a unique identity. This is its **corporate culture**—the shared experiences, stories, beliefs, and norms that characterize it. Here are some examples:

- At ING Direct, the culture encourages employees to challenge the status quo, both within the company and the banking industry.[39]
- The culture of the Toronto Blue Jays organization is designed to make employees feel like they are part of a family. To facilitate the culture, employees have "snacks with the president" so they can talk about how the organization is operating.
- Google creates a culture of "yes" in order to encourage innovation. Employees focus on what is right with a new idea rather than what is wrong.[40]

CORPORATE CULTURE The shared experiences, stories, beliefs, and norms that characterize a firm.

- Magna International, a large Canadian producer of auto parts, is a firm with a strong culture. Its founder, Frank Stronach, is well known for his views about employees, working conditions, daycare centres, unions, the free-enterprise system, and profit distribution.[41]
- Mountain Equipment Co-op's new headquarters in Vancouver reflects its corporate culture. It includes space for yoga and CrossFit classes, a bouldering room, bike lockers, and a view of the mountains.[42]

Companies that focus largely on one type of product (e.g., Starbucks Coffee) may have a fairly homogeneous culture throughout the organization. But companies with many different divisions and many different types of customers (e.g., the Royal Bank of Canada) are likely to have several different subcultures, because the various divisions pursue different goals and because different types of people are found in the different divisions.

A strong corporate culture guides everyone to work toward the same goals and helps newcomers learn accepted behaviours. In a strong culture where financial success is the key issue, newcomers quickly learn that they are expected to work long, hard hours and that the "winner" is the one who brings in the most revenue. But if quality of life is more fundamental to the culture, newcomers learn that it's acceptable to balance work and non-work activities. Cameron Herold—a Vancouver entrepreneur who has had a string of successes in franchising, including College Pro Painters, Boyd Autobody, and 1-800-GOT-JUNK—says that a cult-like culture is crucial for attracting great employees. He says what's needed is a culture that is "more than a business and slightly less than a religion."[43]

Every year, Waterstone Human Capital conducts in-depth interviews with senior managers at many different Canadian companies and asks them which corporate cultures they admire most. The 2014 winners included AltaGas (Calgary), Monsanto Canada (Winnipeg), and Starbucks Coffee (Toronto).[44] Although many companies do not systematically monitor their corporate cultures, Starbucks is one company that does. Once every 18 months, employees fill out a Partner View Survey containing questions that are designed to help the company determine whether it is making progress toward one of its key values—providing a work environment where people treat one another with respect and dignity. The survey is voluntary, but about 90 percent of employees fill it out (on company time). One reason the participation rate is so high is that the company actually pays attention to what employees say in the survey. For example, when one survey showed that employees were not clear about career progression possibilities in the company, Starbucks held career fairs in several Canadian cities, where company managers spoke with employees about management opportunities at Starbucks.[45]

Communicating the Culture and Managing Change

Managers must carefully consider the kind of culture they want for their organization, then work to nourish that culture by communicating with everyone who works there. Walmart, for example, assigns veteran managers to lead employees in new territories. Royal Bank of Canada and Four Seasons Hotels and Resorts also survey their employees to determine how well they are progressing toward their corporate culture goals.[46]

If a problem arises with a company's products, it may create pressure for change in the company's culture. For example, General Motors recalled 2.6 million cars with bad ignition switches that sometimes shut off the car engine and made it difficult to steer. Accidents that were caused by this problem resulted in the deaths of 13 people. An investigation revealed that the culture at GM (which emphasized cost-cutting) was partly to blame for the problem. Even though fixing the problem would have cost very little money, nothing was done.[47]

COMMUNICATING THE CULTURE

To use a company's culture to full advantage, its managers must accomplish several tasks, all of which hinge on effective communication. First, managers themselves must have a clear understanding of the culture. Second, they must transmit the culture to others in the organization. Communication is a key aim in training and orienting newcomers. A clear and meaningful statement of the organization's mission is also a valuable communication tool. Finally, managers can maintain the culture by rewarding and promoting those who understand it and work toward maintaining it.

MANAGING CHANGE

Organizations must sometimes change their cultures. Ontario Hydro, for example, had an "engineering" culture for many years. That meant that everything was planned and analyzed down to the last detail before any action was taken. But Ontario Hydro's culture has changed to a more consumer-oriented, risk-taking culture as it tries to cope with large debt and changes in its markets.

Changing an organization's culture can be difficult, so just because someone recognizes the need for cultural change does not mean that it will actually be implemented. For example, when several RCMP officers alleged that there were problems with senior management, lawyer David Brown was appointed by the government to look into the matter. His report concluded that the Commissioner had exercised absolute power, that no one questioned his management style, and that there was a "tone" at the top of the organization that resulted in little respect for employees. The report also said that whistle-blowers within the RCMP were punished when they pointed out that there were problems. The report concluded that the culture and management structure at the RCMP were "horribly broken."[48] These developments were discouraging, because just a few years earlier the RCMP had completed a "visioning" process that resulted in a new mission statement, a new set of core values, and a commitment to the communities where it worked. At that time, it was reported that the culture of the RCMP was quite different than it had been in the days when military tradition dominated the organization, but subsequent events suggested that the culture had not actually changed much.

MyBizLab

Study, practise, and explore real business situations with these helpful resources:
- **Interactive Lesson Presentations:** Work through interactive presentations and assessments to test your knowledge of business concepts.
- **Study Plan:** Check your understanding of chapter concepts with self-study quizzes.
- **Dynamic Study Modules:** Work through adaptive study modules on your computer, tablet, or mobile device.
- **Simulations:** Practise decision-making in simulated business environments.
- **Videos:** Learn more about the business practices and strategies of real companies.

SUMMARY OF LEARNING OBJECTIVES

LO-1 DESCRIBE THE FOUR ACTIVITIES THAT CONSTITUTE THE *MANAGEMENT PROCESS*.

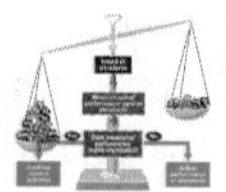

Management is the process of planning, organizing, leading, and controlling an organization's financial, physical, human, and information resources to achieve the organization's goals. *Planning* means determining what the company needs to do and how best to get it done. *Organizing* means determining how best to arrange a business's resources and the necessary jobs into an overall structure. *Leading* means guiding and motivating employees to meet the firm's objectives. *Controlling* means monitoring the firm's performance to ensure that it is meeting its goals.

LO-2 IDENTIFY *TYPES OF MANAGERS* BY LEVEL AND AREA.

Managers can be differentiated in two ways: by level and by area. By level, *top managers* set policies, formulate strategies, and approve decisions. *Middle managers* implement policies, strategies, and decisions. *First-line managers* usually work with and supervise employees. By area, managers focus on *marketing*, *finance*, *operations*, *human resource*, and *information*. Managers at all levels may be found in every area of a company.

LO-3 DESCRIBE THE FIVE BASIC *MANAGEMENT SKILLS*.

Most managers agree that five basic management skills are necessary for success. *Technical skills* are needed to perform specialized tasks ranging from typing to auditing. *Human relations skills* are needed to understand and get along with other people. *Conceptual skills* allow managers to think in the abstract, to diagnose and analyze various situations, and to see beyond present circumstances. *Decision-making skills* allow managers to define problems and to select the best course of action. *Time management skills* refer to managers' ability to make productive use of the time available to them.

LO-4 EXPLAIN THE IMPORTANCE OF *GOAL SETTING* AND *STRATEGIC MANAGEMENT* IN ORGANIZATIONAL SUCCESS.

Goals—the performance targets of an organization—can be *long-term*, *intermediate*, and *short-term*. They provide direction for managers, they help managers decide how to allocate limited resources, they define the corporate culture, and they help managers assess performance. *Strategic management* involves three major activities: setting strategic goals, analyzing the organization and its environment, and matching the organization and its environment. The strategies that are decided upon are then translated into *strategic*, *tactical*, and *operational* plans.

LO-5 DISCUSS *CONTINGENCY PLANNING* AND *CRISIS MANAGEMENT* IN TODAY'S BUSINESS WORLD.

To deal with crises or major environmental changes, companies develop contingency plans and plans for crisis management. *Contingency planning* tries to identify in advance the important aspects of a business or its markets that might change and how the company will respond if such changes actually occur. *Crisis management* means developing methods and actions for dealing with an emergency that requires an immediate response. To prepare for such emergencies, organizations develop crisis plans.

LO-6 EXPLAIN THE IDEA OF *CORPORATE CULTURE* AND WHY IT IS IMPORTANT.

Corporate culture is the shared experiences, stories, beliefs, and norms that characterize an organization. A strong, well-defined culture can help a business reach its goals and can influence management styles. Culture is determined by several factors, including top management, the organization's history, stories and legends, and behavioural norms. If carefully communicated and flexible enough to accommodate change, corporate culture can be managed for the betterment of the organization.

QUESTIONS AND EXERCISES

QUESTIONS FOR ANALYSIS

1. How are the four *functions* of management related to the five *skills* of management? Use examples to clarify your answer.
2. What is the relationship between Mintzberg's *roles* of management and the more traditional *functions* of management? Use examples to clarify your answer.
3. Identify the managers by level and area at your college or university.
4. Can you identify any organizations where the technical skills of top managers are more important than human relations or conceptual skills? Can you identify organizations in which conceptual skills are not important at all?
5. What differences might you expect to find in the corporate cultures of a 100-year-old manufacturing firm based in Winnipeg and a 5-year-old e-commerce firm based in Ottawa?
6. Consider the various corporate-level strategies discussed in the chapter (concentration, growth, integration, diversification, investment, reduction). What is the relationship between these various strategies? Are they mutually exclusive? Complementary? Explain.

APPLICATION EXERCISES

7. Interview a manager at any level of a local company. Identify the manager's job according to level and area. Explain what planning, organizing, directing, and controlling mean in terms of the manager's job. Give examples. Also indicate which management skills are most important for the manager's job.
8. Review the example of the decisions made by Airbus and Boeing regarding new large aircraft. Then research the most current information on the status of the two planes. Which company seems to have made the better decision?
9. Interview an administrator at your college or university and get that person's views on the school's strengths and weaknesses and on the threats and opportunities the school is facing. Then use this information to write up a SWOT analysis for the school.
10. Select any organization of which you are a member (your company, your family, your place of worship, or a club). Explain the relevance of the management functions of planning, organizing, directing, and controlling for that organization.

TEAM EXERCISES

BUILDING YOUR BUSINESS SKILLS

SPEAKING WITH POWER

GOAL

To encourage students to appreciate effective speaking as a critical human relations skill.

BACKGROUND

A manager's ability to understand and get along with supervisors, peers, and subordinates is a critical human relations skill. At the heart of this skill, says Harvard University professor of education Sarah McGinty, is the ability to speak with power and control. McGinty defines "powerful speech" in terms of the following characteristics:

- the ability to speak at length and in complete sentences
- the ability to set a conversational agenda
- the ability to deter interruption
- the ability to argue openly and to express strong opinions about ideas, not people
- the ability to make statements that offer solutions rather than pose questions
- the ability to express humour

Taken together, says McGinty, "all this creates a sense of confidence in listeners."

METHOD

Step 1 Working alone, compare your own personal speaking style with McGinty's description of powerful speech by taping yourself as you speak during a meeting with classmates or during a phone conversation.

(Tape both sides of the conversation only if the person to whom you are speaking gives permission.) Listen for the following problems:

- unfinished sentences
- an absence of solutions
- too many disclaimers ("I'm not sure I have enough information to say this, but …")
- the habit of seeking support from others instead of making definitive statements of personal conviction (saying "As Emily stated in her report, I recommend consolidating the medical and fitness functions," instead of "I recommend consolidating the medical and fitness functions")
- language fillers (saying "you know," "like," and "um" when you are unsure of your facts or uneasy about expressing your opinion)

Step 2 Join with three or four other classmates to evaluate each other's speaking styles.

- Have a 10-minute group discussion on the importance of human relations skills in business.
- Listen to other group members, and take notes on the "power" content of what you hear.
- Offer constructive criticism by focusing on what speakers say rather than on personal characteristics (say "Bob, you sympathized with Paul's position, but I still don't know what you think," instead of "Bob, you sounded like a weakling.").

FOLLOW-UP QUESTIONS

1. How do you think the power content of speech affects a manager's ability to communicate? Evaluate some of the ways the effects may differ among supervisors, peers, and subordinates.
2. How do you evaluate yourself and group members in terms of powerful and powerless speech? List the strengths and weaknesses of the group.

3. Do you agree or disagree with McGinty that business success depends on gaining insight into your own language habits? Explain your answer.
4. In our age of computers and email, why do you think personal presentation continues to be important in management?
5. McGinty believes that power language differs from company to company and that it is linked to the corporate culture. Do you agree, or do you believe that people express themselves in similar ways no matter where they are?

EXERCISING YOUR ETHICS

CLEAN UP NOW OR CLEAN UP LATER?

THE SITUATION

The top management team of a medium-sized manufacturing company is on a strategic planning "retreat" where it is formulating ideas and plans for spurring new growth in the company. As one part of this activity, the team, working with the assistance of a consultant, has conducted a SWOT analysis. During this activity, an interesting and complex situation has been identified. Next year, the federal government will be issuing new—and much more stringent—pollution standards for the company's industry. The team sees this as a potential threat in that the company will have to buy new equipment and change some of its manufacturing methods in order to comply.

THE DILEMMA

One member of the team, James Smith, has posed an interesting option—not complying. His logic can be summarized as follows:

1. The firm has already developed its capital budgets for the next two years. Any additional capital expenditures will cause major problems with the company's cash flow and budget allocations.
2. The company has a large uncommitted capital budget entry available in three years; those funds might be used to upgrade pollution control systems at that time.
3. Because the company has a spotless environmental record so far, James Smith argues that if the company does not buy the equipment for three years, the most likely outcomes will be (a) a warning in year 1; (b) a small fine in year 2; and (c) a substantial fine in year 3. However, the total amounts of the years 2 and 3 fines will be much lower than the cost of redoing the company budgets and complying with the new law next year.

TEAM ACTIVITY

Assemble a group of four students and assign each group member to one of the following roles:

- management team member
- lower-level employee at the company
- company customer
- company investor

ACTION STEPS

1. Before hearing any of your group's comments on this situation and from the perspective of your assigned role, decide whether James Smith's suggestion regarding ignoring pollution standards is a good one. Write down the reasons for your position.
2. Before hearing any of your group's comments on this situation and from the perspective of your assigned role, determine what the underlying ethical issues are in this situation.
3. Gather your group together and reveal, in turn, each member's comments on James Smith's suggestion. Next, reveal the ethical issues listed by each member.
4. Appoint someone to record main points of agreement and disagreement within the group. How do you explain the results? What accounts for any disagreement?
5. From an ethical standpoint, what does your group conclude would be the most appropriate action by the company in this situation?
6. Develop a group response to the following question: What are the respective roles of profits, obligations to customers, and obligations to the community for the firm in this situation?

BUSINESS CASE 6

CORPORATE CULTURE

Corporate culture is sometimes defined simply as "the way we do things around here." A corporate culture can emphasize a variety of things. Consider the following examples:

- At Telus Corp., *customer service* is the cornerstone of its culture; during one quarter in 2014, the company attracted 113 000 new customers, more than either BCE or Rogers.
- At competitor Rogers Communications, the culture emphasizes the *well-being of employees*; this includes offering employees discounts on products.
- At CIBC, the culture includes three core values: teamwork, trust, and accountability; these three values create a culture of providing high quality service to *customers*.
- At MEG Energy, the corporate culture encourages all employees to share *innovative ideas*; this leads to advancements in sustainable technology.

nikitos77/Fotolia

Two interesting questions arise regarding corporate culture:

1. What happens if two companies with widely differing cultures merge?
2. What happens if there is a culture clash within an organization? That is, what if top managers disagree with lower-level employees about the kind of culture the organization should have?

MERGING COMPANIES WITH DIFFERENT CULTURES

During the past few years, there have been several high-profile mergers between companies with different cultures, and these combinations often caused difficulties.

Vale and Glencore Plc. In 2014, the Brazilian mining company Vale and the Swiss miner Glencore Plc discussed merging their nickel assets in Sudbury. But the idea was finally abandoned when it became clear that the two companies had significantly different corporate cultures. One point of concern was each company's view of risk: Vale's culture was risk-averse, while Glencore's culture was much more risk-seeking. There were also disagreements about how to share the costs of the merger. This is an interesting situation, because a few years earlier Inco and Falconbridge had talked about combining their Sudbury assets, but then Inco was purchased by Vale, and Xstrata purchased Falconbridge. Then Glencore bought Xstrata.

Vale and Inco. When Vale bought Inco, there was also a "culture clash." Shortly after the purchase, there was a meeting of executives of both companies, but the meeting ended suddenly when one of the Brazilian managers lost his temper. That was the first sign the cultures of the companies were different enough that problems were going to be evident. Over the next few months, many Canadian managers, engineers, and operating staff left the company. For example, of 29 managers who were involved in a strategy session shortly after the merger, only 6 were still there a few months later.

In retrospect, it is clear that the cultures of the companies were quite different prior to the takeover. At Inco, there was a constant exchange of ideas, and decentralized decision making was encouraged by top management. But at Vale, top managers gave orders and expected them to be followed. Not surprisingly, Vale encountered resistance from Inco executives who did not agree with that approach. There were also differences in the products the companies focused on before Vale bought Inco. Vale's focus was on iron ore, a basic commodity mined using a relatively simple technology. But the underground mining of nickel, a key ingredient in stainless steel, is a more complex undertaking. One Inco manager likened nickel mining to having a PhD, while iron ore mining was like having a high school diploma. Canadian managers obviously felt some disdain for their new Brazilian bosses.

The cultural differences between the two companies were not limited to the top level of management. Some years earlier, the miner's union had given up annual wage increases in return for a bonus based on the price of nickel. When the price of nickel soared, workers received large bonuses. Vale wanted to raise the threshold at which the bonus kicked in, and also wanted to convert the defined benefit pension plan to a defined contribution plan. The union strongly resisted. Vale is seen as a company with an "attitude," and Vale's management has been very aggressive in dealing with the Canadian workers it inherited from Inco.

One of the most visible signs of the culture difference was a strike by the United Steelworkers union. Workers rejected an offer to settle by a wide margin, saying that Vale's offer fell far short of what the union members expected. Vale then took legal action against the union, accusing it of vandalism, assaults, and death threats. It also laid off many employees and shut down various projects because of the uncertain economic environment. Vale then announced it was going to bring in replacement workers in order to get two of the nickel mines back up to full production. The federal government did not get involved in the dispute, in spite of claims by the union that Vale was a foreign company trying to change the culture of Canadian union–management relations.

Vale's CEO said that the cultures of the two companies would simply have to adjust. But Vale also removed the name "Inco" from its nickel business. (*Note:* The Vale takeover of Inco did not go nearly as smoothly as the Xstrata takeover of Falconbridge, partly because Xstrata gave Canadian managers a lot more say in changes made after the takeover.)

China National Offshore Oil Corp. (CNOOC) and Nexen. In 2012, the China National Offshore Oil Corp. (CNOOC) announced its intention to purchase Nexen, a Canadian oil producer. There was concern that a communist government was buying a Canadian oil company, but CNOOC made a public commitment to boost capital expenditures in Canada, maintain Nexen's workforce, and keep all of Nexen's senior executives. The federal government of Canada approved the sale, but said no more sales to organizations controlled by foreign governments would be allowed.

Soon after the takeover, CNOOC started laying off Nexen employees and introducing cost-cutting programs. The unexpected fall in oil prices during 2014 also caused CNOOC to substantially reduce its capital budget. Many current and former employees said that the cultures of the two companies were very different, and that a climate of fear had developed among Nexen employees worried about even more layoffs. They also claimed that the Chinese viewed Canadians as lazy. About half of the former Nexen executives are no longer at the new company (now called Nexen Energy ULC).

Some planned mergers never happen, because concerns about a possible culture clash inhibit negotiations. For example, when two Japanese companies (Kirin Holdings Co. and Suntory Holdings Ltd.) announced plans to merge in order to create one of the world's largest beverage companies, it was thought a merger would create a company that could break out of the domestic Japanese market and become a major player on the international scene. But it never took place, partly because of differences in management styles. Kirin (a member of the Mitsubishi group) had solid, traditional management, but Suntory had a unique style influenced by the fact that families owned about 90 percent of the company's shares. During negotiations, the companies simply could not reconcile the differences and the merger was called off.

A planned acquisition of Sun Microsystems by IBM also fell through. When rumours of the takeover started circulating, a Sun vice-president warned there would be a culture clash. He said the developer staff at Sun were "weirder" than those at IBM. In fact, Sun did have a somewhat radical culture, because it had been pushing open systems like Unix. This contrasted with IBM's more proprietary approach. The talks eventually broke off because the two companies could not agree on terms.

A similar-looking situation was evident when Kraft Foods tried to acquire Cadbury. The finance director at Cadbury (the maker of such well-known brands as Caramilk candy bars and Bubblicious gum), warned that Cadbury's unique corporate culture would be lost if Kraft acquired it. He said that the Cadbury "magic" was important for the brands it markets. The company's CEO also weighed in, saying Cadbury's culture of "principled capitalism" was what made it great. The British public was concerned about losing one of its icons, and Warren Buffett sold off almost one-quarter of his Kraft stock when he heard about the plan. The two companies did, in fact, have quite different histories and cultures. Cadbury had tried to build a socially benign business and had launched a fair trade initiative with its Dairy Milk brand; Kraft was a much more traditional multinational business firm. In spite of these concerns, after protracted negotiations Kraft did acquire Cadbury.

CULTURE CLASHES WITHIN AN ORGANIZATION

Culture clashes don't happen only when two independent companies try to merge. They can also happen when a top manager's vision for a culture comes into conflict with the culture lower-level employees prefer. Consider the situation that arose at the DeGroote School of Business at McMaster University when Paul Bates, a former Bay Street brokerage executive, was hired as dean of the business school. When he sought reappointment for a second term, he was opposed by 80 percent of the faculty, but the views of faculty members were overruled by the board of governors and Bates was reappointed. Many professors were unhappy with Bates's corporate management style; they accused him of bullying and intimidation, and of not understanding the academic culture of the school. Those who supported the dean said he had done good things for the school, and that the faculty members were biased against anyone not "academic" enough. A report issued by the McMaster Office of Human Rights and Equity Services concluded that the business school had a dysfunctional work environment, and that immediate action should be taken to resolve the problem. The report also noted that the school had a history of conflict between deans and faculty members.

Sometimes a new top executive is brought in to change the corporate culture in response to a crisis the company is facing. Edward Whitacre, the former CEO of General Motors, was one such person. He was recruited in 2009 and given the mandate to turn the company around and change GM's plodding culture. But he did not have an easy job: GM was going to have to introduce massive changes to dig itself out of the financial hole it was in. He tried to reduce bureaucracy and push decision-making authority down into GM's many management layers so that decisions were made more quickly and the company would be more responsive to changes in the marketplace. Prior to Whitacre's arrival, decisions were not made until approved by many different committees. For example, a few years earlier the company had introduced a program to stamp out bureaucracy, but the committee guiding the effort had trouble deciding how many committee meetings were necessary to achieve the goal. That kind of dithering was not what Whitacre had in mind. One of the things he did to change the culture was to be more hands-on and accessible than his predecessors (who spent most of their time in the executive suite). He had some success with that strategy, as GM employees began talking about "Ed sightings" in the hallways and cafeteria. He also visited GM manufacturing plants to talk to workers. But Whitacre is no longer the CEO of GM.

QUESTIONS FOR DISCUSSION

1. What is corporate culture? Compare and contrast the companies described in this case in terms of their corporate culture.
2. Can the CEO of a company really influence the culture of an organization in a substantial way?
3. Consider the following statement: *The idea that a culture clash is important is overstated. People generally are so focused on doing their own jobs that abstract issues like "culture" don't influence their behaviour very much.* Do you agree or disagree? Defend your answer.

micromonkey/Fotolia

LO

AFTER READING THIS CHAPTER, YOU SHOULD BE ABLE TO:

LO-1 Discuss the elements that influence a firm's *organizational structure*.

LO-2 Explain how *specialization* and *departmentalization* are the building blocks of organizational structure.

LO-3 Distinguish between *responsibility* and *authority* and explain the differences in decision making in *centralized* and *decentralized organizations*.

LO-4 Explain the differences between *functional*, *divisional*, *project*, and *international organization structures*, and describe the most popular forms of organizational design.

LO-5 Understand how the *informal organization* is different from the formal organization.

Time to Reorganize!

In our fast-paced modern economy, business organizations must constantly change their organization structures in order to remain competitive. Listed below are just some of the companies that changed their structures in 2014:

- Bombardier Inc. changed its organization structure after experiencing many delays in the development of the CSeries jet. The company previously had just two business units (Transportation and Aerospace), but now it will have four (Transportation, Aerostructures and Engineering Services, Business Aircraft, and Commercial Aircraft). The new structure is designed to reduce costs, increase profitability, increase responsiveness to customer needs, and focus attention on Bombardier's growth areas.
- After experiencing a decline in sales, McDonald's announced that it was changing its organization structure in order to more effectively respond to consumer needs in the diverse markets that it serves. The new organization structure is based on four geographic zones: Northeast, South, Central, and West. It will give local managers more autonomy to develop menu items that consumers in their area prefer.
- In response to declining sales, Sears Canada laid off hundreds of employees and changed its organizational structure in order to reduce the number of people at the vice-presidential level.

Julio Cortez/AP/Canadian Press Images

Organizing *the* Business Enterprise

CHAPTER 07

- BlackBerry changed its structure by dropping the Chief Operating Officer (COO) and Chief Marketing Officer (CMO) positions from its organization chart. These were the two most important consumer-oriented executives in the company, and the move shows that BlackBerry is going to focus on business customers, not individual consumers.
- Nissan Canada Inc. streamlined its organizational structure as part of a larger effort to increase sales. Formerly, Nissan dealers reported to a regional general manager, who reported to a sales director, who reported to a regional vice-president. The new structure eliminates the sales director position and shortens the chain of command so decisions can be made more quickly.
- Coty Inc., the cosmetics company, has introduced a new organizational structure that is based on four product categories (fragrance, skin care, colour cosmetics, and body care) in four distinct regions (North America, Europe, Latin America, and Asia-Pacific/Middle East, Africa). The new structure replaces one that had just two divisions (Coty Prestige and Coty Beauty).
- Hewlett-Packard announced plans to split into two companies, one focusing on computers and printers, and the other focusing on corporate hardware and service operations. The change was made to reduce inefficiencies that are often evident in large conglomerate businesses.

HOW WILL THIS HELP ME?

Companies frequently introduce changes to improve their organizational structures. By understanding the material in this chapter, as an *employee*, you'll understand your "place" in the organization that employs you. As a *boss* or *owner*, you'll be better equipped to decide on the optimal structure for your own organization.

When companies decide to reorganize, they may face certain dilemmas. Three of the most common are: (1) whether to emphasize centralization or decentralization, (2) whether to use geographical or product departmentalization, and (3) whether to split a single company into two (or more) companies.

Centralization vs. Decentralization

It may not be easy to decide whether to operate with a centralized structure (where decision-making authority is concentrated at the top of the organizational hierarchy) or a decentralized structure (where decision-making authority is pushed down to lower levels in the hierarchy). This dilemma can clearly be seen in the long history of General Motors. In the 1920s, GM's president, Alfred Sloan, introduced a decentralized structure that gave each car division considerable autonomy to produce what the division managers thought would attract whatever market segment the division was pursuing. It worked so well that GM became the largest automobile manufacturer in the world by the middle of the twentieth century. But all this autonomy resulted in widely differing car designs that were very expensive to produce. As decades passed, costs soared and competition from cost-conscious Japanese automakers became ferocious. GM's sales and overall profitability plummeted. In response, GM then took away much of the autonomy that managers in various international divisions had, and instituted a requirement that its worldwide units work much more closely together to design cars that could be sold (with modest variations) worldwide. A "Global Council" in Detroit made key decisions about how much would be spent on new car development. But even these actions were not sufficient to stem GM's decline, and in 2008 the company was bailed out by the U.S. and Canadian governments and entered bankruptcy protection as it tried to recover.

Geographic vs. Product Departmentalization

Some firms use geographic departmentalization (organizing on the basis of geographic regions) and some use product departmentalization (organizing on the basis of products that are sold). But it is not always easy to decide which form is best. In recent years, increased global competition and reduced impediments to cross-border communication have led some companies to switch from geographic to product departmentalization. For example, Heinz abandoned geographical departmentalization in favour of product departmentalization.

Managers in various countries work with each other to apply the best ideas from one region to all the others. Exide Corp.'s structure formerly consisted of several "country organizations" that had considerable latitude to make decisions that were best for that country. But it adopted a new product structure with global business units to oversee the company's various product lines such as car and industrial batteries.

Either approach—products or geography—can cause problems if taken to an extreme. If a company organizes by products, it can standardize manufacturing, introduce new products around the world faster, and eliminate overlapping activities. But if too much emphasis is put on product and not enough on geography, a company is likely to find that local decision making is slowed and products are not tailored to a specific country's customers. When Ford Motor Co. moved to product departmentalization, the reorganization saved the company $5 billion in its first few years of operation, but Ford's market share declined during the same period. Ford responded by giving executives in various regions more authority to decide what types of vehicles were best for their local market. In other words, it moved back a bit toward the geographical model.

Radu Razvan/Fotolia

Splitting a Single Company into Two (or More) Companies

In 2014, the German utility E.ON SE reorganized into two separate companies, one focusing on renewables and one on fossil fuels. A spokesperson said that the missions of the two new companies are so fundamentally different that they need to have different structures.

Kraft Foods also decided to split into two distinct companies, one focusing on worldwide snacks (including brand names like Oreo and Lu cookies, Cadbury chocolate, and Trident gum), and the other on the North American grocery business (including brands like Velveeta cheese and Maxwell House coffee). The North American grocery business was launched as a publicly traded company, but both companies retained the Kraft Foods name. One reason for the restructuring was the realization that sales revenue in the grocery business was growing more slowly than in the snacks business. The decision to create two companies required Kraft managers to make interesting decisions about which products would go where. They decided, for example, that Planters Peanuts would go with the grocery company and move from its current home in snack foods. But for Philadelphia Cream Cheese—whose sales revenue is about evenly split between North America and the rest of the world—one company would license the brand from the other.

Tyco International is another company that split up. It now focuses on selling security and fire-suppression systems to businesses. Tyco's two other divisions, which sold ADT residential alarms and industrial valves and pipes, were spun off. This restructuring may allow all three units to be more easily acquired by other companies, or for them to pursue other takeovers on their own.

Sobeys split into two units, but both will continue to operate under the umbrella of a single company. The IGA Operations unit includes IGA, IGA Extra, Les Marchés Tradition, Marché Bonichoix, and Rachelle-Béry in Quebec. The Multi-Format Operations includes Sobeys, Thrifty Foods, Sobeys Urban Fresh, Foodland, FreshCo, Needs, Fast Fuel, Sobeys liquor operations, and IGA stores in western Canada.

Other Issues in Reorganizing

For many years there were three separate professional accounting organizations in Canada—Chartered Accountants, Certified General Accountants, and Certified Management Accountants. When the three merged, a new organization was created—Chartered Professional Accountants of Canada. The new organization structure is less complicated than the previous separate organizations, because now there is only one group in each province instead of three.

Sometimes a dispute in a family business necessitates a change in a company's organizational structure. Consider the Irving family of New Brunswick, which owns nearly 300 businesses in areas as diverse as oil refining, forestry, shipbuilding, food processing, publishing, transportation, and home improvement. The company was founded by J.D. Irving in 1882 and expanded dramatically under his son K.C. He then passed it on to his three sons—J.K., Arthur, and Jack. These brothers then had five sons. But tensions developed between two of the five regarding the strategic direction of the company. The brothers wanted to avoid a bitter family feud, so they reorganized the company and let the two main parts (forestry and oil) go their separate ways.

QUESTIONS FOR DISCUSSION

1. In your own words, explain the dilemma that exists when managers are trying to decide whether to use a geographic or product basis for departmentalization. Do the same for the centralization/decentralization dilemma.
2. Why would a company decide to split up into two (or more) companies?
3. Consider the following statement: *We should not pay too much attention to what an organization's structure looks like. It is far more important to have a good corporate strategy and leaders who can motivate employees who work well together than it is to worry about the mechanical structure of an organization.* Do you agree or disagree? Explain your reasoning.

WHAT IS ORGANIZATIONAL STRUCTURE?

Organizational structure is the specification of the jobs to be done within a business and how those jobs relate to one another. To understand what organizational structure is all about, consider an analogy—a business is like an automobile. All automobiles have an engine, four wheels, fenders and other structural components, an interior compartment for passengers, and various operating systems including those for fuel, brakes, and climate control. Each component has a distinct purpose, but must also work in harmony with all the others. Automobiles made by competing firms all have the same basic components, although the way they look and fit together may vary. Similarly, all businesses have common structural and operating components, each of which has a specific purpose. Each component must fulfill its own purpose while simultaneously fitting in with the others. And, just like automobiles made by different companies, how these components look and fit together varies from company to company.

Every institution—be it a for-profit business like Frantic Films, a not-for-profit organization like the University of Saskatchewan, or a government agency like the Competition Bureau—must develop an appropriate structure for its own unique situation. What works for Air Canada is not likely to work for Canada Revenue Agency. Likewise, the structure of the Red Cross will not likely work for the University of Toronto.

LO-1 Determinants of Organizational Structure

How is an organization's structure determined? Does it happen by chance or is there some strategy that managers use to create structure? Or is it a combination of the two? Ideally, managers should assess a variety of factors as they plan for and then create a structure that will make their organization effective. But with the busyness evident in most organizations, structure may often develop without much planning.

What factors influence structure? The organization's purpose, mission, and strategy are obviously important. A dynamic and rapidly growing enterprise, for example, needs a structure that contributes to flexibility and growth, while a stable organization with only modest growth will function best with a different structure. Size, technology, and changes in environmental circumstances also affect structure. A large manufacturing firm operating in a strongly competitive environment requires a different structure than a local barbershop or convenience store.

Whatever structure an organization adopts, it is rarely fixed for long. Indeed, most organizations change their structures almost continually. Since it was first incorporated in 1903, for example, Ford Motor Co. has undergone literally dozens of major structural changes, hundreds of moderate changes, and thousands of minor changes. In just the past 15 years, Ford has initiated several major structural changes designed to eliminate corporate bureaucracy, speed up decision making, and improve communication and working relationships among people at different levels.

ORGANIZATIONAL STRUCTURE The specification of the jobs to be done within a business and how those jobs relate to one another.

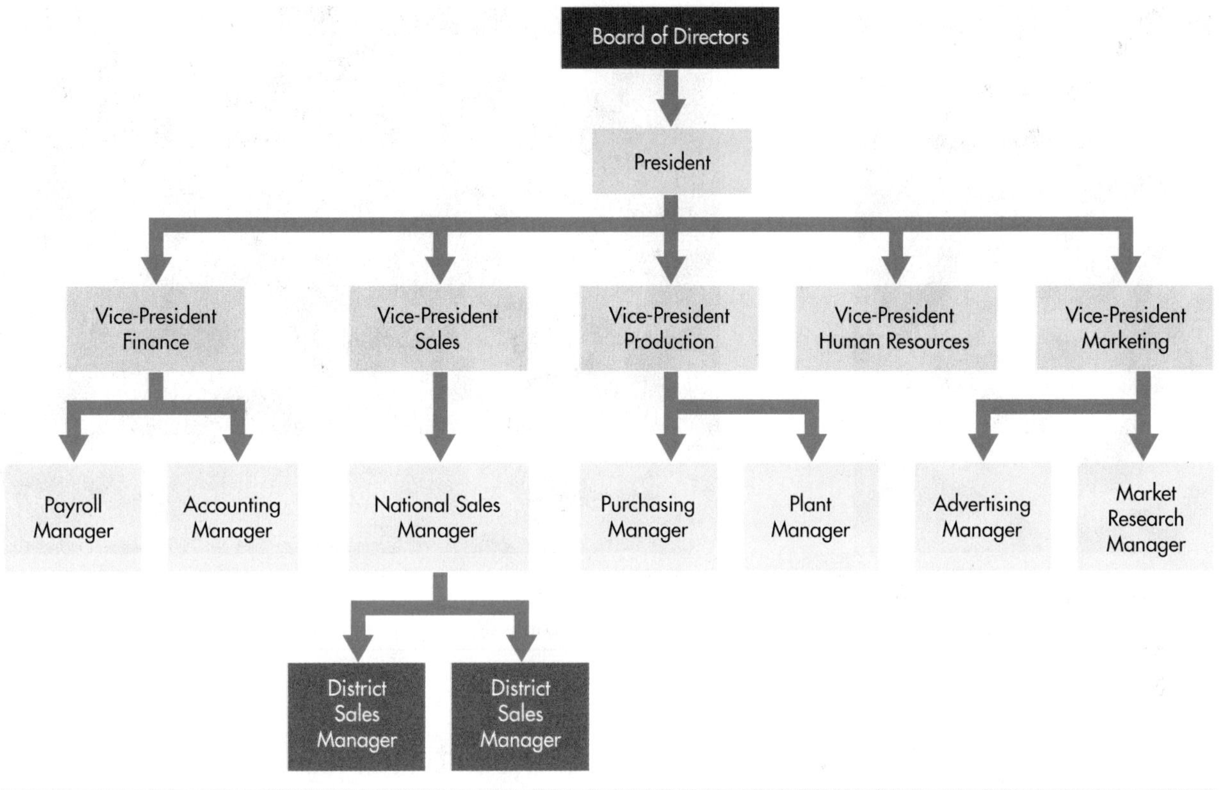

FIGURE 7.1 An organization chart

An organization chart shows key positions in the organization and interrelationships among them. An actual organization chart would, of course, be far more complex and include individuals at many more levels. Indeed, because of their size, larger firms cannot easily draw a diagram with everyone on it.

The Chain of Command

Most businesses prepare **organization charts** that illustrate the company's structure and show employees where they fit into the firm's operations. Figure 7.1 shows the organization chart for a hypothetical company. Each box represents a job within the company. The solid lines that connect the boxes define the *chain of command*, or the reporting relationships within the company. Thus, each plant manager reports directly to the vice-president of production who, in turn, reports to the president. When the chain of command is not clear, many different kinds of problems can result. An actual organization chart would, of course, be far more complex and include individuals at many more levels. Large firms cannot easily draw an organization chart with everyone on it. The chart might also show unusual features. For example, until recently, the organization chart of BlackBerry showed two CEOs and two chairs of the board. But in 2011, investor pressure caused the company to change the structure so that just one person did each job.[1]

ORGANIZATION CHART A physical depiction of the company's structure showing employee titles and their relationship to one another.

THE BUILDING BLOCKS OF ORGANIZATIONAL STRUCTURE

The most fundamental building blocks of organizational structure are *specialization* (determining who will do what) and *departmentalization* (determining how people performing certain tasks can most appropriately be grouped together).

In a sense, all businesses have only one major "job"—making a profit by selling products and services to consumers. But this big job must be broken into smaller components which are then assigned to individuals. Consider the manufacturing of men's shirts. Because several

LO-2 Specialization

Job specialization is the process of identifying the specific jobs that need to be done and designating the people who will perform them.

JOB SPECIALIZATION The process of identifying the specific jobs that need to be done and designating the people who will perform them.

When Walt Disney was just starting out, he did most of the work on his animated features all by himself. But today's features like Disney's 2013 hit *Monsters University* require the work of hundreds of people doing very specialized tasks.

Pictorial Press Ltd/Alamy (left); Disney-Pixar/AP Images (right)

steps are required to produce a shirt, each job is broken down into its components—that is, into a set of tasks to be completed by a series of individuals or machines. One person, for example, cuts material for the shirt body, another cuts material for the sleeves, and a third cuts material for the collar. Components are then shipped to a sewing room, where a fourth person assembles the shirt. In the final stage, a fifth person sews on the buttons.[2]

SPECIALIZATION AND GROWTH

In a very small organization, the owner may perform every job. As the firm grows, however, so does the need to specialize jobs so that others can perform them. When Mrs. Fields Cookies began, Debbi Fields did everything herself: bought the equipment, negotiated the lease, baked the cookies, operated the store, and kept the records. As the business grew, however, she found that her job was becoming too much for one person. She first hired a bookkeeper to handle her financial records, then an in-store manager and a cookie baker. Her second store required another set of employees—another manager, another baker, and some salespeople. While Fields focused on other expansion opportunities, she turned promotions over to a professional advertising director. Thus, the job that she once did all by herself was increasingly broken down into components and assigned to different individuals.

Job specialization is a natural part of organizational growth. It is neither a new idea nor limited to factory work. It carries with it certain advantages—individual jobs can be performed more efficiently, the jobs are easier to learn, and it is easier to replace people who leave the organization. But if job specialization is carried too far and jobs become too narrowly defined, people get bored, become less satisfied with their jobs, and lose sight of how their contributions fit into the overall organization.

DEPARTMENTALIZATION The process of grouping jobs into logical units.

Departmentalization

Departmentalization is the process of grouping specialized jobs into logical units. Departmentalization improves control and coordination because managers can see more easily how various units are performing. It allows

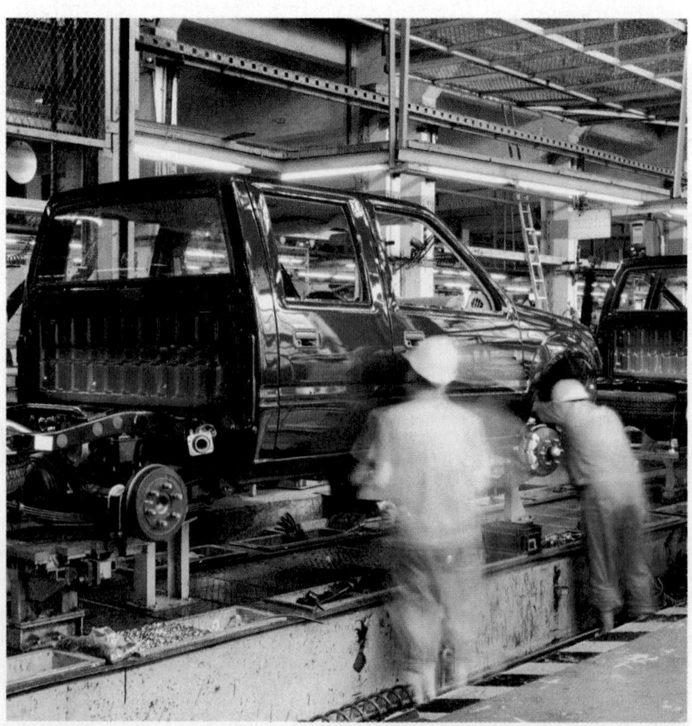

A key factor in the efficiency of truck and automobile production is the organization of the workstations. At some stations, workers install just about everything that the driver touches inside the vehicle. Other stations take care of the vehicle frame, the entire electrical system, or completed doors.

gui yong nian/Fotolia

the firm to treat a department as a *profit centre*—a separate unit responsible for its own costs and profits. Thus, by assessing profits from sales in a particular area—for example, men's clothing—Sears can decide whether to expand or curtail promotions in that area. Departmentalization may occur along *functional*, *customer*, *product*, *geographic*, or *process* lines (or some combination of these).

FUNCTIONAL DEPARTMENTALIZATION

Functional departmentalization means organizing departments according to the function they perform—marketing, finance, production, human resources, and so on. Each of these departments might be further subdivided; for example, the marketing department might be divided geographically or into separate staff for market research and advertising.

CUSTOMER DEPARTMENTALIZATION

Customer departmentalization involves setting up departments or divisions that focus on meeting the needs of specific customers. Some retail stores actually derive their generic name—department stores—from the manner in which they are structured. Stores like HMV are divided into departments—a classical music department, an R&B department, a pop department, and so on. Each department targets a specific customer category (people who want a certain genre of music). Customer departmentalization makes shopping easier by providing identifiable store segments. Thus, a customer shopping for Shania Twain's latest CD can bypass World Music and head straight for Country. Stores can also group products in locations designated for deliveries, special sales, and other service-oriented purposes. In general, the store is more efficient and customers get better service—in part because salespeople tend to specialize and gain expertise in their departments.[3]

PRODUCT DEPARTMENTALIZATION

Product departmentalization means dividing an organization according to the specific products or services that are being created. 3M Corp., which makes both consumer and industrial products, operates different divisions for Post-it brand tape flags, Scotch-Brite scrub sponges, and the Sarns 9000 perfusion system for open-heart surgery. In 2011, home improvement giant Lowe's reorganized its merchandising operations into two product divisions: (1) building and outdoor products and (2) kitchen, bath, and home decor products.[4]

PROCESS DEPARTMENTALIZATION

Process departmentalization means dividing the company according to the production process used. Vlasic, a pickle maker, has separate departments that transform cucumbers into fresh-packed pickles, relishes, or pickles cured in brine.

Many department stores are departmentalized by product. Concentrating different products in different areas of the store makes shopping easier for customers.

fiphoto/123RF

GEOGRAPHIC DEPARTMENTALIZATION

Geographic departmentalization means creating departments based on the area of the country—or even the world—they serve. In 2011, Lowe's created three divisions: north, south, and west.[5] In 2009, Nike introduced a new structure that was organized around six geographic regions: North America, Western Europe, Eastern/Central Europe, Greater China, Japan, and emerging markets.[6]

Because different forms of departmentalization offer different advantages, larger companies tend to adopt different types of departmentalization at various levels of the corporation. For example, the company illustrated in Figure 7.2 uses functional departmentalization at the top level, geographic departmentalization at the mid-level, and product departmentalization at the lowest level.

FUNCTIONAL DEPARTMENTALIZATION Departmentalization according to functions or activities.

CUSTOMER DEPARTMENTALIZATION Departmentalization according to the types of customers likely to buy a given product.

PRODUCT DEPARTMENTALIZATION Departmentalization according to the products being created or sold.

PROCESS DEPARTMENTALIZATION Departmentalization according to the production process used to create a good or service.

GEOGRAPHIC DEPARTMENTALIZATION Departmentalization according to the area of the country or world supplied.

ESTABLISHING THE DECISION-MAKING HIERARCHY

A major question that must be asked about any organization is this: Who makes which decisions? This leads to a consideration of the decision-making hierarchy, which generally results from a three-step process:

1. *Assigning tasks.* Determining who can make decisions and specifying how they should be made
2. *Performing tasks.* Implementing decisions that have been made
3. *Distributing authority.* Determining whether the organization is to be centralized or decentralized

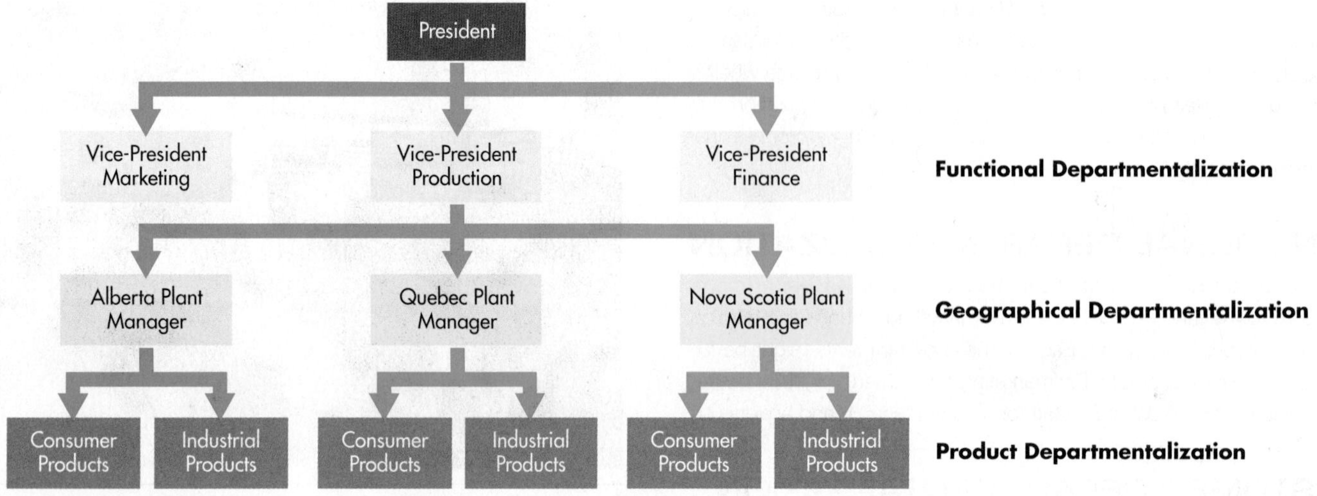

FIGURE 7.2 Multiple forms of departmentalization

Most organizations use multiple bases of departmentalization. This organization, for example, is using functional, geographic, and product departmentalization.

LO-3 Assigning Tasks

Authority is the power to make the decisions necessary to complete a task. **Responsibility** is the duty to perform an assigned task. These ideas may seem simple, but two distinct problems may arise when they are applied in practice. First, authority and responsibility may not be balanced. For example, suppose a buyer for a department store has an unexpected opportunity to make a large purchase of inventory at an extremely good price, but does not have the authority to make the purchase without confirmation from above. The company's policies on authority and responsibility are inconsistent because the buyer is responsible for purchasing the clothes that will be sold in the store, but lacks the discretion (authority) to make the needed purchases. Second, when things go wrong, there is often debate about who is responsible. In the *News of the World* phone-hacking scandal, Rupert Murdoch said he wasn't responsible for the phone hacking that some of his reporters engaged in. But observers say that top managers *were* responsible because they put pressure on reporters to get "scoops" so the paper's circulation would increase, and this drove the reporters to take extreme measures to get stories.[7]

Performing Tasks

Delegation means assigning a task to a subordinate. Once authority has been delegated, **accountability** falls to the subordinate, who must then complete the task. When Winnipeg-based Frantic Films first began operations, the principal shareholders made all the decisions. But the CEO, Jamie Brown, thought that it was important to delegate more authority to lower-level workers so they would gain experience in making decisions that affected the company. So he gave lower-level managers the authority to spend up to $5000 without having to get the approval of top management. This change was also made because the top managers were spending too much time dealing with requests for small amounts of money.[8] Table 7.1 lists some common

AUTHORITY The power to make the decisions necessary to complete a task.

RESPONSIBILITY The duty to perform an assigned task.

DELEGATION Assignment of a task, a responsibility, or authority by a manager to a subordinate.

ACCOUNTABILITY Liability of subordinates for accomplishing tasks assigned by managers.

TABLE 7.1 Learning to delegate effectively

I'm afraid to delegate because . . .	Solution
My team doesn't know how to get the job done.	If members of your team are exhibiting opportunities for improved performance, offer them the training necessary for them to become more effective at their jobs.
I like controlling as many things as possible.	Recognize that trying to accomplish everything yourself while your team does nothing only sets you up for burnout and failure. As you begin to relinquish control, you will come to trust your team more as you watch your team members succeed.
I don't want anyone on my team outperforming me.	High-performing team members are a reflection of your success as a manager. Encourage them to excel, praise them for it, and share the success of your team with the rest of the organization.
I don't know how to delegate tasks effectively.	Consider taking a management training course or reading some books on the topic of delegating effectively.

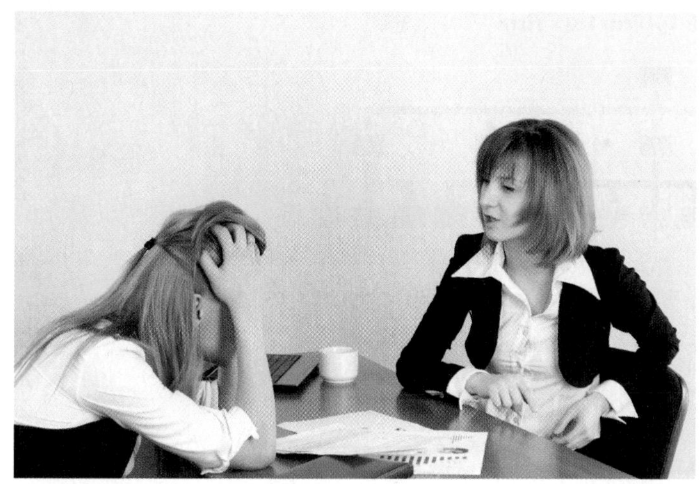

When managers do not properly delegate tasks to subordinates, or when there are disagreements about how much authority should be delegated, both managers and workers become frustrated.

nikomi/Fotolia

obstacles that hinder the delegation process, along with strategies for overcoming them.

Managers who fail to delegate don't have time to do long-range planning, and they may be uninformed about important industry trends and competitive products because they are too involved in day-to-day operations. Jeffrey Kindler, the former CEO of Pfizer Inc., quit after he lost the support of other executives who were frustrated with his focus on detail and his micromanaging style.[9]

Managers should keep the following points in mind when they are delegating authority:

- Decide on the nature of the work to be done.
- Match the job with the skills of subordinates.
- Make sure the person chosen understands the objectives he or she is supposed to achieve.
- Make sure subordinates have the time and training necessary to do the task.

Distributing Authority

In a **centralized organization**, top management retains the right to make most decisions that need to be made. Most lower-level decisions must be approved by upper management before they can be implemented.[10] McDonald's, for example, uses centralization as a way to standardize its operations. All restaurants must follow precise steps in buying products and making and packaging burgers and other menu items. Most advertising is handled at the corporate level, and any local advertising must be approved by a regional manager. Restaurants even have to follow prescribed schedules for facilities' maintenance and upgrades like floor polishing and parking-lot cleaning.[11]

In a **decentralized organization**, more decision-making authority is delegated to managers at lower levels in the hierarchy. The purpose of decentralization is to make a company more responsive to its environment by giving lower-level managers more autonomy. At FedEx, for example, the commitment to decentralization promotes innovation. Managers are encouraged and rewarded for questioning, challenging, and developing new ideas, which are always given serious consideration. Developments have included teaming up with Motorola and Microsoft to create a proprietary pocket-size PC, sending package information to cell phones, and creating software products for small business logistics.[12]

TALL AND FLAT ORGANIZATIONS

Decentralized firms tend to have a *flat* organizational structure with only a few layers, such as the one shown in Figure 7.3a. In contrast, centralized organizations usually have multiple layers of management and a *tall* organizational structure (see Figure 7.3b).

SPAN OF CONTROL

As shown in Figure 7.3, the **span of control** refers to how many people are supervised by an individual manager. The span of control may be wide (many subordinates reporting to a boss) or narrow (few subordinates reporting to a boss). Factors influencing the span of control include employees' abilities, the supervisor's managerial skills, the nature of the tasks being performed, and the extent to which tasks are interrelated. For example, when many employees perform the same simple task or a group of interrelated assembly-line tasks, a wide span of control is possible. Because all the jobs are routine, one supervisor may well control an entire assembly line with 40 or more workers. Since tasks are interrelated—if one workstation stops, they all stop—having one supervisor ensures that all stations receive equal attention. In contrast, when jobs are not routine, or when they are unrelated, a narrower span of control is preferable.

Downsizing—the planned reduction in the scope of an organization's activity—affects the span of control. When downsizing involves cutting large numbers of managers, entire layers of management are eliminated. When this happens, the remaining managers often end up with larger spans of control. Because spans of control are wider, corporate structures are flatter after downsizing.

Three Forms of Authority

As individuals are delegated responsibility and authority, a complex web of interactions develops. These interactions may take one of three forms of authority: line, staff, or committee and team. All three may be found in a single company, especially a large one.

LINE AUTHORITY

Line authority flows up and down the chain of command (refer back to Figure 7.1). Most companies rely on *line departments*, those directly linked to the production and sale of specific products. For example,

CENTRALIZED ORGANIZATION Top managers retain most decision-making rights for themselves.

DECENTRALIZED ORGANIZATION Lower- and middle-level managers are allowed to make significant decisions.

SPAN OF CONTROL The number of people managed by one manager.

DOWNSIZING The planned reduction in the scope of an organization's activity.

LINE AUTHORITY Authority that flows in a direct chain of command from the top of the company to the bottom.

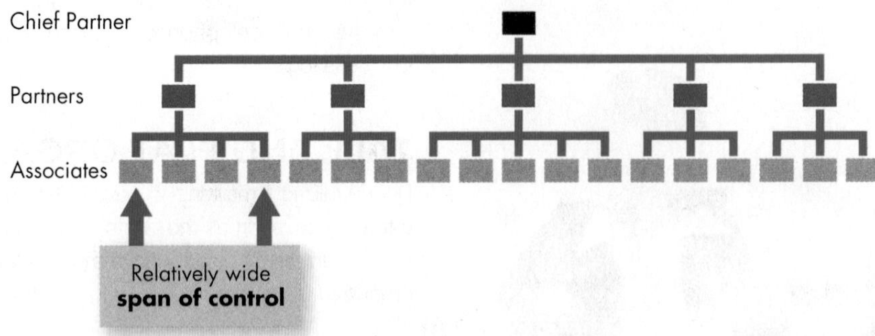

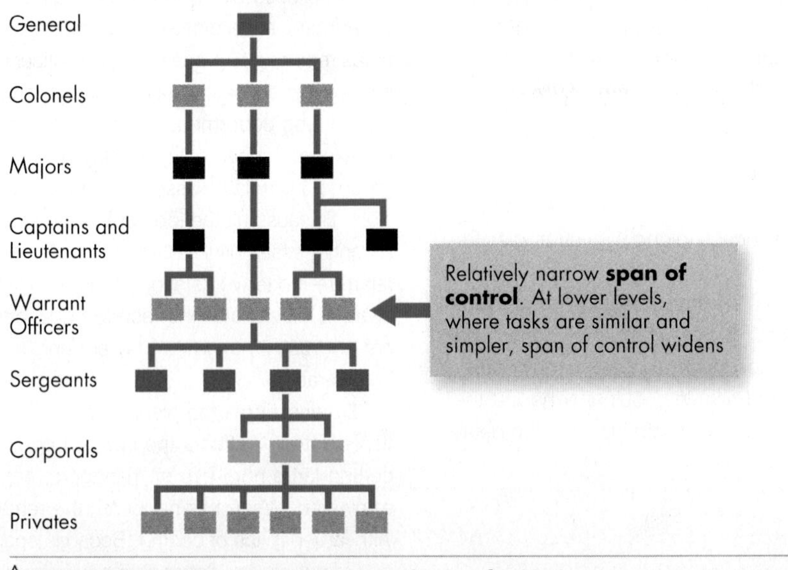

FIGURE 7.3 Organizational structures and span of control

Clark, an equipment manufacturer, has a division that produces forklifts and small earthmovers (see Figure 7.4). In this division, line departments include purchasing, materials handling, fabrication, painting, and assembly (all of which are directly linked to production), along with sales and distribution (both of which are directly linked to sales).

Each line department is essential in achieving the goals the company has set. Line employees are the "doers" and producers in a company. If any line department fails to complete its task, the company cannot sell and deliver finished goods. Thus, significant authority is usually delegated to line departments.

STAFF AUTHORITY

Companies often employ individuals with technical expertise in areas like law, accounting, marketing research, and human resources. These

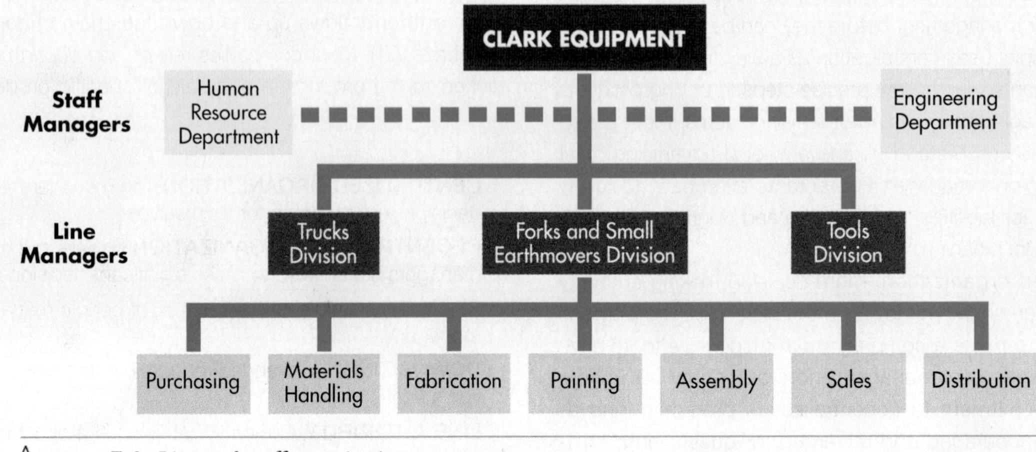

FIGURE 7.4 Line and staff organization

experts may be given **staff authority**; that is, they help line departments in making decisions, but they do not have the authority to make the final decision. For example, if the fabrication department at Clark has an employee with a drinking problem, the line manager of the department might consult a human resource staff expert for advice on how to handle the situation. The staff expert might suggest that the worker stay on the job, but enter a counselling program. But if the line manager decides that the job is too dangerous to be handled by a person whose judgment is impaired by alcohol, the line manager's decision will most likely prevail.

Typically, line authority is represented on organization charts by solid lines, while staff authority is shown by dotted lines. Line managers are directly involved in producing the firm's products or services, while staff members generally provide services to management. But remember, the goals of the organization influence the distinction between line and staff authority. At Aluminum Company of Canada, for example, the director of personnel has staff authority because the personnel department supports the primary function of the company (the production and marketing of aluminum). But at Office Overload, the director of personnel is a line manager because the primary goal of that firm is to provide personnel to other firms.

Business firms are increasingly using work teams and allowing groups of employees to plan and organize their own work with a minimum of supervision. This contributes to employee empowerment.

Andres Rodriguez/Fotolia

COMMITTEE AND TEAM AUTHORITY

More and more organizations have started to use **committee and team authority**—authority granted to committees or work teams that play central roles in the firm's daily operations. A committee, for example, may consist of top managers from several major areas of the company. If the work of the committee is especially important, and if the committee will be working together for an extended time, the organization may even grant it special authority as a decision-making body that goes beyond the individual authority possessed by each of its members.

Firms are also increasingly using work teams at the operating level. These teams are made up of workers (not managers) and are empowered to plan, organize, and perform their work with a minimum of supervision. Organizations usually find it beneficial to grant special authority to work teams so that they will function more effectively.[13] More information about teams is presented in Chapter 9.

STAFF AUTHORITY Authority based on expertise and that usually involves advising line managers.

COMMITTEE AND TEAM AUTHORITY Authority granted to committees or work teams involved in a firm's daily operations.

LO-4 BASIC ORGANIZATIONAL STRUCTURES

A glance at the organization charts of many organizations reveals what appears to be an almost infinite variety of structures. However, closer examination shows that most of them fit into one of four basic categories: functional, divisional, project, or international.

The Functional Structure

In the **functional structure**, the various units in the organization are formed based on the key functions that must be carried out to reach organizational goals. The functional structure—an example of which was shown in Figure 7.1—makes use of departmentalization by function. The advantages and disadvantages of the functional structure are summarized in Table 7.2. To overcome one of the disadvantages of the

FUNCTIONAL STRUCTURE Various units are included in a group based on functions that need to be performed for the organization to reach its goals.

TABLE 7.2 Advantages and disadvantages of a functional structure

Advantages	Disadvantages
1. It focuses attention on the key activities that must be performed.	1. Conflicts may arise among the functional areas.
2. Expertise develops within each function.	2. No single function is responsible for overall organizational performance.
3. Employees have clearly defined career paths.	3. Employees in each functional area have a narrow view of the organization.
4. The structure is simple and easy to understand.	4. Decision making is slowed because functional areas must get approval from top management for a variety of decisions.
5. It eliminates duplication of activities.	5. Coordinating highly specialized functions may be difficult.

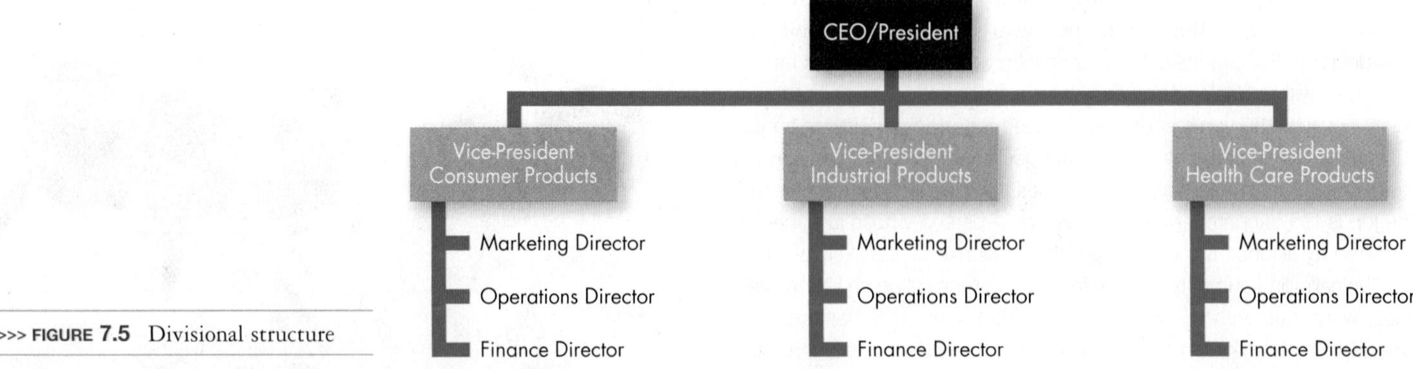

>>> **FIGURE 7.5** Divisional structure

functional structure—poor interdepartmental communication—some companies have established *customer innovation centres* that have expertise on product development, brand management, and sales. At these centres, key customers provide feedback on product performance and brainstorm new ideas for products that will better satisfy customers.[14]

The Divisional Structure

The **divisional structure** divides the organization into several divisions, each of which operates as a semi-autonomous unit and profit centre. An example of a divisional structure is shown in Figure 7.5. Divisions in organizations can be based on products, customers, or geography. For example, Winnipeg-based Frantic Films has three product divisions: live action (which produces programs like *Pioneer Quest* and *Til Debt Do Us Part*), TV commercials (which produces television commercials for national and international clients), and software (which creates new, stand-alone software to enhance certain visual effects).[15] Bell Canada created three customer-based divisions: consumers, small and medium-sized businesses, and large corporations. This structure replaced the former divisional structure that was geographically based.[16] Sometimes a company reorganizes divisions in order to be more effective. Yahoo Inc. established three divisions—consumers, regions, and technology—in order to focus its activities and to increase growth prospects.[17]

Whatever basis is used, divisional performance can be assessed because each division operates almost as a separate company. Divisionalized companies can buy, sell, create, and disband divisions without disrupting the rest of their operations. Different divisions can sponsor separate advertising campaigns and foster different corporate identities. They can also share certain corporate-level resources (such as market research data). But sometimes unhealthy competition develops between divisions, or the efforts of one division may be duplicated by those of another. At PepsiCo, for example, each of the company's three major beverage brands—Pepsi, Gatorade, and Tropicana—formerly operated as independent divisions. But this became a problem because the brands were competing for the same resources and there was very little coordination and sharing of information. Now, all three brands are in one division so that a unified approach to brand management is achieved. The advantages and disadvantages of the divisional structure are summarized in Table 7.3.

Project Organization

A typical organization is characterized by unchanging vertical authority relationships because the organization produces a product or service in a repetitive and predictable way. Procter & Gamble, for example, produces millions of tubes of Crest toothpaste every year using standardized production methods. The company has done this for years and intends to do so indefinitely. But some organizations find themselves faced with new product opportunities, or with projects that have a definite starting and ending point. These organizations often use a project structure to deal with the uncertainty encountered in new situations. **Project organization** involves forming a team of specialists from different functional areas of the organization to work on a specific project.[18] A project structure may be temporary or permanent; if it is temporary, the project team disbands once the project is completed and team members return to their regular functional area or are assigned to a new project.

Project organization is used extensively by Canadian firms in the construction of hydroelectric generating stations like those developed by Hydro-Quebec on the La Grande River and by Manitoba Hydro on the Nelson River. Once the generating station is complete, it becomes part of the traditional structure of the utility. Project organization is also

DIVISIONAL STRUCTURE Divides the organization into divisions, each of which operates as a semi-autonomous unit.

PROJECT ORGANIZATION An organization that uses teams of specialists to complete specific projects.

>>> **TABLE 7.3** Advantages and disadvantages of a divisional structure

Advantages	Disadvantages
1. It accommodates change and expansion.	1. Activities may be duplicated across divisions.
2. It increases accountability.	2. A lack of communication among divisions may occur.
3. It develops expertise in the various divisions.	3. Adding diverse divisions may blur the focus of the organization.
4. It encourages training for top management.	4. Company politics may affect the allocation of resources.

The project organization structure is very useful for construction projects like this hydroelectric generating station on the La Grande River in Quebec. The construction of installations like this has a specific beginning and ending point. Once completed, the generating station becomes part of the traditional organization structure of the provincial utility.

set/Shutterstock

used at Genstar Shipyards Ltd. in Vancouver. Each ship built is treated as a project and supervised by a project manager, who is responsible for ensuring that the ship is completed on time and within budget.[19] Project organization has also proven useful for coordinating the many elements needed to extract oil from the tar sands.

A *matrix organization* is a variation of the project structure in which the project manager and the regular line managers share authority. When a project is concluded, the matrix is disbanded. Ford, for example, uses a matrix organization to design new car models. A design team composed of people from engineering, marketing, operations, and finance is created to design the new car. After the team's work is completed, team members move back to their permanent functional jobs.

Martha Stewart Living Omnimedia, Inc., has created a permanent matrix organization for its lifestyle business. The company is organized broadly into media and merchandising groups, each of which has specific products and product groups. Layered on top of this structure are teams of lifestyle experts organized into groups such as cooking, crafts, weddings, and so forth (see Figure 7.6). Although each group targets specific customer needs, they all work across all product groups. A wedding expert, for example, might contribute to an article on wedding planning for a Martha Stewart magazine, develop a story idea for a Martha Stewart cable television program, and supply content for a Martha Stewart website. This same individual might also help select fabrics suitable for wedding gowns that are to be retailed.[20]

CEO
Area specialists
Media group
Merchandising group
Magazines
Books
Internet
Radio/ newspapers
Network/ cable TV
Kmart line
Catalogue online
Sears paint
Specialty retailing
Cooking
Entertainment
Weddings
Crafts
Gardening
Home
Holidays
Children

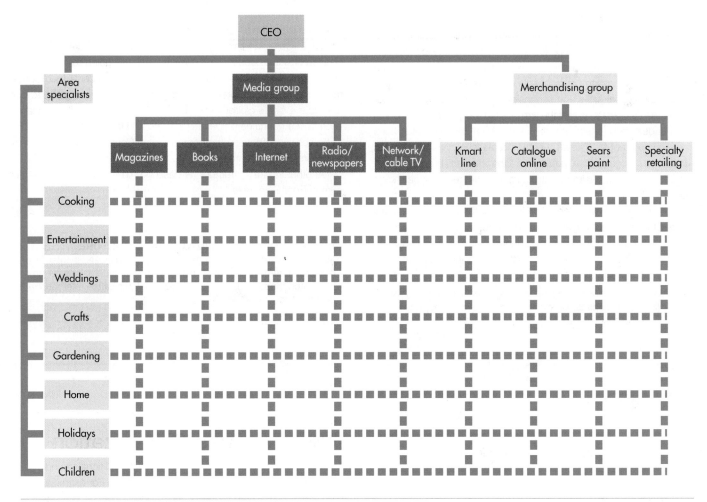

FIGURE 7.6 Matrix organization of Martha Stewart

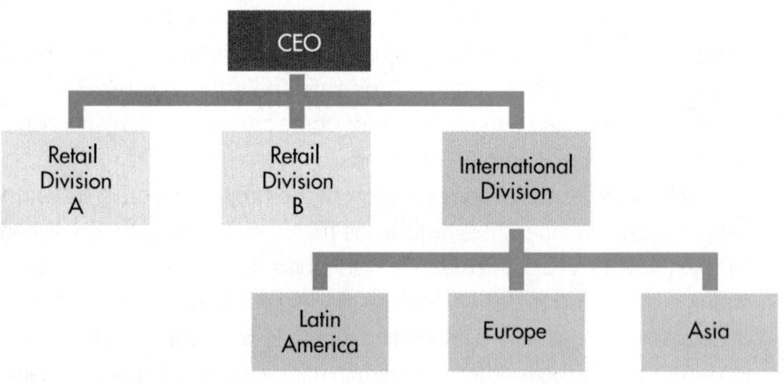

FIGURE 7.7 International division structure

All the signs at this 8000 square metre store in Numazu identify it as a Seiyu outlet run by Japan's fifth-largest supermarket chain. However, Walmart owns 38 percent of Seiyu, and this giant store is part of Walmart's effort to enter the world's second-largest retail market.

Chiaki Tsukumo/AP Images

The matrix structure is not always effective. In 2009, Carol Bartz—then-CEO at Yahoo—announced a restructuring that was designed to make managers more accountable and to speed up decision making. The new structure essentially did away with the matrix structure and workers no longer report to multiple bosses.[21]

International Organization Structures

Several types of **international organizational structures** have emerged as competition on a global scale becomes more intense and companies experiment with the ways in which they might respond. For example, when Walmart opened its first store outside the United States in the early 1990s, it set up a special projects team to handle the logistics. As more stores were opened during the next decade, the firm created a small international department to handle overseas expansion. By then, however, international sales and expansion had become such a major part of Walmart's operations that the firm created a separate international division headed up by a senior vice-president. International operations are now so important to Walmart that the international division has been further divided into geographic areas where the firm does business, such as Mexico and Europe. Walmart's structure is of the general type shown in Figure 7.7.

Other companies have adopted variations of the basic international structure. The French food giant Danone Group, for instance, has two major product groups: dairy products (Danone yogurt) and bottled water (Evian). Danone's structure does not differentiate internationally, but rather integrates global operations within each product group.[22]

Some companies adopt a truly global structure in which they acquire resources (including capital), produce goods and services, engage in research and development, and sell products in whatever local market is appropriate, without any consideration of national boundaries. Until a few years ago, for example, General Electric (GE) kept its international business operations as separate divisions. Now, however, the company functions as one integrated global organization. GE businesses around the world connect and interact with each other constantly, and managers freely move back and forth among them.[23]

When Canadian firms "go global," they need to address three organization structure questions: (1) Is the business going to be centralized in the home base in Canada or is going to allow decentralized decision making in its various foreign offices? (2) Is the business going to communicate a single global message or is it going to tailor its message to each of the countries it operates in? and (3) How is collaboration going to be achieved between the home office in Canada and the company's offices in foreign countries?[24]

Another kind of "structure" is described in the boxed insert entitled "Green Roof Structures."

INTERNATIONAL ORGANIZATIONAL STRUCTURE An organizational structure designed to help a company succeed in international markets. International departments, international divisions, or an integrated global organization are all variations of the international organizational structure.

ORGANIZATIONAL DESIGN FOR THE TWENTY-FIRST CENTURY

As the world grows increasingly complex and fast-paced, companies continue to seek new forms of organization that permit them to compete effectively. Among the most popular of these new forms are the boundaryless organization, the team organization, the virtual organization, and the learning organization.

Boundaryless Organization

The boundaryless organization is one in which traditional boundaries and structures are minimized or eliminated altogether. For example, General Electric's fluid organizational structure, in which people, ideas, and

THE GREENING OF BUSINESS

Green Roof Structures

The term "organizational structure" is commonly used to explain *theoretical* concepts like departmentalization, authority, responsibility, and the hierarchical patterns within organizations. But organizations also need actual *physical* structures like office buildings and factories to do their work, and managers are beginning to realize that their physical structures present significant opportunities to be eco-friendly. The roofs of buildings present two interesting possibilities: green roofs and solar panels.

Green rooftops—which means planting trees and vegetation on the roofs of buildings—are an increasingly popular feature, as shown in these examples:

- The green roof on the Manulife Centre parkade in Toronto has been there for 25 years, and the trees are now three storeys high. In 2009, the Toronto city council passed a bylaw that mandates green roofs on new commercial buildings and high-rise residential buildings.
- In the Fremont Village Shopping Centre in Port Coquitlam, British Columbia, the roofs of Walmart and Canadian Tire are covered with thousands of plants that provide insulation that reduces energy costs and storm water runoff.
- Esri Canada's green-roof building in the Toronto suburb of Don Mills contains 53 types of trees, shrubs, and flowers; employees benefit from having access to the natural world while at work.

Solar panels are the second possibility. Both businesses and individuals are adopting this rooftop structure. The Toronto-Dominion Bank, for example, has installed solar panels in 94 of its locations across North America. Many homeowners want to do the "green thing" by installing solar panels on their roofs, but the $30 000 price tag seems pretty steep. But SolarCity, a provider of solar-energy systems, is making solar panels available by leasing them instead of selling them. Buyers put just $1000 down and agree to a 15-year lease. The cost for a typical installation is around $75 per month, but the consumer saves about $95 a month in electricity costs and recoups their $1000 within a year. SolarCity didn't just solve the problem of high initial investment cost. The company also realized that consumers were reluctant to install solar panels because of the hassle involved, so it arranges for building permits, financing, and tax breaks. SolarCity has also streamlined costs by using innovative computer automation to custom-design consumer installations. SolarCity even compiled utility-rate data to estimate the consumer's return on their solar investment.

CRITICAL THINKING QUESTIONS

1. What are the advantages of "green" initiatives such as green roofs and solar panels? Are there any disadvantages? Explain.
2. Consider the following statement: *It is very expensive to build green roofs or install solar panels, so expenditures like these should generally not be made. Rather, companies should focus on upgrading their production facilities so they can make higher-quality, lower-priced products for consumers and more profits for their shareholders.* Do you agree or disagree? Explain your reasoning.

information flow freely between businesses and business groups, approximates this concept. Similarly, as firms partner with their suppliers in more efficient ways, external boundaries disappear. Some of Walmart's key suppliers are tied directly into the retailer's information system. As a result, when Walmart distribution centres start running low on, say, Wrangler blue jeans, the manufacturer receives the information as soon as the retailer does. Wrangler proceeds to manufacture new inventory and restock the distribution centre without Walmart having to place a new order.

Team Organization

Team organization relies almost exclusively on project-type teams, with little or no underlying functional hierarchy. People "float" from project to project as dictated by their skills and the demands of those projects. At Cypress Semiconductor, units or groups that become large are simply split into smaller units. Not surprisingly, the organization is composed entirely of small units. This strategy allows each unit to change direction, explore new ideas, and try new methods without having to deal with a rigid bureaucratic superstructure. Although few large organizations have actually reached this level of adaptability, Apple and Xerox are among those moving toward it.

Virtual Organization

Closely related to the team organization is the virtual organization. A virtual organization has little or no formal structure. Typically, it has only a handful of permanent employees, a very small staff, and a modest administrative facility. As the needs of the organization change, its managers bring in temporary workers, lease facilities, and outsource basic support services to meet the demands of each unique situation. As the situation changes, the temporary workforce changes in parallel, with some people leaving the organization and others entering it. Facilities and subcontracted services also change. In other words, the virtual organization exists only in response to its own needs.

Global Research Consortium (GRC) is a virtual organization. GRC offers research and consulting services to firms doing business in Asia. As clients request various services, GRC's staff of three permanent employees subcontracts the work to an appropriate set of several dozen independent consultants and/or researchers with whom it has relationships. At any given time, therefore, GRC may have several projects under way and 20 or 30 people working in various capacities. As the projects change, so does the composition of the organization. Figure 7.8 illustrates the basic structure of a virtual organization.

Learning Organization

A learning organization facilitates the lifelong learning and personal development of all of its employees while continually transforming itself to respond to changing demands and needs. The most frequent goals are improved quality, continuous improvement, and performance measurement. The idea is that the most consistent and logical strategy for achieving continuous improvement is to constantly upgrade employee talent, skill, and knowledge. For example, if each employee in an organization learns one new thing each day and can translate that knowledge into work-related practice, continuous improvement will logically follow.

In recent years, many different organizations have implemented this approach on various levels. Shell, for example, purchased an executive conference centre called the Shell Learning Centre. The facility boasts state-of-the-art classrooms and instructional technology, lodging facilities, a restaurant, and recreational amenities such as a golf course, swimming pool, and tennis courts. Line managers at the firm rotate through the centre and serve as teaching faculty. All Shell employees routinely attend training programs, seminars, and related activities, gathering the latest information they need to contribute more effectively to the firm.

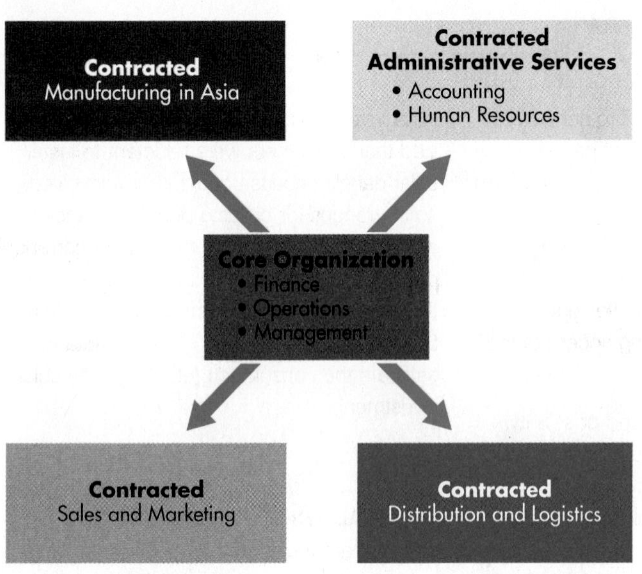

<<< **FIGURE 7.8** The virtual organization

LO-5 THE INFORMAL ORGANIZATION

The formal organization of a business is the part that can be seen and represented on the organization chart. The structure of a company, however, is not limited to the organization chart and the formal assignment of authority. Frequently, the **informal organization**—the everyday social interactions among employees that transcend formal jobs and job interrelationships—effectively alters a company's formal structure. Indeed, the informal organization is sometimes more powerful than the formal structure. The power of the informal organization was evident in the highly publicized rescue of the Chilean miners in 2010. In the underground cavern where they were trapped, there were no top managers, so much of what the miners did was informal (dividing up chores, singing, providing mutual support, and so on). These activities kept the miners' hopes alive until they were rescued.[25] The team ethics exercise at the end of this chapter presents an interesting situation that illustrates the informal organization.

Is the informal organization good or bad? On the positive side, the informal organization can help employees feel that they "belong," and it gives them an outlet for "letting off steam" in a safe environment. It also provides information that employees are interested in hearing. On the negative side, the informal organization can reinforce office politics that put the interests of individuals ahead of those of the company. Likewise, a great deal of harm can be caused by distorted or inaccurate information communicated without management input or review. For example, if the informal organization is generating false information about impending layoffs, valuable employees may act quickly (and unnecessarily) to seek other employment. Two important elements of the informal organization are informal groups and the organizational grapevine.

Informal Groups

Informal groups are simply groups of people who decide to interact among themselves even though they may not be required to do so by the formal organization. They may be made up of people who work together in a formal sense or who simply get together for lunch, during breaks, or after work. They may talk about business, the boss, or non-work-related topics such as families, movies, or sports. For example, at the New York Metropolitan Opera, musicians and singers play poker during the intermissions. Most pots are in the $30 to $40 range. The late Luciano Pavarotti, the famed tenor, once played (he lost).[26]

INFORMAL ORGANIZATION A network of personal interactions and relationships among employees unrelated to the firm's formal authority structure.

^^^ The grapevine is a powerful communications network in most organizations. These workers may be talking about any number of things—an upcoming deadline on an important project, tonight's hockey game, the stock market, rumours about an impending takeover, or gossip about who's getting promoted.

EastWest Imaging/Fotolia

The Organizational Grapevine

The **grapevine** is the informal communication network that runs through the entire organization.[27] The grapevine is found in all organizations, and it does not always follow the same patterns as formal channels of authority and communication. Formerly, when people gathered around the water cooler or on the golf course to exchange gossip and pass on information, they had names and faces. But with the internet (a worldwide grapevine), you may not know who you are talking to, or how reliable the person providing the information is.[28] The boxed insert entitled "Gossip on the Grapevine" provides information on the pros and cons of gossip in the workplace.

Because the grapevine typically passes information orally, messages may get distorted in the process. In addition to miscommunication and attempts by some people to manipulate it for their own ends, it may carry rumours with absolutely no basis in fact. This is most common when there is a complete lack of information. Human nature abhors a vacuum, and the grapevine will fill it with something, even if just rumours. Baseless rumours can be very hard to kill.

Attempts to eliminate the grapevine are fruitless, so managers shouldn't waste their time trying to do so. Rather, they should maintain open channels of communication and respond vigorously to inaccurate information, because this will minimize the damage. In fact, the grapevine can actually be an asset. By getting to know the key people who are part of it, the manager can partially control the information received and use the grapevine to determine reactions to new ideas (e.g., a change in human resource policies or benefit packages). Wise managers will tune in to the grapevine's message, because it is often a corporate early-warning system. Ignoring this valuable source of information can cause managers to be the last to know that they are about to get a new boss, or that they have a potentially fatal image problem.

GRAPEVINE An informal communications network that carries gossip and other information throughout an organization.

THERE'S AN APP FOR THAT!

APP DETAILS	PLATFORMS
1. **Let's Get Organized** **Source:** AppWarrior **Key Features:** Provides tips for individuals to be more organized at home and in the workplace.	Apple, Android
2. **My Teams** **Source:** Davis Fredenvals **Key Features:** Helps you pick, manage, and communicate with workplace teams.	Android
3. **SAP Business One** **Source:** SAP AG **Key Features:** Designed for enterprise resource planning applications for small business.	Apple, Android, Windows

APP DISCOVERY EXERCISE

Since app availability changes, conduct your own search for the "Top Three" business organization apps and identify the key features.

MANAGING IN TURBULENT TIMES

Gossip on the Grapevine

When you hear the word "gossip," the term likely has a negative connotation. But it's also true that within the context of a company, gossip and the grapevine are an important part of the organization's culture. Given that, it is important that you, as an *employee*, understand several things when you participate in gossip, either as a sender or receiver. First, recognize that there are some benefits of gossip. For example, it may be the first place you hear important information, such as a new job opening up or a major contract that your company is about to sign. Second, as you pass along information, remember that what you say will reflect upon you as a person. If you share negative information about a co-worker, it is very likely that others may come to distrust you and therefore keep information from you. Third, you must carefully consider the people with whom you share gossip, making sure that they will keep confidential information private. Fourth, your supervisor will likely be unhappy if you develop a reputation as a gossip, since you will be perceived as a person who can't keep departmental matters confidential. Finally, be very careful about the medium that you use to share information. An email is never private and should not be used for any communication that you would not want shared publicly.

As a *manager*, you will have a somewhat different perspective on gossip. You may, for example, want to encourage the grapevine and "good" gossip that increases employee engagement, facilitates networking among employees, and makes everyone feel like they're part of the "in-group." But you will also encounter situations where gossip is very annoying: when it limits your ability to control the sharing of information, or when it limits your power, or when it creates rumours that you have to spend time refuting. Holly Green, a contributor to *Forbes* magazine, makes several suggestions that can help managers effectively manage gossip on the grapevine: (1) remember that vigorous grapevine activity may be the sign of boredom on the part of your subordinates (so make sure that all members of your work group are fully engaged in their work); (2) remember that the grapevine is very active when information is scarce, and that employees turn to the grapevine when they believe that they are not getting enough information from the formal channels of communication (so make sure you share as much information as possible); (3) remember that the grapevine can warn you about big issues that are on the minds of employees (so keep your ears open for employee complaints or concerns). If the grapevine is managed correctly, it can benefit both employees and managers.

CRITICAL THINKING QUESTIONS

1. What kind of information is typically conveyed through the grapevine at your college or university? How often is the information accurate?
2. Does a flat organization structure (one with few hierarchical levels) encourage or discourage gossip? Explain your reasoning.

SUMMARY OF

LEARNING OBJECTIVES

LO-1 DISCUSS THE ELEMENTS THAT INFLUENCE A FIRM'S *ORGANIZATIONAL STRUCTURE.*

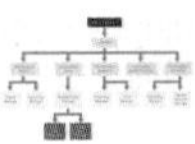

Every business needs structure to operate. *Organizational structure* varies according to a firm's mission, purpose, and strategy. Size, technology, and changes in environmental circumstances also influence structure. In general, while all organizations have the same basic elements, each develops the structure that contributes to the most efficient operations.

LO-2 EXPLAIN HOW *SPECIALIZATION* AND *DEPARTMENTALIZATION* ARE THE BUILDING BLOCKS OF ORGANIZATIONAL STRUCTURE.

As a firm grows, it usually has a greater need for people to perform specialized tasks (specialization). It also has a greater need to group types of work into logical units (departmentalization). Common forms of departmentalization are *customer*, *product*, *process*, *geographic*, and *functional*. Large businesses often use more than one form of departmentalization.

LO-3 DISTINGUISH BETWEEN *RESPONSIBILITY* AND *AUTHORITY* AND EXPLAIN THE DIFFERENCES IN DECISION MAKING IN *CENTRALIZED* AND *DECENTRALIZED ORGANIZATIONS.*

Responsibility is the duty to perform a task, while *authority* is the power to make the decisions necessary to complete tasks. *Delegation* begins when a manager assigns a task to a subordinate; *accountability* means that the subordinate must complete the task. *Span of control* refers to the number of people who work for a manager. The more people supervised by a manager, the wider his or her span of control. Wide spans are usually desirable when employees perform simple or unrelated tasks. When jobs are diversified or prone to change, a narrower span is generally preferable.

In a *centralized organization*, only a few individuals in top management have real decision-making authority. In a *decentralized organization*, much authority is delegated to lower-level management. Where both *line* and *line-and-staff authority* exist in an organization, *line departments* generally have authority to make decisions while *staff departments* have a responsibility to advise. *Committee and team authority* empowers committees or work teams to make decisions about various aspects of operations.

LO-4 EXPLAIN THE DIFFERENCES BETWEEN *FUNCTIONAL, DIVISIONAL, PROJECT*, AND *INTERNATIONAL ORGANIZATION STRUCTURES*, AND DESCRIBE THE MOST POPULAR FORMS OF ORGANIZATIONAL DESIGN.

In a *functional organization*, authority is usually distributed among such basic functions as marketing and finance. In a *divisional organization*, the various divisions operate in a relatively autonomous fashion. In *project organization*, a company creates project teams to address specific problems or to complete specific projects. A company that has divisions in many countries may require an additional level of *international organization* to coordinate those operations. Four of the most popular forms of organizational design are *boundaryless organizations* (traditional boundaries and structures are minimized or eliminated), *team organizations* (relying on project-type teams, with little or no functional hierarchy), *virtual organizations* (which have little formal structure and only a handful of permanent employees, a small staff, and a modest administrative facility), and *learning organizations* (which facilitate employees' lifelong learning and personal development while transforming the organization to meet changing demands and needs).

LO-5 UNDERSTAND HOW THE *INFORMAL ORGANIZATION* IS DIFFERENT FROM THE FORMAL ORGANIZATION.

The *informal organization* consists of the everyday social interactions among employees that transcend formal jobs and job interrelationships. The informal organization exists within the formal structure of every organization and cannot be suppressed. Effective managers work with the informal organization and try to harness it for the good of the formal organization.

QUESTIONS AND EXERCISES

QUESTIONS FOR ANALYSIS

1. Explain the significance of organizational size as it relates to organizational structure. Describe the changes likely to occur as an organization grows.
2. Why do some managers have difficulties in delegating authority? Why do you think this problem might be more pronounced in small businesses?
3. In your own words, explain how a functional structure differs from a divisional structure.
4. Compare and contrast the matrix and divisional approaches to organizational structure. How would you feel personally about working in a matrix organization in which you were assigned simultaneously to multiple units or groups *and* had multiple bosses?
5. If a company has a formal organization structure, why should managers pay attention to the informal organization?
6. The argument has been made that the divisional structure does a better job than the functional structure of training managers for top-level positions. Do you agree or disagree with this argument? Explain your reasoning.

APPLICATION EXERCISES

7. Draw up an organization chart for your college or university.
8. Think about the organization where you currently work (or one where you previously worked). Which of the four basic structural types was it most consistent with (functional, divisional, project, international)? What was the basis of departmentalization in the organization? Why was that particular basis used?
9. Interview the manager of a local service business (e.g., a fast-food restaurant). What types of tasks does this manager typically delegate? Is the appropriate authority also delegated in each case? What problems occur when authority is not delegated appropriately?
10. Review the discussion of intrapreneurs in Chapter 4. Then identify a person who is an intrapreneur. In what ways did the structure of the intrapreneur's company help this individual succeed? In what ways did the structure pose problems?

TEAM EXERCISES

BUILDING YOUR BUSINESS SKILLS

GETTING WITH THE PROGRAM

GOAL

To encourage students to understand the relationship between organization structure and a company's ability to attract and keep valued employees.

SITUATION

You are the founder of a small but growing high-tech company that develops new computer software. With your current workload and new contracts in the pipeline, your business is thriving, except for one problem—you cannot find computer programmers for product development. Worse yet, current staff members are being lured away by other high-tech firms. After suffering a particularly discouraging personnel raid in which competitors captured three of your most valued employees, you schedule a meeting with your director of human resources to plan organizational changes designed to encourage worker loyalty. You already pay top dollar, but the continuing exodus tells you that programmers are looking for something more.

METHOD

Working with three or four classmates, identify some ways in which specific organizational changes might improve the working environment and encourage employee loyalty. As you analyze the following factors, ask yourself the obvious question, *If I were a programmer, what organizational changes would encourage me to stay?*

- *Level of job specialization.* With many programmers describing their jobs as tedious because of the focus on detail in a narrow work area, what changes, if any, would you make in job specialization? Right now, for instance, few of your programmers have any say in product design.
- *Decision-making hierarchy.* What decision-making authority would encourage people to stay? Is expanding employee authority likely to work better in a centralized or decentralized organization?
- *Team authority.* Can team empowerment make a difference? Taking the point of view of the worker, describe the ideal team.
- *Intrapreneuring.* What can your company do to encourage and reward innovation?

FOLLOW-UP QUESTIONS

1. With the average computer programmer earning nearly $70 000, and with all competitive firms paying top dollar, why might organizational issues be critical in determining employee loyalty?
2. If you were a programmer, what organizational factors would make a difference to you? Why?
3. As the company founder, how willing would you be to make major organizational changes in light of the shortage of qualified programmers?

EXERCISING YOUR ETHICS

TO POACH OR NOT TO POACH

THE SITUATION

The Hails Corporation has recently moved toward an all-team-based organization structure. That is, all workers are divided into teams. Each team has the autonomy to divide up the work assigned to it among its individual members. In addition, each team handles its own scheduling for members to take vacations and other time off. The teams also handle the interviews and hiring of new team members when the need arises. Team A has just lost one of its members, who moved to another city to be closer to his ailing parents.

THE DILEMMA

Since moving to the team structure, every time a team has needed new members, it has advertised in the local newspaper and hired someone from outside the company. However, Team A is considering a different approach to fill its opening. Specifically, a key member of another team (Team B) has made it known that she would like to join Team A. She likes the team members, sees the team's work as being enjoyable, and is somewhat bored with her team's current assignment.

The concern is that if Team A chooses this individual to join the team, several problems may occur. For one thing, her current team will clearly be angry with the members of Team A. Further, "poaching" new team members from other teams inside the plant is likely to become a common occurrence. On the other hand, though, it seems reasonable that she should have the same opportunity to join Team A as an outsider would. Team A needs to decide how to proceed.

TEAM ACTIVITY

Assemble a group of four students and assign each group member to one of the following roles:

- member of Team A
- member of Team B
- manager of both teams
- Hails investor

ACTION STEPS

1. Before hearing any of your group's comments on this situation and, from the perspective of your assigned role, decide whether you think that the member of Team B should be allowed to join Team A. Write down the reasons for your position.
2. Before hearing any of your group's comments on this situation and from the perspective of your assigned role, determine the underlying ethical issues, if any, in this situation. Write down the issues.
3. Gather your group together and reveal, in turn, each member's comments on the situation. Next, reveal the ethical issues listed by each member.
4. Appoint someone to record main points of agreement and disagreement within the group. How do you explain the results? What accounts for any disagreement?
5. From an ethical standpoint, what does your group conclude is the most appropriate action Hails should take in this situation? Should Team B's member be allowed to join Team A?
6. Develop a group response to the following questions: (a) Assuming Team A asks the Team B member to join its team, how might it go about minimizing repercussions? (b) Assuming Team A does not ask the Team B member to join its team, how might it go about minimizing repercussions?

BUSINESS CASE 7

WHAT HAPPENED TO THE "OCCUPY WALL STREET" MOVEMENT?

In September 2014, members of unions, religious groups, and global economic reformers marched in New York City using the latest hashtag slogan: #floodwallstreet Stop Capitalism! End the Climate Crisis!" The march brought back memories of the "Occupy Wall Street" movement that received so much publicity in 2011.

Occupy Wall Street started at Vancouver-based Adbusters, an organization that publishes a magazine critical of excessive consumer consumption. Inspired by the so-called Arab Spring in the Middle East earlier in 2011, the Adbusters staff had a brainstorming session and came up with the image of a ballerina balanced on Wall Street's iconic charging-bull sculpture. A simple Twitter hashtag was chosen: #OccupyWallStreet. Thousands grew excited about the idea and before long a big protest was planned for New York City. By mid-October, protests were also taking place in major Canadian and European cities. Protest groups set up camp in many places, including city parks, the Vancouver Art Gallery, Zuccotti Park in New York City, and the Toronto Stock Exchange. People met in large and small groups, played drums, and sang together. Unions and community groups also joined in, and a website called "Occupy Together" was started. The movement appeared leaderless, and stood for open, participatory, non-hierarchical decision making, with everyone entitled to provide input and push their own ideas. As one protestor said, "No one is a leader because everyone is a leader."

Robert Mecea/AP/The Canadian Press

The Occupy Wall Street movement struck a chord in both Canadians and Americans frustrated with a political/economic system they saw as favouring corporations and rich individuals. The movement had many goals, the most general one being an end to economic inequality. The central slogan was "We are the 99%," but that message was combined with a dizzying array of other demands: raise taxes on corporations, offer free college education, stop climate change, stop unfair treatment of Muslims, stop home foreclosures, reduce high unemployment, and nationalize the banks. While the situation seemed rather chaotic, there was actually *some* structure. For example, daily meetings (called assemblies) were held, which planned the occupation, decided where marches would be held, developed communications with the media, and organized donated supplies. Anyone could participate in the assemblies, and their minutes were posted online. Since a New York bylaw prevented use of bullhorns without a permit, protestors adopted a "people's microphone" system in which someone shouted a message a few words at a time to the crowd, then people who heard that message repeated it for others who were further away.

But opposition to the camps soon developed. City officials, for example, grew frustrated by the movement's occupation of public spaces. As police moved protestors out of public parks, and as winter approached, things started to fizzle out. A few camps were still occupied in January 2012, and a few others reappeared in May 2012, but the movement had lost a great deal of momentum.

Why the decline? Observers cited many reasons: (1) the movement was not as egalitarian as generally assumed (the camps exhibited a hierarchy, and a few people dominated everyone else), (2) it had no central message and no clear goal, (3) assemblies were very inefficient and time-consuming, (4) the movement lacked an endgame (under what conditions would protestors end their protest?), (5) the movement's culture was one of entitlement (the protests were dominated by the younger generation, who expected to be handed the wealth of their parents), (6) it cost money (city officials wanted the encampments dismantled because costs were being incurred to control the protestors), and (7) internal dissension developed as the tent camps became havens for the disenfranchised members of society.

The anti-hierarchical nature of Occupy Wall Street was supposed to help it succeed. Kalle Lasn, one of the founders of Adbusters, said critics didn't understand that Occupy was a new-style revolution. It was not vertical, and it didn't have (or want) a designated leader; instead, it was horizontal, because it grew out of the culture of the internet. When asked about the future of the movement, Lasn said it would adopt a different strategy for 2012, one which involved "surprise attacks" in diverse settings like university economics departments and banks, rather than continuous occupations of city parks.

As interest in Occupy Wall Street declined, attention turned to a website called Leadnow.ca, which some thought would become the focal point for a leaderless organization. The website was used to organize "vote mobs" on university and community college campuses, and in just a few months it attracted 60 000 members.

QUESTIONS FOR DISCUSSION

1. What are the key features of organizational structure? Which are evident in the Occupy Wall Street movement? Which are absent?
2. Consider the following statement: *In order to be effective, every organization needs a hierarchical structure with bosses and subordinates. Without such a structure, there is no one in charge, no one knows how much authority they have, and people can't be held accountable for their work.* Do you agree or disagree? Explain your reasoning.

micromonkey/Fotolia

CHAPTER 08

Managing Human Resources *and* Labour Relations

LO

AFTER READING THIS CHAPTER, YOU WILL BE ABLE TO:

LO-1 Define *human resource management*, discuss its strategic significance, and explain how managers plan for human resources.

LO-2 Identify the issues involved in staffing a company, including *internal* and *external recruiting* and *selection*.

LO-3 Discuss different ways in which organizations go about developing the capabilities of employees and managers.

LO-4 Discuss the importance of *wages and salaries*, *incentives*, and *benefit programs* in attracting and keeping skilled workers.

LO-5 Describe some of the key legal issues involved in hiring, compensating, and managing workers in today's workplace.

LO-6 Discuss *workforce diversity*, the *management of knowledge workers*, and the use of *contingent* and *temporary workers* as important changes in the contemporary workplace.

LO-7 Trace the evolution of, and discuss trends in, *unionism* in Canada.

LO-8 Describe the *major laws governing unionism*.

LO-9 Identify the steps in the *collective bargaining process*.

Can Different Generations Work Together?

Iculig/Fotolia

Recently, there has been a lot of publicity about the different "generations" (i.e., people born in different eras) that work in business organizations. It is commonly assumed that these generations differ in a lot of areas, and that these differences complicate working relationships in business firms. The conclusion is then made that human resource managers must cater to the various characteristics and demands of three different generations: Baby Boomers (who were born in the "baby boom" of 1946–1964 in the U.S. and 1947–1966 in Canada), GenXers (born between 1965 and 1980), and Millennials (born between 1980 and 1999).

Various characteristics (real or imagined) are attributed to members of these three groups. Baby Boomers, for example, are the oldest group in the workforce, and are now beginning to retire. They are often in senior management positions, and therefore manage and interact with younger generations of employees of lower rank. GenXers are in the middle of their careers, and some studies show that they are the least happy about their situation. They feel stuck between the Baby Boomers (who have more authority) and the Millennials (who get too much attention). Millennials, the most recent generation to join the workforce, have been portrayed by some as disloyal, lazy, uninterested in their work, and too interested in pay and perks. Millennials want to work differently (perhaps remotely) and have more flexibility than workers have traditionally had. They also expect employers to accommodate their lives, and when employers don't they may well look for an employer who will.

HOW WILL THIS HELP ME?

Effectively managing human resources is critical to the success of organizations. A firm that handles this activity well has a better chance for success than a firm that simply goes through the motions. After reading the material in this chapter, you'll be better able to understand—from the perspective of a *manager*—the importance of properly managing human resources in a department or business you own or supervise. You'll also understand—from the perspective of an *employee*—why your employer has adopted certain approaches to dealing with issues like hiring, training, compensation, and benefits.

While each of the three age groups has been criticized, the fact is that each group has certain realities it has had to deal with, and that have influenced their attitudes and behaviour. Baby Boomers, for example, are often criticized for not leaving the workforce at the "normal" retirement age and thereby causing problems for GenXers, who therefore can't move up in the management hierarchy. But one reason Baby Boomers resist retirement is they feel they cannot afford to retire. Millennials are often criticized for their tendency to put their personal preferences ahead of work. But many Millennials are in a shaky financial situation that demands attention. Some of the oldest Millennials (who were in their early 30s in 2015) are still living with their parents, because they cannot afford to be on their own. The 2014 Yconic/Abacus Data Survey of 1538 Canadian Millennials generated the following interesting findings:

- 43 percent of those aged 30–33 felt they had not achieved financial independence from their parents (18 percent of this age group still lived at home).
- 37 percent of all respondents said their parents had paid off their student loans.
- 17 percent of those aged 30–33 said their parents helped pay their bills.
- 25 percent of all respondents said their parents had helped with a down payment on a home they had purchased.

Jennifer Deal, a researcher at the San Diego Center for Creative Leadership, says there are several misconceptions about Millennials. First, they supposedly don't want to be told what to do; but in a study of 5000 respondents, Deal found them *more* willing to defer to authority than either Baby Boomers or GenXers. Second, Millennials supposedly lack organizational loyalty; Deal's study found that they had about the same level of loyalty to their organization as other groups. Third, Millennials supposedly aren't interested in their work; the study found that Millennials had about the same level of interest in their work as Baby Boomers and GenXers. Fourth, Millennials supposedly are motivated by perks and high pay; Deal's study found no relationship between a person's age and the extent to which they were motivated by perks and high pay. Deal argues that these misconceptions cause human resource managers and other corporate leaders to unnecessarily bend over backwards to please them.

Other human resource experts also support the notion that the difference between the generations is overblown,

Kurhan/Fotolia

and that it is a mistake to try to manage them differently. They argue that the stereotypes floating around about the various generations are not only not helpful, but in fact damaging to business firms. Linda Schweitzer, an associate professor at Carleton University's Sprott School of Business, says that "women" can't be managed as a group, and neither can Millennials. Every person has to be treated as an individual.

Penny Masear, a former director of human resources at Toronto-based Trotter Morton Group, says that companies now have to be more flexible when dealing with the various generations. Older supervisors, for example, who worked their way up through the ranks in the 1970s and 1980s, lived in a very different world than the one that exists today. They have to be more flexible in accommodating the preferences of younger workers.

The human resource implications of Baby Boomers, GenXers, and Millennials are very interesting, but don't forget that a new generation is poised to enter the workforce. The so-called Gen Z (individuals born after 2000) will begin entering by the year 2018 or so. This group of future workers cannot remember a time without the internet, cell phones, and social media. How are they going to get along with the other three generations? Time will tell.

QUESTIONS FOR DISCUSSION

1. Which category do you fit into? Do the characteristics normally described for your age group fit you? How useful do you think the categories are?
2. Consider the following statement: *All the hype about the differences between Millennials, Baby Boomers, and GenXers is meaningless. The fact is that every generation has a mixture of both hard-working, career-oriented individuals and slackers. Human resource managers shouldn't pay much attention to the alleged differences between the generations.* Do you agree or disagree? Explain your reasoning.

LO-1 THE FOUNDATIONS OF HUMAN RESOURCE MANAGEMENT

Human resource management (HRM) is the set of organizational activities directed at attracting, developing, and maintaining an effective workforce. Human resource management takes place within a complex and ever-changing environmental context and is increasingly being recognized for its strategic importance.[1]

The Strategic Importance of HRM

Human resources are critical for effective organizational functioning. Just as financial capital is an indicator of a firm's financial resources, *human capital* is a tangible indicator of the value of the people who work in an organization.[2] HRM (or personnel) was once relegated to second-class status in many organizations, but its importance has grown dramatically in the past two decades, stemming from increased legal complexities, the recognition that human resources are a valuable means for improving productivity, and an awareness of the costs associated with poor human resource management.

Managers now realize that the effectiveness of their HR function has a substantial impact on a firm's bottom-line performance. Poor human resource planning can result in spurts of hiring followed by layoffs—a process that is costly in terms of unemployment compensation payments, training expenses, and morale. Haphazard compensation systems do not attract, keep, and motivate good employees, and outmoded recruitment practices can expose the firm to expensive and embarrassing legal action. Consequently, the chief human resource executive of most large businesses is a vice-president directly accountable to the CEO, and many firms are developing strategic HR plans that are integrated with other strategic planning activities.

Human Resource Planning

Planning is the starting point in attracting qualified human resources. Human resource (HR) planning involves job analysis, forecasting the demand for and supply of labour, and matching supply and demand.

JOB ANALYSIS

Job analysis is a systematic analysis of jobs within an organization. A job analysis is made up of two parts:

1. The **job description** lists the duties of a job; its working conditions; and the tools, materials, and equipment used to perform it.
2. The **job specification** lists the skills, abilities, and other credentials needed to do the job.

HUMAN RESOURCE MANAGEMENT (HRM) Set of organizational activities directed at attracting, developing, and maintaining an effective workforce.

JOB DESCRIPTION The objectives, responsibilities, and key tasks of a job; the conditions under which it will be done; its relationship to other positions; and the skills needed to perform it.

JOB SPECIFICATION The specific skills, education, and experience needed to perform a job.

Job analysis information is used in many HR activities. For instance, knowing about job content and job requirements is necessary to develop appropriate selection methods and job-relevant performance appraisal systems, and to set equitable compensation rates.

FORECASTING HR DEMAND AND SUPPLY

After managers fully understand the jobs to be performed within an organization, they can start planning for the organization's future HR needs. The manager starts by assessing trends in past HR usage, future organizational plans, and general economic trends. A good sales forecast is often the foundation, especially for smaller organizations. Historical ratios can then be used to predict demand for types of employees, such as operating employees and sales representatives. Large organizations use much more complicated models to predict HR needs.

Forecasting the supply of labour involves two tasks:

- forecasting internal supply—the number and type of employees who will be in the firm at some future date
- forecasting external supply—the number and type of people who will be available for hiring from the labour market at large

The simplest approach in forecasting *internal* supply simply adjusts present staffing levels for anticipated turnover and promotions. Large organizations often use extremely sophisticated models to keep track of the present and future distributions of professionals and managers. This allows the company to spot areas where there will eventually be too many qualified professionals competing for too few promotions or, conversely, too few good people available to fill important positions.

Replacement Charts

At higher levels of the organization, managers plan for specific people and positions. The technique most commonly used is the *replacement chart*, which lists each important managerial position, who occupies it, how long he or she will probably stay in it before moving on, and who is now qualified or soon will be qualified to move into it. This technique allows ample time to plan developmental experiences for people identified as potential successors to critical managerial jobs.

EMPLOYEE INFORMATION SYSTEMS (SKILLS INVENTORIES) Computerized systems that contain information on each employee's education, skills, work experience, and career aspirations.

Skills Inventories

To facilitate planning and to identify people for transfer or promotion, some organizations also have **employee information systems**, or **skills inventories**. These systems are usually computerized and contain information on each employee's education, skills, work experience, and career aspirations. Such a system can quickly locate every employee in the company who is qualified to fill a position requiring, say, a degree in chemical engineering, three years of experience in an oil refinery, and fluency in French.

Forecasting the *external* supply of labour is more difficult. For example, how does a manager predict how many electrical engineers will be seeking work in Ontario or British Columbia three years from now? To get an idea of the future availability of labour, planners must rely on information from outside sources, including population and demographic statistics and figures supplied by colleges and universities on the number of students in major fields. Some people argue that these statistics suggest that Canada is soon likely to face a severe labour shortage because so many Baby Boomers are reaching retirement age.[3] But others disagree, noting that people now have healthier lifestyles and are therefore more able and willing to work past the traditional retirement age.[4]

MATCHING HR SUPPLY AND DEMAND

After comparing future demand and internal supply, managers can make plans to navigate predicted shortfalls or overstaffing. If a shortfall is predicted, new employees can be hired, present employees can be retrained and transferred into understaffed areas, individuals approaching retirement can be persuaded to stay on, or labour-saving or productivity-enhancing systems can be installed.

If the organization needs to hire, the external labour-supply forecast helps managers plan how to recruit according to whether the type of person needed is readily available or scarce in the labour market. The use of temporary workers also helps managers by giving them extra flexibility in staffing. If overstaffing is expected to be a problem, the main options are transferring the extra employees, not replacing individuals who quit, encouraging early retirement, and laying people off.

LO-2 RECRUITING HUMAN RESOURCES

Once managers have decided what positions they need to fill, they must find and hire individuals who meet the job requirements. Staffing a business with qualified individuals is one of the most complex and important aspects of good human resource management. A study by the Canadian Federation of Independent Business found that the top three characteristics employers are looking for are a good work ethic, reliability, and willingness to stay on the job.[5]

Recruiting is the process of attracting qualified people to apply for available jobs. **Internal recruiting** means considering present employees as candidates for openings. Promotion from within can help build morale and keep high-quality employees from leaving. In unionized firms, the procedures for notifying employees of internal job-change opportunities are usually spelled out in the union contract. For higher-level positions, a skills inventory system may be used to identify internal candidates, or managers may be asked to recommend individuals who should be considered.

External recruiting means attracting people outside the organization to apply for jobs. External recruiting methods include advertising, campus interviews, employment agencies or executive search firms, union

RECRUITING The phase in the staffing of a company in which the firm seeks to develop a pool of interested, qualified applicants for a position.

INTERNAL RECRUITING Considering present employees as candidates for job openings.

EXTERNAL RECRUITING Attracting people outside the organization to apply for jobs.

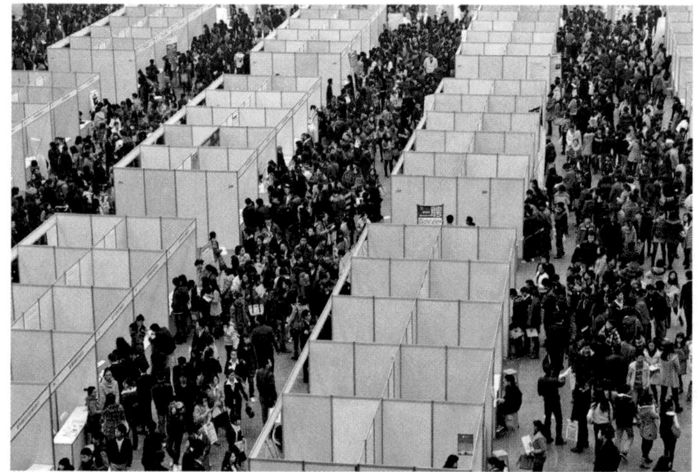

At this job fair in Novosibirsk, Russia, students and recruiters talk face to face about jobs that are available, and the characteristics and training that applicants must have to secure a job.

ChinaFotoPress/The Canadian Press

hiring halls, referrals by present employees, and hiring "walk-ins" (people who show up without being solicited). Private employment agencies can be a good source of clerical and technical employees, and executive search firms specialize in locating top-management talent. Newspaper and job-search website ads are often used, because they reach a wide audience and thus allow minorities "equal opportunity" to learn about and apply for job openings.

At a *job fair*, candidates browse through the positions available and talk face to face with recruiters. Job fairs are cheaper than posting jobs with an employment agency. More than 10 000 people signed up for a *virtual job fair* that was run by Monster.ca. Unlike campus job fairs, individuals from all career stages were involved. Participants clicked on the virtual booths of employers they were interested in. Employers interviewed candidates via video.[6]

Internships are short-term paid or unpaid positions where students focus on a specific project. Hari Pemasani, who came to Canada from India, completed a pharmacy program at the University of Toronto and went through an internship with Loblaw Companies. He was then hired for a full-time position and soon became the pharmacy manager for the store where he worked.[7] The Canadian Undergraduate Survey Consortium found that 55 percent of graduating students had completed an internship.[8]

The biggest change in recent years has been the advent of online recruiting. Companies post positions on websites like Monster, Workopolis, or LinkedIn, and interested applicants respond. Internet recruiting gives employers and those seeking employment a fast, easy, and inexpensive way of interacting. But there are drawbacks. Employers receive huge numbers of applications, and many are from unqualified people. Starbucks, for example, gets millions of applications every year. Many companies now use résumé-filtering software that searches out keywords on applications. If the words aren't there, the applicant is not contacted.[9] IGN Entertainment, a gaming and media company, doesn't even ask for a résumé. Instead, candidates respond to challenges on IGN's website designed to assess thought processes.[10]

Whatever approach to external recruiting is used, it is important to give potential employees a real picture of what it would be like doing the job the company is trying to fill. Failure to provide a *realistic job preview* means that any person hired may soon become dissatisfied. The boxed insert entitled "'Green' Jobs in Surprising Places" illustrates the increasing importance of environmental considerations in external recruiting.

Selecting Human Resources

Once the recruiting process has attracted a pool of applicants, the next step is to select someone to hire. The intent of the selection process is to gather information from applicants that will predict their job success and then to hire the candidates likely to be most successful. The process of determining the predictive value of information is called *validation*.

To reduce the element of uncertainty, managers use a variety of selection techniques, the most common of which are shown in Figure 8.1. Each organization develops its own mix of selection techniques and may use them in almost any order.

APPLICATION FORMS

The first step in selection is asking the candidate to fill out an application form. An application form is an efficient method of gathering information about the applicant's previous work history, educational background, and other job-related demographic data. It should not contain questions about areas unrelated to the job, such as gender, religion, or national origin. Application-form data are generally used informally to decide whether a candidate merits further evaluation, and interviewers use application forms to familiarize themselves with candidates before interviewing them.

TESTS

Employers sometimes ask candidates to take tests during the selection process. Tests of ability, skill, aptitude, or knowledge relevant to a particular job are usually the best predictors of job success, although tests of general intelligence or personality are occasionally useful as well. At

THERE'S AN APP FOR THAT!

APP DETAILS	PLATFORMS
1. **HR Management** **Source:** Smart Media Innovations and WAGmob **Key Features:** Highlights key HR management strategies and HR-based news and information.	Apple, Android, BlackBerry, Windows
2. **Search Jobs Beyond.com** **Source:** Beyond.com **Key Features:** Users can locate thousands of jobs across more than 25 industries by area and keyword.	Apple, Android, BlackBerry
3. **CanadianJobForce.com** **Source:** Beyond.com **Key Features:** Enables users to search for jobs in over 25 industries in the Canadian job market.	BlackBerry

APP DISCOVERY EXERCISE

Since app availability changes, conduct your own search for the "Top Three" human resources apps and identify the key features.

THE GREENING OF BUSINESS

"Green" Jobs in Surprising Places

Younger Canadians have become increasingly concerned about the environment, so it is not surprising that many of them want to work for companies that share their concerns. ECO Canada, a non-profit resource for finding environmental jobs, hosted a Green Careers Summit in Calgary that helped Grade 11 and 12 students explore possible career paths with several business leaders who worked in various environmental fields. The head of ECO says that environmental jobs are available in virtually every sector of the economy, including the oil and gas industry. That might be surprising, as that industry is not generally perceived as environmentally friendly. But the companies are looking for ways to become more sustainable. Green jobs are available for environmental researchers and scientists, health and safety inspectors, control system operators, and quality assurance experts. Consider the jobs of the following individuals:

- After Elizabeth Watterworth received her degree in international business, she worked for a time in Hong Kong, but then returned to Canada to work at ECO. She now works at Nexen as a sustainability and assurance analyst.
- Ariane Bourassa, an environmental advisor at Cenovus Energy Inc., has an undergraduate degree in international law and a master's degree in environmental sciences. Part of her work is planning mitigation measures to limit Nexen's footprint and to minimize wildlife disturbance.
- Christine Daly is a wetland and reclamation research and development coordinator at Suncor Energy Inc. She works with biologists, wetland ecologists, foresters, and engineers to construct new ecosystems. One interesting project she has worked on was transforming an oil-sands tailing pond into a surface that was solid enough to be reforested.

Well over half a million Canadians are now employed in environment-related jobs (e.g., consultants who assess homes to see how energy-efficient they are). Many of these jobs didn't even exist a generation ago. According to the Environmental Careers Organization of Canada, the top five green careers are environmental engineer, environmental technologist, conservation biologist, geographic information system analyst, and environmental communications officer. There are actually more people now working in green jobs in Canada than the total number of people working in the oil sands.

In a survey conducted by Monster.ca, 78 percent of respondents said they would quit their current job if they could get one at a company that had an environmentally friendly focus. In a second survey, 81 percent of the respondents said that their current employer was not environmentally friendly. Only 18 percent said their employer was "extremely green."

There are several websites that provide employment information on green jobs. They include WorkCabin.ca, GoodWork.ca, ECO.ca, and Green-Jobs.ca.

CRITICAL THINKING QUESTIONS

1. What are the advantages of working for an environmentally friendly company? Are there any disadvantages?
2. Consider the following statement: *All the publicity about graduates looking for jobs at environmentally friendly companies is exaggerated. Many graduates are merely claiming they want to work for an environmentally friendly company, even though most of them really don't care that much about the environment.* Do you agree or disagree? Explain your reasoning.

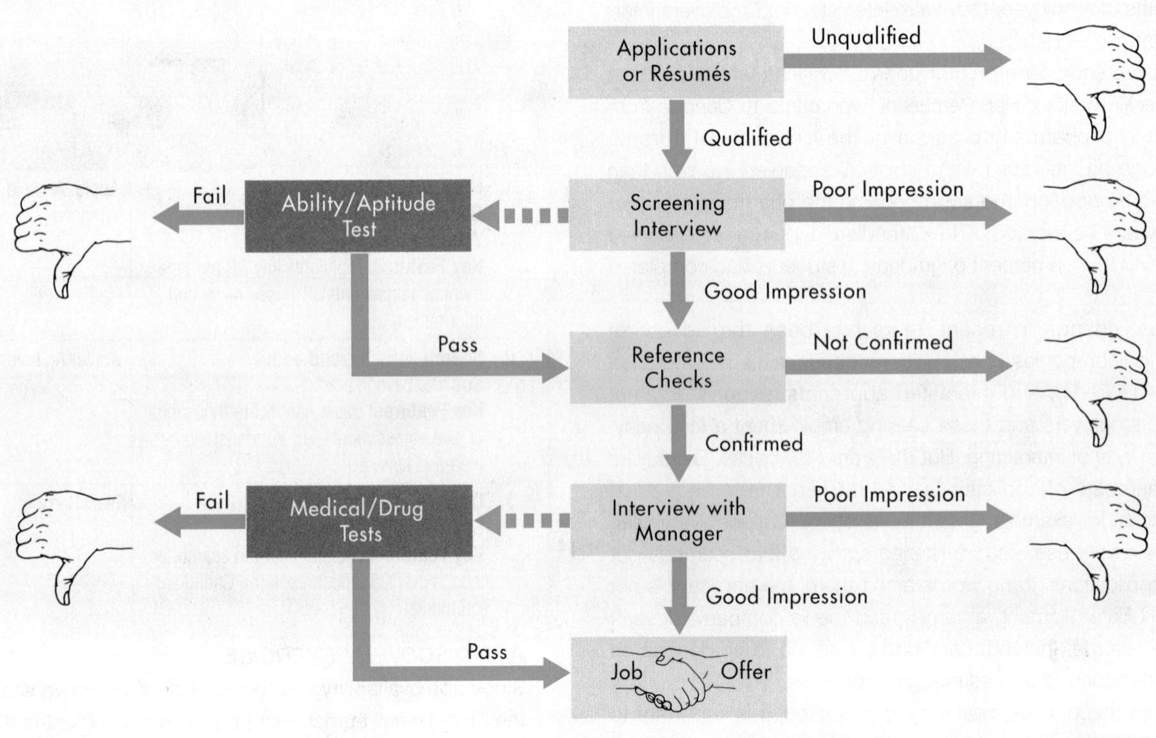

FIGURE 8.1 General steps in the selection process

Astral Media, job candidates are required to take a series of tests that measure verbal and numerical skills and psychological traits.[11] Some companies administer tests to determine how well applicants score on the "big five" personality dimensions discussed in Chapter 9. These scores are used to help make hiring decisions. In addition to being validated, tests should be administered and scored consistently. All candidates should be given the same directions, allowed the same amount of time, and offered the same testing environment, including temperature, lighting, and distractions.

An **assessment centre** is a series of exercises in which candidates perform realistic management tasks under the watchful eye of expert appraisers. During this time, potential managers take selection tests, engage in management simulations, make individual presentations, and conduct group discussions. Assessors check to see how each participant reacts to stress or to criticism by colleagues. A relatively new type of test is *video assessment*, which involves showing potential hires videos of realistic work situations and asking them to choose a course of action to deal with the situation.

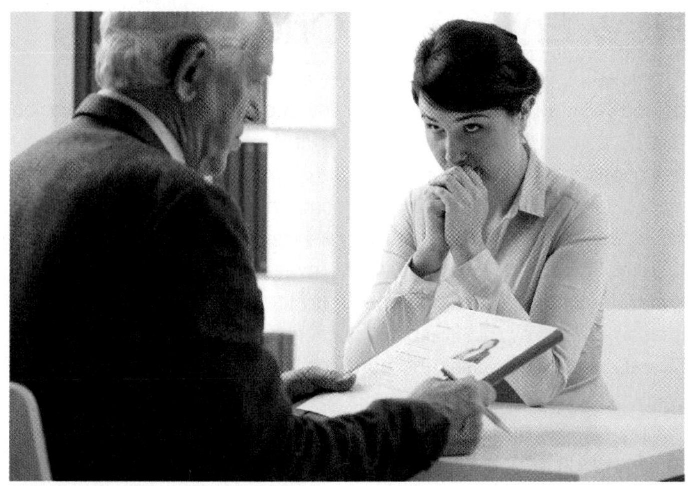

The job interview can be a stressful time for job candidates.

Photographee.eu/Fotolia

INTERVIEWS

The interview is a popular selection device, but it is sometimes a poor predictor of job success because biases inherent in the way people perceive and judge others on first meeting affect subsequent evaluations. Many companies are placing more emphasis on testing and less emphasis on interviewing because job candidates are becoming clever at giving all the "right" answers during interviews.[12] Interview validity can be improved by training interviewers to be aware of potential biases, and by writing out questions in advance and asking all interviewees the same set of questions.

Interviewers can also increase interview validity by asking "curveball" questions—ones job applicants would never expect—to make them think on their feet. Examples might be "How would you move Mount Fuji?" or "How would you sell me a glass of water?"[13]

Another approach to improving interview validity is **behaviour-based interviewing**, which focuses on behaviour rather than on what a person says. It can be used to test for technical skills (e.g., accounting, welding, or computer programming), management skills (e.g., organizing, motivating others, or communicating), and individual skills (e.g., dependability, discipline, or the ability to work on a team). Behaviour-based interviewing—which is based on the assumption that a person's past behaviour is a good predictor of his or her future behaviour—requires the interviewer to first identify the characteristics, skills, and behaviours important in the job to be filled. This can be done by carefully observing current employees who excel, and then identifying the key behaviours necessary for effectiveness. Then, instead of asking a traditional interview question like "Do you often take the initiative?," behaviour-based interviewing asks questions like "Tell me about a situation where you took action to solve a problem that you were facing," or "Tell me how you dealt with a customer who you thought was being unreasonable." Individuals who cannot satisfactorily answer questions like these are not likely to be hired.

OTHER TECHNIQUES

Organizations also use other selection techniques that vary with the circumstances. A manufacturer afraid of injuries to workers on the job might require new employees to have a physical examination. This gives the company some information about whether the applicants are physically fit to do the work and any pre-existing injuries they might have.

Drug tests are also used, but when they can be used is a matter of debate. According to the Canadian Human Rights Commission policy, pre-employment drug testing and random drug testing are not permitted. In 2013, the Supreme Court ruled that companies can use random drug testing if the workplace is inherently dangerous and there is an existing problem with drug use.[14] But in 2014, the Alberta Arbitration Board ruled that Suncor could not introduce random drug testing at one of its locations. These conflicting rulings create much uncertainty for human resource managers.

Reference checks with previous employers are also used, but they may be of limited value because individuals are likely to provide the names of only those references who will give them positive recommendations. It is also getting harder to get good reference information because many HR people are worried about legal rulings in the United States that have been as high as $1.4 million. But many legal experts see the fear as unwarranted, saying that the law upholds honest information, even if negative.[15]

ASSESSMENT CENTRE A series of exercises in which management candidates perform realistic management tasks while being observed by appraisers.

BEHAVIOUR-BASED INTERVIEWING An approach to improving interview validity by asking questions that focuses the interview much more on behaviour than on what a person says.

LO-3 DEVELOPING HUMAN RESOURCES

After a company has hired new employees, it must acquaint them with the firm and their new jobs. This process begins with a formal orientation to welcome the employee and provide information about the company history, structure, culture, benefits programs, and much more. Managers also take steps to train employees and develop necessary job skills. In addition, every firm has some system for performance appraisal and feedback.

New Employee Orientation

A new employee's first 30 days have a big influence on whether the person will stay.[16] An Ipsos Reid survey of over 1000 workers revealed that 50 percent felt they didn't always fit in well.[17] Thus, orientation of new workers is a very important activity. **Orientation** is the process of introducing new employees to the company's policies and programs, the co-workers and supervisors they will interact with, and the nature of their job. Orientation allows new employees to feel like part of a team and to become effective contributors to the organization more rapidly. It also plays a key role in job satisfaction, performance, and retention. Overall, orientation eases the transition from outsider to insider. Poor orientation, on the other hand, can result in disenchantment, dissatisfaction, anxiety, and turnover. The dating website PlentyOfFish uses its matchmaking techniques to find appropriate employees. Just as a friend would recommend a potential partner, employees are encouraged to refer people they may know that would be a great fit for the company as well.[18]

Videoconferencing has become an important part of the training function. Travel costs are reduced, and interactions between the trainer and the trainees are facilitated.

Andrey Popov/Fotolia

Training and Development

Beyond orientation, employees must be trained and developed to improve the quality of their work. The starting point in assessing training and development is a *needs analysis*, which determines the organization's needs and the training programs necessary to satisfy those needs. The needs analysis focuses on two things: the organization's job-related needs and the capabilities of the current workforce. Some of the most popular training and development techniques and methods are described below.

On-the-job training means placing the employee in an actual work situation and having a supervisor or experienced employee demonstrate how to perform the task. Much on-the-job training is informal, as when one employee shows another how to operate the photocopy machine. Training may also be formal, as when a trainer shows employees how to operate a new software program.

In *job rotation*, employees learn a wide array of tasks and acquire more abilities as they are moved from one job to another. This method is most likely to be used for lower-level managers or for operating employees who are being groomed for promotions to supervisory or management positions. The employee learns a wider array of tasks, acquires more abilities, and develops a more comprehensive view of the work of an organization or a particular sub-unit.

Off-the-job training is performed at a location away from the work site. It might be in a classroom within the same facility or at a different location altogether. For example, *vestibule training* involves employees performing work under conditions closely simulating the actual work environment. Montreal-based CAE is famous for building flight simulators that enable airline pilots to learn how to fly a new jet without ever leaving the ground. CAE also develops mock-up operating rooms where medical students can learn in a simulated environment.[19] Another example is McDonald's Hamburger University, where management trainees learn how to grill a burger and how to maintain good customer service.

Management development programs try to enhance conceptual, analytical, and problem-solving skills. Most large companies run formal in-house management development programs or send managers to programs on university campuses. In the Build for the Future program at TD Bank, top managers meet once a month to plan leadership training and coaching of subordinates.[20] But in many companies, training for managers is not so systematic. In one survey of over 1000 managers, 57 percent said they had to learn how to manage by trial and error, and 89 percent said they had not been groomed to be a leader.[21]

Some management development takes place informally, often through processes such as networking and mentoring. **Networking** refers to informal interactions among managers for the purpose of discussing mutual problems, solutions, and opportunities. Networking takes place in a variety of settings, both inside and outside the office. The boxed insert entitled "LinkedIn: Strengthening Your Ability to Connect" provides more information about networking.

Mentoring means having a more experienced manager sponsor and teach a less experienced manager. Men still occupy the majority of top management positions, and they are important in mentoring women who aspire to such jobs.[22]

In 2014, a mentoring program called Ten Thousand Coffees was launched. It gives aspiring leaders access to experienced leaders for conversations over a cup of coffee.[23] For both men and women, *reverse mentoring* is becoming common as well—in which younger, more tech-savvy employees mentor senior staff members on everything from viral marketing to blogging to the use of Facebook and YouTube.[24]

ORIENTATION The process of introducing new employees to the company's policies and programs, the co-workers and supervisors they will interact with, and the nature of their job.

ON-THE-JOB TRAINING Development programs in which employees gain new skills while performing them at work.

OFF-THE-JOB TRAINING Development programs in which employees learn new skills at a location away from the normal work site.

MANAGEMENT DEVELOPMENT PROGRAMS Development programs in which managers' conceptual, analytical, and problem-solving skills are enhanced.

NETWORKING Informal interactions among managers, both inside and outside the office, for the purpose of discussing mutual problems, solutions, and opportunities.

MENTORING Having a more experienced manager sponsor and teach a less experienced manager.

ENTREPRENEURSHIP AND NEW VENTURES

LinkedIn: Strengthening Your Ability to Connect

If you're out of work, looking for a job, and wondering where to turn, help is as close as your computer, tablet, or smartphone. While popular entertainment sites, including Facebook, YouTube, and Twitter, began as cyber highways for recreational and friendship interactions, social networking today is used for much more than simply entertainment. In today's economy, there's a different kind of traffic—professional networking for career transition—among the list of cyber networking products for job-hunting assistance. Leading the way in this regard is LinkedIn.

The company was started by five people (Reid Hoffman, Allen Blue, Konstantin Guericke, Eric Ly, and Jean-Luc Vaillant) in Reid Hoffman's living room back in 2002, and had 4500 members after just one month.

Today LinkedIn serves professionals in over 200 countries. Profiles are posted from more than 364 million members, including executives from all Fortune 500 companies. Users can post résumés, search for companies, and find job openings. The jobs directory allows searching by industry, function, geographic region, title, or company. However, the key attraction is personal connections: one member knows other LinkedIn users, who link with still others, and so on as information flows to those looking for candidates until they find a word-of-mouth prospect that looks good. The system is based on trusted relationships and connections, and it works; LinkedIn is the world's largest business network, and it connects a huge pool of talent that keeps on growing.

In addition to professionals looking for jobs, there are also business members, some searching for prospective employees, industry experts, potential clients, or new business opportunities. Others are interested in sharing the latest business developments within their networks of contacts. LinkedIn Groups, for example, consists of specialty network groups of businesses and professionals focused on particular industries, including Social Media Marketing, Finance and Accounting Professionals, or Business in Japan, to name just three of many. Group members may share industry-specific information on performance-enhancing practices, legal issues, and current events, and even participate in determining new directions for their industry.

LinkedIn's growth is due to meeting its members' needs relative to professional fulfillment. But its industry-leading innovations are yielding attractive financial results as well: in 2014 revenue stood at $2.2 billion.

CRITICAL THINKING QUESTIONS

1. Entrepreneurs are constantly seeking opportunities to get their organization and products noticed in the marketplace. List all the ways LinkedIn can be used to achieve that goal, and explain how entrepreneurs can use other social media tools to support their LinkedIn profiles. In answering this question assume that you are, in turn, (a) a financial advisor and (b) a music producer.

Team Building and Group-Based Training

Since more and more organizations are using teams as a basis for doing their jobs, it should not be surprising that many of the same companies are developing training programs specifically designed to facilitate cooperation among team members. For example, Eagle's Flight is an innovative leader in the development and delivery of practical training programs for the global business community. Their offering of training programs includes team and training experiences, as well as leadership development and learning.[25]

Evaluating Employee Performance

Performance appraisals are designed to show how well workers are doing their jobs. Typically, the appraisal process involves a written assessment issued on a regular basis. As a rule, however, the written evaluation is only one part of a multi-step process. The appraisal process begins when a manager defines performance standards for an employee. The manager then observes the employee's performance. If the standards are clear, the manager should have little difficulty comparing expectations with performance. The process is completed when the manager and employee meet to discuss the appraisal. The process sounds fairly straightforward, but for it to work properly managers must clearly state performance measures, track performance in real time, use multiple measures of performance, use peer recognition, and stick to the evaluation schedule. [26]

It is best to rely on several information sources when conducting appraisals. A system called *360-degree feedback* gathers information from supervisors, subordinates, and co-workers. The most accurate information comes from individuals who have known the person being appraised for one to three years. Eight or ten individuals should take part in the evaluation.[27] The use of social media in appraisal is increasing. When Facebook decided that traditional appraisals were not suited to its employees, it turned to Toronto-based Rypple, a company that specializes in software tools to provide real-time feedback using a Facebook-style interface. Managers can "like" tasks, ask for feedback, and monitor employee progress toward goals.[28]

PROVIDING PERFORMANCE FEEDBACK

Many managers are not effective when providing performance feedback, partly because they don't understand how to do it properly and partly because they don't enjoy it. As a result, managers may have a tendency to avoid giving negative feedback because they know that an employee who receives it may be angry, hurt, discouraged, or argumentative. But if employees are not told about their shortcomings, they will have no concrete reason to try to improve and will receive no guidance as to how to improve. Because of the problems with performance appraisals, some companies have abandoned them. Australian-based Atlassian Inc., for example, replaced annual appraisals with weekly one-on-one meetings between managers and workers. Discussions focus on goals and performance.[29]

PERFORMANCE APPRAISALS A formal program for evaluating how well an employee is performing the job; helps managers determine how effective they are in recruiting and selecting employees.

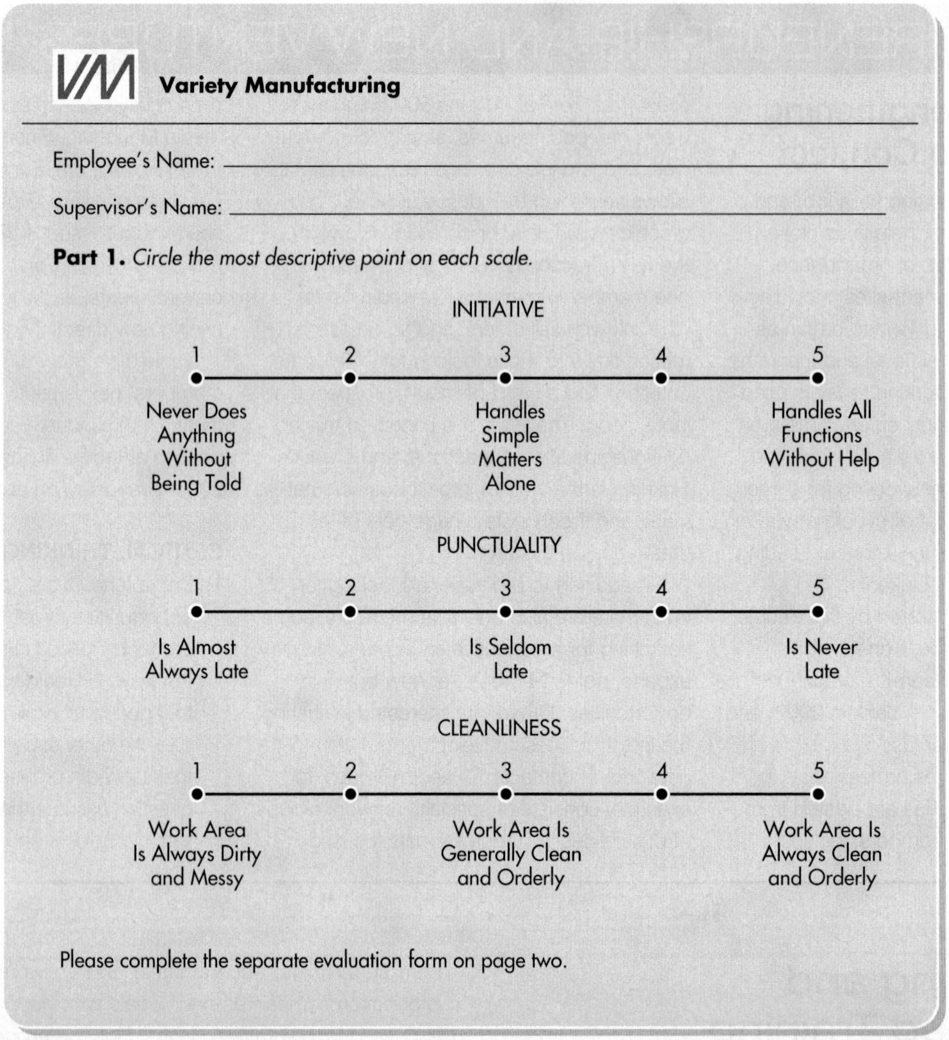

VM **Variety Manufacturing**

Employee's Name: ______________________

Supervisor's Name: ______________________

Part 1. *Circle the most descriptive point on each scale.*

INITIATIVE

1	2	3	4	5
Never Does Anything Without Being Told		Handles Simple Matters Alone		Handles All Functions Without Help

PUNCTUALITY

1	2	3	4	5
Is Almost Always Late		Is Seldom Late		Is Never Late

CLEANLINESS

1	2	3	4	5
Work Area Is Always Dirty and Messy		Work Area Is Generally Clean and Orderly		Work Area Is Always Clean and Orderly

Please complete the separate evaluation form on page two.

FIGURE 8.2 Performance rating scale

METHODS FOR APPRAISING PERFORMANCE

The *simple ranking method* requires a manager to rank-order from top to bottom or from best to worst each member of a particular workgroup or department. The one ranked first is the top performer, the one ranked second is the second-best performer, and so forth. Another method, *forced distribution*, involves grouping employees into predefined frequencies of performance ratings. Those frequencies are determined in advance and are imposed on the rater. A decision might be made, for instance, that 10 percent of the employees in a workgroup will be categorized as outstanding, 20 percent as very good, 40 percent as average, 20 percent as below average, and the remaining 10 percent as poor. The forced distribution method will be familiar to students—it is the principle used by professors who grade on a so-called "bell curve" or "normal curve."

One of the most popular and widely used methods is the *graphic rating scale*, which consists simply of a statement or question about some aspect of an individual's job performance. Figure 8.2 shows a sample graphic rating scale.

The *critical incident method* focuses attention on an example of especially good or poor performance on the part of the employee. Raters then describe what the employee did (or did not do) that led to success or failure. This technique not only provides information for feedback but also defines performance in fairly clear behavioural terms.

LO-4 COMPENSATION AND BENEFITS

Compensation refers to rewards organizations provide in return for employees' willingness to perform various jobs and tasks. It can consist of any of a number of things, such as base salary, incentives, bonuses, benefits, and other rewards.

The compensation received by CEOs can be extremely large, especially when bonuses are included. For example, Nadir Mohamed

COMPENSATION What a firm offers its employees in return for their labour.

(Rogers Communications Inc.) got $26.7 million in total compensation in 2013, and Michael Wilson (Agrium Inc.) $23.8 million.[30] The top 100 Canadian CEOs were paid an average of $9.2 million in 2013, about 195 times what the average Canadian worker earned (about $47 000). Critics have frequently questioned the wisdom of giving executives such large amounts of money, but most attempts to rein in executive salaries have failed. During the recession of 2008, shareholders at CIBC and the Royal Bank of Canada passed motions demanding that the companies give them a voice in executive compensation through non-binding shareholder votes.[31] In Sweden, Norway, and the Netherlands, shareholders have a binding vote on executive pay packages. Whether binding or non-binding, investor feedback may help boards of directors rein in executive compensation that is perceived as too high.[32]

Determining Basic Compensation

Wages generally refer to hourly compensation paid to operating employees. Most of the jobs paid on an hourly-wage basis are lower-level and/or operating-level ones. The average wage in manufacturing is about $20 per hour, while in retailing it is less than $17. But the manufacturing sector is shrinking, and retailers are now the biggest employers in Canada.[33] Rather than expressing compensation on an hourly basis, the organization may instead describe compensation on an annual or monthly basis. Many college and university graduates, for example, compare job offers on the basis of annual **salary**, such as $40 000 versus $38 000 a year.

Companies often use *pay surveys* to determine pay levels. These surveys show the compensation being paid to employees by other employers in a particular geographic area, an industry, or an occupational group. For example, the Canadian Federation of Business School Deans publishes an annual summary of salaries for professors teaching in business schools in Canadian universities. The internet allows job seekers and current employees to more easily get a sense of what their true market value is. If they can document the claim that their value is higher than what their current employer now pays or is offering, they are in a position to demand a higher salary.

Another means of determining basic compensation is *job evaluation*, a method for determining the relative value or worth of a job to the organization, so that individuals who perform it can be compensated appropriately. In other words, it is concerned with establishing internal pay equity. There should be a logical rank-ordering of compensation levels from the most valuable to the least valuable jobs throughout the organization.

Incentive Programs

Employees feel better about themselves and their company when they believe they are being fairly compensated. But money motivates employees only if tied directly to performance, and the most common method of establishing this link is the use of *incentive programs*—special pay programs designed to motivate high performance. These programs can be applied to individuals or teams. A survey by the Conference Board of Canada found that while 80 percent of Canadian companies offer incentive programs, 69 percent of them don't measure their effectiveness.[34]

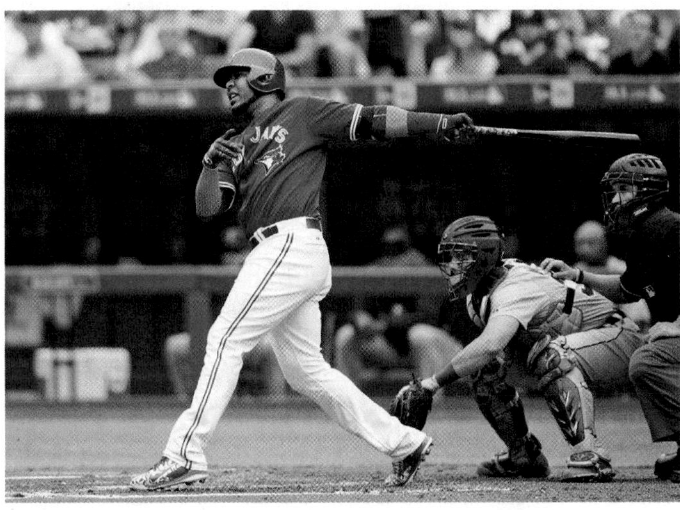

Individual incentive plans have been a big part of professional sports for many years. Players received multimillion-dollar annual compensation for outstanding individual performance.

Darren Calabrese/The Canadian Press

INDIVIDUAL INCENTIVES

Individual incentive plans reward individual performance on a real-time basis. Rather than increasing a person's base salary at the end of the year, an employer gives an individual a salary increase or some other financial reward for outstanding performance immediately or shortly after the performance occurs. Individual incentive systems are most common where performance can be assessed objectively (e.g., by number of units produced or by sales revenues that are generated).

Under a **piece-rate incentive plan**, employees get a certain amount of money for every unit they produce. An assembly-line worker might be paid $1 for every 12 units successfully completed. Sales employees are often paid a *bonus*—a special payment above their salaries—when they sell a certain number or certain dollar amount of goods for the year. Bonuses are also given in non-sales jobs. For example, many baseball players have contract clauses that pay them bonuses for hitting over .300, making the all-star team, or being named most valuable player.

Pay-for-knowledge plans encourage workers to learn new skills and to become proficient at different jobs. These workers receive additional pay for each new skill or job they master. With *pay for performance* (or *variable pay*) schemes, managers are rewarded for especially productive output—for producing earnings that significantly exceed the cost of bonuses. Such incentives go to middle managers on the basis of company-wide performance, business-unit performance, personal record, or all three factors. Eligible managers must often forgo merit or entitlement raises (increases for staying on and reporting to work every day), but many firms say that variable pay is a better motivator

WAGES Dollars paid based on the number of hours worked.

SALARY Dollars paid at regular intervals in return for doing a job, regardless of the amount of time or output involved.

PIECE-RATE INCENTIVE PLAN A compensation system in which an organization pays an employee a certain amount of money for every unit produced.

because the range between generous and mediocre merit raises is usually quite small.

Other forms of individual incentives are also used, such as more time off or recognition in the form of points awarded on a supervisor's recommendation. In the latter case, recipients might convert their points into money and buy merchandise or trips from a special online catalogue. Some retailers have adopted workforce management systems, which schedule the most productive staff to work at the store's busiest times. When employees type their code into the cash register, it displays their "performance metrics" such as average sales per hour and dollars per transaction. Less productive employees are given fewer or less desirable hours.[35] Not surprisingly, this system is disliked by many workers.

TEAM AND GROUP INCENTIVES

Some incentive programs apply to all the employees in a firm. Under **profit-sharing plans**, profits earned above a certain level are distributed to employees. At the Great Little Box Company in Richmond, British Columbia, 15 percent of company profits are split evenly among staff. The company also has an "open book" policy of providing financial information to employees so they can relate financial performance of the company to their share of the profits.[36]

Gainsharing plans distribute bonuses to employees when a company's costs are reduced through greater employee efficiency and/or productivity. The underlying assumption in gainsharing is that employees and the employer have the same goals and should therefore share in incremental economic gains. Palliser Furniture introduced such a plan, rewarding employees for increased production; any profit resulting from production above a certain level was split 50-50 between the company and its employees.[37]

Benefits

Benefits are rewards, incentives, and other things of value that an organization gives to employees in addition to wages, salaries, and other forms of direct financial compensation. Because these benefits have tangible value, they represent a meaningful form of compensation even though they are not generally expressed in financial terms. According to a PricewaterhouseCoopers survey, some of the top benefits sought, other than money, were gift cards, extra vacation days, and being fast-tracked for promotion.[38]

MANDATED PROTECTION PLANS

Protection plans assist employees when their income is threatened or reduced by illness, disability, unemployment, or retirement. *Employment insurance* provides a basic subsistence payment to employees who are unemployed but are actively seeking employment. Both employers and employees pay premiums to an employment insurance fund. The 2015 premium rate cannot exceed $1.88 per $100 of insurable earnings.[39] The insurance also covers maternity leave of 55 percent of a new mother's annual earnings (to a maximum of $49 500).[40]

The *Canada Pension Plan* (CPP) provides income for retired individuals to help them supplement their personal savings, private pensions, part-time work, etc. It is funded through employee and employer taxes withheld from payroll. In 2014, the value of the CPP surpassed $200 billion for the first time.[41]

Workers' compensation is mandated insurance that covers individuals who suffer a job-related illness or accident. Employers bear the cost of workers' compensation insurance. The premium is related to each employer's past experience with job-related accidents and illnesses. For example, a steel company might pay $20 per $100 of wages, while an accounting firm might pay only $0.10 per $100 of wages.

OPTIONAL PROTECTION PLANS

Health insurance, the most important type of coverage, has expanded in recent years to include vision care, mental health services, dental care, and prescription drugs. Employee prescription drug plan costs are doubling about every five years, and companies are increasingly concerned about their ability to offer this kind of coverage.[42] Pension liabilities are also a problem.

PAID TIME OFF

Paid vacations are usually for periods of one, two, or more weeks. Most organizations vary the amount of paid vacation with an individual's seniority, but some companies are reducing the time required to qualify for paid vacations. At Carlson Wagonlit Travel Canada, employees get four weeks of paid vacation after working at the company for just five years. Formerly, ten years of service was required.[43]

Another common paid time-off plan is sick leave, which is provided when an individual is sick or otherwise physically unable to perform his or her job. Sometimes an organization will allow an employee to take off a small number of days simply for "personal business." The Catholic Children's Aid Society provides its child protection workers with time off when they need it, because they routinely face high-stress situations.[44]

OTHER TYPES OF BENEFITS

In addition to protection plans and paid time off, many organizations offer a number of other benefit programs. *Wellness programs*, for example, concentrate on preventing illness in employees rather than simply paying their expenses when they become sick. **Cafeteria-style benefit plans** allow employees to choose the benefits they really want. The organization typically establishes a budget, indicating how much it is willing to spend, per employee, on benefits. Employees are then presented with a list of possible benefits and the cost of each. They are free to put the benefits together in any combination they wish.

PROFIT-SHARING PLANS An incentive program in which employees receive a bonus depending on the firm's profits.

GAINSHARING PLANS An incentive program in which employees receive a bonus if the firm's costs are reduced because of their greater efficiency and/or productivity.

BENEFITS What a firm offers its workers other than wages and salaries in return for their labour.

PROTECTION PLANS A plan that protects employees when their income is threatened or reduced by illness, disability, death, unemployment, or retirement.

CAFETERIA-STYLE BENEFIT PLANS A flexible approach to providing benefits in which employees are allocated a certain sum to cover benefits and can "spend" this allocation on the specific benefits they prefer.

LO-5 THE LEGAL CONTEXT OF HRM

HRM is influenced by federal and provincial law, so managers must be aware of the most important and far-reaching areas of HR regulation. These include *equal employment opportunity*, *comparable worth*, *sexual harassment*, *employee safety and health*, and *retirement*.

Equal Employment Opportunity

The basic goal of all **equal employment opportunity regulations** is to protect people from unfair or inappropriate discrimination in the workplace. Note that differentiating between employees—for example, giving one person a raise and denying the raise to another person—is not illegal. As long as the basis for this distinction is purely job-related (i.e., based on performance or qualifications) and is applied objectively and consistently, the action is legal and appropriate. Problems arise when distinctions among people are not job-related. In such cases, the resulting discrimination is illegal.

ANTI-DISCRIMINATION LAWS

The key federal anti-discrimination legislation is the *Canadian Human Rights Act* of 1977 (each province has also enacted human rights legislation). The goal of the Act is to ensure that any individual who wishes to obtain a job has an equal opportunity. The Act applies to all federal agencies, federal Crown corporations, any employee of the federal government, and business firms that do business interprovincially. The Act prohibits a wide variety of practices in recruiting, selecting, promoting, and dismissing personnel. It specifically prohibits discrimination on the basis of age, race and colour, national and ethnic origin, physical handicap, religion, gender, marital status, or prison record (if pardoned). Some exceptions to these blanket prohibitions are permitted. Discrimination cannot be charged if a blind person is refused a position as a bus driver or crane operator. Likewise, a firm cannot be charged with discrimination if it does not hire a deaf person as an audio engineer.

Difficulties in determining whether discrimination has occurred are sometimes dealt with by using the concept of **bona fide occupational requirement**. That is, an employer may choose one person over another on the basis of overriding characteristics of the job in question. If a fitness centre wants to hire only women to supervise its women's locker room and sauna, it can do so without being discriminatory because it established a bona fide occupational requirement.

Enforcement of the Human Rights Act is carried out by the Canadian Human Rights Commission. The commission can either respond to complaints from individuals who believe they have been discriminated against or launch an investigation on its own if it has reason to believe discrimination has occurred. If a claim of discrimination is substantiated, the offending organization or individual may be ordered to compensate the victim.

The *Employment Equity Act of 1986* addresses the issue of discrimination in employment by designating four groups as employment-disadvantaged—women, visible minorities, Aboriginal people, and people with disabilities. These four groups contain six of every ten individuals in the Canadian workforce, and it is estimated that their underemployment costs the Canadian economy around $50 billion each year.[45] Companies covered by the Employment Equity Act are required to publish statistics on their employment of people in the four designated groups. For example, women at RBC now occupy nearly 40 percent of executive roles in the company, and this figure is growing.[46]

Comparable Worth

Comparable worth is a legal concept that aims at paying equal wages for jobs that are of comparable value to the employer. This might mean comparing dissimilar jobs, such as those of secretaries

EQUAL EMPLOYMENT OPPORTUNITY REGULATIONS Regulations to protect people from unfair or inappropriate discrimination in the workplace.

BONA FIDE OCCUPATIONAL REQUIREMENT When an employer may choose one applicant over another based on overriding characteristics of the job.

COMPARABLE WORTH A legal concept that aims to pay equal wages for work of equal value.

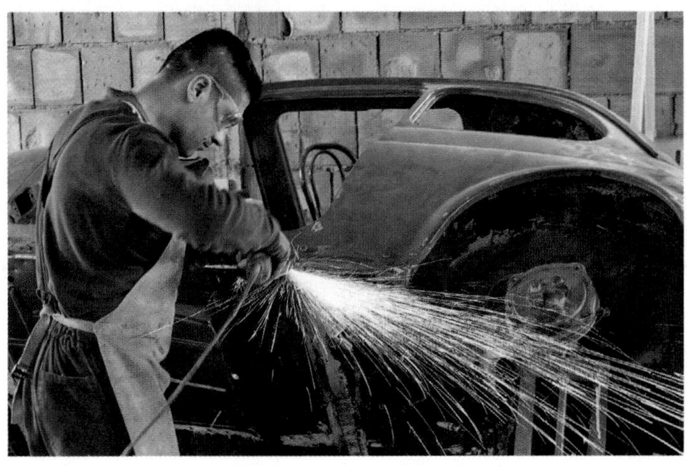

The idea behind comparable worth is to pay equal wages for jobs that are of comparable value to the employer. This may require a comparison of jobs that are quite different.

michaeljung/Fotolia (left); oneinchpunch/Fotolia (right)

and mechanics or nurses and electricians. Proponents of comparable worth say that all the jobs in a company must be evaluated and then rated in terms of basic dimensions such as the level of skill they require. All jobs could then be compared on the basis of a common index. People in different jobs that rate the same on this index would be paid the same. Experts hope that this will help to reduce the gap between men's and women's pay. In a long-standing comparable worth dispute, the Supreme Court of Canada ruled that flight attendants at Air Canada—who have been trying for years to achieve pay equity with male-dominated groups of employees—could compare their pay with the pay of ground crews and pilots because all these employees work for the same company.[47]

Critics of comparable worth object on the grounds that it ignores the supply and demand aspects of labour. They say that legislation forcing a company to pay people more than the open market price for their labour (which may happen in jobs where there is a surplus of workers) is another example of unreasonable government interference in business activities. They also say that implementing comparable worth will cost business firms too much money.

Sexual Harassment

Within the job context, **sexual harassment** refers to requests for sexual favours, unwelcome sexual advances, or verbal or physical conduct of a sexual nature that creates an intimidating or hostile environment for a given employee. The Canadian Human Rights Act takes precedence over any policies that a company might have developed on its own to deal with sexual harassment problems.

Quid pro quo harassment is the most blatant form of sexual harassment. It occurs when the harasser offers to exchange something of value—for example, a promotion—for sexual favours. The creation of a *hostile work environment* is a subtler form of sexual harassment. For example, a group of male employees who continually make off-colour jokes may create a hostile work environment for female employees. Other situations are harder to assess. For example, an employee sued Citibank, claiming she was fired because she dressed too provocatively and was, therefore, a workplace distraction. But some of her co-workers said she was just an attention-seeking gold digger fired for poor performance.[48] She eventually dropped her lawsuit and did not receive any money.[49]

Regardless of the details of a particular case, the same strict rules apply—sexual harassment is illegal, and the organization is responsible for controlling it. If a manager is found guilty of sexual harassment, the company is liable because the manager is an agent of the company.

Employee Safety and Health

Employee health and safety programs help to reduce absenteeism and turnover, raise productivity, and boost morale by making jobs safer and more healthful. In Canada, each province has developed its own workplace health and safety regulations. The *Ontario Occupational Health and Safety Act* illustrates current legislation in Canada. It requires all employers to ensure that equipment and safety devices are used properly. Employers must also show workers the proper way to operate machinery. At the job site, supervisors are charged with the responsibility of ensuring that workers use equipment properly. The Act also requires workers to behave appropriately on the job. Employees have the right to refuse to work on a job if they believe it unsafe; a legal procedure exists for resolving any disputes in this area. In most provinces, the Ministry of Labour appoints inspectors to enforce health and safety regulations. If the inspector finds a sufficient hazard, he or she has the authority to clear the workplace. Inspectors can usually arrive at a firm unannounced to conduct an inspection.

Some industrial work—logging, construction, fishing, and mining—can put workers at risk of injury in obvious ways. But other types of work—such as typing or lifting—can also cause painful injuries. *Repetitive strain injuries (RSIs)* occur when workers perform the same functions over and over again. These injuries disable more than 200 000 Canadians every year and account for nearly half of all work-related lost-time claims.

Retirement

Until the 1990s, Canadian courts generally upheld 65 as the mandatory retirement age, but most Canadian provinces have now abolished mandatory retirement. New rules also took effect in December 2012 abolishing mandatory retirement at federally regulated employers like Air Canada.[50] Some managers fear that the abolition of mandatory retirement will allow less productive employees to remain at work after age 65, but research shows that the employees who stay on the job past 65 are usually the most productive ones. It is true that workers over age 65 are nearly four times as likely to die from work-related causes as younger workers, and older workers have double the health-care costs of workers in their 40s.[51] Since mandatory retirement has been abolished, there have been more lawsuits filed by older workers who claim they were removed from their job because of their age.[52]

In the 1970s, the average retirement age in Canada was 65, but by 2008 it had dropped to 62. The financial crisis that began in 2008 meant lower returns on investments, so more and more workers began delaying their retirement because they thought they weren't going to have enough money to retire. That caused the retirement age to start increasing again. A Sun Life poll of 3000 Canadian workers in 2015 found that about one-third of them expected to be working full-time at age 66. The same survey in 2008 showed that only 16 percent expected to still be working full-time at age 66.[53]

The 2015 Natixis Global Retirement Security Index—which analyzes factors such as health, finances, and quality of life in retirement—ranked Switzerland #1 in the world. Canada ranked #12 and the United States ranked #19.

The federal Pooled Registered Pension Plan Act became law in 2012. It allows individuals to contribute to a defined contribution pension plan even if their employer does not offer a pension plan. There is considerable debate about how pensions should be structured (see the boxed insert entitled "Defined Benefit Versus Defined Contribution Pension Plans").

SEXUAL HARASSMENT Requests for sexual favours, unwelcome sexual advances, or verbal or physical conduct of a sexual nature that creates an intimidating or hostile environment for a given employee.

MANAGING IN TURBULENT TIMES

Defined Benefit Versus Defined Contribution Pension Plans

There are two basic types of pension plans offered by Canadian public- and private-sector organizations. *Defined benefit* (DB) pension plans guarantee employees a certain annual income when they retire. Employees like DB plans, because they get a guaranteed income, and because they don't have to make investment decisions during retirement. But employers don't like DB plans, because they are forced to make guaranteed payments to retirees even if the company runs into financial difficulties.

In contrast, *defined contribution* (DC) pension plans require companies to contribute a certain amount of money each year for employee pensions. The value of the pension upon the employee's retirement depends on how much the pension fund has earned over the years. Employees don't like DC plans, because they don't know how much income they will get when they retire, and because they must make decisions about their investments during retirement. Employers like DC plans, because they put a ceiling on how much money the company must pay out.

Because of low investment returns and increasing life expectancy, many companies have been replacing DB plans with DC plans. For example, the Royal Bank of Canada stopped offering a DB plan to new hires, and Air Canada decided to offer only a DC plan. In 2013, Toyota announced that new hires would have a defined contribution pension plan.

Supporters of DB plans argue that they should not be replaced. They point to the experience of countries like Australia, which abandoned DB plans but are now having problems (e.g., increased senior poverty rates). One study showed that, for public-sector employees, DC plans would be less efficient and more costly than sticking with DB plans. Financial expert Charles Ellis says that DB plans were one of the greatest financial services ever offered to employees, and their loss is a "social tragedy." He argues that retirees don't realize how much money they will need in retirement. For example, if a person has $150 000 in a retirement fund, that will only earn $6000 annually at a 4 percent withdrawal rate.

A hybrid DB/DC model has been proposed to resolve the tension between DB and DC pension plans. In the CAW/Air Canada dispute, for example, a Target Benefit Pension Plan (TBPP) was proposed. Under this system, an expected (target) benefit is defined and the contribution necessary to get such a benefit is calculated. Since the investment environment regularly changes, every year a "new" expected benefit is communicated to workers. The benefit is not guaranteed, but rises and falls depending on returns in financial markets.

CRITICAL THINKING QUESTIONS

1. In your own words, explain the advantages and disadvantages of DB and DC pension plans.
2. Consider the following statement: *Given low investment returns and increased life expectancy, a defined contribution plan is really the only type of pension that is financially feasible.* Do you agree or disagree? Defend your reasoning.

LO-6 NEW CHALLENGES IN THE CHANGING WORKPLACE

As we have seen throughout this chapter, HR managers face various challenges in their efforts to keep their organizations staffed with effective workers. To complicate matters, new challenges arise as the economic and social environments of business change. Several of the most important HRM issues facing business today are managing workforce diversity, managing knowledge workers, and managing contingent and temporary workers.

Managing Workforce Diversity

One extremely important set of human resource challenges centres on **workforce diversity**—the range of workers' attitudes, values, beliefs, and behaviours that differ by gender, race, age, ethnicity, physical ability, and other characteristics. The situation for visible minorities is currently one of the most publicized aspects of diversity. Consider these facts:

- By 2015, 20 percent of Saskatchewan's population will be Aboriginal.
- In 2001, approximately 4 million Canadians were visible minorities; by 2017, that number could increase to as much as 8.5 million.
- Visible minorities currently make up more than 40 percent of the population of Vancouver.
- By 2017, visible minorities will form more than 50 percent of the populations of Toronto and Vancouver.
- By 2017, 22 percent of the total Canadian population will be visible minorities.[54]

Many Canadian companies are actively pursuing the management of diversity. At Procter & Gamble Canada, employees come from 40 different countries and speak at least 30 different languages. Diversity is recognized through "affinity groups" whose goal is to help employees feel comfortable about participating in corporate life.[55] At the Royal Bank of Canada (RBC), 64 percent of the employees are women, 4.6 percent are people with disabilities, 31 percent are visible minorities, and 1.5 percent are Aboriginals. These percentages match pretty well with the composition of the Canadian labour force as a whole.[56]

WORKFORCE DIVERSITY The range of workers' attitudes, values, beliefs, and behaviours that differ by gender, race, age, ethnicity, physical ability, and other relevant characteristics.

In their recruiting and hiring activities, HR managers must take into account the increasing diversity of Canada's workforce.

WavebreakmediaMicro/Fotolia

Organizations are increasingly recognizing that diversity can be a competitive advantage. By hiring the best people available from every group—rather than from just one or a few groups—a firm can develop a higher-quality workforce. A diverse workforce can bring a wider array of information to bear on problems and can provide insights on marketing products to a wider range of consumers. But progress is often slow, even in companies that have great reputations. For example, in 2014 Google said that it was not where it wanted to be with regard to diversity because its workforce was still dominated by white males.[57] And at Suncor, white males also dominate (just 23 percent of the employees are women, 11.1 percent are visible minorities, and 2.7 percent are Aboriginals).

Managing Knowledge Workers

Traditionally, employees added value to organizations because of what they did or because of their experience. In the "information age," however, many employees add value because of what they know.[58]

THE NATURE OF KNOWLEDGE WORK

These employees are usually called **knowledge workers**, and the skill with which they are managed is a major factor in determining which firms will be successful in the future. Knowledge workers, including computer scientists, engineers, and physical scientists, provide special challenges for the HR manager. They tend to work for high-tech firms and are usually experts in some abstract knowledge base. They often prefer to work independently and tend to identify more strongly with their profession than with the organization that pays them—even to the extent of defining performance in terms recognized by other members of their profession.

As the importance of information-driven jobs grows, the need for knowledge workers increases. But these employees require extensive and highly specialized training, and not every organization is willing to make the human capital investments necessary to take advantage of these employees. Even after knowledge workers are on the job, training updates are critical to prevent their skills from becoming obsolete. The failure to update such skills not only results in the loss of competitive advantage, but also increases the likelihood that knowledge workers will move to another firm more committed to updating their knowledge.

KNOWLEDGE WORKER MANAGEMENT AND LABOUR MARKETS

Organizations that need knowledge workers must introduce regular market adjustments (upward) to pay them enough to keep them. This is especially critical in areas in which demand is growing, as even entry-level salaries for these employees are skyrocketing. Once an employee accepts a job with a firm, the employer faces yet another dilemma. Once hired, workers are subject to the company's internal labour market, which is not likely to be growing as quickly as the external market for knowledge workers as a whole. Consequently, the longer knowledge workers remain with a firm, the further behind the market their pay falls—unless it is regularly adjusted upward.

Managing Contingent Workers

A contingent worker is one who works for an organization on something other than a permanent or full-time basis. Categories of contingent workers include part-time workers, independent contractors (freelancers), on-call workers, temporary employees (usually hired through outside "temp" agencies), contract workers, and guest workers (foreigners working in Canada for a limited time).

TRENDS IN CONTINGENT EMPLOYMENT

There are some interesting trends in contingent employment in Canada. While part-time employment was 7.75 percent higher in 2011 than in 2007, that may have been caused by the recession of 2008–2009 (companies make more use of part-timers during times of economic uncertainty).[59] When the economy improves, companies hire more full-time workers. There is also demand for temporary workers in top management positions because there is a lot of turnover at this level. These "temps at the top" usually stay for a year or less until a permanent person is found.[60]

The number of guest workers in Canada—one category of contingent workers—is increasing. They work in all kinds of industries, including agriculture, manufacturing, and services. In any given year there are over 150 000 guest workers in Canada. The number is predicted to rise.[61]

MANAGEMENT OF CONTINGENT WORKERS

The effective management of contingent workers requires consideration of three issues. First, careful planning must be done so the organization brings in contingent workers only when they are actually needed and in the quantity needed to complete necessary tasks. Second, the costs and benefits of using contingent workers must be understood. Many firms bring in contingent workers in order to reduce labour costs, but if contingent workers are less productive than permanent workers, there may be no gain for the organization. Third, contingent workers should be integrated into the mainstream activities of the organization as much as possible. This involves deciding how they will be treated relative to permanent workers. For example, should contingent workers be invited to the company holiday party? Should they have the same access to employee benefits? Managers must develop a strategy for integrating contingent workers according to some sound logic and then follow that strategy consistently over time.[62]

KNOWLEDGE WORKERS Workers who are experts in specific fields like computer technology and engineering, and who add value because of what they know, rather than how long they have worked or the job they do.

LO-7 DEALING WITH ORGANIZED LABOUR

A **labour union** is a group of individuals working together to achieve shared job-related goals, such as higher pay, shorter working hours, greater benefits, or better working conditions.[63] When people think of unions, they often picture modestly paid production workers in a factory who have joined a union in an attempt to improve their wages and benefits. But some highly paid workers also belong to unions. For example, *all* professional athletes in the four major professional sports in North America—hockey, baseball, football, and basketball—belong to unions.

Labour relations refers to the overall process of dealing with employees who are represented by a union. **Collective bargaining** is the process by which union leaders and company management negotiate terms and conditions of employment for those workers represented by unions. We discuss the role of collective bargaining in detail below.

The Development of Canadian Labour Unions

The labour movement was born with the Industrial Revolution, which also gave birth to the factory-based production system that carried with it enormous economic benefits. Job specialization and mass production allowed businesses to create ever-greater quantities of goods at ever-lower costs. But there was also a dark side, as some owners treated their workers as simply resources to be deployed, with little or no regard for the well-being of workers. Employees often worked 60-hour weeks, pay was minimal, there was no job security, workers received few benefits, and safety standards were virtually non-existent. Mining and textile companies employed large numbers of children at poverty wages, and if people complained they were fired. Unions developed to compel management to listen to the complaints of all their workers rather than to just the few brave enough to speak out.

The earliest evidence of labour unions in Canada comes from the Maritime provinces in the nineteenth century. These unions typically included individuals with a specific craft (e.g., printers, shoemakers, barrel makers). Most of these unions were small and had only limited success. However, they laid the foundation for the rapid increase in union activity that occurred during the late nineteenth and early twentieth centuries.

A succession of labour organizations sprang up and just as quickly faded away during the years 1840–1870. In 1873, the first national labour organization was formed—the Canadian Labour Union. By 1886, the Knights of Labour (a U.S.-based union) had over 10 000 members in Canada. The Canadian labour movement began to mature with the formation of the Trades and Labour Congress (TLC) in 1886. The TLC's purpose was to unite all labour organizations and to work for the passage of laws that would ensure the well-being of the working class.

The growth of labour unions began in earnest early in the twentieth century, but sometimes disputes arose within the ranks. For example, there was concern that U.S.-based unions would have a detrimental effect on Canadian ones, so the Canadian Federation of Labour was formed in 1908 to promote national (Canadian) unions over U.S. ones. These and other disputes—such as how communists in the movement should be handled—often led to the creation of rival union organizations that competed for membership. By 1956, these disputes had been largely resolved, and the two largest congresses of affiliated unions—the Trades and Labour Congress and the Canadian Congress of Labour—merged to form the Canadian Labour Congress. This amalgamation brought approximately 80 percent of all unionized workers into one organization.

Unionism Today

In 2013, 4.7 million Canadian workers belonged to unions, but union membership as a proportion of the non-agricultural workforce (called *union density*) is less than one-third. Union density varies widely across countries. In Canada, union density is about 30 percent; in the United States 11 percent; in France 9 percent; and in Sweden 82 percent.[64] Density also varies across occupations. In some occupations, like teaching and nursing, over 80 percent are unionized. In other occupations, like management and food and beverage services, less than 10 percent belong to a union.[65]

Unions are not restricted to the private sector. In fact, the public sector is far more unionized (72.7 percent) than the private sector (18.1 percent).[66] There has been controversy recently about the perceived "rich" compensation and benefits available to public-sector workers (whether or not unionized). For example, federal workers usually have a defined benefit pension that, after 35 years, pays 70 percent of the worker's highest five-year earning average. By contrast, in the private sector, two-thirds of workers don't even have a pension. Mark Ferguson, president of a Toronto branch of the Canadian Union of Public Employees, says that the public hates unions. And Ken Georgetti, president of the Canadian Labour Congress, says that unions are increasingly seen as "out for themselves" and no longer have the respect of the general public in Canada.[67]

Many years ago, unions routinely won certification votes. But in recent years, they have had less success. One reason is that today's workforce is increasingly diverse. Women and ethnic minorities have weaker traditions of union affiliation than white males (who dominated the blue-collar jobs in the past). The workforce is also increasingly employed in the service sector, which traditionally has been less heavily unionized.

Another reason for declining unionization is that companies have become far more aggressive in opposing unions. Federal and provincial labour legislation restricts what management of a company can do to keep out a union, but companies are free to pursue certain strategies to minimize unionization, such as creating a more employee-friendly work environment. For example, Japanese and European manufacturers who have set up shop in North America have so far avoided unionization efforts by providing job security, higher wages, and a work environment in which employees are allowed to participate and be actively involved in plant management.[68]

LABOUR UNION A group of individuals who work together to achieve shared job-related goals.

LABOUR RELATIONS The overall process of dealing with employees who are represented by a union.

COLLECTIVE BARGAINING The process through which union leaders and management personnel negotiate common terms and conditions of employment for those workers represented by the union.

TRENDS IN UNION–MANAGEMENT RELATIONS

The problems that have been experienced by unions have caused significant changes in union–management relations. Not so long ago, most union–management bargaining was very adversarial, with unions making demands for dramatic improvements in wages, benefits, and job security. But with organizational downsizing and a decade of low inflation in Canada, many unions today find themselves able to achieve only modest improvements in wages and benefits. A common goal of union strategy is, therefore, to preserve what has already been won.

Today, unions must cooperate with employers if both companies and unions are to survive and prosper. The goal is to create win-win partnerships in which managers and workers share the same goals: profitability, growth, and effectiveness, with equitable rewards for everyone. Even in those sectors of the economy where unions remain quite strong—most notably in the automobile and steel industries—unions have changed their tactics. In the automobile industry, Buzz Hargrove, former president of the Canadian Auto Workers, has urged members of the union bargaining team to come up with new ideas for improving quality and productivity so that Canadian factories will be more attractive for new investment.[69]

The Future of Unions

Unions face some serious challenges. In the *private sector*, companies have become much more aggressive when negotiating with unions. For example, in 2012, Electro-Motive Canada moved production from its London, Ontario, plant to the United States when workers wouldn't agree to a 50 percent wage cut.[70] In the *public sector*, the federal and provincial governments are looking for ways to save money because of large budget deficits, so there will be pressure to hold the line on wages and benefits.

Unions are facing other challenges as well: the decline of the so-called "smokestack industries" (where union power was formerly very strong), the globalization of business (which has caused the movement of jobs to areas of the world with lower labour costs), technological change (which often reduces the number of workers needed), and the increasing importance of contract and part-time workers (who are difficult to organize). Unions are responding to these challenges in a variety of ways. For example, in 2013, two of Canada's largest unions—the Canadian Auto Workers and the Communications, Energy and Paperworkers—merged to form a new union called Unifor.[71]

LO-8 THE LEGAL ENVIRONMENT FOR UNIONS IN CANADA

Political and legal barriers to collective bargaining existed until well into the twentieth century (see Table 8.1). Courts held that some unions were conspirators in restraint of trade. Employers viewed their employees' efforts to unionize as attempts to deprive the employers of their private property. The employment contract, employers contended, was between the individual worker and the employer—not between the employer and employees as a group. The balance of bargaining power was very much in favour of the employer.

The employer–employee relationship became much less direct as firms grew in size. Managers were themselves employees, and hired managers dealt with other employees. Communication among owners, managers, and workers became more formalized. Big business had more power than workers. Because of mounting public concern, laws were passed to put workers on a more even footing with employers.

The *Constitution Act* (originally called the BNA Act), passed in 1867, has also affected labour legislation. This Act allocated certain activities to the federal government (e.g., labour legislation for companies operating interprovincially) and others to individual provinces (labour relations regulations in general). Thus, labour legislation comes from both the federal and provincial governments, but is basically a provincial matter. That is why certain groups of similar employees might be allowed to go on strike in one province but not in another.

Federal Legislation—The Canada Labour Code

The **Canada Labour Code** is a comprehensive piece of legislation that applies to the labour practices of firms operating under the legislative authority of parliament. The Canada Labour Code has been under review by the federal Minister of Labour. The Canada Labour Code has been under review by the federal Minister of Labour. One of the issues that the review is focusing on is whether managers and supervisors should also

CANADA LABOUR CODE Legislation that applies to the labour practices of firms operating under the legislative authority of parliament.

TABLE 8.1 Key Canadian labour legislation

Date	Legislation	Accomplishments/Goals
1900	Conciliation Act	• Designed to help settle labour disputes through voluntary conciliation • First step in creating more favourable labour conditions
1907	Industrial Disputes Investigation Act	• Compulsory investigation of labour disputes by a government-appointed board before any strike action (found to violate a provision of the British North America Act)
1943	Privy Council Order 1003	• Recognized the right of employees to bargain collectively • Prohibited unfair management labour practices • Established a labour board to certify bargaining authority • Prohibited strikes and lockouts (except in collective bargaining agreements)

be protected by labour code restrictions on the number of hours they work each week, and whether they should receive overtime pay. The issue came to the forefront after the Manitoba Labour Board ruled that Sharon Michalowski, a manager at Nygard International, was entitled to overtime pay, even though she was a manager and had signed a contract stipulating that she would work whatever hours were required to earn her annual salary of $42 000.[72] Managers are still not covered by the provisions of the Canada Labour Code.

The Canada Labour Code has four main sections: fair employment practices; standard hours, wages, vacations, and holidays; safety of employees; and industrial relations regulations.

FAIR EMPLOYMENT PRACTICES

This section of the Code prohibits an employer from either refusing employment on the basis of a person's race or religion or using an employment agency that discriminates against people on the basis of their race or religion. These prohibitions apply to trade unions as well, but not to non-profit, charitable, and philanthropic organizations. Any individual who believes a violation has occurred may make a complaint in writing to Labour Canada. The allegation will then be investigated and, if necessary, an Industrial Inquiry Commission will be appointed to make a recommendation in the case. Since 1982, fair employment practices have been covered by the Canadian Human Rights Act; they are also covered by the Canadian Charter of Rights and Freedoms.

STANDARD HOURS, WAGES, VACATIONS, AND HOLIDAYS

This section of the Code deals with a wide variety of mechanical issues such as standard hours of work (eight-hour day and 40-hour week), maximum hours of work per week (48), overtime pay (at least one and a half times the regular pay), minimum wages, equal wages for men and women doing the same jobs, vacations, general holidays, and parental leave. The specific provisions are changed frequently to take into account changes in the economic and social structure of Canada, but their basic goal is to ensure consistent treatment of employees in these areas.

SAFETY OF EMPLOYEES

This section of the Code requires that every person running a federal work project do so in a way that will not endanger the health or safety of any employee. It also requires that safety procedures and techniques be implemented to reduce the risk of employment injury. The section requires employees to exercise care to ensure their own safety; however, even if it can be shown that the employee did not exercise proper care, compensation must still be paid. The section also makes provisions for a safety officer whose duty it is to ensure the provisions of the code are fulfilled. The safety officer has the right to enter any federal project "at any reasonable time."

INDUSTRIAL RELATIONS REGULATIONS

The final major section of the Canada Labour Code deals with all matters related to collective bargaining.

Provincial Labour Legislation

Each province has enacted legislation to deal with the personnel practices covered in the Canada Labour Code. These laws vary across provinces and are frequently revised; however, their basic approach and substance is the same as in the Canada Labour Code. Certain provinces may exceed the minimum requirements on some issues (e.g., minimum wages).

Union Organizing Strategy

There are several reasons a union might try to organize workers: when a firm is trying to move into a new geographical area or when some workers in a firm are members and the union wants to represent other workers or when it is attempting to outdo a rival union or when it wants to increase the number of workers who belong to the union. For example, the United Auto Workers saw its membership drop sharply in recent years due to layoffs at companies like General Motors and Chrysler. So the UAW launched a campaign to unionize workers of foreign auto manufacturers like Toyota, Honda, Nissan, Hyundai, and Volkswagen. In 2014, Unifor launched a drive to unionize 6500 workers at two Toyota assembly plants in Ontario.[73] The United Food and Commercial Workers (UFCW) union conducted organizing drives at Shoppers Drug Mart (after it was acquired by Loblaw Companies Limited), and at Sobeys Inc. (after it acquired Safeway).[74]

Over the past decade, one of the most visible organizing efforts has been conducted by the United Food and Commercial Workers (UFCW) at Walmart, but Walmart has aggressively fought every UFCW attempt. Until the mid-1990s, the company had never had a union in any of its stores in the United States, Canada, Puerto Rico, Argentina, Brazil, or Mexico. In 1996, management first began hearing rumours that the Canadian Auto Workers (CAW) union was approaching employees at the Windsor, Ontario, store about unionizing. During the organizing drive, there was much squabbling among employees, and when the certification vote was held, the workers voted 151–43 against joining the union. In spite of this, the Ontario Labour Relations Board (OLRB) certified the union as the employees' bargaining agent on the grounds that the company had intimidated employees during the drive. A first collective agreement was approved, but in April 2000 the union was officially decertified.[75]

More recently, each side has had both victories and defeats. In 2009, for example, the UFCW failed in its attempt to be certified as the bargaining agent for Walmart employees in Saguenay, Quebec, but in 2008 the Quebec Labour Relations Board certified the UFCW as the sole bargaining agent for about 150 workers at a Walmart store in Gatineau. That required Walmart to negotiate with the union regarding a collective agreement. In 2005, the UFCW was certified as the sole bargaining agent for nine tire and lubrication workers at another Walmart store in Gatineau. When the UFCW and Walmart failed to negotiate a collective agreement, an arbitrator imposed an agreement that raised workers' wages. Walmart then closed the shop,[76] but in 2014 the Supreme Court ruled the closure illegal.

Management often becomes aware of a union-organizing drive through the grapevine. When management discovers a drive is under way, it may try to counteract it. However, it must know what it can legally do. In Quebec, McDonald's has been the target of organizing drives at several of its restaurants. After a McDonald's restaurant in Saint-Hubert closed (when it appeared that the Teamsters union might be successful getting certified), critics called for a government investigation into the possibility of unfair labour practices on the part of the company.[77]

Each province has somewhat different rules for certifying unions. For example, suppose a union is trying to organize employees of a Manitoba company. If it can show that at least 50 percent of the employees are members of the union, it can apply to the Manitoba Labour Board (MLB)

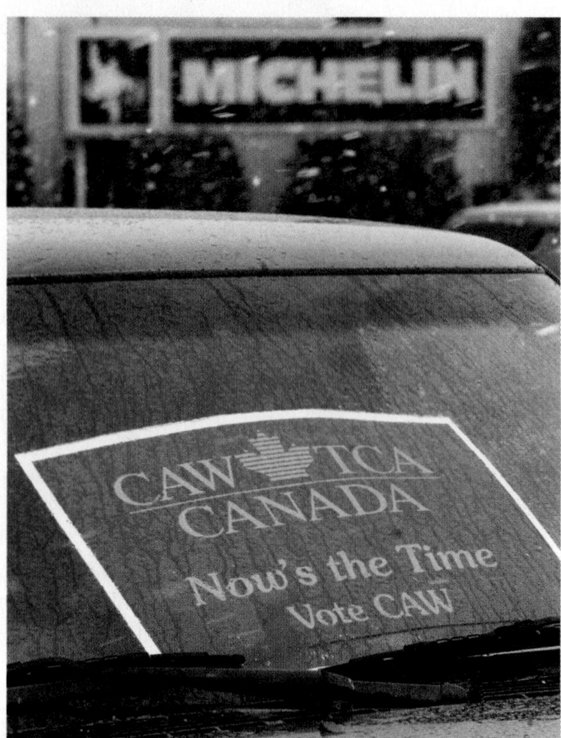

The outcome of this certification vote will determine whether these workers at Michelin will be represented by the CAW.

Andrew Vaughan/Canadian Press Images

for certification as the sole bargaining agent for the employees. During the process, there may be an issue regarding the right of different types of workers to join or not join. For example, supervisors may or may not be included in a bargaining unit along with non-management workers. The **bargaining unit** includes those individuals deemed appropriate by the province, and the MLB has final authority in determining the appropriateness of the bargaining unit. Once the MLB has determined that the unit is appropriate, it may order a **certification vote**. If a majority of those voting are in favour of the union, it is certified as the sole bargaining agent for the unit.

The same law that grants employees the right to unionize also allows them to cease being represented by a union. **Decertification** is the process by which employees legally terminate their union's right to represent them. This happened during a labour dispute over job security and safety that arose at Goldcorp Inc.'s mine near Red Lake, Ontario, which led to a strike involving 100 workers. The strike was settled when workers agreed to decertify their union in return for severance pay at four times the rate mandated by Ontario law.[78]

Union Security

The greatest union security exists in the **closed shop**, in which an employer can hire only union members. For example, a plumbing or electrical contractor who hires workers through a union hiring hall can hire only union members. In a **union shop**, an employer may hire non-union workers even if the employer's current employees are unionized. But newly hired workers must join the union within a stipulated period of time (usually 30 days). In an **agency shop**, all employees for whom the union bargains must pay union dues, but they need not join the union. In an **open shop**, an employer may hire union and/or non-union labour. Employees need not join a union or pay dues to one.

Types of Unions

There are two basic types of unions: craft and industrial. *Craft unions* are organized by crafts or trades—plumbers, barbers, airline pilots, and so forth. Craft unions restrict membership to workers with specific skills. In many cases, members of craft unions work for several different employers during the course of a year. For example, many construction workers are hired by their employers at union hiring halls. When the job for which they are hired is finished, these workers return to the hall to be hired by another employer. Craft unions have a lot of power over the supply of skilled workers, because a person who wants to become a member of a plumbers union, for example, must go through a training (apprenticeship) program. After sufficient training, the apprentice is qualified as a journeyman plumber.

Industrial unions are organized according to industry, for example, steel, auto, and clothing. Industrial unions include semi-skilled and unskilled workers and were originally started because industrial workers were not eligible to join craft unions. Industrial union members typically work for a particular employer for a much longer period of time than do craft union members. An industrial union has a lot of say regarding pay and human resource practices within unionized firms.

The *local union* is the basic unit of union organization in a specific geographical area. A local of a craft union is made up of artisans in the same craft, whereas a local of an industrial union is made up of workers in a given industry or manufacturing plant. Thus, plumbers may be members of the local plumbers (a craft union), while truck drivers in that same area may be members of the Teamsters (an industrial union).

An *independent local union* is one that is not formally affiliated with any labour organization. It conducts negotiations with management only at a local level, and the collective agreement is binding at that location only. The faculty associations at many Canadian universities are examples of independent local unions.

A *national union* has members across Canada, while an *international union* has members in more than one country. There are many national unions in Canada, including the Canadian Union of Public Employees, the National Railway Union, and the Canadian Airline Pilots Union. The United Steelworkers of America is an international union made up of locals in the United States and Canada. National unions represent about two-thirds of unionized Canadian workers and international unions about one-third.[79]

BARGAINING UNIT Individuals grouped together for purposes of collective bargaining.

CERTIFICATION VOTE A vote supervised by a government representative to determine whether a union will be certified as the sole bargaining agent for the unit.

DECERTIFICATION The process by which employees legally terminate their union's right to represent them.

CLOSED SHOP A union–employer relationship in which the employer can hire only union members.

UNION SHOP A union–employer relationship in which the employer can hire non-unionized workers, but they must join the union within a certain period.

AGENCY SHOP A union–employer relationship in which all employees for whom the union bargains must pay dues, but they are not required to join the union.

OPEN SHOP A union–employer relationship in which the employer may hire union or non-union workers.

LO-9 COLLECTIVE BARGAINING

People often associate collective bargaining with the specific act of signing a contract between a union and a company or industry. In fact, collective bargaining is an ongoing process involving both the drafting and administration of the terms of a labour contract.

Reaching Agreement on the Contract's Terms

The collective bargaining process begins when the union is recognized as the exclusive negotiator for its members. The bargaining cycle begins when union leaders meet with management representatives to begin working on a new contract. By law, both parties must negotiate "in good faith." When each side has presented its demands, sessions focus on identifying the bargaining zone. This process is shown in Figure 8.3. For example, although an employer may initially offer no pay raise, it may expect that it may eventually have to grant a raise of up to 6 percent. Likewise, the union may initially demand a 10 percent pay raise while expecting to accept a raise as low as 4 percent. The bargaining zone, then, is a raise between 4 and 6 percent. Obviously, compromise is needed on both sides if agreement is to be reached. The new tentative agreement is then submitted for a ratification vote by union membership. In 2014, the United Steelworkers union reached a tentative agreement with U.S. Steel Canada that covered workers in Hamilton.[80]

Fundamental differences may be evident when labour and management try to develop a new collective agreement. At the Great Blue Heron Charity Casino in Port Perry, Ontario (operated by the Mississaugas of Scugog Island First Nation), a collective agreement was in place with the Canadian Auto Workers union that covered 1000 casino workers (very few of whom were band members). The band wanted to replace the collective agreement with its own labour agreement, which would have denied employees the right to strike. The band felt it could drop the collective agreement with the CAW because it had Aboriginal treaty and self-government rights. When it tried to implement the new labour agreement, the CAW filed a grievance. Eventually, the Ontario Court of Appeal rejected the band's arguments on the grounds that the band had not proven that a labour code was part of its tradition, nor that it was integral to its ancestral culture.[81]

Contract Issues

Most of the issues in the labour contract arise from demands that unions make on behalf of their members. Issues that are typically most important to union negotiators include *compensation, benefits*, and *job security*. Certain management rights issues are also negotiated in most bargaining agreements.

COMPENSATION

The most common issue is compensation. Unions want their employees to earn higher wages immediately, so they try to convince management to raise wages for all or some employees. Of equal concern to unions is future compensation that is to be paid during subsequent years of the contract. One common tool for securing wage increases is a *cost-of-living adjustment (COLA)*. Most COLA clauses tie future raises to the Consumer Price Index (CPI), a government statistic that reflects changes in consumer purchasing power. A *wage reopener clause*—which allows wage rates to be renegotiated at preset times during the life of the contract—is sometimes included in labour contracts where a union is uncomfortable with a long-term contract based solely on COLA wage increases.

BENEFITS

Benefits commonly addressed during negotiations include insurance, retirement benefits, paid holidays, working conditions, and the cost of supplementary health care (prescription drugs, eye care, dental care, and so on). The health-care issue is becoming increasingly contentious during negotiations because the cost of such care is rapidly increasing.

Union's Demand
Employer's Maximum Limit
Union's Expectation
Bargaining Zone
Employer's Expectation
Union's Minimum Limit
Employer's Desired Result

FIGURE 8.3 The bargaining zone

Elementary school teachers protest in Toronto against Bill 115, which froze teacher salaries and reduced their benefits.

Alex Bainbridge/Newzulu STRNEWZ/The Canadian Press

JOB SECURITY

In some cases, a contract may dictate that if the workforce is reduced, seniority will be used to determine which employees keep their jobs. Unions are also increasingly setting their sights on preserving jobs for workers in Canada in the face of business efforts to outsource production in some sectors to countries where labour costs are cheaper. For example, Gildan Activewear outsources much of its production to low-wage countries in the Caribbean.

OTHER UNION ISSUES

Other issues might include such details as working hours, overtime policies, rest periods, differential pay plans for shift employees, the use of temporary workers, grievance procedures, and allowable union activities (dues collection, union bulletin boards, and so on). In addition, some contracts are beginning to include formal mechanisms for greater worker input into management decisions.

MANAGEMENT RIGHTS

Management wants as much control as possible over hiring policies, work assignments, and so forth. Unions, meanwhile, often try to limit management rights by specifying hiring, assignment, and other policies. At one Chrysler plant the contract stipulates that three workers are needed to change fuses in robots: a machinist to open the robot, an electrician to change the fuse, and a supervisor to oversee the process. Such contracts often bar workers in one job category from performing work that falls within the domain of another. Unions try to secure jobs by defining as many different categories as possible (the Chrysler plant has over 100). Of course, management resists this practice, which limits flexibility and makes it difficult to reassign workers.

When Bargaining Fails

An impasse occurs when, after a series of bargaining sessions, management and labour are unable to agree on a first-time contract or a contract to replace an agreement that is about to expire. Both union and management may try various tactics to support their demands until the impasse is resolved.

UNION TACTICS

A **strike** occurs when employees temporarily walk off the job and refuse to work. In 2014, for example, truckers went on strike at the port of Vancouver. The strike crippled the port and caused great concern that Canada's reputation for reliability would be damaged.[82] During a strike, unions may picket or launch a boycott. *Picketing* involves having workers march at the entrance to the company with signs explaining their reasons for striking. *Sympathy strikes* (also called *secondary strikes*) occur when one union strikes in sympathy with a strike initiated by another union. *Wildcat strikes*—those that are not authorized by the union or that occur during the life of a contract—deprive strikers of their status as employees and thus of the protection of labour laws. In 2012 Air Canada ground crews engaged in a wildcat strike that caused hundreds of flights to be delayed or cancelled.[83]

Unions are more reluctant to use the strike weapon than they used to be. One reason is that more and more workers are in profit-sharing plans, meaning they receive a portion of company profits. Going on strike has a negative effect on profits, so workers are hurting themselves if they go on strike. Other reasons are the decline in union power, the bad publicity generated by strikes, and the fact that technology and globalization mean companies can easily displace highly paid but low-skilled workers.[84]

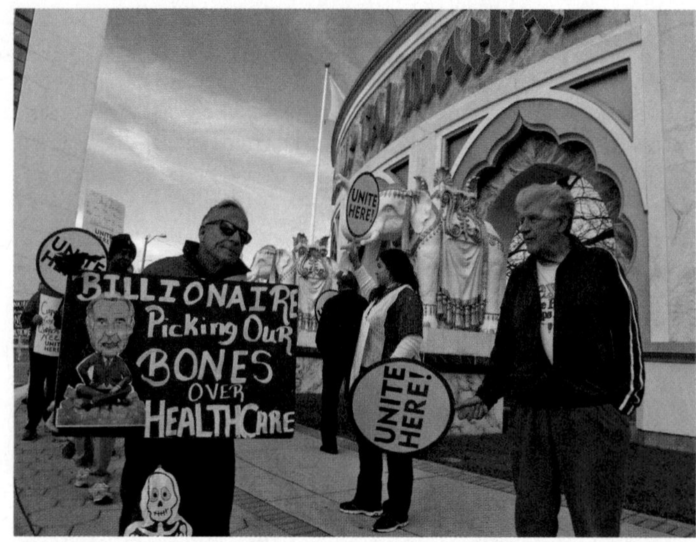

A member of the teacher's union holds a picket sign while on strike in Abbotsford, B.C., in 2014.

Wayne Parry/AP/The Canadian Press

In some situations, unions are not permitted to strike. In 2011, for example, Air Canada flight attendants were not allowed to go on strike after the Labour Minister referred the dispute to the Labour Board.[85] The Province of Nova Scotia passed a law that forbids strikes by health-care workers in that province.[86] Hospital workers cannot strike in Alberta, Prince Edward Island, or Ontario either. Strikes may also be illegal if the union does not go through certain necessary steps before striking.

Union workers have other options they can pursue if they don't want to go on strike. A *boycott* occurs when union members agree not to buy the products of the firm that employs them. Workers may also urge other consumers to shun their firm's products. In a *work slowdown*, workers perform their jobs at a much slower pace than normal. A variation is the *sickout*, during which large numbers of workers call in sick in order to disrupt the company's activities.

MANAGEMENT TACTICS

Management can also respond forcefully to an impasse. A **lockout** occurs when employers physically deny employees access to the workplace. In 2012, Rio Tinto Alcan Inc. locked out 780 workers for six months when the union voted to go on strike.[87] In 2012, National Hockey League owners locked out the players for four months, and in 2011, the National Football League locked out its players. As an alternative to a lockout, firms can hire temporary or permanent replacements (*strikebreakers*) for the absent employees. However, the use of replacement workers is illegal in Quebec and British Columbia.

STRIKE A tactic of labour unions in which members temporarily walk off the job and refuse to work, in order to win concessions from management.

LOCKOUT A tactic of management in which the firm physically denies employees access to the workplace to pressure workers to agree to the company's latest contract offer.

Members of CUPE protest being locked-out by the Southern Railway of B.C. in 2015.

Jacques Boissinot/The Canadian Press

Companies can also lessen the impact of unions by contracting out—to non-union contractors—a lot of assembly work they used to do themselves. This results in fewer union workers within the company. Companies can also join *employers' associations*—groups of companies that get together to plan strategies and exchange information about how to manage their relations with unions. The British Columbia Maritime Employers Association—which includes 67 companies that employ longshoremen in Vancouver and other seaports in B.C.—is an example of an employers' association. In extreme cases, management may simply close down a plant if an agreement cannot be reached with the union. For example, Maple Leaf Foods closed its Edmonton hog processing plant when the workers went on strike there. That cost 850 workers their jobs.

CONCILIATION A method of settling a contract dispute in which neutral third party helps the two sides clarify the issues that are separating them.

MEDIATION A method of settling a contract dispute in which a neutral third party is asked to hear arguments from both the union and management and offer a suggested resolution.

ARBITRATION A method of settling a contract dispute in which a neutral third party imposes a binding settlement on the disputing parties.

Conciliation, Mediation, and Arbitration

Rather than using their weapons on one another, labour and management can agree to call in a third party to help resolve a dispute. In **conciliation**, a neutral third party (the *conciliator*) helps the two sides clarify the issues that are separating them. The conciliator cannot impose a settlement on the disputing parties. In 2012, the Canadian Press asked the federal government to appoint a conciliator to help with negotiations with the Canadian Media Guild, whose contract expired at the end of 2011.[88]

In **mediation**, a neutral third party (the mediator) goes beyond conciliation and advises the disputing parties about specific steps they might take to reach a settlement. The mediator, however, cannot impose a settlement either. In 2012, when the Air Canada Pilots Association received support from its members for a strike, a mediator was appointed to assist in the negotiations between Air Canada and the union in the hope of reaching a negotiated settlement without a strike occurring.[89]

In **arbitration**, a neutral third party (the arbitrator) imposes a settlement on the disputing parties. Arbitration may be either voluntary or compulsory. When *voluntary arbitration* is used, the disputing parties agree to submit the dispute to outside judgment. For example, when union employees at Canadian Pacific Railway went on strike in 2015, the negotiators in the dispute agreed to arbitration.[90] A pension dispute between Air Canada and the Canadian Auto Workers was also sent to an arbitrator for resolution. The arbitrator ruled in favour of the union's proposal for a hybrid pension plan that included elements of both defined benefit and defined contribution pension plans.[91] In some cases, arbitration is legally required to settle bargaining disputes. This *compulsory arbitration* is often used to settle disputes between government and public employees such as firefighters and police officers.

MyBizLab

Study, practise, and explore real business situations with these helpful resources:

- **Interactive Lesson Presentations:** Work through interactive presentations and assessments to test your knowledge of business concepts.
- **Study Plan:** Check your understanding of chapter concepts with self-study quizzes.
- **Dynamic Study Modules:** Work through adaptive study modules on your computer, tablet, or mobile device.
- **Simulations:** Practise decision-making in simulated business environments.
- **Videos:** Learn more about the business practices and strategies of real companies.

SUMMARY OF LEARNING OBJECTIVES

LO-1 DEFINE *HUMAN RESOURCE MANAGEMENT*, DISCUSS ITS STRATEGIC SIGNIFICANCE, AND EXPLAIN HOW MANAGERS PLAN FOR HUMAN RESOURCES.

Human resource management, or *HRM*, is the set of organizational activities directed at attracting, developing, and maintaining an effective workforce. HRM plays a key strategic role in organizational performance. Planning for human resource needs entails several steps: (1) conducting a job analysis, (2) forecasting demand and supply, and (3) matching HR supply and demand.

LO-2 IDENTIFY THE ISSUES INVOLVED IN STAFFING A COMPANY, INCLUDING *INTERNAL* AND *EXTERNAL RECRUITING* AND *SELECTION*.

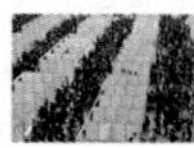

Recruiting is the process of attracting qualified people to apply for open jobs. *Internal recruiting* involves considering present employees for new jobs. It builds morale and rewards the best employees. *External recruiting* means attracting people from outside the organization. Key *selection techniques* include application forms, tests, and interviews. The techniques must be valid predictors of expected performance.

LO-3 DISCUSS DIFFERENT WAYS IN WHICH ORGANIZATIONS GO ABOUT DEVELOPING THE CAPABILITIES OF EMPLOYEES AND MANAGERS.

Nearly all employees undergo some initial *orientation* process. Many employees are also given the opportunity to acquire new skills through various *work-based* and/or *instructional-based programs*.

LO-4 DISCUSS THE IMPORTANCE OF *WAGES AND SALARIES*, *INCENTIVES*, AND *BENEFIT PROGRAMS* IN ATTRACTING AND KEEPING SKILLED WORKERS.

Wages and salaries, *incentives*, and *benefit packages* may all be parts of a company's *compensation program*. By providing competitive compensation levels, a business can attract and keep qualified personnel. *Incentive programs* can also motivate people to work more productively. *Indirect compensation* also plays a major role in effective and well-designed compensation systems.

LO-5 DESCRIBE SOME OF THE KEY LEGAL ISSUES INVOLVED IN HIRING, COMPENSATING, AND MANAGING WORKERS IN TODAY'S WORKPLACE.

Managers must obey a variety of federal and provincial laws in the areas of *equal opportunity* and *equal pay*, *sexual harassment*, and *comparable worth*. Firms are also required to provide employees with safe working environments, as per the guidelines of provincial occupational health and safety acts.

LO-6 DISCUSS *WORKFORCE DIVERSITY*, THE *MANAGEMENT OF KNOWLEDGE WORKERS*, AND THE USE OF *CONTINGENT* AND *TEMPORARY WORKERS* AS IMPORTANT CHANGES IN THE CONTEMPORARY WORKPLACE.

Workforce diversity refers to the range of workers' attitudes, values, beliefs, and behaviours that differ by gender, race, ethnicity, age, and physical ability. Many firms now see diversity as a source of competitive advantage and work actively to achieve diversity in their ranks. Additional challenges exist in *managing knowledge workers* (rapidly increasing salaries and high turnover). *Contingent workers* are hired to supplement an organization's permanent workforce. The use of contingent workers gives managers flexibility; also, these workers are usually not covered by employers' benefit programs—two reasons why their numbers are growing.

LO-7 TRACE THE EVOLUTION OF, AND DISCUSS TRENDS IN, *UNIONISM* IN CANADA.

The first unions were formed in the early nineteenth century in the maritime provinces. Labour organizations sprang up and faded away during the nineteenth century and unions began to develop in the twentieth century. Since the mid-1970s, labour unions in Canada have had difficulty attracting new members. Membership as a percentage of total workforce has declined. Increasingly, unions recognize that they have lost significant power and that it is in everyone's best interests to work with management instead of against it.

LO-8 DESCRIBE THE *MAJOR LAWS GOVERNING UNIONISM.*

Privy Council Order 1003 gave unions the right to bargain collectively in Canada. The *Constitution Act, 1867* allows the federal government to pass labour legislation (e.g., the *Canada Labour Code*) for companies that operate interprovincially, and allowed the provincial governments to pass legislation (e.g., the Ontario Labour Relations Act) for companies that operate in only one province.

LO-9 IDENTIFY THE STEPS IN THE *COLLECTIVE BARGAINING PROCESS.*

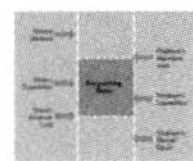

Once certified, the union engages in collective bargaining with the organization. The initial step is reaching agreement on a *labour contract*. Contract demands usually involve wages, job security, or management rights. Both labour and management have several tactics that can be used against the other if negotiations break down. Unions may attempt a *strike*, a *boycott*, or a *work slowdown*. Companies may hire *strikebreakers* or *lockout* workers. Sometimes *mediation* or *arbitration* may be used to settle disputes.

QUESTIONS AND EXERCISES

QUESTIONS FOR ANALYSIS

1. Why is the formal training of workers so important to most employers? Why don't employers simply let people learn about their jobs as they perform them?
2. Why is a good employee–job match important? Who benefits more, the organization or the employee? Explain your reasoning.
3. How is it possible for unemployment to be high while at the same time companies are complaining that they are having trouble hiring people?
4. Obtain a copy of an employment application. What are its strengths and weaknesses in terms of helping a company to decide whether to hire the applicant?
5. Why do you think the unionization rate in the public sector is so much higher than in the private sector? Do you think this will change in the foreseeable future? Explain your reasoning.
6. Consider the following statement: *In a union shop, newly hired employees must join the union within 30 days of starting work. Forcing workers to join a union in order to keep their job is unreasonable and violates their freedom of choice. Workers should be allowed to decide whether they want to join a union or not. Union shops should therefore not be allowed.* Do you agree or disagree? Explain your reasoning.

APPLICATION EXERCISES

7. Interview a human resource manager at a local company. Select a position for which the firm is currently recruiting applicants and identify the steps in the selection process. Do the steps match those shown in Figure 8.1? Why or why not?
8. Survey ten of your acquaintances and determine (a) how important benefits are to them as opposed to salary, (b) the benefits they think are the least and most important in attracting and keeping workers, (c) the extent to which their opinions about benefits versus salary will influence their choice of an employer after graduation.
9. Select a job currently held by you or a close friend. Draw up a job description and job specification for this position.
10. Interview the managers at two local companies, one unionized and one non-unionized. Compare the wage and salary levels, benefits, and working conditions at the two firms. Do you find any differences? If so, what are they?

TEAM EXERCISES

BUILDING YOUR BUSINESS SKILLS

STARTING FROM SCRATCH

GOAL

To help you understand job analysis and the process of recruiting and selecting employees.

THE SITUATION

You are an employee at a growing home improvement contractor. The company has recently moved to a new office space, complete with a showroom highlighting some of the company's work. There are 15 employees, including the president, sales staff, and accounting department. The company has decided to hire a receptionist who can greet prospective customers and assist in social networking and other marketing activities.

ASSIGNMENT

Form groups of three to five students who will play the role of "co-workers" on a hiring committee. The committee's task is to complete the process of job analysis, creating a job description and job specification for the receptionist position. Because this is a completely new position, you are starting from scratch. As a group, develop a job description that clearly explains the duties of the job; its working conditions; and the tools, materials, and equipment that are used to do the job. Be specific. Once this is complete, your group must agree on a job specification which lists the skills, abilities, and other credentials the person needs to do the job.

QUESTIONS FOR DISCUSSION

1. What is the most difficult part of developing a job description? Do you feel that you needed any additional information?
2. When developing the job specification, how did your group determine the education and experience necessary for the job?
3. Because this is an entry-level position, it is likely that you will receive a large number of applications. How will you screen the applications and decide who to interview? What knowledge, skills, or abilities will be most important in the person that you hire?

EXERCISING YOUR ETHICS

HANDLING THE LAYOFFS

THE SITUATION

The CEO of a moderate-sized company is developing a plan for laying off employees. He wants each manager to rank his or her employees according to the order in which they should be laid off, from first to last.

THE DILEMMA

One manager has just asked for help. He is new to his position and has little experience to draw from. The members of the manager's team are as follows:

- *Tony Jones.* White male, 10 years with the company, average performer, reportedly drinks a lot after work.
- *Amanda Wiggens.* White female, very ambitious, 3 years with the company, above-average performer, puts in extra time at work; is known to be abrasive when dealing with others.
- *George Sinclair.* Aboriginal, 20 years with the company, average performer, was previously laid off but called back when business picked up.
- *Dorothy Henderson.* White female, 25 years with the company, below-average performer, has filed five sexual harassment complaints in the last 10 years.
- *Wanda Jackson.* Black female, 8 years with the company, outstanding performer, is rumoured to be looking for another job.
- *Jerry Loudder.* White male, single parent, 5 years with the company, average performer.
- *Martha Strawser.* White female, 6 years with company, excellent performer but spotty attendance, is putting husband through university.

TEAM ACTIVITY

Assemble a group of four students. Your group has agreed to provide the manager with a suggested rank ordering of the manager's employees.

ACTION STEPS

1. Working together, prepare this list, ranking the manager's employees according to the order in which they should be laid off, from first to last. Identify any disagreements that occurred along the way, and indicate how they were resolved.
2. As a group, discuss the underlying ethical issues in this situation and write them down.
3. As a group, brainstorm any legal issues involved in this situation and write them down.
4. Do the ethical and legal implications of your choices always align?
5. Do the ethical and performance implications of your choices always align?

BUSINESS CASE 8

IS A NEW ERA OF LABOUR RELATIONS DAWNING AT AIR CANADA?

In 2014, Air Canada and one of its unions, the Air Canada Pilots Association (ACPA), signed a new, ten-year collective agreement. The signing came after a decade of very poor labour relations between Air Canada and ACPA. There were also confrontations with several other unions representing Air Canada's employees during that period. The agreement with the pilots was surprising, since it was signed 18 months before their existing contract expired. The president of the union said that over the previous decade, the union had learned that confrontation had not benefited either the union or the company.

The disputes between Air Canada and its unions became very public in 2003 when Air Canada was losing money at the rate of $5 million each *day*. To reduce costs, Air Canada laid off large numbers of people, reduced employee benefits, and increased the number of required work hours. Not surprisingly, union workers didn't take kindly to these actions. Robert Milton, who was the CEO of Air Canada at that time, blamed the unions for the mess the company found itself in, and claimed that the unions did not take seriously his warnings that major reductions in labour costs were necessary in order for Air Canada to survive. Union leaders complained that Milton had "put a gun to their heads" by telling them to surrender their contract rights or the company would be put in bankruptcy protection. Air Canada went through bankruptcy proceedings in 2004. As part of those proceedings, the unions made a variety of concessions to the company.

Over the next few years, a series of highly public confrontations took place between Air Canada and its unions. In 2005, unionized ground crews at Air Canada were involved in a wildcat (unauthorized) strike over allegations that some employees were punching out the time cards of their co-workers. The strike grounded or delayed more than 60 flights.

In 2008, members of the International Association of Machinists and Aerospace Workers (IAMAW) wore buttons with the message "Prepare to walk the line in '09" as the expiry date of their collective agreement neared. Air Canada management accused the union of trying to prejudice the bargaining process and ordered workers to stop wearing the buttons when they were in view of Air Canada's customers. The union then filed a grievance, saying the buttons were simply an attempt to promote solidarity among union members. The union also created a combative song which they sang to the tune of Johnny Cash's famous 1950's hit "I Walk the Line."

Also in 2008, management and labour could not reach an agreement about severance packages that would be given to Air Canada employees who lost their job when the company cut 2000 jobs. An arbitrator therefore imposed a decision that was binding on both parties.

Carolyn Franks/Shutterstock

In the summer of 2011, the unions representing flight attendants and service employees reached agreement with Air Canada on the terms of a new collective agreement, but both unions rejected the company's proposal to put new hires into a defined contribution pension plan, rather than a defined benefit plan that was standard at that time. That matter also went before an arbitrator for resolution.

The confrontation between management and labour really heated up in 2012. In March, Air Canada's dispute with its machinists union was sent to binding arbitration after the machinists voted to go on strike. Also in March, three Air Canada workers were fired after they heckled the Labour Minister while she was walking through the Toronto airport. The workers were upset that the federal government had just passed back-to-work legislation that prevented the machinists from going on strike. A wildcat (unauthorized) strike then ensued which grounded flights across the country.

In April 2012, numerous pilots called in sick and did not report for work, so Air Canada got an order from the Canadian Industrial Relations Board declaring that job action to be illegal. The sickout forced Air Canada to cancel flights across the country.

Also in April 2012, Air Canada threatened to fire the president of the pilots' union, alleging that he had questioned the safety of Air Canada's maintenance operations in a televised interview on CBC. The president of the union made the remarks after a dispute developed about Air Canada's plan to outsource some maintenance work.

In May 2012, the federal Minister of Labour appointed arbitrators to impose a settlement in Air Canada's disputes with both pilots and machinists. The arbitrator eventually accepted Air Canada's offer in its entirety. That resolution allowed Air Canada to pursue the formation of a new low-cost carrier called Rouge. That new airline pays its employees less than union members at Air Canada.

A 2013 survey conducted by the Air Canada Pilots Association in the aftermath of the tense situation in 2012 showed that 86 percent of the pilots did not trust Air Canada. More surprisingly, 77 percent said they didn't trust their own union either. The results of this survey were similar to another survey conducted by CUPE, which represents Air Canada's flight attendants. On a more positive note, 58 percent of the pilots said they wanted a more cooperative and less combative relationship with Air Canada.

On January 1, 2013, Craig Blandford was elected president of the ACPA. He recognized that some union members were still resentful about the concessions made to Air Canada during the restructuring in 2004, but he also said members would have to realize that the union would not be successful unless Air Canada was a profitable company. He noted that the success of the new, low-cost carrier Rouge was an important element in Air Canada's profitability because it would help Air Canada expand its markets.

QUESTIONS FOR DISCUSSION

1. What proportion of the blame for Air Canada's difficulties rests with the top management of Air Canada, and what proportion rests with the company's unions? Defend your answer.
2. Air Canada has had a difficult relationship with its unions in the past. What can management and labour do to increase the chance that the two groups will work together more smoothly in the future? Describe both general and specific actions that might be taken.
3. As a result of the 2004 bankruptcy proceedings at Air Canada, workers reluctantly agreed to job cuts in various areas so that Air Canada could reduce its labour costs. Do you think agreements like that may cause workers in Canada to be less likely to join unions because they fear the union will not be able to protect their jobs if times get tough at a company?
4. Consider the following statement: *If a company encounters financial difficulties, it should be allowed to change the provisions of a collective agreement with its labour unions.* Do you agree or disagree? Explain your reasoning.

micromonkey/Fotolia

Motivating, Satisfying, *and* Leading Employees

CHAPTER 

LO

AFTER READING THIS CHAPTER, YOU SHOULD BE ABLE TO:

- LO-1 Identify and discuss the basic *forms of behaviour* that employees exhibit in organizations.
- LO-2 Describe the nature and importance of *individual differences* among employees.
- LO-3 Explain the meaning and importance of *psychological contracts* and the person–job fit in the workplace.
- LO-4 Identify and summarize the most important models of *employee motivation*.
- LO-5 Describe the *strategies* used by organizations to improve job satisfaction and employee motivation.
- LO-6 Define *leadership* and distinguish it from *management*.
- LO-7 Summarize the *approaches to leadership* that developed during the twentieth century.
- LO-8 Describe the most recent ideas about effective leadership.

Satisfaction, Productivity, and Employee Engagement

Managers would like answers to two important questions: (1) Are *satisfied* (happy) employees more productive than unsatisfied (unhappy) employees? (2) How important is *employee engagement* in generating satisfaction and productivity?

ragsac/123RF

Are Satisfied Employees More Productive?

There is a "chicken and egg" element to this question, so we have to ask what comes first: employee satisfaction or employee productivity? Some managers think that satisfied employees are more productive *because* they are satisfied (i.e., satisfaction causes productivity), while others think that employees are satisfied *because* they are productive (i.e., productivity causes satisfaction). Managers who hold the "satisfaction causes productivity" belief argue that employees who are not happy doing their daily work tasks will not be very productive because they'll just be working because they have to. Alexander Kjerulf, the founder and Chief Happiness Officer of Spoing!, a Danish consulting firm, says "The productivity gurus out there will tell you that it's all about having the right system . . . [But] no system, no tool, or methodology in the world can beat the productivity boost you get from really, really enjoying your work. Happiness at work is the #1 productivity booster." Kjerulf cites a number of reasons why this is true: happy people work better with others, fix problems rather than complaining about them, make better decisions, are more optimistic, are more motivated, have more energy, and get sick less often. But Kjerfulf does admit that causation goes both ways to some extent. But he thinks the strongest flow is from happiness to productivity.

One person who disagrees with this view is Paul Larson, a veteran of operations management in a variety of industries. "The legend that happy workers are productive employees has been a part of our organizational thinking for so long that many just take for granted that it has to be true." He agrees that productive workers seem happier than unproductive ones, but concludes that "productivity leads to satisfaction, not the other way around. This is because people who do a good job tend to feel intrinsically good about it."

HOW WILL THIS HELP ME?

The connections employees have with their jobs can go a long way toward determining how happy they are with their work. Some people love their jobs, while others hate theirs. Most people, however, fall somewhere in between. After studying the information in this chapter, you'll be better able to understand (1) your own feelings toward your work from the perspective of an *employee*, (2) the feelings of others toward their work from the perspective of a *manager* or an *owner*, (3) how you can more effectively function as a *leader*, and (4) how your manager or boss strives to motivate you through his or her own leadership.

It is obvious that the relationship between happiness and productivity is complicated. Because of that, we need to consider another factor that might help to clarify the situation. This is where *engagement* comes in. Charles Kerns, a professor at the Graziado School of Business and Management at Pepperdine University, says that managers should focus on both happiness and productivity, and this can be accomplished by emphasizing employee engagement. Engagement can be measured by the extent to which an individual has more happy or positive experiences than negative ones, and the key to increasing positive experiences is engaging an employee's strengths. "An employee's level of engagement . . . and subsequent happiness is likely boosted when he or she has the opportunity to do what he or she does best at work. Utilizing one's strengths is a positive experience." Thus, engagement is not about making employees happy. Rather, it's about having employees who are committed to being highly productive.

How Important Is Employee Engagement?

In a recent Psychometrics Canada poll of 368 Canadian HR managers, 69 percent of respondents said that low employee engagement was a problem in their organization, and 82 percent felt that company management should be doing more to increase employee engagement. The respondents also expressed the opinion that managers should give employees more recognition and praise (58 percent), should listen more to employee opinions (71 percent), and should provide employees with more learning and development opportunities (57 percent).

Another survey—this one involving 30 000 workers in 17 different countries—also found reason for concern about employee engagement. The survey, which was conducted by the global consulting firm Mercer, defined employee engagement as a situation where employees have a vested interest in a company's success, and are motivated to perform at levels that exceed stated job requirements. The survey found that one-third of workers are seriously considering leaving their current employer, and that there has been a decline in employee engagement since 2005 when a similar survey was conducted. Declines were evident in (1) the sense of commitment employees felt to their organization, (2) the pride they had in their organization, (3) employee willingness to go beyond stated job requirements, and (4) the feeling of accomplishment that employees got from their job.

A 2013 Gallup poll that included the results of several different studies showed that businesses that scored in the top half of an employee-engagement ranking system were nearly twice as likely to be successful than companies in the bottom half of the ranking. Telus Corp.'s experience is illustrative. Its score increased from 53 percent in 2007 to 85 percent in 2014. The increase in the score was accompanied by lower turnover rates among its employees, higher customer satisfaction, and a boost in the company's stock price.

A lack of employee engagement is a serious problem, because employees are a great source of ideas for improving company productivity. Consider these examples:

- At Algoma Steel, a shop floor employee came up with a more efficient process for producing heat-treated steel plates that resulted in $90 million in additional revenue for the company.
- At ISL Engineering and Land Services, a senior urban designer was interested in making the company "greener," but he didn't want to force the idea on employees from the top down. Rather, he wanted them to help develop ideas. So 25 employees known to be particularly keen about sustainability were named "green champions." They were encouraged to spend up to 10 percent of their time every day working on environmental issues.
- When Razor Suleman, the CEO of I Love Rewards, noticed employee morale and motivation issues in his company, he decided to directly involve 10 to 12 current employees to interview prospective new employees. The process means that employees essentially "sell" the company to applicants, and by having staff members directly involved in hiring, it helps ensure that new hires will be a "fit" with the company culture. Employee engagement also extends to participation in objective setting, reinforced by an employee share ownership program. Employees are also privy to the company's financial statements and can query management on any budget line expense.

Brad Hams, an organizational change expert, says that employee engagement is typically low because business owners and employees have different perspectives. Owners are concerned about things like profit, cash flow, and cost control, while employees are concerned about things like pay, benefits, and job security. Employee engagement can be increased by giving employees the right incentives (so that they benefit when company performance improves), providing the right education for employees (so that they understand how the business works), and adopting the right performance measures (to help employees accurately monitor their performance).

Another way to increase employee engagement is to use social media. When social media first came on the scene, businesses saw it as a tool for marketing the company's products and services to external groups like customers. But now managers are realizing that social media can be helpful in connecting workers with each other. A survey by International Association of Business Communicators found that 70 percent of companies use social media for internal communications (up from 45 percent the previous year).

About 75 percent of Canadian workers now use social networking sites while on the job. A poll conducted by Robert Half Technology of Canada asked information officers at 270 companies about their company's policy on the use of social media at work. Forty-four percent of the companies allowed employees to use social media sites such as Twitter, Facebook, and LinkedIn for business purposes (up from 22 percent a year earlier). About one-third of the companies still prohibit the use of social media in the office (down from 58 percent a year earlier).

Many companies are taking very specific actions to capitalize on the employee engagement characteristics of social media. At Toronto-Dominion bank, the company's internal website has been made into a social media platform that includes blogs, chat forums, surveys, and a feature that allows employees to leave comments on blog pages, news items, and memos. Wendy Arnott, the vice-president of social media and digital communications, says social media are a great way to increase employee engagement.

mocker bat/Fotolia

Sun Life Financial Inc. also uses social media—blogs, online communities, and wikis—to get ideas from employees, and the company has pilot-tested a social media feature that allows employees to respond to the ideas of colleagues. Sun's social media site also allows each employee to develop a personal profile, and this helps managers find people with certain skills that are needed for specific projects. Managers have also noticed that the more casual nature of social media encourages timid employees to speak up and become engaged, whereas they often wouldn't do so in formal meetings.

QUESTIONS FOR DISCUSSION

1. How do you think happiness and productivity relate to one another? Defend your answer.
2. What factors influence your happiness on the job?
3. Consider the following statement: *The use of social media by employees is harmful to productivity because employees are distracted from their work and spend too much time on personal matters instead.* Do you agree or disagree? Support your position.
4. Consider the following statement: *Since companies provide jobs for people, the company has every right to expect that employees will do things like sharing their job knowledge with their co-workers and with management, because doing so will make the company more successful and allow it to continue to provide jobs.* Do you agree or disagree? Explain your reasoning.

LO-1 FORMS OF EMPLOYEE BEHAVIOUR

Employee behaviour is the pattern of actions by the members of an organization that directly or indirectly influences the organization's effectiveness. Performance behaviours are those that are directly involved in performing a job. An assembly-line worker who sits by a moving conveyor and attaches parts to a product as it passes by has relatively simple performance behaviours, but a research-and-development scientist who works in a lab trying to find new scientific breakthroughs that have commercial potential has much more complex performance behaviours.

Other behaviours—called organizational citizenship—provide positive benefits to the organization in more indirect ways. An employee who does satisfactory work in terms of quantity and quality, but refuses to work overtime, won't help newcomers learn the ropes, and is generally

EMPLOYEE BEHAVIOUR The pattern of actions by the members of an organization that directly or indirectly influences the organization's effectiveness.

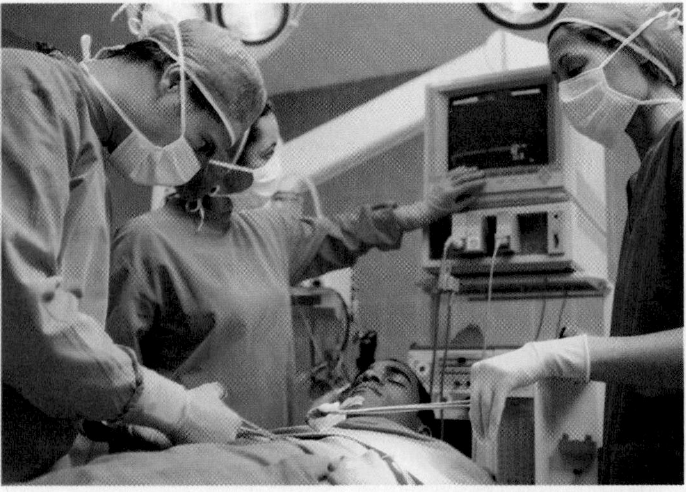

For some jobs (e.g., assembly-line work), performance behaviours can be narrowly defined and easily measured. For many other jobs (e.g., research scientists or doctors), performance behaviours are less objective, more diverse, and more difficult to assess.

Ryan Remiorz/The Canadian Press; wavebreakmedia/Shutterstock

unwilling to make any contribution beyond the strict performance requirements of the job is not a good organizational citizen. In contrast, an employee with a satisfactory level of performance who works late when the boss asks and takes time to help newcomers learn their way around is a good organizational citizen.

Counterproductive behaviours are those that detract from organizational performance. Absenteeism occurs when an employee does not show up for work. When an employee is absent, legitimately or not, that person's work does not get done and a substitute must be hired to do it, or others in the organization must pick up the slack. Tardiness is also a counterproductive behaviour. A survey conducted by CareerBuilder.com revealed that 19 percent of workers admitted being late for work at least once a week.[1]

Turnover occurs when people quit their jobs. It results from a number of factors, including the nature of the job, the nature of supervision, a poor person–job fit, the external labour market, and family influences. One survey of 660 workers showed that 84 percent who worked for a "kind" manager planned to stay with their company a long time, while only 47 percent of those who worked for a "bully" said they planned to stay.[2]

Other forms of counterproductive behaviour are also costly. Theft and sabotage, for example, result in direct financial costs for an organization. Sexual and racial harassment also cost an organization, both directly (through financial liability if the organization responds inappropriately) and indirectly (by lowering morale, producing fear, and driving off valuable employees). Workplace aggression and violence are also counterproductive.

COUNTERPRODUCTIVE BEHAVIOURS Behaviours that detract from organizational performance.

LO-2 INDIVIDUAL DIFFERENCES AMONG EMPLOYEES

Individual differences are physical, psychological, and emotional attributes that vary from one person to another. The individual differences that characterize a specific person make that person unique. Personality and attitudes are two main categories of individual differences.

Personality

Personality is the relatively stable set of psychological attributes that distinguish one person from another. In recent years, researchers have identified five fundamental traits that are especially relevant to organizations. These "big five" traits (shown in Figure 9.1) can be summarized as follows:

- *Agreeableness* is a person's ability to get along with others. A person with a high level of agreeableness is gentle, cooperative, forgiving, understanding, and good-natured in their dealings with others. A person with a low level of agreeableness is often irritable, short-tempered, uncooperative, and generally antagonistic toward other people. Highly agreeable people are better at developing good working relationships with co-workers, whereas less agreeable people are not likely to have particularly good working relationships.
- *Conscientiousness* refers to the number of things a person tries to accomplish. Highly conscientious people tend to focus on relatively few tasks at one time; as a result, they are likely to be organized, systematic, careful, thorough, responsible, and self-disciplined.

INDIVIDUAL DIFFERENCES Personal attributes that vary from one person to another.

PERSONALITY The relatively stable set of psychological attributes that distinguish one person from another.

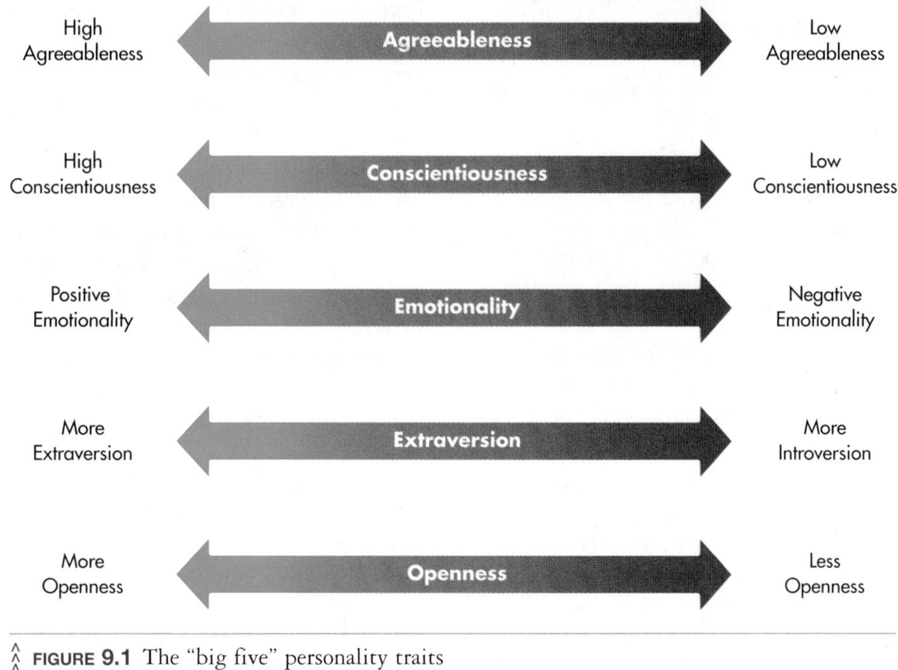

FIGURE 9.1 The "big five" personality traits

Less conscientious people tend to pursue a wider array of tasks; as a result, they are often more disorganized and irresponsible, as well as less thorough and self-disciplined. Highly conscientious people tend to be relatively higher performers in a variety of different jobs.

- *Emotionality* refers to the degree to which people tend to be positive or negative in their outlook and behaviours toward others. People with positive emotionality are relatively poised, calm, resilient, and secure; people with negative emotionality are more excitable, insecure, reactive, and subject to mood swings. People with positive emotionality are better able to handle job stress, pressure, and tension. Their stability might also cause them to be seen as more reliable than their less stable counterparts.
- *Extraversion* refers to a person's comfort level with relationships. Extroverts are sociable, talkative, assertive, and open to establishing new relationships, while introverts are much less sociable, talkative, and assertive, and more reluctant to begin new relationships. Extroverts tend to be higher overall job performers than introverts and are more likely to be attracted to jobs based on personal relationships, such as sales and marketing positions.
- *Openness* reflects how open or rigid a person is in terms of his or her beliefs. People with high levels of openness are curious and willing to listen to new ideas and to change their own ideas, beliefs, and attitudes in response to new information. People with low levels of openness tend to be less receptive to new ideas and less willing to change their minds. People with more openness are often better performers due to their flexibility and the likelihood that they will be better accepted by others in the organization.

EMOTIONAL INTELLIGENCE

Emotional intelligence, or **emotional quotient (EQ)**, refers to the extent to which people possess social skills, are self-aware, can manage their emotions, can motivate themselves, and can express empathy for others.[3] Research suggests that people with high EQs may perform better than others, especially in jobs that require a high degree of interpersonal interaction and that involve influencing or directing the work of others. EQ appears to be something that isn't biologically based, but that can be developed.[4] A survey of 2660 managers conducted by CareerBuilder.com found that 34 percent of hiring managers put a high priority on emotional intelligence when making hiring decisions. Seventy-one percent of the respondents placed a higher priority on emotional intelligence than on mental intelligence when making hiring decisions.[5]

Other Personality Traits

Several other personality traits influence behaviour in organizations: locus of control, self-efficacy, authoritarianism, Machiavellianism, self-esteem, and risk propensity.

Locus of control is the extent to which a person believes that their behaviour has a real effect on what happens to them.[6] Individuals with an *internal locus of control* believe that they control what happens to them. For example, they believe that if they work hard they will get a promotion. Individuals with an *external locus of control* believe that fate or luck controls what happens to them. For example, an employee who does not get a promotion may attribute it to the manipulative political behaviour of others.

Self-efficacy is a person's belief about his or her capabilities to perform a task. People with high self-efficacy believe that they can perform well on a specific task, but people with low self-efficacy have doubts about their ability to perform a specific task. A person's belief in their ability to perform a task results in their being more self-assured and better able to focus their attention on performance.[7]

Authoritarianism is the extent to which a person believes that power and status differences are appropriate within social systems such as organizations.[8] An employee who is highly authoritarian may accept directives or orders from someone with more authority purely because the other person is "the boss." But an employee who is not highly authoritarian is more likely to question things or express disagreement with the boss. A highly authoritarian boss will expect subordinates to follow orders, but a less highly authoritarian boss may encourage subordinate input into decisions.

Machiavellianism refers to behaviour designed to gain power and control.[9] Individuals high in Machiavellianism tend to be rational and nonemotional, may be willing to lie to attain their personal goals, put little emphasis on loyalty and friendship, and enjoy manipulating other people. Individuals low in Machiavellianism have the opposite characteristics.

Self-esteem is the extent to which a person believes that he or she is a worthwhile and deserving individual. A person with high self-esteem is more likely to seek higher-status jobs, be more confident in his or her ability to achieve higher levels of performance, and focus on intrinsic satisfaction like feeling good about doing useful work. By contrast, a person with low self-esteem may be more content to remain in a lower-level job, be less confident of his or her ability, and focus more on extrinsic rewards such as money. Research suggests that the role of self-esteem is important in organizations in many different cultures.

Risk propensity is the degree to which a person is willing to take chances and make risky decisions. A manager with a high risk propensity is willing to experiment with new ideas, gamble on new products, and take financial risks. If these initiatives are successful, the organization will benefit, but if they are not, the organization will suffer. By contrast, a manager with low risk propensity is reluctant to experiment with new ideas, gamble on new products, or take financial risks. This may result in a lack of new initiatives, which may either maintain organizational stability or cause the organization to fail because it does not change with the times.

Attitudes at Work

People's attitudes affect their behaviour in organizations. **Attitudes** reflect our beliefs and feelings about specific ideas, situations, or other people. People in organizations have attitudes about many different things: their salary, their promotion possibilities, their boss, their employee benefits, and so on.

Attitudes are formed by a variety of forces, including our personal values, our experiences, and our personalities. For example, if an employee values honesty and integrity, that employee may develop a favourable attitude toward managers who are honest and moral. Or, if an employee has an unpleasant experience with a co-worker, that employee is likely to develop a negative attitude toward that co-worker.

Attitudes contain three components: cognition, affect, and intention. *Cognition* is the knowledge a person has about someone or something. For example, you may like a class because the textbook is interesting, the

EMOTIONAL INTELLIGENCE (EMOTIONAL QUOTIENT [EQ]) The extent to which people are self-aware, can manage their emotions, can motivate themselves, express empathy for others, and possess social skills.

ATTITUDES A person's beliefs and feelings about specific ideas, situations, or people.

class meets at a convenient time for you, the instructor is knowledgeable, and the workload is light. Cognitions are based on perceptions about reality, and perceptions agree with reality to varying degrees. When two sets of cognitions or perceptions are contradictory or incongruent, a person experiences *cognitive dissonance*. Cognitive dissonance also occurs when people behave in a way that is inconsistent with their attitudes. For example, a person who thinks that smoking and overeating are dangerous may nevertheless do both because the person finds the behaviour pleasurable. The person may try to reduce the associated anxiety and discomfort by, for example, deciding to go on a diet (but not until next week!).

A person's *affect* is his or her feelings toward someone or something. For example, you may like one of your classes and dislike another one. If the class you dislike is an elective, you may not be particularly concerned about your participation or your final grade. But if the class you like is required for your major, you may work very hard to get a good grade.

Intention guides a person's behaviour. If you like a certain instructor, you may intend to take another class from that instructor next term. But intentions are not always translated into actual behaviour. If the instructor's course next term is scheduled for 8:30 a.m., you may decide that it is not convenient for you take it.

Two key attitudes are job satisfaction and organizational commitment.

- **Job satisfaction** reflects the extent to which people have positive attitudes toward their jobs. (A related concept—morale—refers to the overall attitude people have toward their workplace.) A Workopolis survey of 577 Canadians showed that 53 percent loved their jobs, 16 percent kept their job simply because it helped pay the bills, and 14 percent felt their current job might lead to something better.[10] A survey of workers in 23 countries found that workers in Norway, Denmark, and Canada were the most satisfied with their current employer.[11] Satisfied employees tend to be absent less often, to be good organizational citizens, and to stay with the organization. Dissatisfied employees may be absent more often, may experience stress that disrupts co-workers, and may be continually looking for another job. Contrary to what a lot of managers believe, however, high levels of job satisfaction do not automatically lead to high levels of productivity.
- **Organizational commitment** (also called *job commitment*) reflects an individual's identification with the organization and its mission. Highly committed employees see themselves as true members of the firm, overlook minor sources of dissatisfaction, and see themselves remaining members of the organization. Less committed employees are more likely to see themselves as outsiders, to express more dissatisfaction about the work situation, and to not see themselves as long-term members of the organization. One way to increase employee commitment is to give employees a voice. BBVA, Spain's second-largest bank, accomplishes this by including employees in the performance evaluation process. Not only is the employee's own self-evaluation considered, but co-workers also answer questions about each employee's performance. Infosys Technologies in Bangalore, India, started a Voice of Youth program, which gives top-performing young employees a seat on its management council.[12]

Sometimes employees make disparaging comments about the company they work for, or about their co-workers or managers. Even if this happens when the employee is not at work, managers may see it as a sign of poor organizational commitment. The boxed insert entitled "Employers Are Judging Your Social Life" describes several of these incidents.

JOB SATISFACTION The extent to which people have positive attitudes toward their jobs.

ORGANIZATIONAL COMMITMENT An individual's identification with the organization and its mission.

E-BUSINESS AND SOCIAL MEDIA SOLUTIONS

Employers Are Judging Your Social Life

In May 2015, there was a high-profile reminder that what you say and do outside your workplace can affect your career. While attending a Toronto FC soccer match, Shawn Simoes was caught on TV making obscene comments to a CityTV news reporter. The incident went viral and within hours Simoes had been dismissed from his job at Hydro One. Mr. Simoes was not at the game in an official work capacity, nor was he there with a client. The on-camera comments were very offensive and juvenile. His employer made a clear statement that such behaviour would not be tolerated no matter what the setting. This incident shows that your behaviour can negatively influence your work, even if the incident does not occur while you are at work.

Not every immature comment gets broadcast on the news, but every day people post comments on social media sites like Facebook and Twitter that can damage their job prospects. An estimated 93 percent of recruiters check the social media profiles of potential recruits. A potential employer may not tell you that you didn't get the job because of the drunken, embarrassing picture you posted (from that wild party three years ago), but make no mistake, quite often these images are a determining factor. While the dangers are particularly clear for younger workers who have embraced this technology, this is a cautionary note for all workers.

- A British teen was fired from a marketing job after describing it as extremely "dull," even though she didn't mention the name of the company she worked for. Her colleagues and boss saw the post on Facebook and that was enough to relieve her of her "boring" job.
- Two employees at a car dealership near Vancouver were fired after they posted extremely negative comments about their employer and the managers at the company. The workers complained about the legitimacy of the decision, but the British Columbia Labour Relations Board upheld their dismissal.

Employer interests seem to be well protected in Canada. Up to this point the labour tribunals have supported the management position and indicated that such acts violate the legal "duty of loyalty." Of course, this is a new and quickly evolving area of labour relations, so the challenges will continue. However, watch what you say in public and what you write in your social media posts because you may be judged.

CRITICAL THINKING QUESTION

1. Do you believe that employers should have the right to terminate an employee based on comments the employee made in a private setting or on Twitter or Facebook posts?

LO-3 MATCHING PEOPLE AND JOBS

Given the array of individual differences that exist across people and the many different forms of employee behaviour that can occur in organizations, it is important to have a good match between people and the jobs they are performing. Two key methods for facilitating this match are psychological contracts and the person–job fit.

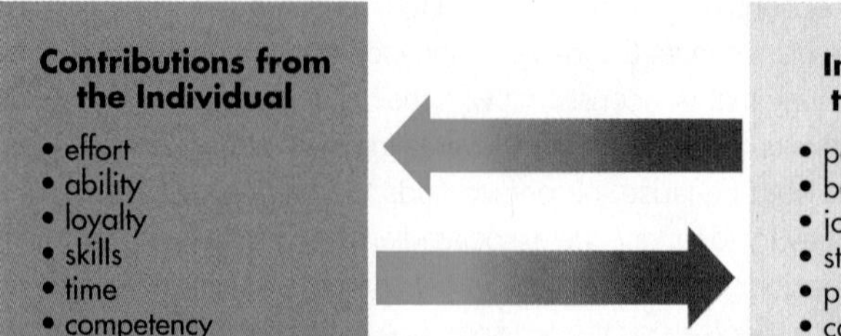

FIGURE 9.2 The psychological contract

Psychological Contracts

A **psychological contract** is the set of expectations held by an employee concerning what he or she will contribute to an organization (referred to as *contributions*) and what the organization will provide to the employee (referred to as *inducements*). If either party perceives an inequity in the contract, that party may seek a change. The employee, for example, might ask for a pay raise, a promotion, or a bigger office, or might put forth less effort or look for a better job elsewhere. The organization can also initiate change by training workers to improve their skills, transferring them to new jobs, or terminating them. Unlike a business contract, a psychological contract is not written on paper, nor are all of its terms explicitly negotiated. Figure 9.2 illustrates the essential features of a psychological contract.

The downsizing and cutbacks that have occurred in Canadian businesses in recent years have complicated the process of managing psychological contracts. Many organizations, for example, used to offer at least some assurance of job security as a fundamental inducement to employees. Now, however, because job security is lower, alternative inducements (like improved benefits, more flexible working hours, bonuses, and so on) may be needed.

The Person–Job Fit

The **person–job fit** refers to the extent to which a person's contributions and the organization's inducements match one another. Each employee has a specific set of needs that he or she wants fulfilled, and a set of job-related behaviours and abilities to contribute. If the organization can take perfect advantage of those behaviours and abilities and exactly fulfill those needs, it will have achieved a perfect person–job fit. A good person–job fit can result in higher performance and more positive attitudes, whereas a poor person–job fit can have just the opposite effect.

PSYCHOLOGICAL CONTRACT The set of expectations held by an employee concerning what he or she will contribute to an organization (contributions) and what the organization will provide the employee (inducements) in return.

PERSON–JOB FIT The extent to which a person's contributions and the organization's inducements match one another.

Person–job fit is an important consideration when hiring people for specific jobs. Some might thrive working in extreme weather, travelling most of the time, or performing risky tasks (like this window washer), but others will prefer far less "exciting" jobs.

Sergey Smirnov/Alamy

MOTIVATION IN THE WORKPLACE

Motivation means the set of forces that causes people to behave in certain ways. While one worker may be motivated to work hard to produce as much as possible, another may be motivated to do just enough to get by. As we saw in the opening case, effective managers recognize that different employees have different needs and are motivated by different things. One company that stopped handing out T-shirts with the company logo on them found that professional workers didn't much care, but immigrant workers in entry-level jobs were unhappy because the T-shirts had symbolic value for them (the shirts apparently made them feel like they belonged in Canada).[13] This example, and thousands more, show that managers must think very carefully about how to motivate employees.

MOTIVATION The set of forces that causes people to behave in certain ways.

Over the past century, many theories have been proposed to explain the complex issue of motivation. In this section, we will focus on three major approaches that reflect a chronology of thinking in the area of motivation: classical theory, early behavioural theory, and contemporary motivational theories.

Classical Theory

In the **classical theory of motivation**, it is assumed that workers are motivated solely by money. In his book *The Principles of Scientific Management* (1911), industrial engineer Frederick Taylor proposed a way for both companies and workers to benefit from this view of life in the workplace.[14] If workers are motivated by money, Taylor reasoned, then paying them more would prompt them to produce more. Meanwhile, the firm that analyzed jobs and found better ways to perform them would be able to produce goods more cheaply, make higher profits, and thus pay—and motivate—workers better than its competitors.

Taylor's approach is known as scientific management, and his ideas captured the imagination of many managers in the early twentieth century. Soon, plants across Canada and the United States were hiring experts to perform time-and-motion studies, which were the first "scientific" attempts to break jobs down into easily repeated components and to devise more efficient tools and machines for performing them.[15] The results were impressive. For example, studies of workers loading iron onto rail cars showed that productivity tripled when scientific management principles were used.

Early Behavioural Theory

In 1925, a group of Harvard researchers began a study at the Hawthorne Works of the Western Electric Company. Their intent was to examine the relationship between changes in the physical environment and worker output, with an eye to increasing productivity. The results of the experiment at first confused, then amazed, the scientists. Increasing lighting levels improved productivity, but so did lowering lighting levels. And, against all expectations, raising the pay of workers failed to increase their productivity. Gradually, they pieced together the puzzle—the explanation for the contradictory findings lay in workers' response to the attention being paid to them. In essence, the researchers determined that almost any action on the part of management that made workers believe they were getting special attention caused their productivity to rise. This result, known as the **Hawthorne effect**, convinced many managers that paying attention to employees is indeed good for business.

The Hawthorne studies were an important step in developing an appreciation for the human factor at work. These women worked under different lighting conditions as researchers monitored their productivity. The researchers were amazed to find that productivity increased regardless of whether lighting levels increased or decreased.

Courtesy of AT&T Archives and History Center

Following the Hawthorne studies, managers and researchers alike focused more attention on how good *human relations*—the interactions between employers and employees and their attitudes toward one another—helped in motivating employees. Researchers eventually developed several now-classic motivation theories, including the *human resources model*, the *hierarchy of needs model*, *two-factor theory*, and *acquired needs theory*.

CLASSICAL THEORY OF MOTIVATION A theory of motivation that presumes workers are motivated almost solely by money.

HAWTHORNE EFFECT The tendency for workers' productivity to increase when they feel they are getting special attention from management.

LO-4 THE HUMAN RESOURCES MODEL: THEORIES X AND Y

Behavioural scientist Douglas McGregor concluded that managers had different beliefs about how best to use the human resources at a firm's disposal. He classified these beliefs into sets of assumptions that he labelled "Theory X" and "Theory Y."[16] Managers who subscribe to **Theory X** tend to believe that people are naturally lazy and uncooperative and must therefore be either punished or rewarded to be made productive. Managers who subscribe to **Theory Y** tend to believe that people are naturally energetic, growth-oriented, self-motivated, and interested in being productive.

McGregor generally favoured Theory Y beliefs, and argued that Theory Y managers are more likely to have satisfied, motivated employees. Of course, the model's distinctions are somewhat simplistic and offer little concrete basis for action. Their value lies primarily in their ability to highlight and analyze the behaviour of managers as a result of their attitudes toward employees.

THEORY X A management approach based on the belief that people must be forced to be productive because they are naturally lazy, irresponsible, and uncooperative.

THEORY Y A management approach based on the belief that people want to be productive because they are naturally energetic, responsible, and cooperative.

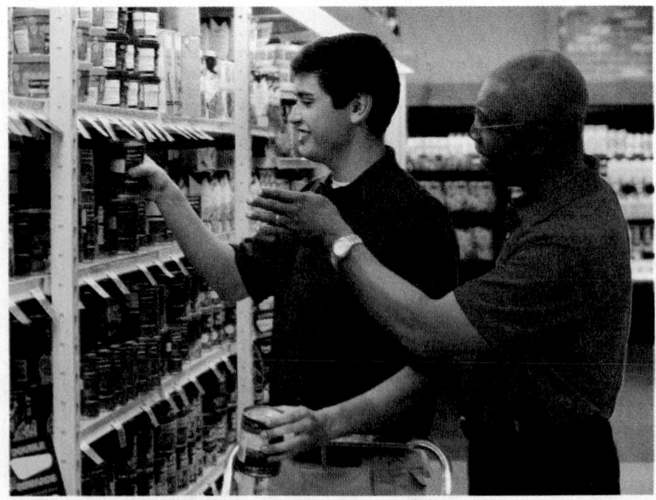

Treating employees with respect and recognizing that they are valuable members of the organization can go a long way toward motivating employees to perform at a high level.

Ariel Skelley/Blend Images/Alamy

MASLOW'S HIERARCHY OF HUMAN NEEDS MODEL

Psychologist Abraham Maslow's **hierarchy of human needs model** proposed that people have a number of different needs that they attempt to satisfy in their work.[17] He classified these needs into five basic types and suggested that they are arranged in a hierarchy of importance, in which lower-level needs must be met before a person will try to satisfy those on a higher level (see Figure 9.3).

- *Physiological needs* are those concerned with survival; they include food, water, shelter, and sleep. Businesses address these needs by providing both comfortable working environments and salaries sufficient to buy food and shelter.
- *Security needs* include the needs for stability and protection from the unknown. Many employers thus offer pension plans and job security.
- *Social needs* include the needs for friendship and companionship. Making friends at work can help to satisfy social needs, as can the feeling that you "belong" in a company.
- *Esteem needs* include the needs for status, recognition, and self-respect. Job titles and large offices are among the things that businesses can provide to address these needs.
- *Self-actualization needs* are needs for self-fulfillment. They include the needs to grow and develop one's capabilities and to achieve new and meaningful goals. Challenging job assignments can help satisfy these needs.

According to Maslow, once needs at one level have been satisfied, they cease to motivate behaviour. For example, if you feel secure in your job, a new pension plan will probably be less important to you than the chance to make new friends and join an informal network among your co-workers. If, however, a lower-level need suddenly becomes unfulfilled, most people immediately refocus on that lower level. For example, if you are trying to meet your esteem needs by working as a divisional manager at a major company and you learn that your division and your job may be

HIERARCHY OF HUMAN NEEDS MODEL Theory of motivation describing five levels of human needs and arguing that basic needs must be fulfilled before people work to satisfy higher-level needs.

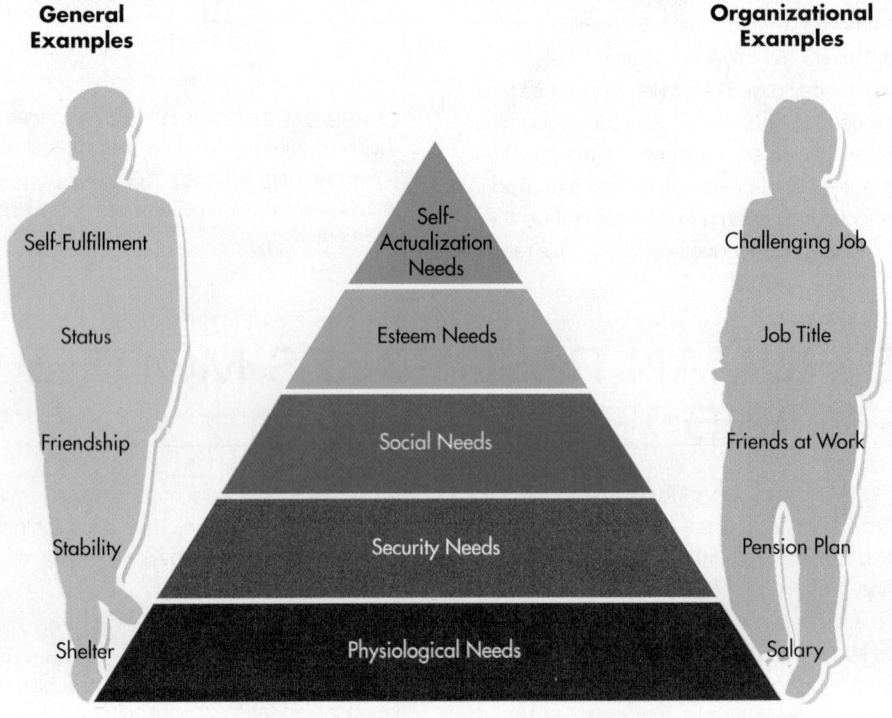

FIGURE 9.3 Maslow's hierarchy of human needs

Source: Maslow, Abraham H., Frager, Robert D., and Fadiman, James, *Motivation and Personality*, 3rd edition, © 1987. Adapted and electronically reproduced by permission of Pearson Education, Inc., Upper Saddle River, NJ.

eliminated, you might very well find the promise of job security at a new firm very motivating.

TWO-FACTOR (MOTIVATOR–HYGIENE) THEORY

After studying a group of accountants and engineers, psychologist Frederick Herzberg proposed the **two-factor theory**, which says that job satisfaction and dissatisfaction depend on two separate factors: *hygiene factors* (such as working conditions, quality of supervision, interpersonal relations, pay, and job security) and *motivating factors* (such as recognition, responsibility, advancement, and achievement).[18] Motivation factors cause movement along a continuum from no satisfaction to satisfaction. For example, if workers receive no recognition for successful work, they may not be satisfied, but neither will they be dissatisfied. If recognition is provided, they will likely become more satisfied. *Hygiene factors* cause movement along a different continuum, one from no dissatisfaction to dissatisfaction. For example, workers will be dissatisfied if they feel that working conditions are poor, but if working conditions are improved, workers will not become satisfied; rather, they will no longer be dissatisfied. Overall, motivation factors are directly related to the work that employees actually perform, while hygiene factors refer to the environment in which they perform it (see Figure 9.4). This theory suggests that managers must first ensure that hygiene factors are acceptable (to avoid worker dissatisfaction) and then offer motivating factors (to improve satisfaction and motivation).

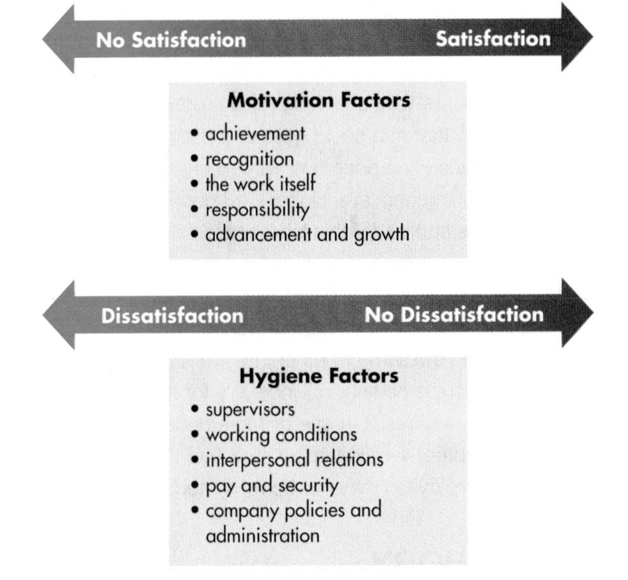

^^ **FIGURE 9.4** Two-factor theory of human motivation

MCCLELLAND'S ACQUIRED NEEDS THEORY

There are three needs in David McClelland's acquired needs theory: achievement, affiliation, and power.[19] One of these typically dominates a given individual's need structure. People who are high in *need for achievement* have a strong desire to accomplish a goal or task as effectively as possible. They tend to set moderately difficult goals and to make moderately risky decisions. They are preoccupied with work, and they take personal responsibility for getting things done. They want immediate feedback on their performance, so they often take sales jobs because they get immediate feedback from customers. They avoid jobs in areas like research and development where feedback comes much more slowly.

Individuals with a high *need for affiliation* focus on human companionship.[20] They want reassurance and approval from others, and are genuinely concerned about others' feelings. They are likely to act and think as they believe others want them to, especially those with whom they strongly identify with and want their friendship. They most often work in jobs with a lot of interpersonal contact, such as teaching.

Individuals with a high *need for power* are driven by the desire to control their environment (including the financial, material, information, and human resource aspects).[21] People with a high need for power can be successful managers if they (1) seek power in order to help the organization perform better, (2) have a fairly low need for affiliation (because their power need may alienate others), and (3) have good self-control and are not excessive in their use of power.[22]

TWO-FACTOR THEORY A theory of human relations developed by Frederick Herzberg that identifies factors that must be present for employees to be satisfied with their jobs and factors that, if increased, lead employees to work harder.

EXPECTANCY THEORY The theory that people are motivated to work toward rewards that they want and that they believe they have a reasonable chance of obtaining.

Contemporary Motivation Theory

In recent years, other, more complex models of employee behaviour and motivation have been developed. Two of the more interesting and useful ones are *expectancy theory* and *equity theory*.

EXPECTANCY THEORY

Expectancy theory suggests that people are motivated to work toward rewards they want and which they believe they have a reasonable chance—or expectancy—of obtaining.[23] A reward that seems out of reach, for example, is not likely to be motivating even if it is intrinsically positive (see Figure 9.5). Suppose that an assistant department manager

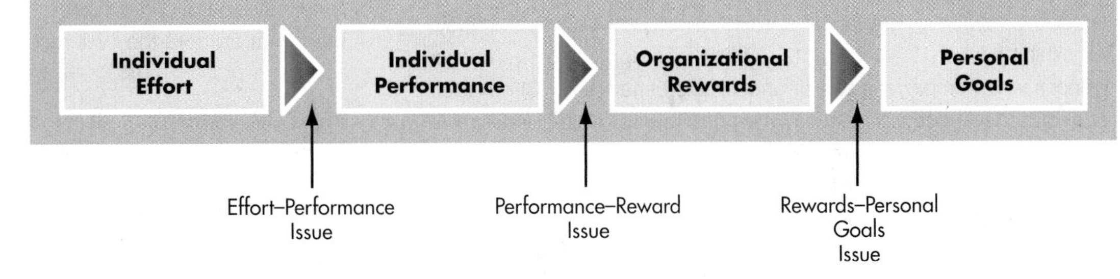

>>> **FIGURE 9.5** Expectancy theory model

learns that a division manager has retired and that the firm is looking for a replacement. Even though she wants the job, the assistant manager does not apply for it because she doubts that she would be selected. Then she learns that the firm is looking for a production manager on a later shift. She thinks that she could get this job but does not apply for that one either, because she does not want to change shifts. But when she learns of an opening one level higher—full department manager—in her own division, she applies for this job because she both wants it and thinks she has a good chance of getting it.

Expectancy theory helps to explain why some people do not work as hard as they can when their salaries are based purely on seniority. Because they are paid the same whether they work very hard or just hard enough to get by, there is no financial incentive for them to work harder. Similarly, if hard work will result in one or more undesirable outcomes—say, a transfer to another location or a promotion to a job that requires unwanted travel—employees may not be motivated to work hard.

EQUITY THEORY

Equity theory focuses on social comparisons—people evaluating their treatment by the organization relative to the treatment of others. This approach says that people begin by analyzing what they contribute to their jobs (time, effort, education, experience, and so forth) relative to what they get in return (salary, benefits, recognition, security). The result is a ratio of contribution to return. Employees compare their own ratios to those of "comparison others" (employees who are similar in terms of experience and training). Depending on their assessments, they experience feelings of equity or inequity.[24]

For example, suppose a new college graduate gets a starting job at a large manufacturing firm. His starting salary is $38 000 per year, he gets a compact company car, and he shares an office with another new employee. If he later learns that another new employee has received the same salary, car, and office arrangement, he will feel equitably treated. But if he finds out that another newcomer received $40 000, a full-size company car, and a private office, he may feel he has been inequitably treated.

When people think they are being inequitably treated, they might do various things to restore fairness. For example, they might ask for a raise, reduce their work effort, work shorter hours, or complain to their boss. They might also rationalize their situation, find a different comparison person, or simply quit.

EQUITY THEORY The theory that people compare (1) what they contribute to their job with what they get in return and (2) their input/output ratio with that of other employees.

LO-5 STRATEGIES FOR ENHANCING MOTIVATION

Understanding what motivates workers and provides job satisfaction is only part of the manager's job. The other part is to apply that knowledge. Experts have suggested—and many companies have instituted—a wide range of programs designed to make jobs more interesting and rewarding and the work environment more pleasant. Six of the most common strategies are reinforcement/behaviour modification, goal setting, participative management and empowerment, team management, job enrichment and redesign, and modified work schedules.

Reinforcement/Behaviour Modification

Reinforcement is a two-step process. The first step is to define the specific behaviours managers want their employees to exhibit (working hard, being courteous to customers, stressing quality, and so on), and the specific behaviours they want to eliminate (wasting time, being rude to customers, ignoring quality, and so on). The second step is to "shape" employee behaviour by using reinforcement.

Reinforcement means applying (or withholding) positive (or negative) consequences in order to motivate employees to exhibit behaviour the manager wants. A manager has four basic reinforcement options: (1) *positive reinforcement* (apply positive consequences when employees exhibit desired behaviours), (2) *punishment* (apply negative consequences when employees exhibit undesirable behaviours), (3) *omission* (withhold positive consequences when employees exhibit undesirable behaviours), and (4) *negative reinforcement* (withhold negative consequences when employees exhibit desired behaviours).

Managers generally prefer positive reinforcement, because it contributes to good employer–employee relationships. They generally dislike punishing employees, partly because workers may respond with anger, resentment, hostility, or even retaliation. Most people think of monetary rewards when they think of positive reinforcement, but one of the simplest, though uncommon, ways for managers to motivate workers is to praise them. A *Globe and Mail* web poll showed that 27 percent of the 2331 respondents had *never* received a compliment from their boss. Another 10 percent had not received a compliment in the past year, and 18 percent had not received a compliment in the past month.[25] Other non-monetary rewards are also useful. Calgary-based Pacesetter Directional and Performance Drilling rewards top employees with time off, and Markham, Ontario–based Nobis, a manufacturer of hats and apparel, rewards employees by allowing them to name hats after family and friends.[26]

The boxed insert entitled "Carrot or Stick?" presents some interesting ideas about the use of rewards and punishment in motivating employees.

Goal-Setting Theory

Goal-setting theory focuses on setting goals that will motivate employees. Research has shown that SMART goals (Specific, Measurable, Achievable, Relevant, and Time-framed) are most likely to result in increased employee performance. It is also true that on occasion, goal setting may lead to bad behaviour on the part of managers. For example, if managers are told they will receive a bonus if they achieve a certain

REINFORCEMENT Controlling and modifying employee behaviour through the use of systematic rewards and punishments for specific behaviours.

GOAL-SETTING THEORY The theory that people perform better when they set specific, quantified, time-framed goals.

MANAGING IN TURBULENT TIMES

Carrot or Stick?

Assume for a moment that you are the general manager of a supermarket, and that you've just finished a department-by-department year-end performance review of your managers. You observe that all departments have performed well except one: the produce department fell 12 percent short of management's forecast. You therefore decide to reward all your managers with bonuses, except for your produce manager.

According to Daniel Kahneman, a psychologist who won the Nobel Prize in economics for his work on behavioural and decision-making models, your decision can be challenged on logical grounds. Here's how he sees the logic you apparently used in making your decision:

> Manager's department performs well → you reward manager → you expect the department to continue to perform well in the future
>
> Managers' department performs poorly → you punish manager → you expect the department to perform better in the future

Kahneman argues that your logic is flawed. The key to his criticism is a concept called *regression to the mean*: the principle that, from one performance measure to the next, the change in performance will be toward the overall average level of performance. To see how this works, consider the following example.

Say you're an avid runner and you run a kilometre along the same route every morning. On average, it takes you 7 minutes to run your kilometre. If you run it on Monday in 6 minutes and 10 seconds, on Tuesday your time will probably be longer, that is closer to 7 minutes. You *might* run even faster on Tuesday, but most of the time, if you run faster than your average one day, you will run slower than your average the next day. Likewise, if you run slower than your average one day, you are very likely to run faster than your average the next day. Regression to the mean occurs because there are many factors that determine any outcome. Factors that influence your running speed, for example, include how much sleep you got and what you ate for dinner the night before, the air temperature while you run, your motivation level on a particular day, and so on.

Now, let's return to our example of the produce manager. It's not likely that the manager's performance was the sole (or even the primary) factor in the department's poor performance. Other factors might include variations in competition, economic and other market conditions, and decisions made by other managers. If we take these things into account, we can develop a model that more accurately reflects reality:

> Manager's department performs above average in one period → department will probably not perform as well in the next period
>
> Manager's department performs below average in one period → department will probably perform better in the next period

Kahneman says that the failure to recognize regression to the mean causes people to reward others when they perform well and punish others when they perform poorly. But even without the reward or punishment, the performance of others is likely to change simply because regression to the mean is operating.

CRITICAL THINKING QUESTION

1. Consider the following statement: *Given the reality of the regression to the mean concept, it is clear that rewards and punishments should not be applied in the workplace.* Do you agree or disagree? Explain.

level of sales revenue, they may focus all their attention on generating sales revenue, and not pay any attention to profits. At Enron, managers got large bonuses for achieving revenue goals even though the company was failing.[27]

One of the most popular methods for setting performance goals is **management by objectives (MBO)**, which involves managers and subordinates in setting goals and evaluating progress. The motivational impact is perhaps the biggest advantage of MBO. When employees meet with managers to set goals, they learn more about company-wide objectives, feel that they are an important part of a team, and see how they can improve company-wide performance by achieving their own goals.

Investors Group Financial Services has used MBO for many years to motivate its sales force in selling financial services. The MBO process begins when the vice-president of sales develops general goals for the entire sales force. Sales reps review their financial accomplishments and think through their personal and financial goals for the coming year. They then meet with their division managers and reach a consensus about the specific goals the sales reps will pursue during the next year. Each division manager then forwards the proposed objectives for his or her division to the appropriate regional manager. This process continues all the way up to the vice-president of sales, who gives final approval to the overall sales objectives of the company for the coming year.[28]

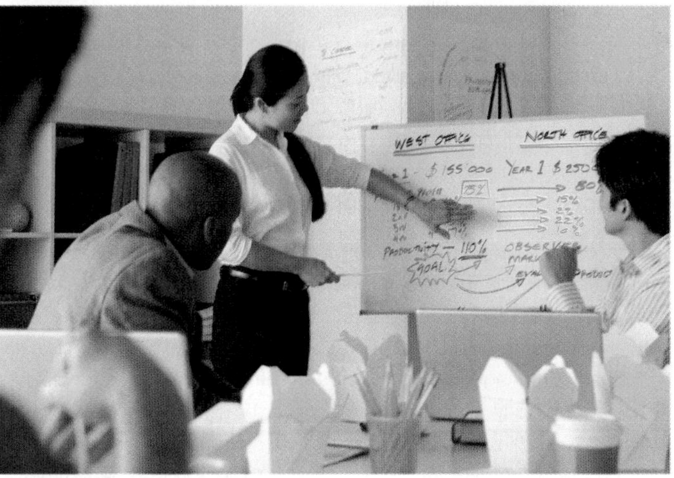

Research has shown that goals that are specific, measurable, and moderately difficult to achieve result in high performance for employees.

Tetra Images/Shutterstock

MANAGEMENT BY OBJECTIVES (MBO) A system of collaborative goal setting that extends from the top of an organization to its bottom.

Participative Management and Empowerment

Participative management and empowerment involves tapping into workers' knowledge about the job, encouraging them to be self-motivated and to make suggestions for improvements, and giving them more authority and responsibility so that they feel they are a real part of the company's success. Some companies try to operate without the usual hierarchy and give workers a large amount of discretion. For example, at Morning Star Company—the world's largest tomato processor—workers write up a mission statement that describes how they will contribute to the overall goals of the company. Employees are expected to propose the hiring of new people if they are overloaded or if they see a need that should be met. Each employee also develops a "Colleague Letter of Understanding" with other employees who are affected by the person's work. At the end of the year, employees receive feedback on their performance from colleagues with whom they have a Letter of Understanding. Pay is determined by an elected committee. All business units are ranked (on the basis of performance), and those that rank poorly have to explain what happened. One employee said that "nobody is your boss, everyone is."[29]

There are many other examples of empowerment in Canadian and international businesses:

- At WestJet, front-line staff have the right to issue travel credits to customers they feel have not been treated properly. WestJet thinks that the goodwill generated by the practice will increase repeat business.[30]
- At Toronto's Delta Chelsea Hotel, employees noticed that in the summer months there were fewer business guests and more vacationers' children in the hotel. As a result of employee suggestions, the hotel installed a waterslide, appointed a "kids' concierge," and set up a game room for teens to better serve this market segment.[31]
- At ING Direct Canada, a webpage has been set up that allows employees to submit ideas for peers to vote on. An innovation team then evaluates the ideas.[32]
- AES Corporation is a large energy company where multifunctional teams manage themselves without the assistance of any legal, human resources, or other functional department, or any written policies or procedures. No one person is in charge of the teams. As a result of this structure (some call it "empowerment gone mad"), employees exhibit flexibility and continuous learning.[33]

To enhance employee productivity, some companies are now using wikis—websites that allow employees to add content on issues that are of interest to the business. This is part of a move to "mass collaboration" that is going on in businesses.[34] Another technique to encourage participative management is the **quality circle**, a group of employees who meet regularly to consider solutions for problems in their work area. At Great-West Life Assurance Company, for example, quality circles are made up of volunteers who meet once a week (on company time) to consider ways to do higher quality, more effective work.

PARTICIPATIVE MANAGEMENT AND EMPOWERMENT Method of increasing job satisfaction by giving employees a voice in the management of their jobs and the company.

QUALITY CIRCLE A technique for maximizing quality of production. Employees are grouped into small teams that define, analyze, and solve quality and other process-related problems within their area.

Empowerment is not desired by all employees. Some will be frustrated by responsibilities they are not equipped to handle, and others will be dissatisfied if they see the invitation to participate as more symbolic than real. A good approach is to invite participation if employees want to have input and if participation will have real value for an organization.

Team Management

Companies have traditionally given individual employees the responsibility to complete certain tasks, but in recent years, an emphasis on teams has become increasingly common. These teams take a variety of forms. Problem-solving teams focus on developing solutions to specific problems. They are based on the idea that the best solutions to problems are likely to come from the employees who actually do the work. For example, at the Bowmanville, Ontario, plant of St. Mary's Cement Inc., members of various departments joined a problem-solving team whose goal was to find ways to reduce the company's energy bills. After analyzing the situation, the committee developed a list of energy-saving initiatives and created plans to implement them. Over a recent three-year period, the initiatives saved the company $800 000.[35]

The problem-solving idea is developed even further in self-managed teams, which set their own goals, select their own team members, evaluate their own performance, and generally manage themselves. At Johnsonville Foods, self-managing teams recruit, hire, evaluate, and terminate low performers on their own.[36]

Project teams (also called *venture teams*) work on specific projects like developing new processes, new products, or new businesses. The classic example of a project team is the one that developed IBM's first personal computer many years ago. Transnational teams, composed of members from many different countries, have also become common. For example, Fuji-Xerox sent 15 engineers from Tokyo to New York to work with U.S. engineers as they developed a "world copier," a product that became a big success.[37] Virtual teams are groups of geographically dispersed co-workers that are assembled to accomplish a specific task, using a combination of telecommunications and information technologies. These teams are becoming increasingly popular because of globalization.

This pit crew has to work as a team in order to minimize the time the race car is in the pit. Coordination among team members is crucial, since even a few wasted seconds can make the difference between victory or defeat in the race.

Terry Renna/AP/The Canadian Press

Teams provide monetary benefits for companies that use them, but they can also provide non-monetary benefits such as increasing motivation and job satisfaction levels for employees, enhancing company-wide communication, and making members feel like they are an integral part of the organization.[38] But, as with participative management, managers must remember that teams are not for everyone, nor are they effective in every situation.[39] At Levi Strauss, for example, individual workers who performed repetitive tasks like sewing zippers into jeans were paid according to the number of jobs they completed each day. In an attempt to boost productivity, company management reorganized everyone into teams of 10 to 35 workers and assigned tasks to the entire team. Each team member's pay was determined by the team's level of productivity. But faster workers became resentful of slower workers because they reduced the group's total output. Slower workers, meanwhile, resented the pressure put on them by faster-working co-workers. As a result, motivation, satisfaction, and morale all dropped, and Levi Strauss eventually abandoned the teamwork plan altogether.[40]

Teams work best when successful task completion requires input from several people, when there is interdependence between tasks (as in team sports), and when working together can accomplish tasks that an individual could not do alone (as in a hospital surgical team).[41]

Job Enrichment and Redesign

While MBO programs and participative management can work in a variety of settings, job enrichment and job redesign programs can increase satisfaction only if a job lacks motivating factors to begin with.[42] **Job enrichment** means adding one or more motivating factors to a job. In a now-classic study, a group of eight typists worked in isolated cubicles taking calls from field sales representatives and then typing up service orders. They had no client contact, so if they had a question about the order, they had to call the sales representative. They also received little performance feedback. Interviews with these workers suggested that they were bored with their jobs and did not feel valued. As part of a job enrichment program, each typist was paired with a small group of designated sales representatives and became a part of their team. Typists were also given permission to call clients directly if they had questions about the order. Finally, a new feedback system was installed to give the typists more information about their performance. As a result, their performance improved and absenteeism decreased markedly.[43]

Job enrichment is accomplished by job redesign, which involves combining tasks to increase job variety, forming natural work groups, and establishing client relationships. By redesigning work to achieve a more satisfactory person–job fit, job redesign motivates individuals who have a high need for growth or achievement.[44]

COMBINING TASKS

This involves enlarging jobs and increasing their variety to make employees feel that their work is more meaningful. In turn, workers are more motivated. For example, the job done by a computer programmer who maintains computer systems might be redesigned to include some system design and development work. The programmer is then able to use additional skills and is involved in the overall system package.

FORMING NATURAL WORKGROUPS

People who do different jobs on the same project are good candidates for natural workgroups. These groups help employees get an overview of their jobs and see their importance in the total structure. They also help managers, and the firm in general, because the people working on a project are usually the most knowledgeable about it and are thus able to solve problems related to it. Consider a group where each employee does a small part of the job of assembling iPhones. One worker may see his job as working on the internal components, while another worker may see her job as working on the external components. The jobs could be redesigned to allow the group to decide who does what and in what order. The workers can exchange jobs and plan their work schedules. Now they all see themselves as part of a team that assembles iPhones.

ESTABLISHING CLIENT RELATIONSHIPS

A third way of redesigning a job is to establish client relationships, that is, to let employees interact with customers. This approach increases the variety of a job. It also gives workers greater feelings of control over their jobs and more feedback about their performance. Instead of responding to instructions from marketing managers on how to develop new products, software writers at Lotus are encouraged to work directly with customers. Similarly, software writers at Microsoft watch test users work with programs and discuss problems with them directly rather than receive feedback from third-party researchers.

Modified Work Schedules

Several types of modified work schedules have been developed to increase job satisfaction, including *flextime*, *compressed workweeks*, *telecommuting*, and *workshare programs*.

FLEXTIME

Flextime allows people to pick their working hours. Figure 9.6 illustrates how a flextime system might be arranged and how different people might use it. The office is open from 6 a.m. until 7 p.m. Core time is 9 a.m. until 11 a.m. and 1 p.m. until 3 p.m. Joe, being an early riser, comes in at 6 a.m., takes an hour lunch between 11 a.m. and noon, and finishes his day by 3 p.m. Sue, on the other hand, prefers a later day. She comes in at 9 a.m., takes a long lunch from 11 a.m. to 1 p.m., and then works until 7 p.m. Pat works a more traditional day from 8 a.m. until 5 p.m.

One survey found that 88 percent of Canadian businesses offer some form of flexible work arrangements (but many businesses offer them to only the most senior employees).[45] Since many employees work more than 40 hours per week, more and more companies are offering flexible working schedules to help them cope.[46] Flextime options are provided at organizations like Next Level Games Inc. (Vancouver), the National Energy Board (Calgary), and the Office of the Auditor General (Ottawa).[47] Alexandra Jacobs, a single mother who works for the Royal Bank of Canada, works three days a week from home. Jacobs manages a staff of five, and each of those people also has a flexible work schedule.[48]

JOB ENRICHMENT A method of increasing employees' job satisfaction by extending or adding motivating factors such as responsibility or growth.

FLEXTIME A method of increasing employees' job satisfaction by allowing them some choice in the hours they work.

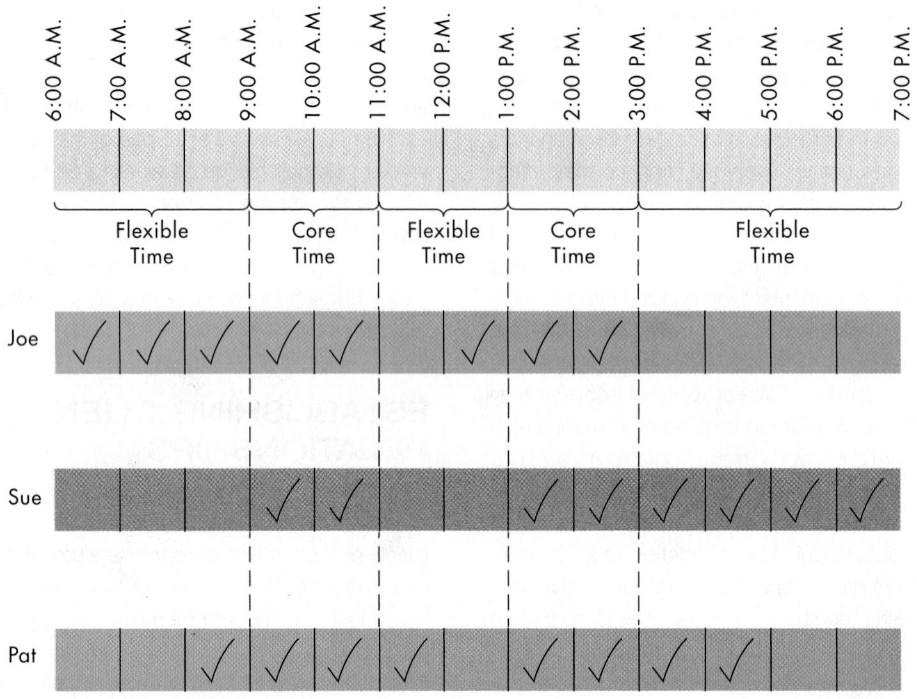

FIGURE 9.6 Flextime schedules

Flextime schedules include core time, when everyone must be at work, and flexible time, during which employees can set their own working hours.

COMPRESSED WORKWEEKS

In the **compressed workweek**, employees work fewer days per week but more hours on the days they do work. The most popular compressed workweek is four days, ten hours per day, which is used in many companies and municipalities. Companies providing a compressed workweek option include Chubb Insurance Company of Canada (Toronto), Next Level Games Inc. (Vancouver), and Cameco Corp. (Saskatoon).[49] The Catholic Children's Aid Society of Toronto has introduced the compressed workweek to help staff cope with long, unpredictable hours.[50]

TELECOMMUTING

A third variation in work design is **telecommuting**, which allows people to do some or all of their work away from their office. The availability of networked computers, fax machines, smartphones, tablets, email, and overnight delivery services makes it possible for many independent professionals to work at home or while travelling. About one-third of the world's labour force now works wherever they are, not just in the office.[51] Many Canadian organizations offer telecommuting as an option. At BC Biomedical Laboratories, 15 percent of the administrative staff work from home, and at LoyaltyOne, 50 percent of call centre representatives don't commute.[52] At Cisco Systems, 90 percent of internal meetings are conducted using virtual meeting software. While 500 people work out of the downtown Toronto office, there are only 200 desks there.[53] In some business functions like customer service and telemarketing, most employees are telecommuters.[54]

Telecommuting has advantages and disadvantages for individual workers and for the organization (see Table 9.1).

In 2013, Marissa Mayer, the CEO of Yahoo Inc., surprised everyone by ending the practice of telecommuting for its employees. The decision provoked a debate in business papers, some praising the decision and others roundly criticizing it.[55] One research study showed that telecommuters are 50 percent less likely to get a promotion than employees who are in the office every day.[56] For this and other reasons, telecommuting may not be for everyone. Would-be telecommuters must ask themselves several important questions: Can I meet deadlines even when I'm not being closely supervised? What will it be like to be away from the social context of the office five days a week? Can I renegotiate family rules so my spouse doesn't come home expecting to see dinner on the table just because I've been home all day?

The boxed insert entitled "The Four-Day Workweek and Telecommuting: Are They Really Green?" presents some interesting information on the environmental impact of compressed workweeks and telecommuting.

WORKSHARE PROGRAMS

A fourth type of modified work schedule, **worksharing** (also called **job sharing**), benefits both employees and the employer. This approach allows two (or more) people to share one full-time job. For example, two people might share a position advising the human resources department. One person works Mondays through Wednesdays, and the other works Wednesdays through Fridays. Or five people might share one

COMPRESSED WORKWEEK Employees work fewer days per week, but more hours on the days they do work.

TELECOMMUTING Allowing employees to do all or some of their work away from the office.

WORKSHARING (JOB SHARING) A method of increasing employee job satisfaction by allowing two people to share one job.

TABLE 9.1 Advantages and Disadvantages of Telecommuting

Advantages of Telecommuting	Disadvantages of Telecommuting
For Employees	
• health benefits (lower stress levels) • lower costs (reduced car expenses) • better use of time (no commuting long distances) • better use of time (no interruptions)	• feeling "out of the loop" (not being knowledgeable about important business issues or interesting personal gossip) • having difficulty separating personal and professional life (work intrudes at home) • feeling ill suited for telework (lack of discipline and feeling lonesome) • finding it difficult to work closely with colleagues when necessary • fear of career derailment
For the Organization	
• increases productivity (two-thirds of employers surveyed said that employee productivity went up) • cost savings (fewer offices and office supplies are needed; lower vehicle expenses) • lower electric bills (fewer lights and computers are turned on in offices) • access to qualified staff (who otherwise wouldn't be available because they don't live in the area or don't want to drive so far to work) • lower travel expenses (teleconferencing, email, networking systems take the place of travel) • lower employee turnover	• requires a change in management thinking (forces managers to adopt an attitude of trust regarding employees) • many managers still think if they can't see employees, they aren't working (may threaten the control of bosses who are used to having employees in sight) • bosses have to spend more time with subordinates on the phone or other media (they may prefer face-to-face communication) • bosses don't know when employees are actually working • telecommuting may not work well for companies where customers are frequently in the office • telecommuting may not work well if colleagues frequently need intense face-to-face collaboration to complete rush jobs on time

THE GREENING OF BUSINESS

The Four-Day Workweek and Telecommuting: Are They Really Green?

The four-day workweek has been touted as good not only for employee morale and satisfaction, but also for the environment. Two main points are usually made in support of the argument. First, since workers will be driving to work only four days each week instead of five, they will be using less gas and will therefore reduce the amount of greenhouse gas emissions. But whether the four-day workweek really saves gas depends on what workers do on the fifth day. If they drive their SUV 400 kilometres to go visit relatives, they will burn more gas than they would have by simply driving to and from work. On the other hand, maybe they would have taken such a trip on the weekend if they had to work a traditional five-day workweek.

Second, a four-day workweek should mean that less electricity will be used by businesses because machines, computers, and heating systems will be running at very low levels on the fifth day. While it is true that factory machines will not be running on the fifth day, there may be no actual savings because those machines have already run for 40 hours as a result of the four previous days at 10 hours. Other electricity savings may also be elusive unless the company is committed to turning down the heat and turning off the lights on the fifth day. But that may be impossible, because there always seem to be people that need to be at work on the fifth day. Even if workers do stay at home on the fifth day, they may do other tasks that require the equivalent amount of electricity or gas that they would have consumed at work (e.g., renovating their home).

You can see why it might be difficult to determine if the *four-day workweek* is better for the environment than the five-day workweek. But *telecommuting* may indeed be a more effective strategy, because workers who telecommute don't come in to the office very much. If they are at home working, they will not be driving their car, so that should save gas. As well, companies that encourage telecommuting may save considerable money on real estate and other operating costs. But even here, we need to analyze what individual workers do as alternative activities before we can conclude that telecommuting is good for the environment.

CRITICAL THINKING QUESTIONS

1. Using material contained in this insert as well as other material that you find, develop a list of arguments that the *four-day workweek* is better for the environment than the five-day workweek. Then develop a list of arguments that the four-day workweek is no better for the environment than the five-day workweek. Which list is more persuasive?
2. Using material contained in this insert and other material you can find, develop a list of arguments that *telecommuting* is better for the environment than the four-day workweek. Then develop a list of arguments that telecommuting is not better for the environment. Which list is more persuasive?

reservationist's job at Air Canada, each working one day a week. Each person earns some money, remains in the job market, and enjoys some travel benefits. Worksharing programs can also help ease experienced workers into retirement while training their replacements, and they allow co-op students to combine academic learning with practical experience. The worksharing option is used in organizations as diverse as the Ontario Public Service and the National Hockey League, where two goalies often share duties during the high-stress playoffs.[57]

LO-6 LEADERSHIP AND MOTIVATION

Leadership refers to the processes and behaviours used by managers to motivate, inspire, and influence subordinates to work toward certain goals. People often assume that "leadership" and "management" mean the same thing, but there are important differences. A person can be a manager, a leader, or both.[58] Consider a hospital setting. The chief of staff (chief physician) of a large hospital is clearly a manager by virtue of the position the person occupies. But this individual may or may not be respected or trusted by others and may have to rely solely on the authority vested in the position to get people to do things. Thus, being a manager does not ensure that a person is also a leader. In contrast, an emergency-room nurse with no formal authority may be quite effective at taking charge of a chaotic situation and directing others in how to deal with specific patient problems. Others in the emergency room may respond because they trust his or her judgment and have confidence in his or her decision-making skills. In this case, the nurse is a leader, but not a manager. Finally, the head of pediatrics, supervising a staff of 20 other doctors, nurses, and attendants, may also enjoy the staff's complete respect, confidence, and trust. They readily take the head's advice, follow directives without question, and often go far beyond what is necessary to help carry out the unit's mission. In this case, the head of pediatrics is both a manager and a leader. The key distinctions between leadership and management are summarized in Table 9.2.[59]

Organizations need both management and leadership if they are to be effective. Leadership is necessary to create and direct change and to help the organization get through tough times, and management is necessary to achieve coordination and systematic results and to handle administrative activities during times of stability and predictability.[60] Management—in conjunction with leadership—can help achieve planned orderly change. Leadership—in conjunction with management—can keep the organization properly aligned with its environment. Both managers and leaders play a major role in establishing the moral climate of the organization and in determining the role of ethics in its culture.[61]

Leadership and Power

To fully understand leadership, it is also necessary to understand *power*, which is the ability to affect the behaviour of others. There are several different types of power. *Legitimate power* is the power granted through the formal organizational hierarchy. Managers have legitimate power because of the specific position they occupy in the hierarchy. This power gives them the right to assign tasks to subordinates. A subordinate who refuses to do the tasks can be reprimanded or fired. Legitimate power is synonymous with authority, as discussed in Chapter 7. Keep in mind that the mere possession of legitimate power does not make a manager a leader.

LEADERSHIP The process of motivating others to work to meet specific objectives.

TABLE 9.2 Kotter's Distinctions Between Management and Leadership

Activity	Management	Leadership
Creating an agenda	Planning and budgeting. Establishing detailed steps and timetables for achieving needed results; allocating the resources necessary to make those needed results happen.	Establishing direction. Developing a vision of the future, often the distant future, and strategies for producing the changes needed to achieve that vision.
Developing a human network for achieving the agenda	Organizing and staffing. Establishing some structure for accomplishing plan requirements, staffing that structure with individuals, delegating responsibility and authority for carrying out the plan, providing policies and procedures to help guide people, and creating methods or systems to monitor implementation.	Aligning people. Communicating the direction by words and deeds to all those whose cooperation may be needed to influence the creation of teams and coalitions that understand the vision and strategies and accept their validity.
Executing plans	Controlling and problem solving. Monitoring results versus plan in some detail, identifying deviations, and then planning and organizing to solve these problems.	Motivating and inspiring. Energizing people to overcome major political, bureaucratic, and resource barriers to change, by satisfying very basic, but often unfulfilled, human needs.
Outcomes	Produces a degree of predictability and order and has the potential to consistently produce major results expected by various shareholders (e.g., for customers, always being on time; for stockholders, being on budget).	Produces change, often to a dramatic degree, and has the potential to produce extremely useful change (e.g., new products that customers want, new approaches to labour relations that help make a firm more competitive).

Asked to identify important leaders, people often mention influential historical figures such as Winston Churchill, Abraham Lincoln, Martin Luther King, and Mother Teresa.

(Left to right) Bettmann Premium/Corbis; MPVHistory/Alamy Stock Photo; GL Archive/Alamy Stock Photo; Dinodia Photo/AGE Fotostock

Reward power is the power to give or withhold rewards like salary increases, bonuses, promotions, praise, and interesting job assignments. The greater the number of rewards a manager controls, and the more valued these rewards are to subordinates, the greater the manager's reward power.

Coercive power is the power to force another person to comply by means of psychological, emotional, or physical threat. In most organizations today, coercion is limited to verbal or written reprimands, layoffs, demotion, or termination. The more punitive the elements under a manager's control, the more power the manager possesses.

Expert power is derived from information or expertise that the manager possess. Managers who know how to interact with important customers, or scientists who achieve an important technical breakthrough have expert power. The more important the information and the fewer the people who have access to it, the greater the degree of expert power possessed by a manager or leader.

Referent power is the most abstract form of power. It is based on identification, imitation, loyalty, or charisma of the leader (see the discussion of charisma later in this chapter). Because followers highly value what the leader stands for, the leader gains power over the followers. Followers might choose to imitate a leader by wearing the same kind of clothes, working the same hours, or supporting the same management philosophy that the leader uses.

LO-7 Approaches to Leadership

Political, religious, and business leaders have influenced the course of human events throughout history, but careful scientific study of leadership began only about a century ago. In the following paragraphs, we briefly summarize the development of this research.

THE TRAIT APPROACH

The **trait approach**—which was emphasized by researchers in the first two decades of the twentieth century—was based on the idea that leaders had unique traits that distinguished them from non-leaders. Many traits were thought to be important, including intelligence, dominance, self-confidence, energy, height, and knowledge about the job. As time passed, the list became so long that it lost any practical value. The trait approach was all but abandoned by the middle of the twentieth century, but in recent years it has resurfaced. Some researchers now argue that certain traits (e.g., intelligence, drive, motivation, honesty, integrity, and self-confidence) provide the potential for effective leadership, but only if the person is really motivated to be a leader. The implication is that people without these traits are not likely to be successful leaders even if they try.[62] Recall that the emotional intelligence idea discussed earlier in this chapter identified five somewhat different traits of successful leaders.[63]

THE BEHAVIOURAL APPROACH

Because the trait approach was a poor predictor of leadership success, attention shifted from managers' traits to their behaviours. The goal of the **behavioural approach** was to determine how the behaviours of effective leaders differed from the behaviours of less effective leaders. This research led to the identification of two basic forms of leader behaviour: task-oriented (the manager focuses on how tasks should be performed in order to achieve important goals) and employee-oriented (the manager focuses on the satisfaction, motivation, and well-being of employees). Task-oriented managers tend to have higher-performing subordinates, while employee-oriented managers tend to have more satisfied subordinates.

Researchers have also identified three main leadership styles: the autocratic style (the manager issues orders and expects them to be obeyed without question), the democratic style (the manager requests input from subordinates before making decisions, but retains final decision-making power), and the free-rein style (the manager serves as an advisor to subordinates who are given a lot of discretion when making decisions). Most leaders tend to regularly use one style, and may, in fact, find it difficult to change from one style to another. But some leaders do manage to change their style. For example, Andrall (Andy) Pearson was an abrasive, numbers-oriented, hard-to-please manager when he was president and COO of PepsiCo. But

TRAIT APPROACH A leadership approach focused on identifying the essential traits that distinguished leaders.

BEHAVIOURAL APPROACH A leadership approach focused on determining what behaviours are employed by leaders.

as director of Yum Brands, he softened and transformed, and truly cared about employees.[64]

THE SITUATIONAL APPROACH TO LEADERSHIP

The **situational approach to leadership** assumes that appropriate leader behaviour varies from one situation to the next (see Figure 9.7). The trait and behavioural approaches to leadership were both "universal" in nature, because they attempted to prescribe leader traits and behaviours that worked in every situation. Supporters of these universal perspectives might argue, for example, that tall and intelligent people or people who are always employee-focused will always be effective leaders. But leadership research has found this is not true. So the situational approach to leadership attempts to identify various forms of leader behaviour that result in contingent outcomes and consequences. By "contingent," we mean that they depend on elements of the situation and characteristics of the leader and the followers.

Leadership characteristics include the manager's value system, confidence in subordinates, personal inclinations, feelings of security, and actual behaviour. Subordinate characteristics include the subordinate's need for independence, readiness to assume responsibility, tolerance for ambiguity, interest in the problem, understanding of goals, knowledge, experiences, and expectations. Situational characteristics that affect decision making include the type of organization, group effectiveness, the problem itself, and time pressure.

Many different contingency theories have been developed. Briefly described below are the path-goal theory, the decision tree approach, and the leader-member exchange (LMX) model.

The *path-goal theory* of leadership is an extension of the expectancy theory of motivation discussed earlier in this chapter.[65] Recall that the primary components of expectancy theory include the likelihood of attaining various outcomes and the value associated with those outcomes. The path-goal theory of leadership suggests that the primary functions of a leader are to make valued or desired rewards available in the workplace and to clarify for the subordinates the kinds of behaviours that will

Universal Approach

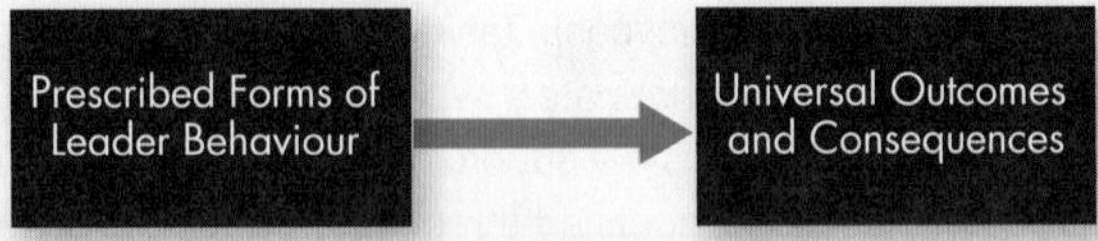

Situational Approach

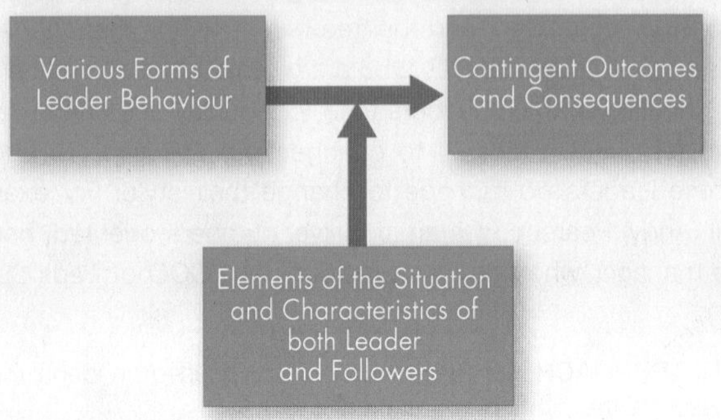

FIGURE 9.7 The situational approach to leadership

THERE'S AN APP FOR THAT!

APP DETAILS	PLATFORMS
1. **Leadership Qualities** **Source:** Bigo **Key Features:** Learn 12 winning leadership qualities of a competent and influential leader.	Apple, BlackBerry
2. **Toastmaster Magazine** **Source:** Toastmaster International **Key Features:** Covers a variety of subjects related to communication and leadership. Toastmasters is the leading organization dedicated to communication and leadership skill development.	Apple, Android, Windows
3. **Quotes** **Source:** Skol Games LLC **Key Features:** A collection of motivational quotes to inspire.	Apple, Android

APP DISCOVERY EXERCISE

Since app availability changes, conduct your own search for the "Top Three" motivational and leadership apps and identify the key features.

lead to goal accomplishment and valued rewards. The leader clarifies the paths to goal attainment and can use four kinds of behaviours to achieve this, depending on the situation. *Directive leader behaviour* lets subordinates know what is expected of them, gives guidance and direction, and schedules work. *Supportive leader behaviour* is being friendly and approachable, showing concern for subordinates' welfare, and treating members as equals. *Participative leader behaviour* means consulting with subordinates, soliciting suggestions, and allowing participation in decision making. *Achievement-oriented behaviour* sets challenging goals, expects subordinates to perform at high levels, encourages subordinates, and shows confidence in subordinates' abilities.

Like the path-goal theory, the *decision tree approach* attempts to prescribe a leadership style that is appropriate in different situations. It also assumes that the leader is able to display different leadership styles. This approach concerns itself with only a single aspect of leader behaviour: subordinate participation in decision making. It assumes that the degree to which subordinates should participate in decision making depends on the characteristics of the situation, and that no one decision-making process is best for all situations. After evaluating a variety of problem attributes, the leader determines an appropriate decision style that specifies the amount of subordinate participation.

The *leader-member exchange (LMX) model* focuses on the differential relationships leaders often establish with different subordinates.[66] Each superior-subordinate pair represents a "vertical dyad." The model suggests that supervisors establish a special relationship with a small number of trusted subordinates (the "in-group"). The in-group usually receives special duties and special privileges. Subordinates who are not a part of this group are called the "out-group," and they receive less of the supervisor's time and attention.

SITUATIONAL (CONTINGENCY) APPROACH TO LEADERSHIP A leadership approach in which appropriate leader behaviour varies from one situation to another.

LO-8 RECENT TRENDS IN LEADERSHIP

During the late twentieth and early twenty-first centuries, many new ideas about leadership have been developed. We conclude this chapter with a brief discussion of several of these ideas.

TRANSFORMATIONAL LEADERSHIP

Transformational leadership is the set of abilities that allows a leader to recognize the need for change, to create a vision to guide that change, and to execute the change effectively. In contrast, **transactional leadership** involves routine, regimented activities that are necessary during periods of stability.

Many leaders may find it difficult to exercise both types of leadership. For example, when Michael Eisner took over the Walt Disney organization, the company was stagnant and was heading into decline. Relying on transformational skills, Eisner turned things around in dramatic fashion. Among many other things, he quickly expanded the company's theme parks, built new hotels, improved Disney's movie business, created a successful Disney cruise line, launched several other major initiatives, and changed the company into a global media powerhouse. But when the firm began to plateau and needed some time to let the changes all settle in, Eisner was unsuccessful at changing his own approach from transformational leadership to transactional leadership and was pressured into retiring.

CHARISMATIC LEADERSHIP

Charismatic leadership is a type of influence based on the leader's personal charisma. Figure 9.8 portrays the three key elements of charismatic leadership that most experts acknowledge today.[67]

Charismatic leaders have a high level of self-confidence and a strong need to influence others. They also communicate high expectations about follower performance and express confidence in their followers. A highly charismatic supervisor will generally be more successful in influencing a subordinate's behaviour than a supervisor who lacks charisma. The late Steve Jobs, the legendary CEO of Apple, commanded a cult-like following from both employees and consumers. He exhibited charisma, confidence, originality, brilliance, and vision. He was clearly a leader who could deliver success in businesses that were rapidly changing, highly technical, and demanding. Yet he also was portrayed as intimidating, power-hungry, and an aggressive egotist.[68]

Charismatic leadership ideas are popular among managers today and are the subject of numerous books and articles.[69] One concern is that some charismatic leaders will inspire such blind faith in their followers that the followers may engage in inappropriate, unethical, or even illegal behaviours simply because the leader instructs them to do so. This tendency likely played a role in the collapse of both Enron and Arthur

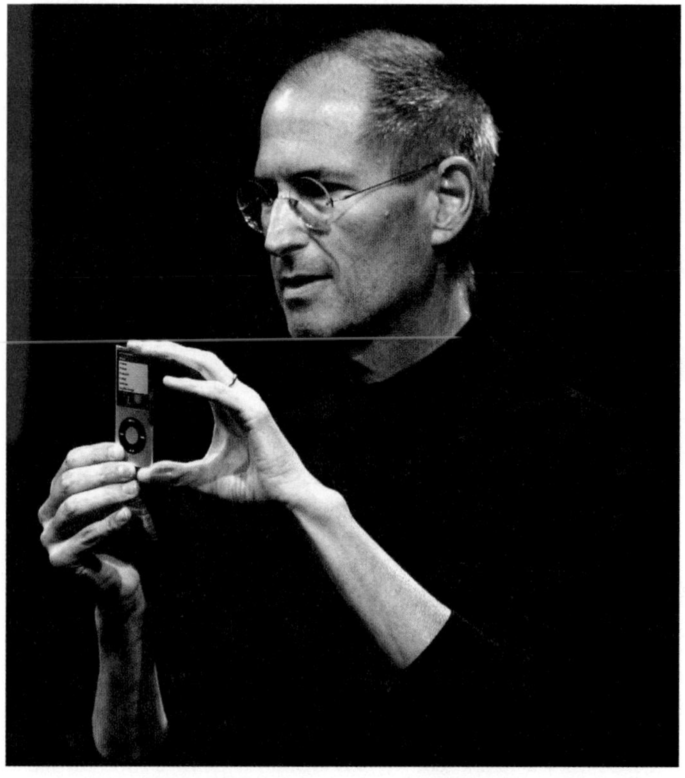

The late Steve Jobs, former CEO of Apple, was a prime example of a charismatic leader.

Monica M. Davey/EPA/Newscom

TRANSFORMATIONAL LEADERSHIP The set of abilities that allows a leader to recognize the need for change, to create a vision to guide that change, and to execute the change effectively.

TRANSACTIONAL LEADERSHIP The set of abilities that involves routine, regimented activities that are necessary during periods of stability.

CHARISMATIC LEADERSHIP Type of influence based on the leader's personal charisma.

The Charismatic Leader

Envisioning	Energizing	Enabling
• articulating a compelling vision • setting high expectations • modelling consistent behaviours	• demonstrating personal excitement • expressing personal confidence • seeking, finding, and using success	• expressing personal support • empathizing • expressing confidence in people

FIGURE 9.8 Charismatic leadership

Andersen, as people followed orders from their charismatic bosses to hide information, shred documents, and mislead investigators. The film *Enron: The Smartest Guys in the Room* documents this problem.

LEADERS AS COACHES

Many organizations are now attempting to become less hierarchical—that is, to eliminate the old-fashioned command-and-control mentality often inherent in bureaucratic organizations—and to motivate and empower individuals to work independently. This changes the role of leaders. Whereas leaders were once expected to control situations, direct work, supervise people, closely monitor performance, make decisions, and structure activities, many leaders today are being asked to become coaches instead of overseers.[70]

Consider the parallel with an athletic team. The coach selects the players for the team and decides on the general direction to take (such as emphasizing offence versus defence). The coach also helps develop player talent and teaches team members how to execute specific plays. But at game time, it's up to the players to execute plays and get the job done. While the coach may get some of the credit for the victory, he or she didn't actually score any of the points.

For business leaders, a coaching perspective calls for the leader to help select team members and other new employees, to provide overall direction, to help train and develop the team and the skills of its members, and to help the team get the information and other resources it needs. The leader may also have to help resolve conflict among team members and mediate other disputes that arise. And coaches from different teams need to link the activities and functions of their respective teams. But beyond these activities, the leader is expected to keep a low profile and let the group get its work done without overly close supervision.

GENDER AND LEADERSHIP

Another factor that is altering the face of leadership is the growing number of women advancing to the highest levels in organizations. Given that most leadership theories and research studies have focused on male leaders, developing a better understanding of how women lead is clearly an important next step. For example, do women and men lead differently? Some early observers, for instance, predicted that (consistently with prevailing stereotypes) female leaders would be relatively warm, supportive, and nurturing as compared to their male counterparts. But research suggests otherwise. Likewise, male leaders are not systematically more harsh, controlling, or task focused than female leaders. Women do seem to have a tendency to be more democratic when making decisions, whereas men have a tendency to be somewhat more autocratic.[71]

CROSS-CULTURAL LEADERSHIP

Culture is a broad concept that encompasses both international differences and diversity-based differences within one culture. For instance, when a Japanese firm sends an executive to head up the firm's operation in Canada, that person will need to be sensitive to the cultural differences that exist between the two countries and consider changing his or her leadership style accordingly. Japan is generally characterized by collectivism (group before individual), whereas Canada is based more on individualism (individual before group). The Japanese executive, then, will find it necessary to recognize the importance of individual contributions and rewards and the differences in individual and group roles that exist in Japanese and Canadian businesses.

Cross-cultural factors also play a growing role in organizations as their workforces become more diverse. Most leadership research, for instance, has analyzed white male leaders because those individuals

Women occupy top management positions in many companies. For example, Elyse Allan (left) is President and CEO of GE Canada. Liz Rodbell (right) is President and CEO of The Bay and Lord & Taylor.

J.P. Moczulski/Canadian Press/AP Images; Jennifer Graylock/Sipa USAJennif/Newscom

dominated leadership positions in North America. But as Asians, Blacks, Aboriginals, and Hispanics achieve leadership positions, it will be necessary to reassess how applicable current models of leadership are when applied to an increasingly diverse pool of leaders.

Canadian versus American Management Styles

The management styles of Canadian managers might look a lot like that of Americans, but there are several notable differences. In general, Canadian managers are more subtle and subdued than American managers, more committed to their companies, less willing to mindlessly follow the latest management fad, and more open to different cultures because of the multicultural nature of Canada.[72] The Global Leadership and Organizational Behavior Effectiveness study found that Canadian managers are very oriented toward fairness, are less likely to protect their own interests above those of their teams, and put more emphasis on long-term goals rather than short-term gratification.[73] All of these characteristics are advantageous for Canadian companies that increasingly compete in global markets.

Many Canadian-born managers have achieved significant success in companies that operate internationally. These include Bob Kelly (CEO of the Bank of New York Mellon Corp.), Henry McKinnell (former CEO of Pfizer), Steven McArthur (president of Expedia), Patricia Arnold (vice-president of Credit Suisse First Boston), Clara Furse (former CEO of the London Stock Exchange), Simon Cooper (CEO of Ritz-Carlton Hotel), and Dominic Barton (chairman of McKinsey & Company's Asia Region).[74]

STRATEGIC LEADERSHIP

Strategic leadership—which focuses on leadership in top management—is a leader's ability to understand the complexities of both the organization and its environment in order to lead change toward enhanced competitiveness. Steve Jobs was an effective strategic leader. For example, he recognized the potential growth of MP3 players and the fact that those devices used technology similar to that found in computers. He therefore directed the development of the Apple iPod, the iPhone, and iTunes, which have become enormously successful and profitable products.

ETHICAL LEADERSHIP

In the wake of corporate scandals at firms like AIG, Enron, and WorldCom, faith in business leaders has been shaken. Business leaders are now being called on to maintain high ethical standards for their own conduct, to unfailingly exhibit ethical behaviour, and to hold others in their organizations to the same standards—in short, to practise ethical leadership. Those responsible for hiring new leaders are looking more closely at the backgrounds of candidates. The emerging pressure for stronger corporate governance models is likely to further increase the commitment to select for leadership positions only those individuals with high ethical standards and to hold them more accountable for both their actions and the consequences of those actions.

VIRTUAL LEADERSHIP

Virtual leadership involves carrying out leadership activities when the leader does not have regular personal contact with followers. This contrasts with earlier times, when leaders and their employees worked together in the same physical location and engaged in personal (i.e., face-to-face) interactions on a regular basis. The challenges of virtual leadership have confronted Alexey Saltykov, the CEO of InsureEye Inc., a company that helps consumers understand their insurance costs. Alexey is located in Toronto, but he has two employees in Russia, one in Montreal, and a business advisor in Australia. The company uses Skype and web-based collaboration software, but neither approach works as well as Alexey would like. He wants more in-person communication with all the people in one room.[75]

Under virtual leadership, communication between leaders and their subordinates still occurs, but it may be largely by videoconferencing, telephone, and email. In these situations, leaders have to work harder at creating and maintaining relationships with their employees. Nonverbal communication is not possible with email, for example, so managers have to make a special effort to convey appreciation, reinforcement, and constructive feedback to subordinates.

MyBizLab

Study, practise, and explore real business situations with these helpful resources:

- **Interactive Lesson Presentations:** Work through interactive presentations and assessments to test your knowledge of business concepts.
- **Study Plan:** Check your understanding of chapter concepts with self-study quizzes.
- **Dynamic Study Modules:** Work through adaptive study modules on your computer, tablet, or mobile device.
- **Simulations:** Practise decision-making in simulated business environments.
- **Videos:** Learn more about the business practices and strategies of real companies.

SUMMARY OF LEARNING OBJECTIVES

LO-1 IDENTIFY AND DISCUSS THE BASIC *FORMS OF BEHAVIOUR* THAT EMPLOYEES EXHIBIT IN ORGANIZATIONS.

Employee behaviour is the pattern of actions by the members of an organization that directly or indirectly influences the organization's effectiveness. *Performance behaviours* are the total set of work-related behaviours that the organization expects employees to display. *Organizational citizenship* refers to the behaviour of individuals who make a positive overall contribution to the organization. *Counterproductive behaviours* are those that detract from, rather than contribute to, organizational performance.

LO-2 DESCRIBE THE NATURE AND IMPORTANCE OF *INDIVIDUAL DIFFERENCES* AMONG EMPLOYEES.

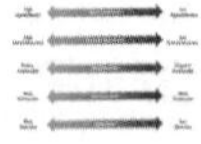

Individual differences are personal attributes that vary from one person to another. *Personality* is the relatively stable set of psychological attributes that distinguish one person from another. The *"big five" personality traits* are agreeableness, conscientiousness, emotionality, extraversion, and openness. *Emotional intelligence*, or emotional quotient (EQ), refers to the extent to which people are self-aware, can manage their emotions, can motivate themselves, express empathy for others, and possess social skills. *Attitudes* reflect our beliefs and feelings about specific ideas, situations, or other people. Especially important attitudes are *job satisfaction and organizational commitment.*

LO-3 EXPLAIN THE MEANING AND IMPORTANCE OF *PSYCHOLOGICAL CONTRACTS* AND THE PERSON–JOB FIT IN THE WORKPLACE.

A *psychological contract* is the overall set of expectations held by employees and the organization regarding what employees will contribute to the organization and what the organization will provide in return. A good *person–job fit* is achieved when the employee's contributions match the inducements the organization offers. Having a good match between people and their jobs can help enhance performance, job satisfaction, and motivation.

LO-4 IDENTIFY AND SUMMARIZE THE MOST IMPORTANT MODELS OF *EMPLOYEE MOTIVATION*.

Motivation is the set of forces that cause people to behave in certain ways. Early approaches to motivation were first based on the assumption that people work only for money, and then on the assumption that social needs are the primary way to motivate people. The *hierarchy of human needs* model holds that people at work try to satisfy one or more of five different needs. The *two-factor theory* argues that job satisfaction is influenced by motivation factors such as recognition for a job well done, while job dissatisfaction depends on hygiene factors such as working conditions. *Expectancy theory* suggests that people are motivated to work toward rewards that they desire and have a reasonable expectancy of obtaining. *Equity theory* focuses on social comparisons—people evaluating their treatment by the organization relative to the treatment of others.

LO-5 DESCRIBE THE *STRATEGIES* USED BY ORGANIZATIONS TO IMPROVE JOB SATISFACTION AND EMPLOYEE MOTIVATION.

Reinforcement involves applying (or withholding) positive (or negative) consequences in an attempt to motivate employees to exhibit behaviour the manager wants. *Goal setting* involves setting SMART goals that will motivate workers to high performance. *Participative management and empowerment* involves tapping into workers' knowledge about the job, encouraging them to be self-motivated, and giving them more authority and responsibility so that they feel they are a real part of the company's success. *Team management* means forming teams of employees and empowering the team to make decisions on issues like production scheduling, work procedures, work schedules, and the hiring of new employees. *Job enrichment* means adding motivating factors to job activities. *Modified work schedules*—such as *work sharing* (job sharing), *flextime*, and *telecommuting*—increase employee satisfaction by providing increased flexibility for workers.

LO-6 DEFINE *LEADERSHIP* AND DISTINGUISH IT FROM *MANAGEMENT*.

Leadership refers to the processes and behaviours used by a person in order to motivate, inspire, and influence the behaviours of others. Leadership and management are not the same thing. Leadership involves such things as developing a vision, communicating that vision, and directing change. *Management* focuses more on following procedures, monitoring results, and working toward outcomes.

LO-7 SUMMARIZE THE *APPROACHES TO LEADERSHIP* THAT DEVELOPED DURING THE TWENTIETH CENTURY.

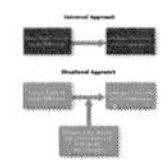

The *trait approach* to leadership focused on identifying the traits of successful leaders. Recent research has focused on traits such as emotional intelligence, drive, honesty and integrity, self-confidence, and charisma. The *behavioural approach* identified two common leader behaviours: *task-focused* and *employee-focused* behaviours. Three leadership styles—*autocratic*, *democratic*, and *free-rein*—were also identified. The *situational approach* to leadership assumes that factors in the leader, factors in the followers, and factors in the situation determine which leadership behaviour is most effective.

LO-8 DESCRIBE THE MOST RECENT IDEAS ABOUT EFFECTIVE LEADERSHIP.

Transformational leadership (as distinguished from *transactional leadership*) focuses on the set of abilities that allows a leader to recognize the need for change, to create a vision to guide that change, and to execute the change effectively. *Charismatic leadership* is influence based on the leader's personal charisma. Leaders are often expected to play the role of *coach*, which involves selecting team members; providing direction, training, and developing; and allowing the group to function autonomously. Research on *gender and leadership* is reexamining assumptions about how men and women lead. *Cross-cultural leadership* is becoming increasingly important as companies become more diverse in a globalized economic system. *Strategic leadership* is the leader's ability to lead change in the organization so as to enhance its competitiveness. *Ethical leadership* requires that leaders maintain high ethical standards for their own conduct, and to hold others in their organizations to the same standards. *Virtual leadership* is becoming important as more leaders and their followers work in physically separate places.

QUESTIONS AND EXERCISES

QUESTIONS FOR ANALYSIS

1. Describe the psychological contract you currently have or have had in the past with an employer. If you have never worked, describe the psychological contract that you have with the instructor in this class.
2. Explain how each of the "big five" personality traits influence leadership effectiveness.
3. How is the job enrichment/job redesign approach to motivation different from the modified work schedules (flextime, compressed workweek) approach to motivation? Are there similarities between the two approaches? Explain.
4. How can participative management programs enhance employee satisfaction and motivation? Why do some employees not want to get involved in participative management?
5. What is the relationship between performance behaviours and organizational citizenship behaviours? Which are more important to an organization?
6. Describe the type of circumstance in which it would be appropriate to apply each of the theories of motivation discussed in this chapter. Which theory would be easiest to use? Which one would be hardest? Why?

APPLICATION EXERCISES

7. Interview your employer or an administrator at your college. Ask the person what they believe motivates their employees. Identify one or more theories of motivation that seem consistent with this person's approach.
8. Ask a manager what traits he or she thinks are necessary for success. How does the manager's list compare with the "big five" list in this chapter? How many differences are there? Why would these differences exist?
9. Interview the human resource manager of a local company and ask what strategies the company uses to enhance employee job satisfaction.
10. Think of the job you now have or a job you had in the past. How many of the five kinds of power did your boss use? Give examples.

BUILDING YOUR BUSINESS SKILLS

LEARNING TO LEAD

GOAL

To encourage you to understand your own strengths and weaknesses as they relate to critical leadership skills.

BACKGROUND INFORMATION

Most large businesses devote considerable resources to identifying those managers with the most leadership potential, and then providing training and development opportunities for those managers to enhance and refine their leadership skills. One company, for instance, has identified the following traits, characteristics, and skills, as important in leadership:

- personal integrity
- decision-making skills
- interpersonal skills
- communication skills
- strategic thinking skills
- global awareness skills
- financial management skills

METHOD

Step 1 Working with three other students (as assigned by your instructor), develop and describe indicators and measures a business could use to *assess* each of the traits, characteristics, and skills listed above in managers, so the company could select those managers with the strongest potential for leadership. In other words, describe how you would go about selecting managers for special leadership training and development.

Step 2 Work with your group to develop or describe the techniques and methods that would *enhance* the traits, characteristics, and skills listed above. In other words, after you have identified the managers with the strongest potential for growth as leaders in Step 1, in Step 2 describe how you would go about teaching and developing those individuals so as to enhance their leadership potential and capacity.

FOLLOW-UP QUESTIONS

1. Comment on the traits, characteristics, and skills in the above list. Do you agree or disagree that these would differentiate between those who are both managers and leaders and those who are simply managers? Are there others items that should be added to the list?
2. How easy do you think it would be to select managers for leadership and development in a company?
3. Do you believe that leadership can be taught? What are the assumptions underlying your answer?
4. If you personally were selected for a leadership development program, what would you expect to encounter during the training and development? How do you think you might be different after the training and development were completed?

EXERCISING YOUR ETHICS

TAKING ONE FOR THE TEAM

THE SITUATION

You are a skilled technician who has worked for a major electronics firm for the past ten years. You love your job—it is interesting, stimulating, and enjoyable, and you are well paid. The plant where you work is one of five manufacturing centres your firm operates in a major metropolitan area. The firm is currently developing a new prototype for one of its next-generation products. To ensure that all perspectives are reflected, the company has identified a set of technicians from each plant who will work together as a team for the next two months.

THE DILEMMA

You have just met with your new teammates and are quite confused about what you might do next. As it turns out, the technicians from two of the manufacturing centres have heard rumours that your company is planning to close at least three of the centres and move production to a lower-cost factory in another country. These individuals are very upset. Moreover, they have made it clear that they (1) do not intend to put forth much extra effort on this project and (2) are all looking for new jobs. You and the other technicians, though, have heard none of these rumours. Moreover, these individuals seem as excited as you about their jobs.

TEAM ACTIVITY

First, working alone, write a brief summary of how you would handle this situation. For instance, would you seek more information or just go about your work? Would you start looking for another job, would you try to form a sub-group just with those technicians who share your views, or would you try to work with everyone?

Second, form a small group with some of your classmates. Share with each other the various ideas you each identified. Then, formulate a group description of what you think most people in your situation would do. Finally, share your description with the rest of the class.

BUSINESS CASE 9

SEARCHING FOR A GREAT PLACE TO WORK

Every year a list of Canada's Top 100 places to work is co-published by the *Globe and Mail* and MediaCorp. The 2015 winners include 3M Canada, The Aboriginal Peoples Television Network, and Telus Corp. The criteria that are used to rate companies include human resource practices, the atmosphere of the workplace, health benefits offered to employees, vacation and time off, encouragement of employee feedback to management, and effective performance management. More detail about the study and the companies that made the list can be found at www.CanadasTop100.com.

Other international companies have also been recognized in various surveys as great places to work. Two of the most well known are Google and Netflix.

Nathalie Madore/The Canadian Press

GOOGLE

Larry Page met Sergey Brin when he visited Stanford University as a prospective graduate student in computer science. Although they did not initially hit it off, a year later they were collaborating on a new search engine. By 1998, they had investors, and had incorporated both Google—the name of their search engine—and the name of their business venture. From the beginning, Page and Brin realized that happy, motivated employees were at the centre of successful organizations. Karen May, vice-president of People Development at Google, shares their vision: "Imagine a world where most organizations were the best place to work. Imagine what we could be getting done on the planet if this were true."

Google has grown quickly, from a two-person operation to a company with more than 37 000 employees in 40 countries. Google has become famous for its over-the-top perks, such as on-site bowling alleys and pools tables, free haircuts during work hours, and Lego rooms. Unlike other companies, Google is analytical about the perks it offers, using complex metrics to evaluate which are most valued by employees. Google is also a pay leader, offering salaries well above the market average.

Google executives believe it essential that people love what they do. Every employee has the opportunity to spend at least 20 percent of work time on a project of his or her choice using Google's extensive resources. For example, Chade-Meng Tan, an engineer at Google, has been working on a project to achieve world peace in his lifetime. Although this goal is not likely to be attained, Tan has been encouraged to spend time on the project. He has developed a course on mindfulness for Google employees and has written on the topic, all while working to create Google's mobile search engine.

Prasad Setty, vice-president of People Analytics and Compensation, is a strong supporter of Google's flexible work hours policy. Employees are given a lot of freedom to decide when to work or when to go to the gym, play volleyball, or get a free massage. Setty says, "One of the tenets we strongly believe in is if you give people freedom, they will amaze you." However, to make this autonomy idea work, Google has a highly selective and deliberate hiring process directed at employing people who are ambitious and achievement-oriented.

Finally, Google employees are given a voice in company decision making. The company gets feedback from employees on issues as diverse as compensation and the types of bikes available to ride around the campus. Every Friday, Brin and Page hold employee forums to respond to commonly asked questions. Employees are also given access to detailed company information that is often a closely guarded secret. Google's revolutionary approach to the workplace has paid off—the company's stock has significantly outperformed the Dow Jones index.

NETFLIX

Selling movies to consumers is a dynamic and challenging industry. In order to cope with the complex and rapidly evolving nature of the industry, Netflix CEO and founder Reed Hastings recruited a team of top performers in fields such as marketing, content management, and website operations. But then he had to find a way to motivate these stars to fulfill their potential. Netflix does use monetary rewards as a motivator ("We're unafraid to pay high," says Hastings), but the company achieves its greatest results by focusing on employee needs.

One important set of needs Netflix fulfills is the desire to work with friends, to be part of a team, and to "belong." The atmosphere is casual and collaborative, but as Michelle Conlin of BusinessWeek puts it, "Netflix is no frat party with beer bashes and foosball tables." The values statement says, "The benefit of a high-performance culture is that you work with consistently outstanding colleagues, which is exhilarating. We're a high-performance team, not a family. A strong family is together forever, no matter what. A strong company, on the other hand, is more like a professional sports team, which is built to win."

Netflix works to fulfill employees' needs for esteem by being an employer that is well liked. The job pages of the company's website say, "It is satisfying to work at a company that people love. We're ranked number one in customer satisfaction across the entire Internet, narrowly besting such great companies as Apple and Amazon."

Another need is employees' passion to achieve. The "best in class" personnel at this firm of just 400 workers are attracted by the opportunity to have a significant impact on a successful and ever-changing company. The Netflix values statement summarizes Hastings' viewpoint as follows: "Rules inhibit creativity and entrepreneurship, leading to a lack of innovation. Our solution to increased complexity is to increase talent density. Great people make great judgment calls, despite ambiguity. We believe in freedom and responsibility, not rules."

The Netflix motivation scheme is not for everyone. "At most companies, average performers get an average raise," says Hastings. "At Netflix, they get a generous severance package." Netflix is getting maximum performance from its workers in order to gain a competitive advantage over its key competitors.

QUESTIONS FOR DISCUSSION

1. Describe how Maslow's needs hierarchy could be applied to Google's approach to employee motivation.
2. Use Herzberg's two-factor theory to explain how Google motivates employees.
3. What types of people are best and least suited for work at Google? At Netflix?
4. Consider the following statement: *Trying to motivate employees by focusing on their needs is a frustrating and not very workable idea, because it is hard to find out just what employee needs are. Even if you do find out, that doesn't tell you specifically what you should do to satisfy those needs.* Do you agree or disagree? Defend your answer.

PART 2(A): THE BUSINESS OF MANAGING

GOAL OF THE EXERCISE

In Part 1 of the business plan project, you formulated a basic identity for your business. Part 2(a) asks you to think about the goals of your business, some internal and external factors affecting the business, and the organizational structure of the business.

EXERCISE BACKGROUND: PART 2(A) OF THE BUSINESS PLAN

As you learned in Chapter 6, every business sets goals. In this part of the plan, you'll define some of the goals for your business. Part 2(a) also asks you to perform a basic SWOT analysis for your business. As you'll recall from Chapter 6, a SWOT analysis looks at the business's Strengths, Weaknesses, Opportunities, and Threats. The strengths and weaknesses are internal factors—things the business can control. The opportunities and threats are generally external factors that affect the business:

Socio-cultural forces. Will changes in population or culture help your business or hurt it?

Economic forces. Will changes in the economy help your business or hurt it?

Technological forces. Will changes in technology help your business or hurt it?

Competitive forces. Does your business face much competition or very little?

Political–legal forces. Will changes in laws help your business or hurt it?

Each of these will affect different businesses in different ways, but some may not apply to your business at all.

Part 2(a) of the business plan also asks you to determine how the business is to be run. One thing you'll need to do is create an organizational chart to get you thinking about the different tasks needed for a successful business. You'll also examine various factors relating to operating your business.

YOUR ASSIGNMENT

MyBizLab

STEP 1

Open the saved Business Plan file you began working on in Part 1. You will continue to work from this file.

STEP 2

For the purposes of this assignment, you will answer the questions in Part 2(a): The Business of Managing:

1. Provide a brief mission statement for your business.

   Hint: *Refer to the discussion of mission statements in Chapter 6. Be sure to include the name of your business, how you will stand out from your competition, and why a customer will buy from you.*

2. Consider the goals for your business. What are three of your business goals for the first year? What are two intermediate-to-long-term goals?

   Hint: *Refer to the discussion of goal setting in Chapter 6. Be as specific and realistic as possible with the goals you set. For example, if you plan on selling a service, how many customers do you want by the end of the first year, and how much do you want each customer to spend?*

3. Perform a basic SWOT analysis for your business, listing its main strengths, weaknesses, opportunities, and threats.

   Hint: *We explained previously which factors you should consider in your basic SWOT analysis. Look around at your world, talk to classmates, or talk to your instructor for other ideas in performing your SWOT analysis.*

4. Who will manage the business?

   Hint: *Refer to the discussion of managers in Chapter 6. Think about how many levels of management and what kinds of managers your business needs.*

5. Show how the "team" fits together by creating a simple organizational chart for your business. Your chart should indicate who will work for each manager, and each person's job title.

   Hint: *As you create your chart, consider the different tasks involved in the business. To whom will each person report? Refer to the discussion of organizational structure in Chapter 7 for information to get you started.*

Note: Once you have answered the questions, save your Word document. You'll be answering additional questions in later chapters.

PART 2(B): THE BUSINESS OF MANAGING

GOAL OF THE EXERCISE

At this point, your business has an identity and you've described the factors that will affect your business and how you will operate it. Part 2(b) of the business plan project asks you to think about your employees, the jobs they will be performing, and the ways in which you can lead and motivate them.

EXERCISE BACKGROUND: PART 2(B) OF THE BUSINESS PLAN

To complete this part of the plan, you need to refer to the organizational chart you created in Part 2(a). In this part of the business plan exercise, you'll take the different job titles you created in the organizational chart and give thought to the skills that employees will need to bring to the job before they begin. You'll also consider training you'll need to provide after they are hired, and how you'll compensate your employees. Part 2(b) of the business plan also asks you to consider how you'll lead your employees and keep them happy and motivated.

YOUR ASSIGNMENT

MyBizLab

STEP 1

Open the Business Plan file you have been working on.

STEP 2

For the purposes of this assignment, you will answer the questions in Part 2(b): The Business of Managing:

1. What do you see as the "corporate culture" of your business? What types of employee behaviours, such as organizational citizenship, will you expect?

   Hint: *Will your business demand a casual environment or a more professional environment? Refer to the discussion on employee behaviour in this chapter for information on organizational citizenship and other employee behaviours.*

2. What is your philosophy on leadership? How will you manage your employees on a day-to-day basis?

   Hint: *Refer to the discussion on leadership in this chapter to help you formulate your thoughts.*

3. Looking back at your organizational chart in Part 2(a), briefly create a job description for each team member.

   Hint: *As you learned in Chapter 8, a job description lists the duties and responsibilities of a job; its working conditions; and the tools, materials, equipment, and information used to perform it. Imagine your business on a typical day. Who is working, and what are each person's responsibilities?*

4. Next, create a job specification for each job, listing the skills and other credentials and qualifications needed to perform the job effectively.

   Hint: *As you write your job specifications, consider what you would write if you were making an ad for the position. What would the new employee need to bring to the job in order to qualify for the position?*

5. What sort of training, if any, will your employees need once they are hired? How will you provide this training?

   Hint: *Refer to the discussion of training in Chapter 8. Will you offer your employees on-the-job training? Off-the-job training? Vestibule training?*

6. A major factor in retaining skilled workers is a company's compensation system—the total package of rewards that it offers employees in return for their labour. Part of this compensation system includes wages/salaries. What wages or salaries will you offer for each job? Why did you decide on that pay rate?

   Hint: *Refer to Chapter 8 for more information on forms of compensation.*

7. As you learned in Chapter 8, incentive programs are special programs designed to motivate high performance. What incentives will you use to motivate your workforce?

   Hint: *Be creative and look beyond a simple answer, such as giving pay increases. Ask yourself: Who are my employees and what is important to them? Refer to Chapter 8 for more information on the types of incentives you may want to consider.*

Note: Once you have answered the questions, save your Word document. You'll be answering additional questions in later chapters.

CBC VIDEO CASE 2-1

CBC

NEALE'S SWEET 'N NICE ICE CREAM

THE COMPANY

Entrepreneurs Stafford Attsz and Andrew McBarnett are cousins who have started a specialty ice cream business. Their grandfather was well known in the Caribbean nation of Trinidad in the 1940s for selling "ice cream, sweet and nice." He handed down his secret recipe to his grandchildren, and they want to sell in Canada what they say is the world's best-tasting ice cream. Their product is currently sold in 40 retail outlets across Ontario. For more details on the company, go to www.sweetnnice.ca.

THE PITCH

As they enter Dragons' Den, Attsz and McBarnett pedal an old-fashioned ice cream cart that was commonly seen on the streets of Canada many years ago. As part of their pitch to the dragons, Attsz and McBarnett tell the story of their grandfather. They are asking for $100 000 for a 25 percent share of their business (valued at $400 000). If they convince the dragons to invest, they will use the money to expand their business across Canada. The cousins give samples to the dragons to try. The response is very positive. The dragons are impressed with the taste, and also the product's velvety and creamy texture.

THE DRAGONS' POINT OF VIEW

The dragons want to hear more details about the company. Attsz and McBarnett say that so far their sales are $20 000, but that's just from a phase 1 test launch in local ethnic stores. They plan to test their product on a small basis first, to determine market acceptance. They want to eventually achieve the success and visibility of a company like Ben & Jerry's. Two dragons decline to make an offer. Vikram Vij is concerned about two large competitors who have a big market share. He doesn't think Attsz and McBarnett can win that battle, so he says he is out. So is Robert Herjavec, even though he loves the ice cream.

Three of the dragons do make an offer. Michael Wekerle, an investor in tech and media companies, wants the cousins to be as successful as Ben & Jerry's. He wants 25 percent of the company and a 10 percent royalty on sales. Arlene Dickinson, CEO of Venture Communications, asks about the business strategy. The entrepreneurs say their strategy is to initially sell to ethnic groups, but they want to eventually get into the big stores and sell across Canada. Dickinson says they should stay in the ethnic market. She offers $100 000 for 50 percent of the business. She also wants a 5 percent royalty starting one year later and she wants that to continue until she gets her money back. She likes their story, but says they'll need more money and have to expend a lot of effort to be successful. Jim Treliving (Boston Pizza) wants 50 percent of the business plus a 5 percent royalty until the money is paid back. He also wants a say in running the business.

(continued)

THE OUTCOME

After hearing these three individual offers, the entrepreneurs ask if the three dragons would agree to work together. The three finally agree. They will each get 15 percent of the business plus a 2 percent royalty on sales.

QUESTIONS FOR DISCUSSION

1. If you were the two entrepreneurs, would you take the joint offer made by the three dragons? Explain your reasoning.
2. What management issues must the entrepreneurs deal with at this stage in their company's life? In what ways can the dragons help them manage through this expansion phase?
3. What lessons about organizing and financing a business can you take away from this video? If Attsz and McBarnett were given a second opportunity to make this pitch, what advice would you give them?

Source: "Neale's Sweet 'n Nice Ice Cream," *Dragons' Den,* Episode 14, Season 9 (February 11, 2015).

BUSINESS TODAY VIDEO CASE 2-1

PIZZA HUT

Pizza Hut is part of the Yum! Brands family of companies. There are three basic levels of management in the organization. Top managers work for Yum! Brands, which is Pizza Hut's parent company. First-line managers run the individual Pizza Hut restaurants (which are mostly franchisee owned). Middle managers work at head office. Chris Fuller is the Director of Public Relations and Social Media for Pizza Hut. His job is to keep Pizza Hut in the news in a positive way. He focuses on publicizing the brand and he does this by integrating the Pizza Hut name into movies and TV scenes. Chris has to balance parent companies expectations with the needs of franchisees in different markets.

The basic functions of planning, organizing, leading, and controlling are important in an organization like Pizza Hut. Controlling is particularly important, and specific standards are set for all franchisees, regardless of the geographical region in which their particular outlet is located. While control at the top is important to ensure standard product quality, brand image, and menu choices, head office managers must also respect the needs and opinions of franchisees.

To be effective, managers need various skills. For example, time management skills are important for Chris Fuller, because he must quickly react to changes in market conditions. He also has to have technical skills in order to write good public relations material. Interpersonal skills are important because ideas need to be effectively communicated to workers. Decision-making skills and technical skills are required when he chooses new techniques to get Pizza Hut's message out to customers. For example, traditional media may not be as effective as it used to be, because social media is now much more important (and because consumers are tweeting, posting, and blogging things that may negatively affect Pizza Hut's public image).

Strategic management is an important activity at an organization like Pizza Hut. Recently, the company noticed that sales were declining and margins were getting tighter. A SWOT analysis showed that a pizza-centred menu was a weakness because many other food options were being made available to customers by Pizza Hut's competitors. But a bright spot was that the demand for pasta was increasing. So there was an opportunity to expand food offerings, and this countered the threat of losing customers to other businesses. Top managers put together a strategic plan that included an increased emphasis on pasta. At the operational level, Chris Fuller's team introduced Tuscani Pasta, and, as part of a large public relations campaign, announced (on April Fool's Day) that the company's name was being changed to Pasta Hut. The company even made a new logo to reflect the change. Since there was concern that consumers might not get the joke, a contingency plan was drawn up to deal with that potential problem. But consumers went along with the (fake) change, the news media gave it big coverage, and Pizza Hut benefited.

QUESTIONS FOR DISCUSSION

1. Describe the three levels of management at Pizza Hut.
2. What are the four functions of management? How are these evident at Pizza Hut?
3. What specific skills must managers possess? How are these skills evident at Pizza Hut?

BUSINESS TODAY VIDEO CASE 2-2

CH2MHILL

CH2MHill was founded in 1946 by a civil engineering professor and several of his students. It is now an employee-owned global engineering and project delivery firm with 30 000 employees and $6 billion in annual revenues. The company manages complex engineering and construction projects like the expansion of the Panama Canal.

Kurt Workman, Digital Communication Manager at CH2MHill, sees leadership as a continuum. At one end is a leader who is liked, and at the other end is one who is feared. But he thinks a great leader is in the middle and is respected. Workman says a leader can be found at any level in an organization. A leader inspires others to be better. A leader must be adaptable; when things get tough, the leader encourages everyone to see a way to solve the problem. A leader has a calming presence on others and cares about the people around them. He or she also takes an interest in people and makes them feel part of the team. A leader must be able to make tough decisions but must also be friendly and fun to work with (tough but caring). Leaders must be willing to tell low performers that their performance is not up to par, but must also have empathy for followers. In short, the leader must exhibit a balance between being liked and being tough.

QUESTIONS FOR DISCUSSION

1. What is the difference between a leader and a manager? Is Kurt Workman talking about a leader or a manager? Explain.
2. What is the difference between task-oriented and employee-oriented behaviour? How do those ideas fit into the comments made by Kurt Workman?
3. What is the trait approach to leadership? How is it relevant for Workman's view of leaders?

PART 3 MANAGING OPERATIONS AND INFORMATION

LO

AFTER READING THIS CHAPTER, YOU WILL BE ABLE TO:

LO-1 Explain the meaning of the term *production* (or *operations*) and describe the four kinds of *utility* it provides.

LO-2 Identify the characteristics that distinguish *service operations* from *goods production* and explain the main differences in the *service focus*.

LO-3 Describe two types of *operations processes.*

LO-4 Describe the factors involved in *operations planning* and *operations control.*

LO-5 Explain the connection between *productivity* and *quality*.

LO-6 Understand the concept of *total quality management* and describe nine tools that companies can use to achieve it.

LO-7 Explain how a *supply-chain strategy* differs from traditional strategies for coordinating operations among businesses.

Big Changes in Canadian Manufacturing

The Ontario and Minnesota Paper Co. paper mill in Fort Frances, Ontario, produced its first roll of paper in 1914. Over the years, the mill provided good jobs for thousands of workers, and multiple generations of workers from the same family had careers there. One of the construction workers who helped build the mill saw his son, grandson, and great-grandson work there.

But the mill was shut down in 2014, and it is just one of many paper mills that have met the same fate. During the period 2005–2014, 17 pulp and paper mills in Canada ceased operations. These mills span the country from sea to sea, from the West Fraser Timber mill in Kitimat, British Columbia, to the AbitibiBowater mill in Stephenville, Newfoundland. These shutdowns resulted from major changes that have swept through the forestry sector in Canada.

What happened? For pulp and paper mills, the emergence of the internet was a game changer. As more and

hxdyl/Fotolia

more people went online, newspapers and magazines struggled to cope with declining readership and advertising revenues. Many newspapers and magazines went out of business and the demand for newsprint and fine papers

Operations Management, Productivity, *and* Quality

CHAPTER 10

declined. The numbers below give some indication of the magnitude of the decline in the forestry sector:

- In 2004, the forestry sector provided employment for over 308 000 workers; by 2014, that number had declined to 190 000.
- In 2000, the forestry sector generated a positive balance of trade ($38 billion); by 2013, that had declined to $19 billion.
- In 1994, the forestry sector generated 3 percent of Canada's GDP; in 2013, it was just 1 percent.
- In 2000, there were 50 paper mills in Canada; in 2014, there were 30.

Automobile manufacturing is another part of the manufacturing sector that has faced big challenges in recent years. In the 1990s, the industry generated an annual trade surplus of $20 billion, but now it shows an annual *deficit* of $12 billion. Canada's share of North American production has dropped to a record low 14 percent (Mexico's share is about 20 percent). Wages for workers in Mexico are about one-tenth those paid to workers in Canadian automobile plants. In 2000, 198 000 people worked in the Canadian auto industry, but the number has declined to about 125 000. Canada produces 2 million cars now compared with 3 million in 2000.

And the future looks uncertain. When General Motors Canada received bailout money from the federal government during the recession of 2008–2009, it had to guarantee it would keep a certain number of jobs in Canada. But that requirement ends in 2016, so GM may shift even more production elsewhere. It has already closed manufacturing plants in Toronto, Windsor (Ontario), and St. Thérèse (Quebec).

The challenges that have confronted the forestry and automobile industries have also caused many manufacturing operations that formerly made products like microwave ovens, refrigerators, washers, dryers, and televisions to cease. During the past 30 years or so, factory *output* increased nearly 60 percent, but factory *employment* fell 16 percent. During the last decade, 500 000 manufacturing jobs vanished, and factory employment in Canada dropped to its lowest level on record. As of October 2014, manufacturing accounted for 10.6 percent of GDP, and for 10 percent of the jobs in Canada (down from 16 percent in 2000). Manufacturing was the biggest sector in the Canadian economy from 1976 to 1990, but it is now third behind two service-producing industries (real estate/rental leasing and health care/social assistance).

By mid-2014, some improvements were evident. The capacity utilization rate (the proportion of Canada's capacity to produce that is actually being used) had risen to 82.7 percent, the highest since 2007. The transportation sector was running at 93.7, which is an extremely high level. Petroleum products and food processing made big gains, but traditional manufacturing in the automotive and forest products industries are still below their pre-recession levels. The gains made in other sectors in manufacturing came as a result of a weaker Canadian dollar and improved economic performance in the United States (leading to higher Canadian exports). But Canada's total manufacturing capacity is still less than it was in 2007. This reflects the large number of factory shutdowns that have occurred since the recession of 2008–2009.

Three factors explain much of the change that has affected manufacturing companies. First, in an attempt to increase their competitiveness, manufacturers have introduced new technologies and automation. This led to increased output, but fewer workers. For example, Maple Leaf Foods closed five old food processing factories that were inefficient and replaced them with *one* new, highly efficient factory in Hamilton, Ontario, that produces more than the five old plants combined. But about 1500 jobs were lost in the process.

Second, other countries have been very aggressive in attracting manufacturing plants to their jurisdictions. Some

HOW WILL THIS HELP ME?

You will benefit in three ways by reading and understanding methods that managers use for managing production operations and improving quality: (1) as an *employee*, you'll get a clearer picture of why everyone in a business should be concerned about productivity and quality, and how your job depends on the goods and services your company provides; (2) as a *manager*, you'll understand that, if companies want to remain competitive, they must continually analyze their production methods so they can efficiently produce high-quality products and services; and (3) as a *consumer*, you'll gain an appreciation of the significant efforts that companies expend in order to efficiently produce high-quality goods and services for consumers.

U.S. states, for example, have been giving automobile companies millions of dollars in incentives to encourage them to open manufacturing facilities there. Volkswagen received more than $500 million from the state of Tennessee, and Mexico convinced both Honda and Nissan to build new plants there. Representatives of foreign organizations have also come to Canada to tout the benefits of their location. For example, the CEO of the Economic Development Coalition of Southwest Indiana came to Canada to encourage Canadian auto parts makers to set up shop in the state.

Third, the fluctuating Canadian dollar has created uncertainty. In the 1970s and 1980s, when the dollar was worth 65–70 cents compared to the U.S. dollar, Canadian manufacturers found ready markets in the United States, because Canadian products could effectively compete on price. But when the value of the Canadian dollar soared above par several years ago, Canadian manufacturers found it much more difficult to compete on price. In 2015, the Canadian dollar dropped again to about 75 cents, so the situation may improve somewhat.

All these developments sound pretty ominous, but keep in mind that manufacturing's declining share of GDP was not sudden; the trend began shortly after the end of World War II. During the war, the manufacturing-to-GDP ratio was nearly 30 percent, but by the 1960s it had declined to 23 percent, and then to just 14 percent during the most recent decade. Over the past 60 years, most developed economies have also experienced declines in manufacturing's share of GDP, so Canada has lots of company. For example, in the United States, manufacturing's share of GDP has dropped from 24 percent in 1970 to just 13 percent at present.

There is good news on the manufacturing front. There have actually been increases in manufacturing activity, particularly in the energy industry. Consider the Nisku industrial complex south of Edmonton, which is the second-biggest energy park in North America (the biggest being in Houston, Texas). Pipes are the building blocks of refineries, petrochemical plants, and oil-sands extraction sites, and they are fitted together at Nisku into the necessary configurations. Manufacturing here is not mass production; rather, it is engineered-to-order modules made one at a time. The oil-sands boom has drastically increased the number of jobs available for welders, pipefitters, and electricians. In Edmonton, manufacturing jobs are up 50 percent since the recession ended.

Odua Images/Fotolia

There are also success stories in the automobile industry. Magna International's Newmarket, Ontario, factory—which makes door latches for automobiles—has become a world-class manufacturing plant. It defies the claim that low-cost countries automatically kill manufacturing in advanced industrial countries. The Newmarket plant is so efficient that it ships door latches to automakers in China. Linamar Corp., another auto parts company, has become a global competitor since Linda Hasenfratz took over as CEO in 2002. Linamar has 45 manufacturing plants, sales of $3.6 billion, and 19000 employees.

QUESTIONS FOR DISCUSSION

1. Explain in your own words how developments during the past few decades have presented challenges for Canadian manufacturing.
2. Consider the following statement: *The Canadian government should have intervened even more aggressively in the automobile industry (and in other manufacturing industries) in order to maintain employment.* Do you agree or disagree? Explain your reasoning.

LO-1 WHAT DOES "OPERATIONS" MEAN TODAY?

Everywhere you go, you encounter businesses that provide goods and services to their customers. You wake up in the morning, for example, to the sound of your favourite radio station. You stop at the corner store for a newspaper on your way to the bus stop, where you catch the bus to work or school. Your instructors, the bus driver, the clerk at the 7-Eleven, and the morning radio announcer are all examples of people who work in **service operations**. They provide you with tangible and intangible service products, such as entertainment, transportation, education, and food preparation. Firms that make tangible products—radios, newspapers, buses, textbooks—are engaged in **goods production**. The term *operations* includes all of the activities involved in making goods and providing services for customers. All businesses are service operations to some extent. For example, General Electric is well known as a maker of consumer appliances and jet engines, but its fastest-growing areas of business are its service operations (insurance, real estate, commercial finance, transportation services, and health-care information).

In Canada's early years, agriculture, trapping, and fishing were the dominant sectors in the economy. In the late nineteenth and early twentieth century, manufacturing became important. In the middle of the twentieth century, the service sector began to grow rapidly, and it now provides the majority of the jobs in Canada (although manufacturing is still important). Many of the things that we need or want—from health care to fast food—are produced by service operations.

SERVICE OPERATIONS Production activities that yield tangible and intangible service products.

GOODS PRODUCTION Production activities that yield tangible products.

Changes in Operations

Over the past 300 years, there have been several industrial revolutions. The first occurred in Britain in the 1800s, and the second in the United States in the early 1900s. Now, a third one is under way, based on new technologies, software, robots, and miniaturization.[1] For example, 3-D printing produces goods like car parts and dresses using successive layers of plastic ink, and Ford Motor Company is using this process to design and test new engineering ideas.[2] The technology means that new product prototypes can be developed within a day or two of the development of a new design, rather than the three-to-four-month time frame required with traditional methods. Other new technologies allow machines to run more cleanly, quickly, and safely, and to operate on a global scale. In a modern factory with online manufacturing, machines can log on to the internet, adjust their own settings, and make minor decisions without human help. They can communicate with other machines in the company (via an intranet) and with other companies' machines (via the internet). So-called "smart" equipment stores performance data that becomes available on desktops around the world, where designers can click on machine data, simulate machine action, and evaluate performance, before the machines themselves ever swing into action. With the internet, producers of both services and goods are integrating their production activities with those of far-off suppliers and customers.

CREATING VALUE THROUGH OPERATIONS

Products (both goods and services) provide customers with **utility** (want satisfaction). By making a product available at a time when consumers want it, production creates *time utility*, as when a company turns out ornaments in time for Christmas. By making a product available in a place convenient for consumers, production creates *place utility*, as when a local department store creates a "Trim-a-Tree" section. By making a product that consumers can take pleasure in owning, production creates *ownership (possession) utility*, as when you take a box of ornaments home and decorate your tree. By turning raw materials into finished goods, production creates *form utility*, as when an ornament maker combines glass, plastic, and other materials to create tree decorations.

Operations (or **production**) **management** is the systematic direction and control of the processes that transform resources into finished goods and services. As Figure 10.1 shows, *operations managers* must bring raw materials, equipment, and labour together under a production plan that effectively uses all the resources available in the production facility. As the demand for a product increases, managers must schedule and control work to produce the amount required. Meanwhile, they must control costs, quality levels, inventory, and plant and equipment. The impact of production activity on the environment must also be considered. The boxed insert entitled "Producing Green Energy" describes the dilemma that exists in the production of energy.

Some operations managers work in service "factories" like FedEx package-sorting depots, whereas others work in traditional factories that make physical products like cell phones. Still others work in offices, restaurants, hospitals, and stores. Farmers are operations managers who create utility by transforming soil, seeds, fuel, and other inputs into soybeans, milk, and other outputs. They may hire crews of workers to plant and harvest, or they may opt instead for automated machinery, or prefer some combination of workers and machinery.

LO-2 Differences Between Service and Manufacturing Operations

Both service and manufacturing operations transform raw materials into finished products. In service operations, however, the raw materials, or inputs, are not things like glass or steel. Rather, they are people who

UTILITY The power of a product to satisfy a human want; something of value.

OPERATIONS (OR PRODUCTION) MANAGEMENT A set of methods and technologies used in the production of a good or a service.

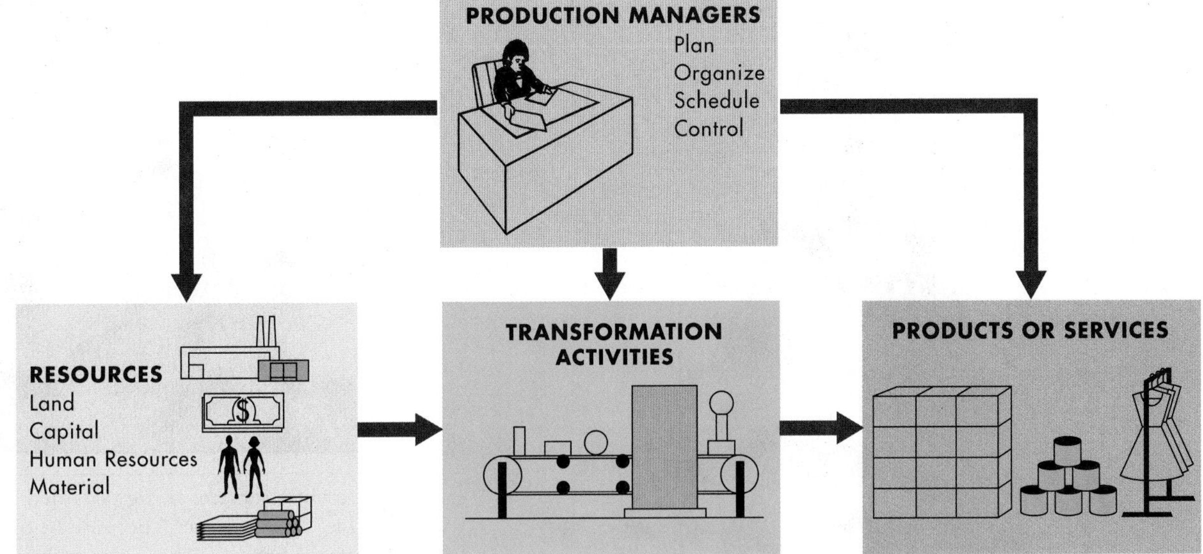

>>> **FIGURE 10.1** The transformation system

have either unsatisfied needs or possessions needing care or alteration. The output of service operations is not physical products, but people with needs met and possessions serviced. Service operations are more complicated than goods production in four ways: (1) the interaction with consumers, (2) the intangible and unstorable nature of some services, (3) the customer's presence in the process, and (4) service quality considerations.

INTERACTING WITH CONSUMERS

Manufacturing operations emphasize outcomes in terms of physical goods—for example, a new jacket. But the outcomes of most service operations are really combinations of goods and services—both making a pizza and serving (or delivering) it. Service workers need human relations skills. For example, gas company employees may need to

THE GREENING OF BUSINESS

Producing Green Energy

When people think about the production of goods, they usually think of products like automobiles, home appliances, computers, toothpaste, and so forth. But the production of *energy* is also a crucial activity in our society, and, in recent years, there has been a big push to produce "greener" forms of energy, like wind and solar. But it is also becoming clear that making green decisions about energy is very complicated, because each type of energy (oil, coal, gas, nuclear, hydroelectric, wind, solar, geothermal, and biofuel) has both advantages and disadvantages.

The dilemma is very clear—the most abundant and cheapest sources of energy (coal, oil, and natural gas) create significant environmental pollution when they are burned, while the least available and most expensive sources of energy (wind, solar, geothermal, and nuclear) create very little pollution. The fact that consumers want to pay the lowest price possible for energy likely means that there will continue to be a reliance on coal, oil, and natural gas for most of our energy needs.

Several other factors complicate decisions about the production of energy. First, some scientists are now questioning whether carbon dioxide is really the driver of global warming. If their views become dominant, that will reduce the push for "greener" energy sources like wind and solar. Second, critics have noted that without large government subsidies, wind and solar power are not competitive with coal and oil, and, as a result, wind and solar will not constitute a significant proportion of total energy for many years. Third, technological advances in the extraction of traditional fossil fuels have increased the supply of those fuels, which, in turn, lowers their price and makes them more attractive than wind and solar power. The sharp drop in gasoline prices in 2014 illustrates this phenomenon.

Biofuel—energy produced from sources like corn (used to make ethanol) and palm oil (used to make biodiesel)—looked promising at one time, but several unanticipated problems have arisen with this idea. For example, the increased demand for corn to make ethanol has driven up corn prices and increased the costs for all businesses that use corn. That, in turn, resulted in higher prices paid by consumers. Poor people have been hurt the most, because they spend a larger proportion of their total income on food.

It seems that everywhere we turn there are problems.

CRITICAL THINKING QUESTIONS

1. Consult the sources listed for this boxed insert (found at the end of this book), and then develop a list of the advantages and disadvantages of each type of energy. On the basis of the list, which source of energy do you think is best? What problems did you encounter as you tried to make your decision about which form is best?
2. Consider the following statement: *It is unwise to continue spending large amounts of money to develop wind and solar power because these sources are too unreliable and too expensive. Instead, emphasis should be put on developing technologies to make traditional fossil fuels less polluting.* Do you agree or disagree? Defend your reasoning.

The decorations for a Christmas tree illustrate the importance of the concepts of time, place, ownership, and form utility to consumers.

Lucky Business/Shutterstock

calm frightened customers who have reported gas leaks. Thus, their job includes more than just repairing pipes. In contrast, factory workers who install gas pipes in manufactured homes have no contact with customers and don't need such skills.

SERVICES CAN BE INTANGIBLE AND UNSTORABLE

Often, services can't be touched, tasted, smelled, or seen. An important satisfier for customers, therefore, is the intangible value they receive in the form of pleasure, gratification, or a feeling of safety. For example, when you hire an attorney, you purchase not only the intangible quality of legal expertise, but also the equally intangible reassurance that help is at hand. Many services—such as trash collection, transportation, child care, and house cleaning—can't be produced ahead of time and then stored for high-demand periods. If a service isn't used when available, it is usually wasted. Services, then, are typically unstorable. Airline companies try to cope with unstorability by scheduling more aircraft maintenance during the slower winter months, when consumer demand for seats is lower.[3]

The hair-styling services being provided to this customer are classified as "high-contact," because he or she must be part of the operations process. The services also illustrate the three key features of service operations: intangibility, customization, and unstorability.

Syda Productions/Fotolia

THE CUSTOMER'S PRESENCE IN THE OPERATIONS PROCESS

The customer is often present in the operations process. To get a haircut, for example, most of us have to go to the barbershop or hair salon. As they participate in the operations process, consumers can affect it. As a customer, you expect the salon to be conveniently located (place utility), to be open for business at convenient times (time utility), to provide safe and comfortable facilities, and to offer quality grooming (form utility) at reasonable prices (value for money spent). Accordingly, the manager sets hours of operation, available services, and an appropriate number of employees to meet customer requirements. But what happens if a customer, scheduled to receive a haircut, also asks for additional services, such as highlights or a shave, when he or she arrives? In this case, the service provider must balance customer satisfaction with a tight schedule. High customer contact has the potential to significantly affect the process.

The growth of e-commerce has introduced a "virtual presence," as opposed to a physical presence, of the customer. Consumers interact electronically and in real time with sellers, collecting information about product features, delivery availability, and after-sales service. Many companies have invited "the virtual customer" into their service systems by building customer-communications relationships. For example, the online travel agency Expedia.ca responds to your personalized profile with a welcome email, presents you with a tailor-made webpage the next time you sign in, offers chat rooms in which you can compare notes with other customers, and notifies you of upcoming special travel opportunities.

SERVICE QUALITY CONSIDERATIONS

Consumers use different measures to judge services and goods because services include intangibles, not just physical objects. Service managers know that quality of *work* and quality of *service* are not necessarily the same thing. Your car, for example, may have been flawlessly repaired (quality of work), but you'll probably be unhappy with the service if you're forced to pick it up a day later than promised (quality of service).

LO-3 Operations Processes

An **operations process** is a set of methods and technologies used in the production of a good or a service. Banks, for example, use two processes—document shredding and data encryption—to protect confidential information. Automakers use precision painting methods to produce a glittering paint finish.

GOODS-PRODUCING PROCESSES

At the most general level, operations processes for the production of physical products are either *make-to-order* (producing custom-designed products for special order) or *make-to-stock* (producing standard items in large quantities for consumers in general). More specifically, operations processes in manufacturing firms can be classified on the basis of (1) the kind of transformation technology that is used and (2) whether the operations process combines resources or breaks them into component parts.

Types of Transformation Technologies

Manufacturers use the following types of transformation technologies to turn raw materials into finished goods:

- In *chemical* processes, raw materials are chemically altered. Such techniques are common in the aluminum, steel, fertilizer, petroleum, and paint industries.
- *Fabrication* processes mechanically alter the basic shape or form of a product. Fabrication occurs in the metal forming, woodworking, and textile industries.
- *Assembly* processes put together various components. These techniques are common in the electronics, appliance, and automotive industries.
- In *transport* processes, goods acquire place utility by being moved from one location to another. For example, bicycles are routinely moved from manufacturing plants to consumers by truck and through warehouses and discount stores.
- *Clerical* processes transform information. Combining data on employee absences and machine breakdowns into a productivity report is a clerical process. So is compiling inventory reports at a retail outlet.

Analytic versus Synthetic Processes

An *analytic process* breaks down basic resources into their component parts. For example, Rio Tinto Alcan manufactures aluminum by extracting it from an ore called bauxite. The reverse approach, a *synthetic process*, combines a number of raw materials to produce a finished product such as fertilizer or paint.

SERVICE-PRODUCING PROCESSES

One useful way of classifying services is to determine whether a given service can be provided without the customer being part of the production system. In **high-contact systems**, the customer is part of the process. For example, when you purchase transportation, you must board a bus, train, or airplane. Transportation managers, therefore, must pay attention to the cleanliness of the trains, buses, and airplanes. Dental and medical services, hair salons, and guided tours are also high-contact systems. By contrast, in **low-contact systems**, the customer is not

OPERATIONS PROCESS A set of methods and technologies used in the production of a good or a service.

HIGH-CONTACT SYSTEM A system in which the service cannot be provided without the customer being physically in the system (e.g., transit systems).

LOW-CONTACT SYSTEM A system in which the service can be provided without the customer being physically in the system (e.g., lawn-care services).

age fotostock/SuperStock

Stockbyte/Getty Images

Kim Steele/Getty Images

Comstock/Stockbyte/Getty Images

© jovannig-Fotolia.com

<<< The various types of transformation technologies used by businesses provide an impressive array of products and services to consumers. The basic technologies shown here are *chemical* (top left), *fabrication* (top centre), *assembly* (top right), *transport* (bottom left), and *clerical* (bottom right).

TABLE 10.1 Business Strategies That Win Customers for Four Companies

Company	Strategy for Attracting Customers	What the Company Does to Implement Its Strategy
Toyota	Quality	Cars perform reliably, have an appealing fit and finish, and consistently meet or exceed customer expectations at a competitive price
No Frills	Low price	Foods and everyday items offered at prices significantly lower than conventional food chains
3M	Flexibility	Innovation, with more than 55 000 products in a constantly changing line of convenience items for home and office
FedEx	Dependability	Every delivery is fast and on time, as promised

physically present. The cheque-processing centre at a bank is a low-contact system, because customers are not in contact with the bank while the service is being performed. Gas and electric utilities, auto repair shops, and lawn-care services are also low-contact systems.

Business Strategy As the Driver of Operations

Production is a flexible activity that can be moulded into many shapes to give quite different capabilities for different purposes. The kind of production that is best for a particular company should be decided from above by the firm's business strategy.[4] In the following paragraphs, we present examples of four firms—two in goods production and two in services—that have different business strategies and, therefore, different operations capabilities. As shown in Table 10.1, each company has identified a business strategy it can use to attract customers in its industry. Toyota chose quality as their strategy for competing in selling cars. No Frills Grocery (owned by Loblaw Companies) emphasizes discount prices. The flexibility strategy at 3M prioritizes new product development in an ever-changing line of products for home and office, and FedEx captures the overnight delivery market with delivery dependability. Firms design their operations to support the company's business strategy.

Since the four firms have different business strategies, we should expect to see differences in their operations. The top-priority *operations capability* (*production capability*)—the activity or process that production must do especially well, with high proficiency—is listed for each firm in Table 10.2, along with key operations characteristics for implementing that capability. Each company's operations capability matches up with its business strategy, so that the firm's activities—from top to bottom—are focused in a particular direction. For example, Toyota's top priority is quality, so its operations—inputs, transformation activities, and outputs—are devoted first and foremost to quality. All production processes, equipment, and training are designed to build better cars. The entire culture supports a quality emphasis among employees, suppliers, and dealerships.

TABLE 10.2 Operations Capabilities and Characteristics for Four Companies

Operations Capability	Key Operations Characteristics
Quality (Toyota)	• High-quality standards for materials suppliers. • Just-in-time materials flow for lean manufacturing. • Specialized, automated equipment for consistent product buildup. • Operations personnel expert on continuous improvement of product, work methods, and materials.
Low Cost (No Frills)	• Avoids excess overhead and costly inventory (no floral departments, sushi bars, or banks that drive up costs). • Originally provided a limited assortment of "No Name" products and only the most basic customer service (more recently, stores have expanded both products and customer services). • Customers are required to pack their own groceries and provide their own bags. • Low labour costs are achieved by minimum staffing. • Labour and shelving costs are reduced by selling merchandise out of custom shipping cartons (in recent years, more conventional product displays have been introduced).
Flexibility (3M)	• Maintains some excess (expensive) production capacity available for fast start-up on new products. • Adaptable equipment/facilities for production changeovers from old to new products. • Hires operations personnel who thrive on change. • Many small-to-medium-sized facilities in diverse locations to enhance creativity.
Dependability (FedEx)	• Customer automation: uses electronic and online tools with customers to shorten shipping time. • Wireless information system for package scanning by courier, updating of package movement, and package tracking by customer. • Maintains a company air force, global weather forecasting centre, and ground transportation for pickup and delivery, with backup vehicles for emergencies. • Each of 30 automated regional distribution hubs processes up to 45 000 packages per hour for next-day deliveries.

LO-4 OPERATIONS PLANNING

Managers from many departments contribute to the firm's decisions about operations management. As Figure 10.2 shows, however, no matter how many decision makers are involved, the process can be described as a series of logical steps. The business plan and forecasts developed by top managers guide operations planning. The business plan outlines goals and objectives, including the specific goods and services that the firm will offer. Managers also develop long-range production plans through *forecasts* of future demand for both new and existing products. Covering a period of two to five years, the production plan specifies the number of plants or service facilities and the amount of labour, equipment, transportation, and storage that will be needed to meet demand. It also specifies how resources will be obtained. There are five main categories of operations planning: *capacity*, *location*, *layout*, *quality*, and *methods planning*.

Capacity Planning

The amount of a product a company can produce under normal working conditions is its **capacity**. A firm's capacity depends on how many people it employs and the number and size of its facilities. A supermarket, for instance, has far more cash registers than it needs on an average day. But on a Saturday morning or during the three days before Christmas, all registers will be running at full speed.

Long-range capacity planning considers both current and future requirements. If capacity is too small for demand, the company must turn away customers, a situation that cuts into profits and alienates both customers and salespeople. If capacity greatly exceeds demand, the firm wastes money by maintaining facilities that are too large, or employing too many workers. In goods-producing operations, capacity planning means ensuring that a firm's capacity just slightly exceeds the normal demand for its product. In low-contact service-producing operations, capacity should be set at the level of average demand. Orders that arrive faster than expected can be set aside in a "to be done" file and processed later, during a slower period. In high-contact service producing systems, managers must plan capacity to meet peak demand. When Alaska Airlines introduced self-service check-in machines and staffed "bag drop" stations, it doubled its capacity, halved its staffing needs, and cut costs, all while speeding travellers through the check-in process.[5]

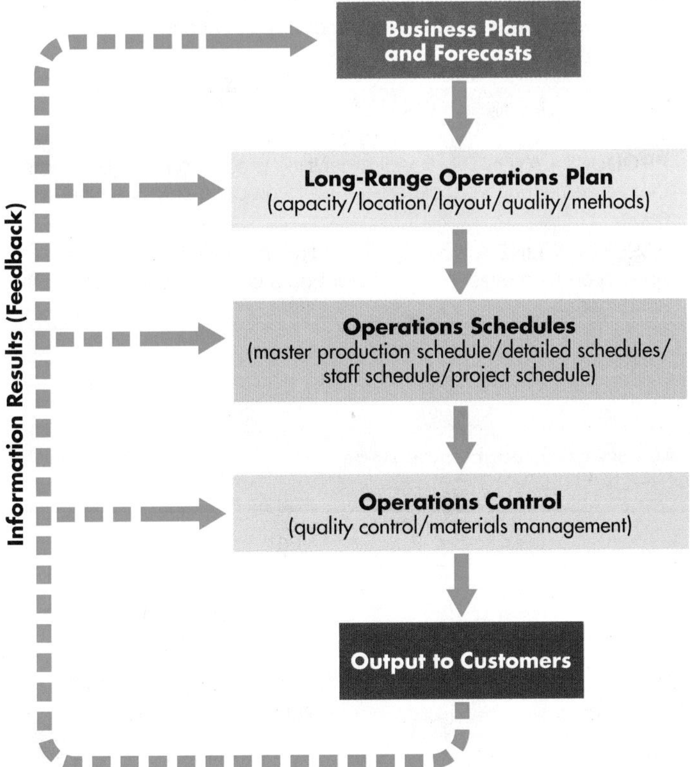

FIGURE 10.2 Operations planning and control

Location Planning

Because the location of a factory, office, or store affects its production costs and flexibility, sound location planning is crucial. Companies that locate in high-cost areas will find themselves at a cost disadvantage relative to their competitors.

In goods-producing operations, location decisions are influenced by proximity to raw materials and markets, availability of labour, energy and transportation costs, local regulations and taxes, and community living conditions. In low-contact systems, service can be located near resource supplies, labour, or transportation outlets. For example, the typical Walmart distribution centre is located near the hundreds of Walmart stores it supplies, not near the companies that supply the distribution centre. Distribution managers regard Walmart stores as their customers. By contrast, high-contact services must locate near the customers who are a part of the system. Thus, fast-food restaurants such as Taco Bell and McDonald's locate near areas with high traffic, such as college campuses, hospital cafeterias, and shopping malls.

Layout Planning

Once a site has been selected, managers must decide on plant layout. Layout of machinery, equipment, and supplies determines whether a company can respond quickly and efficiently to customer requests for more and different products and services, or whether it will find itself unable to match competitors' production speed or convenience of service. Three of the most widely used layouts are *process*, *product*, and *fixed position*.

PROCESS LAYOUTS

In a **process layout** (also called **custom-product layout**), equipment and people are grouped according to function. This layout is well suited to make-to-order shops (or job shops) that specialize in custom work. FedEx Office stores (formerly Kinko's Copy Centers) use custom-product layouts to accommodate a variety of custom jobs. Specific activities or processes, such as photocopying, faxing, computing, binding, and laminating are performed in separate specialized areas of the store. Walk-in

CAPACITY The amount of a good a firm can produce under normal working conditions.

PROCESS LAYOUT (CUSTOM-PRODUCT LAYOUT) A way of organizing production activities such that equipment and people are grouped together according to their function.

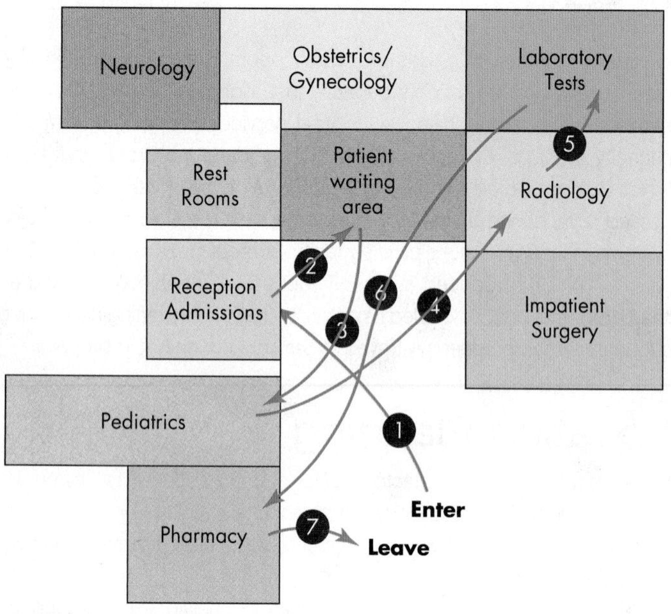

FIGURE 10.3 Process layout for a service provider—a medical clinic

With the Kiva MFS system, operators stand still while products come to them. Pallets, cases, and orders are stored on inventory pods that are picked up and moved by mobile robotic drive units (the small orange device under the shelves in the centre of the picture).

Chris Mueller/Redux

customers move from area to area using the self-service they need. In a woodworking shop, machines cut the wood in one area, sanding occurs in another area, and jobs that need painting are taken to a dust-free area where all the painting equipment is located. The job shop produces many one-of-a-kind products, and each product requires different kinds of work.

The main advantage of process layouts is flexibility. At any time, the shop can process individual customer orders, each requiring a different kind of work. Depending on its work requirements, a client being served or a job being processed may flow through three activity areas, another through just one area, and still others through four or more work areas. Figure 10.3 shows the process layout of a service provider (a medical clinic). The path taken through the facility reflects the unique treatments for one patient's visit.

Product Layouts

A **product layout** (also called a *same-steps* or **assembly line** *layout*) is set up to provide one type of service or to make one type of product in a fixed sequence of production steps. All units go through the same set of steps. It is efficient for large-volume make-to-stock operations that mass produce many units of a product. A partially finished product moves step by step through the plant on conveyor belts or other equipment, often in a straight line, as it passes through each stage until the product is completed. Automobile, food processing, and television assembly are examples of the use of the same-steps layout, as is mail processing at UPS and FedEx facilities. Figure 10.4 shows a product layout at a service provider (an automatic car wash), while Figure 10.5 shows a goods producer assembling parts needed to make storm windows.

PRODUCT LAYOUT A way of organizing production activities such that equipment and people are set up to produce only one type of good.

ASSEMBLY LINE A type of product layout in which a partially finished product moves through a plant on a conveyor belt or other equipment.

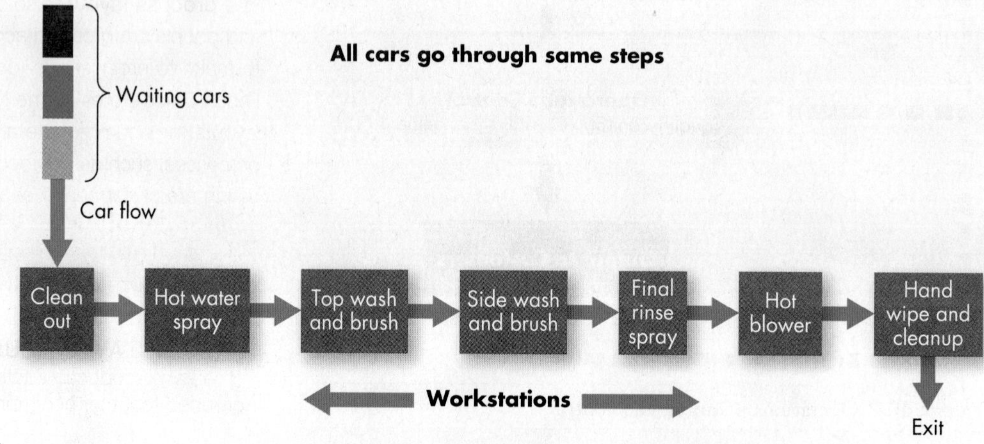

FIGURE 10.4 Product layout for a service—automated car wash

Same assembly steps for all frames

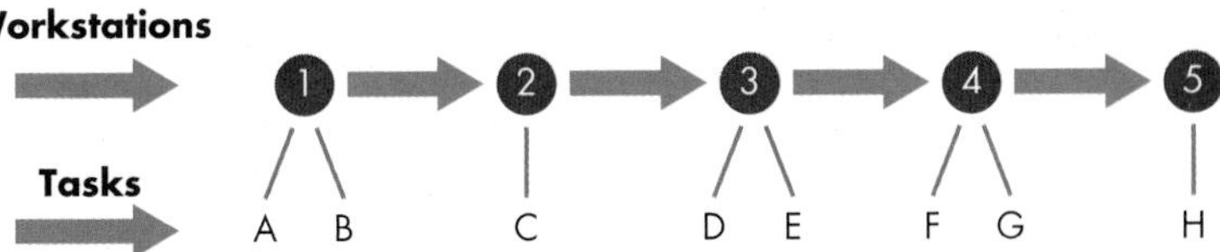

A: Assemble window frame
B: Install frame latch
C: Install rubber moulding
D: Insert frame screws
E: Cover frame screws
F: Install frame handle
G: Install glass pane
H: Pack window unit

FIGURE 10.5 Product layout for goods production—storm window assembly

FIXED POSITION LAYOUT

A **fixed position layout** is necessary when, because of size, shape, or other reasons, managers cannot move the service or product to another production facility. In fixed positon layouts, the product or customer remains at one location and equipment, materials, and human skills are moved to that location as needed. For example, physical rehabilitation specialists go to the home of patients who are recovering from knee replacement surgery. Plumbers also come to consumers' homes to make repairs when the pipes leak. The fixed position layout is also used for building huge ships that can't be moved; for constructing buildings; and for agricultural operations like plowing, fertilizing, and harvesting.

In any one of these three basic types of layout, both goods-producing and service-producing organizations may use *robots* to perform repetitive operations quickly and accurately. At Amazon.com, robots are used to locate items in customers' orders and to move products around the warehouse.[6] In agriculture, robots are used to pick fruit and to milk cows,[7] and hospitals use "service robots" to carry trays of medication or loads of laundry.[8] The boxed insert entitled "Will Robots Take Your Job?" raises some interesting issues about the effect of robots on employment levels.

Recent Developments in Layout Planning For goods-producing operations, there have been several recent developments that have increased the flexibility of operations. With a **flexible manufacturing system (FMS)**, a single factory can produce a wide variety of products. Automobile manufacturers, for example, now build several models of cars using the same basic "platform" (the underbody of the car). Nissan, Toyota, and Honda make the majority of their cars using FMS, and North American carmakers are now rapidly adopting the strategy.[9] The Oakville, Ontario, Ford plant was the first flexible assembly plant in Canada.[10]

Some companies have experimented with so-called **soft manufacturing**—reducing huge FMS operations to smaller, more manageable

FIXED POSITION LAYOUT A way of organizing production activities in which labour, equipment, materials, and other resources are brought to the geographic location where all operations work is done.

FLEXIBLE MANUFACTURING SYSTEM (FMS) A production system that allows a single factory to produce small batches of different goods on the same production line.

SOFT MANUFACTURING Emphasizes computer software and computer networks instead of production machines.

MANAGING IN TURBULENT TIMES

Will Robots Take Your Job?

Industrial robots have been used for years on assembly lines, where they tirelessly and efficiently perform highly specific tasks such as arc welding. Most of them are very expensive and are not very flexible in what they can do, but a new generation of robots that are cheaper, smarter, and more mobile are being developed. Consider just a few examples:

- A bakery in Switzerland uses robots to grab pretzels off a production line and bag them while they are still hot.
- Kitchener, Ontario–based Clearpath Robotics makes unmanned Kingfisher vehicles that measure tailings in potash mines so that humans are not exposed to harsh chemicals.
- At one New York City hotel, robots deliver guests' luggage to their rooms.
- A German beer maker has increased production efficiency, reduced production bottlenecks, and reduced delivery times by using robots that can sort through 30 000 bottles each hour.
- One Lowe's store has a robot that functions as the store greeter; it knows where every item in the store is located, and it converses in English or Spanish.
- Amazon.com is using robots made by Kiva Systems to reduce the cost of filling orders in its warehouses.

There are already about a million industrial robots in use around the world, and their numbers will increase in the coming years. But there is concern that this trend will reduce employment opportunities for human workers. A recent survey by the Pew Research Center found that 48 percent of the respondents felt automation (such as provided by robots) will destroy more jobs than it will create. Some experts claim that almost half of all jobs will be automated, and that unemployment will be very high in the future.

Those who are concerned about automation point to the obvious fact that when robots do the work of humans, jobs are lost. Those who disagree with this argument take the more moderate view that while some types of jobs are indeed likely to become automated (e.g., telemarketers, bank tellers, and bookkeepers), others are much less likely to be (e.g., occupational therapists, scientists, and managers). They also point out that many of the jobs that provide employment today did not even exist 50 years ago.

While there is much debate about the effects of robots on *employment*, there does seem to be a general consensus that automation may increase *income inequality*. Those who have a high level of technological skills will have high-paying jobs, but those who don't will receive much lower wages for their work.

CRITICAL THINKING QUESTION

1. Do you think that developments in automation and robotics will lead to higher levels of unemployment in society? Explain your reasoning.

groups of machines. Automation is less likely to fail when relegated to jobs it does best, while human workers perform the assembly-line jobs that require dexterity and decision making. Both are supported by networks of computers programmed to assist in all sorts of tasks.

The latest development is the *movable factory*. Because FMS is so expensive, some developing countries with lots of labour, but little capital, are buying up equipment from industrialized countries that is still relatively modern and then using it to produce new and untested products in their own country. For example, a used press from the Buffalo-Niagara region, capable of shaping steel with its 14 000 tons of pressure per square inch, is used to manufacture the internal workings of new Chinese nuclear power plants.[11]

Quality Planning

In planning production systems and facilities, managers must keep in mind the firm's quality goals.[12] Thus, any complete production plan includes systems for ensuring goods are produced to the firm's quality standards. The issue of quality is discussed in more detail later in this chapter.

Methods Planning

In designing production systems, managers must clearly identify all production steps and the specific methods for performing them. They can then work to reduce waste, inefficiency, and poor performance by examining procedures on a step-by-step basis, an approach sometimes called *methods improvement*.

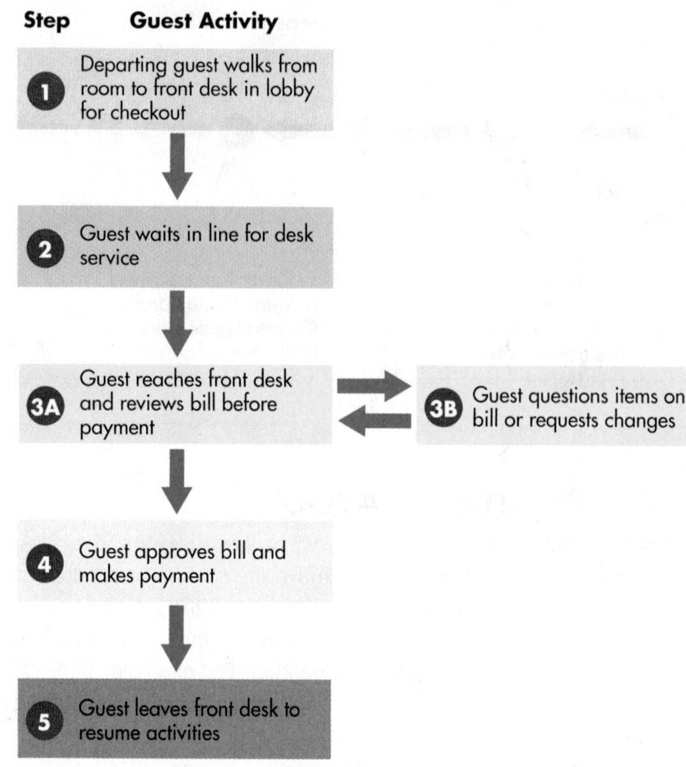

Step
Guest Activity
1 Departing guest walks from room to front desk in lobby for checkout
2 Guest waits in line for desk service
3A Guest reaches front desk and reviews bill before payment
3B Guest questions items on bill or requests changes
4 Guest approves bill and makes payment
5 Guest leaves front desk to resume activities

FIGURE 10.6 Flowchart of a traditional guest checkout

IMPROVING PROCESS FLOWS

Improving process flows at goods-producing operations begins by documenting current production practices. A detailed description using a diagram called a *process flowchart* is helpful in organizing and recording information. The flowchart identifies the sequence of production activities, movement of materials, and work performed at each stage of the process. It can then be analyzed to isolate wasteful activities, sources of delays, and other inefficiencies. The final step is implementing improvements.

Similar procedures are useful in designing and evaluating service systems. In a low-contact service system like a bank, the cash-management unit collects accounts receivable for corporate clients; the sooner cheques are collected and deposited, the sooner the client begins collecting interest. In high-contact services, the demands of systems analysis are somewhat different. Here, the steps in the process must be analyzed to see where improvements can be made. Consider the traditional checkout method at hotels. The process flowchart in Figure 10.6 shows five stages of customer activities. A more efficient method eliminates Steps 1, 2, 3A, and 5. Customers now scan their bills on the TV in their rooms before departure. If the bill is correct, no further checkout is required, and the hotel submits the charges against the credit card the customer showed at check-in.

OPERATIONS SCHEDULING

Referring again to Figure 10.2, we see that once plans have been developed, operations managers must develop timetables for implementing the plans. This aspect of operations is called *scheduling*. There are four different kinds of schedules: (1) the master operations schedule (the "game plan" for deciding the volume of upcoming activities over a period of months), (2) detailed schedules (which show day-to-day activities of production), (3) staff schedules (which identify how many employees will be working and when), and (4) project schedules (which provide coordination for completing large-scale projects).

The Master Operations Schedule

A **master production schedule** shows which products will be produced, when production will occur, and what resources will be used during the scheduled time period. Consider the case of Logan Aluminum Inc., which makes coils of aluminum for companies that make beverage cans. Logan's master schedule (with a format like the partial schedule shown in Figure 10.7) covers production for 60 weeks in which more than 300 000 tons (about 272 tonnes) will be produced. For various types of coils (products), the master schedule specifies how many tonnes will be produced every week, which helps managers determine the kinds of material, equipment, and other resources needed for each upcoming week.

The master schedule for a service provider, such as a regional food retailer, may begin with the planned number of retail stores to

MASTER PRODUCTION SCHEDULE Schedule showing which products will be produced, when production will take place, and what resources will be used.

Coil # (Product)	8/4/14	8/11/14	8/18/14	...	11/3/14	11/10/14
TC016	1500	2500			2100	600
TC032	900		2700		3000	
TR020	300		2600			1600

FIGURE 10.7 Example of partial master operations schedule

be operating in each quarter of the coming two years. Then, key resources needed in each quarter to provide customer services for all stores are estimated (see Figure 10.8). It provides information for planning on how many people the company will have to hire and train, planning for purchases of food products and the financing needed for those purchases, and planning for construction requirements of new stores.

Detailed Schedules

Although the master production schedule is the backbone for overall scheduling, additional information comes from *detailed schedules* that show daily work assignments with start and stop times for assigned jobs at each workstation. At Logan Aluminum, for example, production personnel need to know the locations of all the coils in the plant and their various stages of completion. Managers must assign start and stop times, and employees need scheduled work assignments daily, not just weekly. Detailed short-term schedules allow managers to use customer orders and information about equipment status to update sizes and the variety of coils to be made each day.

Staff Schedules and Computer-Based Scheduling

Scheduling is useful for employee staffing in service companies, too, including restaurants, hotels, and transportation and landscaping companies. Staff schedules, in general, specify assigned working times in upcoming days, perhaps for as many as 30 days or more, for each employee on each work shift. Staff schedules consider employees' needs and the company's efficiency and costs, including the ebb and flow of demand for production.

Computer-based scheduling, using tools such as the ABS Visual Staff Scheduler PRO (VSS Pro) software, can easily handle multi-shift activities for many employees, both full- and part-time. It accommodates vacation times, holiday adjustments, and daily adjustments in staffing for unplanned absences and changes in production schedules.

Project Scheduling

Special projects, such as plant renovations or relocations, often require close coordination and precise timing. In these cases, special tools, such as Gantt and PERT charts, facilitate scheduling.

GANTT CHARTS

A **Gantt chart** diagrams steps to be performed and specifies the time required to complete each step. The manager lists all activities needed

GANTT CHART Scheduling tool that diagrams steps to be performed and specifies the time required to complete each step.

KEY RESOURCES	Quarter/Year							
	1/2014	2/2014	3/2014	4/2014	1/2015	2/2015	3/2015	4/2015
Number of Stores	17	17	18	19	20	20	21	22
Staffing Level (no. of employees)	1360	1360	1530	1615	1700	1700	1653	1827
Fresh Vegetables (tonnes)	204	204	192	228	240	240	230	260
Canned Goods (case loads)	73 950	77 350	80 100	80 100	83 000	84 500	88 600	90 200
Fresh Meats Etc.	–	–	–	–	–	–	–	–
–								
–								
–								

FIGURE 10.8 Food retailer's partial operations schedule

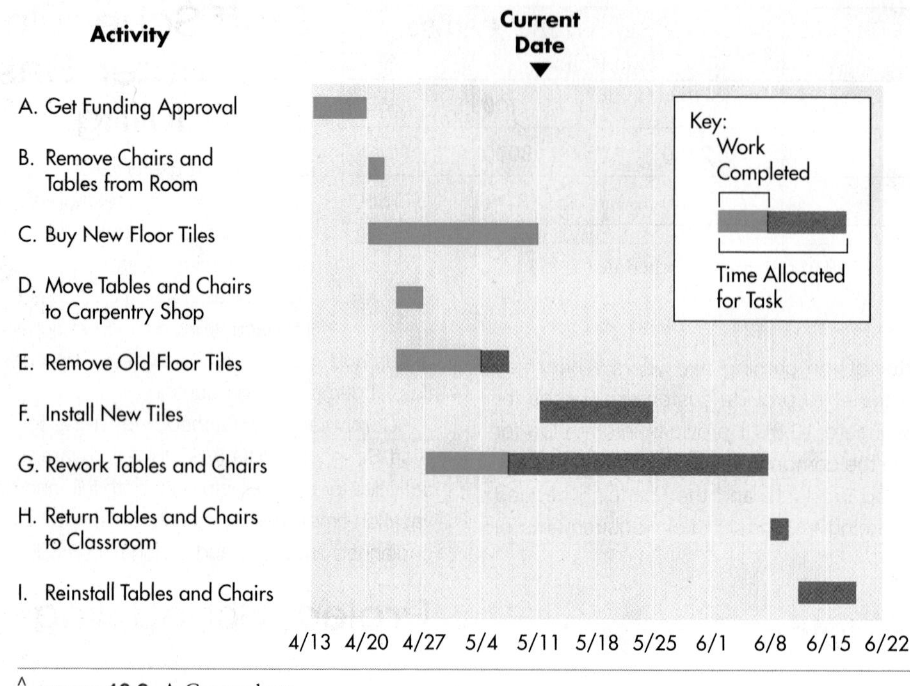

FIGURE 10.9 A Gantt chart

to complete the work, estimates the time required for each step, and checks the progress of the project against the chart. If it is ahead of schedule, some workers may be shifted to another project. If it is behind schedule, workers may be added or completion delayed.[13]

Figure 10.9 shows a Gantt chart for the renovation of a college classroom. It shows progress to date and schedules for the remaining work. The current date is 11/5. Note that workers are about half a week behind in removing old floor tiles and reworking tables and chairs.

PERT CHARTS

The *program evaluation and review technique (PERT)* is useful for customized projects in which numerous activities must be coordinated. Like Gantt charts, **PERT charts** break down large projects into steps and specify the time required to perform each. Unlike Gantt charts, however, PERT charts not only show the necessary sequence of activities, but also identify the critical path for meeting project goals.[14] Figure 10.10 shows a PERT chart for the classroom renovation we reviewed above. The critical path consists of activities A, B, D, G, H, and I. It is critical because any delay in completing any activity will cause workers to miss the completion deadline (nine and a half weeks after start-up). No activity along the critical path can be started until all preceding activities are done. Chairs and tables can't be returned to the classroom (H) until after they've been reworked (G) and after new tiles are installed (F). The chart also identifies activities that will cause delays unless special action is taken at the right time. By reassigning workers and equipment, managers can speed up potentially late activities and keep on schedule.

PERT CHART Production schedule specifying the sequence and critical path for performing the steps in a project.

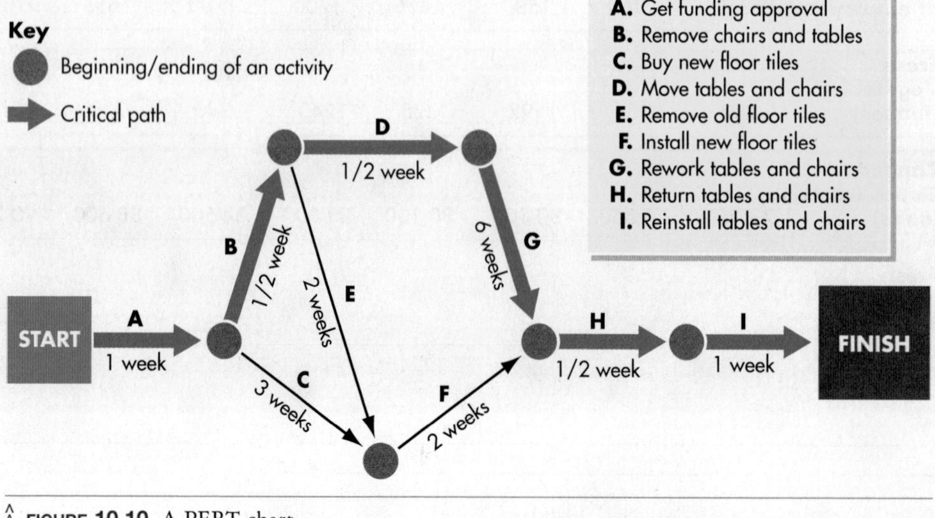

FIGURE 10.10 A PERT chart

OPERATIONS CONTROL

Operations control requires production managers to monitor production performance by comparing results with detailed plans and schedules. If schedules or quality standards are not met, these managers must take corrective action. *Follow-up*—checking to ensure that production decisions are being implemented—is an essential and ongoing facet of operations control. Operations control involves *materials management* and *production process control*. Both activities ensure that schedules are met and that production goals are fulfilled, both in quantity and in quality.

Materials Management

Materials management involves planning, organizing, and controlling the flow of materials. Even before production starts, materials management focuses on product design by emphasizing materials *standardization*—the use, where possible, of standard and uniform components, rather than new or different components. Standardization simplifies paperwork, reduces storage requirements, eliminates unnecessary material flows, and saves money, by reducing the number of different parts that are needed. The five major areas of materials management are as follows:

- *Transportation.* Includes the means of transporting resources to the company and finished goods to buyers.
- *Warehousing.* Storage of both incoming materials for production and finished goods for physical distribution to customers.
- *Inventory control.* Includes the receiving, storing, handling, and counting of all raw materials, partly finished goods, and finished goods. It ensures that enough material inventories are available to meet production schedules.
- *Supplier selection.* Finding and choosing suppliers of services and materials to buy from. It includes evaluating potential suppliers, negotiating terms of service, and maintaining positive buyer–seller relations.
- *Purchasing.* Acquisition of all the raw materials and services a company needs to produce its products. Most large firms have purchasing departments to buy proper materials in the amounts needed.

Production Process Control

Companies use various tools for process control, including *worker training*, *just-in-time production systems*, *material requirements planning*, and *quality control*.

OPERATIONS CONTROL Managers monitor production performance by comparing results with plans and schedules.

MATERIALS MANAGEMENT Planning, organizing, and controlling the flow of materials from purchase through distribution of finished goods.

JUST-IN-TIME (JIT) PRODUCTION SYSTEMS A method of inventory control in which materials are acquired and put into production just as they are needed.

MATERIAL REQUIREMENTS PLANNING (MRP) A method of inventory control in which a computerized bill of materials is used to estimate production needs, so that resources are acquired and put into production only as needed.

BILL OF MATERIALS Production-control tool that specifies the necessary ingredients of a product, the order in which they should be combined, and how many of each are needed to make one batch.

WORKER TRAINING

When providing services, employees are both producers and salespeople. Thus, human relations skills are vital for anyone who has contact with the public. Service employees with poor attitudes reduce sales, but the right attitude is a powerful sales tool. Disney World has a team of sweepers constantly at work picking up bits of trash as soon as they fall to the ground. When visitors have questions about directions or time, they often ask one of the sweepers. Because their responses affect visitors' overall impressions of Disney World, sweepers are trained to respond in appropriate ways. Their work is evaluated and rewarded based on strict performance appraisal standards.[15]

JUST-IN-TIME PRODUCTION SYSTEMS

To minimize manufacturing inventory costs, many companies use **just-in-time (JIT) production systems**. JIT brings together all the needed materials and parts at the precise moment they are required for each production stage, and not before. JIT reduces inventory of goods in process to practically nothing and saves money by replacing stop-and-go production with smooth movement. Sobeys, for example, has invested in more efficient inventory management that has allowed it to reduce the size of storage rooms by 10 percent, because products now move more quickly to the shelves.[16]

MATERIAL REQUIREMENTS PLANNING

Material requirements planning (MRP) uses a **bill of materials** that is basically a "recipe" for the finished product. It specifies the necessary raw materials, the order in which they should be combined, and the quantity of each ingredient needed to make one "batch" of the product (say 2000 finished telephones). The recipe is fed into a computer that controls inventory and schedules each stage of production. The result is fewer early arrivals, less frequent stock shortages, and lower storage costs.

Just-in-time (JIT) production, a type of lean manufacturing, brings together all needed materials at the precise moment they are required for each stage in the production process.

Nathan Denette/The Canadian Press

Manufacturing resource planning, or MRP II, is an advanced version of MRP that ties together all parts of the organization into the company's production activities. For example, MRP inventory and production schedules are translated into cost requirements for the financial management department and personnel requirements for the human resources department. Information on capacity availability for new customer orders goes to the marketing department.

QUALITY CONTROL

Quality control refers to the management of the production process so as to manufacture goods or supply services that meet specific quality standards. McDonald's, for example, is a pioneer in quality control in the restaurant industry. The company oversees everything from the farming of potatoes for french fries to the packing of meat for Big Macs. Quality-assurance staffers even check standards for ketchup sweetness and french-fry length. We discuss quality control in more detail in the following section.

MANUFACTURING RESOURCE PLANNING (MRP II) An advanced version of MRP that ties together all parts of the organization into the company's production activities.

QUALITY CONTROL The management of the production process so as to manufacture goods or supply services that meet specific quality standards.

LO-5 THE PRODUCTIVITY–QUALITY CONNECTION

Productivity measures how much is produced relative to the resources used to produce it. By using resources more efficiently, the quantity of output will be greater for a given amount of input. But unless the resulting goods and services are of satisfactory quality, consumers will not want them. **Quality**, then, means fitness for use—offering features that consumers want. We will look at quality in detail later, but let's first examine the concept of productivity a bit more.

Meeting the Productivity Challenge

A country that efficiently uses its resources can increase the wealth of all its inhabitants. Conversely, a decline in productivity shrinks a nation's total wealth. Additional wealth from higher productivity can be shared among workers (as higher wages), investors (as higher profits), and customers (as stable or declining prices).

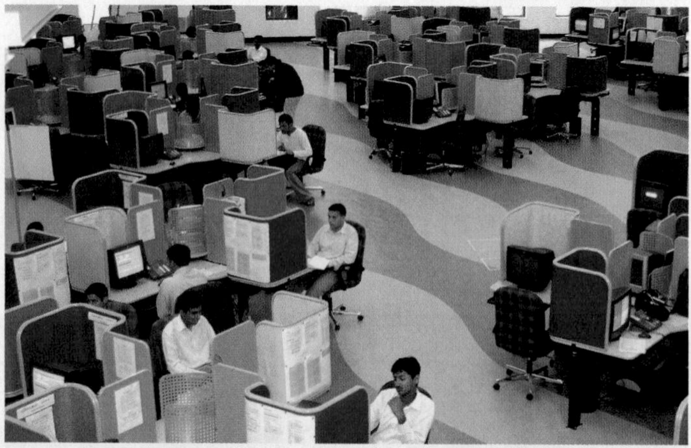

Workers at this call centre in Bangalore, India, field calls from the customers of multinational firms headquartered in North America and Europe. Many jobs like these are outsourced to service suppliers in India, because workers there receive lower wages than their North American counterparts. This translates into higher productivity, since costs are lower for a given level of output.

Newscom

MEASURING PRODUCTIVITY

How do we know how productive a country is? Most countries use **labour productivity**, which compares the amount of labour used with the benefits (the country's GDP) that results from using that resource. Labour productivity is computed by using the following formula:

$$\text{Labour productivity} = \frac{\text{GDP for the year}}{\text{Total number of labour hours worked for the year}}$$

PRODUCTIVITY AMONG GLOBAL COMPETITORS

A nation's productivity determines how large a piece of the global economic-resource pie it gets. A country whose productivity fails to increase as rapidly as that of other countries will see its people's standard of living fall relative to the rest of the world. A 2012 study by the Organisation for Economic Co-operation and Development (OECD) reported on productivity levels in selected countries (see Figure 10.11).[17] Output per hour worked was the highest in Norway and Luxembourg, and lowest in Mexico and Russia.

Why such productivity differences across nations? There are many reasons: differences in technologies, human skills, economic policies, natural resources, and even traditions. In Japan, for example, the food-production industry is fragmented and highly protected, and, compared with Canadian and U.S. food production, extremely inefficient (the average U.S. worker produces 3.5 times as much food as a Japanese worker).[18]

According to Michael Porter, a Harvard University expert on international competitiveness, Canada's international competitiveness is a concern because we have been living off our rich diet of natural resources. Porter criticizes Canadian business, government, and labour for failing to abandon outdated ways of thinking regarding productivity and innovation.[19] Other critics say Canada is stuck in a "productivity trap," meaning we are collectively working harder and using up more natural resources but the benefits and outputs we receive aren't proportional. The productivity trap is reducing Canada's ability to compete in international markets.[20]

QUALITY A product's fitness for use in terms of offering the features that consumers want.

LABOUR PRODUCTIVITY Partial productivity ratio calculated by dividing gross domestic product by total number of workers.

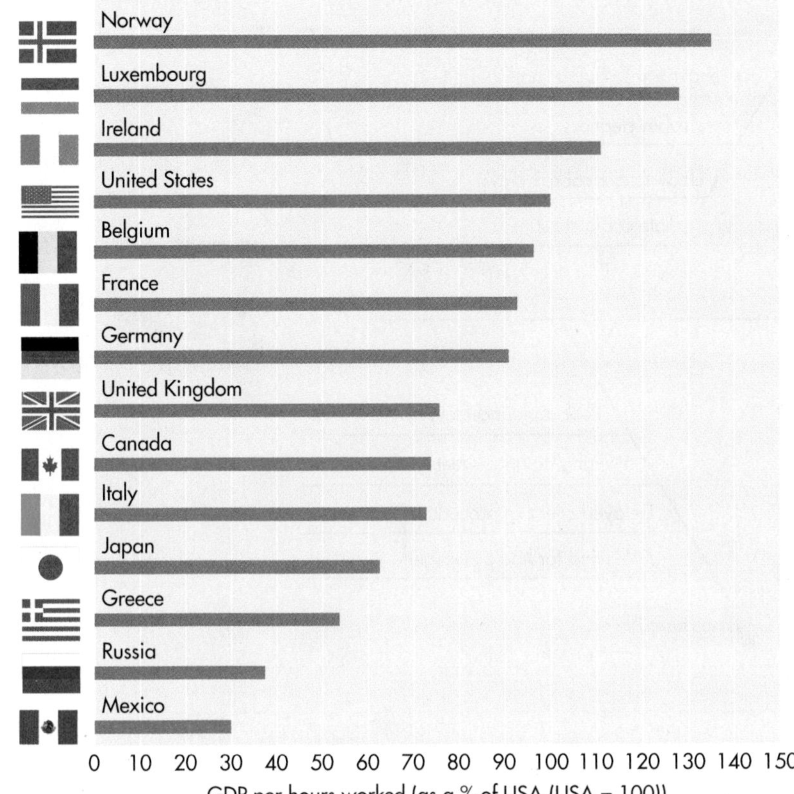

FIGURE 10.11 International productivity comparisons (selected countries, 2012)

Source: Organisation for Economic Co-operation and Development (OECD).

MANUFACTURING VERSUS SERVICE PRODUCTIVITY

Manufacturing productivity is higher than service productivity. It is important to improve service productivity, because the service sector is an important and growing part of the Canadian economy. For many years, it was believed the service sector suffered from "Baumol's Disease." Economist William Baumol argued that, since the service sector focused more on hands-on activity that machines couldn't replace, it would be more difficult to increase productivity in services. But the Opera Company of Brooklyn is challenging that notion. It now puts on the opera *The Marriage of Figaro* with only 12 musicians and a technician who oversees a computer program that plays all the other parts. The orchestra's productivity has increased sharply because it does not have to pay for the usual complement of musicians.[21]

INDUSTRY PRODUCTIVITY

Productivity varies across industries, and within any given industry it also varies across countries (e.g., Canadian agriculture is more productive than agriculture in many other nations, because we use more sophisticated technology and possess superior natural resources). The productivity of many industries has increased over time. In the steel industry, for example, about ten hours of labour were required to produce a tonne of steel in the 1980s, but now only about four hours of labour are needed. In forestry, Canfor Corporation developed a strategic planning tool called Genus to manage its forestry operations, using it to determine how the company should adjust its logging plans to reflect market demand.[22]

COMPANY PRODUCTIVITY

The productivity of individual companies is important to investors, workers, and managers. High productivity gives a company a competitive edge because its costs are lower. As a result, it can offer its product at a lower price (and gain more customers), or it can make a greater profit on each item sold. Some companies have found they can increase their productivity by monitoring employee interactions. At Cubist Pharmaceutical, for example, sales and marketing employees wore badges that collected data on their conversational patterns and movements. The company discovered that more face-to-face interactions among employees were associated with higher levels of productivity. It, therefore, remodelled its cafeteria and provided better food, so that employees would be more likely to have lunch together.[23]

MEETING THE QUALITY CHALLENGE

It is not enough for a company to be highly productive. It must also create products and services that have the level of quality consumers want. Consider just one example. In 2014, automobile companies had to recall millions of vehicles because airbags made by Takata Corp. sometimes exploded and killed or injured drivers and their passengers.[24]

The importance of quality was recognized many years ago by American business consultant W. Edwards Deming. In the decades after World War II, he tried to persuade U.S. firms that they needed to improve the quality of their products. Like many prophets, he was not honoured in his homeland. But his arguments won over the Japanese. Through years of meticulous hard work, Japan's manufacturers changed "Made in Japan" from a synonym for cheap, shoddy merchandise into a hallmark of reliability. Eventually, North American businesses came to understand that Deming was right.

Quality advocates such as Joseph Juran and Kaoru Ishikawa introduced methods and tools for improving quality. Ishikawa, for example, developed "fishbone diagrams" (also known as "cause-and-effect diagrams" or "Ishikawa diagrams") that help employees figure out the causes of quality problems in their work areas. The diagram in Figure 10.12, for instance, was developed to help an airport manager find out why the facility had so many delayed departures. Focusing on five major categories of possible causes, the manager then noted several possible causes of the problem in each. It turned out there weren't enough tow trucks to handle baggage transfers.[25]

LO-6 Managing for Quality

Total quality management (TQM) includes all the activities necessary for getting high-quality goods and services into the marketplace. TQM emphasizes that no defects are tolerable, and that employees are responsible for maintaining quality standards. For example, at Toyota's Cambridge, Ontario, plant, workers can push a button or pull a rope to stop the production line when something is not up to standard.[26]

TOTAL QUALITY MANAGEMENT (TQM) A concept that emphasizes that no defects are tolerable and that all employees are responsible for maintaining quality standards.

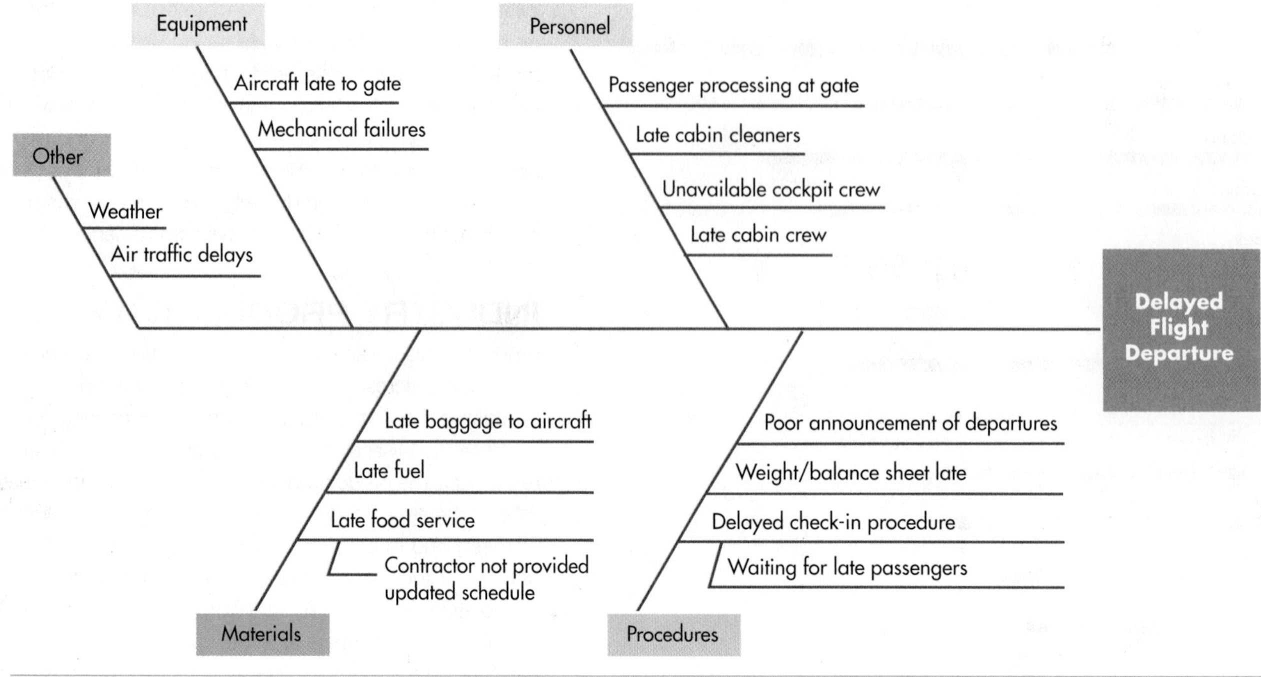

FIGURE 10.12 "Fishbone" or "cause-and-effect" diagram

A customer focus is the starting point for TQM. It includes using methods for determining what customers want and then making sure that all the company's activities and people are focused on fulfilling those needs. Total participation is critical; if all employees are not working toward improved quality, the firm is wasting potential contributions from its human resources and is missing a chance to become a stronger competitor in the marketplace. TQM in today's competitive markets demands continuous improvement of products; after-sales service; and all of the company's internal processes, such as accounting, delivery, billing, and information flow.

Consider the example of Standard Aero in Winnipeg, which is in the business of aircraft overhaul. When the company instituted TQM, the process began with the formation of a "change council" consisting of the CEO and five senior managers. Next, a nine-person task force was formed that consisted of employees who had done the full range of jobs on one of Standard's major overhaul contracts. The task force's first job was to find out what the customer wanted. It did this by designing a questionnaire and visiting customer plants around the world to gather information. It also worked within Standard Aero to determine exactly how the company did its aircraft overhaul work. After weeks of analysis, the task force was able to reduce the time required for overhaul work significantly. The number of times a certain gearbox was handled as it moved through the repair process, for example, was reduced by 84 percent.[27]

THERE'S AN APP FOR THAT!

APP DETAILS	PLATFORMS
1. **Quality Management** **Source:** WAGmob **Key Features:** On-the-go learning tool for quality management issues.	Android, BlackBerry, Windows
2. **Productivity Wizard** **Source:** Success Wizard Inc. **Key Features:** A powerful tool to help you plan and create results.	Apple
3. **Pert Estimator** **Source:** Burriss Consulting Group LLC **Key Features:** Takes the best, worst, and most likely estimates along with the hourly cost to provide an accurate estimate for a given task.	Android

APP DISCOVERY EXERCISE

Since app availability changes, conduct your own search for the "Top Three" operations management apps and identify the key features.

PLANNING FOR QUALITY

Planning for quality should begin before products are designed or redesigned. **Performance quality** refers to the features of a product and how well it performs. For example, Maytag gets a price premium because its washers and dryers offer a high level of performance quality. Customers perceive Maytag products as having more advanced features and being more durable than other brands.

Quality reliability refers to the consistency or repeatability of performance. At Courtyard by Marriott hotels, for example, consistency is achieved by maintaining the same features at all of Marriott's nearly 700 locations (high-speed internet access, meeting space, access to an exercise room and swimming pool, and 24-hour access to food).

ORGANIZING FOR QUALITY

Having a separate "quality control" department is no longer enough. Everyone, from the chair of the board to the part-time clerk, must work to

PERFORMANCE QUALITY The overall degree of quality; how well the features of a product meet consumers' needs and how well the product performs.

QUALITY RELIABILITY The consistency of quality from unit to unit of a product.

assure quality. At Germany's Messerschmitt-Boelkow-Blohm aerospace company, for example, all employees are responsible for inspecting their own work. The goal is to minimize problems by making the product correctly from the beginning.

LEADING FOR QUALITY

Leading for quality means that managers must inspire and motivate employees throughout the company to achieve quality goals. They need to help employees see how they affect quality and how quality affects their jobs and their company. If managers succeed, employees will ultimately accept **quality ownership**—the idea that quality belongs to each person who creates or destroys it while performing a job.

CONTROLLING FOR QUALITY

By closely monitoring its products and services, a company can detect mistakes and make corrections. To do so, however, managers must first establish specific quality standards and measurements. Companies that pay attention to quality standards and measurements typically provide high-quality products and services to customers. In 2012, Alaska Airlines and Delta Air Lines were top-rated in a study published by *The Middle Seat*, a company that ranks air carriers on key quality measures like on-time arrivals, cancelled flights, and mishandled bags. Both Alaska and Delta had ranked poorly in previous years, but both had instituted major operational overhauls that focused on improving quality.[28]

Tools for Quality Assurance

Many tools exist for achieving the desired level of quality: *competitive product analysis*, *value-added analysis*, *statistical process control*, *quality/cost studies*, *quality improvement teams*, *benchmarking*, *getting closer to the customer*, *ISO 9000*, *re-engineering*, and *adding value through supply chains*.

COMPETITIVE PRODUCT ANALYSIS

Ideas for improving both the product and the production process may come from **competitive product analysis**. For example, Toshiba will take apart a Xerox photocopier and test each component to see how it compares with its own competing product. It can then decide which of its own product features are satisfactory, which need to be upgraded, and whether production processes need improvement.

VALUE-ADDED ANALYSIS

Value-added analysis means evaluating all work activities, material flows, and paperwork to determine the value that they add for customers. Value-added analysis often reveals wasteful or unnecessary activities that can be eliminated without harming customer service. For example, when Hewlett-Packard reduced its customer contracts from 20 pages to as few as 2, computer sales rose by more than 18 percent.

STATISTICAL PROCESS CONTROL

Companies can improve uniformity in their outputs by understanding the sources of variation. **Statistical process control (SPC)** methods—especially process variation studies and control charts—allow managers to analyze variations in production data.

Process Variation While some amount of *process variation* is acceptable, too much can result in poor quality and excessive operating costs. Consider the box-filling operation for Honey Nuggets cereal. Each automated machine fills two 400-gram boxes per second. Even under proper conditions, slight variations in cereal weight from box to box are normal. Equipment and tools wear out, the cereal may be overly moist, and machinists make occasional adjustments. But how much variation is occurring? How much is acceptable?

Information about variation in a process can be obtained from a process capability study. Boxes are taken from the filling machines and weighed. The results are plotted, as in Figure 10.13, and compared with the upper and lower specification limits (quality limits) for weight. These limits define good and bad quality for box filling. Boxes with more than 410 grams are a wasteful "giveaway." Underfilling has a cost because it is unlawful.

In Figure 10.13, we see that none of Machine A's output violates the quality limits, and it is fully capable of meeting the company's quality standards. But Machines B and C have problems and cannot reliably meet Honey Nuggets' quality standards. The company has to take special—and costly—actions to sort the good boxes from the bad before releasing the cereal for shipment.

Control Charts Knowing a process is capable of meeting quality standards is not enough. Managers still have to monitor the process to prevent its going astray. To detect the beginning of bad conditions, managers can check production periodically and plot the results on a **control chart**. For example, several times a day, a machine operator at Honey Nuggets might weigh several boxes together to ascertain the average weight.

QUALITY/COST STUDIES FOR QUALITY IMPROVEMENT

Quality/cost studies identify a firm's current costs and also reveal areas with the largest cost-saving potential.[29] For example, Honey Nuggets must determine its costs for *internal failures*. These are expenses—including the costs of overfilling boxes and the costs of sorting out bad boxes—incurred during production and before bad product leaves the plant. *External failures* occur when bad boxes get out of the factory and reach the customer. The costs of correcting them—refunds to customers, transportation costs to return bad boxes to the factory, possible lawsuits, factory recalls—are also tabulated in a quality/cost study.

QUALITY OWNERSHIP The concept that quality belongs to each employee who creates or destroys it in producing a good or service; the idea that all workers must take responsibility for producing a quality product.

COMPETITIVE PRODUCT ANALYSIS Process by which a company analyzes a competitor's products to identify desirable improvements.

VALUE-ADDED ANALYSIS The evaluation of all work activities, material flows, and paperwork to determine the value they add for customers.

STATISTICAL PROCESS CONTROL (SPC) Statistical analysis techniques that allow managers to analyze variations in production data and to detect when adjustments are needed to create products with high-quality reliability.

CONTROL CHART A statistical process control method in which results of test sampling of a product are plotted on a diagram that reveals when the process is beginning to depart from normal operating conditions.

QUALITY/COST STUDIES A method of improving product quality by assessing a firm's current quality-related costs and identifying areas with the greatest cost-saving potential.

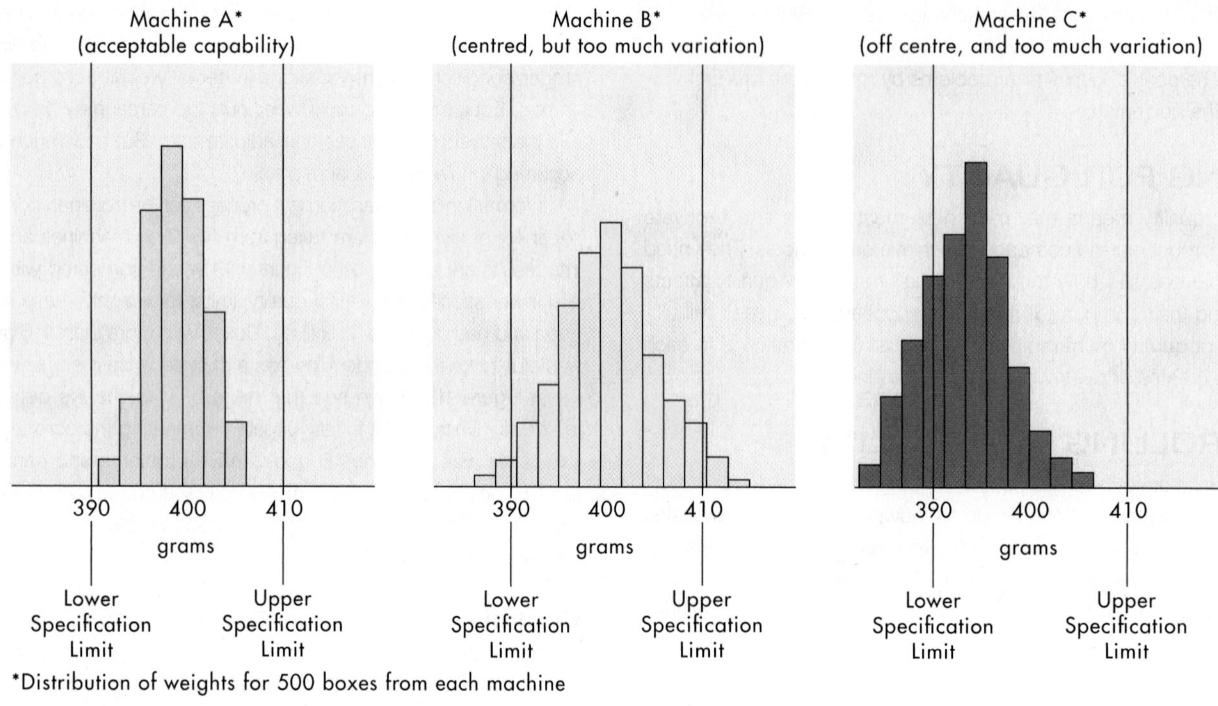

FIGURE 10.13 Process variation in box filling for Honey Nuggets cereal

QUALITY IMPROVEMENT TEAMS

Quality improvement (QI) teams are groups of employees from various work areas who meet regularly to define, analyze, and solve common production problems. Their goal is to improve both their own work methods and the products they make.[30] Many QI teams organize their own work, select leaders, and address problems in the workplace. Motorola, for example, sponsors company-wide team competitions to emphasize the value of the team approach, to recognize outstanding team performance, and to reaffirm the team's role in the company's continuous-improvement culture. Teams get higher marks for dealing with projects closely tied to Motorola's key initiatives.[31]

BENCHMARKING

With **benchmarking**, a company compares its current performance against its own past performance (internal benchmarking), or against the performance of its competitors (external benchmarking). As an example of the former, the percentage of customer phone calls last month requiring more than two minutes of response time may be compared to the required response time the month before that. As an example of the latter, Toronto Hospital gathered performance data on 26 indicators from various Canadian hospitals so it could determine how well it was performing compared to other organizations in the health-care industry.[32]

BENCHMARKING Comparing the quality of the firm's output with the quality of the output of the industry's leaders.

ISO 9000 Certification program attesting to the fact that a factory, a laboratory, or an office has met the rigorous quality management requirements set by the International Organization for Standardization.

BUSINESS PROCESS RE-ENGINEERING Redesigning of business processes to improve performance, quality, and productivity.

GETTING CLOSER TO THE CUSTOMER

Successful businesses take steps to know what their customers want in the products or services they buy. For example, the Coast Capital Savings Credit Union branch in Surrey, British Columbia, simplified the banking experience of its customers and developed an innovative new service called "You're the Boss Mortgage" which was named Mortgage of the Year by CanadianMortgageTrends.com.[33]

ISO 9000

DuPont had a problem—a moulding press used to make plastic connectors for computers had a 30 percent defect rate. Efforts to solve the problem went nowhere until, as part of a plant-wide quality program, press operators were asked to submit detailed written reports describing how they did their jobs. After comparing notes, operators realized that they were incorrectly measuring the temperature of the moulding press; as a result, temperature adjustments were often wrong. With the mystery solved, the defect rate dropped to 8 percent.

The quality program that led to this solution is called **ISO 9000**—a certification program attesting to the fact that a factory, a laboratory, or an office has met the rigorous quality management requirements set by the International Organization for Standardization. ISO 9000 (pronounced "ICE-o nine thousand") originated in Europe as an attempt to standardize materials received from suppliers in high-tech industries such as electronics, chemicals, and aviation. To get certified, companies must document the procedures followed by workers during every stage of production. The purpose is to ensure a manufacturer's product is exactly the same today as it was yesterday and as it will be tomorrow. Ideally, standardized processes would ensure goods are produced at the same level of quality, even if all employees were replaced by a new set of workers.

BUSINESS PROCESS RE-ENGINEERING

Business process re-engineering is the fundamental rethinking and radical redesign of business processes to achieve dramatic improvements as measured by cost, quality, service, and speed.[34] It requires rethinking of each of the steps in a process, starting from scratch. For example, when Caterpillar Financial Services changed to an online system for customers, it re-engineered the whole payments and financing process by improving equipment, retraining employees, and connecting customers to its databases.[35]

LO-7 ADDING VALUE THROUGH SUPPLY CHAINS

Companies usually belong to a network of firms that must coordinate their activities. As each firm performs its transformation processes, it relies on others in the network. A **supply chain** (or **value chain**) for any product is the flow of information, materials, and services that starts with raw-materials suppliers and continues adding value through other stages in the network of firms until the product reaches the end customer.[36]

Figure 10.14 shows the supply-chain activities involved in supplying baked goods to consumers. Each stage adds value for the final customer, and each stage depends on the others for success in getting fresh-baked goods to consumers.

Supply-chain management (SCM) tries to improve the overall flow through a system composed of companies working together. The smooth flow of accurate information along the chain reduces unwanted inventories, avoids delays, and cuts supply times. Materials move faster to other businesses and, ultimately, consumers, and the efficiency of SCM means faster deliveries and lower costs than customers could get if each member acted only according to its own operations requirements. Because customers ultimately get better value, SCM gains competitive advantage for each supply-chain member.[37] A traditionally managed bakery, for example, would focus simply on getting production inputs from flour millers and paper suppliers and supplying baked goods to distributors. Unfortunately, this approach limits the chain's performance and doesn't allow for possible improvements when activities are more carefully coordinated. Supply-chain management can improve performance and, as a result, provide higher quality at lower prices.

Supply-chain management is also important for services. As was mentioned in Chapter 6, Port Metro Vancouver developed a supply-chain strategy that reduced container "dwell time"—the time containers sit on the dock—from 3.7 days to 2.5 days, after managers determined that the port had to become more competitive with American ports. This reduction also improved the port's relationships with operators like Canadian National Railway and Canadian Pacific Railway Ltd.[38] Supply chains are also becoming increasingly global. For example, an architect from Malaysia might sketch out a new office tower for the city of London, an architect from the Philippines might do the detailed renderings, and an engineer from China might assess the structural soundness of the building.[39]

Supply-Chain Disruption

Many supply chains were disrupted during the frigid winter of 2013–2014 because transporting goods became more difficult. To avoid a repeat of that problem, many companies stockpiled inventories in the fall of 2014 so they could keep their operations going even if the weather was bad during the winter of 2014–2015.[40] But this strategy increased supply-chain costs, since it violated a fundamental tenet of just-in-time inventory (hold very little inventory). Companies continue to use JIT, but many are starting to hold larger stocks of inventory in case of supply-chain disruptions.

Supply chains may be disrupted for reasons other than weather. In 2014 the Bombardier factory in Thunder Bay had to lay off about 50 workers because it could not get enough parts to manufacture streetcars for the city of Toronto. The parts, made in another Bombardier factory in Mexico, did not arrive in a timely fashion, so the plant could not meet the delivery deadlines Bombardier had promised Toronto.[41] Some workers at the Thunder Bay plant also said the parts were defective or not built to the right size.

The devastating earthquake and tsunami that struck northeastern Japan in 2011 disrupted the production of automobiles, automobile parts, and electronic components like flash memory and dynamic random-access memory for computing devices and smartphones. Advanced Semiconductor Engineering Inc., a Taiwan-based chip-packaging company, had to look for new suppliers in China and South Korea after its Japanese supplier was unable to deliver supplies of plastic moulding compounds used to wrap semiconductors.[42]

SUPPLY CHAIN (VALUE CHAIN) Flow of information, materials, and services that starts with raw-materials suppliers and continues through other stages in the operations process until the product reaches the end customer.

SUPPLY-CHAIN MANAGEMENT (SCM) Principle of looking at the chain as a whole to improve the overall flow through the system.

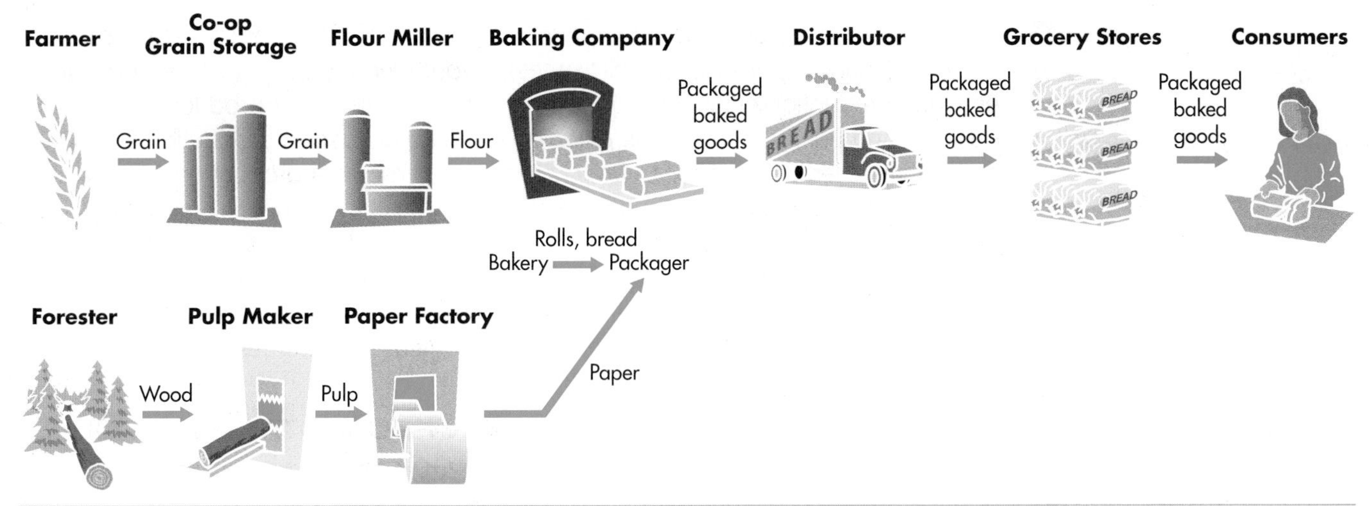

FIGURE 10.14 Supply chain for baked goods

MyBizLab

Study, practise, and explore real business situations with these helpful resources:

- **Interactive Lesson Presentations:** Work through interactive presentations and assessments to test your knowledge of business concepts.
- **Study Plan:** Check your understanding of chapter concepts with self-study quizzes.
- **Dynamic Study Modules:** Work through adaptive study modules on your computer, tablet, or mobile device.
- **Simulations:** Practise decision-making in simulated business environments.
- **Videos:** Learn more about the business practices and strategies of real companies.

SUMMARY OF LEARNING OBJECTIVES

LO-1 EXPLAIN THE MEANING OF THE TERM *PRODUCTION* (OR *OPERATIONS*) AND DESCRIBE THE FOUR KINDS OF *UTILITY* IT PROVIDES.

Production (or *operations*) refers to the processes and activities for transforming resources into finished services and goods for customers. Production creates *time utility* (products are available when customers want them), *place utility* (products are available where they are convenient for customers), *ownership utility* (customers benefit from possessing and using the product), and *form utility* (products are in a form that is useful to the customer).

LO-2 IDENTIFY THE CHARACTERISTICS THAT DISTINGUISH *SERVICE OPERATIONS* FROM *GOODS PRODUCTION* AND EXPLAIN THE MAIN DIFFERENCES IN THE *SERVICE FOCUS.*

In service production, raw materials are not things but rather people, so services are performed, while goods are produced. Also, services are largely *intangible*, more likely than physical goods to be *customized* to meet the purchaser's needs, and more *unstorable* than most products. Because services are intangible, for instance, providers work to ensure that customers receive value in the form of pleasure, satisfaction, or a feeling of safety. Service providers also focus on the *customer–service link*, often acknowledging the customer as part of the operations process.

LO-3 DESCRIBE TWO TYPES OF *OPERATIONS PROCESSES.*

In manufacturing, *analytic processes* break down resources into component parts and *synthetic processes* combine raw materials to produce a finished product. Services use either *high-contact processes* (the customer is in the system while the service is being performed) or *low-contact processes* (the customer is not in the system while the service is being performed).

LO-4 DESCRIBE THE FACTORS INVOLVED IN *OPERATIONS PLANNING* AND *OPERATIONS CONTROL.*

Operations planning involves *forecasting* (determining future demand for products), *capacity planning* (calculating how much of a product can be produced), *location planning* (analyzing proposed facility sites), *layout planning* (designing a facility to enhance production efficiency), *quality planning* (ensuring that products meet a firm's quality standards), and *methods planning* (identifying specific production steps and methods for performing them). *Operations control* requires production managers to monitor production performance (by comparing results with detailed plans and schedules) and then to take corrective action as needed. *Materials management* involves the planning, organizing, and controlling of the flow of materials. There are several tools for helping managers control operations processes, including *worker training programs*, *just-in-time (JIT) production systems*, *material requirements planning (MRP)*, and *quality control*.

LO-5 EXPLAIN THE CONNECTION BETWEEN *PRODUCTIVITY* AND *QUALITY.*

Productivity is a measure of economic performance; it compares how much is produced with the resources used to produce it. *Quality* is a product's fitness for use. However, an emphasis solely on productivity or solely on quality is not enough. Profitable competition in today's business world demands high levels of both productivity and quality.

LO-6 **UNDERSTAND THE CONCEPT OF *TOTAL QUALITY MANAGEMENT* AND DESCRIBE NINE TOOLS THAT COMPANIES CAN USE TO ACHIEVE IT.**

Total quality management (TQM) includes all the activities necessary for getting high-quality goods and services into the marketplace. Tools that are available to managers include *value-added analysis*, *statistical process control methods*, *quality/cost studies*, *quality improvement teams*, *benchmarking*, *getting closer to the customer*, *ISO 9000*, *re-engineering*, and *supply-chain management*.

LO-7 **EXPLAIN HOW A *SUPPLY-CHAIN STRATEGY* DIFFERS FROM TRADITIONAL STRATEGIES FOR COORDINATING OPERATIONS AMONG BUSINESSES.**

The *supply-chain strategy* is based on the idea that members of the supply chain can gain competitive advantage by working together as a coordinated system of units. Sharing information allows companies to reduce inventories, improve quality, and speed the delivery of products to consumers.

QUESTIONS AND EXERCISES

QUESTIONS FOR ANALYSIS

1. What are the resources needed and the finished "products" produced in the following services: real-estate firm, child-care facility, bank, city water and electric department, and hotel?
2. Is your college a "make-to-order" or make-to-stock" operation? Explain your reasoning.
3. Pick three physical products (not services) that you regularly use. Which of the basic production processes are used to produce these products (chemical, fabrication, assembly, transport, or clerical processes)? To what extent are multiple processes used in the production of the product?
4. Pick three services (not physical products) that you regularly use. Explain what customization, unstorability, and intangibility mean for each of the services. How do these factors influence the way the service is delivered to customers?
5. Develop a service-flow analysis for some service that you use frequently, such as buying lunch at a cafeteria, having your hair cut, or riding a bus. Identify areas of potential quality or productivity failures in the process.
6. Describe three high-contact service operations and three low-contact service operations. Do the concepts of intangibility and unstorability have different implications for low- and high-contact service operations?

APPLICATION EXERCISES

7. Interview the manager of a local service business, such as a restaurant or hair salon. Identify the major decisions involved in planning the business's service operations. Determine how the factors of intangibility and unstorability affect the business.
8. Choose a product that you regularly use and trace its supply chain. Can you see areas where improvements might be made?
9. Interview a production manager in a local firm and determine which of the tools for total quality management the company is using. Also determine why the company has chosen not to use some other tools.
10. Think of an everyday activity—either personal or professional—that you would like to do more efficiently (e.g., going to work or school, enrolling in classes, or filling up your car at the gas station). Describe how you would use methods planning to achieve increased efficiency in that activity. Draw a process flowchart that shows the stages in the activity you chose, and then explain how you would use it.

TEAM EXERCISES

BUILDING YOUR BUSINESS SKILLS

THE IMPACT OF EFFICIENCY

PURPOSE OF THE ASSIGNMENT

To encourage students to think critically about the idea of productivity and its effects on people and organizations.

THE SITUATION

In 1865 (yes, 1865), William Jevons published a book entitled *The Coal Question*. In it, he argued that increased efficiency in the use of coal in iron-making would not lead to less consumption of coal (as most people would think), but to more consumption of coal. He gave the following example to support this seemingly counterintuitive argument. If some technological improvement allowed more iron to be made with less coal than previously, the iron company's profits would increase and new investment dollars would flow into the company. The company's reduced costs would allow it to reduce the price of its products. That price reduction, in turn, would cause increased demand from customers. Over time, as more and more companies efficiently produced more and more iron, the total consumption of coal needed to make all that iron would be greater than it was before the increase in efficiency occurred. The most general point that Jevons made was that increased economy in the use of fuel would actually lead to increased consumption of that fuel. This is because increasing energy efficiency really means increasing the productivity of energy. And when you increase the productivity of something, its price goes down.

In 2011, David Owen wrote a book entitled *The Conundrum* (New York: Riverhead Books) that contains many examples of how Jevons' basic idea works in modern society. He notes, for example, that improving roads (i.e., making them more efficient) does not reduce traffic congestion, but makes it worse over time. Why? Because better roads attract more drivers, and this increases congestion. All of these extra cars also produce a large amount of air pollution. If governments want to reduce air pollution by attracting more people to public transit, they must increase the cost of driving. That can be accomplished by providing poor (i.e., congested) roads for drivers, who will then get so fed up with driving that they will be motivated to use public transit.

ASSIGNMENT

Step 1 Get together with three other students. Assign one or two of the chapters in Owen's 2011 book to each group member (the chapters are very short). Chapters 1, 2, 6, 12, 13, 19, 20, and 21 are particularly recommended.

Step 2 Gather the group together for a discussion of the idea that increased efficiency actually results in increased use, rather than decreased use of some resource. Use the Follow-up Questions below as a starting point.

Step 3 Write a brief report summarizing your group's conclusions.

FOLLOW-UP QUESTIONS

1. Is Jevons' idea sound? Defend your answer.
2. Briefly describe several areas where Jevons' ideas apply. Are there areas where his ideas do not apply?
3. Assume for a moment that you agree with the argument that increased efficiency means more consumption rather than less. If you wanted to decrease consumption, give a specific example of the actions you would take. Also note whether you think the actions are politically feasible.

EXERCISING YOUR ETHICS

CALCULATING THE COST OF CONSCIENCE

THE SITUATION

Product quality and cost affect every firm's reputation and profitability, as well as the satisfaction of customers. This exercise will expose you to some ethical considerations that pertain to certain cost and service decisions that must be made by operations managers.

THE DILEMMA

As director of quality for a major appliance manufacturer, Ruth was reporting to the executive committee on the results of a program for correcting problems with a newly redesigned compressor that the company had recently begun putting in its refrigerators. Following several customer complaints, the quality lab had determined that some of the new compressor units ran more loudly than expected. One corrective option was to simply wait until customers complained and responding to each complaint if and when it occurred. Ruth, however, decided that this approach was inconsistent with the company's policy of being the high-quality leader in the industry. Insisting on a proactive, "pro-quality" approach, Ruth initiated a program for contacting all customers who had purchased refrigerators containing the new compressor.

Unfortunately, her "quality and customers first" policy was expensive. Service representatives across Canada had to phone every customer, make appointments for home visits, and replace original compressors with a newer model. Because replacement time was only 30 minutes, customers were hardly inconvenienced, and food stayed refrigerated without interruption. Customer response to the replacement program was overwhelmingly favourable.

Near the end of Ruth's report, an executive vice-president was overheard to comment, "Ruth's program has cost this company $400 million in service expenses." Two weeks later, Ruth was fired.

TEAM ACTIVITY

Assemble a group of four students and assign each group member to one of the following roles:

- Ruth
- Ruth's boss
- a customer
- a company investor

ACTION STEPS

1. Before hearing any of your group's comments on this situation and from the perspective of your assigned role, take a moment to consider whether Ruth's firing is consistent with the company's desire for industry leadership in quality. Write down the reasons for your position.
2. Before hearing any of your group's comments on this situation and from the perspective of your assigned role, consider what underlying ethical issues, if any, exist in this situation. Write down the issues.
3. Gather your group together and reveal, in turn, each member's comments on Ruth's firing. Next, reveal the ethical issues listed by each member.
4. Appoint someone to record the main points of agreement and disagreement within the group. How do you explain the results? What accounts for any disagreement?
5. From an ethical standpoint, what does your group conclude is the most appropriate action the company could have taken in this situation?
6. Develop a group response to the following question: What are the respective roles of profits, obligations to customers, and employee considerations for the firm in this situation?

BUSINESS CASE 10

SOME GLITCHES IN THE PROVISION OF SERVICES

When consumers purchase a tangible product like a lawn mower, washing machine, or automobile, it is generally not difficult for them to tell whether the product is working as well as expected. But is the same thing true for intangible services such a hair care, air travel, legal services, or financial services? That's a bit more complicated, because of the intangible nature of services. What we do know is that consumers are very vocal about unsatisfactory services.

Consider air travel. Consumer unhappiness with this service is often in the news (think of the highly publicized cases of passengers being forced to sit in an aircraft on the tarmac for hours with no food, water, or air conditioning and overtaxed bathrooms). In recent years, commercial airlines have gotten a lot of negative publicity about many aspects of the services they provide. The list is long: higher fares, less in-flight service, extra baggage fees, lost baggage (airlines lose 26 million passengers' bags each year due to theft, mishandling, and labelling errors), cramped seats, inconvenient scheduling, discourteous airline personnel, overbooked flights, long waits, cancelled flights, and late flights—to name just a few. All this has led to a decline in customer satisfaction with commercial airlines.

Ben Stansall/Newscom

Skytrax, a U.K.-based consulting firm, conducts surveys of international travellers to determine which airlines have the best airport lounges, cabin staff, and in-flight entertainment. It also publishes the annual World Airline Star Ranking, which is based on a quality analysis system that assesses airline products and services. There are five Star Ranking levels in the system:

5-star. "High" level of quality (e.g., Singapore Airlines)
4-star. "Good" level of quality (e.g., Air Canada)
3-star. "Acceptable" level of quality (e.g., Air China)
2-star. "Poor" level of quality (e.g., Air Italy)
1-star. "Very poor" level of quality (e.g., Air Koryo)

The rankings are *not* based on customer feedback, but on a systematic audit of the activities of airline companies. Obvious factors such as late arrivals, cancelled flights, mishandled bags, passengers being bumped from flights, and so on are included in the assessment, but so are less obvious ones like seat comfort and seating arrangements. Every year, Skytrax publishes a list of the best international airlines. In 2014, Cathay Pacific ranked first, Qatar Airways second, and Singapore Airlines third. Many of the top ten airlines are located in Southeast Asia. The lowest-rated were Kulula Airlines, Croatia Airlines, and S7 Airlines.

Commercial airlines constitute only one part of the travel industry. Others, such as travel companies and booking agents, have also come under fire in recent years. For example, when Conquest Vacations suddenly ceased operations, many Canadian travellers were left stranded in hotels in Mexico, the Dominican Republic, and Cuba. Many of them were told by hotel officials that they had to pay for their rooms, because the bill had not been paid by the travel company.

The Ontario government established the Travel Industry Council of Ontario (TICO) to ensure that fair business practices and ethical behaviour are adhered to, and that Canadian travellers are not scammed or taken advantage of. But Conquest's sudden shutdown meant that TICO was not given proper notice and therefore could not provide sufficient information to travellers. The outcome left many critics questioning the usefulness of the Council.

Complaints about poor service are not limited to the travel business. To observe consumer dissatisfaction in action, go to Complaints.com, a forum for people who have had bad experiences as consumers. Enter "missed appointment" or "late repairman" in the search engine and you will get pages of hits. Typical is this complaint about a failed window installation: "I then made an appointment for [an] employee to come to my house the next day between 2 p.m. and 4 p.m. . . . I took a day off from work and stayed home to wait for the [company] truck. Four p.m. came and went. No one from [the company] showed up or called."

ConsumerAffairs.com, an advocacy group for customers who have received poor service or purchased shoddy merchandise, also details numerous incidents in which people were left waiting helplessly for repair people who were late for scheduled appointments. Part of the problem is that the company that manufactures a product might not be the same one that provides service for it. This is often the case with mass-produced products purchased in department stores or wholesale outlets. For example, General Electric might make a refrigerator, but a GE repair person is not located in every town where that refrigerator is sold. Outside contractors must therefore be hired, some of whom may lack the specific expertise required to do the job well and quickly.

It's not only products in need of installation or repair that can cause frustration over missed appointments. How many hours have you spent waiting in crowded doctors' offices, overbooked salons, and slow-service restaurants? In every case, even if the quality of the product or service turns out to be excellent, you may still be dissatisfied with the overall experience. For service providers in particular, that failure can be as costly as producing a defective product.

QUESTIONS FOR DISCUSSION

1. In your own words, explain the similarities and differences between manufacturing and service operations. How do the examples presented above illustrate your points?
2. How do the service factors of intangibility, customization, and unstorability generally influence the provision of services? How do these factors specifically impact the air travel and home repair industries?
3. Describe how process flowcharts may be helpful for methods improvement in airline service operations. What kinds of information would you hope to gain from the flowcharts?
4. Consider the following statement: *It is well known that airlines have had difficulty making profits during the past few years. Increased fees and the decline in service quality that consumers are experiencing are the direct result of airlines having to decrease their costs in order to increase their profitability.* Do you agree or disagree? Defend your answer.

LO

AFTER READING THIS CHAPTER, YOU SHOULD BE ABLE TO:

LO-1 Explain the *role of accountants*, distinguish between the three traditional *professional accounting designations* in Canada, and understand the new unified role of the *Canadian Chartered Professional Accounting (CPA) designation*.

LO-2 Explain how the *accounting equation* is used.

LO-3 Describe three basic *financial statements* and show how they reflect the activity and financial condition of a business.

LO-4 Explain the key *standards* and *principles* for *reporting financial statements*.

LO-5 Explain how computing *financial ratios* can help in analyzing the financial strengths of a business.

LO-6 Discuss the role of *ethics in accounting*.

LO-7 Describe the *evolving role of the modern accountant*.

Searching for Stolen Maple Syrup: Accounting for Missing Inventory

You might think accountants spend all their time sitting in comfortable offices, but that picture fails to consider many important functions. For example, auditing inventory levels is a vital business task conducted by accountants. The goal of this exercise is to ensure that the numbers on paper match the real numbers. This process requires different (often complicated) methods depending on the industry. Some young accountants are surprised to find themselves boarding tiny airplanes and flying to remote northern regions where they will manually measure mineral reserves. To complete these tasks, accountants have to roll up their sleeves or even climb onto stockpiles (e.g., coal, dolomite, and so on) in order to estimate reserves.

Christian Delbert/Fotolia

© Web Pix/Alamy

Understanding Accounting

CHAPTER 11

When Michel Gauvreau was assigned the task of auditing the Global Strategic Maple Syrup Reserve, he probably expected it to be just another job. There were 16 000 barrels listed in the storage facility, and as he entered the complex and saw row after row of barrels, he had no reason for concern. As he manoeuvred through the warehouse, however, Michel quickly realized that this task was anything but routine; his audit would lead to the discovery of a major theft and organized fraud. First, Michel found a series of empty barrels. As he continued the audit, he found more empty barrels, and then realized that many of the "full" containers did not contain maple syrup at all; they were filled with water. At $32 per gallon, each missing barrel represented $1800 of missing maple syrup inventory. What Mr. Gauvreau had discovered was no error; it was an unbelievable, systematic theft of approximately $20 million worth of maple syrup. Enough to put a tablespoon on 183 million pancakes!

HOW WILL THIS HELP ME?

For most of us, the words and ideas in accounting can seem like a foreign language, and the specialized terminology can be used to mask fraud and corruption. However, accounting terminology is a necessary tool that allows professionals in every industry to analyze growth, understand risk, and communicate detailed ideas about a firm's financial health. This chapter will cover the fundamental concepts of accounting and apply them to familiar business situations. By grasping the basic accounting vocabulary, you—as an employee, taxpayer, or owner—will be able to participate when the conversation turns to the financial matters that constitute so great a part of a firm's daily operations.

What exactly is the Global Strategic Maple Syrup Reserve? Quebec produces about 70 percent of the world's maple syrup supply. A few years ago, this federation was created to help manage the supply. Overproduction leads to lower prices, and this can be countered by keeping a strategic reserve stockpile in good years. These reserves help to balance supply and meet demand in bad years (years with poor production). Ultimately, this creates more stable (usually inflated) prices, so that producers have a steadier income stream. However, like all managed supply systems, it requires cooperation from all local producers. The federation has had many legal run-ins with rogue producers. But this case was something much more eye-opening and devious. True, the storage facility did not have a sophisticated security system; however, since it would take about 100 truckloads to move this amount of maple syrup, the theft had to be an inside job. This scenario became all the more likely when it was revealed that the thieves had taken the time to transfer some of the contents from the original barrels with bar codes (to identify their origins) into seemingly untraceable containers.

Now that Michel had done his job, the theft was a police matter. Was there any hope of recovering the stolen inventory? Isn't maple syrup untraceable? Well, you might think that this was a perfect crime. But, taking the inventory is just phase one; selling it is another challenge. How do you unload this much product discreetly? Selling such a huge quantity of maple syrup within Canada would raise suspicions, but if the thieves tried to cross the border with their syrup, they would leave a major paper trail behind. So, although phase one went off without a hitch (until the accountants uncovered it), phase two was another matter.

Officers from various agencies (the RCMP, Canada Border Services Agency, U.S. Immigration, and the QPP) interviewed over 300 people in Quebec, New Brunswick, Ontario, and the northeastern United States. They reviewed export documents and statistics, and conducted forensic

se media/Fotolia

analysis of syrup kettles, forklifts, and scales. They eventually traced two-thirds of the stolen goods before the arrests and accusations were made public.

- Twenty-six people were arrested.
- Companies and individuals in three provinces were implicated.
- Twelve tanker trucks worth of stolen maple syrup were found at a Vermont candy producer's factory.

Regardless of your beliefs about the appropriateness of an organized supply system, it is clear that Michel Gauvreau helped to protect all the legal stakeholders. He alerted everyone that the numbers on the paper did not match the numbers in the warehouse, thus ensuring the integrity of this system, flawed as it may be. This whole strange story may soon be in movie theatres. A Hollywood film starring Jason Segel is in the works and rumoured to begin production in late 2015.

QUESTIONS FOR DISCUSSION

1. How does the case of the maple syrup robbery demonstrate the important role of accountants?
2. Conduct some research and find articles discussing this case. What are the latest findings? What have investigators revealed by looking at the accounting paper trail?

WHAT IS ACCOUNTING, AND WHO USES ACCOUNTING INFORMATION?

Accounting is a comprehensive information system for collecting, analyzing, and communicating financial information. It measures business performance and translates the findings into information for management decisions. Accountants prepare performance reports for owners, the public, and regulatory agencies. To perform these functions, accountants keep records of transactions such as taxes paid, income received, and expenses incurred—a process called **bookkeeping**—and they analyze the effects of these transactions on business activities. By sorting, analyzing, and recording thousands of transactions, accountants can determine how well a business is being managed and how financially strong it is.

Because businesses engage in many thousands of transactions, ensuring that financial information is consistent and dependable is mandatory. This is the job of the **accounting information system (AIS)**: an organized procedure for identifying, measuring, recording, and retaining financial information so that it can be used in accounting statements and management reports. The system includes all of the people, reports, computers, procedures, and resources for compiling financial transactions.[1]

Users of accounting information are numerous:

- *Business managers* use accounting information to set goals, develop plans, set budgets, and evaluate future prospects.
- *Employees and unions* use accounting information to get paid and to plan for and receive benefits such as health care, insurance, vacation time, and retirement pay.
- *Investors and creditors* use accounting information to estimate returns to stockholders, determine a company's growth prospects, and determine whether it is a good credit risk before investing or lending.
- *Tax authorities* use accounting information to plan for tax inflows, determine the tax liabilities of individuals and businesses, and ensure that correct amounts are paid on time.
- *Government regulatory agencies* rely on accounting information to fulfill their duties. Provincial securities regulators, for example, require firms to file financial disclosures so that potential investors have valid information about a company's financial status.

If a company does not produce accurate accounting information, all of these groups may be hurt. As we saw in the opening case, inventory counts at the Global Strategic Maple Syrup Reserve were inaccurate. Standard accounting procedures identified the inconsistency, thus revealing the theft. The discovery had important implications for maple syrup producers, government agencies, and customers who ultimately may have purchased stolen products unknowingly. A few years ago, General Motors warned its investors that it did not yet have an effective

ACCOUNTING A comprehensive system for collecting, analyzing, and communicating financial information.

BOOKKEEPING Recording accounting transactions.

ACCOUNTING INFORMATION SYSTEM (AIS) organized procedure for identifying, measuring, recording, and retaining financial information for use in accounting statements and management reports.

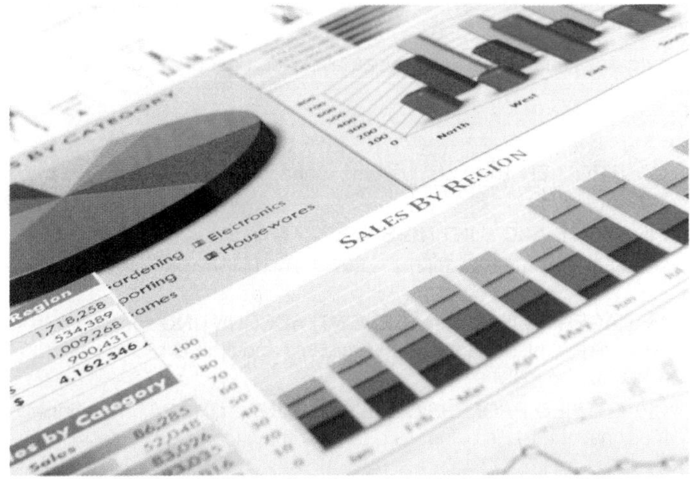

A financial report is an integral component of the financial accounting system.

Damir Karan/E+/Getty Images

accounting control system in place, and that it could not guarantee the reliability of its financial statements.[2] The Sarbanes-Oxley Act (passed in the U.S. in 2002) required senior managers in companies to certify that their company had an effective internal control system in place. In Canada, this idea was partially adopted two years later through National Instrument 52-109. Critics of this type of legislation argue that it has been very expensive to implement and has not achieved the goal of more reliable accounting information.[3]

LO-1 WHO ARE ACCOUNTANTS AND WHAT DO THEY DO?

The **controller**, or chief accounting officer, manages a firm's accounting activities by ensuring that the AIS provides the reports and statements needed for planning, decision making, and other management activities. This range of activities requires different types of accounting specialists. In this section, we begin by distinguishing between the two main fields of accounting: *financial* and *managerial*. Then, we discuss the different functions and activities of the three traditional professional accounting groups in Canada and the new, unified CPA designation.

Financial Versus Managerial Accounting

In any company, the two fields of financial and managerial accounting can be distinguished by the users they serve: those outside the company and those within.[4]

FINANCIAL ACCOUNTING

A firm's **financial accounting system** is concerned with external users of information such as consumer groups, unions, stockholders, and government agencies. Companies prepare and publish income statements and balance sheets at regular intervals, as well as other financial reports that are useful for stockholders and the general public. All of these documents focus on the activities of the company as a whole, rather than on individual departments or divisions.

MANAGERIAL ACCOUNTING

In contrast, **managerial (or management) accounting** serves internal users. Managers at all levels need information to make decisions for their departments, to monitor current projects, and to plan for future activities. Other employees also need accounting information. Engineers, for instance, want to know the costs for materials and production so they can make product operation improvements. To set performance goals, salespeople need data on past sales by geographic region. Purchasing agents use information on material costs to negotiate terms with suppliers.

CONTROLLER The individual who manages all the firm's accounting activities.

FINANCIAL ACCOUNTING SYSTEM The process whereby interested groups are kept informed about the financial condition of a firm.

MANAGERIAL (OR MANAGEMENT) ACCOUNTING Internal procedures that alert managers to problems and aid them in planning and decision making.

CHARTERED PROFESSIONAL ACCOUNTANT (CPA) The banner (designation) that is being used to unify the accounting profession in Canada.

CHARTERED ACCOUNTANT (CA now referred to as **CPA, CA)** An individual who has met certain experience and education requirements and has passed a licensing examination; acts as an outside accountant for other firms.

Professional Accountants

Over the years, three accounting organizations developed in Canada to certify accounting professionals. The three designations they created are chartered accountant (CA), certified management accountant (CMA), and certified general accountant (CGA). Below, we discuss each of these and its traditional strengths and roles; however, the three organizations have now agreed to unite them under the banner of **chartered professional accountant (CPA)**. In fact, as of October 2014, there are over 190 000 CPAs in Canada.[5] We will discuss the unification as well as the transition process after a brief explanation of their three traditional roles.

CHARTERED ACCOUNTANTS

The Canadian Institute of Chartered Accountants (CICA) managed the **chartered accountant (CA)** designation (now known as **CPA, CA**). To achieve this designation, a person earned a university degree, then completed an educational program and passed a national exam. About half of all CAs work in CA firms that offer accounting services to the public; the other half work in government or industry. CA firms typically provide audit, tax, and management services. CAs focus on external

TABLE 11.1 Top 10 Accounting Firms in Canada, 2014

	Company	Annual Revenues (millions of dollars)
1	Deloitte LLP	1776
2	PricewaterhouseCoopers LLP	1211
3	KPMG LLP	1203
4	Ernst & Young LLP	968
5	Grant Thornton Canada	582
6	MNP LLP	487
7	BDO Canada LLP	465
8	Collins Barrow National Cooperative Inc.	177
9	Richter LLP	80
10	Mallette	64

Source: Based on *The Bottom Line*, April 2014, "Canada's Top 30 Accounting Firms," p. 13.

financial reporting, that is, certifying for various interested parties (stockholders, lenders, the Canada Revenue Agency, and so on) that the financial records of a company accurately reflect the true financial condition of the firm.

CERTIFIED GENERAL ACCOUNTANTS

The Certified General Accountants Association of Canada managed the **certified general accountant (CGA)** designation (now known as **CPA, CGA**). To become a CGA, a person completed an education program and passed a national exam; to be eligible, a person also required an accounting job within a company. CGAs can audit corporate financial statements in most provinces. Most work in private companies, but there are a few CGA firms. Some also work in CA firms. CGAs also focus on external financial reporting and emphasize the use of the computer as a management accounting tool.

Take a look at the feature called "There's an App for That!" as it outlines three accounting apps.

CERTIFIED MANAGEMENT ACCOUNTANTS

The Society of Management Accountants of Canada managed the **certified management accountant (CMA)** designation (now known as **CPA, CMA**). To achieve the designation, a person required a university degree, passed a two-part national entrance examination, and completed a strategic leadership program while gaining practical experience in a management accounting environment. CMAs work in organizations of all sizes and focus on applying best management practices in all of the operations of a business. CMAs bring a strong market focus to strategic management and resource deployment, synthesizing and analyzing financial and non-financial information to help organizations maintain a competitive advantage. They emphasize the role of accountants in the planning and overall strategy of the firm in which they work.

THERE'S AN APP FOR THAT!

APP DETAILS	PLATFORMS
1. **QuickBooks App** **Source:** Intuit **Key Features:** Allows you to manage customers, invoices, sales receipts, estimates, and small business finances.	Apple, Android, BlackBerry, Windows
2. **Kashoo Accounting App** **Source:** Kashoo (Vancouver) **Key Features:** Permits small business owners to keep track of receipts, invoices, and bank balances on the go.	Apple, Android
3. **Learn Accounting by GoLearningBus** **Source:** WAGmob **Key Features:** Provides a summary of key accounting concepts through videos, tutorials, quizzes, and flashcards.	Apple, Android, Windows

APP DISCOVERY EXERCISE

Since app availability changes, conduct your own search for the "Top Three" accounting apps and identify the key features.

THE NEW RULES: TRANSITION FROM CA, CGA, AND CMA TO CPA

Students who begin their studies in the future will earn a CPA designation once all of the requirements are met and the final legislation is approved in all jurisdictions. All of the accounting professionals currently in the workforce (as well as individuals who complete their studies during the transition period) will refer to themselves as CPA, CA; CPA, CMA; CPA or CGA; CPA until November 2022. After that they can simply refer to themselves as CPAs.

The new CPA structure borrows some of the best practices from all three former organizations. It gives students a well-rounded accounting education but also permits them to specialize in another area such as strategy, auditing, finance and tax.[6] For the most up-to-date information on the transition process take a look at the following site: www.cpacanada.ca.

Accounting Services

CPA, CAs and CPA, CGAs usually perform several accounting services for their clients. The most common of these are auditing, tax services, and management services.

AUDITING

In an **audit**, accountants examine a company's AIS to ensure that it follows **generally accepted accounting principles (GAAP)**. An audit involves examination of receipts such as shipping documents, cancelled cheques, payroll records, and cash receipts records. In some cases, an auditor may physically check inventories, equipment, or other assets, even if it means descending 200 metres into a mine. The opening case about stolen maple syrup provides some concrete evidence as to why accountants must be thorough in their evaluations of assets. At the end of an audit, the auditor will certify whether the client's financial reports comply with GAAP.

International Accounting Standards In a globalized economy, users of financial information want assurances that accounting procedures are comparable from country to country. So the International Accounting Standards Board (IASB) has developed International Financial Reporting Standards (IFRS), a sort of "global GAAP," which is now being used by more than 120 countries.[7] Canadian companies adopted the IFRS on January 1, 2011, but it required a lot of work to determine how to present accounting information in a way that satisfies the new standards.[8] IASB financial statements require an income statement, balance sheet, and statement of cash flows, which are similar to those that have

CERTIFIED GENERAL ACCOUNTANT (CGA, now referred to as **CPA, CGA)** An individual who has completed an education program and passed a national exam; works in private industry or a CGA firm.

CERTIFIED MANAGEMENT ACCOUNTANT (CMA, now referred to as **CPA, CMA)** An individual who has completed a university degree, passed a national examination, and completed a strategic leadership program; works in industry and focuses on internal management accounting.

AUDIT An accountant's examination of a company's financial records to determine if it used proper procedures to prepare its financial reports.

GENERALLY ACCEPTED ACCOUNTING PRINCIPLES (GAAP) Standard rules and methods used by accountants in preparing financial reports.

historically been developed by Canadian accountants; but a variety of formats are used since a uniform format has not been developed. Some experts argue that IFRS gives managers too much leeway to report the figures they want, which means less protection for investors.[9] The United States has resisted the adoption of IFRS, but the standard has been adopted by three-quarters of the powerful G20 nations.[10]

The new IASB standards may have a noticeable impact on the way Canadian companies report some financial results. For example, suppose a company has a customer loyalty plan that gives customers points for purchases they make, and then these points can be redeemed for free products. If a customer makes $1000 in purchases and earns points that can be redeemed for $25 worth of merchandise, the company may have historically counted the $1000 as sales revenue and then also counted the $25 as sales revenue when the points were redeemed. But under the new IFRS, companies cannot add the $25 to the original $1000. The new rules will reduce the apparent same-stores sales growth numbers for these companies.[11]

Detecting Fraud In recent years, there has been much publicity about the failure of auditors to detect fraud. Therefore, when audits are being conducted, **forensic accountants** may be used to track down hidden funds in business firms. Because of the increase in white-collar crime, forensic accounting is one of the fastest-growing areas in the field. Forensic accountants must be good detectives. They look behind the corporate walls instead of accepting financial records at face value. In combining investigative skills with accounting, auditing, and the instincts of a bloodhound, they assist in the investigation of business and financial issues that may have application to a court of law. Forensic accountants may be called upon by law enforcement agencies, insurance companies, law firms, and business firms. They may conduct criminal investigations of internet scams and misuse of government funds. Forensic accountants also assist business firms in tracing and recovering lost assets from employee business fraud or theft.

Fraud examiners interview high-level executives, pursue tips from employees or outsiders, and search through emails, looking for suspicious words and phrases. The CA designation in investigative and forensic accounting (CA IFA) provides in-depth knowledge and experience in investigative and forensic accounting. You can get more information on the topic at the website for the Association of Certified Fraud Examiners (CFE) at www.acfe.com.

TAX SERVICES

Tax services include helping clients not only with preparing their tax returns, but also in their tax planning. Tax laws are complex, and an accountant's advice can help a business structure (or restructure) its operations and investments and save millions of dollars in taxes. To serve their clients best, of course, accountants must stay abreast of changes in tax laws—no simple matter.

MANAGEMENT CONSULTING SERVICES

Management consulting services range from personal financial planning to planning corporate mergers. Other services include plant layout and design, marketing studies, production scheduling, computer feasibility studies, and design and implementation of accounting systems. Some CA firms even assist in executive recruitment. Small wonder that the staffs of CA firms include engineers, architects, mathematicians, and even psychologists.

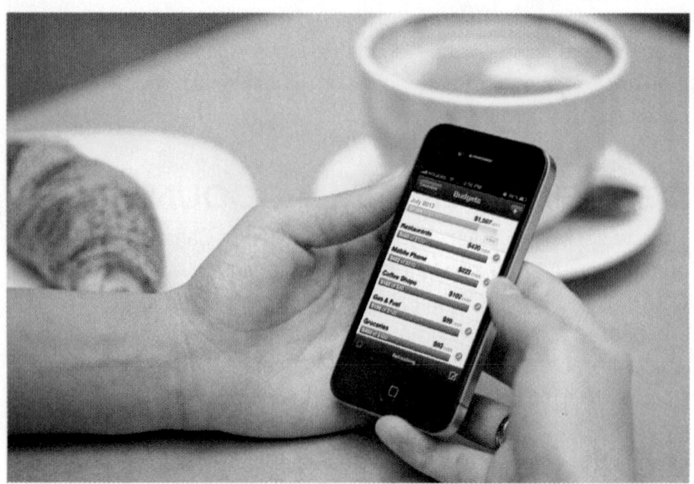

Thanks to smartphones, financial information is now much more accessible wherever you might be located.

pizuttipics/Fotolia

Private Accountants

Private accountants are salaried employees who deal with a company's day-to-day accounting needs. Large businesses employ specialized accountants in such areas as budgets, financial planning, internal auditing, payroll, and taxation. In a small firm, a single individual may handle all accounting tasks. The work of private accountants varies, depending on the nature of the specific business and the activities needed to make that business a success. An internal auditor at Petro-Canada, for example, might go to an oil platform off the coast to confirm the accuracy of oil-flow meters on the offshore drilling platform. But a supervisor responsible for $200 million in monthly accounts payable to vendors and employees may travel no further than the executive suite.

THE ACCOUNTING CYCLE

Private accountants use a six-step process to develop and analyze a company's financial reports (see Figure 11.1). The first step is to analyze data generated as a result of the company's regular business operations (sales revenue, income tax payments, interest income, inventory purchases, and so on). These transactions are entered in a journal (which lists them in chronological order) and then in a ledger (which shows the increases and decreases in the various asset, liability, and equity accounts). Then, the ledger amounts for each account are listed in a trial balance (which assesses the accuracy of the figures). Financial statements (balance sheet, income statement, and statement of cash flows) are then prepared using GAAP. The last step in the process involves analyzing the financial statements (e.g., by using ratio analysis). Many years ago, these steps were done laboriously by hand, but now computers are used to help private accountants efficiently work through the six steps.

FORENSIC ACCOUNTANT Accountants who track down hidden funds in business firms.

MANAGEMENT CONSULTING SERVICES Specialized accounting services to help managers resolve a variety of problems in finance, production scheduling, and other areas.

PRIVATE ACCOUNTANT An accountant hired as a salaried employee to deal with a company's day-to-day accounting needs.

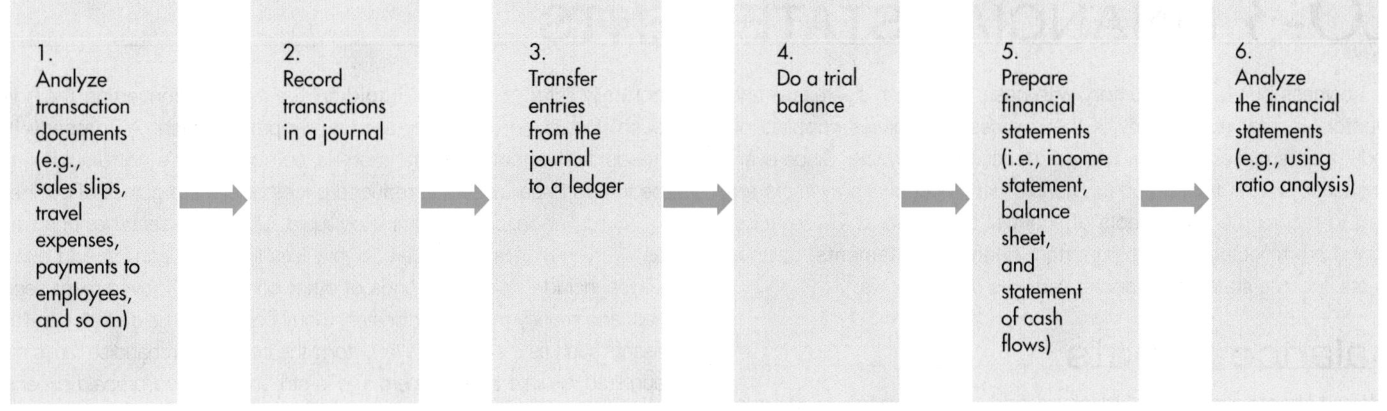
1.
Analyze transaction documents (e.g., sales slips, travel expenses, payments to employees, and so on)
2.
Record transactions in a journal
3.
Transfer entries from the journal to a ledger
4.
Do a trial balance
5.
Prepare financial statements (i.e., income statement, balance sheet, and statement of cash flows)
6.
Analyze the financial statements (e.g., using ratio analysis)

FIGURE 11.1 The accounting cycle

LO-2 THE ACCOUNTING EQUATION

All accountants, whether public or private, rely on record keeping. Underlying all record-keeping procedures is the most basic tool of accounting: the **accounting equation**. At various points in the year, accountants use the following equation to balance the data pertaining to financial transactions:

Assets = Liabilities + Owners' equity

After each transaction (e.g., payments to suppliers, sales to customers, wages to employees), the accounting equation must be in balance. To understand the importance of this equation, we must understand the terms *assets, liabilities*, and *owners' equity*.[12]

Assets and Liabilities

An **asset** is any economic resource that is expected to benefit a firm or an individual who owns it. Assets include land, buildings, equipment, inventory, and payments due to the company (accounts receivable). A **liability** is a debt that the firm owes to an outside party.

Owners' Equity

You may have heard of the equity that a homeowner has in a house—that is, the amount of money that could be made by selling the house and paying off the mortgage. Similarly, **owners' equity** is the amount of money that owners would receive if they sold all of a company's assets and paid all of its liabilities. We can rewrite the accounting equation to highlight this definition:

Assets − Liabilities = Owners' equity

If a company's assets exceed its liabilities, owners' equity is positive; if the company goes out of business, the owners will receive some cash (a gain) after selling assets and paying off liabilities. If liabilities outweigh assets, owners' equity is negative; assets are insufficient to pay off all debts. If the company goes out of business, the owners will get no cash and some creditors won't be paid. Owners' equity is meaningful for both investors and lenders. Before lending money to owners, for example, lenders want to know the amount of owners' equity in a business. Owners' equity consists of two sources of capital:

1. the amount the owners originally invested
2. profits earned by and reinvested in the company

When a company operates profitably, its assets increase faster than its liabilities. Owners' equity, therefore, will increase if profits are retained in the business instead of paid out as dividends to stockholders. Owners' equity also increases if owners invest more of their own money to increase assets. However, owners' equity can shrink if the company operates at a loss or if owners withdraw assets.

ACCOUNTING EQUATION Assets = Liabilities + Owners' equity; the formula used by accountants to balance data for the firm's financial transactions at various points in the year.

ASSET Anything of economic value owned by a firm or individual.

LIABILITY Any debt owed by a firm or individual to others.

OWNERS' EQUITY Any positive difference between a firm's assets and its liabilities; what would remain for a firm's owners if the company were liquidated, all its assets were sold, and all its debts were paid.

drive
away
today

The inventory at this car dealership is part of the company's assets. The cars constitute an economic resource because the firm will benefit financially as it sells them. After they are sold and at the end of the company's accounting period, the dealership will convert the cost of the cars as expenses and show them as costs of goods sold.

Alex Segre/Alamy

LO-3 FINANCIAL STATEMENTS

If a business purchases inventory with cash, then cash decreases and inventory increases. Similarly, if the business purchases supplies on credit, then supplies increase and so do accounts payable. Since every transaction affects two accounts, *double-entry accounting systems* are used to record the dual effects of financial transactions. These transactions are reflected in three important **financial statements**: balance sheets, income statements, and statements of cash flows.[13]

Balance Sheets

Balance sheets supply detailed information about the accounting equation factors: assets, liabilities, and owners' equity. Figure 11.2 shows the balance sheet for Perfect Posters.

ASSETS

As we have seen, an asset is any economic resource that a company owns and from which it can expect to derive some future benefit. Most companies have three types of assets: current, fixed, and intangible.

Current Assets **Current assets** include cash, money in the bank, and assets that can be converted into cash within a year. The act of converting something into cash is called *liquidating*. Assets are normally listed in order of **liquidity**, the ease of converting them into cash. Debts, for example, are usually paid in cash. A company that needs but cannot generate cash—a company that's not "liquid"—may be forced to sell assets at reduced prices or even to go out of business.

By definition, cash is completely liquid. *Marketable securities* purchased as short-term investments are slightly less liquid but can be sold quickly. These include stocks or bonds of other companies, government securities, and money market certificates. Many companies hold other non-liquid assets such as *merchandise inventory*, the cost of merchandise that's been acquired for sale to customers and is still on hand and *prepaid expenses* (supplies on hand and rent paid for the period to come). Figure 11.2

FINANCIAL STATEMENTS Any of several types of broad reports regarding a company's financial status; most often used in reference to balance sheets, income statements, and/or statements of cash flows.

BALANCE SHEET A type of financial statement that summarizes a firm's financial position on a particular date in terms of its assets, liabilities, and owners' equity.

CURRENT ASSETS Cash and other assets that can be converted into cash within a year.

LIQUIDITY The ease and speed with which an asset can be converted to cash; cash is said to be perfectly liquid.

Perfect Posters, Inc.
555 Riverview, Toronto, Ontario

Perfect Posters, Inc.
Balance Sheet
As of December 31, 2015

Assets			
Current Assets:			
Cash		$7 050	
Marketable securities		2 300	
Accounts receivable	$26 210		
Less: Allowance of doubtful accounts	(650)	25 560	
Merchandise inventory		21 250	
Prepaid expenses		1 050	
Total current assets			**$57 210**
Fixed Assets:			
Land		18 000	
Building	65 000		
Less: Accumulated depreciation	(22 500)	42 500	
Equipment	72 195		
Less: Accumulated depreciation	(24 815)	47 380	
Total fixed assets			**107 880**
Intangible Assets:			
Patents	7 100		
Trademarks	900		
Total intangible assets			**8 000**
Total assets			**$173 090**

Liabilities and Owners' Equity		
Current liabilities:		
Accounts payable	$16 315	
Wages payable	3 700	
Taxes payable	1 920	
Total current liabilities		**$21 935**
Long-term liabilities:		
Notes payable, 8% due 2018	10 000	
Bonds payable, 9% due 2020	30 000	
Total long-term liabilities		**40 000**
Total liabilities		**$61 935**
Owners' Equity:		
Common stock, $5 par	40 000	
Additional paid-in capital	15 000	
Retained earnings	56 155	
Total owners' equity		**111 155**
Total liabilities and owners' equity		**$173 090**

FIGURE 11.2 Perfect Posters' balance sheet

This balance sheet shows clearly that the firm's total assets equal its total liabilities and owners' equity.

shows that Perfect Posters' current assets as of December 31, 2015, totalled $57 210.

Fixed Assets **Fixed assets** (e.g., land, buildings, and equipment) have long-term use or value. As buildings and equipment wear out or become obsolete, their value depreciates. Various methods can be used to calculate depreciation, but, in its simplest sense, **depreciation** means determining an asset's useful life in years, dividing its worth by that many years, and then subtracting the resulting amount each year. The asset's remaining value therefore decreases each year. In Figure 11.2, Perfect Posters shows fixed assets of $107 880 after depreciation.

Intangible Assets Although their worth is hard to set, intangible assets have monetary value. **Intangible assets** usually include the cost of obtaining rights or privileges such as patents, trademarks, copyrights, and franchise fees. **Goodwill** is the amount paid for an existing business beyond the value of its other assets. Perfect Posters has no goodwill assets, but it does own trademarks and patents for specialized storage equipment. These intangible assets are worth $8000. Larger companies have intangible assets that are worth much more.

LIABILITIES

Current liabilities are debts that must be paid within one year. These include **accounts payable** (unpaid bills to suppliers for materials, as well as wages and taxes that must be paid in the coming year). Perfect Posters has current liabilities of $21 935.

Long-term liabilities are debts that are not due for at least one year. These normally represent borrowed funds on which the company must pay interest. Perfect Posters' long-term liabilities are $40 000.

OWNERS' EQUITY

The final section of the balance sheet in Figure 11.2 shows owners' equity broken down into *common stock, paid-in capital*, and *retained earnings*. When Perfect Posters was formed, the declared legal value of its common stock was $5 per share. By law, this $40 000 ($5 multiplied by 8000 shares) cannot be distributed as dividends. **Paid-in capital** is additional money invested in the firm by its owners. Perfect Posters has $15 000 in paid-in capital.

Retained earnings are net profits minus dividend payments to shareholders. Retained earnings accumulate when profits, which could have been distributed to shareholders, are kept instead for use by the company. At the close of 2015, Perfect Posters had retained earnings of $56 155.

LO-4 Income Statements

The **income statement** is sometimes called a profit-and-loss statement, because its description of revenues and expenses results in a figure showing the firm's annual profit or loss. In other words,

Revenues − Expenses = Profit (or loss)

Profit or loss, popularly known as "the bottom line," is probably the most important figure in any business enterprise. Figure 11.3 shows the 2015 income statement for Perfect Posters, whose bottom line that year was $12 585. The income statement is divided into three major categories: revenues, cost of goods sold, and operating expenses. Unlike a balance sheet, which shows the financial condition at a specific *point in time*, an income statement shows the financial results that occurred during a *period of time*, such as a month, quarter, or year.

Perfect Posters, Inc.
555 Riverview, Toronto, Ontario

Perfect Posters, Inc.
Income Statement
Year ended December 31, 2015

Revenues (gross sales)			**$256 425**
Costs of goods sold:			
Merchandise inventory, January 1, 2015	$22 380		
Merchandise purchases during year	103 635		
Goods available for sale		$126 015	
Less: Merchandise inventory, December 31, 2015		21 250	
Cost of goods sold			**104 765**
Gross profit			**151 660**
Operating expenses:			
Selling and repackaging expenses:			
Salaries and wages	49 750		
Advertising	6 380		
Depreciation—warehouse and repackaging equipment	3 350		
Total selling and repackaging expenses		59 480	
Administrative expenses:			
Salaries and wages	55 100		
Supplies	4 150		
Utilities	3 800		
Depreciation—office equipment	3 420		
Interest expense	2 900		
Miscellaneous expenses	1 835		
Total administration expenses		71 205	
Total operating expenses			**130 685**
Operating income (income before taxes)			20 975
Income taxes			8 390
Net income			**$12 585**

FIGURE **11.3** Perfect Posters' income statement

The final entry on the income statement, the bottom line, reports the firm's profit or loss.

FIXED ASSETS Assets that have long-term use or value to the firm, such as land, buildings, and machinery.

DEPRECIATION accounting method for distributing the cost of an asset over its useful life.

INTANGIBLE ASSETS Non-physical assets, such as a patent or trademark, that have economic value in the form of expected benefit.

GOODWILL The amount paid for an existing business beyond the value of its other assets.

CURRENT LIABILITIES debt that must be paid within one year.

ACCOUNTS PAYABLE Amounts due from the firm to its suppliers for goods and/or services purchased on credit; a form of current liability.

LONG-TERM LIABILITIES Any debts owed by the firm that are not due for at least one year.

PAID-IN CAPITAL Any additional money invested in the firm by the owners.

RETAINED EARNINGS A company's net profits less any dividend payments to shareholders.

INCOME STATEMENT (PROFIT-AND-LOSS STATEMENT) A type of financial statement that describes a firm's revenues and expenses and indicates whether the firm has earned a profit or suffered a loss during a given period.

REVENUES

When a law firm receives $700 for preparing a will or when a supermarket collects $100 from a customer buying groceries, both are receiving **revenues**—the funds that flow into a business from the sale of goods or services. In 2015, Perfect Posters reported revenues of $256 425 from the sale of art prints and other posters.

Take a look at some particular considerations in the Entrepreneurship and New Ventures box entitled "Accounting Practices for the Small Business."

Revenue Recognition and Matching

Revenue recognition is the formal recording and reporting of revenues in the financial statements. Although any firm earns revenues continuously as it makes sales, earnings are not reported until the earnings cycle is completed. Revenues are recorded for the accounting period in which sales are completed and collectible (or collected).

The **matching principle** states that expenses will be matched with revenues to determine net income for an accounting period.[14] This principle is important, because it permits the user of the statement to see how much net gain resulted from the assets that had to be given up to generate revenues during the period covered in the statement.

COST OF GOODS SOLD

In Perfect Posters' income statement, the **cost of goods sold** category shows the costs of obtaining materials to make the products sold during the year. Perfect Posters began 2015 with posters valued at $22 380. Over the year, it spent $103 635 to purchase posters. During 2015, then, the company had $126 015 worth of merchandise available to sell. By the end of the year, it had sold all but $21 250 of those posters, which remained as merchandise inventory. The cost of obtaining the goods sold by the firm was thus $104 765.

REVENUES Any monies received by a firm as a result of selling a good or service or from other sources such as interest, rent, and licensing fees.

REVENUE RECOGNITION The formal recording and reporting of revenues in the financial statements.

MATCHING PRINCIPLE Expenses should be matched with revenues to determine net income for an accounting period.

COST OF GOODS SOLD Any expenses directly involved in producing or selling a good or service during a given time period.

ENTREPRENEURSHIP AND NEW VENTURES

Accounting Practices for the Small Business

This chapter's accounting fundamentals apply to all businesses, large and small alike. However, some additional considerations are relevant for small firms, especially for start-ups. Most new firms are started by entrepreneurs who are not accountants, many of whom know little about accounting. Fortunately, experienced help is available from firms specializing in small business accounting to guide start-ups on "things to avoid" and "things to do" while getting acquainted with accounting-related tasks.

Five Things for the Start-up Owner to Do

- Do as many of the accounting and bookkeeping chores yourself, as time allows, rather than delegating them to others. First-hand experience is the best way to improve your knowledge of accounting for your business.
- Get acquainted with a small business accounting firm that is accessible for answering questions and providing guidance with special accounting needs in your industry.
- Focus your initial efforts on learning the most basic reporting practices—balance sheets, income statements, statements of cash flows—so that you understand what information each report contains, how to interpret that information, and how to explain to others the purposes of the reports.
- Always keep your personal records and transactions separated from the records and transactions of the business. Mixing personal and business data creates serious tax problems and raises questions of credibility about your firm's financial condition.
- Establish internal procedures to ensure that all of the firm's bills are paid, all income is received, and all financial transactions are accounted for. Knowing the true financial status of the business depends on controlling and verifying all its transactions.

Five Things for the Start-up Owner to *Not* Do

- Do not use the money you have set aside for taxes, including payroll and sales taxes, for other purposes. Governments set tax due dates and tax rates, and are unforgiving when those requirements are not met. Chances increase for not meeting your obligations when set-asides are used for other purposes.
- Do not rely on verbal agreements. They should be treated as a source of disagreement. Memories can be short, so instead of verbal agreements with suppliers, employees, lenders, local officials, and others, put everything in writing.
- Do not overestimate how much money you will be earning, especially early on. For planning purposes, be conservative in estimating future incomes and expenses. Avoid overestimating future incomes from sales, and avoid underestimating outflows for payments on rent, supplies, salaries, and other expenses.
- Do not allow anyone else to write cheques on behalf of the business. Many start-ups become shut-downs when the bank account is suddenly emptied by a trusted employee who can no longer be located.
- Don't be careless with billing. Before paying any bill, be sure to have evidence that the amount billed to you by the supplier matches the purchase order that was sent to that supplier. It is not unusual to be over- or undersupplied, without corresponding offsets in payments due.

CRITICAL THINKING QUESTION

1. Conduct online research about the specific challenges of small businesses accounting, and come up with two additional things to do and two additional things to avoid.

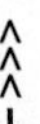

Gross Profit (or Gross Margin) To calculate **gross profit** (or **gross margin**), subtract the cost of goods sold from revenues. Perfect Posters' gross profit in 2015 was $151 660 ($256 425 minus $104 765). Expressed as a percentage of sales, gross profit is 59.1 percent ($151 660 divided by $256 425 times 100).

Gross profit percentages vary widely across industries. In retailing, Home Depot reports 34 percent; in manufacturing, Harley-Davidson reports 36 percent; and in pharmaceuticals, Pfizer Inc. reports 80 percent. For companies with low gross margins, product costs are a big expense. If a company has a high gross margin, it probably has low cost of goods sold, but high selling and administrative expenses.

OPERATING EXPENSES

In addition to costs directly related to acquiring goods, every company has general expenses ranging from erasers to the president's salary. Like cost of goods sold, **operating expenses** are resources that must flow out of a company for it to earn revenues. As you can see in Figure 11.3, Perfect Posters had operating expenses of $130 685 in 2015. This figure consists of $59 480 in selling and repackaging expenses and $71 205 in administrative expenses.

Selling expenses result from activities related to selling the firm's goods or services. These may include salaries for the sales force, delivery costs, and advertising expenses. *General and administrative expenses*, such as management salaries, insurance expenses, and maintenance costs, are expenses related to the general management of the company.

Operating Income and Net Income Sometimes managers calculate **operating income**, which compares the gross profit from business operations against operating expenses. This calculation for Perfect Posters ($151 660 minus $130 685) reveals an operating income, or income before taxes, of $20 975. Subtracting income taxes from operating income ($20 975 minus $8390) reveals **net income** (also called **net profit** or **net earnings**). In 2015, Perfect Posters' net income was $12 585.

Statements of Cash Flows

In order to survive, a business must earn a profit (i.e., its sales revenues must exceed its expenses), but it must also make sure it has cash available when it needs it (e.g., to pay employees). Cash-flow management requires the development of a **statement of cash flows**, which describes a company's yearly cash receipts and cash payments. It shows the effects on cash of three important business activities:

- *Cash flows from operations.* This part of the statement is concerned with the firm's main operating activities: the cash transactions involved in buying and selling goods and services. It reveals how much of the year's profits result from the firm's main line of business (e.g., Ferrari's sales of automobiles), rather than from secondary activities (e.g., licensing fees that a clothing firm paid to Ferrari to use their logo).
- *Cash flows from investing.* This section reports net cash used in or provided by investing. It includes cash receipts and payments from buying and selling stocks, bonds, property, equipment, and other productive assets.
- *Cash flows from financing.* The final section reports net cash from all financing activities. It includes cash inflows from borrowing or issuing stock, as well as outflows for payment of dividends and repayment of borrowed money.

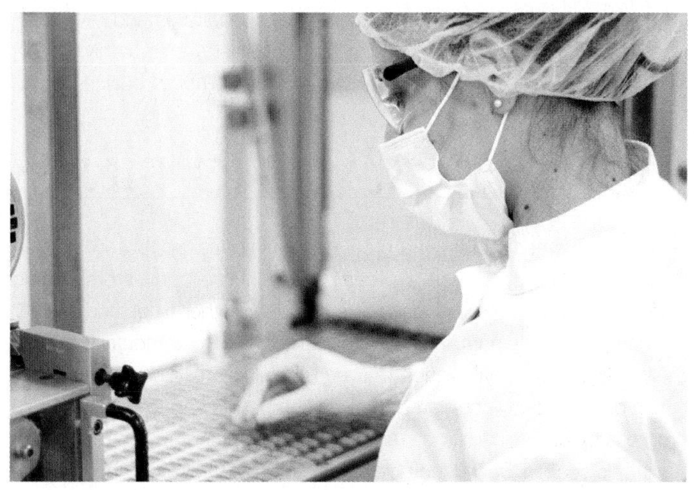

At the end of its accounting period, this pharmaceuticals company will subtract the cost of making the goods that it sells from the revenues it receives from sales. The difference will be its gross profit (or gross margin).

RGtimeline/Fotolia

The overall change in cash from these three sources provides information to lenders and investors. When creditors and stockholders know how firms obtained and used their funds during the course of a year, it is easier for them to interpret the year-to-year changes in the firm's balance sheet and income statement.

The Budget: An Internal Financial Statement

For planning, controlling, and decision making, the most important internal financial statement is the **budget**, a detailed report on estimated receipts and expenditures for a future period of time. Although that period is usually one year, some companies also prepare three- or five-year budgets, especially when considering major capital expenditures. The budget differs from the other statements we have discussed in that budgets are not shared outside the company; hence the "internal financial statement" title.

Although the accounting staff coordinates the budget process, it needs input from many areas regarding proposed activities and required resources. In preparing next year's budget, accounting must obtain projections from the sales group about units to be sold and expected expenses for the coming year. Then, accounting draws up the final budget and,

GROSS PROFIT (GROSS MARGIN) A firm's revenues (gross sales) less its cost of goods sold.

OPERATING EXPENSES Costs incurred by a firm other than those included in cost of goods sold.

OPERATING INCOME Compares the gross profit from business operations against operating expenses.

NET INCOME (NET PROFIT OR **NET EARNINGS)** A firm's gross profit less its operating expenses and income taxes.

STATEMENT OF CASH FLOWS A financial statement that describes a firm's generation and use of cash during a given period.

BUDGET Detailed statement of estimated receipts and expenditures for a future period of time.

throughout the year, compares it to actual expenditures and revenues. Budgets are also useful for keeping track of weekly or monthly performance. For example, Procter & Gamble evaluates all of its business units monthly, by comparing actual financial results with monthly budgeted amounts. Discrepancies in "actual versus budget" totals signal potential problems and initiate action to get financial performance back on track.

LO-5 ANALYZING FINANCIAL STATEMENTS

Financial statements present a great deal of information, but what does it all mean? How, for example, can statements help investors decide what stock to buy or help managers decide whether to extend credit? Statements provide data, which in turn can be used to compute solvency, profitability, and activity ratios that are useful in analyzing the financial health of a company compared to other companies and to check a firm's progress by comparing its current and past statements.

In this section we will look closely at some of the key financial ratios, but to get a sense of the difficulty of evaluating true value read the Managing in Turbulent Times box entitled "The Fairness Dilemma: What Is an Asset's Real Value?"

Solvency Ratios: Borrower's Ability to Repay Debt

What are the chances that a borrower will be able to repay a loan and the interest due? This question is first and foremost in the minds of bank lending officers, managers of pension funds and other investors, suppliers, and the borrowing company's own financial managers. **Solvency ratios** measure the firm's ability to meet its debt obligations.

SHORT-TERM SOLVENCY RATIOS

Short-term solvency ratios measure a company's liquidity and its ability to pay immediate debts. The most commonly used ratio is the **current ratio**, which reflects a firm's ability to generate cash to meet obligations through the normal, orderly process of selling inventories and collecting revenues from customers. It is calculated by dividing current assets by current liabilities. The higher a firm's current ratio, the lower the risk it represents to investors. For many years, the guideline was a current ratio of 2:1 or higher—which meant that current assets were at least double current liabilities. More recently, many firms that are financially strong operate with current ratios of less than 2:1.

How does Perfect Posters measure up? Look again at the balance sheet in Figure 11.2. Judging from its current assets and current liabilities at the end of 2015, we see that the company looks like a good credit risk:

$$\frac{\text{Current assets}}{\text{Current liabilities}} = \frac{\$57\,210}{\$21\,935} = 2.61$$

LONG-TERM SOLVENCY

Stakeholders are also concerned about long-term solvency. Has the company been overextended by borrowing so much that it will be unable

SOLVENCY RATIOS Ratios that estimate the financial risk that is evident in a company.

SHORT-TERM SOLVENCY RATIO Financial ratio for measuring a company's ability to pay immediate debts.

CURRENT RATIO Financial ratio for measuring a company's ability to pay current debts out of current assets.

MANAGING IN TURBULENT TIMES

The Fairness Dilemma: What Is an Asset's Real Value?

Think of a personal possession such as your car or house. What is its value? Is it the amount you paid for it, or perhaps the market price you could sell it for in a couple of years? A consumer who buys a house for $475 000 just before a recession hits is likely to discover that the house's value has dropped significantly. If the consumer cannot make the payments on the house, it may be foreclosed by the bank. But what value should the bank assign to the house on its balance sheet? The original purchase price? The current market price? What the house will be worth when the recession ends?

This example demonstrates that when businesses try to value assets on their balance sheets, the state of the economy can complicate their task. In a deep recession, for example, the market for goods and services has essentially shut down, so it is difficult to know what a fair market price is. With few or no buyers, once-valuable properties and financial investments may become unsellable "toxic assets."

A procedure called "mark-to-market accounting"—or "fair value accounting"—requires that assets be priced on balance sheets at current market value. But this can create problems when the economy turns down because it will force a major write-down for toxic assets and forces losses that may cause companies to fold. Advocates for relaxing mark-to-market accounting argue that since presently distressed assets may eventually become more valuable as time passes and the economy recovers, currently depressed values are not actually "fair" indicators of their worth. Instead, they say, mark-to-market exaggerates the scale of losses in an economic downturn.

In the United States, the housing crash of 2006–2012 caused pressure to develop for relief from mark-to-market accounting. That relief came when the U.S. Financial Accounting Standards Board (FASB) relaxed mark-to-market accounting for financial institutions and gave banks more flexibility for valuing toxic assets. But opponents of the change warned that relaxing the rules might let banks hide the true (i.e., low) value of assets they held, and that would deceive investors at a time when trust in financial reporting is really needed.

CRITICAL THINKING QUESTIONS

1. Make a case for rigid adherence to the idea of mark-to-market accounting. Then make a case for flexibility in applying mark-to-market rules. Which case is more compelling? Defend your answer.

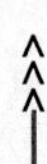

to repay debts in future years? A firm that can't meet its long-term debt obligations is in danger of collapse or takeover, a risk that makes creditors and investors quite cautious. To evaluate a company's risk of running into this problem, creditors turn to the balance sheet to see the extent to which a firm is financed through borrowed money. Long-term solvency is calculated by dividing **debt** (total liabilities) by owners' equity. The lower a firm's debt, the lower the risk to investors and creditors. Companies with **debt-to-equity ratios** above 1.0 may be relying too much on debt. Companies with more debt may find themselves owing so much that they lack the income needed to meet interest payments or to repay borrowed money. In the case of Perfect Posters, we can see from the balance sheet in Figure 11.2 that the debt-to-equity ratio calculates as follows:

$$\frac{\text{Debt}}{\text{Owners' equity}} = \frac{\$61\ 935}{\$111\ 155} = \$0.56$$

Sometimes, high debt can not only be acceptable, but also desirable. Borrowing funds gives a firm **leverage**—the ability to make otherwise unaffordable investments. In leveraged buyouts, firms have sometimes taken on huge debt in order to get the money to buy out other companies. If owning the purchased company generates profits above the cost of borrowing the purchase price, leveraging makes sense. Unfortunately, many buyouts have caused problems because profits fell short of expected levels or because rising interest rates increased payments on the buyer's debt.

Profitability Ratios: Earnings Power for Owners

Although it is important to know that a company is solvent, safety or risk alone is not an adequate basis for investment decisions. Investors also want some measure of the returns they can expect. Return on equity, return on sales, and earnings per share are three commonly used **profitability ratios** (sometimes these are called shareholder return ratios or performance ratios).

RETURN ON EQUITY

Owners are interested in the net income earned by a business for each dollar invested. **Return on equity** measures this performance by dividing net income (recorded on the income statement, Figure 11.3) by total owners' equity (recorded on the balance sheet, Figure 11.2). For Perfect Posters, the return-on-equity ratio in 2015 is:

$$\frac{\text{Net income}}{\text{Total owners' equity}} = \frac{\$12\ 585 \times 100}{\$111\ 155} = 11.3\%$$

Is this ratio good or bad? There is no set answer. If Perfect Posters' ratio for 2015 is higher than in previous years, owners and investors should be encouraged. But if 11.3 percent is lower than the ratios of other companies in the same industry, they should be concerned.

RETURN ON SALES

Companies want to generate as much profit as they can from each dollar of sales revenue they receive. The **return on sales** ratio is calculated by dividing net income by sales revenue (see Figure 11.3). For Perfect Posters, the return on sales ratio for 2015 is:

$$\frac{\text{Net income}}{\text{Sales revenue}} = \frac{\$12\ 585 \times 100}{\$256\ 425} = 4.9\%$$

Is this figure good or bad? Once again, there is no set answer. If Perfect Posters' ratio for 2015 is higher than in previous years, owners and investors should be encouraged, but if 4.9 percent is lower than the ratios of other companies in the same industry, they will likely be concerned.

EARNINGS PER SHARE

Earnings per share—calculated by dividing net income by the number of shares of common stock outstanding—influences the size of the dividend a company can pay to its shareholders. Investors use this ratio to decide whether to buy or sell a company's stock. As the ratio gets higher, the stock value increases because investors know that the firm can better afford to pay dividends. The market value of a stock will typically decline if the latest financial statements report a decline in earnings per share. For Perfect Posters, we can use the net income total from the income statement in Figure 11.3 to calculate earnings per share as follows:

$$\frac{\text{Net income}}{\text{Number of common shares outstanding}} = \frac{\$12\ 585}{8000} = \$1.57 \text{ per share}$$

Activity Ratios: How Efficiently Is the Firm Using Its Resources?

The efficiency with which a firm uses resources is linked to profitability. As a potential investor, you want to know which company gets more mileage from its resources. Information obtained from financial statements can be used to calculate **activity ratios.** For example, suppose that two firms use the same amount of resources or assets. If Firm A generates greater profits or sales, it is more efficient, and thus has a better activity ratio.

One of the most important activity ratios is the **inventory turnover ratio**, which calculates the average number of times that inventory is sold and restocked during the year.[15] Once a company knows its average inventory (calculated by adding end-of-year inventory to beginning-of-year inventory and dividing by 2), it can calculate the inventory turnover

DEBT A company's total liabilities.

DEBT-TO-EQUITY RATIOS A form of debt ratio calculated as total liabilities divided by owners' equity.

LEVERAGE Using borrowed funds to make purchases, thus increasing the user's purchasing power, potential rate of return, and risk of loss.

PROFITABILITY RATIOS Measures of a firm's overall financial performance in terms of its likely profits; used by investors to assess their probable returns.

RETURN ON EQUITY A form of profitability ratio calculated as net income divided by total owners' equity.

RETURN ON SALES Ratio calculated by dividing net income by sales revenue.

EARNINGS PER SHARE A form of profitability ratio calculated as net income divided by the number of common shares outstanding.

ACTIVITY RATIOS Measures of how efficiently a firm uses its resources; used by investors to assess their probable returns.

INVENTORY TURNOVER RATIO An activity ratio that measures the average number of times inventory is sold and restocked during the year.

<<< The inverntory turnover ratio measures the average number of times that a store sells and restocks its inventory in one year. The higher the ratio, the more products get sold and the more revenue comes in. Zara had a 28.56 inventory turnover ratio in 2015—far superior to the industry average.[16]

Bjanka Kadic/Alamy

ratio, which is expressed as the cost of goods sold divided by average inventory:

$$\frac{\text{Cost of goods sold}}{\text{Average inventory}} = \frac{\text{Cost of goods sold}}{(\text{Beginning inventory} + \text{Ending inventory}) \div 2}$$

To calculate Perfect Posters' inventory turnover ratio for 2015, we take the merchandise inventory figures for the income statement in Figure 11.3. The ratio can be expressed as follows:

$$\frac{\$104\ 765}{(\$22\ 380 + \$21\ 250) \div 2} = 4.8$$

In other words, new merchandise replaces old every 76 days (365 days divided by 4.8). The 4.8 ratio is below the industry average of 7.0 for comparable wholesaling operations, indicating that the business is somewhat inefficient.

LO-6 BRINGING ETHICS INTO THE ACCOUNTING EQUATION

The ultimate purpose of strong ethical standards in accounting is to maintain public confidence in business institutions, financial markets, and the products and services of the accounting profession. Without ethics, all accounting tools and methods would be meaningless, because their usefulness depends ultimately on their honest application.

Why Accounting Ethics?

In recent years, we have seen many corporations demonstrate poor judgment and ethical lapses. In some cases, this has led to a minor problem; in others (like Nortel), it has contributed to the demise of a company. Ethics remains an area where one person who is willing to "do the right thing" can make a difference—and people do, every day.

With the unification process of the accounting designations, a new Canadian Chartered Professional Accounting Code of Ethics is being developed that will borrow from the best practices of the three current designations. In Table 11.2, you can see the existing CPA code of ethics in the United States.

A code of ethics is a good start; it clearly outlines good practices and points out improper behaviour. Ultimately, the actions of conscientious

TABLE 11.2 Highlights from the CPA Code of Ethics[17]

The new Canadian CPA designation is merging best practices from the previous designations to form a similar code to the one found south of the border for American Certified Public Accountants.
Responsibilities as a Professional Exercise their duties with a high level of morality and in a manner that is sensitive to bringing credit to their profession.
Serving the Public Interest Demonstrate commitment to the profession by respecting and maintaining the public trust and serving the public honorably.
Maintaining Integrity Perform all professional activities with highest regards for integrity, including sincerity and honesty, so as to promote the public's confidence in the profession.
Being Objective and Independent Avoid conflicts of interest, and the appearance of conflicts of interest, in performing their professional responsibilities. They should be independent from clients when certifying to the public that the client's statements are true and genuine.
Maintaining Technical and Ethical Standards Exercise "due care," through professional improvement, abiding by ethical standards, updating personal competence through continuing accounting education, and improving the quality of services.
Professional Conduct in Providing Services In public practice abide by the meaning and intent of the Code of Professional Conduct when deciding on the kinds of services and the range of actions to be supplied for clients.

accountants will maintain and improve the level of faith investors have in accounting reports. As discussed earlier in the chapter, legislation to improve clarity and increase accountability, the Sarbanes-Oxley Act in the U.S. and the National Instrument 52-109 in Canada, has been developed to ensure public confidence.

LO-7 THE EVOLVING ROLE OF THE MODERN ACCOUNTANT

Lessons from the most recent global recession along with evolving information technologies are among the prominent forces shaping the future for accounting professionals. However, the accountant's knowledge of business aided by analytical and technical skills, although essential, are not sufficient capabilities for meeting current and future market demands in this changing profession. The traditional accountant's role was centred on analyzing historical financial data, creating financial statements, and providing interpretations of financial data and documents to facilitate business decisions. The expectations for the modern CPAs, increasingly, call for the more intimate role of leadership in demonstrating financial implications for many additional facets of the business including its overall operations, strategy, data management, human resources, and technical resources. The accountant, in this increasing participation with client firms, uses additional competencies beyond those of the traditional financial accounting expert.

In consultative roles, accountants are being asked for guidance on broad issues including business development; evaluating strategic opportunities; assessments of risks and threats; and strategies for using massive databases to identify promising directions for developing new products, improving customer service, and evaluating new lines of business to gain competitive advantage. Beyond just technical expertise, these kinds of participation require thorough knowledge of the client's business and the markets in which it operates.

The following trends have emerged and are contributing to the additional roles of the modern accountant:

- *Fewer restrictions from physical and geographic boundaries.* With increasing globalization many foreign-based firms are interacting with firms based elsewhere around the world. Coupled with modern technology, accountants and clients in other countries are working together remotely. Today, an accountant based at a company office, or at an office-in-the-home, in Calgary, Alberta, can provide services to a client in Singapore.
- *Social-media-driven changes in relationships and the way business is conducted.* Modern accountants establish professional relationships through active participation through social media. No longer do CPAs rely solely on face-to-face interactions at occasional professional meetings. Social media such as LinkedIn provide at-your-fingertips platforms for remote interactions allowing exchanges of (non-critical) information, professional advice, and temporary collaborations among accountants to serve clients in need of particular skill sets. New business opportunities arise, too, when accountants use a social networking presence to establish their business reputations.
- *Need for the accountant to be an effective communicator.* Communication skills are vital in the modern accountant's role in advising clients on global business trends and strategic perspectives. The accountant's thorough knowledge, to be leveraged into meaningful advice, must be communicated to clients on time, clearly and convincingly, both verbally and in writing. Effectiveness can be critical in a variety of communications contexts, ranging from formal presentations, to interactive group meetings, to one-to-one informal conversations, either face to face or remotely.
- *Project management in the accountant's expanded role.* Serving as project manager is becoming commonplace for accountants, because they provide guidance on the client's strategy, overall operations, and business development. These broad-based issues typically involve large-scale teams of specialists requiring long-term participation in activities such as financial forecasting, product and process engineering, financial interpretation, cost estimation, and human resource analysis. Success depends on the project manager's ability to decompose the project into manageable tasks, gain acceptance of task assignments, encourage timely reporting by task groups, and merge the project's many steps into coherent conclusions.

It is evident, then, that tomorrow's accountant needs to be prepared with more than just traditional skills. He or she needs to know the nature of the client's business and its competitive environment, and understand how to assist that client in gaining greater competitive advantage.[18]

MyBizLab

Study, practise, and explore real business situations with these helpful resources:

- **Interactive Lesson Presentations:** Work through interactive presentations and assessments to test your knowledge of business concepts.
- **Study Plan:** Check your understanding of chapter concepts with self-study quizzes.
- **Dynamic Study Modules:** Work through adaptive study modules on your computer, tablet, or mobile device.
- **Simulations:** Practise decision-making in simulated business environments.
- **Videos:** Learn more about the business practices and strategies of real companies.

SUMMARY OF

LEARNING OBJECTIVES

LO-1 EXPLAIN THE *ROLE OF ACCOUNTANTS*, DISTINGUISH BETWEEN THE THREE TRADITIONAL *PROFESSIONAL ACCOUNTING DESIGNATIONS* IN CANADA, AND UNDERSTAND THE NEW UNIFIED ROLE OF THE *CANADIAN CHARTERED PROFESSIONAL ACCOUNTING (CPA) DESIGNATION*.

By collecting, analyzing, and communicating financial information, accountants provide business managers and investors with an accurate picture of a firm's financial health. Traditionally, *chartered accountants (CAs) and certified general accountants (CGAs)* provide accounting expertise for client organizations that must report their financial condition to external stakeholders. *Certified management accountants (CMAs)* provide accounting expertise for the firms that employ them. However, these three separate designations have joining forces to create the *Canadian chartered professional accountant (CPA) designation*.

LO-2 EXPLAIN HOW THE *ACCOUNTING EQUATION* IS USED.

Accountants use the following equation to balance the data pertaining to financial transactions:

$$\text{Assets} - \text{Liabilities} = \text{Owners' equity}$$

After every financial transaction (e.g., payments to suppliers, sales to customers, wages to employees), the *accounting equation* must be in balance. If it isn't, an accounting error has occurred. The equation also provides an indication of the firm's financial health. If assets exceed liabilities, owners' equity is positive; if the firm goes out of business, owners will receive some cash (a gain) after selling assets and paying off liabilities. If liabilities outweigh assets, owners' equity is negative and assets aren't enough to pay off debts. If the company goes under, owners will get no cash; and some creditors won't be paid, thus losing their remaining investments in the company.

LO-3 DESCRIBE THREE BASIC *FINANCIAL STATEMENTS* AND SHOW HOW THEY REFLECT THE ACTIVITY AND FINANCIAL CONDITION OF A BUSINESS.

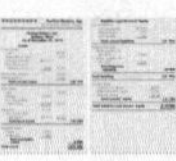

The *balance sheet* summarizes a company's assets, liabilities, and owners' equity at a given point in time. The *income statement* details revenues and expenses for a given period of time and identifies any profit or loss. The *statement of cash* flows reports cash receipts and payment from operating, investing, and financial activities.

LO-4 EXPLAIN THE KEY *STANDARDS* AND *PRINCIPLES* FOR *REPORTING FINANCIAL STATEMENTS* .

Accountants follow standard reporting practices and principles when they prepare financial statements. Otherwise, users wouldn't be able to compare information from different companies, and they might misunderstand—or be led to misread—a company's true financial status. *Revenue recognition* is the formal recording and reporting of revenues in financial statements. The *earnings cycle* is complete when the sale has been made, the product is delivered, and the sale price has been collected or is collectible. This practice assures interested parties that the statement gives a fair comparison of what was gained for the resources that were given up. The *matching principle* states that expenses will be matched with revenues to determine net income for an accounting period. This permits the user of the statement to see how much net gain resulted from the assets that had to be given up to generate revenues during the period covered in the statement.

LO-5 EXPLAIN HOW COMPUTING *FINANCIAL RATIOS* CAN HELP IN ANALYZING THE FINANCIAL STRENGTHS OF A BUSINESS.

Drawing upon data from financial statements, ratios can help creditors, investors, and managers assess a firm's finances. The *current, short-term solvency (liquidity)*, and *debt-to-owners' equity ratios* all measure solvency, a firm's ability to pay its debt in both the short and long terms. Return on sales, return on equity, and earnings per share are all ratios that measure profitability. The inventory turnover ratio shows how efficiently a firm is using its funds.

LO-6 DISCUSS THE ROLE OF *ETHICS IN ACCOUNTING*.

The purpose of *ethics in accounting* is to maintain public confidence in business institutions, financial markets, and the products and services of the accounting profession. Without ethics, all of accounting's tools and methods would be meaningless, because their usefulness depends, ultimately, on truthfulness in their application. Accordingly, professional accounting associations enforce codes of professional conduct that include ethics-related areas, such as the accountant's responsibilities, the public interest, integrity, and so on. The associations include ethics as an area of study to meet requirements for certification. The codes prohibit, among other things, misrepresentation and fraud in financial statements.

LO-7 DESCRIBE THE EVOLVING ROLE OF THE MODERN ACCOUNTANT.

The role of accounting professionals is evolving. The traditional accountant's role was centred on analyzing historical financial data, creating financial statements, and providing interpretations of financial data and documents to facilitate business decisions. The expectations for the modern CPAs, increasingly, call for a more intimate role of leadership in demonstrating financial implications for many additional facets of the business including its overall operations, strategy, data management, human resources, and technical resources. The following trends have emerged and are contributing to the additional roles of the modern accountant: *fewer restrictions from physical and geographic boundaries*, *changed relationships and the way business is conducted due to the influence of social media*, *the need for the accountant to be an effective communicator*, and *project management in the accountant's expanded role*.

QUESTIONS AND EXERCISES

QUESTIONS FOR ANALYSIS

1. Balance sheets and income statements are supposed to be objective assessments of the financial condition of a company. But the accounting scandals of the last few years show that certain pressures may be put on accountants as they audit a company's financial statements. Describe these pressures. To what extent do these pressures make the audit more subjective?
2. If you were planning to invest in a company, which of the three types of financial statements would you want most to see? Why?
3. A business hires a professional accountant to assess the financial condition of the company. Why would the business also employ a private accountant?
4. How do financial ratios help managers to monitor their own efficiency and effectiveness?
5. Explain the difference between financial and managerial accounting. In your answer, describe the different audiences for the two types of accounting and the various individuals involved in the process.
6. Use the accounting equation to determine your net worth. Identify your assets and liabilities. With this information, how would you increase your net worth in the future?

APPLICATION EXERCISES

7. Suppose that Inflatables Inc., makers of air mattresses for swimming pools, has the following transactions in one week:
   - sold three deluxe mattresses to Al Wett (paid cash $50, remaining $25 on credit) on 7/16
   - received cheque from Ima Flotein as payment for mattresses bought on credit ($120) on 7/13
   - received new shipment of 200 mattresses from Airheads Mfg. (total cost $3000, paid 50 percent cash on delivery) on 7/17

   Construct a journal for Inflatables Inc.
8. Flynn Plastics Company reports the following data in its September 30, 2015, financial statements:
   - Gross sales $225 000
   - Current assets $50 000
   - Long-term assets $130 000
   - Current liabilities $33 000
   - Long-term liabilities $52 000
   - Net income $11 250

   a. Compute the owners' equity.
   b. Compute the current ratio.
   c. Compute the debt-to-equity ratio.
   d. Compute the return on sales.
   e. Compute the return on owners' equity.
9. Interview an accountant at a local manufacturing firm. Trace the process by which budgets are developed in that company. How does the firm use budgets? How does budgeting help its managers plan business activities? How does budgeting help them control business activities? Give examples.
10. >>> Interview the manager of a local business and ask about the role of ethics in the company's accounting practices. How important is ethics in accounting? What measures does the firm take to ensure that its internal reporting is ethical? What steps does the company take to maintain ethical relationships in its dealing with external accounting firms?

TEAM EXERCISES

BUILDING YOUR BUSINESS SKILLS

PUTTING THE BUZZ IN BILLING

GOAL

To encourage students to think about the advantages and disadvantages of using an electronic system for handling accounts receivable and accounts payable.

METHOD

Step 1 As the CFO of a utility company, you are analyzing the feasibility of switching from a paper-based system to an electronic one. You decide to discuss the potential results of the choice with three associates (choose three classmates to take on these roles). Your discussion requires that you research existing electronic payment systems. Specifically, using online and library research, you must find out as much as you can about the electronic bill-paying systems by companies like Visa International, Intuit, IBM, and the CheckFree Corporation.

Step 2 After you have researched this information, brainstorm the advantages and disadvantages of switching to an electronic system.

FOLLOW-UP QUESTIONS

1. What cost savings are inherent in the electronic system for both your company and its customers? In your answer, consider such costs as handling, postage, and paper.
2. What consequences would your decision to adopt an electronic system have on others with whom you do business, including manufacturers of cheque-sorting equipment, Canada Post, and banks?
3. Switching to an electronic system would mean a large capital expense for new computers and software. How could analyzing the company's income statement help you justify this expense?

EXERCISING YOUR ETHICS

GIVE AND TAKE WITH ACCOUNTING CLIENTS

THE SITUATION

Accountants provide valuable services for their clients, both businesses and individuals. Although it's important to make clients happy, accountants have additional considerations when preparing financial statements and tax returns.

THE DILEMMA

Aaron Ault is the owner of a small contracting business. In late January 2016, he delivered original expense and income records so that his CPA, Katrina Belinski, could prepare 2015 financial statements and tax returns for Ault's small business firm. Several weeks later, Belinski delivered the completed financial statements and tax return to Ault. Ault was pleased with the financial statements but realized that he was going to owe a lot of money in taxes. His business is just recovering from tough times and he can't afford to pay such a large tax bill. One particularly large job was completed at the end of the year, and Ault has decided that he'd like to record this during the current year. This would result in a much lower taxable income for 2015. However, Ault is disappointed with Belinski. She tells him that she's not able to make this change and he's threatening to take his business elsewhere. Belinski is torn because Ault has been a long-time client and she doesn't want to lose his business.

FOLLOW-UP QUESTIONS

1. What are the ethical issues in this situation?
2. What are the basic arguments for and against Aaron Ault's position in this situation? for and against Katrina Belinski's position?
3. What do you think that Ault and Belinski should do in this situation?

BUSINESS CASE 11

CSI: STOCK MARKET EDITION

In the aftermath of a flurry of financial scandals, many companies are showing an urgent interest in the field of forensic accounting, the use of accounting for legal purposes. The expansion of the forensic accounting field—the Association of Certified Fraud Examiners (ACFE) has experienced a huge increase in membership, with more than 75 000 professionals—is the result of increased attention against various kinds of financial scams, including a strong desire on the part of companies to protect themselves from accounting fraud.

Fraud examiners typically begin an investigation of a company by interviewing high-level executives. Team members pursue tips from employees or outsiders, then comb through emails, searching for suspicious words and phrases. The combination of interviews and emails may lead investigators to specific accounting files or ledger entries. According to Al Vondra, partner in Forensic Services and a Certified Fraud Examiner at PricewaterhouseCoopers, some of the most common fraudulent practices involve hiding revenues and expenses under phony categories, such as "Total Noncurrent Assets" or "Other Current Liabilities." At India's Satyam Computer Services Ltd., founder and former CEO Ramalinga Raju was arrested after admitting he falsified accounts that deceived investors for years. The Indian government's Serious Fraud Investigation Office is searching to identify collaborators who falsely reported more than $1 billion in cash and assets that didn't exist at India's fourth-largest software company.

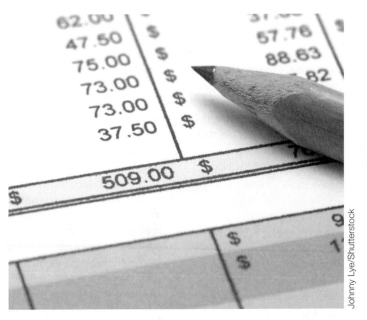

Johnny Lye/Shutterstock

Although accounting scandals have always existed, they spike in economic downturns. According to data from the ACFE, more than 3000 fraud-related reports and whistle-blowing tips were reported in the United States alone, in a four-year span during and after the most recent recession. ACFE members believe the increase stems from heavier financial pressures: when employees feel less secure, they may falsify data to show better performance, or they may take greater risks that need to be covered up to show financial success. Forensic accounting professor Tommie Singleton states, "The cases of fraud will only climb as a country sinks into recession, and with that so will the demand for highly skilled, specialized forensic accountants to help prevent, detect and prosecute those looking to cheat the system."

Fraud exists also among the public at large. Fraudulent insurance claims are increasing. A private investigator films an injury victim throwing the neck brace into the back seat of his car after leaving the doctor's office, a homeowner inflates the cost of articles stolen in an alleged burglary, and victims of car wrecks from years past suddenly submit injury claims. Employees, too, are a source of fraud; it is estimated that one-third of business shutdowns are the result of employee theft. Inventory stolen from the firm's warehouse is resold; the company's strategic inside information is stolen and sold to a competitor; and employees receive reimbursement for falsely inflated business expenses.

The broad scope of fraud—its costs, who commits it and how, and how it is detected—is revealed in Global Fraud Studies conducted by the ACFE. Fraud typically costs organizations 5 percent of their annual revenues, but small businesses are especially vulnerable because they usually have fewer internal controls for protecting their resources. Global fraud loss is estimated at $3.5 trillion annually. Employees commit more cases of fraud than do managers, and top-level executives and owners are least involved. However, it comes as no surprise that financial losses by higher-level perpetrators is typically ten times that of other employees. The most common kind of fraud is asset theft—stealing cash, falsifying business expenses, forging cheques, and stealing noncash assets. For example, the chief financial officer of a tree farm falsified cheques and misused company credit cards to embezzle $10 million, which got him a 96-month prison sentence and a $14 million fine. The least common organizational fraud, and the costliest by far, is financial statement manipulation. How do these thieves get caught? Most commonly, detection starts from employee-supplied tips. Although internal audits are somewhat effective, external audits are less effective than commonly believed. The ACFE study concludes any organization's number-one safeguard is employee education in recognizing, reporting, and preventing fraud.

At the beginning of this chapter you read about CFEs and their role in fighting various kinds of fraudulent accounting practices, especially during troubled economic times. Using the information presented in this chapter, you should now be able to answer the following questions.

QUESTIONS FOR DISCUSSION

1. What factors do you think are most important in choosing among various methods to protect against fraud in a firm?
2. Suppose you are hoping for a career as a CFE. How do recent trends in fraud provide new opportunities for such a career?
3. An external auditor, such as a CPA firm's accountant, may suspect irregularities in a client firm's accounting practices. In what ways might a CFE be of assistance?
4. Consider the anti-fraud training for a company's employees. Which four (or more) topics should be included in that training?
5. What ethical issues, if any, are involved in a decision to investigate a suspected case of fraud in a firm's accounting activities?

CHAPTER SUPPLEMENT 03

Using Technology to Manage Information in the Internet and Social Media Era

Throughout the text, we examine how the internet and the emergence of social media have improved communications, revolutionized distribution, augmented human resource practices, revolutionized industries (and threatened others), developed new marketing communication channels, and changed the most basic business systems. In this supplement, we will begin by providing additional information about the internet and social media. We will also examine the evolving role of technology in managing information.

INTERNET USAGE

Before we look into the specific impact of the internet on business, let's examine some of the key Canadian internet statistics. As regards speed, Hong Kong has the fastest internet connections in the world; Canada ranks 17th.[1] However, Canada ranks ninth among G20 countries in terms of internet contribution to GDP. Canadian also spend an average of 36.3 hours per month on their computers (not including the vast amount of time spent on mobile devices) which ranks first in the world.[2] In addition, 94 percent of Canadians who live in households with incomes above $85 000 are connected (only 56 percent for households with incomes below $30 000 per year).[3] These figures will continue to increase for the next few years.

The federal government has also set its sights on increasing and improving the connectivity in rural settings. The improved infrastructure will help increase rural access, build further opportunities for companies wishing to sell to rural Canadian clients, and provide more incentive and opportunity for small businesses to operate in rural settings.[4]

THE IMPACT OF INFORMATION TECHNOLOGY (IT)

No matter where we go, we can't escape the impact of **information technology (IT)**—the various devices for creating, storing, exchanging, and using information in diverse modes, including images, voice, multimedia, and business data. We see ads all the time for the latest smartphones, laptops, iPads and other tablets, and software products, and most of us connect daily to the internet (many of you never disconnect).

INFORMATION TECHNOLOGY (IT) The various devices for creating, storing, exchanging, and using information in diverse modes, including visual images, voice, multimedia, and business data.

E-COMMERCE Buying and selling processes that make use of electronic technology.

INTERNET MARKETING The promotional efforts of companies to sell their products and services to consumers over the internet.

Email, texting, and instant messaging have become staples in business, and even such traditionally "low tech" businesses as hair salons and garbage collection companies are becoming dependent on the internet, computers, and networks. As consumers, we interact with databases every time we withdraw money from an ATM, order food at McDonald's, use an Apple or Android application to order food or movie tickets, or check on the status of a package at UPS or FedEx.

IT has had an immense effect on businesses—in fact, the growth of IT has changed the very structure of business organizations. Its adoption has altered workforces in many companies, contributed to greater flexibility in dealing with customers, and changed how employees interact with each other. E-commerce has created new market relationships around the globe.

We begin by looking at how businesses are using IT to bolster productivity, improve operations and processes, create new opportunities, and communicate and work in ways not possible before.

THE IMPACT OF THE INTERNET ON MARKETING

E-commerce refers to buying and selling processes that make use of electronic technology, while **internet marketing** refers to the promotional efforts of companies to sell their products and services to consumers over the internet.[5]

Photoshot/Newscom

In 2015, Barack Obama was still an avid BlackBerry user. Despite calls for him to join the iPhone crowd, he resisted. The BlackBerry provides a superior encryption system for secure messaging with advisors and colleagues.

While internet marketing has some obvious advantages for both buyers (access to information, convenience, and so on) and sellers (reach, direct distribution, and so on), it also has weaknesses, including profitability problems (many internet marketers are still unprofitable and the failure rates are high), and information overload (consumers may not know what to do with all the information available to them). In addition to these weaknesses, internet marketers must also cope with consumer concerns about security-related issues.

Consumers also object to *spyware* software, which monitors websites they visit and observes their shopping habits. Spyware is often implanted on their personal computers as they wander through the web, generating advertisements targeted to them specifically.

CREATING PORTABLE OFFICES: PROVIDING REMOTE ACCESS TO INSTANT INFORMATION

IT devices such as Samsung mobile phones and Apple iPhones, along with IBM wireless internet access and PC-style office applications, save businesses time and travel expenses by enabling employees, customers, and suppliers to communicate from any location. Mobile messaging capabilities mean that a geographic separation between the workplace and headquarters is more common.

Employees no longer work only at the office or the factory, nor are all a company's operations performed at one place; employees take the office with them. When using such devices, off-site employees have continuous access to information, instead of being forced to be at a desk to access their files and the internet. Client project folders, email, and voice messaging are accessible from any location. Such benefits currently attract 85 million enthusiastic subscribers worldwide to BlackBerry smartphones.[6]

Looking to the future, a possible next step for office portability is Google Glass, a head-mounted, internet-connected information display that may someday be blended into everyday eyeglasses. It will respond to voice commands to give rapid visual access to the internet's ocean of digital information, while the user on the move.[7]

© dpa picture alliance/Alamy Stock Photo

Google Glass has captured the imagination of the consumer market. Will this lead one day to yet another mandatory tool for doing business?

ENABLING BETTER SERVICE BY COORDINATING REMOTE DELIVERIES

With access to the internet, company activities may be geographically scattered, but remain coordinated through a networked system that provides better service for customers. Many businesses, for example, coordinate activities from one centralized location, but their deliveries flow from several remote locations, often at lower cost. When you order furniture from an internet storefront—a chair, a sofa, a table, and two lamps—the chair might come from a warehouse in Toronto, the lamps from a manufacturer in China, and the sofa and table from a supplier in North Carolina. In response to the customer's order, activities are coordinated through the company's network, as if the whole order were being processed at one place. This avoids the expensive in-between step of first shipping all the items to a central location.

In 2014, approximately 35 percent of holiday gifts were bought online (up from 20 percent two years earlier) and, with improved shipping and easy deliveries, Canadian retailers have surely felt the impact of their U.S. counterparts like Macy's, Neiman Marcus, and Nordstrom making it much easier for Canadians to shop online and bypass their traditional local retailers.[8]

CREATING LEANER, MORE EFFICIENT ORGANIZATIONS

Networks and technology are also leading to leaner companies with fewer employees and simpler structures. Because networks enable firms to maintain information linkages between employees and customers, more work and customer satisfaction can be accomplished with fewer people. Bank customers can access 24-hour information systems and monitor their accounts without employee assistance. Instructions that once were given to assembly workers by supervisors are now delivered to workstations electronically. IT communications provide better use of employee skills and greater efficiencies from physical resources. For example, truck drivers used to return to a shipping terminal to receive instructions from supervisors on reloading freight for the next delivery. Today, one dispatcher using IT has replaced several supervisors. Instructions to the fleet arrive on electronic screens in trucks on the road so drivers know in advance the next delivery schedule, and satellite navigation services such as the XM NavTraffic alert drivers of traffic incidents ahead so they can reroute to avoid delays.

ENABLING INCREASED COLLABORATION

Interaction among internal units and with outside firms is greater when firms use collaboration software and other IT communication devices (which we discuss below). Companies are learning that complex problems can be better solved through IT-supported collaboration, either with formal teams or spontaneous interaction among people and departments. The design of new products was once largely an engineering responsibility. Now it is a shared activity using information from people in marketing, finance, production, engineering, and purchasing, who, collectively determine the best design. For example, the design of Boeing's 787 Dreamliner aircraft is the result of collaboration, not just among engineers, but also from passengers (who wanted electronic outlets to recharge personal electronic devices), cabin crews (who wanted more bathrooms and wider aisles), and air traffic controllers (who wanted larger, safer airbrakes). Although recent performance problems grounded the 787, solutions involved a worldwide network of Boeing engineers, suppliers, customers, and NASA.[9]

ENABLING GLOBAL EXCHANGE

The global reach of IT is enabling business collaboration on a scale unheard of just a few years ago. Consider Lockheed Martin's contract for designing the Joint Strike Fighter and supplying thousands of the planes in different versions for Canada, the United States, Britain, Italy, Denmark, and Norway. Lockheed can't do the job alone. Over the project's 20-year life, more than 1500 companies will supply everything from radar systems to engines to bolts. Web collaboration on a massive scale is essential for coordinating design, testing, and construction, while avoiding delays, holding down costs, and maintaining quality.[10]

IMPROVING MANAGEMENT PROCESSES

IT has also changed the nature of the management process. At one time, upper-level managers didn't concern themselves with all the detailed information filtering upward from the workplace, because it was expensive to gather, slow in coming, and quickly outdated. Workplace management was delegated to middle and first-line managers. With databases, specialized software, and networks, however, instantaneous information is accessible and useful to all levels of management.

For example, consider *enterprise resource planning* (ERP), a system for organizing and managing a firm's activities across product lines, departments, and geographic locations. An ERP stores real-time information on work status and upcoming transactions and notifies employees when action is required if certain schedules are to be met. It coordinates internal operations with activities of outside suppliers and notifies customers of upcoming deliveries and billings.

Consequently, more managers use it routinely for planning and controlling operations. A manager at Hershey Foods might use ERP to check on the current status of any customer order for Hershey Kisses, inspect productivity statistics for each workstation, and analyze the delivery performance on any shipment. Managers can better coordinate company-wide performance because they can identify departments that are working well together and those that are lagging behind schedule and creating bottlenecks.

In addition, high-tech processes have replaced many simple functions in the name of better management oversight and better decisions. Prestotea Co. Ltd., a tea retailer with 12 locations in Toronto, moved away from the traditional customer reward punchcard and replaced it with an electronic service that allows consumers to tap into a digital program, thus avoiding an extra card in their wallet. From the company's point of view, it is a great way to gather information on their customers and actually track loyalty.[11]

PROVIDING FLEXIBILITY FOR CUSTOMIZATION

IT has also created new manufacturing capabilities that enable businesses to offer customers greater variety and faster delivery cycles. Whether it's a personal computer from Dell, one of Samsung's smartphones, or Vaughn goalie pads, today's design-it-yourself world has become possible through fast, flexible manufacturing using IT networks. At Timbuk2's website, for example, you can "build your own" custom messenger bag at different price levels with choices of size, fabric, colour combinations, accessories, liner material, strap, and even left- or right-hand access.[12] The principle is called **mass customization**—although companies produce in large volumes, each unit features the unique options the customer prefers. As shown in Figure IT.1, flexible production and speedy delivery depend on an integrated network of information to coordinate all the activities among customers, manufacturers, suppliers, and shippers.

>>> Vaughn goalie pads are used by some of the top goaltenders in the NHL, like Tukka Rask of the Boston Bruins and Jonathan Quick of the LA Kings. You can purchase the gear off the rack, but Vaughn offers a mass customization series that permits you to adjust your gear to your needs (for colour, size, and so on).

PROVIDING NEW BUSINESS OPPORTUNITIES

Not only is IT improving existing businesses, but it is also creating entirely new ones. For big businesses, this means developing new products, offering new services, and reaching new clients. Only a few years ago, Google was a fledgling search engine. In 2015, the company had nearly $65 billion in cash and short-term investments, and it was no longer simply a search engine; Google had email (Gmail) and other productivity software (Google Docs, and so on), the Android cell phone platform, and YouTube.[13]

The IT landscape has also presented small business owners with new e-business opportunities. To assist start-up businesses, eBay's services network is a ready-made online business model, not just an auction market. Services range from credit financing to protection from fraud and misrepresentation, information security, international currency exchanges, and post-sales management. These features enable users to complete sales transactions, deliver merchandise, and get new merchandise for future resale, all from the comfort of their homes.

Technology continues to provide new and improved business models. For example, Instinet Inc. was a pioneer in electronic trading. It recently launched a service called Meet the Street, which matches companies with potential investors. This service competes directly with investment companies like the Royal Bank of Canada (RBC) and Goldman Sachs that are known for creating "road shows" (days packed with meetings with potential investors). The service enables business owners to book their own meetings, make travel arrangements, suggest dining spots, and use GPS technology to organize meetings efficiently to save time.[14]

MASS CUSTOMIZATION Although companies produce in large volumes, each unit features the unique options the customer prefers.

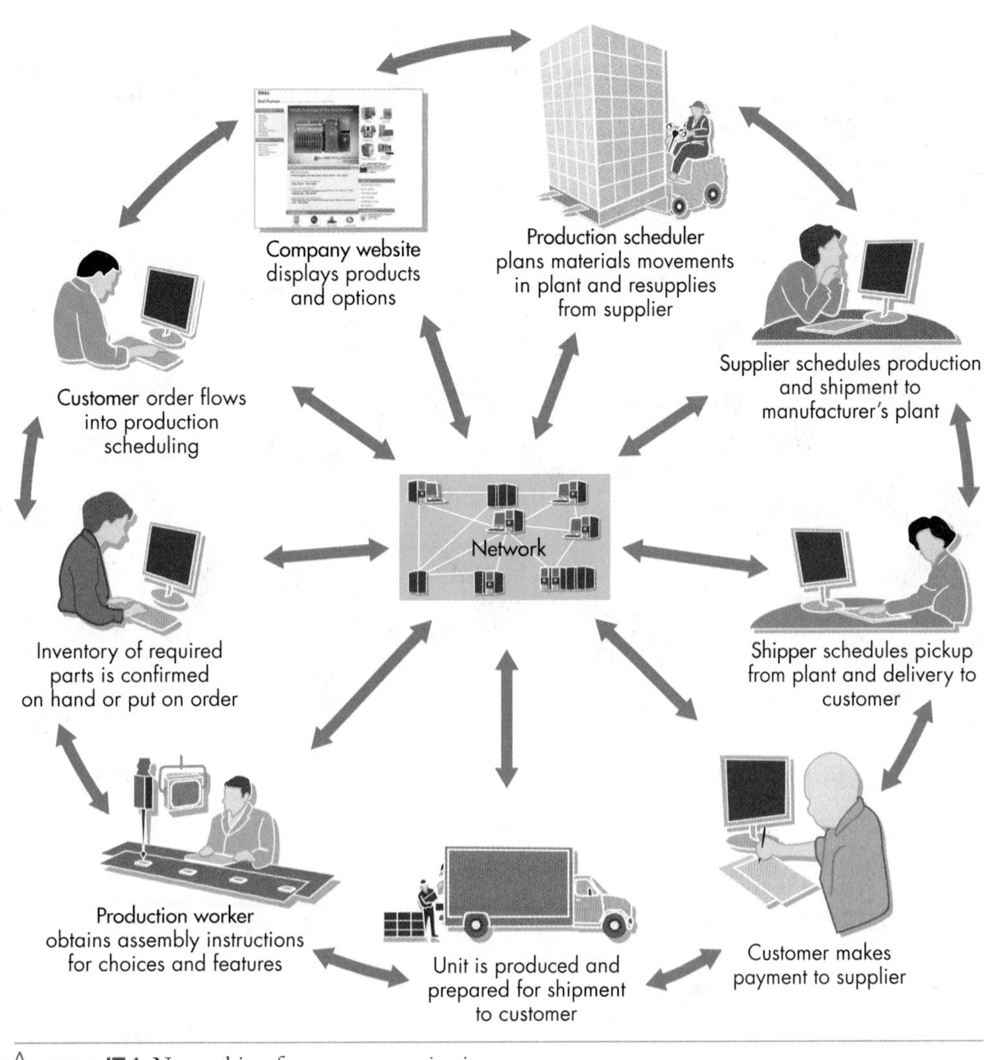
Company website displays products and options
Production scheduler plans materials movements in plant and resupplies from supplier
Customer order flows into production scheduling
Supplier schedules production and shipment to manufacturer's plant
Network
Inventory of required parts is confirmed on hand or put on order
Shipper schedules pickup from plant and delivery to customer
Production worker obtains assembly instructions for choices and features
Unit is produced and prepared for shipment to customer
Customer makes payment to supplier

FIGURE IT.1 Networking for mass customization

IMPROVING THE WORLD AND OUR LIVES

Can advancements in IT really make the world a better place? Developments in smartphones, social networking, home entertainment, automobile safety, and other applications have certainly brought enjoyment and convenience to the everyday lives of millions around the globe. Extending technology beyond previous-model cell phones and PCs, new technologies provide access to endless choices of *apps* (shorthand for *application software*), allowing each user to "build it your way," depending on what you want your device to do and how and where you'll be using it. Apps for computers and smartphones include *programs* for learning languages, music, work, games, travel, art, and almost any other area of interest. Just two years after its opening, Apple's App Store had supplied more than 40 billion downloads worldwide to users of Macs, iPhones, iPads, and iPod Touches. As we described in Chapter 4's E-Business and Social Media Solutions box "Teenage Innovator, Entrepreneur, and Multimillionaire" the range of current applications is immense and increasing to meet the needs of business and consumers. We have also included a feature in this text called "There's an App for That!" to encourage you to use your smartphone or tablet to access resources related to all the functions of business.

Organizations, too, including hospitals and medical equipment companies, are embracing IT advancements. For example, when treating combat injuries, surgeons at Walter Reed Army Medical Center rely on high-tech imaging systems that convert 2-D photographs of their patients' anatomies into 3-D physical models for pre-surgical planning. These mockups of shoulder and facial bones and femurs give doctors the opportunity to see and feel the anatomy as it will be seen in the

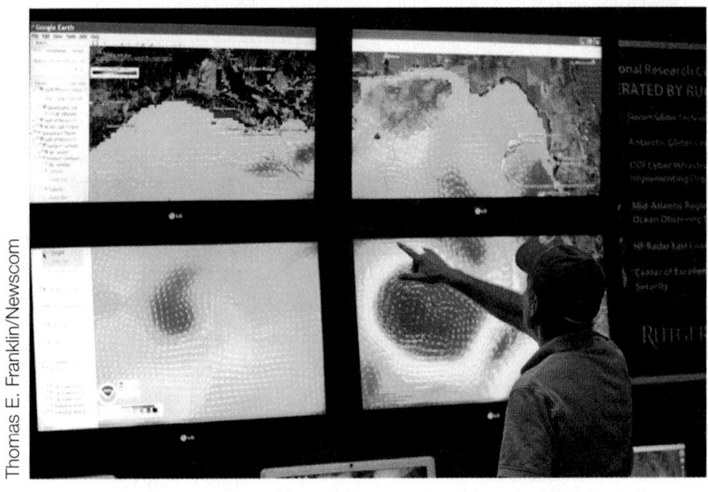

Thomas E. Franklin/Newscom

3-D computer modelling software gives engineers a better idea of where oil might be located.

Karen Bleier/Newscom

In this map of the internet, from the OPTE Project, each line represents a connection between computers or other network devices.

operating room, before they even reach for their scalpels. Meanwhile, pill-sized cameras that patients swallow are providing doctors with images of the insides of the human body, helping them to make better diagnoses for such ailments as ulcers and cancer.[15]

THE IMPACT OF THE INTERNET ON YOUR POCKETBOOK

Many people complain that the cost of internet service is yet another expense in their lives that did not exist in the past. However, these complaints fail to recognize the cost-saving benefits. A recent study conducted by the Internet Innovation Alliance (IIA) indicates that the average person saves approximately $9000 per year because of the internet (comparing with those not connected). See Table IT.1.[16]

TABLE IT.1 Source of Internet Savings

Typical Sources of Savings from Internet Connections	Result
1. Online comparison shopping	• Better-negotiated deals based on online research (savings of hundreds or even thousands of dollars) • Savings on fuel (less running around)
2. Paying bills online	• Savings on fuel • No stamps, envelopes, and so on
3. Accessing cheaper inventory (deals)	• Easy access to online aggregator sites (discount retailers, coupons, and so on)

SOCIAL NETWORKING: PROVIDING A SERVICE

The many forms of social media—blogs and networks such as LinkedIn, Twitter, and Facebook—are no longer just playthings for gossips and hobbyists. Today, job seekers turn to online networking—tapping leads from friends, colleagues, and acquaintances—for contacts with companies that may be hiring. Peers and recruiters are networking using a combination of social media sites, company website tools, professional associations and trade groups, technical schools, and alumni organizations. Some social sites provide occupation-specific career coaching and job tips. For example, scientists are connecting with Epernicus, while top managers use Meet the Boss.[17]

IT BUILDING BLOCKS: BUSINESS RESOURCES

Businesses today have a wide variety of IT resources at their disposal. In addition to the internet and email, these include communications technologies, networks, hardware devices, and software as shown at technology media sites such as TechWeb.com.

THE INTERNET AND OTHER COMMUNICATION RESOURCES

The **internet** is a gigantic system of interconnected computer networks belonging to millions of collaborating organizations and agencies—government, business, academic, and public—linked by voice, electronic,

INTERNET Gigantic system of interconnected computer networks linked together by voice, electronic, and wireless technologies and wireless technologies.[18] Computers within the networks are connected by various communications *protocols*—standardized coding systems—such as the *hypertext transfer protocol (HTTP)*, which is used for the *World Wide Web*, a branch of the internet consisting of interlinked hypertext documents, or webpages. Other protocols serve a variety of purposes such as sending and receiving email. The World Wide Web and its protocols provide the common language that allows information sharing on the internet. For thousands of businesses, the internet has replaced the telephone, fax machine, and standard mail as the primary communication tool.

The internet has spawned a number of other business communications technologies, including *intranets, extranets, electronic conferencing*, and *VSAT satellite communications*.

Intranets Many companies have extended internet technology by maintaining internal websites linked throughout the firm. These private networks or **intranets**, accessible only to employees, may contain confidential information on benefits programs, a learning library, production management tools, or product design resources. For firms such as Ford Motor Company, whose intranet is accessible by 200 000 people daily, sharing information on engineering, distribution, and marketing has reduced the lead time for getting new models into production and has shortened customer delivery times.[19]

Extranets **Extranets** allow outsiders limited access to a firm's internal information network. The most common application allows buyers to enter a system to see which products are available for sale and delivery, thus providing convenient product availability information. Industrial suppliers are often linked into customers' information networks so that they can see planned production schedules and prepare supplies for customers' upcoming operations.

Electronic Conferencing **Electronic conferencing** allows groups of people to communicate simultaneously from various locations via email, phone, or video, thereby eliminating travel time and saving money. One form, called *data conferencing*, allows people in remote locations to work simultaneously on one document. *Videoconferencing* allows participants to see one another on video screens while a conference is in progress. For example, Lockheed Martin's Joint Strike Fighter project, discussed earlier, uses internet collaboration systems with both voice and video capabilities. Although separated by oceans, partners can communicate as if they were in the same room while redesigning components and creating production schedules. Electronic conferencing is attractive to many businesses, because it eliminates travel and saves money.

VSAT Satellite Communications Another internet technology businesses use to communicate is **VSAT satellite communications**. VSAT (short for "very small aperture terminal") systems have a transmitter-receiver (transceiver) that sits outdoors with a direct line of sight to a satellite. The hub—a ground-station computer at the company's headquarters—sends signals to and receives signals from the satellite, exchanging voice, video, and data transmissions. An advantage of VSAT is privacy. A company that operates its own VSAT system has total control over communications among its facilities, no matter their location, without dependence on other companies. A firm might use VSAT to exchange sales and inventory information, advertising messages, and visual presentations between headquarters and store managers at remote sites.

NETWORKS: SYSTEM ARCHITECTURE

A *computer network* is a group of two or more computers linked, either hardwired or wirelessly, to share data or resources (e.g., a printer). The most common type of network used in businesses is a **client-server network**. In client-server networks, clients are usually the laptop or desktop computers through which users make requests for information or resources. Servers are the computers that provide the services shared by users. In big organizations, servers are usually assigned a specific task. For example, in a local university or college network, an application server stores the word-processing, spreadsheet, and other programs used by all computers connected to the network. A print server controls the printers, stores printing requests from client computers, and routes jobs as the printers become available. An email server handles all incoming and outgoing email. With a client-server system, users can share resources and internet connections—and avoid costly duplication.

Networks can be classified according to geographic scope and means of connection (either wired or wireless).

Wide Area Networks (WANs) Computers that are linked over long distances—province-wide or even nationwide—through telephone lines, microwave signals, or satellite communications make up what are called **wide area networks (WANs)**. Firms can lease lines from communications vendors or maintain private WANs. Walmart, for example, depends heavily on a private satellite network that links thousands of U.S. and international retail stores to its Bentonville, Arkansas, headquarters.

Local Area Networks (LANs) In **local area networks (LANs)**, computers are linked in a smaller area, such as an office or a building. For example, a LAN unites hundreds of operators who enter call-in orders at Home Shopping Network's facility. The arrangement requires only one computer system with one database and one software system. *Virtual private networks (VPNs)* connect two or more LANs through a public network like the internet. This saves companies money, because they don't have to pay for private lines; but it is important that strong security measures be in place, so that unauthorized persons can't gain access.

INTRANET An organization's private network of internally linked websites accessible only to employees.

EXTRANET A system that allows outsiders limited access to a firm's internal information network.

ELECTRONIC CONFERENCING IT that allows groups of people to communicate simultaneously from various locations via email, phone, or video.

VSAT SATELLITE COMMUNICATIONS A network of geographically dispersed transmitter-receivers (transceivers) that send signals to and receive signals from a satellite, exchanging voice, video, and data transmissions.

CLIENT-SERVER NETWORK A common business network in which clients make requests for information or resources and servers provide the services.

WIDE AREA NETWORK (WAN) Computers that are linked over long distances through telephone lines, microwave signals, or satellite communications.

LOCAL AREA NETWORK (LAN) Computers that are linked in a small area, such as all of a firm's computers within a single building.

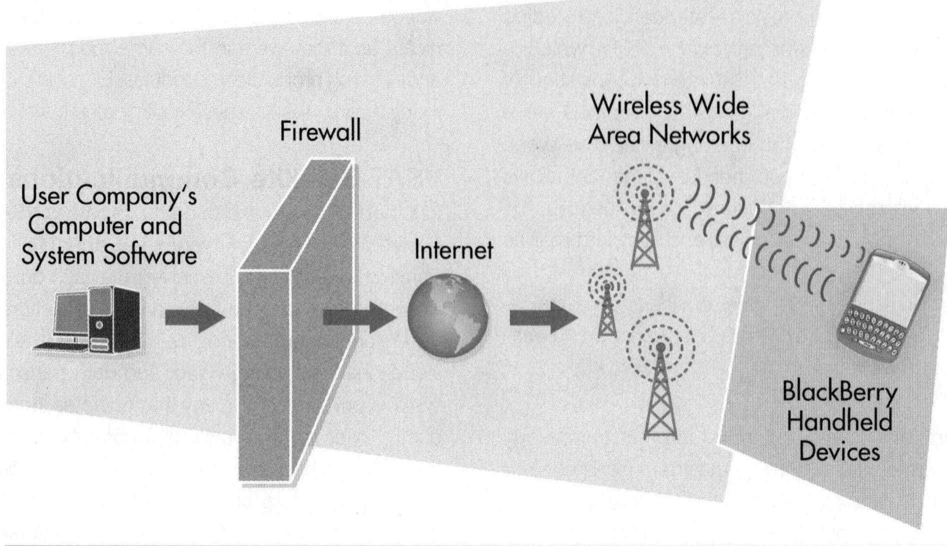

FIGURE IT.2 BlackBerry wireless internet architecture

Wireless Networks Wireless networks use airborne electronic signals to link network computers and devices. Like wired networks, wireless networks can either reach across long distances or exist within a single building or small area. For example, the BlackBerry system shown in Figure IT.2 consists of devices that send and receive transmissions on the **wireless wide area networks (WWANs)** of more than 100 service providers—such as Rogers (Canada), T-Mobile (United Kingdom and United States), and Vodafone (Italy)—in countries throughout the world. The wireless format that the system relies on to control messaging is supplied by BlackBerry and installed on the user company's computer.[20] In such a system, a firewall provides privacy protection. We'll discuss firewalls in more detail later in this supplement.

Wi-Fi hotspots are locations such as coffee shops, hotels, and airports that provide wireless internet connections for people on the go. Each hotspot, or **Wi-Fi** (short for "wireless fidelity") access point, uses its own small network, called a *wireless local area network (wireless LAN or WLAN)*. Although wireless service is free at some hotspots, others charge a daily or hourly rate. For example, in an attempt to find new revenue sources, airlines are scrambling to provide in-flight Wi-Fi service through ground-based or satellite connections. To this end, WestJet is working with a U.S.-based air-to-ground service provider named Gogo LLC.[21]

HARDWARE AND SOFTWARE

Any computer network or system needs **hardware**—the physical components, such as keyboards, monitors, system units, and printers. In addition to laptops, desktop computers, tablets, and smartphones are also used in businesses. For example, Walmart employees roam store aisles using handheld devices to identify, count, and order items, track deliveries, and update backup stock at distribution centres to keep the shelves stocked.

The other essential component in any computer system is **software**—programs that tell the computer how to function. Software includes system software, such as the latest version of Microsoft Windows, which tells the computer's hardware how to interact with the software. It also includes application software, which meets the needs of specific users (e.g., Adobe Photoshop). Some application programs are used to address common, long-standing needs such as database management and inventory control; others have been developed for a variety of

WIRELESS WIDE AREA NETWORK (WWAN) A network that uses airborne electronic signals instead of wires to link computers and electronic devices over long distances.

WI-FI Short for "wireless fidelity"; a wireless local area network.

HARDWARE The physical components of a computer network, such as keyboards, monitors, system units, and printers.

SOFTWARE Programs that tell the computer's hardware what resources to use and how.

After conquering the consumer market (taking sales away from other major players including Apple), Samsung is pushing its smartphone hardware platform and trying to carve out a bigger share of the business market by emphasizing features and security.

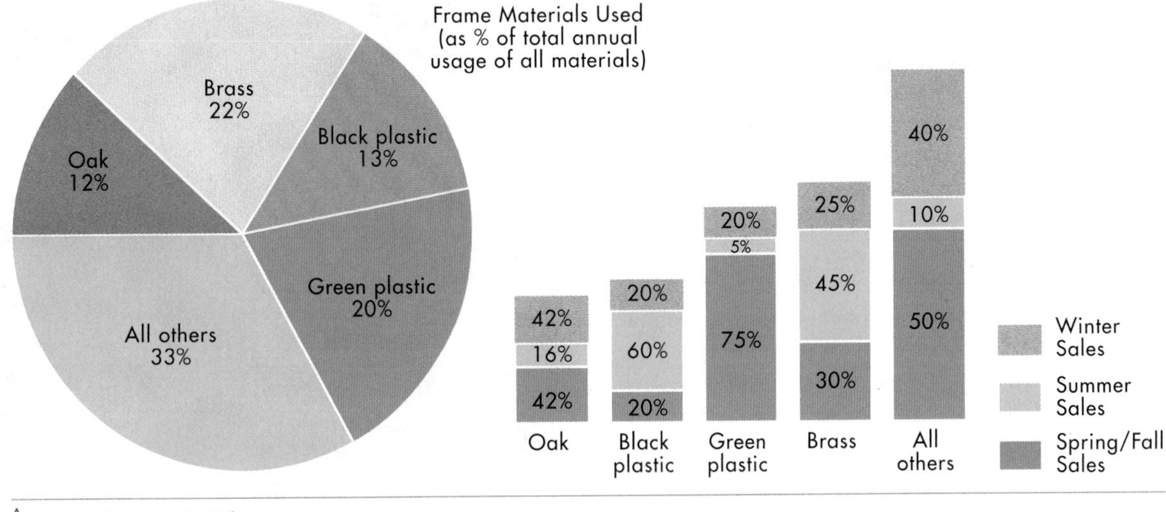

FIGURE **IT.3** Artists' frame service

specialized tasks such as mapping the structure of underground oil fields or the anatomy of the human body.

Computer graphics convert numeric and character data into pictorial information like charts and graphs. They allow managers to see relationships more easily and generate clearer and more persuasive reports and presentations. As Figure IT.3 shows, both types of graphics can convey different kinds of information—in this case, the types of materials that should be ordered by a picture framing shop like Artists' Frame Service.

Groupware—software that connects group members for email distribution, electronic meetings, message storing, appointments and schedules, and group writing—allows people to collaborate from their own desktop PCs, even if they're remotely located. It is especially useful when people work together regularly and rely heavily on information sharing. Groupware systems include IBM Domino, Microsoft Exchange Server, and Novell GroupWise.

INFORMATION SYSTEMS: HARNESSING THE COMPETITIVE POWER OF INFORMATION TECHNOLOGY

Business today relies on information management in ways that no one could foresee even a decade ago. Managers now treat IT as a basic organizational resource for conducting daily business. At major firms, every activity—designing services, ensuring product delivery and cash flow, evaluating personnel—is linked to information systems. An **information system (IS)** uses IT resources and enables managers to take *data*—raw facts and figures that by themselves may not have much meaning—and turn that data into *information*—the meaningful, useful interpretation of data. Information systems also enable managers to collect, process, and transmit that information for use in decision making.

One of the most widely publicized examples of the strategic use of information systems is Walmart. Their IS drives down costs and increases efficiency, because the same methods and systems are applied for all 5000-plus stores in Europe, Asia, and North America. Data on the billions of sales transactions—time, date, place—flows to company headquarters in Bentonville, Arkansas. Keeping track of nearly 700 million stock-keeping units (SKUs) weekly, the information system enforces uniform reordering and delivery procedures—on packaging, timing, and quantities—for more than 30 000 suppliers. It also regulates the flow of more than five billion cases through its distribution centres and deliveries by nearly 8000 Walmart truck drivers to its stores. Beyond the firm's daily operations, information systems are also crucial in planning. Managers routinely use the IS to decide on products and markets for the next five to ten years. The company's vast database enables marketing managers to analyze demographics, and it is also used for financial planning, materials handling, and electronic funds transfers with suppliers and customers.

Like most businesses, Walmart regards its information as an asset that is planned, developed, and protected. Therefore, it's not surprising that businesses have *information systems managers* who operate the systems used for gathering, organizing, and distributing information, just as they have production, marketing, and finance managers. These managers use many of the IT resources we discussed earlier to sift through this information and apply it to their jobs. The effective use of information is so critical that many companies have appointed *chief information officers* who are responsible for managing all aspects of information resources and information processes.

There are so many new challenges and opportunities for IT managers! For example, **cloud computing** is a major buzzword in those circles. The term has different meanings to different people, but in essence cloud computing is the internet-based, as opposed to locally based, development and use of computer technology. Individuals have been using this approach for years with email and photo sharing (think Google and Flickr). Organizations are now taking a closer look.

At the conceptual level, cloud computing means placing some infrastructure online and having someone else run it rather than doing

COMPUTER GRAPHICS Programs that convert numeric and character data into pictorial information like charts and graphs.

GROUPWARE Software that connects group members for email distribution, electronic meetings, message storing, appointments and schedules, and group writing.

INFORMATION SYSTEM (IS) A system that uses IT resources to convert data into information and to collect, process, and transmit that information for use in decision making.

CLOUD COMPUTING Internet-based development and use of computer technology; at the conceptual level, placing some infrastructure online and having someone else run it rather than doing it in-house.

it in-house. Some of the major advantages promised by this approach include lower costs, quicker set-up, easy scalability, easier software integration, reduced financial risk, less downtime, potential services for small business (that otherwise could not afford them), automatic updates that don't disrupt or endanger other systems, and empowered users.[22]

While many of you routinely use such services (e.g., iCloud), the question remains whether major companies will adopt this approach in large numbers. According to a Telus survey of IT managers, 71 percent of large Canadian companies want nothing to do with it.[23] In another study of 476 executives (conducted by Northstar for Microsoft), 45 percent of respondents believe that storing the company's information online would be unsafe.[24] However, other firms are embracing the approach in its various forms and reaping the benefits. Cadillac Fairview, the Toronto-based commercial real-estate company, switched its email service to Gmail and reduced its costs to $50 per person from $210 with their previous provider. In addition, the company gets an impressive amount of storage for the service. Cadillac Fairview is also looking at adopting Salesforce.com, a customer relationship management provider that would allow the company to eliminate in-house servers for its customer relationship needs.[25]

Serp/Shutterstock

>> Many data warehouses are setting up or relocating to countries like Canada, Finland, and Sweden to take advantage of the natural cooling provided by the weather (during winter) and because of inexpensive electricity.

LEVERAGING INFORMATION RESOURCES: DATA WAREHOUSING, BIG DATA, AND DATA MINING

Almost everything you do leaves a trail of information about you. Preferences in movie rentals, television viewing, internet sites, and groceries; the destinations of phone calls, credit-card charges, financial status; and personal information about age, gender, marital status, and even health are just a few of the items about each of us that are stored in scattered databases. The behaviour patterns of millions can be traced by analyzing files gathered over time from their internet usage and in-store purchases.

Data Warehousing The collection, storage, and retrieval of such data in electronic files is called **data warehousing**. In recent years, many data warehouses have been locating or relocating existing facilities to Canada. This is partly because of our climate: data warehouses generate a lot of heat and the natural environment in a northern climate helps cool facilities. But the natural cooling effect of our winters is only part of the story; cheaper, clean energy sources are another important consideration. According to Mike O'Neil, president of IT Market Dynamics, "It is far cheaper and easier to set up a data center next to a hydro dam." Finland and Sweden are also popular destinations.[26]

Big Data and Data Mining Companies are increasingly faced with larger and larger sets of data collected about their consumers. Every single day we create 2.5 quintillion bits' worth of it. If that sounds like a big number, it is! According to IBM, 90 percent of the data in the world has been created in the past two years alone. This data originates from purchase transaction records, sensors, pictures and video posts on social media sites, and smartphone GPS signals, to name just a few.[27] This surge is forcing IT specialists to change their perspective and adapt. *Big data* can be defined as "high-volume, high-velocity and high-variety information assets that demand cost-effective, innovative forms of information processing for enhanced insight and decision making."[28] In other words, we have more data than ever before, and our processes are now quicker than ever. The real test for businesses is to create systems to extract this information in a fast, cost-effective manner. Some firms are actively using this information in real time, while others' information resources remain untapped.

According to market researcher IDC, in Canada alone businesses are expected to produce over 90 trillion gigabytes by 2020. Even so, Canadian businesses lag behind in the use of big data. Internet retailers like Shop.ca have been early adopters. According to Trevor Newell, president of Shop.ca, sales of a projector increased by 800 percent after the company sent automated targeted emails to members and promoted the product on social media sites.[29]

Trying to access the gold mine of information in company databases is nothing new. In order to make sense of the mountains of information, companies have used **data mining**—the application of electronic technologies for searching, sifting, and reorganizing pools of data to uncover useful information—for years. Data mining helps managers plan for new products, set prices, and identify trends and shopping patterns. By analyzing what consumers actually do, businesses can determine what subsequent purchases they are likely to make and then send them tailor-made ads. For example, a grocery chain can collect data on customer shopping habits to find ways to gain greater customer loyalty. It can accumulate information from its shopper cards, analyze the data to uncover shopping patterns, and send money-saving coupons to regular customers for the specific products they usually buy. One supermarket chain in the US, analyzing data, realized that men coming to buy baby diapers were also buying beer. So the supermarket decided to place beer and diapers side by side, stimulating more sales.[30]

Philosophically, "big data" is replacing "data mining," moving users from a perspective of searching for that golden nugget of information after the fact (data mining) to a quick-moving, interactive, systematic flow of real-time (or near-time) information (the big data approach).[31]

DATA WAREHOUSING The collection, storage, and retrieval of data in electronic files.

DATA MINING The application of electronic technologies for searching, sifting, and reorganizing pools of data to uncover useful information.

Information Linkages with Suppliers The top priority for Walmart's IS—improving in-stock reliability—requires integration of Walmart's and suppliers' activities with store sales. That is why Procter & Gamble, Johnson & Johnson, and other suppliers connect into Walmart's information system to observe up-to-the-minute sales data on individual items, by store. They can use the system's computer-based tools—spreadsheets, sales forecasting, and weather information—to forecast sales demand and plan delivery schedules. Coordinated planning avoids excessive inventories, speeds up deliveries, and holds down costs throughout the supply chain, while keeping shelves stocked for retail customers.

TYPES OF INFORMATION SYSTEMS

Since employees have a variety of responsibilities and decision-making needs, a firm's information system may actually be a set of several information systems that share data, while serving different levels of the organization, different departments, or different operations. One popular information system is called the **transaction processing system (TPS)**, which processes information for many different, day-to-day business transactions like customer order-taking by online retailers, approval of claims at insurance companies, receiving and confirming reservations by airlines, and payroll processing.

Because they work on different kinds of problems, managers and their subordinates need access to the specialized information systems that satisfy their different information needs. In addition to different types of users, each business function—marketing, human resources, accounting, production, finance—has its own information needs, as do groups working on major projects. Each user group and department, therefore, may need a special IS. Two important groups are knowledge workers and managers.

Information Systems for Knowledge Workers As we discussed in Chapter 8, knowledge workers are employees for whom information and knowledge are the raw materials of their work, such as engineers, scientists, and IT specialists who rely on IT to design new products or create new processes. These workers require **knowledge information systems** that provide resources to create, store, use, and transmit new knowledge for useful applications—for instance, databases to organize and retrieve information, and computational power for data analysis.

Specialized support systems have also increased the productivity of knowledge workers. **Computer-aided design (CAD)** helps knowledge workers design products ranging from cell phones to jewellery to auto parts, by simulating them and displaying them in 3-D graphics. The older method—making handcrafted prototypes from wood, plastic, or clay—is replaced with faster, cheaper prototyping. The CAD system electronically transfers instructions to a computer-controlled machine that builds the prototypes.

Jochen Tack/Alamy

Quick communication within an organization is more important than ever. New tools are available to managers to help deal with the flood of data and exchanges of information. Companies are always looking for cost-effective ways to manage the sharing of knowledge.

Information Systems for Managers Each manager's information activities and IS needs vary according to his or her functional area (accounting, marketing, and so on) and management level. The following are some popular information systems used by managers for different purposes.

Management information systems (MISs) support managers by providing reports, schedules, plans, and budgets that can then be used for making decisions, both short- and long-term. For example, at a publishing company, managers rely on detailed information—current customer orders, staffing schedules, employee attendance, production schedules, equipment status, and materials availability—for moment-to-moment decisions during the day. They require similar information to plan mid-range activities such as personnel training, materials movements, and cash flows. They also need to anticipate the status of the jobs and projects assigned to their departments. Many MISs—cash flow, sales, production scheduling, and shipping—are indispensable for helping managers complete these tasks.

For longer-range decisions involving business strategy, managers need information to analyze trends in the publishing industry and overall company performance. They need both external and internal information, current and future, to compare current performance data to data from previous years and to analyze consumer trends and economic forecasts.

Managers who face a particular kind of decision repeatedly can get assistance from **decision support systems (DSSs)**—interactive systems that create virtual business models and test them with different data to see how they respond. When faced with decisions on plant capacity, managers can use a capacity DSS. The manager inputs data on anticipated sales, working capital, and customer-delivery requirements. The data flows into the DSS processor, which then simulates the plant's performance under the proposed conditions. After experimenting with various conditions, the DSS makes recommendations on the best levels of plant capacity for each future time period.

TRANSACTION PROCESSING SYSTEM (TPS) Applications of information processing for basic day-to-day business transactions.

KNOWLEDGE INFORMATION SYSTEMS Information system that supports knowledge workers by providing resources to create, store, use, and transmit new knowledge for useful applications.

COMPUTER-AIDED DESIGN (CAD) IS with software that helps knowledge workers design products by simulating them and displaying them in 3-D graphics.

MANAGEMENT INFORMATION SYSTEM (MIS) Computer system that supports managers by providing information—reports, schedules, plans, and budgets—that can be used for making decisions.

DECISION SUPPORT SYSTEM (DSS) Interactive system that creates virtual business models for a particular kind of decision and tests them with different data to see how they respond.

Artificial intelligence (AI) refers to the development of computer systems to imitate human behaviour—in other words, systems that perform physical tasks, use thought processes, and learn. In developing AI systems, business specialists, modellers, and information-technology experts try to design computer-based systems capable of reasoning, so that computers, instead of people, can perform certain activities. For example, a credit-evaluation system may decide which loan applicants are creditworthy and which are too risky, and it may then compose acceptance and rejection letters accordingly. Some AI systems possess sensory capabilities, such as lasers that "see," "hear," and "feel."

The *expert system* is designed to imitate the thought processes of human experts in a particular field.[32] Expert systems incorporate the rules that an expert applies to specific types of problems, such as the judgments a physician makes when diagnosing illnesses. In effect, expert systems supply everyday users with "instant expertise."

IT RISKS AND THREATS

As with other technologies throughout history, IT has attracted abusers intent on mischief, of severity ranging from a small annoyance to outright destruction. Eager IT users everywhere are finding that even social networking and cell phones have a "dark side"—privacy invasion. Facebook postings of personal information about users can be intercepted and misused. Beacon, a now-defunct part of Facebook's advertising system, caused a public uproar when it published peoples' online purchases in their Facebook newsfeeds. Maintaining privacy is a problem with cell phone advancements. Bluetooth connections allow savvy intruders to read a victim's text messages, listen in on live conversations, and even view users' photos.[33] With the tremendous rise in the use of smartphones, the threat of information theft is that much higher today.

Businesses, too, are troubled with IT's dark side. Hackers break into computers, stealing personal information and company secrets, and launching attacks on other computers. Meanwhile, the ease of information sharing on the internet has proven costly for some companies, which are having increasing difficulty protecting their intellectual property; and viruses that crash computers have cost companies millions. In this section, we'll look at these and other IT risks.

HACKERS

Breaking and entering no longer refers only to physical intrusion. Today, it applies to IT intrusions as well. **Hackers** are cybercriminals who gain unauthorized access to a computer or network, either to steal information, money, trade secrets, or property or to tamper with data. One of the most famous cases occurred in 2014 when hackers succeeded in penetrating Sony's systems. They caused major problems, releasing sensitive information including personal details and embarrassing emails. They also made threats of violence if Sony released the satirical movie *The Interview* (about the fictional assassination of North Korean leader Kim Jong-Un) into movie theatres. Eventually, Sony decided to release the movie online rather than in theatres (the movie was downloaded two million times in its first few days). In an interesting twist, Sony also decided to pull their old BlackBerry devices out of storage (that they had not used in years) in order to protect their information during the crisis. That was a nice image boost for BlackBerry; although they have lost a tremendous amount of market share, their smartphones are still considered the safest because of their advanced encryption technology.[34]

Another common hacker activity is to launch *denial of service (DoS)* attacks—which flood networks or websites with bogus requests for information and resources, shutting the networks or websites down and preventing legitimate users from accessing them.

Accessing unsecured wireless networks is a profitable industry for cyber criminals. Once inside, hackers can commit identity theft and steal credit-card numbers, among other things. When police officers try to track down these criminals, they're long gone, leaving the network host exposed to criminal prosecution.

IDENTITY THEFT

Once inside a computer network, hackers are able to commit **identity theft**, the unauthorized stealing of personal information (such as social insurance numbers and addresses) to get loans, credit cards, or other monetary benefits by impersonating the victim. Clever crooks get information on unsuspecting victims by digging in trash, stealing mail, or using phishing or pharming schemes to lure internet users to bogus websites. For instance, a cyber criminal might send TD Bank online customers an email notifying them of a billing problem with their accounts. When the customers click on the link, they are transferred to a spoofed (falsified) webpage, modelled after TD Bank's site. The customers then submit the requested information—credit-card number, social insurance number, and PIN—into the hands of the thief. Today, consumers are more aware of these scams, but many are still victimized. Major organizations like the Canadian Bankers Association and the Competition Bureau are working with organizations to identify patterns and inform consumers.[35]

In Canada, the federal government has created new privacy legislation in the Personal Information Protection and Electronic Documents Act (PIPEDA), designed to promote e-commerce while protecting personal information. The Act outlines the rules for managing personal information in the private sector.[36]

INTELLECTUAL PROPERTY THEFT

Nearly every company faces the dilemma of protecting product plans, new inventions, industrial processes, and other **intellectual property**—something produced by the intellect or mind that has commercial value. Its ownership and the right to its use may be protected by patent, copyright, trademark, and other means. Intellectual property theft is evident when, for example, individuals illegally download unpaid-for movies, music, and other resources from file-swapping networks. But the activities are not limited to illegal entertainment downloads. For example, according to the U.S. Intelligence Agency, Chinese

ARTIFICIAL INTELLIGENCE (AI) The development of computer systems to imitate human thought and behaviour.

HACKER Cyber criminal who gains unauthorized access to a computer or network, either to steal information, money, trade secrets, or property or to tamper with data.

IDENTITY THEFT Stealing of personal information (such as social insurance number and address) to get loans, credit cards, or other monetary benefits by impersonating the victim.

INTELLECTUAL PROPERTY A product of the mind that has commercial value.

cyber spies steal about $40 to $50 billion worth of intellectual property each year.[37]

COMPUTER VIRUSES, WORMS, AND TROJAN HORSES

Another IT risk facing businesses is rogue programmers who disrupt IT operations by contaminating and destroying software, hardware, or data files. Viruses, worms, and Trojan horses are three kinds of malicious programs that, once installed, can shut down any computer system.

A computer *virus* exists in a file that attaches itself to a program and migrates from computer to computer as a shared program or as an email attachment. It does not infect the system unless the user opens the contaminated file, and users typically are unaware they are spreading the virus by file sharing. It can, for example, quickly copy itself over and over again, using up all available memory and effectively shutting down the computer.

Worms are a particular kind of virus that travel from computer to computer within networked computer systems, without the need for any software to be opened. In a matter of days, the notorious Blaster worm infected some 400 000 computer networks, destroying files and even allowing outsiders to take over computers remotely. The worm replicated rapidly, sending out thousands of copies to other computers in the network. Travelling through internet connections and email address books in the network's computers, it absorbed system memory and shut down network servers, web servers, and individual computers.

Unlike viruses, a *Trojan horse* does not replicate itself. Instead, it most often comes into the computer, at your request, masquerading as a harmless, legitimate software product or data file. Once installed, the damage begins. For instance, it may simply redesign desktop icons or, more maliciously, delete files and destroy information.

SPYWARE

As if forced intrusion isn't bad enough, internet users unwittingly invite spies masquerading as friendly files available as a giveaway or shared among individual users on their PCs. This so-called **spyware** is downloaded by users who are lured by "free" software. Once installed, it crawls around to monitor the host's computer activities, gathering email addresses, credit-card numbers, passwords, and other inside information that it transmits back to someone outside the host system. Spyware authors assemble incoming stolen information to create their own "intellectual property" that they then sell to other parties to use for marketing and advertising purposes or for identity theft.[38]

Spam **Spam**—junk email sent to a mailing list or a *newsgroup* (an online discussion group)—is a greater nuisance than postal junk mail, because the internet is open to the public, email costs are negligible, and massive mailing lists are accessible through file sharing or by theft. Spam operators send unwanted messages. In addition to wasting users' time, spam also consumes a network's bandwidth, reducing the amount of data that can be transmitted in a fixed amount of time for useful purposes.

IT PROTECTION MEASURES

Security measures against intrusion and viruses are a constant challenge. Businesses guard themselves against intrusion, identity theft, and viruses by using firewalls, special software, and encryption.

FIREWALLS

Firewalls are security systems with special software or hardware devices designed to keep computers safe from hackers. A firewall is located where two networks—for example, the internet and a company's internal network—meet. It contains two components for filtering each incoming data:

1. *The company's security policy.* Access rules that identify every type of message that the company doesn't want to pass through the firewall.
2. *A router.* A table of available routes or paths, a "traffic switch" that determines which routes or paths on the network to send each message to after it is tested against the security policy.

Only those messages that meet the conditions of the user's security policy are routed through the firewall and permitted to flow between the two networks. Messages that fail the test are blocked.

PREVENTING IDENTITY THEFT

Internet privacy experts say that a completely new identity verification system is needed to stop the rising tide of internet identity theft. One possibility is an "infocard," which would act like a credit card and would allow websites to verify a customer's identity without keeping personal information on the customer. While foolproof prevention is impossible, steps can be taken to reduce the chance that you will be victimized. A visit to the Identity Theft Resource Center (www.idtheftcenter.org) is a valuable first source of information on everything from scam alerts to victim issues (assistance on lost and stolen wallets, and so on) to media resources, current laws, and prevention of identity theft in the workplace.

PREVENTING VIRUSES: ANTI-VIRUS SOFTWARE

Many viruses take advantage of weaknesses in operating systems in order to spread. Network administrators must make sure that the computers on their systems are using the most up-to-date operating system that includes the latest security protection. Combating viruses, worms, and Trojan horses has become a major industry for systems designers and software developers. Installation of **anti-virus software** products protects systems by searching incoming email and data files for "signatures" of known viruses and files with virus-like characteristics. Contaminated files are discarded or placed in quarantine for safekeeping.

SPYWARE Program unknowingly downloaded by users that monitors their computer activities, gathering email addresses, credit-card numbers, and other information that it transmits to someone outside the host system.

SPAM Junk email sent to a mailing list or a newsgroup.

FIREWALL Security system with special software or hardware devices designed to keep computers safe from hackers.

ANTI-VIRUS SOFTWARE Product that protects systems by searching incoming emails and data files for "signatures" of known viruses and files with virus-like characteristics.

PROTECTING ELECTRONIC COMMUNICATIONS: ENCRYPTION SOFTWARE

Unprotected email can be intercepted, diverted to unintended computers, and opened, revealing contents to intruders. Protective software is available to guard against those intrusions, adding a layer of security by encoding emails so that only intended recipients can open them. An **encryption system** works by scrambling an email message so that it looks like garbled nonsense to anyone who doesn't possess the key.

AVOIDING SPAM AND SPYWARE

To help their employees avoid privacy invasion and to improve productivity, businesses often install anti-spyware and spam-filtering software on their systems. Dozens of anti-spyware products provide protection—software such as Webroot's Spy Sweeper—but they have to be continually updated to keep pace with new spyware techniques. While it cannot be prevented entirely, spam is reduced by many internet service providers (ISPs) that ban the spamming of ISP subscribers.

ENCRYPTION SYSTEM Software that assigns an email message to a unique code number (digital fingerprint) for each computer, so only that computer, not others, can open and read the message.

CRAFTING A BUSINESS PLAN PART 3:

MANAGING OPERATIONS AND INFORMATION

GOAL OF THE EXERCISE

This part of the business plan project asks you to think about your business in terms of both accounting concepts and information technology (IT) needs and costs. See Chapter Supplement 03 for material on IT.

MANAGING OPERATIONS AND INFORMATION

An increasingly important part of a business plan is a consideration of how IT—computers, the internet, social media, software, and so on—influences businesses. This part of the business plan asks you to assess how you will use technology to improve your business. Will you, for example, use a database to keep track of your customers? How will you protect your business from hackers and other IT security risks?

This part of the business plan also asks you to consider the costs of doing business, such as salaries, rent, and utilities. You'll also be asked to complete the following financial statements:

- *Balance sheet.* The balance sheet is a foundation for financial reporting. This report identifies the valued items of the business (its assets) as well as the debts that it owes (its liabilities). This information gives the owner and potential investors a snapshot revealing the health of the business.
- *Income statement (or profit-and-loss statement).* This is the focus of the financial plan. This document will show you what it takes to be profitable and successful as a business owner for your first year.

YOUR ASSIGNMENT

MyBizLab

STEP 1

Open the saved Business Plan file you have been working on.

STEP 2

For the purposes of this assignment, you will answer the following questions:

1. What kinds of IT resources will your business require?

   Hint: Think about the employees in your business and what they will need in order to do their jobs. What computer hardware and software will they need? Will your business need a network and an internet connection? What type of network? Refer to Chapter Supplement 03 for a discussion of IT resources you may want to consider.

2. How will you use IT to keep track of your customers and potential customers?

   Hint: Many businesses—even small ones—use databases to keep track of their customers. Will your business require a database? What about other information systems? Refer to Chapter Supplement 03 for more information on these topics.

3. What are the costs of doing business? Equipment, supplies, salaries, rent, utilities, and insurance are just some of these expenses. Estimate what it will cost to do business for one year.

   Hint: The Business Plan Student Template file provides a table for you to insert the costs associated with doing business. Note that these are just estimates—just try your best to include accurate costs for the expenses you think will be a part of doing business.

4. How much will you charge for your product? How many products do you believe you can sell in one year (or how many customers do you think your business can attract)? Multiply the price you will charge by the number of products you hope to sell or the amount you hope each customer will spend. This will give you an estimate of your revenues for one year.

   Hint: You will use the amounts you calculate in the costs and revenues questions in this part of the plan in the accounting statements in the next part, so be as realistic as you can.

5. Create a balance sheet and an income statement (profit-and-loss statement) for your business.

   Hint: You have two options for creating these reports. The first is to use the Microsoft Word versions that are found within the Business Plan Student Template itself. The second is to use the specific Microsoft Excel templates created for each statement, which can be found on this book's MyBizLab. These Excel files are handy, because the worksheet calculations are preset—all you have to do is plug in the numbers and the calculations will be performed automatically for you. If you make adjustments to the different values in the Excel worksheets, you'll automatically see how changes to expenses, for example, can improve the bottom line.

6. Create a floor plan of the business. What does it look like when you walk through the door?

   Hint: When sketching your floor plan, consider where equipment, supplies, and furniture will be located.

7. Explain what types of raw materials and supplies you will need to run your business. How will you produce your good or service? What equipment do you need? What hours will you operate?

   Hint: Refer to the discussion of operations in Chapter 10 for information to get you started.

8. What steps will you take to ensure that the quality of the product or service stays at a high level? Who will be responsible for maintaining quality standards?

   Hint: Refer to the discussion of quality improvement and total quality management in Chapter 10 for information to get you started.

Note: Once you have answered the questions, save your Word document. You'll be answering additional questions in later chapters.

CBC VIDEO CASE 3-1

CBC

ZERONEXT

THE COMPANY

Mathieu Desjardins and Claude Pinet, entrepreneurs from Montreal, are trying to change the look—indeed the very thinking—behind wine cooler technology. The Renoir is a design-driven, wall-mounted, silent fridge that stores 30 bottles and displays them like a piece of artwork. This is not like the standard appliance it attempts to replace. It is unique not only in aesthetic design but also in functional design, with side access panels and cutting-edge electronic cooling that does not require a compressor. It is silent . . . it is beautiful . . . and it comes with five optional art frames to complete the look. The Renoir retails for about $4500. For more details on the company, go to zeronext.com.

THE PITCH

The owners of Zeronext asked for $500 000 in return for 20 percent ownership of the company (valued at $2 500 000). Zeronext has projected sales of approximately $1 million dollars (by year-end). Mathieu and Claude are seeking the investment and the support of the dragons to help them expand and to address existing interest in Europe and the United States.

THE DRAGONS' POINT OF VIEW

The dragons seemed very interested in the product, and they loved the design, but the consensus was that Zeronext should have charged a higher price in order to increase the margins after Mathieu revealed that the Renoir had a 40 percent markup (when sold to distributors). Arlene was concerned; she indicated that they probably only ended up with 10 percent on the bottom line. Claude said that the margins were going to improve in the coming months because of the economies of scale, which are associated with higher sales volume. However, the dragons insisted that they should increase the price by a few hundred dollars. This is a premium product and charging $4999 rather than $4499 would probably not make a huge difference to consumer demand but it would mean a lot to the company's bottom line.

Vikram Vij began the process of negotiation by offering to pay the $500 000 asking price for a 35 percent stake rather than 20 percent. He also seemed confident that this product would be a good fit for luxury condo builders in Vancouver. Soon after, Michael Wekerle increased the stakes when he offered $1 000 000 for 40 percent; he also asked Jim Treliving to join him on the deal. He believed that this product should be targeted at high-end hotels. Jim Treliving agreed to join forces with Michael. Arlene Dickinson said she loved the product but only as a potential consumer not as an investor. Finally, Dave Chilton told the owners not to give up the extra equity; he offered exactly what they asked: $500 000 for 20 percent.

THE OUTCOME

After discussing the pros and cons of the offers, the entrepreneurs decided that they would indeed give up 40 percent of the company for $1 million to Jim Treliving and Michael Wekerle. They believed that giving up the higher percentage was worth it if the extra funding could help them expand quicker into the U.S. market.

QUESTIONS FOR DISCUSSION

1. In this section of the course we cover key accounting terms such as *revenues, expenses, margins,* and *markups*. Trace the discussion that the owners had with the dragons, and highlight the key accounting terms and how they were used by the dragons to help them make their points and analyze the situation.
2. Do you think the owners did a good job in this pitch? (From an accounting point of view? From an operations point of view?) What was the high point and what was the low point from the owners' perspective?
3. Do you think it was wise for the owners of Zeronext to sell 40 percent equity in the company? In the short term? In the long term? (Support your answers.)

Source: "ZeroNext," *Dragons' Den*, Season 9, Episode 19 (April 22, 2015).

BUSINESS TODAY VIDEO CASE 3-1

RUDI'S BAKERY

Rudi's Organic Bakery operates a state-of-the-art, small-batch bakery. The company bakes about 16 million loaves of bread annually and ships its products across the country. When Hanno Holm, the chief operating officer, first started working at Rudi's, there was a lot of discussion among employees that there was a quality problem due to excessive variation in the colour of the loaves being made. In one three-month period, about 4.5 million loaves were produced, and the company received just 60 complaints. But none of those complaints were actually about the *colour* of the bread; they were about *bubbles* in the bread.

Holm realized that the company had to define quality the same way consumers defined it, and in this case it meant that Rudi's had to focus on reducing the number of bubbles instead of the colour. Since the bubbles could be seen in uncut loaves, they had to develop a system for solving the problem. With some research they found they could buy a machine that broke air bubbles as the loaves were being produced. The result was a more uniform mass of dough and far fewer bubbles. This reduced consumer complaints. Holm says that quality management means focusing on how to solve quality problems that consumers talk about, not just ones that workers talk about.

QUESTIONS FOR DISCUSSION

1. How is "quality" defined in the text? Is Hanno Holm's definition of quality consistent with the text definition? Explain.
2. How is the concept of total quality management relevant here?
3. What different tools for quality assurance are available to managers? Which ones would be most appropriate for Rudi's bakery?

BUSINESS TODAY VIDEO CASE 3-2

DID BURGER KING DEFECT TO CANADA TO SAVE TAX MONEY?

Burger King is merging with Tim Hortons to become the third-largest fast-food company in the world. When the merger was announced, it caused major shock waves both in the U.S. and in Canada.

For Canadians the fear was that another Canadian brand was losing its core identity (even if Tim Hortons has already been down this path with Wendy's). For Americans it was surprising to see a top U.S. brand move its headquarters north of the border to save tax dollars and it did not go unnoticed (with the president making condemning statements about tax shielding games). If Burger King moves its headquarters from Miami, Florida, to Canada, it will save about $50 million in taxes. As Canadians we are accustomed to the notion that we always pay more taxes than Americans; but in this corporate case it appears to be different.

In this age of globalization it should be no surprise to see such mergers. Burger King is already a global brand, so the location of its home office is really not a big deal, is it? Tim Hortons is primarily a Canadian brand (with a respectable number of stores in the U.S.) but it is also actively expanding in the Middle East. Will this merger allow Tim Hortons to grow more effectively with an experienced partner (especially in the U.S.)? The two organizations can share expertise to help improve their understanding of the foreign economic environment in the countries they serve. In addition, Tim Hortons is a strong breakfast destination, whereas Burger King thrives in the afternoon and evenings. So it seems there is potential for learning and sharing on both sides.

QUESTIONS FOR DISCUSSION

1. Why might Burger King's recent merger save the company tax money?
2. Burger King's CEO said, "Tax really wasn't the driver for this deal." If not, why do you think Burger King sought to merge with Tim Hortons?
3. How does this merger benefit Tim Hortons? Be specific.

PART 4 PRINCIPLES OF MARKETING

Jakub Jirsák/Fotolia

LO

AFTER READING THIS CHAPTER, YOU SHOULD BE ABLE TO:

- LO-1 Explain the concept of *marketing* and identify the five forces that constitute the *external marketing environment*.
- LO-2 Explain the purpose of a *marketing plan* and identify the four components of the *marketing mix*.
- LO-3 Explain *market segmentation* and how it is used in *target marketing* and *positioning*.
- LO-4 Discuss the purpose of *marketing research*, and compare marketing research methods.
- LO-5 Describe the *consumer buying process* and the key factors that influence that process.
- LO-6 Discuss the three categories of *organizational markets*, and the characteristics of business-to-business (B2B) buying behaviour.
- LO-7 Explain the definition of a product as a *value package*, and classify *goods and services*.
- LO-8 Describe the key considerations in the new *product development process*, and explain the importance of *branding and packaging*.

P&G Marketing: Dealing with a Shrinking Middle Class

DragonImages/Fotolia

Kristoffer Tripplaar/Alamy

Tide, Pampers, Bounty, Gillette, Crest, Scope, and Febreze. What do they all have in common? They are just a few of the brands owned by Procter & Gamble (P&G), the iconic marketer of household products. The company was established in 1837 and today serves over five billion people in over 70 countries. In 2014, sales were over US$83 billion. Of the large collection of brands, 23 actually have annual sales above US$1 billion. It is estimated that 98 percent of North

Understanding Marketing Principles *and* Developing Products

CHAPTER 12

American households use at least one P&G product, a position that has grown largely by targeting middle-class consumers. However, P&G is facing a puzzling marketing dilemma because the number of mid-range shoppers is shrinking.

The source of the problem is the reduction in middle-class purchasing power. Many families are now pinched with rising prices for housing, food, gasoline, and medical products but little or no wage increases. This economic condition has been described as the "Consumer Hourglass Theory." Advocates of the theory believe that purchasing power has shifted away from the once-massive middle and is concentrated now at the bottom and top. That's where consumer action is now, at the high-end market and the low-end market.

HOW WILL THIS HELP ME?

Adjusting its marketing strategy is an example of how a company can apply marketing basics to appeal to the forces of the external marketing environment. This chapter examines the marketing plan, components of the marketing mix, and the roles of targeting, market segmentation, and positioning. It also explores the fundamentals of market research and the key factors that influence the consumer and organizational buying processes. The chapter concludes with a look at how new products are developed and how they are defined by branding and packaging. By grasping the marketing methods and ideas in this chapter, you will be better prepared not only as a marketing professional, but also as an informed consumer.

Is this simply a short-term issue? Based on P&G's research, Melanie Healey, group president for P&G's North America business, expects middle-class downsizing will be a continuing trend. Accordingly, P&G and other companies are rethinking their target markets. Aiming at the high-end segment, the company introduced its more expensive Olay Pro-X skin-care product. Previously, P&G introduced Gain, the bargain-priced dish soap, which is aimed at the growing lower portion of the previous middle-class market following a dip in sales of the mid-priced Tide brand. During the previous recession, P&G's lower-priced Luvs diapers gained market share from their higher-priced Pampers brand. Following a path similar to that of P&G, H. J. Heinz has developed more food products for the lower-priced markets. Meanwhile, retailers focusing on lower-income consumers, such as Winners and Dollarama, are attracting customers from higher-priced retailers.

Refocusing away from the mainstream middle onto high- and low-end consumers is a new marketing experience at P&G. They have increased market research on lower-income households, often using face-to-face interviews to gain in-depth understanding of these consumers. So far, the low-end and the high-end segments each are generally smaller than the former massive middle-class market, which means P&G is splitting its marketing efforts. As one company official noted, historically they have been good at doing things on a larger scale, but now they are learning how to deal with smaller sales volumes for products in each of two segments. New product development is affected, too, because the high-end segment often involves fewer products with attractive extra features that will sell profitably at higher prices. P&G is betting that the Hourglass Theory has set the course for the company's future.

auremar/Fotolia

QUESTIONS FOR DISCUSSION

1. How would you best describe P&G's marketing strategy for the situation presented in this case?
2. What elements of P&G's external marketing environment are influencing the company's marketing strategy? Explain your reasoning.
3. P&G's marketing research includes face-to-face interviews for the situation described in this case. Would other forms of marketing research also be useful in this situation? Explain your reasoning.
4. Explain the roles of target marketing and market segmentation as they apply in this case.
5. In what ways are the components of P&G's marketing mix being affected by the situation described in this case? Give examples.

LO-1 WHAT IS MARKETING?

What comes to mind when you think of marketing? Most people think of advertisements designed for detergents, and soft drinks. Or they think of promoting products to customers through social networking. However, marketing covers a much wider range of activities. **Marketing** can be defined as "an organizational function and a set of processes for creating, communicating, and delivering value to customers and for managing customer relationships in ways that benefit the organization and its stakeholders."[1]

A company that employs the **marketing concept** is coordinated to achieve one goal—to serve its present and potential customers at a profit. This concept means that a firm must get to know what customers really want and closely follow evolving tastes. The various departments of the firm—marketing, production, finance, and human resources—must operate as a well-coordinated system that is unified in the pursuit of customer satisfaction.

Delivering Value

What attracts buyers to one product instead of another? Although our desires for the many goods and services available to us may be unlimited, financial resources force most of us to be selective. Accordingly, customers buy products that offer the best value when it comes to meeting their needs and wants.

VALUE AND BENEFITS

The **value** of a product compares its benefits with its costs. Benefits include not only the functions of the product, but also the emotional satisfaction associated with owning, experiencing, or possessing it. But every product has costs, including sales price, the expenditure of the buyer's time, and even the emotional costs of making a purchase decision. A satisfied customer perceives the benefits derived from the purchase to be greater than its costs. Thus, the simple but important ratio for value is derived as follows:

Value = Benefits/Costs

The marketing strategies of leading firms focus on increasing value for customers. Marketing resources are deployed to add benefits and decrease costs of products to provide greater value. To satisfy customers, a company may do any of the following:

- develop an entirely new product that performs better (provides greater performance benefits) than existing products
- keep a store open longer hours during a busy season (adding the benefit of greater shopping convenience)
- offer price reductions (the benefit of lower costs)
- offer information that explains how a product can be used in new ways (the benefit of new uses at no added cost)

VALUE AND UTILITY

To understand how marketing creates value for customers, we need to know the kind of benefits that buyers get from a firm's goods or services. As we discussed in Chapter 10, those benefits provide customers with **utility**—the ability of a product to satisfy a human want or need. Marketing strives to provide four kinds of utility in the following ways:

- *Form utility.* Marketing has a voice in designing products with features that customers want.
- *Time utility.* Marketing creates a time utility by providing products when customers will want them.
- *Place utility.* Marketing creates a place utility by providing products where customers will want them.
- *Possession utility.* Marketing creates a possession utility by transferring product ownership to customers by setting selling prices, setting terms for customer credit payments, if needed, and providing ownership documents.

Because they determine product features, and the timing, place, and terms of sale that provide utility and add value for customers, marketers must understand customers' wants and needs. Their methods for creating utility are described in this and the following chapter.

Goods, Services, and Ideas

The marketing of tangible goods is obvious in everyday life. It applies to two types of customers: those who buy consumer goods and those who buy industrial goods. Think of the products that you bought the last time you went to the mall or the grocery store or on the internet. In a department store, an employee asks if you'd like to try a new brand of cologne. Your local auto dealer offers an economy car at an economy price. These products are **consumer goods**: tangible goods that you can buy for personal use. Firms that sell goods to consumers for personal consumption are engaged in consumer marketing, also known as B2C (business-to-consumer) marketing.

Marketing also applies to **industrial goods**: physical items used by companies to produce other products. Surgical instruments and bulldozers are industrial goods, as are many components and raw materials such as integrated circuits, steel, and plastic. Firms that sell goods to other companies are involved in industrial marketing, also known as B2B (business-to-business) marketing.

But marketing techniques are also applied to **services**—products with intangible (non-physical) features, such as professional advice, timely information for decisions, or arrangements for a vacation. Service marketing—the application of marketing for services—continues to be a major growth area in Canada. Insurance companies, airlines, public accountants, and health clinics all engage in service marketing, both to individuals (consumer markets) and to other companies (industrial markets).

Finally, marketers also promote ideas. Ads in theatres, for example, warn us against copyright infringement and piracy. Other marketing

MARKETING An organizational function and a set of processes for creating, communicating, and delivering value to customers, and for managing customer relationships in ways that benefit the organization and its stakeholders.

MARKETING CONCEPT The idea that the whole firm is directed toward serving present and potential customers at a profit.

VALUE A relative comparison of a product's benefits versus its costs.

UTILITY The ability of a product to satisfy a human want or need.

CONSUMER GOODS Physical products purchased by consumers for personal use.

INDUSTRIAL GOODS Physical products purchased by companies to produce other products.

SERVICES Products with non-physical features, such as information, expertise, or an activity that can be purchased.

Fairmont Hotels actively use CRM techniques to satisfy customers in over 60 luxury properties around the globe, including the scenic Fairmont Chateau Lake Louise.

Achinthamb/Shutterstock

campaigns may stress the advantages of avoiding fast foods, avoiding texting while driving, or quitting smoking—or they may promote a political party or candidate.

Relationship Marketing and Customer Relationship Management

Although marketing often focuses on single transactions for products, services, or ideas, marketers also take a longer-term perspective. Thus, **relationship marketing** emphasizes building lasting relationships with customers and suppliers. Stronger relationships—including stronger economic and social ties—can result in greater long-term satisfaction, customer loyalty, and customer retention.[2] A recent survey, by Northstar, indicated that 74 percent of consumers reported switching from one brand to another in the previous year.[3] Clearly, companies must find more effective ways to connect with consumers. Like many other marketing areas, the ways that marketers go about building relationships with customers are evolving. Tim Hortons has a traditional rewards card known as the Tim Card and a modern version known as the TimmyME app that attracts return customers with free coffee refills and other extras.

Customer relationship management (CRM) is an organized method that enterprises use to build better information connections with clients. The power of internet communications, coupled with the ability to gather and assemble information on customer preferences, allows marketers to better predict what clients will want and buy. Compiling and storing customers' data, known as *data warehousing*, provides the raw materials from which marketers can gather information that allows them to find new clients. It also identifies their best customers who can then be informed about upcoming new products and supplied with special information such as post-purchase service reminders. *Data mining* automates the massive analysis of data by using computers to sort and search for previously undiscovered clues about what customers look at and react to, and how they might be influenced.[4]

Toronto-based Fairmont Resort Hotels first used data mining to rebuild its customer-relations package by finding out what kinds of vacations their customers prefer, and then placing ads where they were more likely to reach those customers. When data mining revealed the worldwide destinations of Fairmont customers, it helped determine Fairmont's decision to buy their customers' number-one preference—the Savoy in London.[5] More recently, Fairmont's enhanced CRM is attracting new guests, along with heightening relationships and loyalty among existing clients, through web-based promotions and incentives. Using profiles of guest information, Fairmont identifies target traveller segments and supplies travellers with personalized price discounts and special hotel services.[6] For a more detailed discussion on data warehousing and data mining refer to Chapter Supplement 03: Using Technology to Manage Information in the Internet and Social Media Era.

The Marketing Environment

Marketing strategies are not determined unilaterally by any business—rather, they are strongly influenced by powerful outside forces. As you see in Figure 12.1, every marketing program must recognize the factors in a company's external environment, that is, everything outside an organization's boundaries that might affect it. In this section, we will discuss how these external forces affect the marketing environment in particular.

POLITICAL–LEGAL ENVIRONMENT

Political activities, both global and domestic, have a major influence on marketing. For example, environmental legislation has determined the destinies of entire industries. The political push for alternative energy sources is creating new markets and products for emerging companies, such as India's Suzlon Energy Limited (large wind turbines), wind-powered electric generators from Germany's Nordex AG, and wind farms and power

RELATIONSHIP MARKETING A marketing strategy that emphasizes building lasting relationships with customers and suppliers.

CUSTOMER RELATIONSHIP MANAGEMENT (CRM) Organized methods that a firm uses to build better information connections with clients, so that stronger company–client relationships are developed.

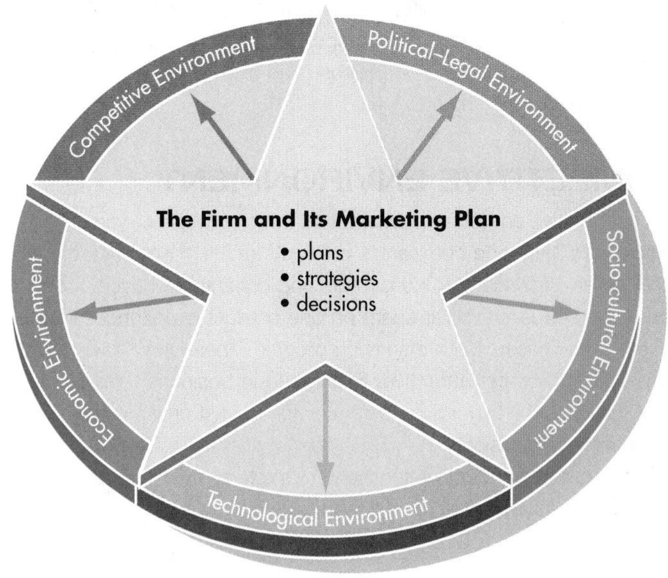

FIGURE 12.1 The external marketing environment

plants created by Spain's Gamesa Corporation. Marketing managers try to maintain favourable political and legal environments in several ways. To gain public support for products and activities, marketers use ad campaigns to raise public awareness of important issues, and companies contribute to political candidates.

SOCIO-CULTURAL ENVIRONMENT

Changing social values force companies to develop and promote new products. Just a few years ago, organic foods were available only in specialty food stores like Whole Foods. Today, in response to a growing demand for healthy foods, we see new organic lines in traditional supermarkets like Loblaws (notably the PC Organics line). In addition, Whole Foods and other grocers like it are expanding. In 2015, Whole Foods had 417 stores in Canada, the United States, and the United Kingdom, but it had plans to reach 1200 stores in short order. With same-store sales increases of 10 percent during that fiscal year, it is clear that consumers are becoming more willing to pay higher prices for better quality food.[7] For another interesting look at environmentally friendly products and practices, read the boxed feature entitled "Feeling the Pressure for 'Green.'"

TECHNOLOGICAL ENVIRONMENT

New technologies create new goods and services. New products make existing products obsolete, and many products change our values and lifestyles. In turn, lifestyle changes often stimulate new products not directly related to the new technologies themselves. For example, smartphones facilitate business communication just as prepackaged meals

THE GREENING OF BUSINESS

Feeling the Pressure for "Green"

Marketing managers face the challenge of "going green" in each of the external environments of marketing: political–legal, socio-cultural, technological, economic, and competitive. Consumers are looking for green alternatives to gas-guzzling cars, home buyers want energy-efficient heating and cooling in their homes, provincial utilities are offering incentives for construction that uses environmentally sensitive building designs that conserve energy, and environmentalists are pushing for alternative energy sources, notably wind and solar power, to replace fossil fuels.

Here are just a few of the new "green" products and services that have come on the market as a result of these environmental pressures:

- Quebec-based Cascades Inc. developed a new technology that will make it possible to produce toilet paper from recycled paper that is as soft as that produced from new wood.
- PepsiCo introduced a new bottle that is fully recyclable. It is made from switchgrass, corn husks, and pine bark—by-products from the company's food business.
- Bridgestone, Goodyear, Michelin, and Pirelli have developed new tires that reduce fuel consumption (and therefore exhaust emissions).
- Canadian National Railways has made sustainability an integral part of its business. The company estimates that it can now move 1 tonne of freight 317 kilometres using only 1 litre of diesel fuel.

Pressures from the external environment of marketing present challenges (and opportunities) for all areas of marketing: identifying new target markets, designing new products and services for those markets, and finding new technologies to make new products. Success depends on coordinating the "Four P's" of marketing (product, pricing, place, and promotion) with an integrated marketing strategy. For example, marketers need to present a convincing rationale for a product's pricing and demonstrate how the product provides the benefits sought by the target market. Distribution methods have to match up with promises made in promotional messages.

The marketing blueprint for Toyota's Prius automobile illustrates how an integrated marketing strategy can meet the challenge of going green. While developing the fuel-efficient hybrid technology, Toyota identified niche target markets of users in some 40 countries and determined a price range compatible with the company's performance reliability and quality reputation. Promotion started two years before the car was released so that customers could view and purchase a Prius. In one high-visibility pre-launch promotion, Toyota teamed up with the Sierra Club and lent the car to Hollywood superstars to provide exposure and allow car testing in the target market. The main advertising campaign to general audiences emphasized that consumers can still have speed and comfort along with environmental friendliness. Pre-ordered cars were delivered on time to buyers. As a result, the Prius became a very successful hybrid automobile.

CRITICAL THINKING QUESTION

1. What other environmentally friendly products and services are you aware of from your own experience?

New technologies lead to new products, such as the electric car. The long-term success of this product category will depend largely on the creation of proper infrastructure. These stations enable customers to recharge their vehicles. As cities and businesses increase investment in such stations the electric car will become more practical for the mass consumer.

Sopotnicki/Shutterstock

provide convenience for busy household cooks. Both kinds of products also free up time for recreation and leisure.

ECONOMIC ENVIRONMENT

Because they determine spending patterns by consumers, businesses, and governments, economic conditions influence marketing plans for product offerings, pricing, and promotional strategies. Marketers are concerned with such economic variables as inflation, interest rates, and recession. Thus, they monitor the general business cycle to anticipate trends in consumer and business spending. Subtle consumer shifts in attitude can affect all areas of business and must be taken into account when building marketing strategies.[8]

COMPETITIVE ENVIRONMENT

In a competitive environment, marketers must convince buyers that they should purchase one company's products rather than those of some other seller. Because both consumers and commercial buyers have limited resources, every dollar spent on one product is no longer available for other purchases. Each marketing program, therefore, seeks to make its product the most attractive. Expressed in business terms, a failed program loses the buyer's dollar forever (or at least until it is time for the next purchase decision).

To promote products effectively, marketers must first understand which of three types of competition they face:

- *Substitute products* may not look alike or they may seem very different from one another, but they can fulfill the same need. For example, your cholesterol level might be controlled with either of two competing products: a physical fitness program or a drug regimen. The fitness program and the drugs compete as substitute products.
- *Brand competition* occurs between similar products and is based on buyers' perceptions of the benefits of products offered by particular companies. For internet searches do you turn to the Google or Bing search engine? Brand competition is based on users' perceptions of the benefits offered by each product.
- *International competition* matches the products of domestic marketers against those of foreign competitors. The intensity of international competition has been heightened by the formation of alliances, such as the European Union, NAFTA and the Trans-Pacific Partnership.

Having identified the kind of competition, marketers can then develop a strategy for attracting more customers.

LO-2 DEVELOPING THE MARKETING PLAN

The **marketing plan** identifies the marketing objectives stating what marketing will accomplish in the future. It contains a strategy that identifies the specific activities and resources that will be used to meet the needs and desires of customers in the firm's chosen target markets, so as to accomplish the marketing objectives.

A marketing manager at a major home appliance manufacturing company explains the concept of *developing the marketing plan* by using the analogy of planning for a trip:

- "First, you decide where you want to go and what you want to happen when you get there. Why take this trip and not others, instead?"
  [Identify the *objective* or *goal* to be achieved.]
- "At some stage you decide when the trip will happen and how you'll get to the destination."
  [*Plan* for *when* it will happen, and for the *paths* (or *routes*) that will be taken to get there.]
- "Every trip requires resources so you identify the requirements, and compare them against resources that are available."
  [*Evaluate resource* requirements and availabilities.]
- "If available resources are too expensive, then you adjust the trip so it becomes more affordable."
  [*Adjust plans* as needed to become *realistic* and *feasible*.]
- "During and after the trip, you assess the successes (what went right) and the drawbacks (what went wrong) and consider them to make the next trip even better."
  [Keep notes and data about what happened because *learning* from this experience increases the chances for *greater success on the next*.]

First and foremost, marketing plans are futuristic, showing what will be happening with marketing's upcoming activities. Every well-founded marketing plan, as shown in Figure 12.2, begins with objectives or goals setting the stage for everything that follows. **Marketing objectives**, the goals the marketing plan intends to accomplish, are the foundation that guides all of the detailed activities in the plan. The marketing objectives themselves, however, exist solely to support the company's overall business mission (at the top in Figure 12.2) and typically focus on maintaining or enhancing the organization's future competitive position in its chosen

MARKETING PLAN Detailed strategy for focusing marketing efforts on consumers' needs and wants

MARKETING OBJECTIVES the things marketing intends to accomplish in its marketing plan

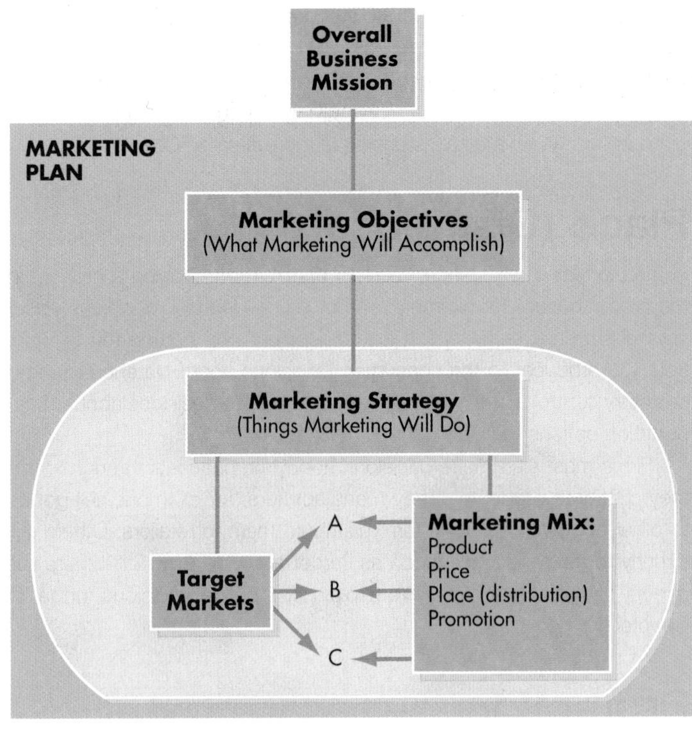

FIGURE 12.2 Components of the marketing plan

THERE'S AN APP FOR THAT!

APP DETAILS	PLATFORMS
1. **Marketing 101** **Source:** WAGmob **Key Features:** Offers online tutorials to help you learn marketing concepts.	Apple, Android, BlackBerry, Windows
2. **Icon Pop Brand** **Source:** Alegrium **Key Features:** A logos quiz game that challenges players to name products, brands, companies, and organizations using imaginative, handcrafted visual clues inspired by each answer.	Apple, Android, Windows
3. **Personal Branding Course** **Source:** Udemy **Key Features:** A series of transformative exercises designed to reveal every element of your ideal personal brand positioning.	Android

APP DISCOVERY EXERCISE

Since app availability changes, conduct your own search for the "Top Three" marketing apps and identify the key features.

markets. Hypothetically, Starbucks' overall business mission could aim at being the world's leading retailer of specialty coffee. Two supporting marketing objectives, then, could be (1) achieve a 5 percent increase in its worldwide market share by 2017 and (2) become the leading retailer (in dollar sales) of specialty coffee in China by 2020.

Strategy: The Marketing Mix

The marketing team can develop a strategy once they have clarified the marketing objectives. Specifically, **marketing strategy** identifies the planned marketing programs, all the marketing activities that a business will use to achieve its marketing goals and when those activities will occur. If planned activities are not affordable, then marketers need to adjust the activities or goals until realistic plans emerge. Finally, marketing planning is an ongoing process; it can be improved through experience by learning from past triumphs and mistakes.

Marketing managers are the people responsible for planning, organizing, leading, and controlling the organization's marketing resources toward supporting and accomplishing the organization's overall mission. To meet these responsibilities marketing managers, rely on mapping out a clear strategy for planning and implementing all the activities that result in the transfer of goods or services to customers. As you can see in Figure 12.2, the marketing strategy focuses on the needs and wants of customers in the company's chosen target markets. Marketing strategy also includes four basic components (often called the "Four P's") of the marketing mix: *product, pricing, place*, and *promotion*, that marketing managers use to satisfy customers in target markets. The specific activities for each of the Four P's will be designed differently to best meet the needs of each target market.

You can learn more about many of the key terms and concepts in this chapter by examining and downloading the contents from the box entitled "There's an App for That!"

Product

Marketing begins with a **product**—a good, a service, or an idea designed to fill a customer's need or want. Conceiving and developing new products is a constant challenge for marketers, who must always consider: changing technology, changing wants and needs of customers, and changing economic conditions.

Producers often promote particular features of products in order to distinguish them in the marketplace. **Product differentiation** is the creation of a feature or image that makes a product differ enough from existing products to attract customers. For example, Lululemon has a clear identity based on a yoga-inspired theme and has carved out a strong presence in the athletic clothing market. We cover the development process and the branding of products in detail in the final section of the chapter.

Pricing

Pricing a product—selecting the best price at which to sell it—requires consideration of several variables. Determining the best price at which

MARKETING STRATEGY all the marketing programs and activities that will be used to achieve the marketing goals

MARKETING MIX A combination of product, pricing, promotion, and place (distribution) strategies used to market products.

PRODUCT Good, service, or idea that is marketed to fill consumers' needs and wants.

PRODUCT DIFFERENTIATION Creation of a product feature or product image that differs enough from existing products to attract customers.

PRICING The process of determining the best price at which to sell a product.

Lululemon has a clear identity based on a yoga-inspired theme; it has carved out a strong presence in the athletic clothing market.

RosaBetancourt 0 people images/Alamy

to sell a product is a difficult balancing act. From a manufacturer's point of view, prices must support the organization's operating, administrative, research, and marketing costs. On the other hand, prices cannot be so high that consumers turn to competing products. Successful pricing means finding a profitable middle ground between these two requirements.

Both low- and high-price strategies can be effective, depending on the situation. For example, Canadian Tire maintained healthy sales in patio furniture and barbecues during the most recent recession by stocking additional lower-priced items and scaling back their stock of more expensive items.[9] At the same time, de Grisogono was launching its The Meccanico watch in style, by winning the Prix du Public at a prestigious competition in Geneva. The company proclaims that The Meccanico is the world's most complicated watch, and it retails for about $200 000—roughly as much as a Ferrari.[10] Low prices will generally lead to a larger volume of sales. High prices will usually limit the size of the market, but will increase a firm's profits per unit. In some cases, however, high prices may actually attract customers by implying that the product is especially good or rare. We will discuss pricing in more detail in Chapter 13.

Place (Distribution)

In the marketing mix, **place** refers to **distribution**. Placing a product in the proper outlet—for example, a retail store—requires decisions about several activities, all of which are concerned with getting the product from the producer to the consumer. Decisions about warehousing and inventory control are distribution decisions, as are decisions about transportation options.

Firms must also make decisions about the channels through which they distribute products. Many manufacturers, for example, sell goods to other companies that, in turn, distribute them to retailers. Others sell directly to major retailers, such as Target and The Bay. Still others sell directly to final consumers. We explain distribution decisions further in Chapter 13.

Promotion

The most visible component of the marketing mix is, no doubt, **promotion**, which refers to techniques for communicating information about products. The most important promotional tools include advertising, personal selling, sales promotions, publicity/public relations, and direct or interactive marketing. Promotion decisions are discussed further in Chapter 13.

PLACE (DISTRIBUTION) The part of the marketing mix concerned with getting products from producers to consumers.

PROMOTION The aspect of the marketing mix concerned with the most effective techniques for communicating information about products.

LO-3 MARKETING STRATEGY: MARKET SEGMENTATION, TARGET MARKETING, AND POSITIONING

Market segmentation refers to dividing a market into categories of customer types or "segments." Marketers have long known that products cannot be all things to all people. The emergence of the marketing concept and the recognition of customers' needs and wants has led marketers to think in terms of **target markets**—groups of people or organizations with similar wants and needs, who can be expected to show interest in the same products.

Once they have identified segments, companies may adopt a variety of strategies. Some firms target more than one segment (with different offers). For example, General Motors offers a wide variety of automobiles with various features and price points. Actually, GM's old strategy was to provide an automobile for nearly every segment of the market. The financial crisis, however, forced GM's changeover to fewer target markets and associated brands by closing Saturn, phasing out Pontiac, and selling or shutting down Hummer and Saab.

In contrast, some businesses offer a narrower range of products, such as Ferrari's high-priced sports cars, aiming at a narrow segment. Note that segmentation is a strategy for analyzing consumers, not products. Once a target segment is identified, the marketing of products for that segment begins.

The process of fixing, adapting, and communicating the nature of the product itself is called **product positioning**. In the Canadian

MARKET SEGMENTATION The process of dividing a market into categories of customer types or "segments."

TARGET MARKET A group of people who have similar wants and needs and can be expected to show interest in the same products.

PRODUCT POSITIONING The process of fixing, adapting, and communicating the nature of a product to appeal to the selected target market.

coffee-house landscape, two companies stand out with very different value propositions and positioning approaches. Tim Hortons emphasizes a standardized product and provides fast service to people in a hurry, while Starbucks provides more customized products in more leisurely surroundings.

Identifying Market Segments

By definition, members of a market segment must share some common traits that affect their purchasing decisions. In identifying consumer segments, researchers look at several different influences on consumer behaviour. The next section examines five of the most important segmentation approaches: demographic, geographic, geo-demographic, psychographic, and behavioural segmentation.

DEMOGRAPHIC SEGMENTATION

Demographic variables describe populations by identifying characteristics such as age, income, gender, ethnic background, marital status, race, religion, and social class as detailed in Table 12.1. Note that these are objective criteria that cannot be altered. Marketers must work with or around them.

Depending on the marketer's purpose, a segment can be a single classification (e.g., age 20 to 34) or a combination of categories (e.g., age 20 to 34, married with children, earning \$40 000 to \$59 999). Hot Topic is a California-based chain that specializes in clothes, accessories, and jewellery designed to appeal to the youth market, whereas the Bank of Montreal is paying particular attention to the large Baby Boomer population (born between 1947 and 1966), which represents approximately 40 percent of the working population. Specialized services and products are being developed to serve the growing retirement needs of this group.[11]

In Canada, the two dominant cultures—English and French—have historically shown significant differences in consumer attitudes and behaviour. Researchers have found that compared with English Canadians, French Canadians are more involved with home and family, attend the ballet more often, travel less, eat more chocolate, and are less interested in convenience food.

Canada's great ethnic diversity requires companies to pay close attention to ethnicity as a segmentation variable. These consumers can be precisely targeted using one of the 358 media outlets geared toward 93 ethnic groups in Canada. Ethnic TV stations include the Fairchild Network (Cantonese and Mandarin) and ATN (South Asian).[12] In another sign of the growing consumer power and potential of the multibillion-dollar ethnic marketing segment, Metro purchased a 55 percent stake in Adonis, a Montreal-based ethnic grocery store, for an undisclosed sum. This deal was made not only to acquire a piece of a very successful chain, but also to gain expertise and access to supplier networks to increase the profile of ethnic foods in Metro's regular grocery stores.[13]

TABLE 12.1 Demographic Variables

Age	Under 5; 5–11; 12–19; 20–34; 35–49; 50–64; 65+
Education	Elementary school or less; some high school; graduated high school; some college or university; college diploma or university degree; advanced degree
Family Life Cycle	Young single; young married without children; young married with children; older married with children under 18; older married without children under 18; older single; other
Family Size	1, 2–3, 4–5, 6+
Income	Under \$20 000; \$20 000–\$39 999; \$40 000–\$59 999; \$60 000–\$79 999; \$80 000 and over
Nationality	Including but not limited to English, French, Irish, Italian, Latin American, Middle Eastern, and Scandinavian
Race	Including but not limited to Aboriginal, Asian, black, and white
Religion	Including but not limited to Buddhist, Catholic, Hindu, Jewish, Muslim, and Protestant
Gender	Male, female, trans

GEOGRAPHIC SEGMENTATION

Many buying decisions are affected by the places people call home. **Geographic variables** are the geographical units, from countries to neighbourhoods that may be important in a segmentation strategy. For example, the heavy rainfall in British Columbia prompts its inhabitants to purchase more umbrellas than people living in Arizona's desert climate. Urban dwellers have less demand for pickup trucks than their rural counterparts. Sailboats sell better along both coasts than they do in the Prairie provinces. These patterns affect marketing decisions about what products to offer, at what price to sell them, how to promote them, and how to distribute them. Consider the marketing of down parkas in rural Saskatchewan. Demand will be high, price competition may be limited, local newspaper advertising may be very effective, and the best location may be one easily reached from several small towns.

GEO-DEMOGRAPHIC SEGMENTATION

Geo-demographic variables are a combination of geographic and demographic traits, and they are becoming the most common segmentation tool. An example would be Young Urban Professionals—well-educated, 25-to-34-year-olds with high-paying professional jobs living in the "downtown" core of major cities. This type of segmentation is more-effective because the greater number of variables defines the market more precisely.

PSYCHOGRAPHIC SEGMENTATION

Members of a market can also be segmented according to **psychographic variables** such as lifestyles, opinions, interests, and attitudes. Psychographics variables help us understand why two demographically identical people (i.e. male, 28 years old, with one child, earning \$55 000 per year) may make totally different purchases. One person may be very environmentally friendly and prefer to purchase an electric car and the other may be more of a thrill-seeker who prefers performance and is not

DEMOGRAPHIC VARIABLES Characteristics of populations that may be considered in developing a segmentation strategy.

GEOGRAPHIC VARIABLES Geographic units that may be considered in developing a segmentation strategy.

GEO-DEMOGRAPHIC VARIABLES A combination of geographic and demographic traits used in developing a segmentation strategy.

PSYCHOGRAPHIC VARIABLES Consumer characteristics, such as lifestyles, opinions, interests, and attitudes that may be considered in developing a segmentation strategy.

particularly concerned with environmental issues. In other words, statistics alone are not enough.

Psychographics are also important to marketers because, unlike demographics and geographics, they can sometimes be changed by marketing efforts. Many companies have succeeded in changing some consumers' opinions by running ads highlighting products that they have improved directly in response to consumer desires.

BEHAVIOURAL SEGMENTATION

Behavioural segmentation refers to dividing a market into groups based on consumer knowledge, use, or response to a product.[14] **Behavioural variables** include *benefits sought* (e.g., Head and Shoulders shampoo addresses dandruff control), *user status* (i.e., ex-users, current users, non-users etc.), *usage rate* (i.e., heavy users vs. light users), *loyalty status* (i.e., highly brand-loyal vs. brand-promiscuous), and *occasion for use* (e.g., time of day, special occasion, etc.).

BEHAVIOURAL VARIABLES Behavioural considerations, such as benefits sought, loyalty status, usage rate, user status, and occasion for use that may be used in developing a segmentation strategy.

LO-4 MARKETING RESEARCH

Marketing decisions are seldom perfect, yet the consequences of a firm's choices of marketing mix and segmentation strategy can be long-lasting. Effective decisions must be customer-focused and based on timely information about marketplace trends. **Marketing research**, the study of what customers need and want and how best to meet those needs and wants, is a powerful tool for gaining decision-making information.

The relationship of research to the overall marketing process is shown in Figure 12.3. Ultimately, its role is to increase competitiveness

MARKETING RESEARCH The study of what customers need and want and how best to meet those needs and wants.

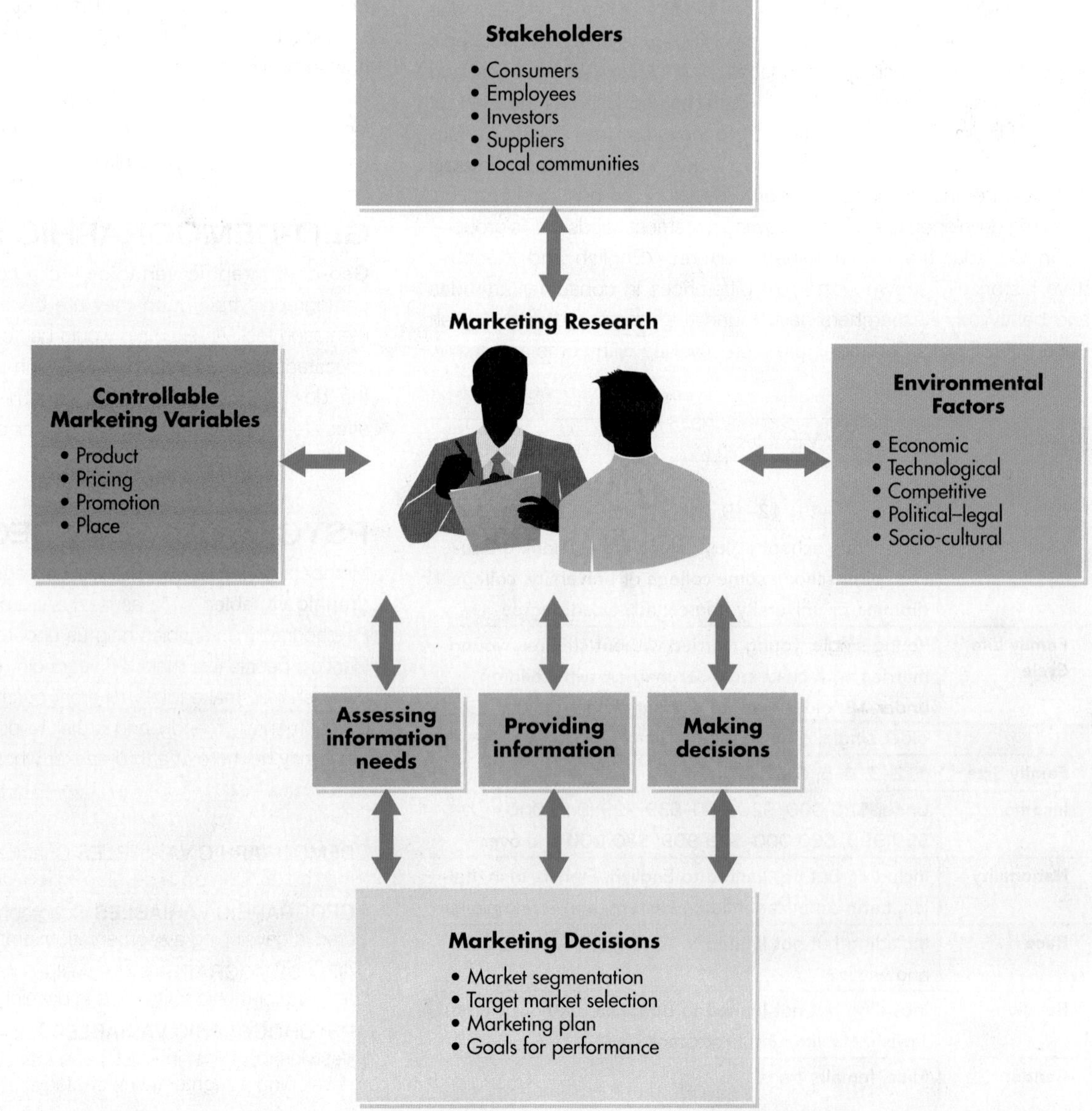

>>> FIGURE 12.3 Market research and the marketing process

by clarifying the interactions among a firm's stakeholders (including customers), marketing variables, environmental factors, and marketing decisions. Researchers use several methods to obtain, interpret, and apply information about customers. They determine the kinds of information needed for decisions on marketing strategy, goal setting, and target-market selection. In doing so, they may conduct studies on customer responses to proposed changes in the marketing mix. One researcher, for example, might study response to an experimental paint formula (new product). Another might explore the response to a price reduction (new price) on condominiums. Still a third might check responses to a proposed advertising campaign (new promotion). Marketers also try to learn whether customers will more likely purchase a product in a specialty shop or on the internet (new place).

The Research Process

Market research can occur at almost any point in a product's existence, but it is most frequently used when a new or altered product is being considered. There are five steps to performing market research:[15]

1. *Study the current situation*. What is the need and what is currently being done to meet it?
2. *Select a research method.* In choosing a method, marketers must bear in mind the effectiveness and costs of different methods.
3. *Collect secondary data. Secondary data* refers to information already available as a result of previous research by the firm or other organizations. For example, Statistics Canada publishes a great deal of useful data for business firms. Using secondary data can save time, effort, and money. But in some cases, secondary data is unavailable or inadequate, so *primary data*—new research by the firm or its agents—must be obtained.
4. *Analyze the data.* Data is not useful until it has been organized into clear information.
5. *Prepare a report.* This report normally includes a summary of the study's methodology and findings, various alternative solutions (where appropriate), and recommendations for an appropriate course of action.

Research Methods

The four basic types of methods used by market researchers are *observation, survey, focus groups*, and *experimentation*.

OBSERVATION

Probably the oldest form of market research is simple **observation**. It is also a popular research method because it is relatively low in cost, often drawing on data that must be collected for some other reason, such as reordering. In earlier times, when a store owner noticed that customers were buying red children's wagons, not green ones, the owner reordered more red wagons, the manufacturer's records showed high sales of red wagons, and the marketing department concluded that customers wanted red wagons. But observation is now much more sophisticated. For example, retail guru Paco Underhill collects approximately 50 000 hours of video every year for customers like Walmart, Best Buy, and Gap. It is analyzed and used to guide decisions by identifying patterns of behaviour.[16]

For an interesting modern look at the subject, take a close look at the E-Business and Social Media Solutions box entitled "Retailers Are Watching and Tracking You."

SURVEY

Sometimes observation of current events is not enough, and marketers need to conduct a **survey** to find out what consumers want. The heart of any survey is a questionnaire carefully designed to give the company honest answers about specific research issues. Surveys can be expensive to carry out and may vary widely in their accuracy. Because no firm can afford to survey everyone, marketers must carefully select a representative group of respondents. In the past, surveys have been mailed to individuals for their completion, but online surveys are now extremely popular.

FOCUS GROUPS

Many firms also use **focus groups**, in which 6 to 15 people are brought together to talk about a product or service. A moderator leads the group's discussion, and employees from the sponsoring company may observe the proceedings from behind a one-way mirror. People's comments are taped, and researchers go through the data looking for common themes. The group are not usually told which company is sponsoring the research.

EXPERIMENTATION

Experimentation compares the responses of the same or similar individuals under different circumstances. For example, a firm that is trying to decide whether to include walnuts in a new candy bar probably would not learn much by asking people what they thought of the idea. But if it made some bars with nuts and some without and then asked people to try both, the responses could be very helpful.[17]

OBSERVATION A market research technique involving viewing or otherwise monitoring consumer buying patterns.

SURVEY A market research technique based on questioning a representative sample of consumers about purchasing attitudes and practices.

FOCUS GROUP A market research technique involving a small group of people brought together and allowed to discuss selected issues in depth.

EXPERIMENTATION A market research technique in which the reactions of similar people are compared under different circumstances.

LO-5 UNDERSTANDING CONSUMER BEHAVIOUR

Market research in its many forms can help marketing managers understand how common traits of a market segment affect consumers' purchasing decisions. It helps with fundamental questions: Why do people buy a certain product? What desire are they fulfilling with the product? Is there a psychological or sociological explanation for why they purchase one product and not another? These questions and

E-BUSINESS AND SOCIAL MEDIA SOLUTIONS

Retailers Are Watching and Tracking You

Can a retailer track your daily movements and know if you recently visited a yoga studio or coffee shop? The short answer is yes. Technically, that sort of technology exists and many of you are willing participants (based on your smartphone settings) whether you know it or not.

Understanding what consumers want and providing it when they want it has always been good business practice for retailers. In small towns, general stores carry a variety of goods, and the owner's ability to understand individual customer needs goes a long way in satisfying customers. Today, big-city retailers may not have a personal relationship with you, but they have a wealth of information to help them understand who you are and what you buy. In addition, they can track your location, monitor your actions in high definition, and see how much time you spend in certain departments. Retailers are only beginning to scratch the surface of what is possible with modern technology, but you might be surprised to find out just how far they have already come. Here are a few examples:

Retailers are tracking you via surveillance cameras and tracking you through your smartphone. So next time you are posing for a "selfie" don't forget to smile for the camera above your shoulder as well.

william87/Fotolia

- Retailers and malls have set up Wi-Fi networks to satisfy customer needs, but that same technology permits them to track you. Toronto-based Turnstyle Solutions Inc. has placed a few hundred data recording beacons in downtown Toronto businesses. Boingo Wireless Inc. is testing a system that monitors traffic patterns in malls. Nearbuy Systems is pushing a system that is supposed to enable retailers to cross-reference the websites shoppers visit on their phones with their location in the outlet.
- Mac's and Couche-Tard outlets will take this technology even further in an attempt to turn your smartphone into a mini-billboard. Using a technology from iSign Media Solutions Inc., Couche-Tard will strategically send ads to anyone within a 300 metre radius of one of their stores. The messages will request your permission, but the reminder of the location proximity is automatic and potentially quite effective.
- Many retailers are tapping into their video surveillance to track customer behaviour and analyze buying patterns. Alexander Fernandes founded Vancouver-based QImaging for medical and industrial use, but has found a great market in shopping-mall and retail-store surveillance. Fernandes and his team developed High Definition Stream Management, which makes it less expensive and easier to store and send images. His customers include shopping malls, arenas, banks, and many other outlets.
- The most traditional tool to track consumers is actual sales data. Charles Brown, president of The Source, noticed that shoppers were buying more headphones. Armed with this information, he started stocking more upscale lines (e.g., Beats by Dr. Dre) and sales in this category increased by 40 percent. Many chains, like The Source, supplement this data by analyzing real-time chatter on social media sites and examining online consumer product reviews and commentary.

All of this brings up questions of privacy, but the companies pushing the intrusive cell phone technology point out that you could always turn off your phone or the tracking capability. But, of course, most consumers are oblivious to all that is going on around them. Even if they were aware, would they really care? Retailers will argue that they are just trying to understand your needs to meet demands efficiently. Is this any different than the digital greeter named Anna that says hello to shoppers as they enter The Bay's flagship store in Toronto? What do you think? Is this all bordering on creepy, or is it just the way things are today?

QUESTIONS FOR DISCUSSION

1. Which of the techniques described above do you find the most effective? Which do you find least effective?
2. Do you believe retailers are crossing ethical lines with some of this new technology?

many others are addressed in the study of **consumer behaviour**—the study of the decision process by which people buy and consume products.

Influences on Consumer Behaviour

To understand consumer behaviour, marketers draw heavily on such fields as psychology and sociology. The result is a focus on four major influences on consumer behaviour: psychological, personal, social, and cultural. By identifying which influences are most active in certain circumstances, marketers try to explain consumer choices and predict future buying behaviour.

- *Psychological influences* include an individual's motivations, perceptions, ability to learn, and attitudes.
- *Personal influences* include lifestyle, personality, and economic status.
- *Social influences* include family; opinion leaders (people whose opinions are sought by others); and such reference groups as friends, co-workers, and professional associates.
- *Cultural influences* include culture (the way of living that distinguishes one large group from another); subculture (smaller groups with shared values); and social class (the cultural ranking of groups according to such criteria as background, occupation, and income).

CONSUMER BEHAVIOUR The study of the decision process by which people buy and consume products.

The Consumer Buying Process

When consumers are in the process of buying a new product (especially a big purchase) they pass through five key stages: (1) problem/need recognition, (2) information seeking, (3) evaluation of alternatives, (4) purchase decision, (5) post-purchase evaluation. Marketers are always trying to understand what makes consumers tick; they are looking for ways to provide information and solutions to help consumers see the benefits of buying their products at every stage. Let's take a closer look.

PROBLEM/NEED RECOGNITION

This process begins when the consumer recognizes a problem or need. Need recognition also occurs when you have a chance to change your buying habits. After an exercise workout, you recognize that you are thirsty and in need of a refreshment. When you obtain your first job after graduation, your new income may let you buy things that were once too expensive for you. You may find that you need professional clothing, apartment furnishings, and a car. RBC and Scotiabank cater to such shifts in needs when they market credit cards to recent graduates.

INFORMATION SEEKING

Having recognized a need, consumers often seek information. The search is not always extensive. When you are thirsty you may simply look for the nearest vending machine; however, before making major purchases, most people seek information from personal sources, public sources, and experience. When buying a new car you may take months to gather information from various sources (online, from friends, mechanics, and so on) before you even consider a purchase.

EVALUATION OF ALTERNATIVES

People who are in the market for skis probably have some idea of who makes skis and how they differ. By analyzing product attributes (price, prestige, quality) of the consideration set (the group of brands they will consider buying), consumers compare products before deciding which one best meets their needs.

PURCHASE DECISION

Ultimately, consumers make purchase decisions. "Buy" decisions are based on rational motives, emotional motives, or both. *Rational motives* involve the logical evaluation of product attributes: cost, quality, and usefulness. *Emotional motives* involve non-objective factors and include sociability, imitation of others, and aesthetics. For example, you might buy the same brand of jeans as your friends to feel accepted in a certain group, not because your friends happen to have the good sense to prefer durable, comfortable, low-priced jeans (usually it is the opposite scenario).

POST-PURCHASE EVALUATION

Marketing does not stop with the sale of a product. What happens after the sale is just as important. Marketers want consumers to be happy after buying products so that they are more likely to buy them again. Because consumers do not want to go through a complex decision process for every purchase, they often repurchase products. Dissatisfied consumers may complain, file a lawsuit, or publicly criticize the product and the company on social media.

LO-6 ORGANIZATIONAL MARKETING AND BUYING BEHAVIOUR

In the consumer market, buying and selling transactions are visible to the public. Equally important, though far less visible, are organizational (or commercial) markets. Marketing to organizations that buy goods and services used in creating and delivering consumer products involves various kinds of markets and buying behaviours different from those in consumer markets.

Business Marketing

Business marketing involves organizational or commercial markets that fall into three B2B categories: industrial, reseller, and government/institutional markets. Taken together, B2B markets account for more than two times the sales amount of the consumer market.[18]

INDUSTRIAL MARKET

The **industrial market** includes businesses that buy goods to be converted into other products or that are used up during production. It includes farmers, manufacturers, and some retailers. For example, clock-making company Seth Thomas buys electronics, metal components, and glass from other companies to make clocks for the consumer market. The company also buys office supplies, tools, and factory equipment—items never seen by clock buyers—that are used during production.

RESELLER MARKET

Before products reach consumers, they pass through a **reseller market** consisting of intermediaries, including wholesalers and retailers that buy and resell finished goods. For example, as a leading distributor of parts and accessories for the pleasure boat market, Coast Distribution System buys lights, steering wheels, and propellers and resells them to marinas and boat-repair shops.

GOVERNMENT AND INSTITUTIONAL MARKET

Federal, provincial, and municipal governments are very important, not only for the laws they create and maintain, but also for their economic spending power. The Canadian federal government, for example, spent an estimated $235 billion in 2015. A new website enables Canadians

INDUSTRIAL MARKET An organizational market consisting of firms that buy goods that are either converted into products or used during production.

RESELLER MARKET An organizational market consisting of intermediaries that buy and resell finished goods.

to track this spending at www.tbs-sct.gc.ca/ems-sgd/edb-bdd/index-eng.html.[19] The **institutional market** consists of non-governmental organizations, such as religious organizations, museums, and charities, that also use supplies and equipment as well as legal, accounting, and transportation services.

INSTITUTIONAL MARKET An organizational market consisting of such non-governmental buyers of goods and services as hospitals, religious organizations, museums, and charitable organizations.

B2B Buying Behaviour

In some respects, organizational buying behaviour bears little resemblance to consumer buying practices. Consumer–seller relationships are often impersonal, short-lived, one-time interactions. In contrast, B2B situations often involve frequent and long-term buyer–seller relationships. Unlike most consumers, organizational buyers purchase in large quantities and are professional, specialized, and well informed. They make decisions based on rational motives such as relative performance, cost, efficiency, and maintenance costs.

LO-7 WHAT IS A PRODUCT?

In developing the marketing mix for any product, whether goods or services, marketers must consider what customers really want when they purchase products. Only then can these marketers plan strategies effectively.

The Value Package

Whether it is a physical good, a service, or some combination of the two, customers get value from the various benefits, features, and even intangible rewards associated with a product. **Product features** are the qualities, tangible and intangible, that a company builds into its products. However, as we discussed earlier, to attract buyers, features must also provide benefits.

For example, Gibson Guitars sells more than just the sum of the features for its legendary Les Paul guitars (mahogany headstock and neck, nickel and silver frets, rosewood fingerboard, solid mahogany back and body, and maple top); it also sells a powerful package linked to the very history of rock and roll. Some of the greatest legends of music have used this guitar, including Jimmy Page of Led Zeppelin. Consumers ultimately purchase based on the benefits that are provided by those features. In the case of the Les Paul, it is not simply the maple top or the fact that Gibson carefully glues the necks of the guitars onto the main bodies (a more expensive, time-consuming process than simply bolting them on, as most other makers do). It is also the results and ultimate benefits that guitar enthusiasts seek; Gibson believes this approach leads to a warmer tone and a more resonant sound. According to Jimmy Vivino, bandleader of the TV show *Conan*, "The mahogany-necked Gibson creates a lingering sound, with more 'fur' around the notes. That's the sound I want."[20]

Today's customer regards a product as a bundle of attributes—benefits and features—that, taken together, marketers call the *value package*. Increasingly, buyers expect to receive products with greater value—with more benefits and features at reasonable costs—so firms must compete on the basis of enhanced value packages.

Classifying Goods and Services

We can classify products according to expected buyers, who fall into two groups: buyers of consumer products and buyers of organizational products. As we saw earlier in this chapter, the consumer and industrial buying processes differ significantly. Similarly, marketing products to consumers is vastly different from marketing products to companies and other organizations.

CLASSIFYING CONSUMER PRODUCTS

Consumer products are commonly divided into three categories that reflect buyer behaviour: **convenience goods and services**, **shopping goods and services**, and **specialty goods and services**. These are outlined in Table 12.2.

PRODUCT FEATURES Tangible and intangible qualities that a company builds into its products.

CONVENIENCE GOOD/CONVENIENCE SERVICE An inexpensive good or service purchased and consumed rapidly and regularly.

SHOPPING GOOD/SHOPPING SERVICE A moderately expensive, infrequently purchased good or service.

SPECIALTY GOOD/SPECIALTY SERVICE An expensive, rarely purchased good or service.

>>> **TABLE 12.2** Categories of Consumer Products

Category	Description	Examples
Convenience Goods and Services	• Consumed rapidly and regularly • Inexpensive • Purchased often and with little input of time and effort	• Milk • Newspaper • Fast food
Shopping Goods and Services	• Purchased less often • More expensive • Consumers may shop around and compare products based on style, performance, colour, price, and other criteria	• Television set • Tires • Car insurance
Specialty Goods and Services	• Purchased infrequently • Expensive • Consumer decides on a precise product and will not accept substitutions, and spends a good deal of time choosing the "perfect" item	• Jewellery • Wedding gown • Catering

>>> **TABLE 12.3** Categories of organizational products

Category	Description	Examples
Production Items	• Goods or services used directly in the production process	• Loads of tea processed into tea bags • Information processing for real-time production
Expense Items	• Goods or services that are consumed within a year by firms producing other goods or supplying other services	• Oil and electricity for machines • Building maintenance • Legal services
Capital Items	• Permanent (expensive and long-lasting) goods and services • Life expectancy of more than a year • Purchased infrequently so transactions often involve decisions by high-level managers	• Buildings (offices, factories) • Fixed equipment (water towers, baking ovens) • Accessory equipment (computers, airplanes)

CLASSIFYING ORGANIZATIONAL PRODUCTS

Depending on how much they cost and how they will be used, organizational products can be divided into three categories: *production items, expense items*, and *capital items*. These are explained in Table 12.3.

The Product Mix

The group of products that a company makes available for sale, whether consumer, industrial, or both, is its **product mix**. Black+Decker makes toasters, vacuum cleaners, electric drills, and a variety of other appliances, tools and, more recently (based on the popular Bob the Builder wave), children's toys.

Many companies begin with a single product. Over time, they find that the initial product fails to suit every customer shopping for the product type. To meet market demand, they introduce similar products. For example, Starbucks, expanded their line of coffees by adding various Italian-style espresso beverages, including mochas, cappuccinos, lattes (hot and iced), and flavoured blended cremes. A group of products that are closely related because they function in a similar manner (e.g., flavoured coffees) or are sold to the same customer group (e.g., stop-in coffee drinkers) who will use them in similar ways is a **product line**.

PRODUCT MIX A group of products that a firm makes available for sale.

PRODUCT LINE A group of products that are closely related because they function in a similar manner or are sold to the same customer group who will use them in similar ways.

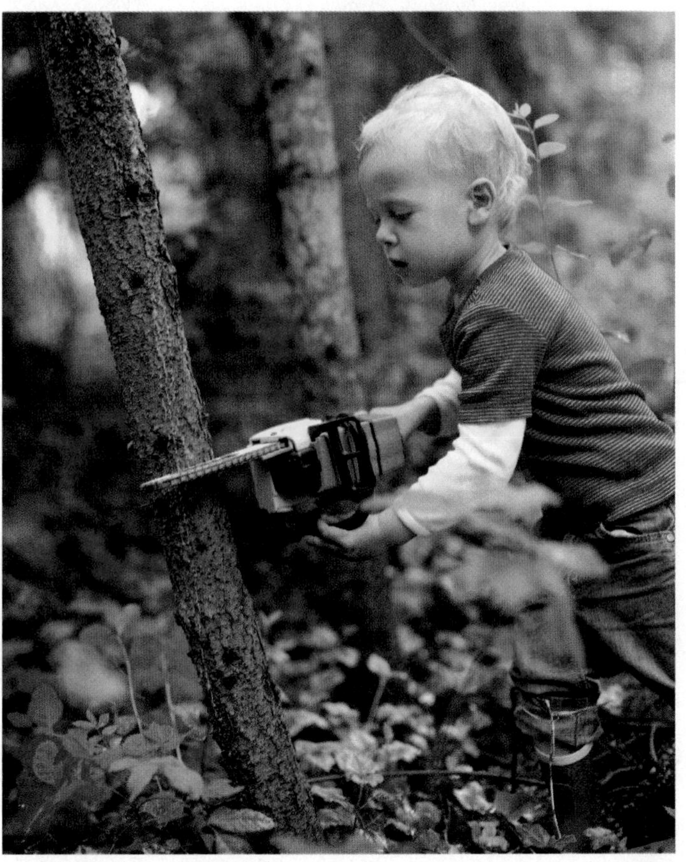

Black+Decker has a wide range of product categories, but one fairly recent addition has proven quite successful. The company now sells branded toy replicas to kids so they can catch the do-it-yourself bug at a young age.

Stephen Lux/Cultura/Alamy

LO-8 DEVELOPING NEW PRODUCTS AND BRANDING

To expand or diversify product lines—in fact, just to survive—firms must develop and introduce streams of new products. Faced with competition and shifting customer preferences, no firm can count on a single successful product to carry it forever.

Famous Product and Brand Failures	Reasons for Failure
Qwikster	Is this the biggest product failure since New Coke? When Netflix announced that it was splitting its online streaming and DVD mail service, consumers were outraged. The DVD-by-mail service was going to be called Qwikster, but the outrage over the loss of convenience and increased prices led to the loss of about 800 000 customers. Netflix ultimately reversed the decision and killed the Qwikster brand.
Pepsi Blue	Despite a good marketing campaign linked to hip-hop artists, the X-games, and the March Madness Basketball tournament, Pepsi Blue was a failure. The ultimate test for any product is consumer response; Pepsi's Blue cola did not taste or look right and consumers rejected it.
Toshiba's HD DVD	Consider the battle between Toshiba (HD DVD) and Sony (Blu-ray) for global dominance in the format of high-definition DVDs. Both companies invested millions of dollars, and experts predicted that there would be a long fight between the two companies. But in less than two years, Toshiba gave up and stopped producing its product. Why? Because Sony was successful in convincing movie studios like Warner to release movies only in Blu-ray. Major retail outlets like Walmart and Netflix also announced they would only sell Blu-ray. [4]
New Coke	This example dates back over 30 years but teaches a big lesson in marketing research. At the time, Coke reformulated its century-old flagship brand to deal with the threat of Pepsi. The new beverage tested well in research labs but consumers did not realize that Coke was going to replace its original formula. The new formula was launched, the public was outraged, and the company quickly came back with Coca-Cola Classic.
XFL	Vince McMahon (the founder of WWE wrestling) founded the XFL to compete indirectly with the NFL. There were great gimmicks and exciting camera angles but consumers were not fooled. The league quickly folded because the ultimate product was inferior.

FIGURE 12.4 Recent and classic product failures

The New Product Development Process

Product development is a long and expensive process. Many top firms invest heavily in their research and development (R&D) departments to explore new product possibilities. One company is consistently at the top of that list. It is estimated that 3M has invented over 50 000 products ranging from Scotch Tape to stethoscopes.[21] Of course, it is not alone. Cisco Systems recently invested approximately $4 billion into its R&D facilities in Ontario (creating an expected 1700 jobs in the process).[22]

It is estimated that it takes 50 new ideas to generate one product that finally reaches the market. Even then, only a few products become successful. Those with the best chances are innovative and deliver unique benefits ("me too" products often fade into the background). In addition, by introducing new products ahead of competitors, companies can establish market leadership. How important is *speed to market*? One study reports that a product that is only three months late to market (three months behind the leader) loses 12 percent of its lifetime profit potential. At six months, it will lose 33 percent.

Take a look at Figure 12.4 for some recent and some classic examples of spectacular product failures.

THE SEVEN-STEP DEVELOPMENT PROCESS

To increase their chances of developing successful new products or services, many firms use a basic seven-step process. Steps 2, 3, 4, 6, and 7 are the same for both products and services, but there are some differences in Steps 1 and 5.

1. *Product ideas.* Product development begins with a search for ideas for new products. Product ideas can come from consumers, the sales force, research and development, or engineering. As we saw in the opening case, Procter & Gamble has invented hundreds of products including many category firsts: household detergent, fluoride toothpaste (Crest), stackable chips (Pringles), and a time-saving cleaning system (Swiffer). The company has over 1000 PhDs among its 8000 employees located in 26 research facilities around the world.[23]

2. *Screening.* This stage is an attempt to eliminate all product ideas that do not mesh with the firm's abilities, expertise, or objectives. Representatives from marketing, engineering, and production must have input at this stage.
3. *Concept testing.* Once ideas have been initially reviewed, companies use market research to solicit consumers' input. Firms can identify benefits that the product must provide, as well as an appropriate price level for the product.
4. *Business analysis.* This involves developing a comparison of costs and benefits for the proposed product. Preliminary sales projections are compared with cost projections from finance and production to determine whether the product can meet minimum profitability goals.
5. *Prototype development.* Using input from the concept-testing phase, engineering and/or research and development produce a preliminary version of the product. Prototypes can be extremely expensive, often requiring extensive hand crafting, tooling, and development of components, but this phase can help identify potential production problems.
6. *Product testing and test marketing.* The company begins limited production of the item. If the product meets performance requirements, it is made available for sale in limited areas (test markets). This stage is very costly, since promotional campaigns and distribution channels must be established. Test marketing gives a company its first information on how consumers will respond to a product under real market conditions.
7. *Commercialization.* If test-marketing results are positive, the company will begin full-scale production and marketing of the product. Gradual commercialization, with the firm moving the product into more and more areas over time, reduces stress on the firm's initial production capabilities, but delays in commercialization may give competitors a chance to bring out their own version.

For a modern look on new product development take a look at the Entrepreneurship and New Ventures box entitled "This Business is Appsolutely Booming."

Product Life Cycle

When a product reaches the market, it enters the **product life cycle (PLC)**, a series of stages through which it passes during its commercial

PRODUCT LIFE CYCLE (PLC) A series of stages in a product's commercial life.

ENTREPRENEURSHIP AND NEW VENTURES

This Business Is Appsolutely Booming

"Hamburger buttons," "swipe," "edge gesture," and "pull to refresh" are just a few of the features provided by application (app) developers to make it easier to use your favourite apps. With an untold number of apps already available, a still-growing demand has created a genuine cottage industry. With product development underway at large firms such as Google and Apple, other smaller, home-based app developers and high- and low-tech entrepreneurs are making successful careers in this booming industry.

Jean Whitehead

For example, 28-year-old Loren Brichter has quietly risen to a position of renown—"a high priest of app design"—among app developers. In 2007 he started his own app-development company—Atebits. He is credited with creating user-friendly features that are now standard in many apps, such as the "cell swipe" that uncovers hidden buttons, sliding panels from the side of the screen, and the "pull to refresh" feature, among others. With a degree in electrical engineering, Brichter started his career at Apple working on the iPhone technology. He later created the Tweetie app (including the "pull to refresh" feature), which along with Brichter's Atebits was purchased by Twitter. The selling price Brichter received for Atebits was reported to be in the "single millions." Most recently, Brichter is focusing on the gaming side of app development.

In contrast to Brichter's high-tech orientation, others with "non-tech" backgrounds also have become apps entrepreneurs. From his many travels, Mike Vichich, a 28-year-old business consultant, saw the possibilities for a new iPhone app to track credit-card rewards and to get the most value from his accumulated credit-card points. Although he understood the business side of the apps industry (Vichich has a business education), he had no technical background for understanding how to develop an app.

He soon discovered several sources for getting started. For beginners, simple apps can be built using online tools, such as Appypie.com, ViziApps.com, and AppMakr by reading text and data into online templates. A more technical getting-started option is attending one of the intensive short courses to learn computer coding for developing mobile apps. Another, more expensive option is to hire a professional programmer or coding language specialist on contract, or as an employee.

Vichich started on his own three-month crash course, enough to learn the basics. He then recruited an app developer and found investors who provided $500 000 start-up capital—and Glyph, the iPhone app he envisioned, became available at the App Store.

The successes of Brichter and Vichich illustrate that visions for new products can stem from two different orientations, one technology-based, the other business- or user-based. Entrepreneurship occurs with the awareness that, by combining both orientations, innovative products will emerge for eager consumers.

CRITICAL THINKING QUESTIONS

1. Does the product development process differ from the traditional process we would use in creating a new type of physical product?

life. Depending on the product's ability to attract and keep customers, its PLC may be a matter of months, years, or decades. Strong, mature products (such as Coca-Cola and H&R Block) have had long, productive lives.

STAGES IN THE PLC

The life cycle for both goods and services is a natural process in which products are born, grow in stature, mature, and finally decline and die. Look at the two graphics in Figure 12.5. In (a), the four phases of the PLC are applied to several products with which you are familiar:

1. *Introduction.* This stage begins when the product reaches the marketplace. Marketers focus on making potential customers aware of the product and its benefits. Because of extensive promotional and development costs, profits are nonexistent. But the use of modern media tools like Twitter and YouTube is providing cost-efficient alternatives for companies to generate attention and buzz.
2. *Growth.* If the new product attracts and satisfies enough consumers, sales begin to climb rapidly. During this stage, the product begins to show a profit. Other firms in the industry move speedily to introduce their own versions. Heavy promotion is often required to build brand preference over the competition.
3. *Maturity.* Sales growth starts to slow. Although the product earns its highest profit level early in this stage, increased competition eventually forces price-cutting, increasing advertising and promotional expenditures and lowering profits. Toward the end of the stage, sales start to fall.
4. *Decline.* Sales and profits continue to fall, as new products in the introduction stage take away sales. Firms end or reduce promotional support (ads and salespeople), but may let the product linger to provide some profits.

Figure 12.5(b) plots the relationship of the PLC to a product's typical profits or losses. Although the early stages of the PLC often show financial losses, increased sales for successful products recover earlier losses and continue to generate profits until the decline stage. For many products, profitable life spans are short—hence the importance put by so many firms on the constant replenishment of product lines.

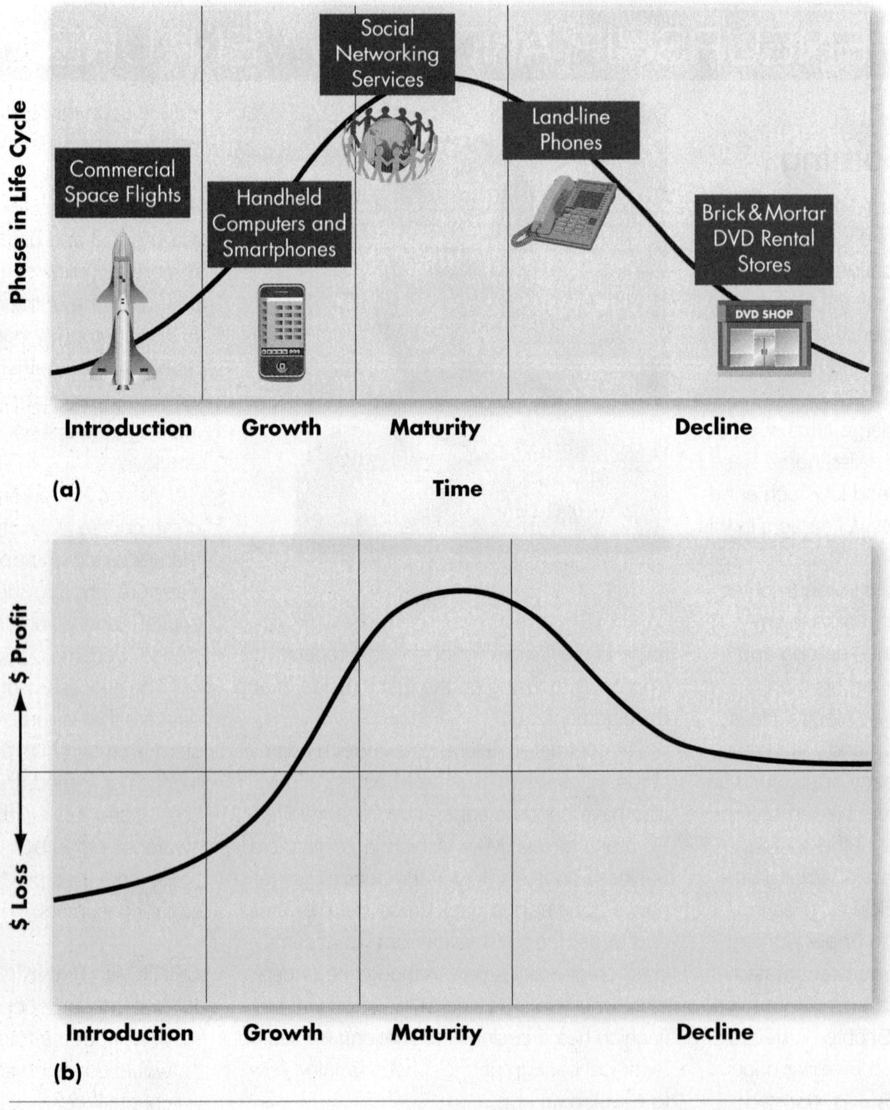

FIGURE 12.5 Products in the life cycle: (a) phases and (b) profit (or loss)

EXTENDING PRODUCT LIFE: AN ALTERNATIVE TO NEW PRODUCTS

Companies try to keep products in the maturity stage as long as they can. Over the years, sales of TV sets, for example, have been revitalized by such feature changes as colour, portability, miniaturization, stereo capability, high definition, and 3-D. Companies can extend product life through a number of creative means. Foreign markets offer three possibilities for lengthening product life cycles:

1. In *product extension*, an existing product is marketed globally; Coca-Cola is a prime example of international product extensions.
2. With *product adaptation*, the product is modified for greater appeal in different countries. In Germany, a McDonald's meal includes beer; in Japan, Ford puts the steering wheel on the right side. After Kraft Foods changed the shape of the traditional round Oreo Cookie to be long and thin (and coated the cookie in chocolate), it became the best-selling cookie in China. The new shape is also sold in Canada.[24]
3. *Reintroduction* means reviving, for new markets, products that are becoming obsolete in older ones. NCR has reintroduced manually operated cash registers in Latin America.

Identifying Products: Branding and Packaging

Marketers must also identify products so that consumers recognize them. Two important tools for this task are branding and packaging/labelling.

BRANDING PRODUCTS

Branding is the use of symbols to communicate the qualities of a particular product made by a particular producer. Coca-Cola might be the best-known brand in the world. Some Coke executives claim that if all the company's other assets were destroyed, they could go to the bank and borrow $100 billion on the strength of the brand name alone. According to Millward Brown Optimor, which creates the BrandZ Top 100 Global Brands Ranking, the Coke brand is worth over $80 billion.[25] Industry observers regard brands as a company's most valuable asset.[26] In 2014, technology companies were at the top of the brand value list: #1 Google, #2 Apple, and #3 IBM. Three Canadian brands made the Top 100: #38 RBC, #47 TD, and #89 Scotiabank.[27]

Kellogg's recently purchased the Pringles potato chip brand and its assets from Procter & Gamble for US$2.7 billion. Procter & Gamble is turning its focus to household goods and beauty and personal care products; Pringles was the last remaining asset in its food business. For Kellogg's, the purchase helps solidify the company as the fourth-largest maker of sweet and savoury snacks in the world. Having a powerful brand like Pringles on its roster will help as the company tries to gain more sales in international markets.[28]

^ The Coca-Cola brand has been consistently at or near the top of brand rankings. It is instantly recognizable worldwide.

Jens Kalaene/picture alliance/ZB/Newscom

ADDING VALUE THROUGH BRAND EQUITY

Brand equity is the added value a brand name provides to a product beyond its basic functional benefits. Widely known and admired brands are valuable because of their power to attract customers. Those with higher brand equity generate greater brand awareness and loyalty on the part of consumers, have larger market shares than competing brands, and are perceived to have greater quality.

GAINING BRAND AWARENESS

The expensive, sometimes fierce, struggle for brand recognition is a growing concern in most industries. Today, marketers are finding more effective, less expensive ways to gain brand awareness. Recent successes have been found with several methods, including product placement, buzz marketing, and viral marketing and social networking.

Product Placement Television commercials can be a real turn-off for many viewers, but entertainment programming gets our full attention. And that's when marketers are turning up the promotional juice with **product placement**—a promotional tactic for brand exposure in which characters in television, film, music, magazines, or video games use a real product with a brand visible to viewers. A couple of years ago, Canada Goose was thrilled to be front and centre in the *Sports Illustrated* Swimsuit Edition as model Kate Upton posed in one of their jackets for a shoot in Antarctica.[29]

Product placements are effective because the message is delivered in an attractive setting that holds the customer's interest. When used in successful films and TV shows, the brand's association with famous performers is an implied celebrity endorsement. The idea is to legitimize the brand in the mind of the customer. In all, nearly $5 billion is spent annually on product placements, especially on television, and major marketers are putting more into product placements than advertisements in that medium.

Buzz Marketing One method for increasing brand awareness is **buzz marketing**, which relies on word of mouth to spread "buzz" about

BRANDING A process of using symbols to communicate the qualities of a product made by a particular producer.

BRAND EQUITY The added value a brand name provides to a product beyond its basic functional benefits.

PRODUCT PLACEMENT A promotional tactic for brand exposure in which characters in television, film, music, magazines, or video games use a real product with its brand visible to viewers.

BUZZ MARKETING Marketing that relies on word of mouth to spread "buzz" about a particular product or idea.

The very nature of GoPro's durable, high-tech video recorders (crash cams) makes them perfect for creating content and generating buzz for organizations (not to mention for GoPro itself).

JULIAN STRATENSCHULTE/dpa/Alamy

a particular product or idea. Buzz marketing agencies provide volunteer participants with new products to try and ask them to share the buzz with their friends, family, co-workers, and others in their social network. Here's the key—most companies running word-of-mouth campaigns require full disclosure, which means the participants should let people know they are participating in a campaign. This is essential so that those on the receiving end of the "buzz" don't feel tricked or taken advantage of.

Viral Marketing and Social Networking **Viral marketing** is buzz that relies on social networking on the internet to spread information "like a virus" from person to person. Messages about new cars, sports events, and numerous other goods and services flow via networks among potential customers who pass the information on to others. Using various social network formats—games, contests, blogs, and so on—marketers encourage potential customers to try out products and tell other people about them.

How effective can it be? Viral marketing can lead to consumer awareness faster and with wider reach than traditional media messages—and at lower cost. It works for two reasons. First, people rely on the internet for information they used to get from newspapers, magazines, and television. Equally important, however, is the interactive element: the customer becomes a participant in the process of spreading the word by forwarding information to other internet users.

TYPES OF BRAND NAMES

National brands are those produced and distributed by the manufacturer across an entire country (e.g., Chips Ahoy). When a company with a well-known brand sells another company the right to place that brand on its products, these are called *licensed brands*. Harley-Davidson's famous logo—emblazoned on boots, eyewear, gloves, purses, lighters, and watches—brings the motorcycle maker more than $210 million annually. Along with brands such as Coors and Ferrari, licensing for character-based brands like Spider-Man is equally lucrative.

Private brands carry the retailer's own brand name, even though they are manufactured by another firm. Loblaw Companies Ltd. created a line of upscale products under the private brand President's Choice (PC). If you want Loblaws' famous PC Decadent chocolate chip cookies, you need to visit a Loblaws outlet or one of its subsidiaries. These brands are often 25 percent cheaper for consumers and yet the profit margins tend to be 15 percent higher for the company. This is a clear win-win scenario.[30]

Generic brands are also gaining more shelf space; they are the products that you see in grocery stores that simply state a category name like "bacon" or "peanut butter." If you've been to Costco recently, you may have picked up its very popular generic chocolate chip cookies. Major retailers are carrying fewer national brands and more of their own private brands as well as these less-expensive, no-frills generic brands.

Packaging Products

Except for products like fresh fruits and vegetables and structural steel, almost all products need some form of **packaging** so they can be transported to the market. Packaging also serves several other functions—it is an in-store advertisement that makes the product attractive; it clearly displays the brand; it identifies product features and benefits; and it reduces the risk of damage, breakage, or spoilage. The package is the marketer's last chance to say "buy me" to the consumer. Maison Orphée, a Quebec City–based maker of oils, mustards, sea salts, and vinegars, took the advice of consultants and redesigned their packaging with slimmer bottles and a high-end label design. The result was a 70 percent increase in sales without a dime spent on traditional advertising.[31] Packaging counts!

Labelling Products

Every product has a **label** on its package. Like packaging, labelling can help market the product. First, it identifies the product or the brand, such as the name "Campbell" on a can of soup or "Chiquita" on a banana. Labels also promote products by getting consumers' attention. Attractive colours and graphics provide visual cues to products that otherwise might be overlooked on the shelf. Finally, the label describes the product by providing information about nutritional content, directions for use, proper disposal, and safety.

The federal government regulates the information on package labels. The *Consumer Packaging and Labelling Act* has two main purposes: first, to provide a comprehensive set of rules for packaging and labelling of consumer products; second, to ensure that manufacturers provide full and factual information on labels. All pre-packaged products must state in French and English the quantity enclosed in metric units, as well as the name and description of the product.

VIRAL MARKETING Buzz that relies on social networking on the internet to spread information "like a virus" from person to person.

NATIONAL BRANDS Products distributed by and carrying a name associated with the manufacturer.

PRIVATE BRANDS Products promoted by and carrying a name associated with the retailer or wholesaler, not the manufacturer.

GENERIC BRANDS No-frills products sold under the general category name rather than a specific company name.

PACKAGING Physical container in which a product is sold, advertised, or protected.

LABEL That part of a product's packaging that identifies the product's name and contents and sometimes its benefits.

MyBizLab

Study, practise, and explore real business situations with these helpful resources:

- **Interactive Lesson Presentations:** Work through interactive presentations and assessments to test your knowledge of business concepts.
- **Study Plan:** Check your understanding of chapter concepts with self-study quizzes.
- **Dynamic Study Modules:** Work through adaptive study modules on your computer, tablet, or mobile device.
- **Simulations:** Practise decision-making in simulated business environments.
- **Videos:** Learn more about the business practices and strategies of real companies.

SUMMARY OF LEARNING OBJECTIVES

LO-1 EXPLAIN THE CONCEPT OF *MARKETING* AND IDENTIFY THE FIVE FORCES THAT CONSTITUTE THE *EXTERNAL MARKETING ENVIRONMENT*.

Marketing is responsible for creating, communicating, and delivering value and satisfaction to customers at a profit. Marketing manages customer relationships to benefit the organization and its stakeholders. After identifying customers' needs and wants, it develops plans to satisfy them by creating products, and establishing their prices, methods for distributing them, and ways of promoting them to potential customers. Marketing is successful if satisfied buyers perceive that the benefits derived from each purchase outweigh its costs, and if the firm, in exchange for providing the products, meets its organizational goals. Five outside factors make up a company's external environment and influence its marketing programs: (1) *political and legal actions,* (2) *socio-cultural factors,* (3) *technological changes,* (4) *economics, and* (5) *competition.*

LO-2 EXPLAIN THE PURPOSE OF A *MARKETING PLAN* AND IDENTIFY THE FOUR COMPONENTS OF THE *MARKETING MIX*.

The marketing plan is a detailed strategy for focusing marketing efforts on meeting consumer needs and wants. The plan defines the organization's marketing goals, and identifies all the activities for reaching those goals that will result in the successful transfer of goods and services to its customers. In planning and implementing strategies, marketing managers focus on the four elements (Four P's) of the marketing mix: (1) *products for consumers*, (2) *pricing of products*, (3) *place (distribution) of products to consumers*, *and* (4) *promotion of products.*

LO-3 EXPLAIN *MARKET SEGMENTATION* AND HOW IT IS USED IN *TARGET MARKETING* AND *POSITIONING*.

Marketers think in terms of target markets—groups of people or organizations with similar wants and needs and who can be expected to show interest in the same products. Target marketing requires *market segmentation*—dividing a market into categories of customer types or "segments." Members of a market segment must share some common traits that influence purchasing decisions. Once they identify segments, companies adopt a variety of strategies for attracting customers in one or more of the chosen target segments. The following are *five variables used for segmentation:* (1) *Demographic variables* describe populations by identifying such traits as age, income, gender, ethnic background, and marital status. (2) *Geographic variables* are the geographical units that may be considered in developing a segmentation strategy. (3) *Geo-demographic variables* combine demographic variables with geographic variables, such as an age category coupled with urban areas. (4) *Psychographic variables* include lifestyles, interests, and attitudes. (5) *Behavioural* variables include benefit sought, user status, usage rate, loyalty status, and occasion for use.

LO-4 DISCUSS THE PURPOSE OF *MARKETING RESEARCH*, AND COMPARE MARKETING RESEARCH METHODS.

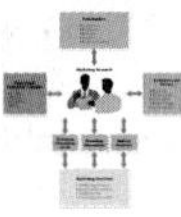

Market research is the study of what buyers need and the best ways to meet those needs. This process involves (1) *studying the current situation*, (2) *selecting a research method*, (3) *collecting and analyzing data, and* (4) *preparing the report*. The four most common research methods are *observation*, *surveys*, *focus groups*, *and experimentation*.

LO-5 DESCRIBE THE *CONSUMER BUYING PROCESS* AND THE KEY FACTORS THAT INFLUENCE THAT PROCESS.

One consumer behaviour model considers five influences that lead to consumption: (1) *Problem/need recognition:* The buying process begins when the consumer recognizes a problem or need. (2) *Information seeking:* Having recognized a need, consumers seek information. The information search leads to a consideration set—a group of products they will consider buying. (3) *Evaluation of alternatives:* By analyzing product attributes (price, prestige, quality) of the consideration set, consumers compare products to decide which product best meets their needs. (4) *Purchase decision:* "Buy" decisions are based on rational motives, emotional motives, or both. (5) *Post-purchase evaluations:* Consumers continue to form opinions after their purchase. Marketers want consumers to be happy after the consumption of products so that they are more likely to buy them again.

LO-6 DISCUSS THE THREE CATEGORIES OF *ORGANIZATIONAL MARKETS*, AND THE CHARACTERISTICS OF BUSINESS-TO-BUSINESS (B2B) BUYING BEHAVIOUR.

(1) The *industrial market* consists of businesses that buy goods to be converted into other products or that are used during production. This market includes farmers, manufacturers, and some retailers. (2) Before products reach consumers, they pass through a *reseller market* consisting of intermediaries—wholesalers and retailers—that buy finished goods and resell them. (3) The government and *institutional market* includes federal, provincial, and local governments, and non-governmental buyers—hospitals, religious organizations, and charities—that purchase goods and services needed for serving their clients. Taken together, these organizational markets annually do more than twice the business of the consumer markets.

LO-7 EXPLAIN THE DEFINITION OF A PRODUCT AS A *VALUE PACKAGE*, AND CLASSIFY *GOODS AND SERVICES*.

Customers buy products to receive value that satisfies a want or a need. Thus, a successful product is a *value package*—a bundle of attributes that, taken together, provides the right features and offers the right benefits that satisfy customers' wants and needs. Features are the qualities, tangible and intangible, that are included with the product. To be satisfying, features must provide benefits that allow customers to achieve the end results they want. The value package has services and features that add value by providing benefits that increase the customer's satisfaction.

Products (both *goods and services*) can be classified according to expected buyers as either *consumer products (convenience*, *shopping*, *and specialty goods)* or *organizational products (production items*, *expense items*, *or capital items)*.

LO-8 DESCRIBE THE KEY CONSIDERATIONS IN THE NEW *PRODUCT DEVELOPMENT PROCESS*, AND EXPLAIN THE IMPORTANCE OF *BRANDING AND PACKAGING*.

To expand or diversify product lines, new products must be developed and introduced. Many firms have research and development (R&D) departments for continuously exploring new product possibilities, because high mortality rates for new ideas result in only a few new products reaching the market. Even then, only a few of these survivors become successful products. *Speed to market*—how fast a firm responds with new products or market changes—determines a product's profitability and success. A continuous product development process is necessary because every product has a product life cycle—a series of stages through which it passes during its commercial life. The development of new products, then, is the source for renewal of the firm's product offerings in the marketplace.

Branding and *packaging* identify products so that consumers recognize them. Branding is the use of names and symbols, like "Coca-Cola" or McDonald's golden arches, to communicate the qualities of a particular product made by a particular producer. The goal in developing a brand is to distinguish a product from others so that consumers develop a preference for that particular brand name. Most products need some form of packaging—a physical container in which it is sold, advertised, or protected. A package makes the product attractive, displays the brand name, and identifies features and benefits. It also reduces the risk of damage, breakage, or spoilage, and it lessens the likelihood of theft.

QUESTIONS AND EXERCISES

QUESTIONS FOR ANALYSIS

1. What does *brand equity* mean and how do companies like Apple take advantage of their strong brand equity?
2. Select a good or service that you have purchased recently. Try to retrace the relevant steps in the buyer decision process as you experienced it. Which steps were most important to you?
3. What are the various classifications of consumer and industrial products? Give an example of a good and a service for each category other than those discussed in this text.
4. How is the concept of the value package useful in marketing to consumers and industrial customers?
5. Why has the in-store use of hidden cameras become so popular? Is this "video mining" ethical? If not, how could it be made more acceptable?
6. Some companies have very narrow product mixes, producing just one or two products, while others have many different products. What are the advantages of each approach?

APPLICATION EXERCISES

7. Identify a company with a product that interests you. Consider ways the company could use customer relationship management (CRM) to strengthen relationships with its target market. Specifically, explain your recommendations on how the company can use each of the four basic components of the marketing mix in its CRM efforts.
8. Select a product made by a foreign company and sold in Canada. What is the product's target market? What is the basis on which the target market is segmented? Do you think that this basis is appropriate? How might another approach, if any, be beneficial? Why?
9. Choose a product that could benefit from word-of-mouth buzz marketing. Then create a marketing campaign kit for participants to spread the word about this product.
10. Interview the manager of a local manufacturing firm. Identify the company's different products according to their positions in the product life cycle.

TEAM EXERCISES

BUILDING YOUR BUSINESS SKILLS

THE GREAT OUTDOORS

GOAL

To understand the product and pricing strategy decisions made by marketers.

BACKGROUND INFORMATION

You and your team have been hired as consultants by a manufacturer that has been making camping equipment for more than a century. Although their original target market was gold miners and loggers, they primarily sell to recreational campers. The company has a long history of quality, long-lasting products with few frills, including tents, sleeping bags, lanterns, and camp stoves.

METHOD

Step 1 Working with your group, brainstorm how the company might make their products more appealing to recreational campers today. Be creative and think outside the box. How could the company make their tents, sleeping bags, lanterns, and camp stoves more exciting and desirable?

Step 2 The company's marketing manager has suggested that the company branch out into other products for camping beyond the company's long established product line. Work with your group to develop a list of products that the company should consider selling. Don't filter your suggestions; try to develop a long and detailed list.

Step 3 As a group, determine which new products as well as modifications to existing products hold the most promise and develop a recommendation that you present to your client.

FOLLOW-UP QUESTIONS

1. How do you think the market for camping equipment has changed over the last 50 years? How did this influence your decision making?
2. As you developed your list of new products, which wants and needs of the target market were most important?
3. What pricing strategy should the company use for their existing products?
4. What pricing strategy should the company use for their new products? Is skimming or penetration more appropriate?

EXERCISING YOUR ETHICS

MAKING A TOUGH CALL

THE SITUATION

You are the quality control manager for a major dietary supplement company. Because your products are sold over the counter as nutritional supplements rather than as medications, you are not regulated by Health Canada. Researchers have worked for years to develop a weight-loss product that is safe and effective. Several years ago, researchers identified a naturally occurring compound that was effective in appetite suppression. Your company has done several years of testing, and you have found that 85 percent of people using the supplement were able to lose at least 20 pounds in the first year of use. Additionally, those who continued to take the supplement were able to maintain their weight loss for an additional year. Company executives believe that this drug can bring billions of dollars in revenues in the first year of sales. Obesity has become an epidemic, and much of the developed world and people who are obese are at a significantly greater risk of stroke, heart attack, and diabetes.

THE DILEMMA

You are reviewing the results of the clinical trials and pleased to see the product is effective. Just as you become ready to recommend that the company introduce the product to the market, you uncover upsetting information. A small group of people who took the supplement during testing, actually less than 1 percent, developed a rare neurological disorder. It's not clear that the supplement was the cause, but the disorder was not observed in the control group that took a placebo. Because the risk is so small, the marketing manager is recommending that the company go ahead with introducing the supplement and monitor to see if consumers report a similar side effect. Commercialization of this product could make your company profitable and could save thousands of lives by helping consumers lose weight, but you are unsure if this is the right thing to do.

QUESTIONS TO ADDRESS

1. How would you characterize the particular ethical issues in this situation?
2. From an ethical standpoint, what are the obligations of the quality control manager and the marketing manager regarding the introduction of the product in this situation?
3. If you were the quality control manager, how would you handle this matter?

BUSINESS CASE 12

THE CAR BRANDING GAME: TWO COMPANIES, TWO BRANDS, ONE PLATFORM

© Jim West/Alamy

AP Photo/Richard Drew

The Scion FRS outsells the Subaru BRZ by a ratio of approximately two to one. Why is that significant? They are essentially identical twins. What's in a brand name? Why do people choose one product over another? When you choose between two items, how much of your decision is based on the brand's reputation and how much is based on the actual features? If you had to choose between two cars with identical features, how would the brand make the difference?

In order to reduce new product development costs, companies are using many techniques, including outsourcing and even partnerships with competing brands. This is especially true in the automobile sector, where development is long and costs are high. Recently, Toyota (which owns the Scion brand) and Subaru teamed up their engineering capabilities to create one new sports car and sell it under two different brand names: the Subaru BRZ and the Scion FRS.

OUTSOURCING

Outsourcing is a popular cost- and time-reduction technique in the auto sector; it involves farming out some or all of the development and manufacturing process to external companies. Magna International (headquartered in Aurora, Ontario) is a company that many manufacturers turn to for solutions. Magna was founded in 1957, but today has 316 manufacturing and 87 product development facilities in 29 countries. Here are just a few examples of Magna's product content solutions in the car industry:

- *Dodge Caravan.* Door panels and transmission components
- *Mercedes Benz M-Class.* Body structure stamping and assembly
- *Lincoln MKZ.* Engine, underbody stamping, and assembly
- *BMW X3.* Full vehicle assembly, original engineering design

DIRECT PARTNERSHIPS

Some companies have created joint ventures and built common manufacturing plants with competitors to assemble their vehicles (e.g., Toyota and Peugeot Citroen in the Czech Republic). In order to truly leverage strengths, some companies even make the ultimate commitment and merge (Renault-Nissan). This latest "project" partnership between Subaru and Toyota (Scion) enables these companies to share their expertise to build a better car. Scion is strong in design, geared for Generation Y drivers, and Subaru is famous for its advanced technology and the symmetrical all-wheel-drive system.

BRAND EQUITY

Why do people pay premium prices for a Louis Vuitton purse or a Mercedes car? The material is top quality, but we all know that the cost to manufacture does not fully justify the extra price. People are willing to pay extra for a brand logo, for the positive association, for the status granted, and for the image. In the case of Toyota and Subaru, the two cars are the same, so which would you buy if you had the choice, the Subaru or the Scion? Most consumers will never know the truth about these cars, but you do. Your answer will be based on the brand you value more. There is no other rational basis for comparison in this case. However, if you did not know the truth, your perception of each brand might blur your opinions. One thing is clear: both companies believed they could produce a better product at a lower base cost by teaming up. However, the market will decide their long-term fate.

QUESTIONS FOR DISCUSSION

1. What lessons about product development does this case demonstrate?
2. Why might it be advantageous for competitors to cooperate in the development of new products? Provide additional product examples.
3. Why would consumers be willing to pay a higher price for a product that is essentially identical to one with a lower price?

Jakub Jirsák/Fotolia

AFTER READING THIS CHAPTER, YOU SHOULD BE ABLE TO:

LO-1 Identify the various *pricing objectives* that govern pricing decisions, and describe the *price-setting tools* used in making these decisions

LO-2 Discuss *pricing strategies* that can be used for different competitive situations and identify the *pricing tactics* that can be used for setting prices.

LO-3 Identify the important *objectives of promotion* and discuss the considerations in selecting a *promotional mix*.

LO-4 Define the *role of advertising* and describe the key *advertising media*.

LO-5 Outline the tasks involved in *personal selling*, describe the various types of *sales promotions*, describe *direct (or interactive) marketing*, and distinguish between *publicity* and *public relations*.

LO-6 Explain the *distribution mix* and identify the different *channels of distribution*.

LO-7 Describe the role of *intermediaries*. Explain the functions of *wholesalers* and identify the types of *retailers* and *e-intermediaries*.

LO-8 Describe the *physical distribution process*.

Premium Pricing, Rising Market Share

In the past decade Canadian yogurt consumption has been increasing by approximately 3.3 percent per year, according to the Dairy Farmers of Canada. In the fight for supremacy, something interesting has been occurring and it is not exactly a new product that is leading the way (unless you believe products that have been around for centuries are new). What's old is now new in yogurt aisles, and leading the revolution is the Greek yogurt category. Greek yogurt already accounted for 25 percent of the Canadian market, by volume, at the beginning of 2014. Capturing one-quarter of the market in only a few years is staggering. In in its first year alone, the President's Choice Greek brand became the number-one seller at Loblaws.

To truly understand the potential for additional growth, we can look south of the border, where the Greek yogurt craze started two years earlier than in Canada and achieved a 13 percent market share in just three years (it took energy drinks twice as long to get an equivalent share of the beverage market). At the time, Consumer Edge Research predicted that the category could actually capture as much as half of the U.S. market, worth $9 billion by 2015. They were wrong! Sales reached that milestone in 2014. These numbers are all impressive, but what is even more spectacular is that this product is usually sold in smaller packages for significantly higher premium prices than regular yogurt.

With all this potential, it seems like everyone is trying to take advantage of the trend. Even Ben & Jerry's

Pricing, Promoting, *and* Distributing Products

CHAPTER 13

Darrin Henry/Fotolia

Africa Studio/Fotolia

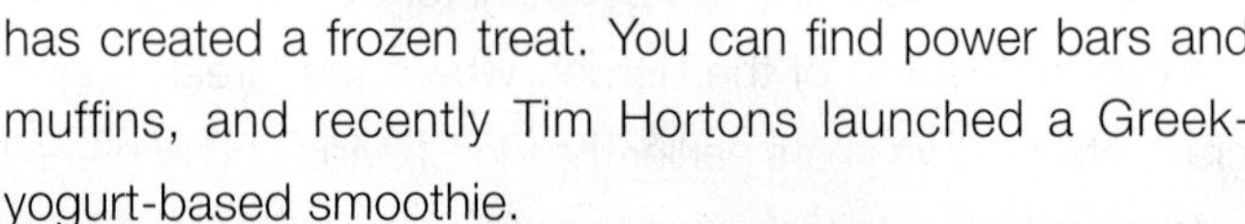

has created a frozen treat. You can find power bars and muffins, and recently Tim Hortons launched a Greek-yogurt-based smoothie.

It All Starts with a Good Product

The success of this subcategory is based on some very solid fundamentals. The product fits in well with the increased trend toward healthy living and eating habits. People are willing to pay more for good, healthy products, and, in this case, the creamier taste is not created by artificial flavours or unhealthy ingredients. Rather, Greek yogurt is unique because it is strained using a cheesecloth filter to remove the liquid. That is why it is thicker and has a different texture that consumers seem to appreciate.

Spreading the Word

As for any great launch, marketing has been a key ingredient in the product's success. In Canada, the President's Choice brand was supported by a significant marketing campaign. Liberté brand launched with an emphasis on health and conducted sampling events and taste tests in gyms and other health-related venues. The Skotidakis brand invested in billboard ads to get the word out. Down south, Chobani is the market leader ahead of Fage (an authentic imported Greek brand). Chobani used a truck it called the "Chomobile," which travelled around promoting the health benefits of its yogurt and supplying samples.

These approaches built up the initial buzz, but it is clear that the stakes are rising along with the popularity. Danone (the French multinational) recently invested in a mass-marketing campaign for a Super Bowl advertisement (featuring John Stamos) for its Oikos Greek yogurt brand. This was a clear signal that this niche had transformed into a major multibillion-dollar segment.

HOW WILL THIS HELP ME?

To become the number-one brand or retailer in any market takes a solid understanding of how best to set prices, reach market-share objectives, promote and distribute products to customers, and, ultimately, achieve profits. This chapter examines those topics, and the different types of intermediaries involved with an emphasis on wholesalers and retailers. It also highlights how the online marketplace has changed the nature of how companies do business. By understanding methods for pricing, distributing, and promoting products, you'll be more prepared to evaluate a company's marketing programs, distribution methods, and competitive potential.

As we saw in Chapter 12, product development managers decide which products a company will offer to its customers. In this chapter, we'll look at three of the four P's of the marketing mix. We'll start by looking at the concept of pricing and the tools used in making pricing decisions. Then we'll look at promotion and discuss the considerations in selecting a promotional mix. We will also describe the tasks involved in personal selling, sales promotions, publicity, and public relations. Finally, we'll discuss place—the distribution mix and the different channels and methods of distribution.

Who will win the battle of the Greek yogurt brands? Time will tell, but, after centuries in existence, this "new" segment in the North American market appears to be here to stay.

QUESTIONS FOR DISCUSSION

1. What are the primary features and benefits that help explain the successful commercialization of this yogurt category in the North American market?
2. In the case, we identified both private brands and national brands. Categorize each of the brands mentioned, and explain the difference between national and private brands (as discussed in Chapter 12).
3. If you were involved in launching a new brand of Greek yogurt for a major food manufacturer, what strategy would you employ?
4. If you were in charge of creating a new campaign for the President's Choice Greek yogurt brand, what elements of the promotion mix would you employ? How would you use social media tools to get the message out?

LO-1 DETERMINING PRICES

After *product*, the second major component of the marketing mix is **pricing**—determining what the customer pays and the seller receives in exchange for a product. Setting prices involves understanding how they contribute to achieving the firm's sales objectives.

Pricing to Meet Business Objectives

Pricing objectives are the goals that sellers hope to achieve in pricing products for sale. Some companies have profit-maximizing pricing objectives, while others have market-share pricing objectives. Pricing decisions are also influenced by the need to compete in the marketplace, by social and ethical concerns, and even by corporate image. eBay, the popular internet auction site, has a straightforward pricing structure: Let buyers make offers until a price is finally settled. While eBay sellers hope for a high price, they are sometimes willing to give up some profit in return for a quick sale. Unfortunately, the eBay pricing model, one-on-one price setting, isn't feasible for all companies with lots of customers and products.

PROFIT-MAXIMIZING OBJECTIVES

The seller's pricing decision is critical for determining the firm's revenue, which is calculated using the following formula:

$$\text{Revenue} = \text{Selling price} \times \text{Units sold}$$

Companies that set prices to maximize profits want to set the selling price to sell the number of units that will generate the highest possible total profits. If a company sets prices too low, it will probably sell many units, but may miss out on additional profits on each unit (and may even lose money on each exchange). If a company sets prices too high, it will make a large profit on each item, but will sell fewer units. Again, the firm loses money, and it may also be left with excess inventory.

In calculating profits, managers weigh sales revenues against costs for materials and labour, as well as capital resources (plant and equipment) and marketing costs (such as maintaining a large sales staff). To use these resources efficiently, many firms set prices to cover costs and achieve a targeted level of return for owners.

MARKET-SHARE (MARKET PENETRATION) OBJECTIVES

In the long run, a business must make a profit to survive. Because they are willing to accept minimal profits, even losses, to get buyers to try products, companies may initially set low prices for new products to establish **market share** (or **market penetration**)—a company's percentage of the total industry sales for a specific product type. In some cases, companies set strategic objectives based on events and on declining share.

PRICING FOR E-BUSINESS OBJECTIVES

When pricing for online sales, marketers must consider different kinds of costs and different forms of consumer awareness. Many e-businesses reduce both costs and prices because of the internet's unique marketing capabilities. Because the web provides a more direct link between producer and customer, buyers often avoid the added costs of wholesalers and retailers. Another factor is the ease of comparison shopping. Obviously, point-and-click shopping can be much more efficient than driving from store to store in search of the best price. Moreover, both consumers and business buyers can get lower prices by joining together for greater purchasing power.

Price-Setting Tools

Whether a company's central objective is maximizing profits or market share, managers like to measure the potential impact of price before finalizing what they will charge for their product. Two tools used for this purpose are cost-oriented pricing and breakeven analysis. Although each can be used alone, both are often used because they provide different kinds of information for determining prices that will allow the company to reach its objectives.

COST-ORIENTED PRICING

Cost-oriented pricing considers a firm's desire to make a profit and its need to cover production costs.

$$\text{Selling price} = \text{Seller's costs} + \text{Profit}$$

PRICING Process of determining what a company will receive in exchange for its products.

PRICING OBJECTIVES The goals that sellers hope to achieve in pricing products for sale.

MARKET SHARE (MARKET PENETRATION) A company's percentage of the total industry sales for a specific product type.

COST-ORIENTED PRICING Pricing that considers the firm's desire to make a profit and its need to cover production costs.

For example, a T-shirt store manager would price shirts by calculating the cost of making them available to shoppers. Thus, price would include the costs of store rent, employee wages, utilities, product displays, insurance, and the shirt manufacturer's price. If the manufacturer's price is $8 per shirt and the store sells shirts for $8, the store won't make any profit. Nor will it make a profit if it sells shirts for $8.50 each—or even $10 or $11. To be profitable, the company must charge enough to cover product and other costs. Together, these factors determine the **markup**—the amount added to an item's purchase cost to sell it at a profit. In this case, a reasonable markup of $7 over the purchase cost means a $15 selling price. The following equation calculates the markup percentage and determines what percent of every dollar of revenue is gross profit:

$$\text{Markup percentage} = \frac{\text{Markup}}{\text{Sales price}}$$

For our T-shirt retailer, the markup percentage is 46.7:

$$\text{Markup percentage} = \frac{\$7 \times 100}{\$15} = 46.7\%$$

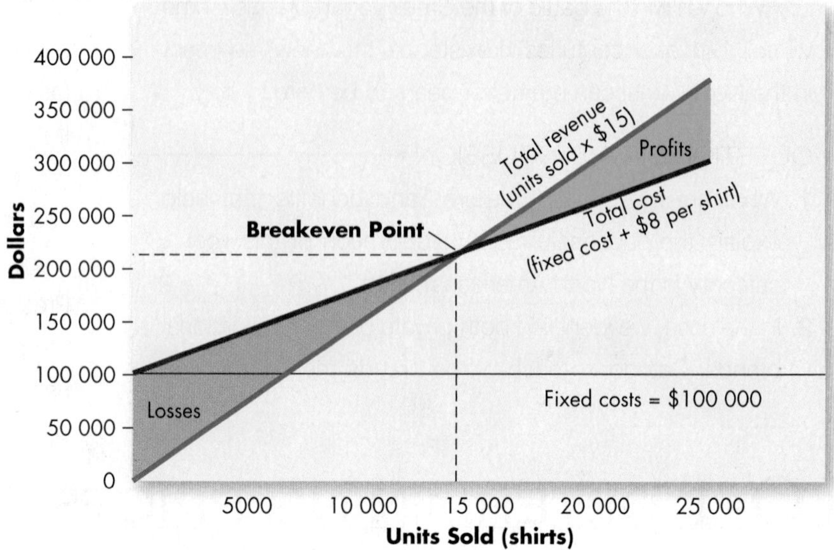

FIGURE 13.1 Breakeven analysis

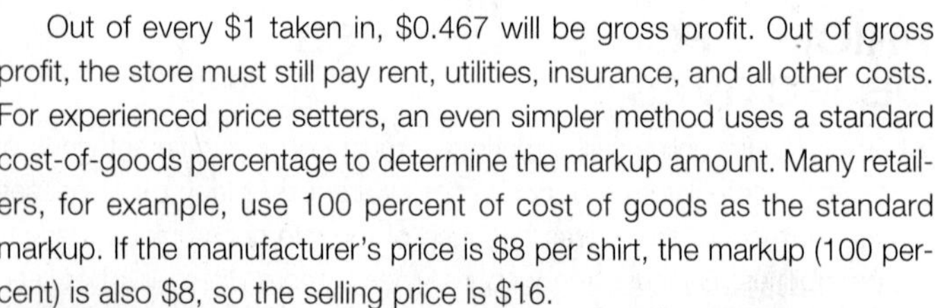

Out of every $1 taken in, $0.467 will be gross profit. Out of gross profit, the store must still pay rent, utilities, insurance, and all other costs. For experienced price setters, an even simpler method uses a standard cost-of-goods percentage to determine the markup amount. Many retailers, for example, use 100 percent of cost of goods as the standard markup. If the manufacturer's price is $8 per shirt, the markup (100 percent) is also $8, so the selling price is $16.

BREAKEVEN ANALYSIS: COST-VOLUME-PROFIT RELATIONSHIPS

Using cost-oriented pricing, a firm will cover **variable costs**—costs that change with the number of units of a product produced and sold, such as raw materials, sales commissions, and shipping. Firms also need to pay **fixed costs**—costs, such as rent, insurance, and utilities, that must be paid *regardless of the number of units produced and sold.*

Costs, selling price, and the number of units sold determine how many units a company must sell before all costs, both variable and fixed, are covered, and it begins to make a profit. **Breakeven analysis** assesses costs versus revenues for various sales volumes and shows, at any particular selling price, the amount of loss or profit for each possible volume of sales.

If you were the manager of a T-shirt store, how would you determine how many shirts you needed to sell to break even? We know that the *variable cost* of buying each shirt from the manufacturer is $8. This means that the store's annual variable costs depend on how many shirts are sold, the number of shirts sold times the $8 cost for each shirt. Say that *fixed costs* for keeping the store open for one year are $100 000 (no matter how many shirts are sold). At a selling price of $15 each, how many shirts must be sold *so that total revenues exactly cover both* fixed and variable costs? The answer is the **breakeven point**, which is 14 286 shirts:

$$\text{Breakeven point (in units)} = \frac{\text{Total fixed cost}}{\text{Price} - \text{variable cost}}$$

$$= \frac{\$100\ 000}{\$15 - \$8} = 14\ 286 \text{ Shirts}$$

Look at Figure 13.1. If the store sells fewer than 14 286 shirts, it loses money for the year. If sales go over 14 286, profits grow by $7 for each additional shirt. If the store sells exactly 14 286 shirts, it will cover all its costs, but earn zero profit.

Zero profitability at the breakeven point can also be seen by using the profit equation:

$$\text{Profit} = \begin{matrix}\text{Total}\\\text{revenue}\end{matrix} - \left(\begin{matrix}\text{Total}\\\text{fixed}\\\text{cost}\end{matrix} + \begin{matrix}\text{Total}\\\text{variable}\\\text{cost}\end{matrix}\right)$$

$$= (14\ 286 \text{ shirts} \times \$15) - (\$100\ 000 \text{ Fixed cost}$$

$$+ [14\ 286 \text{ shirts} \times \$8 \text{ Variable cost}])$$

$$\$0 = (\$214\ 290) - (\$100\ 000 + \$114\ 288)$$

(rounded to the nearest whole shirt)

Of course, this is a simplistic example with only one product and one price. Under that situation the store would need to sell approximately 1200 t-shirts per month, approximately 40 t-shirts per day (assuming they are open 7 days a week). Is that realistic? In reality, they would probably carry some higher margin products to up-sell customers while pushing accessories to reduce the unit sales requirements and improve their chances for success.

MARKUP Amount added to an item's purchase cost to sell it at a profit.

VARIABLE COST Cost that changes with the quantity of a product produced and sold.

FIXED COST Cost that is incurred regardless of the quantity of a product produced and sold.

BREAKEVEN ANALYSIS For a particular selling price, assessment of the seller's costs versus revenues at various sales volumes.

BREAKEVEN POINT The sales volume at which the seller's total revenue from sales equals total costs (variable and fixed) with neither profit nor loss.

LO-2 PRICING STRATEGIES AND TACTICS

The pricing tools discussed in the previous section help managers set prices on specific goods. They do not, however, help them decide on pricing philosophies for diverse competitive situations. In this section, we discuss pricing strategy (pricing as a planning activity) and some basic pricing tactics (ways in which managers implement a firm's pricing strategies).

Pricing Strategies

Pricing is an extremely important element in the marketing mix, as well as a flexible marketing tool—it is certainly easier to change prices than to change products or distribution channels. This section will look at how pricing strategies can result in widely differing prices for very similar products.

PRICING EXISTING PRODUCTS

A firm has three options for pricing existing products:

1. Pricing *above* prevailing market prices for similar products to take advantage of the common assumption that higher price means higher quality
2. Pricing *below* market prices while offering a product of comparable quality to higher-priced competitors
3. Pricing *at* or near market prices

Godiva chocolates and Patek Philippe watches price high by promoting prestige and quality images. In contrast, both Budget and Dollar car-rental companies promote themselves as low-priced alternatives to Hertz and Avis. Pricing below prevailing market price works if a firm offers a product of acceptable quality while keeping costs below those of higher-priced competitors.

PRICING NEW PRODUCTS

When introducing new products, companies must often choose between very high prices or very low prices. **Price skimming**—setting an initial high price to cover development and introduction costs and generate a large profit on each item sold—works only if marketers can convince customers that a new product is truly different from existing products and there is no foreseeable major competition on the horizon. Apple's iPod is a good example. With no strong competitors entering the market for several years, Apple was able to maintain a high retail price with little discounting, even at Walmart. In contrast, **penetration pricing**—setting an initial low price to establish a new product in the market—seeks to create customer interest and stimulate trial purchases. This is the best strategy when introducing a product which has or expects to have competitors very quickly.

FIXED VERSUS DYNAMIC PRICING FOR ONLINE BUSINESS

The digital marketplace has introduced a highly variable pricing system as an alternative to conventional fixed pricing for both consumer and business-to-business (B2B) products. At present, fixed pricing is still the most common option for cyber shoppers. E-commerce giant Amazon.com has maintained this practice as its pricing strategy for its millions of retail items. In contrast, dynamic pricing, like eBay's auction bidding, uses flexibility between buyers and sellers in setting a price and uses the web to instantly notify millions of buyers of product availability and price changes.

Another kind of dynamic pricing—the reverse auction—allows sellers to alter prices privately on an individual basis. At Priceline.com, for example, consumers set a price (below the published fixed price) they are willing to pay for airfare (or a rental car or a hotel room); then an airline can complete the sale by accepting the bid price.[1]

PRICE SKIMMING Setting an initially high price to cover new product costs and generate a profit.

PENETRATION PRICING Setting an initially low price to establish a new product in the market.

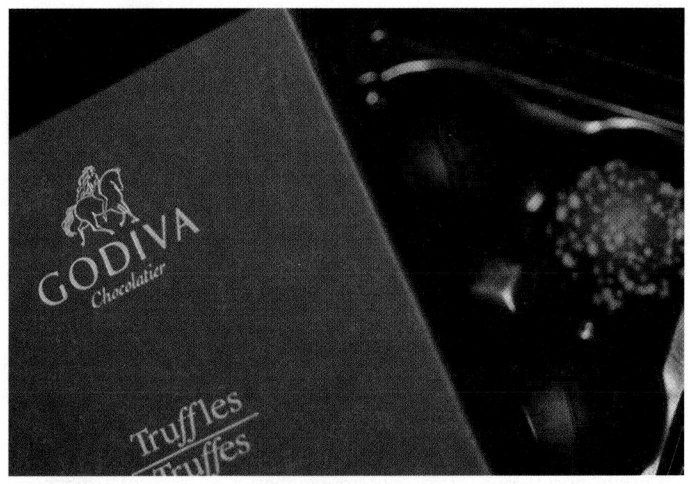

Godiva chocolates are definitely not the cheapest on the market; the company chooses to provide quality for a premium price.

Helen Sessions/Alamy

Pricing Tactics

Regardless of its pricing strategy, a company may adopt one or more pricing tactics. Companies selling multiple items in a product category

THERE'S AN APP FOR THAT!

APP DETAILS	PLATFORMS
1. **Marketing Hoopla** **Source:** 3H Communications **Key Features:** Regular posts on marketing, branding, advertising, social media, and design trends.	Apple, Android
2. **Price Check Guru** **Source:** Big Bang Partners **Key Features:** Puts comparative costs at your fingertips, giving you information to make an informed decision to save money.	Apple, Android, BlackBerry
3. **Adzi—Advertising Expert** **Source:** WannaBiz **Key Features:** Use the power of professional advertising campaigns for your small business.	Android

APP DISCOVERY EXERCISE

Since app availability changes, conduct your own search for the "Top Three" marketing apps and identify the key features.

often use **price lining**—offering all items in certain categories at a limited number of prices. A clothing retailer, for example, might predetermine $199, $299, $399, and $499 as the price points for men's suits, so all men's suits would be set at one of these four prices. This allows the store to have a suit for the different customer segments it hopes to attract. Grocery stores utilize this strategy as well; for example, in canned goods they will carry a national brand, a store brand, and a generic brand at different price points.

Psychological pricing takes advantage of the fact that customers are not completely rational when making buying decisions. One type, *odd-even pricing*, is based on the theory that customers prefer prices that are not stated in even dollar amounts. Thus, customers regard prices of $1000, $100, $50, and $10 as significantly higher than $999.95, $99.95, $49.95, and $9.95, respectively. Finally, sellers must often resort to price reductions—**discounts**—to stimulate sales.

PRICE LINING Setting a limited number of prices for certain categories of products.

PSYCHOLOGICAL PRICING A pricing tactic that takes advantage of the fact that consumers do not always respond rationally to stated prices.

DISCOUNT A price reduction offered as an incentive to purchase.

LO-3 PROMOTING PRODUCTS AND SERVICES

Promotion refers to techniques for communicating information about products and is part of the communication mix—the total message any company sends to customers about its product. Promotional techniques, especially advertising, must communicate the uses, features, and benefits of products, and marketers use an array of tools for this purpose.

The ultimate objective of promotion is to increase sales. However, marketers also use promotion to increase consumer awareness of their products, to make consumers more knowledgeable about product features, and to persuade consumers to prefer their brand over others. Today's value-conscious customers gain benefits when the specific elements in the promotional mix are varied so as to communicate value-added benefits. Burger King shifted its promotional mix by cutting back on advertising and using those funds for customer discounts. Receiving the same food at a lower price is "value added" for Burger King's customers. Many companies, like Hallmark Cards, experience seasonal sales patterns. By increasing their promotional activities in slow periods, they can achieve a more stable sales volume throughout the year. As a result, they can keep their production and distribution systems running evenly. Tim Hortons achieves the same goal with its annual Roll up the Rim contest.

Promotional Strategies

Once a firm's promotional objectives are clear, it must develop a promotional strategy to achieve these objectives. Promotional strategies may be of the push or pull variety. A company with a **push strategy** will "push" its product to wholesalers and retailers, who then persuade customers to buy it. In contrast, a company with a **pull strategy** appeals directly to customers, who demand the product from retailers, who in turn demand the product from wholesalers, who in turn demand the product from the manufacturer. Advertising "pulls," while personal selling "pushes."

Makers of industrial products often use a push strategy, while makers of consumer products often use a pull strategy. Many large firms use a combination of the two. For example, Coca-Cola uses advertising to create consumer demand (pull) for its various beverages—Coke, Fruitopia, Dasani, and Powerade. It also pushes wholesalers and retailers to stock these products. In total, the company has over 3500 products worldwide.[2]

The Promotional Mix

Five of marketing's most powerful promotional tools are advertising, personal selling, sales promotions, direct or interactive marketing, and publicity and public relations. The best combination of these tools—the best **promotional mix**—depends on many factors. The most important is the target audience.

PROMOTION Aspect of the marketing mix concerned with the most effective techniques for communicating information about and selling a product.

PUSH STRATEGY A promotional strategy in which a company aggressively pushes its product through wholesalers and retailers, which persuade customers to buy it.

PULL STRATEGY A promotional strategy in which a company appeals directly to customers, who demand the product from retailers, which demand the product from wholesalers.

PROMOTIONAL MIX the combination of tools used to promote a product.

Beats by Dre has been built though a non-traditional approach; the message and reputation has spread through online buzz, YouTube videos, and more traditional techniques like cinema ads. This modern approach is revolutionizing the whole business of promotion.

S K D/Alamy

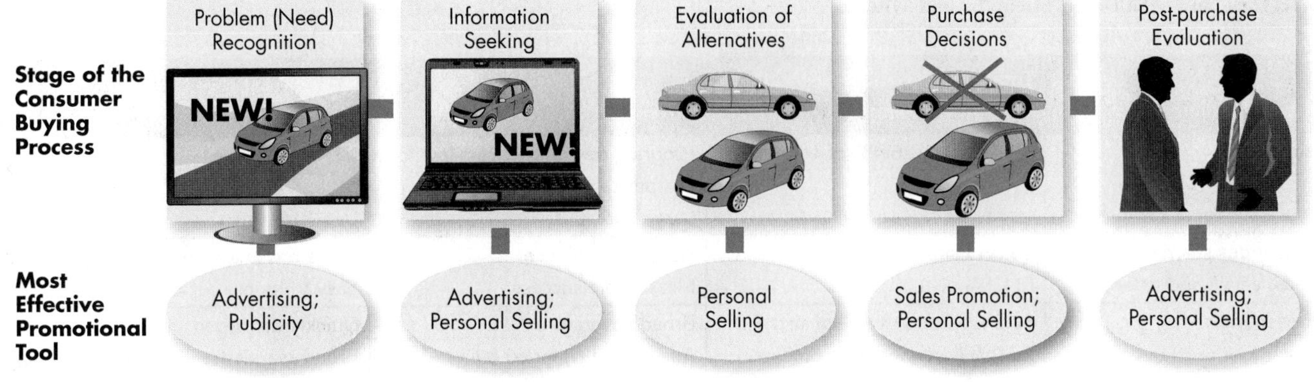

FIGURE 13.2 The consumer buying process and the promotional mix

In establishing a promotional mix, marketers match promotional tools with the five stages in the buyer decision process:

1. When consumers first recognize the need to make a purchase, marketers use advertising and publicity, which can reach many people quickly, to make sure buyers are *aware of their products*.
2. As consumers search for information about available products, advertising and personal selling are important methods *to educate them*.
3. Personal selling can become vital as consumers compare competing products. Sales representatives can *demonstrate product quality, features, benefits, and performance* in comparison with competitors' products.
4. When buyers are ready to purchase products, sales promotion can give consumers *an incentive to buy*. Personal selling can help by bringing products to convenient purchase locations.
5. After making purchases, consumers evaluate products and note (and remember) their strengths and deficiencies. At this stage, advertising and personal selling can *remind customers that they made wise purchases.*

Figure 13.2 summarizes the effective promotional tools for each stage in the consumer buying process.

LO-4 ADVERTISING PROMOTIONS AND MEDIA

Advertising is paid, non-personal communication by which an identified sponsor informs an audience about a product. You can probably remember many jingles and slogans from your early childhood. If a friend tells you that he or she has dandruff, you might instinctively tell them to use Head and Shoulders shampoo. Companies have been planting messages in your mind for years. Like it or not, we are all a little bit brainwashed. Consumers remember brand names more easily if the company has a catchy advertising slogan. Buckley's Mixture is well known in Canada. You remember the slogan, don't you? "It tastes awful. And it works." Advertising can convince customers to try a company's product or service, but it has limits. It is the customers' experience with the product or service that determines whether they will make repeat purchases.

Advertising Media

Consumers tend to ignore the bulk of advertising messages that bombard them; they pay attention to what interests them. Marketers must find out, then, who their customers are, which media they pay attention to, what messages appeal to them, and how to get their attention. Thus, marketers use several different **advertising media**—specific communication devices for carrying a seller's message to potential customers. The combination of media through which a company advertises is called its media mix. Table 13.1 shows the strengths and weaknesses of various media and below we analyze each form in some detail.

NEWSPAPERS

Newspapers offer excellent coverage, since each local market has at least one daily newspaper. This medium offers flexibility (ads can change from day to day) and believability (ads are presented next to news items). In addition, a larger percentage of individuals with higher education and income level tend to read newspapers on a daily basis. However, the focus in the newspaper business is definitely changing; papers are adopting a "digital first" strategy to change with the times, because traditional print daily newspaper ad revenues have declined in the last decade from approximately 30 percent of spending, in Canada, to just 15 percent.[4]

TELEVISION

National advertising is usually done on television, because it still reaches more people than any other medium. Television allows advertisers to combine sight, sound, and motion, thus appealing to almost all of the viewer's senses. Information on viewer demographics for a particular program allows advertisers to promote to their target audiences.

ADVERTISING Paid, non-personal communication by which an identified sponsor informs an audience about a product.

ADVERTISING MEDIA The specific communication device—television, radio, online, newspapers, direct mail, magazines, outdoor, mobile—used to carry a firm's advertising message to potential customers.

TABLE 13.1 Total Media Usage, Strengths, and Weaknesses

Advertising Medium	Total $ Spent and Percentage of Total Advertising[3]	Strengths	Weaknesses
Television	$3.4 billion (26.4% of total)	Program demographics allow for customized ads Large audience	Most expensive
Online (includes search, display, classifieds, email, and video)	$3.08 billion (24.1% of total)	Targeted audience Measurable success	Some forms are annoying for consumers Easy to ignore
Daily newspapers	$1.91 billion (14.9% of total; 25.2% if you include community papers)	Broad coverage Ads can be changed daily	Quickly discarded Broad readership limits ability to target specific audience
Radio	$1.6 billion (12.5% of total)	Inexpensive Large audience Fairly easy to identify segments	Easy to ignore Message quickly disappears
Magazines	$558 million (4.4% of total)	Often reread and shared Fairly easy to identify segments	Require advanced planning Little control over ad placement
Outdoor	$514 million (4% of total)	Inexpensive Difficult to ignore Repeat exposure	Presents limited information Little control over audience
Mobile	$443 million (3.5% of total)	Accessibility Relative cost Ability to personalize	Sometimes difficult to read Lack of standardization

However, TV advertising can be expensive. In 2015, a 30-second commercial on U.S. television during the NFL Super Bowl cost over $4.5 million.[5] A national 30-second spot in Canada during the Super Bowl costs approximately $130 000.[6] A comparable 30-second Grey Cup spot costs about $65 000.[7] Another disadvantage of this medium is that there are too many commercials, which causes viewers to confuse products. In addition, viewers who record programs on DVRs (digital video recorders) often fast-forward through the ads appearing on the TV shows they have recorded. That is why product placement, which involves using brand-name products as part of the actual storyline, is gaining in popularity. Shows like *Survivor* and *American Idol* are noticeably full of placements. Finally, the brevity of TV ads also makes television a poor medium to educate viewers about complex products.

RADIO

According to BBM research, more than 90 percent of Canadians aged 12 years and over listen to the radio more than 19 hours a week.[8] Radio ads are fairly inexpensive and, since most radio is programmed locally, this medium gives advertisers a high degree of customer selectivity. For example, radio stations are already segmented into listening categories such as classic rock, country and western, jazz, talk, news, and religious programming. On the negative side, radio only permits an audio presentation and ads are over quickly. As well, people tend to use the radio as "background" while they are doing other things, so they may pay little attention to advertisements. Subscriber-based satellite radio also poses a significant long-term threat to the traditional radio model.

MAGAZINES

The many different magazines on the market provide a high level of consumer selectivity. The person who reads *Popular Photography* is more likely to be interested in the latest specialized lenses from Canon than a *Gourmet* magazine subscriber. Magazine advertising allows for excellent reproduction of photographs and artwork that not only grab buyers' attention, but also may convince them of the product's value. Magazines also provide advertisers with plenty of space for detailed product information. Magazines have a long life and tend to be passed from person to person, doubling and tripling the number of exposures.

OUTDOORS

Outdoor advertising—billboards, signs, and advertisements on buses, taxis, and subways—is relatively inexpensive, faces little competition for customers' attention, and is subject to high repeat exposure. Many billboards now feature animation and changing images, and today's billboard messages are cheaper because they can be digitally printed in colour in large quantities. On the downside, outdoor ads can present only limited information, and sellers have little control over who sees their advertisements.

ONLINE

The power of online advertising is unquestionable and it encompasses various forms including: search, display, classifieds, email, and video. Online advertising offers advantages such as flexibility, feedback (sellers can measure the success of messages by counting how many people see each ad and track the number of people that click-through to their websites), reach, and a capacity for relationship building (with customers on interactive websites).[9] Online ad revenues are up approximately 1300 percent in the past decade and the overall figures are set to surpass the reigning advertising king (TV) as the most important medium in terms of overall spending.[10]

WestJet has been able to maximize the power of online campaigns by using various forms of online advertising to make an impact.

Leonard Ortiz/ZUMA Press, Inc/Alamy

ONLINE CONSUMER ENGAGEMENT

Online communications have changed how companies interact with customers. The engagement is now more likely to be two-way as more companies ask consumers to get involved with the brand and actually influence marketing decisions. You can include Starbucks (name a flavour), Crayola (new colours), and Frito-Lay (flavour ideas and ad themes) in the growing crowd.[11]

Advertisers are observing consumer behaviour and as a result they are spending more online. For example, a survey conducted by the Solutions Research Group indicated that Canadians are truly hooked on YouTube. They asked respondents: When was the last time you visited YouTube? The results: 57 percent within 24 hours, 25 percent within the last week, 9 percent within the last month, and only 8 percent within more than a month and 12 percent answering never.[12]

To truly highlight the transformational power of this medium, consider the strategic fortress of TV advertising—the Super Bowl. Even this sacred advertising event has changed. Instead of tightly guarding secret campaigns for the big day, companies are now creating teaser campaigns on YouTube and Facebook to build interest weeks before the big day and encouraging consumers to participate in events. In addition, the immense audience is being directed from TV to the internet during the game. For example, Budweiser Canada used the Super Bowl to drive people to its Facebook page in order to enter a live contest that concluded at the end of the game.[13] In another example, the media check-in service Get Glue worked with Pepsi to help the company maximize its expensive halftime show sponsorship (starring Beyoncé). The result was that 95 747 virtual stickers were unlocked (and could be posted by the participants) reaching an estimated 36 million people (who saw those messages).[14]

MOBILE AND OTHER ADVERTISING MEDIA

Mobile phone ads are growing in importance, for obvious reasons. Some of the advantages of this medium include accessibility (always handy), cost (a fraction of TV), timeliness (great to push out messages about current sales for example), and the ability to personalize

Sean Combs, the entertainment artist and entrepreneur, does not miss a chance to promote Ciroc on social media, and as a result the brand is a strong beneficiary of PR and publicity. This is the precise reason why Diageo, the world's largest producer of alcohol products, teamed up with and made him a brand ambassador leveraging his power to engage consumers.

Scott Gries/Getty Images

messages. On the negative side, the format can be difficult to read or appreciate (small size), and it suffers from a lack of standardization of mobile device technology and privacy issues. According to eMarketer, worldwide mobile ad spending is expected to reach US$23.6 billion in 2016.[15]

A combination of many additional media—including catalogues, sidewalk handouts, Yellow Pages, skywriting, special events, and door-to-door communications—make up the remaining advertising vehicles. Advergaming is also a major new venue for advertising since there are approximately 170 million impressionable console and computer gamers in North America.[16]

Read the Entrepreneurship and New Ventures box called "Promoting Music Artists" to get a glimpse of a company that has been successful in the music industry for over 25 years.

ENTREPRENEURSHIP AND NEW VENTURES

Promoting Music Artists

Eric Lawrence and Rob Lanni are the founders of Coalition Music; they have been successfully promoting artists for over 25 years. In that time, they have seen the highs and they have also come face to face with an ever-changing digital music environment. While they are still executing many of the same tasks that helped them launch the careers of bands like Simple Plan and Our Lady Peace, they are also acutely aware that they must continuously evolve with the times. That means constantly connecting the audience to the artists through all new forms of social media communication. It also means understanding the new model and providing expertise to young budding artists.

Entrepreneurs identify opportunities, access resources, improve on, or build something from scratch. Their creations must provide value that other people can appreciate and support through purchases of goods or services. When you think of that entrepreneurial spirit, you might imagine an old traditional manufacturer or retailer or a new high-tech start-up. However, that entrepreneurial spirit can be found in all types of organizations. The people behind Coalition Music are a prime example.

For all their hard work, Coalition Music was awarded the honour of Company of the Year by the Canadian Music and Broadcast Industry Awards. This was a nice acknowledgment, but, in this business, long-term success comes down to a few important statistics to prove your worth. Coalition has plenty to be proud of:

- over 30 commercial albums released
- over 12 million artist albums sold worldwide
- loyal and successful clients (partner relationships):

Simple Plan is one of the successful acts represented by Coalition Music.

n8n photo/Alamy

  - Our Lady Peace (21 years)
  - Finger Eleven (17 years)
  - Simple Plan (12 years)

Success in the music business is not just about numbers, but clearly these statistics point to Eric's and Rob's ability to identify opportunities and manage talent. Dealing with artists requires the skill set to handle egos, provide valuable input, and to manage expectations. After spending over a quarter-century building a wealth of industry knowledge, the two entrepreneurs took their passion to a new level.

Canada's Music Incubator (Artist Entrepreneur Program)

While Coalition Music is a distinct business, they represent music artists who have their own brands, unique identities, fan bases, promotional efforts, and so on. In other words, they are in the business of helping each artist manage his or her own distinct business identity. It's the artists' music and their ability to connect with their fans (sell music, tickets, and merchandise) that determines their survival. The second you visit the website and read about the company, this core principle is highlighted—Coalition develops "artist-entrepreneurs" and helps them build long-standing careers in both the arena and studio.

So in 2012, Rob and Eric took this idea and created the Artist Entrepreneur Program. It allows the firm to leverage their core knowledge and teach diverse music industry topics like production, songwriting, music law, tour logistics, social media networking, marketing, and publicity. By 2015, the concept had evolved into a separate entity (still located in the Coalition Music building) as a not-for-profit incubator called Canada's Music Incubator (CMI). It allows program participants direct access to a community of artists across all genres of music, to touring professionals, artist managers, and industry experts, and to decades of experience and expertise. CMI partners and sponsors include Bell Media, City of Toronto, TD Bank Group, Newcap Radio, Sennheiser, D'Addario, Stingray Music, and Warner Music Canada.

As Coalition Music celebrated its many years in business it was operating in a refurbished facility in Toronto, complete with great rehearsal spaces and a new recording studio (featuring a vintage Neve console) and a classroom. In its quarter-century it has been involved directly in the evolution of the Canadian music scene. With the creativity and passion of the founders it should continue to thrive for years to come.

CRITICAL THINKING QUESTION

1. Describe the greatest challenges of promoting music today as opposed to ten years ago. How has music promotion changed?
2. Conduct some research on CMI. What are the benefits for the students? Are there any secondary benefits for Coalition Music?

LO-5 PERSONAL SELLING, SALES PROMOTIONS, DIRECT (OR INTERACTIVE) MARKETING, PUBLIC RELATIONS, AND PUBLICITY

In this section, we outline the tasks involved in personal selling, describe the various types of sales promotions, look at direct (or interactive) marketing, and distinguish between publicity and public relations.

Personal Selling

Virtually everyone has done some selling. Perhaps you have had a lemonade stand or sold candy for the drama club. Or you may have gone on a job interview, selling your abilities and services as an employee to the interviewer's company. **Personal selling**—the oldest form of it—provides the personal link between seller and buyer. It adds to a firm's credibility, because it gives buyers a contact person who will answer questions. Because it involves personal interaction, personal selling requires a level of trust between the buyer and the seller. When a buyer feels cheated by the seller, that trust has been broken and a negative attitude toward salespeople in general can develop.

Personal selling is the most expensive form of promotion per contact, because presentations are generally made to one or two individuals at a time. Personal-selling expenses include salespeople's compensation and their overhead (travel, food, and lodging). The average cost of an industrial sales call has been estimated at $300 to $500.[17] Costs have prompted many companies to turn to telemarketing, using telephone solicitations to conduct the personal-selling process. Such savings are stimulating the growth of telemarketing, which provides 150 000 jobs in Canada and generates $25 billion in annual sales. Telemarketing returns $6.25 for every dollar spent.[18]

Sales Promotions

Sales promotions are short-term promotional activities designed to stimulate consumer buying or cooperation from distributors, sales agents, or other members of the trade. They are important because they increase the likelihood that buyers will try products. They also enhance product recognition and can increase purchase size and amount. For example, soap is often bound into packages of four with the promotion "Buy three and get one free."

To be successful, sales promotions must be convenient and accessible when the decision to purchase occurs. If Harley-Davidson has a one-week motorcycle promotion and you have no local dealer, the promotion is neither convenient nor accessible to you, and you will not buy. But if Herbal Essences offers a 20 percent–off coupon that you can save for use later, the promotion is convenient and accessible. Like anything else, too much of a good thing can be destructive. The Bay has been criticized for holding too many scratch-and-save "Bay Days." The goal of such programs is to generate immediate sales, as people are given an incentive to buy now or buy before the end of the weekend. But in the case of The Bay, many customers have been conditioned to expect these sales. The end result is that some customers delay purchases, waiting for the next sale. This is clearly not the goal of a sales promotion program.

TYPES OF SALES PROMOTIONS

Most consumers have taken part in a variety of sales promotions, such as free samples (giveaways), which let customers try products without risk, and **coupon** promotions, which use certificates entitling buyers to discounts in order to encourage customers to try new products, lure them away from competitors, or induce them to buy more of a product. **Premiums** are free or reduced-price items, such as pencils, coffee mugs, and six-month low-interest credit cards, given to consumers in return for buying a specified product. Contests can boost sales by rewarding high-producing distributors and sales representatives with vacation trips to Hawaii or Paris.

To grab customers' attention in stores, companies use **point-of-purchase** (or **sale**) **displays** at the ends of aisles or near checkout counters to ease finding products and to eliminate competitors from consideration. In addition to physical goods, point-of-purchase pedestals also provide services, namely information for consumers. Bank lobbies and physicians' waiting rooms, for example, might have interactive kiosks inviting clients to learn more about bank products or educational information about available treatments on consumer-friendly touchscreen displays. For B2B promotions, industries sponsor **trade shows** where companies rent booths to display and demonstrate products to customers who have a special interest or who are ready to buy.

Direct (or **interactive**) **marketing** is one-on-one non-personal selling that tries to get consumers to make purchases away from retail stores and, instead, to purchase from home, at work, or by using a mobile device while travelling. This fast-growing selling method includes non-store retailers (catalogues, telemarketing, home video shopping), direct mail, direct response advertising (such as infomercials and direct-response magazine and newspaper ads), and targeted emails. When used by B2B businesses, direct marketing is primarily lead generation so a salesperson can close the sale where interest has been shown. In B2C businesses, it has primarily a selling goal. The advantage of direct marketing is that you can target the message to the individual and you can measure the results. For example, Amazon knows when you sign in who you are and what you have purchased in the past and makes recommendations based on your purchases. When you select a certain title or product, they can suggest titles that other buyers of your selection have also purchased and in that way, increase the value of the sale to you.

Read the Managing in Turbulent Times box entitled "Direct Mail: Back from a Slow Death?"

Publicity and Public Relations

Much to the delight of marketing managers with tight budgets, **publicity** is free. Moreover, because it is presented in a news format, consumers see publicity as objective and believable. However, marketers may have little control over bad publicity, and that can have a very negative impact. For example, a Twitter post associated to Digiorno Pizza (Delissio in Canada) got the brand into trouble when a post seemed to make light of or joke about an incident of domestic abuse committed by former NFL player Ray Rice. The comment was immediately removed, but people saw the message and reacted swiftly and the mainstream media also

PERSONAL SELLING Promotional tool in which a salesperson communicates one to one with potential customers.

SALES PROMOTIONS Short-term promotional activities designed to stimulate consumer buying or cooperation from distributors and other members of the trade.

COUPON A method of sales promotion featuring a certificate that entitles the bearer to stated savings off a product's regular price.

PREMIUM A method of sales promotion in which some item is offered free or at a bargain price to customers in return for buying a specified product.

POINT-OF-PURCHASE (OR **SALE**) A method of sales promotion in which a product display is located in a retail store in order to encourage consumers to buy the product.

TRADE SHOW A method of sales promotion in which members of a particular industry gather for displays and product demonstrations designed to sell products to customers.

DIRECT (OR **INTERACTIVE**) **MARKETING** One-on-one non-personal selling by non-store retailers and B2B sellers using direct contact with prospective customers, especially via the internet.

PUBLICITY Information about a company, a product, or an event transmitted by the general mass media (with no direct cost to the company).

MANAGING IN TURBULENT TIMES

Direct Mail: Back from a Slow Death?

A few years ago, some marketing experts were predicting the "slow death" of direct mail marketing because of the growth of the internet. But direct mail might not disappear just yet, because a new driver of direct mail's growth has appeared on the scene: new data technologies. Thousands of online sources accumulate information about every internet user and household, including their purchasing transactions, social networking interactions, their choices of information sources and content, television viewing habits, and casual internet surfing. The result is an explosion of data that enables businesses to target potential customers in specific ways. Analytic software can search through mounds of data in microseconds and identify individuals, households, and their locations, and match refined specifications for targeted potential customers. Instead of just demographics, data mining identifies potential qualitative characteristics of customers, such as different lifestyle patterns.

An added stimulus for smarter direct mail marketing is new developments in digital printing technology. Greater flexibility and speed allow for rapid runs of small volume, specialized advertising content. A toy company, for example, can create a catalogue of upscale toys that targets households who (1) live in upperincome neighbourhoods, (2) have a specific income range, (3) have made recent purchases of high-end toys, and (4) have 5-to-10-year olds. That same toy company can also create a catalogue of lower-end toys that targets households with who (1) live in lower-income geographical areas, (2) have a specific income range, (3) have made recent purchases of lower-end toys, and have 1-to-5-year-olds.

Today's digital printers can quickly produce both catalogues with different graphics and printed content, and expedite mailings that begin to rival emails. Printing capabilities make it economically feasible to personalize catalogue messages to dozens of smaller groupings of targeted customers, instead of just two or three groups. As a result, sharply targeted direct mail is becoming more economical by refocusing with messages tailored to detailed profiles of a limited number of recipients who are more likely to buy, rather than wasting mass mailings of a single message to everyone, most of whom will ignore it.

CRITICAL THINKING QUESTIONS

1. How does the development of new technology make it difficult to make predictions about future trends?

picked up the story. The apology was also botched. In the social media age with instant access, an error can very quickly escalate.[19]

In contrast, **public relations** is a term that describes company-influenced publicity. It attempts to create goodwill between the company and its customers through public-service announcements that enhance the company's image. For example, a bank may announce that senior citizens' groups can have free use of a meeting room for their social activities. As well, company executives may make appearances as guest speakers representing their companies at professional meetings and civic events. They also may serve as leaders in civic activities, like the United Way campaign and university fundraising.

In 2012, in a surprising but interesting move, McDonald's talked honestly about their food to any customer willing to ask questions in an online campaign called "Our Food, Your Questions." In recent years, the company has made an effort to improve quality and offer healthier choices, but clearly they opened themselves up to some difficult answers. For example, they confirmed that a strawberry milkshake has 1100 calories! Not all the questions led to unfavourable responses, though, and McDonald's clearly felt that this dialogue was already occurring in cyberspace, especially since the film *Super Size Me* was released a few years ago. Why not address the point directly and also dismiss some myths as well?[20]

PUBLIC RELATIONS Company-influenced information directed at building goodwill with the public or dealing with unfavourable events.

>>> Kate Upton wore a Canada Goose jacket on the cover of the *Sports Illustrated* Swimsuit Edition and generated a lot of attention at no cost to the company.

maximimages.com/Alamy

LO-6 THE DISTRIBUTION MIX

In addition to a good product mix and effective pricing and promotion, the success of any product also depends on its **distribution mix**—the combination of distribution channels by which a firm gets products to end users. In this section, we look at intermediaries and different kinds of distribution channels. Then, we discuss some benefits consumers reap from services provided by intermediaries.

Intermediaries and Distribution Channels

Intermediaries, once called "middlemen," help to distribute goods, either by moving them or by providing information that stimulates their movement from sellers to customers. **Wholesalers** are intermediaries who sell products to other businesses for resale to final consumers. **Retailers** sell products directly to consumers.

DISTRIBUTION OF GOODS AND SERVICES

A **distribution channel** is the path a product follows from producer to end user. Figure 13.3 shows how four popular distribution channels can be identified according to the channel members involved in getting products to buyers.

Channel 1: Direct Distribution In a **direct channel**, the product travels from the producer to the consumer or organizational buyer without intermediaries. Dell built its name using this channel approach. Most business goods, especially those bought in large quantities, are sold directly by the manufacturer to the industrial buyer.

Channel 2: Retail Distribution In Channel 2, producers distribute consumer products through retailers. Goodyear, for example, maintains its own system of retail outlets. Levi's has its own outlets, but also produces jeans for other retailers. Large outlets, such as Walmart, buy merchandise directly from producers. Many industrial buyers, such as businesses buying office supplies at Staples, rely on this channel.

Channel 3: Wholesale Distribution Channel 2, once the most widely used method of non-direct distribution, requires a large and costly amount of floor space for storing and displaying merchandise. Wholesalers relieve the space problem by using Channel 3—that is, storing merchandise and restocking store displays frequently. With approximately 90 percent of its space used to display merchandise and only 10 percent left for storage and office facilities, the combination convenience store/gas station's use of wholesalers is an example of this channel.

Channel 4: Distribution by Agents or Brokers Sales agents or brokers represent producers and receive commissions on the goods they sell to consumers or industrial users. **Sales agents**, including many travel agents, generally deal in the related product lines of a few producers, such as tour companies, to meet the needs of many customers. Vancouver-based Uniglobe Travel International, a travel agency representing airlines, car rental companies, hotels, and tour companies, books flight reservations and arranges complete recreational travel services for consumers. The firm also services companies whose employees need lodging and transportation for business travel. In contrast to agents, **brokers**, in industries such as real estate and stock exchanges, match numerous sellers and buyers as needed to sell properties, often without knowing in advance who they will be.

DISTRIBUTION MIX The combination of distribution channels by which a firm gets its products to end users.

INTERMEDIARY An individual or firm that helps to distribute a product.

WHOLESALER An intermediary who sells products to other businesses for resale to final consumers.

RETAILER An intermediary who sells products directly to consumers.

DISTRIBUTION CHANNEL The network of interdependent companies through which a product passes from producer to end user.

DIRECT CHANNEL A distribution channel in which a product travels from producer to consumer without intermediaries.

SALES AGENT An independent intermediary who generally deals in the related product lines of a few producers and forms long-term relationships to represent those producers and meet the needs of many customers.

BROKER An independent intermediary who matches numerous sellers and buyers as needed, often without knowing in advance who they will be.

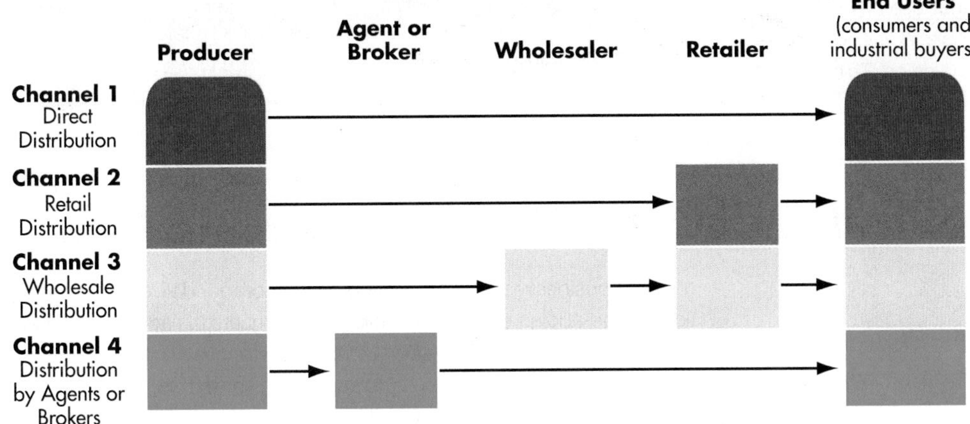

<<< FIGURE 13.3 Channels of distribution

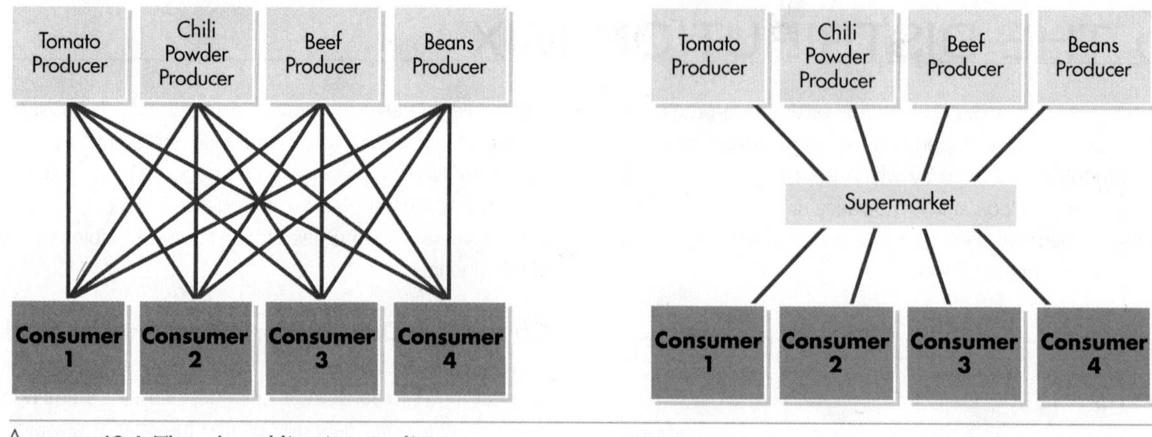

FIGURE 13.4 The value-adding intermediary

THE PROS AND CONS OF NON-DIRECT DISTRIBUTION

One problem with non-direct distribution is higher prices. The more members there are in the channel—the more intermediaries making a profit by charging a markup or commission—the higher the final price. Intermediaries, however, can provide added value by providing time-saving information and making the right quantities of products available where and when consumers need them. Figure 13.4 illustrates the problem of making chili without the benefit of a common intermediary—the supermarket. As a consumer, you would obviously spend a lot more time, money, and energy if you tried to gather all the ingredients from separate producers. In short, intermediaries exist because they provide necessary services that get products efficiently from producers to users.

Distribution Strategies

The choice of a distribution strategy determines the amount of market exposure the product gets and the cost of that exposure. **Intensive distribution** occurs when a product is distributed through as many channels and channel members as possible. Doritos chips flood the market through many different outlets. Intensive distribution is normally used for low-cost consumer goods, such as candy and magazines. In contrast, **exclusive distribution** occurs when a manufacturer grants the exclusive right to distribute or sell a product to one wholesaler or retailer in a given geographic area. For example, Jaguar automobiles are sold by only a single dealer servicing a large metropolitan area. **Selective distribution** falls between intensive and exclusive distribution. A company that uses this strategy selects only wholesalers and retailers who will give special attention to the product in terms of sales efforts, display position, and so on. This method is usually embraced by companies like Black+Decker, whose product lines do not require intense market exposure to increase sales.

Channel Conflict and Channel Leadership

Channel conflict occurs when members of the distribution channel disagree over the roles they should play or the rewards they should receive. John Deere, for example, would no doubt object if its dealers began distributing Russian and Japanese tractors. Channel conflict may also arise if one member has more power than the others or is viewed as receiving preferential treatment. Such conflicts defeat the purpose of the system by disrupting the flow of goods to their destinations. Usually, one channel member—the *channel captain*—is the most powerful in determining the roles and rewards of other members. The channel captain might be a manufacturer, or it might be a large retailer like Walmart that generates large sales volumes.

INTENSIVE DISTRIBUTION A distribution strategy in which a product is distributed in nearly every possible outlet, using many channels and channel members.

EXCLUSIVE DISTRIBUTION A distribution strategy in which a product's distribution is limited to only one wholesaler or retailer in a given geographic area.

SELECTIVE DISTRIBUTION A distribution strategy that falls between intensive and exclusive distribution, calling for the use of a limited number of outlets for a product.

CHANNEL CONFLICT Conflict arising when the members of a distribution channel disagree over the roles they should play or the rewards they should receive.

LO-7 THE ROLE OF INTERMEDIARIES

Wholesaling

The roles differ among the various intermediaries in distribution channels. As noted earlier, most wholesalers are independent operations that buy products from manufacturers and sell them to various consumers or other businesses. They usually provide storage, delivery, and additional value-adding services, including credit, marketing advice, and merchandising services, such as marking prices and setting up displays. Merchant wholesalers take title to merchandise; that is, they buy and own the goods they resell to other businesses.

Unlike wholesalers, agents and brokers do not own their merchandise. Rather, they serve as sales and merchandising arms for producers or sellers who do not have their own sales forces. The value of agents and brokers lies in their knowledge of markets and their merchandising expertise. They show sale items to potential buyers and, for retail stores, they provide such services as shelf and display merchandising and advertising layout. They remove open, torn, or dirty packages; arrange products neatly; and generally keep goods attractively displayed.

Retailing

You may not have had much contact with wholesalers, but, like most Canadians, you buy nearly all the goods and services you consume from retailers. Most retailers are small operations, often consisting of just the owners and part-time help. Retailers also include huge operations, such as Walmart, the world's largest corporate employer, as well as other global players like Carrefour in France, Daiei in Japan, and domestic players like Canadian Tire. Retailers are adapting with the times. Even the most fundamental elements of consumer interaction are changing. Take a look at the E-Business and Social Media Solutions box entitled "Bye-Bye Cash Registers, Hello Tablets!"

TYPES OF BRICK-AND-MORTAR RETAIL OUTLETS

Canadian retail operations vary widely by type as well as size. They can be classified by their pricing strategies, location, range of services, or range of product lines. Choosing the right types of retail outlets is a crucial aspect of distribution strategy. Table 13.2 describes retail stores using three classifications: *product-line retailers*, *bargain retailers*, and *convenience stores*.

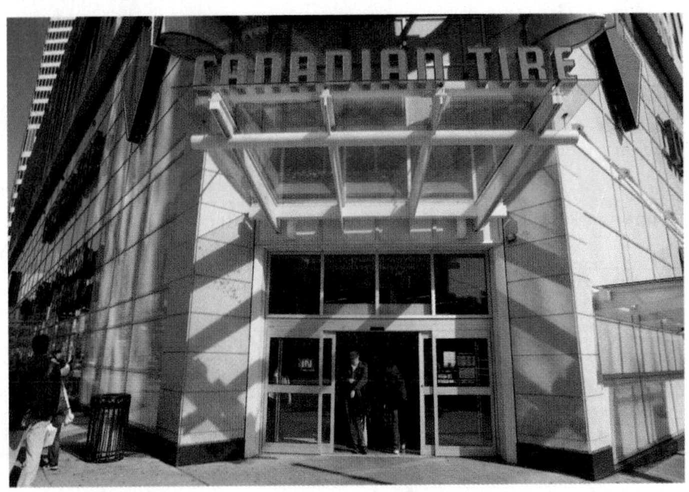

Canadian Tire has 487 stores serving consumers from coast to coast.

TheStoreGuy/Alamy

NON-STORE RETAILING

Some of the largest retailers sell all or most of their products without brick-and-mortar stores. Certain types of products—snack foods and candy—sell well from card- and coin-operated machines. For all products, global annual sales through vending are projected to reach $200 billion in 2015. But this is still a very small percentage (1 to 2 percent) of total retail sales.[21] Non-store retailing also includes **direct-response retailing**, in which firms contact customers directly to inform them about

DIRECT-RESPONSE RETAILING A form of non-store retailing in which firms directly interact with customers to inform them of products and to receive sales orders.

E-BUSINESS AND SOCIAL MEDIA SOLUTIONS

Bye-Bye Cash Registers, Hello Tablets!

In the late 1800s a saloon keeper found a better way to prevent sales clerks from stealing from the cash drawer. Thus, the cash register began its long career among retailers. Today, the cash register's future looks bleak as more and more stores are using smartphones and tablets instead of the heavy, awkward, now-unattractive machines poised at the end of check-out lines.

Mobile devices are on the rise because they are faster, simpler, more attractive, more flexible, and more convenient for shoppers and store owners. They also are far less expensive. An iPad that includes credit-card readers costs $1500, whereas a cash register costs $4000. Urban Outfitters claims to have ordered its last register, planning instead to go entirely mobile at its chain of clothing stores, after a two-year trial run with iPod Touch devices that was well received by customers.

In modernizing their stores, some are planning to ring up sales on iPods and iPads mounted on swivels stationed at counters. Others, including Walmart, are testing "scan and go" apps enabling customers to digitally "ring up" items using their smartphones as they move through the store, instead of in line at checkout. A doughnut store hangs iPad registers on a track on the wall, allowing employees to slide iPads to customers for quick signing of their bills. Other stores equip cashiers with mobile devices to approach customers waiting in line, where they scan purchases and tally sales totals to improve service by reducing waiting time.

Because payment technology continues to change, industry innovators are anticipating the emergence of other new methods. They foresee receipt printers disappearing, along with exchanges of cash that are no longer needed when the use of smartphones and other devices becomes more prominent for electronic payments. Retail shopping is expected, eventually, to involve no checkout, no cash, and no unwanted waiting, all for a better customer shopping experience.

CRITICAL THINKING QUESTION

1. How comfortable are you with going totally digital with your payments? Surely you appreciate quicker checkouts, but are you also OK with a totally paperless process? Are you concerned about security issues?

TABLE 13.2 Types of Retailers

Product-Line Retailers	Description	Examples
Department Stores	Organized into specialized departments (e.g., shoes, furniture, women's petite sizes, and so on); usually large, handle a wide range of goods, and provide a variety of services.	The Bay, Sears
Supermarkets	Organized and divided into departments of related products (e.g., food products, household products, and so on); stress low prices, self-service, and wide selection.	Loblaws, Sobeys, Safeway, Metro
Specialty Stores	Serve specific market segments with full product lines and knowledgeable sales personnel in narrow product fields.	Aldo Shoes, Sunglass Hut
Category Killers	Very large form of specialty store; focuses on particular categories on a giant scale and often dominates retail sales in the category.	Toys "Я" Us, Staples
Bargain Retailers	**Description**	**Examples**
Discount Stores	Provide a wide variety of merchandise with minimal service at low prices.	Walmart
Factory Outlets	Large discount stores; usually sell last season's merchandise, discontinued items, and factory seconds at a low price.	Nike Outlet Store
Wholesale Clubs	Offer large discounts on a wide range of brand-name merchandise to customers who pay annual membership.	Costco
Convenience Stores	**Description**	**Examples**
Convenience Stores	Characterized by easily accessible locations, extended store hours, and speedy service; in recent years, more than 2300 convenience stores closed across Canada, partly because contraband cigarettes eliminated about $2.5 billion in sales.*	Couche-Tard, Mac's

*Bertrand Marotte, "Contraband Killing Convenience Stores," *Globe and Mail*, April 7, 2010, B9.

products and to receive sales orders. Take a look at Table 13.3 for a description of certain forms of direct-response retailing.

E-INTERMEDIARIES

The ability of e-commerce to bring together millions of widely dispersed consumers and businesses has changed the types and roles of intermediaries. **E-intermediaries** are internet-based channel members who perform one or both of two functions: (1) collect information about sellers and present it to consumers or (2) help deliver products to buyers. Over 85 percent of the world's online population—over one billion consumers—have made purchases online. *Electronic retailing (online retailing)* allows sellers to inform, sell to, and distribute to consumers via the web. Amazon.com is the world's largest online retailer, with annual sales of $89 billion.[23]

In addition to large companies, millions of small businesses around the globe have their own websites. Online spending in Canada is expected to top $30.9 billion in 2015.[24] More than 30 000 Canadians are "small retailers" who make a significant portion of their annual income by selling goods and services on sites like Kijiji. But they often do not pay income or sales tax on their sales, so both the Canada Revenue Agency and the federal government are losing millions of dollars in tax revenues every year. A few years ago, the Federal Court of Appeal ordered eBay to provide information on people who sell more than $1000 per month on its site.[25]

E-INTERMEDIARY An internet distribution channel member that assists in delivering products to customers or that collects information about various sellers to be presented to consumers.

TABLE 13.3 Non-Store and Direct-Response Retailing

Direct-Response	Description
Mail Order Catalogue Marketing	A form of non-store retailing in which customers place orders for merchandise in catalogues and receive orders by mail.
Telemarketing	Uses telephone calls to sell directly to consumers. Telemarketing also includes inbound toll-free calls, which most catalogue and other retail stores make available.
Direct Selling	The oldest form of retailing, selling door to door or through home-selling parties. Avon Products, the world's largest direct seller, has 6 million door-to-door sales representatives in more than 100 countries.[22]
Video/TV	A form of retailing that lets viewers shop at home from special channels on their TVs. For example, QVC displays and demonstrates products on TV, as well as on Facebook, YouTube, and Twitter, and allows viewers to phone in or email orders.

LO-8 PHYSICAL DISTRIBUTION

Physical distribution refers to the activities needed to move products from manufacturer to customer and includes warehousing and transportation operations. Its purpose is to make goods available when and where customers want them, keep costs low, and provide services to satisfy customers. Because of its importance for customer satisfaction, some firms have adopted distribution as their core marketing strategy of choice. Companies are constantly seeking efficient solutions. For example, Maersk Line and Aqualife AS have partnered to create a transport system to ship seafood from Canada's east coast aquaculture companies to customers in Europe. Specialized tanks on board the ships oxygenate water without having to use pumps. The new system will help to open new markets for aquaculture products grown in Canada.[26]

Warehousing Operations

Warehousing is the physical distribution operation concerned with the storage of goods. In selecting a distribution strategy, managers must keep in mind both the different characteristics and costs of warehousing operations. Warehouses may be owned by a single manufacturer, wholesaler, or retailer, which deals in mass quantities and needs regular storage (such as The Brick). Other warehouses are independently owned and rent space to companies as required (e.g., during peak periods).

Transportation Operations

Physically moving a product creates the highest cost many companies face. In addition to transportation methods, firms must also consider the nature of the product, the distance it must travel, the speed with which it must be received, and customer wants and needs.

Differences in cost among the major transportation modes—trucks, railroads, planes, digital transmission, water carriers, and pipelines—are usually most directly related to delivery speed. See Table 13.4 for more details about transportation modes.

For more information on transportation modes, take a look at the next boxed feature entitled "Unexpected Outcomes." It discusses a major project that has been in the news quite a bit lately.

FedEx has over 140 000 employees worldwide and operates a fleet of 654 airplanes that help the company deliver speedy service to clients around the world.

Hady Khandani/vario images GmbH & Co.KG/Alamy

TABLE 13.4 Pros and Cons of the Various Modes of Transporting Goods

Mode of Transport	Pros and Cons
Trucks	+ Flexibility, fast service, and dependability – Increased truck traffic is raising safety concerns
Planes	+ Fastest traditional method (potential for lower-inventory costs; reduces the need to store items that might spoil) – Most expensive approach
Digital Transmission	+ Newest, fastest, and least expensive method – Restricted to certain products (e.g., music, movies, software, and so on)
Water Carriers	+ Least expensive traditional mode – Slowest method
Railroads	+ Economically transport high-volume, heavy, bulky items (e.g., cars, steel) – Delivery routes are limited by fixed railway lines
Pipelines	+ Good for specialized products (liquids and gases); economical and reliable – Slow, lack of flexibility

Distribution Through Supply Chains as a Marketing Strategy

Instead of just offering advantages in product features, quality, price, and promotion, many firms have turned to supply chains that depend on distribution as a cornerstone of business strategy. This approach means assessing, improving, and integrating the entire stream of activities—upstream suppliers, wholesaling, warehousing, transportation, delivery, and follow-up services—involved in getting products to customers.

Walmart built its distribution system utilizing the best practices of both just-in-time and supply chains (as discussed in Chapter 10), instead of the industry practice of relying on outside freight companies and wholesalers. When you buy a product (like Tide) at Walmart, the checkout scanner reads the barcode on the box and Walmart's inventory system is updated instantly, showing that a replacement is needed on the shelf. Once the supply of Tide dwindles to its automatic triggering number, Walmart's distribution centre receives a digital signal notifying that this store needs more Tide and, at the same time, the system also notifies the manufacturer (in this case, Procter & Gamble) that this location needs a replenishment supply—a predetermined number of boxes. Walmart's data mining system determines the reorder number for every product based on sales (daily, weekly, and even by time of the year). Because of Walmart's constant rapid restocking from upstream sources, its store shelves are resupplied

PHYSICAL DISTRIBUTION Activities needed to move a product efficiently from manufacturer to consumer.

WAREHOUSING A physical distribution operation concerned with the storage of goods.

THE GREENING OF BUSINESS

Unexpected Outcomes

On July 6, 2013, a runaway train carrying crude oil from the Bakken formation in North Dakota derailed in Lac-Mégantic, Quebec. The resulting explosion and fire killed 47 people and destroyed almost the entire town centre. Several other large-scale oil train explosions have also occurred recently in the United States. As a result of these accidents, both the Canadian and U.S. governments have required changes to tank cars that make it less likely that they will be punctured in an accident. The rail industry has expressed concerns that the new restrictions will cause further disruptions in getting oil to markets.

Behind these rail tragedies lies a story of how the activities of different groups can lead to unexpected negative outcomes. The story begins with the fact that oil is Canada's largest export, and it has a significant positive effect on our balance of trade and on our national wealth. The U.S. imports more oil from Canada than from any other country, and to facilitate the exporting of even more oil, TransCanada Corp. wanted to build the Keystone XL pipeline to carry oil from Alberta to Houston, Texas (where many oil refineries are located). During the past several years, environmental groups objected to the pipeline on the grounds that it posed an environmental threat, and several well-publicized pipeline leaks seemed to support their claims. Canadian activists—led by Greenpeace Canada, the Council of Canadians, and the Indigenous Environmental Network—also organized a protest in Ottawa to raise awareness of the problem and stop approval for the pipeline. After several years of debate and delay, in 2015 U.S. president Barack Obama vetoed a bill that would have allowed the pipeline to be built. The U.S. Senate failed to override the veto.

These delays were very frustrating to oil companies, because current pipeline capacity is not sufficient to move the increased amounts of oil being produced in Alberta's oil sands and in the Bakken formation in North Dakota. The oil companies therefore decided to ship their oil to market using railroad tank cars because they didn't need any additional approval to do that. The result has been a dramatic increase in the amount of oil carried on trains (each train can carry up to 60 000 barrels of oil). But that decision also led to increased accidents, oil spills, fires, and deaths.

CRITICAL THINKING QUESTION

1. How has the external environment of business impacted companies like TransCanada Corp.?
2. Consider the following statement: *Since it is safer to transport oil in pipelines than in rail cars, the Keystone XL pipeline should be approved. This will reduce the problem of oil spills as a result of railroad accidents.* Do you agree or disagree? Explain your reasoning.

without the company's having to keep large inventories in its warehouses and retail stores, thus reducing inventory costs and providing lower prices.

Walmart's JIT system has allowed it to achieve a short (as low as two-day) turnaround from manufacturer to store shelf, providing cost control and product availability. It maintains lower levels of inventory, meets customer demand, and keeps the lowest prices in the retail industry.

These close partnership relationships also have other benefits when competitors try to enter their territory. For example, as Target began to open stores across Canada in 2013 (before ultimately failing in its quest), it complained of difficulty in finding vendors for certain products in Canada. For smaller vendors that receive 80 to 90 percent of their business from companies like Walmart and HBC, there may have been capacity issues, but there also may have been direct verbal or implied pressure to stay loyal and avoid the new player on the block.[27]

SUMMARY OF LEARNING OBJECTIVES

LO-1 IDENTIFY THE VARIOUS *PRICING OBJECTIVES* THAT GOVERN PRICING DECISIONS, AND DESCRIBE THE *PRICE-SETTING TOOLS* USED IN MAKING THESE DECISIONS.

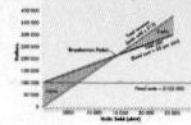

Two major pricing objectives are (1) pricing to maximize profits—set the price to sell the number of units that will generate the highest possible total profits and (2) market-share objectives—pricing is used for establishing market share. The seller is willing to accept minimal profits, even losses, to get buyers to try products. Two basic tools are used: (1) cost-oriented pricing begins by determining total costs for making products available to shoppers, then a figure for profit is added in to arrive at a selling price, and

(2) breakeven analysis assesses total costs versus revenues for various sales volumes. It shows, at each possible sales volume, the amount of loss or profit for any chosen sales price. It also shows the breakeven point, the number of sales units for total revenue to equal total costs.

LO-2 DISCUSS *PRICING STRATEGIES* THAT CAN BE USED FOR DIFFERENT COMPETITIVE SITUATIONS AND IDENTIFY THE *PRICING TACTICS* THAT CAN BE USED FOR SETTING PRICES.

Pricing for existing products can be set above, at, or below market prices for similar products. High pricing is often interpreted as meaning higher quality and prestige, while low pricing may attract greater sales volume. Strategies for new products include price skimming, setting an initially high price to cover costs and generate a profit, and penetration pricing, setting a low price to establish a new product in the market. Strategies for e-businesses include dynamic versus fixed pricing. Dynamic pricing establishes individual prices by real-time interaction between the seller and each customer on the internet. Fixed pricing is the traditional one-price-for-all arrangement.

Three tactics are often used for setting prices: (1) With price lining, any product category (such as ladies' shoes) will be set at three or four price levels, and all shoes will be priced at one of those levels. (2) Psychological pricing acknowledges that customers are not completely rational when making buying decisions, as with odd-even pricing in which customers regard prices such as $10 as being significantly higher than $9.95. (3) Discount pricing uses price reductions to stimulate sales.

LO-3 IDENTIFY THE IMPORTANT *OBJECTIVES OF PROMOTION* AND DISCUSS THE CONSIDERATIONS IN SELECTING A *PROMOTIONAL MIX*.

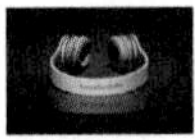

Although the ultimate goal of any promotion is to increase sales, other goals include communicating information, positioning a product, adding value, and controlling sales volume. In deciding on the appropriate promotional mix, the best combination of promotional tools (e.g., advertising, personal selling, sales promotions, direct [or interactive] marketing, public relations), marketers must consider the good or service being offered, characteristics of the target audience, the buyer's decision process, and the promotional mix budget.

LO-4 DEFINE THE *ROLE OF ADVERTISING* AND DESCRIBE THE KEY *ADVERTISING MEDIA*.

Advertising is paid, non-personal communication, by which an identified sponsor informs an audience about a product. Marketers use several different advertising media—specific communication devices for carrying a seller's message to potential customers—each with its specific advantages and drawbacks. The most common media—television, newspapers, direct mail, radio, magazines, outdoor advertising, online, mobile—differ in their cost and their ability to segment target markets.

LO-5 OUTLINE THE TASKS INVOLVED IN *PERSONAL SELLING*, DESCRIBE THE VARIOUS TYPES OF *SALES PROMOTIONS, DESCRIBE DIRECT* (*OR INTERACTIVE*) *MARKETING*, AND DISTINGUISH BETWEEN *PUBLICITY* AND *PUBLIC RELATIONS*.

Personal selling is a promotional tool in which a salesperson communicates one to one with potential customers; it provides the personal link between seller and buyer. Sales promotions include point-of-purchase (or sale) displays to attract consumer attention, help them find products in stores and offices, and provide product information. Other sales promotions give purchasing incentives, such as samples (customers can try products without having to buy them), coupons (a certificate for price reduction), and premiums (free or reduced-price rewards for buying products). At trade shows, B2B sellers rent booths to display products to industrial customers. Contests intend to stimulate sales, with prizes to high-producing intermediaries and consumers who use the seller's products.

Direct (or interactive) marketing is one-on-one non-personal selling that tries to get consumers to make purchases away from retail stores and, instead, to purchase from home, at work, or by using a mobile device. It includes non-store retailers (catalogues, telemarketing, home video shopping), direct mail, direct response advertising (such as infomercials and direct response magazine and newspaper ads), and targeted emails.

Publicity is information about a company, a product, or an event transmitted by the general mass media to attract public attention. Control of the message's content is determined by outside writers and reporters. In contrast to publicity, public relations is company-influenced information that seeks to either build good relations with the public or to deal with unfavourable events.

LO-6 EXPLAIN THE MEANING OF *DISTRIBUTION MIX* AND IDENTIFY THE DIFFERENT *CHANNELS OF DISTRIBUTION*.

The combination of distribution channels for getting products to end users—consumers and industrial buyers—is the distribution mix. Intermediaries help to distribute a producer's goods by moving them from sellers to customers; wholesalers sell products to other businesses, which resell them to final users. Retailers, sales agents, and brokers sell products directly to end users. In Channel 1, the simplest of the four distribution channels, the producer sells directly to users. Channel 2 includes a retailer, Channel 3 involves both a retailer and a wholesaler, and Channel 4 includes an agent or broker.

LO-7 DESCRIBE THE ROLE OF *INTERMEDIARIES*. EXPLAIN THE FUNCTION OF *WHOLESALERS* AND IDENTIFY THE DIFFERENT TYPES OF *RETAILERS* AND *E-INTERMEDIARIES*.

The roles differ among the various intermediaries in distribution channels. Wholesalers provide a variety of services, including delivery, credit arrangements, and product information. In buying and reselling an assortment of products, wholesalers provide storage, marketing advice, and assist customers by marking prices and setting up displays. Retail stores range from broad product-line department stores and supermarkets, to small specialty stores for specific market segments seeking narrow product lines. Non-store retailing includes direct-response retailing, mail order (or catalogue marketing), telemarketing, and direct selling.

E-intermediaries are internet-based channel members who perform one or both of two functions: (1) they collect information about sellers and present it to consumers and (2) they help deliver internet products to buyers. For example, electronic retailers interact online with customers and add value by informing, selling to, and distributing products to them.

LO-8 DESCRIBE THE *PHYSICAL DISTRIBUTION PROCESS*.

Physical distribution activities include providing customer services, warehousing, and transportation of products. Warehouses provide storage for products, whereas transportation operations physically move products from suppliers to customers. Trucks, railroads, planes, water carriers (boats and barges), digital transmission, and pipelines are the major transportation modes used in the distribution process.

QUESTIONS AND EXERCISES

QUESTIONS FOR ANALYSIS

1. Discuss the goal of price skimming and penetration pricing.
2. How do cost-oriented pricing and breakeven analysis help managers measure the potential impact of prices? What general factors motivate marketing managers to price their products at, above, or below prevailing market prices?
3. From the manufacturer's point of view, what are the advantages and disadvantages of using intermediaries to distribute products? How about from the end user's point of view?
4. Describe the three levels of market coverage. When is each one most appropriate?
5. Select four advertising media and compare the advantages and disadvantages of each.
6. Give three examples (other than those provided in the chapter) of products that use intensive distribution. Do the same for products that use exclusive distribution and selective distribution. What are the characteristics of the products in each category? For which category was it easiest to find examples? Why?

APPLICATION EXERCISES

7. Select a product and analyze pricing objectives for it. What information would you want if you were to adopt a profit-maximizing objective or a market-share objective?
8. Consider the various kinds of non-store retailing. Give examples of two products that typify the kinds of products sold through each form of non-store retailing. Are different products best suited to each form of non-store retailing? Explain.
9. Identify a company that is a member in a supply chain. Explain how its presence in the chain affects the company's marketing decisions for pricing, promoting, and distributing its products.
10. Choose two advertising campaigns that have recently been conducted by business firms in your area. Choose one that you think is effective and one that you think is ineffective. What differences in the campaigns make one better than the other? Why would a business use a push strategy rather than a pull strategy?

TEAM EXERCISES

BUILDING YOUR BUSINESS SKILLS

A BIG PUSH FOR PUBLICITY

GOAL

To encourage you to work in teams to develop a promotional campaign aimed at the specific needs of an organization.

BACKGROUND INFORMATION

A new theme park is opening just a few kilometres away from your campus. It will feature lots of rides and roller coasters as well as a water park. There will be lots of food options, from fast food to fine dining, and something for everyone in the family. There are two other theme parks within a 200 kilometre radius of your college, but this new park will be significantly closer than the competition.

The developers of the park have been so impressed with your college that they have invited teams of students to develop proposals. Your group is one of several that have been charged with developing the promotional mix for the new park. You will present your proposal to the company and company executives will select the one they think is most appropriate. Although this is, at the time, an activity for your class, it could turn into a full-time job with the company, so the stakes are high.

METHOD

Step 1 Assemble a group of four students and assign each group member to one of the following components of the promotional mix: Advertising, Personal Selling, Sales Promotion, Publicity, and Public Relations. As a group, develop your promotional objectives. What are the initial objectives of your promotional campaign?

Step 2 Each group member will work on ideas (based on the agreed upon objectives) from the perspective of their assigned role. What specific promotional activities within your category would you recommend?

Step 3 Get together again and share your ideas and make decisions; don't forget to make sure that there is a good match between the activities. Develop a 1–2-page recommendation that you could present to the company's executives.

QUESTION FOR DISCUSSION

1. Do you think that the promotional mix will change over time? How might it be different in three years?
2. What role will online communications play for this theme park: (a) before the launch, (b) during the launch, and (c) on an ongoing basis?

EXERCISING YOUR ETHICS

THE CHAIN OF RESPONSIBILITY

THE SITUATION

Because several stages are involved when distribution chains move products from supply sources to end consumers, the process offers ample opportunity for ethical issues to arise. This exercise encourages you to examine some of the ethical issues that can emerge during transactions among suppliers and customers.

THE DILEMMA

A customer bought an expensive wedding gift at a local store and asked that it be shipped to the bride in another province. Several weeks after the wedding, the customer contacted the bride, who had not confirmed the arrival of the gift. It hadn't arrived. Charging that the merchandise had not been delivered, the customer requested a refund from the retailer. The store manager uncovered the following facts:

- All shipments from the store are handled by a well-known national delivery firm.
- The delivery firm verified that the package had been delivered to the designated address two days after the sale.
- Normally, the delivery firm does not obtain recipient signatures; deliveries are made to the address of record, regardless of the name on the package.

The gift giver argued that even though the package had been delivered to the right address, it had not been delivered to the named recipient. It turns out that, unbeknownst to the gift giver, the bride had moved. It stood to reason, then, that the gift was in the hands of the new occupant at the bride's former address. The manager informed the gift giver that the store had fulfilled its obligation. The cause of the problem, she explained, was the incorrect address given by the customer. She refused to refund the customer's money and suggested that the customer might want to recover the gift by contacting the stranger who received it at the bride's old address.

TEAM ACTIVITY

Assemble a group of four students and assign each group member to one of the following roles:

- customer (the person who had originally purchased the gift)
- employee (of the store where the gift was purchased)

- bride (the person who was supposed to receive the gift)
- customer service manager (of the delivery company)

QUESTIONS FOR DISCUSSION

1. Before hearing any of your group's comments and from the perspective of your assigned role, decide whether there are any ethical issues in this situation. If so, write them down.
2. Before hearing any of your group's comments and from the perspective of your assigned role, decide how this dispute should be resolved.
3. Together with your group, share the ethical issues that were identified. What responsibilities does each party—the customer, the store, and the delivery company—have in this situation?
4. What does your group recommend be done to resolve this dispute? What are the advantages and disadvantages of your recommendations?

BUSINESS CASE 13

HOLLYWOOD'S NEW MARKETING CAMPAIGN: REVIVING CLASSIC MOVIES

As film columnist Pete Hammond notes, "In Hollywood they say 'everything old is new again' and that has never been more true . . ." Consider, for example, the 50th anniversary digital remake of the movie *The Great Escape* starring Steve McQueen and Disney's animated *Peter Pan*. Hundreds of classic films from Hollywood (and from studios around the world) are finding renewed popularity. The revival of these so-called "catalogue titles" is no accident; because disc sales of new movies have been on a ten-year decline, studios have been on the hunt for new revenue sources. The result is an industry-wide marketing campaign for reviving classic movies or, restated in marketing terms, it's an example of "product extension, or reintroduction of old brands." Although the campaign has not solved all of the industry's sales issue, it is helping.

© Jeff Gilbert/Alamy Stock Photo

Sales of DVDs (and CDs) in Canada were down from a total of $1.6 billion in 2010 to $1.1 billion in 2014. However, the biggest decline came in the area of new releases; classic films were still putting up a good fight. Sales of catalogue titles were increasing as they account for nearly 45 percent of the industry's film disc (DVD and Blu-ray) revenues. In other words, they are a minor positive sign in a very negative landscape.

A core demographic for the revival is older movie fans who remember and re-watch catalogue titles, including many who want upgraded Blu-ray remakes of classic films such as *Rebel Without a Cause* (1955) with James Dean. These Blu-ray releases are especially important, because they generate higher profit margins than standard DVDs. While most younger viewers turn to Netflix or other on-demand video outlets, some are turning to illegally downloaded options.

It is estimated that 80 percent of catalogue-title disc purchases are made by price-conscious impulse shoppers, including younger viewers, at mass-market retail stores such as Walmart. Thus, two contrasting groups of buyers have emerged: (1) older viewers buying Blu-ray and other kinds of upgraded discs and (2) buyers, both younger and older, seeking very-low-priced DVDs. Accordingly, large retail stores are placing bins in the aisles packed with inexpensively packaged DVDs priced as low as $5 for movies like *Home Alone*.

Along with Blu-ray upgrades, the marketing campaign includes increased retailer display space for classic films, eye-catching online marketing images, and newer packaging to interest the classic audience. Distributors are packaging thematic boxed sets of multiple disks, some with films starring a particular actor, such as Tom Hanks, others grouping together one type of films, such as famous musicals. Prominent firms Warner Bros. and the Paramount Pictures Library (Viacom Inc.), for example, are collaborating in combining related movies from different studios together in one package, including several John Travolta thrillers. Similarly, a few years ago, MGM promoted *Bond 50: The Complete 22 Film Collection*, the 50th anniversary Blu-ray collection. These marketing efforts are having a visible public impact; Blu-ray discs of *Jaws*, and the *Bond 50 Collection* broke onto Rentrak Corp.'s Top 10 list.

The trend to revive classic films is moving internationally, too, with India's online retailers, Flipkart and Moviemart.com, experiencing an increased number of customers and more DVD sales of old and classic movies than new films. Reaching beyond DVDs and Blu-ray, Warner Bros. has launched a subscription streaming service for classic TV shows and movies. In addition to films and TV, the impact of the classic-movie trend appears to be stretching into seemingly unrelated industries; PureCostumes.com, purveyor of Halloween costumes, carries licensed costumes of such classic movies as *Breakfast at Tiffany's* and *Grease*. Who knows? Perhaps the industry's marketing campaign itself may someday be considered a classic.

QUESTIONS FOR DISCUSSION

1. Describe the advertising mix being used in Hollywood's new marketing campaign.
2. What are the main reasons for the new campaign? How do you recommend they measure results?
3. How might the marketing campaign benefit from a revised advertising mix? Explain your reasoning.
4. Identify the distribution channels that exist in the new marketing campaign. How might they become more effective?
5. Describe the target market(s) for the new marketing campaign. Are the advertising and distribution mixes well suited to the target market(s)? Explain.

MANAGING MARKETING

GOAL OF THE EXERCISE

So far, your business has an identity, you've described the factors that will affect your business, and you've examined your employees, the jobs they'll be performing, and the ways in which you can motivate them. Part 4 of the business plan project asks you to think about marketing's 4 P's—product, price, place (distribution), and promotion—and how they apply to your business. You'll also examine how you might target your marketing toward a certain group of consumers.

EXERCISE BACKGROUND: PART 4 OF THE BUSINESS PLAN

In Part 1, you briefly described what your business will do. The first step in Part 4 of the plan is to more fully describe the product (good or service) you are planning to sell. Once you have a clear picture of the product, you'll need to describe how this product will stand out in the marketplace—that is, how will it differentiate itself from other products?

In Part 1, you also briefly described who your customers would be. The first step in Part 4 of the plan is to describe your ideal buyer, or target market, in more detail, listing their income level, education level, lifestyle, age, and so forth. This part of the business plan project also asks you to discuss the price of your products, as well as where the buyer can find your product.

Finally, you'll examine how your business will get the attention and interest of the buyer through its promotional mix—advertising, personal selling, sales promotions, and publicity and public relations.

This part of the business plan encourages you to be creative. Have fun! Provide as many details as you possibly can, as this reflects an understanding of your product and your buyer. Marketing is all about finding a need and filling it. Does your product fill a need in the marketplace?

YOUR ASSIGNMENT

MyBizLab

STEP 1

Open the saved Business Plan file you have been working on.

STEP 2

For the purposes of this assignment, you will answer the following questions in Part 4: Managing Marketing:

1. Describe your target market in terms of age, education level, income, and other demographic variables.

   Hint: Refer to Chapter 12 for more information on the aspects of target marketing and market segmentation that you may want to consider. Be as detailed as possible about who you think your customers will be.

2. Describe the features and benefits of your product or service.

   Hint: As you learned in Chapter 12, a product is a bundle of attributes—features and benefits. What features does your product have—what does it look like and what does it do? How will the product benefit the buyer?

3. How will you make your product stand out in the crowd?

   Hint: There are many ways to stand out in the crowd, such as having a unique product, outstanding service, or great location. What makes your great idea special? Does it fill an unmet need in the marketplace? How will you differentiate your product to make sure that it succeeds?

4. What pricing strategy will you choose for your product, and what are the reasons for this strategy?

   Hint: Refer to this chapter for more information on pricing strategies and tactics. Since your business is new, so is the product. Therefore, you probably want to choose between price skimming and penetration pricing. Which will you choose and why?

5. Where will customers find your product or service? (That is, what issues of the distribution mix should you consider?)

   Hint: If your business does not sell its product directly to consumers, what types of retail stores will sell your product? If your product will be sold to another business, which channel of distribution will you use? Refer to this chapter for more information on aspects of distribution you may want to consider.

6. How will you advertise to your target market? Why have you chosen these forms of advertisement?

   Hint: Marketers use several different advertising media—specific communication devices for carrying a seller's message to potential customers—each with advantages and drawbacks. Refer to this chapter for a discussion of the types of advertising media you may wish to consider here.

7. What other methods of promotion will you use and why?

   Hint: There's more to promotion than simple advertising. Other methods include personal selling, sales promotions, and publicity and public relations. Refer to the discussion of promotion for ideas on how to promote your product that go beyond just advertising.

Note: Once you have answered the questions, save your Word document. You'll be answering additional questions in later chapters.

CBC VIDEO CASE 4-1

CBC

COLT HOCKEY

THE COMPANY

Almost every child in Canada grows up dreaming about scoring the gold medal goal or the overtime winner in the Stanley Cup finals. But in recent years, the daydreaming has been rudely interrupted by the horrible sound of an expensive carbon fibre stick breaking in half. There is no denying that the technology has made hockey sticks lighter and provided added velocity. But anyone who watches hockey can tell you that the performance benefits of composite sticks are accompanied by a major weakness in terms of durability. This is exactly the reason why three young Toronto-based entrepreneurs named Daniel Lucchesi, Daniel Palumbo, and Mario Cieslak created Colt Hockey; they wanted to revolutionize the hockey stick to combine performance with durability. To find a solution, they turned to Integran Technologies (a leader in the aerospace industry). Colt's carbon fibre sticks are coated with Nanovate Nickel Cobalt (Nico), which makes the sticks last two to three times longer.

Where do entrepreneurs find great ideas? In this case, one of the partners had read about the benefits and strength of Nico technology in the *National Post*, and the idea for Colt Hockey sticks was born. Sometimes it really pays to read and discover. For more details on the company, go to colthockey.com.

THE PITCH

The entrepreneurial team from Colt Hockey asked for $500 000 in return for 20 percent ownership of the company (valued at $2 500 000).

THE DRAGONS' POINT OF VIEW

Arlene Dickinson began by telling them she was keeping her protective eye glasses on because she thought their valuation (at $2.5 million) was dangerous. Vikram Vij asked them about their sales. They informed the dragons that Colt Hockey had initial sales of over $255 000 in just three months, with projected sales of over half a million by the end of the season and projected profit of $100 000. Jim Treliving was impressed, but pointed out that the evaluations were still quite high. He also asked about the potential for NHL endorsement deals, and was informed that they had received some interest but the company had not pursued it because they were not yet ready to meet the specifications. However, NHL endorsements were part of their plans moving forward. Michael Wekerle asked them about their relationship with Integran Technologies. Colt Hockey has a 15-year exclusivity deal. When David Chilton asked them if they had pre-negotiated an automatic renewal, they said no.

Michael and Vikram bowed out. Michael said, "I never buy anything with an expiry date and you only have 15 years." However, Jim Treliving did not hesitate; he offered them $500 000 for 50 percent. Within a few seconds there was a second joint offer from Arlene Dickinson and David Chilton at $500 000 for 49 percent.

THE OUTCOME

After speaking to their advisor, the three young entrepreneurs emerged from their huddle and respectfully turned down Jim's offer in favour of Arlene and Dave's. In their brief discussion, Arlene's marketing expertise was cited as an important consideration in their choice.

QUESTIONS FOR DISCUSSION

1. How would you describe this consumer product? What category does it fall under? Explain.
2. Good entrepreneurs see opportunities that others miss. Describe the product development process. As you list the steps, try to imagine what the main issues were for Colt Hockey at each stage for this revolutionary product.
3. If you were the CEO or director of marketing of Colt Hockey, describe how you would market this product. Make sure to provide a detailed explanation for all the elements of the marketing mix. Develop a slogan, and (time permitting) create a storyboard for an ad for this product.

Source: "Colt Hockey," *Dragons' Den*, Season 9, Episode 11 (January 22, 2015).

BUSINESS TODAY VIDEO CASE 4-1

KID TOY TESTERS MAKE BIG BUCKS ON YOUTUBE

Have you ever seen YouTube videos showing kids playing and testing their toys? If not, you are probably too old and/or do not have young children or young siblings. Toy-testing videos are all the rage in the online world.

Why are they so popular? Children love to play. They also love to imagine themselves in fun situations. When they see videos of other children playing it is a win-win scenario. So it is not uncommon for a child to demand that their parents play a certain toy-testing video countless times over the course of a week, month, or year. It is also a way for the companies to expose their toys to the youth of today. The end result is that many of these popular testers are transforming from fans to paid representatives.

Specific laws in Canada restrict advertising to children. However, clearly the standards are not nearly as effective in this new age, in which eyeballs are probably more likely to be tuned to an iPad than a TV. When you conduct a search for "Thomas the Train" or "Angry Birds" or "Cars" or any other beloved animated character, you also get countless videos of young children playing and testing toys. What may have started as a fun activity for some parents has turned into a major business for many. Typical 3-to-6-year-olds might have just as much fun watching another child play with "Thomas the Train" and creating scenarios as they do when they watch the actual videos. Many parents are allowing their young children to surf to such sites at a very young age. In fact, some of these videos are viewed millions of times and earn their young stars approximately $1 million per year.

One prominent example is presented in this video, in the form of family members Maya and Hulyan. Their father indicated that their downloaded videos earned the family over $1.5 million dollars in the previous year. As he says in the video, they are "living the dream."

QUESTIONS FOR DISCUSSION

1. How have young children like Maya, Hulyan, and Evan found success on YouTube?
2. If you were a marketer of children's toys, how would this form of promotion fit into your promotion mix? Talk about the pros and cons of this approach.
3. Why do you think these toy testers are making millions of dollars via YouTube videos?

BUSINESS TODAY VIDEO CASE 4-2

MATTHEW MCCONAUGHEY'S LINCOLN COMMERCIALS GENERATE LOTS OF BUZZ

How do car companies generate buzz? Building a great car is a good start, but they also must find effective ways to cut through the advertising clutter to get noticed. In recent years, the Lincoln brand (owned by Ford) has not been very good at creating positive buzz, generating sales, or building market share. In fact, the brand was ranked eighth among luxury brands at the time this video was made.

However, the decision to build a strange, quirky campaign around a popular actor, Matthew McConaughey, seems to be providing much-needed visibility and a slight boost in sales. The ads are described as "bizarre, surreal, and strange," but despite that description—or maybe because of it—the campaign has gone viral.

Many believe that Lincoln is seeking younger buyers. Does McConaughey reach that audience? Is he a good representative? The commercials have been famously spoofed by Ellen DeGeneres, South Park, and Jim Carrey. How might these spoofs help reach a younger audience? Will they continue to increase sales? Time will tell if this choice of spokesperson will lead to a long-term upswing in sales or just a short-term blip. Clearly, Lincoln is counting on McConaughey's appeal to rub off on a generation of consumers who may have previously ignored the brand but might now take a second look.

QUESTIONS FOR DISCUSSION

1. Describe the Lincoln commercials featuring Matthew McConaughey. Do you think the ads effectively communicate the message? What's the message? Why do you think Lincoln chose to air commercials featuring a celebrity?
2. In this part of the text you learned about segmentation, targeting, and positioning. Based on what you saw in the video and the selected ad content and format, describe Lincoln's positioning. How does the apparent positioning relate to their segmentation and targeting approach?
3. Why might Lincoln welcome commercial spoofs from well-known comedians?

PART 5 MANAGING FINANCIAL ISSUES

Rawpixel/Fotolia

CHAPTER 14

Money and Banking

LO

AFTER READING THIS CHAPTER, YOU SHOULD BE ABLE TO:

LO-1 Define *money* and identify the different forms it takes in Canada's money supply.

LO-2 Understand the different kinds of *financial institutions* that make up the *Canadian financial system* and explain the services they offer.

LO-3 Explain the functions of the *Bank of Canada* and describe the tools it uses to control the money supply.

LO-4 Explain the role of *alternate banks, specialized lending and savings intermediaries*, and *investment dealers* in the Canadian financial system.

LO-5 Discuss some of the institutions and activities in *international banking and finance*.

Canadian Mortgages: Bulls, Bears, and Banks

Low rates, lower rates, even lower rates. . . . Will rates ever rise? Is there a real estate bubble? When will it burst? Depending on who you listen to, you can get some conflicting responses; but clearly the extended period of low interest rates has encouraged Canadians to take on more debt. The average Canadian debt-to-income ratio hit a record high of 163 percent in 2015. The Americans and the British reached levels above 160 percent before it caught up to them in the form of a major housing market crisis. When rates finally do rise, the average Canadian will encounter big increases in financing costs that many home owners may not be ready to handle.

In 2015, potential home buyers were facing a difficult question: To buy or not to buy? They had seen home prices soar for years with the help of cheap mortgage rates. For anyone considering this question in the previous decade, the correct answer was clearly to buy. But could the positive upward trend continue? The average price for a home in Canada stood at $439 144 at the beginning of 2015; this figure had more than doubled in a decade. Check out the average prices of homes in these major cities: Vancouver ($870 207), Toronto ($601 554), Calgary ($447 974), and Montreal ($337 530). These numbers have been steadily increasing; but trends can quickly reverse, as many found out the hard way in the United States. Some homeowners who have seen their equity rise sharply were asking the opposite question: To sell or not to sell? Some experts were calling for a major correction in prices, including the Governor of the Bank of Canada, Stephen Poloz, who said that the Canadian housing market was overvalued by 10 to 30 percent. Strong words from a very influential person.

In the past decade, if you examined these rising valuations and thought this large increase could not be sustained because the trend in salaries and inflation was not keeping pace with housing price increases, you had a very sound traditional argument. However, if you acted on this logic and took a conservative approach, you may have missed out on the wealth accumulation trend. The majority have bought into the following train of thought: "The prices will

cherezoff/Fotolia

keep rising, and if I wait I will have to pay more. So I might as well buy as much house as I can and get the maximum loan the bank is offering." But what happens when the music stops?

Investors who have been waiting on the sidelines for a market correction have been punished. Of course, the housing market, like other investment vehicles, goes in cycles. At times it can be flat and at others it booms. The long-term trend is up, but not at this pace. A significant correction will probably hit the housing market at some point. The real question is: What should you do today? In order to answer this, you have to look at the fundamentals, despite their poor performance in predicting the market lately: the regulators, the role of the banks, the lessons from history and the U.S crisis, and, ultimately, your long-term ability to pay. With new warnings being issued daily, it looks like the pendulum may soon swing back in favour of the conservative home buyer.

HOW WILL THIS HELP ME?

Dealing in matters of money is far more complicated than counting the cash and coins in your pocket, especially when technology and globalization come into play. At its core are questions about where money comes from, how national economies depend on it, and the public's trust in its value. This chapter will give you a solid understanding of the different forms of money and how its supply is created and controlled by different kinds of financial institutions and government regulations.

The Role of the Banks

When it comes to mortgages, banks are in the business of making money by lending to people who can pay back their loans and the interest. Canadian banks have traditionally been quite conservative, but in recent years there has been a shift. The big banks (with the support of the Bank of Canada) have been severe enablers in the rise of housing prices. Low rates and great terms have made it possible for more people to buy homes and for all potential customers to buy bigger (and/or more expensive) homes than they could rationally afford. Many industry experts (including banking officials) were alarmed a few years ago when some banks started offering five-year mortgages at 2.99 percent. It seemed like this low rate, locked in for five years, was irresponsible. What happened? Three years later those same banks were offering rates as low as 2.69 percent for the same term.

The Regulators

Part of the finance minister job is to cool down the economy when it is too hot. However, this task is difficult. On the one hand, we see a major bubble forming in the housing market. The appropriate response is to raise rates to dampen consumer appetite for debt. On the other hand, the drop in oil prices has led to a weakening of the Canadian economy (Canada being an oil-producing nation). So an increase would not be a good response to that issue.

What can be done? Ottawa has made some adjustments through the Canada Mortgage and Housing Corporation (CMHC), which provides mortgage insurance to financial institutions, determining which mortgages are insurable and which not. For years, mortgages in Canada had a maximum amortization period of 25 years. But ten years ago, this policy changed to allow mortgages to be granted for 40 years with very little or no down payment. This meant that people's monthly payments were now much lower (they could pay back the same amount over 40 years instead of 25) and it also meant people could take on much more debt. In response to this concern, Ottawa lowered the amortization maximum to 35 years, later to 30 years, and more recently back to 25 years (under CMHC).

Checking the Numbers

The sustained low-interest-rate environment has encouraged people to purchase more house than they can probably afford. Some people believe that these low rates will last forever or do not understand what even a small increase can mean. Let's take a look at an example.

John and Mary buy a home for $500 000. They make a down payment of $150 000 and take out a mortgage for $350 000. They lock in their $350 000 mortgage for five years at a rate of 2.69 percent, with an amortization of 30 years.

Rate	2.69
Period	5 years
Amortization	30 years
Monthly payment	$1414.99

What would that same house cost in monthly payments under traditional terms?

They lock in their mortgage rate for five years at an amortization of 25 years:

Rate	5.99 (historically a very good rate)
Period	5 years
Amortization	25 years (traditional approach)
Monthly payment	$2237.24

The same house costs $822.25 more per month and that is with a fairly conservative 5.99 percent figure. Nobody expects to see rates above double digits in the foreseeable future, but reasonable rates should be part of your long-term "what if" planning. If you can afford the home either way, then you are probably okay. If not, maybe you should take some time to think about it before you sign.

Conclusion

Time will tell if the housing market was spinning out of control in 2015, but, as investors and homeowners, you should know the facts. There are great opportunities in real estate, but do your homework and understand the implications of interest rates and the functions of the banking system.

Sergey Nivens/Fotolia

QUESTIONS FOR DISCUSSION

1. How has the change in government policy with regard to amortization periods and down payments influenced the housing market?
2. Visit the TD Canada Trust website at www.tdcanadatrust.com and access the Mortgage Calculator tool. How much is the posted rate for a five-year mortgage? How much will it cost you (monthly) to get a mortgage of $250 000 with a 25-year amortization? What is the total cost of your interest payments over the lifetime of the loan?
3. Visit the Canadian Real Estate Association (CREA) website (www.crea.ca/content/national-average-price-map) and find out the average price of homes in Canada, in your province, and in your city. Also, search for some of the other major markets listed in the case. Have prices increased or decreased since 2015? Figure out the percentage increase and decrease in each market.

LO-1 WHAT IS MONEY?

When someone asks you how much money you have, what do you say? Do you count the bills and coins in your pockets? Do you mention the funds in your chequing and savings accounts? What about stocks, or bonds, or your car? Taken together, the value of everything you own is your personal wealth. Not all of it, however, is money.

The Characteristics of Money

Modern money generally takes the form of stamped metal or printed paper issued by governments (e.g., dollars or euros). The Chinese were using metal money to represent the objects they were exchanging as early as 1100 BCE. However, many different objects (cows, shells, stones, and dolphin teeth) have been used as money in different societies. Theoretically, just about anything *portable, divisible, durable*, and *stable* can serve as **money**. To appreciate these qualities, imagine using something that lacks these characteristics:

- *Portability.* Try lugging 500-kilos of cow as a unit of exchange from shop to shop, as was done in ancient agrarian economies. In contrast, modern currency is light and easy to handle.
- *Divisibility.* How would you divide your cow if you wanted to buy a hat, a book, and a radio from three different stores? Is a kilo of head worth as much as a kilo of leg? Modern currency is easily divisible into smaller parts with fixed values a 500-kilo—for example, a dollar for ten dimes.
- *Durability.* Your cow will lose value every day (and eventually die). Modern currency, however, neither dies nor spoils, and, if it wears out, it can be replaced. The Canadian government recently converted paper bills into polymer plastic bills to increase durability. However, just months after the release, there were questions about the bills' ability to withstand heat when a family claimed that the bills shrivelled and melted after being placed close to a heater.[1]
- *Stability.* If cows were in short supply, you might be able to make quite a deal for yourself. In the middle of a year with an abundant cow supply, however, the market would be flooded with cows, so their value would fall. The value of our paper money also fluctuates, but it is considerably more stable and predictable.

The Functions of Money

Imagine, for a moment, a successful cow rancher who needs a new fence. In a *barter economy*—one in which goods are exchanged directly for one another—he or she would have to find someone willing to exchange a fence for a cow (or parts of it). If no fence maker wants a cow, the rancher must find someone else—for example, a wagon maker—who does want a cow. Then, the rancher must hope that the fence maker will trade for a new wagon. In a money economy, the rancher would sell his or her cow, receive money, and exchange the money for goods, like a new fence.

Cattle are not portable, durable, or stable, making them an unsuitable medium of exchange in the modern monetized economy.

Thinkstock Images/Stockbyte/Getty Images

Thus, the barter economy is relatively inefficient. This example demonstrates the three functions of money:

1. *It is a medium of exchange.* Like the rancher "trading" money for a new fence, money is used to buy and sell things. Without money, we would be stuck in a system of barter in a system of barter.
2. *It is a store of value.* Pity the rancher whose cow gets sick on Monday and who wants to buy some clothes on the following Saturday, by which time the cow may have died and lost its value. In the form of currency, however, money can be used for future purchases, since it "stores" value.
3. *It is a unit of account.* Money lets us measure the relative values of goods and services. It acts as a measure of worth because all products can be valued and accounted for in terms of money. For example, the concepts of $1000 worth of clothes or $500 in labour costs have universal meaning.

As you can see, money adds convenience and simplicity to our everyday lives, for consumers and businesses alike. Employees, consumers, and businesses use money as the measure of worth for determining wages and for buying and selling products—everything from ice cream to housing rentals. Consumers with cash can make purchases wherever they go because businesses everywhere accept money as a medium for exchange. As long as money is stable, businesses and individuals save their money, trusting that its value will be available for future use.

The Spendable Money Supply: M-1

For money to serve as a medium of exchange, a store of value, or a unit of account, buyers and sellers must agree on its value. The value of money depends in part on its supply (how much money is in circulation). When the money supply is high, the value of money drops. When the money supply is low, the value of money increases.

It is not easy to measure the supply of money, nor is there complete agreement on exactly how it should be measured. The "narrow" definition of the money supply is called **M-1**, which includes only the most liquid forms of money—currency and demand deposits (chequing accounts) in banks. As of January 2015, M-1 totalled $730.3 billion in Canada.[2]

Currency is paper money and coins issued by the Canadian government. It is widely used to pay small bills. Canadian currency—which clearly states, "This note is legal tender"—is money the law requires a creditor to accept in payment of a debt. Counterfeiting of paper currency is now a worldwide problem, partly because new technologies allow counterfeiters to make real-looking bills rather easily. To reduce counterfeiting, the Bank of Canada has issued new, high-tech polymer $20, $50, and, $100 bills.[3]

MONEY Any object generally accepted by people as payment for goods and services.

M-1 Only the most liquid forms of money (currency and demand deposits).

CURRENCY Paper money and coins issued by the government.

A **cheque** is an order instructing the bank to pay a given sum to a specified person or firm. Cheques enable buyers to make large purchases without having to carry large amounts of cash. Money in chequing accounts, known as *demand deposits*, is counted in M-1 because such funds may be withdrawn at any time without notice.

M-1 Plus the Convertible Money Supply: M-2

M-2 includes everything in M-1 plus items that cannot be spent directly, but that are easily converted to spendable forms: time deposits, money market mutual funds, and savings deposits. M-2 accounts for nearly all the nation's money supply. As this overall supply of money increases, more is available for consumer purchases and business investment. When this supply decreases, less is available for consumer purchases and business investment. As of January 2015, M-2 totalled $1270 billion in Canada up approximately 5 percent during the year.[4]

Unlike demand deposits, **time deposits** require prior notice of withdrawal and cannot be transferred by cheque. The supply of money in time deposits—such as *certificates of deposit (CDs)* and *savings certificates*—are not nearly as popular today in a low-interest rate environment as they were when 10 to 15 percent interest rates were common.

Money market mutual funds are operated by investment companies that bring together pools of assets from many investors. The fund buys a collection of short-term, low-risk financial securities. Ownership of and profits (or losses) from the sale of these securities are shared among the fund's investors.

Credit Cards and Debit Cards: Plastic Money?

The use of credit and debit cards has become so widespread that many people refer to them as "plastic money." Credit cards, however, are not money and, accordingly, are not included in M-1 or M-2 when measuring the nation's money supply. Why? Because spending with a credit card creates a debt, but does not move money until later when the debt is paid by cash or cheque. Credit cards are a money substitute; they serve as a temporary medium of exchange, but are not a store of value. Debit card transactions, in contrast, transfer money immediately from the consumer's bank account, so they affect the money supply the same way as spending with a cheque or cash, and are included in M-1.

With growing fears of rising debt as an incentive, the Canadian government is planning to adopt a new code of conduct to further regulate credit and debit cards.[5] Canadians hold 76.3 million MasterCard and Visa credit cards. The value of goods and services bought with credit cards in Canada amounts to approximately US$30 billion annually.[6] Worldwide, the total value of goods purchased with Visa cards is above $3 trillion annually.[7] Banks like the Bank of Montreal, the Canadian Imperial Bank of Commerce, the Bank of Nova Scotia, and TD Canada Trust are the biggest issuers of Visa cards in Canada. Every time a card is used, the banks receive an "interchange" fee, a percentage of the purchase value of the transaction.

Although consumers enjoy the convenience of credit cards, they are also finding that irresponsible use of the cards can be hazardous to your financial health. Credit-card fraud is another major concern for both consumers and retailers. To deal with this problem, credit-card companies have developed new chip encryption technology that requires an additional password. A discussion on managing the use of credit cards is presented in Chapter Supplement 04, "Managing Your Personal Finances: A Synopsis."

Chip encryption technology was introduced to reduce credit-card fraud.

Freebird/Fotolia

CHEQUE An order instructing the bank to pay a given sum to a specified person or firm.

M-2 Everything in M-1 plus savings deposits, time deposits, and money market mutual funds.

TIME DEPOSIT A deposit that requires prior notice to make a withdrawal; cannot be transferred to others by cheque.

MONEY MARKET MUTUAL FUNDS Funds operated by investment companies that bring together pools of assets from many investors to buy short-term, low-risk financial securities.

LO-2 THE CANADIAN FINANCIAL SYSTEM

Many forms of money, especially demand deposits and time deposits, depend on the existence of financial institutions to provide a broad spectrum of services to both individuals and businesses. In this section, we describe the major types of financial institutions, explain how they work, and describe some of the special services they offer. We also explain their role as creators of money and discuss the regulation of the Canadian banking system.

Financial Institutions

There are several types of financial institutions in Canada, but the main function of all of them is to facilitate the flow of money from sectors with surpluses to those with deficits, by attracting funds into chequing and savings accounts. Incoming funds are loaned to individuals and businesses and, perhaps, invested in government securities.

For many years, the financial community in Canada has been divided rather clearly into four distinct legal areas. These "four financial pillars" are (1) chartered banks, (2) alternate banks (e.g., trust companies and credit unions/caisses populaires), (3) life insurance companies and other specialized lending and saving intermediaries (e.g., factors, finance companies, venture capital firms, mutual funds, and pension funds), and (4) investment dealers. We will discuss each of these in detail in this chapter, but it is important to understand that many changes have taken place in the financial services industry in the past couple of decades, and the lines between the four pillars have blurred. For example, banks are now permitted to own securities dealers, to establish subsidiaries to sell mutual funds, and to sell commercial paper (see Chapter 15). Trust companies have declined in importance, and many of them have been bought by banks or insurance companies.

FINANCIAL PILLAR #1—CHARTERED BANKS

A **chartered bank** is a privately owned, profit-seeking financial intermediary that serves individuals, businesses, and non-business organizations. Chartered banks are the largest and most important financial institutions in Canada. In January 2015, Canadian chartered banks had assets totalling \$2.29 trillion.[8] Chartered banks offer chequing and savings accounts, make loans, and provide many services to their customers. They are the main source of short-term loans for business firms.

Unlike in the United States, where there are hundreds of banks each with only a few branches, in Canada, there are only a few banks, each with hundreds of branches. The five largest Canadian banks account for about 90 percent of total bank assets. *The Guardian* referred to Canadian banks as the envy of the world, and *The Economist* referred to them as the primary reason for Canada's economic resilience.[9]

Schedule I banks are those that are Canadian-owned and have no more than 10 percent of voting shares controlled by a single interest. Schedule II banks are those that may be domestically owned, but do not meet the 10 percent limit, or may be foreign-controlled. Several foreign banks have set up Schedule II subsidiaries in Canada. The *Bank Act* limits foreign-controlled banks to deposits that do not exceed 8 percent of the total domestic assets of all banks in Canada. The largest chartered banks in Canada are shown in Table 14.1, ranked based on revenues.

Services Offered by Banks

The banking business is highly competitive; therefore, banks no longer just accept deposits and make loans. Most now offer pension services, trust services, international services, financial advice, and electronic money transfer.

TABLE 14.1 Top 10 Banks in Canada (ranked by revenues)[10]

Company	Sales Revenue (billions of dollars)
1. Royal Bank of Canada	35.9
2. Toronto-Dominion Bank	30.7
3. Bank of Nova Scotia	28.8
4. Bank of Montreal	20.8
5. Canadian Imperial Bank of Commerce	17.1
6. National Bank of Canada	7.1
7. HSBC Bank Canada (Schedule II bank)	3.0
8. Laurentian Bank	1.5
9. Canadian Western Bank	0.88
10. Pacific & Western Bank of Canada	0.063

PENSION SERVICES

Most banks help customers establish savings plans for retirement. Banks serve as financial intermediaries by receiving funds and investing them as directed by customers. They also provide customers with information on investment possibilities.

TRUST SERVICES

Many banks offer trust services—the management of funds left "in the bank's trust." In return for a fee, the trust department will perform such tasks as making your monthly bill payments and managing your investment portfolio. Trust departments also manage the estates of deceased persons.

INTERNATIONAL SERVICES

The three main international services offered by banks are currency exchange, letters of credit, and banker's acceptances. Suppose that a Canadian company wants to buy a product from a French supplier. For a fee, it can use one or more of three services offered by its bank:

1. It can exchange Canadian dollars for euros at a Canadian bank and then pay the French supplier in euros.
2. It can pay its bank to issue a *letter of credit*—a promise by the bank to pay the French firm a certain amount if specified conditions are met.
3. It can pay its bank to draw up a *banker's acceptance*, which promises that the bank will pay some specified amount at a future date.

FINANCIAL ADVICE

Many banks, both large and small, help their customers manage their money. Depending on the customer's situation, the bank may recommend different investment opportunities. The recommended mix might include guaranteed investment certificates, mutual funds, stocks, and bonds. Today, bank advertisements often stress the growing role of banks as financial advisors.

Take a look at the following "There's an App for That!" feature that outlines three banking and financial investment apps.

CHARTERED BANK A privately owned, profit-seeking firm that serves individuals, non-business organizations, and businesses as a financial intermediary.

THERE'S AN APP FOR THAT!

APP DETAILS	PLATFORMS
1. **TD (Canada)** **Source:** TD Bank Group **Key Features:** Provides quick, easy, secure access to accounts, helpful information, and convenient tools.	Apple, Android, BlackBerry
2. **Mint.com Personal Finance** **Source:** Mint.com **Key Features:** Allows you to track, budget, and manage your money in one place.	Apple, Android, BlackBerry
3. **Globe Investor** **Source:** The Globe and Mail **Key Features:** A guide to help you take control of your investments; Canada's authoritative source of business news and of up-to-the minute market data.	Apple, BlackBerry

APP DISCOVERY EXERCISE

Since app availability changes, conduct your own search for "Top 3" finance apps and identify the key features.

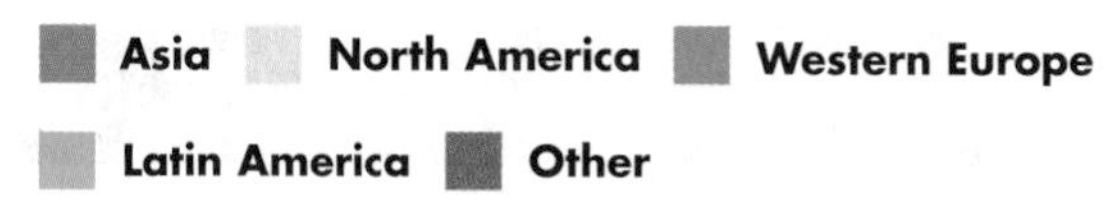

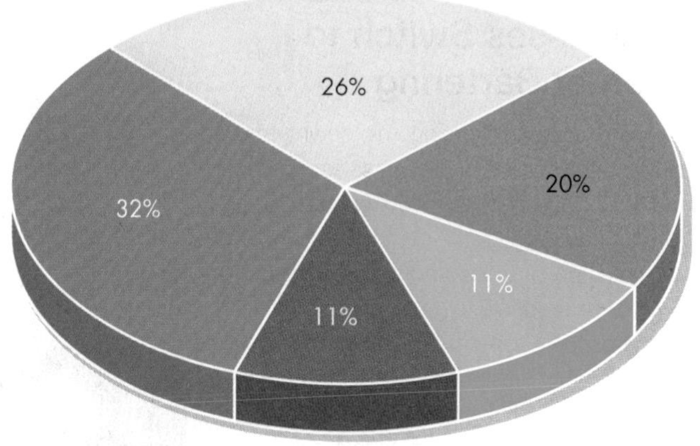

FIGURE 14.1 Global dispersion of ABMs (ATMs)

ELECTRONIC FUNDS TRANSFER

Electronic funds transfer (EFT) provides for payments and collections by transferring financial information electronically. Such systems can help a businessperson close an important business deal by transferring money from Vancouver to Halifax within seconds. In a sign of the times, the Canadian federal government (the largest issuer of cheques in the country) has announced that it will go paperless and switch totally to direct deposit by April 2016. In addition to internet and telephone banking, other examples include:[11]

- *Automated banking machines/automated teller machines (ABMs/ATMs)***.** These let you bank at almost any time of day or night. There are over 60 000 ABMs (also known as ATMS) in Canada and more than 17 500 are bank-owned.[12] FirstOntario Credit Union recently launched a new version it calls the Personal Assistant Teller (PAT). This system provides a video link with a teller who can talk to the consumer about loans or listen to complaints in addition to offering the traditional ABM transactions.[13] (See Figure 14.1 for more about ABMs/ATMs.)
- *Direct deposits and withdrawals.* These enable a user to authorize, in advance, specific, regular deposits and withdrawals. You can arrange to have paycheques and social assistance cheques automatically deposited and recurring expenses, such as insurance premiums and utility bills, automatically paid.
- *Debit cards.* Unlike credit cards, **debit cards** do not increase the funds at an individual's disposal but allow users only to transfer money between accounts to make retail purchases. Debit cards are used more than credit cards as payment for consumer transactions. Approximately 94 percent of Canadians have a debit card and they are accepted in over 450 000 retail establishments across the nation. Over four billion transactions are completed annually using the Interac network (by which you can access your money anywhere).[14]
- *Smart cards.* A **smart card** has an embedded computer chip that can be loaded with "electronic money"—they are also known as *electronic purses* or *stored-value cards*. Such cards have existed for many years. They are most popular in gas-pump payments, prepaid phone service, self-operated checkouts, and vending machines.[15]
- *Mobile (digital) wallet.* At a recent meeting of the Canadian Bankers Association, the country's largest banks agreed to standards to set the tone for the transition from plastic cards to mobile wallets. CIBC and Rogers Communications were among the first to sign a deal to provide the service.[16] For example, Tim Hortons recently launched an app that allows customers to pay for their "double-double" with their mobile phones.[17]

DEBIT CARD Plastic card that allows an individual to transfer money between accounts.

SMART CARD Credit-card-sized plastic card with an embedded computer chip that can be loaded with "electronic money."

Most of Tim Hortons' 4000+ outlets across Canada now accept payment via mobile app.

Hand-out/TIM HORTONS/Newscom

E-BUSINESS AND SOCIAL MEDIA SOLUTIONS

When Cash Gets Scarce, Businesses Switch to Internet Bartering

For many companies, economic downturns involve tighter credit, a drop in sales revenues, and a shortage of cash for doing business. Without cash and credit, companies can't buy the materials, services, and supplies needed to produce products for customers, so business prospects suffer.

Or do they? Enter an unexpected liberator—barter. This ancient trade practice survives even today, but in an internet-enhanced form with global reach and instant access to a vast network of swap agreements. And best of all, it can be done without cash. For example, Firm A provides an advertising program for Firm B that, in return, has vacant building space needed by Firm A. Thus, the needs of both are met, and a cashless swap is born. During the most recent recession, BarterQuest.com had more than 50 000 monthly visitors from Australia, the United States, Canada, and elsewhere. Activity tripled at U-Exchange.com, where its "Barter 101" gets you started, and you can swap as much as you like at no cost. Worldwide, the electronically based barter business has grown into a megabillion-dollar industry.

Shutterstock

Whether it's B2B (business-to-business) or B2C (business-to-consumer), online bartering is an efficient way around the economy's credit crunch, because it enables companies and individuals to get goods and services without using cash. Restaurants, for example, can trade meals or catering for advertising or for cooking equipment. Bartering can also be a good way to move excessive inventory and get needed benefits in return. An unemployed electrician bartered with homeowners who needed electrical wiring; in return, the homeowners gave up unneeded furniture and laptops that the electrician later sold to make mortgage payments.

For loyal swappers of services, websites such as PeopleTradingServices.com make it easy for small business owners to find barter matchups with hundreds of kinds of services, ranging from gardeners to songwriters to clergy. As a barter matchmaker, PeopleTradingServices.com posts members' profiles, lists services they trade, and provides a convenient way to contact member professionals online. Along with endless trading possibilities, the cash conservation can be a lifesaver for any cash-strapped small business during troubled times.

CRITICAL THINKING QUESTIONS

1. What are the advantages and disadvantages of the internet bartering services discussed in this boxed feature?

Bank Loans

Banks are the major source of short-term loans for business. Although banks make long-term loans to some firms, they prefer to specialize in providing short-term funds to finance inventories and accounts receivable. A *secured* loan is one backed by collateral (e.g., accounts receivable); if the borrower cannot repay, the bank sells the collateral. An unsecured loan is backed only by the borrower's promise. Only the most creditworthy borrowers can get unsecured loans.

Borrowers pay interest on their loans. Large firms with excellent credit records pay the **prime rate of interest**, which is the lowest rate charged to borrowers. This rate changes often because of changes in the demand and supply of loanable funds, as well as Bank of Canada policies. The so-called "Big Six" Canadian banks (Royal Bank, CIBC, Bank of Montreal, Bank of Nova Scotia, TD Canada Trust, and National Bank of Canada) typically act in concert with respect to the prime rate.

Banks as Creators of Money

Financial institutions provide a special service to the economy—they create money. They don't mint bills and coins, but by taking in deposits and making loans, they expand the money supply. We will first look at how this expansion process works, assuming that banks have a *reserve requirement*, which means they must keep a portion of their chequable deposits in vault cash or as deposits with the Bank of Canada. (The reserve requirement was dropped over two decades ago, and the implications of this change are described later.)

Suppose you saved $100, took it to a bank, and opened a chequing account. Let's assume, for the moment, that there is a reserve requirement, and that it is 10 percent. Your bank must therefore keep $10 of your $100 deposit in reserve, so it has only $90 to lend to other borrowers. Now, suppose a person named Jennifer Leclerc borrows $90 from your bank. She now has $90 added to her chequing account. Assume that she writes a cheque for $90 payable to Canadian Tire. Canadian Tire's bank ends up with a $90 deposit, and that bank is also required to keep $9 in reserve. It therefore has $81 to lend out to someone else. This process of deposit expansion can continue as shown in Figure 14.2, and your original deposit of $100 could result in an increase of $1000 in new deposits for all banks in the system.

But what happens if there is no reserve requirement? At the extreme, it means that banks could (theoretically) create infinite amounts of money, because they wouldn't have to keep any in reserve. But banks will not do this because it is risky. So, in practice, the dropping of the reserve requirement simply means that banks will be able to create more money than they did when there was a reserve requirement.

PRIME RATE OF INTEREST The lowest rate charged to borrowers.

Deposit	Money Held in Reserve by Bank	Money to Lend	Total Supply
$100.00	$10.00	$90.00	**$190.00**
90.00	9.00	81.00	**271.00**
81.00	8.10	72.90	**343.90**
72.90	7.29	65.61	**409.51**
65.61	6.56	59.05	**468.56**

FIGURE 14.2 How the chartered banking system creates money

In Oakville, Ontario, for example, Royal Bank of Canada consumers who enter the branch will notice the RBC bank on the right and RBC Insurance on the left. The two operations are separated by a glass wall. Dan Danyluk, the CEO of the Insurance Brokers Association of Canada, says that RBC's strategy is ignoring the intent of the law. He argues that credit-granting institutions like banks should not be allowed to sell insurance in their branches, because they might try to tie, say, approval of a loan to buy a car to the purchase of car insurance.[20] The government agrees, and it recently sent a message by banning banks from selling unauthorized insurance on their websites.[21]

All of this activity is transforming the profit base of banks. In the past, they made most of their money from the spread between interest rates paid to depositors and the rates charged on loans. Investment banking, on the other hand, is fee-based. Banks are making a larger proportion of their profits from fees, and this is blurring the traditional boundary between banks and securities firms.

Other Changes in Banking

Substantial changes in addition to those already described are taking place in banking, including *deregulation, changes in customer demands*, and *changes in international banking*.

DEREGULATION

Deregulation has allowed banks to alter their historical role as intermediaries between depositors and borrowers. Canada's banks have been diversifying to provide more financial products to their clients. Training bankers to be effective in this environment is necessary, and over 100 executives at TD Canada Trust attended a Harvard University course that taught them to think like investment bankers. They have learned the lessons well and have embraced their new role. In fact, the major Canadian banks recently petitioned U.S. regulators to exempt them from the Volker Rule (part of the Dodd Frank Wall Street Reform Consumer Protection Act), which would prevent them from investing in private equity funds and other speculative investments because they are deposit-taking banks.[18]

CHANGES IN CONSUMER DEMANDS

Many consumers refuse to keep their money in a traditional bank when they can get more elsewhere. They are turning to electronic banks like Tangerine (formerly ING Direct) that pay higher interest on savings accounts. Such companies can pay higher rates because they don't incur the costs associated with having branches like traditional banks do. Traditional banks are responding to this new competition by selling more services in their branches. Banks are finding new ways to attract and serve their clientele in order to remain competitive and attract a new generation that does not have the same loyalties as previous generations. In addition, Scotiabank actually purchased Tangerine (from ING) and has shown every intention of capitalizing on this new segment.[19]

Banks also want to get much more involved in selling insurance, but the Bank Act has prohibited them from selling insurance in their branch offices (they are allowed to sell it elsewhere). Consequently, Canadian banks are finding creative ways to keep insurance and banking activities separate (but not too separate).

CHANGES IN INTERNATIONAL BANKING

Canada's banks are going to experience increased competition, because foreign banks are now allowed to do business in Canada. Canadian banks are responding with a variety of tactics, including attempts to merge with one another. But bank mergers have been blocked by the federal government because it fears the mergers will reduce competition and harm consumers. However, as we saw in Chapter 5 (and, in particular, the closing case on Scotiabank), Canadian banks have grown and strengthened through acquisitions overseas and improved efficiencies in their home market.

LO-3 The Bank of Canada

The **Bank of Canada**, formed in 1935, is Canada's central bank. It has a crucial role in managing the Canadian economy and in regulating certain aspects of chartered bank operations. The Bank is managed by a board of governors composed of a governor, a deputy governor, and 12 directors appointed from different regions.

The rate at which chartered banks can borrow from the Bank of Canada is called the **bank rate**, or **rediscount rate**. It serves as the basis for establishing the chartered banks' prime interest rates. In practice, chartered banks seldom have to borrow from the Bank of Canada. However, the bank rate is an important instrument of monetary policy as a determinant of interest rates. In recent years, the Bank of Canada and central banks across the globe have kept rates very low. As we saw in the opening case, this extended period of low rates has led citizens to increase their debt load and has fuelled housing price booms, but there are loud calls for the governor of the Bank to increase rates and restore some order. With the U.S. Federal Reserve moving in that direction, the Bank will feel pressure to follow, and will do so if it feels the economy is strong enough to handle an increase.[22]

BANK OF CANADA Canada's central bank; formed in 1935.

BANK RATE (REDISCOUNT RATE) The rate at which chartered banks can borrow from the Bank of Canada.

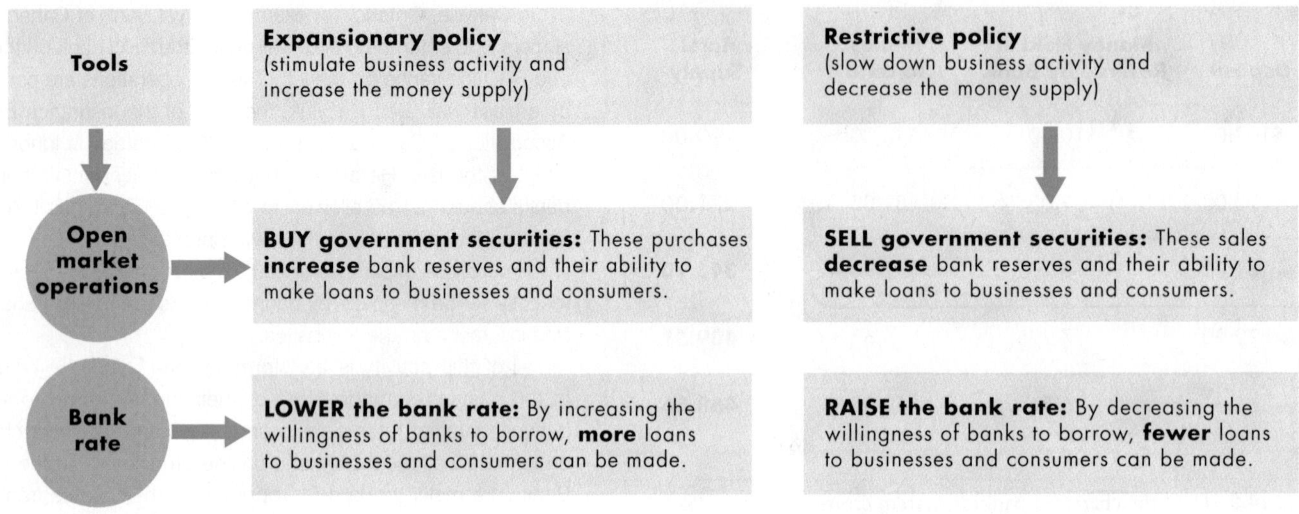

Tools
Expansionary policy
(stimulate business activity and increase the money supply)
Restrictive policy
(slow down business activity and decrease the money supply)
Open market operations
BUY government securities: These purchases increase bank reserves and their ability to make loans to businesses and consumers.
SELL government securities: These sales decrease bank reserves and their ability to make loans to businesses and consumers.
Bank rate
LOWER the bank rate: By increasing the willingness of banks to borrow, more loans to businesses and consumers can be made.
RAISE the bank rate: By decreasing the willingness of banks to borrow, fewer loans to businesses and consumers can be made.

FIGURE 14.3 Bank of Canada monetary policy actions

THE MONEY SUPPLY AND THE BANK OF CANADA

The Bank of Canada plays an important role in managing the money supply in Canada (see Figure 14.3). If it wants to increase the money supply, it can buy government securities. The people who sell these bonds then deposit the proceeds in their banks. These deposits increase banks' reserves and their willingness to make loans. The Bank can also lower the bank rate; this action will cause increased demand for loans from businesses and households, because these customers borrow more money when interest rates drop.

If the Bank of Canada wants to decrease the money supply, it can sell government securities. People spend money to buy bonds, and these withdrawals bring down banks' reserves and reduce their willingness to make loans. The Bank of Canada can also raise the bank rate; this action will cause decreased demand for loans from businesses and households because these customers borrow less money when interest rates rise.

The federal government and the Bank of Canada got strong endorsements of their management of the money supply when it was reported that Iceland was considering adopting the Canadian dollar as its official currency. So far Iceland has not made major steps in that direction but the idea was still floated based on a well-earned reputation.[23] In another sign of the approval of the Canadian system, Mark Carney, former governor of the Bank of Canada, was hired by the Bank of England. According to George Osborne, chancellor of the Bank of England, Mark Carney is "simply the best, most experienced and most qualified person in the world" to handle that country's economic challenges.[24]

Will the Canadian loonie be seen swimming in Icelandic waters?

Bloomberg via Getty Images; © maximimages.com/Alamy

LO-4 FINANCIAL PILLAR #2—ALTERNATE BANKS

Trust Companies

A **trust company** safeguards property—funds and estates—entrusted to it. It may also serve as trustee, transfer agent, and registrar for corporations, and provide other services.

For example, a corporation selling bonds to investors appoints a *trustee*, usually a trust company, to protect the bondholders' interests. A *transfer agent* records changes in ownership of a corporation's shares of stock, and a *registrar* certifies to the investing public that stock issues are correctly stated and comply with the corporate charter. *Other services* include preparing and issuing dividend cheques to stockholders and serving as trustee for employee profit-sharing funds. Trust companies also accept deposits and pay interest on them. As noted previously, however, trust companies have declined in importance.

Credit Unions/Caisses Populaires

One in every three Canadians is a member of a credit union (called a *caisse populaire* in Quebec), with 5 million members in Quebec and 5.1 million in the rest of Canada.[25] **Credit unions** and **caisses populaires** are cooperative savings and lending associations formed by a group with common interests. They are important because they lend money to businesses and to consumers who use the money to buy durable goods such as cars and furniture from businesses. Members (owners) can add to their savings accounts by authorizing deductions from their paycheques or by making direct deposits. They can borrow short-term, long-term, or mortgage funds from the credit union. Credit unions invest substantial amounts of money in corporate and government securities and sell certificates of deposits to the general public. According to a Moody's Investor Services report, credit unions are gaining in popularity, because they offer many services available at banks and tend to pay dividends to members when they make profits. Table 14.2 identifies the top 10 credit unions in Canada ranked by total members.

TABLE 14.2 Top 10 Credit Unions/Caisses Populaires in Canada, 2015 (ranked by number of members)[26]

Company	Members
1. Mouvement des Caisses Desjardins	5 581 000
2. Coast Capital Savings Credit Union	522 867
3. Vancouver City Savings Credit Union	496 068
4. Servus Credit Union Ltd.	376 655
5. Meridian Credit Union Ltd.	266 264
6. First West Credit Union	167 856
7. Conexus Credit Union	117 290
8. Affinity Credit Union	114 442
9. Assiniboine Credit Union	112 806
10. Alterna Credit Union	101 090

TRUST COMPANY Safeguards funds and estates entrusted to it; may also serve as trustee, transfer agent, and registrar for corporations.

CREDIT UNIONS (CAISSES POPULAIRES) Cooperative savings and lending association formed by a group with common interests.

FINANCIAL PILLAR #3—SPECIALIZED LENDING AND SAVINGS INTERMEDIARIES

Life Insurance Companies

A **life insurance company** shares risk with its policyholders in return for payment of a premium from them. It lends some of the money it collects from premiums to borrowers. Life insurance companies are substantial investors in real estate mortgages and in corporate and government bonds. Next to chartered banks, they are the largest financial intermediaries in Canada. The industry as a whole has over $647 billion invested in Canada with 51 percent invested in bonds (provincial, federal, and corporate bonds), 6.6 percent invested in mortgages, 3 percent in real estate, 16 percent in stocks and mutual funds, and the rest in cash. The industry also employs over 150 100 people.[27]

Factoring Companies

An important source of short-term funds for many firms is factoring companies. A **factoring company** (or **factor**) buys accounts receivable (amounts due from credit customers) from a firm. It pays less than the face value of the accounts, but collects the entire face value of the accounts. The difference, minus the cost of doing business, is the factor's profit. A firm that sells its accounts receivable to a factor shifts the risk of credit loss to the factor. If an account turns out to be uncollectible, the factor suffers the loss. Canada Factoring Company is an example of a domestic factoring company.

Financial Corporations

A **sales finance company** specializes in financing installment purchases made by individuals and firms. When you buy durable goods from a retailer on an installment plan with a sales finance company, the loan is made directly to you. The item itself serves as security for the loan.

LIFE INSURANCE COMPANY A mutual or stock company that shares risk with its policyholders for payment of premiums.

FACTORING COMPANY (OR FACTOR) Buys accounts receivable from a firm for less than their face value and then collects the face value of the receivables.

SALES FINANCE COMPANY Specializes in financing installment purchases made by individuals or firms.

Sales finance companies enable firms to sell on credit, even though the firms could not afford to finance credit sales on their own. General Motors Acceptance Corporation (GMAC) is a sales finance company that finances installment contracts resulting from sales made by General Motors. Industrial Acceptance Corporation is a large Canadian sales finance company.

A **consumer finance company** makes personal loans to consumers. Often, the borrower pledges no security (collateral) for the loan. For larger loans, collateral may be required. These companies do not make loans to businesses, but they do provide the financing that allows consumers to buy goods and services from businesses. Household Finance Corporation is an example of a consumer finance company.

Venture Capital Firms

A **venture capital firm** provides funds for new or expanding firms that seem to have significant potential. Venture capital firms may demand an ownership stake of 50 percent or more before they will buy into a company. Because financing new, untested businesses is risky, venture capital firms also want to earn a higher-than-normal return on their investment. They may insist that they be given at least one seat on the board of directors to observe how their investment is faring. Venture capital firms look for companies with growth potential that could lead to substantial increases in stock value.

Venture capital firms obtain their funds from initial capital subscriptions, from loans from other financial intermediaries, and from retained earnings. The amount of venture capital that is raised varies according to economic conditions. In 2014, venture capital firms raised a total of $1.9 billion in Canada from 379 deals.[28]

Many of you are quite familiar with TV programs like *Dragon's Den* and *Shark Tank* that provide a simplified, made-for-TV version of the venture capital process.

Leon Switzer/ZUMAPRESS/Newscom

CONSUMER FINANCE COMPANY Makes personal loans to consumers.

VENTURE CAPITAL FIRM Provides funds for new or expanding firms thought to have significant potential.

PENSION FUND Accumulates money that will be paid out to plan subscribers in the future.

Pension Funds

A **pension fund** accumulates money that will be paid out to plan subscribers at some time in the future. The money collected is invested in corporate stocks and bonds, government bonds, or mortgages until it is to be paid out. Many private pension funds are being evaluated, and there are great concerns about funding and management in this area.

FINANCIAL PILLAR #4—INVESTMENT DEALERS

Investment dealers (stockbrokers or underwriters) are the primary distributors of new stock and bond issues (the underwriting function). They also facilitate secondary trading of stocks and bonds, both on stock exchanges and on over-the-counter stock and bond markets (the brokerage function).

For example, when in the spring of 2015 both GoDaddy and Cara (Owner of Swiss Chalet, Harvey's, and other fast-food outlets) decided to sell stock for the first time (i.e., make an initial public offering), they turned to investment dealers to underwrite them. GoDaddy's stock price valued the company at approximately $4 billion.[29] These functions of investment dealers are described in more detail in Chapter 15.

OTHER SOURCES OF FUNDS

Government Financial Institutions and Granting Agencies

In Canada, a number of government suppliers of funds are important to business. In general, they supply funds to new and/or growing companies; however, established firms can also use some of them.

The *Business Development Bank of Canada (BDC)* makes term loans, primarily to smaller firms judged to have growth potential but unable to secure funds at reasonable terms from traditional sources. It provides proportionally more equity financing and more management counselling services. A variety of provincial industrial development corporations also provide funds to developing business firms in the hope that they will provide jobs in the province. A number of federal and provincial programs are specifically designed to provide loans to agricultural operators. Most of these, with the exception of farm improvement loans that guarantee bank loans to farmers, are long-term loans for land purchase.

The federal government's *Export Development Corporation (EDC)* finances and insures export sales for Canadian companies. The *Canada*

Mortgage and Housing Corporation (*CMHC*) is involved in providing and guaranteeing mortgages. The CMHC is particularly important to the construction industry. Governments are also involved in providing grants to business operations.

International Sources of Funds

The Canadian capital market is just one part of the international capital market. Canadian provinces borrow extensively in foreign markets, such as those in London and New York. Canadian corporations likewise find it attractive to borrow in foreign markets. Foreign sources of funds have been important throughout the economic development of Canada. Although many groups and individuals have expressed concern about foreign ownership of Canadian businesses, projections of Canada's future capital requirements indicate that we will continue to need these funds. Canadian financial institutions will continue to play a large role in making these funds available.

LO-5 INTERNATIONAL BANKING AND FINANCE

Electronic technologies permit nearly instantaneous financial transactions around the globe. These business exchanges—the prices asked and paid—are affected by *values of the currencies* among the various nations involved in the transactions. Once agreements are reached, the *international payments process* that moves money between buyers and sellers on different continents is not subject to any worldwide policy system beyond loosely structured agreements among countries.

Currency Values and Exchange Rates

Euros, pesos, yuan, dollars, and yen—money comes in all sizes and stripes. With today's global activities, travellers, shoppers, investors, and businesses often rely on banks to convert their dollars into other currencies. When it comes to choosing one currency over others, the best choice changes from day to day. Why? Because every currency's value changes, reflecting global supply and demand—what traders are willing to pay—for one currency relative to others.

STRONG CURRENCY OR WEAK: WHICH IS BETTER?

Most people would prefer a "strong" currency, right? Well, not so fast. It depends on how it will be used.

A good case in point is the fluctuation of the Canadian dollar relative to the American dollar. As we entered the new millennium, Canadians had grown accustomed to a weak dollar, in the 65-to-70-cent range against the U.S. dollar. A dollar at parity with the American dollar was almost unthinkable. Yet, on November 9, 2007, the dollar reached US$1.09, a level that had not been seen for decades. That movement and strength encouraged Canadians to cross the border and purchase everything from clothing to cars. After years of near-parity, the Canadian dollar retreated and stood at approximately US$0.75 in December 2015 with a further decline predicted by many.[30]

These fluctuations have a huge impact on businesses. When the Canadian dollar was at par with or stronger than the U.S. dollar, Canadian companies found it more difficult to compete internationally since they could no longer rely on a cheap Canadian dollar to make their products more affordable. According to chairman and CEO of Clearwater Seafoods Income Fund, "The way to deal with a stronger Canadian dollar is to increase the efficiency of your operations."[31] However, other companies, like Nova Scotia–based High Liner Foods, which buys most of its raw fish on the world markets in U.S. dollars, actually saw a net benefit. The rise in the Canadian dollar helped that company increase profits by 40 percent in one year.[32]

THE LAW OF ONE PRICE

When a country's currency is overvalued, its exchange rate is higher than warranted by its economic conditions, and its high costs make it less competitive. In contrast, an undervalued currency means low costs and low prices. When a currency becomes overvalued, a nation's economic authorities may devalue the nation's currency (deliberate efforts to lower its value) to make their goods less expensive for other countries to buy.

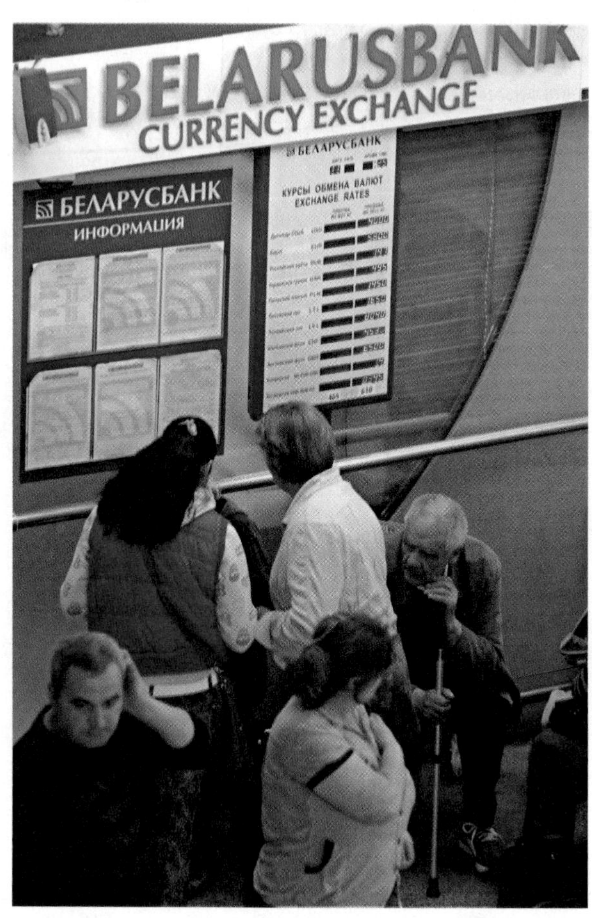

Citizens of the Republic of Belarus, along with visitors from other countries, rely on information about current exchange rates between the Belarusian ruble (Br) and currencies of other countries. The Belarus Bank is a local provider of currency exchange services.

Tatyana Zenkovich/Photoshot License Limited

TABLE 14.3 The Big Mac Index

Country	Price of a Big Mac in $US
Ukraine	1.20
Russia	1.36
India	1.89
Malaysia	2.11
South Africa	2.22
Canada	4.64
United States	4.79
Sweden	4.97
Brazil	5.21
Denmark	5.38
Norway	6.30
Switzerland	7.54

But how do we know whether a currency is overvalued or undervalued? One method involves a simple concept called the **law of one price**: the principle that identical products should sell for the same price in all countries. In other words, if the different prices of a Rolex watch in different countries were converted into a common currency the price should be the same everywhere.

A simple example that illustrates over- and undervalued currencies is the Big Mac Index, published annually in *The Economist*. The index lists a variety of countries and their Big Mac prices in terms of U.S. dollars (see Table 14.3).[33] In 2015, a Big Mac cost $4.79 in the United States. If a Big Mac in another country costs more than $4.79, the currency is overvalued; if it costs less than $4.79, the currency is undervalued.

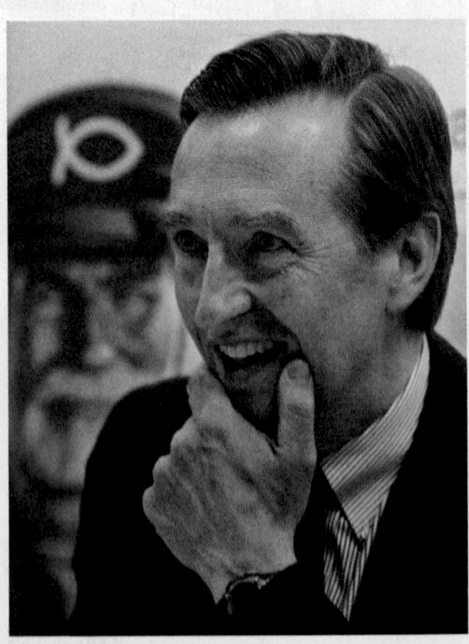

While many Canadian companies found it more difficult to compete or earn high margins because of the increase in the value of the Canadian dollar, High Liner Food was a beneficiary because it buys most of its fish in U.S. dollars on the world market. The recent decline in the value of the Canadian dollar has had the opposite effect.

Andrew Vaughan/Canadian Press Images

In 2015, the most overvalued currencies were Switzerland ($7.54), and Norway ($6.30). The Canadian currency was slightly undervalued at $4.64. Ukraine ($1.20), Russia ($1.36), and India ($1.89) were considered to have the most undervalued currencies.

The International Payments Process

Financial settlements between buyers and sellers in different countries are simplified through services provided by banks. For example, payments from Canadian buyers start at a local bank that converts them from dollars into the seller's currency, such as into euros to be sent to a seller in Spain. At the same time, payments and currency conversions from separate transactions also are flowing between Spanish businesses and Canadian sellers in the other direction.

If trade between the two countries is in balance—if money inflows and outflows are equal for both countries—then *money does not actually have to flow between the two countries*. If inflows and outflows are not in balance at the Canadian bank (or at the Spanish bank), then a flow of money—either to Spain or to Canada—is made to cover the difference.

As you will see in the Managing in Turbulent Times box entitled "What's the Deal with Bitcoin?" virtual currency is adding another dimension to the exchange process as the model tries to capture widespread acceptance.

The International Bank Structure

No worldwide banking system is comparable, in terms of policymaking and regulatory power, to the system of any single industrialized nation. Rather, worldwide banking stability relies on a loose structure of agreements among individual countries or groups of countries. In addition, local standards and laws vary greatly.

Two United Nations agencies, the World Bank and the International Monetary Fund, help to finance international trade. Unlike true banks, the **World Bank** actually provides only a very limited scope of services. For instance, it funds national improvements by making loans to build roads, schools, power plants, and hospitals. The resulting improvements eventually enable borrowing countries to increase productive capacity and international trade. The **International Monetary Fund (IMF)** is a group of 188 nations that have combined their resources for the following purposes:

- to promote the stability of exchange rates
- to provide temporary, short-term loans to member countries
- to encourage members to cooperate on international monetary issues
- to encourage development of a system for international payments

LAW OF ONE PRICE The principle that identical products should sell for the same price in all countries.

WORLD BANK A United Nations agency that provides a limited scope of financial services, such as funding national improvements in undeveloped countries.

INTERNATIONAL MONETARY FUND (IMF) United Nations agency consisting of 188 nations that have combined resources to promote stable exchange rates, provide temporary short-term loans, and serve other purposes.

MANAGING IN TURBULENT TIMES

What's the Deal with Bitcoin?

Bitcoin is a "virtual" currency created by computers that solve complex mathematical problems for the Bitcoin network. The computer owners are called "miners" and their specialized computer equipment is called "mining equipment." Miners don't have to identify themselves.

They receive new *bitcoins* as payment for contributing their computing power to the bitcoin network. The computer network is estimated to have 13 000 times more computing power than the world's 500 largest supercomputers.

Bitcoin can be traded on currency exchanges or used as money to buy goods and services. People who want to buy bitcoins install a virtual wallet on their computer and then pay for the bitcoins with a credit card or with cash. Some retailers accept bitcoin as payment for goods and services, because it allows them to avoid credit-card charges. Some big companies are beginning to accept bitcoin; they include Dell Computers, Expedia, Microsoft, Dish Network Corp., The United Way, and Overstock.com. Most firms don't actually accept bitcoin directly. Rather, they use bitcoin processing companies like Bitpay and Coinbase, who accept bitcoin and convert it into dollars that are then sent to the retailers.

Supporters of bitcoin say that since transactions are anonymous, people who use the currency have privacy in their purchases. Bitcoin users also save money since they don't pay credit-card fees. Because the total number of bitcoins is limited to 21 million, supporters say that the currency is inflation-proof.

But there are also several serious concerns about bitcoin. First, traditional currencies are issued by central governments and are relatively stable in value. But bitcoin is not backed by any central government and its value can change dramatically in a short period of time. At one point in December 2013, one bitcoin was worth over $1000, but by January 2015 the value had dropped to just $179. The Bank of Canada has expressed concern that consumers do not realize how risky bitcoins are, and the Consumer Protection Finance Bureau has issued a warning about the bitcoin concept. Carolyn Wilkins, the senior deputy governor of the Bank of Canada, told students at Wilfred Laurier University that while e-money has benefits, it also presents risks to the Canadian financial system.

Second, there is concern that bitcoin is being used for "laundering" drug money or for supporting terrorist organizations. This is possible because of the anonymous nature of the currency.

Third, the currency can be stolen by hackers. In 2014, a bitcoin exchange called Mt. Gox declared bankruptcy after losing $425 million in bitcoins to hackers. Flexcoin Inc., which called itself a bitcoin bank, ceased operations in 2014 after hackers stole 896 bitcoins worth $670 000. In 2015, Slovenia-based Bitstamp lost about 19 000 bitcoins worth $5.1 million when its "wallets" were compromised.

CRITICAL THINKING QUESTIONS

1. What are the four basic characteristics of money? How well does bitcoin fit these characteristics?
2. What are the three functions of money? How does bitcoin rate in terms of each of these functions?

In 2015, the IMF had about $327 billion available for loans.[34] With the recent economic turmoil created by the housing and commercial paper crisis in the United States and the European debt crisis, economists and governments are openly questioning the efficiency of these international structures. By 2015, the IMF itself was being criticized for its handling of the European debt crisis by preaching austerity at all costs. The IMF's top economists Olivier Blanchard and Daniel Leigh drafted a document that highlighted errors in predicting the impact of austerity (cuts) in the European economies. In particular, they pointed to a very large underestimation of the increase in unemployment and the decline in domestic demand that would result from such policies.[35]

It is now clearly up to the group of 20 major economies (G20), the IMF, and the other major economic bodies to improve the clarity of rules and reexamine and improve the overall international financial structure.[36]

SUMMARY OF

LEARNING OBJECTIVES

LO-1 DEFINE *MONEY* AND IDENTIFY THE DIFFERENT FORMS IT TAKES IN CANADA'S MONEY SUPPLY.

Any item that is portable, divisible, durable, and stable satisfies the four basic *characteristics of money*. Money also serves three functions: a *medium of exchange*, a *store of value*, and a *unit of account*. The nation's money supply is often determined by two measures. *M-1* includes liquid (or spendable) forms of money: currency (bills and coins), demand deposits, and other "chequable" deposits. *M-2* includes M-1 plus items that cannot be directly spent but that can be easily converted to spendable forms: time deposits, money market funds, and savings deposits. Credit must also be considered as a factor in the money supply.

LO-2 UNDERSTAND THE DIFFERENT KINDS OF *FINANCIAL INSTITUTIONS* THAT MAKE UP THE *CANADIAN FINANCIAL SYSTEM* AND EXPLAIN THE SERVICES THEY OFFER.

There are four financial pillars in Canada: *chartered banks, alternate banks, life insurance companies*, and *investment dealers*. Chartered banks are the most important source of short-term funds for business firms. They create money in the form of expanding demand deposits. The four types of institutions offer services like financial advice, brokerage services, electronic funds transfer, pension and trust services, and lending of money. Some of the differences between these institutions are disappearing. The financial services industry continues to evolve in Canada.

LO-3 EXPLAIN THE FUNCTIONS OF THE *BANK OF CANADA* AND DESCRIBE THE TOOLS IT USES TO CONTROL THE MONEY SUPPLY.

The Bank of Canada manages the Canadian economy, controls the *money supply*, and regulates certain aspects of chartered banking operations. If the Bank of Canada wants to increase the money supply, it can buy government securities or lower the *bank rate*. If it wants to decrease the money supply, it can sell government securities or increase the bank rate.

LO-4 EXPLAIN THE ROLE OF *ALTERNATE BANKS, SPECIALIZED LENDING AND SAVINGS INTERMEDIARIES*, AND *INVESTMENT DEALERS* IN THE CANADIAN FINANCIAL SYSTEM.

Alternate banks include trust companies and credit unions. *Trust companies* safeguard property that is entrusted to them. *Credit unions* are co-operative savings and lending associations formed by a group with common interests. They lend money to both businesses and consumers. *Specialized lending and savings intermediaries* include life insurance companies (which share risks with their policyholders in return for payment of a premium), *factoring companies* (which buy accounts receivable from businesses at a discount and then collect the face value of the account receivable), *financial corporations* (which specialize in financing installment purchases made by businesses and individuals), *venture capital firms* (which provide funds for new or expanding businesses), and *pension funds* (which accumulate and invest money that will be paid out to plan subscribers at some time in the future).

LO-5 DISCUSS SOME OF THE INSTITUTIONS AND ACTIVITIES IN *INTERNATIONAL BANKING* AND *FINANCE*.

Changes in currency values and exchange rates reflect global supply and demand for various currencies. Policies by central banks on money supplies and interest rates influence the values of currencies on the foreign currency exchange markets. Electronic technologies now permit speedy global financial transactions to support the growing importance of international finance. Country-to-country transactions rely on an *international payments process* that moves money between buyers and sellers in different nations. If trade between two countries is in balance—if money inflows and outflows are equal for both countries—money does not have to flow between the two countries. If inflows and outflows are not in balance, then a flow of money between them is made to cover the difference. The *World Bank* and the *International Monetary Fund* were developed by the United Nations with the goal of providing stability to encourage international trade.

QUESTIONS AND EXERCISES

QUESTIONS FOR ANALYSIS

1. What specific changes in banking are shifting banks away from their historical role?
2. Do we really need all the different types of financial institutions we have in Canada? Could we make do with just chartered banks? Why or why not?
3. Should credit cards be counted in the money supply? Why or why not? Support your answer by using the definition of money.
4. Should banks be regulated, or should market forces be allowed to determine the money supply? Defend your answer.
5. Customers who deposit their money in online-only chequing and savings accounts can often get higher interest rates than at brick-and-mortar banks. Why do you think that online banks can offer these rates? What might be some drawbacks to online-only banking?
6. What is the logic behind the "law of one price" concept? Give an example using Switzerland and China.

APPLICATION EXERCISES

7. Start with a $1000 deposit and assume a reserve requirement of 15 percent. Now trace the amount of money created by the banking system after five lending cycles.
8. Interview several consumers to determine which banking services and products they use (debit cards, ATMs, smart cards, online brokerage, and so on). If interviewees are using these services, determine the reasons. If they are not, find out why.
9. Interview the manager of a local chartered bank branch. Identify the ways in which the Bank of Canada helps the bank and the ways in which it limits the bank.
10. Consider historical currency exchange rates for the Canadian dollar versus the U.S. dollar and the euro. If you had bought those currencies with Canadian dollars five years ago, what would their Canadian-dollar values be today?

TEAM EXERCISES

BUILDING YOUR BUSINESS SKILLS

FOUR ECONOMISTS IN A ROOM

GOAL

To encourage you to understand the economic factors considered by the Bank of Canada in determining current interest rates.

BACKGROUND INFORMATION

One of the Bank of Canada's most important tools in setting monetary policy is the adjustment of the interest rates it charges member banks to borrow money. To determine interest rate policy, the Bank of Canada analyzes current economic conditions. Its findings are published on their website and are contained in a quarterly *Monetary Policy Report*.

METHOD

Step 1 Working with three other students, access the Bank of Canada's website at www.bankofcanada.ca. Access the most recent *Monetary Policy Report* and read it carefully.

Step 2 Working with group members, pick out three key economic highlights. Discuss the ways each factor influences the Bank of Canada's decision to raise, lower, or maintain interest rates, and what the implications are for regular consumers.

Step 3 Find articles published in the *Globe and Mail* or the *National Post* or another major newspaper. Look for articles published immediately following the appearance of the most recent report. Discuss with group members what the articles say about current economic conditions and interest rates.

Step 4 Based on your research and analysis, what factors do you think the Bank of Canada will take into account to control inflation? Working with group members, explain your answer in writing.

Step 5 Working with group members, research what the governor of the Bank of Canada says about interest rates. Do reasons for raising, lowering, or maintaining rates agree with your team's analysis?

FOLLOW-UP QUESTIONS

1. What are the most important factors in the Bank of Canada's interest-rate decisions?
2. Consider the old joke about economists that goes like this: *When there are four economists in a room analyzing current economic conditions, there are at least eight different opinions.* Based on your research and analysis, why do you think economists have such varying opinions?

EXERCISING YOUR ETHICS

TELLING THE ETHICAL FROM THE STRICTLY LEGAL

THE SITUATION

When upgrading services for convenience to customers, chartered banks are concerned about setting prices that cover all costs so that, ultimately, they make a profit. This exercise challenges you to evaluate one banking service—ABM transactions—to determine if there are also ethical issues that should be considered in a bank's pricing decisions.

THE DILEMMA

Assume that a bank has more than 300 ABMs serving the nearly 400 000 chequing and savings accounts of its customers. Customers are not charged a fee for their 30 million ABM transactions each year, so long as they use their bank's ABMs. For issuing cash to non-customers, however, the bank charges a $2 ABM fee. The bank's officers are reexamining their policies on ABM surcharges because of public protests.

In considering its current policies, the bank's vice-president for community relations is concerned about more than mere legalities. She wants to ensure that her company is "being a good citizen and doing the right thing." Any decision on ABM fees will ultimately affect the bank's customers, its image in the community and industry, and its profitability for its owners.

TEAM ACTIVITY

Assemble a group of four students and assign each group member to one of the following roles:

- a bank customer
- the bank's vice-president for community relations
- a bank shareholder
- the bank's CEO

QUESTIONS FOR DISCUSSION

1. Before discussing the situation with your group and from the perspective of your assigned role, do you think there are any ethical issues in this situation? If so, write them down.
2. Before discussing the situation with your group and from the perspective of your assigned role, decide how this dispute should be resolved.
3. For the various ethical issues that were identified, decide as a group which one is the most important for the bank to resolve. Which issue is second in importance?
4. From an ethical standpoint, what does your group recommend be done to resolve the most important ethical issue? To resolve the second-most-important ethical issue? What are the advantages and disadvantages of your recommendations?

BUSINESS CASE 14

MASTERING THE CREDIT CARD GAME

Have you noticed that many of the skyscrapers in major cities bear the names of banks and insurance companies at the top? The financial services industry is very healthy; the top five banks in Canada earned combined profits of $35 Billion in 2015. The industry is governed by the rules of the Bank Act and supported by internal company policies. In recent years, banks have expanded their services to meet a wider range of consumer investment needs, and service fees have grown and added to the bottom line. Credit cards are another major source of revenues.

© Deklofenak/Fotolia

How many bank-issued credit cards do you possess? How responsible are you with those cards? How much interest do you pay every year? Do you even know the answer to these questions? Look around your lecture hall. Let's say there are 100 people in your class and they are all clients of your local bank. Your classmates deposit money in their accounts (thus providing funds) and receive a very low interest rate in return (in recent years it has been below the 1 percent range). You use your bank-issued credit card to charge $1000 to pay for your spring break vacation. You don't have the money to pay it back, so you have contractually agreed to pay back interest of 20 percent.

Most people won't think twice about how much interest they pay every year because the credit-card issuers allow individuals to pay back borrowed money slowly with the help of minimum payments. If you only pay the minimum, it will take you years—and hundreds of dollars—to pay off even this minor debt.

BUYER BEWARE: THE DANGEROUS AND ALLURING MINIMUM PAYMENT

It might seem like you are getting a great deal by being generously allowed to make only the minimum payment of $50 (or 2 to 3 percent of the balance); but, of course, this deal comes with a major price. If you are carrying $10 000 of credit-card debt at 20 percent interest, for example, you are paying about $2000 in interest per year. Can you think of anything else you could do with an extra $2000 (a trip, a better music system, new furniture)? For many, the whole credit-card experience is like getting onto a defective treadmill that actually starts off slowly, and then gets progressively quicker before the button gets stuck on high speed. In that situation, you would need to find an effective way to jump off or get someone to pull the plug for you. Unfortunately, many people do not know how to help themselves get out of the trap.

Some even delude themselves into thinking that their situation is better than it actually is. They make the minimum payments and may carry a debt load of, say, $10 000 on their credit cards, but in the meantime they have the same amount of money sitting in a bank account. Why would someone collect 1 percent on a $10 000 bank-account balance and simultaneously pay 20 percent interest on a credit-card debt? It's illogical. Under these circumstances, it is costing you $1900 annually (–$2000 cost of credit + $100 interest from the account) to fool yourself.

Some people just never do the math. They can't be bothered or they just don't understand. (You have been warned!) Others are fearful that if they pay off their bills, they will just load their cards up again. If that is the case for you, you need to grab scissors and cut up the cards. Discipline is required.

If you don't have the money to pay for previous debts, you can use other sources of lower-interest borrowing to pay off the bills.

Here are *some short-term options*:

- A home-equity line of credit (HELOC) can be used to pay down your debt. These days you can get a rate of 3 to 5 percent (total savings: $1500 to $1600 per year on the same $10 000 debt). So why not transfer the credit-card debt to this lower-rate option and use the savings to pay down your debt quicker?
- Credit-card issuers often offer cheque transfers at, say, 0.99 to 3.99 percent for six to nine months. You can transfer the 20 percent debt on your Visa, for example, to your MasterCard, when it is offering a temporary 1.99 percent deal. This sort of offer can save you hundreds of dollars and give you extra funds to pay off principal. The catch is that, at the end of the six to nine months, you will be charged a high rate again. (Remember, this is only a short-term solution. Don't add to your debt; instead, use the time to pay it off).
- If you must take on debt by credit card, there are products that charge more reasonable rates. According to the Canadian Bankers Association (CBA), there are over 70 low-interest credit cards on the market. The CBA define low interest as below 12 percent (which is still very high). RBC launched a credit card called the RBC My Project Credit MasterCard. It provides as much as $40 000 with 0 percent interest for six months and interest of 4.99 percent above prime after that.

The real solution: Buy what you can afford and pay cash. Then there is no need for long-term calculations and financially troubling interest payments.

KEY BENEFITS AND SOUND ADVICE

Credit cards are still a great way to make purchases conveniently without carrying large sums of money—if you act responsibly. They provide a 21-to-30-day interest-free loan if you pay on time. In addition, you can earn points that can lead to free travel and free products.

If you are responsible, you can take advantage of the benefits without overcontributing to the construction of another downtown high-rise building. In this chapter, we learned about the definition of money. Credit cards are not money. They can be used as a medium of exchange, but they must be used wisely or they will have a very negative effect on your personal wealth.

QUESTIONS FOR DISCUSSION

1. Identify and explain two of the fundamental warnings about credit cards that are contained in this case.
2. Do you believe the typical consumer understands the full extent of the "credit-card trap"? What elements of the credit game are most difficult to comprehend for consumers?
3. Do you believe the government should put tighter controls on interest rates and ban credit-card companies from charging rates above 15 percent? Why? Why not?

CHAPTER SUPPLEMENT 04

Managing Your Personal Finances: A Synopsis

Below are some important personal finance tips and practical hands-on examples. For a more detailed description, complete with additional worksheets and analysis of these tips, visit the online appendix in MyBizLab.

DEVELOPING A PERSONAL FINANCIAL PLAN

Like it or not, dealing with personal finances is a lifelong job. As a rule, it involves rational management of your personal finances—controlling them as a way of life and helping them grow. Figure F.1 provides a summary of the key steps in developing a financial plan.

THE TIME VALUE OF MONEY AND THE RULE OF 72

The time value of money is perhaps the single most important concept in personal finance. It's especially relevant for setting financial goals and evaluating investments. The concept of *time value* recognizes the basic fact that, while it's invested, money grows by earning interest or yielding some other form of return. Thus, whenever you make everyday purchases, you're giving up interest that you could have earned with the same money if you'd invested it instead. From a financial standpoint, "idle" or uninvested money is a wasted resource.

How long does it take to double an investment? A handy rule of thumb is "The Rule of 72." You can find the number of years needed to double your money by dividing the annual interest rate (in percent) into 72. If, for example, you reinvest annually at 8 percent, you'll double your money in about 9 years.

Take a look at Table F.2 for a clearer picture of the importance of this simple rule.

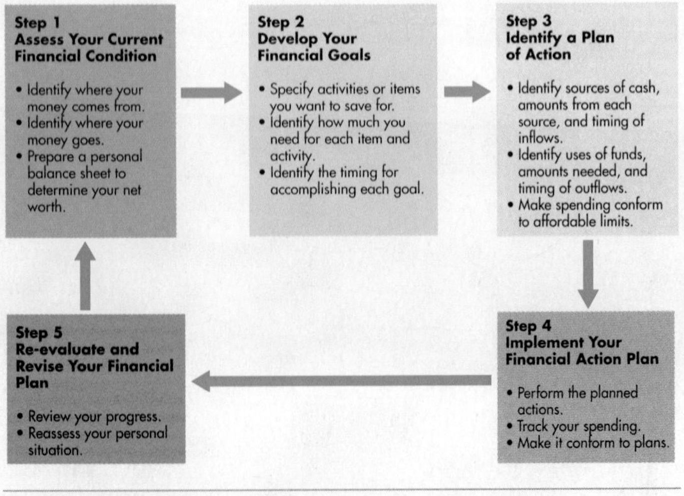

Step 1
Assess Your Current Financial Condition
- Identify where your money comes from.
- Identify where your money goes.
- Prepare a personal balance sheet to determine your net worth.

Step 2
Develop Your Financial Goals
- Specify activities or items you want to save for.
- Identify how much you need for each item and activity.
- Identify the timing for accomplishing each goal.

Step 3
Identify a Plan of Action
- Identify sources of cash, amounts from each source, and timing of inflows.
- Identify uses of funds, amounts needed, and timing of outflows.
- Make spending conform to affordable limits.

Step 4
Implement Your Financial Action Plan
- Perform the planned actions.
- Track your spending.
- Make it conform to plans.

Step 5
Re-evaluate and Revise Your Financial Plan
- Review your progress.
- Reassess your personal situation.

FIGURE F.1 Developing a personal financial plan

How does a $10 000 investment grow under different interest-rate scenarios? These days most banks pay 1 percent interest (if you're lucky). You would have to live another 72 years to see your money double at that rate. Thirty years later that $10 000 initial investment would only be worth $13 800, whereas the same investment would be worth $174 000 if you earned 10 percent. On average, the stock market has earned an average return of 10 percent in the last 75 years. However, if you are risk-averse, you could still put the money in something safer (like bonds) and still turn that $10 000 into $32 430 or more. More detailed explanations and examples are available in the online appendix.

Where you invest your money counts! Never forget the rule of 72 and the time value of money!

USE CREDIT CARDS RESPONSIBLY

Although some credit cards don't charge annual fees, all of them charge interest on unpaid (outstanding) balances. Because credit-card debt is one of the most expensive sources of funds, you need to understand the costs before you start charging.

For example, if you have $5000 worth of credit-card debt on a Visa that charges 18 percent, you are paying $960 in interest per year for that debt. You could probably think of better ways to spend that money (fancy clothes or a weekend getaway perhaps). Most people never make that calculation, because the credit-card companies allow you to make the "minimum payment" and are happy collecting the interest from you (especially as you increase your debt from $5000 to $10 000 to $20 000 over time). If you only make the minimum payment, that *$5000 credit-card debt (at 18 percent) will take 115 months to pay off.* Guess what, the rule of 72 also applies to your debts. So be smart.

Don't destroy your personal wealth by ignoring the cost of your interest payments. If you are stuck with debt, try to transfer it to lower-cost sources of financing and pay it off as soon as possible!

TABLE F.1 Tips for Personal Financial Wealth

Tips for Personal Financial Wealth
1. Develop a Financial Plan
2. Understand the Time Value of Money & Never Forget the Rule of 72!
3. Use Credit Cards Responsibly
4. Invest Wisely in Real Estate
5. Cash Out from (Legal) Tax Avoidance
6. Protect Your Net Worth

>>> **TABLE F.2** The Rule of 72 and the Time Value of Money

The Number 72	Interest Rate	Number of Years for Money to Double	How Much a $10 000 Investment Is Worth After 30 Years
72	1	72	**$13 800**
72	4	18	$32 430
72	6	12	$57 430
72	8	9	$100 620
72	10	7.2	**$174 490**

INVEST CAREFULLY IN REAL ESTATE

Should you rent or buy? The answer to that question involves a variety of considerations, including life stage, family needs, career, financial situation, and preferred lifestyle. If you decide to buy, you have to ask yourself how much house you can afford. To answer that question, you need to ask a number of questions about your personal financial condition and your capacity for borrowing. Buy wisely.

Step 1: Don't spend beyond your means!
Step 2: When signing a mortgage deal, look around and compare; an interest rate even 0.25 percent lower translates into significant savings.

CASHING OUT FROM (LEGAL) TAX AVOIDANCE

Take advantage of all of the various government programs and rules to cut your tax bill. Some of the most important methods for tax relief and/or untaxed accumulation of funds include *registered retirement savings plans (RRSPs), tax-free savings accounts (TSFAs), and registered education savings plans (RESP).*

Lower your tax bill, increase your personal equity.

PROTECT YOUR NET WORTH

With careful attention, thoughtful saving and spending, and skillful financial planning (pus a little luck), you can build up your net worth over time. However, every financial plan should consider steps for preserving it. One approach involves the risk–return relationship. Do you prefer to protect your current assets, or are you willing to risk them in return for greater growth? At various life stages, and whenever you reach a designated level of wealth, you should adjust your asset portfolio to conform to your risk and return preferences—conservative, moderate, or aggressive.

Another approach is life insurance. From a personal-finance perspective, the purpose of life insurance is to replace income upon the death of the policyholder. Accordingly, the amount of insurance you need depends on how many other people rely on your income. Insurance, for example, is crucial for the married parent who is a family's sole source of income. On the other hand, a single person with no financial dependents needs little or no insurance and will probably prefer to put money into higher-paying investments.

Buy the right life insurance and the right amount. For an explanation of the difference between term and whole life insurance, refer to the online site.

Rawpixel/Fotolia

LO

AFTER READING THIS CHAPTER, YOU SHOULD BE ABLE TO:

LO-1 Describe the responsibilities of a *financial manager*.

LO-2 Distinguish between *short-term* (operating) and *long-term* (capital) expenditures.

LO-3 Identify three sources of *short-term financing* for businesses.

LO-4 Identify three sources of *long-term financing* for businesses.

LO-5 Discuss the value of *common stock and preferred stock* to stockholders, and describe the secondary market for each type of security.

LO-6 Explain the process by which securities are bought and sold.

LO-7 Describe the investment opportunities offered by mutual funds, *exchange-traded funds, hedge funds*, and *commodities*.

LO-8 Explain how *risk* affects business operations and identify the five steps in the *risk management process*.

Piles of Cash

Until recently, most financial managers in business organizations felt that they should not hoard cash but instead should invest it to earn a good return for their company.

alswart/Fotolia

But in the past few years many financial managers seem to be rethinking the traditional view, and this change can be observed on company balance sheets.

In 2014, the International Monetary Fund said that Canadian companies were accumulating cash faster than any companies in the G7 group. In the last quarter of 2013, Canadian corporations held $626 billion dollars of cash. Large holders of cash included Sun Life Financial ($6 billion), Power Corp. of Canada ($4.9 billion), and Suncor Energy ($4.8 billion). Technology companies in the United States also held large amounts of cash—Apple ($97 billion), Microsoft ($41 billion), Cisco Systems ($40 billion), and Google ($34 billion). Worldwide, corporations in developed countries held over $8 *trillion* dollars, according to the Institute of International Finance.

Many companies are maintaining so-called "fortress balance sheets," because they vividly remember the

Financial Decisions *and* Risk Management

CHAPTER 15

financial crisis of 2008 and they don't want to be short on cash if another such episode occurs. Although this sounds reasonable, cash hoarding is viewed as a bad thing by many people. Critics say that companies made the financial crisis of 2008 worse because they hoarded cash instead of spending it on job creation. They argue that spending some of that cash would have constituted a "second stimulus" beyond the government's stimulus spending.

There were many specific critical comments. For example, *The Wall Street Journal* said that it would be good if cash-rich companies stepped up their hiring so that the high unemployment rate would be reduced. David Bianco, the chief equity strategist at Merrill Lynch criticized chief financial officers of companies for holding too much cash, and said that cash hoarding was depressing share prices. He noted that shareholders were unhappy because dividend payout ratios were near historical lows. Some critics went so far as to suggest a 2 percent tax on corporation cash balances. A study of 25 companies that had $10 billion or more cash on hand showed that their stock prices were underperforming compared to the general market, and that they had slow growth rates. Mark Carney, the former Bank of Canada governor, called cash hoards "dead money," and said that businesses should either spend their cash or give it back to shareholders in the form of dividends. If shareholders received more dividends, perhaps they would boost the economy because they would have more money to spend.

HOW WILL THIS HELP ME?

The material in this chapter will benefit you in two ways: (1) you will be better able to use your knowledge about finance in your career as both an *employee* and as a *manager* and (2) you will be a more informed *consumer*, with greater awareness of how businesses use financial instruments to support their activities.

But financial managers have a different perspective on the appropriateness of holding large amounts of cash. Even though the economic downturn of 2008 is now in the rearview mirror, financial managers are still wary. They see many possible problems on the horizon—the possibility of another recession, a slowdown in China's economy, and volatility in commodity markets, to name just a few. Financial managers are therefore being very conservative in how they manage cash. Cost-cutting and cash hoarding have become key strategies, and financial managers have adopted a wait-and-see attitude before spending large amounts of money on things like hiring more staff.

The view that it is bad for financial managers to hoard cash is also challenged by Alan Reynolds, a senior fellow at the U.S.-based Cato Institute. He says that such a view reveals ignorance about basic financial realities. (He analyzed data from U.S. corporations, but the same principles apply to Canadian companies.) Reynolds makes four key points. First, net worth indicates the health of a corporation, not the *form* in which assets are held (e.g., cash, accounts receivable, fixed assets, and so on). The net worth of U.S. nonfinancial corporations dropped from $15.9 trillion in 2007 to $12.6 trillion in 2011. The ratio of cash to total assets rose because the value of total assets fell, not because the corporation was hoarding large amounts of cash.

Second, liquid assets like cash serve as a safety cushion to deal with unexpected business difficulties. To characterize the holding of cash as "hoarding" without also considering the level of risk and short-term debt is meaningless. U.S. corporations hold nearly $2 trillion in cash, but that is far less than the $3.67 trillion in short-term debt on their books.

Third, there is a big difference between the assets a corporation owns (which are shown on the balance sheet) and the money it disburses and receives (which is shown on the income statement). Companies don't draw down assets (liquid or otherwise) to meet payroll expenses; rather, they add workers when they think that they can increase their after-tax revenues by doing so.

Fourth, the idea that investing in liquid assets (e.g., bonds, time deposits, and mutual funds) somehow reduces hiring is simply wrong. Corporations can, and do, make capital expenditures (e.g., in buildings and inventories) at the same time they are making investments in liquid assets. It's also true that even if cash-rich technology companies like Apple spend some of their cash, it would likely create jobs in foreign countries, not North America.

Here is another consideration in this debate. It is possible that when Canadian corporations hold large amounts of cash they may inadvertently be suppressing inflation. During 2012–2014, inflation levels in Canada were consistently below the 2 percent target set by the Bank of

Duckman76/Fotolia

Canada. This was surprising, because low interest rates during that period should have resulted in a greater money supply, which in turn should have led to a higher rate of inflation. This did not occur, possibly because the velocity of money—the rate at which money changes hands—also declined. So, an increase in the money supply isn't automatically inflationary if the extra money isn't being passed around. And the money isn't passed around when corporations hoard cash.

Companies aren't alone in holding large amounts of cash. Individual and institutional investors are doing the same thing. A 2014 survey by State Street found that, worldwide, investors are holding about 40 percent of their portfolios in cash. That's up from 31 percent in 2012.

QUESTIONS FOR DISCUSSION

1. What are three main responsibilities of financial managers? How do these responsibilities influence the amount of cash that companies hold?
2. If companies paid out more money in dividends, do you think that consumers would spend more money and thereby boost the economy? Defend your answer.
3. Which of the two claims—that companies are unreasonably hoarding cash or companies are not unreasonably hoarding cash—do you think is most persuasive? Explain.

LO-1 THE ROLE OF THE FINANCIAL MANAGER

Financial managers plan and control the acquisition and dispersal of the company's financial assets. The business activity known as **finance** (or corporate finance) typically involves four responsibilities:

1. determining a firm's long-term investments
2. obtaining funds to pay for those investments
3. conducting the firm's everyday financial activities
4. managing the risks that the firm takes

In recent years, more and more chief financial officers (CFOs) have been appointed as chief executives officers (CEOs). For example, at Pepsico, Indra Nooyi was promoted from CFO to CEO. About 20 percent of CEOs were formerly CFOs.[1] The skill set of CFOs is expanding because they have access to a great deal of information about the internal workings of companies, and because they are responsible for setting budgets and dealing with regulatory agencies.[2] Rowan O'Grady, president of Hays Canada, a recruiting firm, says that CFOs do much more than simply focus on financial documents like spreadsheets; they also work extensively with people, and they have a significant leadership role to play in their organization.[3]

FINANCE The business function involving decisions about a firm's long-term investments and obtaining the funds to pay for those investments.

Objectives of the Financial Manager

A financial manager's overall objective is to increase a firm's value and stockholders' wealth. Financial managers do many specific things to increase a firm's value: collect funds, pay debts, establish trade credit, obtain loans, control cash balances, and plan for future financial needs. Whereas accountants create data to reflect a firm's financial status, financial managers make decisions for improving that status. Financial managers must ensure that a company's revenues exceed its costs—in other words, that it earns a profit. In sole proprietorships and partnerships, profits translate directly into increases in owners' wealth. In corporations, profits translate into an increase in the value of common stock.

Responsibilities of the Financial Manager

The various responsibilities of the financial manager in increasing a firm's wealth fall into three general categories: *cash-flow management, financial control*, and *financial planning*.

CASH-FLOW MANAGEMENT

To increase a firm's value, financial managers must ensure that it always has enough funds on hand to purchase the materials and human resources that it needs to produce goods and services. Funds that are not needed immediately must be invested to earn more money. This activity—**cash-flow management**—requires careful planning. If excess cash balances are allowed to sit idle instead of being invested, a firm loses the interest that it could have earned. One study revealed that companies averaging $2 million in annual sales typically hold $40 000 in non-interest-bearing accounts. Larger companies hold even larger sums. By putting idle cash to work, firms gain additional investment income.

FINANCIAL CONTROL

Because things never go exactly as planned, financial managers must be prepared to make adjustments for actual financial changes that occur each day. **Financial control** is the process of checking actual performance against plans to ensure that the desired financial outcome occurs. For example, planned revenues based on forecasts usually turn out to be higher or lower than actual revenues. Why? Simply because sales are unpredictable. Control involves monitoring revenue inflows and making appropriate financial adjustments. Higher-than-expected revenues, for instance, may be deposited in short-term interest-bearing accounts, or they may be used to pay off short-term debt. Otherwise earmarked resources can be saved or put to better use. In contrast, lower-than-expected revenues may necessitate short-term borrowing to meet current debt obligations.

Budgets are important in financial control (see Chapter 11) and provide the "measuring stick" against which performance is evaluated. The cash flows, debts, and assets, not only of the whole company, but also of each department, are compared at regular intervals against budgeted amounts. Discrepancies indicate the need for financial adjustments so that resources are used to the best advantage.

FINANCIAL PLANNING

The cornerstone of effective financial management is the development of a **financial plan**, which describes a firm's strategies for reaching some future financial position. In 2012, for example, Canadian Pacific Railway Ltd. announced that it would make strategic investments totalling $1.2 billion in order to improve its operating ratio (which, in 2011, was the worst among North America's Big Six railways).[4] In the energy industry, the sharp drop in the price of oil in 2014 caused companies to cut their capital spending. For example, Canadian Natural Resources cut $2.4 billion from its budget. That meant that the company would drill far fewer wells than it had previously planned.[5] Crescent Point Energy Corp. also cut $1.45 billion from its capital budget. That meant that the company would produce fewer barrels of oil in 2015 than it did in 2014.[6]

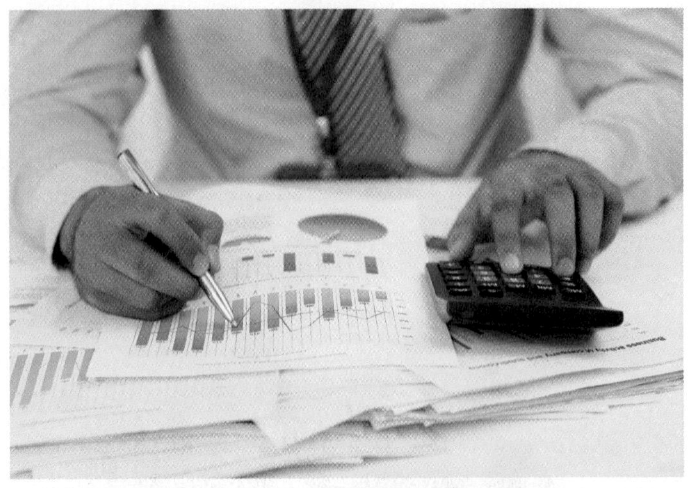

Financial managers have the responsibility of ensuring that the financial assets of their company are used effectively. This includes the performance of investments the company may have in other companies in the form of shares of stock. Regular assessment of how these investments are performing is an important responsibility of financial managers.

DragonImages/Fotolia

When constructing a financial plan, several questions must be answered:

- What funds are needed to meet immediate plans?
- When will the firm need more funds?
- Where can the firm get the funds to meet both its short- and its long-term needs?

To answer these questions, a financial manager must develop a clear picture of why a firm needs funds. Managers must also assess the relative costs and benefits of potential funding sources. In the following sections, we examine the main reasons why companies generate funds and describe the main sources of business funding, both for the short and long term.

CASH-FLOW MANAGEMENT Managing the pattern in which cash flows into the firm in the form of revenues and out of the firm in the form of debt payments.

FINANCIAL CONTROL The process of checking actual performance against plans to ensure that the desired financial status is achieved.

FINANCIAL PLAN A description of how a business will reach some financial position it seeks for the future; includes projections for sources and uses of funds.

LO-2 WHY BUSINESSES NEED FUNDS

Every company needs money to survive. Failure to make a contractually obligated payment can lead to bankruptcy and the dissolution of the firm. Financial managers must distinguish between short-term (operating) expenditures and long-term (capital) expenditures. The time frame for short-term expenditures is typically less than one year, while for long-term expenditures the time frame is greater than one year.

Short-Term (Operating) Expenditures

A firm incurs short-term expenditures regularly in its everyday business activities. To handle these expenditures, financial managers must pay attention to *accounts payable*, *accounts receivable*, and *inventories*.

ACCOUNTS PAYABLE

In Chapter 11, we defined accounts payable as unpaid bills owed to suppliers plus wages and taxes due within a year. For most companies, this is the largest single category of short-term debt. To plan for funding flows, financial managers want to know in advance the amounts of new accounts payable, as well as when they must be repaid. For information about such obligations and needs—say, the quantity of supplies required by a certain department in an upcoming period—financial managers must rely on other managers. The Exercising Your Ethics section at the end of this chapter presents an interesting dilemma regarding accounts payable.

ACCOUNTS RECEIVABLE

Accounts receivable refer to funds due from customers who have bought on credit. Because accounts receivable represent an investment in products for which a firm has not yet received payment, they temporarily tie up its funds. Clearly, the seller wants to receive payment as quickly as possible. A sound financial plan requires financial managers to project accurately both how much credit is advanced to buyers and when they will make payments. For example, managers at Kraft Foods must know how many dollars' worth of cheddar cheese Safeway supermarkets will order each month; they must also know Safeway's payment schedule.

Credit Policies Predicting payment schedules is a function of *credit policy*—the rules governing a firm's extension of credit to customers. This policy sets standards as to which buyers are eligible for what type of credit. Typically, credit is extended to customers who have the ability to pay and who honour their obligations. Credit is denied to firms with poor payment histories.

Credit policy also sets specific payment terms. For example, credit terms of "2/10, net 30" mean that the selling company offers a 2 percent discount if the customer pays within 10 days. The customer has 30 days to pay the regular price. Under these terms, the buyer would have to pay only $980 on a $1000 invoice on days 1 to 10, but all $1000 on days 11 to 30. The higher the discount, the more incentive buyers have to pay early. Sellers can thus adjust credit terms to influence when customers pay their bills.

INVENTORIES

Between the time a firm buys raw materials and the time it sells finished products, it ties up funds in **inventory**—materials and goods that it will sell within the year. Failure to manage inventory can have grave financial consequences. Too little inventory of any kind can cost a firm sales, while too much inventory means tied-up funds that cannot be used elsewhere. In extreme cases, a company may have to sell excess inventory at low prices simply to raise cash.

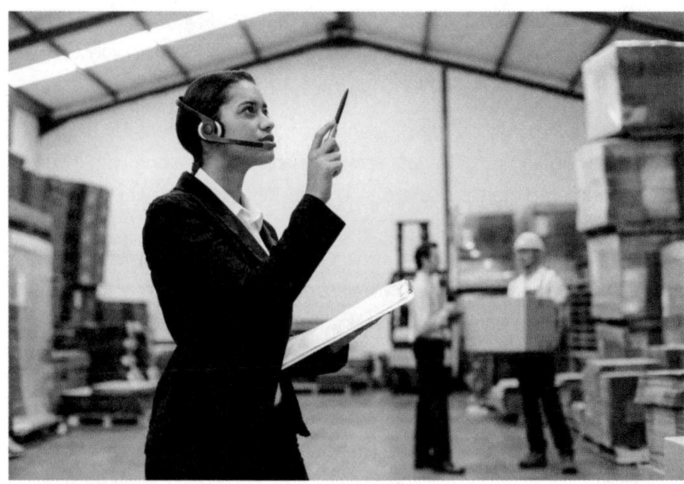

This warehouse manager is checking inventory levels in a large warehouse.

Wavebreak Media Ltd /123RF

The basic supplies a firm buys to use in its production process are its *raw-materials inventory*. Levi Strauss's raw-materials inventory includes huge rolls of denim. *Work-in-process inventory* consists of goods partway through the production process. Cut-out but not-yet-sewn jeans are part of the work-in-process inventory at Levi's. Finally, *finished-goods inventory* refers to items that are ready for sale (completed blue jeans ready for shipment to Levi's dealers).

Long-Term (Capital) Expenditures

Companies need funds to cover long-term expenditures for fixed assets like land, buildings, and machinery. In 2012, for example, Walmart Canada spent $750 million on remodelling, expanding, or relocating 73 different retail outlets.[7] Long-term expenditures are more carefully planned than short-term outlays because they pose special problems. They differ from short-term outlays in the following ways, all of which influence the ways that long-term outlays are funded:

- Unlike inventories and other short-term assets, they are not normally sold or converted to cash.
- Their acquisition requires a very large investment.
- They represent a binding commitment of company funds that continues long into the future.

INVENTORY Materials and goods currently held by the company that will be sold within the year.

LO-3 SOURCES OF SHORT-TERM FUNDS

Firms can call on many sources for the funds they need to finance day-to-day operations and to implement short-term plans. These sources include *trade credit*, *secured short-term loans*, and *unsecured short-term loans*.

Trade Credit

Accounts payable are not merely an expenditure. They are also a source of funds to the company, which has the use of both the product purchased and the price of the product until the time it pays its bill. **Trade credit**, the granting of credit by one firm to another, is effectively a short-term loan. Trade credit can take several forms.

- The most common form, *open-book credit*, is essentially a "gentlemen's agreement." Buyers receive merchandise along with invoices stating credit terms. Sellers ship products on faith that payment will be forthcoming.
- When sellers want more reassurance, they may insist that buyers sign legally binding *promissory notes* before merchandise is shipped. The agreement states when and how much money will be paid to the seller.
- The *trade draft* is attached to the merchandise shipment by the seller and states the promised date and amount of payment due. To take possession of the merchandise, the buyer must sign the draft. Once signed by the buyer, the document becomes a *trade acceptance*. Trade drafts and trade acceptances are useful forms of credit in international transactions.

Secured Short-Term Loans

For most firms, bank loans are a vital source of short-term funding. Such loans almost always involve a promissory note in which the borrower promises to repay the loan plus interest. In **secured loans**, banks also require the borrower to put up collateral—to give the bank the right to seize certain assets if payments are not made. Inventories, accounts receivable, and other assets (e.g., stocks and bonds) may serve as *collateral* for a secured loan. Secured loans allow borrowers to get funds when they might not qualify for unsecured credit. Moreover, they generally carry lower interest rates than unsecured loans.

INVENTORY AS COLLATERAL

When a loan is made with inventory as a collateral asset, the lender lends the borrower some portion of the stated value of the inventory. Inventory is more attractive as collateral when it can be readily converted into cash. Boxes full of expensive, partially completed lenses for eyeglasses are of little value on the open market, but a thousand crates of canned tomatoes might well be convertible into cash.

ACCOUNTS RECEIVABLE AS COLLATERAL

When accounts receivable are used as collateral, the process is called *pledging accounts receivable*. In the event of non-payment, the lender may seize the receivables (funds owed the borrower by its customers). If these assets are not enough to cover the loan, the borrower must make up the difference. This option is especially important to service companies such as accounting firms and law offices. Because they do not maintain inventories, accounts receivable are their main source of collateral. Typically, lenders that will accept accounts receivable as collateral are financial institutions with credit departments capable of evaluating the quality of the receivables.

Factoring Accounts Receivable A firm can also raise funds by *factoring* (i.e., selling) its accounts receivable. The purchaser of the receivables (called a factor) might, for example, buy $50 000 worth of receivables for 80 percent of that sum ($40 000). The factor then tries to collect on the receivables and profits to the extent that the money it eventually collects exceeds the amount it paid for the receivables. Usually the factor ends up with a profit of 2 to 4 percent, depending on the quality of the receivables, the cost of collecting them, and interest rates. Factoring essentially means outsourcing the collection process. About $4 billion worth of goods are factored each year in Canada, but this is far below the $300 billion in the U.S. Toronto-based Liquid Capital Advance Corp., a factoring company, had revenues of almost $2 billion in 2011.[8]

Unsecured Short-Term Loans

With an **unsecured loan**, the borrower does not have to put up collateral. In many cases, however, the bank requires the borrower to maintain a compensating balance—the borrower must keep a portion of the loan amount on deposit with the bank in a non-interest-bearing account.

The terms of an unsecured loan—amount, duration, interest rate, and payment schedule—are negotiated. To receive such a loan, a firm must ordinarily have a good banking relationship with the lender. Once an agreement is made, a promissory note will be executed and the funds transferred to the borrower. There are three common types of unsecured loans: *lines of credit, revolving credit agreements*, and *commercial paper*.

LINES OF CREDIT

A standing agreement with a bank to lend a firm a maximum amount of funds on request is called a **line of credit**. With a line of credit, the firm knows the maximum amount it will be allowed to borrow if the bank has sufficient funds. The bank does not guarantee that the funds will be available when requested. For example, suppose that RBC gives Sunshine Tanning Inc. a $100 000 line of credit for the coming year. By signing promissory notes, Sunshine's borrowings can total up to $100 000 at any time. The bank may not always have sufficient funds when Sunshine needs them. But Sunshine benefits from the arrangement by knowing in advance that the bank regards the firm as creditworthy and will lend funds to it on short notice.

REVOLVING CREDIT AGREEMENTS

Revolving credit agreements are similar to bank credit cards for consumers. Under a **revolving credit agreement**, a lender agrees to make some amount of funds available on demand to a firm for continuing short-term loans. The lending institution guarantees that funds will be available when sought by the borrower. In return, the bank charges a commitment fee—a charge for holding open a line of credit for a customer even if the customer does not borrow any funds. The commitment fee is often expressed as a percentage of the loan amount, usually 0.5 to 1 percent of the committed amount. For example, suppose that RBC

TRADE CREDIT The granting of credit by a selling firm to a buying firm.

SECURED LOANS A short-term loan in which the borrower is required to put up collateral.

UNSECURED LOAN A short-term loan in which the borrower is not required to put up collateral.

LINE OF CREDIT A standing agreement between a bank and a firm in which the bank specifies the maximum amount it will make available to the borrower for a short-term unsecured loan; the borrower can then draw on those funds, when available.

REVOLVING CREDIT AGREEMENT A guaranteed line of credit for which the firm pays the bank interest on funds borrowed, as well as a fee for extending the line of credit.

agrees to lend Sunshine Tanning up to $100 000 under a revolving credit agreement. If Sunshine borrows $80 000, it still has access to $20 000. If it pays off $50 000 of the debt, reducing its debt to $30 000, then $70 000 is available. Sunshine pays interest on the borrowed funds and also pays a fee on the unused funds in the line of credit.

COMMERCIAL PAPER

Commercial paper, which is backed solely by the issuing firm's promise to pay, is an option for only the largest and most creditworthy firms. Here's how it works: Corporations issue commercial paper with a face value. Companies that buy commercial paper pay less than that value. At the end of a specified period (usually 30 to 90 days, but legally up to 270 days), the issuing company buys back the paper—at the face value. The difference between the price the buying company paid and the face value is the buyer's interest earned. For example, if Air Canada needs to borrow $10 million for 90 days, it might issue commercial paper with a face value of $10.2 million. If an insurance company with $10 million in excess cash buys the paper, after 90 days Air Canada would pay $10.2 million to the insurance company. So the insurance company earns $200 000 for its $10 million investment (an annual interest rate of approximately 2 percent).

COMMERCIAL PAPER A method of short-run fundraising in which a firm sells unsecured notes for less than the face value and then repurchases them at the face value within 270 days; buyers' profits are the difference between the original price paid and the face value.

LO-4 SOURCES OF LONG-TERM FUNDS

Firms need long-term funding to finance expenditures on fixed assets like the buildings and equipment that is necessary for conducting business. They may seek long-term funds through *debt financing*, *equity financing*, or *hybrid financing*.

Debt Financing

Long-term borrowing from outside the company—**debt financing**—is a major component of most firms' long-term financial planning. Debt financing is most appealing to companies that have predictable profits and cash-flow patterns. For example, demand for electric power is quite steady from year to year and predictable from month to month. Thus, provincial hydroelectric utilities rely heavily on debt financing. There are two primary sources of debt financing: *long-term loans* and the sale of *bonds*.

LONG-TERM LOANS

Most corporations get their long-term loans from a chartered bank, usually one with which the firm has developed a long-standing relationship. Long-term loans are usually matched with long-term assets. Interest rates for the loan are negotiated between the borrower and lender. Although some bank loans have fixed rates, others have floating rates tied to the prime rate that they charge their most creditworthy customers (see Chapter 14). For example, a company might negotiate a loan at "prime + 1 percent." If prime is 3 percent at that particular time, the company will pay 4 percent. Credit companies, insurance companies, and pension funds also grant long-term business loans.

Long-term loans have several advantages. They can be arranged quickly, the duration of the loan is easily matched to the borrower's needs, and if the firm's needs change, the loan usually contains clauses making it possible to change the terms. But long-term loans also have some disadvantages. Large borrowers may have trouble finding lenders to supply enough funds. Long-term borrowers may also have restrictions placed on them as conditions of the loan. They may have to pledge long-term assets as collateral. And they may have to agree not to take on any more debt until the borrowed funds are repaid.

BONDS

A **corporate bond** is a contract—a promise by the issuing company or organization to pay the bondholder a certain amount of money (the principal) on a specified date, plus interest in return for use of the investor's money. The *bond indenture* spells out the terms of the bond, including the interest rate that will be paid, the maturity date of the bond, and which of the firm's assets, if any, are pledged as collateral. Alibaba Group Holdings Ltd. began planning to sell bonds just two months after its very successful IPO (see Business Case 15 at the end of this chapter).[9]

Bonds are the major source of long-term debt financing for most large corporations. Bonds are attractive when companies need large amounts of funds for long periods of time; in many cases, bonds may not be redeemed for 30 years. But bonds involve expensive administrative and selling costs, and they may also require high interest payments if the issuing company has a poor credit rating. If a company fails to make a bond payment, it is in *default*.

Sovereign nations also issue bonds, and just like businesses and individuals, they must make sure that their debt does not exceed their capacity to pay it back. Well, sort of. Greece has been trying for several years to resolve its massive debt problems and pay back other countries in the European Union that loaned it money. Some observers think that Greece may default on its bond payments and stop using the euro as its currency.[10]

Registered bonds register the names of holders with the company, which then mails out cheques to the bondholders. *Bearer (or coupon) bonds* require bondholders to clip coupons from certificates and send them to the issuer to receive payment. Coupons can be redeemed by anyone, regardless of ownership. With **secured bonds**, borrowers can reduce the risk of their bonds by pledging assets to bondholders in the event of default. If the corporation does not pay interest when it is due, the firm's assets can be sold and the proceeds used to pay the bondholders. Unsecured bonds are called *debentures*. No specific property is pledged as security for these bonds. Holders of unsecured bonds generally have claims against property not otherwise pledged in the company's

DEBT FINANCING Raising money to meet long-term expenditures by borrowing from outside the company; usually takes the form of long-term loans or the sale of corporate bonds.

CORPORATE BOND A promise by the issuing company to pay the holder a certain amount of money on a specified date, with stated interest payments in the interim; a form of long-term debt financing.

SECURED BONDS Bonds issued by borrowers who pledge assets as collateral in the event of non-payment.

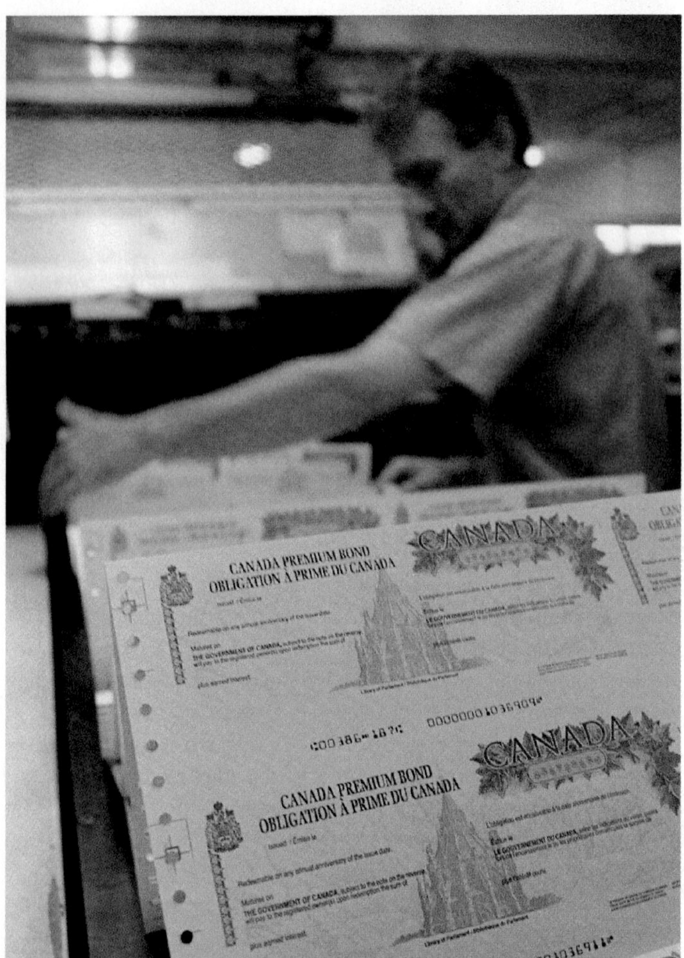

<<< Corporations aren't the only organizations that sell bonds. The government of Canada also sells bonds to finance its activities.

Tom Hanson/The Canadian Press

other bonds. Accordingly, debentures have inferior claims on the corporation's assets. Financially strong corporations often use debentures.

The boxed insert entitled "Green Bonds" describes a new development in the selling of bonds.

With regard to maturity dates, there are three types of bonds: *callable, serial*, and *convertible*.

Callable Bonds The issuer of *callable bonds* may call them in and pay them off before the maturity date at a price stipulated in the indenture. Usually the issuer cannot call the bond for a certain period of time after issue, often within the first five years. Issuers usually call in existing bonds when prevailing interest rates are lower than the rate being paid on the bond. The issuer must still pay a *call* price to call in the bond. The call price usually gives a premium to the bondholder. The premium is merely the difference between the face value and call price. For example, a bond that bears a $100 face value might be callable by the firm for $108.67 any time during the first year after issue. The call price (and therefore the premium) decreases annually as the bonds approach maturity.

Callable bonds are often retired by the use of *sinking-fund provisions*. The issuing company is required to put a certain amount of money into a special bank account annually. At the end of a certain number of years, the money (including interest) will be sufficient to redeem the bonds. Failure to meet the sinking-fund provision places the issue in default. Such bonds are generally regarded as safer investments than many other bonds.

THE GREENING OF BUSINESS

Green Bonds

Green bonds are much like regular bonds except that the funds generated by them are directed toward projects that are environmentally friendly. They were pioneered by the World Bank as a way of raising capital for projects with specific environmental benefits. But now these types of bonds are increasingly appealing to both individual and institutional investors concerned about the environment. And the market for them is growing rapidly.

More green bonds were issued in Canada in 2013 than in the entire period 2007–2012, and twice as many were issued in 2014 as in 2013. Climate Bonds Initiative, a British research group, says the worldwide market for these bonds is about $500 billion.

During 2014, there were four large green bond issues in Canada: the Ontario government, TD Bank, Export Development Canada, and North Island Hospital Project. The Ontario bonds will fund environmentally friendly infrastructure projects around the province like Eglinton Crosstown Light Rail Transit, a partially underground rail system that will replace buses. The North Island Hospital Project is a public–private partnership, and the funds will be used to finance a hospital in Campbell River and another in Comox Valley, British Columbia. Corporate green bonds have also been issued by energy companies like NextEra Energy Inc., Enerfin Energy Co. of Canada, and Brookfield Renewable Energy Partners. SolarShare, an Ontario co-op, has raised $5 million over the past three years from members who get a stake in a variety of rooftop and ground-mounted solar projects. Bondholders get a 5 percent guaranteed interest rate.

Some bonds are explicitly called *green bonds*, but others are unlabelled (e.g., bonds issued by hydroelectric utilities). Their increasing popularity means that agreement will have to be reached on what actually qualifies as a green bond. Such an agreement should also include follow-up measures to ensure that the money raised by the bonds is actually spent on legitimate green projects. If follow-up is not done, "greenwashing" (claiming that a project is green when it really isn't) may become a problem. Ceres, a non-profit organization, has published guidelines that green bond issues should adhere to, but the guidelines are voluntary.

CRITICAL THINKING QUESTIONS

1. Do you think green bonds might encounter the same problems that the "cap and trade" system did? (Review the "cap and trade" material in Chapter 3 before answering this question.)
2. Consider the following statement: *Green bonds are just a gimmick to attract investors who think they will be doing the right thing by buying bonds that support environmentally friendly projects.* Do you agree or disagree? Explain your reasoning.

If bond rating agencies like Moody's, Standard & Poor's, or Fitch downgrade a company's ratings to low enough levels, its bonds become junk bonds. When that happens, investors demand higher interest rates to reflect the increased risk of investing in the company.

Henny Ray Abrams/Dapd/AP Images

Serial Bonds Some corporations issue serial or convertible bonds. With a *serial bond*, the firm retires portions of the bond issue in a series of different preset dates. For example, a company with a $100 million issue maturing in 20 years may retire $5 million each year.

Convertible Bonds *Convertible bonds* can be converted into the common stock of the issuing company. For example, suppose that Bell Canada Enterprises sold a $100 million issue of 4.5 percent convertible bonds in 2010. The bonds were issued in $1000 denominations, and they mature in 2020. At any time before maturity, each bond of $1000 is convertible into 19.125 shares of the company's common stock. Suppose that between October 2010 and March 2017, the stock price ranged from a low of $28 to a high of $67. In that time, then, 19.125 common shares had a market value ranging from $535 to $1281. The bondholder could have exchanged the $1000 bond in return for stock to be kept or sold at a possible profit (or loss).

Bonds differ from one another in terms of their level of risk. To help bond investors make assessments, several services rate the quality of bonds from different issuers. Table 15.1 shows ratings by Moody's and Standard & Poor's (S&P). The rating measures the bond's default risk—the chance that one or more promised payments will be deferred or missed altogether. The financial crisis of 2008 revealed some significant problems with bond rating agencies. The credibility of those companies declined because they gave overly favourable ratings to certain securities that were actually very risky. People who made investments based on the ratings lost billions of dollars when bonds they thought were safe turned out not to be.[11] In 2015, S&P paid a $1.5 billion fine after the U.S. Justice Department said the company breached its duty to investors.[12]

EQUITY FINANCING Raising money to meet long-term expenditures by issuing common stock or by retaining earnings.

LO-5 Equity Financing

Sometimes, looking inside the company for long-term funding is preferable to looking outside. In most cases, **equity financing** takes the form of *issuing stock* or *retaining the firm's earnings*. Both options involve putting the owners' capital to work. In 2014, Canadian corporations raised just over $40 billion in equity capital. That was a 25 percent increase over the $32 billion that was raised in 2013.[13] Banks and energy companies were the dominant players; they raised 63 percent of the total ($25 billion).

TABLE 15.1 Bond Ratings

	High Grade	Medium Grade (Investment Grade)	Speculative	Poor Grade
Moody's	Aaa Aa	A Baa	Ba B	Caa C
Standard & Poor's	AAA AA	A BBB	BB B	CCC D

ISSUING COMMON STOCK

By selling shares of common stock, the company obtains the funds it needs to buy land, buildings, and equipment. Individuals and companies buy a firm's stock, hoping that it will increase in value (a capital gain) and/or will provide dividend income. Let's look at an example. Suppose that Sunshine Tanning's founders invested $10 000 in buying the original 500 shares of common stock (at $20 per share) in 2003. If the company used these funds to buy equipment and succeeded financially, by 2012 it may have needed further funds for expansion. A pattern of profitable operations and regularly paid dividends enabled Sunshine to raise $50 000 by selling 500 new shares of stock for $100 per share. This additional paid-in capital would increase the total shareholders' equity to $60 000, as shown in Table 15.2.

Common stock values are expressed in three ways. The face value of a share of stock—its **par value**—is set by the issuing company's board of directors. The **book value** of common stock represents stockholders' equity (the sum of a company's common stock par value, retained earnings, and additional paid-in capital) divided by the number of shares. A stock's real value is its **market value**—the current price of a share in the stock market. For successful companies, the market value is usually greater than its book value. Thus, when market price falls to near book value, some investors buy the stock on the principle that it is underpriced and will increase in value in the future. The price of a share of stock can be influenced by both objective factors (company profits) and by subjective factors such as *rumours* (e.g., claims that a company has made a big gold strike), *investor relations* (publicizing the positive aspects of a company's financial condition to financial analysts and financial institutions), and *stockbroker recommendations* (a recommendation to buy a stock may increase demand and cause its price to increase, while a recommendation to sell may decrease demand and cause the price to fall).

The **market capitalization** of a company's stock is computed by multiplying the number of a company's outstanding shares times the market value of each share. Because stock prices change every day, so do market capitalizations. In Canada, banks and resource companies dominate the top-10 list of companies with the largest market capitalizations.

The use of equity financing via common stock can be expensive because paying dividends is more expensive than paying bond interest. This is because interest paid to bondholders is tax-deductible, but dividends paid to stockholders are not. Even though equity financing is expensive, financial managers cannot rely totally on debt capital, because long-term loans and bonds carry fixed interest rates and represent a promise to pay regardless of the profitability of the firm. If the firm defaults on its obligations, it may lose its assets and even go into bankruptcy.

In 2012, for example, Yellow Media Inc. was trying to pay off a $1.5 billion debt it had accumulated. To get money to pay bondholders, the company cut off dividends for preferred shareholders, but that caused the value of those shares to drop by up to 55 percent. Common shares dropped in value by 97 percent.[14]

TABLE 15.2 Stockholders' Equity for Sunshine Tanning

Common Stockholders' Equity, 2003	
Initial common stock (500 shares issued @ $20 per share, 2003)	$10 000
Total stockholders' equity	$10 000
Common Stockholders' Equity, 2012	
Initial common stock (500 shares issued @ $20 per share, 2003)	$10 000
Additional paid-in capital (500 shares issued @ $100 per share, 2012)	50 000
Total stockholders' equity	$60 000

RETAINING THE FIRM'S EARNINGS

Another approach to equity financing is to use retained earnings. These earnings represent profits not paid out in dividends. Using retained earnings means that the firm will not have to borrow money and pay interest on loans or bonds. A firm that has a history of reaping much higher profits by successfully reinvesting retained earnings may be attractive to some investors. But the smaller dividends that can be paid to shareholders as a result of retained earnings may decrease demand for—and thus the price of—the company's stock.

Let's revisit our Sunshine Tanning example. If the company had net earnings of $50 000 in 2012, it could pay a $50-per-share dividend on its 1000 shares of common stock. But if it plans to remodel at a cost of $30 000 and retains $30 000 of earnings to finance the project, only $20 000 is left to distribute for stock dividends ($20 per share).

Hybrid Financing: Preferred Stock

Preferred stock is a hybrid because it has some of the features of corporate bonds and some features of common stock. As with bonds, payments on preferred stock are for fixed amounts. Unlike bonds, however, preferred stock never matures. It can be held indefinitely, like common stock. And dividends need not be paid if the company makes no profit. If dividends are paid, preferred stockholders receive them first in preference to dividends on common stock. A major advantage of preferred stock to the issuing corporation is its flexibility. It secures funds for the firm without relinquishing control, since preferred stockholders have no voting rights. It does not require repayment of principal or the payment of dividends in lean times.

Preferred stock is usually issued with a stated par value, such as $100. Dividends paid on preferred stock are usually expressed as a percentage of the par value. For example, if a preferred stock with a $100 par value pays a 6 percent dividend, stockholders would receive an annual dividend of $6 on each share.

Some preferred stock is *callable*, meaning that the issuing firm can require the preferred stockholders to surrender their shares in exchange for a cash payment. The amount of this cash payment, known as the call price, is specified in the agreement between the preferred stockholders and the firm.

PAR VALUE The arbitrary value of a stock set by the issuing company's board of directors and stated on stock certificates; used by accountants but of little significance to investors.

BOOK VALUE The value of a common stock expressed as total stockholders' equity divided by the number of shares of stock.

MARKET VALUE The current price of one share of a stock in the secondary securities market; the real value of a stock.

MARKET CAPITALIZATION The dollar value (market value) of stocks listed on a stock exchange.

Choosing Between Debt and Equity Financing

Financial planning involves striking a balance between debt and equity financing to meet the firm's long-term need for funds. The mix of debt and equity a firm uses is called its **capital structure**. Financial plans contain targets for the capital structure, but choosing a target is not easy. A wide range of debt-versus-equity mixes is possible.

The most conservative strategy is to use all-equity financing and no debt, because a company has no formal obligations for financial payouts. But as we have noted, equity is a very expensive source of capital. The riskiest strategy would be to use all debt financing. While less expensive than equity funding, indebtedness increases the risk that a firm will be unable to meet its obligations and will go bankrupt. Financial managers try to find a mix somewhere between these two extremes that will maximize stockholders' wealth. Figure 15.1 summarizes the factors management takes into account when deciding between debt and equity financing.

The Risk–Return Relationship

Every investor has a personal preference for safety versus risk. Investors generally expect only modest returns for secure investments such as government-insured bonds, but expect higher returns for riskier investments. Each type of investment, then, has a **risk–return relationship**.

CAPITAL STRUCTURE Relative mix of a firm's debt and equity financing.

RISK–RETURN RELATIONSHIP Shows the amount of risk and the likely rate of return on various financial instruments.

Debt financing	Equity financing
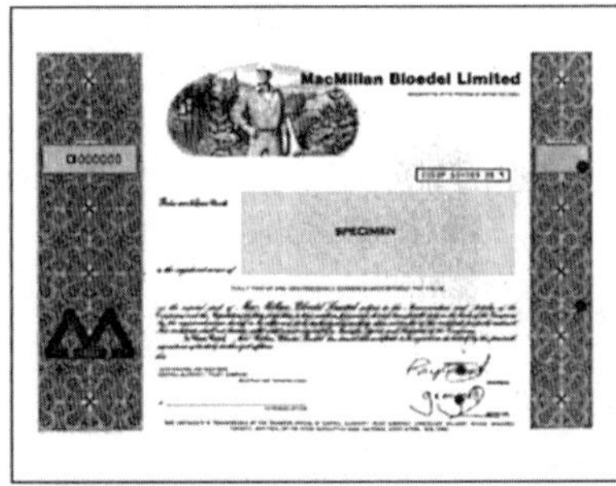	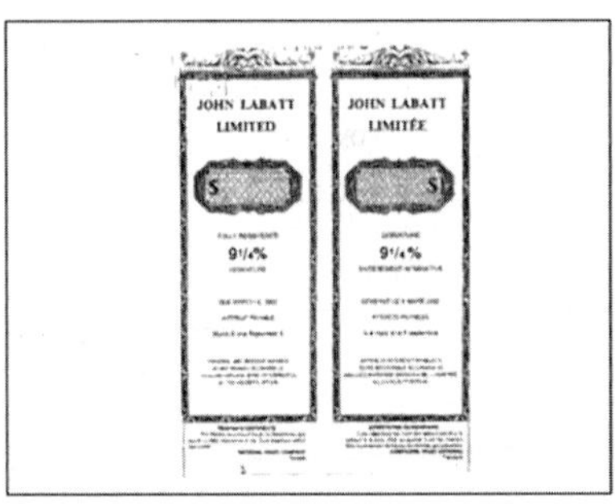
When must it be repaid?	
Fixed deadline	No limit
Will it make claims on income?	
Yes, regular and fixed	Only residual claim
Will it have claims on assets?	
In liquidation, creditors come first	In liquidation, shareholders must wait until creditors are paid and preferred equity precedes common equity
Will it affect management control?	
No	May cause challenge for corporation control
How are taxes affected?	
Bond interest is deductible	Dividends are not deductible
Will it affect management flexibility?	
Yes, many constraints	No, few constraints

FIGURE 15.1 Comparing debt and equity financing

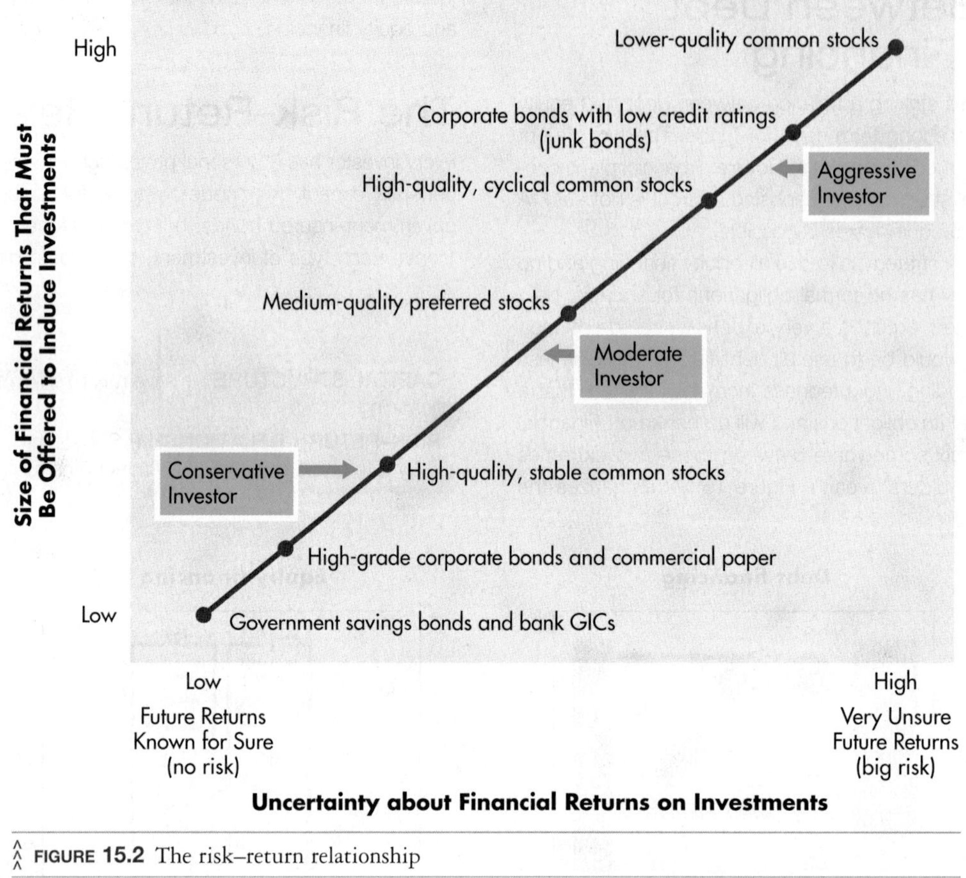

FIGURE 15.2 The risk–return relationship

Figure 15.2 shows the general risk–return relationship for various financial instruments. High-grade corporate bonds, for example, rate low in terms of risk, but they also provide low returns. Junk bonds, on the other hand, rate high in terms of risk (because the company might default), but they also provide high returns to attract investors.

Risk–return differences are recognized by financial planners, who try to gain access to the greatest funding at the lowest possible cost. By gauging investors' perceptions of their riskiness, a firm's managers can estimate how much it must pay to attract funds to its offerings. Over time, a company can reposition itself on the risk continuum by improving its record on dividends, interest payments, and debt repayment.

MANAGING RISK WITH DIVERSIFCATION AND ASSET ALLOCATION

Investors seldom take an extreme approach (total risk or total risk avoidance) when selecting their investments. Instead, most investors select a mix of investments, with some being riskier and some being more conservative. *Diversification* means buying several different kinds of investments rather than just one. For example, as applied to common stocks, diversification means that you invest in the stocks of several different companies in different industries and in different countries. This reduces the risk of loss because although any one stock may tumble, the chances are slim that all of them will decline at the same time. Diversification is furthered when a variety of investments is used (stocks, bonds, mutual funds, real estate, and so on).

Asset allocation is the proportion of funds invested in each of the investment alternatives. Young investors may decide to allocate, say, 50 percent of their funds to common stocks, 25 percent to bonds, and 25 percent to guaranteed investment certificates (GICs). But older investors would typically have a larger proportion in more conservative investments (like bonds and GICs) and a smaller proportion in stocks.

RETURN ON INVESTMENT

In evaluating investments, investors look at returns from dividends (or interest), returns from price appreciation, and total return.

Dividends The rate of return from dividends paid to shareholders is commonly referred to as the *current dividend yield* (or in the case of interest from a loan, the *current interest yield*). It is calculated by dividing the yearly dollar amount of dividend income by the investment's current market value. For example, if each share of stock in Western Star Mining receives an annual dividend of $1.80, and on a given day the share price is $35.67, the current yield would be 5.05 percent ($1.80/$35.67 × 100). This dividend can then be compared against current yields from other investments to see which one is better.

Price Appreciation Another source of returns depends on whether the investment is increasing or decreasing in dollar value. *Price appreciation* is an increase in the dollar value of an investment. Suppose, for example, that you purchased a share of Western Star Mining for $35.67, and then sold it one year later for $37.45. The price appreciation is $1.78 ($37.45 – $35.67). This profit, realized from the increased market value of the stock, is known as a *capital gain*.

Total Return The sum of an investment's current dividend (or interest) yield, plus any capital gain, is its total return. Total return cannot be computed until it is compared to the investment that was required to get that return. Total return as a percentage of investment is calculated as follows:

Total return (%) = (Current dividend payment + Capital gain)/ Original investment × 100

To complete our Western Star Mining example, the total return as a percentage of our one-year investment would be 10.04 percent [($1.80 + $1.78)/$35.67 × 100].

THE TIME VALUE OF MONEY

The most proven "road to wealth" lies in a strategy of saving and investing over a period of many years. Although the "I want it all right now" mentality might sound good, it rarely leads to wealth. The time value of money is one of the most important concepts in business finance. It recognizes the fact that when it's invested over time, money grows by earning interest. Time value stems from the principle of compound growth, which is the cumulative growth from interest paid to the investor over various time periods. With each additional time period, the investment grows as interest payments accumulate and earn more interest, thus multiplying the earning capacity of the investment.

The Rule of 72 How long does it take to double an investment? You can use the Rule of 72 to easily determine the number of years needed to double your money. Simply divide the annual interest rate (in percent) into 72. If, for example, you invest at 8 percent, you'll double your money in about 9 years (72/8 = 9 years). By the same reasoning, if you invest at 4 percent, your money will double in about 18 years. The Rule of 72 can also calculate how much interest you must get if you want to double your money in a given number of years. Simply divide 72 by the desired number years. For example, if you want to double your money in 10 years, you need to get 7.2 percent annual interest (72/10 = 7.2 percent interest rate).

FANTASY STOCK MARKETS

Enthusiasts of baseball, football, and hockey aren't the only fans who are energized by fantasy games. Fantasy stock markets are all the rage for learning how securities markets work, for trying your hand at various investment strategies, and for earning a fantasy fortune (or going broke!). Internet-based games, including free ones such as *How the Market Works*, provide an investment experience that is educational, challenging, and entertaining. Participants start with an initial sum in virtual cash that is used to manage their own fantasy portfolio of real companies, and they must live with real market results. It's a learn-by-doing experience using web-based symbol lookups, searching various sources for information on companies of interest, making buy and sell decisions, and then discovering the financial results as real market prices change for the portfolio holdings. Many students are finding these games to be a valuable resource for learning the "how to" of online investing.

SECURITIES MARKETS

Stocks and bonds are known as **securities** because they represent a secured (asset-based) claim on the part of investors. Collectively, the market in which stocks and bonds are sold is called the securities market. *Primary securities markets* handle the buying and selling of new shares (initial public offerings or IPOs) of stocks and bonds by firms or governments. When new securities are sold to one buyer or a small group of buyers, these *private placements* allow the businesses that use them to keep their plans confidential. But new securities represent only a small portion of securities traded. The market for existing stocks and bonds—the *secondary securities market*—is handled by organizations like the Toronto Stock Exchange. Companies do not receive any money when shares of stock are bought and sold in the secondary securities market.

Corporate financial managers (and individual investors) need to be knowledgeable about securities markets if they hope to be successful. In this section, we look at the following aspects of securities markets: *investment banking, stock exchanges, buying and selling securities*, and *financing securities purchases*. We also describe several other investments that investors may purchase.

Investment Banking

Most new stocks and some bonds are sold to the public market. To bring a new security to market, the issuing corporation must obtain approval from a provincial securities commission. It also needs the services of an investment banker. **Investment bankers** serve as financial specialists in issuing new securities. Well-known institutions like RBC Dominion Securities and TD Securities provide the following services:

1. They advise companies on the timing and financial terms for a new issue.
2. By underwriting (buying) the new securities, they bear some of the risk of issuing a new security.
3. They create the distribution network that moves the new securities through groups of other banks and brokers into the hands of individual investors.

Stock Exchanges

A **stock exchange** is composed of individuals (stockbrokers) and organizations (investment banks) that provide a setting in which shares of stock can be bought and sold. The exchange enforces certain rules to govern its members' trading activities. Most exchanges are non-profit corporations established to serve their members. To become a member, an individual must purchase one of a limited number of "seats" on the exchange. Only members (or their representatives) are allowed to trade on the exchange. In this sense, because all orders to buy or sell must flow through members, they have a legal monopoly. Memberships can be bought and sold like other assets.

A **stockbroker** receives buy and sell orders from those who are not members of the exchange and executes the orders. In return, the

SECURITIES Stocks, bonds, and mutual funds representing secured, or asset-based, claims by investors against issuers.

INVESTMENT BANKERS Financial specialists in issuing new securities.

STOCK EXCHANGE A voluntary organization of individuals formed to provide an institutional setting where members can buy and sell stock for themselves and their clients in accordance with the exchange's rules.

STOCKBROKER An individual licensed to buy and sell securities for customers in the secondary market; may also provide other financial services.

broker earns a commission from the person who placed the order. Like many products, brokerage assistance can be purchased at either *full-service* or *at discount* prices. *Full-service brokers* offer services to clients who are either not very well informed about investment possibilities, or who are simply not interested in the details of investing. These brokers offer services such as consulting advice for personal financial planning, estate planning, and tax strategies, along with a wider range of investment products. In addition to delivering and interpreting information, full-service brokers can identify investments that clients might not otherwise notice in the large amount of online financial data that is available.

By contrast, *discount brokers* offer well-informed individual investors a fast, low-cost way to participate in the market. Discount brokerage services cost less because sales personnel receive fees or salaries, not commissions. Discount brokers do not offer investment advice or person-to-person sales consultations. However, they do offer automated online services: stock research, industry analysis, and screening for specific types of stocks. Online trading is popular because of convenient access, fast, no-nonsense transactions, and the opportunity for self-directed investors to manage their own investments while paying low fees. For example, buying 200 shares of a $20 stock might cost an investor up to $100 at a full-service broker, but as little as $6.99 at a discount broker. Price differences are evident even among the discount brokers. For example, you could buy 100 shares of a $50 stock and pay just $1 in brokers' commissions if you use Virtual Brokers, because they charge only $0.01 per share with a minimum charge of $0.99.[15]

CANADIAN STOCK EXCHANGES

The TMX Group owns and operates the Toronto Stock Exchange (TSX) and the TSX Venture Exchange. The TSX is the largest stock exchange in Canada. It is made up of about 110 individual members who hold seats. The securities of most major corporations are listed here. A company must pay a fee before it can list its security on the exchange.

FOREIGN STOCK EXCHANGES

Many foreign countries also have active stock exchanges, and several foreign stock exchanges—most notably those in the United States and the United Kingdom—trade far more shares every day than the TSX does. For many people, "the stock market" means the New York Stock Exchange (NYSE). In 1980, the U.S. stock market accounted for more than half the value of the *world* market in traded stocks. Market activities, however, have shifted as the value of shares listed on foreign exchanges continues to grow rapidly. The annual dollar value of trades on exchanges in London, Tokyo, and other cities is now in the trillions. In fact, the London Stock Exchange exceeds even the NYSE in the number of stocks listed.

THE OVER-THE-COUNTER MARKET

The **over-the-counter (OTC) market** is so called because its original traders were somewhat like retailers—they kept supplies of shares on hand and, as opportunities arose, sold them over the counter to interested buyers. Even today, the OTC market has no trading floor. It consists of many people in different locations who hold an inventory of securities that are not listed on any of the major exchanges. The OTC market consists of independent dealers who own the securities that they buy and sell at their own risk.

NASDAQ

The *National Association of Securities Dealers Automated Quotation (NASDAQ)* is the world's first electronic stock market.[16] The NASDAQ telecommunications system operates the NASDAQ Stock Market by broadcasting trading information on an intranet to over 350 000 terminals worldwide. NASDAQ orders are paired and executed on a computer network. The stocks of nearly 3700 companies are traded by NASDAQ. Many newer firms are listed here when their stocks first become available in the secondary market. Highly traded listings include Apple, Microsoft, Intel, BlackBerry, Baidu, and Netflix.[17]

LO-6 Buying and Selling Securities

When buying and selling stocks, bonds, and other financial instruments, financial managers and individuals need to gather information about possible investments and match them to their investment objectives.

USING FINANCIAL INFORMATION SERVICES

Have you ever looked at the financial section of your daily newspaper and found yourself wondering what all those tables and numbers mean? Fortunately, this skill is easily mastered.

Stock Quotations Figure 15.3 shows the type of information newspapers provide about daily market transactions of individual stocks. The corporation's name is shown along with the number of shares sold, the high and low prices of the stock for that trading day, the closing price of the stock, and the change from the closing price on the previous day.

Bond Quotations Bond prices also change daily. These changes form the coupon rate, which provides information for firms about the cost of borrowing funds. Prices of domestic corporation bonds, Canadian government bonds, and foreign bonds are reported separately. Bond prices are expressed in terms of 100, even though most have a face value of $1000. Thus, a quote of 85 means that the bond's price is 85 percent of its face value, or $850.

A corporate bond selling at 155¼ would cost a buyer $1552.50 ($1000 face value multiplied by 1.5525), plus commission. The interest (coupon) rate on bonds is also quoted as a percentage of par, or face, value. Thus "6½s" pay 6.5 percent of par value per year. Typically, interest is paid semi-annually at half of the stated interest or coupon rate.

The market value (selling price) of a bond at any given time depends on three things: its stated interest rate, the "going rate" of interest in the market, and its redemption or maturity date. A bond with a higher stated interest rate than the going rate on similar quality bonds will probably sell at a premium above its face value—its selling price will be above its redemption price. A bond with a lower stated interest rate than the going rate on similar quality bonds will probably sell at a discount—its selling price will be below its redemption price. How much the premium or discount is depends largely on how far in the future the maturity date is. The maturity date is shown after the interest rate. Figure 15.4 shows the type of information daily newspapers provide.

Suppose you bought a $1000 par-value bond in 1995 for $650. Its stated interest rate is 6 percent, and its maturity or redemption date is 2015. You therefore receive $60 per year in interest. Based on your

OVER-THE-COUNTER (OTC) MARKET Organization of securities dealers formed to trade stock outside the formal institutional setting of the organized stock exchanges.

H. Armstrong Roberts/ClassicStock/Alamy

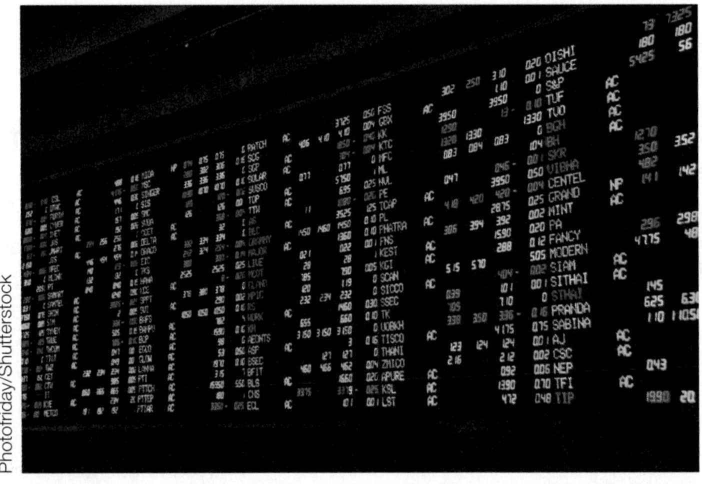

Photofriday/Shutterstock

Stock-market procedures and tools have changed a lot over the years, but the fundamentals remain the same. Investors must do their homework and conduct careful research before shares of stock are purchased.

Company	Volume	High	Low	Close	Change
Bombardier	5875	3.82	3.66	3.67	−0.11
Goldcorp	**6203**	**41.52**	**38.70**	**40.93**	**+3.23**
Royal Bank	3664	50.89	49.84	49.99	−1.56
Magna Intl.	892	41.30	39.14	39.50	−2.25
IAMGold	4615	12.26	11.36	12.15	+1.08
Kinross	3232	8.41	8.94	8.88	+0.59

- *Stock*
  Goldcorp Inc. (Name of Company).
- *Volume*
  6203 (total number of shares traded on this date [in 100s]).
- *High and Low*
  During the trading day, the highest price was $41.52 and the lowest price was $38.70.
- *Close*
  At the close of trading on this date, the last price paid per share was $40.93.
- *Net Change*
  Difference between today's closing price and the previous day's closing price. Price increased by $3.23 per share.

FIGURE 15.3 How to read a daily stock quotation

Issuer	Coupon	Maturity	Price	Yield
		GOVERNMENT OF CANADA		
Canada	4.20	June 1, 18	117.45	3.57
Canada	3.5	June 1, 20	115.40	3.03
		PROVINCIALS		
Hy Que	6.50	Feb. 15, 35	147.09	4.42
BC	4.7	June 18, 37	124.83	3.76
		CORPORATE		
Telus	**4.95**	**Mar. 3, 17**	**101.92**	**4.86**
Bank of Mon.	5.10	Apr. 21, 21	109.38	4.66

- *Issuer*
  Company name is Telus.
- *Coupon*
  The annual rate of interest at face value is 4.95 percent.
- *Maturity*
  The maturity date is March 3, 2017.
- *Price*
  On this date, $101.92 was the price of the last transaction.
- *Yield*
  The yield is computed by dividing the annual interest paid by the current market price. (*Note:* Yield to maturity [YTM] would also take into account duration and capital repayment.)

FIGURE 15.4 How to read a bond quotation

actual investment of $650, your *bond yield* is 9.2 percent. If you hold it to maturity, you get $1000 for a bond that originally cost you only $650. This extra $350 increases your true, or effective, yield.

Market Indexes Although they do not indicate how specific securities are doing, **market indexes** provide a useful summary of trends in specific industries and the stock market as a whole. Such information can be crucial in choosing investments. For example, market indexes reveal bull and bear market trends. **Bull markets** are periods of upward-moving stock prices. The years 1981 to 1989, 1993 to 1999, and 2004 to 2006 were bull markets. Periods of falling stock prices are called **bear markets**. The years 1972 to 1974, 1991 to 1992, 2000 to 2002, and 2008 to 2009 were bear markets.

The most widely cited market index is the *Dow Jones Industrial Average (DJIA)*, which is the sum of market prices for 30 of the largest industrial firms listed on the NYSE. By tradition, the Dow is an indicator of blue-chip (top-quality) stock price movements. Because of the small number of firms it considers, however, it is a limited gauge of the overall stock market. The Dow increased sharply in the 1990s. It reached 11 000 early in 2000 but dropped to less than 6500 in 2009. By mid-2015, it exceeded 18 000.

The *S&P/TSX index* is an average computed from 225 large Canadian stocks from various industry groups.[18] The index has also been very volatile during the last few years. It moved sharply upward during the bull market of the 1990s and topped 11 000 in the summer of 2000. It dropped below 8000 by 2009, but increased to 15 400 by mid-2015.

The *S&P 500* (Standard & Poor's Composite Index) consists of 500 stocks, including 400 industrial firms, 40 utilities, 40 financial institutions, and 20 transportation companies. The index average is weighted according to market capitalization of each stock, so the more highly valued companies exercise a greater influence on the index.

Some stock-market observers regard the *NASDAQ Composite Index* as the most important of all market indexes. Unlike the Dow and the S&P 500, all NASDAQ-listed companies are included in the index. The NASDAQ market has been very volatile. In early 2000, it reached 5000, but by 2001 had dropped to just 1300. In mid-2015 it had risen again to just over 5000.

BUYING AND SELLING STOCKS

Based on your own investigations and/or recommendations from your stockbroker, you can place many types of orders. A *market order* requests the broker buy or sell a certain security at the prevailing market price at the time. A *limit order* authorizes the purchase of a stock only if its price is less than or equal to a given limit. For example, a limit order to buy a stock at $80 per share means that the broker is to buy it if and only if the stock becomes available for a price of $80 or less. Similarly, a stop order instructs the broker to sell a stock if its price falls to a certain level. For example, a *stop order* of $85 on a particular stock means that the broker is to sell it if and only if its price falls to $85 or below.

You can also place orders of different sizes. A *round lot* order requests 100 shares or some multiple thereof. Fractions of a round lot are called *odd lots*. Trading odd lots is usually more expensive than trading round lots, because an intermediary called an odd-lot broker is often involved, which increases brokerage fees.

The business of buying and selling stocks is changing rapidly. Formerly, a person had to have a broker to buy and sell stocks. More and more individuals are now buying and selling stocks on the internet, and traditional brokers are worried that before long customers will avoid using their services. More information is contained in the boxed insert entitled "Stock Trading at Your Fingertips."

STOCK OPTIONS

A **stock option** is the right to buy or sell a stock. A *call option* gives its owner the right to buy a particular stock at a certain price, with that right lasting until a particular date. A *put option* gives its owner the right to sell a particular stock at a specified price, with that right lasting until a particular date. These options are traded on several stock exchanges.

Here's how stock options work: If you thought the price of Goldcorp Inc. (G) (which sold for $40 per share in June 2012) was going to go up, you might buy a call option giving you the right to buy 100 shares any time in the next two months at a so-called strike price of $50. If the stock rose to $60 before July, you would exercise your call option. Your profit would be $10 per share ($60 – $50) less the price you paid to buy the option. However, if the stock price fell instead of rising, you would not exercise your call option, because Goldcorp shares would be available on the open market for less than $50 per share. Your stock option would be "under water"; that is, it would be worthless. You would lose whatever you paid for the option. In recent years, there has been much negative publicity about stock options given to executives to motivate them to work hard for the company.

Financing Securities Purchases

When you place a buy order of any kind, you must tell your broker how you will pay for the purchase. You might maintain a cash account with your broker. Then, as stocks are bought and sold, proceeds are added into the account and commissions and costs of purchases are withdrawn by the broker. You can also buy shares on credit.

MARGIN TRADING

Shares of stock can be purchased on **margin**—putting down only a portion of the stock's price. You borrow the rest from your broker, who, in turn, borrows from the banks at a special rate and secures the loans with stock. Suppose you purchase $100 000 worth of stock in WestJet. Let's also say that you paid $50 000 of your own money and borrowed the other $50 000 from your broker at 10 percent interest. Valued at its market price, your stock serves as your collateral. If shares have risen in value to $115 000 after one year, you can sell them and pay your broker $55 000 ($50 000 principal + $5000 interest). You will have $60 000 left over. Your original investment of $50 000 will have earned a 20 percent profit of $10 000. If you had paid the entire price out of your own pocket, you would have earned only a 15 percent return.

Although investors often recognize possible profits to be made in margin trading, they sometimes fail to consider that losses can be

MARKET INDEX A measure of the market value of stocks; provides a summary of price trends in a specific industry or of the stock market as a whole.

BULL MARKET A period of rising stock prices; a period in which investors act on a belief that stock prices will rise.

BEAR MARKET A period of falling stock prices; a period in which investors act on a belief that stock prices will fall.

STOCK OPTION The purchased right to buy or sell a stock.

MARGIN The percentage of the total sales price that a buyer must put up to place an order for stock or a futures contract.

E-BUSINESS AND SOCIAL MEDIA SOLUTIONS

Stock Trading at Your Fingertips

Trading stocks was once a fairly difficult chore. Information was not instantly available, and there were time lags before the general public could access information such as market trends, daily high and low prices, and current trading prices. Moment-to-moment information was available only by calling a stockbroker or by visiting a brokerage where data were visible for each transaction on an overhead screen. Many investors relied on newspaper reports summarizing the most recent day's market transactions before making buy or sell decisions.

Today's trading environment is different. Instead of reading the *Globe and Mail* to see what happened yesterday, mass communication and online networks provide current market information nearly anywhere. Financial television networks, such as BNN, display transactions and market conditions as they occur at the TSX or NYSE or NASDAQ exchanges. Investors and traders seeking financial opportunities abroad have access to developments in global financial markets as well as currency exchange rates.

Investors seeking market information on specific stocks can visit sites like www.theglobeandmail.com/globe-investor. Going beyond mere information gathering, web trading has become a popular tool for investors. You can place trades—buying and selling stocks, bonds, and commodities—by establishing an account with one of the many online brokers.

pictoores/Fotolia

Online trading has also increased the popularity of something called *day trading*. As contrasted with investing, in which a buyer intends to hold the stock (or other financial instrument) into the future before selling for a long-term profit, a trader holds a stock for only a brief period of time before selling to capture a short-term profit. Day trading is an even more specialized form of trading, because the buying and selling is accomplished within one day, without holding the stock overnight. Day traders rely on speedy transactions to profit from small difference between buying and selling prices during the day, sometimes holding a stock for only a few seconds or minutes before selling.

More recently, Mobile investing has emerged as an important investment tool. Basic mobile banking has been around for a while, but most Canadian institutions have been slower to build mobile investing apps (trading platforms designed for your smartphone). However, that is changing. According to an informal *Globe and Mail* poll, 22 percent of individuals claimed that they were either currently conducting mobile trading or were open to it.

Easy access and speed does not necessarily lead to successful trades. In fact, it can be quite the opposite, so do your homework. Investment blogs found on sites such as Money Index (moneyindex.org/Canada) and the *Wall Street Journal*'s Deal Journal (wsj.com/deals) are a good place to start.

CRITICAL THINKING QUESTIONS

1. Have you ever bought or sold securities using an online or mobile investing platform? Are you open to this approach? Explain your response.
2. Consider the following statement: *Mobile investing is dangerous. People need to carefully analyze investment data and not make quick on-the-go decisions. This approach may cause inexperienced investors to feel a false sense of security and will lead to more foolish impulse investments.* Do you agree with the statement? Defend your answer.

amplified. If the value of your initial WestJet investment of $100 000 had instead fallen to $85 000 after one year, you would have lost 15 percent if you had paid out of pocket. However, if you had used margin trading, you would have lost $20 000 ($5000 interest payment + $15 000 share decrease) on a $50 000 investment, which amounts to a 40 percent loss.

>>> When the stock market is volatile, there are often spreads between bid prices (what traders pay for a share of stock) and ask prices (what they charge for it). The difference isn't necessarily large, but if you can make a number of quick hits during the day, you can make money. That strategy appeals to traders at large firms, but also to individual traders working on their own.

Monkey Business/Fotolia

The rising use of margin credit by investors was a growing concern during the bull market of 2004–2006. Investors focused on the upside benefits but were not sensitive enough to the downside risks. Especially at online brokerages, inexperienced traders were borrowing at an alarming rate, and some were using the borrowed funds for risky and speculative day trading. Day traders (see above) visited websites online to buy and sell a stock in the same day (so-called *intraday trades*), seeking quick in-and-out fractional gains on large volumes (many shares) of each stock. While some day traders were successful, most ended up losers.

SHORT SALE Selling borrowed shares of stock in the expectation that their price will fall before they must be replaced, so that replacement shares can be bought for less than the original shares were sold for.

SHORT SALES

In addition to money, brokerages also lend buyers securities. A **short sale** involves borrowing a security from your broker and selling it (one of the few times it is legal to sell what you do not own). At a given time in the future, you must restore an equal number of shares of that issue to the brokerage, along with a fee.

For example, suppose that in June you believe the price of Bombardier stock will soon fall. You order your broker to sell short 1000 shares at the market price of $5 per share. Your broker will make the sale and credit $5000 to your account. If Bombardier's price falls to $3.50 per share in July, you can buy 1000 shares for $3500 and give them to your broker, leaving you with a $1500 profit (before commissions). The risk is that Bombardier's price will not fall but will hold steady or rise, leaving you with a loss. The boxed insert entitled "Short Selling: Herbalife and Sino-Forest" describes two recent cases of short selling that caused a lot of controversy.

LO-7 OTHER INVESTMENTS

Although stocks and bonds are very important, they are not the only marketable securities for businesses. Financial managers are also concerned with investment opportunities in *mutual funds*, *exchange-traded funds*, *hedge funds*, and *commodities*.

MUTUAL FUND Any company that pools the resources of many investors and uses those funds to purchase various types of financial securities, depending on the fund's financial goals.

Mutual Funds

Mutual funds pool investments from individuals and other firms to purchase a portfolio of stocks, bonds, and short-term securities. For example, if you invest $1000 in a mutual fund that has a portfolio worth $100 000, you own 1 percent of the portfolio. Mutual funds usually have portfolios worth many millions of dollars. Investors in *no-load funds* are not charged a sales commission when they buy into or sell out of the mutual fund. *Load funds* carry a charge of between 2 and 8 percent of the invested

MANAGING IN TURBULENT TIMES

Short Selling: Herbalife and Sino-Forest

In July 2014, William Ackman, the head of Pershing Square Capital Management, made a three-hour presentation that summarized his investigation into Herbalife International Inc., a company that sells energy drinks, vitamins, and body-care products. Ackman claimed that Herbalife was running a pyramid scheme, and that its CEO was a predator exploiting minorities (i.e., Hispanics) trying to make a better life for themselves. This very public conflict between Herbalife and Ackman began in 2012, when Ackman publicly announced he was "shorting" Herbalife's stock. He had concluded the company was running a pyramid scheme after he read a report that claimed Herbalife's distributors were buying the company's products so they could earn commissions, not so they could actually sell products to consumers.

Herbalife's stock price dropped soon after Ackman made his claim, but then some other prominent investors said that they thought Ackman's claims were nonsense, and that they were buying Herbalife stock. That drove the price up, and in January 2014, the stock's price was $81 per share. But by February 2015, the price had dropped to $31.

Ackman has not yet proven his charges. But the Federal Trade Commission and the Securities and Exchange Commission are both investigating Herbalife, and so is Canada's Competition Bureau. These investigations may or may not find anything incriminating. Both Herbalife and Ackman have spent about $50 million each during the fight.

Another highly publicized case of short selling occurred in Canada in 2011 when a company called Muddy Waters released a report critical of the accounting practices of Sino-Forest Corp., a company that owned timber lands in China. The report essentially questioned whether the company actually owned the timber assets it claimed, and whether it was actually receiving the revenue it claimed. The report had an immediate and negative effect on the stock price of Sino-Forest, causing shares to drop from $18.21 on June 1 to just $1.29 by June 21. In 2012, Sino-Forest filed for bankruptcy.

The incentives for short sellers are very high if they can demonstrate that there are problems in a company. For example, if you had borrowed 1000 shares of Sino-Forest from your broker on June 1, 2011, and sold them, you would have received $18 210 (1000 × $18.21). You could then have purchased 1000 replacement shares on June 21 for just $1290 (1000 × $1.29). Your profit would have been $16 920 ($18 210 minus $1290).

Short sellers are often able to spot problems regulatory agencies miss. One study of 454 companies that had been disciplined for misrepresenting their finances found that short sellers were active long before the regulatory agencies.

CRITICAL THINKING QUESTION

1. Consider the following statement: *Short selling should be banned, because it creates instability in the price of a company's stock*. Do you agree or disagree? Defend your reasoning.

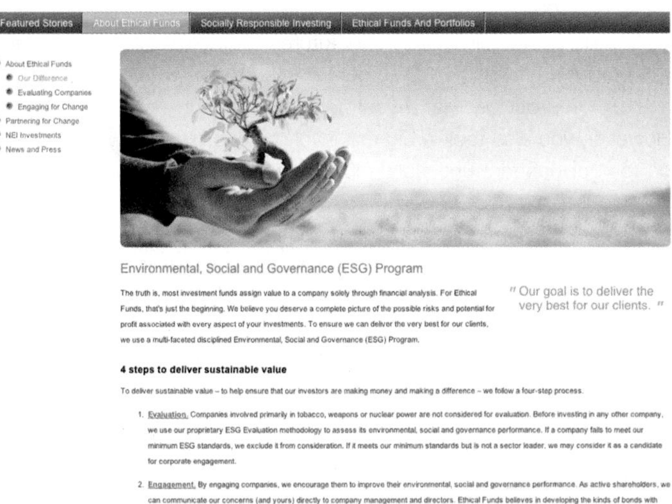

Home | Advisor Site | Investor Trax | Contact us | Français
Search
Search
MAKE MONEY. MAKE A DIFFERENCE.
Featured Stories
About Ethical Funds
Socially Responsible Investing
Ethical Funds And Portfolios
About Ethical Funds
Our Difference
Evaluating Companies
Engaging for Change
Partnering for Change
NEI Investments
News and Press
Environmental, Social and Governance (ESG) Program
The truth is, most investment funds assign value to a company solely through financial analysis. For Ethical Funds, that's just the beginning. We believe you deserve a complete picture of the possible risks and potential for profit associated with every aspect of your investments. To ensure we can deliver the very best for our clients, we use a multi-faceted disciplined Environmental, Social and Governance (ESG) Program.
" Our goal is to deliver the very best for our clients. "
4 steps to deliver sustainable value
To deliver sustainable value – to help ensure that our investors are making money and making a difference – we follow a four-step process.
1. Evaluation. Companies involved primarily in tobacco, weapons or nuclear power are not considered for evaluation. Before investing in any other company, we use our proprietary ESG Evaluation methodology to assess its environmental, social and governance performance. If a company fails to meet our minimum ESG standards, we exclude it from consideration. If it meets our minimum standards but is not a sector leader, we may consider it as a candidate for corporate engagement.
2. Engagement. By engaging companies, we encourage them to improve their environmental, social and governance performance. As active shareholders, we can communicate our concerns (and yours) directly to company management and directors. Ethical Funds believes in developing the kinds of bonds with corporate leaders that transform "communications" into conversations. We talk to the people who have the power to break new ground and encourage them to be corporate leaders, showing others in their industry the way to sustainability.

Ethical Funds, a division of NEI Investments, does not invest in companies involved primarily in the production of tobacco, weapons, or nuclear power.

NEI Investments

funds. Mutual funds give small investors access to professional financial management. Their managers have up-to-date information about market conditions and the best large-scale investment opportunities.

Mutual funds vary by the investment goals they stress. Some stress safety and invest in Treasury bills and other safe issues that offer income (liquidity). Other funds seek higher current income and are willing to sacrifice some safety. Still other mutual funds stress growth. Aggressive-growth mutual funds seek maximum capital appreciation; they sacrifice current income and safety and invest in new companies and other high-risk securities.

There are mutual funds that stress socially responsible investing. They will not invest in cigarette manufacturers or companies that make weapons, for example, and instead focus on investing in companies that produce safe and useful products and show concern for their employees, for the environment, and for human rights. While many companies offer such investments, the company Ethical Funds is dedicated to this mission.

Most mutual funds are actively managed by "experts" who pick the stocks the fund holds in order to (hopefully) provide the fund's income. But research suggests that most mutual funds do not perform as well as the average return of the overall stock market. For example, Standard & Poor's SPIVA 2014 Canada Scorecard showed that only one-third of mutual funds beat the S&P/TSX index over the past three years. In the United States, only 1 in 70 mutual funds beat the S&P 500 index over the past three years.[19] This poor performance is the result of high management fees and poor stock picking by the "experts." This has motivated many investors to drop mutual funds and buy into exchange-traded funds.

EXCHANGE-TRADED FUND (ETF) A bundle of stocks (or bonds) that is in an index that tracks the overall movement of the market.

HEDGE FUNDS Private pools of money that try to give investors a positive return regardless of stock-market performance.

FUTURES CONTRACTS Agreement to purchase specified amounts of a commodity (or stock) at a given price on a set future date.

Exchange-Traded Funds

An **exchange-traded fund (ETF)** is a bundle of stocks (or bonds) that is in an index that simply tracks the overall movement of the market. Unlike mutual funds—which are priced only at the end of each day—you can buy or sell ETFs at any time during the day when the market reaches your target price. Also unlike mutual funds—which incur the costs of active management—ETFs have lower operating expenses because they are bound by rules that specify what stocks will be purchased and when. Once the rule is established, active management is not needed, and this reduces expenses. Annual fees for mutual funds average 1.4 percent of assets, but for ETFs the rate is as low as 0.04 percent.[20]

Hedge Funds

Hedge funds are private pools of money that try to give investors a positive return regardless of stock-market performance. Hedge funds often engage in risky practices like short selling (essentially betting that a company's stock price will go down) and leveraging (borrowing money against principal). Historically, interest in hedge funds has been limited to wealthy people (called *accredited investors*) assumed to be very knowledgeable about financial matters and able to weigh the risks. But recently, hedge funds have begun marketing their products to the average investor with something called *principal-protected notes*. They guarantee that investors will get their original investment back at a certain time, but they do not guarantee that any additional returns will be forthcoming.

Some hedge funds have been in the news for all the wrong reasons. For example, an Ontario Securities Commission panel ruled that two executives from the now-defunct Norshield Asset Management Ltd. knowingly misled their clients and investigators and failed to keep proper books. Losses are estimated at $159 million.[21]

Commodities

Futures contracts—agreements to purchase a specified amount of a commodity at a given price on a set date in the future—are available for

THERE'S AN APP FOR THAT!

APP DETAILS	PLATFORMS
1. Bloomberg Finance **Source:** Bloomberg Finance LP **Key Features:** Offers news, stock quotes, company descriptions, market leaders, price charts, and more.	Apple, Android, BlackBerry, Windows
2. CFA Institute **Source:** CFA Institute **Key Features:** Provides summaries and blog posts on the latest developments in finance and investing.	Apple, Android
3. Financial Terms **Source:** Winjit **Key Features:** A guide for beginners to key definitions, and a quick reference for the most frequently used terms and ratios; easy navigation.	Apple, Android, BlackBerry

APP DISCOVERY EXERCISE

Since app availability changes, conduct your own search for the "Top Three" finance and insurance apps and identify the key features.

commodities ranging from coffee beans and live hogs to propane and platinum, as well as for stocks. Since selling prices reflect traders' beliefs about the future, prices of such contracts are very volatile, and futures trading is very risky.

For example, on January 3, 2012, the price of gold was $1625 per ounce. If futures gold contracts for July 2013 were selling for $1575 per ounce, this price would reflect investors' judgment that gold prices would be slightly lower in July. Now, suppose that you purchased a 100 ounce gold futures contract in January for $157 500 ($1575 × 100). If, in March 2013, the July gold futures sold for $1700, you could sell your contract for $170 000. Your profit after the two months would be $12 500. Of course, if the futures contract had been selling for less than $1575, you would have lost money. Usually, buyers of futures contracts need not put up the full purchase amount; rather, they post a smaller amount—the margin—that may be as little as $3000 for contracts of $100 000.

Let us look again at our gold futures example. If you had posted a $4250 margin for your July gold contract, you would have earned a $12 500 profit on that investment of $4250 in only two months. However, you also took a big risk involving two big ifs. If you had held on to your contract until July and if gold had dropped, say to $1525, you would have lost $5000 ($157 500 – $152 500). And if you had posted a $4250 margin to buy the contract, you would have lost that entire margin and would owe an additional $750. Between 75 and 90 percent of all small-time investors lose money in the futures market.

SECURITIES REGULATION

Unlike the United States, Canada does not have comprehensive federal securities legislation or a federal regulatory body. Government regulation is primarily provincial and emphasizes self-regulation through the various provincial securities exchanges. A report by a government-appointed committee that studied Canada's system of securities regulation noted that Canada is the only country in the industrialized world with a patchwork of provincial regulations, and it recommended a single regulator for Canada. The main concerns the committee noted were a lack of meaningful enforcement of securities laws, unnecessary costs, and delays that make Canada's capital markets uncompetitive internationally.

But some progress is being made. By early 2015, four provinces (Saskatchewan, New Brunswick, Ontario, and British Columbia) had signed an agreement-in-principle on the Co-operative Capital Markets Regulatory System.[22] These four provinces represent about 50 percent of market capitalization of Canadian companies listed on the Toronto Stock Exchange, and the annual economic output of the financial sector in these provinces represents two-thirds of the Canadian total. But two other big provinces—Quebec and Alberta have not signed on. Their big concern is that the new regulator will be too focused on Ontario.

Ontario is generally regarded as having the most progressive securities legislation in Canada. The Ontario Securities Act contains disclosure provisions for new and existing issues, prevention of fraud, regulation of the Toronto Stock Exchange, and takeover bids. It also prohibits insider trading. The Toronto Stock Exchange provides an example of self-regulation by the industry. The TSX has regulations concerning listing and delisting of securities, disclosure requirements, and issuing of prospectuses for new securities.

In 1912, the Manitoba government pioneered Canadian laws applying mainly to the sale of new securities. Under these **blue-sky laws**, corporations issuing securities must back them up with something more than the "blue sky." Similar laws were passed in other provinces. Provincial laws also generally require that stockbrokers be licensed and securities be registered before they can be sold. In each province, issuers of proposed new securities must file a *prospectus* with the provincial securities exchange. The prospectus must be made available to investors who might want to invest. The province of Ontario wants to relax some of the rules regarding the prospectus for individual investors with at least $1 million in financial assets; this should make it easier for small businesses to raise capital. But critics argue that some investors will get involved in ventures that are excessively risky.[23] The boxed insert entitled "Crowdfunding: Some Changes in the Works" provides information on a similar (and controversial) new type of fund-raising that relies on social media.

BLUE-SKY LAWS Laws regulating how corporations must back up securities.

FINANCIAL MANAGEMENT FOR SMALL BUSINESSES

Most new businesses have inadequate funding. Why are so many start-ups underfunded? Entrepreneurs often underestimate the value of establishing bank credit as a source of funds and use trade credit ineffectively. In addition, they often fail to consider venture capital as a source of funding, and they are notorious for not planning cash-flow needs properly. Many of them are also not aware of government programs available for support. For example, programs like the Canada Small Business Funding Program enable entrepreneurs to receive up to $350 000 worth of loans and up to $500 000 for the purchase of real property. Every year, the program provides approximately 10 000 loans for over $1 billion of financing.[24] Of course, companies that do not apply, or are unaware of the program, get $0 even if they are good potential candidates.

Establishing Bank Credit and Trade Credit

Some banks have liberal credit policies and offer financial analysis, cash-flow planning, and knowledgeable advice. Some provide loans to small businesses in bad times and work to keep them going. Obtaining credit, therefore, begins with finding a bank that can—and will—support a small firm's financial needs. Once a line of credit is obtained, the small business

ENTREPRENEURSHIP AND NEW VENTURES

Crowdfunding: Some Changes in the Works

Crowdfunding means raising money online through internet sites like Kickstarter or Indiegogo, usually by getting a small amount of money from a large number of investors. For example, the producers of the movie *Veronica Mars* used Kickstarter to get a lot of publicity and raised US$5.7 million for their project. Kickstarter has also attracted Canadian projects, like the one to raise seed money for the Peachy Printer, an inexpensive ($100) 3-D printer made by Saskatoon-based Rinnovated Design. A spokesperson for Indiegogo said that crowdfunding gives entrepreneurs in Canada's remote North a new opportunity to compete for start-up funds.

Prior to 2014, Canadian provincial securities regulations did not allow crowdfunding to be used to raise *equity* funds from investors. Crowdfunding *was* legal if the company gave investors a product rather than an equity stake. For example, when Calgary native Eric Migicovsky could not get financial backing from venture capitalists for the high-tech watch he was developing, he turned to Kickstarter. He did not violate the "no equity funding" rule, because he offered a watch to each investor instead of an equity stake in his company. In 2015, Migicovsky raised more than $6 million dollars in just eight hours for his latest smartwatch.

The restrictive rules in place before 2014 protected contributors from fraud, but they also kept people who contributed from sharing in any financial gains the company made. Oculus VR Inc. (a maker of virtual reality hardware) raised funds on Kickstarter, but when Facebook bought Oculus, the people who had contributed money to Oculus did not make any gains because they didn't hold an equity stake in Oculus. Because of situations like this, the National Crowdfunding Association of Canada and the Canadian Advanced Technology Alliance both supported the idea of relaxing some of the restrictive rules governing crowdfunding.

In 2014, some changes were finally proposed by Canadian provincial securities regulators. In Ontario, for example, the new regulations would allow companies to raise up to $1.5 million in equity funds in a one-year period, but individuals couldn't invest more than $10 000 in a given year, and no more than $2500 in a single project. The changes in British Columbia were even more modest: a $150 000 maximum in equity funds, and investors would be limited to a $1500 investment.

Proponents of crowdfunding say that it is a way to turn social media enthusiasts into venture capitalists. But critics argue that crowdfunding will lead to fraud, because unscrupulous operators will see an opportunity to fleece unsophisticated investors. They point out that if a start-up is really promising, it will attract the attention of venture capital firms. They conclude that if the rules are relaxed, most of the companies doing crowdfunding will be those that are not good investment options.

CRITICAL THINKING QUESTION

1. Consider the following statement: *Crowdfunding websites should not be allowed to raise equity funds, because con artists will be able to fleece unsophisticated investors*. Do you agree or disagree? Explain your reasoning.

can seek more liberal credit policies from other businesses. Sometimes suppliers give customers longer credit periods—say 45 or 60 days rather than 30 days. Liberal trade credit terms with their suppliers lets firms increase short-term funds and avoid additional borrowing from banks.

Start-up firms without proven financial success usually must present a business plan to demonstrate creditworthiness.[25] As we saw in Chapter 4, a business plan is a document that tells potential lenders why the money is needed, the amount needed, how the money will be used to improve the company, and when it will be paid back.

Venture Capital

Many newer businesses—especially those undergoing rapid growth—cannot get the funds they need through borrowing alone. They may, therefore, turn to venture capital—outside equity funding provided in return for part ownership of the firm (see Chapter 4).

Planning for Cash-Flow Requirements

All businesses should plan for their cash flows, but it is especially important for small businesses to do so. Success or failure may hinge on anticipating times when cash will be short and when excess cash is expected. Figure 15.5 shows possible cash inflows, cash outflows, and net cash position (inflows minus outflows), month by month, for Slippery

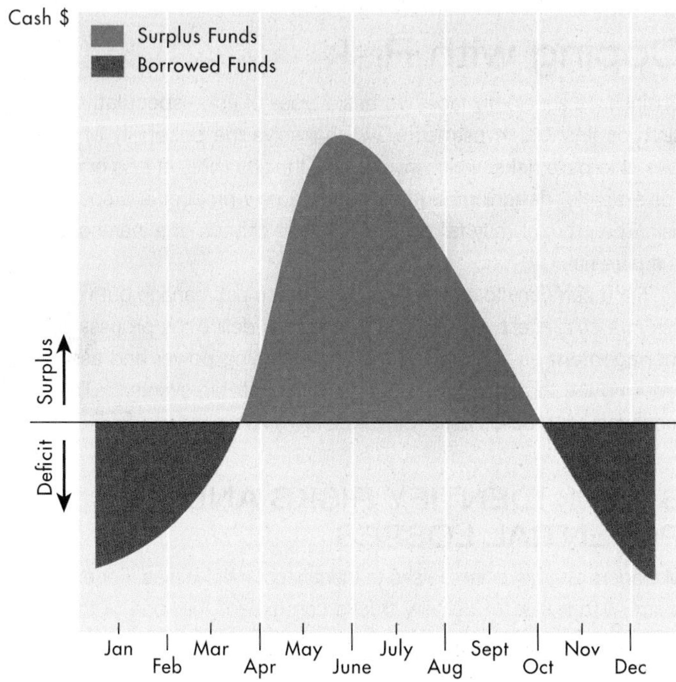

FIGURE 15.5 Cash flow for Slippery Fish Bait Supply Company

Fish Bait Supply. In this highly seasonal business, bait stores buy heavily from Slippery during the spring and summer months. Revenues outpace expenses, leaving surplus funds that can be invested. During the fall and winter, expenses exceed revenues. Slippery must borrow funds to keep going until sales revenues pick up again in the spring. Comparing predicted cash inflows from sales with outflows for expenses shows the firm's monthly cash-flow position.

By anticipating shortfalls, a financial manager can seek advance funds and minimize their cost. By anticipating excess cash, a manager can plan to put the funds to work in short-term, interest-earning investments.

LO-8 RISK MANAGEMENT

Risk—uncertainty about future events—is a factor in every manager's job because nearly every managerial action raises the possibility for either positive or negative outcomes. Risk management is therefore essential.[26] Firms devote considerable resources not only to recognizing potential risks, but also to positioning themselves to make the most advantageous decisions regarding risk.

The financial crisis that erupted in 2008 caused many firms to take a second look at their risk-management practices. For example, the Caisse de dépôt et placement du Québec incurred heavy losses in 2008 as a result of its involvement in currency and stock-related derivatives and the commercial paper crisis.[27] The Bank of Montreal (BMO) also had problems and reported write-downs of $490 million. That was on top of the $850 million charge it incurred as the result of fraud committed by one of its traders. As a result of the losses, BMO did a complete review of its risk-management systems and procedures. Bill Downe, the CEO, admitted that BMO got involved in some business activities that were beyond the company's risk tolerance and strategic plan.[28]

According to a survey of 600 executives conducted by Toronto-based recruitment firm Watson Gardner Brown, the most difficult jobs to staff are in the risk management and compliance areas. Why? Firms are increasing the size of these divisions because of the scandals and the meltdown in some securities in recent years. Institutional investors are demanding more attention to risk oversight before they will trust their funds to such organizations. Finding enough highly qualified people to fill these spots, even with generous salaries, has been a challenge.[29]

Coping with Risk

Businesses constantly face two basic types of risk—**speculative risks**, such as financial investments, which involve the possibility of gain or loss, and **pure risks**, which involve only the possibility of loss or no loss. For example, designing and distributing a new product is a speculative risk. The product may fail or succeed. The chance of a warehouse fire is a pure risk.

For a company to survive and prosper, it must manage both types of risk in a cost-effective manner. We can thus define the process of **risk management** as "conserving the firm's earning power and assets by reducing the threat of losses due to uncontrollable events."[30] The risk-management process usually involves five steps.

STEP 1: IDENTIFY RISKS AND POTENTIAL LOSSES

Managers analyze a firm's risks to identify potential losses. For example, a firm with a fleet of delivery trucks can expect that one of them will eventually be involved in an accident. The accident may cause bodily injury to the driver or others, and may cause physical damage to the truck or other vehicles as well as damage to any goods being carried by the truck.

STEP 2: MEASURE THE FREQUENCY AND SEVERITY OF LOSSES AND THEIR IMPACT

To measure the frequency and severity of losses, managers must consider both past history and current activities. How often can the firm expect the loss to occur? What is the likely size of the loss in dollars? For example, our firm with the fleet of delivery trucks may have had two accidents per year in the past. If it adds more trucks to its fleet, it may reasonably expect the number of accidents to increase.

STEP 3: EVALUATE ALTERNATIVES AND CHOOSE TECHNIQUES THAT WILL BEST HANDLE LOSSES

Having identified and measured potential losses, managers are in a better position to decide how to handle them. They generally have four choices: *avoidance*, *control*, *retention*, or *transfer*.

Risk Avoidance A firm opts for **risk avoidance** by declining to enter or by ceasing to participate in a risky activity. For example, the firm with the delivery trucks could avoid any risk of physical damage or bodily injury by closing down its delivery service. Similarly, a pharmaceutical maker may withdraw a new drug for fear of liability lawsuits.

Risk Control When avoidance is not practical or desirable, firms can practise **risk control**—say, the use of loss-prevention techniques to minimize the frequency of losses. A delivery service, for instance, can prevent losses by training its drivers in defensive-driving techniques, mapping out safe routes, and conscientiously maintaining its trucks.

Risk Retention When losses cannot be avoided or controlled, firms must cope with the consequences. When such losses are manageable and predictable, they may decide to cover them out of company funds. The firm is thus said to "assume" or "retain" the financial

RISK Uncertainty about future events.

SPECULATIVE RISK An event that offers the chance for either a gain or a loss.

PURE RISK An event that offers no possibility of gain; it offers only the chance of a loss or no loss.

RISK MANAGEMENT Conserving a firm's (or an individual's) financial power or assets by minimizing the financial effect of accidental losses.

RISK AVOIDANCE Stopping participation in or refusing to participate in ventures that carry any risk.

RISK CONTROL Techniques to prevent, minimize, or reduce losses or the consequences of losses.

consequences of the loss: hence the practice known as **risk retention**. For example, the firm with the fleet of trucks may find that each vehicle suffers vandalism totalling $300 per year. Depending on its coverage, the company may find it cheaper to pay for repairs out of pocket rather than to submit claims to its insurance company.

Risk Transfer When the potential for large risks cannot be avoided or controlled, managers often opt for **risk transfer**. They transfer the risk to another firm—namely, an insurance company. In transferring risk to an insurance company, a firm pays a premium. In return, the insurance company issues an insurance policy—a formal agreement to pay the policyholder a specified amount in the event of certain losses. In some cases, the insured party must also pay a deductible—an agreed-upon amount of the loss that the insured must absorb prior to reimbursement. Thus, the truck company may buy insurance to protect itself against theft, physical damage to trucks, and bodily injury to drivers and others involved in an accident.

STEP 4: IMPLEMENT THE RISK-MANAGEMENT PROGRAM

The means of implementing risk-management decisions depend on both the technique chosen and the activity being managed. For example, risk avoidance for certain activities can be implemented by purchasing those activities from outside providers, such as hiring delivery services instead of operating delivery vehicles. Risk control might be implemented by training employees and designing new work methods and equipment for on-the-job safety. For situations in which risk retention is preferred, reserve funds can be set aside out of revenues. When risk transfer is needed, implementation means selecting an insurance company and buying the right policies.

STEP 5: MONITOR RESULTS

Because risk management is an ongoing activity, follow-up is always essential. New types of risks emerge with changes in customers, facilities, employees, and products. Insurance regulations change, and new types of insurance become available. Consequently, managers must continually monitor a company's risks, reevaluate the methods used for handling them, and revise them as necessary.

RISK RETENTION The covering of a firm's unavoidable losses with its own funds.

RISK TRANSFER The transfer of risk to another individual or firm, often by contract.

MyBizLab

Study, practise, and explore real business situations with these helpful resources:

- **Interactive Lesson Presentations:** Work through interactive presentations and assessments to test your knowledge of business concepts.
- **Study Plan:** Check your understanding of chapter concepts with self-study quizzes.
- **Dynamic Study Modules:** Work through adaptive study modules on your computer, tablet, or mobile device.
- **Simulations:** Practise decision-making in simulated business environments.
- **Videos:** Learn more about the business practices and strategies of real companies.

SUMMARY OF

LEARNING OBJECTIVES

LO-1 DESCRIBE THE RESPONSIBILITIES OF A FINANCIAL MANAGER.

A financial manager's overall objective is to increase a firm's value and stockholders' wealth. They must ensure that earnings exceed costs, so that the firm generates a profit. The responsibilities of the financial manager fall into two general categories: (1) *cash-flow management* and (2) *financial control*.

LO-2 DISTINGUISH BETWEEN *SHORT-TERM* (OPERATING) AND *LONG-TERM* (CAPITAL) EXPENDITURES.

Short-term (operating) expenditures are incurred in a firm's everyday business activities. To handle these expenditures, managers must pay attention to accounts payable, accounts receivable, and inventories. *Long-term* (capital) expenditures are required to purchase fixed assets.

LO-3 IDENTIFY THREE SOURCES OF *SHORT-TERM FINANCING* FOR BUSINESSES.

Trade credit is really a short-term loan from one firm to another. *Secured short-term loans*, like bank loans, usually involve promissory notes in which the borrower promises to repay the loan plus interest. These loans require collateral, which can be seized if payments are not made as promised. *Unsecured short-term loans* are those in which a borrower does not have to put up collateral. The bank may, however, require the borrower to maintain a compensating balance—a portion of the loan amount kept on deposit with the bank.

LO-4 IDENTIFY THREE SOURCES OF *LONG-TERM FINANCING* FOR BUSINESSES.

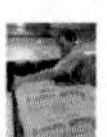

The three sources of long-term financing for businesses are debt financing, equity financing, and hybrid financing. *Debt financing* involves long-term borrowing from outside the company; it is a major component of most firms' long-term financial planning. The most common forms of debt financing are long-term loans and the issuing of bonds. A *bond* is a contract—a promise by the issuing company or organization to pay the bondholder a certain amount of money (the principal) on a specified date, plus interest, in return for use of the investor's money. *Equity financing* takes the form of issuing stock or retaining the firm's earnings. Both options involve putting the owners' capital to work. By selling shares of common stock, the company obtains the funds it needs to buy land, buildings, and equipment. The use of preferred stock is a *hybrid* approach; it has features of both corporate bonds and common stocks.

LO-5 DISCUSS THE VALUE OF *COMMON STOCK* AND *PREFERRED STOCK* TO STOCKHOLDERS, AND DESCRIBE THE SECONDARY MARKET FOR EACH TYPE OF SECURITY.

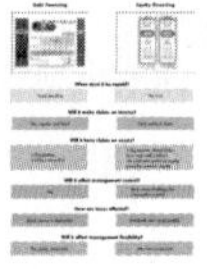

Common stock gives investors the prospect of capital gains and dividend income. Common stock values are expressed in three ways: *par value* (the value set by the issuing company's board of directors), *market value* (the current price of a share on the stock market), and *book value* (stockholders' equity divided by the number of shares). *Preferred stock* is less risky than common stock, because dividends are paid before common shareholders receive any returns. Both common and preferred stock are traded on stock exchanges (and in over-the-counter [OTC] markets).

LO-6 EXPLAIN THE PROCESS BY WHICH SECURITIES ARE BOUGHT AND SOLD.

Investors generally use such financial information services as newspapers and online stock, bond, and OTC quotations. Market indexes such as the Toronto Stock Exchange index, the Dow Jones Industrial Average, Standard & Poor's Composite Index, and the NASDAQ Composite provide useful summaries of trends. Investors can then place different types of orders. Market orders are orders to buy or sell at current prevailing prices. Investors can issue limit or stop orders that are executed only if prices rise or fall below specified levels. Round lots are purchased in multiples of 100 shares. Odd lots are purchased in fractions of round lots. Securities can be bought on margin or as part of short sales.

LO-7 DESCRIBE THE INVESTMENT OPPORTUNITIES OFFERED BY MUTUAL FUNDS, *EXCHANGE-TRADED FUNDS*, *HEDGE FUNDS*, AND *COMMODITIES*.

Mutual funds offer investors different levels of risk and growth potential. Load funds require investors to pay commissions of 2 to 8 percent; no-load funds do not charge commissions when investors buy in or out. *Hedge funds* are private pools of money that try to give investors a positive return, regardless of stock-market performance. Futures contracts (agreements to buy specified amounts of *commodities*, like coffee, at given prices on preset dates) are traded in the commodities market. Commodities traders often buy on margin, which means that only a percentage of the total sales price is put up to order futures contracts. A *stock option* gives the holder the right to buy or sell a stock at a certain price until a specific date.

LO-8 EXPLAIN HOW *RISK* AFFECTS BUSINESS OPERATIONS AND IDENTIFY THE FIVE STEPS IN THE *RISK MANAGEMENT PROCESS*.

Businesses face both *speculative risks* (where a gain or loss is possible), and *pure risks* (where only a loss or no loss is possible). Risk management means conserving earning power and assets by reducing the threat of losses due to uncontrollable events. The five-step *risk management process* requires managers to (1) identify risks and potential losses, (2) measure the frequency and severity of losses and their impact, (3) evaluate alternatives, (4) implement the risk management program, and (5) monitor results.

QUESTIONS AND EXERCISES

QUESTIONS FOR ANALYSIS

1. In what ways do the two sources of debt financing differ from each other? How do they differ from the two sources of equity financing?
2. Explain how an investor might make money in a commodities trade. Then explain how an investor might lose money in a commodities trade.
3. What is the basic relationship between the amount of risk associated with a project and the likelihood of gains (or losses) on the project? Explain how several financial instruments (GICs, common stocks, preferred stocks, corporate bonds) illustrate this basic relationship.
4. Which of the three measures of common stock value is most important? Why?
5. Suppose that you are a business owner and you need new equipment and immediate funds to meet short-term operating expenses. From what sources could you gain the capital you need, and what are some of the characteristics of those sources?
6. What are the risks and benefits associated with the sources of short-term funds (trade credit, secured loans, and unsecured loans)? How do these risks and benefits compare with those associated with sources of long-term funds (debt and equity)?

APPLICATION EXERCISES

7. Interview the financial manager of a local business. What are the investment goals of the organization? What mix of securities does it use? What advantages and disadvantages do you see in its portfolio?
8. Contact a stock broker for information about setting up a personal account for trading securities. Prepare a report on the broker's requirements for placing buy/sell orders, credit terms, cash account requirements, services available to investors, and commissions/fees schedules.
9. Go to Sedar.com and find the balance sheets of two corporations operating in the same industry. Determine the relative emphasis each company has placed on raising money through debt versus equity. Why might these differences exist?
10. Do an online search to find a case involving insider trading. Who was accused of insider trading and what was their relationship to the company? Were they convicted of insider trading, and if so, what was the penalty? How could the person accused of insider trading have avoided these charges?

TEAM EXERCISES

BUILDING YOUR BUSINESS SKILLS

MARKET UPS AND DOWNS

GOAL

To encourage students to understand the forces that affect fluctuations in stock prices.

SITUATION

Investing in stocks requires an understanding of the various factors that affect stock prices. These factors may be intrinsic to the company itself or part of the external environment.

- Internal factors relate to the company itself, such as an announcement of poor or favourable earnings, earnings that are more or less than expected, major layoffs, labour problems, management issues, and mergers.
- External factors relate to world or national events, such as a threatened war in the Persian Gulf, the BP oil spill in the Gulf of Mexico, weather conditions that affect sales, the Bank of Canada's adjustment of interest rates, and employment figures that were higher or lower than expected. By analyzing these factors, you will often learn a lot about why a stock did well or why it did poorly. Being aware of these influences will help you anticipate future stock movements.

METHOD

>>> Step 1 Working alone, choose a common stock that has experienced considerable price fluctuations in the past few years. Here are several examples (but there are many others): IBM, Amazon.com, BlackBerry, and Apple Computer. Find the symbol for the stock and the exchange on which it is traded.

>>> Step 2 Visit the Globe Investor website (or a similar site) and gather information on the particular stock and study its trading pattern. You can also visit your library and find the *Daily Stock Price Record*, a publication that provides a historical picture of daily stock closings. There are separate copies for the various stock exchanges.

>>> Step 3 Find four or five days over a period of several months or even a year when there have been major price fluctuations in the stock. (A two-or-three-point price change from one day to the next is considered major.) Then research what happened on that day that might have contributed to the fluctuation. The best place to begin is the *Globe and Mail* or the *Wall Street Journal*.

>>> Step 4 Write a short analysis linking changes in stock price to internal and external factors. As you analyze the data, be aware that it is sometimes difficult to know why a stock price fluctuates.

Step 5 Get together with three other students who studied different stocks. As a group, discuss your findings, looking for fluctuation patterns.

FOLLOW-UP QUESTIONS

1. Do you see any similarities in the movement of the various stocks during the same period? For example, did the stocks move up or down at about the same time? If so, do you think the stocks were affected by the same factors? Explain your thinking.
2. Based on your analysis, did internal or external factors have the greater impact on stock price? Which factors had the longer-lasting effect? Which factors had the shorter effect?
3. Why do you think it is so hard to predict changes in stock price on a day-to-day basis?

EXERCISING YOUR ETHICS

DOING YOUR DUTY WHEN PAYABLES COME DUE

THE SITUATION

Sarah Keats is the vice-president of finance at Multiverse, a large firm that manufactures consumer products. On December 15 (two weeks before the end of the fiscal year), she attends an executive committee meeting at which Jack Malvo, the CEO, expresses concern that the firm's year-end cash position will be less favourable than projected. The firm has exceeded analysts' performance expectations in each of his eight years at the helm, and Malvo is determined that stockholders will never be disappointed as long as he is CEO. The purpose of the meeting is to find solutions to the cash problem and decide on a course of action.

THE DILEMMA

To open the meeting, Malvo announces, "We have just two weeks to reduce expenses or increase revenues. We need a $100 million swing to get us where market analysts predicted we'd be on cash flows for the year. Any suggestions?"

In the discussion that ensues, it is noted that Multiverse owes $150 million to about 80 companies that supply component parts and other operating supplies to Multiverse. The money is due before year-end. Sarah Keats says, "Our cash outflows for the year will be lower if we delay paying suppliers, which will help the bottom line. And, it's like getting a free loan." The procurement director, Julie Levin, expresses the following concern: "Our agreements with suppliers call for faithful payments at designated times, and many of the smaller firms depend on receiving that cash to meet their obligations. Also, we've worked hard for two years at improving relationships with all suppliers, and that effort could go down the drain if we don't meet our financial commitments as promised."

As the meeting draws to a close, Malvo announces, "Keep me posted on any unexpected developments, but if nothing helpful comes up in the next few days, let's go ahead and withhold supplier payments for three weeks."

TEAM ACTIVITY

Assemble a group of four students and assign each group member to one of the following roles:

- Jack Malvo (CEO of Multiverse)
- Sarah Keats (vice-president of finance)
- Julie Levin (procurement director)
- A stockholder of Multiverse

ACTION STEPS

1. Before discussing the situation with your group and from the perspective of your assigned role, decide whether there are any ethical issues here.
2. Before discussing the situation with your group and from the perspective of your assigned role, decide what action you think should be taken. Write down your recommended action.
3. Gather your group together and reveal, in turn, each member's comments and recommendations.
4. Appoint someone to record the main points of agreement and disagreement within the group. How do you explain the results? What accounts for any disagreements?
5. From an ethical standpoint, what does your group recommend?

BUSINESS CASE 15

HOW ARE WE DOING WITH OUR IPO?

The initial public offering (IPO) is a key moment in the life of a business. The launching of an IPO is an exciting (and sometimes tense) time for three interested groups: the owners of the company, the investment bank that facilitates the IPO, and the investors (both individuals and institutions) who want to buy shares in the company. All of these people are interested in one thing: making money out of the deal. And there is a great deal of money to be made if the market judges the company to be a winner. But there is no guarantee that an IPO will be successful.

Over 200 companies went public in the United States in 2014, but more than half of them saw their share price underperform compared to the S&P 500 stock index. In Canada, 243 IPOs were launched between 2010 and 2014. Of the 15 biggest IPOs, eight had negative returns (the average was –28 percent). One research study showed that the number of IPO's in Canada has declined over time. Between 1993 and 2000, there were an average of 42 IPO's on the Toronto Stock Exchange each year, but after 2000, the average dropped to just 18 per year. Some highly publicized examples of IPOs are described below.

ALIBABA

In 2014, the Chinese e-commerce firm Alibaba raised US$25 *billion* with its IPO. That was the biggest IPO in U.S. history, which is saying quite a lot. The stock was offered at $68 per share, which some analysts thought was too high to create much interest for investors. But the stock immediately surged in value when it was made available to the public.

By January 2015, the price was just over $96 per share. As part of the IPO, Alibaba chairman Jack Ma sold some of his shares and received over $800 *million* dollars.

© Christopher Penler/Alamy

SEVEN GENERATIONS

This Calgary-based natural gas producer raised $810 million in its 2014 IPO. The initial price was $18 per share. The declining price of oil and gas reduced the value of each share to about $15 by January 2015.

PRAIRIESKY ROYALTY

In 2014, Encana Corp. spun off its PrairieSky Royalty business with an IPO that initially generated $1.67 billion. A second equity offering yielded another $2.6 billion. The investment banks that managed the original IPO earned 5 percent for their work (about $170 million) and 3.25 percent for the second equity offering. Due to a sharp decline in the price of oil, PrairieSky's share price had dropped to about $26 by January 2015.

GOPRO INC.

GoPro makes cameras that allow surfers, skiers, and skydivers to photograph their exploits. The stock was offered at $24, but surged to over $100 per share within a few weeks. By January 2015, the price had declined to about $47 per share, but that was still significantly higher than the original issue price.

FACEBOOK AND TWITTER

Two social media stocks got a lot of attention in 2012 and 2013. In 2012, Facebook was making all the headlines with its highly anticipated IPO. While the market believed in Facebook's growth potential, some experts felt that the initial offering price was too high ($38). Two weeks after the IPO, Facebook shares had lost 25 percent of their value, and by September 2012, their price had dropped to about $17 per share. Part of the reason was that investors had concerns about the cost of running the business. They were also concerned that new competitors might emerge that would threaten Facebook's future revenue streams. But as time passed, those concerns declined, and by January 2015 the price had risen to $75. Founder Mark Zuckerberg is often mentioned as the world's youngest billionaire.

Twitter's IPO took place in 2013. The initial offering price was set at $26 per share, but the price of the stock immediately rose to over $45. By January 2015, the stock had settled back to a price of about $37 per share.

GROUPON

In its IPO, this online daily discount website launched its stock at a price of $20 per share, and over the next few weeks the stock rose over 30 percent. However, problems emerged when Groupon restated some of its financial statements. By 2013, amid a new round of financial irregularities, Groupon's stock price dropped to just $4.43 a share because investors were starting to think that Groupon's business model (which is focused on daily coupon deals) was fundamentally flawed. A survey of merchants who had used daily deals found that nearly 40 percent of them were not likely to run another Groupon promotion. Their reasons included commission rates that were too high, repeat business that was too low, and the belief that other forms of marketing were more effective than coupons. By January 2015, Groupon's stock price had risen slightly to just over $7, but that was still significantly below its issue price of $20.

LINKEDIN

Employers pay LinkedIn to post job openings and career pages as they search for candidates on the site. At the time of its IPO, LinkedIn had 202 million users. While this number paled in comparison to the 900 million users on Facebook, it was LinkedIn's revenue potential that the investment community was impressed with. LinkedIn had a growing number of paid subscribers and the company was increasing revenues in the area of "hiring solutions." LinkedIn went public in 2011 with an issue price of $45 per share. Within a day the stock price rose to over $90. In January 2015, it had risen to just over $214.

AFTER THE IPO

The hype surrounding an IPO results in a lot of publicity, and may cause frenzied trading of a company's stock in the short run. But in the long run, the price of any stock is based on fundamentals such as revenue, growth prospects, and profitability. The newly minted public companies described above must compete in the "real world" of stock evaluations and it can be a brutal world since unexpected events can occur that boost or suppress the value of a company's stock. In 2014, for example, the steep drop in oil prices depressed the stock prices of companies like Seven Generations and PrairieSky Royalty. But the public's continuing interest in companies like Facebook and LinkedIn has boosted their stock prices.

The complexity of the business world makes it difficult to predict which companies will be successful and which companies will have problems. But that does not stop optimistic entrepreneurs from starting new companies and issuing IPOs. In 2015, several new IPOs were in the works. For example, Shopify (not to be confused with Spotify), an e-commerce firm that provides retailers with a system to collect payments and process credit card transactions, planned to raise about US$100 million in Canada and the United States. And Canada Jetlines Ltd., a new company that wants to offer bargain airfares 30–40 percent lower than those charged by WestJet and Air Canada, planned to raise $50 million in an IPO.

QUESTIONS FOR DISCUSSION

1. Why is it difficult to predict which IPO's will be long-term successes?
2. What factors influence the market price of a share of stock? Which factors were most important for each of the companies mentioned above?
3. What other IPO's have taken place beyond those companies mentioned above? How have they performed during their first year of public ownership?

CHAPTER SUPPLEMENT 05

Insurance as Risk Management

To deal with some risks, both businesses and individuals may choose to purchase one or more of the products offered by insurance companies. Buyers find insurance appealing for a very basic reason—in return for a relatively small sum of money, they are protected against specific losses, some of which are potentially devastating. With insurance, individuals and businesses share risks by contributing to a fund out of which those who suffer losses are paid. Insurance companies are willing to accept these risks for other companies because they make profits by taking in more in **premiums** than they pay out to cover policyholders' losses. Although many policyholders are paying for protection against the same type of loss, it is unlikely that all of them will suffer such a loss.

INSURABLE VS. UNINSURABLE RISKS

Like every other business, insurance companies must avoid certain risks. Insurers thus divide potential sources of loss into *insurable* and *uninsurable risks*.[31] Obviously, they issue policies only for insurable risks, which must satisfy the four criteria of *predictability*, *casualty*, *unconnectedness*, and *verifiability*.

Predictability The insurer must be able to use statistical tools to forecast the likelihood of a loss. For example, an auto insurer needs information about the number of car accidents in the past year to estimate the expected number of accidents for the following year. With this knowledge, the insurer can translate expected numbers and types of accidents into expected dollar losses. The same forecast also helps insurers determine premiums charged to policyholders. Cyber attacks on companies like Sony and Target are difficult for insurance companies to deal with, since it is very difficult to determine the likelihood of a cyber attack and the costs that will be incurred by one.[32]

Casualty A loss must result from an accident, not from an intentional act by the policyholder. For example, an insurer does not have to cover damages if a policyholder deliberately sets fire to a business. To avoid paying in cases of fraud, insurers may refuse to cover losses when they cannot determine whether policyholders' actions contributed to them.

Unconnectedness Potential losses must be random and must occur independently of other losses. No insurer can afford to write insurance when a large percentage of those exposed to a particular kind of loss are likely to suffer such a loss. One insurance company, for instance, would not want all the hail coverage in Saskatchewan or all the earthquake coverage in Vancouver. By carefully choosing the risks it will insure, an insurance company can reduce its chances of a large loss.

Verifiability Finally, insured losses must be verifiable as to cause, time, place, and amount. Did an employee develop emphysema because of a chemical to which she was exposed or because she had smoked 40 cigarettes per day for 30 years? Did the policyholder pay the renewal premium before the fire destroyed his factory? Were the goods stolen from the company's office or from the president's home? What was the insurable value of the destroyed inventory? When all these points have been verified, payment by the insurer goes more smoothly.

THE INSURANCE PRODUCT

Some insurers offer only one area of coverage—life insurance, for example—while others offer a broad range. In this section, we briefly describe three major categories of business insurance—*liability, property*, and *life*.

Liability Insurance Liability means responsibility for damages in case of accidental or deliberate harm to individuals or property. **Liability insurance** covers losses resulting from damage to people or property when the insured party is judged liable. A business is liable for any injury to an employee when the injury arises from activities related to occupation. When workers are permanently or temporarily disabled

PREMIUMS Money paid to an insurance company by customers in return for being covered for certain types of losses should they occur.

LIABILITY INSURANCE Covers losses resulting from damage to people or property when the insured party is judged liable.

Losses are reduced or prevented when this security specialist uses electronic surveillance (left), when valuables are stored under lock and key (middle), and when workers are reminded to wear safety gear at this construction site (right).

David R. Frazier Photolibrary, Inc./Alamy Stock Photo; Mile Atanasov/Shutterstock; Morgan Rauscher/Fotolia

by job-related accidents or disease, employers are required by law to provide **workers' compensation coverage** for medical expenses, loss of wages, and rehabilitation services.

Every year in Canada, well over $1 billion is lost to insurance fraud. The insurance industry estimates that between $10 and $15 of every $100 you pay in premiums goes to cover fraud losses. The Insurance Bureau of Canada (IBC) is an industry association that represents Canadian companies that provide car, home, and business insurance. The IBC protects honest policyholders by monitoring insurance claims and determining which ones are fraudulent. Two areas of particular concern are organized crime rings and fraudulent injury claims. One popular scam is the "staged accident." The swindler purposely (but carefully) runs into, say, a telephone pole, and then everyone in the car claims they are suffering from whiplash. After the accident is reported, the insurance company contacts the car's occupants and sends them accident benefit packages. Sometimes people who aren't even insured are paid benefits because they use counterfeit "proof of insurance" cards.[33] The IBC also lobbies the government to make legislative changes that will deter insurance fraud. Visit the IBC website at www.ibc.ca.

Property Insurance Firms purchase **property insurance** to cover injuries resulting from physical damage to real estate or personal property. Property losses may result from fire, lightning, wind, hail, explosion, theft, vandalism, or other destructive forces, such as hurricanes. In 2005, insurance companies received claims exceeding $55 billion as a result of several hurricanes that hit the southern United States and flooded New Orleans. That figure was double the previous record (set in 2004). Canadian insurers were expected to pay out about $570 million of the 2005 total.

In some cases, loss to property is minimal in comparison with loss of income. A manufacturer, for example, may have to close down for an extended time while fire damage is being repaired. During that time, the company is not generating any income, but certain expenses—such as taxes, insurance premiums, and salaries for key personnel—may continue. To cover such losses, a firm may buy *business interruption insurance*.

Life Insurance Insurance can also protect a company's human assets. As part of their benefits packages, many businesses purchase **life insurance** for employees. Life insurance companies receive premiums in return for the promise to pay beneficiaries after the death of insured parties. As with other types of insurance, a portion of the premium is used to cover the insurer's own expenses.

Life insurance can, of course, also be purchased by individuals. For many years, Canadian life insurance companies have sold insurance policies to Canadians, but now they are rapidly expanding overseas, particularly in China and India. Sun Life Financial, for example, has formed a joint venture with Aditya Birla Group to sell life insurance and mutual funds in India. As a result of this partnership, Sun Life is the second-largest privately owned life insurance company in India.[34] But in 2011, both Sun Life and Standard Life Assurance decided to stop selling individual life insurance policies in the United States, because low interest rates and volatile stock markets made it difficult to make a profit selling such policies.[35] In some areas of the world, unstable and dangerous situations have motivated entrepreneurs to sell special kinds of insurance. For example, the Al-Ameen Insurance Co. pays out $3500 to beneficiaries of people killed as a result of insurgent activity in Iraq. The annual premium is about $35.[36]

Most companies buy **group life insurance**, which is underwritten for groups as a whole rather than for each individual member. The insurer's assessment of potential losses and its pricing of premiums are based on the characteristics of the entire group.

Catastrophic losses like those caused by fire are avoided when a business buys property insurance. The cost of the rebuilding will be paid by the insurance company. But interruption of the firm's normal operations will also be harmful, so many businesses buy business interruption insurance as well.

Cary Ulrich Photography/Alamy

SPECIAL FORMS OF BUSINESS INSURANCE

Many forms of insurance are attractive to both businesses and individuals. For example, homeowners are as concerned about insuring property from fire and theft as businesses are. Businesses, however, have some special insurable concerns—the departure or death of key employees or owners.

Key Person Insurance Many businesses choose to protect themselves against loss of the talents and skills of key employees. If a salesperson who brings in $2.5 million of sales revenue dies or takes a new job, the firm will suffer loss. It will also incur recruitment costs to find a replacement and training expenses once a replacement is hired. **Key person insurance** is designed to offset both lost income and additional expenses.[37]

Business Continuation Agreements Who takes control of a business when a partner or an associate dies? Surviving partners are often faced with the possibility of having to accept an inexperienced heir as a management partner. This contingency can be handled in **business continuation agreements**, whereby owners make plans to buy the ownership interest of a deceased associate from his or her heirs. The value of the ownership interest is determined when the agreement is made. Special policies can also provide survivors with the funds needed to make the purchase.

WORKERS' COMPENSATION COVERAGE Compensation for medical expenses, loss of wages, and rehabilitation services for injuries arising from activities related to occupation.

PROPERTY INSURANCE Covers injuries to firms resulting from physical damage to or loss of real estate or personal property.

LIFE INSURANCE Insurance that pays benefits to survivors of a policyholder.

GROUP LIFE INSURANCE Life insurance underwritten for a group as a whole rather than for each individual member.

KEY PERSON INSURANCE Insurance that protects a company against loss of the talents and skills of key employees.

BUSINESS CONTINUATION AGREEMENT An agreement in which owners of a business make plans to buy the ownership interest of a deceased associate from his or her heirs.

MANAGING FINANCIAL ISSUES

GOAL OF THE EXERCISE

In this final part of the business plan project, you'll consider how to finance your business and create an executive summary for your plan.

EXERCISE BACKGROUND: PART 5 OF THE BUSINESS PLAN

In a previous part of the business plan, you discussed the costs of doing business, as well as how much revenue you expect to earn in one year. It's now time to think about how to finance the business. To get a great idea off the ground requires money. But how will you get these funds?

You'll then conclude this project by creating an executive summary. The purpose of the executive summary is to give the reader a quick snapshot of your proposed business. Although this exercise comes at the end of the project, once you're done writing it, you'll end up placing the executive summary at the beginning of your completed business plan.

YOUR ASSIGNMENT

STEP 1

Open the saved Business Plan file you have been working on.

STEP 2

For the purposes of this assignment, you will answer the following questions, shown in Part 5: Managing Financial Issues.

1. How much money will you need to get your business started?

   Hint: *Refer to Part 3 of the plan, in which you analyzed the costs involved in running your business. Approximately how much will you need to get your business started?*

2. How will you finance your business? For example, will you seek a bank loan? Borrow from friends? Sell stocks or bonds initially or as your business grows?

   Hint: *Refer to this chapter for information on securities such as stocks and bonds. Refer to this chapter and Chapter 4 for more information on sources of short-term and long-term funds.*

3. Now, create an executive summary for your business plan. The executive summary should be brief—no more than two pages—and cover the following points:

   - the name of your business
   - where your business will be located
   - the mission of your business
   - the product or service you are selling
   - who your ideal customers are
   - how your product or business will stand out in the crowd
   - who the owners of the business are and what experience they have
   - an overview of the future prospects for your business and industry

   Hint: *At this point, you've already answered all of these questions, so what you need to do here is put the ideas together into "snapshot" format. The executive summary is really a sales pitch—it's the investor's first impression of your idea. Therefore, as with all parts of the plan, write in a clear and professional way.*

Congratulations on completing the business plan project!

CBC VIDEO CASE 5-1

T CAPS INTERNATIONAL

THE COMPANY

People often wear baseball caps with sunglasses perched on top. The trouble is, people forget the sunglasses are up there and move their head in such a way that the glasses fall off—and then perhaps get stepped on. Thierry Annez has come up with a solution he calls the "t-cap." The sunglasses are firmly connected to the baseball hat, but there is a slit in the bill that allows the glasses to be easily slipped down into the wearing position. There are various t-caps in Thierry's product line: t-caps for children, for sports activity, and for corporate promotional uses. They range in price from $14.95 to $49.95. For more details on the company, go to www.tcapsinternational.com.

THE PITCH

In the Dragons' Den, Thierry demonstrates how the product works, saying "Now you see me, now you don't" as he moves the glasses up and down in the slit. Thierry briefly explains his innovative idea, and then gives each dragon their own t-cap to try on. Thierry says that he has spent about $330 000 so far in developing his product. About $70 000 of that was spent getting international patent protection. So far, Thierry has sold 6000 of the sunglasses to promotional companies. He is asking for $100 000 for 25 percent of his company (valued at $400 000).

THE DRAGONS' POINT OF VIEW

Jim Treliving says it will work well with golfers. But Arlene Dickinson thinks the product will be easy to counterfeit, and Thierry will find himself involved in a lot of legal wrangling as he tries to protect his patents. For that reason, she doesn't want to invest. Vikram Vij is also out. Jim Treliving says he likes the idea, but he too is leaning toward dropping out. Michael Wekerle thinks it's a great product, but is concerned it will have a short life span. He therefore offers $500 000 for 100 percent of the business, and he will give Thierry a 3 percent royalty on all sales. He also says that if he sells the company within five years, he'll give Thierry 20 percent of the sale price.

THE OUTCOME

Thierry says he never thought that one of the dragons would offer to actually buy his company, so he hesitates as he thinks about the offer. Michael Wekerle wonders whether Jim would partner with him. Thierry is asked if he actually wants to sell his company outright. He says it's a tough decision. Finally, Thierry asks if Wekerle will give him $750 000 plus a 5 percent royalty on sales. Wekerle says no. Then Thierry asks for a 5 percent royalty on Wekerle's original $500 000 offer. Jim Treliving says he's out, then Michael says he won't accept Thierry's latest offer either. Finally Thierry accepts Wekerle's original offer of $500 000 and a 3 percent royalty on sales.

QUESTIONS FOR DISCUSSION

1. What has Thierry Annez learned about negotiating deals from this experience?
2. Could Thierry Annez have obtained the needed funds on his own by selling stocks or bonds? Explain.
3. What lessons about financing a business can you take away from this video? If Thierry Annez were given a second opportunity to make a pitch to the dragons, what advice would you give him?

Source: "T Caps International," *Dragons' Den*, Episode 19, Season 9 (April 2, 2015).

BUSINESS TODAY VIDEO CASE 5-1

JOHNNY CUPCAKES

Johnny Earle started a company called Johnny Cupcakes when he was just 18 years old. The company sells T-shirts with cupcakes on them. Johnny always wanted to work for himself, and as a kid operated a lemonade stand and organized yard sales. He started the company as something of a joke. He starting wearing a cupcake T-shirt to work and people wanted to know where they could get such a shirt. When he saw how interested people were, he decided to quit his regular job and start Johnny Cupcakes. He says that risk taking is what separates entrepreneurs from everyday people.

Lorrain Earle (Johnny's mother) is the chief financial officer and business manager of the company. Her job is to obtain financing for the making and selling of T-shirts. She originally gave her credit card to her son and advice on how to use the money wisely. He started purchasing shirts, rolling the $30 000 on the credit card over and over again. He rented a modest retail outlet for $700 a month, but eventually he decided to open a new store in Boston where the customer traffic would be much higher.

But the rent went up from $700 to $7000 per month. To open the store, he had to convince a bank to lend him the money. He finally found a willing bank, and on the first day he took in enough revenue to pay the rent for three months. So he began hiring to help meet the demand. In his first year, he sold $1.2 million worth of t-shirts, and in the second year that increased to $2.7 million. He was recognized by *Inc.* magazine as one of fastest-growing small businesses. The company now has 32 employees, three retail stores, and an online store. Estimated revenue for next year is $4 million.

Johnny and his mother want the company to remain a family-type firm, but they also recognize that they need to publicize their products. The next big project is opening a store in London, England. Lorrain says it takes money to make money, and she is therefore trying to figure out where the $250 000 needed to open the London store is going to come from. She says banks won't lend money to make rent payments, so she is trying to finance from profits instead.

Lorrain says that planning ahead is critical in the finance area and she is always thinking "What will my accountant think of my financial transactions"? She remembers that Johnny went over budget when he opened the Los Angeles store (he spent $750 000) and she doesn't want that to happen again. The L.A. store will put a big strain on finances and she will have to play catch-up. She knows not to dip into operating funds to finance new store openings.

Johnny and his mother want the business to grow steadily, not by leaps and bounds. Johnny likes the idea of the online store, because he doesn't have to pay rent and the online store makes money while he sleeps. It turns a simple idea into a multimillion-dollar business.

QUESTIONS FOR DISCUSSION

1. What type of financing has Johnny Cupcakes relied upon so far?
2. What are the financial objectives of Johnny Cupcakes?
3. How does Johnny Cupcakes manage cash flows?

BUSINESS TODAY VIDEO CASE 5-2

FIND FRESH FLOWERS

The controversial currency bitcoin is exploding in popularity as more retailers accept it in payment for goods and service. But lawmakers don't know what to make of bitcoin and how to regulate and tax it, because they often don't understand how it works. Critics also say it is used for drug smuggling and money laundering.

Farbod Shoraka is the CEO of BloomNation, an online florist that partners with 3000 local businesses around the country who are part of the BloomNation system. Consumers in many places can go to their local florist and purchase flowers using bitcoins. He says BloomNation is trying to tap into tech-savvy young people who want to buy flowers online. He says people should be happy to send flowers using bitcoin because it uses a sophisticated encryption system to verify transactions. It is therefore more secure than credit cards or cash. The system also gives local businesses a chance to tap into the tech-savvy world. He says that more businesses are going to accept bitcoin, and it's going to be disruptive to the cash and credit card industry.

Asked about the risk of bitcoin fluctuating in value more than dollars, Shoraka says that BloomNation has partnered with Coinbase, a company that immediately converts bitcoin into regular dollars that are then sent to the selling company. That reduces the chance of a consumer or a company being hurt by fluctuations in the value of bitcoins.

For Shoraka it's important to be a first mover like BloomNation because it is an innovative company that wants to connect with tech-savvy consumers. He says that consumers spend 50 percent more with bitcoin than they do with credit cards.

QUESTIONS FOR DISCUSSION

1. In your own words, explain what bitcoin is and how it can be used by consumers to buy products and services.
2. Why does BloomNation accept bitcoin?
3. How does partnering with BloomNation help local florists?

ENDNOTES AND SOURCE NOTES

ENDNOTES

CHAPTER 1

1. "Best Country for Business: Canada," *The Globe and Mail*, October 5, 2011, B2.
2. Robert A. Collinge and Ronald M. Ayers, *Economics by Design: Principles and Issues*, 2nd ed. (Upper Saddle River, NJ: Prentice Hall, 2000), 41–42; Michael J. Mandel, "The New Economy," *Businessweek*, January 31, 2000, 73–77.
3. Sean Wise, "Social Networks Reshaping Economics," *Winnipeg Free Press*, May 18, 2011, A11.
4. Richard I. Kirkland Jr., "The Death of Socialism," *Fortune*, January 4, 1988, 64–72.
5. Andres Oppenheimer, "Latin America Is Skeptical," *Orlando Sentinel*, February 20, 2006, A19.
6. James Kynge, "Private Firms' Growth in China Striking: Report," *National Post*, May 11, 2000, C14.
7. "Cuba Allows Private Ads in Phone Book," *The Globe and Mail*, December 9, 2011, B7.
8. Karl E. Case and Ray C. Fair, *Principles of Economics*, 5th ed. (Upper Saddle River, NJ: Prentice Hall, 1999), 69–74; Robert A. Collinge and Ronald M. Ayers, *Economics by Design: Principles and Issues*, 2nd ed. (Upper Saddle River, NJ: Prentice Hall, 2000), 51–52.
9. Andres Oppenheimer, "While Latin America Nationalizes, India Opens Up," *Orlando Sentinel*, January 22, 2007, A11.
10. Barry Critchley, "Canada Post Should Be Privatized: OECD; Productivity Issue," *National Post*, March 11, 2010, FP2.
11. John Greenwood, "Study Cites Privatization in Productivity Gains," *National Post*, June 26, 2009, FP1.
12. News.go.ca/web/article-en.do?nid=819829.
13. Claire Brownell, "CRTC Wipes Netflix from Hearing Record; Chooses to Ignore Its and Google's Submissions Rather Than Take Companies to Court for Refusing to Provide User Data," *National Post*, September 30, 2014, FP1.
14. Terence Corcoran, "Power Grab; CRTC Uses Vertical Integration as Excuse to Expand Its Authority," *National Post*, September 23, 2011, FP11.
15. Jim Middlemiss, "Don't Get Caught Offside in Rules Changes; Wrong Advice on Competition Act Could Be Costly," *National Post*, March 23, 2009, FP6. For an analysis of the current situation in the U.S. regarding resale price maintenance, see Joseph Pereira, "Price-Fixing Makes Comeback After Supreme Court Hearing," *Wall Street Journal*, August 18, 2008, A1, A12.
16. Hollie Shaw, "Bogus Ads: If You Mislead the Consumer, Be Ready to Suffer the Financial Fallout," *National Post*, May 22, 2009, FP12.
17. Marina Strauss, "Competition Bureau Sets Stiff Limits in Loblaw's Deal for Shoppers," *The Globe and Mail*, March 22, 2014, B1.
18. Eric Atkins, "Keurig Fights Back over Competition Filing: After Complaint to Competition Bureau, Coffee Company Argues It Has to 'Control the Experience,'" *The Globe and Mail*, November 18, 2014, B3.
19. Tara Perkins, "Top Court Move Reignites Toronto Real Estate Board Battle," *The Globe and Mail*, July 25, 2014, B1.
20. John Gray, "Texas Fold 'Em," *Canadian Business*, October 9–22, 2006, 44–46.
21. "Video Gaming: The Next Level," *Venture*, March 20, 2005.
22. "Alberta Film, TV Production Faces Decline," May 19, 2010, CBC News, www.cbc.ca/arts/film/story/2010/05/18/alberta-film-production-decline.html.
23. Kristine Owram, "Aftermath; The Five-Year Legacy of Canada's Auto Bailout," *National Post*, July 19, 2014, FP6.
24. Barrie McKenna, "The Costly Seduction of Private–Public Partnerships," *The Globe and Mail*, December 15, 2014, B1.
25. Parker Gallant, "A Liberal Decade of Disaster; Irrational Energy Planning in Ontario Is Tripling Power Rates Under the Liberals' Direction," *National Post*, June 3, 2014, FP9.
26. Jennifer Allen, "New Lobby Rules Mean More Work for Lawyers," *The Globe and Mail*, August 13, 2008, B5.
27. Some people argue that new technological developments mean that some products are not really subject to market forces; see Guy Dixon, "On the Verge of a New Era, Where Electricity Flows Free," *The Globe and Mail*, June 24, 2014, B16.
28. Andy Hoffman, "Global Demand for Maple Syrup Keeps Rising. Sweet!" *The Globe and Mail*, March 12, 2009, B1.
29. Alexandra Wexler, "Gastronomes Foraging for Bargain Truffles Are in Luck," *The Wall Street Journal*, December 27–28, 2014, A1.
30. Shirley Won, "Why Demand for Palladium Is Looking White Hot," *The Globe and Mail*, March 7, 2011, B9; also Peter Koven, "Rare-Earth Share Bonanza: Increase Sharp as U.S. Seeks Secure Supply," *National Post*, October 19, 2010, FP4.
31. Joel Millman, "Metal Is So Precious That Scrap Thieves Now Tap Beer Kegs," *Wall Street Journal*, March 14, 2006, A1, A15.
32. Paul Heyne, Peter J. Boettke, and David L. Prychitko, *The Economic Way of Thinking*, 10th ed. (Upper Saddle River, NJ: Prentice Hall, 2003), 190, 358–359.
33. Karl E. Case and Ray C. Fair, *Principles of Economics*, 6th ed., upd. (Upper Saddle River, NJ: Prentice Hall, 2003), 300–309.
34. *Hoover's Handbook of World Business 2002* (Austin: Hoover's Business Press, 2002), 74–75.
35. Timothy Aeppel, "Show Stopper: How Plastic Popped the Cork Monopoly," *Wall Street Journal*, May 1, 2010, A1.
36. Barrie McKenna, "Canada Post's Losses Mount," *The Globe and Mail*, May 6, 2014, B3.
37. Vincent Geloso and Youri Chassin, "Postal Monopoly Is Becoming a Dead Letter," *National Post*, June 2, 2011, FP11.
38. Concerns about the supply management system have also caused problems for Canada with respect to trade issues; see Barrie McKenna, "Ottawa Faces Renewed Pressure on Dairy, Poultry Protection," *The Globe and Mail*, August 4, 2014, B1.

CHAPTER 2

1. Bertrand Marotte, "Bauer Aims to Rebound from NHL Lockout with Lacrosse Power Play," *The Globe and Mail*, October 8, 2012, B1.
2. See Jay B. Barney and William G. Ouchi, eds., *Organizational Economics* (San Francisco: Jossey-Bass, 1986), for a detailed analysis of linkages between economics and organizations.
3. Marina Strauss, "Grocers Scramble to Offset Higher Food Costs," *The Globe and Mail*, May 2, 2011, B4.
4. Matthew Levin, "Dollarama Profit Rises 23% on Higher Sales," *Financial Post*, December 6, 2012; Manya Venkatesh, Reuters, Canoe.Ca Website,

www.canoe.ca/Canoe/Money/News/2014/09/11/21934456.html, accessed March 19, 2015.

5. Karl E. Case and Ray C. Fair, *Principles of Economics*, 6th ed., upd. (Upper Saddle River, NJ: Prentice Hall, 2003), 432–433.

6. Karl E. Case and Ray C. Fair, *Principles of Economics*, 6th ed., upd. (Upper Saddle River, NJ: Prentice Hall, 2003), 15.

7. Ibid, 15.

8. Ibid.

9. *Bank of Canada Banking and Financial Statistics*, Table H1 (February 2015): S98; Trading Economics Website, www.tradingeconomics.com/canada/gdp, accessed March 19, 2015.

10. World Bank Website, GDP statistics, search.worldbank.org/data?qterm=gdp&language=&format=, accessed March 18, 2015.

11. Bertrand Marotte, "Bombardier Setting Up Shop in Morocco," *The Globe and Mail*, September 6, 2012.

12. Matthew McLearn, "Our Dangerous Addiction to GDP," *Canadian Business*, October 12, 2009, 23.

13. World Bank Website, GDP statistics, search.worldbank.org/data?qterm=gdp%20per%20capita&language=EN, accessed March 14, 2015.

14. Olivier Blanchard, *Macroeconomics*, 3rd ed. (Upper Saddle River, NJ: Prentice Hall, 2003), 24–26.

15. OECD Website, stats.oecd.org/Index.aspx?DataSetCode=PDB_LV, accessed March 19, 2015.

16. Statistics Canada Website, www.statcan.gc.ca/tables-tableaux/sum-som/l01/cst01/gblec02a-eng.htm, accessed March 19, 2015..

17. CTV News, www.ctvnews.ca/politics/ottawa-s-cash-surplus-will-be-1-9b-in-2015-oliver-1.2098147, accessed March 19, 2015; Canadian Press, "Canada Urged to 'Get Act Together' as National Debt to Hit $600-Billion Saturday," *Financial Post*, November 23, 2012.

18. Celia Dugger, "Life in Zimbabwe: Wait for Useless Money, Then Scour for Food," *New York Times*, October 2, 2008, A1, A14.

19. Geoffrey York, "How Zimbabwe Slew the Dragon of Hyperinflation," *The Globe and Mail*, March 23, 2009, B1.

20. Trading Economics Website, www.tradingeconomics.com/south-africa/inflation-cpi, accessed March 19, 2015; Mike Cohen and Franz Wild, "South Africa Holds Rate as Rand Sparks Inflation Fears," Bloomberg Website, January 24, 2013.

21. Tavia Grant, "A Snapshot of How We Spend," *The Globe and Mail*, April 20, 2010, B2; Tavia Grant, "Lard in 1913, Plasma TV Now: CPI Tracks Changes," *The Globe and Mail*, April 21, 2005, B1, B15.

22. Tavia Grant, "Food Prices to Rise in 2013, Report Says," *The Globe and Mail*, December 6, 2012, B8; Rita Trichur, "Maple Leaf Takes on Challenge of Food Inflation," *The Globe and Mail*, April 29, 2011, B9.

23. Figure 2.3: Bank of Canada website, CPI Statistics, www.bankofcanada.ca/rates/price-indexes/cpi/?page_moved=1, March 19, 2015.

24. Eric Atkins, "Food to Become More Expensive in 2015, Report Says," *The Globe and Mail*, December 2, 2014, B4.

25. *Bank of Canada Banking and Financial Statistics*, Series H5, Labour Force Status of the Population, January 2015, S102.

26. Gordon Isfeld, "Canada's Unemployment Rate Hits Five-Month High, but Job Loss Less Than Feared," *Financial Post*, March 13, 2015.

27. Statistics Canada, Labour Force Report, www.statcan.gc.ca/tables-tableaux/sum-som/l01/cst01/labor07a-eng.htm, accessed March 19, 2015.

28. Statistics Canada. "Spending on Research and Development," www.statcan.gc.ca/daily-quotidien/120113/dq120113d-eng.htm, accessed February 2, 2013.

29. Statistics Canada, "Industrial Research and Development: Intentions," Catalogue No. 88-202-X, Table 4, "Concentration of Total Intramural Research and Development Expenditures by Top Performing Companies," 2008, www.statcan.gc.ca/pub/88-202-x/2012000/t050-eng.htm, accessed February 2, 2013.

30. Marina Strauss, "Starbucks Rolls Out Smart Phone Payments," *The Globe and Mail*, November 11, 2011, B4.

31. Nathan Vanderklippe, "Yukon's Golden Dilemma," *The Globe and Mail*, February 2, 2013, B1.

32. Marina Strauss and Kevin Howlett, "Ontario Cuts Generic Drug Payments Again," *The Globe and Mail*, April 24, 2012, B4; Michael Babad, "How Ontario's Drug Reforms Could Hit Shoppers Drug Mart," *The Globe and Mail*, April 8, 2010, B1.

33. Brenda Boum, "No Regrets From the Capitalist Miner Who Built Bridges to Communist Cuba," *The Globe and Mail*, November 25, 2011, B1.

34. Angelina Chapin, "Under Cover Economy," *Canadian Business*, September 26, 2011, 50–52.

35. Ira Boudway, "Labour Disputes: The Wal-Mart Way," *Bloomberg Businessweek*, 57–60.

36. CBC Website, "Wal-Mart Runs Afoul of Sask. Labour Laws," www.cbc.ca/news/canada/saskatchewan/story/2012/10/23/sk-weyburn-wal-mart-union-121023.html, accessed February 2, 2013.

37. UFCW Canada Website, "Wal-Mart found guilty of unfair labour practices by BC Labour Relations Board," www.ufcw.ca/index.php?option=com_content&view=article&id=424&catid=&lang=en, accessed March 20, 2015.

38. Richard Blackwell, "The Greening of the Corner Office," *The Globe and Mail*, March 26, 2007, B1, B4.

39. Michael Porter, *Competitive Strategy: Techniques for Analyzing Industries and Competitors* (New York: The Free Press, 1980).

40. Jeff Beer, "Fresh Trouble for the Double-Double," *Canadian Business*, February 18, 2013, 11.

41. Marina Strauss, "Nordstrom Content to Tread Carefully," *The Globe and Mail*, March 5, 2015, B5.

42. "Bauer Expects Price Pressure as Big Customers Merge," *The Globe and Mail*, August 19, 2011, B5.

43. Barrie McKenna, "Canada Post in the Red for First Time in 16 Years," *The Globe and Mail*, May 2, 2012, B1, B8.

44. Diane Peters, "Setting the Bar High for Outsourcing," *The Globe and Mail*, November 29, 2011, B15.

45. Judy Strauss and Raymond Frost, *E-Marketing* (Upper Saddle River, NJ: Prentice Hall, 2001), 245–246.

46. Lee J. Krajewski and Larry P. Ritzman, *Operations Management: Strategy and Analysis*, 6th ed. (Upper Saddle River, NJ: Prentice Hall, 2002), 3–4.

47. Lee J. Krajewski and Larry P. Ritzman, *Operations Management: Strategy and Analysis*, 6th ed. (Upper Saddle River, NJ: Prentice Hall, 2002), ch. 3.

48. Marina Strauss, "HBC Finds a Bargain with Saks Deal," *The Globe and Mail*, November 25, 2015, B6.

49. Financial Post Website, "Wall Street Titans Dominate Canadian M&A Activity in 2014, RBC Slips to Third Spot," *Financial Post*, December 14, 2014, business.financialpost.com/2014/12/30/wall-street-titans-dominate-canadian-ma-activity-in-2014-rbc-slips-to-third-spot, accessed March 20, 2015.

50. Bertrand Marotte, "Couche-Tard Steps on the Gas," March 18, 2015, B4, *The Globe and Mail*, secure.globeadvisor.com/servlet/ArticleNews/story/gam/20150318/RBCDCOUCHETARDDEALFINAL.

51. Ross Marowits, "Air Canada Adopts Poison Pill," *The Globe and Mail*, March 31, 2011, B1.

52. Dana Cimilluca, Jonathan Rockoff, and Anupreeta Das, "Nestlé Wins Pfizer's Baby Food Division," *The Globe and Mail*, April 24, 2012, B11.

53. "Culture of Fun Benefits Clients, Staff," *National Post*, October 27, 2008, FP12.

54. Susan Krashinsky, "Rogers and Wal-Mart to Launch Magazine," *The Globe and Mail*, December 6, 2012, B3.

55. Company fact sheet, Rona Website, www.rona.ca/corporate, accessed March 20, 2015; David Milstead, "Rona Forecast Remains Cloudy Despite Sunny Days Ahead," *The Globe and Mail*, May 24, 2011, B13.

CHAPTER 3

1. Chris MacDonald, "Sweeping Ethics Under the Rug," *Canadian Business*, January 23, 2012, 12.

2. Ronald Ebert and Ricky Griffin, *Business Essentials*, 7th ed. (Upper Saddle River, NJ: Prentice Hall, 2009).

3. Thomas Donaldson and Thomas W. Dunfee, "Toward a Unified Conception of Business Ethics: An Integrative Social Contracts Theory," *Academy of Management Review* 19(2) (1994): 252–284.

4. "Drug Companies Face Assault on Prices," *Wall Street Journal*, May 11, 2000, B1, B4.

5. John Saunders, "Bitter Air Carrier Dogfight Heads to Court," *The Globe and Mail*, July 8, 2004, B3.

6. Andrew Crane, "Spying Doesn't Pay; Intelligence Gathering Is Still an Ethical and Legal Minefield," *National Post*, November 11, 2008, FP12.

7. G. McArthur, "New Corruption Allegations Hit SNC-Lavalin," *The Globe and Mail*, December 19, 2012, B1.

8. Yadullah Hussain, "SNNC-Lavalin Charged with Fraud, Bribery; 'Another Cloud' over SNC's Head," *National Post*, February 20, 2015, FP1.

9. "China Fines Glaxo US$489-Million as Bribery Probe Ends," *National Post*, September 20, 2014, FP7.

10. Joel Schectman and Brent Kendall, "Alstom to Pay $772 Million In Bribery Case," *The Wall Street Journal*, December 23, 2014, B3.

11. Claire Brownell, "Perception of Corruption Grows," *National Post*, June 12, 2014, FP1.

12. Julian Sher, "OECD Slams Canada's Record on Prosecuting Bribery," *The Globe and Mail*, March 28, 2011, B4.

13. Various other models have been proposed. See J. Rest, "Background Theory and Research," in J. Rest and T. Narvaez, eds., *Moral Development in the Professions: Psychology and Applied Ethics* (New Jersey: Lawrence Earlbaum Associates Inc., 1991), 1–26. Also T. Jones, "Ethical Decision Making by Individuals in Organizations: An Issue-Contingent Model," *Academy of Management Review* 16 (1991): 366–395. Rest's model, for example, includes four phases: *moral sensitivity* (awareness that a situation contains a moral issue), *moral judgment* (determining which possible solutions can be morally justified), *moral motivation* (the intention to make a moral decision), and *moral action* (the action the individual takes).

14. Bertrand Marotte, "Victims Unmoved by Fraudster's Courtroom Tears," *The Globe and Mail*, January 16, 2010, A16.

15. These three factors were included as part of a "fraud triangle" (see Donald R. Cressey, *Other People's Money* [Montclair: Patterson Smith, 1973, p. 30]). The factors were originally described in terms of financial fraud carried out by a trusted individual, but the factors can be applied to both financial and non-financial issues.

16. Mark Schwartz, "Heat's On to Get an Effective Code," *The Globe and Mail*, November 27, 1997, B2.

17. Mary Gentile, *Giving Voice to Values* (New Haven: Yale University Press, 2010).

18. Jeffrey S. Harrison and R. Edward Freeman, "Stakeholders, Social Responsibility, and Performance: Empirical Evidence and Theoretical Perspectives," *Academy of Management Journal* 42(5) (1999): 479–485. See also David P. Baron, *Business and Its Environment*, 5th ed. (Upper Saddle River, NJ: Prentice Hall, 2006), ch. 18.

19. "A Wake-up Call for Canadian Consumers," *Winnipeg Free Press*, April 26, 2013, A15.

20. "Parent Company of Victoria's Secret to Probe Claims of Child Labour," *National Post*, December 16, 2011, FP6.

21. Laura Pratt, "Sustainability Reporting," *CGA Magazine*, September/October, 2007, 18–21; also Sharda Prashad, "Good Green Goals," *The Toronto Star*, April 27, 2007, www.thestar.com/printArticle/205855; also Ralph Shaw, "Peak Performance (Mountain Equipment Co-op)," *Alternatives Journal* 31(1) (2005): 19–20.

22. John Lyons, "Skin-Deep Gains for Amazon Tribe," *Wall Street Journal*, May 5, 2011, A1.

23. Jeffrey S. Harrison and R. Edward Freeman, "Stakeholders, Social Responsibility, and Performance: Empirical Evidence and Theoretical Perspectives," *Academy of Management Journal* 42(5) (1999): 479–485. See also David P. Baron, *Business and Its Environment*, 3rd ed. (Upper Saddle River, NJ: Prentice Hall, 2000), Chapter 17.

24. See SROI Canada Website, www.sroi-canada.ca/about/index.html, accessed July 22, 2013; see also SROI Network International Website, www.thesroinetwork.org/publications, accessed July 22, 2013.

25. An idea of the conflicting ideas that exist in this debate can be seen in two articles: Peter Foster, "Milton's Loophole," *National Post*, June 22, 2011, FP15; and Eleanor Vaughan, "Just What Milton Would Have Wanted?" *National Post*, June 24, 2011, FP11.

26. Steve Ladurantaye, "Maple Leaf Battered by Meat Recall Costs," *The Globe and Mail*, October 30, 2008, B3.

27. Nicholas Casey, Nicholas Zamiska, and Andy Pasztor, "Mattel Seeks to Placate China with Apology on Toys," *Wall Street Journal*, September 22–23, 2007, A1, A7.

28. Martin Cash, "Icemaker Facing Heat over Finances," *Winnipeg Free Press*, July 20, 2011, B5.

29. Paul Waldie, "Chocolate Bar Makers Probe over Prices," *The Globe and Mail*, November 28, 2007, B1, B10.

30. Christine Dobby, "Three Gas Retailers Fined in Price Fixing," *National Post*, March 22, 2012, FP4.

31. Brian Milner, "Sausage Sellers Linked to Price-Fixing to Fork Over 338 Million in Penalties," *The Globe and Mail*, July 16, 2014, B8.

32. Jacquie McNish and Jeff Gray, "'Quaint' Canada Called No Match for Price-Fixers," *The Globe and Mail*, January 27, 2010, B11.

33. Jonathan Cheng, "False Ads: Chinese Consumers Awaken to a Western Problem," *Wall Street Journal*, July 8, 2005, B9.

34. Jeanne Whalen and Benoit Faucon, "Counterfeit Cancer Medicines Multiply," *Wall Street Journal*, December 31, 2012, B1.

35. "These Just Won't Fly," *Winnipeg Free Press*, September 1, 2011, B1.

36. Jeff Gray, "Lululemon Cracks Down on Knockoffs," *The Globe and Mail*, July 19, 2014, B4.

37. Carlos Tejada, "China Raps Alibaba for Fakes," *The Wall Street Journal*, January 29, 2015, A1.

38. Louise Watt, "Fake Apple Stores Pop Up in China," *Winnipeg Free Press*, July 22, 2011, B11; also "Apple Hits New York's Fake Stores with Lawsuit," *The Globe and Mail*, August 6, 2011, B2.

39. Melanie Lee, "Blue, Yellow and Fake; China's Penchant for Fake Products Expands to the Whole Brand Experience," *National Post*, August 2, 2011, FP3.

40. Marjo Johne, "Counterfeiting: When Imitation Isn't Flattery: Companies Doing Business Abroad Are Vulnerable to Having Their Brands Knocked Off. Here Are Ways They Can Protect Themselves," *The Globe and Mail*, November 25, 2014, B7.

41. Jeanne Whalen and Benoit Faucon, "Counterfeit Cancer Medicines Multiply," *Wall Street Journal*, December 31, 2012, B1; also Daryl-Lynn Carlson, "The Costly Reality of Fakes," *National Post*, December 5, 2007.

42. Marjo Johne, "Counterfeiting: When Imitation Isn't Flattery: Companies Doing Business Abroad Are Vulnerable to Having Their Brands Knocked Off. Here Are Ways They Can Protect Themselves," *The Globe and Mail*, November 25, 2014, B7.

43. Holly Shaw, "Buzzing Influencers," *National Post*, March 13, 2008, FP12.

44. Tim Barker, "Word-of-Mouth Advertising Grows in Influence, Concern," *Orlando Sentinel*, March 17, 2006, A1, A19.

45. Shona McKay, "Willing and Able," *Report on Business*, October 1991, 58–63.

46. J. Southerst, "In Pursuit of Drugs," *Canadian Transportation*, November 1989, 58–65.

47. Steve Lambert, "Pushing Boundaries: Keeping an Eye on Employees," *The Globe and Mail*, August 20, 2011, B15.

48. Joshua Gallu and Dawn Kopecki, "Whistleblower Awarded Record US$5.1 Million," *National Post*, September 4, 2009, FP3.

49. Brent Jang and Patrick Brethour, "This WestJet Staffer Blew the Whistle on His Employer's Corporate Spying: He's Still Waiting for Someone to Say Thanks," *The Globe and Mail*, October 18, 2006, A1, A12.

50. Cora Daniels, "'It's a Living Hell,'" *Fortune*, April 15, 2002, 367–368.

51. Boyd Erman, "Whistleblower Hotline Opens," *The Globe and Mail*, May 26, 2009, B5.

52. Grant McCool and John Poirier, "Madoff Mess Manoeuvres," *National Post*, December 18, 2008, FP3.

53. Laurel Brubaker Calkins and Andrew Harris, "Stanford Gets 110 Years for Ponzi Scheme," *National Post*, June 15, 2012, FP12.

54. Jeff Gray, "BMO Lawsuit Targets 'Cheque-Kiting' Scheme," *The Globe and Mail*, July 4, 2012, B6.

55. Janet McFarland, "Five Grand Cache Executives Accused of Insider Trading," *The Globe and Mail*, December 9, 2011, B5.

56. David Glovin, Patricia Hurtado, and Bob Van Voris, "Galleon Boss Gets 11-Year Term; Rajaratnam Stays Silent in Facing Prison Time," *National Post*, October 14, 2011, FP1.

57. Joanna Slater, "Biggest Insider-Trading Trial Ends with Guilty Verdict," *The Globe and Mail*, February 7, 2014, B1.

58. Janet McFarland, "Insider Trading 'Pervasive' Before Deals: Study," *The Globe and Mail*, July 15, 2014, B4.

59. Janet McFarland and Jeff Gray, "Insider Trading Cases Prove Difficult," *The Globe and Mail*, September 25, 2014, B6.

60. Laura Calabrese, "Telus Celebration of Giving Donates $46 Million This Year," *National Post*, November 15, 2014, FP2.

61. "AltaGas Puts Stock in Social Value," *National Post*, February 2, 2015, SC5.

62. "Looking Good in Green," *Maclean's*, May 9, 2011, 47.

63. Diane McLaren, "Doing Their Part—with Goals in Mind," *The Globe and Mail*, December 10, 2008, B7.

64. Bruce Owen, "Camp Tim on Its Way," *Winnipeg Free Press*, May 28, 2010, A6.

65. Diana McLaren, "Spirit of Philanthropy Is Thriving," *The Globe and Mail*, December 10, 2008, B7.

66. "Survey Shows Canadian Businesses Engaged in Meeting Community Need," *Canada NewsWire*, February 7, 2008, 1.

67. Neil Reynolds, "The Dirty Truth of China's Energy," *The Globe and Mail*, March 28, 2007, B2.

68. Bill Curry, "Ottawa Wants Kyoto Softened," *The Globe and Mail*, May 12, 2006, A1, A7.

69. Jeffrey Ball, "U.N. Effort to Curtail Emissions in Turmoil," *Wall Street Journal*, April 12–13, 2008, A1, A5.

70. K. Dougherty, "Cap and Trade Comes into Force; Quebec, California," *National Post*, January 2, 2013, FP4.

71. Patricia Adams, "The Next Big Scam," *National Post*, January 13, 2010, FP15.

72. Gabrielle Bauer, "The Future of Energy: Alternative," *Canadian Business* 87(9) (September 2014), 56.

73. Lauren Etter, "For Icy Greenland, Global Warming Has a Bright Side," *Wall Street Journal*, July 18, 2006, A1, A12.

74. "Going Green Losing Its Shine Among World's Citizens: Poll," *Winnipeg Free Press*, November 28, 2008, A20.

75. "Syncrude Guilty in Duck Deaths," *Winnipeg Free Press*, June 26, 2010, A10; also Tim Shufelt, "Trial Goes Far Beyond Ducks," *National Post*, March 19, 2010, FP1.

76. Brian Morton, "Green Practices Are Both Right and Profitable," *National Post*, June 11, 2012, FP8.

77. Elisa Birnbaum, "Banking on Recycling," *National Post*, February 17, 2015, FP6.

78. Egle Procuta, "One Man's Garbage Is Another's Gold," *The Globe and Mail*, April 11, 2006, B7.

79. Geoffrey Scotton, "Cleanups Can Hurt, Companies Warned," *Financial Post*, June 25, 1991, 4.

80. Marc Huber, "A Double-Edged Endorsement," *Canadian Business*, January 1990, 69–71.

81. Daniel Machalaba, "As Old Pallets Pile Up, Critics Hammer Them as New Eco-Menace," *Wall Street Journal*, April 1, 1998, A1.

82. Claudia Cattaneo, "Talisman Braces for Jungle Standoff: Threats of Violence," *National Post*, November 14, 2008, FP1.

83. Emily Steel, "Nestlé Takes a Beating on Social Media Sites," *Wall Street Journal*, March 29, 2010, B5.

84. Daniel Stoffman, "Good Behaviour and the Bottom Line," *Canadian Business*, May 1991, 28–32.

85. Sandra Waddock and Neil Smith, "Corporate Responsibility Audits: Doing Well by Doing Good," *Sloan Management Review*, (Winter 2000): 75–85.

86. Derek Sankey, "Green Careers Available in Every Sector," *National Post*, November 7, 2012, FP11.

87. Marjo Johne, "Sustainability Performance a New Essential," *The Globe and Mail*, May 19, 2011, B8.

88. "Looking Good in Green," *Maclean's*, May 9, 2011, 47.

89. Alison Arnot, "The Triple Bottom Line," *CGA Magazine*, January/February 2004, 27–32.

90. Richard Blackwell, "The Double-Edged Sword of Corporate Altruism," *The Globe and Mail*, November 10, 2008, B5.

91. "Global 100 Most Sustainable Corporations 2015," www.rankingthebrands.com/The-Brand-Rankings.aspx?rankingID=107&year=895.

92. "Mega Brands Wins Case over Lego," *The Globe and Mail*, November 13, 2008, B3.

93. Canadian Intellectual Patent Office (CIPO) Website, www.cipo.ic.gc.ca/eic/site/cipointernet-internetopic.nsf/eng/Home, accessed April 25, 2010; Canadian Western Diversification Canada Website, www.wd.gc.ca/eng/7133.asp, accessed April 25, 2010.

94. Paul Waldie, "How RIM's Big Deal Was Done," *The Globe and Mail*, March 6, 2006, B1, B14.

95. *The Globe and Mail* Website, "Judge Rules for RIM in Patent Dispute," February 3, 2010, www.theglobeandmail.com, accessed April 25, 2010.

96. Avery Johnson, "Pfizer Buys More Time for Lipitor," *Wall Street Journal*, June 19, 2008, B1.

97. "Google to Pay US$125 Million to Settle Copyright Lawsuits Over Book Project," *National Post*, October 29, 2008, FP6.

CHAPTER 4

1. "Oh, to Be Young, and An Entrepreneur," *USA Today*, February 8, 2013, 8B.

2. David Parkinson, "Growing Self-Employed Muddies Canadian Labour Picture," *The Globe and Mail*, February 12, 2015, B2; Statistics Canada Website, www.statcan.gc.ca/pub/71-001-x/2015001/part-partie1-eng.htm, accessed February 21, 2015.

3. "Business Dynamics in Canada," Statistics Canada Website, Catalogue No. 61-534-XIE (Ottawa: Minister of Industry, 2006).

4. P.D. Reynolds, S.M. Camp, W.D. Bygrave, E. Autio, and M. Hay, *Global Entrepreneurship Monitor: 2001 Executive Report* (Kansas City, MO: Kauffman Center for Entrepreneurial Leadership, 2001); P.D. Reynolds, M. Hay, W.D. Bygrave, S.M. Camp, and E. Autio, *Global Entrepreneurship Monitor: 2000 Executive Report* (Kansas City, MO: Kauffman Center for Entrepreneurial Leadership, 2000).

5. Industry Canada, *Key Small Business Statistics.* (Ottawa: Public Works and Government Services Canada, 2006), 24.

6. Industry Canada, *Labor Force Information*, www.statcan.gc.ca/pub/71-001-x/2014012/t002-eng.pdf, accessed February 1, 2015.

7. Industry Canada, *Key Small Business Statistics*, (August 2013), www.ic.gc.ca/eic/site/061.nsf/eng/02812.html, accessed January 5, 2015.

8. "Best Small and Medium Sized Employers in Canada," www.aon.com/canada/attachments/human-capital-consulting/news_aon_BSME-2015EN.pdf, accessed January 5, 2015.

9. Nancy M. Carter, William B. Gartner, and Paul D. Reynolds, "Firm Founding," in W.B. Gartner, K.G. Shaver, N.M. Carter, and P.D. Reynolds, eds., *Handbook of Entrepreneurial Dynamics: The Process of Business Creation* (Thousand Oaks, CA: Sage, 2004), 311–323.

10. William D. Bygrave and C.W. Hofer, "Theorizing About Entrepreneurship," *Entrepreneurship Theory and Practice* 16(2) (Winter 1991): 14; Donald Sexton and Nancy Bowman-Upton, *Entrepreneurship: Creativity and Growth* (New York: Macmillan, 1991), 7.

11. Jim Edwards, "'Facebook Inc.' Actually Has 2.2 Billion Users Now—Roughly One Third of the Entire Population of Earth," July 24, 2014, www.businessinsider.com/facebook-inc-has-22-billion-users-2014-7#ixzz3QWVFZTXf, accessed February 1, 2015.

12. Roy MacGregor, "Kicking Horse: Brewing a Small Town Success," *The Globe and Mail*, September 20, 2014, B4.

13. Heritage Foundation Index of Economic Freedom Website, www.heritage.org/index/ranking, accessed February 1, 2015.

14. Angela Dale, "Self-Employment and Entrepreneurship: Notes on Two Problematic Concepts," in Roger Burrows, ed., *Deciphering the Enterprise Culture* (London: Routledge, 1991), 45, 48; Holt 1992, 11.

15. Donald Sexton and Nancy Bowman-Upton, *Entrepreneurship: Creativity and Growth* (New York: Macmillan, 1991), 11; Kao, 1991, 21.

16. Allan A. Gibb, "The Enterprise Culture and Education: Understanding Enterprise Education and Its Links with Small Business, Entrepreneurship and Wider Educational Goals," *International Small Business Journal* 11(3) (1993): 13–34; Donald Sexton and Nancy Bowman-Upton, *Entrepreneurship: Creativity and Growth* (New York: Macmillan, 1991).

17. Chitra Anand, "Act Like a Startup: Telus Nurtures the Intrapreneurial Spirit," *The Globe and Mail*, January 15, 2015, B3.

18. Industry Canada, Small Business Research and Policy, *Key Small Business Statistics*, Table 2 (August 2013), www.ic.gc.ca/eic/site/061.nsf/eng/02804.html, accessed February 1, 2015.

19. Ibid.

20. Statistics Canada Website, "Employment by Class of Worker and Industry," www.statcan.gc.ca/pub/71-001-x/2014012/t002-eng.pdf, accessed February 1, 2015.

21. Industry Canada, Small Business Research and Policy, *Key Small Business Statistics* (Ottawa: Public Works and Government Services Canada, August 2013), www.ic.gc.ca/eic/site/061.nsf/eng/02805.html, accessed February 2, 2015.

22. Industry Canada, Small Business Research and Policy, *Key Small Business Statistics* (Ottawa: Public Works and Government Services Canada, August 2013), 10.

23. Lauren McKeon, "Tied to Home," *Canadian Business*, April 14, 2008, 33.

24. Women of Influence, RBC Female Entrepreneur Awards, www.womenofinfluence.ca/rbc-cwea-2014/Baby, accessed February 2, 2015.

25. Roma Luciw, "Stay-at-Home Moms Stay the Business Course," *The Globe and Mail*, March 3, 2007, B10.

26. "Canadian Small Business Week, 2011 Young Entrepreneur Awards," *BDC Newsletter*, P8.

27. Donald F. Kuratko and Richard M. Hodgetts, *Entrepreneurship: Theory, Process, Practice*, 7th ed. (Mason, OH: Thomson South-Western, 2007), 118–125; John A. Hornday, "Research About Living Entrepreneurs," in *Encyclopedia of Entrepreneurship*, Calvin Kent, Donald Sexton, and Karl Vesper, eds. (Englewood Cliffs, NJ: Prentice Hall, 1982), 26–27; Jeffry A. Timmons and Stephen Spinelli, *New Venture Creation: Entrepreneurship for the 21st Century* (Boston: McGraw-Hill Irwin, 2007), 9.

28. J.D. Kyle, R. Blais, R. Blatt, and A.J. Szonyi, "The Culture of the Entrepreneur: Fact or Fiction," *Journal of Small Business and Entrepreneurship*, 1991: 3–14.

29. R.H. Brockhaus and Pam S. Horwitz, "The Psychology of the Entrepreneur," in *The Art and Science of Entrepreneurship*, D.L. Sexton and Raymond W. Smilor, eds. (Cambridge, MA: Ballinger, 1986); William B. Gartner, "What Are We Talking About When We Talk About Entrepreneurship?" *Journal of Business Venturing* 5(1) (1990): 15–29; Allan A. Gibb, "The Enterprise Culture and Education: Understanding Enterprise Education and Its Links with Small Business, Entrepreneurship and Wider Educational Goals," *International Small Business Journal* 11(3) (1993): 13–34; J.C. Mitchell, "Case and Situation Analysis," *Sociological Review* 31(2) (1983): 187–211.

30. Donald Sexton and Nancy Bowman-Upton, *Entrepreneurship: Creativity and Growth* (New York: Macmillan, 1991); Karl H. Vesper, *New Venture Strategies* (Englewood Cliffs, NJ: Prentice Hall, 1990); W.D. Bygrave and C.W. Hofer, "Theorizing About Entrepreneurship," *Entrepreneurship Theory and Practice* 16(2) (Winter 1991): 14.

31. Lizette Chapman, "'Pivoting' Pays Off for Tech Entrepreneurs," *The Globe and Mail*, April, 26, 2012, B11.

32. Walter Good, *Building a Dream* (Toronto: McGraw-Hill Ryerson, 1998), 40.

33. Wayne A. Long and W. Ed McMullan, *Developing New Ventures* (San Diego: Harcourt Brace Jovanovich, 1990), 374–375.

34. Polar Mobile Website, polar.me/customers#customers, accessed February 15, 2015; May Jeong, "Fast-Growing Apps Developer Polar Mobile Looks East," *The Globe and Mail*, August 24, 2011, B4; Omar El Akkad, "Nokia Picks Polar to Build 300 Mobile Apps," *The Globe and Mail*, August 27, 2011, B3.

35. Michael E. Porter, "Know Your Place," *Inc.* 13(9) (September 1992): 90–93.

36. Invivo Website, www.invivocorp.com/SentinellebyInvivo.php, accessed February 15, 2015; Rasha Mourtada, "Tested to the Limit," *The Globe and Mail*, April 14, 2009, B4.

37. Howard H. Stevenson, H. Irving Grousbeck, Michael J. Roberts, and Amarnath Bhide, *New Business Ventures and the Entrepreneur* (Boston: Irwin McGraw-Hill, 1999), 19.

38. Ibid., 21.

39. Marc J. Dollinger, *Entrepreneurship: Strategies and Resources* (Upper Saddle River, NJ: Prentice Hall, 1999), 94–101.

40. Thomas W. Zimmerer and Norman M. Scarborough, *Essentials of Entrepreneurship and Small Business Management*, 4th ed. (Upper Saddle River, NJ: Pearson Prentice Hall), 359.

41. Michael E. Porter, "Know Your Place," *Inc.* 13(9) (September 1992): 90–93.

42. Gordon Pitts, "Two Deals, $1 Billion and 50 Millionaires," *The Globe and Mail*, October, 17, 2011, B1, B6; Quentin Casey, "Moncton CEO Named Top Angel Investor," *Telegraph-Journal*, January, 30, 2013.

43. Shane Dingman, "Who Needs Silicon Valley? Canadian Startups Scoring Bigger Deals," *The Globe and Mail*, February 10, 2015, B1; Canada's Venture Capital and Private Equity Website, news.cvca.ca, accessed February 15, 2015.

44. Regus Website, www.regus.ca, accessed February 15, 2015]; Wallace Immen, "Co-work Spaces Help Businesses Blossom," *The Globe and Mail*, June 18, 2011, B21.

45. Business Development Bank of Canada Website, www.bdc.ca, accessed February 15, 2015.

46. Humaira Irshad, Alberta Agriculture and Rural Development, "Business Incubation in Canada," June 2014, www1.agric.gov.ab.ca, accessed December 29, 2014; Canadian Association of Business Incubation Website, www.cabi.ca/docs/Incubators-in-Canada.pdf, accessed March 30, 2013.

47. Karl H. Vesper, *New Venture Mechanics* (Englewood Cliffs, NJ: Prentice Hall, 1993), 105.

48. Jeffry A. Timmons, *New Venture Creation* (Boston: Irwin McGraw-Hill, 1999), 277.

49. George Anders, Carol Hymowitz, Joann Lublin, and Don Clark, "All in the Family," *Wall Street Journal*, August 1, 2005, B1, B4.

50. Harvey Schacter, "Honey, You're Fired," *The Globe and Mail*, October 18, 2010, E5.

51. Kal Tire website, info.kaltire.com, accessed February 15, 2015; Tom Maloney, "Burnin' Rubber," *Report on Business*, December 2014, P32–33.

52. Canadian Franchise Association Website, www.cfa.ca/tools_resources/franchise-research-facts, accessed February 15, 2015.

53. Anita Elash, "Frogbox Needs a Plan to Jump into the US Market," *The Globe and Mail*, June 15, 2011, B17.

54. Tony Wilson, "Legal Advice on Starting a Franchise," *The Globe and Mail*, March 16, 2010.

55. Julie Jargon, "Burger King Franchisees Begrudge Coaching," *The Globe and Mail*, October 27, 2014, B4.

56. Cara Website, www.carafranchising.com/harveys/investment-options/harveys-2200-sq-ft.html, accessed February 15, 2015.

57. Tony Wilson, "A Hodge-Podge Mix of Provincial Franchise Laws Cries Out for a Fix," *The Globe and Mail*, October 19, 2011, E10.

58. Industry Canada, Small Business Research and Policy, *Key Small Business Statistics* (Ottawa: Public Works and Government Services Canada, July 2012), 3.

59. Kevin Marron, "Want to Succeed? Read This," *The Globe and Mail*, October 19, 2005, E1, E5. Several excellent articles on starting and operating a small business are found in Section E, "Report on Small Business," in The *Globe and Mail*, October 19, 2005.

60. See Norman M. Scarborough and Thomas W. Zimmerer, *Effective Small Business Management: An Entrepreneurial Approach*, 7th ed. (Upper Saddle River, NJ: Prentice Hall, 2003).

61. "Canada's 100 Biggest Companies by Revenue in 2014," *The Globe and Mail*, June 27, 2014.

62. "Board Games 2014: The Best and Worst Governed Companies in Canada," *The Globe and Mail*, November 23, 2014.

63. Advisor.ca Website, "IPO Market Triumphed in 2014," January 5, 2015, www.advisor.ca/news/industry-news/ipo-market-triumphed-in-2014-172429, accessed February 20, 2015.

64. Terry Pedwell, "Income Trusts Face Tough Rules," *Winnipeg Free Press*, November 1, 2006, B7.

65. Marzena Czarnecka, "Income Trusts Are Back," *Canadian Business*, December 8, 2012.

66. "An Overview of Available Business Structures," www.umanitoba.ca/afs/agric_economics/MRAC/structures.html#Cooperatives, accessed July 22, 2013.

CHAPTER 5

1. World Trade Organization Website, www.wto.org/english/res_e/statis_e/statis_bis_e.htm?solution=WTO&path=/Dashboards/MAPS&file=Map.wcdf&bookmarkState={%22impl%22:%22client%22,%22params%22:{%22langParam%22:%22en%22}}, accessed April 26, 2015.

2. "Best Buy, Home Depot Find China Market a Tough Sell," *USA Today*, February 23, 2011, 5B.

3. Peter Wonascott, "U.S. Takes Notice of China's Expanding Ties to Africa," *The Globe and Mail*, September 2, 2011, B9.

4. John W. Miller and Marcus Walker, "China Passes Germany as Top Exporter," *The Globe and Mail*, January 6, 2010, B8.

5. World Bank website, data.worldbank.org/about/country-and-lending-groups#Low_income, accessed April 26, 2015; Ricky Griffin and Michael W. Pustay, *International Business: A Managerial Perspective*, 5th ed. (Upper Saddle River, NJ: Prentice Hall, 2007).

6. Thomas Friedman, *The World Is Flat* (New York: Farrar, Straus, and Giroux, 2005).

7. "World's Largest Economies," CNN Monet Website, money.cnn.com/news/economy/world_economies_gdp, accessed May 3, 2015.

8. Paul Brent, "A Few BRICS Short of a Load," *Canadian Business*, November 23, 2009, 21; Courtland L. Bovee, John V. Thill, and George Dracopoulos, *Business in Action*, 2nd Canadian ed. (New York: Pearson Education, 2008), ch. 2; Shirley Won, "BRIC May Cure Any Resource Sector Ills," *The Globe and Mail*, November 22, 2007, B17; Andrew Mills, "The Face of Brazil's Ascent," *The Globe and Mail*, March 12 2010, B11.

9. Tom Krishner, "Indian Car Maker May Land Jaguar, Land Rover," *The Globe and Mail*, January 4, 2008, B3.

10. *The Guardian* Website, www.guardian.co.uk/world/2011/apr/19/south-africa-joins-bric-club, accessed September 10, 2011.

11. Jeffrey T. Lewis, "BRICS Put Money Behind Their Rhetoric," *The Globe and Mail*, July 16, 2014, B9.

12. Dominic Barton, "A $30-Trillion Opportunity," *Canadian Business*, November 15, 2012, P25.

13. Ricky W. Griffin and Michael W. Pustay, *International Business: A Managerial Perspective*, 2nd ed. (Reading, MA: Addison-Wesley, 1999), ch. 3; Dominick Salvatore, *International Economics*, 6th ed. (Upper Saddle River, NJ: Prentice Hall, 1998), 27–33; Karl E. Case and Ray C. Fair, *Principles of Economics*, 5th ed. (Upper Saddle River, NJ: Prentice Hall, 1999), 813–817.

14. John J Wild, Kenneth L. Wild, and Jerry C. Han, *International Business: The Challenges of Globalization*, 4th ed. (Upper Saddle River, NJ: Prentice Hall, 2008), 159–160.

15. Dexter Roberts. "Made in Cambodia—For Now," *Bloomberg Businessweek*, January 16–22, 2012, 16.

16. Syed Zain Al-Mahmood, "Bangladesh Garment Plants Still Hazardous," *The Globe and Mail*, October 15, 2014, B9.

17. This section is based on Michael Porter, *The Competitive Advantage of Nations* (Boston: Harvard Business School Press, 1990), chs. 3 and 4; Warren J. Keegan, *Global Marketing Management*, 6th ed. (Upper Saddle River, NJ: Prentice Hall, 1999), 312–321; John J. Wild, Kenneth L. Wild, and Jerry C.Y. Han, *International Business: An Integrated Approach* (Upper Saddle River, NJ: Prentice Hall, 2000), 175–178.

18. World Economic Forum website, Global Competitiveness Report, www3.weforum.org/docs/WEF_GlobalCompetitivenessReport_2014-15.pdf, accessed May 3, 2015.

19. Bank of Canada, Banking and Financial Statistics, Series J2, Canadian Balance of Payments, January 2011, S116–S117; Table 5.1: Statistics Canada Website, www.statcan.gc.ca/tables-tableaux/sum-som/l01/cst01/gblec02a-eng.htm, accessed April 14, 2013.

20. Statistics Canada Website, www.statcan.gc.ca/tables-tableaux/sum-som/l01/cst01/gblec02a-eng.htm, accessed May 3, 2015.

21. Statistics Canada Website, www.statcan.gc.ca/tables-tableaux/sum-som/l01/cst01/econ01a-eng.htm, accessed May 3, 2015.

22. Karl E. Case and Ray C. Fair, *Principles of Economics*, 5th ed. (Upper Saddle River, NJ: Prentice Hall, 1999), 818–821.

23. Gordon Pitts, "How Captain High Liner Beat the Dollar Odds," *The Globe and Mail*, March 16, 2010, B1–B4.

24. Geoffrey York, "McCain Laying Down Its Chips on African Strategy," *The Globe and Mail*, December 22, 2009, B3.

25. Carolyne Wheeler, "Yum Brands' Recipe for Fast-Food Success in China? Adapt to Local Tastes," *The Globe and Mail*, May 11, 2011, B5.

26. Yum Brands Financial Report, www.yum.com/investors/restcounts.asp, accessed May 4, 2015; Dianne Brady, "Yum's Big Game of Chicken," *Bloomberg Businessweek*, March 29, 2012, 63–69.

27. Barrie McKenna, "Rise as Auto-Parts Power Reflects New Manufacturing Edge," *Wall Street Journal*, August 1, 2006, A1, A6.

28. Nick Rockel, "B.C. Caviar Farmer Takes Over Where Russia Left Off," *The Globe and Mail*, February 11, 2015, B9.

29. The Hershey Company Website, www.thehersheycompany.com/about-hershey.aspx, accessed May 4, 2015.

30. Ray August, *International Business Law: Text, Cases, and Readings*, 3rd ed. (Upper Saddle River, NJ: Prentice Hall, 2000), 192–197.

31. Fortune 500 Website, Global500 Rankings 2014, fortune.com/global500/wal-mart-stores-1, accessed May 4, 2015.

32. Warren J. Keegan, *Global Marketing Management*, 6th ed. (Upper Saddle River, NJ: Prentice Hall, 1999), 290–292; Ricky W. Griffin and Michael W. Pustay, *International Business: A Managerial Perspective*, 2nd ed. (Reading, MA: Addison-Wesley, 1999), 427–431; John J. Wild, Kenneth L. Wild, and Jerry C.Y. Han, *International Business: An Integrated Approach* (Upper Saddle River, NJ: Prentice Hall, 2000), 454–456.

33. Ricky W. Griffin and Michael W. Pustay, *International Business: A Managerial Perspective*, 2nd ed. (Reading, MA: Addison-Wesley, 1999), 431–433; John J. Wild, Kenneth L. Wild, and Jerry C.Y. Han, *International Business: An Integrated Approach* (Upper Saddle River, NJ: Prentice Hall, 2000), 456–458.

34. Shirley Won, "Small Firms Beating a Path to the Middle Kingdom," *The Globe and Mail*, August 31, 2004, B7.

35. James R. Haggerty, "Whirlpool Strikes Deal to Boost Chinese Market Share," *Wall Street Journal*, March 20, 2012, B7.

36. John J. Wild, Kenneth L. Wild, and Jerry C.Y. Han, *International Business: An Integrated Approach* (Upper Saddle River, NJ: Prentice Hall, 2000), ch. 7; Ricky W. Griffin and Michael W. Pustay, *International Business: A Managerial Perspective*, 2nd ed. (Reading, MA: Addison-Wesley, 1999), 436–439.

37. Ross Marowits, "Bombardier Looking to Morocco for Production," *The Globe and Mail*, May 7, 2011, B8; Bombardier Website, www.bombardier.ca/en/corporate/media-centre/press-releases/details?docID=0901260d8029499b, accessed April 14, 2013.

38. Tim Kiladze, "RBC Turns to U.S. in Quest for Growth," *The Globe and Mail*, January 23, 2015, B1.

39. Dawn Calleja, "Foreign Investment: Opportunity + Danger," *The Globe and Mail*, March 28, 2013, B6.

40. Marcus Gee, "Green Hats and Other Ways to Blow a Deal in China," *The Globe and Mail*, August 27, 2007, B1.

41. Elizabeth Holmes, "The Return of the Luxe Life," *The Globe and Mail*, May 4, 2011, B17.

42. Marina Strauss, "Retailers Warn of Price Hikes as Ottawa Boosts Tariffs," *The Globe and Mail*, March 23, 2013, B1–B5.

43. Barrie McKenna, "In a Bureaucratic Box: Cardboard, Cheetos and the Canadian Border," *The Globe and Mail*, January 10, 2013, B1–B4.

44. Ronald Ebert and Ricky Griffin, *Business Essentials*, 7th ed. (Upper Saddle River, NJ: Prentice Hall, 2009).

45. Richard Blackwell, "Free Trade Abroad But Not at Home?" *The Globe and Mail*, April 25, 2013, B4.

46. Gary McWilliams, "Wal-Mart Era Wanes amid Big Shifts in Retail," *Wall Street Journal*, October 3, 2007, A1, A17.

47. Brian Womack and Sara Forden, "Google to Pay $500 Million in Settlement over Online Drug Ads," *The Globe and Mail*, August 25, 2011, B1.

48. Christopher Curtis, "SNC-Lavalin Paid $160-Million in Libyan Bribes, RCMP Says," *Montreal Gazette*, March 6, 2013.

49. Nicholas Bray, "OECD Ministers Agree to Ban Bribery as Means for Companies to Win Business," *Wall Street Journal*, May 27, 1997, A2.

50. Transparency International Website, www.transparency.org/cpi2014/results, accessed May 4, 2015.

51. Tim Treadgold, "Wave Goodbye to Another Commodity Cartel as Potash Goes the Way of Oil," *Forbes*, March 10, 2015.

52. Canadian Press, "China Decries U.S. Duties on Steel Pipes," *The Globe and Mail*, January 1, 2010, B4.

53. Peter Wonacott, "Downturn Heightens China–India Tension on Trade," *Wall Street Journal*, March 20, 2009, A8.

54. Ibid.

55. "New Global Trade Regulator Starts Operations Tomorrow," *Winnipeg Free Press*, December 31, 1994, A5.

56. Barrie McKenna, "Boeing's WTO Win May Prove a Hollow Victory," *The Globe and Mail*, September 5, 2009, B5.

57. Barrie McKenna, "Aspiring WTO Head Warns Organization Risks Irrelevancy," *The Globe and Mail*, March 28, 2013, B12.

58. Europa Website, europa.eu/index_en.htm, accessed May 1, 2015.

59. Bruce Little, "Free-Trade Pact Gets Mixed Reviews," *The Globe and Mail*, June 7, 2004, B3.

60. Greg Keenan, "Mexico Races as Canada Stalls," *The Globe and Mail*, February 10, 2015, B1.

61. Rachel Pulfer, "NAFTA's Third Amigo," *Canadian Business*, June 15, 2009, 27.

62. Barrie McKenna, "Putting Canada–Mexico Trade in High Gear," *The Globe and Mail*, June 16, 2011, B12.

CHAPTER 6

1. Chris Knight, "McDonald's New Recipe for Success; The Golden Arches Has Fought Its Way Back, Not with the Burger, but with Coffee, Snack Wraps, and a Restaurant Facelift," *National Post*, September 5, 2009, FP1.
2. John Heinzl, "Why I've Lost My Appetite for McDonald's," *The Globe and Mail*, December 17, 2014, B8.
3. Peter Burrows, "The Hottest Property in the Valley?" *Business Week*, August 30, 1999, 69–74.
4. Ben Worthen, "CEO Whitman Tells H-Ps Workers 'Everything Is on Table' in Overhaul," *Wall Street Journal*, March 22, 2012, B7; "Hewlett Packard Reorganizes Under Onslaught from Mobile Devices," *National Post*, March 21, 2012, FP6.
5. Gary Hamel and C.K. Prahalad, "Competing for the Future," *Harvard Business Review*, July/August 1994: 122–128; also Joseph M. Hall and M. Eric Johnson, "When Should a Process Be Art, Not Science?" *Harvard Business Review*, March 2009: 58–65.
6. Drew Hasselback, "Overtime at Issue in Class Rulings," *National* Post, June 27, 2012, FP14.
7. Alex Taylor III, "How a Top Boss Manages His Day," *Fortune*, June 19, 1989, 95–100.
8. Richard Blackwell, "Co-Presidents," *The Globe and Mail*, July 17, 2014, B6.
9. Dan Ovsey, "Will Anyone Repair the C-Suite Brand?" *National Post*, March 13, 2012, FP7.
10. Leah Eichler, "Hey, CEOs, Social Media Is Watching You," *The Globe and Mail*, September 13, 2014, B15.
11. Henry Mintzberg, *The Nature of Managerial Work* (New York: Harper and Row, 1973).
12. Roma Luciw, "No. 1 Employee Not Always Your No. 1 Manager," *The Globe and Mail*, February 17, 2007, B10.
13. Adam Bryant, "Quest to Build a Better Boss: Google Looks at What Makes a Good Manager," *National Post*, March 16, 2011, FP12.
14. Cody Gault, "What It Takes to Be a CEO: Increasingly Those Who Hone Their Soft Skills Beyond Their Hard Skills Are in Demand," *National Post*, March 24, 2015, FP6.
15. "Hands-On from the Top Down: ING Direct," *National Post*, February 3, 2012, JV3.
16. The experiences of these and other bosses are depicted in the CBS television series *Undercover Boss*, which premiered in 2010. CEOs work with entry-level employees (who don't know they are working with the CEO). The program summarizes the lessons the CEOs learned. In 2012, a Canadian edition began on the W network. Another series, the "Big Switcheroo" on CBC, portrays situations where bosses trade jobs with lower-level workers.
17. "Executive Compensation: Canada's 100 Top-Paid CEOs," *The Globe and Mail*, www.theglobeandmail.com/report-on-business/careers/management/executive-compensation/executive-compensation-2014/article18721871.
18. Jerry Useem, "Boeing vs. Boeing," *Fortune*, October 2, 2000, 148–160; "Airbus Prepares to 'Bet the Company' as It Builds a Huge New Jet," *Wall Street Journal*, November 3, 1999, A1, A10.
19. Jon Ostrower, "FAA: 787 Can't Return Until Fire Risks Fixed," *The Wall Street Journal*, February 23–24, 2013, B3.
20. "Office Politics Seen as Key to Advancing," *The Globe and Mail*, March 2, 2012, B15.
21. Charles P. Wallace, "Adidas—Back in the Game," *Fortune*, August 18, 1997, 176–182.
22. Barry M. Staw and Jerry Ross, "Good Money After Bad," *Psychology Today*, February 1988, 30–33.
23. Gerry McNamara and Philip Bromiley, "Risk and Return in Organizational Decision Making," *Academy of Management Journal* 42 (1999): 330–339.
24. Brian O'Reilly, "What It Takes to Start a Startup," *Fortune*, June 7, 1999, 135–140.
25. Brent Jang, "WestJet Sets Sights on Air Canada's Title," *The Globe and Mail*, January 2, 2012, B1.
26. Nick Rockel, "Keeping the Containers Moving," *The Globe and Mail*, November 15, 2011, B15.
27. Sue Shellenbarger, "Making Kids Work on Goals (and Not Just Soccer)," *Wall Street Journal*, March 9, 2011, D1.
28. "Sony CEO Wields Ax, Sets Turnaround Targets," *BNN*, April 12, 2012.
29. Joanna Pachner, "A Perfect Predator," *Canadian Business*, July 20–August 16, 2010, 51.
30. Sinclair Stewart and Derek DeCloet, "It's Mr. Focus v. Mr. Diversification," *The Globe and Mail*, June 3, 2006, B4.
31. Jon Ostrower and Paul Vieira, "Bigger Proves Far from Better for Canadian Jet Maker," *The Wall Street Journal*, January 9, 2015, A1.
32. "Maple Leaf Rolls Out New Five-Year Plan," *National Post*, October 7, 2010, FP6.
33. Brenda Bouw, "Bauer's 'Game Changer' Growth Strategy," *The Globe and Mail*, February 25, 2014, B15.
34. Martin Mittelstaedt, "A Conflicting Moment for Kodak," *The Globe and Mail*, May 24, 2011, B13.
35. For an analysis of this interesting situation, see Hollie Shaw, "The Assault on Target," *National Post*, January 17, 2015, FP1; also Hollie Shaw, "A Case Study of What Not to Do," *National Post*, January 16, 2015, FP1.
36. Michael Porter, *Competitive Strategy: Techniques for Analyzing Industries and Competitors* (New York: The Free Press, 1980).
37. Bertrand Marotte, "Gildan Takes T-Shirt Making to the Cutting-Edge of Casual Apparel," *The Globe and Mail*, July 3, 2004, B3.
38. Brent Jang, "Pearson Strives for Better Preparation," *The Globe and Mail*, January 11, 2014, B6.
39. "Hands-On from the Top Down; ING Direct," *National Post*, February 3, 2012, JV3.
40. Chrystia Freeland, "Americans Struggle to Adjust to New Culture of 'No,'" *The Globe and Mail*, November 26, 2010, B2.
41. Ric Dolphin, "Magna Force," *Canadian Business*, May, 1988.
42. Josh O'Kane, "Inside MEC's Modern, Woodsy HQ: Mountain Equipment Co-op's Vancouver Headquarters Harnesses the Company's 'Bring-It' Culture," *The Globe and Mail*, March 31, 2015, B8.
43. Derek Sankey, "Cult-Like Culture Is Key," *Financial Post*, July 28, 2008, www.nationalpost.com/story-printer.html?id=684225.
44. Waterstone Human Capital Website, "2014 National Winners," www.waterstonehc.com/cmac/about-canadas-10/2011-national-and-regional-winners.
45. Calvin Leung, "Culture Club," *Canadian Business*, October 9–22, 2006, 115.
46. "Golden Rule Is Measure of Success: 10 Most Admired Corporate Cultures," *National Post*, December 3, 2008, FP16; Calvin Leung, "Culture Club," *Canadian Business*, October 9–22, 2006, 115, 116, 118, 120.
47. Tom Krisher and Dee-Ann Durbin, "Nobody Took Responsibility," *Winnipeg Free Press*, June 6, 2014, B9.
48. Meagan Fitzpatrick, "RCMP 'Horribly Broken,' Need Fix Quickly: Report," *Winnipeg Free Press*, June 16, 2007, A9.

CHAPTER 7

1. Tim Kiladze and Iain Marlow, "RIM Shakeup Gets Chilly Welcome," *The Globe and Mail*, January 24, 2012, B1.
2. John A. Wagner and John R. Hollenbeck, *Management of Organizational Behavior* (Englewood Cliffs, NJ: Prentice Hall, 1992), 563–565.
3. Jay Diamond and Gerald Pintel, *Retailing*, 6th ed. (Upper Saddle River, NJ: Prentice Hall, 1996), 83–84.
4. "Lowe's Restructures Its Store and Merchandising Organizations," *National Post*, August 30, 2011, FP5.
5. Ibid.
6. "Nike Redefines Its Regions amid Spending Pullback," *The Globe and Mail*, March 21, 2009, B7.
7. Roger Martin, "Don't Ask, Don't Tell," *The Globe and Mail*, July 22, 2012, A15.
8. Interview with Jamie Brown, CEO of Frantic Films.
9. Tom Randall, "Kindler Quits as Pfizer CEO Before Special Meeting," *National Post*, December 7, 2010, FP2.
10. Michael E. Raynor and Joseph L. Bower, "Lead from the Center," *Harvard Business Review*, May 2001, 93–102.
11. Bruce Horovitz, "Restoring the Golden-Arch Shine," *USA Today*, June 16, 1999, 3B.
12. *Hoover's Handbook of American Business 2006* (Austin, TX: Hoover's Business Press, 2006); Brian Dumaine, "How I Delivered the Goods," *Fortune Small Business*, October 2002.
13. Donna Fenn, "The Buyers," *Inc.* (June 1996): 46–48+.
14. Mitchell Osak, "Customers Always Know Best; Customer Innovation Centres are Designed to Break Down Organizational and Functional Silos," *National Post*, September 7, 2010, FP5.
15. Interviews with Jamie Brown, CEO of Frantic Films.
16. Nelson Wyatt, "Bell Canada Plan Creates 3 Divisions," *The Winnipeg Free Press*, May 8, 2003, B7.
17. "Yahoo Adopts New Structure in Search for Revival Following Layoffs," *National Post*, April 11, 2012, FP5.
18. J. Galbraith, "Matrix Organization Designs: How to Combine Functional and Project Forms," *Business Horizons*, 1971: 29–40; H.F. Kolodny, "Evolution to a Matrix Organization," *Academy of Management Review* 4 (1979): 543–553.
19. Interview with Tom Ward, operations manager for Genstar Shipyards.
20. Diane Brady, "Martha Inc.," *Businessweek*, January 17, 2000, 62–66.
21. Miguel Helft, "Yahoo Chief Rearranges Managers Once Again," *New York Times*, February 27, 2009, B5.
22. Gail Edmondson, "Danone Hits Its Stride," *Businessweek*, February 1, 1999, 52–53.
23. Thomas A. Stewart, "See Jack. See Jack Run," *Fortune*, September 27, 1999, 124–127.
24. Mitchell Osak, "Go Global, Carefully," *National Post*, June 24, 2014, FP5.
25. Wallace Immen, "The Power of Teamwork," *The Globe and Mail*, October 15, 2010, B15.
26. James P. Sterba, "At the Met Opera, It's Not Over till the Fat Man Folds," *Wall Street Journal*, January, 1998, 1, 6.
27. Jerald Greenberg and Robert A. Baron, *Behavior in Organizations: Understanding and Managing the Human Side of Work*, 7th ed. (Upper Saddle River, NJ: Prentice Hall, 2000), 308–309.
28. Tyler Hamilton, "Welcome to the World Wide Grapevine," *The Globe and Mail*, May 6, 2000, B1, B6.

CHAPTER 8

1. See Angelo S. DeNisi and Ricky W. Griffin, *Human Resource Management* (Boston: Houghton Mifflin, 2001) for a complete overview.
2. David Lepak and Scott Snell, "Examining the Human Resource Architecture: The Relationships Among Human Capital, Employment, and Human Resource Configurations," *Journal of Management* 28(4) (2002): 517–543.
3. Patrick Brethour and Heather Scoffield, "Plenty of Work, Not Enough Bodies," *The Globe and Mail*, August 21, 2006, B4.
4. Todd Hirsch, "Labour Crunch Isn't What It's Cracked Up to Be," *The Globe and Mail*, February 28, 2013, B2.
5. Elizabeth Church, "Store Owners Struggle with Staffing," *The Globe and Mail*, November 25, 1996, B6.
6. Wallace Immen, "The Rise of the Virtual Job Fair," *The Globe and Mail*, April 13, 2011, B16.
7. Diane Jermyn, "Internships Lead to Life-Changing Jobs," *The Globe and Mail*, March 14, 2012, B16.
8. Christine Dobby, "Intern Nation," *National Post*, June 11, 2011, FP7.
9. Lauren Weber, "Your Résumé vs. Oblivion," *Wall Street Journal*, January 24, 2012, B1.
10. Rachel Silverman, "No More Résumés, Say Some Firms," *Wall Street Journal*, January 24, 2012, B6.
11. Wallace Immen, "Prospective Hires Put to the Test," *The Globe and Mail*, January 26, 2005, C1, C2.
12. Ibid.
13. Katie Rook, "Curveball Job Questions: How Not to Strike Out," *The Globe and Mail*, September 3, 2005, B9.
14. Julius Melnitzer, "Decision Raises Questions About Random Testing," *National Post*, June 18, 2014, FP10.
15. David Hutton, "Job Reference Chill Grows Icier," *The Globe and Mail*, June 18, 2008, B1.
16. Kira Vermond, "Rolling Out the Welcome Mat," *The Globe and Mail*, April 26, 2008, B19.
17. Wallace Immen, "Half of Workers Don't Fit In," *The Globe and Mail*, October 22, 2008, C2.
18. Tony Wanless, "Picking Employees Like a Matchmaker," *National Post*, December 27, 2011, FP8.
19. Bertrand Marotte, "From the Cockpit to the OR: CAE's Diversification," *The Globe and Mail*, May 25, 2010, B3.
20. Jacqueline Nelson and Kasey Coholan, "Leaders in Leadership," *Canadian Business*, November 8, 2010, 61.
21. Wallace Immen, "Rookie Managers Left to Sink or Swim," *The Globe and Mail*, April 2, 2011, B17.
22. Fiona MacFarlane, "Key to C-Suite May Just Be a Hero," *National Post*, November 30, 2011, FP8; see also Mary Bitti, "From Mentors to Sponsors: Promoting Women," *National Post*, September 27, 2011, FP10.
23. Susan Krashinsky, "Program Connects Mentors with Aspiring Leaders," *The Globe and Mail*, January 21, 2014, B3.
24. Tavia Grant, "Weekend Workout: Reverse Mentoring," *The Globe and Mail*, July 11, 2009, B14.
25. Eagle's Flight Website, www.eaglesflight.com, accessed July 23, 2013.
26. David Ciccarelli, "Why the Annual Performance Review Doesn't Work," *The Globe and Mail*, October 17, 2014, B15.
27. Kira Vermond, "Taking a Full-Circle Look at Work Reviews," *The Globe and Mail*, November 24, 2007, B18.

28. Iain Marlow, "Fixing the Dreaded Performance Review," *The Globe and Mail*, July 15, 2011, B13.

29. Rachel Silverman, "Work Reviews Losing Steam," *Wall Street Journal*, December 19, 2011, B7.

30. "Executive Compensation: Canada's 100 Top-Paid CEOs," *The Globe and Mail*, www.theglobeandmail.com/report-on-business/careers/management/executive-compensation/executive-compensation-2014/article18721871.

31. Boyd Erman, "Shareholders Win Voice on CEO Pay at 3 Big Banks," *The Globe and Mail*, February 27, 2009, B1.

32. Joann Lublin, "Say on the Boss's Pay," *Wall Street Journal*, March 7, 2008, B1–B2.

33. Statistics Canada Website, www.statcan.gc.ca, accessed July 23, 2013.

34. "Plenty of Canadian Companies Offer Incentives but Few Track Their Effectiveness," *National Post*, November 10, 2010, FP14.

35. Vanessa O'Connell, "Retailers Reprogram Workers in Efficiency Push," *The Wall Street Journal*, September 10, 2008, A1.

36. Cathryn Atkinson, "The Total Package: Anatomy of a Great Place to Work," *The Globe and Mail*, July 2, 2008, B6.

37. David Roberts, "A Long Way from Cambodia," *The Globe and Mail*, July 5, 1994, B18.

38. Jennifer Myers, "The Right Way to Reward," *The Globe and Mail*, April 3, 2010, B13.

39. Canada's Economic Action Plan Website, actionplan.gc.ca/initiatives/eng/index.asp?mode=2&initiativeID=329.

40. Service Canada Website, "Employment Insurance: Important Notice About Maximum Insurable Earnings for 2014," www.servicecanada.gc.ca/eng/ei/information/maximum2014.shtml.

41. Janet McFarland, "CPP Fund Tops $200 Billion for First Time," *The Globe and Mail*, February 15, 2014, B2.

42. Virginia Galt, "Companies, Unions, Expect Little Relief," *The Globe and Mail*, September 15, 2004, B4.

43. Virginia Galt, "Gift of Time Pays Off for Savvy Employers," *The Globe and Mail*, December 28, 2004, B3.

44. Ibid.

45. Kamal Dib, "Diversity Works," *Canadian Business*, March 29, 2004, 53–54.

46. Catalyst Website, www.catalyst.org/publication, accessed July 1, 2010.

47. Richard Blackwell and Brent Jang, "Top Court Sides with Airline Attendants," *The Globe and Mail*, January 27, 2006, B1, B6.

48. Jennifer Peltz, "Fired NY Banker's Suit, and Suits, Raise Eyebrows," *The Globe and Mail*, June 29, 2010, B5.

49. Bess Levin, "Citi Would Like to Make It Clear It Did Not Pay Debrahlee Lorenzana a Dime," dealbreaker.com/2012/05, accessed July 24, 2013.

50. Brent Jang, "Air Canada Plans to End Forced Retirement at 60," *The Globe and Mail*, January 28, 2012, B8.

51. Michael Moss, "For Older Employees, On-the-Job Injuries Are More Often Deadly," *Wall Street Journal*, June 17, 1997, A1, A10.

52. Jeff Gray, "The Rise of the Older Worker—and One Type of Lawsuit," *The Globe and Mail*, January 14, 2014, B3.

53. Barry Critchley, "Arrested Retirement; More of Us Expect to Be Working at Age 66; Survey," *National Post*, February 18, 2015, FP2.

54. Jill Mahoney, "Visible Majority by 2017," *The Globe and Mail*, March 23, 2005, A1, A7.

55. Virginia Galt, "P & G Leverages Its Cultural Diversity," *The Globe and Mail*, April 7, 2005, B1, B5.

56. Caitlyn Coverly, "Wanted: Diversity," *National Post*, June 18, 2014, FP6.

57. Ibid.

58. Max Boisot, *Knowledge Assets* (Oxfor, UK: Oxford University Press, 1998).

59. Statistics Canada Website, www.statcan.ca.

60. Tavia Grant, "Financial Crisis Sparks More Demand for Temps at the Top," *The Globe and Mail*, November 14, 2008, B16.

61. Citizenship and Immigration Canada Website, www.cic.gc.ca/english/work/index.asp, accessed July 1, 2010.

62. Aaron Bernstein, "When Is a Temp Not a Temp?" *Businessweek*, December 7, 1998, 90–92.

63. David Lipsky and Clifford Donn, *Collective Bargaining in American Industry* (Lexington, MA: Lexington Books, 1981).

64. Statistics Canada Website, Table 1, www.statcan.gc.ca/pub/75-001, accessed May 3, 2012; Melanie Trottman and Kris Maher, "Organized Labor Loses Members," *Wall Street Journal*, January 24, 2013, A6; UFCW Canada, www.ufcw.ca/index, accessed May 3, 2012.

65. Statistics Canada Website, www.statcan.gc.ca/pub/75001, accessed May 3, 2012.

66. Ibid.

67. Paul Vieira, "Public Spat; The Battle Boiling Over in Wisconsin Simmers in Canada," *National Post*, March 5, 2011, FP1; Terence Corcoran, "Why the Public Sector Is Hanging On for All It's Worth," *National Post*, March 5, 2011, A1.

68. Greg Keenan, "Unifor Applies to Organize Toyota Workers," *The Globe and Mail*, April 1, 2014, B4.

69. Greg Keenan, "CAW Rewriting Playbook to Keep Factories Running," *The Globe and Mail*, September 5, 2006, B3.

70. Jeff Gray, "Rocky Times Loom for Labour," *The Globe and Mail*, January 7, 2012, B6.

71. Alexandra Bosanac, "Evolving Work Force Presents New Challenges to Unions," *The Globe and Mail*, September 1, 2014, B3.

72. Virginia Galt, "Worn-Out Middle Managers May Get Protection," *The Globe and Mail*, January 3, 2005, B1, B8.

73. Greg Keenan, "Unifor Applies to Organize Toyota Workers," *The Globe and Mail*, April 1, 2014, B4.

74. Marina Strauss, "Shoppers Deal Leaves Loblaw Fighting Union Headaches," *The Globe and Mail*, April 30, 2014, B1.

75. "CAW Walks Away from Wal-Mart," *National Post*, April 20, 2000, C5.

76. Terence Corcoran, "Wal-Mart Wins Big Union Battle," *National Post*, April 9, 2009, FP13; Bert Hill, "Another Wal-Mart Unionized; Second for Quebec," *National Post*, December 20, 2008, FP6; Jean-Francois Bertrand, "Union Contract Imposed on Quebec Wal-Mart Store a First," *Winnipeg Free Press*, August 16, 2008, B10.

77. Sarah Binder, "McDonald's Store Closes, Union Wails," *The Globe and Mail*, February 14, 1998, B23.

78. Paul McKie, "Goldcorp Workers Accept Offer, Dismantle Union," *Winnipeg Free Press*, April 22, 2000, A6.

79. "Union Coverage in Canada, 2011," Appendix Table 3, www.hrsdc.gc.ca/eng/labour, accessed May 3, 2012.

80. Greg Keenan, "U.S. Steel, Hamilton Workers Reach Tentative Agreement," *The Globe and Mail*, October 15, 2014, B4.

81. Peter Brieger, "Court Rejects First Nation's Bid For Own Union Pact," *National Post*, November 29, 2007, www.nationalpost.com/story-printer.html?id=130625.

82. Carrie Tait, Eric Atkins, and Justin Giovannetti, "Toll Rises as Vancouver Port Strike Drags On," *The Globe and Mail*, March 19, 2014, B1.

83. Brent Jang, "Labour Board Calls Air Canada Stoppages Illegal," *The Globe and Mail*, April 14, 2012, B7.

84. Jeffrey Ball, Glenn Burkins, and Gregory White, "Why Labor Unions Have Grown Reluctant to Use the S-Word," *The Wall Street Journal*, December 16, 1999, A1, A8.

85. Brent Jang, "Rejected Deal Imposed on Air Canada Attendants," *The Globe and Mail*, November 8, 2011, B9.

86. Alison Auld, "N.S. Nurses Defy Strike Law," *The Globe and Mail*, June 28, 2001, B1.

87. "Rio Tinto Alcan in Tentative Pact with Locked-Out Workers at Its Quebec Smelter," *National Post*, July 3, 2012, FP3.

88. Simon Houpt, "Canadian Press Asks for Conciliator," *The Globe and Mail*, January 19, 2012, B10.

89. Scott Deveau, "Air Canada, Pilots Agree to Mediation," *National Post*, February 16, 2012, FP4.

90. Kristine Owram, "CP Rail Strikers in from the Cold: Sides Agree to Mediate," *National Post*, February 17, 2015, FP1.

91. Brent Jang, "Air Canada Moves to Appeal Arbitrator's Pension Ruling," *The Globe and Mail*, October 24, 2011, B3.

CHAPTER 9

1. "Time Is Money: 1 in 5 Canadians Late for Work at Least Once a Week," *National Post*, February 24, 2011, FP5.

2. "Bosses: Killing Them with Kindness Pays Off," *The Globe and Mail*, October 8, 2008, C3.

3. Daniel Goleman, *Emotional Intelligence: Why It Can Matter More Than IQ* (New York: Bantam Books, 1995); Kenneth Law, Chi-Sum Wong, and Lynda Song, "The Construct and Criterion Validity of Emotional Intelligence and Its Potential Utility for Management Studies," *Journal of Applied Psychology* 89(3) (2004): 78–90.

4. Daniel Goleman, "Leadership That Gets Results," *Harvard Business Review*, March/April 2000, 78–90.

5. Wallace Immen, "Emotional Smarts Sway Hiring Choices," *The Globe and Mail*, August 24, 2011, B17.

6. J.B. Rotter, "Generalized Expectancies for Internal vs. External Control of Reinforcement,"*Psychological Monographs* 80 (1966): 1–28.

7. Jeffrey Vancouver, Kristen More, and Ryan Yoder, "Self-Efficacy and Resource Allocation: Support for a Nonmonotic, Discontinuous Model," *Journal of Applied Psychology* 93(1) (2008): 35–47.

8. T.W. Adorno, E. Frenkel-Brunswick, D.J. Levinson, and R.N. Sanford, *The Authoritarian Personality* (New York: Harper & Row), 1950.

9. The concept is named after Nicolo Machiavelli, the sixteenth-century author who wrote the book *The Prince*, which explained how the nobility could more easily gain and use power.

10. "Half of Canadians Love Their Jobs," *The Globe and Mail*, February 17, 2010, B20.

11. "Canadians Ranked No. 3 in Satisfaction with Their Current Employer," *National Post*, April 14, 2010, FP5.

12. Doris Burke, Corey Hajim, John Elliott, Jenny Mero, and Christopher Tkaczyk, "The Top Ten Companies for Leaders," *Fortune*, October 1, 2007, money.cnn.com/galleries/2007/fortune/0709/gallery.leaders_global_topten.fortune/index.html, accessed July 24, 2013.

13. Barbara Moses, "A Cruise with the Boss? A Box of Timbits? Time to Get Serious About Rewarding Employees," *The Globe and Mail*, April 28, 2010, B16.

14. Frederick W. Taylor, *The Principles of Scientific Management* (New York: Harper and Brothers, 1911).

15. See Daniel Wren, *The History of Management Thought*, 5th ed. (New York: John Wiley & Sons, 2004).

16. Douglas McGregor, *The Human Side of Enterprise* (New York: McGraw-Hill, 1960).

17. Abraham Maslow, "A Theory of Human Motivation," *Psychological Review* (July 1943): 370–396.

18. Frederick Herzberg, Bernard Mausner, and Barbara Bloch Snydeman, *The Motivation to Work* (New York: Wiley, 1959).

19. David McClelland, *The Achieving Society* (Princeton, NJ: Nostrand, 1961).

20. Stanley Schacter, *The Psychology of Affiliation* (Palo Alto, CA: Stanford University Press, 1959.

21. David McClelland and David H. Burnham, "Power Is the Great Motivator," *Harvard Business Review* (March-April 1976): 100–110.

22. Craig Pinder, *Work Motivation in Organizational Behavior*, 2nd ed. (Upper Saddle River, NJ: Prentice-Hall, 2008); also McClelland and Burnham, "Power Is the Great Motivator."

23. Victor Vroom, *Work and Motivation* (New York: Wiley, 1964); Craig Pinder, *Work Motivation* (Glenview, IL: Scott, Foresman, 1984).

24. J. Stacy Adams, "Toward an Understanding of Inequity," *Journal of Abnormal and Social Psychology* 75(5) (1963): 422–436.

25. Jeff Buckstein, "In Praise of Praise in the Workplace," *The Globe and Mail*, June 15, 2005, C1, C5.

26. Deena Waisberg, "Tip of the Hat to Excellence: Employers Get Creative with Rewards to Keep Top Performers," *National Post*, November 19, 2008, FP15.

27. For more information on some of the potential problems with goal setting, see Drake Bennett, "Do Goals Undermine Good Management?" *National Post*, March 24, 2009, FP10; Wallace Immen, "The Goal: To Set Goals That Really Can Be Met," *The Globe and Mail*, March 20, 2009, B12.

28. Interviews with Sterling McLeod and Wayne Walker, senior vice-presidents of sales for Investors Group Financial Services.

29. Harvey Schachter, "Managing Without Managers," *The Globe and Mail*, December 19, 2011, B5.

30. Brent Jang, "High-Flying WestJet Morale Gets Put to the Test," *The Globe and Mail*, November 25, 2005, B3.

31. Virginia Galt, "Change Is a Good Thing When Everyone Is Involved," *The Globe and Mail*, June 25, 2005, B11.

32. Tavia Grant, "Workplace Democracy," *The Globe and Mail*, May 30, 2009, B14.

33. Robert Grant, "AES Corporation: Rewriting the Rules of Management," *Contemporary Strategy Analysis* (Hoboken, NJ: John Wiley & Sons, 2007), www.blackwellpublishing.com/grant/docs/17AES.pdf.

34. Patricia Kitchen, "Tap Your Employees," *Orlando Sentinel*, March 14, 2007, F1.

35. Mary Teresa Bitti, "The Power of Teamwork," *National Post*, December 18, 2009, FP12.

36. Tom Peters, *Liberation Management* (New York: Alfred Knopf, 1992), 238–239.

37. Charles Snow, Scott Snell, Sue Canney Davison, and Donald Hambrick, "Use Transnational Teams to Globalize Your Company," *Organizational Dynamics*, Spring 1996, 61.

38. Gregory Moorhead and Ricky W. Griffin, *Organizational Behavior*, 6th ed. (Boston: Houghton Mifflin, 2001), ch. 7.

39. For a discussion of team effectiveness, see Nancy Langton and Stephen Robbins, *Organizational Behaviour*, 4th Canadian ed. (Toronto: Pearson Canada, 2006), 217–230.

40. Gregory Moorhead and Ricky W. Griffin, *Organizational Behavior*, 6th ed. (Boston: Houghton Mifflin, 2001), ch. 7.

41. A.B. Drexler and R. Forrester, "Teamwork—Not Necessarily the Answer," *HR Magazine*, January 1998, 55–58.

42. Gregory Moorhead and Ricky W. Griffin, *Organizational Behavior*, 6th ed. (Boston: Houghton Mifflin, 2001), ch. 7.

43. Ricky Griffin, *Task Design* (Glenview, IL: Scott, Foresman, 1982).

44. Richard J. Hackman and Greg Oldham, *Work Redesign* (Reading, MA: Addison-Wesley, 1980).

45. "Canadian Businesses World Leaders in Offering Work-from-Home Options," *National Post*, March 16, 2011, FP12.

46. Wallace Immen, "Most Firms Offer Flexible Work," *The Globe and Mail*, July 2, 2011, B11.

47. Diane Jermyn, "Canada's Best Places to Work," *The Globe and Mail*, October 7, 2011, E10; Gail Johnson, "Companies Who Cut the Cost of Education," *The Globe and Mail*, December 8, 2011, B11.

48. Mary Gooderham, "Better Mom Becomes Better Manager," *The Globe and Mail*, October 15, 2010, E6.

49. Diane Jermyn, "Canada's Best Places to Work," *The Globe and Mail*, October 7, 2011, E10; Diane Jermyn, "Keeping Veteran Talent as Key Contributors," *The Globe and Mail*, June 7, 2011, B14; Diane Jermyn, "The GTA's Top Employers for 2012," *The Globe and Mail*, November 16, 2011, E4.

50. Mary Gooderham, "Where It's Not All About the Money," *The Globe and Mail*, November 22, 2010, E2.

51. Jameson Berkow, "Workers of the World DISPERSE," *National Post*, June 20, 2011, FP1.

52. "Looking Good in Green," *Maclean's*, May 9, 2011, 47.

53. Jameson Berkow, "Workers of the World DISPERSE," *National Post*, June 20, 2011, FP1.

54. Joyce Rosenberg, "Out of Sight, On Your Mind: Learning to Trust Telecommuters," *The Globe and Mail*, September 20, 2008, B19.

55. For example, Richard Branson, the founder of Virgin Group PLC, said that forcing workers to come to the office was a bad idea, but the mayor of New York City called telecommuting a dumb idea. An editorial in the *National Post* noted that both supporters and opponents of telecommuting actually have very little evidence on which to base their views. What is needed is systematic research to determine when telecommuting is effective and when it is not. See Omar El Akkad, "Branson Blasts Mayer's Telework Stand," *The Globe and Mail*, March 6, 2013, B7; Omar El Akkad, "Telework or Teamwork? The Office Evolves," *The Globe and Mail*, February 27, 2013, B1; "Yahoo Right on Work: Past Management Allowed Inappropriate Telecommuting," *National Post*, March 6, 2013, FP11.

56. Rachel Silverman and Quentin Fottrell, "The Home Office in the Spotlight," *Wall Street Journal*, February 24, 2013, B6.

57. Diane Jermyn, "The 10 Best to Work For," *The Globe and Mail*, September 30, 2010, B2; Cam Cole, "Flyers' Goalie Carousel Is Norm," *National Post*, June 1, 2010, B9.

58. John Kotter, "What Leaders Really Do," *Harvard Business Review* (December 2001): 85–94.

59. John Kotter, "What Leaders Really Do," *Harvard Business Review*, December, 2001, pp. 85–94.

60. Ronald Heifetz and Marty Linsky, "A Survival Guide for Leaders," *Harvard Business Review* (June 2002): 65–74.

61. Frederick Reichheld, "Lead for Loyalty," *Harvard Business Review* (July/August, 2001): 76–83.

62. S.A. Kirkpatrick and E.A. Locke, "Leadership: Do Traits Matter?" *Academy of Management Executive* (May 1991): 48–60.

63. Daniel Goleman, "What Makes a Leader?" *Harvard Business Review* (November/December 1998): 93–99.

64. David Dorsey, "Andy Pearson Finds Love," *Fast Company*, August 2001, 78–86.

65. Robert J. House and Terence R. Mitchell, "Path-Goal Theory of Leadership," *Journal of Contemporary Business* (Autumn, 1974): 81–98.

66. Fred Dansereau, George Graen, and W.J. Haga, "A Vertical Dyad Linkage Appraoch to Leadership Within Formal Organizations: A Longitudinal Investigation of the Role-Making Process," *Organizational Behavior and Human Performance* 15 (1975): 46–78.

67. David A. Waldman and Francis J. Yammarino, "CEO Charismatic Leadership: Levels-of-Management and Levels-of-Analysis Effects," *Academy of Management Review* 24 (1999): 266–285.

68. Ronald Ebert and Ricky Griffin, *Business Essentials*, 7th ed. (Upper Saddle River, NJ: Prentice Hall, 2009), 129.

69. Jane Howell and Boas Shamir, "The Role of Followers in the Charismatic Leadership Process: Relationships and Their Consequences," *Academy of Management Review* (January 2005): 96–112.

70. J. Richard Hackman and Ruth Wageman, "A Theory of Team Coaching," *Academy of Management Review* (April 2005): 269–287.

71. "How Women Lead," *Newsweek*, October 24, 2005, 46–70.

72. Madelaine Drohan, "What Makes a Canadian Manager?" *The Globe and Mail*, February 25, 1997, B18.

73. Rebecca Walberg, "Canada's Management Dividend," *National Post*, November 17, 2009, FP14.

74. Sinclair Stewart, "Passed By at TD, CEO Hits Stride in New York," *The Globe and Mail*, December 5, 2006, B1, B21; Zena Olijnyk, Mark Brown, Any Holloway, Calvin Leung, Alex Mlynek, Erin Pooley, Jeff Sanford, Andrew Wahl, and Thomas Watson, "Canada's Global Leaders," *Canadian Business*, March 8–April 10, 2005, 37–43.

75. Bryan Borzykowski, "Collaborating with a Far-Flung Team," *The Globe and Mail*, January 18, 2012, B7.

CHAPTER 10

1. Neil Reynolds, "Technology Spurring a New Manufacturing Revolution," *The Globe and Mail*, May 9, 2012, B2.

2. John Shinal, "3-D Printers Wave Their Magic Wands," *USA Today*, March 21, 2013, B1.

3. Susan Carey, "Airlines Lose the Winter Blahs," *Wall Street Journal*, February 29, 2012, B1.

4. Terry Hill, *Manufacturing Strategy*, 3rd ed. (Boston: Irwin McGraw-Hill, 2000), chs. 2–4; James A. Fitzsimmons, Mona J. Fitzsimmons, *Service Management: Operations Strategy, Information Technology*, 6th ed. (Boston: Irwin McGraw-Hill, 2008), 46–48.

5. Susan Carey, "The Case of the Vanishing Airport Lines," *Wall Street Journal*, August 9, 2007, B1.

6. John Letzing, "Amazon Adds That Robotic Touch," *Wall Street Journal*, March 20, 2012, B1.

7. Rita Trichur, "Down on the Farm with Robo-Milker," *The Globe and Mail*, March 17, 2011, B4.

8. Timothy Hay, "The Robots Are Coming to Hospitals," *Wall Street Journal*, March 15, 2012, B12.

9. Neal Boudette, "Chrysler Gains Edge by Giving New Flexibility to Its Factories," *Wall Street Journal*, April 11, 2006, A1, A15.

10. Greg Keenan, "Ford's New Maxim: Flex Manufacturing," *The Globe and Mail*, May 10, 2006, B3.

11. Lou Michel, "WNY's Trash, China's Treasure," *Buffalo News*, July 20, 2008.

12. Don Marshall, "Time for Just in Time," *PIM Review*, June 1991, 20–22; Gregg Stocker, "Quality Function Deployment: Listening to the Voice of the Customer," *APICS: The Performance Advantage*, September 1991, 44–48.

13. Lee J. Krajewski and Larry P. Ritzman, *Operations Management: Strategy and Analysis*, 6th ed. (Upper Saddle River, NJ: Prentice Hall, 2002), 153–154, 828–829; Robert S. Russell and Bernard W. Taylor III, *Operations Management*, 4th ed. (Upper Saddle River, NJ: Prentice Hall, 2003), 221–222, 593–595.

14. Robert S. Russell and Bernard W. Taylor III, *Operations Management*, 4th ed. (Upper Saddle River, NJ: Prentice Hall, 2003), 222–224.

15. "The Disney Institute," April 25, 2000, www.disney.go.com/DisneyWorld/DisneyInstitute/ProfessionalPrograms/DisneyDifference/index.html.

16. Marina Strauss, "Low Fills/High Stakes," *The Globe and Mail*, May 12, 2010, B1.

17. "Labour Productivity Levels in the Total Economy," OECD.Stat, stats.oecd.org/Index.aspx?DatasetCode=LEVEL.

18. Bart VanArk and Robert McGuckin, "International Comparisons of Labor Productivity and Per Capita Income," *Monthly Labor Review* (July 1999): 33–41.

19. Harvey Enchin, "Canada Urged to Stop Living off Fat of the Land," *The Globe and Mail*, October 25, 1991, B1, B6.

20. Barrie McKenna and Tavia Grant, "Canada's Productivity Trap," *The Globe and Mail*, September 15, 2010, B1.

21. Jon Hilsenrath, "Behind Surging Productivity: The Service Sector Delivers," *Wall Street Journal*, November 7, 2003, A1, A8.

22. Peter Kennedy, "Canfor Goes High Tech to Cut Costs," *The Globe and Mail*, July 29, 2000, 3.

23. Rachel Silverman, "Tracking Sensors Invade the Workplace," *Wall Street Journal*, March 7, 2013, B1.

24. Greg Keenan, "Honda Canada in Airbag Recall: Pullback Affects 700,000 Vehicles Under Worldwide Initiative Stemming from Takata's Exploding Bags," *The Globe and Mail*, December 10, 2014, B5.

25. Lee J. Krajewski and Larry P. Ritzman, *Operations Management: Strategy and Analysis*, 5th ed. (Reading, MA: Addison-Wesley, 1999), 229–230.

26. Bruce McDougall, "The Thinking Man's Assembly Line," *Canadian Business*, November 1991, 40.

27. Ted Wakefield, "No Pain, No Gain," *Canadian Business*, January 1993, 50–54.

28. Scott McCartney, "Ranking Airlines by Lost Bags, Canceled Flights," *Wall Street Journal*, January 5, 2012, D3.

29. Thomas Foster Jr., *Managing Quality: An Integrative Approach* (Upper Saddle River, NJ: Prentice Hall, 2001), 325–339.

30. Ibid.

31. James Evans and James Dean Jr., *Total Quality: Management, Organization, and Strategy*, 2nd ed. (Cincinnati, OH: South-Western, 2000), 230.

32. Margot Gibb-Clark, "Hospital Managers Gain Tool to Compare Notes," *The Globe and Mail*, September 9, 1996, B9.

33. "Quality Customer Care," *National Post*, February 3, 2012, JV6.

34. Roberta S. Russell and Bernard W. Taylor III, *Operations Management*, 4th ed. (Upper Saddle River, NJ: Prentice Hall, 2003), 137–140.

35. Del Jones, "Baldrige Award Honors Record 7 Quality Winners," *USA Today*, November 26, 2003, B6.

36. Sunil Chopra and Peter Meindl, *Supply Chain Management: Strategy, Planning, and Operation*, 6th ed. (Upper Saddle River, NJ: Prentice Hall, 2001), 3–6; Lee J. Krajewski and Larry P. Ritzman, *Operations Management: Strategy and Analysis,* 5th ed. (Reading, MA: Addison-Wesley, 1999), ch. 11; Roberta S. Russell and Bernard W. Taylor III, *Operations Management*, 4th ed. (Upper Saddle River, NJ: Prentice Hall, 2003), ch. 7; Thomas Foster Jr., *Managing Quality: An Integrative Approach* (Upper Saddle River, NJ: Prentice Hall, 2001), ch. 9.

37. Sunil Chopra and Peter Meindl, *Supply Chain Management: Strategy, Planning, and Operation*, 6th ed. (Upper Saddle River, NJ: Prentice Hall, 2001), ch. 20.

38. Nick Rockel, "Keeping the Containers Moving," *The Globe and Mail*, November 15, 2011, B15.

39. Joseph Sternberg, "Now Comes the Global Revolution in Services," *Wall Street Journal*, February 10, 2011, A17.

40. James Kelleher, "GM Among Firms Preparing for Bad Winter," *National Post*, November 21, 2014, FP10.

41. Peter Kuitenbrouwer, "Supply Chain Blues Hit the Line at Bombardier Plant," *National Post*, January 5, 2015, FP1.

42. James Hookway and Aries Poon, "Crisis Tests Supply Chain's Weak Links," *The Wall Street Journal*, March 18, 2011, A8.

CHAPTER 11

1. Ronald Hilton, *Managerial Accounting*, 2nd ed. (New York: McGraw-Hill, 1994), 7.

2. David Milstead, "Accounting Issues Raise Big Red Flag over Reborn GM," *The Globe and Mail*, November 27, 2010, B12.

3. Tim Leech, "Mend our SOX," *National Post*, October 19, 2011, FP15.

4. See Anthony A. Atkinson, Robert S. Kaplan, Ella Mae Matsumura, and S. Mark Young, *Management Accounting*, 5th ed. (Upper Saddle River, NJ: Prentice Hall, 2007), ch. 1.

5. Chartered Professional Accountant Website, unification.cpacanada.ca/blog/2014/10/02/it%e2%80%99s-official-190000-pros-one-designation, accessed March 7, 2015.

6. Janet McFarland, "Canadian Accountants Merge Under CPA Designation," *The Globe and Mail*, June 23, 2014, B1; Gordon Isfeld, "Chartered Accountants Show They Can Get Along," *Financial Post*, December 2, 2014.

7. Hollie Shaw, "Accounting's Big Bang Moment: Switch from GAAP," *National Post*, September 24, 2009, FP1.

8. Virginia Galt, "It's Crunch Time as Accounting Changes Loom," *The Globe and Mail*, June 17, 2010, B10.

9. Al Rosen, "Cooking with IFRS," *Canadian Business*, July 20, 2009, 12.

10. The IFRS Foundation Website, www.ifrs.org/The-organisation/Documents/2015/Who-We-Are-January-2015.pdf, accessed March 8, 2018.

11. David Milstead, "A Close Inspection of Shoppers' Revenue Accounting," *The Globe and Mail*, May 17, 2010, B8.

12. Charles T. Horngren, Walter T. Harrison Jr., and Linda Smith Bamber, *Accounting*, 5th ed. (Upper Saddle River, NJ: Prentice Hall, 2002), 11–12, 39–41.

13. Charles T. Horngren, Walter T. Harrison Jr., and Linda Smith Bamber, *Accounting*, 5th ed. (Upper Saddle River, NJ: Prentice Hall, 2002), 17–20.

14. Billie Cunningham, Loren Nikolai, and John Bazley. *Accounting: Information for Business Decisions* (Fort Worth, TX: Dryden, 2000), 133–134.

15. Charles T. Horngren, Walter T. Harrison Jr., and Linda Smith Bamber, *Accounting*, 4th ed. (Upper Saddle River, NJ: Prentice Hall, 1999), 201–202.

16. "Zara Financials," Investing.com, www.investing.com/equities/zara-investmen-ratios, accessed March 16, 2015.

17. AICPA Website, "Code of Professional Conduct," www.aicpa.org/research/standards/codeofconduct/pages/default.aspx.

18. Iwona Tokc-Wilde, "#AAYP 2013: Modern Accountants—People Who Think Differently," *Accountancy Age*, May 1, 2013, www.accountancyage.com/aa/feature/2265153/-aayp-2013-modern-accountants-people-who-think-differently; "Intuit 2020 Report Depicts Future of the Accounting

Profession: A New Mindset and Model Required to Thrive in a Connected World," Intuit Inc. Website, about.intuit.com/about_intuit/press_room/press_release/articles/2011/Intuit2020ReportDepictsFuture.html, accessed February 2, 2011; Rich Walker, "Intuit 2020 Report Depicts Future of the Accounting Profession," Intuit Accountants News Central, blog.accountants.intuit.com/intuit-news/intuit%C2%AE-2020-report-depicts-future-of-the-accounting-profession, accessed February 2, 2011; "Accountants—the Old and the New," CA Saga, contractaccountants.wordpress.com/2012/08/15/accountants-the-old-and-the-new, accessed August 15, 2012; "The Many Hats of a Modern Accountant," Jobs.net, www.jobs.net/Article/CB-6-Talent-Network-Finance-Ins-The-Many-Hats-of-a-Modern-Accountant, accessed May 14, 2013.

CHAPTER SUPPLEMENT 03

1. Mark Milian, "Where to Find the World's Fastest Internet: Top 20," *Bloomberg Business*, January 14, 2014.
2. CBC News Website, "Desktop Internet Use by Canadians Highest in World, ComScore Says," March 27, 2015, accessed May 8, 2015.
3. Omar El Akkad, "Canadian Internet Usage Grows," *The Globe and Mail*, May 11, 2010, B9.
4. Ian Marlow and Jacquie McNish, "Canada's Digital Divide," *The Globe and Mail*, April 3, 2010, B1, B4.
5. Philip Kotler, Gary Armstrong, and Peggy H. Cunningham, *Principles of Marketing*, 6th Canadian ed. (Toronto: Pearson, 2005), 88.
6. Phil Goldstein, "RIM Unveils BlackBerry Z10 and Q10, but Pushes U.S. Launch to March," *FierceWireless*, January 30, 2013, fiercewireless.com/story/rim-unveils-blackberry-z10-and-q10-pushes-us-launch-march/2013-01-30.
7. Joanna Stern, "Google's Project Glass is Ready, but for Developers' Eyes Only," January 16, 2013, abcnews.go.com/blogs/technology/2013/01/googles-glass-is-ready-but-for-developers-eyes-only.
8. Michael Oliviera, "Canadian Retailers Lag Rivals in Online Selling," The Globe and Mail, November 1, 2012, B1; Melody McKinnon, "4 Holiday Online Shopping Trends in Canada," canadiansinternet.com/4-holiday-online-shopping-trends-canada, November 27, 20149; "Appropriator Asks NASA to Help Boeing Fix Dreamliner Problems," January 13, 2013, fattah.house.gov/latest-news/appropriator-asks-nasa-to-help-boeing-fix-dreamliner-problems.
10. Northrop Grumman, "Northrop Grumman Awards International Contracts for F-35 Joint Strike Fighter," news release, September 29, 2005, www.irconnect.com/noc/pages/news_printer.html?=86963&print=1; Faith Keenan and Spencer E. Ante, "The New Teamwork," *Businessweek Online*, February 18, 2002.
11. Marjo Johne, "High-Tech Options Replace the Lowly Retail Punch Card," *The Globe and Mail*, October 10, 2014, B8.
12. Laura Northrup, "Timbuk2 Really, Really Wants You to Be Happy with Their Bags," *Consumerist*, June 5, 2009, www.consumerist.com/5280357/timbuk2_really-really-wants-you-to-be; Emily Walzer, "Have It Your Way," *SGB* 38(1) (January 2005): 42.
13. "Annual Report," investor.google.com/pdf/2012_google_annual_report.pdf, 77, accessed June 12, 2013; David Milstead, "A Rocket, a Meteor—or a One Trick Pony?" *The Globe and Mail*, January, 29, 2010, B9.
14. Boyd Erman, "Online Brokerage Muscles In on the Road Show," *The Globe and Mail*, March 29, 2010, B5.
15. 3D Systems, "3D Systems Helps Walter Reed Army Medical Center Rebuild Lives," www.3dsystems.com/appsolutions/casestudies/walter_reed.asp, accessed June 15, 2009; Hannah Hickey, "Camera in a Pill Offers Cheaper, Easier Window on Your Insides," January 24, 2008, UWNews.org, uwnews.org/article.asp?articleid=39292.
16. "The Internet Is Saving You Money," *Backbone Magazine*, March/April 2013, 8.
17. David LaGesse, "How to Turn Social Networking into a Job Offer," *U.S. News & World Report*, May 11, 2009, www.usnews.com/articles/business/careers/2009/05/11/how-to.
18. Emily Bazar, "Bartering Booms During Economic Tough Times," *USA Today*, February 25, 2009, usatoday.com/tech/webguide/internetlife/2009-02-25-barter_N.htm; Debbie Lombardi, "Bartering Can Boost Your Budget and Business," www.bbubarter.com/news.aspx?NewsID=18, accessed October 27, 2008; Donna Wright, "Hard Times Create Boom of Local Bartering," BradentonHerald.com, March 8, 2009, www.bradenton.com/874/v-print/story/1277848.html; "The Advantages of Business Bartering," U-Exchange.com, www.u-exchange.com/advantages-business-bartering, accessed February 24, 2011; Bob Meyer, "In-Depth Look at U.S. Trade Exchange Industry's Size," *BarterNews*, April 24, 2012, www.barternews.com.
19. "ABN AMRO Mortgage Group Offers One Fee to Ford Motor Company Employees," *Mortgage Mag*, February 14, 2005, www.mortgagemag.com/n/502_003.htm; also "An Intranet's Life Cycle," morebusiness.com, June 16, 1999, www.morebusiness.com/getting_started/website/d928247851.brc.
20. Figure IT.2 is a modified version of diagrams on the BlackBerry website, Research in Motion Ltd., www.blackberry.com/images/technical/bes_exchange_arthitecture.gif.
21. Guy Dixon and Bert Archer, "WiFi in the Sky: Airlines Seek Web-Based Revenue," *The Globe and Mail*, June 7, 2013, B3.
22. Gayle Balfour, "The Wisdom of the Cloud," *Backbone Magazine*, May 2009, 16–20; SalesForce.com website, www.salesforce.com/cloudcomputing, accessed July 7, 2010.
23. Danny Bradbury, "Flying Cloudless," *Backbone Magazine*, December 2012, P26–30.
24. Jacqueline Nelson, "Businesses Can Get Ahead in the Cloud," *The Globe and Mail*, October 29, 2014, B4.
25. Nick Rockel, "Why Canada Lags in Cloud Computing," *The Globe and Mail*, February 9, 2012, B4.
26. Jonathan Stoller, "It's Cool to Be Cold," *The Globe and Mail*, December 20, 2012, B4.
27. IBM Website, www-01.ibm.com/software/data/bigdata/what-is-big-data.html, accessed May 8, 2015.
28. Gartner Website, www.gartner.com/it-glossary/big-data, accessed June 12, 2013.
29. Marina Strauss, "In Store Aisles, Dr. Dre Meets Big Data," *The Globe and Mail*, March 5, 2013.
30. Harvey Shachter, "Unearthing Big Myths About Big Data," *The Globe and Mail*, March 4, 2015.
31. IT World Website, "How Has Big Data Demonstrated a Shift from Data Mining?" www.itworld.com/answers/topic/business-intelligence/question/how-has-big-data-demonstrated-shift-data-mining, accessed June 12, 2103.
32. Kenneth C. Laudon and Jane P. Laudon, *Essentials of Management Information Systems*, 3rd ed. (Upper Saddle River, NJ: Prentice Hall, 1999), 383–388; E. Wainwright Martin, et al., *Managing Information Technology: What Managers Need to Know*, 3rd ed. (Upper Saddle River, NJ: Prentice-Hall, 1999), 225–227.
33. Phuong Tram, "Facebook and Privacy Invasions," *Imprint Online*, June 15, 2008, imprint.uwaterloo.ca/index.php?option=com_content&task=view&id=2570&Itemid=57; also Jacqui Cheng, "Canadian Group: Facebook a Minefield of Privacy Invasion," May 30, 2008, arstechnica.com/tech-policy/news/2008/05/canadian-group-files-complaint-over-facebook-privacy.ars; also "Cell Phones a Much Bigger Privacy Risk than Facebook," Fox News, February 20, 2009, www.foxnews.com/printer_friendly_story/0,3566,497544,00.html.
34. Kelly Gilblom, "Sony Turned to Blackberry After Hack," *The Globe and Mail*, January 1, 2015, B3; "The Interview: A Guide to the Cyber

Attack on Hollywood," BBC News, www.bbc.com/news/entertainment-arts-30512032, accessed May 8, 2015.

35. "Fraud Prevention," *The Globe and Mail*, March 29, 2010, FP1.

36. Treasury Board of Canada Secretariat.

37. Siobhan Gorman, "The Cold War Goes Digital—and Corporate," *The Globe and Mail*, January 14, 2010, B7.

38. Webopedia Website, www.webopedia.com/TERM/S/spyware.html.

CHAPTER 12

1. American Marketing Association, "Marketing Definitions," December 1, 2010, www.marketingpower.com.

2. Philip Kotler and Gary Armstrong, *Principles of Marketing*, 12th ed. (Upper Saddle River, NJ: Prentice Hall, 2008), 7.

3. Susan Krashinsky, "Losing Loyalty," *The Globe and Mail*, June 6, 2014, B5.

4. "CRM (Customer Relationship Management)," TechTarget.com, search-crm.techtarget.com/definition/CRM, accessed December 8, 2010; "Customer Relationship Management," Wikipedia, en.wikipedia.org/wiki/Customer_relationship_management, accessed December 8, 2010.

5. Poonam Khanna, "Hotel Chain Gets Personal with Customers," *Computing Canada*, April 8, 2005, 18.

6. "Fairmont Hotels & Resorts: Website Development and Enhanced CRM," *Accenture*, www.accenture.com/Global/Services/By_Industry/Travel/Client_Successes/FairmontCrm.htm, accessed December 8, 2010.

7. Whole Foods, "Whole Foods Market Delivers Record Q2 Sales and EPS," press release, May 6, 2015.

8. Shawn McCarthy and Greg Keenan, "Ottawa Demands Lower Auto Worker Costs," *The Globe and Mail*, January 19, 2009, v1business.theglobeandmail.com/servlet/story/RTGAM.20090119.wrautos19/BNStory/Business; McClatchy Newspapers, "Lemons into Lemonade," *Columbia Daily Tribune*, February 2, 2009, 7B.

9. Marina Strauss, "Canadian Tire Targets the Price Sensitive," *The Globe and Mail*, May 15, 2009, B4.

10. Eric Reguly, "Hard Time: Makers of Luxury Watches Clock a Slow Return to Sales Health," *The Globe and Mail*, February 2, 2010, B1.

11. Rasha Moutarda, "Gerontologists Go Beyond the Numbers," *The Globe and Mail*, February 19, 2010, B9.

12. Canadian Media Directors' Council, *Media Digest, 2012/2013* (Toronto: Marketing, 2012), 88, www.yellowhouseevents.com/img/CMDC_images/CMDC_Digital_Ed_2012.pdf.

13. Marina Strauss, "Wal-Mart Expansion Eats into Grocer Growth," *The Globe and Mail*, April 25, 2013, B5; Bertrand Marotte, "Metro Forges into Ethnic Food Market with Stake in Adonis," *The Globe and Mail*, October 27, 2011, B8.

14. Philip Kotler, Gary Armstrong, and Peggy Cunningham, *Principles of Marketing*, 7th ed. (Don Mill, ON: Pearson Education, 2008), 289–290.

15. John Morton, "How to Spot the Really Important Prospects," *Business Marketing*, January 1990, 62–67.

16. Susan Berfield, "Getting the Most out of Every Shopper," *Businessweek*, February 9, 2009, 45.

17. Emily Nelson, "P&G Checks Out Real Life," *Wall Street Journal*, May 17, 2001, B1, B4.

18. Ibid.

19. Global News Website, Joel Eastwood, "New Database Will Allow Canadians to Track Government Spending," April 22, 2013, global-news.ca/news/502224/new-database-will-allow-canadians-to-track-government-spending-data, accessed May 24, 2013.

20. Ben Austen, "Rock N' Roll Will Never Die," *Bloomberg Businessweek*, January 23–29, 2012, 74.

21. James R. Haggerty, "50,000 Products and Counting," *The Globe and Mail*, November 19, 2013, B20.

22. Tavia Grant, "Why Cisco Chose Canada," *The Globe and Mail*, December 18, 2013, B3.

23. "At P&G, the Innovation Well Runs Dry," *Bloomberg Businessweek*, September 10–16, 2012, 23–25.

24. Jeff Beer, "Oreo's Chinese Twist," *Canadian Business*, December 10, 2012, 66–67.

25. Millward Brown Website, "Global Brand Rankings," www.wpp.com/wpp/marketing/brandz/brandz-2014, accessed May 13, 2015.

26. "BP's Brand Value Sinks with Oil Spill," *Columbia Daily Tribune*, September 16, 2010, accessed www.columbiatribune.com/news/2010/sep/16/bps-brand-value-sinks-with-oil-spill.

27. Millward Brown Website, www.millwardbrown.com/BrandZ/Top_100_Global_Brands.aspx, accessed May 27, 2013.

28. "Kellogg to Swallow P&G's Pringles for $2.7-Billion," *The Globe and Mail*, February 16, 2012, B1.

29. Susan Krashinsky, "For Canada Goose, Sports Illustrated Swimsuit Edition Is a Golden Egg," *The Globe and Mail*, February 14, 2013, B3.

30. Courtland Bovee, John V. Thill, and George Dracopoulos, *Business in Action*, 2nd ed. (Don Mills, ON: Pearson Education, 2008), 332.

31. Susan Krashinsky, "A Top-Shelf Transformation," *The Globe and Mail*, May 9, 2013, B4.

CHAPTER 13

1. "Reverse Auction," *Encyclopedia of Management*, 2009, Encyclopedia.com, January 16, 2011, www.encyclopedia.com/doc/1G2-3273100254.html; MediaBids, www.mediabids.com.

2. Coca-Cola Website, www.coca-colacompany.com/investors, accessed June 1, 2013.

3. Canadian Media Directors' Council, *Media Digest, 2014–2015* (Toronto: Marketing, 2015), 7.

4. Ibid.

5. Susan Krashinsky, "P&G's Super Bowl Risk Pays Off," *The Globe and Mail*, February 3, 2015.

6. Susan Krashinsky, "Why Most Super Bowl Ads Get Stopped at the Border," *The Globe and Mail*, February 3, 2012, B8.

7. Marina Strauss, "Super Bowl Clobbers the Grey Cup," *The Globe and Mail*, January 26, 2008, B3.

8. Canadian Media Directors' Council, *Media Digest, 2012–2013* (Toronto: Marketing, 2013), 8.

9. Philip Kotler, Gary Armstrong, and Peggy Cunningham, *Principles of Marketing,* 6th Canadian ed. (Don Mills, ON: Pearson, 2005), 89–91.

10. Canadian Media Directors' Council, *Media Digest, 2014–2015* (Toronto: Marketing, 2015), 8.

11. Susan Krashinsky, "The Next Hot Marketer? You," *The Globe and Mail*, February 8, 2013, B6.

12. Susan Krashinski, "Advertisers Channel YouTube," *The Globe and Mail*, March 29, 2013, B5.

13. Simon Houpt, "Super Bowl Marketers Are Changing Their Game," *The Globe and Mail*, February 5, 2010, B5.

14. Susan Krashinsky, "TV Twitter Connection Takes Flight," *The Globe and Mail*, April 26, 2013, B5.

15. Sam Grobart, "Mobile Ads Are the Future. They're Also Lousy," *Bloomberg Businessweek*, November 5–11, 2012, P42.

16. Canadian Media Directors' Council, *Media Digest, 2009–2010* (Toronto: Marketing, 2009), 76, www.cmdc.ca/pdf/Media_Digest_2009.pdf.

17. Jeff Green, "The New Willy Loman Survives by Staying Home," *Bloomberg Business Week*, January 14–20, 2013, 17.

18. Simon Avery, "Do Not Call List Could Give Boost to Direct Mail," *The Globe and Mail*, September 29, 2008, B3.

19. Susan Krashinsky, "DiGiorno Pizza's Apology Come Fully Baked," *The Globe and Mail*, September 10, 2014.

20. Duncan Hood, "McDonald's Gets Shockingly Honest. I'm Lovin' It," *Canadian Business*, October 29, 2012, 4.

21. "Vending Machines: A Global Strategic Business Report," *CompaniesAndMarkets.com: Market Report*, September 1, 2010, www.companiesandmarkets.com/Market-Report/vending-machines-a-global-strategic-business-report-companiesandmarkets.com.

22. Avon 2009 annual report, phx.corporate-ir.net/phoenix.zhtml?c=90402&p=irol-irhome.

23. Marketwatch Website, "Annual Financials for Amazon.com Inc.," www.marketwatch.com/investing/stock/amzn/financials, accessed May 20, 2015.

24. Marina Strauss, "Wal-Mart's Endless Aisle,'" *The Globe and Mail*, December 5, 2011, B1.

25. Vito Pilieci, "Taxman Eyes Internet Sellers," *Winnipeg Free Press*, November 18, 2008, B5.

26. Bertrand Marotte, "Reeling in Fresh Customers," *The Globe and Mail*, April 20, 2010, B3.

27. Mark Brown, "Target Becomes the Targeted," *Canadian Business*, April 29, 2013, 13–14.

CHAPTER 14

1. Steve Mertl, "Durability of Canada's Plastic Money Being Questioned," ca.news.yahoo.com/blogs/dailybrew/durability-canada-plastic-currency-questioned-201813438.html, accessed May 22, 2012.

2. Statistics Canada Website, "Exchange Rates, Interest Rates, and Money Supply," www.statcan.gc.ca/tables-tableaux/sum-som/l01/cst01/econ07-eng.htm, accessed April 6, 2015.

3. CBC News Website, "Is Canada's New $20 Bill Too 'Pornographic'? accessed May 12, 2012.

4. Statistics Canada Website, "Exchange Rates, Interest Rates, and Money Supply," www.statcan.gc.ca/tables-tableaux/sum-som/l01/cst01/econ07-eng.htm, accessed April 6, 2015.

5. Tara Perkins, "Card Payment Players Clash over Code," *The Globe and Mail*, January 18, 2010, B5.

6. Canadian Bankers Association Website, Credit Card Statistics, www.cba.ca/en/media-room/50-backgrounders-on-banking-issues/123-credit-cards, accessed April 6, 2015.

7. Boyd Erman, "Visa's IPO Taps into the World's Love of Plastic," *The Globe and Mail*, February 26, 2008, B1, B6.

8. *Bank of Canada Banking and Financial Statistics*, Series C1, Chartered Bank Assets, March 2015, S17.

9. Derek DeCloet, "As Canadian as … Banking?" *Canadian Business*, December 2011, P 20.

10. "Top 10 Banks in Canada," *The Globe and Mail*, Report on Business, July/August 2014, 96.

11. "Are the Days of the Paper Cheque Over?" *The Globe and Mail*, May 16, 2012.

12. Canadian Bankers Association Website, "The ABM Market in Canada," www.cba.ca/en/media-room/50-backgrounders-on-banking-issues/118-abm-market-in-canada, accessed January 18, 2013.

13. Tara Perkins and Grant Robertson, "The Bank Machine with a Personal Touch," *The Globe and Mail*, June 3, 2010, B5.

14. Canadian Bankers Association Website, "Canada's Efficient and Secure Payments System," www.cba.ca/en/media-room/50-backgrounders-on-banking-issues/616-canadas-efficient-and-secure-payments-system, accessed May 15, 2012.

15. Smart Card Alliance Website, "About Smart Cards: Introduction: Primer," www.smartcardalliance.org/pages/smart-cards-intro-primer, accessed April 22, 2011.

16. Rita Trichur and Grant Robertson, "CIBC, Rogers Launch Digital Wallet," *The Globe and Mail*, May 16, 2012, B7.

17. "The End of Cash," *Canadian Business*, July/August 2014, 30.

18. Grant Robertson and Tim Kaladze, "Banks Warn Volcker Rule Could Violate NAFTA," *The Globe and Mail*, January 20, 2012, A1, B4.

19. Dana Flavelle, "As ING Direct Becomes Tangerine, Will No Frills Legacy Survive?" *Toronto Star*, April 23, 2014.

20. Tara Perkins, "A Piece of Drywall Away from Being Part of the Branch," *The Globe and Mail*, April 26, 2008, B6.

21. Business News Network Website, "Ottawa Bans Insurance Sales on Bank Websites," May 27, 2010, www.bnn.ca/news/17916.html, accessed July 10, 2010.

22. William Robson, "Why Interest Rates Must Rise," *Canadian Business*, October 29, 2012, P30.

23. Barrie McKenna, "Envoy's Loonie Remarks Spark Krona Controversy," *The Globe and Mail*, March 3, 2012, B5.

24. CTV News Website, www.ctvnews.ca/canada/mark-carney-named-bank-of-england-governor-1.1053945#ixzz2IekqZCH4, accessed January 20, 2012.

25. Special Feature on Cooperatives, "A Force in the Canadian Banking System," *The Globe and Mail*, May 15, 2012, CO 2.

26. Credit Union Central of Canada, "Largest 100 Credit Unions/Caisses Populaires," www.cucentral.ca/FactsFigures/top100-4Q14_18-Mar-15.pdf.

27. Canadian Health Insurance Association Website, www.clhia.ca, accessed April 16, 2015.

28. Canada's Venture Capital and Private Equity Association Website, www.cvca.ca/research-resources/industry-statistics, accessed April 16, 2015.

29. Niall McGee, "Cara IPO Sees Huge Demand," *The Globe and Mail*, April 2, 2015, B10; Corrie Driebusch and Shira Ovide, "GoDaddy Shares Surge in Market Debut," *The Globe and Mail*, April 2, 2015, B8.

30. Jeremy Torobin, "Dollar at Par: The New Normal," *The Globe and Mail*, March 18, 2010, B1, B6; Bank of Canada Website, www.bankofcanada.ca/cgi-bin/famecgi_fdps, accessed April 17, 2015.

31. LuAnn LaSalle, "Clearwater Eyes Productivity to Offset High Loonie," *The Globe and Mail*, March 24, 2010, B1.

32. Gordon Pitts, "How Captain High Liner Beat the Dollar Odds," *The Globe and Mail*, March 16, 2010, B1–B4.

33. *The Economist* Website, "The Big Mac Index," January 22, 2015, www.economist.com/content/big-mac-index, accessed April 17, 2015.

34. International Monetary Fund Website, www.imf.org/external/about.htm, accessed April 17, 2015.

35. "IMF Economists Admit to 'Errors' on Austerity Policy," *EU Observer*, euobserver.com/economic/118644, accessed January 27, 2013.

36. Paul Bluestein, "The Inefficiency of International Financial Institutions," *The Globe and Mail*, November 12, 2013, B4.

CHAPTER 15

1. Stefan Stern," The Rise of the Bean Counters," *National Post*, August 23, 2006, WK5.

2. Derek Sankey, "CFO Positions Demand Ever-Expanding Skill Set; Decision Makers," *National Post*, April 11, 2012, FP10.

3. Brenda Bouw, "The Evolution of the Chief Financial Officer," *The Globe and Mail*, May 10, 2014, B15.

4. Brent Jang, "CP Unveils Strategic Spending Plan," *The Globe and Mail*, January 18, 2012, B9.

5. Geoffrey Morgan, "Canadian Natural Revises Capital Plans; Returns Unmet; Budget Takes 28% Trim," *National Post*, January 13, 2015, FP3.

6. Geoffrey Morgan," Oil Changes," *National Post*, January 7, 2015, FP1.

7. Hollie Shaw, "Walmart Canada to Invest $750 Million in Building Projects in 2012, *National Post*, February 8, 2012, FP4.

8. Barry Critchley, "Trading in Receivables," *National Post*, June 11, 2012, FP1.

9. "Two Months After Record IPO, Alibaba Eyes First Bond Sale," *National Post*, November 14, 2014, FP10.

10. Simon Nixon, "Greece Is Snatching Defeat from Jaws of Victory," *The Wall Street Journal*, December 8, 2014, A9. For a more detailed discussion of the situation in Greece, see Ronald Ebert, Ricky Griffin, Frederick Starke, and George Dracopolous, *Business Essentials*, 7th Canadian ed. (Don Mills, ON: Pearson, 2014), 103.

11. Aaron Lucchetti, "As Housing Boomed, Moody's Opened Up," *Wall Street Journal*, April 11, 2008, A1, A15.

12. Timothy Martin and Andrew Grossman, "U.S. Fires a Few Parting Shots at S&P," *The Wall Street Journal*, February 4, 2015, C2.

13. Barry Critchley, "Energy, Banks Won the Year," *National Post*, December 29, 2014, FP2.

14. Steve Ladurantaye, "Yellow Media Battles Debt Crunch," *The Globe and Mail*, February 10, 2012, B1.

15. Virtual Brokers Website, www.virtualbrokers.com/contents.aspx?page_id=2, accessed June 1, 2012.

16. NASDAQ Website, June 25, 2000, www.nasdaq.com/about/timeline.stm.

17. NASDAQ Website, www.nasdaq.com, accessed May 29, 2010.

18. Richard Blackwell, "TSE 300 Shift Will Shrink Index," *The Globe and Mail*, January 31, 2002, B17.

19. Tim Shufelt, "Actively Managed Funds vs. the Index: Once Again, No Contest," *The Globe and Mail*, November 14, 2014, B10.

20. "Why Exchange-Traded Funds?" *Yahoo Finance*, Exchange-Traded Funds Center, finance.yahoo.com/etf/education/02, accessed June 1, 2012.

21. Janet McFarland, "OSC Rules Norshield Hedge Fund Misled Investors," *The Globe and Mail*, March 9, 2010, B6.

22. Josh Wingrove, "Quebec, Alberta Shun National Regulator," *The Globe and Mail*, July 10, 2014, B3.

23. Jeff Gray, "Looser Rules Would Raise Billions—at a Cost," *The Globe and Mail*, March 27, 2014, B6.

24. Industry Canada Website, www.ic.gc.ca, accessed May 31, 2010.

25. Norman M. Scarborough and Thomas W. Zimmerer, *Effective Small Business Management: An Entrepreneurial Approach*, 6th ed. (Upper Saddle River, NJ: Prentice Hall, 2000), 298–300.

26. Richard S. Boulton, Barry D. Libert, and Steve M. Samek, "Managing Risk in an Uncertain World," *Upside*, June 2000, 268–278.

27. Gordon Pitts and Bertrand Marotte, "Has Sabia Jumped from the Frying Pan into the Fire?" *The Globe and Mail*, March 14, 2009, www.globeinvestor.com/servlet/story/GAM.20090314.RSABIA14/GIStory.

28. Tara Perkins, "BMO Retreats to Its Low-Risk Roots," *The Globe and Mail*, March 5, 2008, B5.

29. Joe Castaldo, "Bay Street Hurt by Talent Deficit," *Canadian Business*, December 9, 2009, 15.

30. Thomas P. Fitch, *Dictionary of Banking Terms*, 2nd ed. (Hauppauge, NY: Barron's, 1993), 531.

31. Mark S. Dorfman, *Introduction to Risk Management and Insurance*, 6th ed. (Upper Saddle River, NJ: Prentice Hall, 2000), ch. 1.

32. For an analysis of this problem, see Luciana Lopez, "Insurers Grapple with Risk Models for Cyber Threats: Sony Latest Case," *National Post*, December 23, 2014, FP10; also Jacqueline Nelson, "Technological Advances Take Insurers into New Territory," *The Globe and Mail*, September 11, 2104, B6.

33. Denyse O'Leary, "The Scams That Drive Up Premiums," *The Globe and Mail*, May 2, 1995, B1; Denyse O'Leary, "Insurers United Against Fraud Face Serious Obstacles," *The Globe and Mail*, May 2, 1995, B1.

34. Sinclair Stewart, "Sun Life's Insurance Policy: The Great Indian Middle Class," *The Globe and Mail*, October 1, 2005, B1, B6.

35. Barbara Shecter, "Sun Life Limits Life Policies, Annuities," *National Post*, December 13, 2011, FP1.

36. Yochi Dreazen, "As Iraq Terror Rises, Businessmen Find Niche in Life Insurance," *Wall Street Journal*, August 19, 2005, A1, A16.

37. Mark S. Dorfman, *Introduction to Risk Management and Insurance*, 6th ed. (Upper Saddle River, NJ: Prentice Hall, 2000), 420–421.

SOURCE NOTES

CHAPTER 1

Combining the Whopper and the Timbit

Hollie Shaw, "Tims Shareholders Give Approval to Burger King's $12.5B Takeover; New Name Selected to Help Brand New Corporate Entity," *National Post*, December 10, 2014, FP4; Jeff Gray, "Tim Hortons Shareholders OK Burger King Deal," *Globe and Mail*, December 10, 2014, B4; Hollie Shaw, "Ottawa Gives OK to BK-Tims Merger, Approval Comes with Detailed List of Conditions," *National Post*, December 5, 2014, FP1; Matthew Campbell, "Inversions Become Political Trip Wire; Debate Swirls Around U.S. Treasury Nominee's Role in Tim Hortons Deal," *National Post*, November 26, 2014, FP3; Nicolas Van Praet, "TIMS-BK Vow to Press on Despite U.S. Clampdown, Merger Driven by Long-Term Growth, Not Taxes, Officials Say in the Face of New Rules," *National Post*, September 24, 2014, FP1; John McKinnon and Damian Paletta, "Corporate News: Burger King–Tim Hortons Plan Raises Heat in Washington," *The Wall Street Journal*, August 26, 2014, B4.

Riversong: Revolutionary Canadian Guitars

Riversong Guitars Website, riversongguitars.com/posts, accessed May 8, 2015; interview with Mike Miltimore, October 26, 2014; "BDC's Young Entrepreneur Award Push Locals to Get Serious About Business," *Kelowna Capital News*, February 28, 2013; Danny Bradbury, "Lee's Music Puts Focus on Innovative Guitar Manufacturing with Riversong Guitars Venture," *Financial Post*, January 14, 2013; EMD Music Website, www.emdmusic.com, accessed May 8, 2015.

Taking a Bite out of Internet Radio

Ed Christman and Alex Pham, "Underwhelming Start to iTunes Radio Lights Fire Under Apple," *Billboard*, www.billboard.com/biz/articles/news/digital-and-mobile/6042224/underwhelming-start-to-itunes-radio-lights-fire-under, accessed May 19, 2015; Nancy Blair, "Apple's iTunes Radio Service: 3 Things to Know," *USA Today*, June 13, 2013, P11; Doug Gross, "Apple Arrives (Late?) to Music Streaming with iTunes Radio," CNN.com, June 11, 2013, Web, June 13, 2013; Glenn Peoples, "Leading from the Front," *Billboard*, May 2013; *EBSCO Business Source Premier*, June 13, 2013; Spotify Website, www.spotify.com/ca-en, accessed May 19, 2015; Mark Stone, "Canadians Take a Beating with Inability to Access Streaming Services like Pandora and Hulu," TechVibes.com, www.techvibes.com/blog/canadians-inability-to-access-streaming-services-2014-01-24, accessed May 19, 2015; CNET, "Samsung Regains Smartphone Sales Crown from Apple," www.cnet.com/news/samsung-regains-smartphone-sales-crown-from-apple, accessed May 19, 2015.

Where Are Gasoline Prices Headed?

Ronald J. Ebert and Ricky W. Griffin, *Business Essentials* (Boston: Pearson, 2015), 5; Gwyn Morgan, "Time to Seize a Prosperous Future Fuelled by Natural Gas," *Globe and Mail*, November 3, 2014, B6; Neil Reynolds, "Methane Hydrate Technology Fuels a New Energy Regime," *Globe and Mail*, May 16, 2012, B2; Gary Hunt, "The New Energy Order; Unconventional U.S. Oil and Gas Change Everything," *National Post*, February 17, 2012, FP13; Claudia Cattaneo, "All Eyes on Tight Oil's Future," *National Post*, February 16, 2012, FP5; Margot Habiby, "North American Oil Output Growth to Soar, IEA says: Behind Only OPEC," *National Post*, June 17, 2011, FP6; "ExxonMobil Makes Big Find of Oil Reserves in Gulf of Mexico," *National Post*, June 9, 2011, FP6; Brian Lee Crowley, "The Running Out of Resources Myth," *National Post*, May 27, 2011, FP11; Matt Ridley, "The Shale Revolution: Huge Supplies of Cheap Gas Shatter Peak Energy Fears," *National Post*, May 6, 2011, FP11; Neil Reynolds, "The Fossil Fuel King of the World," *Globe and Mail*, April 6, 2011, B2; Eric Reguly, "Nuclear's Loss Is Not a Worry," *Globe and Mail*, March 17, 2011, B2; Claudia Cattaneo, "Peak Oil Demand Theory in Vogue," *National Post*, January 26, 2009, FP1; John Lyons and David Luhnow, "Brazil May Be the Globe's Next Big Spigot," *Globe and Mail*, May 23, 2008, B8; "New Method to Extract Gas Hydrates," *Winnipeg Free Press*, April 17, 2008, A6; Neil King, "A Rosy View of Oil Supply," *Globe and Mail*, January 17, 2008, B7; Russell Gold and Ann Davis, "Oil Officials See Limit Looming on Production," *The Wall Street Journal*, November 19, 2007, A1; Shawn McCarthy, "Canada's Oil Boom Has Legs, IEA Says," *Globe and Mail*, July 10, 2007, B1; Neil Reynolds, "Peak Oil Doomsayers Fall Silent as Reserves Grow Ever Larger," *Globe and Mail*, April 11, 2007, B2; Robert Hirsch, "Peaking of World Oil Production: Recent Forecasts," *WorldOil* 228, April 2007; Patrick Brethour, "Peak Oil Theorists Don't Know Jack," *Globe and Mail*, September 6, 2006, B1; Michael Lynch, "Oil Discovery Forecasts Doomed," *Globe and Mail*, May 28, 2005, B6; Haris Anwar, "Supply: Are Saudi Reserves Drying Up?" *Globe and Mail*, May 21, 2005, B19.

CHAPTER 2

Supermarket Battles: Then There Were Three

Canadian Press, "Sobeys Profit Up from Year Ago, Boosted by Canada Safeway Acquisition," *Canadian Business*, March 12, 2015; Linda Nguyen, "Loblaw to Open 50 New Grocery Stores as Part of $1.2 Billion Investment," *Globe and Mail*, March 9, 2015; Ross Marowits, "Metro Says Slumping Oil Prices Driving Spending in Grocery Stores," *Canadian Business*, January 27, 2015; "Metro Hikes Dividend as Profits Rise 13.4%," *Globe and Mail*, January 27, 2015; Sobeys Corporate Website, corporate.sobeys.com, accessed March 21, 2015; Loblaws Corporate Website, www.loblaw.ca/English/About-Us/company-overview/default.aspx, accessed March 21, 2015; Metro Website, corpo.metro.ca/en/about-us.html, accessed March 21, 2015; Marina Strauss and Jeff Gray, "Price Check," *Globe and Mail*, November 18, 2014, B1; Marina Strauss, "Why Groceries Are Going Upscale," *Globe and Mail*, April 16, 2014, B8; Ross Marowits, "Metro Vows Patience Amid Sector Shakeup," *Globe and Mail*, January 29, 2014; Joe Castaldo, "A New Threat for Big Grocery," *Canadian Business*, October 14, 2013, P12; Marina Strauss, "With Safeway Deal Complete, Sobeys Demands Price Cuts," *Globe and Mail*, January 9, 2014, B1.

Here Comes the Hydrogen Fuel Cell ... Again

Jeremy Cato, "So ... Where Are Those Fuel Cell Cars, Exactly?" *Globe and Mail*, March 27, 2014, D6; Shawn McCarthy, "Hyundai Goes Hydrogen with Fuel-Cell Revival," *Globe and Mail*, November 26, 2014, B1; Brenda Bouw, "Hydrogenics Leads the Charge in Fuel Cells," *Globe and Mail*, August 6, 2014, B8; Brenda Bouw, "Plug Power Rides Wave of Enthusiasm for Fuel Cells," *Globe and Mail*, January 3, 2014, B6; Peter Kennedy, "Ballard's Celebrated Drive Hits a Bumpy Road," *Globe and Mail*, July 17, 2004, B6; Chris Nuttall-Smith, "Waiting for the Revolution," *Report on Business* (February, 2003): 44–54; Jeffrey Ball, "Hydrogen Fuel May Be Clean, but Getting It Here Looks Messy," *The Wall Street Journal*, March 7, 2003; Rebecca Blumenstein, "Auto Industry Reaches Surprising Consensus: It Needs New Engines," *The Wall Street Journal*, January 5, 1998, A1, A10.

Selling Magic in a Connected World

Based on a case written by Eric Dolansky, Brock University, Goodman School of Business, Selling Magic Online, Vanier/BDC Case Competition 2015.

The Impact of the Physical Environment

Jacqueline Nelson, "On Ontario's Docks and Patios, a Cool Summer Chills Profits," *Globe and Mail*, August 23, 2014, B1; Greg Keenan, "Essar Algoma Pounded by Winter Weather," *Globe and Mail*, March 28, 2014, B8; Ross Marowits, "Weather Takes Toll on Rona," *Globe and Mail*, February 19, 2014, B4; Eric Atkins, "Bitter Winter Dampens CN's Bottom Line," *Globe and Mail*, January 31, 2014, B3; Susan Krashinsky, "Ice Storm/Deep Freeze/Polar Vortex/Below Zero/Snow Squalls/Arctic Blast/Capitalization on Cold Weather," *Globe and Mail*, January 10, 2014, B6; Jacqueline Nelson, "Insurance Rates to Rise in Weather's Wake," *Globe and Mail*, January 8, 2014, B1; Brent Jang, "Deep Freeze at Pearson," *Globe and Mail*, January 8, 2014, A1; Eric Atkins, "Icy Air Sends Cattle Prices Soaring," *Globe and Mail*, January 8, 2014, B3; Jeffery Jones, "As Polar Vortex Hits, Natural Gas Prices Skyrocket," *Globe and Mail*, January 7, 2014, B3.

Staying Connected in the Skies

Gogo Company Website, gogoair.mediaroom.com; Gogo Air Canada Deal, www.gogoair.com/gogo/cms/aircanada.do, accessed March 20, 2015; Bloomberg Business, www.bloomberg.com/quote/GOGO:US, accessed March 20, 2015; David Koenig, "IPO Shares of Flight Web Service Gogo Fall," *USA Today*, June 22, 2013, www.usatoday.com/story/money/business/2013/06/22/gogo-nasdaq-airlines-wifi/2448083, accessed July 16, 2013; "GOGO: Summary for Gogo Inc.—Yahoo! Finance," *Yahoo Finance*, July 16, 2013; "Gogo—This Recent Public Offering Is Not Going Yet," *Seeking Alpha*, June 28, 2013, seekingalpha.com/article/1526942-gogo-this-recent-public-offering-is-not-going-yet, accessed July 16, 2013.

Netflix: Video Streaming Revolution

Netflix Website, ir.netflix.com, accessed March 20, 2015; James Bradshaw, "Netflix Buys into Canadian Show," *Globe and Mail*, October 21, 2014, B6; James Bradshaw, "Netflix Refuses CRTC Data Request," *Globe and Mail*, September 23, 2014, B3; Gautham Nagesh, "Another Battle Looms over Net Neutrality," *Globe and Mail*, May 1, 2014, B9; David Milstead, "Netflix Drama May Lack Happy Ending for Investors," *Globe and Mail*, September 6, 2012, B15; Samson Okalow, "Why Netflix Won't Conquer Canada, Canadian Business, February 1, 2013; Jennifer Roberts, "Netflix Comes Roaring Back After Price-Hike Miscue," *Globe and Mail*, January 26, 2012, B7; Susan Krashinsky, "Astral Taking HBO over the Top to Fend Off Netflix Threat," *Globe and Mail*, December 14, 2011, B3; Susan Krashinsky, "A New Canadian Player on Hollywood TV Buying Spree," *Globe and Mail*, May 30, 2011, B12; Ronald Grover and Cliff Edwards, "Can Netflix Find Its Future by Abandoning the Past?" *Businessweek*, October 2, 2011, P32; Susan Krashinsky, "Netflix Gets a Pass on Being Regulated—For Now," *Globe and Mail*, October 6, 2011, B5; Steve Laverdure, "For Blockbuster in Canada, The Closing Credits Roll," *Globe and Mail*, May 6, 2011, B1.

CHAPTER 3

What's Happening in the Fair Trade Movement?

Cathryn Atkinson, "The Roots of What We Consume," *Globe and Mail*, August 18, 2014, L6; Carl Mortished, "Fairtrade Certification Fails to Help the Poor, British Report Finds," *Globe and Mail*, May 27, 2014, B6; Ali Morrow, "What's in a Fair-Trade Label?" *Globe and Mail*, January 31, 2013, B12; Daina Lawrence, "Can Fair Trade Goods Get a Fair Shake as U.S. Resigns Pact?" *Globe and Mail*, May 12, 2012, B9; "Slaves Feed World's Taste for Chocolate," Knight Ridder News Service, January 9, 2011; "Chocolate and Slavery: Child Labor in Côte d'Ivoire," *TED Case Studies* 664, 2009; "Abolishing Child Labor on West African Cocoa Farms," SocialFunds.com, April 4, 2009; "Stoop Child Labor: Cocoa Campaign," International Labour Rights Forum, 2008, April 3, 2010; Jennifer Alsever, "Fair Prices for Farmers: Simply Idea, Complex Reality," *New York Times*, March 19, 2006.

Creating Games with a Social Twist

Based on a case written by Mary Charleson, Acsenda School of Management, Silicon Sisters, Vanier/BDC Case Competition. Jason Payne, "Silicon Sisters Interactive, a Vancouver-Based Gaming Company Formed to Address the Lack of Female-Themed Games," *Ottawa Citizen*, November 8, 2013; Kate Taylor, "Outside the Boy Box: Women Are Embracing and Rethinking Video Games," *Globe and Mail*, September 6, 2012; Craig and Marc Kielburger, "What Are Some Kids' Video Games That Carry Positive Messages," *The Globe and Mail*, August 6, 2012, www.theglobeandmail.com/life/giving/what-are-some-kids-video-games-that-carry-positive-messages/article4465504; Silicon Sisters Interactive Website, www.siliconsisters.ca, May 9, 2015; Rachel Webber, "Spielberg, Lucas and Del Toro Talk Game," Games Industry Website, www.gamesindustry.biz/articles/2013-06-13-spielberg-lucas-and-del-toro-talk-games, May 9, 2015.

Should We Pay Whistle-Blowers?

Barbara Shecter, "OSC Says Bounty 'Critical' to Success; Rewards for Whistleblowers Arrive, with Modesty; Financial Crimes," *National Post*, February 4, 2015, FP1; Tara Perkins, "U.S. Whistleblower Rewards Provide a Powerful Incentive," *Globe and Mail*, August 5, 2014, B2; David Gautheir-Villars, "Renault Security Held in Spy Case," *The Wall Street Journal*, March 12–13, 2011, B1; Edward Waitzer, "Should We Pay for Whistle-Blowing?" *National Post*, March 22, 2011, FP11; Dimitri Lascaris, "Speak Truth to Power," *National Post*, March 25, 2011, FP11; David Gauthier-Villars and Sebastian Moffett, "Renault to Yield in l'Affaire d'Espionnage," *The Wall Street Journal*, March 10, 2011, B1.

Some Frustrations in the Green Movement

Bjorn Lomborg, "Green Cars Have a Dirty Little Secret," *Wall Street Journal*, March 11, 2013, A15; Jeremy Cato, "It's Not Easy Buying Green," *Globe and Mail*, July 15, 2011, D1; Peter Foster, "The Coming Green Car Pileup," *National Post*, January 14, 2011, FP11; Veronique Dupont, "Consumer Interest in Green Cars Lags; Still Niche Market," *National Post*, January 12, 2011, FP3; Garry Marr, "We'll Go Green If the Price Is Right," *National Post*, November 17, 2010, FP10; Peter Foster, "Yellow Brick Road to Green Serfdom," *National Post*, November 10, 2010, FP17; Sarah Schmidt, "Public 'Greenwashed' by Eco-Friendly Claims: Study," *Winnipeg Free Press*, October 26, 2010, A2.

The Problem of Consumer Skepticism

Jeremy Cato, "It's Not Easy Buying Green," *Globe and Mail*, July 15, 2011, D1; William Watson, "Green Except When It Costs," *National Post*, March 9, 2011, FP17; Lindsey Wiebe, "Logo La-La Land," *Winnipeg Free Press*, August 23, 2009, A7; Lindsey Wiebe, "Will Consumers Go for True 'Green' Products?" *Winnipeg Free Press*, books section, August 2, 2009, 6; Diane Katz, "The Grocery-Bag Dilemma: Is Paper or Plastic Greener?" *Winnipeg Free Press*, July 26, 2009, A11; Susan Krashninsky, "The Green Gap," *Globe and Mail*, July 17, 2009, B4; "Beyond the Green Marketing Mirage: GoodGuide Supplies Instant Information on a Host of Products," *National Post*, June 22, 2009, FP5; Terrence Belford, "Developers Blue Over Green Roofs," *Globe and Mail*, June 16, 2009, B10; David Ebner, "Coke Will Use the Olympics to Launch Its Latest Environmental Push, but Will a Generation That's Grown Wary of 'Greenwashing' Buy the PlantBottle?" *Globe and Mail*, June 10, 2009, B1; William Watson, "The Uses of Eco-OCD," *National Post*, May 30, 2009, FP19; Jennifer Wells, "How Recession Changed the Green Marketplace," *Globe and Mail*, April 20, 2009, B1; Konrad Yakabuski, "Green Dreams, Unplugged," *Globe and Mail*, April 4, 2009, F1; Lawrence Solomon, "Green Economics: It Just Doesn't Add Up," *National Post*, March 31, 2009, FP11; Alia McMullen, "Will Green Agenda Fade? In Tough Times, Environmental Action May Lose Its Momentum," *National Post*, January 17, 2009, FP1; Joe Castaldo, "Green Counting," *Canadian Business*, October 13, 2008, 27.

CHAPTER 4

Mr. Ma: King of the Canadian Food Court!

MTY Website, www.mtygroup.com/en/home.aspx, accessed February 20, 2015; CNW Newswire, MTY Reports Earnings for Its 2014 Fiscal Period," February 5, 2015, www.newswire.ca/en/story/1486727/mty-reports-earnings-for-its-2014-fiscal-period#, accessed February 20, 2015; Bertrand Marotte, "Quebec Food Court King Ventures into Casual Dining," *Globe and Mail*, April 10, 2014, B1; Nicolas Van Praet, "Keurig Sells Quebec-Based Van Houtte Chain to MTY," *Globe and Mail*, November 7, 2014, B1; Bertrand Marotte, "Montreal's MTY to Buy Extreme Pita," *Globe and Mail*, May 28, 2013, B1; Richard Blackwell, "An Empire Served on a Plastic Tray," *Globe and Mail*, October 8, 2011, B3; Richard Blackwell, "Ravenous MTY Food Group Gobbles Up Mr. Submarine," *Globe and Mail*, April 18, 2011.

Teenage Innovator, Entrepreneur, and Multimillionaire

Kim Lachance Shandrow, "Young Millionaire: Inside the Mind of Yahoo's Teen Sensation Nick D'Aloisio," *Entrepreneur Magazine*, March 24, 2014, www.entrepreneur.com/article/232336 accessed February 4, 2015; Amir Efrati, "Yahoo Snaps Up Teen-Created News App," *Globe and Mail*, March 26, 2013, B10; "Natural Curiosity Pays Off for Yahoo's Teen Millionaire," *Globe and Mail*, March 27, 2013, B10; CBC Website, "Yahoo Buys Teen Developer's Bestselling App," March 26, 2013, www.cbc.ca/news/technology/story/2013/03/26/tech-yahoo.html, accessed April 26, 2013.

Harvard Dropout Turned Billionaire

Brad Stone, "Microsoft Buys Stake in Facebook," *New York Times*, October 25, 2007, p. B1; C.T. Moore, "The Future of Facebook Revenues," *ReveNews*, February 15, 2009, 4–6; "The Facebook IPO Timeline," mashable.com/2012/05/16/facebook-ipo-timeline, accessed April 2, 2013; MarketWatch Website, www.marketwatch.com/investing/stock/fb/financials, accessed February 15, 2015; Steve Hargreaves, CNN Money, money.cnn.com/2014/01/29/technology/facebook-earnings, accessed February 15, 2015;

Small Businesses Go Green

Jessica Leeder, "New Fund Has a Taste for Organic Food," *Globe and Mail*, September 5, 2011, B9; Mark Hume, "It All Depends on Which Way the Wind Blows," *Globe and Mail*, July 26, 2011, S3; Sarah Elton, "A Bicycle Built for Food (and Other Goods)," *Globe and Mail*, June 14, 2011, L3; Erin McPhee, "New Green Software a 'Quick Tax for Carbon,'" *National Post*, March 28, 2011, FP4; Deborah Cohen, "Rising Energy Costs Incentive to Go Greener: Entrepreneurs Finding New Ways to Cut Back," *National Post*, March 21, 2011, FP10; Todd Macintosh, "Small Firms Put Green Focus on Energy: Eco-Survey," *National Post*, June 21, 2010, FP7; Green Enterprise Ontario Website, greenenterprise.net/index.php, accessed June 18, 2010; Laura Ramsay, "Small Firms Can Go Green Too: There's Lots of Help Out There," *Globe and Mail*, October 14, 2008, E1; Burke Campbell, "Entrepreneur's Green Inspiration from the East," *National Post*, September 22, 2008, www.nationalpost.com/story-printer.html?id=812446.

Entrepreneurial Spirit: Beyond the Rack

Tanya Kostiw, "Brands of the Year: Beyond the Rack Gets into Closets," *Strategy Magazine*, strategyonline.ca/2014/10/06/brands-of-the-year-beyond-the-rack-gets-into-canadians-closets/#ixzz3SQLQ9U00, accessed February 20, 2014; Jason Madger, "Montreal's Beyond the Rack Closes a $10 Million Funding Deal," October 27, 2014; Becky Reuber, "Navigating the Shoals of Rapid Growth," *Globe and Mail*, April 15, 2011, B8; Boyd Erman, "Beyond the Rack Lands $12-Million Financing," *Globe and Mail*, July 12, 2010; "Flash Sale E-Tailer Beyond the Rack Expands Its Beauty Business by Adding Membership Base of BeautyStory.com," *Canadian Business*, July 5, 2011, www.canadianbusiness.com/24772, accessed September 27, 2011; Jameson Berkow, "Montreal's Beyond the Rack Named North America's Fastest-Growing Online Retailer," *Financial Post*, June 24, 2011; Sramana Mitra, "The Promise of e-Commerce," *Forbes Magazine*, September 4, 2010; Beyond the Rack Website, www.beyondtherack.com, accessed February 20, 2014.

CHAPTER 5

Not My Cup of Tea

Starbucks Website, "Starbuck Company Timeline," globalassets.starbucks.com/assets/5deaa36b7f454011a8597d271f552106.pdf, accessed May 6, 2015; Adam Jordan and Billy Rigby, "Starbucks Partners Drinks Maker Tingyi to Expand in China," Reuters, March 19, 2015; Burkitt, Laurie. "Starbucks Plays to Local Chinese Tastes," *Wall Street Journal*. Dow Jones Company, Inc., November 26, 2012, accessed June 13, 2013; "Greater China," Starbucks.com. Starbucks Corporation, n.d., accessed June 13, 2013; Helen H. Wang, "Five Things Starbucks Did to Get China Right," Forbes.com, August 10, 2012, accessed June 13, 2013; Teavana Website, www.teavana.com, accessed May 6, 2015.

Bugatti-Sedona: Charting a New Path

Export Development Canada Website, "EDC Financing Helps Propel Montreal's Bugatti-Sedona onto World Stage," February 11, 2015, www.edc.ca/EN/About-Us/News-Room/News-Releases/Pages/bugatti.aspx, accessed May 6, 2015; Bloomberg Business Website, Bugatti-Sedona Overview, www.bloomberg.com/research/stocks/private/snapshot.asp?privcapId=241309589, accessed May 6, 2015; CNW Newswire, "Bugatti An Iconic Brand Trades Hands," June 4, 2013, accessed May 6, 2015; Simon Forsythe, "From Body-Checks to Bugatti Business Bags," February 11, 2015, exportwise.ca/body-checks-bugatti-business-bags, accessed May 6, 2015; Marketers Media Website, "Bugatti at the 2015 Golden Globe Awards," January 12, 2015, marketersmedia.com/bugatti-at-the-2015-golden-globe-awards/71989, accessed May 6, 2015.

The Urge to Move

Ricky W. Griffin and Michael W. Pustay, *International Business: A Managerial Perspective*, 8th ed. (Upper Saddle River, NJ: Prentice-Hall, 2015); "Some Manufacturers Say 'Adios' to China," *USA Today*, March 19, 2013, 7B.

Scotiabank's Global Footprint

Scotiabank Mexico Website, www.scotiabank.com/images/en/filesservicesoutside/19312.pdf, accessed May 5, 2015; Grant Robertson, "Scotiabank's Patience Thins as China Weighs Guangzhou Deal," *Globe and Mail*, January 9, 2013, B1; Grant Robertson, "Scotiabank Sees Bright Future in South America," *Globe and Mail*, January 9, 2013, B1; Grant Robertson, "Shrinking Profit Margins Hit Scotiabank," *Globe and Mail*, May 30, 2012, B3; Grant Robertson, "Scotiabank Takes Stake in Chinese Bank," *Globe and Mail*, September 10, 2011, B9; Grant Robertson, "Scotiabank Finds a Pricier Merger Market," *Globe and Mail*, May 11, 2011, B4; Grant Robertson, "Canada's Banks Make Grade in World Standings," *Globe and Mail*, May 10, 2011, B4; Grant Robertson, "A Once Cautious Bank Takes a Bold Leap South," *Globe and Mail*, August 20, 2011, B6; Grant Robertson, "Scotiabank Profits Jump," *Globe and Mail*, August 30, 2011, B6; Steve Chase, "Scotiabank CEO Optimistic About Brazil Opportunities," *Globe and Mail*, August 9, 2011, B4; Steven Chase, "In Brazil, the Rise of the Mall," *Globe and Mail*, September 2, 2011, B1; Scotiabank Website, www.scotiabank.com/ca/en/0,,464,00.html, accessed May 1, 2015.

CHAPTER 6

Google Keeps Growing

"Google Corporation Information," April 11, 2013, www.google.com; "The Secret to Google's Success," *Businessweek*, March 6, 2008, www.businessweek.com; "In Search of the Real Google," *Time*, February 20, 2007, www.time.com; www.google.com/competition/howgooglesearchworks.html.

The Truth About Your Online Customer Service

"A World with Better Customer Service—Helping Consumers Find It, and Helping Businesses Achieve It," *StellaService*, www.stellaservice.com, accessed May 17, 2015; Dana Mattioli, "Data Firm Attracts Funding," *Wall Street Journal*, February 28, 2013, B5; Don Davis, "StellaService Raises $15 Million and Starts Charging for Its e-Retail Data," *Internet Retailer*, February 28, 2013, www.internetretailer.com/2013/02/28/stellaservice-raises-15-million-and-starts-charging-data; Lyz Welch, "A Solution for Fake Online Reviews," Inc.com, www.inc.com/magazine/201404/liz-welch/stella-service-rates-your-customer-service.html, accessed May 17, 2015.

Challenges Facing Managers

Ronald J. Ebert and Ricky W. Griffin, *Business Essentials* (Boston: Pearson, 2015), 279 ("Leadership Stretched to the Brink"), used with permission; Ronald J. Ebert and Ricky W. Griffin, *Business Essentials* (Boston: Pearson, 2015), 304 ("The Man Behind the Genius"), used with permission.

Some Complications in Setting Green Goals

Konrad Yakabuski, "Electric Cars Missed Their Moment. But Gas Taxes …," *Globe and Mail*, December 15, 2014, A13; Gary Mason, "B.C. Must Not Undo Fuel Standards: As Energy Minister Looks into Low-Carbon Requirements, the Province Risks Its Environmental Reputation," *Globe and Mail*, December 9, 2014, S1; Jeff Lewis, "Oil Sands Group Delays Setting Goals for Emissions," *Globe and Mail*, November 26, 2014, B4; Gwyn Morgan, "Time to Seize a Prosperous Future Fuelled by Natural Gas," *Globe and Mail*, November 3, 2014, B6; "Looking Good in Green," *Maclean's*, May 9, 2011, 47; Alexandra Lopez-Pacheco, "Planet-Friendly Offices," *National Post*, October 2, 2009, FP12; John Murphy, "Honda CEO Vies for Green Mantle," *The Wall Street Journal*, June 16, 2008, B1–B2; Sharda Prashad, "Good Green Goals," TheStar.com, April 22, 2007, www.thestar.com/printArticle/205855.

Corporate Culture

Claudia Cattaneo, "CNOOC Eyes Major Nexen Writedown; Billions May Be Lost to Setbacks After $15B Chinese Takeover," *National Post*, February 4, 2015, FP1; Claudia Cattaneo, "Culture Clash; Two Years After Ottawa Approved the Nexen Takeover, Moves by the Chines Owners Are Raising Hackles in the Oil Patch," *National Post*, December 13, 2014, FP1; "Innovation Propels Rogers," *National Post*, December 4, 2014, FP7; Christina Kramer and Laura Dottori-Attanasio, "Rising to the Challenge: CIBC Winners Exemplify Corporation Commitment to Advancing Gender Diversity," *National Post*, November 28, 2014, SC5; Christine Dobby, "Beyond Price: The Latest Twist in the Wireless Wars," *Globe and Mail*, November 7, 2014, B1; "Nod to Gravity Defying Oil Man," *National Post*, October 27, 2014, FP8; John Izzo, "A Lesson in Leading," *National Post*, September 6, 2014, FP7; Silvia Antonioli, "Glencore, Vale Break Off Talks over Canadian Nickel Deal: Share of Costs," *National Post*, September 3, 2014, FP4; Gordon Pitts, "Kraft CEO Still Digesting Cadbury Takeover," *Globe and Mail*, June 7, 2010, B8; "Vale Resumes Negotiations with Striking Sudbury Nickel Workers," *National Post*, June 5, 2010, FP4; Heidi Ulrichsen, "Vale Inco Plans to Bring in a 'Couple Hundred' Replacement Workers," *Sudbury Northern Life*, April 19, 2010, www.northernlife.ca/news/localNews/2010/04/replacementworkers-190410.aspx; Stacey Lavaillie, "Date Set for USW, Vale Inco Bad Faith Bargaining Hearing," *Sudbury Northern Life*, April 9, 2010, www.northernlife.ca/newes/localNews/2010/04/olrb-090410.aspex; Sharon Terlap, "GM's Plodding Culture Vexes Its Impatient CEO," *The Wall Street Journal*, April 7, 2010, B1; Kristine Owram, "Sudbury Strike Becomes Longest in Inco's History; Little Hope for Resolution," *The Canadian Press*, April 6, 2010, www.google.com/hostednews/canadianpress/article/ALeqM5j90NJ-uvH5ZhfZy08T; Steve Hamm, "IBM–Sun Merger Talks Off," *Bloomberg Businessweek*, April 5, 2009, www.businessweek.com/technology/content/apr2009/tc2009045_914072.htm; Paul Waldie, "Culture Clash Pits Business School Dean Against Faculty," April 1, 2010, www.globecampus.ca/in-the-news/aritcle/culture-clash; Bernard Simon and Jonathan Wheatley, "Heading in Opposite Directions," *Financial Times*, March 11, 2010, 10; "Corporate Culture Clash Took Fizz out of Merger," Asia News Network, www.asianewsnet.net/print.php?id=10019; Michael de la Merced and Chris Nicholson, "Kraft to Acquire Cadbury in Deal Worth $19 Billion," *The New York Times*, January 20, 2010, www.mytimes.com/2010/01/20/business/global/20kraft.html?pagewanted=print; Simon Bowers, "Cadbury Warns of Culture Clash Under Kraft," www.guardian.co.uk/business/2009/oct/21/cadbury-kraft-sales-profits-job-losses; "James Gosling Warns of 'Culture Clash' If IBM Buys Sun," *Computer Business Review*, March 23, 2009, www.businessreviewonline.com/blog/archives/2009/03/james_gosling_w.html.

CHAPTER 7

Time to Reorganize!

Julie Jargon, "Corporate News: McDonald's Sales Drop Worst in Years," *The Wall Street Journal*, December 9, 2014, B2; Natalia Drozdiak, "Germany Joins the Corporate Split Craze," *The Wall Street Journal*, December 1, 2014, B1; Gordon Isfeld, "Accountants Show They Can Get Along and Be a Model for Other Professions," *National Post*, November 29, 2014, FP9; Matthew Braga, "Chen Clears BlackBerry Brass; Cuts Put End to Consumer Push," *National Post*, November 26, 2014, FP1; Julie Jargon, "Corporate News:

McDonald's Hacks at Its Bureaucracy," *The Wall Street Journal*, October 31, 2014, B2; Supantha Mukherjee and Edwin Chan, "Hewlett-Packard to Split into Two Companies; 5,000 Jobs to Go," *National Post*, October 7, 2014, FP10; Jack Clark, "HP to Split Up: Report," *National Post*, October 6, 2014, FP1; Kristine Owram, "Bombardier Aerospace Chief Out in Shakeup: Jet Maker Cites CSeries Delays, Financial Woes," *National Post*, July 24, 2014, FP1; Greg Keenan, "Bombardier Restructures amid CSeries Woes," *Globe and Mail*, July 24, 2014, B1; "Corporate Watch," *Wall Street Journal*, July 10, 2014, B4; Janet McFarland, "Canadian Accountants Merge Under CPA Designation," *Globe and Mail*, June 24, 2014, B3; Hollie Shaw, "Sears Canada Cuts Felt First at Top, CEO Says: VP Ranks Trimmed," *National Post*, April 25, 2014, FP4; Greg Keenan, "Small Ambition: Nissan's Big Northern Bet," *Globe and Mail*, February 11, 2014, B5; Paul Ziobro, "Kraft to Cut Jobs as Part of Split," *The Wall Street Journal*, January 18, 2012, B3; Julie Jargon and Paul Ziobro, "Corporate News: Kraft Picks Leaders for Split—Rosenfeld and Vernon Next Will Hash Out Details on Teams, Sort Smaller Brands," *The Wall Street Journal*, December 6, 2011, B3; Gordon Pitts, "Immigrant, Engineer, Education Junkie: The Outsider at the Helm of Irving Oil," *Globe and Mail*, November 3, 2011, B1; Hollie Shaw, "Sobeys to Split Grocery Chain in Two," *National Post*, October 14, 2011, FP4; Joann Lublin and Bob Tita, "End of an Empire: Tyco Plans Split," *The Wall Street Journal*, September 20, 2011, B1; Paul Ziobro, "Kraft CEO Spent Billions Preparing to Dismantle," *The Wall Street Journal*, August 5, 2011, B1; Dean Jobb, "Tough Times for the Irving Clan," *Canadian Business*, September 13, 2010, 14; Gordon Pitts, "Death, Departure Set Irving on New Path," *Globe and Mail*, July 22, 2010, B1; Lee Hawkins, "Reversing 80 Years of History, GM Is Reining in Global Fiefs," *The Wall Street Journal*, October 6, 2004; Joann Lublin, "Place vs. Product: It's Tough to Choose a Management Model," *The Wall Street Journal*, June 27, 2001, A1, A4; Rekha Bach, "Heinz's Johnson to Divest Operations, Scrap Management of Firm by Region," *The Wall Street Journal*, December, 1997, B10–B12.

Green Roof Structures

Richard Blackwell, "Solar Power's New Wave," *Globe and Mail*, February 18, 2014, B5; David A. Hill, "Solar City Takes Aim at Home Energy Audit Market," *Colorado Energy News*, May 14, 2010, coloradoenergynews.com, accessed April 10, 2013; Rick Needham, "Helping Homeowners Harness the Sun," The Official Google Blog, June 14, 2011, googleblog.blogspot.com, accessed April 10, 2013; Pete Engardio and Adam Aston, "The Next Energy Innovators," *Businessweek*, July 16, 2009, www.businessweek.com, accessed April 10, 2013; "Solar Power for Less Than Your Cable Bill," *Environmental Forum*, April 24, 2008, blogs.reuters.com, accessed April 10, 2013; Julie Schmidt, "SolarCity Aims to Make Solar Power More Affordable," *USA Today*, November 10, 2009, www.usatoday.com, accessed April 10, 2013; Eric Wesoff, "SolarCity Adds Energy Efficiency to Solar Finance, Design and Monitoring" *Greentech Media*, October 14, 2010, www.greentechmedia.com, accessed April 10, 2013; Brenda Dalglish, "Up on the Roof, Green Takes Root," *Globe and Mail*, July 24, 2012, B7; Erica Kelly, "Banking's New Shade of Green," *Globe and Mail*, December 20, 2011, B8; Gail Johnson, "Easy to Be Green When Your Roof Saves You Money," *Globe and Mail*, November 15, 2011, B11; Martin Cash, "Terminal Case of Energy Efficiency," *Winnipeg Free Press*, October 29, 2011, B6; Shelley White, "Part Office Building, Part Power Plant," *Globe and Mail*, September 20, 2011, B10; "Green Buildings," *Canadian Business*, August 16–September 12, 2011, 55; Sarah Boesveld, "The Green Building Impact on Employees," *Globe and Mail*, October 19, 2010, B12; Jay Somerset, "A Building with an Energy All Its Own," *Globe and Mail*, November 11, 2008, B9.

Gossip on the Grapevine

Scaachi Koul, "The Case for … Office Gossip," *Canadian Business*, October, 2014, 28; Amy Gallo, "Go Ahead and Gossip," *Harvard Business Review* (March 2013): 21; Holly Green, "How to Prune Your Organizational Grapevine," *Forbes Magazine*, www.forbes.com/sites/work-in-progress/2012/05/22/how-to-prune-your-organizational-grapevine/?ss=strategies-solutions.

What Happened to the "Occupy Wall Street" Movement?

Terence Corcoran, "Wall St. Will Survive Climate Occupiers," *National Post*, September 23, 2014, FP1; Gordon Crovitz, "Occupy Astro Turf," *The Wall Street Journal*, January 30, 2012, A13; Omar El Akkad, "After the Campaign Put Out the Simple Twitter Hashtag #OccupyWallStreet, 'It Just Went Crazy,'" *Globe and Mail*, December 22, 2011, A12; Kathryn Blaze Carlson, "Utopian Failure; Why the Occupy Movement Is Doomed: Huan Brains Crave Hierarchy," *National Post*, November 26, 2011, A10; Gary Mason, "Founders of Leadnow Strive to Build a Progressive Voice with Real Focus," *Globe and Mail*, November 26, 2011, A18; "Five Reasons Why Occupy Failed," *National Post*, November 19, 2011, A10; Gary Mason, "Sorry, Folks, but This Protest's in Danger of Fizzling Out," *Globe and Mail*, November 3, 2011, A19; "Rogue Senate Page Lends Her Support to the 99ers," *National Post*, October 18, 2011, A8; Kim Mackrael, "Occupy Wall Street: Who They Are, What They Want," *Globe and Mail*, October 7, 2011, A23; Kelly McParland, "Confused Protesters March On; 'Movements' Don't Have Leaders or Clear Goals," *National Post*, October 4, 2011, A2.

CHAPTER 8

Can Different Generations Work Together?

Jessica Barrett, "Shattering Stereotypes; Companies Negotiate Challenges of Multi-Generational Workforce," *National Post*, November 4, 2014, FP3; Rebecca Walberg, "Clash in Styles: To Unlock Millennial Talent, Managers Must First Labour to Earn Their Respect," *National Post*, October 28, 2014, FP9; Shelley White, "Generation Z: The Kids Who'll Save the World?" *Globe and Mail*, September 26, 2014, E1; Rob Carrick, "The Impact of Gen Y on Retirement Plans," *Globe and Mail*, May 29, 2014, B12; Nicole Gallucci, "Five Tips for Motivating Millenials," *Globe and Mail*, January 24, 2014, B12; Zara McAlister, "Making a Living on Part-Time Employment," *National Post*, December 4, 2013, FP9; humanresources.about.com/od/businessmanagement/a/top_ten_trends.htm; humanresources.about.com/od/managementtips/a/millenial_myth.htm; humanresources.about.com/od/managementtips/a/millenials.htm; Fred Vettese, "The Great Generational Divide," *National Post*, December 1, 2012, FP10; Harvey Schachter, "Five Myths About Generation Y Workers," *Globe and Mail*, April 2, 2012, B7; Derek Abma, "GenXers Least Happy at Work," *National Post*, November 30, 2011, FP10.

"Green" Jobs in Some Surprising Places

Richard Blackwell, "Green Jobs Surpass Oil Sands Total: Climate Think Tank Says Ottawa Is 'Really Missing in Action' When It Comes to Support for Clean Energy," *Globe and Mail*, December 2, 2014, B3; Alexandra Lopez-Pacheco, "Green Jobs Tied to Resources Extraction," *National Post*, October 20, 2013, FP10; Derek Sankey, "Green Careers Available in Every Sector," *National Post*, November 7, 2012, FP11; "Looking Good in Green," *Maclean's*, May 9, 2011, 47; Katie Engelhart, "From the Bottom Up," *Canadian Business*, April 27–May 10, 2010, 60; Greg McMillan, "The Greening of the Jobscape," *Globe and Mail*, November 14, 2008, B7; Marjo Johne, "Show Us the Green, Workers Say," *Globe and Mail*, October 10, 2007, C1; "Creating Jobs by Going Green," www.premier.gov.on.ca/news/Product.asp?ProductID=1400.

LinkedIn: Strengthening Your Ability to Connect

"LinkedIn Financial Figures," Google Finance, www.google.ca/finance?q=NYSE: LNKD&fstype=ii, accessed May 9, 2015; McClatchy Newspapers (Minneapolis), "Social Networking Sites Make Powerful Job-Hunting Tools," *Columbia Daily Tribune*, January 21, 2009, 7B; "LinkedIn Launches New Tools to Boost HR Professionals' Efficiency as Responses to Job Postings Double in Challenging Economy," press release, accessed February 2, 2009, press.linkedin.com/linkedin-new-hr-tools, accessed March 3, 2013.

Defined Benefit Versus Defined Contribution Pension Plans

Robert Brown and Craig McInnes, "DB to DC Won't Work: Call for the Conversion of Defined Benefit Public Pensions to Defined Contribution Harms Efficiency and Increases Cost," *National Post*, October 8, 2014, FP11; Mathew McClearn, "High Noon for Canadian Carmaking," *Canadian Business*, March, 2014, 7; Jonathan Chevreau, "PRPPs Will Do Nothing to Address Pension Crisis, Monica Townson Says," *National Post*, December 7, 2011, FP7; Jonathan Chevreau, "Jumping into the Pension Pool: PRPPs Will Only Work If They Are Mandatory," *National Post*, November 23, 2011, FP7; Jonathan Chevreau, "'Social Tragedy' in Pension Loss: Defined Benefit Plans a

Great Value: Author," *National Post*, November 21, 2011, FP2; John Crocker, "Keep Defined-Benefit Pensions," *National Post*, November 15, 2011, FP17; R. Brown, "Air Canada Pioneers Pension Advance," *National Post*, November 4, 2011, FP11; Greg Keenan, "U.S. Steel Union Relents on Key Contract Demands," *Globe and Mail*, October 13, 2011, B3; Barry Critchley, "Big Banks Face Benefit Shortfalls; Hit by Low Rates," *National Post*, September 28, 2011, FP1; "RBC Changing New-Hire Pensions," *Globe and Mail*, September 24, 2011, B11.

Is a New Era of Labour Relations Dawning at Air Canada?

Scott Deveau, "Air Canada Pilots Not Trusting of Union, Executives: Pilots Association Survey," *National Post*, July 24, 2013, FP3; Scott Deveau, "Raitt Appoints Arbitrators to Hear Dispute Between Air Canada, Unions," *National Post*, May 3, 2013, FP4; Scott Deveau, "Air Canada Moves to Prevent More Sick-Outs: Cancelled Flights May Extend into Weekend," *National Post*, April 14, 2012, FP4; Scott Deveau, "Air Canada Warns Union President over Safety Remarks; 'Breach of His Duties,'" *National Post*, April 10, 2012, FP2; Scott Deveau, "Air Canada Labour Disputes Put on Hold; Unions Challenge Government's Back-to-Work Bill," *National Post*, April 3, 2012, FP4; Christine Dobby, "Air Canada Labour Relations Worsen; Wildcat Strike," *National Post*, March 24, 2012, FP4; Scott Deveau, "Air Canada Headed for Arbitration," *National Post*, March 15, 2012, FP4; Scott Deveau, "Air Canada Gets Tentative Deal with Attendants," *National Post*, August 2, 2011, FP2; Scott Deveau, "Air Canada Workers Approve Accord," *National Post*, June 28, 2011, P. FP4; Kristine Owram, "Air Canada Union Deal Sign of New Labour Era: 10-Year Agreement," *National Post*, October 7, 2014, FP4; Brent Jang, "Air Canada Labour Relations Tested," *Globe and Mail*, January 21, 2005, B4; Keith McArthur, "Cuts Take Harsh Toll on Air Canada Employees," *Globe and Mail*, May 2, 2004, B1, B16; "Unions, Airline Give Nod to Deal," *Winnipeg Free Press*, May 25, 2003, A6; Cassandra Szklarski, "Air Canada Reaches Tentative Deal with Machinists," *Winnipeg Free Press*, May 28, 2003, B6, B10; "1,000 AirCan Mechanics Told to Take Summer Off," *Winnipeg Free Press*, May 16, 2003, B7; David Paddon, "Airline Charting New Territory," *Winnipeg Free Press*, April 2, 2003, B4, B5; Keith McArthur, "Air Canada to Fight Hostile Motions," *Globe and Mail*, April 21, 2003, B1, B8; Allan Swift, "Air Canada Unions OK Cuts," *Winnipeg Free Press*, April 1, 2003, B1, B8; David Paddon, "Air Canada to Shed More Jobs," *Winnipeg Free Press*, April 23, 2003, B9.

CHAPTER 9

Satisfaction, Productivity, and Employee Engagement

Jared Lindzon, "How Employee Engagement Can Boost the Bottom Line: Finding Ways to Make Your Staff Happier Generates Better Results for the Company as a Whole," *Globe and Mail*, December 3, 2014, B17; Deborah Aarts, "The Truth About Employee Engagement," *Canadian Business* 87(2), 31–32, 34–35; "Do Happy Workers Mean Higher Profits?" *USA Today*, February 20, 2013, 1B; R. Spence, "Harness Employee Power," *National Post*, June 25, 2012, FP4; "One in Two U.S. Employees Looking to Leave or Checked Out on the Job, Says *What's Working* Research," www.mercer.com/press-releases/1418665, accessed January 3, 2012; Marjo Johne, "Firing on All Cylinders with Social Media," *Globe and Mail*, October 21, 2011, B15; Wallace Immen, "Canadian Companies Warm to Social Media," *Globe and Mail*, June 10, 2011, B16; Darah Hansen, "New Age, New Problems: Social Media No. 1 Concern for Employers," *National Post*, June 8, 2011, FP11; Wallace Immen, "Feeling Unmotivated? HR Managers Say It's the Boss's Fault," *Globe and Mail*, March 23, 2011, B21; Richard Branson, "Don't Leave Employees on the Outside Looking In," *Canadian Business*, July 20–August 16, 2010, 13; Joe Castaldo, "How to Coax Ideas out of a Sheepish Staff," *Canadian Business*, April 27–May 10, 2010, 80; Katie Engelhart, "From the Bottom Up," *Canadian Business*, April 27–May 10, 2010, 60; Leena Rao, "I Love Rewards Raises $5.9 Million for Employee Rewards Program," TechCrunch Website, www.techcrunch.com/2009/05/07/i-love-rewards-raises-59-million-for-employee-rewards-program accessed May 7, 2009; Chris Atchison, "Masters of One," *Profit* 28(2) (May 2009), 18; Charles Kerns, "Putting Performance and Happiness Together in the Workplace," *Graziado Business Report* 11 (2008), gbr.pepperdine.edu, accessed April 13, 2013; Alexander Kjerulf, "Top 10 Reasons Why Happiness at Work Is the Ultimate Productivity Booster," PositiveSharing.com, March 27, 2007, positivesharing.com, accessed April 13, 2013; Ari Weinzweig, "Ask Inc: Tough Questions, Smart Answers," *Inc.* 29(12) (December 2007): 84; Virginia Galt, "Ideas: Employees' Best-Kept Secrets," *Globe and Mail*, June 18, 2005, B11; Frederick A. Starke, Bruno Dyck, and Michael Mauws, "Coping with the Sudden Loss of an Indispensable Worker," *Journal of Applied Behavioral Science* 39(2) (2003): 208–229; Timothy Aeppel, "On Factory Floors, Top Workers Hide Secrets to Success," *The Wall Street Journal*, July 1, 2002, A1, A10; Timothy Aeppel, "Not All Workers Find Idea of Empowerment as Neat as It Sounds," *The Wall Street Journal*, September 8, 1997, A1, A13.

Employers Are Judging Your Social Life

Canadian Press, "Man Fired by Hydro One Apologizes to Reporter for Vulgarities: CityNews," www.thestar.com/news/crime/2015/05/15/man-fired-by-hydro-one-apologizes-to-reporter-for-vulgarities-citynews.html, accessed May 17, 2015; Susie Poppick, "10 Social Media Blunders That Cost a Millennial a Job—or Worse," Time.com Money Website, September 5, 2014, time.com/money/3019899/10-facebook-twitter-mistakes-lost-job-millennials-viral, accessed May 17, 2015; "Think Before You Tweet," *Globe and Mail*, May 25, 2011, B9; Fox News Website, "Twitter Feed F-Word Gets Chrysler Employee Fired," www.foxnews.com/us/2011/03/10/f-word-appears-chryslers-twitter-feed/March 11, 2011, accessed January 4, 2012; Scott Edmonds, "Car Dealership Employees Fired for Facebook Posts," *Globe and Mail*, December 9, 2010, B9.

Carrot or Stick?

David Hall, "Daniel Kahneman Interview," *New Zealand Listener*, January 21, 2012, www.listener.co.nz, accessed April 12, 2013; Steve Miller, "We're Not Very Good Statisticians," *Information Management*, March 26, 2012, www.information-management.com, accessed April 12, 2013; Galen Strawson, "*Thinking, Fast and Slow* by Daniel Kahneman—Review," *The Guardian*, December 13, 2011, www.guardian.co.uk, accessed April 12, 2013; *Judgment Under Uncertainty: Heuristics and Biases*, ed. Daniel Kahneman, Paul Slovic, and Amos Tversky (Cambridge, UK: Cambridge University Press, 1982), 68, books.google.com, accessed April 21, 2013.

Searching for a Great Place to Work

Ronald J. Ebert and Ricky W. Griffin, *Business Essentials* (Boston: Pearson, 2015), 273, used with permission; Canada's Top 100.com, accessed January 2, 2015; Ronald J. Ebert and Ricky W. Griffin, *Business Essentials* (Boston: Pearson, 2013), 248, used with permission.

CHAPTER 10

Big Changes in Canadian Manufacturing

Greg Keenan, "Mexico Shifts into Overdrive," *Globe and Mail*, February 14, 2015, B1; Mary Teresa Bitti, "Linamar Chief Has a Firm Hand on the Wheel," *National Post*, December 15, 2014, FP5; Greg Keenan, David Parkinson, and Brent Jang, "The Fall of Forestry: An Industry in Retreat," *Globe and Mail*, December 6, 2014, B1; David Parkinson, "Canadian Factories Getting Busy," *Globe and Mail*, September 11, 2014, B5; Kristine Owram, "'We're Fighting an Uphill Battle'; With Automakers' Promises Ending Soon, It May Be the End of the Road for Some Canadian Operations," *National Post*, August 23, 2014, FP5; David Parkinson, "Canada's Manufacturers Limping Back to Health," *Globe and Mail*, May 16, 2014, B4; Gordon Isfeld, "Economy's Tectonic Shift Not Over Yet: Studies; Resources Rising," *National Post*, May 8, 2014, A1; Greg Keenan, "Made (Smarter) in Canada: Inside a World-Beating Factory," *Globe and Mail*, March 2, 2013, B6; P. Cross, "Dutch Disease in Canada a Myth; Manufacturers Have Adapted to Higher Loonie," *National Post*, January 16, 2013, FP1; Greg Keenan, "GM to Slash Oshawa Line, Move Production to Tennessee," *Globe and Mail*, June 2, 2012, B4; Livio Di Matteo, "Everybody's Dutch: All G7 Nations Have Seen Manufacturing Declines," *National Post*, May 30, 2012, FP11; Greg Keenan, "Stage Set for Standoff with Unions, Auto Makers," *Globe and Mail*, April 17, 2012, B1; Barrie McKenna, "Manufacturing Hard Hit, but It's Nowhere Near Dead," *Globe and Mail*, March 19, 2012, B1; Gordon Pitts, "In Alberta, Oil Sands Fuel a Factory Boom," *Globe and Mail*, March 6, 2012, B1; Greg Keenan, "Ten Years of High Loonie Takes Big Toll on Country's Factories," *Globe and Mail*,

March 2, 2012, B1; Greg Keenan, "Indiana Beckons Factories Squeezed by Higher Costs," *Globe and Mail*, February 16, 2012, B1; Tavia Grant and Greg Keenan, "Factory Employment Hits a 35-Year Low as More Plants Close," *Globe and Mail*, November 5, 2011, B1; Jacquie McNish, "Maple Leaf's Big Move," *Globe and Mail*, October 20, 2011, B1; Kevin Carmichael, "From a Burst Bubble, a New Brand of Manufacturing Emerges in Ottawa," *Globe and Mail*, June 11, 2011, B11.

Producing Green Energy

Martin Hutchinson, "Solar Firm's Bankruptcy Shines Light on U.S. Policy," *Globe and Mail*, September 15, 2011, B12; Peter Foster, "Scorched by Solar," *National Post*, September 3, 2011, FP17; Neil Reynolds, "The German Irony: Will It Have to Import Nuclear Energy?" *Globe and Mail*, June 15, 2011, B2; Brian McKenna, "McGuinty's Green Energy 'Explosion' More of an Implosion," *Globe and Mail*, June 13, 2011, B2; Claudia Cattaneo, "Consumers Will Opt for Lowest Cost: Report," *National Post*, April 28, 2011, FP8; Lawrence Solomon, "Nuclear Power Extremes; The Problems with Nuclear Support from Both Right and Left," *National Post*, April 9, 2011, FP19; "The New Impossible Energy No-Fly Zone," May 17, 2011, FP11; Richard Blackwell, "Activists Lose Court Challenge over Wind Power Turbines," *Globe and Mail*, March 4, 2011, B5; Todd Woody, "Solar Power Plans Spark Lawsuit Storm," *National Post*, February 25, 2011, FP3; Lawrence Solomon, "Green Collapse: Across the World, Unsustainable Subsidies for Wind and Solar Are Being Cut Back—Ontario Is Next," *National Post*, December 4, 2010, FP19; Lawrence Solomon, "Profitin' in the Wind: Billionaire Energy Tycoon T. Boone Pickens Has a Two-Step Plan to Cash in on Climate Change. Today," *National Post*, July 18, 2009, FP19; "Fossil Fuel Dependency to Continue for Rest of Century, Expert Says," *National Post*, July 16, 2009, FP4; Sigurd Lauge Pedersen, "Wind Power Works," *National Post*, May 12, 2009, FP13; Michael J. Trebilcock, "Wind Power Is a Complete Disaster," *National Post*, April 9, 2009, FP13; Diane Francis, "Canada's Nuclear Power Play," *National Post*, October 25, 2008, FP2; Neil Reynolds, "Wind Turbine Marketers Are Full of Hot Air," *Globe and Mail*, July 11, 2008, B2; Peter Moreira, "Irving Oil Looks to Make Waves with Tidal Power," *Globe and Mail*, May 27, 2008, B7; Rebecca Smith, "New Wave of Nuclear Plants Faces High Costs," *The Wall Street Journal*, May 12, 2008, B1; Patrick Barta, "In Australia, a Wind-Powered Plant Makes Water from Ocean Fit to Drink," *The Wall Street Journal*, March 11, 2008, A1; Lauren Etter, "Ethanol Craze Cools as Doubts Multiply," *The Wall Street Journal*, November 28, 2007, A1; Patrick Barta, "Jatropha Plant Gains Steam in Global Race for Biofuels," *The Wall Street Journal*, August 24, 2007, A1; Patrick Barta and Jane Spencer, "As Alternative Fuels Heat Up, Environmental Concerns Grow," *The Wall Street Journal*, December 5, 2006, A1; Richard Blackwell, "In Ontario and Alberta, How Much Wind Power Is Too Much?" *Globe and Mail*, October 30, 2006, B1.

Will Robots Take Your Job?

Andrew Jackson, "Computers, Jobs and Rising Income Inequality," *Globe and Mail*, January 8, 2015, B2; John Revill, "Robots Keep the Beer Flowing," *The Wall Street Journal*, December 27–28, 2014, B4; Diane Francis, "Silicon Valley Brings Robots to the Masses," *National Post*, December 13, 2014, FP2; Peter Cheney, "Rebirth of a Nation," *Globe and Mail*, December 11, 2014, D1; Leah Eichler, "I, for One, Welcome Our Robot Overlords," *Globe and Mail*, August 30, 2014, B14; Barrie McKenna, "Driverless Cars on a Jobless Street? The Downside of a Robotic Future," *Globe and Mail*, August 7, 2014, B1; Tavia Grant, "Rise of the Affordable Robot: Cheap Robotics Tip into Mass Market," *Globe and Mail*, April 21, 2014, A1; Carl Mortished, "The Robots Are Coming, but Productivity Is Still Slumping," *Globe and Mail*, January 16, 2014, B2; Greg Bensinger, "Before the Drones Come, Amazon Lets Loose the Robots," *The Wall Street Journal*, December 9, 2013, B6.

Some Glitches in the Provision of Services

www.worldairlineawards.com/Awards_2014/Airline2014_top20.htm; Scott McCartney, "Ranking Airlines by Lost Bags, Canceled Flights," *The Wall Street Journal*, January 5, 2012, D3; Karen Howlett, "Ontario Launches Review of Travel Industry Watchdog Due to Conquest's Demise," *Globe and Mail,* April 22, 2009; Keith Leslie, "Other Tour Operators 'Likely' Face Financial Problems: McGuinty," *Globe and Mail*, April 21, 2009.

CHAPTER 11

Searching for Stolen Maple Syrup: Accounting for Missing Inventory

Carolyn Jarvis and Francesca Fionda, "More Arrests in Quebec Maple Syrup Heist," Global News, globalnews.ca/news/1589998/how-did-18-million-dollars-worth-of-maple-syrup-go-missing-from-a-warehouse-in-quebec, accessed March 9, 2015; Brandon Borrell, "Sticky Gold," *Bloomberg Business Week*, January 4, 2013, 58–61; Tina Shufelt, "The Great Canadian Maple Syrup Heist," *Canadian Business*, November 26, 2012, 52–56; Anne Sutherland, "Vermont Firm Implicated in $20-Million Maple Syrup Heist from Quebec Warehouse," *Montreal Gazette*, February 8, 2013; Canadian Press, "Police Make Arrests in Massive Maple Syrup Heist," *CTV News.ca*, December 12, 2012; Graeme Hamilton, "The Maple Syrup Cartel: Quebec's Syrup Monopoly Helped Spawn Smuggling Prohibition Style," *National Post*, February 16, 2013; Bertrand Marotte, "Maple Syrup Delinquents Raided," *Globe and Mail*, April 18, 2013, B3.

Accounting Practices for the Small Business

"10 Do's and Don'ts on Small Business Accounting Practice," BassFishingGuide, bassfishingguide.hubpages. com/hub/10-Dos-And-Donts-On-Small-Business-Accounting-Practice, accessed May 30, 2013.

The Fairness Dilemma: What Is an Asset's Real Value?

Louis R. Woodhill, "One Way to Deal with Toxic assets," *RealClearMarkets*, January 23, 2009, www.realclearmarkets.com/articles/2009/01/one_way_to_deal_with_toxic_ass.html; Patrick F. Gannon, "Demystifying Mark-to-Market," Forbes.com, April 21, 2009, www.forbes.com/2009/04/21mark-to-market-personal-finance-guru-insights-accounting-standards.html; Steven L. Henning, "Controlling the Real-World Risks of Mark-to-Market Valuation," *WebCPA*, June 1, 2009, www.webcpa.com/ato_issues/2009_9/-50466-1.html?pg=3; Jouhn Berlau, "The Mark-to-Market Relief Rally," *OpenMarket.org*, April 2, 2009, www.openmarket.org/2009.04/02/the-mark-to-market-relief-rally; "Instant View: U.S. Eases Mark-to-Market Accounting," "April 2, 2009, *Reuters*, www.reuters.com/article/2009/04/02us-financial-accounting-instant-view-idUKTRE5314PX20090402; Elizabeth Williamson and Kara Scannell, "Momentum Gathers to Ease Mark-to-Market Accounting Rule," WJS.com, October 2008, online.wsj.com/article/SB122290736164696507.html.

CSI: Stock Market Edition

Lison Joseph, C.R. Sukumar, and K. Raghu, "Ramalinga Raju Admits to Accounting Fraud, Resigns," livemint.com, January 31, 2012, www.livemint.com/Companies/ldmclvNdW3Z6dNayVfZSPI/Ramalinga-Raju-admits-to-accounting-fraud-resigns.html; Adam Piore, "Fraud Scene Investigator," *Portfolio*, March 10, 2008, www.portfolio.com/careers/job-of-the-week/2008/03/10/Forensic-Accountant-Al-Vondra; Albert A. Vondra, *LinkedIn*, December 12, 2012, www.linkedin.com/pub/albert-a-vondra/1a/57b/459, accessed February 14, 2013; Kartik Goyal and Subramanian Sharma, "India Orders Fraud Office Probe into Satyam Computer Accounts," Bloomberg.com, January 13, 2009, www.bloomberg.com/apps/news?pid=20601091&refer=india&sid=ayhBmRJs7nh0; ACFE Website, www.acfe.com/canadian-main.aspx#home, accessed March 7, 2015; Adam Smith, "The Reasons Fraud Spikes in a Recession," *Time*, May 20, 2009, www.time.com/time/business/article/0,8599,1899798,00.html; "Recession-Proof Career: Forensic Accounting and IT Auditing Financial Fraud Increases in Economic Recessions," *UAB Media Relations*, November 6, 2008, main.uab.edu/Sites/MediaRelations/articles/54133; www.uab.edu/newsarchive/54133-recession-proof-career-forensic-accounting-and-it-auditing-financial-fraud-increases-in-economic-recessions; Will Kenyon, "Five Tips for Combating Fraud in the Recession," Finance Week, March 23, 2009, www.financeweek.co.uk/risk/five-tips-combating-fraud-recession; Association of Certified Fraud Examiners (ACFE), "2012 Report to the Nations," Austin, TX, 2012, www.acfe.com/rttn-Highlights.aspx; "U.S. Securities and Exchange Commission Annual Report on the Dodd-Frank Whistleblower Program, Fiscal Year 2012," at www.sec.gov/about/offices/owb/annual-report-2012.pdf; Russ Schreiber, "Fighting Fraud: Predictive Analytics & Business Rules Make a Powerful Combination," *Insurance & Technology*, March 19, 2012, www.insurancetech.com/security/fighting-fraud-predictive-analytics-bus/232602826; Katy Stech, "Fighting Fraud: Link Between Bogus Insurance Claims,

Recession Is Murky," *The Post and Courier*, August 9, 2010, www.postandcourier.com/news/2010/aug/09/fighting-fraud; Randy Southerland, "Recession Pressures May Boost Employee Fraud," *Atlanta Business Chronicle*, August 19, 2010, www.bizjournals.com/atlanta/stories/2010/08/23/focus9.html; "Fraud to Thrive Beyond the Economic Downturn," *Lloyd's*, January 18, 2010, www.lloyds.com/News-and-Insight/News-and-Features/Business-Risk/Business-2010/Fraud_to_thrive_beyond_the_economic_downturn; "Examples of Corporate Fraud Investigations—Fiscal Year 2010," *IRS.gov*, www.irs.gov/compliance/enforcement/article/0,,id=213768,00.html; "Examples of Corporate Fraud Investigations—Fiscal Year 2012," IRS.gov, www.irs.gov/uac/Examples-of-Corporate-Fraud-Investigations-Fiscal-Year-2012; Marshall B. Romney and Paul John Steinbart, *Accounting Information Systems*, 11th ed. (Upper Saddle River, NJ: Prentice Hall, 2009), ch. 1.

CHAPTER 12

P&G Marketing: Dealing with a Shrinking Middle Class

"Company Statistics," Procter & Gamble Website, news.pg.com/about, accessed May 15, 2015; Roshni Bhatnagar, "Why Citi's Consumer Hourglass Theory Matters," *Northwestern Business Review*, January 3, 2012, northwesternbusinessreview.org/why-citis-consumer-hourglass-theory-matters, accessed May 15, 2015; Ellen Byron, "As Middle Class Shrinks, P&G Aims High and Low," *Wall Street Journal*, September 12, 2011, A1, A16; Aimee Groth, "The Consumer Hourglass Theory: This Is Why P&G, Saks, and Heinz Are Ignoring the Middle Class," *Business Insider*, September 24, 2011, www.businessinsider.com/hourglass-consumer-theory-pg-citigroup-2011-9.

Feeling the Pressure for "Green"

Ronald J. Ebert and Ricky W. Griffin, *Business Essentials* (Boston: Pearson, 2015), 355; Robert Matas, "B.C. Forecasts Boom Market for Clean-Energy Vehicles," *Globe and Mail*, November 17, 2011, S3; Brent Jang, "Ford Management Looks to Green Technology to Give Brand a Market Edge," *National Post*, June 14, 2011, FP9; "CN Touts the Green Advantage of Rail Shipments," *Globe and Mail*, April 28, 2011, B3; "Pepsico to Begin Testing New Plant-Based Bottle Next Year," *National Post*, March 16, 2011, FP6; Jim Henry, "Prius Hybrid Aimed Small, Stood Tall," *Automotive News*, October 29, 2007, 150.

Retailers Are Watching and Tracking You

Tim Kiladze, "Why Your Smartphone is Telling This Toronto Tech Firm All About You," *Globe and Mail*, January 14, 2014; "Who's Watching Whom," *Report on Business*, February 2013, 12–13; Marina Strauss, "In Store Aisles, Dr. Dre Meets Big Data," *Globe and Mail*, March 5, 2013, B20; Anton Troianovski, "New WiFi Pitch: Tracking Shoppers," *Globe and Mail*, June 19, 2012, B9; Marina Strauss, "Retailers Revamp with a High-Tech Makeover," *Globe and Mail*, February 21, 2012, B3; "Big Brother Arrives at a Store Near You," *Bloomberg Businessweek*, December 19–25, 2011, 41–42; Susan Krashinsky, "Ads That Reach out to the Passing Pedestrian," *Globe and Mail*, February 28, 2012, B3; Bryan Borzykowski, "Are Checkout Counters Headed for Extinction?" *Globe and Mail*, February 22, 2013, B12.

This Business Is Appsolutely Booming

Altebis Website, www.atebits.com/contact, accessed May 13, 2015; Emily Maltby and Angus Loten, "App Building, the Do-It-Yourself Way," *Wall Street Journal*, March 7, 2013, B4; Jessica E. Lessin, "High Priest of App Design, Home in Philly," *Wall Street Journal*, March 18, 2013, B1, B5; "Twitter's Loren Brichter Aims for Patent on Pull-to-Refresh," *MacNN News*, March 27, 2012, www.macnn.com/articles/12/03/27/tech.already.used.in.many.third.party.titles; Romain Dillet, "Tweetie Creator Loren Brichter's Next Act: Atebits 2.0 to 'Make Fun and Useful Things' [Like Games]," *TechCrunch*, October 15, 2012, techcrunch.com/2012/10/15/tweetie-creator-loren-brichters-next-act-atebits-2-0-to-make-fun-and-useful-things-like-games; "Twitter Acquires Atebits, Will Make Tweetie for iPad," *Electronista*, April 9, 2010, www.electronista.com/articles/10/04/09/twitter.hand.picks.tweetie.for.apps; Bryan M. Wolfe, "Glyph Users Can Maximize Their Card Rewards and Protect Their Credit," *AppAdvice*, February 13, 2013, appadvice.com/appnn/2013/02/glyph-users-can-maximize-their-card-rewards-and-protect-their-credit.

The Car Branding Game: Two Companies, Two Brands, One Platform

Patrick George, "Everyone Is Wrong About Subaru BRZ and Scion FR-S Sales," March 11, 2014, accessed May 15, 2015; Jack Baruth, "Clueless Dealers Do the Scion FR-S and Subaru BRZ No Favors," *Road and Track Magazine*, March 7, 2014, www.roadandtrack.com/car-culture/a6313/avoidable-contact-at-dealers-the-frs-brz-story-is-told-by-idiots, accessed May 15, 2015; Marc Hacking, "When Competitors Team Up," *Globe and Mail*, January 24, 2012, B11; Ian Sherr, "Auto Makers Debut 'Intelligent' Car Systems," *Globe and Mail*, January 13, 2012, B8; Magna International Website, Vehicle Content, www.magna.com/about-magna, accessed May 15, 2015; Courtland Bovee, John Thill and George Dracopoulos, "Magna International," *Business in Action* (New York: Pearson Education, 2009), 228.

CHAPTER 13

Premium Pricing, Rising Market Share

Danone Website, "One Yogurt A Day: Improving Consumer Health One Spoonful at a Time," www.danone.ca/sites/default/files/press-pdfs/Press%20kit_ActiviaGreek_EN_final.pdf, accessed May 21, 2015; "Greek Yogurt's Market Share of the U.S. Yogurt Market in 2008 and 2014," www.statista.com/statistics/279746/us-market-greek-yogurts-market-share, accessed May 21, 2015; Susan Krashinsky, "In the War for Healthy Eating, Greek Yogurt Takes Palates by Storm," *Globe and Mail*, March 16, 2012, B5; Chris Nuttall-Smith, "Greek Yogurt Put to the Taste Test," *Globe and Mail*, March 20, 2012; Leslie Beck, "Greek Yogurt Is All the Rage—But Is It Good for Me?" *Globe and Mail*, August 3, 2011; Terence Corcoran, "Canada's Big Fat Chobani Greek Yogurt Drama," *Financial Post*, April 2, 2012; Dominique Vidalon and Noelle Mennella, "Danone Plays Catch-up in Greek Yogurt Race," *Edmonton Journal*, April 7, 2012; Richard Blackwell, "Milking the Yogurt Market," *Globe and Mail*, October 22, 2012, B10.

Promoting Music Artists

Coalition Music Website, www.coalitionent.com, accessed May 9, 2015; Canadian Independent Music Association Website, www.cimamusic.ca/Page.asp?PageID=122&ContentID=2602&SiteNodeID=66, accessed May 1, 2013; Music Managers Forum Canada Website, musicmanagersforum.ca/news/coalition-musics-artist-entrepreneur-program-discounted-for-mmf-members, accessed May 9, 2015; Music Canada Website, www.musiccanada.com/newsitem.aspx?scid=63191, accessed May 9, 2015.

Direct Mail: Back from a Slow Death?

Joel Schectman, "A Smarter Way to Send Junk Mail," *Wall Street Journal*, January 1, 2013, B11; Brian Bradtke, "DRTV: Microtargeted TV," *Target Marketing*, February 2013, www.targetmarketingmag.com/article/microtargeted-tv-addressable-television-emerging-direct-marketing-channel/1; Dianna Dilworth, "Direct Mail, Evolved," *Direct Marketing News*, March 1, 2013, www.dmnews.com/direct-mail-evolved/article/280361.

Bye-Bye Cash Registers, Hello Tablets!

CBC News Website, "Stores Ditch Cash Registers for New Technology," www.cbc.ca/news/business/stores-ditch-cash-registers-for-new-technology-1.1352519, accessed May 19, 2015; "No Sale: 'Cash Registers' Days Are Numbered,' Retail Store Experts Say," *Columbia Daily Tribune*, March 22, 2013, 6B; Anne D'Innocenzio, "Cash Registers Disappearing at Retail Stores," Ohio.com, March 22, 2013, www.ohio.com/business/cash-registers-disappearing-at-retail-stores-1.383688,; Nick Wingfield, "With Tablets, Businesses Ring Up at More Fanciful Cash Registers," *New York Times*, April 21, 2013, www.nytimes.com/2013/04/22/technology/with-tablets-businesses-ring-up-at-more-fanciful-cash-registers.html?pagewanted=all&_r=0.

Unexpected Outcomes

"Republicans Fail to Override Obama's Veto of Keystone Pipeline Bill," *National Post*, March 5, 2015, FP8; Bob Tita, "Railcar Bottleneck Looms over Oil," *The Wall Street Journal*, December 22, 2014, B3; Russell Gold, "Shale Oil's Secret Routes to Market," *The Wall Street Journal*, December 4, 2014, A1; "Canada's Crude Oil Export Shipments by Rail Rise 22% Year over Year in Q3," *National Post*, December 2, 2014, FP3; Eric Atkins, "Regulators 'Overreacted' to Disaster in Lac- Mégantic, CP CEO Says," *Globe and Mail*, October 3, 2014, A1; Nia Williams, "Maiden Voyage for Suncor Crude; Ships First Tanker from East Coast to Europe," *National Post*, September 24, 2014, FP1; Kristine Owram, "New Rules Unlikely to Slow Rail Profits; Safety Regulations," *National Post*, August 20, 2014, FP1; Jeff Lewis, "Bitumen-Only Trains Hit Tracks," *National Post*, August 1, 2014, FP5; Anna Nicolaou, "U.S. Sets New Rules on Shipping Crude by Rail," *Globe and Mail*, July 24, 2014, B1; "Activists Plan 'Civil Disobedience' in Ottawa to Protest Keystone XL Pipeline," *National Post*, August 26, 2011, FP5.

Hollywood's New Marketing Campaign: Reviving Classic Movies

Statistics Canada, "Retail Sales Statistics," www.statcan.gc.ca/tables-tableaux/sum-som/l01/cst01/trad52-eng.htm, accessed May 21, 2015; Ben Fritz, "Hollywood's New Star Has a Classic Look, *Wall Street Journal*, April 22, 2013, B1, B4; U.N. Sushma, "Classic Movies Edge Out Blockbusters in Online Sales," *The Hindu Business Line*, July 6, 2012, www.thehindubusinessline.com/industry-and-economy/info-tech/classic-movies-edge-out-blockbusters-in-online-sales/article3610282.ece, accessed April 25, 2013; "Licensed Halloween Costume Sales Increase Significantly at PureCostumes.com Due to Hollywood Movie Box Office Hits Affecting Costume Trends," *PRWeb*, August 21, 2102, www.prweb.com/releases/prwebPureCostumes/HollywoodMovies/prweb9822338.htm; Pete Hammond, "Hollywood's Proud Past Lives Again This Week with AFI, TCM Classic Film Festival and Danny Kaye Centennial," *Deadline Hollywood*, April 24, 2013, www.deadline.com/2013/04/hollywoods-proud-past-lives-again-this-week-with-afi-tcm-classic-film-festival-and-danny-kaye-centennial.

CHAPTER 14

Canadian Mortgages: Bulls, Bears, and Banks

Tamsin McMahon, "Rate War Signals Heated Housing Market," *Globe and Mail*, March 18, 2015, B1; Ian McGugan, "Poloz's Brave Warning: Will We Listen?" *Globe and Mail*, December 14, 2015, B7; CBC News Website, "Housing Sales Climb 4% in March," March 13, 2015, www.cbc.ca/news2/interactives/housing-canada, accessed April 17, 2015; Business News Network Website, www.bnn.ca/News/2015/3/12/Canadians-debt-to-income-ration-hits-new-high-at-1633.aspx, accessed April 17, 2015; "How Low Will House Prices Go?" *Canadian Business*, February 18, 2013, 52–54; Tara Perkins, "Housing Market Cools but Does Not Freeze," *Globe and Mail*, October 16, 2013, B14; Richard Blackwell and Grant Robertson, "Mortgage Wars May Prompt More People to Buy," *Globe and Mail*, March 9, 2012, B3; Peter Shawn Taylor, "Mortgages for Free," Canadian Business, April 2, 2012, 28; Matthew McLearn, "Putting Out the Fire," *Canadian Business*, May 14, 2012, 38–42; Rob Carrick, "Ready to Be Bold? Sell the House and Rent," *Globe and Mail*, May 1, 2012, B11; Rob Carrick, "Goodbye to Three Irritating Bank Practices," *Globe and Mail*, March 6, 2012, B14; Richard Blackwell and Tara Perkins, "Mortgage Wars Combatants Losing Taste for Blood," *Globe and Mail*, March 24, 2012, B1; "The Housing Market Will Crash," Special Report, *Canadian Business*, February 20, 2012, 26–28.

When Cash Gets Scarce, Businesses Switch to Internet Bartering

Emily Bazar, "Bartering Booms During Economic Tough Times," *USA Today*, February 25, 2009, usatoday.com/tech/webguide/internetlife/2009-02-25-barter_N.htm; Debbie Lombardi, "Bartering Can Boost Your Budget and Business," www.bbubarter.com/news.aspx?NewsID=18, accessed October 27, 2008; Donna Wright, "Hard Times Create Boom of Local Bartering," BradentonHerald.com, March 8, 2009, www.bradenton.com/874/v-print/story/1277848.html; "The Advantages of Business Bartering," U-Exchange.com, www.u-exchange.com/advantages-business-bartering, accessed February 24, 2011; Bob Meyer, "In-depth Look at U.S. Trade Exchange Industry's Size," *BarterNews*, April 24, 2012, www.barternews.com; "What Do Bartering Websites Do?" www.peopletradingservices.com, accessed June 8, 2009; "BarterQuest, the Online Bartering Website, Is out of Beta," press release, *BarterQuest*, January 16, 2010, www.prlog.org/10535364-barterquest-the-online-bartering-website-is-out-of-beta.html.

What's the Deal with Bitcoin?

Michael J. Casey, "Bitcoin's Plunge Bites 'Miners,'" *Wall Street Journal*, January 15, 2015, C1; Michael J. Casey and Amir Mizroch, "Breach Occurs at Bitcoin Exchange," *The Wall Street Journal*, January 7, 2015, C3; Michael Casey, "Microsoft Move Is a Win for Bitcoin," *The Wall Street Journal*, December 12, 2014, C1; Robin Sidel, "Global Finance: Bitcoin Buyer Saw Past Woes—Virtual Currency's Ability to Survive Failure of Mt. Gox Won Over One Investor," *The Wall Street Journal*, December 2, 2014, C3; Gordon Isfeld, "BoC Eyes Risks of E-Money Growth," *National Post*, November 14, 2014, FP2; Barrie McKenna, "Threatened by Bitcoin, Bank of Canada Ponders E-Cash," *Globe and Mail*, November 14, 2014, B1; Greg Bensinger, "EBay Considers Integrating Bitcoin Payments into Subsidiary of PayPal," *The Wall Street Journal*, August 15, 2014, B5; Ethan Lou, "Hacker Stole Thousands in Virtual Currency," *Globe and Mail*, August 12, 2014, A5; Paul Vigna, "Dell Welcomes Bitcoin Payment," *The Wall Street Journal*, July 19, 2014, B2; Ben Moshinsky and Jim Brunsden, "Bitcoin Faces Regulatory Recoil as EU Alerts Banks to Stay Clear; Safeguards Sought," *National Post*, July 5, 2014, FP12; Jeff Gray, "The Bitcoin Believers," *Globe and Mail*, April 5, 2014, B7; Jeff Gray, "Bitcoin Boosters, Convinced of Its Potential, Undaunted by Mt. Gox, Flexcoin Collapse," *Globe and Mail*, March 7, 2014, B7; Jeff Gray, "Alberta-Based Bitcoin Bank Closes After Being 'Robbed' by Hackers," *Globe and Mail*, March 5, 2014, B3.

Mastering the Credit Card Game

Alexandra Posadksi, "Canadian Banks' Profits Top $31.7 Billion in Fiscal Year, but 'Challenges' Loom," *The Huffington Post,* www.huffingtonpost.ca/2014/12/05/canadian-bank-profits-2014_n_6278166.html, accessed April 17, 2015; Canadian Bankers Association Website, www.cba.ca, accessed April 17, 2015; Roma Luciw, "Young and Prey to Debt," *Globe and Mail*, November 8, 2011, L1; Rob Carrick, "Borrowing to Pay for Your Wedding," *Globe and Mail*, May 1, 2012, B1; Canadian Bankers Association Website, www.cba.ca, accessed April 17, 2015; Dianne Nice, "Credit Card Crackdown May Cost Consumers," *Globe and Mail*, August 30, 2010; CBC Website, "Card Costs: Who Pays What to Whom," December 17, 2010, www.cbc.ca/news/story/2009/04/16/f-cardfees.html, accessed May 27, 2012.

CHAPTER 15

Piles of Cash

David Parkinson, "Have Corporate Cash Piles Been Smothering Inflation?" *Globe and Mail*, August 13, 2014, B2; Tim Shufelt, "Forget 'Dead Money'—Cash Is King," *Globe and Mail*, June 23, 2014, B7; Tim Shufelt, "Corporate Canada's Mountains of Cash," *Globe and Mail*, May 27, 2014, B12; Barrie McKenna, "Canadian Companies Increase Cash Hoards," *Globe and Mail*, March 28, 2014, B3; Brady Yauch, "Is Carney Right to Ask Businesses to Spend?" *Business News Network*, August 8, 2012, www.bnn.ca/News/2012/8/24; Stephen Fidler, "Firms' Cash Hoarding Stunts Europe," *The Wall Street Journal*, March 24–25, 2012, A10; David Parkinson, "The Myth of Canada's Cash Mountain," *Globe and Mail*, March 24, 2012, B10; "U.S. Firms Hoarding Large Cash Stockpiles: $1.2T Saved After Bad Credit Crisis Memories," *National Post*, March 15, 2012, FP6; Simon Avery, "Teck Keen to Put Its Cash to Work," *Globe and Mail*, November 8, 2011, B16; Tim Kiladze, "Cash-Hoarding Firms Look Smart Now," *Globe and Mail*, September 27, 2011, B15; Simon Avery, "Billions in the Vault, but Not Much Bang," *Globe and Mail*, August 19, 2011, B10; Greg Keenan, "'Fortress Balance Sheets' Breed a New Kind of Crisis," *Globe and Mail*, August 10, 2011, B1; Paul Wiseman, "Strong Corporate Stats, Lingering U.S. Joblessness," *Winnipeg Free Press*, July 23, 2011, B16; David Parkinson, "Shareholders' Lament: Mountains of Cash, Miserly Payouts," *Globe and Mail*, July 16, 2011, B15; Kevin Carmichael, "Caution Keeps Cash-Rich U.S. Employers from Hiring," *Globe and Mail*, July 9, 2011, B1; Alan Reynolds, "The Myth of Corporate Cash Hoarding," *The Wall Street Journal*, February 23, 2011, A17.

Green Bonds

Richard Blackwell, "Canada Takes a Big Step in Growing Green Bonds Market," *Globe and Mail*, December 8, 2014, B3; Barry Critchley, "How the Green Bond Market Will Grow," *National Post*, November 8, 2014, FP2;

Barry Critchley, "Ontario Green Bond Nets $2.4B," *National Post*, October 10, 2014, FP2; Barry Critchley, "Green Bonds Blossom," *National Post*, September 20, 2014, FP2; Richard Blackwell, "SolarShare Grows as 'Green Bonds' Heat Up," *Globe and Mail*, September 15, 2014, B11; Barry Critchley, "P3s Debut Green Bonds," *National Post*, July 10, 2014, FP2; John Schmuel, "Greening the Bond Market," April 10, 2014, FP6.

Short Selling: Herbalife and Sino-Forest

Ian McGugan, "Why You Should Thank a Short Seller," *Globe and Mail*, July 8, 2014, B2; Joanne Slater, "Ackman's Herbalife Attack Turns Personal," *Globe and Mail*, July 23, 2014, B8; Juliet Chung, "Showdown over Herbalife Spotlights New Wall Street," *The Wall Street Journal*, January 10, 2012, A1; Andy Hoffman and Jeff Gray, "Sino-Forest Files for Bankruptcy Protection," *Globe and Mail*, March 31, 2012, B4; Terence Corcoran, "Sino Kiss-Off Comes Too Late: Woes Take Down Forest of Global Reputations," *National Post*, June 22, 2011, FP1; Peter Koven, "Paulson Dumps Sino Stake: Shares Down 14.4% Before Hedge Fund's Sale Revealed," *National Post*, June 21, 2011, FP1; Peter Koven, "Block Questions Sino-Forest Documents: Shares Slip 4.5%," *National Post*, June 18, 2011, FP4; Peter Koven and David Pett, "Sino Call Fails to Convince; Stock Plunges Further 32% as CEO Tries to Explain Arcane Business Strategy," *National Post*, June 15, 2011, FP1; Jonathan Chevreau, "Investor ED Flags: Due Diligence Is Critical, as Tale of Sino-Forest Shows," *National Post*, June 11, 2011, FP9; David Pett and John Shmuel, "Muddy Waters Research 'Craps': Dundee Blasts Attacker of Sino-Forest," *National Post*, June 8, 2011, FP1; David Pett and John Shmuel, "Sino-Forest Falls 20.6% After Short Seller's Report: Muddy Waters," *National Post*, June 3, 2011, FP7.

Stock Trading at Your Fingertips

Theresa W. Carey, "Cut the Cord," Barrons.com, online.barrons.com/article/SB50001424052748704759704577267660673833538.html#articleTabs_article%3D0, accessed March 12, 2012; "Stock Market: Why Is Stock Market Data Delayed by 20 Minutes (NYSE, NASDAQ) to the General Public?" *QUORA*, August 25, 2010, www.quora.com/Stock-Market/Why-is-stock-market-data-delayed-by-20-minutes-NYSE-NASDAQ-to-the-general-public; "Online Trading Software," *TradeStation*, www.tradestation.com, accessed June 7, 2013; "Where Can I Find Information About Pre- and After-Hours Trading on the NYSE and the Nasdaq?" *Investopedia,* February 26, 2009, www.investopedia.com/ask/answers/06/preaftermarket.asp; Adam Milton, "What Is Day Trading?" About.com, daytrading.about.com/od/daytradingbasics/a/WhatIsDayTradin.htm, accessed June 8, 2013; Rob Carrick, "Have Your Say on the Best Money Blogs," *Globe and Mail*, May 3, 2011, B19; "Poll: How Likely Are You to Conduct Investing on a Mobile Device?" www.theglobeandmail.com/globe-investor/2011-online-broker-rankings/poll-how-likely-are-you-to-conduct-investing-on-a-mobile-device/article2236011, accessed May 9, 2015; Rob Carrick, Mathew Ingram, Howard Lindzon, Boyd Erman, David Berman, and Andrew Willis, "Best of Blogs," www.theglobeandmail.com/report-on-business/best-of-the-blogs/article683468/page2, accessed May 9, 2015.

Crowdfunding: Some Changes in the Works

Shane Dingman, "Smartwatch Maker Raises $1 Million in Less Than an Hour," *Globe and Mail*, February 25, 2015, B1; "There's No Refunding in Crowdfunding," *The Wall Street Journal*, November 26, 2014, B1; Omar El Akkad, "Oculus Deal Shows Crowdfunding's Promise," *Globe and Mail*, March 27, 2014, B3; Tavia Grant, "To Find Seed Money, Canadian Startups Follow the Crowd," *Globe and Mail*, March 24, 2014, B1; Jeff Gray and Janet McFarland, "New Rules Give Boost to Crowdfunding," *Globe and Mail*, March 21, 2014, B3; Richard Blackwell, "Crowdfunding Shows New Promise: Study," *Globe and Mail*, January 29, 2014, B7; Zachary Gubler, "Inventive Funding Deserves Creative Regulation," *The Wall Street Journal*, February 1, 2013, A13; A. Cortese, "CircleUp Helps Small Consumer Goods Firms Round Up Money: An Alternative to Tapping Credit Cards," *National Post*, January 28, 2013, FP7; M. Medley, "Words from Their Sponsors; Authors Cash in on Crowd-Sourced Funding Sites Such as Kickstarter and Indiegogo," *National Post*, January 9, 2013, B5; J. McFarland, "OSC Weighs, 'Crowdfunding' Against Risk of Fraud," *Globe and Mail*, December 15, 2012, B6; C. Dobby, "Ontario to Back Startup Crowdfunding: Fraud Warning," *National Post*, November 30, 2012, FP5; Q. Casey, "Crowd Money," *National Post*, October 22, 2012, FP1; B. Critchley, "Crowd Funds Close the Gap," *National Post*, September 20, 2012, FP2; K. Carmichael, "Facebook Generation Takes on the Regulators," *Globe and Mail*, August 23, 2012, B7; D. Indiviglo, "The Foolishness of Crowds," *Globe and Mail*, March 22, 2012, B11.

How Are We Doing with Our IPO?

Tim Kiladze, "Canada's Top IPOs Largely Sport Ugly Returns," *The Globe and Mail*, February 12, 2015, B7; Claire Brownell, "Shopify Eyes Possible Spring Launch of US$100M Initial Public Offering: Report," *National Post*, January 10, 2015, FP5; David Milstead, "Rounding Up a Year of IPOs: While Biotech's Boom Has Helped Create the Most Offerings Since 2000, Nearly 60 Percent of New U.S. Entrants Trailed the S&P 500," *The Globe and Mail*, January 3, 2015, B9; Barry Critchley, "Energy Banks Won the Year," *National Post*, December 29, 2014, FP2; Greg Keenan, "Jetlines Targets Ultra-Low-Cost Airspace with Order for Five Boeing 737s," *The Globe and Mail*, December 16, 2014, B3; "Seven Generations Rises in IPO Debut," *National Post*, October 31, 2014, FP4; Jessica Toonkel, "Investors Just Not into Alibaba," *National Post*, September 8, 2014, FP3; Bryce C. Tingle, "Collapsing IPO Markets," *National Post*, September 4, 2014, FP9; "GoPro Jumps 31% After IPO Values Camera-Maker at US$3B," *National Post*, June 27, 2014, FP10; Evelyn Rusli, "LinkedIn Rallies While Its Web Peers Lose Luster," *The Wall Street Journal*, February 28, 2013, B1; Evelyn Rusli and John Letzing, "Groupon Lands with a Thud," *The Wall Street Journal*, February 28, 2013, B2; Evelyn Rusli, "Facebook Shares Rally Above $30," *The Wall Street Journal*, January 10, 2013, B4; Nivedita Bhattacharjee and Alexei Oreskovic, "Groupon Fights for Its Life as Daily Deals Fade," *Business News Network*, November 12, 2012, www.bnn.ca/News/2012/11/12; Fabrice Taylor, "Facebook's Hidden Costs," *The Globe and Mail*, May 29, 2012, B9; Andrew Ackerman, "No Violations Found in Facebook IPO," *The Globe and Mail*, May 31, 2012, B8; Douglas MacMillan, "How Mark Zuckerberg Jacked the Valley," *Canadian Business*, May 21–27, 2012, 61–67; "The Facebook Hype Meter," *Canadian Business*, June 11, 2012, 74; Lynn Cowan, "Groupon IPO Cheers Companies Waiting in the Wings," *The Globe and Mail*, November 5, 2011, B6; David Milstead, "As Groupon Shares Soar, It's Time to Discount the Frenzy," *The Globe and Mail*, November 8, 2011, B15; Fabrice Taylor, "Stop and Let It Pop," *Canadian Business*, June 2012, 20; Omar El Akkad and Paul Waldie, "Work Experience: LinkedIn Founder Net Worth: Billions," *The Globe and Mail*, May 10, 2011, B1, B6; David Parkinson, "As Facebook Falls Flat, LinkedIn Adds Friends," *The Globe and Mail*, May 30, 2012, B14.

NAME AND ORGANIZATION INDEX

A
AbitibiBowater Inc., 229
Aboriginal Peoples Television Network, 222
AcceleratorYYC, 84*f*
Accor SA, 106
acfe.com, 260
Ackman, William, 382
Adbusters, 167
Adidas, 62, 133
Aditya Birla Group, 393
Adolph Coors Co., 38
Adonis, 24, 299
Advanced Semiconductor Engineering Inc., 249
Aerospace & Defence Park, 84*f*
AES Corporation, 210
Afeyan, Levon, 36
Affinity Credit Union, 353*f*
Agrium Inc., 179
AIG, 219
Air Canada, 8, 37, 38, 48, 49*f*, 56–57, 89–90, 123*f*, 128, 133, 150, 182, 183, 190, 191, 194–195, 212, 214, 253, 391
Air Canada Pilots Association (ACPA), 191, 194–195
Air China, 253
Air Italy, 253
Air Koryo, 253
Air Miles, 134
Airbus, 111, 131, 132, 132*f*, 136
Aissa, Ben, 110
Al-Ameen Insurance Co., 393
Alaska Airlines, 237, 247
Alberta Arbitration Board, 175
Aldo Shoes, 332*f*
Alegrium, 297
Algoma Steel, 199
Alibaba, 54, 390–391
Alibaba Group Holdings Ltd., 369*n*
Alimentation Couche-Tard, 89*f*
Allan, Elyse, 218*f*
Allergan, 62
Alstom SA, 48
AltaGas, 57–58, 139
Alterna Credit Union, 353*f*
Aluminum Company of Canada (Alcan), 107, 157
Amazon Prime Video, 42
Amazon.com, Inc., 57, 95, 119, 125, 223, 239, 321, 327, 332
American Airlines, 131
American Express, 134
Andersen, Arthur, 217–218
Android, 15, 276
Annez, Thierry, 394–395
Aon Hewitt, 75
App Store, 307
Apple, 15, 32, 32*f*, 42, 54, 99, 124, 126, 129, 137, 161, 217, 217*f*, 219, 223, 275, 277, 280*f*, 307, 309, 321, 365–366, 378
AppMakr, 307
AppWarrior, 163
Appypie.com, 307
Aqualife AS, 333
Arctic Glacier Inc., 53
Armani, 34
Arnold, Patricia, 219
Arnott, Wendy, 199
Artists' Frame Service, 281, 281*f*
Artopex Inc., 61
Assiniboine Credit Union, 353*f*
Association of Certified Fraud Examiners (CFE), 260, 273
Astral Media Inc., 42, 175
Atco Ltd., 133
Atebits, 307
Atlantic Superstore, 23
Atlas Business Solutions, Inc. (ABS), 241
Atlassian Inc., 177
ATN, 299
Attsz, Stafford, 225
Audi, 134
Authors Guild, 70
The Auto West Group, 85
Avant Web Solutions, 104
Avis Rent a Car System, 321
Avon Products, 52, 332*f*

B
Baby Gourmet, 77
Baidu, 378
Ballard Power Systems, 32
Banco Colpatria, 116
Banco Sud Americano, 116
Bank of Canada, 30, 343–344, 346, 350, 351, 352, 352*f*, 357, 358, 366–367
Bank of England, 352
Bank of Guangzhou, 116
Bank of Montreal (BMO), 55, 57, 89, 116, 299, 347, 348*f*, 350, 379*f*, 386
Bank of New York Mellon Corp., 219
Bank of Nova Scotia. *See* Scotiabank
Baron, David P, 51*n*
Barrick Gold, 4
Barrick Resources, 127
BarterQuest.com, 350
Barton, Dominic, 219
Bartz, Carol, 160
Bates, Paul, 144
Bauer Performance Sports Limited, 26, 26*f*, 36, 136
Baumol, William, 245
Baxter Corp., 61
The Bay. *See* Hudson's Bay Company (HBC)
BBM, 324
BBVA, 203
BC Biomedical Laboratories, 212
BC Labour Relations Board, 34
BDC Venture Capital Inc., 95
BDO Canada LLP, 258*f*
Beats by Dre, 302, 322*f*
Beats Music, 15
Beatty, Perrin, 110
BeautyStory.com, 95
Beddoe, Clive, 124
Belerus Bank, 355*f*
Bell Canada Enterprises (BCE), 42, 137, 143, 158, 373
Bell Media, 326
Ben & Jerry's, 225, 317–318
Ben-Artzi, Eric, 56
Best Buy, 99, 301
Better Business Bureau, 62
Beyoncé, 325
Beyond the Rack (BTR), 75, 84, 94–95

Beyond.com, 173
Bianco, David, 366
Big Bang Partners, 321
Bigo, 216
Bing, 296
BIO | FOOD | TECH, 84*f*
Biogen Idec, 62
Bitpay, 357
Bitstamp, 357
Black, Conrad, 57
BlackBerry, 5, 8*f*, 15, 70, 130, 148, 151, 274*f*, 275, 280, 284, 378
Black+Decker, 305, 305*f*, 330
Blanchard, Olivier, 357
Blandford, Craig, 195
Blockbuster, 42
Bloomberg Finance LP, 383
BloomNation, 395
Blue, Allen, 177
BMW, 8, 85, 315
BNN, 381
Boeing, 111, 131, 132, 132*f*, 136, 138, 275, 275*f*
Boingo Wireless Inc., 302
Bombardier, 4, 28, 62, 66, 89–90, 99, 107, 109, 136, 147, 249, 379*f*, 382
Bond Street, 107
BoniCholx, 24
Boston Bruins, 276*f*
Boston Consulting Group, 66
Boston Pizza, 225
The Bottom Line, 258*n*
Bourassa, Ariane, 174
Bourgoyne, Doug, 86
Box, 23
Boyd Autobody, 139
BP, 59, 138
Brichter, Loren, 307
The Brick, 333
Bridgestone, 295
Bright Beam, 53
Brin, Sergey, 5, 121–122, 223
Bristol Aerospace, 128
British Airways, 131
British Columbia Labour Relations Board, 203
British Columbia Maritime Employers Association, 191
Brock University, 33*n*
Brookfield Asset Management, 134
Brookfield Renewable Energy Partners, 372
Brown, Charles, 302
Brown, David, 139
Brown, Jamie, 154
Bryant, Samuel, 29*f*
Buckingham, Cathy, 77
Buckley's, 323
Budget Rent a Car, 321
Budweiser Canada, 325
Buffett, Warren, 144
Bugatti-Sedona, 107, 107*f*
Burger King, 3–4, 38, 86, 289, 322
Burriss Consulting Group LLC, 246
Business Development Bank of Canada (BDC), 6, 77–78, 77*f*, 83, 354
BusinessWeek, 223

C

C-Suite, 34
Cadbury, 53, 144
Cadillac Fairview, 282
CAE, 176
Cahan, Adam, 79
Caisse de depot et placement du Quebec, 386
Cameco Corp., 212
Campbell, 310
Can-Eng Manufacturing, 106
Canada Border Services Agency, 109, 256–257
Canada Business Network, 83
Canada Deposit Insurance Corporation, 51
Canada Factoring Company, 353
Canada Goose, 309, 328*f*
Canada Jetlines Ltd., 391
Canada Mortgage and Housing Corporation (CMHC), 344, 354–355
Canada Post, 8, 9, 16, 36
Canada Revenue Agency, 150, 259, 332
Canada's Music Incubator (CMI), 326
Canada's Oli Sands Innovation Alliance (COSIA), 134
Canadian Advanced Technology Alliance, 385
Canadian Airline Pilots Union, 188
Canadian Angel Investor, 82, 85*f*
Canadian Association of Business Incubation (CABI), 83
Canadian Association of Consulting Engineers, 11–12
Canadian Auto Workers (CAW), 183, 186, 188*f*, 189, 191
Canadian Bankers Association, 284, 349, 361
Canadian Cancer Society, 12
Canadian Centre for Policy Alternatives, 3–4
Canadian Chamber of Commerce, 110
Canadian Congress of Labour, 185
Canadian Federation of Business School Deans, 179
Canadian Federation of Independent Business, 172
Canadian Federation of Labour, 185
Canadian Human Rights Commission, 175, 181
Canadian Imperial Bank of Commerce (CIBC), 347, 348*f*, 349, 350
Canadian Industrial Relations Board, 195
Canadian Institute of Chartered Accountants, 51, 150, 258
Canadian Institute of Hamburgerology, 87*f*
Canadian Labour Congress, 185
Canadian Labour Union, 185
Canadian Media Guild, 191
Canadian National Railway (CN), 4, 8, 55, 127, 136, 249, 295
Canadian Natural Resources, 368
Canadian Pacific Railway (CP), 191, 249, 368
The Canadian Press, 191, 372*n*
Canadian Radio-television and Telecommunications Commission (CRTC), 9, 15, 42
Canadian Real Estate Association (CREA), 10
Canadian Standards Association (CSA), 59
Canadian Tire, 35, 36, 53, 86, 160, 161, 298, 331, 331*f*
Canadian Undergraduate Survey Consortium, 173
Canadian Union of Public Employees (CUPE), 185, 188, 191*f*, 195
Canadian Western Bank, 348*f*
Canadian Wheat Board, 9
CanadianMortgageTrends.com, 248
Canfor Corporation, 245
Canon, 324
Cara, 354
Caramba App Development, 29*f*
CareerBuilder, 201, 202
Carleton University, 171
Carlson, Jennifer, 77
Carlson Wagonlit Travel, 68
Carlson Wagonlit Travel Canada, 180
Carney, Mark, 352, 366
Carnival Corp., 138
Carrefour, 331
Carrey, Jim, 341
Casabella, 112
Cascades Inc., 295
Case, Karl E., 13*n*
Cash, Johnny, 194
Castro, Fidel, 33
Caterpillar Financial Services, 249
Caterpillar Inc., 48, 137
Cathay Pacific, 253
Catholic Children's Aid Society, 180
Catholic Children's Aid Society of Toronto, 212

Cato Institute, 366
CBC, 195, 339–340
Cenovus Energy Inc., 174
Centerplate, 127
Centre for Corporate Social Performance and Ethics, 60
Ceres, 372
Certified General Accountants Association of Canada, 150, 259
CFA Institute, 383
Chartered Professional Accountants of Canada, 150
Chartwell Technology, 10
CheckFree Corporation, 272
Cheer, 15
Chevrolet, 60, 125
Chez Cora, 86
Chilton, Dave, 118, 288, 340
China National Offshore Oil Corp. (CNOOC), 144
China National Petroleum Corporation, 100
Chipotle Mexican Grill, 118
Chips Ahoy, 310
Chiquita, 310
CH2MHill, 227
Chobani, 318
Chrysler, 8, 66, 187, 190
Chrysler Canada, 11
Chubb Insurance Company of Canada, 212
Churchill, Winston, 215*f*
CIBC, 143, 179
CIBC World Markets Inc., 87
CIC Manitoba, 84*f*
Cieslak, Mario, 340
CIL, 129
Circle-K, 38
Ciroc, 325*f*
Cirque du Soleil, 90, 107
Cisco Systems, 212, 306, 365
Citibank, 182
City National Corp., 107
City of Toronto, 326
CityTV, 203
Clark Equipment Company, 156–157, 156*f*
Clarkson, Max, 60
Clear Skies Solar, 66
Clearpath Robotics, 239
Clearwater Seafoods Income Fund, 355
Climate Bonds Initiative, 372
Club Penguin, 55
CNN, 15
Co-operators Life Insurance Co., 134
Coalition Music, 326, 326*f*
Coast Capital Savings Credit Union, 248, 353*f*
Coast Distribution System, 303
Coca-Cola, 15, 65, 70, 129, 136, 306*f*, 308, 309, 309*f*, 313, 322
Coinbase, 357, 395
College Pro Painters, 139
Collins Barrow National Cooperative Inc., 258*f*
Colt Hockey, 339–340
Combs, Sean, 325*f*
Commercial Alert, 54
Communications, Energy and Paperworkers Union, 186
Competition Bureau, 3, 9–10, 51, 53, 150, 284
Concordia University, 6*n*
Conexus Credit Union, 353*f*
Conference Board of Canada, 9, 179
Conlin, Michelle, 223
Conquest Vacations, 253
Consultancy Solutions Research Group, 42
Consumer and Corporate Affairs Canada, 68
Consumer Edge Research, 317
Consumer Protection Finance Bureau, 357
ConsumerAffairs.com, 253
Cooper, Simon, 219
Coors, 310
Cora Franchise Group, 77
Costco, 27, 332*f*
Coty Inc., 148
Couche-Tard, 38, 302, 332*f*
Council of Canadians, 334
Country Style, 73
Courtyard by Marriott, 246
cpacanada.ca, 259
Crayola, 325
Credit Suisse First Boston, 219
Crescent Point Energy Corp., 368
Crichton, Michael, 70
Croatia Airlines, 253
Crothers, Melvin, 56–57
Crowley, Brian, 19
Cryptologic Inc., 10
Cubist Pharmaceutical, 245
Cultures, 73
Cybertech Automation Inc., 75*f*
Cypress Semiconductor, 161

D

D'Addario, 326
Daiei, 331
Daimler, 58, 100
DaimlerChrysler, 133
Dairy Farmers of Canada, 317
Dairy Mart, 38
Dairy Milk, 144
Dallaire, Christian, 107
D'Aloisio, Nick, 79
Daly, Christine, 174
Danier Leather, 109, 109*f*
Danone Group, 38, 160, 318
David's Tea, 98
Davis, Scott, 36
DDI Canada, 130
de Grisogono, 298
De Pinto, Joseph, 130
Deal, Jennifer, 170
Dean, James, 338
Déco Découverte, 136
Deep Fried Entertainment, 55
DeGeneres, Ellen, 341
DeGroote School of Business, 144
Dejardins, Mathieu, 288
Delaney, Ian, 33
Delissio Pizza, 327
Dell, Michael, 5, 329
Dell Computers, 357
Deloitte LLP, 258*f*
Delta Air Lines, 37, 247
Delta Chelsea Hotel, 210
Deming, W. Edwards, 245
Department of Foreign Affairs and International Trade (DFAIT), 11
Desjardins, 107
Detroit Red Wing, 107
Deutsche Bank, 56
DevFacto Technologies Inc., 75*f*
Diageo, 325*f*
Dickinson, Arlene, 118, 225, 288, 340, 394
Digiomo Pizza, 327
Dillon Consulting Ltd., 134
Dish Network Corp., 42, 357
Disney, Walt, 152*f*
Disney World, 243
D.L.G.L. Ltd., 75*f*
Dodge, 315
Dolansky, Eric, 33*n*

Dollar Rent a Car, 321
Dollarama, 27, 292
Dominion, 23
Doritos, 330
DoubleClick, 122
Dow Jones, 134, 223, 380, 388
Downe, Bill, 386
Drabinsky, Garth, 57
Dragon's Den, 118*n,* 288*n,* 340*n,* 395*n*
DuPont, 248
Dushnisky, Kelvin, 127

E

Eagle's Flight, 177
Earle, Johnny, 395
Earle. Lorrain, 395
Earth 911 Inc., 53
Eastman Kodak, 137
Easton, 26, 136
Eaton's, 71
eBay, 276, 319, 321, 332
ECO Canada, 174
Ecolabelling.org, 66
Economic Development Coalition of Southwest Indiana, 231
The Economist, 8*f,* 28, 29*f,* 79, 348, 356
Eisner, Michael, 217
Electro-Motive Canada, 186
11 Furniture, 54
Ellis, Charles, 183
eMarketer, 325
Embraer, 109
EMD music, 6
Empire Co. Ltd., 24
Enbridge Inc., 89*f*
Encana Corp., 391
Enerfin Energy Co. of Canada, 372
Energy Information Administration (EIA), 20
Enron, 51, 57, 71, 209, 217–218, 219
Ensyn Corp., 59
Entertainment Software Association of Canada, 55
Entrepreneur Media, 83
Environmental Careers Organization of Canada, 174
Environmental Protection Agency(EPA), 49
E.ON SE, 149
Epernicus, 278
EPIX, 42
Ernst & Young LLP, 258*f*
Esri Canada, 161
Essar Steel Algoma Inc., 35
Esso, 108
Ethical Funds, 383, 383*f*
Europol, 58
Exide Corp., 149
Expedia, 219, 357
Expensify, 83
Export Development Canada (EDC), 11, 95, 107, 354–355, 372
Extra Foods, 23
Extreme Pita, 74
ExxonMobil, 58

F

Facebook, 5, 37, 55, 59–60, 75, 76, 78, 80, 95, 176, 177, 199, 203, 278, 284, 332*f,* 385, 391
Fadiman, James, 206*n*
Fage, 318
Fair, Ray C., 13*n*
Fair Trade USA, 47
Fairchild Network, 299
Fairmont Resort Hotels, 294, 294*f*
Fairtrade Foundation, 52
Fairtrade Labelling Organizations International(FLO), 45–47
Falconbridge, 143–144
Fallon, John, 123*f*
Fast Fuel, 149
Featherstone Two Wheels Green Delivery, 85
Federal Communications Commission (FCC), 42
Federal Court of Appeal, 332
Federal Trade Commission, 382
FedEx (Federal Express), 16, 129, 155, 232, 236, 236*f,* 238, 274, 333*f*
FedEx Office, 237
Ferguson, Mark, 185
Fernandes, Alexander, 302
Ferrari, 265, 298, 310
Ferrari, Bruno, 111
Fields, Debbi, 152
Fiorina, Carly, 124
First West Credit Union, 353*f*
FirstOntario Credit Union, 349
Fitch, 373*f*
Flexcoin Inc., 357
Flickr, 281
Flipkart, 338
Food Basics, 24
Foodland, 24, 149
Foord, Tom, 85–86
Forbes, 5, 79, 163
Forbes, Kristen, 55
Ford, Henry, 21
Ford Motor Co., 7–8, 54*f,* 60, 100, 101, 106, 149, 150, 159, 232, 279, 341
Forensic Services, 273
Fortinos, 23
Fortune, 106, 177
Forzani, 36
Four Seasons Hotels and Resorts, 107, 139
Foursquare, 55
Frager, Robert D., 206*n*
Frantic Films, 150, 154, 158
Fraser Inc., 137
Fredenvals, Davis, 163
Fremont Village Shopping Centre, 161
FreshCo., 24, 149
Frito-Lay, 109, 325
FrogBox, 86
Fuji-Xerox, 210
Fuller, Chris, 226
Furse, Clara, 219

G

Gadhafi, Saad, 110
Galleon Group, 57
Gallup, 74, 198
Game Developers Conference of Canada, 55
Gamesa Corporation, 294–295
Gap, 301
Garden.com, 135
Gauvreau, Michel, 256–257
General Electric (GE), 80, 133, 160–161, 232, 253
General Electric (GE) Canada, 218*f*
General Foods, 15
General Mills, 15
General Motors (GM), 8, 25, 66, 100, 139, 144–145, 148, 187, 257–258, 298, 354
General Motors Acceptance Corporation (GMAC), 354
General Motors Canada, 11, 25, 230
Genesis Centre, 84*f*
Genstar Shipyards Ltd., 159
Gentile, Mary, 51
George Weston Ltd., 89*f*
Georgetti, Ken, 185
Gershkovitch, Brenda Bailey, 55
Get Glue, 325

Ghosn, Carlos, 126
Gibson Guitars, 6, 304
Gildan Activewear, 137, 190
Gilt, 94–95
Girl Guides, 61
GlaxoSmithKline, 48
Glencore Plc, 143
Global Institute of Research, 101
Global Research Consortium (GRC), 161
Global Strategic Maple Syrup Reserve, 256–257
The Globe and Mail, 89, 208, 222, 332*n,* 349, 381
GlobeScan, 7
Glyph, 307
Gmail, 282
GmbH & Co., 393*n*
Gobi Carbon Management Solutions, 85
GoDaddy, 354
Godin Guitars, 6
Godiva, 321, 321*f*
Gogo LLC, 37, 280
Gold, Robert, 94
Goldcorp Inc., 188, 379*f,* 380
Goldman Sachs, 100, 276
GoodGuide, 66
Goodman School of Business, 33*n*
GoodWork.ca, 174
Goodyear, 295, 329
Google, 5, 33, 51, 70, 110, 121–122, 125, 130, 138, 184, 223, 275, 275*f,* 276, 281, 296, 307, 309, 365
GoPro Inc., 310*f,* 391
Gottlieb, Myron, 57
Gourmet, 324
Government of Canada, 83, 144
Government of Ontario, 80, 253
Gowans, James, 127
Grand Cache Coal Corp., 57
Grant Thornton Canada, 258*f*
Graziado School of Business, 198
Great Blue Heron Charity Casino, 189
Great Little Box Company, 180
Great-West Life Assurance Company, 210
Green, Holly, 163
Green Gardeners, 85
Green-Jobs.ca, 174
Greenpeace Canada, 334
Groupe Donone. *SEE* Danone Group
Groupon, 391
Grupo Financiero Scotiabank Inverlat, S.A. de C.V., 116
The Guardian, 348
Guericke, Konstantin, 177
Guillemet, Chris, 118
Gunn's Hill Artisan Cheese, 77–78

H

Habanero Consulting Group, 75*f*
Hague, Desmond, 127
Hallmark Cards, 322
Hammond, Pete, 338
Hamp-Gonsalves, David, 53
Hams, Brad, 199
Hanks, Tom, 338
Hanson, Tom, 372*n*
Hargrove, Buzz, 186
Harley-Davidson, 265, 327
Harvard University, 80, 141, 205, 244
Harvey's, 86, 354
Hasenfratz, Linda, 231
Hastings, Reed, 223
Hattem, Andrew, 107
Hays Canada, 367
HBO, 42
Healey, Melanie, 292
Health Canada, 314
Herbal Essences, 327
Herbalife International Inc., 382
Heritage Foundation, 76
Herjavec, Robert, 225
Herold, Cameron, 139
Hershey Foods, 53, 106, 276
The Hertz Corporation, 321
Herzberg, Frederick, 207
Hewlett-Packard (HP), 124, 148, 247
High Liner Foods, 104, 355, 356*f*
Highland Capital Partners LLC, 95
Hillberg & Burk, 78
Hirai, Kazuo, 134
Hisene Kelon Electrical Holdings Co., 106
H.J. Heinz, 148, 292
H&M, 102
HMV, 153
Hockey Experts, 36
Hoffman, Reid, 177
Hollinger International, 57
Holm, Hanno, 288
Holt Renfrew, 35
Home Depot, 99, 265
Home Outfitters, 39, 136
Home Shopping Network, 279
Honda, 102, 187, 231, 239
Horizon Air, 66
Household Finance Corporation, 354
H&R Block, 308
HSBC Bank Canada, 348*f*
Hudson's Bay Company (HBC), 38, 39, 136, 218*f,* 298, 302, 327, 332*f,* 334
Hulu, 15
Hummer, 298
Hunger, J. David, 136*n*
Hurd, Mark, 124
Hydro One, 203
Hydro-Quebec, 9, 158
Hydrogenics Corp., 32
Hyundai Corp., 32, 100, 187

I

i-Gen Solutions Inc., 75*f*
I Love Rewards, 199
IAMGold, 379*f*
IB Smart, 8*f*
Ibis, 106
IBM, 106, 144, 210, 272, 275, 281, 282, 309
iCloud, 282
IDC, 282
idtheftcenter.org, 285
IGA, 24, 149
IGA Extra, 149
iGate Global Solutions, 75*f*
IGN Entertainment, 173
Ikea, 54
Imperial Oil, 5, 51, 89*f,* 128
Inc., 395
Inco, 107, 143–144
Independent City Market, 23
Indiegogo, 385
Indigenous Environmental Network, 334
Industrial Acceptance Corporation, 354
Industry Canada, 11, 75
Infosys Technologies, 203
ING Direct Canada, 130, 138, 210, 351
Innovacorp, 84*f*
Instagram, 76, 78, 80
Instinet Inc., 276

Institute of International Finance, 365
Insurance Bureau of Canada (IBC), 393
InsureEye Inc., 219
Integran Technologies, 340
Intelex Technologies Inc., 75*f*, 378
International Accounting Standards Board (IASB), 259–260
International Association of Business Communicators, 199
International Association of Machinists and Aerospace Workers (IAMAW), 194
International Chamber of Commerce, 54
International Monetary Fund (IMF), 356–357, 359, 365
International Organization for Standardization (ISO), 247, 248, 251
Internet Innovations Alliance (IIA), 278
Intuit, 259, 272
Investeco Capital Corp., 85
Investment Canada, 107
Investment Industry Regulatory Organization of Canada (IIROC), 56, 57
Investors Group Financial Services, 209
Invivo, 80
Ipsos Reid, 85, 176
Irving, Arthur, 150
Irving, J. D., 150
Irving, J. K., 150
Irving, Jack, 150
Irving, K. C., 150
Ishikawa, Kaoru, 245
iSign Media Solutions Inc., 302
ISL Engineering and Land Services Ltd., 75*f*, 199
IT Market Dynamics, 282
iTunes, 122, 135

J

J.-Armand Bombardier Incubator, 84*f*
Jacobs, Alexandra, 211
Jaguar, 101, 330
JAL, 131
J.D. Power, 60
Jell-O, 70
Jevons, William, 251–252
Joanel Inc., 107
Jobs, Steve, 124, 126, 217, 217*f*, 219
Joe Fresh, 51
John Deere, 330
John Molson School of Business, 6*n*
Johnny Cupcakes, 395
Johnson, Leo, 76, 76*f*
Johnson & Johnson, 283
Johnsonville Foods, 210
Jugo Juice, 73
Jung, Oliver, 95
Juran, Joseph, 245

K

Kahneman, Daniel, 209
Kal Tire, 75, 85–86, 86*f*
Kaleeswaran, K., 135
Kashoo, 259
Katz, Lothar, 104
Kellogg, 15, 309
Kelly, Bob, 219
Kelsall, Zane, 78
Kerns, Charles, 198
Keurig Green Mountain Coffee, 10
KFC, 38, 105
Kicking Horse Coffee, 76, 76*f*, 76*n*
Kickstarter, 385
Kijiji, 332
KimChi, 73
Kindler, Jeffrey, 155
King, Martin Luther, 215*f*
Kinko's Copy Centers, 237
Kinross, 379*f*
Kirin Holdings Co., 144
Kiva Systems, 238*f*, 239
Kjerulf, Alexander, 197–198
Klick Health, 75*f*
KLM, 131
Kmart, 159*f*
Knights of Labour, 185
Kopchinski, John, 56
Koryo Korean BBQ, 74
KPMG LLP, 125, 258*f*
Kraft Foods, 52, 144, 149, 309, 369
Kulula Airlines, 253

L

L.A. Kings, 276*f*
La Fleche, Eric, 25
La Senza, 34, 34*f*
La Vie en Rose, 34
Labour Canada, 187
Lafreniere, Phil, 77*f*
Land Rover, 101
Lanni, Rob, 326
Larose, Benoit, 107
Larson, Paul, 198
Lasn, Kalle, 167
Laurentian Bank, 348*f*
Lawrence, Eric, 326
Lay, Ken, 57
Lazaridis, Mike, 5
Led Zeppelin, 304
Lee's Music, 6
LEGO, 70
Leigh, Daniel, 357
Les Marchés Tradition, 24, 149
Levi Strauss, 61, 106, 211, 329, 369
Limited Brands, 15
Linamar Corp., 231
Lincoln, 315, 341
Lincoln, Abraham, 215*f*
LinkedIn, 173, 177, 199, 269, 278, 391
Lion's Club, 62, 128
Lions Gate, 5, 42
Liquid Capital Advance Corp., 369*n*
Lis, Julius, 107
Livent Inc., 57
Liz Claiborne, 15
Loblaw Companies Limited, 9–10, 23, 24–25, 89*f*, 123*f*, 173, 187, 236, 295, 310, 317, 332*f*
Loblaws City Market, 23
Lockheed Martin, 276, 279
Logan Aluminum Inc., 240–241
London Stock Exchange, 219, 378
London University, 47
Lord & Taylor, 218*f*
Louis Vuitton, 315
Lowe's, 153, 239
LoyaltyOne, 212
Lucas, George, 55
Lucchesi, Daniel, 340
Lululemon, 54, 298

M

Ma, Jack, 391
Ma, Stanley, 73–74
Macdonald-Laurier Institute, 19
Mac's, 38, 302, 332*f*
Macy's, 275
Mad Science, 86
Madoff, Bernie, 57

Maersk Line, 333
Magna International, 25, 89*f*, 139, 231, 315, 379*f*
Maison Orphée, 310
Malaysian Airlines, 138
Mallette, 258*f*
Manchu Wok, 74
Manitoba Hydro, 158
Manitoba Labour Board (MLB), 187–188
Manufacturing Marvel, 112
Manulife Centre, 65, 161
Maple Leaf Foods, 30, 53, 136, 138, 191, 230
Maple Leaf Gardens Ltd., 137
Marché Ami, 24
Marché Bonichoix, 149
Marché Extra, 24
Marché Richelleu, 24
Marotte, Bertrand, 332*n*
Mars, 53
Mars Canada, 58
Martell, Dan, 85*f*
Martha Stewart Living Omnimedia, Inc., 159, 159*f*
Martin, Boris, 118
Martin Guitar, 6
Martoma, Matthew, 57
Marx, Karl, 7
Masear, Penny, 171
Maslow, Abraham, 206, 206*f*, 206*n*
MasterCard, 347, 361
Mattel Inc., 53
Maxi & Cle, 23
May, Karen, 223
Mayer, Marissa, 126, 212
Mazda, 102
McArthur, Steven, 219
McBarnett, Andrew, 225
McCain Foods Limited, 105–106
McClelland, David, 207
McConaughey, Matthew, 341
McDonald's, 32, 34, 35, 61, 62*f*, 86, 87*f*, 99, 105, 106, 118, 124, 126, 136, 147, 155, 187, 237, 244, 274, 309, 313, 328
McDonald's Hamburger University, 176
McGill University, 129
McGinty, Sarah, 141
McGregor, Douglas, 205
McKinnell, Henry, 219
McKinsey and Company, 135, 219
McMahon, Vince, 306*f*
McMaster University, 144
McQueen, Steve, 338
MediaCorp, 222
Meet the Boss, 278
MEG Energy, 143
Mega Brands Inc., 70
Mercedes-Benz, 137, 315
Meridian Credit Union Ltd., 353*f*
Merrill Lynch, 366
Messenger, 76
Messerschmitt-Boelkow-Blohm, 247
MET Fine Printers, 59
Metro, 23, 24, 25, 299, 332*f*
Meyer, Marissa, 79
MGM, 42, 338
Michalowski, Sharon, 187
Michelin, 100, 188*f*, 295
Microsoft, 80, 121, 155, 211, 281, 282, 357, 365, 378
The Middle Seat, 247
Mielke, Rachel, 78
Migicovsky, Eric, 385
Millward Brown Optimor, 309
Miltimore, Mike, 6
Milton, Robert, 194
Ministry of Labour, 127, 182, 186
Mint.com, 349
Mintzberg, Henry, 129
Mitsubishi, 144
MNP LLP, 258*f*
Mohamed, Nadir, 178–179
Molson Inc., 38
Mompreneur, 77
Mompreneur Networking Group, 77
Money Index, 381
Monsanto Canada, 139
monster.ca, 173, 174
Moody's Investor Services, 353, 373, 373*f*
Morning Star Company, 210
Moser, Roger, 112
Mother Teresa, 215*f*
MotoMaster, 35
Motor Trend, 60
Motorola, 70, 155, 248
Mouffon, 107
Mountain Equipment Co-op (MEC), 50, 51, 90, 139
Mouvement des Caisses Desjardins, 353*f*
Moviemart.com, 338
Mr. Burrito, 74
Mr. Gas Ltd., 53
Mr. Sub, 73
Mrs. Fields Cookies, 152
MSurf Lab, 135
Mt. Gox, 357
MTY Group (MTY), 73–75
Muddy Waters, 382
Murad, Philip, 33
Murdoch, Rupert, 154
MyHabit.com, 95

N

NASA, 275, 275*f*
National Association of Music Merchants (NAMM), 6
National Bank of Canada, 348*f*, 350
National Crowdfunding Association of Canada, 385
National Energy Board, 211
National Football League (NFL), 190, 327
National Hockey League (NHL), 190, 214, 276*f*, 340
National Post, 340
National Railway Union, 188
Natixis Global Asset Management, 182
Natural Resources Canada, 11
NCR, 309
Nearbuy Systems, 302
Needs, 149
NEI Investments, 383*f*, 383*n*
Neiman Marcus, 275
Neligan, James, 6
Nestlé, 38, 53, 59–60, 100, 106
Netflix, 4, 9, 42–43, 223, 306*f*, 338, 378
Netsweeper, 47
New Development Bank, 101, 101*f*
New York Metropolitan Opera, 162
New York Stock Exchange (NYSE), 378, 380, 381
New York Yankees, 133
Newcap Radio, 326
Newell, Trevor, 282
Newman, Rick, 118
News of the World, 154
Newton, Chris, 82
Nexen Energy ULC, 144, 174
Nexfor, 137
Next Level Games Inc., 211, 212
NextEra Energy Inc., 372
Nike, 133, 153
Nike Outlet Store, 332*f*

Nippon Steel, 100
Nisku, 231
Nissan, 60, 100, 102, 126, 187, 231, 239
Nissan Canada Inc., 148
No Frills, 23, 236, 236*f*
Nobis, 208
Nooyi, Indra, 367
Nordex AG, 294–295
Nordstrom Inc., 35, 36*f*, 275
Norshield Asset Management Ltd., 383
Nortel, 268
North Island Hospital Project, 372
Northstar, 282
Novell, 281
Novotel, 106
NTP Inc., 70
Nygard International, 187

O

OACIQ, 75*f*
Obama, Barack, 274*f*, 334
Oculus VR Inc., 385
Odgers Berndston, 130
O'Donnell, Larry, 130
Office Overload, 157
O'Grady, Rowan, 367
Olympia & York, 71
1-800-GOT-JUNK, 139
O'Neil, Mike, 282
Ontario and Minnesota Paper Co., 229
Ontario Human Rights Commission, 51
Ontario Hydro, 139
Ontario Labour Relations Board (OLRB), 127, 187
Ontario Public Service, 214
Ontario Securities Commission, 56, 383
Opera Company of Brooklyn, 245
OPTE Project, 278*f*
Organisation for Economic Co-operation and Development (OECD), 8, 29, 49, 110, 244
Organization of the Petroleum Exporting Countries (OPEC), 19
O'Rourke, Dara, 66
Orser, Adam A., 77*f*
Orser, Daisy Leslie, 77*f*
Osborne, George, 352
Our Lady Peace, 326
Overstock.com, 357
Owen, David, 252

P

Pacesetter Directional and Performance Drilling, 208
Pacific & Western Bank of Canada, 348*f*
Pad Thai, 74
Page, Jimmy, 304
Page, Larry, 5, 121–122, 223
Palliser Furniture, 180
Palumbo, Daniel, 340
Pandora, 15
Paramount, 42
Paramount Pictures Library, 338
Patek Phillippe, 321
Pattison Outdoor Advertising, 89*f*, 90
Pavarotti, Luciano, 162
PayPal, 80
Pearson, Andrall (Andy), 215–216
Pearson International Airport, 35, 137–138
Pearson PLC, 123*f*
Pemasani, Harl, 173
Pendola, Rocco, 15
People Analytics and Compensation, 223
PeopleTradingServices.com, 350
Pepperdine University, 198
PepsiCo, 15, 38, 135, 158, 215–216, 295, 306*f*, 325, 367
Pershing Square Capital Management, 382
Petro-Canada, 89–90, 129, 260
Peugeot Citroen, 315
Pew Research Center, 239
Pfizer Inc., 38, 56, 70, 155, 219, 265
Philip & Henry Productions, 33
Philips, 80
Phillippe, Patek, 108
Pincus, Mark, 79
Pinet, Claude, 288
Pioneer Energy, 53
Pirelli, 295
Piron, Cameron, 80
Pizza Hut, 38, 106, 226
Plastic Bank, 59
PlentyOfFish, 176
Plug Power Inc., 32
Polar Mobile, 79
Poloz, Stephen, 343–344
Pond, Gerry, 82, 85*f*
Pontiac, 298
Popular Photography, 324
Porsche, 134
Port Metro Vancouver, 133, 190, 249
Porter, Michael, 34, 35*f*, 137, 244
Postini, 122
Power Corp. of Canada, 89*f*, 365
PrairieSky Royalty, 391
President's Choice (PC), 24–25, 27, 310, 317, 318
Prestotea Co. Ltd., 276
Price Chopper, 24
Priceline.com, 321
PricewaterhouseCoopers LLP (PwC), 90, 180, 258*f*, 273
Pringles, 309
Procter & Gamble (P&G), 53, 66, 76, 100, 129, 158, 183, 261, 283, 291–292, 306, 309, 333
Profit, 75
Protegra Inc., 75*f*
Provigo, 23
Province of British Columbia, 11
Province of Ontario, 11
Province of Quebec, 11
Psychometrics Canada, 198
PureCostumes.com, 338

Q

Q1 Labs, 82
Qatar Airways, 253
QImaging, 302
QPP (Quebec Provincial Police), 256–257
Quaker Oats, 15
Quebec Labour Relations Board, 187
Queen's Centre for Business Venturing, 75
Quick, Jonathan, 276*f*
Quinn, Rob, 130
QVC, 332*f*
Qwikster, 306*f*

R

Rachelle-Béry, 149
Radian6, 82
Radical Entertainment, 55
Rainforest Alliance, 52
Rajaratnam, Raj, 57
Raju, Ramalinga, 273
Ralph Lauren, 125
Ralph Lauren Polo, 15
Rask, Tukka, 276*f*
RBC Dominion Securities, 377

RCMP, 48, 53, 139, 256–257
RE/MAX, 86
Real Canadian Superstore, 23
Red Cross, 138*f*, 150
Reebok, 26, 133
Reebok-CCM, 107
Regus PLC, 82
Renault, 56, 100, 126
Rentrak Corp., 338
Repsol SA, 38
Restaurant Brands International, 3
Reynolds, Alan, 366
Rice, Ray, 327
Richter LLP, 258*f*
Rinnovated Design, 385
Rio Tinto Alcan Inc., 190, 235
Ritz-Carlton Hotel, 219
Riversong, 5, 6
Robert Half Technology of Canada, 199
Rodbell, Liz, 218*f*
Rogers Communications Inc., 39, 42, 55, 143, 178–179, 280, 349
Rolex, 134, 356
Rolling Stone, 79
Rona Inc., 35, 41
Ronald McDonald House, 61, 62*f*
Root Cellar Village Green Grocer, 77*f*
Rosenfeld, Elena, 76, 76*f*
Ross, Christopher, 6*n*
Rouge, 195
Rovinescu, Calin, 123*f*
Roy, Stefane, 110
Royal Bank of Canada (RBC), 55, 77, 83, 89*f*, 107, 135, 139, 179, 181, 183, 211, 276, 303, 309, 348*f*, 350, 361, 379*f*
Royal Dutch Shell, 100, 106
Rudi's Organic Bakery, 288
Rypple, 177

S

S7 Airlines, 253
Saab, 298
SAC Capital Advisors, 57
Safeway, 23, 24, 187, 332*f*, 369
Saks Fifth Avenue, 38
Saks Inc., 38
Salesforce.com, 282
Saltykov, Alexey, 219
Samsung, 15, 100, 275, 280*f*
San Diego Center for Creative Leadership, 170
Sanago, Massimo, 127
SAP AG, 163
Saturn, 298
Satyam Computer Services Ltd., 273
Save Easy, 23
Savoy, 294
Scania, 134
School of Oriental and African Studies(SOAS), 47
Schultz, Howard, 6*f*, 126
Schweitzer, Linda, 171
Scion, 314*f*, 315
Scotch, 70
Scotiabank, 89, 100, 111, 115–116, 134, 303, 309, 347, 348*f*, 350, 351
Scotiabank Inverlat, 116
Scotiabank Inverlat Casa de Bolsa, 116
Sealply Products Inc., 36
Sears, 15, 153, 159*f*, 332*f*
Sears Canada, 147
Securities and Exchange Commission, 382
Segel, Jason, 257
Seiyu, 160*f*
Sennheiser, 326
SenseAsian, 74
Sentinelle Medical, 80
Serious Fraud Investigation Office (India), 273
Servus Credit Union Ltd., 353*f*
Seth Thomas, 303
Setty, Prasad, 223
7-Eleven, 130, 232
Seven Generations, 391
SFU Venture Connections, 84*f*
Shaw Communications, 42
Shazam, 15
Shell Oil, 126, 136, 162
Sherritt International, 33
SHIFT Urban Cargo Delivery, 85
Shomi, 42
Shop.ca, 282
Shopify, 391
Shoppers Drug Mart, 4, 9–10, 23, 24, 33, 41, 187
Shoraka, Farbod, 395
Shtern, Yona, 94–95
Siemens, 100
Sierra Club, 295
Silicon Sisters Interactive, 55
Simoes, Shawn, 203
Simple Plan, 326, 326*f*
Singapore Airlines, 131, 253
Singleton, Tommie, 273
Sino-Forest Corp., 382
Skoda, 134
Skol Games LLC, 216
Skotidakis, 318
Skype, 219
Skytrax, 253
Sloan, Alfred, 148
Smart Media Innovations, 173
Smith, Adam, 102
Snapchat, 37, 37*f*
SNC-Lavalin Group, 48, 110
Sobeys Inc., 23, 24, 149, 187, 243, 332*f*
Sobeys Urban Fresh, 149
Social Logix, 55–56
Society of Management Accountants of Canada, 150, 259
Sofitel, 106
SolarCity, 161
SolarShare, 372
Solutions Research Group, 325
Songza, 15
Sony, 29*f*, 128, 134, 284, 284*f*, 306*f*, 392
Sony Ericsson, 54
The Source, 302
Southern Railway, 191*f*
Spiring, Charlie, 39
Spoing!, 197
Sport Chek, 36
Sports Illustrated, 309, 328*f*
Spotify, 391
Springboard West Innovations, 84*f*
Sprott School of Business, 171
SRV Network, 15
St. Mary's Cement Inc., 210
Stamos, John, 318
Standard & Poor's, 373, 373*f*, 380, 383, 388, 390
Standard Aero, 246
Standard Life Assurance, 393
Stanford, R. Allen, 57
Stanford University, 121, 223
Staples, 329, 332*f*
Starbucks, 6*f*, 35, 52, 52*f*, 97–99, 97*f*, 126, 132, 173, 297, 299, 305, 325
Starbucks Canada, 32, 139
State Street, 367

Statistics Canada, 11, 75, 77, 301
Statoil, 38
Stebco, 107
Steelcase, 128
StellaService Inc., 125
Stingray Music, 326
Stratos Inc., 61
The Street, 15
Stronach, Frank, 139
Student Workforce, 54
Subaru, 314*f*, 315
Success Partners, 83
Success Wizard Inc., 246
Sukiyaki, 74
Suleman, Razor, 199
Summly, 79
Sun Ice, 129
Sun Life Financial Inc., 89, 182, 200, 365, 393
Sun Microsystems, 144
Suncor Energy Inc., 89*f*, 130, 174, 175, 184, 365
Sunglass Hut, 332*f*
Suning Appliance Co., 107
Suntory Holdings Ltd., 144
SuperC, 24
Sushi Shop, 74
Suzlon Energy Limited, 294–295
Swarovski, 78
Swiss Chalet, 354
Syncrude, 59
Systrom, Kevin, 78

T

T Caps International, 394–395, 395*n*
T-Mobile, 280
Taco Bell, 38, 237
Takata Corp., 245
Talisman Energy, 38, 59
Tan, Chade-Meng, 223
Tandori, 74
Tangerine, 351
Target, 35, 137, 137*f*, 298, 334, 392
Target Maine Hatcheries, 106
Tata, 101
Taylor, Frederick, 205
Taylor Guitars, 6
TD Bank Group, 326, 349
TD Canada Trust, 347, 350, 351
TD Securities, 377
Teamsters, 188
Teavana, 98–99
TechWeb.com, 278
Teck Resources, 62
Telus, 57, 62, 76, 89, 282, 379*f*
Telus Corp., 143, 198, 222
Ten Thousand Coffees, 176
TerraChoice, 60
Thai Express, 73
Theft Resource Center, 285
Thiel, Peter, 80
3G Capital, 4
3H Communications, 321
3M Canada, 222
3M Corp., 76, 133, 153, 236, 236*f*, 306
Thrifty Foods, 24, 149
Tide, 15
Tiki-Ming, 73–74
Tim Hortons, 3–4, 35, 38, 58, 62, 86, 124, 289, 294, 299, 318, 322, 349, 349*f*
Timex, 134
Tingyi Holdings, 98
TMX Group, 378
TNR Industrial Doors, 77
TNT Post Group N.V., 8
Toastmaster International, 216
Tobacco Institute, 12
Toronto Blue Jays, 138
Toronto-Dominion Bank (TD), 89*f*, 116, 135, 161, 176, 199, 284, 309, 348*f*, 372
Toronto Fashion Incubator, 84*f*
Toronto FC, 203
Toronto General Hospital, 248
Toronto Maple Leafs, 137
Toronto Raptors, 137
Toronto Real Estate Board (TREB), 10
Toronto Stock Exchange (TSX), 74, 167, 377, 378, 381, 384, 388, 390
Toshiba, 100, 247, 306*f*
Toyota Motor Co., 8, 32, 57, 100, 102, 138, 183, 187, 236, 236*f*, 239, 245, 295, 315
Toys "R" Us, 332*f*
Trades and Labour Congress (TLC), 185
TransCanada Corp., 334
Transparency International (TI), 110
Travel Industry Council of Ontario (TICO), 253
Traveller-Sedona GbbH, 107
Travolta, John, 338
Treliving, Jim, 118, 225, 288, 340, 394
Trotter Morton Group, 171
Troy-Bilt, 35
Tscheltzoff, Oleg, 95
Tsouflidou, Cora, 77
TSX Venture Exchange, 378
Turnstyle Solutions Inc., 302
TVI Pacific Inc., 59
Twain, Shania, 153
Twitter, 59–60, 177, 199, 203, 278, 307, 308, 327, 332*f*, 391
Two If by Sea Café, 78
Tyco International, 149

U

U-Exchange.com, 350
Ubisoft, 11
Udemy, 297
Ugo Santini, 107
Underhill, Paco, 301
Unifor, 186, 187
Uniglobe Travel, 329
Unilever, 100
Unilever Canada, 58
United Auto Workers, 187
United Food and Commercial Workers (UFCW), 187
United Nations, 46, 58, 100, 356, 359
United Steelworkers of America, 144, 188, 189
United Way, 57, 62, 328, 357
University of Saskatchewan, 150
University of Toronto, 60, 150
Unix, 144
UPS, 16, 238, 274
Upton, Kate, 309, 328*f*
Uralkali, 110
Urban Outfitters, 331
U.S. Federal Aviation Administration (FAA), 132
U.S. Federal Reserve, 351
U.S. Financial Accounting Standards Board (FASB), 266
U.S. Government, 56
U.S. Immigration, 256–257
U.S. Intelligence Agency, 285
U.S. Justice Department, 373
U.S. Securities and Exchange Commission (SEC), 56
U.S. Steel Canada, 189
U.S. Treasury Secretary, 4

V

Vaillant, Jean-Luc, 177
Vale, 68, 143–144
Valu-mart, 23
Van Houtte Coffee, 74
Vancouver Art Gallery, 167
Vancouver City Savings Credit Union (Vancity), 61, 90, 353*f*
Vanelli's, 74
Vaughn Hockey, 276*f*
Velofix, 118
Vente-privee, 94
Venture Communications, 225
Vert Catering, 85
Viacom Inc., 338
Vichich, Mike, 307
Victoria's Secret, 51, 54
Videotron, 42
Vij, Vikram, 225, 288, 340, 394
Virtual Brokers, 378
Visa, 272, 347, 361
Vivino, Jimmy, 304
ViziApps.com, 307
Vlasic, 153
Vodafone, 280
Volkman, Ken, 15
Volkswagen, 49, 100, 134, 187, 231
Volvo, 137
Vondra, Al, 273

W

WAGmob, 8*f,* 173, 246, 259, 297
The Wall Street Journal, 79, 366, 381
Walmart, 23, 34, 36, 39, 89, 106, 110, 124, 125, 137, 139, 160, 160*f,* 161, 187, 237, 279, 280, 281, 283, 301, 306*f,* 321, 329, 330, 331, 332*f,* 333–334, 338
Walmart Canada, 34, 369
The Walt Disney Company, 130, 217, 338
Walter Reed Army Medical Center, 277–278
Walton, Sam, 124
Wang, Vera, 126
WannaBiz, 321
Warner Bros., 109*f,* 306*f,* 338
Warner Music Canada, 326
Wasabi Grill and Noodle, 74
Waste Management, 130
Waterstone Human Capital, 139
Watson Gardner Brown, 386
Watterworth, Elizabeth, 174
Wavebreak Media Ltd., 369*n*
The Weather Network, 35
Webroot, 285
Wekerle, Michael, 118, 225, 288, 340, 394–395
Wellington West Holdings Inc., 39
West Fraser Timber Co. Ltd., 229
Western Compensation & Benefits Consultants of Vancouver, 39
Western Electric Company, 205
WestJet, 48, 49*f,* 56–57, 124, 133, 210, 280, 325*f,* 380–381, 391
Weston, Galen Jr., 123*f*
WhatsApp, 76, 80
Wheelen, Thomas L., 136*n*
Whirlpool, 106
Whitacre, Edward, 144–145
White Pages, 137
Whitfield, Simon, 118
Whitman, Meg, 124
Whole Foods Market, 58, 295
Wilfred Laurier University, 357
Wilkins, Carolyn, 357
Williams, Steven, 130
Willowest Hospitality Furnishings, 77
Wilson, Michael, 179
Windsurfer, 70
Winjit, 383
Winks, 38
Winners, 95
Winnipeg Jets, 53
Winterkorn, Martin, 134
WorkCabin.ca, 174
Worker Rights Consortium, 51
Workman, Kurt, 227
Workopolis, 173
World Bank, 100, 101, 356, 359, 372
World Economic Forum, 102
World Trade Organization (WTO), 71, 109, 110–111, 114
WorldCom, 219
Wrangler, 161
wsj.com, 381
WWE, 306*f*

X

XE.COM Inc., 104
Xerox, 70, 76, 161, 247
XFL, 306*f*
Xi'an City Commercial Bank, 116
Xiaochen, Cheng, 98
XM, 275
Xstrata, 143–144

Y

Yahoo Finance, 118
Yahoo Inc., 79, 121, 126, 160, 212
Yconic/Abacus, 170
Yellow Media Inc., 374
Yellow Pages, 137, 325
Yigit, Kaan, 42
Yogen Früz, 73
Your Independent Grocer, 23
YouTube, 59–60, 122, 176, 177, 276, 308, 322*f,* 325, 332*f,* 340
Ysselstein, Shep, 77–78
Yum! Brands Inc., 38, 215–216, 226

Z

Zara, 268*f*
Zehrs Markets, 23
Zellers, 137*f*
Zeronext, 288
Zhang, Emily (Shi Yu), 77
Zuckerberg, Mark, 5, 76, 80, 391
Zynga, 79

SUBJECT INDEX

boldface page number indicates definition; *f* indicates figure; *t* indicates table

A
Aboriginal peoples, 183
absolute advantage, **102**
accommodative stance, 61
accountability, **154**
accountants, 258–260
  see also accounting
  accounting services, 259–260
  auditing, 259–260
  evolving role, 269
  fraud detection, 260
  management consulting services, 260
  private accountants, 260
  professional accountants, 258–259
  tax services, 260
  transition to CPA, 259
accounting, **257**
  accountants. *See* accountants
  accounting cycle, 260
  accounting equation, 261, 268–269
  double-entry accounting, 262
  fair value accounting, 266
  financial statements, 262–266
  forensic accounting, 273
  international accounting standards, 259–260
  mark-to-market accounting, 266
  for missing inventory, 255–257
  small businesses, 264
  users of accounting information, 257–258
accounting equation, **261,** 268–269
accounting ethics, 268–269
accounting information system (AIS), **257**
accounting profession, 34
accounts payable, **263,** 369
accounts receivable, 369, 370
achievement-oriented behaviour, 216
acquired needs theory, 207
acquisition, **38**
activity ratios, **267–268**
administrative law, **68**
advertising, **323**
  of counterfeit brands, 53–54
  ethics in, 53–54
  morally objectionable advertising, 54
  stealth (undercover) advertising, 54
  truth in advertising, 53
advertising media, **323–325,** 324*t*
Adzi – Advertising Expert app, 321
affect, 203
affiliation, need for, 207
Afghanistan, 100, 110
Africa, 99, 113
agency-principal relationship, **69**
agency shop, **188**
aggregate output, **27**
agreeableness, 201
agreement, 68
Agreement on Internal Trade (AIT), 110
air pollution, 58–59
Alberta, 86, 109, 190, 384
alternate banks, 353
analytic processes, 235
angels, 82
anti-discrimination laws, 181
anti-virus software, 285–**286**
application forms, 173
applied R&D, 31
apps, 277
  Adzi – Advertising Expert, 321
  Bloomberg Finance, 383
  Business Anywhere APK, 104
  CanadianJobForce.com, 173
  CFA Institute, 383
  demand for, 307
  The Eco Activist, 53
  Economics App, 8
  The Economist App, 8
  The Economist World in Figures, 29
  Entrepreneur Magazine, 83
  Ethical Barcode, 53
  Expensify, 83
  Financial Terms, 383
  Globe Investor, 349
  Goal Tracker: SmartGoals, 135
  Gross Domestic Product, 29
  HR Management, 173
  IB Smart Economics, 8
  International Business Guide, 104
  iRecycle, 53
  Kashoo Accounting App, 259
  Leadership Qualities, 216
  Learn Accounting by GoLearningBus, 259
  Let's Get Organized, 163
  Marketing Hoopla, 321
  McKinsey Insights, 135
  Mint.com Personal Finance, 349
  My Teams, 163
  National Debt, 29
  Pert Estimator, 245
  Price Check Guru, 321
  Productivity Wizard, 245
  Quality Management, 245
  QuickBooks App, 259
  Quotes, 216
  SAP Business One, 163
  Search Jobs Beyond.com, 173
  Success Magazine, 83
  SWOT Chart, 135
  TD (Canada), 349
  Toastmaster Magazine, 216
  XE Currency App, 104
arbitration, **191**
Argentina, 100, 112
Armenia, 100
artificial intelligence (AI), **284**
Artist Entrepreneur Program, 326
ASEAN Free Trade Area, 112, 112*f*
Asia Pacific, 58, 112
Asia-Pacific Economic Cooperation, 113
assembly line, **238**
assembly processes, 235
assessment centre, **175**
asset, **261**
  current assets, 262–263
  fixed assets, 263
  intangible assets, 263
  real value, 266
asset allocation, 376

assignment of tasks, 154
attitudes, **202–203**
audit, **259**
auditing, 34, 259–260
Australia, 58, 100, 112
authoritarianism, 202
authority, **154**
  committee and team authority, 157
  distribution of, 155
  forms of authority, 155–157
  line authority, 155–156
  staff authority, 156–157
automated banking machines (ABMs), 349
automated teller machines (ATMs), 349
automobile manufacturing, 230

B
Baby Boomers, 169–170
Bahrain, 113
bailment, 69
bailor-bailee relationship, 69
bailouts, 8, 230
balance of payments, **103**
balance of trade, **29, 103**, 103*t*
balance sheet, **262–263**, 262*f*, 365–366
Bangladesh, 51, 100, 102
Bank Act, 348, 351
bank loans, 350
Bank of Canada, 31, **351–352**, 352*f*
Bank of England, 352
bank rate, **351**
banker's acceptance, 348
bankrupt person (or company), 71
bankruptcy, 71
banks and banking
  alternate banks, 353
  chartered banks. *See* chartered banks
  international banking and finance, 355–357
bargain retailers, 331, 332*t*
bargaining unit, **188**
barriers to international trade, 108–110
  business-practice laws, 110
  economic differences, 108
  legal and political differences, 108–109
  local-content laws, 109–110
  overcoming, 110–113
  quotas, 108
  social and cultural differences, 108
  subsidies, 109
  tariffs, 108–109
barter economy, 346
bartering, online, 350
basic R&D, 31
Baumol's Disease, 245
bear markets, **380**
bearer bonds, 371
behaviour-based interviewing, **175**
behaviour modification, 208
behavioural approach, **215–216**
behavioural segmentation, 300
behavioural variables, **300**
Belarus, 110
bell curve, 178
benchmarking, **248**
benefits, **180**, 189, 293
big data, 282
"big five" personality traits, 201–202, 201*f*
Big Mac Index, 356, 356*f*
"Big Six" banks, 350
bill of materials, **243**
Bills of Exchange Act, 70
biofuel, 233
bitcoins, 357
Bloomberg Finance app, 383
blue-sky laws, **384**
board of directors, **89**
bona fide occupational requirement, **181**
bond indenture, 371
bond quotations, 378–380, 379*f*
bonds, 371–373
  callable bonds, 372
  convertible bonds, 373
  green bonds, 372
  ratings, 373*t*
  serial bonds, 373
book value, **374**
bookkeeping, **257**
bootstrapping, **82**
bottom line, 263
boundaryless organization, 160–161
boycott, 190
branch office, **106**
brand awareness, 309–310
brand competition, 296
brand equity, **309**
brand names, 310
branding, **309**–310
Brazil, 47, 100–101, 112
breach of contract, **69**
breakeven analysis, **320**, 320*f*
breakeven point, **320**
bribery, 48–49
brick-and-mortar retail outlets, 331
BRICS (Brazil, Russia, India, China, and South Africa), 100–**101**
British Columbia, 9, 11, 34, 109, 190, 299, 384
British North America (BNA) Act, 68, 186
brokers, **329**
Brunel Darassalum, 112
budget, **265–266**
budget deficits, **29**
bull markets, **380**
business, **4**
  government, influence son, 11–12
  history of business in Canada, 21
  the idea of business, 4–5
  interactions between business and government, 9–12
business analysis, 307
Business Anywhere APK apps, 104
business cases
  The Car Branding Game: Two Companies, Two Brands, One Platform, 314–315
  Corporate Culture, 143–145
  CSI: Stock Market Edition, 273
  Entrepreneurial Spirit: Beyond the Rack, 94–95
  Hollywood's New Marketing Campaign: Reviving Classic Movies, 338
  How Are We Doing With Our IPO?, 390–391
  Is a New Era of Labour Relations Dawning at Air Canada?, 194–195
  Mastering the Credit Card Game, 360–361
  Netflix: Video Streaming Revolution, 42–43
  The Problem of Consumer Skepticism, 65–66
  Scotiabank's Global Footprint, 115–116
  Searching for a Great Place to Work, 222–223
  Some Glitches in the Provision of Services, 252–253
  What Happened to the "Occupy Wall Street" Movement?, 167
  Where Are Gasoline Prices Headed?, 19–20
business continuation agreements, **393**
business crises, 138
business cycle, **28**, 28*f*
Business Development Bank of Canada, 83, 354
business environment, 34

business ethics, **47**
see also ethics
business goals, 133–134
business insurance, 393
business law, **68**
agency, 69
bailment, 69
bankruptcy, 71
breach of contract, 69
contracts, 68–69
copyrights, 70
international framework of, 71
law of property, 69
negotiable instruments, 70
patent, 70
torts, 70
trademarks, 70
transfer of property, 69
warranty, 69
business-level (competitive) strategy, **136**, 137
business marketing, 303–304
business ownership. *See* forms of business ownership
business plan, **81**, 81*t*, 117, 224–225, 287, 339, 394
business-practice laws, **110**
business process management, 37–**38**
business process re-engineering, **248**–249
Business Register, 75
business resources, 278
business strategy, 236
business-to-business (B2B) transactions, 7
business-to-consumer (B2C) transactions, 7
buyers, 36
buying an existing business, 85
buzz marketing, **309**–310

C

cafeteria-style benefit plans, **180**
caisses populaires, **353**
California, 58
call option, 380
callable bonds, 372
callable preferred stock, 374
Cambodia, 102
Canada
Asia-Pacific Economic Cooperation, 113
balance of payments, 103
balance of trade, 103, 103*t*
banking system, 348
bicycles in, 34
bribery, 48–49
chartered banks. *See* chartered banks
on corruption index, 110
ethnic diversity, 299
exports, 103*f*, 106
global economy, role in, 100
gross domestic product (GDP), 28
imports, 103*f*
international competitiveness, 102
job satisfaction, 203
local-content laws, 109–110
management styles, 219
manufacturing, 229–231
maple syrup, 14*f*
mergers and acquisitions in, 38
mortgages, 343–345
NAFTA, 111
per capital income, 100
potash cartel, 110
price increases, 30*f*
research and development (R&D), 31–32
securities regulation, 384
small and medium-sized employers, 75*t*
stock exchanges, 378
top accounting firms, 258*t*
top corporations in Canada, 89*f*
Trans-Pacific Partnership, 112
two dominant cultures, 299
Canada Business Corporations Act, 90
Canada Business program, 11
Canada Consumer Product Safety Act, 10
Canada-European Union Comprehensive Economic and Trade Agreement (CETA), 112
Canada Labour Code, **186**–**187**
Canada Mortgage and Housing Corporation (CMHC), 355
Canada Pension Plan (CPP), 180
Canada Water Act, 11
Canadian Charter of Rights and Freedoms, 187
Canadian Chartered Professional Accounting Code of Ethics, 268, 268*t*
Canadian dollar, 231
Canadian economy, 31
Canadian financial system, 347–348
alternate banks, 353
chartered banks, 348–352
investment dealers, 354
specialized lending and savings intermediaries, 353–354
Canadian Human Rights Act, 181, 182, 187
Canadian Intellectual Property Office, 70
Canadian market economy, 12–14
demand, 12–14, 13*f*
demand and supply schedule, 12, 13*f*
demand curve, 13
laws of supply and demand, 12
shortages, 14
supply, 12–14, 13*f*
supply curve, 13
surplus, 14
Canadian Radio-television and Telecommunications Commission (CRTC), 9
CanadianJobForce.com app, 173
cap and trade system, 58
capacity, **237**
capacity utilization rate, 230
capital, 5
capital expenditures, 369
capital items, 305, 305*t*
capital structure, **375**
capitalism, **8**
carbon dioxide emissions, 59*f*
carbon footprint, 61
caring, 49
cartel, **110**
cases. *See* business cases; video cases
cash-flow management, **368**
cash flow statement, 265
cash flows from financing, 265
cash flows from investing, 265
cash flows from operations, 265
cash registers, 331
category killers, 332*t*
cause-and-effect diagrams, 245
centralized organization, 148, **155**
certificates of deposit (CDs), 347
certification vote, **188**
certified general accountant (CPA, CGA), 258, **259**
certified management accountant (CPA, CMA), 258, **259**
CFA Institute app, 383
chain of command, 151
change management, 139
channel conflict, **330**
channel leadership, 330
charismatic leadership, 217–218, 217*f*
charitable donations, 57–58

chartered accountant (CPA, CA), **258–259**
chartered banks, **348**–352
bank loans, 350
"Big Six" banks, 350
as creators of money, 350, 351*f*
deregulation, 351
electronic funds transfer, 349
financial advice, 348
international banking, changes in, 351
international services, 348
and mortgages, 344
pension services, 348
Schedule I bank, 348
services offered by, 348–349
top banks in Canada, 348*t*
trust services, 348
chartered professional accountant (CPA), **258**
chemical processes, 235
cheque, **347**
cheque kiting, 57
chief accounting officer, 258
chief executive officer (CEO), **89**, 127, 367
chief financial officer (CFO), 367
child labour, 51
Chile, 112
China, 58, 100–101
automobile sales, 14
bicycles in, 34
bribery fines, 48
counterfeit products, 54
dumping, 110
gross domestic product (GDP), 28
manufacturing jobs, 102, 112
market economy, support for, 7
per capital income, 100
pollution in, 58*f*
and product safety, 53
social and cultural differences, 108
strategic alliances, 106–107
as trading partner, 99
circular flow in market economy, 8*f*
Civil Code, 68
classical theory of motivation, **205**
classification of goods and services, 304–305
clerical processes, 235
client relationships, 211
client-server network, **279**
closed shop, **188**
cloud computing, **281**
co-operative, **90–91**
Co-operative Capital Markets Regulatory System, 384
codes of ethics, 50, 51, 268–269
coercive power, 215
cognition, 202–203
COLA clause, 189
collaboration, 275
collateral, **82**, 370
collective bargaining, **185**, 189–191
arbitration, 191
benefits, 189
compensation, 189
conciliation, 191
contract issues, 189–190
job security, 190
management rights, 190
management tactics, 190–191
mediation, 191
other union issues, 190
reaching agreement, 189
union tactics, 190
when bargaining fails, 190–191
Colombia, 100
combination of tasks, 211
command economy, **5**, 7
commercial paper, **371**
commercialization, 307
committee and team authority, **157**
commodities, 16, 383–384
common law, **68**
Common Market, 111
see also European Union (EU)
common stock, **89**, 263, 374
communication
accountants, 269
of corporate culture, 139
communism, 7
company productivity, 245
comparable worth, **181–182**
comparative advantage, **102**
compensation, **178**–180
basic compensation, 179
collective bargaining, 189
incentive programs, 179–180
individual incentives, 179–180
team and group incentives, 180
competence, 68
competition
brand competition, 296
degrees of competition, 14–16
and exchange rates, 104
international competition, 296
monopolistic competition, 15
monopoly, 15
oligopoly, 15
perfect competition, 14
private enterprise, 14
promotion of competition, 9–10
rivalry among existing competitors, 35
Competition Act, **9–10**, 10*t*, 16
Competition Bureau, 3, 9–10, 51, 53, 150, 284
competitive advantage, 101–102
competitive environment, 296
competitive product analysis, **247**
competitive strategy, **137**
compressed workweek, **212**
compulsory arbitration, 191
computer-aided design (CAD), **283**
computer-based scheduling, 241
computer graphics, **281**
computer virus, 285–286
concentration strategy, 136
concept testing, 307
conceptual skills, **130**
conciliation, **191**
Conciliation Act, 186*t*
conflict of interest, **48**
conglomerate diversification, 137
conglomerate merger, 38
conscientiousness, 201–202
consideration, 68
consolidation, 23–24
Constitution Act, 186
Consumer and Corporate Affairs Canada, 10
consumer behaviour, 301–303, **302**
consumer buying patterns, 7
consumer buying process, 303, 323*f*
consumer finance company, **354**
consumer goods, **293**, 304
Consumer Packaging and Labelling Act, 10, 310
consumer price index (CPI), **30**, 189
consumer products, 304*t*
consumer protection, 10

consumer rights, 53
consumer skepticism, 65–66
consumerism, **53**
contingency approach to leadership, 216
contingency planning, **137**–138
contingent workers, 184
contracts, **68**–69
contributions, 204
control chart, **247**
control systems, 87
controller, **258**
controlling, **124**–125, 124*f*
  operations control, 243–244
  for quality, 247
convenience goods, **304**, 304*t*
convenience services, **304**, 304*t*
convenience stores, 331, 332*t*
convertible bonds, 373
copyrights, **70**
core principles, 51*f*
corporate bond, **371**–373
  see also bonds
corporate boundaries. *See* organizational boundaries
corporate charitable donations, 57–58
corporate culture, **138**–139, 143–145
corporate-level strategy, **136**–137
corporate social responsibility (CSR), **51**
  accommodative stance, 61
  advertising, ethics in, 53–54
  approaches to social responsibility, 60–61
  consumer rights, 53
  customers, responsibility toward, 53–54
  defensive stance, 61
  employees, responsibility toward, 55–57
  environment, responsibility toward, 58–60
  financial mismanagement, 57
  formal level, 61–62
  implementation of CSR programs, 60–62
  informal level, 62
  international communities, responsibility toward, 57–58
  investors, responsibility toward, 57
  local communities, responsibility toward, 57–58
  management of CSR programs, 61–62
  obstructionist stance, 61
  proactive stance, 61
  small businesses, 62
  stakeholder model of responsibility, 52–60
  suppliers, responsibility toward, 57
  unfair pricing, 53
  whistle-blowers, 56–57
corporation, **89**–90
  advantages and disadvantages of incorporation, 90
  employee-owned corporations, 38–39
  formation of, 90
  parent corporation, 39
  private corporation, 90
  public corporation, 89–90
  subsidiary corporation, 39
  sustainable corporations, 62
  top corporations in Canada, 89*f*
  types of, 89–90
Corruption Perceptions Index, 110
cost leadership, 137
cost of goods sold, **264**
cost-of-living adjustment (COLA), 189
cost-oriented pricing, **319**–320
costs
  exit costs, 80
  fixed costs, 320
  variable costs, 320
counterfeit brands, 53–54
counterproductive behaviours, **201**
coupon, **327**
coupon bonds, 371
court system, 68
CPA, CA, **258**
CPA, CGA, **259**
CPA, CMA, **259**
craft unions, 188
creativity, 76
credit cards, 347, 360–361, 362
credit policy, 369
credit unions, **353**
creditors, 257
crisis management, **138**
critical incident method, 178
cross-cultural leadership, 218–219
crowdfunding, 385
CSR. *See* corporate social responsibility (CSR)
Cuba, 33
cultural differences, 108
cultural influences, 302
currency, 103–104, **346**
currency values, 355–356
current assets, **262**–263
current dividend yield, 376
current interest yield, 376
current liabilities, **263**
current ratio, **266**
custom-product layout, **237**
customer departmentalization, **153**
customer innovation centres, 158
customer relationship management (CRM), **294**
customers
  adaptation to customer needs, 105
  consumer behaviour, 301–303
  consumer rights, 53
  getting closer to, 248
  interaction with, 233–234
  operations process, presence in, 234
  preferences, 34
  responsibility toward, 53–54
  tastes, 34
  tracking customers, 302
  virtual presence, 234
customization, 276
cutbacks, 204
cyclical unemployment, 30

D

data, 281, 301
data mining, **282**
data warehousing, **282**
day trading, 381, 382
debentures, 371
debit cards, 347, **349**
debt, **267**
debt financing, **371–373**, 375, 375*f*
debt-to-equity ratios, **267**
"decade of greed," 21
decentralized organization, 148, **155**
decertification, **188**
decision making
  behavioural aspects of, 132–133
  decision-making hierarchy, 153–157
  decision-making skills, 131–132
  evaluation of alternatives, 132
  evaluation of results, 132
  following up, 132
  identification of alternatives, 131–132

implementation of chosen alternative, 132
rational decision-making process, 131*t*
recognizing and defining the decision situation, 131
selection of best alternative, 132
decision-making hierarchy, 153–157
decision-making roles, 129
decision-making skills, **131–132**
decision support systems (DSSs), **283**
decision tree approach, 216
decline stage, 307
deed, **69**
default, 371
defensive stance, 61
deficit, **103**
defined benefit (DB) pension plans, 183
defined contribution (DC) pension plans, 183
deflation, **30**
degrees of competition, 14–16
delegation, **154**, 154*t*
demand, 12–14, 13*f*, 87
for apps, 307
banks, and changes in consumer demand, 351
international demand, 104–105
labour demand, 172
demand and supply schedule, **12**, 13*f*
demand conditions, 102
demand curve, **13**
demand deposits, 347
demographic segmentation, 299
demographic variables, **299**, 299*t*
Denmark, 104, 110, 203
department stores, 332*t*
departmentalization, 148–149, **152–153**, 154*f*
depreciation, **263**
depression, 28
deregulation, **9**, 351
Designated Public Office Holders (DPOHs), 12
detailed schedules, 241
developed countries, 102
developing countries, 100
development, 176
development of opportunity, 81–82
differentiation strategy, 137
digital marketplace, 321
digital transmission, 333*t*
digital wallet, 349
direct channel, **329**
direct deposits and withdrawals, 349
direct mail, 328
direct marketing, **327**
direct-response retailing, **331**, 332*t*
direct selling, 332*t*
directing, **124**
directive leader behaviour, 216
discharge, 69
discount, **322**
discount brokers, 378
discount stores, 332*t*
distracted driving, 54*f*
distribution, **298**
channel conflict, 330
channel leadership, 330
distribution channels, 329–330
distribution mix, 329–330
distribution strategies, 330
intermediaries, 329, 330–332
physical distribution, 333–334
through supply chain, 333–334
distribution channel, **329**, 329*f*
distribution mix, **329–330**
distribution of authority, 155
distribution strategies, 330
diversification, 137, 376
diversity in the workforce, 183–184
divestitures, **38**
divestment, 137
dividends, 89, **90**, 376
divisional structure, **158**, 158*f*, 158*t*
Dodd Frank Wall Street Reform Consumer Protection Act (U.S.), 351
double-entry accounting, 262
double taxation, **90**
Dow Jones Industrial Average (DJIA), 380
downsizing, **155**, 204
dumping, **110**
duty of loyalty, 203
dynamic pricing, 321

E

e-business objectives, 319
e-commerce, 234, **274**
e-intermediaries, **332**
early behavioural theory, 205
early years of business, 21
earnings per share, **267**
Eastern Europe, 100
The Eco Activist app, 53
economic agents, behaviour toward, 48–49
Economic Community of Central African States, 113
economic differences, 108
economic environment, **26**–31
aggregate output, 27
balance of trade, 29
business cycle, 28, 28*f*
Canadian economy, 31
consumer price index (CPI), 30
deflation, 30
economic growth, 27–29
economic stability, 30–31
GDP per capita, 28
gross domestic product (GDP), 28
gross national product (GNP), 28
inflation, 30
marketing environment, 296
national debt, 29
productivity, 29
purchasing power parity, 28–29
real GDP, 28
real growth rates, 28
standard of living, 27
unemployment, 30–31
economic growth, 27–29
economic stability, 30–31
economic system, **5**–6
Canadian market economy, 12–14
command economy, 5, 7
market economy, 5, 7–8
mixed market economy, 8–9
Economics App, 8
The Economist App, 8
The Economist World in Figures app, 29
effectiveness, 123
efficiency, 123
electronic conferencing, **279**
electronic funds transfer, 349
electronic purses, 349
email, 130
embargo, **108**
emerging markets, 100–101
emotional intelligence, **202**
emotional motives, 303

- emotional quotient (EQ), **202**
- emotionality, 202
- employee behaviour, **200**
- employee engagement, 198–200
- employee information systems, **172**
- employee-owned corporations, 38–39
- employee safety and health, 182, 187
- employee satisfaction, 197–198
- employee stock ownership plans (ESOPs), 38–39
- employees
  - behaviour toward, 48
  - development, 176
  - ethics training, 50, 51
  - individual differences, 201–203
  - orientation, 176
  - responsibility toward, 55–57
  - training, 176, 243
  - as users of accounting information, 257
- employers
  - behaviour toward, 48
  - lawsuits against, 127
  - small and medium-sized employers in Canada, 75*t*
- employers' associations, 190
- Employment Equity Act, 181
- employment insurance, 180
- employment standards, 187
- empowerment, 210
- encryption system, **286**
- endorsement, **70**
- enterprise resource planning (ERP), 276
- entrepreneur, 5, **76**
- *Entrepreneur* Magazine app, 83
- entrepreneur-opportunity fit, 84
- entrepreneur-resources fit, 84
- entrepreneurial era, 21
- entrepreneurial process, 78–85, 78*f*
  - assessment of fit between elements in process, 84
  - building the right team, 83–84
  - financial resources, 82
  - identification of opportunities, 78–82
  - resources, 82–83
- entrepreneurship, **76**
- the environment
  - *see also* the greening of business
  - air pollution, 58–59
  - cap and trade system, 58
  - carbon dioxide emissions, 59*f*
  - carbon footprint, 61
  - environmental protection, 11
  - land pollution, 59–60
  - recycling, 59
  - responsibility toward, 58–60
  - water pollution, 59
- environment of business
  - economic environment, 26–31
  - emerging challenges and opportunities, 36–38
  - external environment, 25
  - marketing environment, 294–296, 295*f*
  - multiple organizational environments, 26
  - organization-environment match, 135–136
  - organizational boundaries, 25
  - physical environment, impact of, 35
  - political-legal environment, 33
  - socio-cultural environment, 34–36
  - technological environment, 31–33
- environmental analysis, 135
- Environmental Contaminants Act, 11
- Environmental Protection Acts, 59
- Environmental Protection and Enhancement Act (Alberta), 59
- equal employment opportunity regulations, **181**
- equilibrium price, **13**
- equity financing, 82, **373**
  - asset allocation, 376
  - common stock, 374
  - *vs.* debt financing, 375, 375*f*
  - diversification, 376
  - hybrid financing, 374
  - preferred stock, 374
  - retained earnings, 374
  - return on investment, 376–377
  - risk management, 376
  - risk-return relationship, 375–376, 376*f*
  - time value of money, 377
- equity theory, **208**
- escalation of commitment, 133
- ESOPs, 38–39
- essential services, 11
- esteem needs, 206
- Ethical Barcode app, 53
- ethical compliance, 34
- ethical funds, 383
- ethical leadership, 219
- ethical sourcing, 50
- ethics, 47
  - accounting ethics, 268–269
  - in advertising, 53–54
  - assessment of ethical behaviour, 49
  - business ethics, 47
  - codes of ethics, 50, 51, 268–269
  - conflict of interest, 48
  - economic agents, behaviour toward, 48–49
  - employees, behaviour toward, 48
  - employers, behaviour toward, 48
  - encouraging ethical behaviour, 50–51
  - ethics director or officer, 51
  - ethics training, 50, 51
  - individual ethics, 47–48
  - managerial ethics, 48–49
  - professional ethics, 34
  - top management commitment to ethical standards, 50–51
  - training, 50
  - in the workplace, 47–51
- Ethiopia, 99
- euro, **104**, 348
- Europe, 100
- European Union (EU), 58, 100, 104, **111**, 111*f*, 112, 371
- evaluation of alternatives, 303, 386–387
- evaluation of employee performance, 177–178
- exchange rates, 103–104, 355–356
- exchange-traded fund (ETF), **383**
- exclusive distribution, **330**
- exit costs, 80
- expectancy theory, 207–208, 207*f*
- expense items, 305, 305*t*
- Expensify app, 83
- experimentation, **301**
- expert power, 215
- expert system, 284
- export, **99**, 103*f*
- Export Development Corporation (EDC), 354
- exporter, 105–106
- express contract, **68**
- express warranty, **69**
- external environment, **25**
  - dimensions of, 27*f*
  - economic environment, 26–31
  - marketing environment, 294–296, 295*f*
  - political-legal environment, 33
  - socio-cultural environment, 34–36
  - technological environment, 31–33

external failures, 247
external locus of control, 202
external recruiting, 172–173
extranets, **279**
extraversion, 202

F

fabrication processes, 235
face-to-face communications, 37
factor, **353**, 370
factor conditions, 102
factoring, 370
factoring company, **353**
factors of production, **5**
  see also specific factors of production
factory outlets, 332*t*
factory system, 21
fair employment practices, 187
fair-trade movement, 45–47, **51–52**
fair value accounting, 266
fairness, 49
family business, 85–86
fantasy stock markets, 377
federal government. *See* government
finance, **367**
  see also financing
finance era, 21
Financial Accounting Standards Board (FASB), 266
financial accounting system, **258**
financial assistance, 11
financial control, **368**
financial corporations, 353–354
financial crisis, 31, 182
financial information services, 378–380
financial institutions, 82, 348
financial management, 57
financial managers, 129, 367–368
financial measures, 52
financial pillars. *See* Canadian financial system
financial plan, 362, **368**, 375
financial reporting, 34
financial resources, 82
financial statements, **262**–266
  analysis of, 266–268
  balance sheet, 262–263, 262*f*, 365–366
  budget, 265–266
  income statement, 263–265, 263*f*
  statement of cash flows, 265
Financial Terms app, 383
financial viability, 80
financing
  cash flows from financing, 265
  debt financing, 371–373
  equity financing, 373–377
  government financial institutions and granting agencies, 354–355
  long-term funds, sources of, 371–377
  need for, 368–369
  other sources, 354–355
  secured short-term loans, 370
  securities purchases, 380–382
  short-term funds, sources of, 369–371
  specialized lending and savings intermediaries, 353–354
  trade credit, 369–370
  unsecured short-term loans, 370–371
finished-goods inventory, 369
Finland, 110
firewalls, **285**
first-line managers, **128**, 130
fiscal policies, **31**
fishbone diagrams, 245
Fisheries Act, 11
five forces model, 34–35, 35*f*
fixed assets, **263**
fixed costs, **320**
fixed position layout, **239**
fixed pricing, 321
flat organizations, 155, 156*f*
flexible manufacturing system (FMS), **239**
flextime, **211**, 212*f*
focus groups, **301**
focus strategy, 137
Food and Drug Act, 10
food courts, 73–74
forced distribution, 178
forecast of HR demand and supply, 172
foreign direct investment (FDI), **107**
foreign stock exchanges, 378
forensic accountants, **260**
forensic accounting, 273
form utility, 232, 293
formal organization, 162
forms of business ownership
  co-operative, 90–91
  comparison of, 91*t*
  corporation, 89–90
  partnership, 88–89
  sole proprietorship, 88
fortress balance sheet, 365–366
four-day workweek, 213
four Ps of marketing, 297–298
France, 28, 100, 108, 111
franchise, **81**, 86, 87*t*
Franchise Disclosure Documents (FDD), 86
franchising agreement, **86**
fraud detection, 260
free trade agreements, 111–113
freedom of choice, 14
frictional unemployment, 30
friendly takeover, 38
full-service brokers, 378
functional departmentalization, **153**
functional strategies, **136**, 137
functional structure, **157**–158, 157*t*
futures contracts, **383**–384

G

G8, 99
G20, 99
GAAP, 259
gainsharing plans, **180**
games with a social twist, 55
gaming consoles, 55
Gantt chart, **241**–242, 242*f*
gasoline prices, 19–20
GDP per capita, **28**
gender, and leadership, 218
General Agreement on Tariffs and Trade (GATT), **110**
general and administrative expenses, 265
general partners, **88**
general partnership, 88
generally accepted accounting principles (GAAP), **259**
generations, 169–171
generic brands, **310**
GenXers, 170
geo-demographic segmentation, 299
geo-demographic variables, **299**
geographic clusters, 100
geographic departmentalization, 148–149, **153**
geographic expansion, 136
geographic segmentation, 299

geographic variables, **299**
Germany, 28, 47, 99, 100, 110, 111
global competitors, 244
global context of business
  barriers to international trade, 108–113
  global economy, 99–104
  international business management, 104–107
global economy, 99–104
  balance of payments, 103
  balance of trade, 103
  competitive advantage, forms of, 101–102
  emerging markets, 100–101
  exchange rates, 103–104
  major world marketplaces, 100
global era, 21
global exchange, 276
global GDP, 28
Global Leadership and Organizational Behaviour Effectiveness study, 219
globalization, **99**, 126
Globe Investor app, 349
"go global," 21
goal setting, 133–134
goal-setting theory, **208**–209
Goal Tracker: SmartGoals app, 135
goals, **133**, 133–134
  business goals, 133–134
  green goals, 134
  SMART goals, 134, 208
  strategic goals, 134–135
goods, 293–294
  classification of, 304–305
  consumer goods, 293, 304
  convenience goods, 304, 304*t*
  distribution of, 329
  industrial goods, 293
  shopping goods, 304, 304*t*
  specialty goods, 304, 304*t*
goods-producing processes, 235
goods production, **232**
goodwill, **263**
gossip, 163
government
  bailouts, 8, 230
  business, influences on, 9–11
  competition, promotion of, 9–10
  as competitor, 9
  consumer protection, 10
  as customer, 9
  environmental protection, 11
  essential services, provider of, 11
  financial assistance, provider of, 11
  incentives, provider of, 11
  interactions between business and government, 9–12
  market, 303–304
  as regulator, 9–11
  regulatory bodies, 9, 257
  securities regulation, 384
  social goals, 10
  suppliers of funds, 354–355
  as taxation agent, 11
grapevine, 162*f*, 163, **163**
graphic rating scale, 178
Greece, 371
green bonds, 372
green energy, 233
green movement, 60, 65
green roof structures, 161
the greening of business
  feeling the pressure for "green," 295
  four-day workweek, 213
  green bonds, 372
  green energy, 233
  green goals, 134
  "green" jobs in surprising places, 174
  green movement, frustrations in, 60
  green roof structures, 161
  hydrogen fuel cells, 32
  small business go green, 85
  telecommuting, 213
  unexpected outcomes, 334
greenwashing, 60, 372
Gross Domestic Product app, 29
gross domestic product (GDP), **28**
gross margin, **265**
gross national product (GNP), **28**
gross profit, **265**
"grossly deceptive product," 28
group-based training, 177
group incentives, 180
group life insurance, **393**
groupware, **281**
growth stage, 307
growth strategy, 136
Guatemala, 100
Gulf Cooperation Council, 113

H

hackers, **284**
Haiti, 100
hardcore unemployed, 55
hardware, **280**–281
Hawthorne effect, **205**
hazardous products, 10, 10*f*
Hazardous Products Act, 10
hedge funds, **383**
Herzberg's two-factor theory, 207, 207*f*
hierarchy of human needs model, **206**–207, 206*f*
high-contact systems, **235**
high-income countries, 100
history of business in Canada, 21
holidays, 187
horizontal integration, 136
horizontal merger, 38
hostile takeover, 38
hostile work environment, 182
hours of work, 187
housing market, 343–345
HR Management app, 173
HRM. *See* human resource management (HRM)
human capital, 171
human relations, 205
human relations skills, **130**
human resource management (HRM), **171**
  anti-discrimination laws, 181
  benefits, 180
  challenges in changing workplace, 183–184
  comparable worth, 181–182
  compensation, 178–180
  contingent workers, management of, 184
  development of human resources, 175–178
  employee safety and health, 182
  equal employment opportunity, 181
  evaluation of employee performance, 177–178
  forecasting HR demand and supply, 172
  group-based training, 177
  human resource planning, 171–172
  job analysis, 171–172
  knowledge workers, management of, 184
  labour relations. *See* labour relations
  legal context, 181–182

matching HR supply and demand, 172
new employee orientation, 176
recruiting, 172–175
retirement, 182
selection process, 173–175, 174*f*
sexual harassment, 182
strategic importance of, 171
team building, 177
training and development, 176
workforce diversity, 183–184
human resource managers, 128
human resource planning, 171–172
hybrid financing, 374
hydrogen fuel cells, 32
hygiene factors, 207
hypertext transfer protocol (HTTP), 279

I

IB Smart Economics app, 8
Iceland, 352
idea generation, 78–79
ideas, 293–294
identification of opportunities, 78–82
identity theft, **284**–285, 285
implied contract, **68**
implied warranty, **69**
import, **99**, 103*f*
importer, **105**–106
improper financial management, 57
in-flight Internet service, 37
in-group, 216
incentive programs, 179–180
incentives, 11
income statement, **263**–265, 263*f*
Income Tax Act, 68
income trust, **90**
incorporation, 90
incubators, **83**, 84*t*
independent agent, **106**
independent local union, 188
India, 100–101, 106, 110
individual differences, **201**
attitudes at work, 202–203
emotional intelligence, 202
other personality traits, 202
personality, 201–202
individual ethics, 47–48
individual incentives, 179–180
individual values and codes, 48
Indonesia, 58, 101
Industrial Disputes Investigation Act, 186*t*
industrial goods, **293**
industrial market, **303**
Industrial Revolution, 21
industrial unions, 188
Industry Canada, 75
industry environment, 34–35
industry productivity, 245
inflation, **30**
infocard, 285
informal groups, 162
informal organization, **162**
grapevine, 162*f*, 163
informal groups, 162
information, 5, 281
information managers, 129
information resources, 282–283
information seeking, 303
information system (IS), **281**–282, 283–284
information technology (IT), 235*f*, **274**, 274–286
business resources, 278
collaboration, 275
cost-saving benefits, 278
electronic conferencing, 279
extranets, 279
flexibility for customization, 276
global exchange, 276
hardware, 280–281
improvements, 277–278
information resources, leveraging, 282–283
information system (IS), 281–282, 283–284
Internet and other communication resources, 278–279
intranets, 279
lean, efficient organizations, 275
management processes, 276
networks, 279–280
new business opportunities, 276
portable offices, 275
protection measures, 285–286
remote access to information, 275
remote deliveries, 275
risks and threats, 284–286
security measures, 285–286
social networking, 278
software, 280–281
system architecture, 279–280
VSAT satellite communications, 279
informational roles, 129
initial public offering (IPO), **90**, 377, 390–391
input market, 7–8
inside directors, 89
insider trading, **57**
insolvent person (or company), 71
institutional market, 303–**304**
insurable risk, 392
insurance, 392–393
intangible assets, **263**
intangible services, 234
integration strategy, 136
intellectual property, 70, **285**
intensive distribution, **330**
intention, 203
intentional tort, **70**
interactive marketing, **327**
intermediaries, **329**, 330–332, 330*f*
e-intermediaries, 332
retailing, 331–332
specialized lending and savings intermediaries, 353–354
wholesaling, 330–331
intermediate goals, 134
internal failures, 247
internal locus of control, 202
internal recruiting, **172**
international accounting standards, 259–260
International Accounting Standards Board (IASB), 259–260
international banking and finance, 351, 355–357
currency values, 355–356
exchange rates, 355–356
international bank structure, 356–357
international payments process, 356
International Business Guide app, 104
international business management, 104–107
exporters, 105–106
going international, 104–105, 105*f*
importers, 105–106
international demand, 104–105
international firms, 106
international organizational structures, 106–107
involvement levels, 105–106
multinational firms, 106

international communities, responsibility toward, 57–58
international competition, 296
international competitiveness, **102**
international division structure, 160*f*
International Financial Reporting Standards (IFRS), 259–260
international firms, **106**
international law, **71**
International Monetary Fund (IMF), **356**–357, 365
international organizational structures, 106–107, **160**
international payments process, 356
international trade barriers. *See* barriers to international trade
international union, 188
Internet, **278**–279
  bartering, 350
  cost-saving benefits, 278, 278*t*
  e-commerce, 234, 274
  fixed *vs.* dynamic pricing, 321
  and global business, 99
  in-flight Internet service, 37
  information technology. *See* information technology (IT)
  Internet era, 21
  Internet radio, 15
  marketing, impact on, 274–275
  online advertising, 324–325, 324*t*
  online consumer engagement, 325
  online customer service, 125
  online trading, 381
  selling Nazi memorabilia online, 47
  small business and entrepreneurship resources, 83
  social media. *See* social media
  usage, 274
  virtual presence of customers, 234
internet marketing, **274**–275
Internet radio, 15
internships, 173
interpersonal roles, 129
interviews, 175
intraday trades, 382
intranets, **279**
intrapreneurs, **76**
introduction stage, 307
intuition, 132–133
inventory, **369**
  as collateral, 370
  merchandise inventory, 262
  missing inventory, 255–257
  types of, 369
inventory control, 243
inventory turnover ratio, **267**–268
investment bankers, **377**
Investment Canada, 107
investment dealers, 354
investment reduction, 137
investments
  bonds. *See* bonds
  cash flows from investing, 265
  commodities, 383–384
  exchange-traded fund (ETF), 383
  hedge funds, 383
  mutual funds, 382–383
  real estate investments, 363
  securities. *See* securities
investor relations, 374
investors
  private investors, 82
  responsibility toward, 57
  as users of accounting information, 257
involuntary bankruptcy, 71
IPO. *See* initial public offering (IPO)
iRecycle app, 53
Ishikawa diagrams, 245
ISO 9000, **248**
Israel, 100
Italy, 100, 108, 111

J

Japan, 28, 58, 100, 102, 104, 112, 245
jeitinho, 47
job analysis, 171–172
job commitment, 203
job description, **171**
job enrichment, **211**
job fair, 173
job redesign, 211
job rotation, 176
job satisfaction, **203**
job security, 190, 204
job sharing, **212**–214
job specialization, **151**–152
job specification, **171**
just-in-time (JIT) production systems, **243**
justice, 49

K

Kashoo Accounting App, 259
key person insurance, **393**
Key Small Business Statistics, 75
knowledge information systems, **283**
knowledge workers, **184**, 283
Kotter's distinctions between management and leadership, 214*t*
Kuwait, 100, 113
Kyoto Summit, 58

L

label, **310**
labour, 5
labour demand, 172
Labour Force Survey, 75
labour markets, 184
labour movement, 185
labour productivity, **244**
labour relations, **185**
  Canada Labour Code, 186–187
  collective bargaining, 185, 189–191
  employee safety, 187
  fair employment practices, 187
  industrial relations regulations, 187
  key Canadian labour legislation, 186*t*
  labour unions, 185–186, 187–188
  legal environment for unions, 186–188
  provincial labour legislation, 187
  standard hours, wages, vacations, and holidays, 187
  trends in union-management relations, 186
  union organizing strategy, 187–188
  union security, 188
labour shortage, 31
labour supply, 172
labour union, **185**
  see also labour relations
  bargaining unit, 188
  certification vote, 188
  decertification, 188
  development of Canadian labour unions, 185
  future of, 186
  legal environment for, 186–188
  types of unions, 188
  union organizing strategy, 187–188
  union security, 188
  union tactics, 190
  unionism today, 185
  as user of accounting information, 257

Lac-Mégantic, Quebec, 334
land pollution, 59–60
law, **68**
  administrative law, 68
  business law. *See* business law
  business-practice laws, 110
  common law, 68
  court system, 68
  international law, 71
  local-content laws, 109–110
  sources of law, 68
  statutory law, 68
law of demand, **12**
law of one price, 355–**356**
law of supply, **12**
layoffs, 171
layout planning, 237–240
leader-member exchange (LMX) model, 216
leadership, **214**
  approaches, 215–216
  behavioural approach, 215–216
  channel leadership, 330
  charismatic leadership, 217–218, 217*f*
  coaches, leaders as, 218
  cross-cultural leadership, 218–219
  decision tree approach, 216
  ethical leadership, 219
  and gender, 218
  leader-member exchange (LMX) model, 216
  vs. management, 214*t*
  and motivation, 214–216
  path-goal theory, 216
  and power, 214–215
  recent trends, 217–219
  situational approach to leadership, 216, 216*f*
  strategic leadership, 219
  trait approach, 215
  transactional leadership, 217
  transformational leadership, 217
  virtual leadership, 219
Leadership Qualities app, 216
leading, **124**
leading for quality, 247
lean, efficient organizations, 275
"lean and mean" organizations, 126
Learn Accounting by GoLearningBus, 259
learning organization, 161–162
lease, **69**
Lebanon, 100
legal differences, 108–109
legal purpose, 69
Let's Get Organized app, 163
letter of credit, 348
leverage, **267**
liability, **261**, 263
liability insurance, **392**–393
licensed brands, 310
licensing arrangement, **106**
life insurance, **393**
life insurance company, **353**
limit order, 380
limited liability, **90**
limited partners, **88**
limited partnership, 88
line authority, **155**–156
line departments, 155
line of credit, **370**
liquidation plan, 71
liquidity, **262**
living standards, 27
load funds, 382–383
loans
  see also financing
  bank loans, 350
  long-term loans, 371
  secured loan, 350, 370
  unsecured loans, 370–371
Lobbying Act, 12
lobbyist, **11**–12
local area networks (LANs), **279**
local communities, responsibility toward, 57–58
local-content laws, **109**–110
local union, 188
location planning, 237
lockout, **190**
locus of control, 202
long-term (capital) expenditures, 369
long-term funds
  debt financing, 371–373
  equity financing, 373–377
long-term goals, 134
long-term liabilities, **263**
long-term loans, 371
long-term solvency, 266–267
love money, 82
low-contact systems, **235**–236
low-income countries, 100
low-middle-income countries, 100
luck, 87

M

M-1, **346**–347
M-2, **347**
Machiavellianism, 202
magazines, 324, 324*t*
mail order catalogue marketing, 332*t*
make-to-order, 235
make-to-stock, 235
Malawi, 100
Malaysia, 58, 112
management, **123**
  see also managers
  areas of, 128–129
  cash-flow management, 368
  competence, 87
  contingency planning, 137–138
  controlling, 124–125, 124*f*
  and corporate culture, 138–139
  crisis management, 138
  vs. leadership, 214*t*
  leading, 124
  levels of, 127–128, 127*f*, 128*t*
  management jobs, 126–127
  management process, 123–125
  organizing, 124
  planning, 123–124
  processes, and information technology, 276
  rights, in collective bargaining, 190
  roles, 129
  science *vs.* art, 125
  skills, 129–133
  strategic management, 133–137
  styles, 219
  tactics, in collective bargaining, 190–191
  in turbulent times. *See* managing in turbulent times
management accounting, **258**
management by objectives (MBO), **209**
management consulting services, **260**
management development programs, **176**
management information systems (MISs), **283**

management process, 123–125
management skills, 129–133
conceptual skills, 130
decision-making skills, 131–132
human relations skills, 130
technical skills, 130
time management skills, 130
managerial accounting, **258**
managerial capitalism, 52
managerial ethics, **48**–49
managers, **123**
see also management
becoming a manager, 125–127
challenges facing, 126
financial managers, 129, 367–368
first-line managers, 128, 130
human resource managers, 128
information managers, 129
information systems for, 283
marketing managers, 129, 297
middle managers, 128
operations managers, 128
service managers, 234
top managers, 50–51, 127
types of, 127–129
as users of accounting information, 257
managing in turbulent times
asset's real value, 266
bitcoins, 357
carrot *vs.* stick, 209
challenges facing managers, 126
direct mail, 328
gossip on the grapevine, 163
pension plans, 183
physical environment, impact of, 35
robots, 239
short selling, 382
urge to move, 112
whistle-blowers, 56
mandated protection plans, 180
Manitoba, 86, 187–188, 384
manufacturing, 229–231
manufacturing operations, 232–234
manufacturing productivity, 245
manufacturing resource planning (MRP II), 244
margin, **380**–382
mark-to-market accounting, 266
market, **7**, **12**
bear markets, 380
bull markets, 380
government and institutional market, 303–304
industrial market, 303
input market, 7–8
labour markets, 184
output market, 7–8
over-the-counter (OTC) market, 378
reseller market, 303
securities markets, 377–382
speed to market, 306
market capitalization, 374
market economy, **5**, 7–8, 8*f*
see also Canadian market economy
market indexes, **380**
market order, 380
market penetration, 136, **319**
market price, **13**
market segmentation, **298**, 299–300
behavioural segmentation, 300
demographic segmentation, 299
geo-demographic segmentation, 299
geographic segmentation, 299
psychographic segmentation, 299–300
market share, **319**
market value, **374**
marketability, 80
marketable securities, 262
marketing, **293**–296
business marketing, 303–304
buzz marketing, 309–310
customer relationship management (CRM), 294
delivering value, 293
direct (interactive) marketing, 327
four Ps of marketing, 297–298
goods, services, and ideas, 293–294
process, 300*f*
relationship marketing, 294
viral marketing, 310
marketing concept, **293**
marketing environment, 294–296, 295*f*
competitive environment, 296
economic environment, 296
political-legal environment, 294–295
socio-cultural environment, 295
technological environment, 295–296
marketing era, 21
Marketing Hoopla app, 321
marketing managers, 129, 297
marketing mix, **297**
marketing objectives, **296**–297
marketing plan, **296**
development of, 296–298
marketing strategy, 297–298
marketing research, **300**–301, 300*f*
marketing strategy, 297–298
distribution through supply chain, 333–334
market segmentation, 298, 299–300
product positioning, 298–299
target markets, 298
markup, **320**
markup percentage, 320
Maslow's hierarchy of human needs model, 206–207, 206*f*
mass customization, **276**
mass production, 21
master production schedule, **240**–241, 241*f*
matching principle, **264**
material requirements planning (MRP), **243**
materials management, **243**
matrix organization, 159, 159*f*
maturity stage, 307
McClelland's acquired needs theory, 207
McGregor's Theory X and Theory Y, 205
McKinsey Insights apps, 135
media mix, 323
mediation, **191**
medium of exchange, 346
meetings, 130
mentoring, **176**
merchandise inventory, 262
Mercosur, 112
merger, **38**
methods planning, 240
Mexico, 100, 111, 112, 113
middle class, 291–292
middle managers, **128**
Migratory Birds Act, 59
Millennials, 170–171
Mint.com Personal Finance app, 349
misrepresentation of finances, 57
missing inventory, 255–257
mission statement, **133**

mixed market economy, **8–9**
mobile advertising, 324*t*, 325
mobile investing, 381
mobile wallet, 349
modified work schedules, 211–214
mompreneurs, 77
monetary policies, **31**, 352*f*
money, **346**
    banks as creators of money, 350, 351*f*
    characteristics of, 346
    divisibility, 346
    durability, 346
    functions of, 346
    M-1, 346–347
    M-2, 347
    as medium of exchange, 346
    "plastic money," 347
    portability, 346
    stability, 346
    as store of value, 346
    supply of, and Bank of Canada, 352
    time value of money, 362, 363*t*, 377
    as unit of account, 346
money market mutual funds, **347**
monopolistic competition, **15**
monopoly, **16**
morale, 203
morally objectionable advertising, 54
mortgages, 343–345
motivating factors, 207
motivation, **204**
    acquired needs theory, 207
    classical theory of motivation, 205
    contemporary motivation theory, 207–208
    early behavioural theory, 205
    equity theory, 208
    expectancy theory, 207–208, 207*f*
    hierarchy of human needs model, 206–207, 206*f*
    and leadership, 214–216
    strategies for enhancing motivation, 208–214
    Theories X and Y, 205
    two-factor theory, 207, 207*f*
motivation strategies
    goal-setting theory, 208–209
    job enrichment and redesign, 211
    modified work schedules, 211–214
    participative management and empowerment, 210
    reinforcement/behaviour modification, 208
    team management, 210–211
motivator-hygiene theory, 207
movable factory, 240
multinational firm, **106**
municipal government, 11
music artists, 326
mutual funds, **382**–383
My Teams app, 163

N

NAFTA, 111
NASDAQ, 378
NASDAQ Composite Index, 380
national brands, **310**
national competitive advantage, **102**, 103*f*
national debt, **29**
National Debt app, 29
national union, 188
nationalization, 8
Natixis Global Retirement Security Index, 182
natural monopolies, 16
natural resources, 5
natural workgroups, 211
need for affiliation, 207
need for power, 207
need recognition, 303
negative reinforcement, 208
negligence, **70**
negotiable instruments, **70**
net earnings, **265**
net income, **265**
net profit, **265**
net worth, 363
networking, **176**
networks, 279–280
New Brunswick, 86, 384
New Development Bank, 101
new product
    development, 305–307
    pricing, 321
new ventures, **76**, 77–78
New Zealand, 110, 112
newspapers, 323
Nigeria, 99
no-load funds, 382
non-direct distribution, 330
non-programmed decisions, 131
non-store retailing, 331–332, 332*t*
normal curve, 178
North America, 100
North American Free Trade Agreement (NAFTA), 111
North Korea, 110
Norway, 203
not-for-profit organizations, **5**
Nova Scotia, 190

O

observation, **301**
obstructionist stance, 61
Occupy Wall Street, 167
odd-even pricing, 322
odd lots, 380
off-the-job training, **176**
oligopoly, **15**
Oman, 100, 113
omission, 208
on-the-job training, **176**
"one best way," 21
online advertising, 324–325, 324*t*
online consumer engagement, 325
online customer service, 125
online trading, 381
Ontario, 9, 11, 59, 86, 190, 384
Ontario Occupational Health and Safety Act, 182
Ontario Securities Act, 384
open-book credit, 370
open shop, **188**
openness, 202
operating expenditures, 368–369
operating expenses, **265**
operating income, **265**
operational plans, **136**
operations
    business strategy, 236
    capabilities and characteristics, 236*t*
    cash flows from, 265
    changes in, 232
    customer's presence in operations process, 234
    meaning of, 232
    operations control, 243–244
    operations processes, 235–236
    scheduling, 240–242

operations (*continued*)
service *vs.* manufacturing operations, 232–234
transformation system, 233
transportation operations, 333
value creation through operations, 232–236
operations capability, 236
operations control, **243–244**
operations management, **232**
operations managers, 128
operations planning, 237*f*
capacity, 237
layout, 237–240
location, 237
methods planning, 240
quality planning, 240
operations process, **235**–236
opportunity, 50
opportunity decisions, 131
opportunity identification, 78–82
opportunity-resources fit, 84
optional protection plans, 180
organization chart, **151**, 151*f*, 162
organization-environment match, 135–136
organizational boundaries, 25, 38–39
organizational buying behaviour, 304
organizational citizenship, 200
organizational commitment, **203**
organizational design
boundaryless organization, 160–161
learning organization, 161–162
team organization, 161
virtual organization, 161
organizational marketing, 303–304
organizational politics, 132
organizational products, 305, 305*t*
organizational stakeholders, **52**, 52*f*
organizational structure, 102, **150**
assignment of tasks, 154
basic organizational structures, 157–160
building blocks of, 151–153
chain of command, 151
committee and team authority, 157
decision-making hierarchy, 153–157
departmentalization, 152–153, 154*f*
determinants of, 150
distribution of authority, 155
divisional structure, 158, 158*f*, 158*t*
flat organizations, 155, 156*f*
forms of authority, 155–157
functional structure, 157–158, 157*t*
influencing factors, 150
international division structure, 160*f*
international organizational structures, 160
line authority, 155–156
matrix organization, 159, 159*f*
performance of tasks, 154–155
project organization, 158–160
span of control, 155, 156*f*
specialization, 151–152
staff authority, 156–157
tall organizations, 155, 156*f*
organizational values, 51*f*
organizing, 124
organizing for quality, 246–247
orientation, **176**
out-group, 216
outdoor advertising, 324, 324*t*
output market, 7–8
outside directors, 89
outsourcing, **36**
over-the-counter (OTC) market, **378**
owners' equity, **261**, 263
ownership utility, 232

P

Pacific Rim, 113
packaging, **310**
paid-in capital, **263**
paid time off, 180
paperwork, 130
par value, **374**
Paraguay, 112
parent corporation, 39
participative leader behaviour, 216
participative management and empowerment, **210**
partnership, **88–89**
patent, **70**
path-goal theory, 216
pay-for-knowledge plans, 179
pay for performance, 179
pay surveys, 179
peak, 28
penetration pricing, **321**
pension funds, **354**
pension plans, 183
per-capita income, 100
perfect competition, 14
performance appraisals, 177–178
performance feedback, 177
performance of tasks, 154–155
performance quality, **246**
performance ratios, 267
person-job fit, **204**
personal competencies, 84
personal finances
credit cards, 362
legal tax avoidance, 363
net worth, protecting, 363
personal financial plan, 362
real estate investments, 363
Rule of 72, 362, 363*t*
time value of money, 362, 363*t*
tips, 362*t*
personal financial plan, 362
personal influences, 302
Personal Information Protection and Electronic Documents Act (PIPEDA), 48, 285
personal property, **69**
personal savings, 82
personal selling, **326–327**
personality, **201–202**
PERT charts, **242**, 242*f*
Pert Estimator app, 245
Peru, 112
Philippines, 58, 100
physical distribution, **333–334**
physical environment, 35
physiological needs, 206
picketing, 190
piece-rate incentive plan, **179**
pipelines, 333*t*
place, **298**
see also distribution
place utility, 232, 293
planes, 333*t*
planning, **123–124**
human resource planning, 171–172
operations planning, 237–240
for quality, 246
plans, 136

"plastic money," 347
pledging accounts receivable, 370
point-of-purchase (sale) displays, **327**
poison pill, **38**
political differences, 108–109
political-legal environment, **33**, 294–295
political stability, 33
pollution, **58**–60
Ponzi schemes, 49, 57
Pooled Registered Pension Plan Act, 182
portable offices, 275
Portugal, 108
positioning, 298–299
positive reinforcement, 208
possession utility, 232, 293
post-purchase evaluation, 303
potential entrants, threat of, 35
power
 and leadership, 214–215
 need for power, 207
 types of power, 215
preferences, 34
preferred stock, 374
premiums, **327**, **392**
prepaid expenses, 262
pressure, 50
price
 appreciation, 376
 equilibrium price, 13
 gasoline prices, 19–20
 increases in Canada, 30*f*
 market price, 13
 unfair pricing, 53
Price Check Guru app, 321
price lining, **322**
price-setting tools, 319–320
price skimming, **321**
pricing, 297–298, **319**
 breakeven analysis, 320, 320*f*
 cost-oriented pricing, 319–320
 dynamic pricing, 321
 existing products, 321
 fixed pricing, 321
 new products, 321
 odd-even pricing, 322
 price-setting tools, 319–320
 pricing strategies, 321
 pricing tactics, 321–322
 psychological pricing, 322
pricing objectives, **319**
pricing strategies, 321
pricing tactics, 321–322
primary data, 301
primary securities markets, 377
prime rate of interest, **350**
Prince Edward Island, 86, 190
principal-protected notes, 383
Principles of Scientific Management (Taylor), 205
privacy, 284
private accountants, **260**
private brands, **310**
private corporation, **90**
private enterprise, 14
private equity firms, **90**
private investors, 82
private placements, 377
private property, 14
private sector, **77**
privatization, **8**
Privy Council Order 1003, 186*t*
proactive stance, 61
problem decisions, 131
problem recognition, 303
process departmentalization, **153**
process flowchart, 240, 240*f*
process layouts, **237**–238, 238*f*
process variation, 247, 248*f*
product, **297**
 branding, 309–310
 classification of goods and services, 304–305
 consumer products, 304, 304*t*
 famous product and brand failures, 306*f*
 ideas, 306
 label, 310
 new product development, 305–307
 organizational products, 305, 305*t*
 packaging, 310
 product adaptation, 309
 product extension, 309
 product life cycle (PLC), 307–309
 reintroduction, 309
 value package, 304
product adaptation, 309
product departmentalization, 148–149, **153**
product development, 136
product differentiation, **297**
product extension, 309
product features, **304**
product layouts, **238**, 238*f*, 239*f*
product liability, **70**
product life cycle (PLC), **307**–309
product line, **305**
product-line retailers, 331, 332*t*
product mix, **305**
product placement, **309**
product positioning, **298**–299
product safety, 53
product technologies, 32–33
product testing, 307
production era, 21
production items, 305, 305*t*
production management, **232**
production process control, 243–244
productivity, **29**, 197–198
 among global competitors, 244
 company productivity, 245
 industry productivity, 245
 international productivity comparisons, 245*f*
 labour productivity, 244
 manufacturing productivity, 245
 measurement of, 244
 meeting the productivity challenge, **244**
 productivity-quality connection, 244–245
 service productivity, 245
productivity-quality connection, 244–245
Productivity Wizard app, 245
professional accountants, 258–259
profit, **5**
 calculation of, 319
 net profit, 265
 private enterprise, 14
profit-and-loss statement, 263–265, 263*f*
profit-maximizing objectives, 319
profit-sharing plans, **180**
profitability ratios, **267**
program evaluation and review technique (PERT), 242
programmed decisions, 131
progressive companies, 55
progressive revenue taxes, 11
project management, 269

project organization, **158–160**
project scheduling, 241–242
project teams, 210
promissory notes, 370
promotion, **298, 322**
advertising promotions and media, 323–325
direct (interactive) marketing, 327
of music artists, 326
personal selling, 326–327
promotional mix, 322–323, 323*f*
promotional strategies, 322
public relations, 327–328
publicity, 327–328
sales promotions, 327
promotional mix, **322**–323, 323*f*
promotional strategies, 322
property, **69**
property insurance, **393**
protection plans, **180**
protectionism, **109**
protocols, 279
prototype development, 307
provincial governments. *See* government; specific provinces and territories
provincial labour legislation, 187
P3s, 11
psychographic segmentation, 299–300
psychographic variables, **299**–300
psychological contracts, **204**, 204*f*
psychological influences, 302
psychological pricing, **322**
public corporation, **89**–90
public-private partnerships (P3s), 11
public relations, 327–**328**
publicity, **327**–328
pull strategy, **322**
punishment, 208
purchase decision, 303
purchase of existing business, 85
purchasing, 243
purchasing power parity, **28**–29
pure R&D, 31
pure risks, **386**
purpose, **133**
push strategy, **322**
put option, 380

Q

Qatar, 113
quality, **244**
benchmarking, 248
business process re-engineering, 248–249
competitive product analysis, 247
controlling for quality, 247
getting closer to the customer, 248
ISO 9000, 248
leading for quality, 247
managing for quality, 245–249
meeting the quality challenge, 245–249
organizing for quality, 246–247
performance quality, 246
planning for quality, 246
productivity-quality connection, 244–245
quality assurance tools, 247
quality improvement teams, 248
statistical process control (SPC), 247
value-added analysis, 247
quality assurance tools, 247
quality circle, **210**
quality control, **244, 246**
quality/cost studies, **247**
quality improvement teams, 248
Quality Management app, 245
quality ownership, **247**
quality planning, 240
quality reliability, **246**
Quebec, 9, 11, 58, 68, 109, 187, 190, 334, 353, 384
QuickBooks App, 259
quid pro quo harassment, 182
quota, **108**
Quotes app, 216

R

radio, 324, 324*t*
railroads, 333*t*, 334
ratio analysis
activity ratios, 267–268
current ratio, 266
debt-to-equity ratios, 267
earnings per share, 267
inventory turnover ratio, 267–268
long-term solvency, 266–267
profitability ratios, 267
return on equity, 267
return on sales, 267
short-term solvency ratios, 266
solvency ratios, 266–267
rational motives, 303
rationalization, 50
raw-materials inventory, 369
real estate investments, 363
real GDP, **28**
real growth rates, 28
real property, **69**
realistic job preview, 173
receiving order, 71
recession, 8, 28
recovery, 28
recruiting, **172–175**
application forms, 173
external recruiting, 172–173
internal recruiting, 172
interviews, 175
selection process, 173–175, 174*f*
tests, 173–175
recycling, **59**
rediscount rate, **351**
redrawing corporate boundaries, 38–39
reference checks, 175
referent power, 215
registered bonds, 371
registered education savings plans (RESP), 363
registered retirement savings plans (RRSPs), 363
registrar, 353
regressive revenue taxes, 11
regulation, 9–11
regulatory bodies, 9, 257
reinforcement, **208**
reintroduction, 309
related diversification, 137
related industries, 102
relationship marketing, **294**
remote access to information, 275
remote deliveries, 275
reorganization, 71, 147–150
repayment plan, 71
repetitive strain injuries (RSIs), 182
replacement chart, 172
report, 301
research. *See* marketing research

research and development (R&D), **31–32**, 306
research method, 301
reseller market, **303**
resources, 82–83
responsibility, **154**
responsible business behaviour, 34
restrictive taxes, 11
retail distribution, 329
retailers, **329**, 331–332, 332*t*
retained earnings, **263**, 374
retirement, 182
retrenchment, 137
return on equity, **267**
return on investment, 376–377
return on sales, **267**
revenue recognition, **264**
revenue taxes, 11
revenues, **264**, 319
revolving credit agreement, **370**–371
reward power, 215
right to be educated about purchases, 53
right to be heard, 53
right to be informed, 53
right to choose what to buy, 53
right to courteous service, 53
right to safe products, 53
rights, 49
risk, **386**, 392
risk avoidance, **386**
risk control, **386**
risk management, 376, **386**–387
    insurance, 392–393
risk-management program, 387
risk propensity, 133, 202
risk retention, 386–**387**
risk-return relationship, **375**–376, 376*f*
risk transfer, **387**
rivalries, 102
rivalry among existing competitors, 35
robots, 239
round lot, 380
router, 285
royalties, 106
Rule of 72, 362, 363*t*, 377
rumours, 374
Russia, 100–101, 110

S

salary, **179**
sales agents, **329**
sales era, 21
sales finance company, **353**–354
sales forecast, **80**
sales promotions, **327**
same-steps layout, 238
SAP Business One app, 163
Saskatchewan, 183, 299, 384
Saudi Arabia, 34*f*, 108, 113
savings certificates, 347
scheduling, 240–242
scientific management, 205
Scientific Management Movement, 21
screening, 78–80, 307
Search Jobs Beyond.com app, 173
seasonal unemployment, 30
secondary data, 301
secondary securities market, 377
secondary strikes, 190
secured bonds, **371**
secured loan, 350, **370**
securities, **377**
    buying and selling, 378–380
    financial information services, 378–380
    financing securities purchases, 380–382
    investment banking, 377
    securities regulation, 384
    short sale, 382
    stock exchanges, 377–378
securities markets, 377–382
security needs, 206
security policy, 285
segmentation. *See* market segmentation
selection process, 173–175, 174*f*
selective distribution, **330**
self-actualization needs, 206
self-efficacy, 202
self-employed Canadians, 75
self-esteem, 202
self-fulfillment, 206
selling expenses, 265
Serbia, 111
serial bonds, 373
service managers, 234
service operations, **232**–234
service-producing processes, 235–236
service productivity, 245
service quality considerations, 234
service technologies, 32–33
services, **293**–294
    accounting services, 259–260
    banks, 348–349
    classification of, 304–305
    consumer services, 304
    convenience goods and services, 304, 304*t*
    distribution of, 329
    essential services, 11
    financial information services, 378–380
    intangible services, 234
    shopping services, 304, 304*t*
    specialty services, 304, 304*t*
    tax services, 260
    unstorable services, 234
sexual harassment, **182**
shareholder return ratios, 267
shareholders, 52, **89**
shopping goods, **304**, 304*t*
shopping services, **304**, 304*t*
short sale, **382**
short-term funds, 369–371
    secured short-term loans, 370
    trade credit, 369–370
    unsecured short-term loans, 370–371
short-term goals, 134
short-term (operating) expenditures, 368–369
short-term solvency ratios, **266**
shortages, 14
sick leave, 180
sickout, 190
simple ranking method, 178
Singapore, 58, 102, 112
sinking-fund provisions, 372
situational (contingency) approach to leadership, **216**, 216*f*
skills inventories, **172**
small and medium-sized employers in Canada, 75*t*
small business, **75**
    accounting practices, 264
    bank credit, 384–385
    cash-flow requirements, 385–386
    employment, 77*f*
    failure, reasons for, 87

small business (*continued*)
financial management, 384–386
going green, 85
role of, in Canadian economy, 76–77
and social responsibility, 62
starting up, 85–86
success, reasons for, 87
trade credit, 384–385
venture capital, 385
smart card, **349**
"smart" equipment, 232
SMART goals, **134**, 208
social audit, **61**
social differences, 108
social goals, 10
social influences, 302
social media
and accountants, 269
growing role of, 37
job prospects, 203
top managers and, 127
social needs, 206
social networking, 278, 310
social responsibility. *See* corporate social responsibility (CSR)
Social Return on Investment (SROI), 52
socio-cultural environment, **34**–36
business environment, 34
buyers, 36
customer preferences and tastes, 34
ethical compliance, 34
industry environment, 34–35
marketing environment, 295
responsible business behaviour, 34
rivalry among existing competitors, 35
substitutes, 36
suppliers, 36
threat of potential entrants, 35
soft manufacturing, **239**
software, **280**–281
sole proprietorship, **88**
solvency ratios, **266**–267
Somalia, 110
sources of law, 68
South Africa, 34, 99, 100, 101
South Korea, 58, 100, 101, 110
sovereign nations, 371
S&P 500, 380
S&P/TSX Index, 380, 383
Spain, 100
spam, **285**, 286
span of control, **155**
specialization, 151–152
specialty goods, **304**, 304*t*
specialty services, **304**, 304*t*
specialty stores, 332*t*
specific performance, 69
speculative risks, **386**
speed to market, 306
spinoff, **38**
spyware, **285**, 286
staff authority, **156**–157
staff schedules, 241
stakeholder model of responsibility, 52–60
customers, responsibility toward, 53–54
employees, responsibility toward, 55–57
environment, responsibility toward, 58–60
international communities, responsibility toward, 57–58
investors, responsibility toward, 57
local communities, responsibility toward, 57–58
suppliers, responsibility toward, 57
stakeholders. *See* organizational stakeholders
standard of living, 27
starting up a small business, 85–86
statement of cash flows, **265**
statistical process control (SPC), **247**
Statistics Canada, 75
statutory law, **68**
stealth (undercover) advertising, 54
stock, **90**
see also securities
stock exchanges, **377**–378
stock option, **380**
stock quotations, 378, 379*f*
stockbroker, **377**–378
stockbroker recommendations, 374
stop order, 380
store of value, 346
stored-value cards, 349
strategic alliances, **39**, 106–107
strategic goals, **134**–135
strategic leadership, 219
strategic management, **133**–137
business goals, 133–134
hierarchy of plans, 136
levels of strategy, 136–137
strategy formulation, 134–136
strategic plans, **136**
strategy, **133**, 136*f*
business-level (competitive) strategy, 136, 137
business strategy, 236
competitive strategy, 137
concentration strategy, 136
corporate-level strategy, 136–137
differentiation strategy, 137
distribution strategies, 330
focus strategy, 137
formulation of, 134–136
functional strategies, 136, 137
growth strategy, 136
integration strategy, 136
marketing strategy, 297–298
motivation strategies, 208–214
pricing strategies, 321
promotional strategies, 322
pull strategy, 322
push strategy, 322
union organizing strategy, 187–188
strategy formulation, **134**–136
strict product liability, **70**
strike, **190**
strikebreakers, 190
strong currency, 355
structural unemployment, 30
structure. *See* organizational structure
subsidiary corporation, 39
subsidy, **109**
substitute products, 296
substitutes, 36
Success Magazine app, 83
Sudan, 110
sue for damages, 69
supermarket battles, 23–25
supermarkets, 332*t*
suppliers, 36
as financial resource, 82
information linkages with, 283
responsibility toward, 57
selection of, 243
supply, 12–14, 13*f*
supply chain, **249**, 249*f*, 333–334

supply-chain disruption, 249
supply-chain management (SCM), **249**
supply curve, **13**
supply management, 16
supporting industries, 102
supportive leader behaviour, 216
surplus, **14**, **103**
survey, **301**
sustainable corporations, 62
sustainable development, **61**
Sweden, 104, 108
Switzerland, 102
SWOT analysis, **135**
SWOT Chart app, 135
sympathy strikes, 190
synthetic processes, 235
system architecture, 279–280

T

tablets, 331
tactical plans, **136**
Taiwan, 58, 108
takeover, 38
tall organizations, 155, 156*f*
target market, **298**
tariff, **108**–109
tastes, 34
tax-free savings accounts (TSFAs), 363
taxation
    accountants, and tax services, 260
    double taxation, 90
    government as taxation agent, 11
    legal tax avoidance, 363
    tax authorities, and accounting information, 257
    types of, 11
TD (Canada) app, 349
team building, 177
team incentives, 180
team management, 210–211
team organization, 161
technical skills, **130**
technological environment, 31–33
    marketing environment, 295–296
    product technologies, 32–33
    research and development (R&D), 31–32
    service technologies, 32–33
technological innovations, 49
technology, 31, 32
    information technology, 235*f*, 274–286
    transformation technologies, 235
technology transfer, 32–33
telecommuting, **212**, 213, 213*t*
telemarketing, 332*t*
telephone, 130
television, 323–324, 324*t*, 332*t*
test marketing, 307
tests, 173–175
Textile Labelling Act, 10
Thailand, 58, 101
Theory X, **205**
Theory Y, **205**
threat of potential entrants, 35
360-degree feedback, 177
time deposits, **347**
time management skills, **130**
time utility, 232, 293
time value of money, 362, 363*t*, 377
title, **69**
Toastmaster Magazine app, 216
Tobacco Act, 10
top managers, **127**
torts, **70**
total quality management (TQM), 245–246
total return, 376–377
toxic wastes, 59
tracking customers, 302
trade associations, **12**
trade credit, 369–**370**, 384–385
trade deficit, 29
trade draft, 370
trade shows, **327**
trademarks, **70**
training, 176, 243
trait approach, **215**
Trans-Pacific Partnership, 112
transaction processing system (TPS), **283**
transactional leadership, **217**
transfer agent, 353
transfer of property, 69
transformation technologies, 235
transformational leadership, **217**
transnational teams, 210
transport processes, 235
transportation, 243
transportation operations, 333
triple-bottom-line reporting, 61
Trojan horse, 285
trough, 28
trucks, 333*t*
trust company, **353**
trustee, 353
truth in advertising, 53
turbulent times. *See* managing in turbulent times
Turkey, 100, 111
turnover, 201
two-factor theory, **207**, 207*f*

U

Ukraine, 100, 101
undercover advertising, 54
unemployment, **30**–31
unemployment rate, 31*f*
unfair pricing, 53
uninsurable risk, 392
union. *See* labour union
union security, 188
union shop, **188**
unit of account, 346
United Arab Emirates, 100, 113
United Kingdom, 100, 104, 111
United States
    Asia-Pacific Economic Cooperation, 113
    counterfeit products, 54
    dumping, 110
    foreign direct investment from, 107
    and GATT, 110
    global economy, role in, 100
    gross domestic product (GDP), 28
    international competitiveness, 102
    management styles, 219
    NAFTA, 111
    per capital income, 100
    selling Nazi memorabilia online, 47
    as trading partner, 99
    Trans-Pacific Partnership, 112
unlimited liability, **88**
unsecured loans, **370**–371
unstorable services, 234
upper-middle-income countries, 100
Uruguay, 112

users of accounting information, 257–258
utility, 49, **232**, **293**

V

vacations, 180, 187
value, **293**
  through branding, 309
  value creation through operations, 232–236
  value package, 304
value-added analysis, 247
value chain, **249**
  see also supply chain
variable costs, **320**
variable pay, 179
Venezuela, 112
venture capital, 385
venture capital firm, **354**
venture capitalists, 82
venture teams, 210
vertical integration, 136
vertical merger, 38
vestibule training, 176
video assessment, 175
video cases
  Amazon Cracks Down on Fake Reviews, 119
  CH2MHill, 227
  Colt Hockey, 339–340
  Did Burger King Defect to Canada to Save Tax Money?, 289
  Find Fresh Flowers, 395
  Johnny Cupcakes, 395
  Kid Toy Testers Make Big Bucks on YouTube, 340
  Matthew McConaughey's Lincoln Commercials Generate Lots of Buzz, 341
  McDonald's Eyeing Natural Chicken, 118
  Neale's Sweet 'N Nice Ice Cream, 225–226
  Pizza Hut, 226
  Rudi's Bakery, 288
  T Caps International, 394–395
  Velofix, 118
  Zeronext, 288
video games, 55
video retailing, 332*t*
Vietnam, 58, 100, 102, 112
viral marketing, 37, 54, **310**
virtual job fair, 173
virtual leadership, 219
virtual organization, 161
virtual private networks (VPNs), 279
virtual teams, 210
virus, 285–286
visible minorities, 183
vision, **133**
Volker Rule, 351
voluntary arbitration, 191
voluntary bankruptcy, 71
voters, 12
VSAT satellite communications, **279**

W

wage reopener clause, 189
wages, **179**, 187
warehousing, 243, **333**
warning labels, 10*f*
warranty, **69**
water carriers, 333*t*
water pollution, 59
weak currency, 355
Weights and Measures Act, 10
wellness programs, 180
Western Europe, 100
whistle-blower, **56**–57, 62, 139
wholesale clubs, 332*t*
wholesale distribution, 329
wholesalers, **329**, 330–331
Wi-Fi, **280**
wide area networks (WANs), **279**
wildcat strikes, 190
wireless local area network (wireless LAN or WLAN), 280
wireless wide area networks (WWANs), **280**
women
  gaming by women, 55
  and leadership, 218
work-in-process inventory, 369
work slowdown, 190
workers' compensation, 180
workers' compensation coverage, **393**
workforce diversity, **183**–184
worksharing, **212**–214
World Bank, 100, 101, **356**
world marketplaces, 100
World Trade Organization (WTO), **110**–111
World Wide Web, 279
worms, 285

X

XE Currency App, 104

Y

Young Urban Professionals, 299
Yukon, 33

Z

Zambia, 99
Zimbabwe, 30